5th Edition

creating MOTION GRAPHICS

with After Effects

Trish & Chris Meyer

ELSEVIER

Amsterdam • Boston • Heidelberg • London
New York • Oxford • Paris • San Diego
San Francisco • Singapore • Sydney • Tokyo

Focal Press is an imprint of Elsevier

Focal Press

DEDICATED

to the memory of Vera McGrath, who always said I could do anything I put my mind to – Trish
and to the memory of Leroy Meyer, who taught me to be curious about how things worked – Chris

Focal Press is an imprint of Elsevier
30 Corporate Drive, Suite 400, Burlington, MA 01803, USA
The Boulevard, Langford Lane, Kidlington, Oxford, OX5 1GB, UK

Library of Congress Cataloging-in-Publication Data
Meyer, Trish
 Creating motion graphics with After Effects / Trish & Chris Meyer.
    p. cm.
 Includes index.
 ISBN 978-0-240-81415-5
 1. Cinematography--Special effects--Data processing. 2. Computer animation. 3. Computer graphics.
 4. Adobe After Effects.
 I. Meyer, Chris   II. Title.
 TR858.M492 2010
 006.6'96--dc22

                           2010019568

British Library Cataloguing-in-Publication Data
A catalogue record for this book is available from the British Library.

For information on all Focal Press publications
visit our website at *www.elsevierdirect.com*

10 11 12 13   5 4 3 2 1

Printed in the United States of America

Table of Contents

PART 1

Animation Techniques

Layer Management

Modes, Masks, & Mattes

Cameras! Lights! Action!

Building Hierarchies

PART
8

Color & Keying

Time & Tracking

Drawing, Painting, & Puppetry

PART
11

Working with Audio

Exporting & Rendering

When the Going Gets Tough…

By Trish and Chris Meyer

As we write this, we are coming through the worst recession most of us have experienced; unemployment is the highest it's been for years. Some may see this as a time to hide under a rock until things get better. Instead, we've seen the opposite happen: Artists are redoubling their efforts to train themselves. They're sharpening their existing skills so they become indispensable to their current employer or clients, or retraining to learn new skills and move into new fields. Fortunately for those wishing to learn, the motion graphics industry has a tradition of users sharing information.

Creating Motion Graphics 5th Edition has been thoroughly updated and expanded to reflect changes in After Effects CS4 and CS5. It includes new chapters on the Roto Brush tool, the third-party tracking utilities mocha and mocha shape, and what we call "parallel worlds": strategies for combining 3D layers in After Effects with 3D renders and plug-in effects. We've reworked several chapters including those on text and 3D cameras, demonstrated new techniques such as creating fake reflections, updated the keying chapter to use high-def source material, increased the number of scenarios covered in Color Management, and more.

When we wrote the first edition of *Creating Motion Graphics with After Effects* over 10 years ago, it was with the goal of helping our fellow artists raise their game to take on the entrenched studios who relied on expensive, exclusive, dedicated machinery. Today, everyone is trying to keep up with ever-changing formats, from high-definition video and digital cinema to mobile devices and the web. But even as technology and design trends evolve, it's more important than ever to have a thorough understanding of essential, core techniques – master those, and you can adapt to whatever an ever-changing world throws at you. And that's the idea behind this book: to provide you with a resource that explains the ins and outs of each feature in After Effects, and how we use them in real-world situations. We hope it becomes your trusted companion as you tackle new challenges.

Trish and Chris Meyer
Crish Design
May 2010

If you prefer a tutorial-oriented approach, check out our other book, *After Effects Apprentice* – it is designed for those new to After Effects, or for those who use it as a secondary or part-time tool in their normal work.

How to Use This Book

Our goal in this book is to give you insight into how After Effects thinks, as well as to let you know how *we* think while using it to solve realworld design and production challenges. We've also crammed in numerous *Tips, Gotchas,* and *Factoids* to give you additional ideas for how to use a feature, as well as warn you about situations where they will *not* work.

If you are new to After Effects, or haven't upgraded for a while, make sure you read Chapter 1 which will give you a good "lay of the land" for both the program and its user interface. The rest of the chapters have been arranged in what we feel is a good sequence to learn the program, grouped by subject. Most chapters assume you have read the ones before it, or are at least familiar with their subject matter; we also cross-reference related material that appears in other chapters (look for the *Connect* boxes at the end of each chapter).

If you already have some experience using After Effects, feel free to jump between chapters and sections to brush up on the subjects that most interest you. In addition to using the *Table of Contents,* don't forget to consult the extensive *Index* to quickly zero in on the tidbit you're looking for. And don't miss the Bonus Chapters and Goodies on the DVD-ROM: They contain additional useful information, such as a huge *Effects Roundup* (Bonus Chapter 23B) as well as a tome on writing more advanced expressions (Bonus Chapter 37B).

In this book, we've tried to share everything we use in After Effects. Despite its size, there are probably a few additional tools, functions, and effects we did not cover. For those, we encourage you to reference the After Effects Help. Press F1 from inside After Effects to open the Community Help Client; we personally set its Preferences > Accessibility Mode to Open Help in Browser.

What's in a Name?

After Effects CS5 (also known as version 10.0) runs on both Mac OS and Windows, and is nearly identical on both platforms. That said, there are numerous elements in an After Effects project to keep straight, such as files, compositions, effects, and expressions. To help indicate what we're talking about, here are a few type conventions and shorthand phrases that we use:

• **Words in bold** refer to the names of files, folders, layers, or compositions you are using, as well as any files on disk.

• "**Words in bold and in quotes**" are text you should enter – such as the name for a new composition or solid.

• Words in this style font indicate code inside an expression.

• Menu items, effects, and parameter names do not get a special font.

• When there is a chain of submenus or subfolders you have to navigate, we separate links in the chain with a > symbol: For example, Effect > Color Correction > Levels. (Hierarchies of folders on disk will also be in bold.)

• After Effects makes a distinction between the normal section of the keyboard and the numeric keypad, especially when it comes to the Enter or Return key. When you see Enter, we mean that big key on the keypad; Return indicates the carriage return key that is part of the normal keyboard.

• The Preferences are located under the After Effects menu on the Mac (and under the Edit menu on Windows). We just say "Preferences" and assume you can find them.

Speaking of preferences, we assume you are using the default preferences as your starting point. Where they are saved depends on your operating system. To be safe, first save your current prefs: Search for "Adobe After Effects 10.0-x64 Prefs" and make a note of where you found them. Copy this file to a safe place so that you can return to them later if desired. Then, to restore the default preference settings, hold down Command+Option+Shift on Mac (Control+Alt+Shift on Windows) while launching the program.

Installation

To use this book, you need to install Adobe After Effects CS5. During this process, it will install the additional bundled fonts and third-party effects for you. If you do not have a licensed copy, Adobe makes a fully functional time-limited Trial version available for download on its website at *www.adobe.com/downloads/*. Note that the Trial version does not install the additional fonts, third-party effects, or template projects that come with the full version of the program. Fortunately, very few of the example projects rely on this additional content. For example, if you don't have a font that we use, don't panic; just pick a new one.

DVD Tech Support

If your DVD becomes *damaged*, contact Focal Press Customer Service at:
usbkinfo@elsevier.com

The phone number is:
1 (800) 545-2522 inside North America and
+44 (0)1865 474010 in Europe.

If you have trouble *operating* the DVD, contact Focal Press Technical Support at:
technical.support@elsevier.com

The phone number is:
1 (800) 692-9010 inside North America and
+1 (314) 872-8370 from overseas.

If you don't already have QuickTime installed on your computer, download it from Apple's website (*www.apple.com/quicktime*). We also assume you have Adobe Reader installed in order to open PDF files on the disc; if not, the latest version may be downloaded from *www.adobe.com*.

Adobe prints the minimum and suggested system requirements on the After Effects or Production Premium box. In addition to Adobe's processor and operating system restrictions, we suggest at least a two-button mouse (a scroll wheel is also nice), at least a 1280×900 pixel display, and preferrably 4 or more gigabytes of RAM. Note that After Effects CS5 *requires* a 64-bit operating system.

We also strongly recommend an extended keyboard, as many great shortcuts take advantage of the function keys and numeric keypad. If you are using a laptop, learn where these extended keys are hidden: Look for the small print on your key caps for their alternate uses, which are accessed by pressing the *fn* key.

If you own a recent-model Mac laptop that does not have the numeric keypad replicated on the normal alphanumeric portion of the keyboard, press Control and then select the equivalent key – for example, Control . (period) will initate a RAM Preview; Control+8 will set a marker (as the "8" key is also used for the asterisk).

Mac users should also be aware that Exposé takes over some of the function keys; free them up by opening Exposé in System Preferences and reassign any shortcuts that use function keys.

The DVD

This book and its DVD-ROM go hand in hand: Virtually every chapter comes with one or more companion project files that encourage you to practice the concepts presented in these pages. Look for the *Example Project* box on the first page of each chapter to verify which project you are to load, as well as any special instructions for that chapter. These projects all access a central, shared **Sources** folder which contains virtually all of the media you will be working with.

We recommend you copy the DVD – or at least the **Chapter Example Projects** and **Sources** folders – to your hard drive. This will speed up file access and allow you to save your own versions of the projects as you work (it will also serve as a backup if the DVD should accidentally break or become lost…you know who you are). If you are tight on disk space, open a chapter's project file from the DVD and use the Files > Collect Files feature (discussed in Chapter 43) to copy just the sources used by that chapter to your hard drive.

If files become "unlinked" for some reason, they will appear in italics in the Project panel. Simply double-click the first missing item: This will bring up a standard file navigation dialog where you can locate that item. Select the missing file from its corresponding **Sources** subfolder and click OK. Provided the folder relationship between the project and the other sources has not changed, After Effects will now search for the other missing items and link them in as well.

After opening any lesson project for the first time, you should use Edit > Save As and give it a new name. This will ensure you can keep the original version intact for future reference. (Indeed, the original project file may be locked – especially if you are accessing it directly off the DVD-ROM.)

Virtually all of the material inside this book and on the DVD-ROM are copyright protected and are included only for your own learning and experimentation. A copy of the End User License Agreement is on the DVD-ROM. Please respect copyrights: Some day, it could be *you* who made that cool graphic that you hope to sell…

For Instructors

If you are an instructor, we hope that you will find this book useful in teaching After Effects and will adapt it to your specific needs. Much of this book has been modeled on the advanced After Effects classes Trish taught through the years as well as sessions we've delivered at numerous conferences and trade shows.

As an instructor, you no doubt appreciate how much time and effort it takes to prepare examples and class materials that both teach and inspire. You can certainly understand that we're interested in protecting our own efforts in creating this book for you and your students. Therefore, it will come as no surprise that the contents of this book and its accompanying disc are copyrighted. If a school, company, or instructor distributes copies of the sources, projects, movies, or PDFs to any person who has not purchased the book, that constitutes copyright infringement. Reproducing pages of this book, or any material included on this book's DVD (including creating derivative works), is also a copyright no-no.

As an extension of this, each student must own his or her own copy of this book. Aside from respecting copyright, this also allows them to review the material covered after class without expending valuable class time writing reams of notes! If you are short on disk space on your workstations, students can open the lesson's project file from their DVD, make changes to it as they practice, and save the edited project to their own disk. At the next class, if they mount the book's DVD *before* opening their modified projects, the sources should relink properly.

If your school has the available disk space, students may copy contents from the DVD to their computers, or you may place the files on a server, but again only as long as each student owns his or her own copy of this book. Provided each student owns the book, you are free to then modify the tutorials and adapt them to your specific teaching situation without infringing copyright. Thank you for helping protect our copyrights, as well as those of the people who contributed sources – your cooperation enables us to write new books and obtain great source materials for your students to learn from.

Qualified teaching professionals can acquire evaluation copies of our books directly from Focal Press: Please email textbook@elsevier.com.

After Effects 101

Moving in and getting comfortable.

Our example project files share footage from a central **Sources** folder on the DVD. If you copy the **Chapter Example Projects** and **Bonus Chapters** folders to your hard drive, be sure to also copy the **Sources** folder. If After Effects cannot find an already-imported source file, it will temporarily replace its icon with color bars in the Project panel. To fix this problem, just double-click this icon and locate the first missing footage item on your drive; After Effects will then automatically find the other missing files.

Example Project

Open the 01-Example Project.aep project file to work through the examples in this chapter. You will find it on this book's DVD in the Chapter Example Projects > 01-After Effects 101 folder.

After Effects can be thought of as a blank canvas – a canvas that comes with hundreds of brushes and tools to create images with. The problem with too many tools is that it can be hard to know where to start. Therefore, in this first chapter we want to give you an overview of the After Effects user interface. We also want to give you an idea of how After Effects "thinks" – how projects are structured, how to import sources, and how everything comes together.

Welcome to After Effects

When you first launch After Effects CS5, you'll see a Welcome screen that includes a searchable Tip of the Day, as well as links to your most recent projects, the Help system, and common tasks such as opening Bridge to browse template projects or other potential source material. It can be re-opened at any time by choosing Help > Welcome and Tip of the Day.

The user interface has received a few tweaks in CS5. Generally it is even darker and more compact, with updated icons that should be easier to read across a wider range of user interface brightness settings. (The User Interface Brightness can be set in Preferences > Appearance.)

The After Effects Project

All of your work occurs inside an After Effects project file (file extension: .aep). You must *import* source material into a project to use it. Importing creates a link to your sources, but does not actually copy the sources into the project file – so the project file itself remains small. When you copy a project to another computer, you need to move its source files with it. If After Effects cannot find an already-imported source file, it creates a placeholder and lists the source as temporarily missing.

Source material is referred to as *footage* and appears in the Project panel. Audio, video, still images, vector artwork, PDF files, and other formats may all be footage. Every footage item has a set of parameters attached to it that determine its alpha channel (transparency), frame rate, and other important information that tells After Effects how to use it. We will go over the Project panel and basic importing a few pages from now; importing and interpreting footage are covered in much more detail in Chapter 38.

Compositions

The next major building block is the *composition* ("comp" for short). In comps, you assemble your footage items into the desired composite image. Each item in a composition is referred to as a *layer*. A layer is usually a footage item that has been added to the current comp. There are other types of layers, including synthetic footage items such as solids, text, and shapes; "null objects" that help group together layers or which can serve as controllers; 3D cameras and lights; and special adjustment layers for applying effects.

You can use the same footage item multiple times in the same composition; you can also use it in multiple compositions inside the same project.

Compositions are sorted in the Project panel alongside your footage items. When you open a composition, it appears in two panels: the *Composition* panel and the *Timeline* panel. The Comp panel is a stage where you can arrange your layers visually; the Timeline panel is where you stack them, sequence them in time, and control most of their animations. Indeed, virtually any property of a layer – including effects you apply to them – can be animated through a process known as *keyframing* (covered in Chapters 3, 4, and beyond).

An important concept is that compositions are always "live" – you can go back later and alter any setting of any layer. This allows you to try new ideas or change your mind while maintaining maximum image quality. All of your edits to layers and footage are also *nondestructive*, which means you can always get back to your original sources.

A composition can contain your final work, which you *render* (compute, then save) to disk. The resulting file – usually a movie or a sequence of stills – can then be used as is, or if it's a title or visual effect, it can be incorporated into the finished program in an editing system. You can also render movies to embed directly in a website.

One After Effects project file can contain as many compositions as you like. Compositions can also be used as layers in other compositions (this is called *nesting*), making it possible to build complex animations that are still easy to understand and edit. The basics of creating a composition are covered in detail in the next chapter. We'll discuss building chains of comps in Chapters 18 and 19.

You can queue up multiple comps to render as a batch while you sleep. (Rendering is covered in Chapters 42 through 44.)

In the rest of this chapter, we will give you an overview of the After Effects Application window and its main panels. We'll then discuss importing files, including using Adobe's centralized media management utility Bridge. Lastly, we'll show you how to rearrange the panels and frames inside the Application window, and create custom *workspaces*.

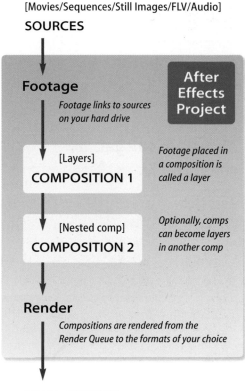

[Movies/Sequences/Still Images/FLV/Audio]
SOURCES

Footage
Footage links to sources on your hard drive

After Effects Project

[Layers]
COMPOSITION 1

Footage placed in a composition is called a layer

[Nested comp]
COMPOSITION 2

Optionally, comps can become layers in another comp

Render
Compositions are rendered from the Render Queue to the formats of your choice

FINAL OUTPUT
[Movies/Sequences/Still Images/FLV/Audio]

This is how an After Effects project is structured: Source files on your computer are imported as footage items; footage is used as layers in a composition. A comp can be rendered directly or used as a layer in other comps (this is called *nesting*).

FACTOID

Importing Projects

You can import an entire project into the current project. After Effects will copy the links to the imported project's source files as well.

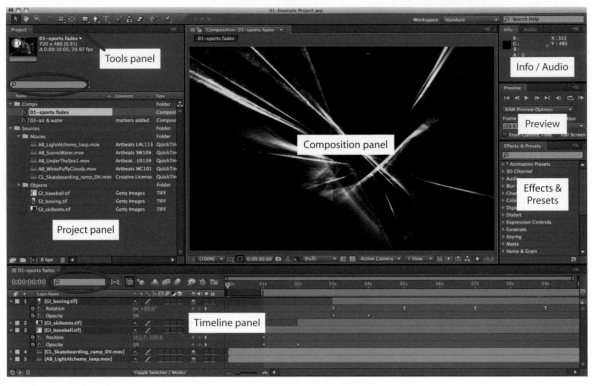

The Standard workspace in After Effects. The active panel is highlighted with a yellow outline. Note the QuickSearch fields (circled in red) which were added to the Project and Timeline panels in CS4. Background courtesy Artbeats/Light Alchemy.

Resize Window

To resize the Application window (or any floating window) to fit inside its current screen, press Command+\ on Mac (Control+\ on Windows). Press this again to expand the window further to fill the screen, with its borders extending beyond the screen.

The Application Window

When you open a project in After Effects, it opens into its Application window. By default, this window occupies your entire main monitor; you can resize it by dragging the lower right corner.

The Application window is divided into *frames* and *panels*. A frame is a major space division inside this window. One or more panels of information may be "docked" into each frame. Panels are dedicated to different types of information, such as the Tools, Project, Composition, Timeline, Audio, Info, Preview, and other panels. Any panels not currently open can be accessed through the Window menu. In some cases, you may have multiple copies of the same type of panel, such as having multiple comps open.

Later in this chapter we will show you how to rearrange these frames and panels, as well as how to save your custom layout as a *workspace*.

QuickSearch fields in the Project and Timeline panels were added in CS4. These make it much easier to find specific sources or parameters, as well as comments in these panels. Related to this, the old Find icon has now disappeared from the bottom of the Project panel; it has been replaced by the QuickSearch field in the Project panel. You can type in the name of the file you are looking for, characteristics of it such as duration or file extension, or the special phrases "**missing**", "**used**", and "**not used**".

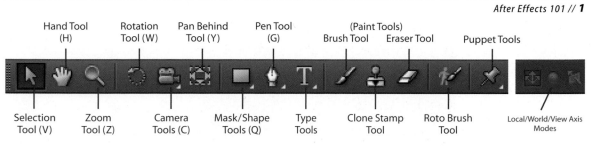

Hand Tool (H) • Rotation Tool (W) • Pan Behind Tool (Y) • Pen Tool (G) • (Paint Tools) Brush Tool • Eraser Tool • Puppet Tools

Selection Tool (V) • Zoom Tool (Z) • Camera Tools (C) • Mask/Shape Tools (Q) • Type Tools • Clone Stamp Tool • Roto Brush Tool • Local/World/View Axis Modes

The Tools Panel

After Effects features a toolbar (known as the Tools panel) that defaults to running as a strip along the top of the Application window. It contains a number of icons you can click to switch between tools; they also visually confirm which tool is currently selected. Many of these tools have popup menus that allow you to choose among variations on that tool – such as different basic shapes for masks and shape layers.

When you select specific tools, additional options may also appear in the middle of the Tools panel (an example would be buttons to define the color and type of Stroke and Fill when you select a Shape tool). Selecting some tools will also automatically open related panels – for example, selecting the Text tool opens its Character and Paragraph panels.

The Selection tool (shortcut = V) is the one you will use most often.

The Rotation and Pan Behind tools are covered in Chapter 3, 10, and 13.

The Pen tool can be used to draw animation motion paths (Chapter 3), but is mostly used to create masks (Chapter 10) and shapes (Chapter 32).

The 3D Camera tools and the Axis Mode buttons are covered in Chapter 13.

The Type tool is covered in Chapter 21. The Paint tools are covered in Chapter 33, Roto Brush (new in CS5) in Chapter 34, and the Puppet tools in Chapter 35.

Panels in Depth

Many tools and functions inside After Effects have dedicated panels. As we cover these tools in future chapters, we will also cover their related panels in depth. Those chapters include:

Composition, Timeline, Layer, and Preview: Chapter 2.

Motion Sketch, Smoother, and Wiggler: Chapter 5.

Align: Chapter 6.

Layer: Chapters 3, 7, 10, 29, 30, 33, 34, and others.

Mask Interpolation: Chapter 10.

Character & Paragraph: Chapter 21.

Effects & Presets plus Effect Controls: Chapter 22.

Tracker: Chapters 29 and 30.

Paint and Brushes: Chapter 33.

Audio: Chapter 36.

Footage: Chapters 6, 38 and 41.

Render Queue, Metadata: Chapters 42 and 43.

We'll cover the Project panel on the next page; the Info panel is used throughout this book. For additional references, see the index, and also check out Help > After Effects Help.

Window	Help	
Workspace		▶
Assign Shortcut to "Standard" Workspace		▶
Align		
Audio	⌘4
Brushes	⌘9
Character	⌘6
✓ Effects & Presets	⌘5
✓ Info	⌘2
Mask Interpolation	
Metadata	
Motion Sketch	
Paint	⌘8
Paragraph	⌘7
✓ Preview	⌘3
Smoother	
✓ Tools	⌘1
Tracker	
Wiggler	
✓ Composition: 01–sports fades	
Effect Controls: GI_baseball.tif	
Flowchart: (none)	
Footage: (none)	
Layer: (none)	
✓ Project	⌘0
Render Queue	⌥⌘0
✓ Timeline: 01–sports fades	

You can open additional panels from the Window menu. Checkmarks indicate which panels are currently open and forward. Note that many of the most common panels have keyboard shortcuts to open them.

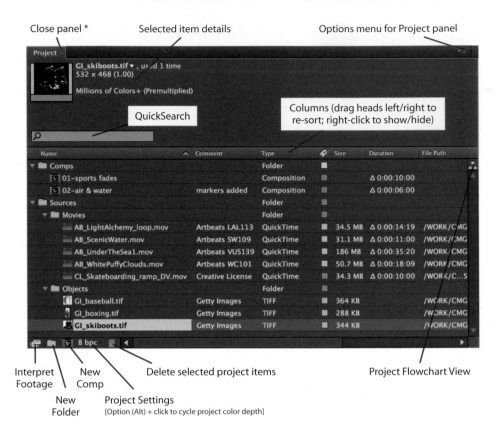

Close panel *

Selected item details

Options menu for Project panel

* Clicking Close for the Project panel does not close the project file. To do so, select File > Close Project. Note that closing the Application window closes not only the project file but also After Effects. If the project was not recently saved, you will be prompted to Save, Don't Save, or Cancel.

QuickSearch

Columns (drag heads left/right to re-sort; right-click to show/hide)

The Project panel, where your imported sources as well as your comps are stored. When you select one of these items, information about it appears at the top of this panel. As a project gets more complex, it pays to create new folders so you can better organize your footage and comps.

Interpret Footage

New Comp

Delete selected project items

Project Flowchart View

New Folder

Project Settings
[Option (Alt) + click to cycle project color depth]

The Project Panel

As we mentioned in the introduction, the Project panel is where all the footage items you import into your project – as well as the compositions you create – reside. It displays information about these items (such as file type, size, and location) in a series of *columns*. The contents of the Project panel are sorted according to the column you select, noted by a sort direction arrow. You can drag the horizontal scroll bar at the bottom of this panel to view the different columns. Columns can be re-ordered by dragging their headers left or right along the top of this panel. To add or subtract a column, right-click on any column header and select or deselect it from the list that appears. Note that the Comment column is now part of the default set, unlike in earlier versions. It initially appears on the far right; scroll over to locate it and drag it to the left until it is next to the Name column. New projects will use your most recent layout.

When you select a footage item in the Project panel, a thumbnail of it will appear at the top of this panel,

along with its vital statistics. If you are already using it in a comp, the name of the comp(s) it appears in will be added to a popup menu to the right of its name. If you need to change some settings for a footage item – such as its frame rate or alpha channel type – select it in the Project panel, then click the Interpret Footage button at the bottom of the Project panel. (Interpret Footage is covered in detail in Chapter 38.)

As projects become more complex, organize the Project panel by creating and sorting items into *folders*. To create a folder, click on the folder icon along the bottom of this panel or use the menu command File > New > New Folder. Then drag items into and out of folders as you like. To expand or collapse a folder, you can either double-click it, use the arrow keys, or click the arrow to its left (also known as its "twirly").

To rename a footage item or a folder, select its name, press Return, type a new name, and press Return again. You can Edit > Duplicate footage items if you need to apply different Interpret Footage settings.

Importing Footage

To import a footage item into your project, use File > Import > File; the shortcut is Command+I on Mac (Control+I on Windows). This will open a dialog where you can browse to the file you want. Pay attention to the area under the file browser, as it contains important options such as whether you want to import the file as a single footage item or as a self-contained composition (handy for layered Photoshop and Illustrator files), plus options to import a single still image, a whole sequence of stills as a movie, or to import an entire folder in one go. When you click OK, this dialog closes; if you chose the File > Import > Multiple Files option instead, the dialog will keep re-opening until you click Done. The intricacies of importing different file types are discussed in detail in Chapter 38.

An alternative to the spartan Import File dialog is using File > Browse, which launches Adobe Bridge. We'll discuss Bridge in greater detail in the next two pages. You can also drag and drop (or copy and paste) footage items from the Finder on Mac or Explorer on Windows directly into the Project panel. Feel free to practice importing a few items into this chapter's example project.

The Footage Panel

When you double-click footage items in the Project panel (or select them and press Enter), they will open into a Footage panel. This allows you to study the footage in greater detail before deciding to use it in a composition. Note that the footage appears with its Interpret Footage settings applied, so you can see the result of choosing a different alpha channel type, field separation order, and the like.

New in CS5: Double-clicking a QuickTime movie in the Project panel now opens the clip in the Footage panel. To open a QuickTime movie in QuickTime Player, press Option (Alt) while double-clicking it. Note that QuickTime Player shows you the footage *before* being processed by the Interpret Footage settings, so alpha channels are not taken into account.

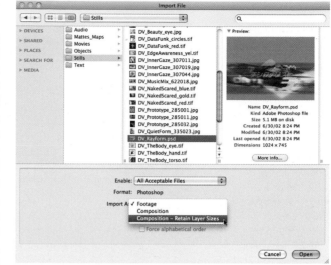

Locate your prospective footage items using the Import File dialog. Additional settings along its bottom help you decide how to interpret different file types including layered files and sequences of files. Image courtesy Digital Vision/Rayform.

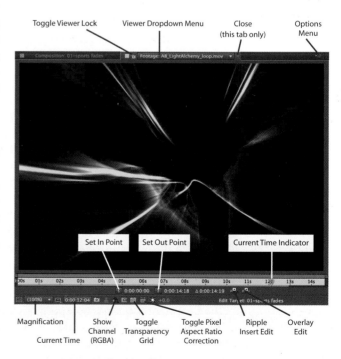

Double-click any footage item in the Project panel (or select it and press Enter) to open it in the Footage panel. If the source is a QuickTime movie, you can also press Option (Alt) while double-clicking to open it in QuickTime Player.

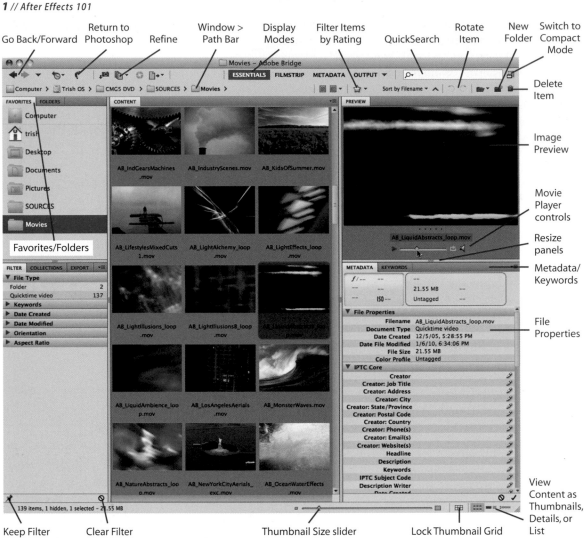

Go Back/Forward · Return to Photoshop · Refine · Window > Path Bar · Display Modes · Filter Items by Rating · QuickSearch · Rotate Item · New Folder · Switch to Compact Mode · Delete Item · Image Preview · Movie Player controls · Resize panels · Metadata/Keywords · File Properties · View Content as Thumbnails, Details, or List · Favorites/Folders · Keep Filter when Browsing · Clear Filter · Thumbnail Size slider · Lock Thumbnail Grid

Adobe Bridge allows you to search, preview, and rank your content as well as import it into After Effects. Footage courtesy Artbeats.

Where Did It Go?

When you import footage or create a new folder or comp, it goes into the folder that is currently selected in the Project panel – except for Bridge, which places it at the top level.

Adobe Bridge

Adobe Bridge is a central application shared by many Adobe programs. It provides a way to search, preview, and rank your content before opening it into your current program. It also gives you access to After Effects Template projects and Animation Presets. As the preview functions of the After Effects Import File dialog are pretty minimal, you may find this becomes your preferred way to import sources.

To access Bridge, select File > Browse from inside After Effects. This will launch Bridge if it isn't already running. To make sure you're looking at the same thing we are, in Bridge select the Essentials display mode, then select Reset Workspace from the same menu. Check that Window > File Bar is enabled, so that you can easily navigate through folders, create a new folder, filter, sort and rotate images, and more.

The Favorites and Folders tabs in the upper left corner of Bridge's Application window help you navigate to different locations on your hard drive. For now, click on the Folders tab and navigate to a folder that contains some video or still image assets. If you've already copied the **Sources** folder on this book's DVD-ROM to your computer, navigate to it and open the **Sources > Movies** folder. (If you like, you can add the **Sources** folder to the Favorites panel.)

The files in the folder you opened will appear in the central Content panel. The default is to display a thumbnail of each file with its name underneath. The size of the thumbnails is controlled by a slider along the bottom right of the Application window; you can show more or fewer details by changing options in the View menu.

Select one of the files in this folder. It will appear in the Preview panel in the upper right corner; if you selected a movie file, you can play it using the Preview transport controls. Below this is a Metadata panel, which shows you some details of the selected file; you can click on the pencil icon to the right of any data field to enter your own details. (This information should then be displayed in After Effects CS5 in the Window > Metadata panel under Files, although the fields don't match exactly.)

Bridge offers extensive options for sorting your assets. Our favorite is the ability to rank individual files so we can remember which were the best takes from a batch video capture or photo memory card. Select a file and use the Label menu to rank clips. Then use Filter Item by Rating menu (the "star" icon in the Path Bar) and the Sort By menu to determine which clips are displayed based on these labels and other criteria. For other choices that determine how to search for and display clips, you can assign keywords to a source (select the Keyword tab docked with the Metadata panel) and take advantage of the Filter panel (lower left corner).

Finally, the payoff: To import one or more files from Bridge into After Effects, select them and either press Enter or Return, or press Command+O (Control+O). If you want to open the file in another application, use the File > Open With command. You can also drag a file from Bridge to an application icon in your dock.

Adobe Bridge is very powerful and is capable of a lot more than we've discussed here. For more details, select Help > Adobe Bridge Help.

You can label your favorite shots in Bridge when you have a lot of clips or photos to choose from. You can then filter and sort by these labels.

TIP

Lost and Found

If you can't find a comp or footage item in your Project panel, use the QuickSearch feature. Type "missing" to have After Effects highlight missing footage items so you can relink.

After Effects & PPI

Print designers and photographers have to pay careful attention to *resolution* (how many pixels are in an inch, or its *ppi*). This resolution is used to determine what size an image will appear when printed to paper. Pixels per inch has no relevance in After Effects – we will be concerned only with the number of pixels in our source layers and comps.

A high-resolution image (one with lots of pixels, regardless of the ppi setting) may appear many times larger than the size of the comp, with most of the image on the pasteboard. This allows you to pan around a large image without having to scale the layer past 100%, as well as move closer to an image when animating in 3D space.

To trade off screen real estate between two panels, hover your cursor over the border between them until you see this special two-headed arrow cursor (above) or corner arrow (below), then click and drag.

Rearranging the Furniture

It is easy to rearrange panels and frames inside the After Effects Application window to suit your monitor resolution and personal tastes. You will find that what works best changes from task to task. We're going to spend the last few pages of this chapter showing you how to rearrange the user interface, plus how to take advantage of workspaces to recall your favorite layouts. You can apply almost everything you learn here across the entire line of Adobe video products.

Resizing Frames

First, let's make sure you're looking at the same panels and frames that we are. We assume that you've opened the project file **01-Example Project.aep**; it's okay if you've already imported additional sources. In the upper right corner of the Application window is a Workspace popup: Select Standard, then select Reset Standard from the same menu; in the dialog that opens, click "Yes" to confirm.

In the Project panel (the one on the left), make sure the **Comps** folder is twirled open; double-click it if it isn't. Then double-click the comp named **01-sports fades** to open it. It will appear in both the Composition and Timeline panels. Click anywhere in either of these panels; a yellow outline indicates it is selected.

Hover the cursor over the border between the Comp and Timeline panels: It will change to a double-headed arrow plus a pair of parallel lines. This indicates you are about to resize a frame. Click and drag up or down to balance off the space between these two frames. The Magnification Ratio in the lower left corner of the Comp panel will tell you how much it is scaling the comp's image to fit into the resized frame. Then hover the cursor between the Comp and Project panels until you see this cursor again; click and drag to balance off their arrangement.

If you hover the cursor over the corner of a frame, the cursor changes to a four-headed arrow, indicating you can resize in any direction. Try dragging the bottom left corner of the Comp panel; this will adjust the Comp, Timeline, and Project panels at the same time.

Some panels can be collapsed into smaller versions of themselves. For example, the default view of the Preview panel displays Options that we rarely change (these are discussed at the end of Chapter 2). Place your cursor between the Preview panel and the Effects & Presets panel underneath it and drag upward until Preview snaps to a smaller size.

Some panels can be collapsed into smaller versions of themselves. Here we're collapsing the bottom of the Preview panel to make more room for Effects & Presets below.

Tabs

Back in the Project panel, double-click the comp named **02-air & water**. It will open into the same frames as your first comp, with a couple of differences. In the Timeline panel, you will see tabs with the names of each of your two comps; clicking on them gives you a quick way to switch between comps. In the Composition panel, there is just one tab; click on it and you will see a popup listing all of your currently open comps. There are additional useful options in this popup, such as closing a specified comp, closing all comps, or locking the current panel so any newly opened comp will be forced to create a panel and frame of its own. (More on these options in Chapter 2.)

The tab along the top of the Comp panel contains a list of all currently open comps, as well as the choice of either closing one or all comps at once or locking this panel and forcing new comps to open into a new panel.

Click on the small "x" on the right side of a tab (circled above) to close that panel. If the tab is for an empty frame, clicking "x" will close the entire frame.

With [**02-air & water**] forward, in the Timeline panel click once on the layer **AB_ScenicWater.mov** to select it. Then select Effect > Effect Controls (shortcut: F3) to open the Effect Controls panel. It defaults to being docked into the same frame as the Project panel. The Project panel tab may be hard to see at this point; click and drag the thin gray horizontal bar above the Effect Controls tab to scroll over to the Project tab, then click on this tab to bring it forward again. You can also use the shortcut Command+0 (Control+0) to bring it forward.

Turn your attention back to the Timeline panel and click on the tab for [**01-sports fades**] to bring it forward. Adjust the height of the Timeline to make sure you can see all of the layers in it. Double-click the layer named **CL_Skateboarding_ramp_DV.mov**. This will open it in its own Layer panel, which will be docked into the same frame as the Comp panel. The Layer panel (discussed in more detail in Chapter 2) provides a direct view of a layer without the distractions of the other layers in the comp; you will put it to work in several later chapters.

When the panel tabs along the top of a frame are wider than the frame itself, a scroll bar will appear allowing you to move those tabs (such as for the Project panel here) back into view.

Improved Help

If After Effects detects an internet connection upon startup, Help will now automatically access a much more extensive, regularly updated web-based Help system instead of the local Help file installed with the program. There are two methods for reaching the After Effects Help system:

• Go to *www.adobe.com/support/aftereffects* and click the link for After Effects Help.

• Choose Help > After Effects Help (or press F1). When the Adobe Help application starts, you can click the URL at the top of the Application window to break out of the AIR application and view the same page in a browser.

To move a panel to a new location, first click on the dots along the left edge of its tab (above).

Then drag and hover your cursor over portions of existing frames; the blue overlays – the "drop zones" – will show you where you are about to place this panel (right, top).

In this case, we moved the Layer panel to its own frame to the left of the Comp panel (right). Footage courtesy Creative License; objects courtesy Getty Images.

Maximize Frame

To expand the current panel or frame to fill the entire Application window, press ~ (the tilde key). Press ~ again to return to your previous arrangement.

Re-docking Panels

You can reorganize panels to create a custom workspace. Since you will often need to see the Comp and Layer panels side by side, try moving the Layer panel.

To move a panel to another frame, click on its tab to bring it forward, then click on the textured dots on the left side of its tab. Drag it around the Application window: You will see blue overlays appear around the borders or in the center of the frames you are hovering over; these will become green rectangles if you are near the edges of the Application window. These are *drop zones*; they give you a visual clue as to where you are about to place this panel. If you drop it on the edge of an existing frame, you will create a new frame at this location; if you drop it into the middle of an existing frame, this panel will be docked with the panel(s) already in that frame.

Drag the Layer panel to the left edge of its current frame and release the mouse. A new frame will be created between the Project and Comp panels for the Layer panel to reside in. (If you accidentally dropped it somewhere else, you cannot undo this; just pick it up again and drag it to its intended location.)

If you have a cramped display, you may want to place a panel into its own floating window that you can move around without disturbing the layout of your existing panels and frames. Click on the arrow in the upper right corner of the Layer panel's frame: This is its Options wing menu. (You can also right-click on a tab to view the Options menu.) The bottom of this menu contains options specific to the current frame. The top of this menu contains options that apply to all frames, including those for manipulating this panel or frame.

Select Undock Panel: The Layer panel will now become its own window (note that the Comp panel will automatically expand to fill in the space you just opened up in that frame). Resize and move this window around as desired; you can also dock other panels into this new window. Note that the textured dots still exist to the left of its tab: Click and drag these dots to the center of the Comp panel to re-dock the Layer panel.

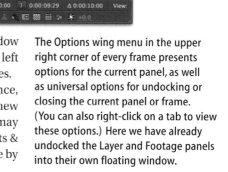

Opening New Panels

The Standard workspace opens only a few of the possible panels in After Effects. As mentioned earlier, the Window menu lists all of the possible panels. Open it; check marks down the left indicate which panels are currently open and forward in their frames.

Panels may not initially open where you want them. For instance, select Window > Tracker. In the Standard workspace, it creates a new frame below Effects & Presets and to the right of the Timeline. You may prefer that the Tracker panel is docked into the same frame as Effects & Presets above; practice moving it around; close it when you are done by clicking in the small **x** on its tab.

The Options wing menu in the upper right corner of every frame presents options for the current panel, as well as universal options for undocking or closing the current panel or frame. (You can also right-click on a tab to view these options.) Here we have already undocked the Layer and Footage panels into their own floating window.

Workspaces

Say you've opened, docked, and sized your panels and frames into an arrangement you like. You can save this for future use. Either click on the Workspace popup along the top right of the Application window or select the menu item Window > Workspace. At the bottom of these menus are choices to delete, reset, or create a new workspace. Select New Workspace and give your workspace a name you'll remember. This new workspace will remember the current arrangement, including floating windows and where currently closed panels should open if you reselect them from the Window menu.

You can continue to modify your current workspace; your changes will be remembered. To see this, close or open a panel after you've saved your workspace. Then open one of Adobe's default workspaces such as Animation. Next, select the name of your saved workspace from the Workspace menu – it will return to where you last left it, *not its state when you saved it*. To return the layout to the point where you saved it, select your workspace and choose Reset. (By the way, this applies to modifications of Adobe's default workspaces as well.)

Pressing Shift+F10, Shift+F11, or Shift+F12 allows you to quickly switch among your three favorites workspaces. To assign which those are, select a workspace and use Window > Assign Shortcut to "Current" Workspace.

Go ahead and practice rearranging, saving, recalling, and deleting workspaces. When you are done, choose Standard and reset it so that you have a known starting point to work through the rest of this book.

After Effects ships with many pre-arranged workspaces. You can save and recall your own; workspaces always remember their most recent layout. Use the Reset menu item to return a workspace to its originally saved state.

Creating a Composition

Procedures and shortcuts for setting up a blank canvas.

When you select a folder in the Project panel (Chapter 1), any new comps you create, or any footage you import, will be automatically placed inside this folder.

Example Project

Explore the 02-Example Project.aep file as you read this chapter; references to [Ex.##] refer to specific compositions within the project file.

Our goal in this chapter is to show you how to create a composition, add source footage as layers, and navigate in both space and time. Mastering these basic concepts, techniques, and shortcuts will prepare you for animating layers in the next few chapters. We'll also cover safe area, grid, guide, and ruler overlays in the Composition panel, as well as the all-important matter of previewing your work. Even if you're a more experienced user, you should skim this chapter to see if there are any shortcuts or tips you've been missing.

The New Composition

In After Effects, the *composition* ("comp" for short) is where you layer your source material, position and size the sources on your virtual canvas, and navigate through time. Open the accompanying **02-Example Project.aep** project file from this book's DVD (open the **Chapter Example Projects** folder, then the **02-Creating a Comp** folder).

To ensure that we are all on the same page, select the Standard workspace from the Workspaces menu (covered in Chapter 1), then select Workspace > Reset "Standard".

In the Project panel, click on the folder **Ex.00-First Comp** to select it; when you create a new comp, it will automatically go into the selected folder. There are several ways to create a new composition:

- select Composition > New Composition;
- use the shortcut Command+N on Mac (Control+N on Windows); or
- click the New Composition button at the bottom of the Project panel.

Whichever method you choose, when you select New Composition, you'll be presented with a dialog to set up the basic working parameters of your blank canvas. It is divided into two main tabbed sections: Basic and Advanced. The parameter settings in the Basic tab are all you need to worry about for now. After Effects remembers the last set of values you entered in Composition Settings and uses those as a starting point when you create a new comp; change them to the following settings:

- The first step is to give your new Composition a meaningful name. For this exercise, call it "**My Creation**".

You can type in pixel dimensions manually or use one of a number of presets from the Preset menu. Selecting the NTSC D1 preset from the Preset popup will set the parameters we'll be using for Width/Height, Pixel Aspect Ratio, and Frame Rate. If you'd rather enter these manually:

In the Basic tab, set the width and height to 720 and 486 pixels respectively. The overall aspect ratio of the comp is calculated to the right; you can lock in the current aspect ratio if you choose. If you do so, typing in one dimension will automatically update the other.

Set the Pixel Aspect Ratio popup to D1/DV NTSC (0.91).

For Frame Rate, we'll be using the NTSC video frame rate of 29.97 frames per second (fps). Other common rates include 25 for PAL video and 23.976 or 24 for high-definition video and film.

Selecting the NTSC D1 preset will set these parameters for you. In future, we will often instruct you to just select a preset.

- Resolution determines how many pixels are processed (more on this later in this chapter). Set its popup to Full for now.

- Leave the Start Timecode at 00:00 and set a relatively short Duration such as 10:00 (10 seconds).

- For the Background Color, click the color swatch and choose Black.

- Click on the Advanced tab just so you know what options it offers. If you must change the comp's size later, the Anchor selector in this section decides which area of the comp it will hold steady – it will expand or shrink the surrounding areas, keeping track of layer positions as it does. When you're making a new comp, the Anchor selector will be grayed out.

The Advanced tab is also where you set the Motion Blur amount (covered in Chapter 8) and the Nesting Options switches (Chapter 18). We won't be using any of these options in this chapter, so you can ignore the Advanced tab for now.

The Composition Settings contain tabbed sections: Basic (left) and Advanced (right). Once you create a comp, you can change any of these settings by selecting Composition > Composition Settings.

After Effects provides a number of preset composition frame sizes for some of the most common media formats. Using a preset automatically sets the Pixel Aspect Ratio to match the frame size and the frame rate, but you can override individual parameters.

Max Comp Size

Comps are limited (if limited is the right word) to a size of 30,000 x 30,000 pixels. Just stock up on RAM first…

TIP

Toggle Panels

Press \ (backslash) to toggle between the Comp and Timeline panels for the current composition.

• Click OK (you can also press Return or Enter), and the comp will be created. After Effects adds the **My Creation** comp to the list in the Project panel; if you selected the **Ex.00-First Comp** folder as we suggested, it will reside in this folder. (If you can't find a new comp, try to remember what was the last item you had selected in the Project panel; you can also search for the comp's name using the QuickSearch field at the top of the Project panel.)

After creating a new comp, two panels will display your comp's name across the top: the *Composition* panel (or "Comp" for short) and the *Timeline* panel. These panels include myriad buttons and switches. We'll discuss the most-used ones here; we'll dive into the tweakier ones later – particularly in Chapter 6.

The Composition Panel

The Comp panel is where you see the image you're creating, displayed at the current point in time, in sync with the Timeline panel. The center region is the active "stage" for your sources; the gray "pasteboard" around the outside is additional working area.

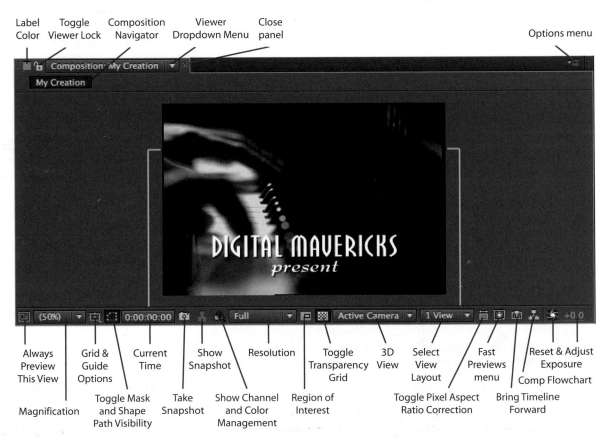

The Comp panel is where you arrange your source material (we've added some layers for added interest). The Comp view gives you a snapshot of the current point in time. Hover your cursor over any icon to see its tooltip. Footage courtesy Lee Stranahan.

Label Color · Time Display · Close (this tab only) · Composition Mini-Flowchart · QuickSearch · Live Update · Draft 3D · Hide Shy Layers · Enable Frame Blending · Enable Motion Blur · Brainstorm · Auto-Keyframe Properties · Graph Editor · Current Time Indicator · Comp Marker Bin · Options menu

Expand or Collapse the In/Out/Duration/Stretch panes

Expand or Collapse the Transfer Controls pane

Expand or Collapse the Layer Switches pane

Zoom out (in time) · Zoom in to frame level, or out to entire comp · Zoom in (in time) · Bring Comp panel forward

The Timeline Panel

The Timeline panel is your "sequencer," where you control the time at which the sources begin and end, and how they animate over time. The current time is displayed numerically in both the Comp and Timeline panels and is indicated by the Current Time Indicator (the yellow time marker) in the Timeline panel.

The Timeline panel contains a number of columns that display different parameters for the *layers* (source material) used in a composition, followed by the time ruler area.

You can right-click (Control+click on the Mac, right-click on Windows) on the top of any column to customize which columns are displayed. For example, After Effects defaults to opening the Parent column, which we won't be using in this chapter. If it's open now, practice closing it by right-clicking on its header, and select Hide This from the popup menu.

You can further customize the look of this panel: The column headers can be resized by dragging their right edges. You can also rearrange the columns by clicking the header and dragging left and right. For example, we prefer the A/V Features column (which includes the Keyframe Navigator arrows, discussed in Chaper 3) to be the rightmost column, closest to the time ruler. Any new comp you create will default to the last arrangement you used.

A companion to the Comp panel is the Timeline panel, where you navigate and arrange your sources in time. Because these panels work as a pair, when you open a comp from the Project panel, both the Comp and Timeline panels are displayed.

Right-clicking on the top of any column allows you to hide and show various columns as needed.

The A/V Features column (which includes the keyframe navigator arrows that appear when you enable animation for a layer) defaults to the far left side of the Timeline panel. Dragging this column closer to the time ruler area reduces mouse movements when editing keyframes.

Get Snappy

To make an already-placed layer snap to the edges of a comp or its center, press Command+Shift (Control+Shift) as you drag it around in the Comp panel.

When you add a new layer by drag-and-dropping it to the Composition panel, it will initially try to snap to the comp's edges and center. Footage courtesy Artbeats/Seascapes.

Adding Footage to a Comp

This chapter concentrates on the Comp and Timeline panels, but since you'll need some footage to practice with, go ahead and add a few sources to the **My Creation** comp. We've already imported various movies and objects in this chapter's example project; you'll find them in subfolders inside the **Sources** folder in the Project panel (twirl these folders open if they aren't already revealed). Feel free to import your own sources to play with. (Importing was discussed in Chapter 1.)

Note that in recent versions of After Effects, sources added to a comp (as well as those you create, such as text, shape and solid layers) *start by default at the beginning of the comp*. In older versions of After Effects, new layers started at the current time; if you preferred this behavior, turn off Preferences > General > Create Layers at Composition Start Time.

There are several ways to add footage to a comp (these methods also work when adding multiple sources at once):

• The obvious one is to drag a source straight from the Project panel to the Composition panel, placing it roughly where you want it on the comp's stage; it will helpfully "snap" to the edges or comp center. The footage will be placed at the top of the layer stack.

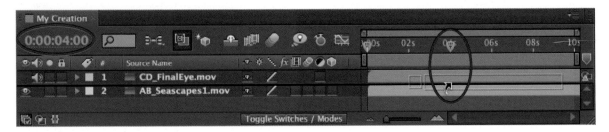

When dragging a new source to the Timeline panel, you can decide where it starts in time by carefully placing it along the timeline in the right side of the panel. You can also place it between existing layers: Note the black horizontal line, which indicates where the new source will be added in the stack. A second yellow time marker (circled in red) follows you as you drag, and the time display (also circled) updates to show the new layer's in point.

• Another way is to drag footage from the Project panel to the left side of the Timeline panel. This allows you to place it anywhere in the layer stack. What's not so obvious is that if you drag it to the timeline area under the ruler, you can also choose to start it at any point in time by dragging it left and right. If you are adding a source that has a fixed duration (such as a movie or a precomp), the Info panel will update in real time showing the in point and duration. Note that still images, solids, shape layers, and text layers have infinite duration.

• You can also drag footage onto a composition's icon in the Project panel; this will add footage at the top of the layer stack, centered in the Comp panel.

• Selecting a source in the Project panel and pressing Command+/ (Control+/) will also add it centered in the comp.

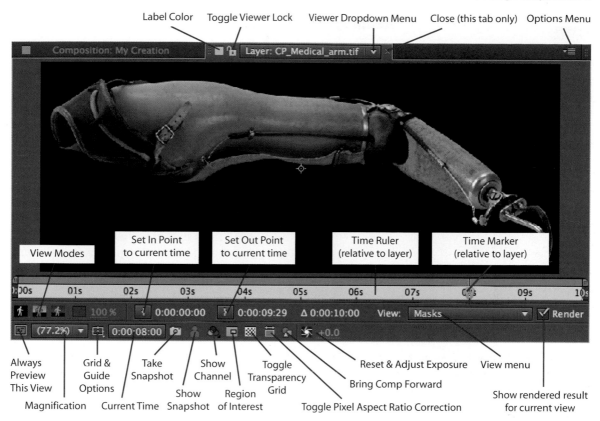

Label Color Toggle Viewer Lock Viewer Dropdown Menu Close (this tab only) Options Menu

View Modes

Set In Point to current time

Set Out Point to current time

Time Ruler (relative to layer)

Time Marker (relative to layer)

Always Preview This View

Magnification

Grid & Guide Options

Current Time

Take Snapshot

Show Snapshot

Show Channel

Region of Interest

Toggle Transparency Grid

Toggle Pixel Aspect Ratio Correction

Reset & Adjust Exposure

Bring Comp Forward

View menu

Show rendered result for current view

More on Layers

Once you add a source to a composition (or create one using the text or shape tools), it becomes known as a *layer*. The Video switch (the eyeball) determines the overall visibility of the layer. You can use the same source in as many comps as you want and as many times as you want in the same composition. Comps can also have an unlimited number of layers.

Layers typically stack with the topmost item in the Timeline panel being the forwardmost layer in the Comp panel. You can re-order this stacking by simply dragging layers up or down the list in the Timeline panel. (In Chapter 6, we will cover how to manage layers efficiently.)

When you double-click a layer*, you open the Layer panel (above), which is not unlike a "clip window" in other applications. We're introducing it here, but you'll be seeing more of it as you trim layers, create masks, use the Roto Brush and Paint tools, and perform other tasks.

Note that the Layer panel defaults to being docked with the Comp panel; you can toggle between the Comp and Layer panels by clicking on their tabs. If you prefer, you can also rearrange these panels to be side by side (see *Workspaces* in Chapter 1, as well as the technique on page 21).

* New in CS5: If the layer is a nested comp layer, the precomp may open – press Option (Alt) + double-click to open its Layer panel. (See Chapter 18.)

Double-click a layer to open it in its own Layer panel.* The Layer panel defaults to being docked with the Comp panel. Footage courtesy Classic PIO/Medical.

The View popup in the Layer panel allows you to preview the layer at any point in its render order (we've added some effects for interest). The None option shows the original source. The Render switch determines whether masks (Chapter 10) create transparency or whether effects are rendered.

Saving Comps

When you save a project, all comps are saved automatically. You don't need to save individual comps before closing their panels.

Keeping Tabs on Multiple Comps

You can create multiple comps in a single project file, and each comp has its own settings (set under Composition > Composition Settings). You can either render compositions separately, or build a hierarchy of comps where one comp becomes a source layer in another comp (this is called "nesting" and is covered in Chapter 18). As you create multiple comps, we strongly encourage you to give your comps useful names and to organize them inside folders inside the Project panel (see Chapter 1).

To review how multiple comps are managed, go ahead and open comps [**Ex.02a**] and [**Ex.02b**] from the Project panel; by default they open in the same Comp and Timeline panels. Multiple tabs start to accumulate along the top of the Timeline panel, each containing the name of a corresponding comp. Clicking on a tab brings the same comp forward in the Comp panel. Drag tabs left and right to reorder them.

Selecting the tab at the top of the Comp panel will drop down a menu where you can select another comp to view, lock the comp view, close the current comp, or close all comps.

Selecting a tab in the Timeline panel will bring forward the partner Composition. You can reorder tabs by dragging them left and right. Footage courtesy Artbeats/Business on the Go.

Closing Comps

To close a composition, in the Timeline panel click on the tiny "close" box near the tab's right edge. Its partner Comp panel will also close. Once all comps are closed (the tabs will say "None"), clicking the close box again will close the Timeline panel itself (oops!). Note that clicking the close box on the Comp panel's tab *will close the entire Comp panel*, not just the current comp (oops again!). Open any comp to restore these panels.

Rather than use the close buttons, we prefer the following shortcuts for closing comps quickly. In both cases, make sure either the Comp or Timeline panel is active (outlined in yellow):

Close comp*	Command+W (Control+W)
Close All comps**	Command+Shift+W (Control+Shift+W)

* closes contents of the active viewer or panel; then closes panel
** closes contents of all viewers of type of active viewer; then closes panel

Selecting the Comp panel's tab will drop down a menu where you can easily close all comps (without closing the Comp panel itself).

If the Project panel is active when you use these shortcuts, After Effects will close the project file if it was recently saved! Try not to panic; if you weren't prompted to Save, then the project hadn't changed since the last time you saved. Use the shortcut Command+Option+Shift+P (Control+Alt+Shift+P) to open the last project you were working on.

Footage = New Comp

If you want to create a new composition that exactly matches the size, duration, and frame rate of a particular source, in the Project panel you can drag that source to the Create a New Composition button at the bottom of the panel. If you drag a still image, the new comp will have the same duration as the last one you entered in the Composition Settings dialog. The new comp will be created in the same folder as the footage item, so you may want to move it later.

You can also drag multiple sources to this button. After Effects will give you the choice of creating an individual comp for each item you selected, or one comp that uses all of the sources. If you choose to create one comp, you can pick which source should be used to decide the comp's dimensions, and optionally sequence the sources one after the other. (Sequencing layers is discussed in detail in Chapter 6.)

A third way to create a comp is to drag a source item directly to the Render Queue panel (discussed in Chapter 42) – After Effects will create comps for them as if you had dragged them individually to the Create a New Composition button.

If you drag multiple sources to the Create a New Composition button, you have the choice of creating one comp per source, or one comp that contains all of the sources either stacked or sequenced one after the other.

Dragging a source to the Create a New Composition button creates a new comp with the same dimensions, duration, and frame rate as the source.

Side-by-Side View

When you have multiple comps open and want to see them side by side, you can use this handy shortcut. Select the Comp panel and press:

**Command+Option+Shift+N
(Control+Alt+Shift+N)**

This splits the frame containing the active viewer and creates a new viewer on the right that is locked. Selecting a different tab in the Timeline panel will load that comp into the left viewer. You can also use the left viewer for the Layer or Footage panels.

The "split frame" shortcut creates two comp viewers side by side, with the right viewer locked (circled above). This is particularly handy when working with nested comps. The Always Preview This View button determines which comp renders when you RAM Preview (covered later in this chapter).

Magnification can be set in the Comp panel popup, with various shortcuts, or with the Zoom tool. The default is to use the "Fit up to 100%" option; the actual zoom level will be displayed in parentheses.

To temporarily toggle to the Hand tool to pan around, hold the spacebar down (tapping the spacebar plays the comp).

Helping Hand

If you have a three-button mouse, use the middle mouse button to temporarily enable the Hand tool. This is especially useful for panning around a Footage or Layer panel for a source that may be much larger than your monitor can handle.

Navigating in Space

It is important to know that you're not stuck viewing the Comp panel at 100% Magnification – you can zoom in to get a detailed view or zoom out to see more of the pasteboard area around your comp's visible stage. The default Magnification is the "Fit up to 100%" option, which means the zoom level varies as the Comp panel is resized.

There are many ways to zoom around the Comp panel; we're going to focus on the ones we use the most. Note that with all these methods, the Comp panel will remain the same size.

To zoom in or out around a specific area, use the Zoom tool in the Tools panel (shortcut: Z). Click in the Comp panel to zoom in on the point where you click, or drag to marquee an area to zoom in on. To zoom out instead, hold down Option (Alt) before clicking.

The disadvantage of this method is that you have to revert to the Selection tool when you are done zooming. To *temporarily* switch to the Zoom tool, press and hold down the Z key (as opposed to tapping it), click to zoom in, then release the Z key. Your previous tool will be reselected automatically. Again, add the Option (Alt) key when clicking to zoom out instead.

Shortcuts for zooming around the center of the Comp panel include:

Zoom in   Command + = (Control + =) (equal sign, on main keyboard) or press the period key (.)

Zoom out   Command + – (Control + –) (hyphen, on main keyboard) or press the comma key (,)

You can use the Hand tool (shortcut: H) to move the image inside the visible area of the panel. Press V to revert to the Selection tool when you're done. Press Option+/ (Alt+/) to recenter the image in the comp.

The Hand tool can be *temporarily* toggled on by pressing and holding down the spacebar, as opposed to tapping the spacebar which starts a Standard Preview (previewing is covered at the end of this chapter).

Mouse Wheel Scrolling

If your mouse includes a scroll wheel, additional options for scrolling in space and time await you:

• To zoom into or out of the *center* of the Comp or Layer panels, roll the mouse wheel normally. In the Timeline, Project, and Render Queue panels or the Effects & Presets panel, this scrolls vertically.

• To zoom into or out of the *area under the mouse pointer*, add the Option (Alt) key. In the Timeline panel, this will zoom in and out of time.

• To scroll horizontally in the Timeline, Project, or Render Queue panels, add the Shift key.

Note: *The panel under the mouse pointer scrolls, even if a different panel is currently active (outlined in yellow).*

Solid Information

You can create Solid layers of a single color to use as graphic elements, as a background layer, or as a container for effects that generate imagery. Solid layers can be any size (up to 30,000 × 30,000 pixels), and once created can have any length.

If you're not familiar with solids, create one to work with:

• Open any comp, and type Command+Y (Control+Y) or select Layer > New > Solid. The Solid Footage Settings dialog opens. It includes a handy button to automatically size it to fill the comp, or you can enter any values in pixels or as a percentage of the Comp. Set the color using the eyedropper or by clicking on the color swatch. The default name is a reflection of the color, but for this exercise, name it "**My Solid**". Click OK; your new solid appears as the top layer in the current comp.

• With this layer selected, select Edit > Duplicate a couple of times so you have three copies.

• In the Project panel, locate and expand the Solids folder. Your new solid is automatically stored in this folder as a single piece of source footage (even though it appears three times in your comp). It can also be dragged to any other comp. If you edit the solid by selecting Layer > Solid Settings when the Project panel is forward, all instances of this solid will be changed.

• When multiple layers are referencing the same solid source, you have the option to change all instances or create a new solid from inside the comp. Select the topmost solid layer, then open Layer > Solid Settings. Take a note of the "Affect all layers that use this solid" switch at the bottom, and then make sure it is off (it defaults to its last state). Change the color of the solid, rename it "**My Solid 2**", and click OK. **My Solid 2** is also created in the Solids folder; the other two layers continue to use the first color.

In the Solid Footage Settings dialog, you can set the Units popup to create solids based on pixels or a percentage of the comp size. Solids also have their own pixel aspect ratio (PAR is covered in Chapter 41).

When you edit Solid Footage Settings while the comp is forward, you can choose whether any changes affect all instances of this solid or whether a new solid is created for this one instance. The Preview switch is new in CS5.

Solids are particularly useful when used as containers for various effects (see *Effects and Solids* in Chapter 22). Solids also form the basis of Adjustment Layers (Chapter 22) and Null Objects (Chapter 17); when you create an adjustment layer or null, they are also stored in the Solids folder in the Project panel.

Pixels or Vectors

Solid layers normally render as pixels, so when you increase their scale value, edges will appear soft and fuzzy. You have the option to treat solids as vector layers by toggling on their Continuously Rasterize switch in the Timeline (see figure, right). With this switch enabled, transformations are applied directly to the  vectors, and edges will appear sharp at any scale value. However, this means that effects will render after transformations and may not animate normally. In some cases, it may be better to resize the solid in Solid Settings and leave this switch off. (Continuous rasterization is covered in detail in Chapter 20.)

Resolution determines how many pixels should be processed. You can set it to Auto, Full, Half, Third, or Quarter from the menu in the Comp panel – or select Custom to set a different number of pixels and lines to be skipped.

Examples of different Resolution settings. Footage courtesy Artbeats/Gears.

Resolution

Separate from a composition's magnification or zoom factor is its *Resolution*. This tells After Effects how many pixels to render when it's calculating images to show in the Comp or Layer panels. The current setting is indicated by the popup along the bottom of the Comp panel; it can be set using this popup, from the menu via View > Resolution, in the Composition Settings dialog, or by using the following shortcuts:

Full Resolution	**Command+J (Control+J)**
Half Resolution	**Command+Shift+J (Control+Shift+J)**
Quarter Resolution	**Command+Shift+Option+J (Control+Shift+Alt+J)**

Full Resolution   Half Resolution   Quarter Resolution

Full Resolution means After Effects calculates every pixel in a composition. Half Resolution calculates only every other horizontal pixel as well as every other vertical line, resulting in only every fourth pixel being rendered – so calculations proceed up to four times as fast. You can experiment with this in [**Ex.01a**]. The other resolutions follow the same scheme. For example, Quarter calculates every fourth pixel and every fourth line, resulting in calculations proceeding up to 16 times as fast.

When Resolution is reduced and Magnification is at 100%, the missing pixels are filled in with duplicates, resulting in a more pixelated look. That's why it's common to set Magnification to 50% when the Resolution is at Half, so that you're displaying only the pixels being calculated. Also, avoid wasting time by having After Effects calculate every pixel (Full Resolution) when the zoom level dictates they will not all be displayed. Setting Resolution to Auto keeps the resolution in sync with magnification in order to boost efficiency, and is a good default to use.

If you are working with larger frame sizes such as film or hi-def, create your comps at the final output size and use reduced resolution to work more efficiently. Screen updates and previews occur much faster, and most effects properly scale to look more or less the same at reduced resolution. (Don't design at a smaller comp size as it will be problematic to resize the comp after you have arranged and animated your sources.)

Another reason to reduce the Resolution setting is to free up more RAM for previewing. For instance, setting the Resolution to Half allows you to render four times as many frames with the same amount of RAM. (More on this in *Preview Possibilities*, at the end of this chapter.)

Auto Resolution

The Auto setting under Resolution was added in CS4. When Auto is selected, changes to the Magnification of the Comp panel will result in the Resolution setting automatically being changed to match. For example, if you set Magnification to 50%, After Effects will set Resolution to Half to ensure that only the pixels you see will be rendered. This is the most efficient way to work. The main gotcha to be aware of is that some effects look radically different at lower Resolution settings, so it is a good idea to always go back to 100% Magnification/Full Resolution to double-check your work before rendering.

Quality

Different from both Magnification and Resolution is Quality. Whereas the first two are parameters that affect an entire composition, Quality is set on a layer-by-layer basis in the Timeline panel. Along the top of the Switches/Modes column, Quality is the switch with the backward-leaning slash. The choices are Best, Draft, and Wireframe. Clicking on the Quality switch for a layer toggles it between Draft and Best.

The default for new layers is to use Best Quality (a forward-leaning slash). In Best Quality, the layer is calculated with the highest precision whenever you change any of its parameters that require pixels to be resampled. Of course, this takes longer to process.

If the switch for a layer is a backward-leaning slash (the same as the column header), the layer is set to Draft mode, where it will render using the faster "nearest neighbor" method. This means it will look pretty crunchy whenever you scale, rotate, or otherwise cause a change to the image that requires resampling pixels. Experiment with this in [**Ex.01b**]; note that Illustrator sources are not antialiased in Draft mode.

In earlier versions the default was to use Draft Quality, which speeds up your workflow. If you'd prefer this behavior, toggle off the Create New Layers at Best Quality switch in Preferences > General.

There is one more Quality option: Wireframe. This reduces a layer to just its outline with an X through its middle – really fast to draw, but not visually informative. It you really need it, you can set a selected layer to this mode with Layer > Quality > Wireframe or by a keyboard shortcut.

To set multiple layers to Best or Draft Quality, click on the first switch and drag down the layer stack, or first select the layers and then change the Quality for one of them. The keyboard shortcuts for Quality are:

Best Quality	Command+U (Control+U)
Draft Quality	Command+Shift+U (Control+Shift+U)
Wireframe Quality	Command+Shift+Option+U (Control+Shift+Alt+U)

Magnification, Resolution, and Quality may seem confusing if you're a beginning user, but you will come to appreciate the flexibility they give you to work more efficiently. If needed, you can optimize your workflow by having After Effects think less while you're editing and previewing, such as by working at 50% Magnification and Half Resolution, with some layers set to Draft Quality. When it comes time to render, you can override these switches in Render Settings and render all comps at Full Resolution and all layers at Best Quality without having to set switches manually (more on these settings in Chapter 42, *Render Queue*).

FACTOID

Smooth Moves

When layers are set to Best Quality, layers use subpixel positioning for smoother moves (more on this in Chapter 3).

Click on the Quality switch to toggle between Draft (broken line) and Best (solid line). When you render a movie, the Render Settings can override these settings and force all layers to render in Best Quality.

The difference between Draft Quality (above) and Best Quality (below) can be seen whenever layers are scaled and rotated. Distortion effects, such as Twirl, also render more smoothly in Best.

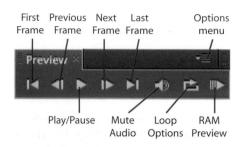

First Frame • Previous Frame • Next Frame • Last Frame • Options menu

Play/Pause • Mute Audio • Loop Options • RAM Preview

The Preview panel can be used for navigation, though we find the shortcuts on an extended keyboard to be more convenient.

In the Timeline panel, you can change the current frame being viewed by either dragging the current time indicator or by scrubbing the current time value (above). New in CS5: Click on the current value and enter a new time directly.

Clicking on the time display in the Comp panel (above) opens the Go To Time dialog (below) where you can enter a specific time to jump to.

Navigating in Time

In After Effects, the concept of the "current time" is very important, as most events such as setting keyframes happen at the frame currently being displayed in the Comp panel. Learning to navigate in time efficiently involves learning a few shortcuts.

Graphically, you can grab and drag the current time indicator (known as the CTI) left and right, which will change the current frame you are viewing in the Comp panel as fast as your computer can render. (This behavior is called Live Update, and is covered in more detail in *Preview Possibilities* at the end of this chapter.) If you want to move the CTI along the timeline without realtime updating, hold down the Option (Alt) key and the Comp panel will render only when you mouse up. You can also simply click in the ruler in the Timeline panel to jump to a new time. Pressing the Shift key as you drag the CTI will force it to snap to layer in and out points, keyframes, and comp and layer markers (Chapter 6).

To move to a new time numerically, you can click on the current time display in the Timeline panel and enter a new time directly (clicking the current time in the Comp or Layer panels will bring up the Go To Time dialog box). The time units used in these displays are set by a preference that we'll discuss later in this chapter in the *Frame Rate = Time Grid* sidebar.

While you can step through time in the Preview panel, the following keyboard shortcuts work great for stepping through time (an extended keyboard is recommended; equivalent commands are listed in the online Help > Keyboard Shortcuts):

Go to beginning	Home
Go to end	End
Forward one frame	Page Down
Forward 10 frames	Shift+Page Down
Backward one frame	Page Up
Backward 10 frames	Shift+Page Up

After Effects' concept of time is such that each frame starts at the frame increments in the Timeline panel and expires just before the next frame increment. If you use the End keyboard shortcut above to jump to the "end" of a composition, the time marker locates to a position just short of all the way to the right. The current time indicator will also seem to be one frame short of the total duration of the comp – for example, 09:29 is the last frame in a 10-second-long, 30-fps comp. After Effects stops here because this is the beginning of the last visible frame; go one frame further, and you would be beyond the last frame.

Zooming in Time

You can also "zoom" in time. The Timeline panel allows you to decide what portion of time it is displaying. This becomes more important when we start animating in future chapters: You may need to zoom in to look at the detail of a set of rapid-fire keyframes, or zoom out and get an overview of how a project flows.

There are a couple of graphical ways to zoom around this panel. One is click on the "mountain" buttons at the bottom of the Timeline panel to zoom in or out. As you drag the pointer between them, the degree of zoom updates in real time, centering the visible portion of time on the current time represented by the current time indicator.

We prefer to use the resizable Time Navigator bar, which appears *above* the time ruler in the Timeline panel. Dragging on the ends of this bar sets the start and end times of the visible portion of the timeline. If the navigator bar does not encompass the entire time ruler, you can then drag the bar left and right to slide the visible area in time.

Of course, there are also keyboard shortcuts for zooming in time:

Zoom in time	**= (equal sign, on main keyboard)**
Zoom out time	**– (hyphen, on main keyboard)**
Zoom to/from frame view	**; (semicolon), or**
	double-click the time navigator bar
Toggle to/from entire composition view	
	Shift + ; (semicolon), or
	Shift+double-click the time navigator bar

If your mouse includes a scroll wheel, refer to Mouse Wheel Scrolling earlier in this chapter for more options for navigating in time.

The Time Navigator bar in the Timeline panel allows you to change what portion of the timeline you are looking at. Slide the navigator's bar left and right to move this zoom area. New in CS5: Clicking on the time navigator displays its start and end times in the Info panel.

TIP

Centering Time

Using = and – to zoom the Timeline view does not center on the current time indicator. To recenter the displayed area of time around the CTI, press the D key after zooming.

The Work Area

You can also define a *work area* time range in a comp. RAM Previewing a comp uses the currently set work area as the section to preview (not the area of the timeline you are zoomed in on); you may also render just the work area portion of a comp in Render Settings.

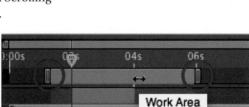

The work area is defined by a resizable bar in the Timeline panel that resides directly *below* the time ruler. It has yellow handles at its ends to adjust its length; you can grab the middle of it and slide it left and right to reposition while maintaining the same duration. The work area's length is visually reinforced by a lighter gray area in the Timeline panel.

When it comes to dragging the work area's start and end points, note that After Effects will not allow you to drag one end point past the other. On the other hand, if the current time is past the end of the work area, pressing the B key will move the work area section to begin at this new time, maintaining the same duration.

Drag the start and end of the work area bar to resize it; grab the center area (where the cursor is) to slide it in time. The keyboard shortcuts B and N set its beginning and end to the current time, respectively. Double-click the bar to reset it to the full length of the comp. New in CS5: Clicking on the work area bar displays its start and end times in the Info panel along with its duration.

Right-clicking on the work area bar brings up a menu with three editing options, which we will cover in Chapter 7, *Trimming Layers*.

There are useful keyboard shortcuts for setting the work area:

Render Lock

To stop the Comp or Layer panel from rendering the current frame, engage the Caps Lock key. If you then try to edit the comp, a red line along the bottom of the panel warns you "Refresh Disabled."

Set work area beginning to current time	B
Set work area end to current time	N
Set work area to length of selected layers	Command+Option+B (Control+Alt+B)
Go to beginning of work area	Shift+Home
Go to end of work area	Shift+End
Reset work area to length of comp	Double-click center of work area bar

The Choose Grid and Guide Options button offers a menu of overlays to help with positioning layers. To simply toggle on/off the Title/Action Safe grid, Option+click (Alt+click) this button.

Visual Aids

After Effects has several ways of adding overlays to the Comp panel that can come in handy when you're positioning layers: Title/Action Safe, Proportional Grid, Grid, Guides, and Rulers. In addition, the 3D Reference Axes are available when working with 3D layers (Chapter 13).

Safe Areas

A significant portion of a composition you are creating for video or film playback may not be visible once it is projected. Video images are "over-scanned" in that they extend beyond the edges of the picture tube's bezel to conceal irregularities in aging or maladjusted sets. Even motion pictures have their edges cropped to neaten up projection. Therefore, it is common to use a "safe area" overlay to remind yourself what portion of the frame is a danger zone.

In normal video, the *action safe* area is considered to be inset 5% from the outer edges all the way around an image (10% in all); assume that some viewers won't see imagery in the action safe zone. Older picture tubes in particular distort an image more around the edges. Therefore, there is also a *title safe* area, which is inset an additional 5% from action safe (for a total of 20% of the image in each dimension). It is considered unwise to put any text or other critical information outside this title safe area, lest it be unreadable to the viewer. We have set up an example in [**Ex.02a**].

The "safe areas" are shown in [**Ex.02a**]. This overlay can be toggled on and off on a comp-by-comp basis.

Safe areas are covered in more detail in Chapter 41, including center-cut safe zones for widescreen content.

You can change the default settings for the safe areas in File > Preferences > Grids & Guides.

There are a couple of shortcuts to toggle the safe areas overlay on and off: Option+click (Alt+click) on the Choose Grid and Guide Options button in the Comp panel, or press the apostrophe key.

Grids

Grids are handy when you need help visualizing the comp in halves or thirds, or you need help delineating a specific number of pixels of spacing. After Effects has two options to overlay a grid of evenly spaced lines onto the Composition panel: Grid and Proportional Grid.

To display the Grid, select Grid from the Choose Grid and Guide Options menu or select View > Show Grid. Once they are on, View > Snap to Grid sets the ability for layers to snap to the grid. The shortcuts are:

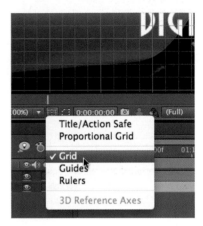

How the various Grids are displayed can be defined in Preferences > Grids & Guides (above). Below is an example of the Grid overlaid on the Comp panel.

Toggle Grid:	Command+' (apostrophe)
Toggle Snap to Grid:	Command+Shift+' (apostrophe)

The Proportional Grid divides the Comp panel into a simple number of divisions, such as thirds. The Proportional Grid cannot be displayed at the same time as safe areas, and layers do not snap to this grid. To display this grid, select Proportional Grid from the Choose Grid and Guide Options menu, or use this keyboard command:

Toggle Proportional Grid: Option+' (apostrophe)

You can set the defaults for both grids in Preferences > Grids & Guides.

Rulers and Guides

Finally, there are rulers and user-definable guides which will be familiar to users of other Adobe applications. Rulers reinforce the X and Y coordinates of a comp (in pixels) and can be displayed by selecting Rulers from the Choose Grid menu or by selecting View > Show Rulers.

If rulers are visible, you may also create guides. To make a new guide, click and hold the mouse button down in the ruler margins, drag the mouse into the Comp panel area, and release where you want the guide. The Info panel will tell you the precise position you are dragging the guides to. Use View > Lock Guides to protect them from being moved accidentally. Drag them back to the rulers to delete them; you can also select View > Clear Guides to delete all guides at once.

Guides are handy aids for lining up multiple layers in the Comp panel, either visually or by turning on the View > Snap to Guides feature. Check out [**Ex.02b**] where we've created some guides and simple Solids for you to experiment with. You can view guides with the rulers turned off, but you can't create guides without rulers. Again, rulers and guides also have keyboard shortcuts:

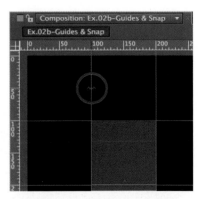

Drag out guides from the rulers that appear around the edges of the Comp panel; enable View > Snap to Guides to help position objects. Their color and appearance can be defined in Preferences > Grids & Guides.

Toggle Rulers:	Command+R (Control+R)
Toggle Guides:	Command+; (Control+;) (semicolon)
Snap to Guides:	Command+Shift+; (Control+Shift+;)
Lock Guides:	Command+Shift+Option+; (Control+Shift+Alt+;)

Frame Rate = Time Grid

Frame rate is an important concept: It defines how often new image frames are read from a source, and how many times per second new frames are calculated during a render. The comp's frame rate does not alter the frame rate of any sources; it sets the time intervals at which sources are sampled and where animation keyframes can be placed.

Each composition can have its own frame rate, set inside Composition > Composition Settings. However, when you render the comp, the frame rate in Render Settings will override the comp's frame rate. (The exception to this is if you enable the Preserve Frame Rate switch under the Advanced Tab in Composition Settings; we'll cover this in Chapter 18.)

For example, if your source material is 23.976 frames per second, setting the frame rate of a comp it is in to 29.97 fps does not speed it up, nor create original frames where there were none before. To see this, open the comp **[Ex.03]** in this chapter's example project. Step through the comp using the Page Up and Down keys. You will see some frames of the source repeated, because the time steps in your comp are smaller than the steps at which new frames appear in the source. Open Composition Settings and change the comp's frame rate to 23.976 fps: Now one frame in the comp equals one frame in the source.

It is usually a good idea to set the composition's frame rate to the rate you intend to render at, so as you step through the timeline, you'll see the points in time that will be rendered. It is usually *not* a good idea to change a comp's frame rate after you have started adding layers, as the layer start and end points – as well as any animation keyframes you set – will remain at the points in time you set them under the old frame rate. If you need to render at a different frame rate, change it in the Render Settings.

Displaying Time

After Effects has three different ways of displaying time: the SMPTE (Society of Motion Picture and Television Engineers) format, the number of frames since the beginning, and the film measurement style of feet and frames. You can set which one you want to use under File > Project Settings or cycle through them by Command+clicking (Control+clicking) on the time displays in the Comp and Timeline panels.

SMPTE timecode is represented as hours:minutes:seconds:frames. Although you can choose any frame rate for a comp, only the most common "timebases" – such as 30, for NTSC video – may be selected in the Timecode Base popup for display (the timebase display has no effect on how you actually *step through* frames in a comp). If possible, use a timebase that matches your comp's frame rate; Auto is correct most of the time.

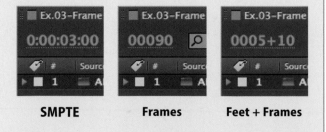

The Project Settings (above) allow you to select the display style, timebase, and frame offset of the counting method throughout the project. You can also Command+click (Control+click) on the time readouts in the Comp and Timeline panels to rotate through these three styles; these different display styles are shown below.

SMPTE	**Frames**	**Feet + Frames**

There is no timebase of 29.97, as fractional frames cannot be easily displayed inside the SMPTE time-code format – 30 is used instead. The NTSC popup brings up a pair of options for counting methods: "Drop Frame" and "Non-Drop Frame."

The Drop Frame timecode attempts to resolve the difference between 29.97 and 30 by skipping certain frame *numbers* (not image frames; just the numbers used to label those frames) in the timeline. It is confusing, and almost never used for projects under a half hour in length. Unless you know precisely why you want drop frame counting, leave this preference at its default setting of Non-Drop Frame. (Note that earlier versions defaulted to Drop Frame.)

In non-drop frame mode, the timecode numbers are separated by colons (if you were to switch to non-drop frame counting, you'll see semicolons instead). After Effects allows you to type in a SMPTE number without the colons; it will fill them in automatically. You also don't need to type in any leading zeroes. As an example, typing a number such as 110 will take you to 0:00:01:10 in the composition. After Effects also supports the common shorthand of typing a period where you want a colon to appear and filling the blanks with zeroes; for example, typing "**1..3**" results in a timecode of 0:01:00:03.

If you type in any two-digit number that is greater than the number of frames in a second, the program will calculate how many seconds and frames it works out to – for example, typing in 70 with a timebase of 30 fps results in the time 2 seconds and 10 frames. Finally, you can type in a positive time offset, such as +15, and After Effects will add this time to the current time and advance 15 frames. To subtract (or back up) 15 frames, you must enter + –15 (typing simply –15 will jump to 15 frames before the beginning).

Most nonvideo animators, and many working with film, prefer the "frames" counting method. It simply refers to which frame you are on from the start of the comp. You can set a frame offset in Project Setting. It is usually used to adjust between those who count "0" as the first frame and those who count "1" as first.

You can skip the colons and leading zeroes when you're typing in SMPTE time code numbers. For example, 110 equals 00:00:01:10.

Many traditional film editors prefer a "feet+frames" counting method, which was initially used to measure the literal physical length of film involved for a shot. Neither options are directly related to film's typical frame rate of 24 per second: 35mm film has 16 frames per foot; 16mm film has 40 frames per foot. Odd yes, but you get used to it. The first frame in each foot is counted as 0; the frame start number parameter also offsets this count.

Each comp can also have its own start offset, which defines what timecode value, frame number, or feet+frame value is used for the first frame in your comp. This offset is for display only, and can be edited in the Composition Settings.

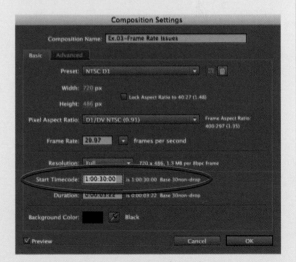

You can enter a custom start time for each comp. This number is used for display only.

Option+click (Alt+click) on the Show Channel button to view the comp's alpha channel; repeat to return to RGB.

RGB Straight may look disconcerting, but is actually the preferred output style when rendering a movie with an alpha.

Show Channel

When After Effects displays an image, internally it is thinking of the Red, Green, Blue, and Alpha channels that make up that image. The Show Channel and Color Management Settings menu at the bottom of the Comp panel lets you view these channels individually.

Of great use is the Alpha Channel, where you can view the comp's overall alpha in isolation. Open comp [**Ex.04**]. If the Opacity property for **solid layer** is not already visible, select the layer and press T to reveal it. Click on the Opacity value, enter "**50**", and press Return. The RGB image will appear darker in the Comp panel, but what's really changed is the value of its alpha channel. Select Alpha from the Show Channel menu and notice that the alpha channel for the solid layer appears as 50% gray (if you drag your mouse cursor over it, the Info panel will display a value of 128 out of a 0-to-255 range).

The Show Channel Colorize option displays channels with their color rather than as grayscale. The RGB Straight option shows how the frame would look if you were to render with a straight alpha channel. (Straight alpha is covered in Chapters 38 and 42.)

The other settings in this menu are covered in Chapter 26, *Color Management*.

Don't forget to return to viewing the regular RGB channels when you're done…

Color Picker

After Effects defaults to using the Adobe Color Picker to select colors. Its interface is modeled after the Photoshop color picker, so many of you will feel right at home. You can enter color values numerically in the appropriate fields (HSB, RGB, or hexademical) or choose colors interactively. The top color swatch shows the latest color choice, while the bottom color swatch shows the original color.

If you are not familiar with choosing and editing colors, press F1 (or select Help > After Effects Help) and search for Adobe Color Picker.

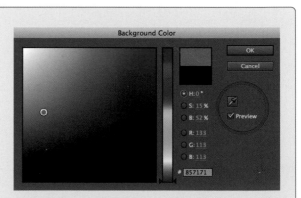

The Color Picker eyedropper can pick up a color from anywhere on the screen; note the interactive Preview switch.

Note: *If you'd prefer to use the color picker that comes with your system, open Preferences > General and toggle on the Use System Color Picker switch.*

The Background Color

The background color is a temporary backplate used to make viewing the contents of a Comp or Layer panel easier. It defaults to black, but there are occasions, such as when masking dark layers or using black text, when a different color would be better. You can change this color on a comp-by-comp basis in Composition > Composition Settings; the shortcut is Command+K (Control+K). Practice changing it with [**Ex.04**]. You can either eyedropper another color from elsewhere on screen, or click the color swatch to bring up the color picker. This color will be used for all new comps you create.

Some programs, such as Photoshop, depict transparent areas as a checkerboard pattern. If you prefer this view, you can set it by clicking the Toggle Transparency Grid button at the bottom of the Comp or Layer panels.

New in CS5: The background color is now set in the Composition Settings dialog, and also sports a handy new Preview button. This color is also used as a background in the Layer panel and for all new comps you create.

Black versus Black

It is important to differentiate between the background color and a color that resides in the comp's RGB color channels. Open [**Ex.05**], where we have placed some black layers against a black background color. The layers are not visible until you toggle the transparency grid on. The black solid and text both exist as pixels in the RGB channels – the black background is "transparency." In later chapters, where you'll nest one comp inside another, you'll also notice that the background color becomes transparent when a comp is nested into another comp.

Set Show Channel to Alpha: The background color will appear as black (fully transparent), and the black layers will appear as white (fully opaque). Change the background color (Composition > Background Color) to blue, and note that the color has no effect on the comp's alpha channel.

If you render as an RGB-only movie, the background color will be used as the background for the movie, so set the color accordingly.

If you render this comp as an RGB+Alpha movie with a Straight alpha channel (the preferred workflow), the background will render as black regardless of the RGB channels; where the background color was visible will result in "transparency" in the alpha. (If you render with a Premultiplied alpha, the background's color will be factored into the semitransparent areas of your objects.) More on these options in Chapter 42.

If you really want a composition's background to consist of pixels in RGB space, create a solid layer the same size as the comp, set to your designed background color, and send it to the bottom of your layer stack.

Black layers on a black background are not visible until you toggle on the transparency grid or change the background color.

CONNECT

Animating transformations: Chapters 3 and 4.

Opacity: Chapter 3.

Working with multiple comp views in 3D space: Chapter 13.

Nesting compositions: Chapter 18.

Continuous rasterization: Chapter 20.

Alpha channels: Chapter 38.

Conforming the frame rate: Chapter 38.

Pixel aspect ratios: Chapter 41.

Render settings: Chapter 42.

Preview Possibilities

After Effects provides several methods for checking your work as you go. Mastering them will help you work much faster and be more confident that your "final" render will indeed be close to final. However, you don't need to master them all right now; we'll tell you what you need to know as you work through this book – so feel free to revisit this section later.

We divide previewing into two general groups:

• **Interactive Previews**, in which After Effects updates the image in the Comp panel as fast as it can while you tweak a parameter or scrub the time indicator.

• **RAM Previews**, in which After Effects renders a portion of your timeline and plays it back at normal speed on your computer screen as a test before you commit to a full render of your composition.

In this section, we'll explain the different options After Effects offers for these techniques. We'll then cover other related issues, including disk caching, previewing audio, multiprocessing, and viewing your work through a true video output.

Interactive Previews

Whenever you update a parameter or the current time indicator in After Effects, it renders the result and displays it in the Comp panel. Because you can move your mouse faster than After Effects can calculate complex images, After Effects employs a few different strategies to keep up the best it can. You can choose between strategies for each comp by selecting the different modes offered in the Fast Previews popup at the bottom of the Comp panel; additional project-wide controls are accessed in Preferences > Previews.

To try out these different modes for yourself, open **[Ex.06]** in this chapter's Example Project. Fast Previews is currently set to Off; drag the current time indicator in the timeline while in this mode to get a feel for your computer's baseline speed. This comp is built in 3D space as 3D is particularly render intensive; the same concepts apply to 2D layers.

Note that if you have already cached frames of your comp into RAM (noted by a green line over portions of the timeline), After Effects will use those

If you don't want After Effects to interactively update the Comp panel while you edit parameters, disable the Live Updates button along the top of the Timeline panel. To temporarily disable live updates as you drag the current time indicator, hold down the Option (Alt) key.

frames instead of generating new ones, which will alter your perception of how fast a particular Fast Preview mode happens to be. For a fairer test, you can clear the RAM cache before previewing by turning a layer off and back on again or by using Edit > Purge > Image Caches.

Here is how each of the Fast Previews modes responds when you scrub the current time indicator or the parameter values for one of the layers:

Off: After Effects tries to render every frame or parameter update requested as fast as it can at the comp's current Resolution. If it can't keep up with your movements, it will skip frames and try to render the most recent frame or value requested. The Fast Previews button appears "deselected" (light gray) when set to Off.

The Fast Previews button at the bottom of every Comp panel decides how After Effects will display an image while you interactively scrub a parameter or drag the time indicator. The lightning bolt will turn yellow while OpenGL is operating. Click on the Fast Previews button to see the list of preview options (below); your selection is made on a comp-by-comp basis. The last entry is a shortcut to Preferences > Previews.

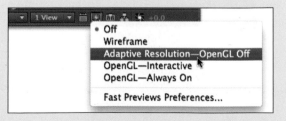

The Fast Previews options are set in Preferences > Previews. Adaptive Resolution Limit decides how many pixels are thrown away in this mode. You can also disable OpenGL on a project-wide basis in this dialog. The Accelerate Effects Using OpenGL option determines whether OpenGL is used to render some effects; the fallback when scrubbing effects parameters while Fast Previews is enabled is Adaptive Resolution mode.

Wireframe: In this seldom-used mode, After Effects skips rendering the pixels for each layer, instead rendering the layers as wireframe outlines. Select this mode with **[Ex.06]** to get a feel for it. RAM Previews are rendered normally.

Adaptive Resolution–OpenGL Off: If After Effects can't keep up with your gestures, in this mode it will temporarily lower the Resolution setting for the Comp panel, meaning it has to calculate fewer pixels (and can therefore render faster). Experiment with this mode by selecting it and dragging the current time indicator in **[Ex.06]** and **[Ex.07]**. Adaptive Resolution may be used in conjunction with OpenGL (set in Preferences > Previews), or by itself.

How low After Effects will go is set by the Adaptive Resolution Limit popup in Preferences > Previews.

The default is 1/4, which means at its slowest After Effects will calculate only every fourth pixel on a line and every fourth line, duplicating pixels and lines as needed to fill out the entire image. Although the image will temporarily look pixelated, the advantage is that everything – all effects, 3D lights and shadows, camera depth of field, et cetera – are calculated. When you release the mouse, After Effects redraws the image at full resolution.

OpenGL–Interactive and **OpenGL–Always On:** To use OpenGL, it must first be enabled in Preferences > Previews, then one of the OpenGL modes must be selected from the Fast Previews popup. When OpenGL mode is engaged, After Effects uses the OpenGL chip included with your video card, bypassing its own software-based rendering engine to take advantage of OpenGL's hardware acceleration. The result is much faster interaction. The downside is that some features are not supported by OpenGL. A full list of what features OpenGL is capable of accelerating can be found in Help > After Effects Help; search for "Render with OpenGL". Features that are not supported are not calculated.

Try scrubbing the time indicator in **[Ex.06]** with either of the OpenGL modes enabled: There will initially be a slight pause as the source images are loaded into the image buffer on the video card, but then After Effects will respond quickly to your movements. This speed comes at the occasional expense of image accuracy.

Continued on next page/

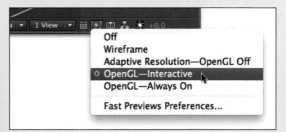

The two OpenGL Fast Preview modes employ the hardware acceleration available on your video card to draw draft versions of your composition faster – especially when you're working in 3D space.

Adaptive Resolution trades off a pixelated image in the name of speed. Footage courtesy Lee Stranahan.

/continued from previous page

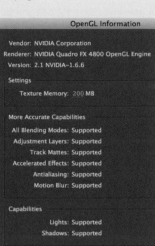

Found via
Preferences >
Previews, the
OpenGL Information
dialog tells you what
forms of accelera-
tion your card
supports and allows
you to reserve
Texture Memory
on your video card.

Faster OpenGL cards can render lights and shadows, although subtle details such as soft shadows can be lost. Images courtesy Digital Vision/Music Mix and All That Jazz.

As different OpenGL chips have different capabili-ties, how accurate the accelerated render is – and how fast it is performed – may vary from computer to computer. Adobe keeps a chart of approved cards, as well as the features they support, online at *www.adobe.com/products/aftereffects/opengl.html*. You can also open Preferences > Previews and click on OpenGL Info to see what your card supports.

The most common performance variable is whether lights (with a limit of eight per composition) and shadows are rendered. To test your system, open **[Ex.06]**. Set Fast Previews to OpenGL–Interactive and drag the time indicator: See if the shadows and vignetted lighting persist or disappear. Even if your system supports lights and shadows, you may not be pleased with the look of OpenGL; for example, Shadow Diffusion (the feathered edges on a 3D light's shadow) are currently ignored. Additionally, in **[Ex.06]** the Light Transmission setting for the layers (which casts shadows based on the image content, rather than a solid black shadow) is also ignored while OpenGL is engaged.

The more memory your video card has, the more elements After Effects can load onto it and acceler-ate. If you have too many layers or if they are too large, After Effects will have to downsample them to get them to fit. You can set the amount of video memory assigned to After Effects in Preferences > Previews > OpenGL Info > Texture Memory; don't set it above 80% of the total memory on the card (you need to leave some aside for the operating system and other applications to use). As After Effects does not tell you how much video RAM your card has, you may need to do some research first.

If your layers consist of movies or precomps that change from frame to frame, performance may still be sluggish while dragging the current time indicator as these new source frames are loaded into OpenGL memory (placing your sources on a faster hard drive will help). You will experience this in **[Ex.07]**.

Selecting OpenGL–Interactive mode results in OpenGL being engaged while you are moving the current time indicator or interactively scrubbing a parameter, providing accelerated performance – at the possible cost of image quality, as mentioned above. If any frames are already rendered to RAM (noted by a green bar above the timeline), After Effects will switch between these frames and the OpenGL render as you scrub the time indicator, which may result in "flashes" as you switch between frames rendered with the normal software engine and those rendered with OpenGL. When you release the mouse, the normal software engine rerenders the frame so you can see it at its best.

If you choose OpenGL–Always On mode, OpenGL is used to render the image at all times, even after you release the mouse. When this mode is engaged, "OpenGL" will be displayed in the upper left corner of the composition. When you perform a render to disk, the software engine is used instead. You can take advantage of OpenGL acceleration while rendering to disk by enabling Use OpenGL Renderer in Render Queue > Render Settings, but given OpenGL's limitations, we recommend against it for critical final renders. (Rendering is covered in detail in Chapter 42.)

When Fast Previews is set to OpenGL–Always On, an OpenGL logo appears in the upper left corner of the Comp panel's pasteboard.

Where OpenGL really comes into its own is when you are moving objects in 3D space. Return to **[Ex.06]** and set Fast Previews to Off. Press C to select the Unified 3D Camera tool. Drag your mouse cursor in the Comp panel and note how slow After Effects is at updating the screen. Repeat with Fast Previews set to Adaptive Resolution. Then change Fast Previews to OpenGL–Interactive and repeat your experiments: After an initial pause to load the images into your video card's memory, After Effects will update the display practically as fast as you can move your mouse! Press V to return to the normal selection tool when you're done.

In Part 4 where we discuss 3D in depth, we have initially set the Fast Previews switch in all the comps to Off so that shifts in image quality won't distract you while you're learning this complex subject. If you've already read this section and now know what to expect, feel free to try out OpenGL previews while working through those chapters.

Viewer Quality and Acceleration

There is one more area where OpenGL can improve performance. If you have a compatible OpenGL card, open Preferences > Display and enable Hardware

Accelerate Composition, Layer, and Footage panels. This will use OpenGL to speed up drawing images in these panels. It defaults to off, just to avoid potential OpenGL driver problems when After Effects is first installed on a new computer.

Speaking of displays, two new Viewer Quality options were added in CS5 under Preferences > Previews. These decide whether Color Management and different zoom levels render faster or more accurately. We prefer to set these to More Accurate. If you have a slow computer, try More Accurate Except RAM Preview (our next topic).

RAM Previews

Next we'll discuss previewing a section of time in your composition. You can continue to use **[Ex.06]** or **[Ex.07]** while trying out these options.

If you tap the spacebar or click on the Play/Pause button in the Preview panel, you will initiate what is called a Standard Preview, where After Effects will render each frame as fast as it can – which usually means playing them much slower than the comp's frame rate. Alternately, initiating a RAM Preview instructs After Effects to render the frames inside the Work Area (described earlier in this chapter), load them into RAM, then attempt to play the result in "real time" (the comp's frame rate).

To initiate a RAM Preview, press 0 on the extended keypad or click on the RAM Preview button in the Preview panel (it's the one on the far right); on a Mac you can also press Control+0 on the normal keyboard. The frames will begin rendering; the Info panel will inform you how many frames you've requested and how many are done. When they're complete, After Effects will play them back. While they're rendering, you can press any key to stop the render and preview the frames calculated so far.

RAM Preview defaults to playing every frame at the comp's frame rate, at its current resolution. You can alter these choices by editing the values in the Preview panel. There is a second set of RAM Preview options available: Click on the RAM Preview Options popup menu and select Shift+RAM Preview Options

Continued on next page/

/continued from previous page

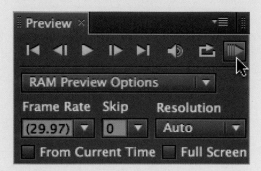

You can customize what After Effects caches and plays back for a RAM Preview or Shift+RAM Preview. It is common to leave the normal RAM Preview options alone and set the Shift+RAM Preview Options for faster calculations – for example, setting Skip to 1, which will cache and play every other frame.

to reveal them. Hold down Shift when you press 0 or click on the RAM Preview button, and these alternate parameters will be used. It's common to set up the Shift+RAM Preview Options for faster processing – for example, setting Skip to 1, which means After Effects will calculate and play back only every other frame, cutting your waiting time in half.

(You can save screen real estate by hiding the RAM Preview Options section of the Preview panel; click on the bottom of the panel and drag it upward until you see just the transport controls.)

After Effects CS5 has added an Alternate Preview option. Pressing Option (Alt) when initiating a RAM Preview will play just the five frames before the current time indicator. This is handy if you just want to check "edge chatter" while keying or using the Roto Brush, for example. The number of frames may be edited in Preferences > Previews.

If After Effects cannot play in real time, the Info panel will display a warning in red and show what the actual playback rate is. If your composition has audio, the audio will play back in real time even if the video can't, which means they may fall out of sync.

Note that setting the project's color depth to 16 or 32 bits per channel in File > Project Settings will slow down your computer. Another problem is when the panel being played straddles across more than one

display. Sometimes, playback is jerky the first time around, then smoother as it loops; if jerky playback persists, your computer is probably dipping into virtual memory to cache the "RAM" Preview – try allocating more RAM to After Effects in Preferences > Memory & Multiprocessing.

While After Effects is calculating any type of preview (Interactive, Standard, or RAM Preview), a green bar will draw along the top of the timeline denoting that the output is cached in RAM. (If you don't see this bar, make sure Show Cache Indicators is enabled in the Timeline panel's Options menu.) If you make a change that causes some of these cached frames to no longer be valid, the green bar will disappear from this section. When you invoke RAM Preview again, only the invalidated frames will be rerendered. After Effects will also do its best to cache frames for each layer in a composition, so rerendering should take less time than the initial render. In a moment, we'll also discuss disk caching, which can save considerable time re-creating frames.

The length of time you can RAM Preview is limited by your Work Area and how much RAM you have free. A big change in CS5 was updating After Effects to be a native 64-bit application; this allows it to access nearly all of the available RAM in your computer, whereas before it was restricted to 2–4 GB.

If you don't have enough free memory to preview the desired length of time, you can use Shift+RAM Preview and set it to skip frames, reduce the bit depth of your project, or reduce the Resolution of your comp. Setting Resolution to Half means After Effects renders just every other pixel on a line, as well as every other line, yielding a frame just a quarter of the original size. For maximum playback performance, Magnification should match Resolution (50% Magnification for Half Resolution and so forth). Set Resolution to Auto for this to happen automatically.

Although we have focused on previewing the Comp panel, RAM Previewing works in the Layer and Footage panels as well. This is especially useful in the Layer panel where you can take advantage of the View popup menu to isolate the results of masks or effects applied to a layer.

When frames are cached in RAM, a green bar appears above the timeline. When they are cached to disk, a blue bar appears. When you request to see frames cached to disk, they will be reloaded more quickly into RAM.

Disk Caching

By default, if the RAM Preview buffer is full and you request new frames to be cached, After Effects will determine which previously cached frames are needed the least and delete them to make room. Things change if you check Enable Disk Cache in Preferences > Memory & Cache: After Effects will then determine if an old frame would take longer to rerender than to save it to disk and retrieve it later. If yes, After Effects copies these frames to the designated folder on disk. Then, if you later perform a RAM Preview or a final render that can reuse those frames, After Effects retrieves them from disk rather than rerenders them. This can result in a significant time savings on render-intensive projects with lots of layers or nested comps.

Frames that are cached to disk are noted with a blue bar (rather than green) in the Timeline panel. As with the RAM cache, individual layers are cached in addition to entire composites; in this case, you won't see a line. The disk cache does not extend the number of frames that you can RAM Preview; it just reduces the amount of time needed to produce the frames requested for previews. As with the RAM cache, the disk cache is erased when you close a project.

Note that the Disk Cache is different from the Conformed Media Cache. The latter is used to store pre-decoded versions of footage items that are otherwise slow to decompress. It is discussed in more detail in Chapter 45.

Saving RAM Previews

To save a RAM Preview to your drive as a movie, press Command+0 (Control+0) on the numeric keypad or Command+click (Control+click) on the RAM Preview button in the Preview panel. You can also select Composition > Save RAM Preview. If the work area has not been fully previewed, this action will initiate the preview. You'll be prompted to name the movie, select a destination, and click Save. The Render Queue will come forward, and "rendering" (in this case saving to disk) will commence immediately.

Saving a RAM Preview to disk uses the Current Settings Template for the Render Settings, as the RAM Preview was calculated using these settings. The size of the resulting movie will be determined by the Resolution of the comp (the Magnification setting is ignored). For example, if you previewed a 720×486 comp at Half Resolution, the preview movie will be 360×243.

By default, the Output Module uses the RAM Preview template. On the Mac, this is set to save a lossless QuickTime Animation movie, RGB only (no alpha). On Windows, it will save an AVI file using Video for Windows (no compression), again RGB only. It is set to import itself into your project when done so you can play the result from inside After Effects.

You can change which template is used by changing the RAM Preview popup in Edit > Templates > Output Module. In this dialog you can also edit the template named RAM Preview. To render the RAM Preview with an alpha channel, make sure that the selected Output Module is set to render RGB+Alpha in the Channels popup and that the codec supports alpha, such as QuickTime Animation set to Millions of Colors+. Because the images created for RAM Preview contain a premultiplied alpha, the output module cannot be set to save as a Straight Alpha. As of CS5, you still cannot render fields using RAM Preview; for interlaced output, you will need to render via the Render Queue. (Chapter 42 covers templates and rendering in more depth.)

Continued on next page/

/continued from previous page

Targeted Preview

There is often more than one way to view what you are working on – be it multiple Views when working in 3D (discussed in Chapter 13) or having both Layer and Comp panels open simultaneously. After Effects provides you with a few options to decide which view gets previewed when you initiate a RAM Preview.

An important feature while working with multiple 3D views is Previews Favor Active Camera. When enabled (the default), RAM Previews are calculated for an Active Camera view, even if that particular view was not selected when you initiated a preview. You can turn this off in the Preview panel's options (click on the arrow in the upper right corner of the panel).

You can enable a chosen Comp, Layer, or Footage panel to always RAM Preview, even if another panel is forward when you start the preview.

A similar idea is embodied in the Always Preview This View button in the lower left corner of the Comp, Layer, and Footage panels. When enabled, the selected panel will always jump to the front when you start a RAM Preview. This is especially useful if you are working on layers in a nested comp (Chapter 18) but want to see the results in the main comp when you preview. Click it again to turn it off; now just the active panel will preview.

Previewing a Region of Interest

When you're working with a large comp size, you can preview less than the full frame by defining a smaller area. This is useful when you wish to preview a particular detail at 100% zoom. To define the area to be previewed, click on the Region of Interest button at the bottom of the Comp panel and use the marquee tool to drag a rectangle around the desired area. To switch back to viewing the full frame, click the button again. To reset the region and start over,

First enable Region of Interest, then drag a marquee around the portion of the Comp panel you wish to preview.

press Option (Alt) and click the Region of Interest button. You can render just the Region of Interest (Chapter 42), although setting up the Crop area in the Output Module is a more reliable method for rendering a portion of a comp. And in case you were wondering, you can't crop the comp size to it…

Previewing Audio Only

There may be occasions when you wish to preview only the audio in a composition. To do this, place the time indicator where you want playback to start, then press the period key (.) on the keypad or select Composition > Preview > Audio Preview (Here Forward). Playback will loop until you stop it by pressing any other key. Practice this with **[Ex.07]**.

After Effects can mix and play back audio tracks in real time, as long as you don't apply effects to them other than Stereo Mixer. Otherwise, you will have to wait for the audio to render before playback begins.

The audio preview quality is set at the bottom of File > Project Settings. The duration for this preview is set in the Preferences > Previews dialog; as of CS5 it defaults to a generous 30:00 seconds.

When you're scrubbing the Timeline panel, add the Command (Control) key to also scrub the audio track. You'll probably find this more useful if the audio waveform is also twirled down (shortcut: select the layer with audio and press LL).

The Window > Audio panel includes a VU (volume unit) meter that displays audio levels during play-back. You can increase the height of the panel for more accurate feedback. On wide monitors, we may drag this panel to the right of the Comp panel. Audio is discussed in more detail in Chapter 36.

You can also set which audio signal path in your computer is used to play back your sound. This is done in Preferences > Audio Hardware and > Audio Output Mapping and is discussed in Chapter 45.

Multiprocessing

If you have multiple processors or processor cores in your computer, After Effects has the ability to launch clones of itself that run in the background. These clones each process their own frames during RAM Previews and final renders, resulting in these renders happening several times faster.

You can enable this feature in Preferences > Memory & Multiprocessing. We tend to reserve 1–2 CPUs for other applications, so that we can still use our computer while After Effects renders in the background. Note that you need a lot of RAM to take advantage of this feature. It is also helpful if your media is on a fast drive, as now several copies of After Effects will be accessing it.

There will be a slight pause when you initiate a preview, as copies of your project have to be transferred to each clone before it can be rendered. Multiprocessing will be disabled for previews or renders if you have chosen to render using the OpenGL engine, or if you are using an effect (such as Stylize > Cartoon) which uses OpenGL to render.

If you like the idea of multiprocessing and want even more options, check out Nucleo Pro by GridIron Software (*www.gridironsoftware.com*). One of its nicer features is the ability to "speculatively" preview a composition, using clones of After Effects running on available processors or cores to fill the RAM cache while After Effects is otherwise idle.

Video Preview

A very useful feature is the ability to have the current view (such as the Comp panel) echoed out through FireWire to a DV device or to video cards that have compatible drivers. (We discuss in Chapter 41 why you sometimes need to preview your work through a real video monitor.)

To enable this feature, open Preferences > Video Preview. If you have a compatible device connected or installed, it will appear in the Output Device menu; select it. Your device may have additional options, such as NTSC or PAL; select the one that matches the

In Preferences > Memory and Multiprocessing, you can set how much of your computers RAM and how many of its CPUs to use for After Effects versus other applications.

video format you are working in from the Output Mode menu. If there is an "RGB" option for your format, choose that one. Note that if you have a video card that acts as a second desktop display, Video Preview takes over that display.

Command+/ (Control+/) on the numeric keypad toggles Video Preview on and off; if it is off, pressing / on the numeric keypad blasts out just the current frame to video. Video Preview obeys the Targeted Preview feature (discussed earlier). This is ideal for sending the final comp out to a video monitor for the client to see, while you're working inside a Layer panel or a nested comp.

You have a good deal of flexibility in deciding when your imagery is echoed to the chosen device and how it is displayed, including compensating for 4:3 or 16:9 aspect monitors. We suggest enabling Scale and Letterbox Output to Fit Video Monitor so odd-shaped comps don't look distorted. There is also a series of checkboxes that let you decide if you want After Effects to automatically update your video output for all normal panel interactions (such as dragging the time indicator through the Timeline or editing an effect parameter) as well as during RAM Previews or final renders.

3

Basic Animation

Animating a layer's transformations along with mastering motion paths.

One of the most important skill sets in motion graphics is learning how to animate *transformations*: Anchor Point, Position, Scale, Rotation, and Opacity. Fortunately, many rules and techniques for creating transform keyframes can be applied to virtually all the other parameters throughout After Effects. And once you learn how to manipulate the handles of a 2D Bezier motion path, you can employ these same skills when using the Pen tool to create vector shapes for masks (Chapter 10) and shape layers (Chapter 32).

Twirl down the layer, then twirl down the Transform section to reveal the transformation properties. In this example, Position is animating (its stopwatch is on); the other properties are at a constant value.

In this chapter, we'll concentrate on the basics, including tips for avoiding many common mistakes. You might be surprised to see how much can be done with just one or two animated properties and just two keyframes per property. You'll notice this if you spend some time studying motion graphics on television: A title moves left to right (two Position keyframes). A title fades in (two Opacity keyframes). A title grows larger (two Scale keyframes). We bet you won't find many titles buzzing around the frame doing figure eights (you know who you are…).

So as not to add to your anxiety, this chapter concentrates on moving layers in 2D space (the X and Y axes), leaving the Z axis to Chapter 13, *3D Space*. After mastering motion in 2D, just one more itsy-bitsy axis shouldn't be too daunting…

In the next chapter, we cover controlling speed (how layers change over time) including how to use the powerful Graph Editor. Don't feel overwhelmed when you start delving into the nitty-gritty of motion paths and velocity curves; more than likely many layers can be animated very simply. However, you will appreciate being able to make a layer move exactly the way you want it to when the project calls for more complex moves and for subtle timing changes.

In Chapter 5, you'll increase your animation skills with tips and techniques for manipulating keyframes and motion paths, as well as explore some of the very useful Keyframe Assistants that ship with After Effects.

Example Project

Explore the 03-Example Project.aep file as you read this chapter; references to [Ex.##] refer to specific compositions within the project file.

Position in Time and Space

Before we delve into creating Position keyframes, it's worth pointing out that Position keyframes exist in both space and time. When you animate Position you create a motion path in the Comp panel. After Effects calls this *spatial* interpolation, or how the layer interpolates between keyframes in *space*. This motion path can be manipulated using Bezier handles; these create different "flavors" of keyframes which we will explore in depth in this chapter.

The overall speed of the layer as it travels along this path is set by two factors: how many pixels the layer travels between keyframes in the Comp panel, and how many frames apart these keyframes are in the Timeline panel. How the layer interpolates between keyframes over *time* is referred to as *temporal* interpolation. To gain more subtle control over its velocity, you can also manipulate a layer's speed graph in the Graph Editor (covered in the next chapter).

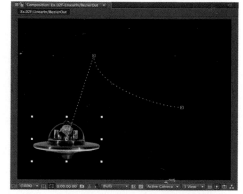

The motion path in the Comp panel determines the direction the layer travels. Spaceman object courtesy Classic PIO/Nostalgic Memorabilia.

Obviously, we're talking about two different concepts here – *space* and *time*. By default, the keyframe flavor you choose for your motion path is independent of the keyframe types available when manipulating the speed in the Graph Editor. And once you are introduced to Roving Keyframes (Chapter 4), you'll see that space and time can even be disconnected from each other for the ultimate in independence!

Besides Position, other properties with values on the X and Y axes are also considered to have a spatial component – such as Anchor Point and Effect Point for 2D and 3D layers, as well as Cameras and Lights in 3D (which add a Z axis, of course). In contrast, properties such as Scale, Rotation, and Opacity do not have a spatial component.

The overall speed of the layer is set by how far the keyframes have to travel in the Comp panel plus the spacing of the keyframes in the Timeline panel (above).

You can then further tweak how the layer travels in time by editing the speed graph in the Graph Editor (below), which is covered in the next chapter. The keyframe interpolation methods used in both time and space are independent of each other.

Step 1: You will create your motion path with the Selection tool (shortcut: V). You will use the Pen tool (circled) later when editing the path.

Stopwatch Shortcut

Option+Shift+P on Mac (Alt+Shift+P on Windows) is the shortcut to turn on the stopwatch for Position and set the first keyframe. This shortcut will also reveal the Position property in the Timeline panel if it is currently twirled up.

Step 2: At 00:00, click the stopwatch to turn it on and set the first Position keyframe.

Animating Position

Open the After Effects file **03-Example Project.aep** from the Chapter Projects folder on your DVD. To get started, create three Position keyframes so you'll have a motion path to play with:

Step 1: Open our first example composition, [**Ex.01_starter**]. We created it at 640×480 pixels, 29.97 frames per second (fps), with a duration of 05:00. We used **CP_Spaceman.tif** from this project's **Sources > Objects** folder, scaled to 40%. For this exercise, you'll be using the Selection tool (shortcut: V), so make sure this is selected.

Step 2: To animate Position, you first need to turn on its animation stopwatch. Rather than twirl all the properties down to find Position, select the **CP_Spaceman** layer and press P to solo the Position property in the Timeline panel. The current value for Position is displayed as a value on the X (left/right, or horizontal) and Y (up/down, or vertical) axes in the Comp panel, computed from the top left-hand corner (which has a value of 0,0). To be precise: The Position value represents the position of the layer's Anchor Point (which defaults to the center of the layer) in relation to the composition.

• Turn on the stopwatch to the left of the word Position to set the first keyframe at 00:00. In the comp panel, click anywhere inside the layer (avoiding the layer's corners) and drag the spaceman to the bottom left-hand corner; this updates the keyframe's XY value. If the Window > Info panel is open, you'll also see the Position value update in real time as you move a layer.

Step 3: Move the current time indicator to 01:00, click anywhere inside the layer, and drag the spaceman to the top of the Comp panel. The second keyframe is created automatically, along with a motion path made up of dots. Each dot indicates the position of the layer on each frame from 00:00 to 01:00.

Step 3: Dragging the layer to a new location creates the second keyframe automatically and draws a motion path between both locations.

Step 4: Move in time to 02:00 and drag the layer to the bottom right-hand corner to create the third keyframe. Notice that the motion path is now rounded at the second keyframe. (The Timeline panel has three diamond-shaped keyframe icons, which we won't worry about for now.) If you got lost, our result is shown in comp [**Ex.01-final**].

Step 5: Press Home to return to time 00:00 and preview the animation by tapping the spacebar; this Standard preview displays the motion path as it plays, unlike RAM Preview. (We explored previewing options in depth at the end of Chapter 2.)

Editing the Motion Path

An important concept is that most editing happens *at the current time*. The position of the current time indicator in the Timeline panel indicates the active frame. If a property is set to animate (its stopwatch is on), changing the value of this property at this point in time either (a) edits a keyframe if one exists on this frame or (b) creates a new keyframe.

The exception to this rule is the motion path: You can select and move keyframe boxes in the Comp panel *without first having to move to that point in time*. Go ahead and practice moving the keyframes around (in Chapter 5, we'll cover moving and scaling the entire motion path).

In the Comp panel, with the Selection tool active, select the keyframes individually by clicking on their keyframe box and notice their associated handles that look not unlike the dots for the motion path. The first keyframe has just one handle, while the middle keyframe, when it's selected, shows a handle on each side. (For now, resist the urge to touch these default handles, or you'll convert them to another keyframe type.) The fact that the handles are drawn simply as "dots," with no connecting lines, indicates that these are all *Auto Bezier* keyframes, the default keyframe in the Comp panel. Because the middle keyframe has both incoming and outgoing characteristics, we'll concentrate on its behavior in the next section.

After Effects identifies its keyframe interpolation types by important-sounding names such as Linear, Auto Bezier, Continuous Bezier, and Bezier. After all, without these names, we would have to refer to Bezier as the "keyframe with handles sticking out in different directions" (or KWHSOIDD for short). Don't get too hung up on the keyframe names – it's more important to know what the Bezier handles are doing and how to edit them. Creating motion paths is easy; making them do exactly what you want them to do takes a little practice! We've provided examples of each keyframe type in the [**Ex.02-spatial keyframes**] folder of comps, so let's take a tour...

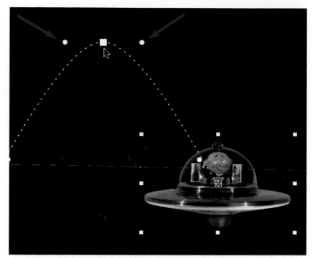

Step 4: The Auto Bezier keyframe is the default spatial keyframe: Select the middle keyframe and you'll see two "dots" on each side of the keyframe box. These dots form an imaginary line. Note that we've increased the size of the keyframe icons in the Comp panel (Preferences > General > Path Point Size) – a new feature in CS5.

FACTOID

Motion Path Color

The color of the motion path is derived from the layer's label color. If you are having trouble seeing the path, try changing the label color (Chapter 6).

TIP

Live Update

When you scrub the current time indicator in the timeline, the Comp panel should update on the fly. If it is not updating until you release the mouse, check that the Live Update button wasn't inadvertently toggled off.

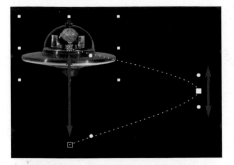

In [Ex.02b], the orientation of the Auto Bezier handles for the middle keyframe appear vertical and parallel to the imaginary line created by the first and last keyframe.

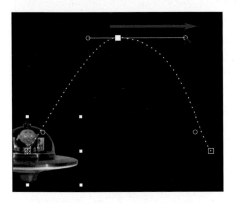

Dragging one of the Auto Bezier dots converts the keyframe to Continuous Bezier, which maintains a straight line through the keyframe.

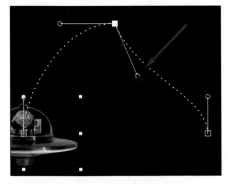

To gain independent control over the incoming and outgoing handles, hold down the G key and drag a Continuous Bezier handle. This technique is a toggle.

Auto Bezier Keyframe: The default keyframe type in the Comp panel is Auto Bezier. Its role is to create a smooth angle into and out of a keyframe, with no hard angles or sudden changes in direction. In [Ex.02a], select the middle keyframe and imagine a line connecting the two dots on each side of the keyframe. Now imagine another line connecting the first and third keyframes. Unless your imagination is playing tricks on you, these two lines should be parallel to each other.

To see what's automatic about Auto Bezier, move the three keyframes around in the Comp panel by selecting their keyframe boxes and dragging them to new positions (again, avoid dragging the keyframe handles themselves). Notice that no matter where you drag the keyframes, the two imaginary lines remain parallel. One result is shown in comp [Ex.02b].

Continuous Bezier Keyframe: More often than not, you'll end up manually editing the default Auto Bezier handles so you can better control the curves of the motion path. You do this by dragging one of the default handle dots, which turns the imaginary line connecting the dots into real direction handles (see [Ex.02c]).

This keyframe type is called Continuous Bezier. You'll notice that as you edit a handle on one side, the opposite handle moves also (similar to a see-saw action). The two direction handles are lengthened or shortened independently of each other, but the handles maintain a continuous straight line through the keyframe.

Note: If you're having trouble finding the default Auto Bezier handle dots amid the motion path dots, press *and hold down* the G key (to *temporarily* toggle to the Pen tool), click on the keyframe in the Comp panel, and drag out new handles. When you release the G key, the Selection tool should be active again. (If you actually changed to the Pen tool, press V to return to the Selection tool.)

Bezier Keyframe: For the ultimate control, you can "break" the incoming and outgoing handles so they operate independently – this is the Bezier keyframe type. You can then create any combination of straight lines and smooth curves, as we did in [Ex.02d].

To break the handles, press *and hold down* the G key (to *temporarily* toggle to the Pen tool) and move the cursor over a handle – the cursor will toggle to the Convert Vertex tool (an upside down V). Click and drag a handle to break it. When you release the G key, the Selection tool should be active again.

To revert back to Continuous Bezier, just repeat the procedure: Hold down the G key, then click and drag on a handle; the opposing handle will jump to form a continuous line again. You can also press G and drag new handles out of the keyframe box.

Note that if you press G and release, it will permanently toggle to the Pen tool. We recommend you stick with the Selection tool for basic editing (see *Using the Pen Tool* on the next page).

Linear Keyframe: Up to now we've dealt with curves and handles, but there are many occasions when you need absolute straight lines and hard angles in your motion path. You can do this by "retracting" the handles into the center of the keyframe:

Press *and hold down* the G key and move your cursor over the keyframe box (the cursor will change to the Convert Vertex tool). Click directly on the keyframe box. The handles will disappear, and the result is a Linear keyframe type with a corner point. To pop out the handles again, just repeat this technique and the Auto Bezier dots will reappear. Note that retracting handles in this manner works across multiple keyframes: Just preselect them first and then edit one of them.

If you hold down the G key and move your cursor over the motion path itself, the cursor will change to the Add Vertex tool. Click to add a new keyframe on the frame represented by that "dot." Release the G key to revert back to the Selection tool, then move and edit the new keyframe as needed.

To change a Linear keyframe directly to Continuous Bezier, press and hold down G to switch to the Pen tool, then click and drag out from the keyframe box.

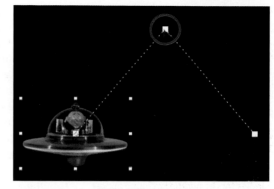

To convert all keyframes to Linear in one go, click on the word Position in the Timeline panel to select all Position keyframes, then hold down the G key and click directly on one of the keyframe boxes.

 TIP

Temporary Tools

You can temporarily toggle to some tools by pressing and holding down the respective shortcut key. This trick works for the Pen (G), Zoom (Z), Rotate (W), and Hand (H) tools.

Using the Pen Tool

We prefer to edit motion paths with the Selection tool, using the Pen tool only to break and retract handles. We use the Pen tool more when creating masks (Chapter 10) and shape paths (Chapter 32). However, feel free to use the Pen tool if you find it more intuitive:

• When the Pen tool is active, dragging a handle will break the handles and convert the keyframe to Bezier. Press Command (Control) to temporarily switch to the Selection tool to move a keyframe box or handle.

• To add a keyframe anywhere along the motion path, select the Pen tool (or Add Vertex tool) and move over the motion path. Click on a motion path dot to create a new keyframe on the frame represented by that dot (see figure to the right).

• When you move over an existing keyframe in the Comp panel, the Pen cursor changes to the Convert Vertex tool, and clicking the keyframe box will toggle it between Linear and Auto Bezier.

Add, delete, and edit keyframes along a motion path directly with the Pen tool; press G to cycle through the various tools (above). Be sure to click directly on the motion path, otherwise you may start drawing either a mask path or a Shape layer! (Undo if so.)

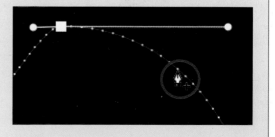

The state of the Keyframe Navigator indicates whether the current time indicator is positioned exactly on a keyframe (left) or between keyframes (right). The left and right arrows are a handy way to navigate among keyframes.

TIP

Skip along the Path

If a property has a motion path, you can double-click a keyframe box in the Comp panel with the Selection tool to jump to that point in time.

A common beginner mistake is to navigate to keyframes by dragging the current time indicator. If you miss by a frame, then edit the layer, you'll have two keyframes one frame apart – and a likely glitch in your animation.

TIP

Sticky Shift

Pressing the Shift key while dragging the current time indicator makes it stick to keyframes, in and out points, and so on.

Keyframe Navigation

Once you've created a few Position keyframes, you'll have noticed that the Keyframe Navigator area in the Timeline panel became active. The navigator consists of a left and right arrow and a diamond-shaped checkbox in the center. When the checkbox is selected (checked), this indicates that the current time indicator is positioned exactly at a keyframe. When the checkbox is empty, it means that you're parked between keyframes.

The keyframe navigator defaults to being grouped with the A/V Features column (Video, Audio, Solo, and Lock) on the left side of the Timeline panel. We prefer to move this column to the far right, beside the timeline area. (Do this by dragging the column header to the right, as covered in Chapter 2.) After Effects will remember this preference for all future comps.

If you prefer to leave the A/V Features column on the left side, we suggest you open the keyframe navigator in its own column: right-click on any column head, and select Columns > Keys from the popup menu. Then move the Keys column to the far right, by the timeline area.

To edit a keyframe value, it's usually necessary to move the current time indicator to that point in time; you can do this either by using the navigator or by double-clicking the keyframe box on the motion path. The natural instinct for beginners is to drag the current time indicator to a keyframe to make it the active frame. The problem with this method is that it's all too easy to drag the time indicator to a frame close to the keyframe, but not *exactly* on top of it. When you move the layer, instead of editing the intended Position keyframe, you create a *new* keyframe just one frame to the left or right. The two keyframes tend to overlap when the timeline is zoomed out; so if you see a glitch in the animation, zoom into the timeline to see if there are two keyframes where there should be one, then delete the unwanted keyframe. You can avoid this problem entirely if you navigate to keyframes using the navigator arrows or shortcuts (see below). If you do prefer to drag the current time indicator, add the Shift key and it will "stick" to keyframes, in and out points, markers, and so on.

Another method for moving the current time indicator to specific keyframes are the following shortcuts (though they become less useful in a complex composition with many visible keyframes):

Go to previous visible keyframe (or layer marker)	J
Go to next visible keyframe (or layer marker)	K

If keyframes are already applied but the layer is currently twirled up, there are a couple of handy shortcuts you'll want to remember. In both cases, select the layer(s) first:

Show all animating values	U
Show all changed values	UU (two Us, in quick succession)

Editing Keyframes Numerically

Up to now we've created Position keyframes interactively by moving the layer around in the Comp panel to set new keyframes or to edit existing ones. Throughout After Effects, however, you also have the choice to scrub parameter values in the Timeline panel, or enter precise values for a keyframe directly.

When you're scrubbing values, press the Shift key to scrub in large increments, or press Command (Control) to scrub in small increments. You can also select multiple keyframes at different points in time (or even across layers) and edit all values simultaneously: Scrub one value, and all the selected values will be edited relative to the value you scrub.

To enter a precise value, click on the text, enter the new value, and press Return to accept it. Again, you can enter values for multiple selected layers. Press Tab to cycle through the various visible parameter entry boxes.

Position values are always displayed as pixel values, and defined by the top left-hand corner of the comp. However, you can enter a Position value using different Units: Right-click on the current value in the Timeline panel, and select Edit Value from the popup. Select from a number of options in the Units popup; the most useful are Pixels and % of Composition. For instance, if you want to center a layer in the comp, set the Units menu to % of Composition, and the X and Y values to 50,50.

To open the Position dialog for a keyframe (without first moving to that point in time), double-click the keyframe icon in the Timeline. If you just want a readout of a keyframe's Position value, right-click on its keyframe box in the Comp panel or its keyframe icon in the Timeline; the first item on the popup menu is the keyframe's numerical value.

Other properties have similar dialog boxes, and the options are context-sensitive: For instance, editing the Anchor Point only gives you the option to set its value to % of Source (not % of Composition), while Rotation and Opacity offer no new options.

Watch out for this gotcha: The numerical value shown in the Timeline panel is the value *at the current time*. A common mistake is to select a keyframe at a different point in time, then either scrub the Position value or type a new value. This does not edit the keyframe you selected – it edits the value at the current time, creating a new keyframe if there wasn't one there already. If you want to edit a specific keyframe, either double-click the keyframe icon to open the Position dialog box, or simply navigate to the keyframe you want to edit so that it now lies at the current time.

Anywhere you see a value that's underlined, you can either scrub the values or click to enter a precise value. Press Shift to scrub in larger increments; press Command (Control) to scrub in finer increments.

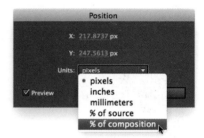

To bring up a dialog to edit numerically, right-click on a value to get the Edit Value option or double-click an existing keyframe. The Position dialog allows you to enter values using various criteria. Note that the subpixel numbers to the right of the decimal point are used when the layer is set to Best Quality (covered in the sidebar at the end of this chapter).

Gotcha! Selecting a keyframe elsewhere on the Timeline, then scrubbing or editing the Position value, does not edit the selected keyframe – it either edits the keyframe at the current time, or adds a new one if none currently exists.

T is for Opacity

Actually, T is for Transparency (the O key was being used already). After Effects uses the concept of *opacity*, rather than *transparency*, so setting the Opacity property to 0% makes a layer 100% transparent.

To practice editing Opacity, close all comps and open [**Ex.03**], select the layer, and type T to reveal this property in the Timeline panel. The easiest way to edit it is to scrub its value in the Timeline panel, watching the result in the Comp panel. You can also edit Opacity by clicking on its value and entering a new number.

New keyboard shortcuts were added in CS4 to alter the Opacity of a selected layer. Hold Control+Option (Control+Alt) and use the + and – keys on the numeric keypad to increase or decrease Opacity in 1% increments. Add the Shift key to jump by 10% increments. (By the way, that's not a typo; the Mac keyboard shortcut really is Control+Option, not Command+Option.)

When you edit Opacity, the layer's alpha channel is being changed, making the layer more or less transparent. In [**Ex.03**], press Option (Alt) and click on the Show Channel button at the bottom of the Comp panel to view the Comp's alpha, and observe the results as you edit Opacity.

You've probably guessed already that turning on the stopwatch for Opacity and setting two keyframes with values of 0% to 100% will fade up a layer. Try it now, and note that the reverse will fade off a layer.

Crossed-up Dissolves

If you crossfade by fading one layer down while the other fades up, as in [**Ex.04a**], you may notice a dip in the middle where both layers are at 50% opacity. If the background is black, the crossfade will result in a dip in brightness as some of the black background becomes visible. In our example, the checkerboard grid is turned on, so it's partially visible.

If both layers are the same size, you need only fade up the top layer from 0 to 100%, as in [**Ex.04b**]. Once the top layer is fully opaque, trim out the bottom layer (even though the bottom layer is obscured, you may waste time retrieving frames from disk).

This does not always work; problems occur when the layers are not the same size, or have their own alpha channels and transparencies. Also, the layer behind might still be partially visible and pop off, as in [**Ex.04c**]. In this case, go ahead and crossfade the two layers.

Opacity Logic

When you stack two layers on top of each other, each with opacity at 50%, you might expect the result would be 100% opaque. But opacity *multiplies* rather than adds. The only way to go fully opaque is to have a layer somewhere in the stack that is at 100% opacity. This fact about opacity can cause problems, such as when two antialiased layers have edges that are supposed to meet seamlessly, or when one layer is fading out while another is fading up on top. Fortunately, After Effects has cures for these two particular cases – the Alpha Add blending mode (Chapter 12) and the Blend effect (Bonus Chapter 23B), respectively.

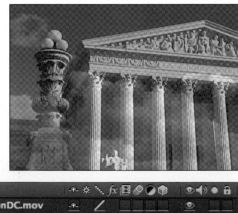

[Ex.04a]: During a "cross" dissolve, both layers are partially transparent, in this case revealing the checkerboard transparency grid behind. This is not always desirable. Footage from Artbeats/White Puffy Clouds and Washington DC.

Fading Layers as a Group

When you fade down multiple layers individually, you will end up with a "staggered" fade-out, as in [**Ex.05a**]. The solution is to fade out the layers as a group *after* they've been composited together. There are two ways to do this:

- [**Ex.05b**]: Add Layer > New > Adjustment Layer and apply Effect > Distort > Transform. Then set keyframes for the Opacity parameter in the Transform effect. This works because the Adjustment Layer gets a copy of the composite of all layers below, and the effect fades it out. (Adjustment Layers are covered in Chapter 22.)

[**Ex.05b**]: One method for fading out multiple layers as a group is to apply the Transform effect to an Adjustment Layer and animate the effect's Opacity value.

- [**Ex.06**]: Composite the layers in one comp (a *precomp*), as we did in [**Ex.06a**]. Then nest this comp into a second comp, [**Ex.06b**]. Animating Opacity in the second comp will apply to the group of layers *after* they've been composited together. Nesting is covered in Chapter 18; you can also use Precomposing (Chapter 19) to move a group of layers to a precomp.

S is for Scale

Next you'll learn how to manipulate the Scale property of a layer in a variety of ways, and pick up a few shortcuts and tips while you're at it. In this chapter's project, close any open comps and open [**Ex.07**]. Select the **AB_WashingtonDC.mov** layer in the Timeline panel, and type S – this is the shortcut to twirling down just the Scale property for a selected layer. You will see two values: the first one is X Scale, representing the layer's width; the second one is Y Scale, representing its height. There are a variety of ways to edit Scale:

- The simplest way to edit Scale is to scrub its value. This works similarly to scrubbing the Position value (discussed earlier in this chapter): scrub to the left or right and the size of the layer will be updated in the Comp panel. If you scrub the value below 0%, the image will flip and start growing again because you are now entering negative Scale values. If you find the values change too fast as you scrub, press the Command (Control) key to scrub in finer increments. Conversely, holding Shift while you're scrubbing will update Scale in increments of 10%.

TIP

Vital Statistics

Hover your cursor over a keyframe in the Timeline panel to display a tooltip containing its time and value. This tooltip does not update if you drag a keyframe in time; keep an eye on the Window > Info panel to verify its new timing.

- You can also edit Scale numerically by clicking on one of the values, entering a new number, and pressing Return.

- If you want to change the X and Y Scale values independently from each other, click on the chain link icon to the left of their values to turn off the aspect ratio lock switch. Clicking again in the empty box where the chain link used to be will turn the aspect lock back on; now changing one of the Scale values will update the other and automatically maintain the same aspect ratio.

To edit Scale in the Timeline, select the layer, type S to expose the Scale property, and scrub its values. The chain link icon indicates that the X and Y Scale values are locked together; the aspect ratio of the layer will be maintained as you change either value.

You can scale a layer directly in the Comp panel by dragging its handles; add the Shift key after you start dragging to maintain the aspect ratio. If the layer displays a colored outline rather than handles, it has a mask applied; if so, turn off the Toggle Mask and Shape Path Visibility button at the bottom of the Comp panel (see arrow).

TIP

Stretch to Fit

Command+Option+F (Control+Alt+F) will force a layer to scale, rotate and position itself to fit the size of the comp exactly. Even more such options can be found under the Layer > Transform menu.

To see this in action, turn off the aspect lock, set the Scale values to some easy-to-remember relationship such as X = 100% and Y = 50%, and turn the aspect lock back on. If you then scrub or change the X Scale value to 60%, the X Scale will automatically change to 30%, keeping the same 2:1 aspect ratio.

Here's a handy shortcut for resetting the X and Y Scale to have the same values: If the chain link icon is on, first turn it off. Then press Option (Alt) as you turn back on the chain link; the Y value will snap to the X value. The aspect ratio will be locked so they continue to stay in sync.

• You can also edit Scale interactively by dragging the handles that appear around a layer's outline in the Comp panel. The trick is to add the Shift key *after* you start dragging to maintain the aspect ratio of the layer as you scale. Note this changes X and Y Scale independently, but does *not* disable the aspect ratio lock switch.

• For even more control, right-click on one of the values and select Edit Value to open the Scale dialog box. Here, you also have the option to change the units you use for Scale to % of Composition or Pixels, as well as the less useful inches or millimeters. There is also a popup menu in this dialog to preserve the aspect ratio of the

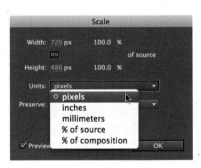

layer as you edit; this mimics the behavior of the chain link icon in the Timeline panel. When the layer has been animated, you can also double-click a Scale keyframe to open this dialog.

• Added in CS4: You can scale in 1% increments holding down Option on Mac (Control – not Alt – on Windows) and using the + and – keys on the numeric keypad (not the regular keyboard). To practice this, make sure the layer is selected, then press Option+ (Control+) to increase Scale by 1% and Option– (Control–) to decrease Scale by 1%. Add the Shift key while you're doing this to change Scale in 10% increments.

Note that no matter which method you use for changing scale, the origin for all scaling (as well as rotation) is the layer's Anchor Point (the icon in the center of the layer that looks like a crosshair). Changing the Anchor Point is covered later in chapter.

Animating Scale

Now that we know several different ways to manipulate Scale, it's time to animate it. You can practice this in [**Ex.08_starter**]:

Step 1: Select the **CP_Spaceman.tif** layer, and type S to reveal the Scale property in the Timeline panel.

Step 2: Make sure the current time indicator is at the beginning of the comp (press Home if it's not), and enable the stopwatch for Scale. This enables animation and sets the first Scale keyframe at the current time using the current size as its value.

Step 3: Still at time 00:00, change the scale of the layer (bearing in mind that values over 100% will blow up pixels and decrease quality).

TIP

Resetting Scale

To return the Scale value of a selected layer back to 100%, double-click the selection arrow in the Tools panel.

Step 4: Move the time indicator later in time and rescale the spaceman to a size different from the first keyframe. Notice that a new keyframe is automatically created in the Timeline panel. Whenever Scale's stopwatch is on, changing the Scale results in a keyframe being created at that point in time, or updated if there was already a keyframe at that point in time, just as with Position keyframes.

As you scrub the time indicator along the timeline, notice that the spaceman changes size between keyframes, as After Effects automatically interpolates the Scale values.

Once you get the hang of animating Scale, try also animating Position and Opacity for the layer if you need the practice. With Scale revealed already in the Timeline panel, select the layer and press Shift+P to also reveal Position, and Shift+T to add Opacity. Remember that the three properties are independent of each other; you don't need to create the same number of keyframes for each property or have them appear at the same points in time. RAM Preview your animation at any time. Our example of all three properties animating is in [**Ex.08-final**].

Steps 1–4: To animate Scale, enable the stopwatch to set the first keyframe, and create at least one more keyframe at a later point in time with a different Scale value. Remember that you can use the keyframe navigator to jump between Scale keyframes, as well as set new keyframes and delete existing ones.

Try animating Position, Scale and Opacity, as we did in [**Ex.08-final**]. Try to avoid scaling a layer above 100%. This forces After Effects to create new pixels without enough information from the source image, resulting in a softer image.

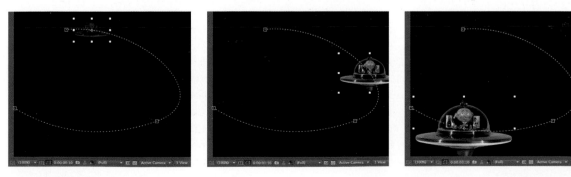

Select a layer and press R to reveal Rotation in the Timeline panel. As you scrub the rightmost parameter – degrees – past 359°, the revolutions value to the left will increase.

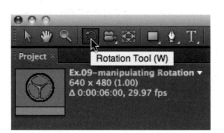

You can rotate 2D layers interactively in the Comp panel using the Rotation tool (shortcut: W). If the Selection tool is active, remember that you can temporarily switch to the Rotation tool by pressing and holding down W; the cursor in the Comp panel will change to the rotate cursor. Rotate the layer and release the W key to return to the Selection tool.

R is for Rotation

The Rotation property has its own set of keyboard shortcuts and alternate methods of manipulation that are worth learning. Close any open comps and open **[Ex.09]**. Select the **CD_bikewheel** layer, and type R on the keyboard – this is the shortcut for revealing just the Rotation property. The value shown is in Revolutions + Degrees, with positive numbers rotating clockwise from 0°. As with Scale, there are a variety of ways to edit Rotation:

• The easiest way to edit Rotation is to scrub its value in the Timeline panel. With the Rotation property revealed, scrub the rightmost value (degrees) to the right or left, watching the wheel rotate in the Comp panel. As you drag past 359°, you will notice that the number of whole revolutions change as the degrees start over again from 0. Holding Command (Control) as you scrub gives you finer control; holding Shift jumps degrees by multiples of 10.

• You can edit Rotation numerically by clicking on its value in the Timeline panel to highlight it, typing in a new value, and pressing Return. The Tab key jumps between the revolutions and degrees values. If you enter a value of 360 or larger, After Effects will automatically convert it to the correct number of full revolutions plus the remaining number of degrees.

• To offset the current Rotation value by 1° increments, make sure the layer is selected, then press the + or – key on the numeric keypad (not the regular keyboard). If you add the Shift key while you're doing this, Rotation will change in 10° increments.

• You can interactively rotate a layer in the Comp panel with the Rotation tool (shortcut: W for Wotate – seriously, that's what they

---

Rotation Rules

After you've rotated a layer a few times in a graphics program such as Adobe Illustrator or Photoshop, it's often difficult to reset the orientation back to the starting position (before it was ever rotated). This is because once rotation is processed, the image reassumes a rotation value of 0.

When you rotate a layer in After Effects, however, the value displayed is always in relation to the original starting value of 0°, and you can always return to this original rotation value at any time. It's also worth pointing out that the Rotation value of a single keyframe *does not indicate how the layer will animate*. For instance, a keyframe value of 90°

does not necessarily mean the layer has just rotated clockwise 90°. That would be true only if the *previous* keyframe had a value of 0°.

In **[Ex.11_starter]**, both wheels rotate from 0° to 180° clockwise over two seconds. If you now wish the wheel to animate counterclockwise by 180°, the third keyframe should be set to 0° (not minus 180° as you might think).

So gauging whether a layer is rotating clockwise or counterclockwise can only be accomplished by checking the values of keyframes before and after the current keyframe, or by consulting the Value Graph in the Graph Editor (Chapter 4).

told us). Add the Shift key after you start dragging to constrain Rotation to 45° increments. If you make a mess, double-click the Rotation tool to revert to 0°.

Animating Rotation

If you'd like to practice animating rotation, follow these steps using [**Ex.10_starter**]:

Step 1: Select the **CD_bikewheel layer** and press R if Rotation is not already revealed in the Timeline panel.

Step 2: Make sure the current time indicator is at 00:00 and click on the stopwatch icon to the left of the word Rotation. This enables animation and sets the first Rotation keyframe at the current time. We'll use the current rotation amount – 0° – for this keyframe.

Step 3: Move the current time indicator to a different point in time and scrub the rotation value in the Timeline panel to create a new keyframe.

Step 4: Move to another point later in time, press *and hold down* the W key to *temporarily* switch to the Rotation tool, and rotate the wheel interactively in the Comp panel to create the third keyframe. (If you accidentally changed tools, press V to revert to the Selection tool.)

Press 0 to RAM Preview the comp to see the effects of your animation. Again, double-clicking on a keyframe is another way to edit a keyframe numerically by opening that property's dialog box.

Our version is [**Ex.10-final**], where we've also animated Scale. RAM Preview; did you notice the animation seamlessly loops? This is because we set the same values for Scale and Rotation at the beginning and end, then placed the last two keyframes one frame after the end of the comp (at 04:00) so that this value wouldn't be repeated when the animation loops. To get to this "extra" frame, press End to jump to the last frame of the comp (03:29), then press Page Down to advance one frame. The Comp panel will be grayed out, but you can still edit the keyframes!

If rotated layers look a bit "sliced" or aliased, check that the Comp panel's Magnification is set to 100%, the layer's Quality switch is set to Best Quality (the default), and the comp's Pixel Aspect Ratio Correction switch is off.

Auto Rotation

Auto-orientation (Chapter 5) can automatically orient a layer along its motion path, with no rotation keyframes necessary!

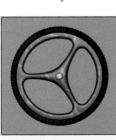
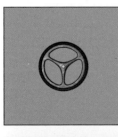

In [**Ex.10-final**], the wheel both rotates and scales (left). The animation creates a seamless loop thanks to the first and last keyframes being identical, and the last two keyframes being placed one frame after the last frame (below).

Ex.10_starter	Ex.10-final

0:00:00:00

#	Source Name		
▼ 1	CD_bikewheel.tif		
	Scale	50.0, 50.0%	◄ ♦ ►
	Rotation	0x +0.0°	◄ ♦ ►

An Orientation in 3D Rotation

When 3D space was added in After Effects, the Rotation property went from having one parameter to having four: Orientation, plus individual X, Y, and Z Rotation. Let's explore how this works.

Open **[Ex.12a]** and make sure the regular 2D Rotation property is exposed for the **CP_MedicalArm.tif** layer. Scrub its value; watch it rotate clockwise and counterclockwise in the Comp panel. Rotation, like Scale, occurs around the layer's anchor point (covered in the next section). Leave Rotation at some value other than 0°, then turn on the layer's 3D Layer switch (the cube icon at the right side of the Switches column).

GOTCHA

3D Terminated

Turning off the 3D Layer switch wipes out the Orientation plus the X and Y Rotation values, keeping just Z Rotation.

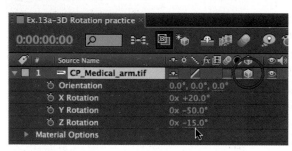

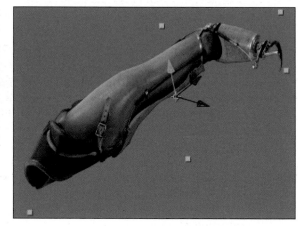

When the 3D Layer switch is enabled (circled in red), you get three Rotation properties plus Orientation (above). The three colored Rotation arrows in the Comp panel (right) show you what axis you are rotating around. Image courtesy Classic PIO/Classic Medical Equipment.

You will now see the four parameters mentioned above: Orientation, X Rotation, Y Rotation, and Z Rotation. Notice that the value you left Rotation at before enabling the 3D Layer switch was copied into Z Rotation. 2D Rotation revolves an object like a pinwheel around the axis pointing out of the layer straight toward you – the Z axis (the blue colored arrow).

• Scrub the Z Rotation value to confirm that it rotates not unlike a 2D layer. The axis it's rotating around (the blue arrow) is hard to see because it's pointing straight toward you. Double-click the Rotation tool to set the Z Rotation back to 0° when you're done.

• Scrub the X Rotation – the layer will tumble around the X axis (red arrow). Undo or set the value back to 0°.

• Scrub the Y Rotation – the layer swivels around the Y axis (green arrow).

• Now rotate the layer using all three Rotation values – X, Y, and Z – and see how any orientation in 3D space is possible.

These three rotational parameters are sometimes referred to as the layer's *Euler* rotation. They are the values you will be keyframing most often when you want to animate a layer's rotation. They each have their own line in the Timeline panel, meaning they each have their own keyframes (and their own graphs in the Graph Editor). This independence

TIP

Solo Selected

To reduce the number of properties revealed in the Timeline, select just the ones you wish to see and press SS to solo them. This is especially useful when you wish to solo parameters that don't have their own shortcuts, such as effect parameters.

allows you to do things like spin a layer like a top 20 times around its Y axis, while you slowly wobble it back and forth along its Z axis.

Double-click the Rotation tool to set all three Rotation parameters back to 0°, and turn your attention to the Orientation property. Notice that it has X, Y, and Z values; as you scrub them, they initially seem to act just like the individual Euler Rotation parameters. But notice the lack of a "number of rotations" value: Orientation is mainly used for posing, rather than animating, a layer. This will become evident when you keyframe these different parameters:

In [**Ex.12b**], two different animations are taking place. (If the keyframes aren't visible, select both layers and press U.) The upper arrow has its X, Y, and Z Rotations animated from 0° to 300° and back. The lower arrow's Orientation property is animated using the same values. If you scrub the current time indicator or RAM Preview the comp, you will notice that the Orientation animation moves only a little, while the Rotation arrow layer gyrates wildly. This is because Orientation uses what is called *Quaternion* interpolation, where it takes the shortest path between keyframes – instead of spinning the exact number of degrees you requested. So in our example, layer 1 rotates 300 degrees between the first and second keyframes, while layer 2 takes the shortest route and rotates negative 60° to arrive at the exact same "pose"!

You'll learn more about working in 3D space in Chapter 13. In the meantime, remember that you can enable the 3D Layer switch any time you need to do a quick swivel and tilt – you don't need to add cameras and lights and create a whole 3D world!

When the Rotation tool is selected, a popup menu appears on the right side in the Tools panel. Here you can toggle the tool's behavior between editing Orientation or Rotation values for a 3D layer.

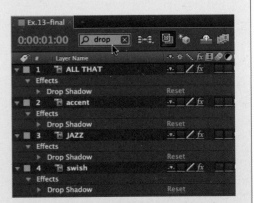

You can rotate the X, Y and Z axes of a 3D layer interactively in the Comp panel (above); place the cursor over the axis you wish to rotate around until the cursor changes to this axis, then click and drag.

Move away from the arrows to rotate freely (inset). That said, be very careful using the Rotate tool to alter Y Rotation or Orientation: There is a nasty anomaly that if you go beyond ±90°, the X and Z values flip by 180° (try it!). That's why we prefer scrubbing the values directly in the Timeline panel.

QuickSearch

QuickSearch fields appear in the Project and Timeline panels. These make it much easier to find specific sources or parameters, as well as comments in these panels. To try this out in the Timeline, open [**Ex.13-final**]; select layers 1–4 and Command (Control) click on the twirly arrow to the left of layer 1. Quite a daunting list of parameters! To search the selected layers for a particular parameter – say, Color – type "**color**" into the QuickSearch field. Try other parameter names, such as "**position**" or "**drop**".

To clear the QuickSearch field, click the X that appears on the right side when a search is active; all layers will twirl up. To search all layers, deselect all layers first (shortcut: F2).

Using QuickSearch allows you to reveal just the parameters you're looking for.

Auto-keyframe Mode

Now that you've had some experience with animating Position, Scale, Rotation, and Opacity, you've seen how important it is to turn on the animation stopwatch for the correct property if you want your actions to be recorded. New users often forget this step and change property values interactively in the Comp panel – only to realize later that After Effects didn't capture any of their changes! Auto-keyframe mode – a new feature in CS5 – aims to solve that problem.

When Auto-keyframe mode is on, modifying a property automatically turns on that property's keyframe animation stopwatch and adds a keyframe at the current time. Try this approach in our next example:

TIP

I Remember U

Pressing U for a selected layer, or layers, twirls down all properties that have their stopwatches set, while UU (two Us in quick succession) also twirls down properties that have changed from their default settings.

• Open [**Ex.13_starter**], where we've already placed four layers that make up the title "All That Jazz" along with a background layer (which is locked). Note that the 3D layer switch is enabled for the four title layers so you can rotate them in 3D (as you practiced on the previous page).

Enable Auto-keyframe mode. Now any changes you make to a layer, either interactively in the Comp panel or by scrubbing values in the Timeline, will create a keyframe automatically.

Once Auto-keyframe mode is enabled, moving the **All That** layer to the pasteboard on the right side will turn on the stopwatch for Position and create the first keyframe. Moving the layer back to its original position will create the motion path (above) and the second keyframe (right).

• Enable Auto-keyframe mode by clicking the large stopwatch icon along the top of the Timeline panel. Its center turns red. Note that Auto-keyframe mode is now on *for all comps in this project*, not just this one.

• At 00:00, select layer 1, **All That**, and drag the X axis arrow (the red one) to move the layer to the right so it resides completely on the pasteboard. (Selecting the X axis means that it won't move up or down accidentally; with a 2D layer you could add the Shift key after you start moving to restrain horizontally.)

• Press U; the stopwatch for Position is on and the first keyframe has been created. Move to 01:00, and scrub the X value in the Timeline to return the layer to its original position. This creates the second keyframe.

• Return to 00:00, and select layer 3, **Jazz**. Select the Rotation tool and check that the Set popup in the Tools panel is set to Rotation (not Orientation). In the Comp panel, rotate the layer around its X, Y, and Z axes. Press R to reveal Rotation in the Timeline; the X, Y, and Z Rotation properties are all set to animate (see figures to the right).

• Press V to return to the Selection tool, move later in time, and set all three values back to 0° – this will create a second set of keyframes.

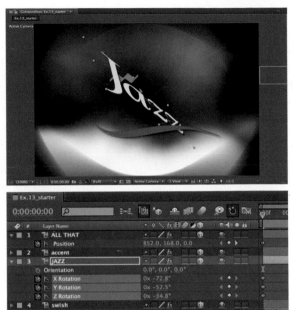

After Auto-keyframe mode is enabled, editing any parameter will add a keyframe for it. However, the act of enabling Auto-keyframe does not create any keyframes at that moment. If you want to create a first keyframe that contains a parameter's current value, it is safer to manually toggle on the stopwatch for that property.

Auto-keyframe mode is set project-wide, not per comp – so remember to turn it off when you're done!

Flip & Flop

Negative scale values are normally used to flip a layer horizontally or vertically (although you can also use 3D Rotation to flip a layer horizontally or vertically). Open **[Ex.90-Flip & Flop]** and make sure its Scale property is exposed in the Timeline panel (select the layer **AB_IndustryScenes.mov** and press S if not).

• Click on the chain link icon to turn off the aspect ratio lock, then click on the X Scale value and type "**–100**" and press Enter. The movie in the Comp panel will flip horizontally and the smoke will now flow out of the smokestack from right to left instead. Turn the aspect lock back on and scrub either value to rescale the flipped image. The shortcut for this technique is to select Layer > Transform > Flip Horizontal.

• To flip a layer vertically, enter a negative value for the Y value, or select Layer > Transform > Flip Vertical.

The Layer > Transform menu commands do not affect existing keyframes. Note that After Effects also has Flip, Flop, and Flip + Flop Animation Presets. These work by adding a Transform effect to the layer, leaving its Scale value – and any existing Scale keyframes – untouched. Animation Presets are covered in Chapter 25.

An image can be flipped horizontally or vertically by entering negative scale values for one or both dimensions. Shortcuts were added to the Layer > Transform submenu in CS4 to perform the same tricks. Footage from Artbeats/Industry Scenes.

A is for Anchor Point

Central – quite literally – to changing the position, scale, and rotation of an image is its *anchor point*. This is the pivot around which these activities take place. Judicious placement and animation of the anchor point will result in more predictable movements. Once you have a good grasp on the anchor point, we will show you how to use it to simulate 2D motion control moves.

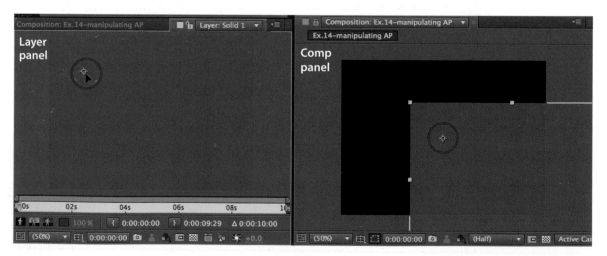

The anchor point is the pivot around which layers scale and rotate; it defaults to the center of the layer. It's important to note that anchor point X and Y values are relative to the layer, while Position's X and Y values refer to the anchor point's position in the Comp panel.

Close your previous comps, and open [**Ex.14**] in this chapter's example project. This comp is 640×480 in size, with a blue solid that is the same size as the comp. Select the solid layer, and notice the anchor point in the center of the layer (it looks like a registration symbol). Press A to solo Anchor Point, and Shift+P to add Position so only these two properties are displayed in the Timeline panel. Make sure that Auto-keyframe mode is turned off.

Both Anchor Point and Position appear to have the same values on the X and Y axes, so how do these numbers differ? Move the layer in the Comp panel and notice that only the value of Position has changed. *The value of Position is the position of the layer's anchor point relative to the comp* (in other words, the Position's X and Y axes are in *comp space*). Undo until the layer returns to the center of the comp.

Because the Layer panel docks with the Comp panel, we suggest you split the Comp viewer for this exercise so you can view both panels side by side: With the Comp panel active, press Command+Option+Shift+N (Control+Alt+Shift+N) to get two viewers. The new viewer on the right side will be locked. Double-click the layer to open the Layer panel (introduced in Chapter 2) in the left viewer (see figure below). In the Layer panel, the anchor point should be visible in the center of the layer.

As you move the anchor point in the Layer panel (left viewer), its value updates in the Timeline, and the layer is offset in the Comp panel (right viewer) in the opposite direction. Notice the position of the anchor point in the Comp panel does not change.

In the Layer panel, grab the anchor point with the mouse and move it around. As you do so, watch the Comp and Timeline panels. You will notice that the anchor point stays in the same place in the Comp panel, but the edges of the layer move to match the distance between the anchor point and the layer edges in the Layer panel. Also note that only the value of the anchor point parameter changes in the Timeline panel. *The anchor point value is the position of the anchor point relative to the layer* (in other words, the anchor point's X and Y axes are in *layer space*).

When you move the anchor point in the Layer panel, the image will appear to move in the opposite direction in the Comp panel. Obviously, this is not very intuitive! But the Position property has no sense of the layer's boundaries; it only keeps track of where the anchor point is in the comp. Considering that the anchor point's location in the Comp panel has not changed, but the position of the anchor point relative to the layer has, it makes sense that the layer is "offset" in the Comp panel. Fortunately, it's easy to reposition the layer in the comp so that your layout appears unchanged. (Chapter 5 covers moving a motion path.)

When working with anchor points, set the Layer panel's View popup to Anchor Point Path. Although you can drag the anchor point in the Masks view (the default), the Anchor Point Path view also allows you to nudge it using the cursor keys, and to see its motion path (if it is animating).

Remember that when you move the anchor point, then scale and rotate the layer, the image will anchor itself around this new position. With some images it'll be obvious that scale and rotation should happen around a certain point – the center of a wheel or gear, for instance. Because of the offset behavior mentioned above, it's best to decide on the location of the anchor point as soon as you drag the layer into the comp – *before* the layer's Position property has been animated over time.

Moving Anchor and Position Together

As you've discovered, in order to change the center of rotation and scale without changing your layout, you have to move the anchor point and then reposition the layer in the Comp panel. But can't we do this in one step? This is where the Pan Behind tool comes in handy: It can edit these two properties at the same time.

To use the Pan Behind tool (shortcut: Y), click directly on the anchor point in the Comp or Layer panel; as you move the anchor point, the layer maintains the same visual position in the comp. It achieves this feat *by changing the value for both Anchor Point and Position at the same time*. Try it in [**Ex.14**] while watching how these parameters update in the Timeline panel. *Beware:* This is of little use if Position is already animating – unless you want to make a mess of your motion path! But, if you set the anchor point in the Comp panel before creating Position keyframes, it sure beats fussing about in the Layer panel.

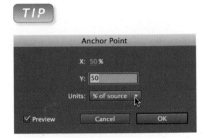
Anchor Point Reset

To set the anchor point back to the center of a layer, right-click on its value in the Timeline panel and select Edit Value. In the Anchor Point dialog, set the Units popup to % of Source, then set both the X and Y values to 50.

Pan Behind What?!

Don't mistake the Pan Behind tool for an innocent "move" tool. It's real purpose is to pan an image behind a window created by a mask (see Chapter 10), while keeping the mask's position stationary in a comp.

To *temporarily* switch to the Pan Behind tool, press *and hold down* the Y key, edit the anchor point, then release the mouse to return to the previous tool.

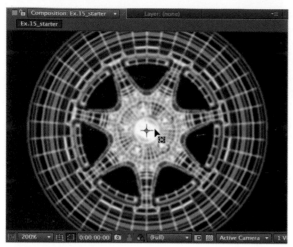

Composition: Ex.15_starter ▾ | Layer: (none) ▾
Ex.15_starter

200% ▾ | 0:00:00:00 | (Full) ▾ | Active Camera ▾ | 1 V

In **[Ex.15_starter]**, you'll need to re-center the anchor point to remove the wobble when the wheel rotates. In the Comp panel, with the Pan Behind tool selected, press Option (Alt) and drag the anchor point to center the wheel.

3D Anchor Point

When the 3D Layer switch is enabled, the anchor point can be offset in Z space as well, allowing 3D orbits. We'll discuss this further in Chapter 13.

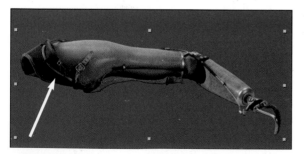

To animate the arm rising and falling using simple rotation, its anchor point should be placed at the shoulder joint (where the arrow is pointing).

It is also possible to edit just the anchor point value in the Comp panel without affecting the value for Anchor Point: Select the Pan Behind tool, then hold the Option (Alt) key while you're dragging the anchor point in the Comp panel. This has the same effect as dragging the anchor point in the Layer panel with the *Selection* tool. To practice this alternate method:

• Close the second (rightmost) comp viewer and open comp **[Ex.15_starter]** which consists of a simple 3D wireframe of a tire and wheel. The Title/Action Safe grid should be enabled. You can see that the anchor point is centered in the comp, but if you press 0 to RAM Preview the animation, you'll see how the tire wobbles as it rotates. This is because the tire is not centered in relation to the source layer.

• To fix this, press Z to select the Zoom tool, then click to zoom into the Comp panel so you can see more detail.

• Press Y to select the Pan Behind tool, then press Option (Alt) and drag the anchor point up and to the right. Notice how the anchor point stays in the same place and the wheel "slides" around behind it. Release the mouse when the wheel is centered in the comp. Because only the Anchor Point value changed, not the value for Position, the wheel continues to rotate around the center of the comp. Preview the animation again and tweak until the wobble is cured, as in **[Ex.15-final]**.

Of course, you could have used the original technique and arrived at the same result: Double-click the layer to open the Layer panel and use the Selection tool to reposition the anchor point to the wheel's center. But it's nice to have options.

Anchor Point Examples

The project file includes several examples of the benefits of manipulating the layer's anchor point:

• Open comp **[Ex.16_starter]** and RAM Preview: An attempt is made to rotate an artificial arm, but the anchor point is centered in the original footage item. The arm pivots about this center, rather than moving from the imaginary shoulder joint, as we would expect it to. To fix this, use the Pan Behind tool (Y) in the Comp panel to reposition the anchor point at the left end where you imagine the joint should be and preview again. Return to the Selection tool (V) when you're done. Our version is in **[Ex.16-final]**.

Remember that you can also position the anchor point outside of the layer's boundary. Then, when you animate Rotation, the layer will rotate in an arc. See **[Ex.17]** for an example.

• To demonstrate how the anchor point works when scaling a layer, open comp [**Ex.18a**] and RAM Preview. We created a series of transitions in which a layer stretches from one corner or side to the other. For instance, if we set the anchor point on the left side of a layer, and animate Scale from 0% width to 100% width, the layer stretches horizontally from the left side.

• [**Ex.18b**] takes this idea further, coordinating keyframes so one layer appears to "push" another off as they scale. Notice that Hold keyframes (discussed in the next chapter) are used for Anchor Point and Position so that a layer can push in from the left side, then be pushed out to the right side later, or even return to scaling from the center.

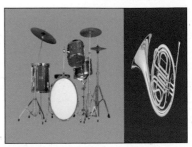

[**Ex.18b**]: Coordinating Anchor Point, Position, and Scale keyframes allows one layer to "push" off another layer. Images courtesy Getty Images.

Orbiting Objects

One of the simplest and most useful things you can do by offsetting an anchor point is to have one object rotate around another, as demonstrated in comp [**Ex.19_orbit-final**]. RAM Preview, then select the top layer and press U to twirl down its keyframes; only Rotation is animating. Let's re-create this effect from scratch:

Step 1: Open comp [**Ex.19_orbit_starter**]. Drag the **CD_sputnik.tif** (found in the Project panel's **Sources > Objects** folder) *to the left side of the Timeline panel* so it defaults to being centered in the Comp panel. Do the same for the **CD_planet_loop.mov** (found in **Sources > Movies**). It's important that both layers share the same Position value.

Step 2: Make sure the sputnik layer is on top of the planet layer in the layer stack. Since it is large in relation to the planet, select the sputnik layer, press S to reveal Scale, and scale it to around 50%.

Step 3: With the **CD_sputnik.tif** layer still selected, press A to reveal its Anchor Point and scrub its X value until the anchor point is centered horizontally in the sphere (about X = 66), then scrub its Y value until the sputnik is positioned above the planet (about X = 320).

Step 4: At time 00:00, press R to reveal Rotation and turn on its stopwatch to set the first keyframe at 0°. For the second keyframe, press End to jump to the end of the comp (05:29), then press Page Down to

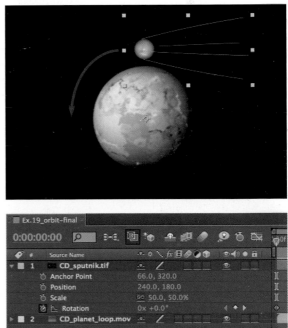

[**Ex.19**]: To make one object orbit another in a perfect circle, it's easier to offset the layer's anchor point and animate its rotation than it is to create a circular motion path with Position keyframes.

advance to 06:00, one frame after the end (the Comp panel will be gray). Click on the value for Rotation, enter a value of −1 Revolutions + 0 Degrees, and press Return. Press 0 to RAM Preview your animation. The sputnik appears to revolve counterclockwise around the planet, using its new anchor point, which just so happens to be the center of the planet. It seamlessly loops because the value of the keyframe one frame after the end is a whole revolution from the starting keyframe.

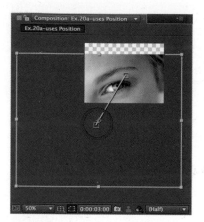

[**Ex.20a**]: Because scaling occurs around the anchor point (circled above), if you animate Position and Scale on an image that is much larger than the comp, the image may appear to drift off toward the pasteboard. Model courtesy Digital Vision/Beauty.

More Than Stills

This technique is not limited to still images – you can use moving sources or a nested comp (see *Size Doesn't Matter* in Chapter 18). Remember that the source should be larger than the output size so you don't need to scale above 100%.

Step 2: Turn on the stopwatches for both Anchor Point and Scale.

Motion Control Moves

The ultimate use for the anchor point is creating 2D motion control moves, popular for panning around photographs. Perhaps the most well-known example of this is the documentary *The Civil War: A Film by Ken Burns*. Traditionally, motion control involved placing photographs on a stand, then having a camera zoom and pan around them.

This technique is easy to replicate – with greater control and higher quality – inside After Effects. It's important to start with an image that's much larger than the comp size so you can avoid scaling past 100% at your tightest zoom, which would result in a softer, lower-quality image.

You could animate Position keyframes, but problems will creep in as soon as you try to simulate a zoom by animating Scale as well: Because layers scale around their anchor point, your image will slide around the frame. An example of what can go wrong when you animate Position and Scale is shown in [**Ex.20a**] – RAM Preview to see how the layer drifts. Select the **DV_Beauty_eye.jpg** layer and press the comma key to reduce the magnification; notice that the anchor point starts on the pasteboard, so scaling occurs around this point, not the center of the Comp panel. Sometimes this problem is barely noticeable, but the larger the image is compared with the comp size or the more off-center the detail you want to zoom in on, the more exaggerated the problem becomes.

How do you keep the anchor point centered? Easy: Center the Position of the layer in the Comp and animate the Anchor Point property instead. The anchor point now becomes the "crosshairs" your virtual camera is aimed at as you pan around an image. Comp [**Ex.20b**] shows the same move and zoom, but with animating the anchor point instead; now the focal point of the image no longer wanders away.

Smooth Operator

If you would like to practice this, re-create a similar motion control move from scratch. Use our image or one of your own:

Step 1: Open [**Ex.21_starter**]. Open the **Sources > Stills** folder in the Project panel, select **DV_AllThatJazz_duo.tif**, and press Command+/ (Control+/) to add it to your comp – this places its Position (and therefore its Anchor Point) at the center of the comp. Don't reposition it!

Step 2: Press A, then Shift+S, to twirl down Anchor Point and Scale in the Timeline panel. At 00:00, turn on the stopwatch for both properties.

Step 3: Select the Comp panel and press Command+Option+Shift+N (Control+Alt+Shift+N) to get two viewers so you can see the Layer and Comp panels side by side. Select the left viewer, then double-click the layer to open the Layer panel. You will be working mainly in the Layer panel, so adjust the magnification to allow you to see the entire image.

Step 4: Our photo consists of two musicians: a pianist and a trumpet player. Our camera move will travel from a close-up on the pianist's hands to a shot that includes both of their faces.

Select Anchor Point Path from the Layer panel's View menu. Now drag the anchor point in the Layer panel and notice that the location of the anchor will be what's centered in the Comp panel (provided the position of the layer is still in the exact center of the comp). Position the Anchor Point so that you nicely frame the pianist's hands.

Step 5: Move the current time indicator later in the comp – say, around 08:00. In the Layer panel, drag the Anchor Point to the faces area so you have a nice initial framing in the Comp panel. Reduce the Scale value to zoom back a bit, and notice that because the Anchor Point is centered in the Comp panel, the image does not slide off toward the pasteboard. In fact, animating Scale results in behavior not unlike zooming in and out with a real camera! Make sure you don't accidentally pan or scale the image so far that part of the comp's background is revealed.

Step 6: RAM Preview. Not a bad start; here are a few improvements:

• The anchor point's motion path in the Layer panel can be edited just like Position; try pulling Bezier handles to introduce a gentle curve.

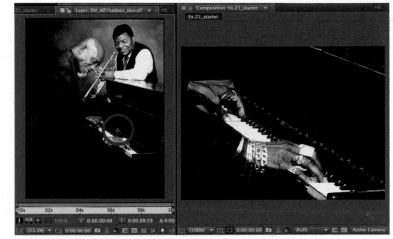

Step 4: Move the anchor point in the Layer panel (left viewer) so the hands on the piano are nicely framed in the Comp panel (right viewer). Image courtesy Digital Vision/All That Jazz.

Step 5: Our second keyframe set zooms back and pans up to their faces

The Kid Stays in the Picture

An update on this technique is to cut objects of interest out of their backgrounds and to perform moves in 3D space. We cover this technique in a column we originally wrote for Artbeats, which is included on the DVD in the **Goodies** folder.

• To smooth out the speed changes, select all the keyframes and press F9 to apply the Easy Ease keyframe assistant (discussed in Chapter 4).

• It can look more realistic if the rate of change is not exactly the same for both the Anchor Point and Scale properties – real camera operators aren't that smooth! In [**Ex.21-JazzGuys_final**], we moved the first anchor point keyframe to 01:00 to linger longer on the hands. You can also adjust their speed graphs in the Graph Editor (Chapter 4) to add variety.

• Add a very slight "wiggle" to the anchor point and scale animations to reduce the ultra-smooth move and better simulate a traditional motion control rig. This is best done with the wiggle expression (Chapter 37).

• If you find the move starts to "strobe" during the faster sections, consider using Motion Blur (Chapter 8).

Transform Keyboard Shortcuts

Here is a handy set of shortcuts to remember when you're working with the transform properties. (Shortcuts in parentheses are the Windows equivalents.)

Reveal property in Timeline panel:

Anchor Point	A	Rotation	R
Position	P	Opacity	T
Scale	S	To add/subtract	Shift + property reveal key

Turn on property stopwatch	Option+Shift (Alt+Shift) + respective reveal key (above)
If stopwatch on, add/delete keyframe	Option+Shift (Alt+Shift) + respective reveal key (above)
Show all animating properties	U
Reveal modified properties	UU
Solo selected properties	SS
Hide property or category	Option+Shift (Alt+Shift) + click property or category name
Select all keyframes for property	Click property name
Set value in dialog box	Command+Shift (Control+Shift) + P, S, or R
Constrain Scale to aspect ratio	Drag layer handle to start scaling, then add Shift
Constrain Rotation to 45° increments	Rotate with tool, then add Shift
Reset Scale to 100%	Double-click Selection tool
Reset Rotation to 0°	Double-click Rotation tool
Nudge Scale + 1% and −1%	Option+ (Control+) and Option− (Control −) (plus and minus keys) on the numeric keypad (add Shift to scale plus/minus 10%)
Nudge Rotation + 1° and −1°	+ (plus) and − (minus) keys on the numeric keypad (add Shift to rotate plus/minus 10°)
Increase/decrease Opacity + and −1%	Control+Option (Control+Alt) + (plus) and − (minus) keys on the numeric keypad (add Shift to rotate plus/minus 10°)
Stretch layer to fit Comp size	Command+Option+F (Control+Alt+F)
Stretch layer to fit vertically only	Command+Option+Shift+G (Control+Alt+Shift+G)
Stretch layer to fit horizontally only	Command+Option+Shift+H (Control+Alt+Shift+H)
Auto-Orient dialog (see Chapter 5)	Command+Option+O (Control+Alt+O)

Keyframe Tips and Gotchas

The concept of *key frames* comes from traditional animation: The master animator would draw the important frames of a scene, while others filled in the frames in-between. In the digital world, you determine the keyframes, and the computer calculates the frames in-between by interpolating intermediate values.

If you are new to animating with keyframes, below are some general tips as well as some common gotchas to help you avoid frustration:

• Be sure to turn on the stopwatch for the specific property you wish to animate (a layer's movement would be Position, to animate its size would be Scale, and so on).

• There is no animation unless you create at least two keyframes with different values at different points in time.

• Turn off Auto-keyframe mode as soon as you are done with it, or you will find extra keyframes all over the place. You've been warned…

• Turning off the stopwatch deletes all the keyframes for that property.

• Don't enable the stopwatch for every property on the first frame of a layer. If you do, you'll be forced to return to the first keyframe at the beginning of the layer to make a global change; you might also create unwanted animation by accidentally adding keyframes later in time.

• When you want a property to animate, the first keyframe does *not* need to occur at the beginning of the layer. For instance, if you want a title to fade out at the end, place two Opacity keyframes (100% and 0%) at the end of the layer. The layer will start out using the value of the first keyframe (100%) until it passes the first keyframe, at which point it will start to interpolate down to 0%. There's no need for a keyframe of 100% at the start of the layer.

• When properties are set to animate, there's no equal-opportunity rule that says they must all have the same number of keyframes all synced to the same points in time! Create keyframes only where needed for each property: The fewer keyframes you have to manage, the easier the animation will be to edit.

• On the other hand, when multiple properties are animating together, it's usually best to apply the same amount of ease in and out to keyframes that do align in time. (Examples of this are in the next chapter.)

Remember: Creating motion graphics begins with *motion*, and manipulating transformation keyframes is a large part of the job. Another very important skill is controlling how layers animate over time, and that is the subject of Chapter 4. We'll cover more animation tips plus some fun and useful keyframe assistants in Chapter 5.

Before you move on, we encourage you to experiment and have fun until you feel comfortable with the basic animation techniques covered so far in this chapter. Create a new comp and design your own animation. Go ahead – it's only software; you can't break anything!

To Keyframe, or Not to Keyframe

Not all animation in After Effects results from creating keyframes:

• Some effects (such as Distort > Wave) self-animate – they create an animation at their default settings.

• Expressions (Chapter 37) can make a property wiggle or loop as well as create more complex animations, all based on JavaScript.

• Behaviors (Chapter 25) use a combination of effects and expressions to automatically animate a layer without using keyframes. For example, the Drift Over Time behavior moves a layer in a certain direction at a certain speed.

• Further examples include the Wiggly Selector for a Text Animator (Chapter 21) and the Wiggle Paths option for Shapes (Chapter 32).

CONNECT

Layer panel, RAM Previewing: Chapter 2.

Graph Editor, hold keyframes: Chapter 4.

Moving and scaling motion paths, auto-orient rotation, keyframe assistants: Chapter 5.

Managing layers: Chapter 6.

Trimming layers: Chapter 7.

Motion blur: Chapter 8.

Anchor point in 3D: Chapter 13.

3D space: Chapters 13–16.

Parenting: Chapter 17.

Nesting compositions: Chapter 18.

Animating effects: Chapter 22.

In Search of the Perfect Pixel

As a motion graphics designer, delivering a high-quality render to your client is of the utmost concern. If you are new to After Effects, however, you may have concerns about why pixels appear less than perfect. Note that many of the solutions involve techniques "not yet in evidence," so feel free to review this checklist when the need arises. We hope it will help you determine if the artifacts you are seeing are temporary, trivial, or really need fixing:

• The image in the Comp panel looks "crunchy." Solution: Check if Magnification is set to less than 100%. This is a temporary display issue and nothing to worry about! See *Navigating in Space*, Chapter 2.

• The Comp panel is at 100%, but images appear "blocky." Solution: Check that the comp's Resolution is set to Auto or Full. See *Resolution*, Chapter 2.

• Magnification is set to 100%, Resolution is at Auto or Full, but images are still "crunchy." Solution: Check if the Pixel Aspect Ratio Correction switch is toggled on at the bottom of the Comp/Layer/Footage panel. See *Working Square*, Chapter 41.

• Layers are not moving smoothly, or they look aliased when rotated or scaled. Solution: Check that the layer's Quality switch is set to Best, which makes layers move smoothly and antialiases them when they are transformed or distorted. See *Subpixel Positioning* (next page), and *Quality*, Chapter 2.

• The layer is set to Best Quality, but you've applied a blur or distortion effect and it doesn't render smoothly. Solution: Check if the effect offers different levels of antialiasing in the Effect Controls panel, and if so, set the Antialiasing popup to High.

• Imported still images look a little softer in After Effects than they do in Photoshop or Illustrator. Solution: Create artwork in other programs where the width and height are an even number of pixels. See *Resampling in Action* (next page).

• Images in the Comp panel look "fat," and circular objects look like eggs. Solution: D1/DV pixels are not square, so this could be correct behavior if you have placed a square pixel image into a D1/DV NTSC or PAL comp. Non-square pixels are discussed in Chapter 41, *Video Issues*, along with correct frame rates and frame sizes for video output as well as working with anamorphic widescreen sources.

• There are horizontal lines running through a movie in the Comp panel. Solution: The movie is interlaced, and you need to separate the fields in the Interpret Footage dialog. See *Fields and Pulldown*, Chapter 38, and *Fields and Interlaced Frames*, Chapter 41.

• Movies in the Comp panel are alternating between sharp and soft. Solution: The source movie's frame rate may not be in sync with the Comp's frame rate. Select the source in the Project panel and open File > Interpret Footage > Main. Then conform the source's frame rate to the correct rate – 29.97 frames per second (fps) for NTSC video, 25 fps for PAL, and so on. (Even if it says the movie is 29.97 already, conform it anyway…) See *Frame Rate*, Chapter 38.

• You play back a rendered movie on a television monitor, and some parts are "flickering" slightly. Solution: You may need to selectively blur these high-contrast areas. See *Field Flicker*, Chapter 41.

• You play back a field-rendered movie on a video monitor, and the flicker is really, *really* bad. Solution: The field order of the movie may not match the hardware chain and the fields therefore may be reversed. See the Field Render options in Chapter 42, *Render Queue*.

• You render a movie with an alpha channel, and when you composite it in your editing program, it has a black "fringe." Solution: Render with a straight alpha channel, not the default premultiplied alpha. This is discussed in the *Color* section of *Output Module Settings*, Chapter 42.

• You render with an alpha channel and the movie looks really ugly when viewed in QuickTime Player. Solution: Congratulations, you successfully rendered a straight alpha channel, but QuickTime Player is showing you only the RGB Channel with the extra "bleed." Import this movie into your editing program – and relax!

Subpixel Positioning

When a layer is set to Best Quality (the default), it will use *subpixel positioning*; this allows a layer to be positioned using less than one pixel for smoother motion. How much less? After Effects resolves to 16 bits of subpixel resolution, so each pixel is divided into 65,536 parts width *and* height. With that kind of resolution, there are more than *4 billion* subpixels. Technically speaking, that's known as "a lot."

When Position is interpolating between keyframes, check out the current value – the subpixel numbers to the right of the decimal point are used when the layer is set to Best Quality (the default).

To see the numerical results of this precision, park the current time indicator between two interpolating Position keyframes, select the layer and press Command+Shift+P (Control+Shift+P) to open the Position dialog. The dialog will show values for the X and Y axes for 2D layers: Numbers to the left of the decimal point are the integer values used by Draft Quality, while the fractional numbers indicate the subpixels used by Best Quality.

When a layer is set to Draft Quality, movement is calculated using whole pixels only. While this lets you set up keyframes and preview them more quickly, you might find the results a little bumpy.

In addition to smoother motion, Best Quality also ensures that effects and transformations are rendered with full antialiasing. Draft Quality renders without antialiasing (this is particularly noticeable with vector artwork such as Text layers, Solid layers, or Illustrator sources).

Resampling in Action

A benefit of Best Quality and subpixel positioning is that layers are antialiased (or resampled) when they are transformed. While good antialiasing is desirable (especially with distortion effects), the softness that resampling adds can be unwanted when you're just placing, say, a non-moving image or title created in Illustrator or Photoshop in your comp at 100%.

To avoid this unwanted resampling, we need to understand why and when it kicks in. As it happens, After Effects resamples a layer whenever it uses subpixel positioning, and that means *whenever the difference between the Anchor Point value and Position value is not a whole number*. Check out the following example comps in this chapter's project:

- **[Ex.99a]:** Your layer is *even* sized, 300 pixels wide by 300 high, which places the Anchor Point in the center at 150,150. You place this image in an even-sized 640×480 pixel comp and Position it in the center (320,240). The difference between 150,150 and 320,240 is a whole number, so the layer does *not* get resampled. Toggle the layer between Draft and Best Quality, and you'll see that there is no change.

- **[Ex.99b]:** Toggle the layer between Draft and Best, and see the image shift and soften slightly. This is because this layer is *odd* sized, 301 pixels wide by 301 high, which places the Anchor Point at

150.5,150.5. When it's positioned in the middle of this even-sized 640×480 pixel comp, the difference between 150.5,150.5 and 320,240 is not a whole number, so the layer will be resampled.

As you can see, you can avoid resampling for non-moving images by creating sources with even sizes in Photoshop or Illustrator. If all else fails, you can always avoid unnecessary resampling by changing the Position of the layer by a half pixel up or down, left or right, until the image pops into sharpness.

4

Keyframe Velocity

The secrets to creating sophisticated animations.

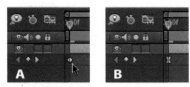

Linear keyframes are denoted by diamonds in the Timeline panel (A). Select one and choose Animation > Keyframe Assistant > Easy Ease (below): This will convert it to a Bezier keyframe that gracefully starts and stops (B).

Example Project

Explore the 04-Example Project.aep file as you read this chapter; references to [Ex.##] refer to specific compositions within the project file.

In the previous chapter, you learned how to animate. In this chapter, you will learn through a series of exercises how to improve your animations by focusing on the timing and speed changes of your movements. We'll start by showing you a few quick tricks, then turn our attention to the Graph Editor: an industrial-strength tool for refining your animations. We'll end our keyframe velocity tour with Roving and Hold keyframes.

Easy Ease

Keyframed values in the timeline default to *linear interpolation*. This means the values they are assigned to – rotation, scale, effect parameters, and such – change by a constant amount from frame to frame in-between keyframes. A side effect of this is an abrupt speed change as you cross a keyframe, which is often perceived as an unrefined animation.

Open this chapter's example project and double-click the comp **[Ex.01_starter]**. RAM Preview it and observe the wheel's animation: It starts spinning suddenly, changes direction abruptly, then suddenly stops. These are telltale signs of linear keyframes. An improvement would be to have the values "ease" into and out of the keyframes.

The Rotation keyframes for **CD_bikewheel.tif** should be revealed in the Timeline panel; select the layer and press R if they aren't.

- Select the first keyframe and apply Animation > Keyframe Assistant > Easy Ease. RAM Preview; the rotation now accelerates smoothly away from the first keyframe.

- Select the last keyframe and press F9, which is the Easy Ease shortcut. Now the wheel also eases to a stop.

- Right-click on the middle keyframe, which will open a contextual menu that provides a third way to apply eases. Select Keyframe Assistant > Easy Ease In and RAM Preview. The rotation will slow down as it approaches this keyframe, then snap away with its normal linear interpolation. Undo and try Easy Ease Out: It has the opposite effect. Select Easy Ease, and rotation will ease in and out.

Just learning to apply Easy Ease and its variations will vastly improve the look of many animations. But it isn't a cure-all, and it certainly isn't all you can do to manipulate keyframe velocity!

Auto Bezier

A trickier challenge is smoothing out changes in values that are supposed to keep moving rather than start and stop. An example would be an animation with multiple Position keyframes such as that in [**Ex.02_starter**]. Open this comp, select **GI_baseball.tif**, and observe its motion path in the Comp panel: Although the path is nicely rounded, notice that the dots along this path are spaced differently between keyframes. Tighter spacing means the layer moves less from frame to frame.

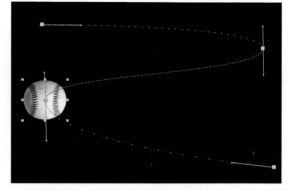

Make sure the baseball's Position property is exposed in the Timeline (shortcut: P). The space between its keyframes in the timeline shows you how much time it takes to get from point to point. A combination of the spacing between keyframes in time and how much the layer moves in the Comp panel determines its *velocity* or *speed*.

RAM Preview and note the sudden speed changes at the middle keyframes. One way to smooth these out is to change the linear keyframes to Auto Bezier: Hold down Command on Mac (Control on Windows) and click on one of the middle keyframes in the Timeline. It will change from a diamond to a circle, and the spacing of the dots will transition more evenly across that keyframe in the Comp panel. Specifically, the incoming velocity and outgoing velocity are being averaged so they are the same value through the keyframe. Change the other middle keyframe to Auto Bezier as well and RAM Preview to see if there's an improvement.

While Auto Bezier smoothes out speed changes right at the keyframe, remember that the speed of the baseball as it moves between keyframes is determined by the number of pixels it has to travel (the distance) and the spacing between keyframes in time. The way to smooth out the overall speed is to slide the middle keyframes in the Timeline panel. Try this yourself while watching the spacing of the dots in the Comp panel: Evenly spaced dots means more constant speed. RAM Preview to check your results.

To ease the baseball into its final position, select the last keyframe and press F9 to apply Easy Ease. RAM Preview again and observe how the baseball speeds up between the last two keyframes before easing to a stop! Adjusting keyframe velocities is a bit of a balancing act: If you're going to slow down one place, you have to speed up in another to cover the same distance in the same amount of time.

The spacing of the dots along a motion path tell you how much the layer moves from frame to frame. Note how the spacing changes on either side of the keyframe; we need to change the timing of the keyframes to smooth out the spacing (and therefore, the layer's velocity). Baseball courtesy Getty Images.

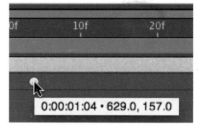

Command+click (Control+click) on a keyframe to change it to the smoother Auto Bezier type, denoted by the circle. Repeat to switch it back to a Linear keyframe.

Comp [**Ex.02-final**] after we converted the middle keyframes to Auto Bezier, spaced the keyframes in time, and applied Easy Ease to the last keyframe.

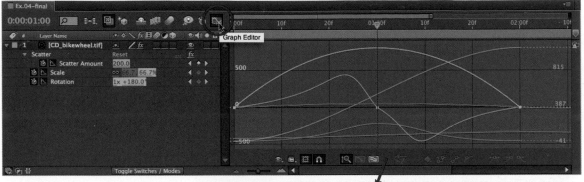

Legend Key

A Choose which properties are shown in Graph Editor

B Choose graph type and options

C Show Transform Box when multiple keys are selected

D Toggle Snap on/off

E Auto-zoom graph height

F Fit selection to view

G Fit all graphs to view

H Separate Dimensions

I Edit selected keyframes

J Convert selected keyframes to Hold

K Convert selected keyframes to Linear

L Convert selected keyframes to Auto Bezier

M Easy Ease

N Easy Ease In

O Easy Ease Out

Show Properties menu

Graph Options menu

The Graph Editor

Easy Ease and Auto Bezier can provide big improvements over using the default linear keyframes, but there quickly comes a time when you need a higher degree of control and refinement. Enter the Graph Editor: It takes over a portion of the Timeline panel to show you precisely what is happening with the values and velocity (speed) of as many parameters as you select, including those across multiple layers.

Value Graphs

We'll start by becoming familiar with viewing and editing keyframes in the Graph Editor. Select Close All from the tab along the top of the Comp panel. Then open [**Ex.03_starter 1**], select **CD_bikewheel.tif**, and if necessary press R to reveal its Rotation keyframes. Click on the Graph Editor switch along the top of the Timeline panel. A graph will replace the layer bars and keyframes on the right side of this panel. Along its bottom are a series of switches that control how the graphs are displayed. These settings are remembered per comp, but let's verify them for practice:

- Click on the eyeball icon to open the Show Properties menu (see figure to the left, above) and make sure Show Selected Properties is enabled; you can leave Show Animated Properties unchecked for now.

- Then click on the next button to the right (Graph Options) and make sure both Edit Value Graph and Show Graph Tool Tips are selected. Leave Show Reference Graph deselected; we'll get to that later.

- Then to the right, make sure the Show Transform Box and Auto-zoom graph height switches are both enabled.

Click once on the word Rotation to select this property. Its keyframes will now appear in the Graph Editor with a line connecting them. Hover the cursor over the line: A tooltip will appear displaying the value of this parameter at this frame. Hover the cursor over a keyframe, and the time

Speed 101

The speed of a layer as it moves along its motion path is determined by the number of pixels it has to travel (the distance) and the amount of time it is allotted for that journey (the spacing between keyframes in time). No amount of fiddling with its graphs is going to make a slowpoke animation suddenly fast and exciting or calm down a frenzied animation.

In After Effects, you set the path of a journey from A to B in the Comp panel, and you set the duration by spacing these two keyframes in the Timeline panel. The default linear interpolation in time results in an average and constant speed for the trip, which ideally is close to the desired speed. If you slow down the takeoff (outgoing from keyframe A), After Effects

will speed up the rest of the journey – otherwise you'd arrive late at keyframe B. Similarly, speeding up your takeoff will slow down the remainder of the trip – or you'd arrive too early. If you slow down both the takeoff and landing, you'll travel much faster than the average speed in the middle. So adjusting the velocity controls is always a balancing act.

Before you adjust the graph, preview the animation using linear keyframes. If your animation is going too fast on average at this point, you may have to deal with the big picture by giving keyframes more time to play out. If the animation seems sluggish, bring the keyframes closer together in time so they have less time to play. Then start tweaking the velocity curves in the Graph Editor.

of the keyframe will also be displayed. Next, click and drag the middle keyframe: Moving it up increases its value, moving it down decreases its value; moving it left and right moves it earlier and later in time. Dragging the keyframe below the 0 line creates a negative rotation value. As you drag, the tooltip will show you the new value and time, as well as the "delta" (change in value and time) from its previous location. Undo to return the keyframe to its previous value.

Click on the word Rotation a second time. This will select all of the Rotation keyframes, which will be surrounded by a bounding box in the Graph Editor (see figure, next page). Drag the handles on the edges of this selection box: You can change the beginning, end, and value range of the entire selection at once; you can even skew the box by dragging its sides between the handles. Feel free to RAM Preview if you want to confirm your edits. To remove your selection, just click outside the selection box. Undo to get back to where you started.

As you drag a keyframe in the Graph Editor, a tooltip tells you how far you are moving a keyframe in time and how much you are changing its value. The straight value graph lines indicate linear keyframe interpolation.

Toggle Graph Editor

The shortcut to open and close the Graph Editor display is Shift+F3.

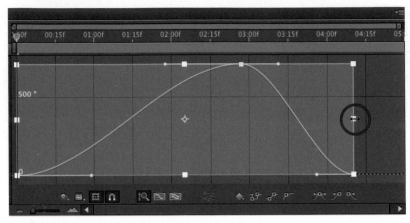

When you select two or more keyframes, they will be surrounded by a bounding box. Dragging the sides and corners of this box edits all of the selected keyframes as a group. Here we've applied Easy Ease to all selected keyframes – note how the value graph is now gently curved.

Scrolling the Graph Editor

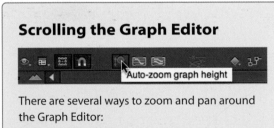

There are several ways to zoom and pan around the Graph Editor:

• The normal Timeline panel Time Navigator bar and Zoom slider work as before (covered in Chapter 2).

• When you're zoomed in, hold down the space-bar to get the Hand cursor, then drag the Graph Editor display horizontally or vertically.

• The Auto-Zoom Graph Height switch along the bottom of the Graph Editor (the magnifying glass icon) automatically zooms and pans the Graph Editor vertically to fit the selected graphs. Note that this overrides your ability to drag the editor vertically with the Hand tool.

• The two buttons to the right of Auto-Zoom Graph Height adjust the Graph Editor horizontally and vertically to fit the selected graphs or keyframes.

Time to see what Easy Ease looks like inside the Graph Editor: Select the first keyframe and either press F9 or click on the Easy Ease switch along the bottom of the Graph Editor. Notice how the graph now ascends much more slowly away from the first keyframe; this shows you how the value changes only a little per frame initially, then changes by larger increments per frame over time. Select the second keyframe and either press Shift+F9 or click on the Easy Ease In icon. Think about what the value graph is telling you: The Rotation value changes slowly as it approaches the second keyframe, then changes more quickly as it leaves it. RAM Preview to affirm the results. Finally, click Rotation again to select all of the keyframes and press F9: All of the selected keyframes will be Easy Eased. Click elsewhere in the graph to deselect the keyframes.

Editing Handles

After you applied Easy Ease to a keyframe, you probably noticed the yellow "influence" handles that suddenly appeared on either side of it. Similar to the Bezier handles for Position path keyframes that you worked with in the previous chapter, these handles give you finer control over how quickly values change as you approach and exit keyframes.

Select the first keyframe, then drag its handle (not the keyframe itself) directly to the right to elongate it. The value graph will stay close to the 0° line even longer in response. If the handle dips below the 0 line, the layer may rotate in reverse; press the Shift key as you drag to constrain its movement to horizontal only. RAM Preview and relate what you see happening in the Comp panel to the shape of the graph: The wheel is even slower to accelerate away from its initial position. (By the way, there's nothing special about an Easy Ease keyframe; it's just a Bezier keyframe with influence handles that default to a particular orientation and length.)

The longer the handle is, the more influence its angle has over how values flow into and out of key-

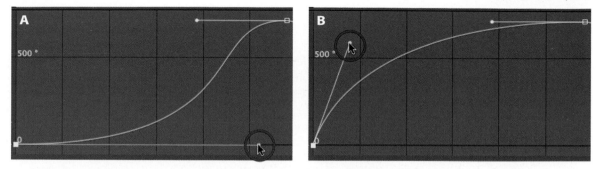

You can lengthen keyframe handles to increase their influence (A), adding Shift to constrain movement to horizontal only. You can also pull them at angles to change how values enter or exit keyframes (B), use them to arc graphs to create value undershoots and overshoots (C), and hold down Option (Alt) as needed to break or rejoin them (D).

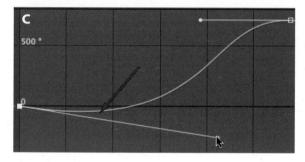

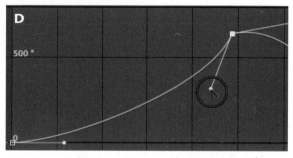

frames. If you want to quickly return a keyframe's interpolation to linear in the Graph Editor, hold down the Option (Alt) key to get the Change Direction tool and click on the keyframe – try this with the first keyframe.

Now drag the same handle upward so that the value graph arcs quickly up and away from the first keyframe. This means that the value will increase more rapidly over the first few frames of the timeline. RAM Preview, and you will see that the wheel spins quickly away from the first keyframe.

Click on the middle keyframe: Handles will appear on either side. You have independent control over how values flow into and out of a keyframe. Play with editing both handles, previewing to check results. To toggle the handles between being joined together and being independent, hold down Option (Alt) to get the Change Direction tool again and drag either one of them.

Finally, turn your attention to the last keyframe. Say you want the wheel's rotation to "overshoot" – meaning, it would spin past its final resting place, then snap back to its final value. Think about what this means value-wise: The value graph line will need to continue down below its final value of 0° before returning. To do this, drag the handle downward so that the curve bends below the 0° line and RAM Preview to check the result. Incidentally, overshooting is one of the keys to creating more realistic character animation movements. In [**Ex.03-overshooting**], we've animated the wheel on the left side to overshoot its final Scale keyframe, while the wheel on the right overshoots its final Rotation keyframe.

FACTOID

You're so Square!

When you enable the stopwatch for a parameter such as a popup menu or a checkbox, After Effects creates a *hold* keyframe. It has a square-shaped icon, indicating that this parameter cannot interpolate over time. You can create more keyframes and assign different values to them, but the values will change abruptly at each new keyframe.

Select Edit Speed Graph from the Choose Graph Type menu to see how fast parameters change over time.

TIP

The Pen and the Graph

You can also use the Pen tool (shortcut: Q) to edit Graph Editor lines.

When displaying speed graphs, the lines in the Graph Editor display velocity at a given frame, with flat lines indicating linear keyframes and constant velocity (top graph).

When Easy Ease is applied to keyframes, the speed graph will return to the "zero" line at each keyframe (bottom graph).

Velocity Graphs

The Graph Editor gives you a second way to see how parameters change over time: By viewing how *fast* they are changing, rather than their absolute values at each frame.

Open comp [**Ex.03_starter 2**], which includes our wheel with linear (constant speed) keyframes. Select **CD_bikewheel.tif**, make sure the Rotation keyframes are visible, and press Shift+F3 to reveal the Graph Editor. Click on the word Rotation once to select it. Then open the Choose Graph Type menu and select Edit Speed Graph.

In contrast to the sloping lines you saw in the previous example, you will see a flat horizontal line connecting your keyframes. Instead of value, this graph is showing you how fast the wheel is rotating at any given frame (note that the unit markings along the vertical axis are in degrees per second). As the first segment is above the 0°/sec line, it tells you that it is rotating in a positive direction (clockwise) during this time; the second segment residing below the 0°/sec line tells you it is rotating in a negative direction (counterclockwise). The distance between this "zero" line and the graph segments tell you how fast the wheel is rotating. Hovering your cursor over a graph line will open a tooltip with this information.

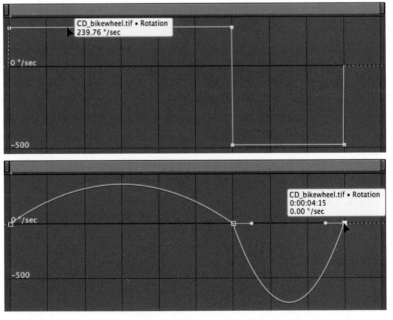

Click Rotation a second time to select all of its keyframes and apply Easy Ease; now it smoothly arcs away from and returns to 0°/sec at each keyframe. RAM Preview and relate it again to the motion of the wheel.

Deselect the keyframes by clicking in the Graph Editor somewhere outside of the selection region. To avoid having to reselect Rotation, set the Choose Properties popup to also enable Show Animated Properties – all keyframes for a selected layer automatically appear. You can edit the influence handles just as you did for the value graph, but with different results as you are affecting how fast the *speed* changes – how quickly the wheel is accelerating and decelerating as it approaches and exits keyframes. For example, lengthen the handles to make the wheel appear sluggish and heavy.

To confirm what is going on, switch back and forth between Edit Value Graph and Edit Speed Graph to see how they relate to each other. To simplify your life, also enable Show Reference Graph so that you can see both graphs at once – although you still need to switch between Edit Value and Edit Speed as you decide which one to tweak.

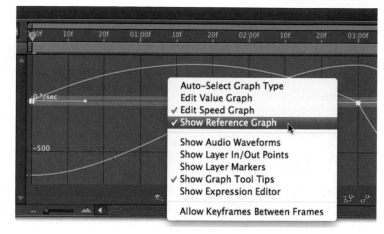

Enable Show Reference Graph allows you to see both the Value and Speed graphs at once – although you can only edit one at a time.

Keyframe Velocity by Numbers

For those more numerically than graphically minded, the Keyframe Velocity dialog offers an alternative way to manipulate the Graph Editor when editing keyframe velocity. To open this dialog:

- If you are in the Graph Editor, double-click a keyframe while in Edit Speed Graph mode.

- If you are in the normal layer bar and keyframe view, right-click on a keyframe and select Keyframe Velocity from the contextual menu that appears; the shortcut is Option+double-clicking (Alt+double-clicking) on a keyframe.

In the Keyframe Velocity dialog you can set the speed at which values are changing when they enter or exit a keyframe (the distance away from the "zero line" in Edit Speed Graph mode), as well as the influence (the length of the Bezier influence handles entering and exiting keyframes). Enabling or disabling the Continuous switch has

In the Graph Editor, double-click a keyframe while in Edit Speed Graph mode to open the Keyframe Velocity dialog.

the same effect as joining or breaking the Bezier handles around a keyframe.

How does this relate to what you've already been doing in this chapter? When you apply Easy Ease to a keyframe, it sets the Incoming and Outgoing Velocity values to 0 and the Influence to 33% – just as you see in the figure here. When you convert a keyframe to Auto Bezier, the Incoming and Outgoing Velocity are left alone, the Continuous switch is set, and the Influence values are set to 16.67% (less influence). Converting a keyframe to linear unchecks Continuous and sets the Influence to 0%.

Autograph

Enabling Auto-Select Graph Type from the Choose Graph Type menu will show the Value Graph for all simple properties such as Rotation; it will display the Speed Graph for position-oriented keyframes.

Multiple Values

An important feature of the Graph Editor is its ability to superimpose multiple values (including values from multiple layers) on the same graph, making it easier to coordinate multiple properties. You can also use Graph Editor Sets to decide which properties you are viewing without worrying about which ones are selected or deselected.

You can close your previous compositions. Then open [**Ex.04_starter**] and RAM Preview. Select **CD_bikewheel.tif** and press U if the keyframes are not visible: This is a busier animation where Scale, Rotation, and a Scatter effect are animated, all using linear keyframes.

Now open the Graph Editor. We've already enabled Show Animated Properties, so all three keyframed parameters will be revealed when the layer is selected. Note how the colored boxes around their values in the Timeline panel's Switches column match the color of their corresponding graph lines; After Effects automatically color-codes properties to help distinguish them.

[Ex.04] animates the Scale, Rotation, and Scatter Amount for a wheel; our goal is to refine and better coordinate it.

It's great to see all parameters at once – but when their value ranges are vastly different (such as Rotation going from 0° to 1080° while Scale goes from 33.3% to 100%), you have a bit of problem: The Scale graph seems to barely change in relation to the steep line of the Rotation graph. You could disable Show Animated Properties and select the properties only you want to see, but when you edit one, the others will be deselected and therefore disappear.

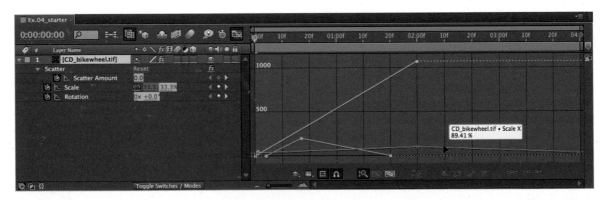

After Effects color-codes the properties being displayed in the Graph Editor. Scale has two values (X and Y); only the red line is visible as the green line (which has the same values) is underneath it.

Graph Editor Sets to the rescue: Click on Choose Properties menu (the eyeball icon along the bottom of the Graph Editor), deselect Show Animated Properties, and enable Show Graph Editor Set. In the Layer Name column of the Timeline panel, you will see a small graph icon to the right of each keyframe stopwatch. These are Graph Editor Set switches. Click on this switch and it will enable this parameter to always be shown. Practice turning parameters on and off to get a feel for how Graph Editor Sets work.

Let's improve our animation:

• Enable the Graph Editor Set switches for Scale and Rotation. Then click on Scale twice to select all of its keyframes. Hold down the Shift key and click on the second Rotation keyframe (the turquoise graph line and dots); note how the selection expands to include it. Then carefully Shift+click on the first Rotation keyframe (under the Scale keyframe) to also include it. Press F9 to convert all to Easy Ease keyframes.

• Next, let's synchronize the Scatter effect with scale and rotation. Giving properties the same start and end times as well as the same keyframe interpolation type synchronizes them together. Enable the Graph Editor Set button for Scatter Amount, then disable Rotation to clean up the display (Scale and Rotation have the same timing so we need to see only one of them, and Scale's parameter range is much closer to that of Scatter Amount).

• Drag the first Scatter Amount keyframe to align in time with the first Scale keyframe. Adding the Shift key after you start dragging will help restrict your movement to one axis as well as reinforce its desire to snap to the timing of the previous keyframe. Drag the last Scatter Amount keyframe to line up with the middle Scale keyframe.

• Ideally, the Scatter Amount should be at its peak when the wheel is rotating its fastest. To better view when this happens, switch the Graph Type to Edit Speed Graph. Then re-enable viewing Rotation in the Graph Editor Set. Drag the middle Scatter Amount keyframe to align with the peak in the Rotation speed graph.

• Finally, to give Scatter Amount the same keyframe velocity as the other parameters, click Scatter Amount again to select all of its keyframes and press F9 to Easy Ease them. RAM Preview to confirm the results of your manipulations.

The Graph Editor Set buttons next to the animation stopwatches (above) help determine which values are shown in the Graph Editor. You must also enable Show Graph Editor Set in the Choose Properties menu (below).

Our final graphs. We've set the Graph Editor to Edit Speed Graphs (the lines with the keyframe dots) and to Show Reference Graph so you can see how both the values and velocity are varying over time.

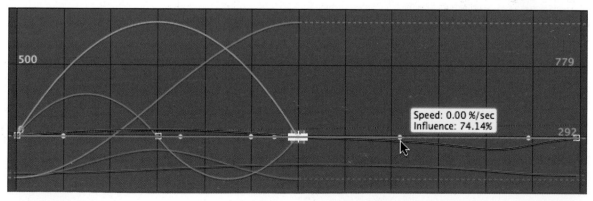

In **[Ex.05]** we started the Twirl before Rotation to make it react more like a spring being wound.

TIP

Right-click for More

Right-clicking in an empty area of the Graph Editor will open a contextual menu with many of the most important options.

This should get you pretty close to a well-coordinated animation, but not all animations feel best when the keyframes are perfectly aligned. **[Ex.05]** contains an example where we used Twirl instead of Scatter on the wheel. We started Twirl before Rotation to make it seem as if the wheel was reacting like a wound spring, and we played with the influence of the later keyframes to make the result feel more natural.

Below is a roundup of keyboard shortcuts that can be used to change keyframe interpolation:

Shortcuts for Graph Editor

Toggle open/closed Graph Editor:	Shift+F3
Toggle interpolation between Linear and Auto Bezier:	Option (Alt) + click keyframe
Constrain movement of handles to horizontal:	Shift + drag handle
In Edit Speed Graph mode, break handles/rejoin handles:	Option (Alt) + drag handle
Open Keyframe Velocity dialog:	Double-click keyframe in Edit Speed Graph mode

Shortcuts for Layer Bar Mode

Toggle interpolation between Linear and Auto Bezier:	Command (Control) + click keyframe
Toggle keyframe interpolation to Hold:	Command+Option (Control+Alt) + click keyframe
Open Keyframe Velocity dialog:	Option (Alt) + double-click keyframe

Shortcuts for Both Modes

Toggle keyframe interpolation to Hold:	Command+Option+H (Control+Alt+H)
Move selected keyframe 1 frame earlier:	Option (Alt) + Left Arrow
Move selected keyframe 1 frame later:	Option (Alt) + Right Arrow
Move selected keyframe 10 frames earlier/later:	Add Shift key to above shortcuts

Position Graphs

Position keyframes are a special case with the Graph Editor. A single Position keyframe contains multiple parameters: X Position, Y Position, and in the case of a 3D Layer (Chapter 13), Z Position. Adjusting the timing of a single Position keyframe affects all of the XYZ values together. This is also true of other multidimensional properties such as Scale.

What makes position-style keyframes unique is that you edit some of their characteristics (the motion path) in the Comp or Layer panel, and the rest (the speed at which you come into and exit these keyframes) in the Timeline panel. As you might expect, this has an impact on how you interact with position-style keyframes in the Graph Editor.

Where's my Motion Path?

Animating the Position property creates a motion path in the Comp panel, as does a Camera or Light's Point of Interest. Animating an Anchor Point or Effect Point creates motion paths in the Layer panel.

Position Value Graphs

Close the previous comps and open [**Ex.06_starter 1**], which is similar to the second comp you encountered earlier in this chapter. Select **QE_Gizmo_loop.mov** and make sure its Position property is exposed (shortcut: P).

Reveal the Graph Editor and make sure the Graph Type popup is set to Edit Value Graph. You should see both a red and a green line: These represent the X and Y Position values respectively. Click and drag one of the independent red or green keyframes in the Graph Editor and observe how the motion path changes in the Comp panel. Feel free to try the opposite: Drag a keyframe in the Comp panel and observe the changes in the Graph Editor.

Now the difference: Unlike the other properties you've worked with in the Graph Editor so far, you won't see Bezier handles by default for the Position value graphs. If you want to edit how the *value* of Position interpolates (without entering a special mode), edit the Bezier handles for the motion path in the Comp panel.

But this doesn't mean you can't edit the *speed* at which these Position values change – we'll do that next.

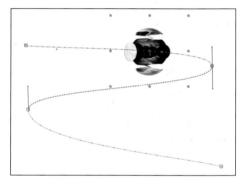

There are two ways to view Position's animation: as a motion path in the Comp panel (above) and as a value graph in the Graph Editor (below). The red and green lines are for the X and Y Position values, respectively. Gizmo courtesy Quiet Earth Design.

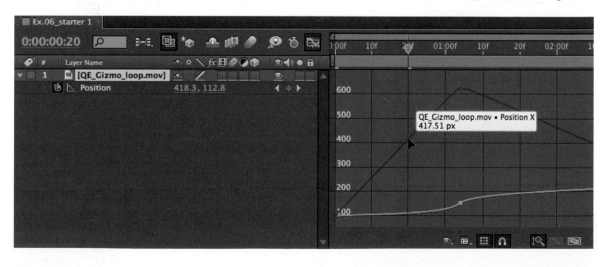

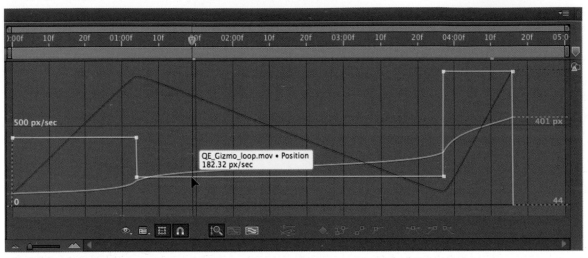

Set the Graph Editor to Edit Speed Graph (the white line) and enable Show Reference Graph (the red and green lines). This will allow you to see how the Position values interpolate as you edit the keyframe velocity for this motion path.

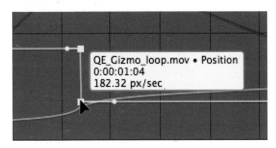

Linear keyframe interpolation means the speed of movement can be different entering and exiting a keyframe – thus the discontinuous break in the graph at the keyframe (above).

Option+click (Alt+click) on a keyframe in the Graph Editor to convert it to Auto Bezier, smoothing the speed change through the keyframe (below).

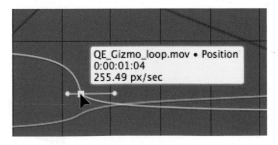

Position Speed Graphs

Open [**Ex.06_starter 2**], which is a copy of the previous comp at the point before you started editing the motion path. We're going to re-create the motion speed edits you performed earlier in this chapter with the baseball, but this time using the Graph Editor to get a more accurate idea of what is going on.

Select **QE_Gizmo_loop.mov**, reveal its Position keyframes, and press Shift+F3 to reveal the Graph Editor. Since we can edit the motion path (Position's values and interpolation) in the Comp panel, switch the Graph Type popup to Edit Speed Graph; you'll see a series of white lines which represent the rate at which the gizmo moves. While you're at it, enable Show Reference Graph; this will overlay the red and green value graphs so you can see how speed and value interact.

Remember that this animation initially has linear temporal keyframes, which results in a constant speed being maintained between them. The flat horizontal segments in the speed graph reflect the constant velocity. Click on the second Position keyframe (on the white speed graph), which is at 01:04 in time. Bezier handles will appear, but they will be disconnected as the speeds coming into and going out of the keyframe are different. To smooth out this sudden speed change, press the "Convert selected keyframes to Auto Bezier" button at the bottom of the Graph Editor. This converts it to an Auto Bezier keyframe (the circle icon in the normal keyframe view), and its Bezier handles will now be joined on the same level, indicating that the object is entering and exiting this keyframe at the same speed. (No prizes for guessing you can click on the "Convert selected keyframes to Linear" button to revert back to Linear.)

There's also a handy shortcut for toggling between Linear and Auto Bezier in the Graph Editor: Hold down the Option (Alt) key to summon the Change Direction tool and click on a keyframe in the Graph Editor. Try this to convert the third keyframe to Auto Bezier.

With both middle keyframes converted to Auto Bezier, spend some time dragging them up and down (which corresponds to the speed through that keyframe) as well as left and right (which corresponds to the time at which that keyframe occurs) until you have as smooth a graph curve as possible. Remember that you can alter the influence handles as well. The spacing between the keyframe dots along the motion path will help provide visual confirmation of what you are doing. RAM Preview regularly to test your results.

That may seem like a lot of work, but it was for a good cause: You can tell how smooth the gizmo's velocity changes are by looking at the graph, which is far more accurate than squinting at dots or watching RAM Previews fly by. (To compare, temporarily return to your finished version of [**Ex.02_starter**] and press Shift+F3 to reveal the Graph Editor: Was your animation as smooth as you thought?)

Just for fun, select all of the Position keyframes and press F9 to apply Easy Ease to them. See how the speed graph returns to zero at each keyframe? Remember: That's what Easy Ease does! You'll find Easy Ease works best at the beginning and end of an animation, and not so well for middle keyframes. Re-tweak the middle keyframes to get a constant speed in the middle of the gizmo's flight. Our version is in [**Ex.06-final**].

In the event you are wondering if there is an easier way to smooth out the speed, there is: They're called *roving keyframes*, and we'll get to them later in this chapter.

Setting all the keyframes to Easy Ease results in the speed graph returning to zero at each keyframe – not necessarily what we wanted (above).

Edit the timing and speed value of the middle keyframes to create as smooth a graph as possible, which will result in a smooth animation (below). Roving keyframes (covered later in this chapter) can achieve this feat more easily.

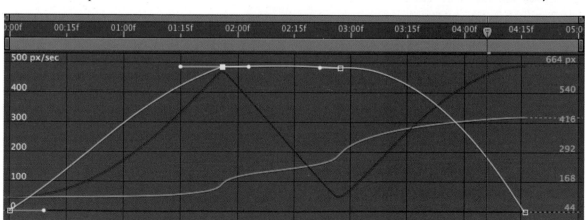

Separate X, Y, and Z

Normally, After Effects bundles the X, Y, and (if the 3D Layer switch is enabled) Z Position values into a single keyframe. A side effect of this approach is that the "value graph" is edited in the Comp panel as the motion path, while the "speed graph" is edited in the Timeline panel. In many cases, this division of labor makes position-style animations easier to manage. However, there are some types of movement – such as bounces, camera crane moves, and others – that it makes more difficult, which frustrates some advanced animators.

To make it easier to edit those types of movements, After Effects CS4 added the ability to separately keyframe the X, Y, and Z values. An example of where this would come in handy is if you were simulating a camera that is on both a dolly and a crane: By separating the dimensions, you can control the camera's height (the Y movement of the crane) independently from its sideways or forward motion (the X or Z movement of the dolly).

Separating these dimensions requires a trip into the Graph Editor. Once they have been separated, you can edit the new independent keyframes in either the Graph Editor or the normal timeline display.

To gain a better understanding of this feature, close your previous comps and work through an example of animating a bouncing ball using **[Ex.07_starter]**:

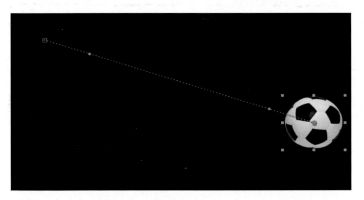

Steps 1–2: Keyframe the position of the soccer ball to travel across the comp panel. Object courtesy iStockphoto, © Deejpilot, Image #10467200.

Step 3: Enable the Graph Editor Set button for Position.

Step 1: Your goal is to make the ball in this composition bounce across the comp's "floor." Select the layer **iS_soccerball.tif** and press P to reveal its Position property in the Timeline panel. Then click on the animation stopwatch icon for Position to enable keyframing for it.

Step 2: Move the current time indicator to the end of the comp (the shortcut is to press End). Drag the soccer ball to the right edge of the Composition panel and about halfway between its top and bottom (roughly a Position of X = 640, Y = 252). You will see a straight motion path in the Composition panel connecting your two keyframes.

Step 3: In the Timeline panel, located between the word Position and its animation stopwatch, is a Graph Editor Set button for this parameter. Enable it. This will ensure that you will always see the Position property in the Graph Editor, even if you accidentally deselect the layer.

Step 4: Reveal the Graph Editor in the Timeline panel by clicking its button along the top of this panel. Then click on the Choose Graph Type button along its bottom (to the right of the eyeball) and make sure Auto-Select Graph Type is enabled.

After doing so, you will see a single horizontal white line in the Graph Editor. This represents the constant speed of the ball as it travels between your two keyframes. You will also notice that there is just one Position parameter along the left side of the Timeline panel.

Step 4: Open the Graph Editor.

Step 5: Make sure the Position parameter is selected. Then click on the Separate Dimensions button underneath the Graph Editor. Two things will happen:

• Along the left, the formerly unified Position value will now be replaced by separate X Position and Y Position parameters, color-coded red and green respectively.

• In the Graph Editor display, the single white velocity graph will be replaced with separate sloping green and red X and Y Position value graphs.

Step 5: Click on the Separate Dimensions button at the bottom of the Graph Editor.

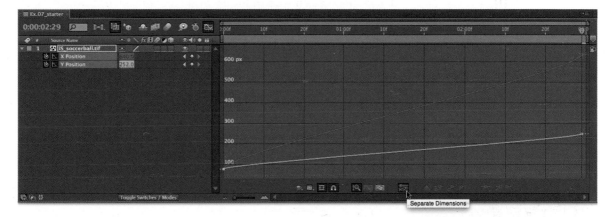

Step 6: The red X Position value graph has slight kinks at its start and end. These are caused by the default Auto Bezier keyframe interpolation that was assigned to it. We want the soccer ball to keep a steady speed as it moves from left to right, so let's convert those to Linear keyframes:

• Deselect the Position parameters by clicking anywhere in the Timeline panel. Then double-click X Position to select just its keyframes. They will be bound by a white rectangle in the Graph Editor (see figure, next page).

• Click the Convert Selected Keyframes to Linear button along the bottom of the Graph Editor. The X Position value graph will straighten out. You might also notice that the motion path changes slightly in the Comp panel; when working with Separate Dimensions, your actions in the Graph Editor directly control your resulting motion path.

• Click outside the white rectangle (or press F2) to deselect the X Position keyframes.

Step 5 *continued*: After enabling Separate Dimensions, separate X and Y Position values will appear. You will also see color-coded lines for the X and Y values and velocities.

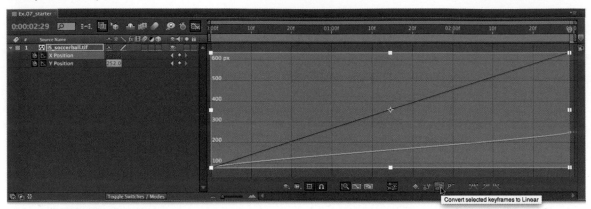

Step 6: To maintain a constant X velocity, convert just the X Position keyframes to linear interpolation.

No Handles?

If your Position keyframes in the Graph Editor do not have any handles, then they currently have an interpolation type of Linear. To pop out the handles, Option+click (Alt+click) on a keyframe to toggle from Linear to Auto Bezier.

Step 7: Next let's work on the bounces, which means editing the Y Position (up and down) graph. First we're going to set the keyframes for where the ball hits the floor, then in the next step edit the Y Position graph to create the flight path between those hits.

• Move the current time indicator to 00:15.

• Scrub the Y Position value until the ball just touches the bottom of the comp (around Y = 433). *Don't* drag the ball in the Comp panel; that would add both X and Y keyframes!

• Make sure just the new Y Position keyframe is selected; it will have a solid yellow box in the Graph Editor, rather than a hollow yellow box. Edit > Copy this keyframe.

• Move the current time indicator to 01:15.

• With Y Position still highlighted along the left of the Timeline, Edit > Paste to create a keyframe at this new time with the same value as the previous keyframe.

• Move the current time indicator to 02:15, and paste again.

Step 8: A bouncing motion is not continuous; the ball reverses direction when it hits the floor. This means you need to create discontinuous motion at the keyframes.

• Bezier handles will be visible in the Graph Editor around each keyframe, reflecting their Auto Bezier interpolation method (the default). Press the Option (Alt) key and drag one of the Bezier handles for the keyframe at 02:15 to "break" them, allowing them to be moved independently.

• Now that the handles are broken for that keyframe, release the Option (Alt) key and drag each handle down until you get a nice arc coming into and leaving this keyframe. You will see this arc in both the Graph Editor and in the resulting motion path in the Comp panel.

• Repeat to also break the handles and create a steep arc at the keyframes at 01:15 and at 00:15.

• Edit the curves for the first and last keyframes to help trace out a nice bounce motion path.

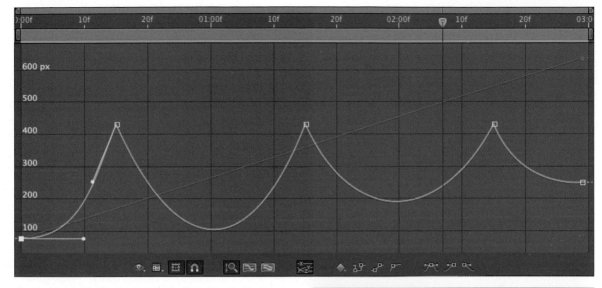

Step 8: Tug on the Bezier handles for Y Position in the Graph Editor to create arcs into and out of each keyframe (above). The results will be reflected in the motion path in the Comp panel (right).

RAM Preview, and continue to tweak until you are happy with your motion. You can also move the Y Position keyframes in time by dragging them left and right in the Graph Editor; press the Shift key after you start dragging to constrain your motion. For example, move the fourth Y Position keyframe later to shorten the "flight time" during the last bounce. Note that this does not alter the ball's speed in the X dimension; it alters only when it bounces in the Y dimension. Compare your results with [Ex.07-final].

Step 9: And now for the magic: Press End and decrease just the X Position value. RAM Preview, and note how the ball doesn't travel as far across the comp, but the up-and-down bounce motion remains the same. Without Separate Dimensions, you would have had to tweak each keyframe by hand.

In general, this animation would have been very difficult to pull off with normal, joined-together Position values – you would be fighting to keep a constant speed in X while you created your bounces in Y. However, using Separate Dimensions does come with a price: You can no longer directly edit the motion path in the Comp panel (note that the Bezier handles disappeared); you have to craft your path in the Graph Editor. The good news is that you can disable Separate Dimensions by selecting Position and then clicking the Separate Dimensions switch along the bottom of the Graph Editor; After Effects will then approximate your final animation using traditional joined Position keyframes.

FACTOID

Seeing Dots

Remember that the spacing between the dots in the motion path indicates how far the object travels between frames in time.

Graph Gotchas

There are no hard and fast rules for how graphs should be manipulated, but there are a few common problems that are easy to spot in the Graph Editor, which makes them easy to work around or avoid. We've built examples of these in the **Ex.08** folder; get some practice by solving them yourself using the Graph Editor. (Note that while the example figures show Position keyframes in the Speed Graph, the concepts apply to other parameters as well.)

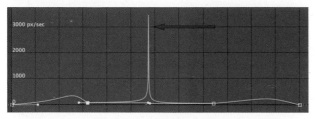

Example of a sharp spike created by handles that are too long – the layer travels very fast for just a frame or two.

• **Influence handles are too long [Ex.08a]:** If you drag opposing influence handles to their maximum length and drag them to the bottom, you'll create a spike in the graph. Spikes indicate that a layer is traveling very fast for just a frame or two, which is also indicated by a gap in the motion path dots.

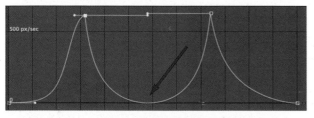

Another problem is created by long handles, which cause a dip in the center where the layer literally stops (hits 0 pixels/sec).

• **Layer slows to a crawl [Ex.08b]:** Similarly, if the handles are so long that they meet higher up the graph, they'll create a large dip in the center of the graph, where the layer is traveling at 0 pixels/sec (it comes to a complete stop). With other parameters such as Rotation, it is possible to dip *below* the 0 line, at which point the parameter will animate in reverse.

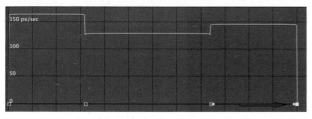

When influence handles are too short, they have no time to work on accelerating or decelerating the layer.

• **Influence handles are too short [Ex.08c]:** If an influence handle is very close to the keyframe, it basically has no effect. Just dragging the handle down to the zero line doesn't add an ease in. If the influence amount is 0%, the layer has *no time* to slow down, so it will appear to stop suddenly. Drag the handle away from the keyframe and watch the curve emerge.

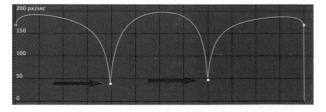

Because speed appears to pick up when objects change direction, you may have to reduce the speed at corners to appear to be maintaining a consistent speed.

• **Phantom speed-up at bends [Ex.08d]:** When an object changes direction, we don't perceive its speed just as the number of pixels it is traveling per second; we also perceive the "tangential velocity" of it rotating around the center of the curve. This makes it appear to pick up speed. To counter this effect, you may need to introduce slight dips in the speed graph for Position when an object is supposed to round a corner at "constant" speed, as we did in [**Ex.08d-fixed**].

Hold Interpolation

After teaching you ways to make your animation as smooth as possible, we're going to switch gears and discuss ways to make your animations start and stop suddenly, or stay in one place for a period of time. The tool for this is the little-known *hold* keyframe interpolation type. If you don't know how to make keyframes "hold," you're creating extra work for yourself as well as possibly encountering motion glitches as you try to employ imperfect workarounds (see the sidebar *Hold It Right There!*).

The hold interpolation's job is to *not* interpolate. When a Position keyframe is set to hold, the layer maintains that Position value until it reaches the next keyframe, and the speed drops to 0 pixels/sec. Hold keyframes are great for creating more rhythmic animations, and they can be used on any property or effect parameter, not just Position.

Open [**Ex.09_starter**]. Select **CP_Spaceman.tif** and press P if his Position keyframes are not already visible. RAM Preview: The spaceman wanders from one corner of the comp to another. Say we want him to suddenly snap to these locations. To make a keyframe hold in place, select any keyframe (except the last) and invoke Animation > Toggle Hold Keyframe; you can also right-click on a keyframe to see this choice. RAM Preview and note the result. Also study what happened to the motion path in the Comp panel: Rather than a curve with keyframe dots, you will see only a thin straight line leading from the keyframe you converted to hold to the next keyframe.

A hold keyframe takes over the entire segment of time until the next keyframe is reached. At this point, the layer will then immediately jump to its new position or value. In the timeline, the incoming ease into the next keyframe is inactive, and that keyframe icon is grayed out on the left side to indicate this. However, the next keyframe could use any keyframe type for its outgoing interpolation because After Effects can freely mix and match interpolation methods.

The hold keyframe is normally indicated by a square icon, but if you started with a linear keyframe the result will be a linear (diamond) icon on the left side and a square on the right. You can still edit the influence handle going into a hold keyframe (unless it follows another hold keyframe, of course), as hold interpolation affects only how you move *out* of a keyframe.

When you tire of visiting the Toggle Hold Keyframe menu, learn the shortcut: press Command+Option (Control+Alt) and click directly on a keyframe in the Timeline panel while in the layer (not Graph Editor) view.

Right-click on a keyframe and Toggle Hold Keyframe from the popup menu.

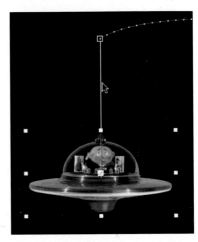

When you convert a keyframe to hold, its normal motion path will be replaced with a thin straight line (above) indicating the layer will jump suddenly to its next position. Spaceman courtesy Classic PIO/Nostalgic Memorabilia.

In the Timeline panel (below), the outgoing keyframe interpolation will be denoted by a square icon, and the following keyframe's incoming interpolation will be grayed out.

Keyframe Icons

Each keyframe in the Timeline panel has an icon indicating the interpolation being used. But what's with these strange icons? If you slice them down the vertical center, you'll see that they're combinations of diamonds, Bezier, and squares (you'll never see half a circle, though). The left half indicates the interpolation coming into the keyframe; the right half indicates the interpolation exiting the keyframe. If one side is grayed out, it means that no interpolation is taking place on that side (such as is the case with the first or last keyframe in an animation).

The regular icons are (left to right): Linear, Auto Bezier, Continuous Bezier/Bezier, and Hold.

Combinations of incoming and outgoing interpolation can create some strange icons. See if you can ID these mutants…

Remember that this feature is a toggle: You can revert back by repeating the Toggle Hold Keyframe on a selected keyframe or by pressing Command (Control) and clicking on the keyframe until the keyframe reverts to the familiar Linear (diamond) icon.

Finally, try using Hold keyframes on other properties besides Position. In [**Ex.09-final**], we used them for Scale and Opacity keyframes as well.

Continuing from Hold

If you need a property to hold on a value and then continue from there, the hold keyframe and the one following should both have the same value, as in [**Ex.10**]. It might also be appropriate to apply an ease out of the second keyframe. Remember that if you later change the value of the first hold keyframe, you'll need to update the following keyframe also. Following are tips for achieving this – in all cases, *be sure to select both keyframes first:*

• Double-click one of the keyframes in the layer bar view or the Graph Editor's Edit Value Graph mode to get the Position dialog box where you can type in a new value. Click OK, and this value will apply to both keyframes.

• Park the current time indicator on one of the keyframes and scrub the value in the Switches column of the Timeline panel.

• Move them as a group in the Graph Editor.

• For Position keyframes only: Park the time indicator on one of the keyframes and use the arrow keys to nudge the layer, or drag the keyframe icon directly in the Comp panel.

Whichever method you use, check that *both* keyframes stay selected afterward, indicating that both Position values have been changed.

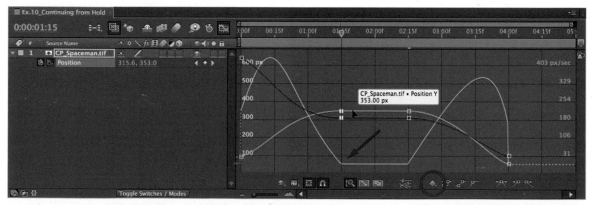

To hold on a value and then continue smoothly from that point, make sure the Hold keyframe (where the current time indicator is parked) is followed by a keyframe with exactly the same value. Notice the speed graph goes flat at zero during the hold period (red arrow). You can also invoke Toggle Hold Keyframe by clicking the "Convert selected keyframes to Hold" button (circled).

Hold It Right There!

The Second Field Glitch Problem

Users who haven't discovered hold keyframes have devised all sorts of workarounds to make a property's value hold in place. The most common one involves duplicating the prior keyframe and placing it one frame in time before the next keyframe, as in comp **[Ex.11_Glitch Problem]**.

Let's say you want a layer to hold at Position A for two seconds from 00:00 to 02:00, then jump to Position B when 02:00 is reached, without interpolating between the two points. You create two linear keyframes, at 00:00 and 02:00. Then, to make the layer hold steady, you duplicate keyframe A at 01:29, one frame before keyframe B is due to occur. When you preview your animation, everything looks fine, and no interpolation occurs.

When you render the animation with field rendering turned on (Chapter 42), you notice a glitch in the motion right around 02:00. Unfortunately, there *is* a position between frame 01:29 and 02:00. It's called the second field. If you examined the movie field by field (or change the comp's frame rate to 59.94 fps), you would see that on frame 01:29, the layer is at Position A for the first field, but has jumped to an interpolated position *between* A and B for the second field.

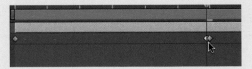

Don't duplicate a keyframe in order to make it "hold" – you'll introduce a glitch when you field render.

Not only does this workaround create a glitch if you field render, but if you edit the value of keyframe A at time 00:00, you have to remember to update the duplicate keyframe at 01:29. There is no reason to use this ugly workaround – this is what the hold keyframe lives and breathes for.

Now that you know better, try changing the first keyframe to a hold keyframe and delete the duplicate keyframe. Position will hold steady until the next keyframe occurs at 02:00, as in **[Ex.11-Glitch Fix]**.

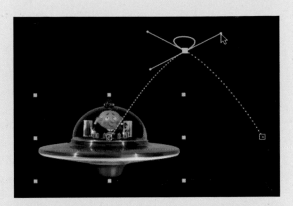

If you manipulate handles then create two Position keyframes with the same value, those handles sticking out will create a loop in the motion path. Convert the first keyframe to a hold keyframe to fix the problem.

The Loop-de-Loop Problem

If in the course of creating a motion path you create two default Position keyframes (let's call them C and D) with exactly the same Position values, After Effects will automatically retract the outgoing Bezier handle from C and the incoming handle for the duplicate keyframe, D. With these handles on the motion path retracted, you'll have the functional equivalent of a hold keyframe for C. (It's not exactly a hold keyframe, but the layer will remain rock steady.)

But have you ever created two Position keyframes with exactly the same values, assuming the layer would hold steady – yet the layer ends up wandering around in a loop instead? This problem occurs because the handles on the motion path at keyframe C were manipulated *before* keyframe D was created. In this situation, After Effects will honor the position you set for the handles and create a small loop in the motion path, as in **[Ex.12_Loop Problem]**. (You can see the loop in the motion path more clearly by zooming in and moving the handles.) To fix this problem, select keyframe C and change it to a hold keyframe. The loop will disappear as the outgoing handle for C and the incoming handle for D are retracted. This won't affect the overall motion path; it will just remove the unwanted loop in the middle, as in **[Ex.12-Loop Fix]**.

In **[Ex.13_starter]**, the motion path has already been created; now the challenge is to smooth out the speed along that path. (The map is from an 1890s edition of *Cram's Unrivaled Family Atlas of the World* and is in the public domain.)

Roving Keyframes

An exciting advantage of the way After Effects separates the motion path and path velocity for Position keyframes is that you can create a complex motion path without thinking about timing, then come later and tweak the overall speed. This is made even easier by employing *roving keyframes*: a lesser-known but extremely valuable feature inside After Effects.

Click on the menu in the Comp panel's tab and select Close All to clean up your display. Then open **[Ex.13_starter]** and select the layer **Blue Star** so you can see its motion path. At this point, we just placed Position keyframes at ten-frame intervals in the timeline while we were crafting the path; press P to reveal these keyframes. However, since the space between the keyframes in the Comp panel varies, the speed between these keyframes varies as well – RAM Preview to verify.

Press Shift+F3 to reveal the Graph Editor. The up-and-down steps of the speed graph confirm how the star's velocity changes suddenly – and often. You know from your experience in working through the other position examples in this chapter that balancing off the speed versus timing of these keyframes is going to be a real challenge. But if all you want is a nice, smooth speed graph (which we do in this case), let After Effects do the work!

Click on Position twice to select all of its keyframes. Then click on the Edit Selected Keyframes button (the diamond icon) along the bottom of the Graph Editor and select Rove Across Time from the menu (you can also right-click on one of the keyframes to bring up the same menu).

Notice what happens to the motion path and the speed graph: The motion path does not change, but the speed path is evened out to a straight line. The first and last keyframes kept their original timing (and still have Bezier influence handles), but all of the remaining keyframes in-between have changed to yellow dots and slid earlier or later in time as needed to flatten out the graph. RAM Preview and observe how the speed is now constant for the entire path.

Click on the Edit Selected Keyframes button along the bottom of the Graph Editor (above). If you have multiple position-style keyframes selected, the option to "rove" them will be active.

After setting a group of linear Position keyframes in the timeline to rove, the speed will be constant across their entire animation (right).

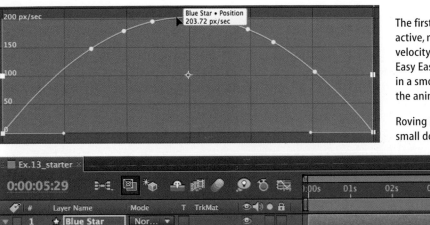

The first and last keyframes are still active, meaning you can edit their velocity influence – including applying Easy Ease to them, which will result in a smooth arc across the length of the animation (left).

Roving keyframes are represented as small dots in the layer bar view (below).

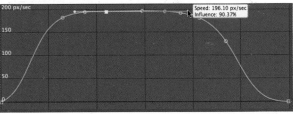

These intermediate keyframes will continue to "rove" as needed as you adjust the first and last keyframes. For example, press F9 to Easy Ease them – now the entire speed graph will be one smooth arc; RAM Preview and the star will smoothly accelerate then decelerate during the course of the entire motion path. You can continue to tweak the Bezier handles on the first and last keyframes, as well as slide them earlier or later in time. For example, select just the first keyframe and slide it later in time, and the same animation will merely take less time.

Equally important is that you can tweak the motion path: The keyframes will continue to rove across time as needed to smooth out the layer's velocity along the entire motion path. Try moving individual keyframes in the Comp panel while watching what happens in the Graph Editor.

To disable roving, simply click and drag any one of the roved keyframes (you might want to deselect the keyframes first so you don't edit them all as a group). You can also marquee multiple roving keyframes to select them, then right-click one and toggle off Rove Across Time from the popup menu. Note you can do this in either the Graph Editor or the normal layer bar view in the Timeline panel.

If you unrove one keyframe in the middle of a group of roving keyframes, the keyframes on either side will continue to rove. This provides a way to "flatten out" the speed graph in the middle of a complex animation. Try this with [Ex.13_starter]: Click and drag one of the middle keyframes, then extend its influence handles to the left and right. Slide this keyframe as needed to create a plateau in the middle of the speed graph. RAM Preview; now you should observe fairly constant speed in the middle of the animation instead of a drawn-out accelerate/decelerate behavior. Our version is in [Ex.13-final].

FACTOID

Exclusive Rove Party

Only properties that create a motion path in Comp or Layer space, such as Position, Anchor Point, and Effect Point (Chapter 22), can be roved.

Our final animation is in [Ex.13-final].

CONNECT

Keyframes, anchor point: Chapter 3.

Pen tool and paths: Chapters 3, 10, and 32.

3D space and cameras: Chapters 13 and 14.

Effects: Chapters 22 and 23B.

Field rendering: Chapter 42.

5

Animation Assistance

A series of tips, tricks, and Keyframe Assistants to make your life easier.

One of the reasons many users love After Effects is because it continually adds switches, shortcuts, and modules to make their lives easier when they're creating an animation. We're going to cover some of our favorite animation helpers here, starting with simple ways to manipulate keyframes then working our way to Auto-Orient Rotation along with more complex Keyframe Assistants including Motion Sketch, Smoother, Wiggler, and Exponential Scale.

Things to Do with Keyframes

It's not always possible to place keyframes in the perfect spot every time, so After Effects provides many options and shortcuts for selecting, deleting, moving, copying, pasting, and changing keyframes:

- To add a new keyframe at the current time using the current value, click in the keyframe navigator diamond for that property. (If there already is a keyframe there, this will delete it instead.)

- If a property's stopwatch is off, an "I-beam" icon will appear at the current time indicator; this signifies that the value is constant for the duration of the layer. While it's not a keyframe per se, it does contain a value that can be selected, copied, and pasted. To include it in a marquee selection, park the time indicator inside the area to be marqueed.

- Select multiple keyframes by Shift+selecting them, or drag a marquee around multiple keyframes. You can even marquee across multiple properties and multiple layers, which is handy when moving many keyframes while maintaining their relationship to each other. To select discontinuous keyframes, press Command on Mac (Control on Windows) while clicking them.

An I-beam icon at the current time indicator indicates that the value is constant for this property; you can select this value for copying by clicking on the I-beam or the property's name.

- Select all keyframes for a property by clicking on the name of the property (for example, click on the word Position to select all Position keyframes). Shift+click multiple property names to select additional keyframes. If a property has no keyframes, its constant value will be selected.

- Select all visible keyframes: Command+Option+A (Control+Alt+A).

- Deselect All Keyframes (leaving layer selected): Shift+F2. (Deselect All is F2.)

- To delete a keyframe, select it and press the Delete key. Delete all keyframes for a property by turning off its stopwatch.

- Right-click on a keyframe to open a contextual menu with additional functions: Select Equal Keyframes (for selecting keyframes on the same property with the same value as the currently selected keyframe); Select Previous Keyframes and Select Following Keyframes (for selecting keyframes on the same property before or after the currently selected keyframe, respectively).

- To move keyframes in time, drag them along the Timeline panel. To make the selected keyframe stick to the time indicator (as well as other keyframes, in and out points, markers and so on), press the Shift key *after* you start dragging. Shift+dragging the time indicator also makes *it* sticky.

- To nudge keyframes in time by one frame, press Option (Alt) and tap the left arrow key to move them earlier in time, or the right arrow key to nudge them later in time. Add the Shift key to nudge ten frames at a time.

- To expand or contract the range of time a group of keyframes extends over, select two or more keyframes and Option+drag (Alt+drag) the first or last keyframe in the timeline. In the Graph Editor, selecting multiple keyframes results in their being contained in a selection box which can be moved, scaled, and skewed by dragging on its edges.

- To move the current time indicator between exposed keyframes in the Timeline, press J to move earlier in time and K to move later in time.

Stupid Math Tricks

In After Effects, all parameter values in the Timeline and Effect Controls panel can be adjusted using simple math tricks that employ the arithmetic expressions +, −, *, and /.

For instance, to move a layer to the right by 64 pixels, place the cursor *after* the current X value, type "+64" and press Return. Subtract amounts by using minus values (100−64), multiply with an asterisk (10*64), and divide with the slash key (100/20).

These math tricks also work in dialog boxes, such as when you right-click on a value and select Edit Value. The exception is the Go To Time dialog: In this dialog you must *replace* the current value and type "**+45**" to jump ahead 45 frames (placing the cursor *after* the current time and typing will result in jumps to unexpected times). However, entering −15 frames will jump to 15 frames before the beginning of the comp. The rule for Go To Time is that to advance 15 frames, type "**+15**"; to rewind 15 frames, type "**+−15**".

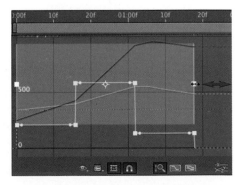

To expand or contract a group of selected keyframes, in the layer bar view, hold down Option (Alt) first, then drag the first or last keyframe (above). In the Graph Editor, drag the edge of the selection rectangle that appears around them (below). All selected keyframes will move accordion-style.

Copying and Pasting Keyframes

You can copy keyframes in the time-honored fashion using the shortcut Command+C (Control+C) or the menu item Edit > Copy. You can then Edit > Paste these keyframes later in time on the same layer or paste them to another layer anywhere inside the program.

After Effects allows you to copy and paste keyframes between related properties (such as Position and Anchor Point). You can also copy/paste multiple properties that have keyframes, as well as paste keyframes to multiple layers. Keyframes for multiple properties can also be stored as Animation Presets – this is the subject of Chapter 25.

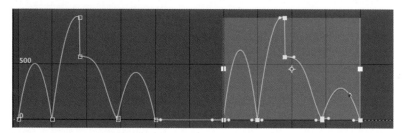

Keyframes do not reference the time from which they were copied; they just remember the spacing (timing) between themselves. When you paste, the first keyframe will appear at the current time, and the others will appear afterward with their original spacing. Keyframes also remember their velocity and interpolation settings.

When you select an entire layer as your paste target, copied keyframes will look for a parameter of the same name to paste into. But as hinted above, keyframes can also be pasted from one property to any other – provided it makes sense to After Effects. You set the destination (or "target") property by first clicking on the property's name in the Timeline panel. For instance, to paste Position keyframes – which normally have two values (for the X and Y axes) – you need to select another property with two channels such as Anchor Point. Click on the words Anchor Point in the Timeline panel to target this property, then Paste.

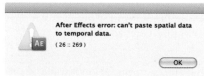

This smart paste feature can sometimes be too smart when you want to copy and paste keyframes between layers. For instance, if you copy Position keyframes from one layer, then adjust the Opacity on the destination layer before pasting, the Opacity property will be the active property. The program will then attempt to paste Position keyframes into Opacity and – as these properties are not compatible – return an error message. Worse yet, it may paste into an unintended, albeit compatible, property. (If pasted keyframes fail to appear, check whether they pasted into the wrong property.) If in doubt, target the intended property by clicking on it before you paste.

When keyframes are pasted, the first keyframe is placed at the current time. Subsequent keyframes follow, maintaining the same relationship as when they were copied. Velocity curves are remembered as well.

If you attempt to paste keyframes to a layer but instead trigger an error message, don't panic; you just have a mismatch between types of properties. In this example, the Opacity I-beam icon was highlighted, and you attempted to paste Position keyframes to Opacity – which is not allowed. Click on the word Position to target that property and try your paste again.

Moving and Nudging Motion Paths

You can move individual keyframes in the Comp panel by selecting the keyframe's box icon and dragging to a new location – you don't need to first navigate in time to where the keyframe occurs. The Info panel gives a running update of the new position as you drag the icon.

To move multiple keyframes (or a motion path) in the Comp panel, first select the keyframes you want to edit, then do one of the following:

- Drag one of the selected keyframe icons in the Comp panel.

- Park the current time indicator on one of the keyframes and scrub the value in the Switches column of the Timeline panel. All selected keyframes will move relative to the current keyframe. *Be sure the time indicator is parked on one of the selected keyframes;* if it isn't, you will instead just add a new keyframe at that point in time.

- You can nudge a layer by using the up/down/left/right cursor keys to move a layer by one screen pixel at a time, or ten screen pixels with Shift pressed. To move a motion path, make sure you are parked on one of the selected keyframes.

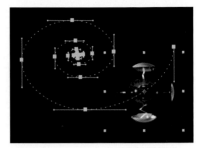

To move an entire motion path, select all the keyframes by clicking on the word Position in the Timeline panel. Drag any of the keyframe icons in the Comp panel to move the path. The Info panel gives you a real-time update. Gizmo courtesy Quiet Earth Design.

Scaling a Motion Path

There is no easy way to scale an overall motion path to make it take up more or less area in a composition, but there is a workaround that involves "parenting" (the subject of Chapter 17). The adventurous can try this exercise now.

Open [**Ex.01_starter**] which contains a gizmo following a spiral path. Say you decide that the spiral needs to be larger so that it will swing out of the comp's boundaries by the end:

Step 1: Add a New > Layer > Null Object. This is a dummy layer that will be used to help us scale the path.

Step 2: Type Shift+F4 to reveal the Parent column in the Timeline panel. Click on the Parent popup for the child layer (**QE_Gizmo_loop.mov**) and select **Null 1** as its parent.

Step 3: Press End so that the gizmo will be at the end of its motion path. Then type S to reveal the null's Scale, and increase the Scale value until the gizmo is pushed off the screen.

Step 4: Set the Parent popup for the child layer back to None. Doing this detaches the gizmo from the null, but After Effects remembers the scaled path.

The downside of this approach is that the target's Scale values will also be altered. If this is an issue, copy the target's Scale keyframes before resizing its motion path, then paste them back into place after you're done.

To nudge a path using the arrow keys, click on the word Position to select all keyframes and make sure the time indicator is parked on one of the selected keyframes (the keyframe navigator will be checked).

TIP

Motion Paths >< Masks

Position motion paths can also be pasted to a mask path, resized using Free Transform Points, and pasted back to Position. See Chapter 10 for info.

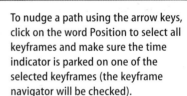

To scale a layer's motion path, parent it to another layer, and change the scale of that second layer.

The Motion Sketch keyframe assistant. The "Capture speed at" setting allows you to sketch more slowly (or more quickly) than the playback speed.

Sketching and Smoothing

Next we're going to move on to using a set of Keyframe Assistants to help create more complex animations. Although After Effects gives you a lot of control over creating and tweaking a motion path, it can still feel like painting with numbers rather than painting with your hand. The Motion Sketch keyframe assistant lets you trace out a motion path with your mouse (or pen, if you're using a digitizing tablet), allowing for more of a human touch. Since it's practically impossible to edit the motion path created by sketching, we often smooth the result to remove some of the bumpiness in the motion as well as reduce the number of keyframes.

Motion Sketch

First, make sure the Motion Sketch panel is open – select Window > Motion Sketch or change the Workspace to Animation. The Motion Sketch panel has several parameters of interest: whether to draw a wireframe of your layer while you are dragging around, whether to make a snapshot of the background layers and keep that onscreen for reference, whether to automatically smooth your results, and the capture speed. Because it can be hard to draw the exact motion we want at the speed we want it to play back at, you can slow down (or speed up) time – for example, a setting of 200% will give you eight seconds to sketch out a path that will take four seconds to play back. If the comp contains an audio layer, you'll hear the sound play as you sketch.

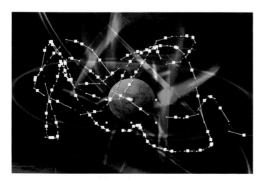

Motion Sketch follows your mouse movements exactly – creating a Position keyframe on numerous frames inside the work area, or until you mouse up. Background courtesy Artbeats/Virtual Intensity.

To practice Motion Sketch, open the comp [**Ex.02_starter**], select layer 1, and use the default settings for Motion Sketch (Speed 100%, Show Wireframe, Smoothing = 1). Enable Show Background if you want the shapes in it to inspire you. Select the Start Capture button and relax – nothing will happen until you're ready to start. Position the cursor in the Comp panel, press the mouse button, and hold it down as you drag it around the Comp panel in time with the music. The timeline progresses, the music plays, and everything stops when the work area finishes. Mousing up also cancels the sketching, so if it stops prematurely, you might be "tapping" to the music – keep the mouse button pressed down.

Once the sketch is complete, you'll notice numerous Position keyframes, depending on how Smoothing was set. Press 0 on the keypad to RAM Preview. If you don't like the results, try again. To delete the old keyframes first, turn off the stopwatch for Position or Undo until they disappear. One possible result is demonstrated in [**Ex.02b**].

Preferences for Position

When working with Position keyframes, there are a few preferences that you should be aware of:

Preferences > General > Default Spatial Interpolation to Linear: If you're constantly retracting the handles on the motion path, temporarily toggle this preference on. Enabling this preference forces all new spatial (motion path) keyframes to be created as linear instead of Auto Bezier, meaning they have sharp rather than rounded corners. This is handy if you're working on a project animating lots of layers that move only in straight line segments such as tracing a maze.

Preferences > Display > Motion Path: The default is to show keyframes for 15 seconds around the current time indicator. However, if the motion path extends over a long duration, the motion path will be cut off – and you'll have to move in time to see and edit the path. If there are a manageable number of keyframes, change the preference to All Keyframes (probably the most useful option).

The Motion Path section of the Display Preferences controls how much of the motion path, or the number of keyframes, are visible at any point in time. Set it to All Keyframes to avoid motion paths being cut off.

On another project, though, you might have hundreds of keyframes on a motion path that crosses over itself, which makes it difficult to distinguish and select individual keyframes easily. In this case, limit the number of keyframes, or the time period, to display keyframes only in an area immediately around the current time indicator.

Motion Sketch can also be used to create nervous text with an organic feel. You can lightly "shake" a layer, then have it jump wildly in one direction when you feel like it. For more manic results, first set Smoothing to 0. Try this with layer 1 in [**Ex.02c**]; turn on layer 2 to see a possible result.

The advantage of using Motion Sketch to create this style of animation is that you're in control: If you use the Wiggler keyframe assistant (discussed later) or the wiggle expression (Chapter 37), the machine-generated results can be less human.

Applying Sketch to Others

Motion Sketch creates Position keyframes only. However, you can copy and paste the keyframes created to any property that also has values on the X and Y axes – such as the effect point parameter of Lens Flare, Write-on, or a particle system plug-in. We usually create the Position keyframes by applying Motion Sketch to a null object or a small solid. Once the keyframes are captured, you can copy them, click on the name of the effect point parameter in the Timeline to "target" it, and Paste.

Practice this in [**Ex.03_starter**]: Motion sketch the solid layer, then paste the Position keyframes to the Lens Flare > Flare Center parameter. Our result is shown in [**Ex.03-final**]. (Refer to the section *Copying and Pasting Keyframes*, page 96, for more on this technique.)

TIP

Range of Motion

Motion Sketch obeys the Work Area (Chapter 2). To limit the range of time you'll be sketching, first set the Work Area to stop and start where you want.

TIP

Effect Point Animation

Applying effects, as well as animating the effect point along a motion path, is covered in more detail in Chapter 22.

Smoother

The problem with the Motion Sketch keyframe assistant is that it creates a multitude of Position keyframes that – as a group – are difficult, if not impossible, to edit as you would a regular motion path. And no matter how smoothly we think we're drawing with the pen or the mouse, sketched paths rarely turn out as nice as we would like. You can set the Smoothing value in Motion Sketch to smooth out these keyframes automatically, or you can decide later how much smoothing you want.

The Smoother keyframe assistant is designed to smooth changes in a property's values; it does this by replacing selected keyframes with a new set of keyframes, taking into account the Tolerance value. When it's applied to a layer that was motion sketched, it can leave behind an editable motion path.

Open Window > Smoother or select Workspace > Animation. Select the Position keyframes you created earlier with Motion Sketch or use our example in [**Ex.04a**]. Remember to click on the word Position in the Timeline to select all of its keyframes. Then select the Smoother panel. One of its parameters is a popup for Spatial or Temporal keyframes. Position keyframes in the Comp panel are Spatial because their values are on the X and Y axes. Properties that change only over time, such as Opacity, would default to Temporal. The meaning of the Tolerance value changes depending on what type of keyframes you are editing – for example, when you're editing Position keyframes, it will define the number of pixels new Position keyframes are allowed to vary from the original path. Larger Tolerance values result in fewer keyframes and therefore generally smoother animation; make sure you don't overdo it, though – a little goes a long way.

Enter a Tolerance value, click Apply, and RAM Preview the results. If the animation requires further smoothing, it's a better idea to Undo and try again with a different setting than to try successive applications. It may take a few tries to get it right, but it'll take far less time than trying to tweak dozens of keyframes by hand.

TIP

Smooth Moves
Smoother can be used on other keyframes as well, such as those generated by Wiggler (later in this chapter) or by motion stabilization and tracking (Chapters 29 and 30).

You will need to have at least three keyframes selected before you can use Smoother.

Motion Sketch with Smoothing set to 0 creates one keyframe per frame (below left). After applying Smoother with a tolerance of 3 (below right), the result is a much more editable path. Baseball courtesy Getty Images.

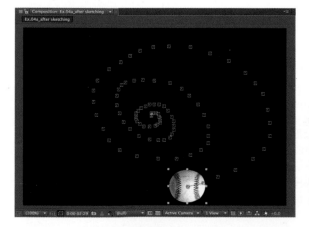
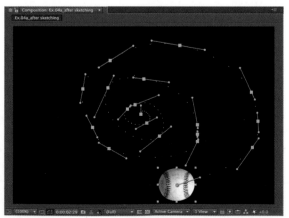

Auto-Orient Rotation

As you create more complex animation paths, you may want to have your layer rotate to always aim along this path. Rather than create a lot of Rotation keyframes to accomplish this, you can take advantage of the Auto-Orient feature in After Effects.

Open comp [**Ex.05_starter**] and either scrub or RAM Preview this simple animation. The butterfly rises up and down along its path but stays level – not exactly realistic. Select the **DP_butterfly 068.tif** layer, and if needed press P to reveal Position keyframes and Shift+R to add the Rotation property. Open the layer's Auto-Orientation dialog: You can either select the menu item Layer > Transform > Auto-Orient, or use the keyboard shortcut Command+Option+O (Control+Alt+O).

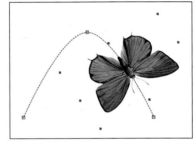

TIP

Reorienting Auto-Orient

If a layer flips upside down when Auto-Orient is enabled, change Rotation to 180° to turn it right side up. Other angles give other alignments. If the 3D Layer switch is enabled, use the Orientation property to make this adjustment.

The Auto-Orientation dialog for a 2D layer presents you with two options: Off or Orient Along Path. (3D layers will also have the option to orient toward the camera.) Select the Orient Along Path option, click OK, and preview the ani-

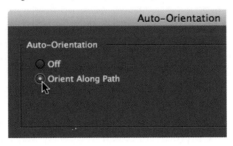

mation again. Now the butterfly rotates to follow its path…but it's sliding sideways. Fortunately, Auto-Orient is separate from the normal Rotation or Orientation values. You may need to offset Rotation to point the layer along a different axis (it defaults to the X axis); in this case, setting Rotation to 90° fixes our problem.

You can't keyframe the Auto-Orient switch. If you need to Auto-Orient during only part of a layer's animation, split the layer (Edit > Split Layer) and enable Orient Along Path only for the segment that needs it.

A problem with Auto-Orient is that there's usually a slight hitch at the beginning and end of the motion path, as seen when you preview [**Ex.05_starter**] after you turn this option on. Zoom into the Comp panel and select the first keyframe's icon (move the time indicator later if the butterfly is in the way). In this example, the spatial keyframes are all of the default Auto Bezier type, whose handles are represented by tiny dots. The handle for the first keyframe does not align with the motion path, so the layer orients itself at a slightly different angle for the first few frames. This results in a twisting motion.

To fix this, drag the handle dot. The direction line will appear (indicating this is now a Continuous Bezier keyframe); align the direction line with the motion path. An alternative is to retract the handle altogether by Command+clicking (Control+clicking) on the keyframe in the Comp panel; try this on the last keyframe as well. Preview again; the motion should be smooth at both ends, as in [**Ex.05-fixed**].

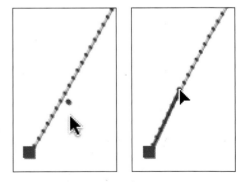

When Auto-Orient Rotation is turned on (left), the layer automatically aligns itself to be tangential to its motion path (above) with no Rotation keyframes added – although you may need to edit Rotation to get the layer to orient properly. Butterfly courtesy Dover.

To avoid rotation twists at the ends of animations, zoom in and grab the dot that represents the Auto Bezier handles (left). Drag the handle so that it is tangential to its path (right).

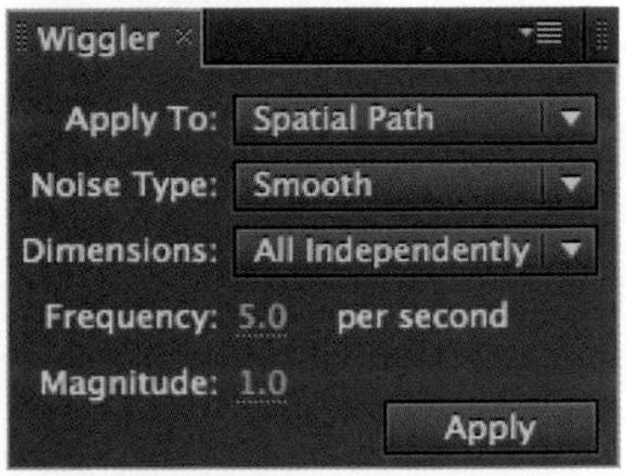

The Wiggler keyframe assistant has several options that determine how a keyframe's parameters are randomized.

Simply Spatial

A common problem in getting Wiggler to work is selecting keyframes that have position values and wiggling with the Temporal option selected – try Spatial Path instead.

Wiggle Expression

The preferred alternative to Wiggler is the wiggle expression discussed in Chapter 37. It allows you to wiggle any parameter without altering or creating keyframes.

A Wiggly World

Wiggler is a nifty keyframe assistant that can impart a nervous – or, when used more subtly, a randomized or less-perfect – quality to animations. It is most often used to automate the creation of jumpy titles by randomizing their position values, but it's also useful for creating random values or deviations for any property or effect.

The Wiggler keyframe assistant creates new keyframes between the first and last selected keyframes, randomly offset in value from where a parameter would normally be at each keyframe's point in time. You could say it adds "bumps in the road" as a value interpolates from one location to the next.

Open Window > Wiggler or choose Workspace > Animation. To use the Wiggler keyframe assistant, make sure you select at least two keyframes (they can even be the same value). Wiggler is not affected by the work area. Options include:

Apply To: The choices are Temporal Graph and Spatial Path. Spatial is available only for properties that have XY or XYZ axes, such as Position, Anchor Point, and Effect Point. Most properties are Temporal – in other words, values that change over time.

Noise Type: Choices are Smooth or Jagged. There is little noticeable difference for many parameters. The biggest change occurs with Position keyframes, where Jagged has "broken" linear path handles in and out of the spatial keyframes, compared with the more rounded motion of the tangential handles you get with Smooth. (We'll see in a moment how to change the keyframes interpolation type after the fact, so don't sweat this option.)

Dimension: Some properties – such as Opacity and Rotation – have only one parameter to change. If this is the case, the Dimension options are ignored. However, many properties – such as Position and Scale – have two dimensions. You can choose if only one of them gets wiggled, if all get wiggled the same (offset by the same amount), or if they get wiggled independently. All Independently is a good default for Position, but for properties such as Scale, All The Same is a better choice as it maintains the layer's aspect ratio.

Frequency: This is how often new keyframes are created, starting from the first selected keyframe. It can be thought of as the frame rate of the inserted keyframes. Note that if Wiggler happens to encounter a keyframe between the first and last keyframes you selected (because it happened to be exactly where a new one would be created by the Frequency's timing), it will offset that middle keyframe's value. Only the values of the first and last keyframes remain unchanged.

Magnitude: How much do you want a parameter randomized by? The amount of change will fall within the range set here, with larger values resulting in bigger changes. If a property has natural limits (such as 0%

and 100% for Opacity), these limits will clip the amount of change. If a property (such as Scale and Rotation) can go negative, Wiggler will swing between positive and negative, rather than getting clipped at zero. The initial value is a tiny 1 unit; you will usually want to increase this.

Wiggly Practice

To practice some wiggler moves, close your previous comps and open [**Ex.06_starter**]. The layer **nervous.ai** has two Position keyframes with the same values applied at the beginning and end (select the layer and press U if these are not already visible). Click on the word Position in the Timeline to select both keyframes and select Window > Wiggler (or click on its tab if it is already open).

After you have set your options, click Apply. If the Apply button is grayed out, make sure that you have at least two keyframes from the same property selected and that no other I-beams or keyframes from other properties are also part of the selection.

After Wiggler calculates the new keyframes, immediately render a RAM Preview. If you don't like the result, Undo, tweak its settings and try again. It often takes a few tries to get it right. (Note that reapplying Wiggler without undoing the first attempt will just further randomize the first set of keyframes, so it's usually best to Undo back to your original keyframes.)

After you apply Wiggler (above), you will have a multitude of keyframes that can be difficult to edit (below).

Be sure to try out some different options. A high Frequency and low Magnitude (such as 15 and 4, respectively) are good starting points for a tight, buzzing nervousness. [**Ex.06-final**] has several pre-wiggled keyframes in 2D and 3D for you to preview, but experimentation is the best path to understanding the effect. If layers are moving rapidly, they will benefit from motion blur (discussed in detail in Chapter 8).

Remember: You can wiggle properties other than position keyframes. [**Ex.07a**] wiggles Scale plus Rotation to bring a zooming alarm clock to life; [**Ex.07b**] wiggles Opacity to get a projector flickering effect; [**Ex.07c**] demonstrates wiggling the Direction and Length parameters for a Directional Blur effect.

Jagged Extreme

If the "jagged" Noise Type isn't jagged enough, select all Wiggler-created keyframes and change them to Hold keyframes (Animation > Toggle Hold Keyframes).

You can apply Wiggler to virtually any parameter. In [**Ex.07a**] we used it on the Scale and Rotation of this alarm clock as it zooms toward you. Motion Blur is also enabled. Clock courtesy Classic PIO/Nostalgic Memorabilia.

Customizing Wiggles

The problem with Wiggler is that the results often look too machine-made. Here are some ideas to introduce further randomness to wiggled animation:

• Consider wiggling with fairly tight values, then manually editing a few keyframes here and there to more extreme values. You can also add keyframes between those created by Wiggler and move some keyframes in time to break up the pattern. These ideas are shown in comp [Ex.08a]; check the Graph Editor view to see what effect this is having.

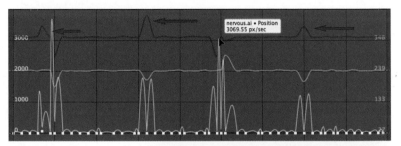

[Ex.08a]: Break up the Wiggler's pattern by editing select keyframes to values outside the Magnitude range, or by moving some keyframes in time.

You can change the keyframe interpolation type after Wiggler has created its new keyframes. If you're applying Wiggler to Position keyframes, a Noise Type of Smooth creates Continuous Bezier spatial keyframes where Jagged creates Bezier keyframes with broken handles. Because both options smoothly interpolate between keyframes, if you want a jagged animation you'll need to change the interpolation type:

• To change the temporal Position keyframes to linear, first select all the keyframes (click on the word Position in the Timeline), then Command+click (Control+click) on any keyframe in the Timeline while in normal layer bar view to change them all to linear.

• To change the spatial keyframes to linear (retracting the handles in the Comp panel), press Command+Option (Control+Alt) and click on any keyframe box in the Comp panel.

• For a really jagged animation, use Hold keyframes for no interpolation: Select all the keyframes in normal layer bar mode, then press Command+Option (Control+Alt) and click on one of them to change them all to Hold keyframes.

You can also change a keyframe's Spatial and/or Temporal interpolation using the Animation > Keyframe Interpolation dialog. Go ahead and experiment on the wiggled text you created in comp [Ex.06_starter].

Moving a Wiggling Layer

If you've wiggled the Position property (or used Motion Sketch), you may have dozens of keyframes to contend with. Try using a Null Object parent (Chapter 17) as a "handle" to easily reposition the layer.

Sketch Your Wiggle!

Instead of using Wiggler on Position keyframes, try using the Motion Sketch keyframe assistant – you'll usually get a more organic result since you're shaking the layer in real time with your hand. One result is shown in [Ex.08b].

You're not limited to the Smooth or Jagged options for Wiggler. Once you've applied the keyframe assistant, select the resulting keyframes and change them in the Keyframe Interpolation dialog.

Time-Reverse Keyframes

Ever built an animation, from the simplest right-to-left move to an involved dervish-like orchestration of Position, Scale, and Rotation, only to decide it would probably work better going the other way? If you haven't, you will. And that's what this no-brainer keyframe assistant is for: flipping a selection of keyframes in time. No values are changed – just their location and order on the timeline. Note that this keyframe assistant works over multiple properties and multiple layers.

The Time-Reverse Keyframes assistant is very straightforward, but we've set up an example for you to practice with anyway. Say you've created a nice animation of a layer scaling and rotating as it moves along a motion path. Now you want it to do this all in reverse:

Step 1: Open **[Ex.09_starter]**, which just happens to have such an animation. Select the layer and press U if the keyframes are not visible. Press 0 on the keypad to RAM Preview. The baseball moves down along the motion path, decreasing in size, and rotating counterclockwise.

Step 2: Click on the word Position in the Timeline to select all its keyframes. Select the Animation menu (or right-click on one of its keyframes) and apply Animation > Keyframe Assistant > Time-Reverse Keyframes. RAM Preview again – the baseball travels along the motion path in the opposite direction, but Scale and Rotation are not affected.

Step 3: If you'd like to reverse these other properties as well, select the keyframes for both properties:

• Click on the word Scale in the Timeline panel, then Shift+click on the word Rotation.

• With these keyframes selected, right-click on any one keyframe and select Keyframe Assistant > Time-Reverse Keyframes from the popup menu. RAM Preview again – the layer will now increase in

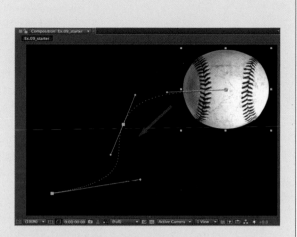

Step 1: The baseball starts off moving down the motion path, decreasing in size and rotating counterclockwise.

Step 2: To reverse the animation, select the keyframes you want to reverse and apply Keyframe Assistant > Time-Reverse Keyframes.

size and rotate clockwise. (Our version is shown in comp **[Ex.09-final]**.)

You don't have to reverse all keyframes on a property; you can be more selective. For example, say you've created a layer fading up, using two Opacity keyframes. Now you want to fade out over the same number of frames at the end of the layer: Copy the first set of Opacity keyframes, move to where you want the fade-out to begin, Paste the two keyframes, and while they're still selected, reverse them.

Note: Time-Reverse Keyframes does not reverse the playback of frames in a movie (reversing layers is covered in Chapter 28).

Exponential Scale

By now, it should be obvious that a lot of After Effects is based on simple math. However, sometimes simple math lets you down. Take keyframing Scale from 0% to 1000% over ten seconds – as we've done in composition [**Ex.10_starter**] in this chapter's example project – using an Illustrator layer that continuously rasterizes. With just two keyframes, After Effects neatly interpolates the scale 100% per second. Reveal the Scale value if it is not already visible (select **at_symbol.ai** and press S) and switch into the Graph Editor (Shift+F3). Study Scale's value as you scrub the current time indicator. From 01:00 to 02:00, it increases from 100% to 200%; from 09:00 to 10:00 it increases from 900% to 1000% as you would expect. Interestingly, the relative increase in the first second is infinite – from 0% to 100% – but the relative increase in the last second is relatively small, from 900% to 1000%.

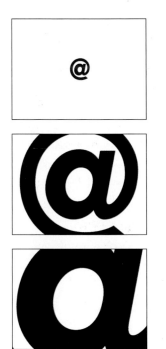

That last little piece of trivia becomes visually important when you RAM Preview this comp: You will quickly see that the result is perceptually wrong. This particular animation starts way too fast, and ends way too slow. Why? Because our perception of scale is relative. Something scaled 200% looks twice as big as something scaled 100%. However, to

A layer that scales using linear keyframes may look like it should scale at a constant rate, but it starts off scaling fast and then slows down as the size increases (sequence, above left). The flat Speed Graph line and steadily rising Value Graph line in the Graph Editor (below) would seem to confirm what we expect, but not what we're seeing. The solution is to apply Keyframe Assistant > Exponential Scale (above right).

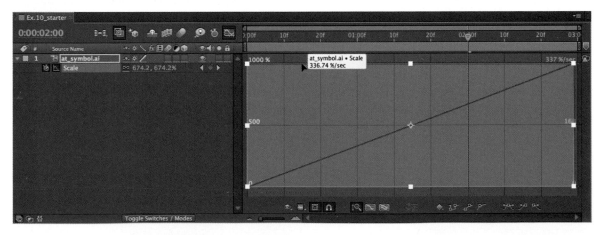

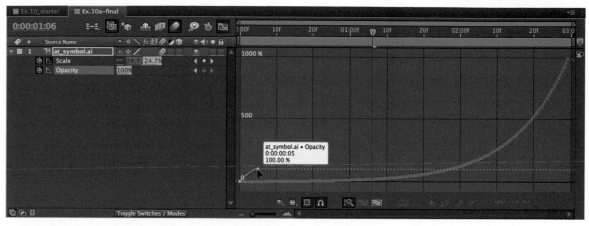

Note the result in the Graph Editor after applying Exponential Scale: This gives a perceptually even zoom when you scale in large amounts. Both the Speed and Value Graphs have the same curve. The first Scale keyframe is at 2% in our final example; to avoid the image appearing to pop on, we've added a five-frame fade-up.

look twice as big again, we need to increase the scale to 400%, not just another 100 to 300%.

The Exponential Scale keyframe assistant was created to cure this specific problem. When you select two Scale keyframes and apply it (Animation > Keyframe Assistant > Exponential Scale or right-click on a Scale keyframe for the same menu), it calculates what the scale should be at each frame to give a perceptually correct zoom. Try it with comp [**Ex.10_starter**]. To get a better idea of what is going on, press Shift+F3 to open the Graph Editor and examine the before and after graphs for Scale.

The only problem you might encounter with Exponential Scale is when you scale up from 0%, as the computer takes an inordinate amount of time to scale from 0% to 1%. After that, it starts to pick up speed. If you're trying to get a layer to zoom toward you for, say, three seconds in sync with a sound effect, the layer will be invisible for all intents and purposes while it scales from 0% to 1% or 2%. RAM Preview [**Ex.10_starter**] after applying Exponential Scale and see for yourself.

To fix this delay, undo the keyframe assistant and use the shortcut Shift+F2 to deselect both keyframes. Change the first keyframe from 0% to some small value like 2%; leave the second keyframe at 1000%. Select both keyframes again and reapply Exponential Scale. Preview the animation, and the apparent dead time at the start of the zoom is removed. If you're bothered by the image popping on at 2%, fade up the layer over a few frames. Our final compromise is shown in [**Ex.10a-final**].

The problem with linear scaling occurs whether you are animating from 0% to 1000% or from 50% to 60% – it's just more obvious at the bigger leaps. You could apply it whenever you scale, if you wanted to be mathematically precise. We usually use it only in extreme zooms where we see a problem. With all of these animation tricks, the real issue is what looks and "feels" right to you when you preview the animation.

TIP

Exponential Editing

To retime the smooth result of an exponential scale, apply Time Remapping (Chapter 28) in a second comp. This is shown in [**Ex.10b**]. (This is not recommended for movie layers, as this will adjust the playback speed of the movie as well.)

CONNECT

Workspaces: Chapter 1.

Keyframing, editing motion paths: Chapter 3.

Keyframe velocity, Graph Editor: Chapter 4.

Split layer: Chapter 7.

Motion blur: Chapter 8.

3D layers, cameras, and lights (including motion paths and auto-orient in 3D): Chapters 13 through 15.

Parenting and null objects: Chapter 17.

Continuous rasterization: Chapter 20.

Animating effects: Chapter 22.

Reverse layer and time remapping: Chapter 28.

Expressions: Chapter 37.

6

The Layer Essentials

Tips for managing multiple layers efficiently, including hot keying, markers, and the layer switches.

By now, you should know how to build a comp and how to animate layers, so let's step up to working with multiple layers efficiently. This chapter covers shortcuts and tips for managing and replacing layers, creating markers and snapshots, and editing images in their original application.

A large portion of using After Effects efficiently is to master some of the keyboard shortcuts. They may seem like brain twisters initially, but learning the most common shortcuts will mean you'll work faster – and therefore, finish work earlier. After Effects usually presents more than one way to do any given task; as before, we'll concentrate on the shortcuts we use regularly. To see the full range of available shortcuts, open the Keyboard Shortcuts (select Help > Keyboard Shortcuts to open After Effects Help). If you wish to practice manipulating layers, open the [**Ex.01**] composition in the accompanying project file, or create your own layered composition.

Selecting Layers

Many editing techniques in After Effects affect all selected layers, so let's start with a roundup of the most useful selection shortcuts. The shortcut for Mac is given first; the shortcut for Windows follows (in parentheses):

Select a range of adjacent layers	Shift+click
Select non-adjacent layers	Command+click (Control+click)
Select All	Command+A (Control+A)
Deselect All	F2, or Command+Shift+A (Control+Shift+A)
Select layer above/below	Command (Control)+up/down arrows
Select specific layer	Type layer number on keypad (for Layer 10 and above, type fast!)
Invert Selection	Use context-sensitive menu (right-click layer name or layer bar)

TIP

Go to In and Out

Press I to move the current time indicator to a selected layer's in point; press O to jump to its out point.

Example Project

Explore the 06-Example Project.aep file as you read this chapter; references to [Ex.##] refer to specific compositions within the project file.

Moving Layers in Time

As you move a layer in time by sliding the layer bar along the timeline, the Info panel (opened by using Command+2 on Mac, Control+2 on Windows) will display the new In and Out times as you drag. If you hold down the Shift key after you start dragging, the layer will snap to the time indicator and other important points in time, such as the in and out points of other layers. This is a great boon in aligning animations. If you're moving multiple layers, only the layer you clicked on to drag the group will exhibit this snapping tendency – so choose your layer wisely.

It is also possible to snap the beginning or end of layers to the current time or to the beginning or end of the comp. Use these simple keyboard shortcuts:

Move layer in point to current time	[(left bracket)
Move layer out point to current time	] (right bracket)
Move layer in point to start of comp	Option+Home (Alt+Home)
Move layer out point to end of comp	Option+End (Alt+End)
Move layer one frame earlier	Option+Page Up (Alt+Page Up)
Move layer one frame later	Option+Page Down (Alt+Page Down)
Move layer ten frames earlier or later	Add Shift key to above shortcut

Moving Layers in the Stack

The way layers are stacked in the Timeline panel directly affects the front-to-back order of 2D layers in the Comp panel; it also influences how mixtures of 2D and 3D layers are sorted. When you drag a footage item from the Project panel to the Timeline panel, you can place it between other layers; if you use a keyboard shortcut such as Command+/ (Control+/) to add a footage item to the forward comp, these new layers are placed at the top of the stack. In either case, you can easily move single or multiple layers up and down the stack by dragging them in the Timeline panel. There is also a set of useful keyboard shortcuts that employ variations of the bracket keys used above:

Bring layer forward one level	Command+] (Control+])
Move layer to front	Command+Shift+] (Control+Shift+])
Send layer back one level	Command+[(Control+[)
Send layer to back	Command+Shift+[(Control+Shift+[)

The Info panel will update in real time to show the new in and out points as you drag a layer along the timeline.

TIP

Scroll Layer to Top

When layers are twirled open and the vertical scroll bar is visible in the Timeline panel, you can select a layer and press X to scroll this layer to the top. (This does not reorder the layer in the stack; it merely auto-scrolls the panel for you.)

TIP

Reverse Layer Stacking Order

If you have multiple layers in the Timeline panel and you want to reverse their stacking order, select the bottom layer, Shift+click the top layer, Edit > Cut, then Edit > Paste – the layers will paste from top to bottom in the reverse order. You can also specify layer order exactly: Command+click (Control+click) layers in the order you want them to stack, then Cut and Paste.

Convert Footage to Layers

If you imported a layered Photoshop or Illustrator file as a single footage item using the Merged Layers option, you can later replace this item with a layered version without having to re-import. Either select the item in the Project panel and use File > Replace Footage > With Layered Comp, or select the layer in a comp and use Layer > Convert To Layered Comp. Importing layered files is covered in more detail in Chapter 38.

Option Paste

Pressing Option (Alt) when you Paste a layer will place the layer's in point at the current time, not the layer's original start time.

The Solo switch temporarily overrides the status of the Video switches of layers in a composition – notice that they are grayed out.

Duplicating Layers and Comps

If you want footage to appear in a composition more than once, you can drag the footage from the Project panel to the composition a second time. However, if you've already animated a layer, you can duplicate a selected layer, or layers, by using Command+D (Control+D) or by selecting Duplicate from the Edit menu. This will duplicate all the attributes assigned to the layer, including keyframes, effects, and so on.

Another possible reason to duplicate a layer is if you want to experiment with attributes but don't want to ruin your original layer. After you duplicate the layer, turn off the visibility for one layer and experiment with the other.

You can also copy and paste layers, even between comps. First, select the layer to copy, making sure that no keyframes are selected by using the shortcut Deselect All Keyframes (Shift+F2). Then Edit > Copy, open or bring forward the comp you want to paste this layer into, and Edit > Paste. If you had any keyframes (or values) selected, then After Effects will copy only the keyframes (or values), and you would either have pasted nothing into the new comp, or have pasted keyframe values into a selected layer. Note that layers paste in the layer stack above any selected layer.

If you plan to experiment with multiple layers, you might want to duplicate the entire comp. To do this, select the comp from the Project panel and Edit > Duplicate. To rename a comp from the Project panel, select it, press Return, type a new name, and press Return again.

If a layer has not been renamed in the Timeline (noted by its name appearing in [brackets] in the Layer Names column), then any duplicate you create will use the same name as the original layer. Therefore, you might want to rename each duplicate to help identify which is which. (See *Renaming Layers* on the next page.)

If a layer has been renamed, the duplicate name will have an incremental number added to it. Duplicating a layer you've named "Blue" will result in a second layer called "Blue 2". If you duplicate either layer again, the third layer will be called "Blue 3". In addition, a layer named "Blue01" will be duplicated as "Blue02". The same convention is used for duplicated compositions and folders.

Soloing Layers

Ever have a complicated composition that you wish you could temporarily simplify so you could focus on what one or two layers were doing? A useful tool is the Solo switch, residing to the right of the Video and Audio switches in the Timeline panel. If the Solo switch is enabled for one or more layers that have visual content, the Video switches for the other layers are temporarily overridden (they will even be grayed out), and only the soloed layers will be rendered in the Comp panel. If you have more than one audio, 3D light, or 3D camera layer, Solo will "mute" the other layers of the same type, previewing just the one(s) you have soloed.

To turn soloing on or off, select the layer or layers you're interested in, and click in the Solo switch column (the hollow circle). You can also drag the mouse down the Solo column to change the status of a number of adjacent layers in one movement. Clicking on the Solo switch for a layer does not automatically turn off the Solo switch for other layers – you must Option+click (Alt+click) if you want to solo a layer exclusively. To see all layers again, turn off all Solo switches (don't just turn on all Solo switches!). The Solo switch is obeyed for RAM Previews and potentially for rendering – make sure you check the Solo Switches popup in Render Settings.

Renaming Layers

Every layer has a *source* name (the name of the source on disk and in the project panel) and a *layer* name (the name of that particular copy of the source in a composition). Clicking on the Source Name column header in the Timeline panel toggles between displaying source and layer names.

The Layer Name defaults to the source's name, but it is easily changed: select the name, press the Return key, type a new name, and press Return to accept. Changing the name of one layer while in Source Name mode automatically toggles the column to Layer Name view; layers that are not renamed will appear in brackets. Selecting a layer and typing Command+Option+E (Control+Alt+E) will display the source name in the Info panel.

Renaming layers is particularly useful if you're using the same source multiple times. It also helps when the source material has an obscure name on disk, such as FAB07FL.TIF, or is named by the timecode it was captured at on a certain reel (common with footage captured by non-linear editing systems). Note that you can also rename footage in the Project panel, plus add descriptive notes in its Comment field.

Replace Source

Here's one you won't want to forget. You spend time animating a layer and are happy with the animation keyframes, effects, and other attributes. But then you decide the source material needs to be changed (you want to swap out the source while keeping everything else). This is called *Replace Source*, and for some reason it's nowhere to be found on any menu. Practice the following steps with [**Ex.02**] to replace the source to a layer:

Step 1: Select the layer (or multiple layers) you want to replace – such as the baseball in [**Ex.02**] – in the Composition or Timeline panel.

Step 2: In the Project panel, select the source you'd like to use instead.

Step 3: With the Option (Alt) key held down, drag and drop the new source into the Comp or Timeline panel. The Info panel will confirm your action. All the attributes of the previous layer(s) will be assigned to the new source.

If the new layer is added to the top of the stack instead of replacing the selected layer, After Effects did not recognize that the Option (Alt) key was held down. Try holding down the Option (Alt) key a little longer after you release the mouse. You can also select the replacement source in the Project panel and use the shortcut Command+Option+/ (Control+Alt+/).

Guide Layers

A handy tool is Guide Layers: layers that appear only in the current composition, but not in compositions further down a chain of nested comps, or (optionally) when you render. Great uses for Guide Layers include scratch audio tracks, grid overlays, or FPO (For Position Only) templates.

To toggle whether or not a layer is a Guide Layer, select it, and choose Guide Layer from either the Layers menu or by right-clicking on it.

 A blue grid icon will appear to the left of its name in the Timeline panel when it is a Guide Layer.

In [**Ex.05**], the topmost layer contains a mask which warns us which parts of a full-frame image might be cut off by film projection. If you render this comp, and you leave the Render Settings popup for Guide Layers to its default Off position, this layer will not appear (see Chapter 42 for more details on rendering).

TIP

Returning to Source Name

If you've renamed a layer and want to return it to the source name, press Return, Delete (so the name is now blank), then Return a second time. This is handy if you've replaced the layer and the original layer name is no longer valid.

Mark That Spot!

Comp and layer markers help you coordinate animations and stay organized.

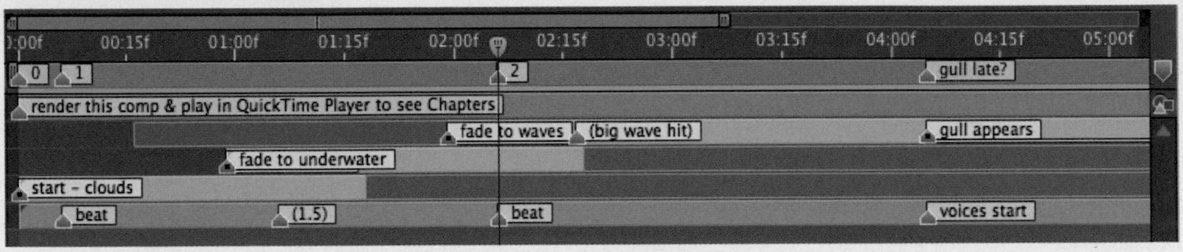

Comp markers appear below the ruler in the Timeline panel; Layer markers appear on individual layers. Both may contain text comments plus other information. The thin bar that appears underneath some markers indicates its duration.

One of the most valuable tools in After Effects is *markers*: tags you can add to a comp or layer in the Timeline panel. These help remind you where major (or even minor) events and other important points in time are. Once you've placed markers, you can use them to quickly navigate in time in a comp, as well as to Shift+drag layers and keyframes to more easily align events.

Markers are an excellent tool for annotating what is happening in the animation in a comp, either to remind yourself later, or before handing a project off to another animator. We've used them extensively in the example projects for this book. The first 63 characters of a marker's comment will appear in the Timeline panel; hover your cursor over a marker to reveal a tooltip with the full text.

To delete a marker, Command+click (Control+click) directly on each marker one at a time. A scissors icon will confirm what you are about to do. To remove all markers on a layer, right-click on one of the markers

and select Delete All Markers from the popup menu. You can also choose to Lock Markers on a layer from the same menu, or open the Settings dialog.

Comp Markers

Comp markers are used to help remember specific points in time in an overall composition. This makes it easier to coordinate multiple layers and keyframes to the same overall time.

Comp markers may be created by locating the current time indicator to the desired point and

Double-click a marker to edit it; Command+click (Control+click) to delete one. Right-click on a marker to get more options, such as one that lets you delete all in one shot. Layer markers have more options, including the ability to lock them.

pressing Shift plus a number from 0 to 9 along the top of the normal keyboard (*not* the numeric keypad). They will appear above the layer bars and below the time ruler in the Timeline panel. Press these numbers without the Shift key to quickly locate back to this time. You can also drag additional comp markers out of the "marker well" at the right edge of the timeline to create additional numbered markers. If no layers are selected, pressing the asterisk key on the numeric keypad will create a blank marker. Double-click a marker to edit its text.

When you nest one composition inside another, any comp markers in the first comp will appear as layer markers on the nested comp's layer in the second comp. Note that layer markers created this way do *not* stay in sync if you later change the comp markers in the first comp. To update nested markers, right-click on a marker in the nested comp, and select Update Markers from Source. This will update all of the markers on this nested layer.

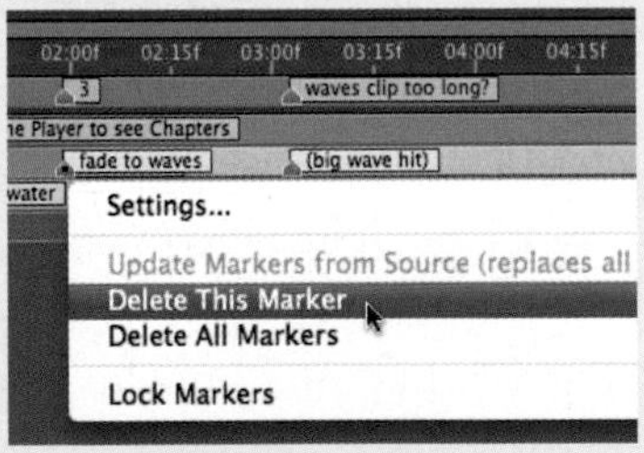

Layer Markers

If you need to mark specific frames in a layer, use layer markers instead. Layer markers attach to the layer, so if you move the footage along the timeline, the markers move with it.

To create a layer marker, select a layer and position the time indicator at the point in time where you'd like a marker to appear. Press the asterisk key (*) on the numeric keypad (not the keyboard), and a triangle-shaped marker will appear on the layer. You can double-click directly on the marker to add a comment to it. If you know you want to add a comment to a marker before you create it, type Option+* (Alt+*) and the Marker dialog will open.

(If you have a Mac laptop without numeric keypad key equivalents, hold Control and press 8 to add a layer or comp marker, depending on whether or not a layer is currently selected. Add Option to open the dialog.)

You can add layer markers while a comp or layer is being RAM or Audio Previewed. This is particularly handy for spotting events in an audio soundtrack. Press the * key when you hear an important beat in the music or phrase in a dialog track. Note that inevitable delays in human and software reaction times will mean that these markers may be placed a couple of frames later than you intended; drag them back to their correct positions when you're done.

Both layer and comp markers allow you to enter comments that appear in the Timeline panel. You can also add Chapters to aid movie navigation and DVD authoring, Web Links for interactive web programming, and Flash Video Cue Point and Parameters information.

Marker Content

In addition to comments, marker start time, and marker duration, markers may also contain Chapter and Web Links, as well as Flash Video Cue Point and Parameters information. Markers with Chapters, Web Links, or Cue Points will have a black dot in their icon in the Timeline panel.

Chapter comments are embedded in QuickTime and AVI files upon rendering. To see these in action, render the comp **[Ex.03]** and open it in QuickTime Player; look for the chapters in its user interface. These markers are also useful for noting chapter breaks for programs such as Adobe Encore DVD.

Web Links are embedded into QuickTime or SWF format output. When played back inside a web page, they will cause a jump to the URL or file name you've entered.

More powerful are Flash Video Cue Point and Parameters. These are embedded in Adobe FLV movies (FLV files) upon rendering. Advanced web authoring is beyond the scope of this book, but experienced web programmers can imagine the interactive possibilities this presents.

Drag to Replace

An alternative to Replace Footage > File is to select an item already in the Project panel, and Option+drag (Alt+drag) it onto the footage item you wish to replace in the Project panel. The original item will not be deleted from the project.

Replace Footage

The Replace Source feature works on a layer-by-layer basis. However, if you have a source in the Project panel that's used multiple times in one comp, or even in multiple comps, you can replace the footage item in the Project panel, which will update all instances in all comps. To Replace Footage, you must select the source in the Project panel. From the File menu, select Replace Footage > File; the shortcut is Command+H (Control+H). Locate the new source on disk, and Import.

If the new source has attributes different from the original footage, select it and click the Interpret Footage button along the bottom of the Project panel to make sure these settings are still appropriate for the new source. The biggest problem usually comes in replacing a footage item that did not have an alpha channel with one that does; you may need to reinterpret the footage and set the alpha to the correct choice.

Replacing Source or Footage does not change any new layer name you might have given a layer in a comp. After replacing, you might want to double-check the layer name to make sure it is still appropriate. If it's not, return it to the source's name (see earlier tip).

Taking Snapshots

After Effects can save a *snapshot* of the Comp, Layer, or Footage panel as an image, which is useful for comparing before and after states, comparing treated and untreated versions of a layer, or for matching up different frames in time.

The usual method for taking a snapshot is to click on the camera button at the bottom of the Comp panel (listen for the camera shutter sound effect). You then make a change to some attribute that updates the composition. Now click on the "man" button to the right of the camera button to display the contents of the snapshot, and quickly do a before-and-after comparison between the snapshot state and the current state.

The camera button allows you to take a snapshot of the current rendered state of a composition. After you make changes, you can compare the new current state to your saved snapshot by clicking and pressing the "man" button (immediately to the right of the camera icon) to display the last snapshot.

A snapshot taken in one panel can be displayed in another panel, so you can temporarily show a snapshot taken in the Comp panel while in the Layer panel or Footage panel, and vice versa. You can also view just one channel from a snapshot by selecting the channel from the Show Channels menu, then recalling the snapshot.

There are four independent snapshots, which are found under the F5 through F8 keys, with F5 being the default snapshot described above. You need to use shortcut keys to access the other three snapshots:

Take snapshot	Shift+F5, F6, F7, or F8
Display snapshot	F5, F6, F7, or F8

The four snapshots are retained in memory during a single After Effects session, even when different projects are opened. However, snapshots cannot be saved or rendered to disk. You can discard individual snapshots using Command+Shift+F5, F6, F7, or F8 (Control+Shift+F5, F6, F7, or F8); you can purge all of them at once using Edit > Purge > Snapshot.

Just remember that snapshots have no power to revert your comp to a previous state (unlike in Photoshop where the History panel allows you to backtrack); only an image is being stored in RAM. But, if you keep track of what each snapshot represents, you can go back through the Edit > History menu or the Undo buffer to revert to that state.

Align Panel

When you're working with multiple layers, the Align & Distribute panel is handy for quickly and accurately tidying up the positions of layers in a composition. It can be opened using Window > Align. To use this panel, select at least two layers for Align or three for Distribute, and click on the icon for the option you want.

Align attempts to line up some feature of the selected layers (*whether they are visible or not* – be careful with your selections), such as their centers or an edge. Distribute spaces out these features equally, rather than forcing them to be the same. In some cases, the relative positions of the selected objects have a big effect on the result. Unlike what you might suspect, it does not look at a user-specified layer to be the reference or "anchor" for an alignment or distribution.

After Effects can "see" the edges of the full dimensions of a layer, or the edges of any masks you created for the layer inside After Effects. However, it cannot detect where the visible edges are for any alpha channel a layer might have (where's the "edge" of a glow or soft feather?). It also does not use the anchor point for any centering-based align or distribute. This reduces its usefulness for irregularly shaped or oddly framed sources.

If you decide to align the top, bottom, left, or right edges of a set of layers, After Effects will look for the topmost, bottommost, leftmost, or rightmost edge of the selected layers and align all the selected layers to that point. For centering, it uses the average center point of all the selected layers.

In the Distribute cases, After Effects has to do a little thinking. It looks at the relevant edges or centers of the selected layers, decides which two are at the furthest extremes in the dimension you have asked to distribute in, then sorts the remaining layers in order of their relevant positions. It will then reposition the layers between the two at the extremes, taking pains not to swap the relative positions of the middle layers.

Comps [Ex.04a] and [Ex.04b] are set up with a few different-shaped objects for you to experiment with. Just remember that you have to select at least two layers for Align or three layers for Distribute to do anything, and that you can always use Command+Z (Control+Z) to Undo.

Finding Sources

To locate the source file for an already-imported footage item, right-click on it in the Project panel and select your preferred "reveal" option, or study its File Path column.

The Align panel is handy for adjusting the positions of 2D layers in a composition. New in After Effects CS5 is the ability to align layers to either the comp's boundaries, or to the other selected layers.

When aligning or distributing layers, After Effects looks at the relative original positions of the selected layers (below left), and only changes the dimensions that it has to. In this case using **[Ex.04]**, aligning their tops vertically maintains their original horizontal positions (below right).

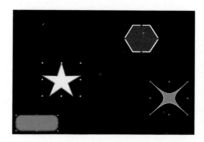

Hot Keying to External Programs

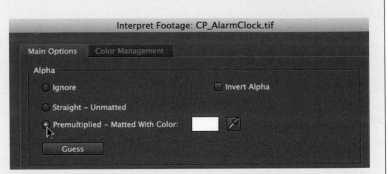

If an original image had no alpha, and you add one when you hot key into Photoshop, the alpha channel will default to being ignored when you return to After Effects. Change its setting in the File > Interpret Footage > Main dialog.

You will find many occasions when a piece of source material needs more work – for example, retouching a photo In Photoshop, or editing some Illustrator art. After Effects lets you directly open the source in the program that created it and track changes when you're done – without having to find the file on your disk. This process is called Edit Original or *hot keying*. These are the steps:

Step 1: Select a source in any panel, then select Edit > Edit Original. The shortcut is Command+E (Control+E).

Step 2: After Effects will look at the file for a "creator" tag, then open the file in the program that created it (assuming you also have this program on your disk). You will need enough RAM to open both programs simultaneously.

Step 3: *Optional:* If you want to maintain a copy of this original file before you start editing, use the Save As > As a Copy feature from the editing application.

Step 4: Make your changes. When the changes are complete, be sure to Save the file.

Step 5: Return to After Effects. As soon as it is brought to the foreground, After Effects checks to see if the file it sent away has been modified since you hot keyed, and if it has, it will automatically reload it for all instances of that file in the project.

If you're having problems, it's worth bearing in mind how After Effects is tracking the file. Let's say you select a Photoshop file and invoke Edit Original. After Effects sends the file to Photoshop and starts "watching" this file on disk. It looks at only this particular file name, which is why protecting the original by doing a regular Save As (instead of Save As > As a Copy) won't work – this modified file is not the one being watched.

Also, the first time you return to After Effects after selecting Edit Original, it checks the source's "last modified date" on the hard drive – if it's been updated, the file is reloaded. Not only that, After Effects checks the status of this particular file only the *first* time you return: If you forgot to save and need to return to Photoshop, then save the file and return to After Effects a *second* time, the file will not be reloaded.

If you need to reload one or more files, select them in the Project panel and use File > Reload Footage; the shortcut is

Command+Option+L (Control+Alt+L). As with the normal Replace Footage command, the previous Interpret Footage settings remain in force. If you add an alpha channel to an image, you will need to change the Alpha settings for the file to match its new state.

Life gets trickier with layered Photoshop and Illustrator files. If you imported them as Merged Layers, you can add and delete layers, and After Effects will properly note the changes. However, if you imported them as a composition, and you then add a layer to a file, After Effects will not recognize it. You will need to import the same file again, either as another composition or by selecting just the new layer. Then, move the new layer into the previous composition you imported. If you re-imported as a composition, also move this new layer's source into the corresponding folder for the composition you imported originally – otherwise, you might accidentally delete its source when you clean up your project.

Color-Coding

You might have noticed that different types of layer sources – such as movies, stills, audio, solids, and other compositions – tend to have different-colored layer bars in the Timeline panel. There is rhyme and reason behind this: After Effects automatically assigns these different types of sources *Labels*. There are sixteen different label colors (including None) with corresponding names. You can override the default label colors in several places throughout the program:

• In the Timeline panel, click on the label for a layer, and select a new color. (If the Labels column is not visible, right-click on any column header in the Timeline panel, and enable Columns > Label.)

• In the Project panel, make sure the Labels column is visible (same procedure as in the Timeline panel); you may need to open the Project panel wide enough or re-sort the columns so the Labels column is accessible. Click on the label for a source, and change its color. This new color will be used when you add the footage to a comp – but footage that has already been used in a comp will retain its original color.

• In the Render Queue, the procedure is the same as above.

If you right-click on a label, you can select all other objects with the same color at once.

You can change the global colors of the labels – and the names assigned to those colors (you're not stuck with wonderful names such as Sea Foam and Pink) – in Preferences > Labels. All objects that use those colors will be updated. You can change the default assignments of which object types gets which color in the same preference panel. Doing this changes the color for any newly imported or newly created layer or source, but does not change the colors already assigned to existing objects.

You can also select all similarly labeled items in the Project panel or Timeline panel through right-clicking on any color icon, which can be a handy shortcut for selecting a group of layers.

In Preferences > Labels, you can override the default colors assigned to the different types of layer sources.

What Does That Switch Do?

If you forget what some of the buttons and switches in the various After Effects panels do, make sure Tool Tips are enabled (Preferences > General > Show Tool Tips), place your mouse cursor over them, and pause a few seconds without clicking. A short line of text explaining it will appear. If you're still stumped, remember the key words it displays, and use them to search the Online Help or the index of this book.

The main layer switches are also covered in the *Beswitched* sidebar on the following pages.

Trimming and splitting layers: Chapter 7.

Nesting compositions: Chapter 18.

Precomposing: Chapter 19.

Interpret Footage dialog: Chapter 38.

Beswitched

The switches are the central hub of the Timeline panel – they control everything from visibility to motion blur.

We've introduced a few of these switches here and in earlier chapters, and will explain more of the simpler switches below. Other switches are so involved that entire chapters will be dedicated to them as noted.

A/V Features Column

This column houses the switches for Video, Audio, Solo, and Lock, as well as the keyframe navigator arrows when a property is set to animate. The column defaults to the left side of the Timeline panel, but we personally prefer to move it to the right, adjacent to the timeline, where the keyframe navigator is more easily accessible.

- **Video:** The Video switch turns on and off visibility for a layer; we will often refer to this as the *eyeball*. Layers that are turned off take no rendering time, unless they are used by another layer as a matte or as a map for a compound effect (Chapter 24).

- **Audio:** The Audio switch turns on and off audio tracks, should the layer be audio-only or have an audio track attached.

- **Solo:** When the Solo switch is set for at least one layer, the Video switch is overridden for all other layers in a comp. You can solo multiple layers; Option+click (Alt+click) to solo one layer and turn off the solo switch for all other layers.

Audio
Video | Solo | Lock

The Video, Audio, Solo, and Lock switches are identified by eyeball, speaker, hollow circle, and padlock icons respectively. The keyframe navigators for exposed, animating properties are also displayed underneath the row of switches for each layer.

- **Lock:** When you lock a layer, you can no longer select it, delete it, move it, or edit any of its keyframes. This is typically used to prevent accidental changes. Layers that are locked will blink in the timeline if you try to select them or move any of their keyframes. You can, however, change the status for many of the switches (such as its visibility and quality), when a layer is locked. The shortcut to lock selected layers is Command+L (Control+L). To Unlock All Layers in a comp use the shortcut Command+Shift+L (Control+Shift+L).

Switches/Modes Column

The Switches column shares space with the Modes column. Press F4 to toggle between them or click on the Switches/Modes button at the bottom of the Timeline panel. You can also right-click along the top of any column and select Modes to be displayed at the same time as Switches. The Modes column is where you select Blending Modes, Track Mattes, Stencils and Preserve Transparency – these are all covered in chapters 9, 11, 12 and 12 respectively.

Back in the Switches column, if there is a gray box under a given column, this switch is available for a given layer. To change the status of a switch, click inside this gray box (all selected layers will change to the new state), or drag the mouse down a row to set. The Layer Switches consist of, from left to right:

- **Shy:** Layers that are set to be shy can be hidden from display in the Timeline panel, though they will still render and behave normally otherwise.

To label a layer as being shy, click on the "Kilroy Was Here" switch and he'll go into hiding. Click the Shy switch again to un-shy the Layer. To hide shy layers from displaying, click on the master Hide Shy Layers switch above the columns. You might want to make layers shy to simplify the Timeline panel, or to hide layers that were failed experiments (in that case, be sure to turn their Video switches off as well!).

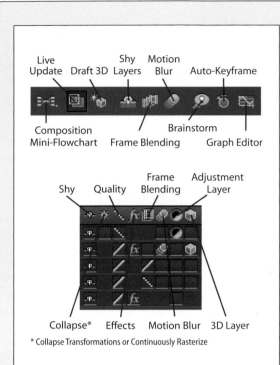

Live Update Draft 3D Shy Layers Motion Blur Auto-Keyframe

Composition Mini-Flowchart Frame Blending Brainstorm Graph Editor

Shy Quality Frame Blending Adjustment Layer

Collapse* Effects Motion Blur 3D Layer

* Collapse Transformations or Continuously Rasterize

Switches define several important rendering and layer management properties, and the current values for any twirled-down properties are displayed in this area. The nine buttons along the top are comp-wide switches. Live Update interacts with Preferences > Previews and is covered at the end of Chapter 2; for Draft 3D, see Chapters 14 and 15.

- **Collapse** (Chapter 20): This switch is available when the layer is a nested composition (where it collapses its contents into the current comp), or contains vector artwork such as text, shape, solid, SWF, PDF, and Illustrator layers (where it determines if the vector art will continuously rasterize).

- **Quality** (Chapter 2): This switch toggles between Draft Quality (dotted line) and Best Quality (solid line). The default is Best Quality, which turns on antialiasing and subpixel positioning.

- **Effects** (Chapter 22): This switch is active only when effects are applied to a layer. You can turn on and off all the effects for a given layer with this one switch – a stylized "*fx*" means effects are on; an

empty gray box means they are off. Switches for individual effects appear in the A/V Column when they are twirled down. Note that the effects switch can be overridden in Render Settings (Chapter 42).

- **Frame Blending** (Chapter 28): This feature will create new frames either by blending together adjacent footage frames (Frame Mix mode, noted by a dotted backslash) or interpolating motion between them (Pixel Motion mode, noted by a solid forward slash). The master Enable Frame Blending switch along the top determines whether enabled layers will display inside the Comp panel with frame blending (which incurs a rendering hit); the comp's master switch can be overridden in Render Settings.

- **Motion Blur** (Chapter 8): Turning on this switch for layers animated by After Effects will render multiple copies of the layer as it moves, creating more natural motion. The master Enable Motion Blur switch determines whether enabled layers will display in the Comp panel with motion blur (which also incurs a rendering hit); as with frame blending, the comp's master display switch is overridden by the rendering controls.

- **Adjustment Layer** (Chapter 22): Effects applied to an adjustment layer will affect all layers below in the stack. This switch decides if a layer behaves normally or becomes an adjustment layer (a black-and-white circle is visible in this column). When enabled, the original content is ignored, and effects applied to the layer affect all layers below, using the adjustment layer's alpha channel and opacity setting.

    You can also use this switch to enable Adjustment Lights, which affect only the layers below them in the Timeline panel's stacking order (see Chapter 15).

- **3D Layer** (Chapter 13): Determines whether a layer is in normal 2D space or is placed in 3D space with an added Z dimension, viewed by a 3D camera and affected by 3D lights. The Draft 3D switch along the top of the Timeline panel disables 3D lighting effects and the camera's depth-of-field blur, which makes After Effects more responsive when you're working with 3D layers. The status of the Draft 3D switch is ignored when you render in Best Quality.

Trimming Layers

Learning how to edit layers through trimming, splitting, and sequencing.

After Effects is stronger vertically – stacking layers to create a single rich image – than horizontally – editing together various layers back to back in a linear fashion. However, there are several tools within the software that aid in editing and sequencing layers. This chapter will cover trimming layers to remove unwanted frames, splitting layers in two so different pieces of time can be manipulated separately, plus the handy Slip, Overlay, and Ripple Insert edit tools. We'll also cover Sequence Layers: a nifty keyframe assistant for automatically arranging multiple layers end to end, with optional overlaps.

Clicking on the "expansion brackets" (circled in red) reveals or hides the columns for In, Out, Duration, and Stretch (speed) of all the layers in a comp. You can also scrub these values directly in the Timeline panel.

The Ins and Outs of In and Out

Before we delve into trimming, let's sort out what we really mean by the terms *in point* and *out point*. They have different meanings, depending on whether you are talking about a layer in relation to its source, or a layer in relation to how it is being used in a composition.

When you add a movie to a comp, its in point defaults to aligning with the start of the composition's timeline (this behavior can be disabled in Preferences > General so that layers start at the current time). Its duration then determines its out point. You can move the layer to a different range of time inside the comp. You can also trim a layer's own in and out points to determine what portion of the layer is going to be used inside a comp.

If you want to numerically check where these end points (and a layer's duration) are in relation to this comp, click on the expansion brackets at the bottom of the Timeline panel. You will now get columns that list In point, Out point, Duration, and Stretch of each layer inside this comp. (We'll deal with Stretch – the speed – in Chapter 28.)

Example Project

Explore the 07-Example Project.aep file as you read this chapter; references to [Ex.##] refer to specific compositions within the project file.

Open the example project for this chapter, and open composition [**Ex.01**]. If the In/Out/Duration/ Stretch columns are not visible, click on the expansion brackets to open them. Click on the layer bar (anywhere on the color bar will do; just avoid the very ends of the bars), and slide the bar left and right to move it in time – notice how both the In and Out point values update while Duration remains the same. The image in the Comp panel will also update, showing which frame of the layer is at the time indicator's current position. Note that when you select the layer, the solid color inside becomes lighter with a slight texture, providing visual feedback while you are moving it.

Now double-click the layer to open the clip in its Layer panel. The Layer panel shows you the original, unedited source. Below the displayed frame is a timeline and another time indicator. Notice that when you move and release the time indicator in the Layer panel, it also moves in the Timeline panel, and vice versa.

Below the Layer panel's timeline is a trio of timecode numbers. These display the in point, out point, and duration of the layer, *regardless of where it is placed in the comp*. If the layer and comp both start at 00:00, the values in the Layer panel and Timeline panel are identical. But don't let that lull you into thinking they are always the same: If any sliding or trimming takes place, the time indicator in the Layer panel shows you where you are in time in the *layer* – not where you are in the comp.

(Note: Editing the In and Out values in the Timeline panel *moves* a clip in time; it does not *trim* it. Similarly, changing the value for Duration also does not trim frames; it time-stretches the clip instead. Notice that as you scrub the Duration value, Stretch changes as well!)

Trimming Layers

Trimming a layer instructs After Effects to temporarily ignore unwanted frames in a video or audio layer. These frames remain as part of the source and can be restored at any time. You can also trim where still images, as well as text, shape, and solid layers, begin and end in the timeline, including extending them to start earlier or end later.

There are two ways to trim a layer – in the Timeline panel or the Layer panel – and the results vary with the method:

The Layer panel displays the original source, before any attributes have been applied; it also shows any trimming you have done, regardless of where it is placed in a comp. If a layer does not line up with the beginning of a comp, note that their relative time indicators – although synchronized – display different numbers, reflecting this offset. Footage courtesy Artbeats/Incarcerated.

Custom Columns

You can also right-click on the In/Out/Duration/Stretch columns to decide which individual parameters to hide or open.

Trim the out point by dragging the end of the layer bar (the cursor will change to a double arrow). Add the Shift key, and the out point will snap to the current time indicator along with other events such as keyframes.

Note that small triangles appear at the in and out points of a layer when its duration is fully extended (except for still images, text, shape and solid layers which have infinite durations).

TIP

Navigating the Layer Panel

The navigation shortcuts for the Timeline panel also work in the Layer panel, including Page Up, Page Down, Home, and End.

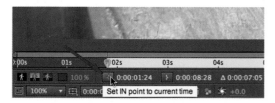

In the Layer panel, clicking on the left curly bracket trims the layer's in point to equal the current time.

Method A: Trimming in the Timeline Panel

This is the more straightforward method. Open [**Ex.02a**] and note the vertical lines at the ends of the layer bar in the Timeline panel. Drag these lines to trim out unwanted frames. Watch the Info panel – opened using Command+2 on the Mac (Control+2 on Windows) – for additional feedback on the new values for In, Out, and Duration (noted with the delta symbol: Δ). The layer bar becomes "empty" to denote the frames that have been trimmed. Add the Shift key as you drag to have the ends snap to the current time indicator. If you have the In/Out/Duration/Stretch columns open, note that the in and out points of the layer in relation to the comp change as you drag the layer bar ends and that the duration updates accordingly.

Most importantly, the frames that you keep appear at the same relative time in the comp's timeline as they did before. (Trimming in this manner does not slide the content of the layer relative to the comp.) You can then drag the trimmed layer anywhere along the timeline, as needed.

The keyboard shortcuts for trimming with this method are so incredibly useful you'll rarely drag the layer bar ends – plus the shortcuts work across multiple layers. The first shortcut is for Mac users (followed by the Windows shortcut in parentheses). Select the layer(s), move the time indicator to the frame you want, and type:

Trim IN point to current time	Option+[(Alt+[)
Trim OUT point to current time	Option+] (Alt+])

Method B: Trimming in the Layer Panel

The second method for trimming requires that you double-click the movie to open it in the Layer panel. Do this with the layer in [**Ex.02a**], find the frame you'd like as the new in point, and click the In point button (the left curly bracket). Similarly, move to the frame you would like for your ending frame, and click the Out button (the right curly bracket).

You can also drag the ends of the layer bar to set the in and out points; the timecode will display the new values in real time as you drag, including its new duration.

So what's the difference between methods A and B? Make a note of the in point of the trimmed movie in the Timeline panel. Now change the in point again in the Layer panel. No matter what frame you pick as your new beginning frame in the Layer panel, the in point in the comp remains the same. In other words, *trimming the in point in the Layer panel honors the in point relative to the comp, as set in the Timeline panel.* If you had determined that a movie needed to start at a specific frame in the entire animation, trimming with this method is the more direct route. However, the frames that you're keeping (and their associated keyframes) will move along the timeline when you edit the in point with this method, meaning the content of the layer will slide relative to the comp.

Comparing Methods

If the subtle differences between trimming methods are still unclear, compare the two methods in the following scenario:

Step 1: Open [**Ex.02b**]. In the layer **CL_SkateSequence.mov**, we've already placed markers at major "hit points" in the footage. We've decided it would be most exciting if the last of these hits synchronized to the final downbeat in the music at 04:00. We've set a comp marker to line up with this point in the music, so press 4 (on the keyboard) to jump to time 04:00.

Step 2: Drag the movie's layer bar to the left until the layer marker named "hit 4" aligns with 04:00 in the timeline. Press Page Up/Down to jog back and forth and check that the landing happens at 04:00.

Step 3: *Method A:* Now trim the movie layer's in point in the Timeline panel to make it start with the musical beat at 01:00. Because you can't see the layer's in point, move the time indicator to 01:00 and use the keyboard shortcut Option+[(Alt+[). Note that the layer marker lined up with 04:00 in the Comp panel does not change; only the in point relative to

TIP

Jumping Around

To jump to a selected layer's in or out point, press I and O respectively. To jump to one frame after the end of the selected layer (to insert a new layer after its end), press O plus Page Down.

the comp does. Double-click the movie to open the Layer panel, and notice that the in point is at 04:14 in relation to the movie (compared with 01:00 in the comp).

Step 4: *Method B:* For comparison, press Command+Z (Control+Z) once: This should Undo the trim so that the in point returns to 00:00 in the Layer panel, and "hit 4" remains aligned with comp marker 4 in the Timeline panel. Now trim the layer's in point directly in the Layer panel to 04:14. However, note that layer marker "hit 4" no longer syncs to 04:00 in the comp! By trimming in the Layer panel, the in point in the comp remained where it was (well before the start of the comp itself), and the movie was forced to slide along the timeline.

Obviously, it's not difficult to slide the layer back so that the trimmed movie starts at 01:00 – locate to this time, and press [to line it up. You could say there's not that much difference between the two methods – except that one method will usually get you where you want to go more directly. So when you trim, try to determine which is more important: keeping the current in point in the Timeline panel (if so, trim in Layer panel), or keeping a specific frame in the movie aligned with a particular point in time (if that's the case, trim in Timeline panel).

If you compare trimming methods in [**Ex.02b**], you'll notice that trimming unwanted frames in the Timeline panel in Step 3 means that the hit point in the movie remained aligned with the downbeat at 04:00. This is not the case when you're trimming frames in the Layer panel (Step 4).

TIP

Out of Bounds

Frames that end up before the start or extend past the end of the composition are automatically ignored – there's no need to trim them.

The head of the clip includes some "dead time" (above). Use Slip Edit to slide the content, revealing the action of the kids sooner (below). Footage courtesy Artbeats/Kids of Summer.

Slip Sliding Away

No matter which trimming method you use, be aware that any keyframes applied to the layer are "attached" to specific frames of the layer, not the comp! The necessity of this should be obvious: If you drag the layer bar in time, the keyframes often need to go along for the ride. The problem is that when you trim a layer, you will also trim out any keyframes attached to the unwanted frames.

One of our favorite features in After Effects is *slip editing*. This allows you to move the content of a layer without moving its keyframes or in and out points in relation to the composition. With a little planning, you can also move some of the keyframes while leaving others in place. Here are a couple of exercises where you can see this in action:

Step 1: Open comp **[Ex.03a]**. It contains two video layers, with the layer on top – **AB_KidsOfSummer.mov** – fading up and then back down again. If you can't see the Opacity keyframes, select the layer and press T to expose them; make sure the keyframes are *not* selected (Shift+F2 is the shortcut to deselect keyframes while keeping a layer selected).

Step 2: RAM Preview the comp. Note that in layer 1, the kids appear a bit late; we waste some "dead time" looking at an empty field.

Step 2: Place the cursor over the "empty" portion of the layer bar, and the dual-arrow Slip Edit tool (circled in red) will appear. This allows you to slide the portion of the layer that is viewed without changing the position of nonselected keyframes, or its in and out points relative to the comp.

Step 3: If the trimmed ends of a layer are not visible in the Timeline panel, place the Pan Behind tool over the main layer bar to bring up the Slip Edit tool.

Place the time indicator at 06:00, at the point where this layer has faded all the way up. Now move the cursor somewhere over the "empty" portions of the layer bar (where the bar is grayer), just beyond its in or out points. Notice how the cursor changes to a double-ended arrow with lines at the ends – this is the Slip Edit tool. Click and drag the layer bar while keeping an eye on the Comp panel. Drag the layer to the left until a few kids are just visible.

RAM Preview again, and note that the fade up and down still happen at the same time in the comp; just a different portion of the clip is used. Go ahead and experiment with different edit choices. Note that the Slip Edit tool will not let you drag the ends of the clip past its current in and out points in the comp (noted by the small black triangles that appear at the ends of the layer bar): This feature ensures that these in and out times cannot be slid by mistake.

Step 3: Now practice slip editing **AB_Transportation.mov**, the underlying clip. The problem is, you can't see any "empty" portions of its layer bar – so how can you use the Slip Edit tool? Press Y to enable the Pan Behind tool: This will bring up the slip cursor regardless of where it is placed over the layer bar. Notice how the texture in the layer bar makes it easier to see how much the layer is sliding by.

Make your edit, and press V to return to the normal Selection tool when you are done (Pan Behind can be a dangerous tool; you don't want it enabled unless you know you need it).

Slipping Keyframes

There are occasions when you will want some of the keyframes applied to a layer to move in sync with its frames as you perform a slip edit. For example, when you spend a lot of time masking or rotoscoping a movie, you want those mask shapes to be tied to the frames they were created for. After Effects allows you to be selective about which keyframes move and which ones don't. Try this out:

Step 1: Open [**Ex.03b**] and RAM Preview. In this animation, a mask has been animated to follow a specific animal as it walks across the landscape. To see this mask more clearly, double-click the **AB_AnimalSafari.mov** layer to open its Layer panel, make sure the Render switch is off, and scrub the time indicator. Opacity has also been animated to fade the clip up and down. (If these keyframes aren't exposed, select the layer and press U to reveal them.)

Step 2: Bring the Comp panel forward again. With this layer selected, press Shift+F2 to deselect all keyframes. Place the current time indicator somewhere in the middle of the animal clip, and slip edit this layer while watching the Comp panel. As you slip, you will see the animal slide outside of the animated mask shape that was created for it. Undo, or slip the layer back to where this animal is centered in its mask again.

Non-Slip Layer

To use the Slip Edit tool, you need to have some material in the layer to slip. Make sure the in and/or out point of the layer is trimmed in from the ends of the clip.

Step 1: An oval mask shape is animated to follow this animal as it walks from left to right in the movie. Inset footage courtesy Artbeats/Animal Safari.

Step 3: In the Timeline panel, click on the words Mask Path for this layer to select its mask keyframes. Now as you slip edit, the mask will move with the layer's contents, but the fade up and down will stay in place relative to the comp's timing.

It is important to remember that any selected keyframes will move with the layer when you slip edit, *even if you can't see them*. It is common for a twirled-up parameter to have a keyframe selected – such as the last keyframe you created or edited. Get in the habit of using Shift+F2 to deselect keyframes before using the Slip Edit tool, just to be safe. Then select any keyframes that you want to move.

Step 3: If certain keyframes need to move with the layer's contents while you slip edit (as with the Mask Path keyframes here), select them before you give them the slip. Unselected keyframes will remain in the same place relative to the comp.

Sequence Layers can help you arrange layers either end to end, or with over-lapping crossfades.

Negative Space

Enter a negative value for Duration and instead of over-lapping layers, Sequence Layers will insert space between layers.

Sequence Layers

An oft-overlooked editing tool in After Effects is the Sequence Layers Keyframe Assistant. Sequence Layers will organize the layers end to end, in the order in which you select them, beginning at the in point of the first layer selected. It can even add automatic crossfades. The layers can consist of movies or stills, and be different sizes and durations. Two common uses include arranging a number of still images in a sequence, and using it to try out different scene orders with a number of video clips.

The easiest way to work with Sequence Layers is to set up the layer stack in the order in which you'd like the layers to sequence, either from the top down or the bottom up (such as in [**Ex.04a**]). Select the layer that will be the first layer in the sequence, then either Shift+click the last layer to select a range, or Command+click (Control+click) to make discontiguous selections. Right-click on one of the layers, or go to the Animation menu and select Keyframe Assistant > Sequence Layers. If you don't need any overlap between the layers, make sure the Overlap button is unchecked and press OK – the layers will be laid out sequentially along the timeline. Go ahead and experiment with different orders of layers, and RAM Preview your results to see which you like best.

To apply an automatic crossfade, turn on the Overlap button and set the overlap Duration. You then have the choice to crossfade the Front layer, or both the Front and Back layers. By *front* and *back*, After Effects is referring to the stacking order in the comp. In [**Ex.04a**], undo your previous Sequence action, and try out the various options, initially with

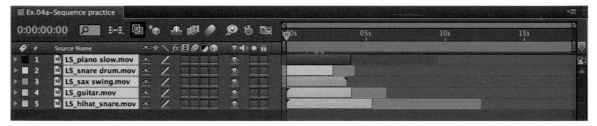

After you have selected a group of layers (above), Sequence Layers will arrange them in time, with defined overlaps and Opacity keyframes (below). In this case, we used Dissolve Front Layer with a 10-frame duration.

about a 10-frame overlap. Twirl down the Opacity keyframes to see what is being done: The shortcut is to use Command+A (Control+A) to Select All and press T. RAM Preview the results to see how the crossfades look. Undo until you're back where you started, and try various dissolve durations. Remember that you can use the Slip Edit tool (covered earlier in this chapter) to slip the contents of trimmed layers after you've sequenced them.

If you choose to dissolve only the front layer, the layer on top in the Timeline panel will have Opacity keyframes applied to where it overlaps in time with a layer underneath, but the layer underneath will not get Opacity keyframes over the same period of time. This is the preferred way to work if all the layers cover the full frame (or the same size and in the same position): The one on top (in front) dissolves to reveal the one underneath, which is already at full opacity.

If you select the Front and Back option, the layer in front (on top) will be set to fade out while the layer in back (underneath) fades in over the same period of time where they overlap. This is preferred when the layers are different sizes or in different positions, if they have alpha channels (for example, text), or if they are otherwise irregularly shaped. Try the two different options with the objects in [**Ex.04b**].

If you plan on using a transition effect (Effect > Transition) set the Transition type to Off and use Sequence Layers to just create the overlaps.

When you're sequencing a series of still images, you may wish for all layers to have the same duration. If so, drag all layers to a new comp, move the time indicator to where the out point should be, and use the shortcut Option+] (Alt+]) to trim all selected layers in one go. Now you can apply the Sequence Layers keyframe assistant to space them out.

Depending on the duration of each individual layer compared with the duration of the comp, some layers may extend beyond the end of the comp. If that's the case, undo, trim, or delete layers as necessary, and reapply Sequence Layers. On the other hand, be careful that the overlap duration is not as long as or longer than the layers; otherwise, Sequence Layers will not work.

If you select more than one footage item in the Project panel and drag the items as a group to the New Composition button, Sequence Layers is presented as an option in creating the new comp (see also Chapter 2).

Trimming by Work Area

In the process of experimenting with trimming and sequencing layers, remember that you can change the length of the comp in Composition Settings as well as change the work area for RAM Previewing. There are some additional menu items and keyboard shortcuts for managing the work area and composition length:

• To automatically set the work area to span the length of the currently selected layers, press Command+Option+B (Control+Alt+B).

• To reset the work area to the entire length of the comp, double-click the work area bar.

• To trim the comp to equal the length of the work area, use Composition > Trim Comp to Work Area. This command – as well as Lift and Extract – are also available by right-clicking on the work area bar.

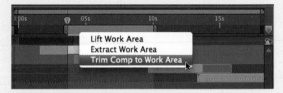

Right-click on the work area bar to gain easy access to these additional trimming options.

• To delete the segments of any selected layers currently inside the work area and to slide any remaining segment(s) up to fill the resulting gap, use Edit > Extract Work Area. If you want to leave a gap behind, use Edit > Lift Work Area. Think of these as advanced Split Layer commands.

The Sequence Layers option will be presented if you drag multiple items to the New Composition button.

Splitting Layers

You can split a layer at any point along the timeline, creating two separate layers from one. To see it in action, select Close All from the tab along the top of the Comp panel to clean up the display, and then open [**Ex.05a**]. Make sure that you can see its keyframes (select the layer and type U if you can't) and that the In and Out columns are exposed (if they aren't, right-click the top of any other column and enable them). Move the time indicator to where you'd like the in point of the second segment to begin, and use either Edit > Split Layer or Command+Shift+D (Control+Shift+D).

Using the Edit > Split Layer command is the same as duplicating a layer and setting in and out points as needed – it's just a lot fewer keystrokes. Figures show before (above) and after (below).

Splitting a layer is the equivalent of duplicating a layer, trimming the first layer's out point, and trimming the second layer's in point. Look at the In and Out values for the two segments after the split, and note that the second one starts one frame after the first one ends. Press U to reveal the keyframes for the new segment, and notice that the keyframes are identical for both layers.

There's nothing special about these two layers at this point – you could overlap the ends or crossfade one section into another if need be, or continue splitting one of the layers again. So why and when would you split a layer? The most obvious reason is when you'd like a layer to change places in the stacking order in the middle of a 2D animation, which allows for an object to appear to go both behind another object and then in front of it.

To see this in action, open comp [**Ex.05b**] which shows a gizmo animating behind a planet from left to right, then right to left. The idea is that the object should go in front of the planet for the right-to-left move:

Step 1: Around time 01:05, the gizmo object (**QE_Gizmo_loop.mov**) is at its rightmost extreme. Select it, and Edit > Split Layer. The layer will split into two sections.

TIP

Splitting Up…or Down

You have a choice of whether the second half of a split layer appears above or below the first half in the Timeline panel. This is set in Preferences > General (Create Split Layers Above Original Layer; on by default).

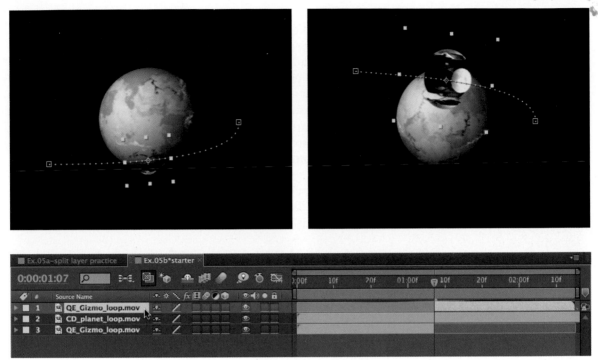

Step 2: Move the second segment to the top of the stack in the Timeline panel. RAM Preview, and now the object passes behind the planet, then in front. If that wasn't clear, check out [**Ex.05c**] for a finished version.

Another important use is to avoid the rendering hit from an effect that's eating time, even though the parameters are set to have zero effect. Most newer, well-written effects don't do this, but there are no doubt a few out there that still do. If the effect doesn't start until the end of the layer, split the layer and apply the effect just to the second part. We also often split layers when we're combining frame blending with time remapping, as blending incurs a render hit even when the speed is normal (100%).

One consequence of splitting a layer is that both resulting layers will contain all the keyframes applied to the original layer. However, because these layers, after splitting, are now completely independent, their keyframes will not remain in sync with each other. If you make a change to one layer, you may have to copy and paste the keyframes to the other segment to avoid an animation glitch where the two segments join. If the changes are extensive, delete the other segment and repeat the split layer step. The same is true when you're slip editing a layer that's been split – the other segment does not automatically follow. For these reasons, it's best to avoid splitting a layer until the animation is locked down.

Advanced Technique: If the animation is constantly changing but you need to split the layer sooner rather than later, you might consider precomposing the layer *before* you split it. Select the layer and Layer >

To have an object first appear to go behind another layer (top left), then in front of it (top right), you need to Edit > Split it and reorder the resulting segments in the Timeline panel (above) so the gizmo is on top of the planet layer when it passes in front. Gizmo courtesy Quiet Earth Design.

GOTCHA

Measure Twice, Cut Once

You can't "rejoin" two layers after you have split them (short of undoing); they are now two separate layers. However, because both retain a full set of their original keyframes, you can usually delete one and retrim the other to cover the original duration.

TIP

Industrial-Strength Editing

If you need stronger editing tools, use a dedicated nonlinear editor. Adobe Premiere Pro integrates very tightly with After Effects (make sure you get the Production Premium bundle). If you use an Avid system or Apple Final Cut Studio, get Automatic Duck's Pro Import AE to export their timelines to After Effects (*www.automaticduck.com*).

Pre-compose; in the Pre-compose dialog, select the second option (Move All Attributes), and press OK. Now all the animation keyframes will reside in the precomp. Split the layer (now a nested comp) in the original comp as many times as necessary. If you need to edit the animation, double-click the nested comp layer to open the precomp, and make your edits there. Any changes you make in the precomp will be updated automatically to all the split segments in the original comp.

Many times, your need to split a layer will disappear once you place the layers in 3D space: You can animate a layer to be closer or farther away than another layer, causing it to pass in front of and then behind this other layer. This also "scales" the apparent size of the object automatically, so it is not necessary to animate the Scale parameter to fake the appearance of distance. We'll discuss 3D in greater detail later in this book; for the intensely curious, we've created a similar animation in [**Ex.05d**].

Overlay and Ripple Insert Edits

The last of the editing tools we'll cover are Overlay and Ripple Insert. These differ from the other tools in that they are accessed from the Footage panel. What they do is allow you to trim a source *before* it has been added to a composition, then place it on top of existing layers in a comp. The Overlay option keeps the timing of all the other layers already in a comp intact; the Ripple Insert option "parts the seas" and scoots all the layers after the point of insertion later in time.

Step 1: Close all other comps, and open [**Ex.06**]. It currently contains one clip of a lucky man going from his Porsche to his private plane. We want to juxtapose this with a clip of an unlucky man, who's in prison. (Homework: How many made-for-TV movie plots can you come up with from just these two shots?) Move the time indicator to some point in the middle of the action – say, around 04:00.

Double-click a footage item in the Project panel to open it in its Footage panel (above). At the bottom right of the Footage panel are icons for the Ripple Insert Edit and Overlay Edit tools (below), plus the name of the comp this footage will be added to if you use them.

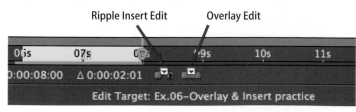

Ripple Insert Edit   Overlay Edit

Step 2: Locate the **AB_Incarcerated.mov** clip in the Project panel's **Sources > Movies** folder. Double-click to open it in the After Effects Footage panel; if necessary, press Option+/ (Alt+/) to center it. Scan it to locate two seconds of action you like, and set its in and out points, using the same techniques as discussed earlier for trimming in the Layer panel.

Step 3: Look along the lower right edge of the Footage panel: It will say "Edit Target:" followed by the name of the current comp (which should be [**Ex.06**]). The two buttons above this text are for the Ripple Insert Edit and Overlay Edit tools. Click on the button on the right: Overlay.

Step 4: Check out the Timeline panel: A copy of **AB_Incarcerated** with your trimmed in and out points has been added to [**Ex.06**], starting at the current time. RAM Preview the comp to see how you like the edit.

Step 3–4: The Overlay Edit tool adds the trimmed footage in the Footage panel to the current comp starting at the current time and at the top of the layer stack. Layers below are not affected.

Step 5: Undo so you are back to a single layer in [**Ex.06**] (or otherwise delete the added layer), and move to time 04:00. Bring **AB_Incarcerated**'s Footage panel forward again, and this time click on the Ripple Insert Edit icon (second from the right). Now study the timeline in [**Ex.06**]: The **AB_BusinessontheGo.mov** layer will be split into two segments. Your trimmed version of **AB_Incarcerated** will start at the current time, and the second segment of **AB_BusinessontheGo** will start after the end of **AB_Incarcerated**. RAM Preview to see if you like this version of the edit better. If you had any keyframes in the **AB_BusinessontheGo** layer, they would be duplicated, just as with the Split Layers command.

Step 5: The Ripple Insert Edit tool adds the trimmed footage to the current comp. Any layers underneath the time indicator are split, with the later segments slid in time to start after the inserted clip.

Be aware that changing the trim points in the Footage panel does not update the composition. However, it does mean that you can retrim the footage and add this second edit to the same or a different comp. Unlike Sequence Layers, you don't get any options to automatically add a cross-fade, but since you have the entire source clip at your disposal in the comp, you can later trim (not to mention Slip Edit) the overlaid or inserted layer and add your own fades.

Remember that the trimmed footage is added to the comp only if you click on the Overlay Edit or Ripple Insert Edit buttons in the Footage panel – if you drag the footage to the comp, or use the Add Footage to Comp command, the entire clip is added.

At the start of this chapter, we warned you that the editing tools in After Effects are not as strong as a dedicated video editing program – but they're pretty decent, allowing you to make a fair number of edit decisions and tweaks with a minimum amount of pain.

CONNECT

Composition settings, time navigation shortcuts: Chapter 2.

Layer management: Chapter 6.

Masking: Chapter 10.

3D space: Chapter 13.

Nesting compositions: Chapter 18.

Precomposing: Chapter 19.

Time stretching, time remapping, frame blending: Chapter 28.

Integration with nonlinear editors: Chapter 39.

8

Motion Blur and More

Life's a blur – at least, to a camera it is.

When images are captured on film or video, objects that are moving appear blurred, while static objects appear sharp. This is due to the fact that the camera is capturing samples of time, and the camera shutter is kept open for some of that time. The faster the object moves, the more distance it will cover while the shutter is open, and the less distinct the image. This *motion blur* makes for smoother motion and is a quality often lacking in computer-generated animation.

The secret to smooth motion blur is increasing the Adaptive Sample Limit (and optionally, Samples Per Frame) setting, found under the Composition Settings > Advanced tab. Adaptive Sample Limit has a maximum value of 256 samples per frame (left). If its value is too low and the motion is fast, the result is a strobed look (right).

Normally, the computer samples the movement of an image at a certain frame rate, and when you view it frame by frame, all frames appear as sharp as nonmoving images. This introduces an unattractive "strobing" effect. And if you're trying to merge computer-generated objects into a live background, the composite will look less than convincing.

With After Effects, you can add motion blur to any layer. It will kick in only when a layer is animated with the Transform properties; a growing number of effects can also add motion blur to their internal animations. By default, After Effects by itself is not capable of analyzing action in a movie or a still, and then adding motion blur just to a car driving past, for example (although there's a trick to fake that). However, if you pan a layer by animating its Position property for example, After Effects can calculate motion blur for your animation.

After Effects creates the illusion of motion blur by calculating intermediate positions of a layer between frames of a render, then blending together these multiple copies of the layer. More copies results in a smoother blur. You have control over how many samples are used in Composition > Composition Settings under the Advanced tab. In this chapter's example project, comp [**Ex.01**] demonstrates the difference between low and high numbers of samples, and no blur at all.

Enabling motion blur does come at the cost of increased rendering times, as After Effects is in essence rendering the same "frame" multiple times to create the effect – so don't just enable it on every layer out of

habit. Think about whether a layer will benefit from motion blur. That said, After Effects employs an adaptive algorithm for most 2D layers, using only the number of samples it thinks it needs – so it is good to set the Adaptive Sample Limit high, and let After Effects do the math. 3D layers, shape layers, and some effects are more render-intensive, and therefore have a separate Samples Per Frame parameter with an upper limit of 64 frames. We usually set this value at its maximum to start, and then decrease it only if we have issues with slow renders.

Be aware that this feature is different from the directional or radial blurs offered by some effects. With those, the same amount of blur is applied to any source, regardless of how it is animating. After Effects takes into account changes in position, scale, and rotation when calculating motion blur, which means the amount of blur is proportional to the amount of movement from frame to frame – including changes in velocity. And as the layer comes to a stop, motion blur is reduced to match.

Applying Motion Blur

To turn on motion blur for a layer, check the Motion Blur switch (the echoed dots) for it in the Switches column of the Timeline panel. Once motion blur has been checked for a layer, the master Enable Motion Blur button along the top of the Timeline panel determines whether the blur is calculated for previewing in the current comp. Try this with the two layers in comp [**Ex.02**]. Note how the faster-moving layer has more blur.

You may want to leave the Enable Motion Blur button off to avoid the rendering hit while you work, but remember to leave the individual Motion Blur switches checked for the layer you want to be blurred.

As you saw in [**Ex.02**], the amount of blur created is proportional to how fast a layer is moving. This becomes more obvious when you don't have smooth speed changes in your layers, particularly where the motion stops and starts. If the animation stops suddenly, the effect is of a blurred image suddenly becoming sharp, often with an unattractive "pop." Add a little ease in and out of a sudden stop so that the motion blur has the time to ramp up or down.

These approaches are compared side by side in [**Ex.03**]; RAM Preview the composition to see the results.

To apply motion blur to a layer, check its Motion Blur switch (circled in red). To view the results in the Comp panel before rendering, turn on the Enable Motion Blur button along the top of the Timeline panel.

In [**Ex.03**], the top planet has no motion blur. The middle one has blur, and pops away from the side at full speed. The bottom planet is easing away from the side, with blur enabled.

The motion blur Shutter Angle (blur amount), Phase (lead/lag), and sample settings (blur smoothness) may be set per comp in the Composition Settings, under the Advanced tab. The new-in-CS5 Preview switch in the lower left corner allows you to inspect the results of different settings while the Composition Settings dialog is still open.

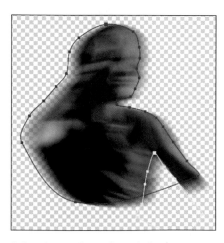

Animating masks can have their edges automatically blurred.

Shutter Angle and Phase

The Shutter Angle parameter controls the amount of time the motion blur samples are spread over, and therefore the length of the blur. It ranges from 0° to a maximum of 720°, simulating the exposure time resulting from the rotating shutter in a film camera. For example, in a 30 fps (frames per second) comp, each frame would play for 1/30th of a second, so a Shutter Angle of 180° would amount to an exposure time of 1/60th of a second (50% of 1/30). Values over 360° extend the blur beyond one frame for special effects. The frame rate has a direct effect on the length of the blur, as lower frame rates result in longer frame durations, which result in longer exposure times and therefore longer blurs.

Shutter Angle can be set per comp in the Composition Settings dialog, under the Advanced tab. When you create a new comp, this value defaults to whatever was the last value you entered. If you need different motion blur lengths for individual layers in the same composition, precompose them and set the Shutter Angle to taste in each precomp. An alternative approach is to animate these layers using Effect > Distort > Transform and to set the Shutter Angle inside this effect.

Shutter Phase determines whether the intermediate frames start after the current time (positive values) or before (negative values). Setting Shutter Phase to be negative half of the value of Shutter Angle will yield the most natural results, with blur spreading before and after the current keyframe. Shutter Phase has a range of ±360°, or up to one full frame of lead or lag. You can create special effects using this parameter, such as a layer whose blur precedes it. An example of this can be found in [Ex.04]: An animating layer is duplicated, with motion blur enabled for one copy, and the comp's Shutter Phase is advanced to 360°.

Blur and Masks

Mask shapes can also have motion blur. This is useful if you are rotoscoping an object which has natural motion blur: You will want your mask's edges to also blur as they move to follow this motion. Masks default to using the layer's Motion Blur switch setting; you can also set the blur for each selected mask to be always on or always off by selecting the layer and going to Layer > Mask > Motion Blur.

Blur and Nested Comps

If you're creating a hierarchy of nested comps, and the motion blur is not working for a layer, check that you turned on the Motion Blur switch for the layer in the comp that contains the animation keyframes. For instance, if you animate a group of individual layers in a precomp, each layer needs to be set to blur. Setting the Motion Blur switch for the nested comp's layer will be of use only for additional animation you perform on this nested comp. This is shown in the [**Ex.05**] folder.

When you're building hierarchies of nested comps, if the Switches Affect Nested Comps checkbox in Preferences > General is set, the master Enable Motion Blur button will behave "recursively" – turning it on also turns on the Enable switch in all nested compositions.

Render Settings

When you render your composition, make sure the Motion Blur popup inside the Render Settings is set to On for Checked Layers. This will ensure that all layers that have their Motion Blur switch checked on will render with motion blur, regardless of whether the Enable button is on in each comp. By doing this, you can turn Enable Motion Blur on or off as needed to preview your blur, but you don't have to worry about leaving it off by accident for your final render.

As we mentioned earlier, frame rate has a direct bearing on blur length. If you were to change the frame rate of a comp from 30 fps to 15 fps, the length of blur would double, as the duration of each frame is now twice as long. Conversely, field rendering effectively doubles the frame rate, cutting the blur length in half. For this reason, you may need to open Composition Settings and double the amount of shutter angle before you field render.

Faux Motion Blur

Sometimes, footage does not have enough natural motion blur. This is often caused by a shutter speed that was too fast when the footage was shot (a real problem with video cameras set on "auto" mode in bright conditions). Or perhaps you want to add more blur for a special effect. But normal Motion Blur in After Effects does not help, as it was designed to blur objects animated inside After Effects – not footage that has already been shot.

The workaround is to apply Effect > Time > Timewarp to the offending shot, set its Speed parameter to 100, and toggle its Enable Motion Blur switch. Set its Shutter Control popup to Manual, and now you can set the Shutter Angle up to 5000°(!), as well as set how many samples to use to smooth any strobing. Check out the results in [**Ex.06**]. We've included a pair of "FauxMotionBlur" Animation Presets for you in the **Goodies** folder on the DVD.

Half the Blur

When you field render a composition, the frame rate is effectively doubled, halving the perceived motion blur. Increase the Shutter Angle setting to compensate.

In the Render Settings, you can decide whether to follow or ignore the set Motion Blur switches.

If fast-moving action does not have enough natural motion blur for your taste (left), apply the Timewarp effect to add additional blur after the fact (right). Footage courtesy Creative License.

Echoed Effects

There are several effect plug-ins that give a result similar to motion blur in that they composite together multiple images from different points in time. They can be used for anything from tacky video effects to faking motion blur in plug-ins that otherwise do not internally support it.

An Original Echo

For many of us, the term "echo effect" conjures images of tacky trails following flying logos in local car ads. Fortunately, After Effects is rarely tacky. Unfortunately, the Echo effect's defaults don't really show off the strength of this effect, and you'll often need to foil the default render order to get it to work at all. First we will give an overview of using Echo; then we'll jump into some fun tricks you can perform with it.

Effect > Time > Echo can be thought of as a multiframe form of frame blending, which gives you control over how many frames are blended together, and how they are blended. Echo can use frames that are either before or after the current one being displayed, depending on whether the Echo Time parameter is negative (frames from the past) or positive (frames from the future).

You can also use the Echo Time parameter to set how far apart the frames are that are used. This parameter is defined in seconds: The number of frames of spacing desired, divided by the frame rate, equals the Echo Time you want in seconds. Longer times start to give a sort of cloning effect; [**Ex.07**] gives an idea of what can be done by carefully setting Echo Time to divisions of how long it takes an object to rotate or an animation to loop.

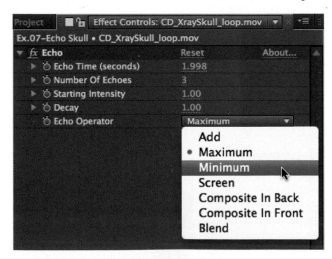

The Echo effect's parameters. It can be approached as a user-adjustable form of frame blending. Most unusual is the Echo Operator popup, which provides a few different forms of blending modes to blend in the echoes.

The Number of Echoes parameter sets how many frames get used. Note that if you have a negative Echo Time, and a large value for Number of Echoes, you'll need to move to a point later in the timeline where the effect has built up some momentum.

Starting Intensity decides how strongly the "original" frame is in the final blend. The Decay parameter decides how much successively weaker the following echoes appear. Decay has a smaller useful range than you might expect, as subsequent echoes get weakened by this amount – they go to being unnoticeable really quickly. The upper half of the range is best.

The opacity of the original image – as opposed to the first echo of that image – is affected by the Starting Intensity parameter. If you want your original image to be 100% strong and your echoes to start at a much reduced level, you will need to duplicate the

original layer on top and play with the opacity of the echoes underneath. Such an echo trail effect is set up in [**Ex.08**].

The most intriguing parameter of the group is Echo Operator; this is similar to "Composite Original" in other effects but with the addition of blending modes. Experiment with this parameter using [**Ex.09**], then swap in your own sources to see how different movies react.

Echoed Animation

If you apply Echo to a layer that is getting its movement from animation keyframes, Echo may not seem to work initially. This is because effects are calculated before transformations, which yield most animation. In this case, you will need to animate the layer in Comp 1, nest this comp in Comp 2, then apply Echo. In the second comp, the animated layer looks like a "movie" with an animated alpha channel, so the effect works as planned.

A lot of fun can be had with extended Echo settings and fast randomly moving objects. [**Ex.10a-Echo-1**] contains a simple object that was animated using a wiggler expression (you could also use Motion Sketch), with Motion Blur turned on. This comp is nested in a second comp – [**Ex.10a-Echo-2**] – with Echo applied. Be aware that render times can quickly stack up when a lot of motion blurred objects are being echoed (as is the case with this example). It also takes a while for the Echo effect to build up at the start, since the echoed frames are taken from earlier in time – and there is no time earlier than 0.

Note that because Echo reaches back to the source for data, animating an object using the Perspective > Transform effect, then applying Echo all on one layer doesn't create an echo trail.

However, you could echo multiple layers in one comp by applying the effect to an adjustment layer. An example of this is in [**Ex.10b**]: A null object is used as a parent to scale and rotate the three baseball objects, while an adjustment layer on top applies Echo to the result of all layers below. (Note that if you want these layers to also have motion blur, you need to turn on motion blur for the individual layers, not the null object, then Enable Motion Blur to display the results.)

The power of Echo comes from its Echo Operator. These three variations show the result of different operators on the same image: Original image (left), the default Add mode (center), and Minimum (right). Footage courtesy Kevin Dole.

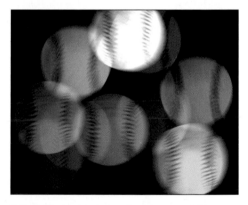

Echo following random animation can yield a complex swirl from a single still image. Baseball image courtesy Getty Images.

A null object parent layer rotates three baseballs, while an adjustment layer on top applies Echo to the result.

Time Continuum

Boris Continuum Complete – BCC for short – from Boris FX (www.borisfx.com) is a massive plug-in package for After Effects that includes several time manipulation effects worth checking out:

Optical Flow is a simpler version of After Effects' Timewarp and RE:Vision Effect's Twixtor (both mentioned in Chapter 28) that creates new in-between frames when varispeeding footage.

Posterize Time is a variation on the After Effects plug-in of the same name, with the advantage of creating crossfades between the final frames.

Sequencer allows you to designate up to 10 source layers that can be played back in a pattern and rhythm you define.

Temporal Blur is a flexible cross between motion blur and an echo effect.

Time Displacement is a variation on the After Effects plug-in of the same name.

Trails creates multiple copies of the source image, which may then be scaled, rotated, and otherwise transformed.

Velocity Remap is a twist on After Effects' Time Remapping (also in Chapter 28) that allows you to define playback speed by percentage, rather than which frame should play at what time.

SEE ALSO

Frame Blending

When you time stretch a clip, After Effects normally skips or duplicates frames, resulting in staggered motion. To create new intermediate frames you can use frame blending, Timewarp, or a third-party effect such as Twixtor. These options are covered in Chapter 28.

Cycore Time Effects

The Cycore FX plug-in package (installed with After Effects CS5) includes a quartet of time-based effects:

CC Force Motion Blur & Wide Time

These effects provide ways to smear time. In both cases, animation should take place in a precomp for the effects to know how the image changes over time. Open **[Ex.11a]**, and RAM Preview it. This contains a fast animation created with CC Kaleida. It's so fast it seems to strobe. CC Kaleida does not support motion blur to smooth this out.

In **[Ex.11a]**, CC Kaleida is used to create a kaleidoscope, but this effect does not support motion blur.

Open [Ex.11b], select layer 1 (the nested [Ex.11a] comp), and select Effect > Effect Controls (the shortcut is F3). We've already applied Time > CC Force Motion Blur and increased the Shutter Angle to 360° so you can see its effect more clearly (its maximum value is 3600°, which is five times normal motion blur's limit). CC Motion Blur samples multiple points in time between two adjacent frames and blends them together. This is similar to normal motion blur, with the exception that normal motion blur works only for transformations and select effects that calculate motion blur internally. CC Force Motion Blur works on any precomp it is applied to (but not movies). The number of points used is determined by the Motion Blur Levels value – if you see distinct echoes, increase it to smooth the result (this will also increase rendering time).

CC Wide Time blends together multiple frames. It does not have the blending mode options of Echo, but it does offer the ability to select how many frames before *and* after the current frame are used. Open [Ex.11c], select layer 1, and press F3: We've already added CC Wide Time, with the number of Forward and Backward Steps increased from their defaults. RAM Preview and compare it with what you observed in

CC Force Motion Blur takes our kaleidoscopic animation and adds interframe blur to smooth it out (left); CC Wide Time blends together multiple frames (right). Underlying image courtesy Digital Vision/Inner Gaze.

[**Ex.11b**]. Note that CC Wide Time can be applied directly to a movie, but if you use transformations or effects, you will still need to precompose.

Both of these effects share a Native Motion Blur popup. When set to Off (the default), these effects will ignore the status of the normal motion blur layer and comp switches. When set to On, they will work only if the layer and comp motion blur switches are enabled.

CC Time Blend & Time Blend FX

A shortcoming of Echo is that it is unable to factor in the result of other effects or transformations applied to a layer. CC Time Blend works around the inability to "see" other effects by keeping a buffer of what previously rendered frames look like. The cost is that you must go to the start of the comp, click on Clear in its Effect Controls panel, then play from the beginning to build this buffer. It's a lot of work, but the results are unique.

Extreme Blur

For more extreme amounts of blur, you may need to add and manually animate the angle and length parameters of the Directional and Radial Blur effects, or use third-party plug-ins.

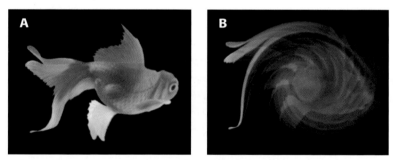

CC Time Blend FX takes a simple distortion (A) and feeds it back upon itself in successive frames (B). Goldfish courtesy Getty Images.

More interesting is CC Time Blend FX. You apply this effect twice to a layer, with the first copy's Instance popup set to Paste, and the second copy's Instance set to Copy. You can then add any effect(s) between these two copies of CC Time Blend FX, resulting in a feedback loop. Open and RAM Preview [**Ex.12a**], which uses Distort > Transform to move our fish across the frame, followed by Distort > Twirl to introduce a wave. Then open and RAM Preview [**Ex.12b**], where the Twirl effect is sandwiched between two copies of CC Time Blend FX: The twirl now builds up over time. Select layer 1, press F3, and study the effect stack in the Effect Controls panel to get a handle on how this chain is built. Note that if you make any adjustment to effect parameters, you will have to press Home, clear the CC Time Blend FX buffers, and perform another RAM Preview.

CONNECT

Composition Settings: Chapter 2.

Masking: Chapter 10.

3D issues: Chapter 13.

Building hierarchies: Chapters 17–20.

Recursive switches: Chapter 20.

Blur effects: Chapters 22–25.

Frame rate manipulation: Chapter 28

Blending Modes

One of the most creative tools After Effects offers is mixing images together using blending modes.

We devoted the previous chapters to stacking multiple objects and moving them around in interesting ways. The next level of motion graphics mastery is combining multiple images together to create an utterly new image. And blending modes (also known as *modes, layer modes* or *transfer modes*) are some of the simplest, yet most tasteful tools for doing so. In this chapter, we'll break down the method behind mode madness, and share a few of our favorite techniques for using them in real-world projects. We'll also cover the two new modes addes in After Effects CS5.

If you use Photoshop or a recent video editing program, you're probably already familiar with how modes work. In the simplest terms, *modes* are different methods for combining images together. They take some properties of one image and combine them with some properties of the underlying image, resulting in a new combination that is often far more intriguing than mere stacking. The results can vary from a relatively subtle enhancement of contrast or color saturation to total retinal burnout. If used with some semblance of taste and restraint, the result is often classy rather than gimmicky and cannot easily be identified as a specific effect. Blending modes render quickly, too.

Many artists use modes through the "happy accident" method: They just try different modes until they find one they like. And that's a valid way to work, because it can be hard to predict exactly what the end result will be. But if you understand what's really going on, you'll find it easier to achieve a desired result – and even create or choose sources more intelligently, based on what you know about how they will blend together.

Modus Operandi

To understand how modes work, a quick refresher course on how After Effects calculates a final image in a composition is in order. After Effects starts with the bottommost layer – in 2D mode, this is the layer at the bottom of the Timeline stack; in 3D, it is the layer farthest from the camera. It calculates the Masks, Effects, and Transformations applied to that layer, and saves the results in a temporary buffer. After Effects then looks at the next layer up, and calculates that layer's Masks/Effects/Transformations. It also looks at the current layer's alpha channel to see what parts of the layer stack underneath are revealed and what parts are covered up by the new layer. After Effects then combines the two layers, and temporarily saves off *that* composite. It then looks at the next layer up from the bottom and repeats the process, a layer at a time, until it reaches the top of the stack.

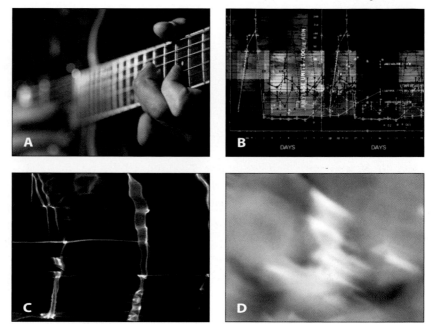

- **Important Concept No. 1:** After Effects is usually thinking about only two images at a time: the current layer, and the combination of everything underneath.

Blending modes modify how this composite takes place. Normally, when the alpha channel of the layer on top is 100% opaque, After Effects replaces the corresponding pixels of the stack underneath with the pixels from the layer it is currently calculating. If the opacity is anything less than 100%, After Effects then mixes the pixels from the current layer and the underlying stack in a straightforward fashion – some of this, some of that. Blending modes say: "Before we mix, let's look at some of the properties of these corresponding pixels (such as their brightness, hue, and so on), change the color values of the pixels of the current layer based on what we found underneath, *then* mix them together."

- **Important Concept No. 2:** Blending modes alter the pixel color values of the layer they are applied to. And these alterations are based on the image (stack of layers) underneath.

Each different mode has a different set of rules (algorithms or math equations) on how it will alter the color value – the red, green, and blue color values – of the pixels in the layer it is working on. In many cases, a mode is applied to just a grayscale layer, to enhance or reinterpret the layer underneath. However, when the red, green, and blue channels are different from each other, these colors further affect the outcome. This means you often see characteristics of the two layers coming through the final composite.

- **Important Concept No. 3:** Differences in colors alter the final effect. Blending modes do not replace or obliterate the normal Masks, Effects, and Transformations calculated for a layer, and most importantly, they normally do not change the transparency of a layer. (See the sidebar *Transparency Modes* on page 150 for exceptions to this rule.)

To demonstrate the effects that different modes have, many of the examples in these pages and their corresponding comps in the **[Ex.00]** folder will use some combination of these four images. The guitar player (A) shot by Lee Stranahan is the main image that we will be treating. The technical chart (B) from Getty Images is a typical detailed, colorful image you may try to blend on top of another. Artbeats/Water Textures (C) – converted to grayscale – is an example of a type of "lighting" movie you might use; the colorful spray (D) from Artbeats/Nature Abstracts is an example of a color "lighting" movie.

Clearer Math

To better understand the math functions being performed by Blending Modes, change the Info panel's display options to Percent or Decimal mode.

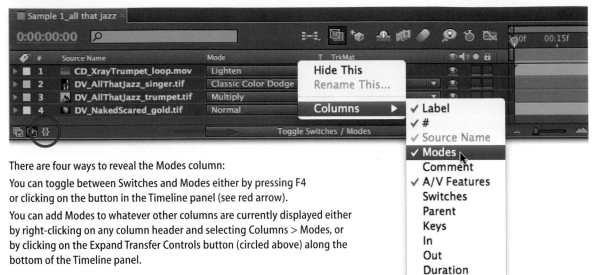

There are four ways to reveal the Modes column:

You can toggle between Switches and Modes either by pressing F4 or clicking on the button in the Timeline panel (see red arrow).

You can add Modes to whatever other columns are currently displayed either by right-clicking on any column header and selecting Columns > Modes, or by clicking on the Expand Transfer Controls button (circled above) along the bottom of the Timeline panel.

Modes and Effects

A number of effect plug-ins (such as those from The Foundry and Boris FX) have blending modes built in, creating interesting results without the need for duplicate layers. Boris Continuum Complete also features several modes not available in the Timeline panel's Modes popup.

Technical Modes

To learn about the algorithms used by blending modes, go to *www.adobe.com* and search for the **PDF Blend Modes Addendum** PDF file.

Mode Swings

Every layer in a composition automatically has a mode applied to it. The default mode is Normal, which means no changes in color value. Each layer can have only one mode, and you cannot animate mode changes on one layer (although we will often stack up multiple copies of the same layer, with different modes set for each, and blend them using opacity). The trick for many users comes in finding the mode switches, so you can indeed change them.

In the Timeline panel, under the layer switches column, is a button labeled Switches/Modes. (If it's not visible, right-click one of the visible columns and select either the Switches or Modes option.) Clicking on the Switches/Modes button toggles the display between Switches and Modes, as does the shortcut F4. If your monitor is wide enough, you can display both the Switches and Modes column at the same time by right-clicking on any column's header and making sure both are selected; if neither is currently displayed, pressing F4 will open them both. Note that the Modes column also includes the T switch (Preserve Underlying Transparency, discussed in Chapter 12) and TrkMat (Track Mattes, discussed in Chapter 11), both of which you can ignore for this chapter.

To change the mode applied to a layer, expose the Modes column, click on the popup menu of modes, and select a new one. To toggle through the different modes, hold the Shift key and use the – and = keys along the top of the keyboard. To change the mode for multiple layers at once, select them and change the mode for any of the selected layers – the others will follow.

Technically, modes alter the color values of the layer they are applied to. You can alter the opacity of this layer and reveal more or less of the otherwise unaltered stack of layers underneath. Despite this, we find it easier to understand modes in terms of "what this layer does to the layers underneath." That's how we'll describe most of them, and you will come to see this as you work with the example projects and look at the illustrations throughout this chapter.

To simplify explanations, we will discuss stacking two layers, with the blending mode always applied to the uppermost layer. If there are additional layers underneath, during rendering they will be composited into what becomes the "lower" layer, anyway. Some modes have the same effect regardless of the order of the layers – that is, of two layers, either one could be on top and have the mode applied to it; the final would be the same. Others look different, depending on which is being "moded" on top of the other.

Experimenting

In this chapter's Example Project, the folder **Ex.00** contains a series of comps which contains the main example of each mode illustrated in this chapter. We have also created additional comps designed for you to experiment with the effects of different modes:

• [**Ex.01a**] has a pair of simple gradients. The background layer goes from black to light blue as it moves from bottom to top; the foreground goes from black to light red as it moves from left to right. Step through this comp to see how the different modes combine these two layers.

• [**Ex.01b**] uses a typical piece of footage as the background layer with a simple black-and-white radial gradient on top, which makes the lighting effects of different modes easier to see. Toggle through the different modes on the upper layer to see each one's effect.

• [**Ex.01c**] uses a typical background, with a colorful layer on top. To get an idea of how colors are mixed by different modes, change the mode for the layer on top. When you're done, set the mode back to Normal and reverse the order of the layers (drag the background layer to be on top) – now try out different modes with this new foreground layer. Experiment with different opacities for the foreground layer; some modes look best when mixed in at less than 100% opacity.

After you've played with these comps, have fun creating your own composites using blending modes. We've loaded a number of examples for you to play with in the Project panel's **Sources > Movies** folder, dividing them into groups of images we think make good backgrounds, good lighting effects to place on top, and other foreground layers with more detail to see how busy images interact.

After Effects offers an extensive list of modes, most of which will be familiar to Photoshop users. The last six have to do with creating transparency and fixing alpha channel problems. We will discuss them in later chapters.

Replacing Layers

To replace a layer's source, select the layer you want to replace in the Timeline, select the replacement layer in the Project panel, and press Command+Option+/ on Mac (Control+Alt+/ on Windows).

Mode Overview

These thumbnail images should give you an idea of how each mode affects the final image. The first two thumbnails are the seed images: The blue gradient is on the bottom; the red gradient is on top and is the layer that has the blending mode applied. The third image to the right shows a simple opacity mix, where the red gradient on top is set to Normal mode with an Opacity of 50%. Color printing being what it is, we encourage you to step through these images for yourself in [**Ex.01a**].

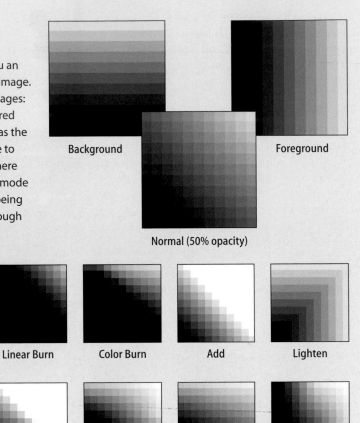

Background

Foreground

Normal (50% opacity)

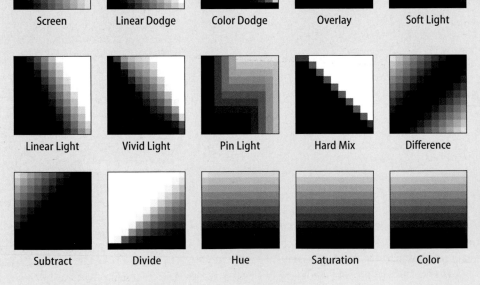

Darken	Multiply	Linear Burn	Color Burn	Add	Lighten
Screen	Linear Dodge	Color Dodge	Overlay	Soft Light	Hard Light
Linear Light	Vivid Light	Pin Light	Hard Mix	Difference	Exclusion
Subtract	Divide	Hue	Saturation	Color	Luminosity

Darkening Modes

The first set of modes all make the final image darker in some way, with varying degrees of usefulness. If the layer they are applied to is pure white, they will have no effect. As a reminder, you'll find examples for these modes in comp [**Ex.00a**].

Darken/Darker Color

These modes compare the color values of the two layers and use the darker pixel's value. Darken takes the lowest value for each individual red, blue, and green channel (often resulting in a color that was in neither source), while Darker Color picks the lower overall value. If either one of the layers is not grayscale, color shifts will usually result. The result often looks slightly posterized. The stacking order does not matter, and both layers contribute somewhat equally to the final result. If one layer is white, the other layer shows through; if one layer is black, the result is black.

Darken mode picks the darkest color channel for each pixel.

Multiply

With this mode, the color values of the selected layer are scaled down by the color values of the layer underneath, resulting in a darkened image, clipping at full black. The order of the two layers does not matter. If one of the images is black, the result will be black (since you will be scaling the other layer with a color value of 0%); if one of the images is white, the result will be no change. Multiply has been likened to stacking two slides together and projecting the result.

Multiply darkens images, with colors coming through the highlights.

Multiply is great for compositing high-contrast black-and-white images over a background. Comp [**Ex.02**] shows what happens when a black-and-white layer is multiplied on top of an image; the white areas drop out, and the original image shows through – sort of like a matte. What makes Multiply different from a matte is that the alpha channel is not changed, and the color – not just the luminance – of the multiplied layer influences the final outcome.

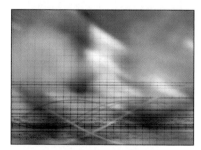

Linear Burn

The three "burn" modes come in handy when you want a more saturated image than Multiply gives, with the trade-off being a darker final image. Photoshop users will be familiar with the concept of "burning" an image: The Burn tool is often used to retouch areas of an image to be darker than before. The difference in After Effects is that the color channels are factored in, resulting in some color shifts as the mix grows darker.

A black-and-white layer overlaid in Multiply mode drops out the white areas, showing the background. Graph courtesy Artbeats/Digital Biz.

Linear Burn darkens an image by using the color information of the layer on top to decrease the brightness of the layer underneath. The order of the two layers does not matter. Any combination that adds up to 100% or less brightness – such as 65% brightness on top and 35% brightness underneath, or 45% brightness on top and 55% brightness underneath – results in black, making the overall impression darker than using Multiply, but with more vivid colors.

Using Linear Burn results in a darker, more saturated image than Multiply.

Color Burn mode also darkens and intensifies the image; it is a compromise between Multiply and Linear Burn.

Choose Your Burn

Color Burn retains black drop shadows; Classic Color Burn looks better at reduced opacity.

Color Burn/Classic Color Burn

Color Burn darkens an image by using the color information in the layer on top to increase the contrast in the layer underneath. A white layer will have no effect when it's color burned onto a layer underneath; a black layer will drive the image toward total black (although the alpha will still be intact); grays will evenly scale the brightness of the underlying image. The result is somewhere between Multiply and Linear Burn: The image is darker than with Multiply, and the colors more saturated, but unlike Linear Burn, the highlights tend to retain their original qualities. Color Burn is sensitive to layer stacking order; the underlying layer tends to come through more in the final composite.

Classic Color Burn has some problems with the way it deals with colors at their extremes; if it's applied to the last layer in a stack, it will turn it nearly all white. Further differences between Color Burn and Classic Color Burn emerge when you reduce the opacity of the layer they are applied to; you may find Classic Color Burn works better at reduced opacity. The exception to this is a black drop shadow: Color Burn retains the shadow, whereas they disappear with Classic Color Burn.

The Math Behind Modes

When we're describing how different modes work internally, we'll be using the terms *add*, *subtract*, *multiply*, *brightness*, and *contrast*. You don't need to understand the details behind these terms to use modes – just apply them and see if you like the results! But for those who want to delve a little deeper, here's a quick course.

When we say a mode *adds* its color values to the layer underneath, the numeric value for each individual color channel – red, green, and blue – is added to the corresponding values of the same color channels underneath. Say a particular pixel in the background layer has 50% strength in the red channel, and the same pixel in the foreground has 25% strength in the red channel. If a mode adds them together, the result is that the pixel has 50 + 25 = 75% strength in the red channel, making it brighter. If the mode instead *subtracts* the value, the result is 50 – 25 = 25% strength in that pixel's red channel, making it darker. *Multiply* follows a similar logic: 0.50 × 0.25 = 0.125, or 12.5% strength in that pixel's red channel.

Some blending modes increase or decrease the brightness or contrast of the layer underneath. *Brightness* works by adding or subtracting from the color values of the pixels. For example, **[Ex.01d]** has a copy of the gradient bars shown earlier in this chapter, with Effect > Color Correction > Brightness & Contrast already applied. The leftmost bar is normally black, with a value of 0 (on a scale of 0 to 255) in each of its color channels. Drag the Brightness parameter up to 100, and this bar now has a value of 100. The color values of each of the other bars will also be increased by 100 (move your cursor over them while you're looking at the Info panel for verification). In other words, all of the colors change by the same amount. Reset Brightness to 0 when you're done.

Contrast scales, rather than adds or subtracts, the color values. Set it to a positive value, and colors lighter than 50% gray get brighter, while at the same time colors darker than 50% gray get even darker. Decrease the contrast, and the darker pixels get lighter, while the lighter pixels get darker. Editing contrast is often more aesthetically pleasing than editing brightness, but each has its uses.

Lightening Modes

The second set of modes all make the final image brighter in some way. They are particularly useful for adding illumination. If the layer they are applied to is pure black, they will have no effect. See [**Ex.00b**] for examples.

Add

This is one of the most useful modes. The color values of the selected layer are added to the values of the layer underneath, resulting in a brightened image, clipping at full white. The order of the two layers does not matter. If one of the images is black, no change will take place; if one is white, the result is white.

Layers set to Add mode brighten the underlying image, often with blown-out areas.

Preview [**Ex.03a**] to see the effect of a white solid in Add mode being faded up over another image – the underlying image goes from looking normal, through an uneven blowout (since brighter parts of the underlying image clip out at full white before the darker parts do), to all white. A favorite technique is to composite a grainy film flash over a transition to hide a cut underneath such a blowout, demonstrated in [**Ex.03b**]. The best flash layers go between all black and all white; you may need to increase the contrast of your "flash" layer with the Color Correction > Levels effect to get the maximum burn.

Many pyrotechnic effects are shot against black, with no alpha channel. Likewise, some plug-ins create synthetic lighting effects against black. Apply the Add or Screen mode to them to drop out the black, and mix the nonblack parts of the image with opacity based on brightness. This is shown in [**Ex.03c**]. If the background is not pure black, bury its black level with the Color Correction > Levels effect. Remember that most modes do not create transparency; if you need a real alpha channel from an image shot against black, "unmultiply" the black out of the image using the Alpha Creation trick in Chapter 22.

An explosion shot on black (left) is composited over another image (center). The Add blending mode is applied to the explosion image to blend them (right). Explosion footage courtesy Artbeats/Reel Explosions 3; background courtesy Lee Stranahan.

Lighten/Lighter Color

These modes are the opposite of Darken and Darker Color: The color values of each pixel for the two layers are compared, and the lighter pixel's value is used. This tends to make the final result look lighter. Lighten picks the higher value for each individual red, green, and blue

Lighten mode is the opposite of darken – the brightest color channel for each pixel is used.

Filmic Glow

To add some of the magical puffiness and glow that film can impart to footage, duplicate the layer. For the top copy, apply a blur effect and select Screen mode; adjust opacity and blur amount to taste. This is demonstrated in **[Ex.04]**.

Screen mode blends images as if projected on the same screen.

Linear Dodge often looks the same as Add mode.

Color Dodge mode can brighten highlights and add overall saturation.

channel; Lighter Color picks the highest overall color value, often with more posterized results. If either one of the layers is not grayscale, color shifts will usually result; if one has light shades of gray, this tends to make it through to the final image. The stacking order does not matter, and both layers contribute more or less equally to the final result. If one layer is black, the other layer shows through unchanged (since it would be lighter by default); if one layer is white, the result is white.

Screen

Screen is the opposite of Multiply: The color values of the selected layer are scaled above their original values based on the color values of the layer underneath, resulting in a brightened image, clipping at full white. (Technically, the inverse brightness values of one are multiplied by the inverse brightness values of the other, then the result is inverted. Got that?) The order of the two layers does not matter. If one of the images is black, no change takes place (the other layer is not scaled up to be any brighter); if one of the images is white, the result is white. Screen has been likened to the result of projecting two slides from different projectors onto the same "screen."

Screen can be thought of as a less intense version of Add, in that Screen does not clip as fast, and it does not approach full white as unevenly. The result can appear washed out, but if you reduce the opacity of the screened layer, it looks more like highlights, or adding light to a scene; depending on your sources, one may be preferable to the other. Go back to the comps in [**Ex.03**] and compare the Screen mode versus the previous Add mode.

Linear Dodge

The technical description of Linear Dodge is that it looks at the color information in each channel of the layer it is applied to and uses this to increase the brightness of the underlying image, clipping at full white. The result looks the same as Add mode if the layer it is applied to is 100% opaque; there are some slight differences as you start to fade a layer down, with Linear Dodge looking more desaturated or gray rather than "hot." The order of the two layers does not matter. If one of the images is black, no change will take place; if one is white, the result is white.

Color Dodge/Classic Color Dodge

This mode scales up the brightness of the underlying layer by decreasing its contrast, based on the color values of the layer it is applied to. If the upper layer is black, the underlying layer will be passed through unaffected; if the upper layer is white, it will usually drive the result to white. The order of the layers matters, with the underlying layer appearing to be more prominent in the result.

Photoshop users will be familiar with the concept of "dodging" an image: It is often used to retouch areas of an image lighter than before by applying a grayscale brush over the original. The fun in After Effects is that the color channels are factored in, resulting in potentially interesting (or jarring) color shifts that the Color Dodged layer will impose on the image underneath.

Classic Color Dodge has an anomaly: If it is applied to the last visible layer of a stack, the final composite will go black. Further differences between Color Dodge and Classic Color Dodge emerge when you reduce the opacity of the layer they are applied to; you might find that Classic Color Dodge works better at reduced opacities.

Lighting Modes

These modes, shown in [**Ex.00c**], have the subjective result of intensifying the contrast and saturation in a scene. If the layer they are applied to is 50% gray, most will have no effect; any lighter, darker, or color variation from this, and things get interesting. Several of them are our favorites for creating a rich image that contains characteristics of both source layers.

Overlay

Technically, parts of the image darker than 50% luminance are *multiplied*, and the parts brighter than 50% are *screened*. In plain English, the lighter areas of the top layer will lighten the corresponding areas of the bottom layer, going to white; darker areas in the top layer will darken the corresponding areas in the bottom layer, going to black; areas that are 50% gray in the overlaid layer have no effect on the underlying layer. The result is increased contrast and particularly saturation, with the shadows and highlights still present, though altered. The stacking order makes a difference: The underlying layer appears to be more prominent in the result.

This mode is as close as they come to an "instant cool" effect, making something interesting out of almost any two layers. Once you get past the gee-whiz factor, start looking for layers that have good contrast between light colorful areas and shadows as being Overlay candidates; those dark areas will end up dark in the result, and the lighter areas will end up with an interesting color mix of both layers.

Comp [**Ex.06**] shows one application: The light playing across the tai chi scene is further infused with the color of the layer above (**AB_LightEffects**), while the dark areas remain in the shadows. Given the increase in saturation Overlay usually brings, you might need to back off the opacity of the moded layer. But depending on your sources, you could also increase the intensity of the effect by duplicating the moded layer.

Altering Lighting

To add the impression of animated lighting to a scene, find a layer that has slowly changing white areas over black, experiment with Opacity, and composite with Overlay mode over your original scene. This effect is demonstrated in [**Ex.05a**], [**Ex.05b**] and [**Ex.06**].

Overlay mode increases contrast, and as a result, apparent saturation.

A colorful animated layer (A) applied in Overlay mode over a movie with strong light and shadows (B) results in the light areas being affected, while the shadows stay dark (C). The Tint effect can also be applied to the lighting layer to convert it to black and white and remove the color cast. Footage courtesy Artbeats/ Light Effects and Lifestyles Mixed Cuts 1.

Soft Light mode is a less intense version of Overlay.

Soft Light

Soft Light often looks like a subdued version of Overlay, with less saturation shift. Areas lighter than 50% gray in the Soft Light layer appear to lighten the underlying image as if it were dodged; areas darker than 50% gray appear to darken the layer underneath as if it were burned in – although in neither case does black or white in the Soft Light layer force the final mix to go completely black or white. Areas that are 50% gray in the upper layer have no effect on how the lower layer shows through. The stacking order makes a difference: The underlying layer appears to be more prominent in the result, but with a more even mix than many other modes.

Adobe likens Soft Light to shining a diffuse spotlight on an image. If you are going for a dramatic effect, you will probably be disappointed and feel that it just looks washed out. However, if you are looking for a more subtle lighting effect without the strong contrast or tendency to go to black or white that several of the other modes have, Soft Light, if you pardon the pun, shines.

Transparency Modes

In general, blending modes alter color values, not transparencies or alpha values. However, a few modes do indeed alter transparency. We will describe the ones we personally find useful in upcoming chapters. Therefore, only a brief summary of these modes will be given here:

Dissolve

Dissolve creates a paint-spatter effect. It's based on a transition that used to be popular in multimedia applications, since they often could not support partial transparency. A percentage of this layer's pixels are made transparent based on their opacity: lower opacity, more transparent pixels. The result overrides normal opacity and alpha channel calculations, since there is no partial transparency with Dissolve. If the layer has no alpha channel or feathered masks and is set to 100% Opacity, this mode will appear to have no effect.

Dancing Dissolve

Like Dissolve, but self-animating. Which pixels are transparent changes every frame, even if their opacity is not changing.

Stencil Alpha/
Stencil Luma/
Silhouette Alpha/
Silhouette Luma

Transparency is cut out of all the layers underneath, based on either the alpha channel or the luminance values of the selected layer. These modes are covered in Chapter 12, including suggestions for using them in a hierarchy of comps.

Alpha Add

This mode is useful when the alpha channels of two layers share an edge or seam. In this case, Alpha Add will then help fill in that seam. We discuss Alpha Add mode in Chapters 10 and 12.

Luminescent Premultiply

Some sources with premultiplied alpha channels can have problems with their edges being overly bright – for example, some synthetic lighting effects (lens flares). Their color information is stronger than it should be for a true "premultiplied" image. If you are having edge problems with these images, Interpret Footage as Straight Alpha, and try using this mode to composite the layer in a comp. This mode is also mentioned in Chapter 40.

Video Projection

Hard Light is perhaps the best mode to use when faking video being "projected" onto another surface. Receiving surfaces that average around 50% gray are the best; their shadows and highlights will affect the contrast of the projected layer without driving them completely to black or white in these areas.

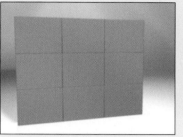

A virtual video-cube wall was rendered in 3D, manipulating the lighting and surface color to average 50% gray (left). A video layer was then "hard lit" onto this surface (right), picking up the shadows in the creases as a result.

Hard Light

Hard Light follows the same general math rules as Overlay, only much more so, with increased contrast and usually more saturation. Although an image can get both brighter and darker depending on the mix, in a similar fashion as Overlay, the result will be more contrasty and saturated. The stacking order makes a difference, but in this case, the Hard Light layer tends to appear more prominent in the final mix than the layer underneath. Interestingly, placing layer "A" in Hard Light mode on top of layer "B" has the same visual result as placing layer "B" in Overlay mode on top of layer "A."

Adobe likens Hard Light to shining a harsh spotlight on an image. If you use Overlay or Soft Light to blend a colorful layer on top of an all-white layer, the result will be all white; if you use Hard Light on this top layer instead, the result will be an overlit version of the Hard Light layer. If the bottom layer is black, Soft Light and Overlay give a black result; Hard Light just increases the shadows, contrast, and in particular, the saturation. With high-contrast sources, it is more likely to be driven into saturation than clip the blacks or whites.

Hard Light is a far more intense version of Overlay, emphasizing the foreground layer.

Linear Light

Mathematically, Linear Light is an amped-up version of Soft Light, although visually it looks like a more intense version of Hard Light. It burns or dodges the layer underneath depending on the colors in the layer it is applied to. If a pixel in the layer it is applied to is lighter than 50% gray, the underlying image is lightened by increasing the brightness; if it is darker than 50% gray, the resulting image is darkened by decreasing the brightness.

As with the rest of these lighting modes, stacking order matters; in this case, the layer on top is more prominent in the final mix. Because of this, if you are trying to use an abstract layer to add color and lighting

Linear Light behaves like an extreme version of Hard Light.

151

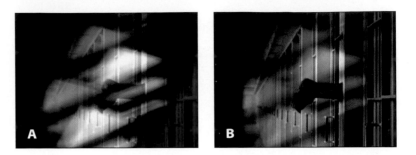

Normally, you place the "effect" layer on top and apply a blending mode to it (A). Some modes – like Linear Light – look better with the main layer on top, and the effect layer underneath (B). Footage courtesy Artbeats/Incarcerated.

Vivid Light has perhaps the most extreme contrast of all the lighting modes.

Pin Light replaces colors depending on the relative brightness of pixels. Here it is applied to the guitar layer, with the lighting layer underneath.

Hard Mix creates a posterized look based on the luminosity of the blend layer and the color of the underlying layer.

effects to another image, instead of putting the "lighting" layer on top, put the normal image on top of the lighting layer, and apply Linear Light to the normal image instead. Experiment with swapping the order of the layers in the series of [Ex.07] comps to see the difference.

Vivid Light

Vivid Light is an even more extreme version of Linear Light. It burns or dodges the layer underneath depending on the colors in the layer it is applied to; in Vivid Light's case, it does this by manipulating the contrast of the layer underneath. The stacking order makes a difference, with the layer on top being more prominent in the final mix. If the layer on top is bright, the overall image will tend to blow out, often with extremely saturated colors. Therefore, Vivid Light works better when applied to darker layers, when you want an intense, high-contrast final image.

Pin Light

Although grouped with the lighting modes, Pin Light has more in common with Darken or Lighten: If a pixel in the layer it is applied to is lighter than 50% gray, underlying pixels darker than this pixel are replaced. If a pixel in the layer is darker than 50% gray, underlying pixels lighter than the pixel in question are replaced. The result can have a bit of a posterized look, borrowing colors from the two images – akin to the modes Darken or Lighten. The stacking order of the layers makes a difference; as with Linear Light, you may get better results if the "lighting" layer is underneath the main image, with Pin Light applied to the main image.

Hard Mix

Applying this unusual mode results in a posterized image that contains up to eight colors: red, green, blue, cyan, magenta, yellow, black, and white. These colors are derived by looking at the luminosity of the layer Hard Mix is applied to plus the color of the underlying layer. Some Photoshop users experiment with Hard Mix to create an unusual sharpening effect: Duplicate a layer, apply Hard Mix to the copy on top, reduce its opacity to taste, apply a blur effect to the Hard Mix layer, and then adjust the blur amount to alter the posterization regions. Large blur amounts create interesting edge and transition region effects (as demonstrated in [Ex.06b]).

Subtraction and Division Modes

These modes, shown in [**Ex.00d**], work by subtracting or dividing the color values of one layer from the layer underneath. They tend to create the strangest-looking (and – unless you're designing a rave party video – arguably least useful) results. However, they do have several utilitarian applications, such as performing math functions for specialized compositing functions.

Difference/Classic Difference

Technically, the color values of one layer are subtracted from the color values of the other layer. You may think this would tend to make the result go toward black. The kink is, if the result is negative (a brighter color value is subtracted from a darker color value), rather than being clipped at black, the positive (or "absolute") value of the color is used instead. The stacking order of the layers does not matter, and both layers contribute to the result more or less equally. If one of the layers is black, the result is unchanged (since black has "zero" difference); if one of the layers is white, the result is an inversion of the other layer. As with Darken and Lighten, these calculations go on per color channel, resulting in often psychedelic color shifts.

If both layers are very similar, however, the final image does indeed shift toward black. This opens the door to a very useful technique known as *difference matting* – when two layers are similar, only the differences between the two show through. An example would be shooting a scene with and without an actor. The result would be nearly black, except where the actor was present; here, the result would be the difference between the person and what was behind him or her. This can be used in conjunction with levels manipulation to pull a matte. It's also handy for comparing two almost identical images to check for differences.

Difference and Classic Difference look essentially identical to each other when the layer they are applied to is at 100% opacity. Their differences (no pun intended) become obvious when you start to reduce the opacity of this layer: Difference tends to have more grays in its blend, where Classic Difference has more color in the transition zones. In [**Ex.08**], change the mode of the **AB_NatureAbstracts** layer between Difference and Classic Difference. As you fade the opacity up and down, the tendency of Difference to go toward gray should become obvious.

Exclusion

This mode is similar to Difference, but with lower contrast and subjectively less saturated colors, resulting in a tendency to drive the final result toward gray. The outcome of this is that the stacking order of the layers does not matter, and both layers contribute more or less equally to the result. If one of the layers is black, the result is still unchanged; if one of the layers is white, the result is still an inversion of the other layer. It differs from Difference in that, when one of the layers is 50% gray, the result is 50% gray and not wildly color-shifted.

Difference mode tends to be the most psychedelic of the modes.

Exclusion mode drives an image more toward gray than Difference.

The new Subtract mode results in less-psychedelic colors when compared with Difference mode.

Dividing our bright, strongly-colored background layer with the dark guitar layer results in a bright composite.

Hue mode combines the hue of the top layer with the luminance and saturation of the layer below.

Subtract

This mode – new in After Effects CS5 – subtracts the color values of the selected layer from the color values of those underneath. Therefore, if you set Subtract mode for a bright layer on top, the result will be dark: Bright layers have high color values, meaning a lot of color will get subtracted out of those underneath. Darker layers set to Subtract mode will have a less drastic effect. Unlike Difference mode, Subtract does not wrap around colors to brighter values, yielding less-psychedelic results.

Divide

Also new in CS5, Divide mode requires a bit of thinking in order to accurately predict its results. Internally, color values can be thought of as having a range of 0.0 (black) to 1.0 (white). Dividing any value by a number less than 1.0 (say, 0.5 for 50% gray) will result in a *larger* final value. Therefore, choosing Divide mode for a 50% gray layer on top will double the brightness of the final composite. The darker the layer on top, the brighter the result. Choosing Divide for a white layer will have no effect.

Property-Replacing Modes

The final set of modes, shown in [**Ex.00e**], takes one particular property of the uppermost layer and uses it in place of the same property for the layer(s) underneath. In this case, being able to think in HSL or HSB colorspace (rather than RGB) will be helpful in visualizing the results.

If you were to break down an image's color into three properties – Hue, Saturation, and Luminance – the following modes select which property to retain from the top layer and which properties to mix in from the layer(s) below.

Hue

With this mode, the hue of the uppermost layer is combined with the luminance and saturation of the underlying layer. The final result gets the basic raw colors of the first layer, but with the brightness and intensity of the second layer. If the layer with Hue applied is a shade of gray (regardless of its brightness), the underlying layer will be shown reduced to grayscale, since the top layer has no hue. The stacking order matters, and the underlying layer will seem to contribute most strongly to the result.

Saturation

The saturation of the uppermost layer is combined with the hue and luminance of the underlying layer. The result gets the basic raw colors and brightness levels of the second layer, but with the saturation pattern of the first layer. If the layer with Saturation applied is a shade of gray (regardless of its brightness), the underlying layer will be shown reduced to grayscale, since the top layer has no saturation regardless of any colors underneath. The stacking order matters, and the underlying layer often seems to contribute most strongly to the final result.

Compared with Hue, Saturation often results in less extreme color shifts, but it can occasionally result in a more posterized look, as can be seen in the example on the previous page.

Color

Technically, the color – the combination of the hue and saturation – of the uppermost layer is combined with just the luminance or brightness levels of the underlying layer. The result is the color wash of the top layer, but with the image details of the underlying layer. The stacking order matters: The underlying image is "repainted" with the colors of the top layer. You will probably find Color mode easier to control and predict than Hue or Saturation, since we often think of "color" as the result of these two properties rather than as individual parameters.

Color mode is most useful for colorizing an underlying image. [Ex.10a*starter] has a movie layer that we want to tint. On the Mac, use the keyboard shortcut Command+Y (Control+Y on Windows) to create a solid, click on the Make Comp Size button, choose the color tint you want with the eyedropper or color picker, and click OK. When you select the Color mode for this new layer, the underlying layer will now be tinted this color, with the highlights and shadows preserved. Vary the color tint layer's opacity, and you'll vary the amount of saturation in the solid's color. This works great for colorizing a stack of layers with a color wash, such as sepia tones. You can also create a linear gradient using a Shape Layer (Chapter 32) to apply a multicolor wash, as we did see [Ex.10b].

Luminosity

Completing our roundup of these color property replacement modes, Luminosity impresses the color (hue plus saturation) of the underlying layer on the luminance or brightness values of the uppermost layer, which it is applied to. The stacking order matters, with the underlying layer stack "repainting" the layer on top that has Luminosity applied to it.

Luminosity is the exact opposite of the Color mode. If you were to swap the layers, and swap these modes, the results would be the same – swap the layers in [Ex.10a_final] if you don't believe us.

Luminosity admittedly has limited uses. However, it does come in handy when you have an image that is essentially grayscale (or that otherwise has a color palette you don't like), and you want to add a color wash to it from another layer: Place the colorful layer underneath, and apply Luminosity to the grayscale layer on top, as shown in [Ex.10c]

Summarizing H, S, L, and Color modes

To summarize the property-replacing modes, the name of the mode describes what is kept from the uppermost layer, which it is applied to. What is used from each layer is described in this table:

Top layer:	Hue	Sat	Color	Luminance
Layers below:	Sat+Lum	Hue+Lum	Lum	Hue+Sat

Color (Hue plus Saturation) mode colorizes the underlying image, keeping the luminance of the layer below.

Punch Up

To increase contrast and saturation in washed-out video or 3D renders, duplicate it and apply Overlay to the uppermost copy. Reduce the opacity of this treated layer to taste.

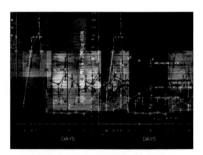

Luminosity inflicts the grayscale values of the layer on top onto the image underneath while retaining the color of the underlying image.

CONNECT

OpenGL previews: Chapter 2.

Stencils: Chapter 12.

Alpha Add mode: Chapter 12.

Adjustment Layers and modes: Chapter 22.

Shape Layers: Chapter 32.

10

All About Masking

Masking tools create transparency using standard or freeform Bezier shapes.

Not all footage items look best full frame. And not all come with their own alpha channels to block out the parts you don't want to see. Therefore, we often use *masks* to "cut out" the alpha channels we require. You can create masks in a variety of ways: You can draw a path using the mask tools in either the Layer or Comp panel, specify the dimensions numerically, or paste a path created in Illustrator or Photoshop.

We'll start this chapter by drawing and editing simple geometric mask shapes, then feathering their edges. We'll continue by drawing Bezier and RotoBezier masks, then offer tips and techniques for animating and modifying masks. We'll be building your expertise until you're comfortable managing multiple masks with Mask Modes. We'll also discuss using effects with masks, rotoscoping techniques, importing paths from Photoshop and Illustrator, interchanging mask and position paths, and extracting masks from images using Auto-trace. We'll also give you a good workout with the Mask Interpolation keyframe assistant.

Masking Basics

You can create and edit masks in either the Composition or Layer panels:

- Editing in the Comp panel has the advantages of seeing your results in the context of other layers and not having to open the Layer panel just to create or tweak a mask. On the other hand, it can be hard to see precisely what you are doing if the layer has been transformed (especially in 3D) or heavily treated with effects. Some also find it distracting for the mask outlines to be drawn in the Comp panel whenever they select a layer – you can turn this off by clicking on the Toggle Mask and Shape Path Visibility button along the bottom of the Comp panel; this also controls whether or not you can manipulate masks in this panel.

- Working in the Layer panel allows you to focus on the layer the mask is applied to, without being distracted by other layers or transformations. If you need to see the other layers for reference, you can open the Comp and Layer panels side by side and see your results in the former while you edit in the latter. The Layer panel sports a View popup and Render switch, which allow you to turn the rendering of masks on or off, as well as see the layer with or without any effects applied.

Shape Tools (Q)   Pen Tool (G)

Tools in the Tools panel used for masking (above): the Shape tools for simple shapes, and the Pen tool for Bezier masking. Click on the current Shape tool to select one of the basic shapes from the menu (below).

	Rectangle Tool	Q
	Rounded Rectangle Tool	Q
	Ellipse Tool	Q
	Polygon Tool	Q
	Star Tool	Q

Example Project

Explore the 10-Example Project.aep file as you read this chapter; references to [Ex.##] refer to specific compositions within the project file.

Masking in the Comp Panel

To get started, open the **10-Example Project.aep** file, then open comp [**Ex.01_starter**]: It contains a movie of a tai chi guru to practice with (but feel free to use your own movie).

You can create either freeform shapes using the Pen tool or one of a series of standardized shapes using the Shape tools. The same tools are used both for creating masks as well as for creating shape layers (discussed in Chapter 32).

To draw a mask, first select the layer that is to receive the mask. If no layer is selected, you will create a new shape layer instead – if you do so while working through this chapter, just Undo, select the layer, and try again. (Incidentally, if you happen to have a shape layer selected, you can draw either a mask or a new shape; a pair of switches that will appear to the right along the Tools panel determine which you will be doing.)

Take note of the Toggle Mask and Shape Path Visibility button along the bottom of the Comp panel (see figure). Verify it is on; it will turn darker when it is. Note that the masking tools are active even when the visibility switch is off; drawing a new mask path will automatically turn the visibility switch back on.

Let's get some practice using the Shape tools to draw mask paths:

Step 1: Select the movie **AB_LifestylesMixedCuts1**. Then select the Rounded Rectangle tool (you can also press Q to select and cycle through the Shape tool options). Making sure the movie is still selected, drag right and down to draw a mask. (If the movie was not selected, the result will be a shape layer – Undo if so.) Observe the result: The image area outside the mask is made transparent (in other words, the layer's alpha channel is modified by the mask shape), and the layer boundary sports a bright yellow border (visible only when Toggle Mask Path Visibility is checked on).

Step 2: After you draw your first mask, the Rounded Rectangle shape tool will remain selected, so press V to switch back to the Selection tool. In the Timeline panel, type MM (two Ms in quick succession) to reveal the mask's properties: Mask Path, Mask Feather, Mask Opacity, and Mask Expansion. The shape you've drawn is the Mask Path; we'll cover the other parameters in due course.

Step 3: Every time you draw a mask, a new mask is created. We'll see later how to manage multiple masks, but at this stage, we suggest you delete the first mask to return to where you started to avoid confusion. The easiest way to do this is to click on the words "Mask 1" in the Timeline and press Delete. (To remove multiple masks at once, select Layer > Mask > Remove All Masks.)

The Toggle Mask and Shape Path Visibility button controls seeing and editing masks directly in the Comp panel. Drawing a mask directly in the Comp panel automatically toggles it on.

Steps 1–2: When you create a mask (above), it gets added to the layer's properties in the Timeline panel (below). With it come several parameters, such as Mask Path, Mask Feather, Mask Opacity, and Mask Expansion. Footage courtesy Artbeats/Lifestyles Mixed Cuts 1.

In the Layer panel (left viewer), note the View menu and the Render checkbox. These decide what part of the rendering chain is displayed. When the Render switch is off, you can see the entire Source in the Layer panel and the results of your masking in the Comp panel (right viewer).

Split Screen

Select the Comp panel and press Command+Option+ Shift+N on Mac (Control+ Alt+Shift+N on Windows) to get two viewers side by side. Now you can use the left viewer for the Layer panel.

TIP

Nudging a Mask

When a mask is selected, the arrow keys nudge the selected points (not the layer) one screen pixel at a time. Add the Shift key to nudge 10 pixels at a time.

Masking in the Layer Panel

This time let's try drawing an oval mask in the Layer panel:

Step 1: Still in [**Ex.01_starter**], double-click the movie to open its Layer panel. It opens docked with the Comp panel; drag its tab outside that panel so it exists as its own panel (see Chapter 1, page 12) and resize it wider until you can see the word Render in the lower right corner. (Depending on the size of your display, you may need to reduce both panels to 50% Magnification or less.)

The View popup at the bottom of the Layer panel decides how far along the rendering chain the Layer panel displays: at the original source, the source after masking, or after a particular effect. You can edit a mask shape in the Layer panel only when View is set to Masks; it automatically switches to Masks whenever you draw a mask in this panel. The Render checkbox to its right decides whether these alterations to the source are visible in this panel. For now, turn Render off.

Step 2: With the Layer panel forward, press Q until you toggle to the Ellipse tool. Click on the movie in the Layer panel and drag right and down to draw an oval-shaped mask. As you do so, you will see just the mask outline in the Layer panel while you see the result of masking in the Comp panel. If you were to switch Render back on, the Layer panel would also cut out the source based on the mask shape. This makes it hard to see what you're doing when you're creating or editing a mask and is why we tend to leave it off when we're working with masks.

When done, press V to return to the Selection tool. If you find the mask outline distracting in the Comp panel, turn off the Toggle Mask and Shape Path Visibility button along its bottom.

Nearly all aspects of masking are the same whether you draw the mask in the Comp or Layer panel. Feel free to re-dock the Layer panel with the Comp panel at any time. Note that the options available under the Layer > Mask submenu are accessible by right-clicking anywhere in the Layer panel or by right-clicking directly on a mask point in the Comp panel.

Shape Shortcuts

Starting on the next page, we will show you how to edit the shape of your masks after you've initially drawn them. However, there are a number of ways you can further manipulate the basic shapes created with the Shape tools while you're initially drawing a mask:

• Select Layer > Mask > New Mask: After Effects will create a Rectangle mask shape that is the same size as the original layer. The shortcut is Command+Shift+N on Mac (Control+Shift+N on Windows). Layer > Mask > Reset Mask will convert any selected mask shape to a rectangle with the same dimensions as the layer, overriding the selected shape.

• Double-click the Shape tools icon to create a mask that uses the currently active shape (Rectangle, Ellipse, Star, and so forth) and that has the same outer dimensions as the layer. Warning: If another mask is selected when you double-click the Shape tool, that mask will be replaced.

• Press the Shift key while you drag to constrain the Rectangle and Rounded Rectangle tools to a square shape, and the Ellipse tool to a circle. Pressing Shift while drawing with the Polygon or Star tools will force them to not rotate.

• The Polygon and Star tools always draw from the center out; Rectangle, Rounded Rectangle, and Ellipse draw from a corner out. To draw rectangles or ellipses from the center out, press Command (Control) *after* you start dragging. When drawing with the Star tool, add the Command (Control) key to change just the outer radius of the star instead of the inner and outer radius together.

To interactively change the mask you are drawing with the Shape tool, add the following keys *after* you start drawing the shape but *before* you release the mouse:

Reset Shape Tools

If you draw a shape and use a modifier key (see table), this shape will become the new default for that tool from then on, even if you quit After Effects. To reset the tool, double-click it (then Undo to delete the shape this creates if you don't need it).

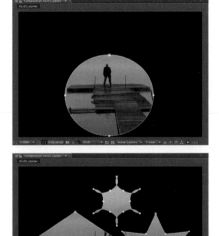

Hold Shift while dragging a rectangle or ellipse to force it to be as tall as it is wide. (It looks slightly fat here because After Effects is compensating for the non-square pixels in this D1 comp.)

Use the Page Up, Page Down, and cursor keys to alter shapes as you drag them, as we did here with the star shape in the middle.

Shape type	up/down cursor keys	left/right cursor keys	page up/down
rounded rectangle	corner roundness	toggle rectangle/ellipse	
polygon	number of sides	outer roundness	
star	number of points	outer roundness	inner roundness

If you have a mouse with a scroll wheel, it will have the same action as the up and down cursor keys. You can also reposition any of the standard mask shapes before releasing the mouse by holding the spacebar and dragging.

The Free Transform Tour

To move, scale, and rotate a mask shape after it has been drawn, use the Free Transform Points feature (also known as Free Transform for short). To access the Free Transform Points, either:

• Double-click the mask path (for this to work in the Comp panel, Toggle Mask Path Visibility will need to be on).

• Select a Mask in the Timeline and press Command+T (Control+T).

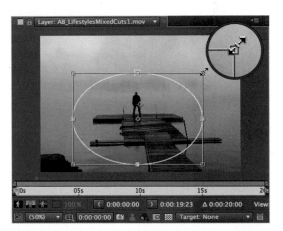

This will select all the points and draw a bounding box. If you want to transform just part of the shape, select individual points and then double-click them. Once the Free Transform box is active, you have the following options:

• You can move the mask shape by dragging anywhere inside the bounding box.

• If you want to resize the mask shape, place the cursor over a corner or side handle; it will change to a Resize symbol (two arrows pointing in opposite directions). Drag a handle to resize; add Shift to maintain the aspect ratio.

• If you want to rotate the mask shape, the cursor changes to the Rotate symbol when it's positioned just outside the bounding box. Drag to rotate; add the Shift key to rotate in 45° increments.

The easiest way to activate the Free Transform bounding box is to double-click the mask path. Moving your mouse over one of the corners will activate the resize tool (inset).

• Press + and – on the keypad to rotate clockwise and counterclockwise in 1° increments, respectively; add Shift to rotate in 10° increments.

• Deselect Free Transform by either double-clicking on the pasteboard or pressing the Enter key on the keypad, or pressing the ESC key. The mask shape will remain selected.

When a mask shape is rotated by using Free Transform, the transformation occurs around the anchor point for the bounding box. This is the tiny "registration" symbol that defaults to the center of the box. (Note that this is completely independent of the layer's anchor point, around which the layer scales and rotates.)

To change the anchor point for the bounding box, drag the symbol to a new position. Now when you rotate the mask, it will rotate around this new point. However, scaling the mask will behave as it did before – if you want to also scale around the anchor point, resize the bounding box with the Command (Control) key pressed. Add the Shift key after you start dragging to keep the same aspect ratio. Note that moving this anchor is temporary – when you reselect Free Transform for this mask in the future, its anchor will have returned to the center of the bounding box.

The registration mark symbol is the center, or anchor, around which free transformations take place. When the cursor changes (it has a second registration symbol at its tail), you can click and drag it to a new location.

There are a few gotchas to watch out for while free transforming:

• If only some mask points are selected when you double-click to switch to Free Transform mode, you will scale or rotate only the selected points. To transform all points, double-click with all (or no) points selected.

• Free Transform is an editing tool rather than a property, meaning that it works only for the current transformation. For instance, if you rotate a mask, then enable Free Transform again some time later, the bounding box will not appear in a rotated position.

• If mask shape keyframes are created using Free Transform to rotate the shape, when After Effects then interpolates between keyframes, the mask won't rotate as a whole; instead, each individual vertex will move independently to its new position. This does not give the same result. (This behavior is explained in more detail in the *More Mask-Animating Advice* section, page 170.)

TIP

Larger Vertex Points

If you find the mask vertices hard to locate or select, you can increase their size in Preferences > General > Path Point Size.

Selection Moves

Sometimes just figuring out the simplest things can reduce your stress level…and so it is with selecting. As you've seen, masks are made up of a collection of points, and editing a mask requires you to select a single point, multiple points, or the entire mask. The following tips assume you have the Selection tool active:

When you use a Shape tool to create a mask, all of its points will

initially be selected (solid squares). Return to the Selection tool and you can now move the entire shape by dragging any point (or line segment). You can also temporarily switch to the Selection tool by pressing Command (Control).

The following tips assume you have the Selection tool active:

Figure A: When a layer is selected but the mask is not, the mask point locations will be represented by dots. Click on a dot to select that point.

Figure B: When a point is selected, its vertex appears as a filled-in square and Bezier handles may appear; the other points appear as hollow squares. You can also use the Selection tool to drag a marquee around all the points

you wish to select. Note that in the Comp panel, once one layer's mask is selected, you can't accidentally select another layer if you marquee around mask points.

Shift+clicking a point will add and subtract points from a selection, as will Shift+marquee.

Figure C: Clicking a line segment will select the points on either end of the line segment.

Figure D: To select all points on a mask path, Option+click (Alt+click) anywhere on the path. To select multiple masks, add the Shift key. You can also select all mask points from the Timeline panel: Press M to twirl down masks and click on the name of the mask or on the words "Mask Path" (Shift+click to select multiple masks).

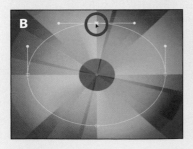

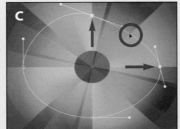

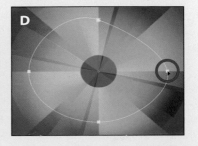

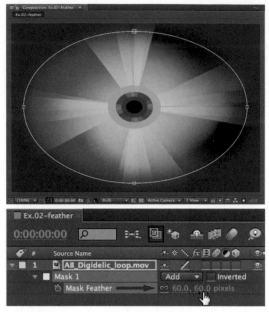

Increasing a mask's Feather parameter above its default of 0 results in a soft edge, centered around the mask's outline. To set independent horizontal and vertical feather amounts, uncheck the link icon.

Mask Expansion expands and contracts the alpha channel created by the mask; it does not change the path itself. Footage courtesy Artbeats/Business World.

Masks of a Feather

Mask outlines may be feathered, creating anything from a slightly wider antialiased edge up through a soft vignette effect. Close the Layer panel to create more space for the Comp panel, and open [**Ex.02-feather**]. We've left Toggle Mask Path Visibility on to help you see how the feather extends both inside and outside the mask shape, but you can turn it off if you find the mask outline distracting.

Select layer 1, and press F to reveal Mask Feather in the Timeline panel (or press MM to twirl open all four Mask properties). Each mask has independent Feather control, and like other properties, it can be set by scrubbing its value or by entering a precise value for horizontal and vertical feather (you can tab between fields for easy entry). These are linked by default, so scrubbing or typing in a new value for one will update the other to match. Uncheck the link icon if you want to set different amounts of horizontal and vertical feather. Option+clicking (Alt+ clicking) on the link icon relinks them, using the X feather value for both X and Y.

Be aware that feathering occurs both inside and outside the mask's edge. If you apply a feather of 20 pixels, the feather attempts to draw roughly 10 pixels inside the edge and 10 pixels outside the edge. (The width is actually wider than 20 pixels; we won't bore you with the reasons why – it has to do with Gaussian distributions.) However, feathering cannot extend outside the dimensions of the layer, so applying a large feather value may cause edges to get clipped by the layer's boundaries. Check the edges with a critical eye, using the Info panel to confirm the that the alpha values drops to 0 before the edge. If you see a problem edge, reduce the feather amount accordingly, inset the mask further, or use the Mask Expansion property.

Mask Expansion

Mask Expansion allows you to expand or contract the mask shape, and is represented in pixels. It is particularly useful when a soft feather results in too much of the desired masked area being cut away – if so, apply positive values to expand the mask. On the other hand, if a mask is drawn close to the layer's edge and using a large feather amount results in a clipped edge, apply negative values to contract the mask. Try this for yourself in [**Ex.03**] by selecting layer 1, pressing MM (two Ms in quick succession) to display all four mask properties, and scrubbing the Mask Expansion amount.

Mask Opacity

Each mask has a separate Mask Opacity control in addition to the layer's main Opacity property. [**Ex.04a**] is an example of different Mask Opacity values applied to three separate masks on the foreground layer. Select layer 1 and type TT (two Ts in quick succession) to twirl down only Mask Opacity for each mask. As with other parameters, you can change the Mask Opacity value either by scrubbing the value, or clicking it and entering a precise value.

Note that in [**Ex.04a**] we changed the Mask Feather value for each mask. Also note that each mask has a different colored outline in the Comp panel; to change the color of the mask, click on the Mask's color swatch in the Timeline and select a new color from the color picker (or set Preference > Appearance > Cycle Mask Colors). We also renamed each mask to describe the area being masked: To rename a mask, select its name (such as Mask 1), press Return, type a new name, and press Return again to accept.

Of course, if you have only one mask shape, you should use the regular Transform > Opacity (covered in Chapter 3) to fade the layer up or down. But with multiple masks, having a separate and animatable fade up/down for each mask opens up lots of possibilities. We reckon this is one of those features you won't know you even need – until you really need it. For instance, you're rotoscoping a man with his arms by his sides, when halfway through the animation he moves his arm – creating a new shape between the arm and body. By animating Mask Opacity for this new shape, you can have a mask shape appear on the first frame it's needed, then turn off later if he moves his arm back down by his side.

A not-so-obvious use for Mask Opacity is to fade up different sections of a logo when all the logo elements exist on one layer. Open [**Ex.04b**] and RAM Preview: We created five masks, one for each logo element. We then used Mask Opacity to fade up each element, offset in time from each other. Because all the elements remain as one layer, moving the layer or animating Scale affects the entire logo, and the regular Opacity control can be used to fade off all the elements together. Also, any effect or Layer Style applied to the layer – such as a bevel alpha or a drop shadow – will apply to all the elements as a group.

In [**Ex.04a**], multiple masks are applied to the same layer. Each mask can have its own separate Mask Opacity in addition to the layer's Transform > Opacity property. Note that each mask also has its own Mask Feather and Expansion values. Background courtesy Artbeats/Alien Atmospheres.

In [**Ex.04b**], Mask Opacity is used to fade up different elements of a logo, where the logo is a single layer. Footage courtesy Lee Stranahan.

The Pen tool (shortcut: G) is used for drawing Bezier paths for masks. Press G to cycle through the Pen tool options. For this exercise, turn off the RotoBezier option (to the right in the Tools panel).

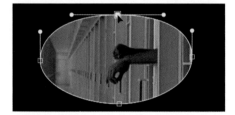

Bezier masks can be open or closed shapes, but only closed shapes can create transparency.

Even when you create a mask with the Ellipse tool, if you click on one of its points, you will see the Bezier path editing handles.

If you're drawing a mask shape with the Pen tool and you pass the cursor back over one of the handles before you've closed the shape, it will turn into the Convert Vertex tool. Use this tool to drag the handle to break the continuous flow of the mask shape through this point.

Freeform Bezier Masking

Now that you've got the basics of how masking works, let's look at the most powerful mask drawing tool: the Pen. This allows you to create masks using Bezier paths. Even when you think you've been creating simple rectangular and oval masks, After Effects has actually been creating Bezier paths to make these masks. You can use these basic shapes as a starting point, or draw a Bezier path directly with the Pen tool.

The Pen can create a Bezier mask of any shape and include a combination of straight and curved segments. The masks can also be open or closed: A closed shape is required to create transparency, but even an open path can be quite useful for effects and text (more on that later).

To draw a Bezier mask, select the Pen tool (shortcut: G), check that the RotoBezier option in the Tools panel is off, select a layer, and draw your path in either the Layer or Comp panels. Practice this in [**Ex.05_starter**], making sure you select layer 1 before drawing.

The Pen tool works similarly to the Bezier drawing tool in other programs such as Photoshop and Illustrator: *A single click with the mouse creates a straight line segment with sharp corners, while a click+drag pulls out handles and creates smooth curves.* To close the path, click back on the first point (or double-click as you draw the last point). To create an open path, switch to the Selection tool (V) when you've finished drawing.

If you're new to Bezier drawing, be aware that it takes a little practice. The secrets are to not use lots of straight lines when you're supposed to be drawing a curve (you know who you are…), and to create as few points as possible while still getting the job done. Don't be worried if the mask shape isn't perfect when you're creating it – it's next to impossible to drag handles perfectly at every point as you draw a path, and it's totally acceptable to just tweak it afterward. If you are already comfortable drawing with a Bezier tool in another program, and/or have completed Chapter 3, the following tips should be all you need to adapt your skills to Bezier masking:

• While you're drawing a mask, if you need to break the continuous handles of a smooth point you've just created, move the cursor over the handle. The Convert Vertex cursor (the upside-down V) will appear. Drag the handle to break it, then continue drawing.

• When you're in the middle of drawing a mask with the Pen tool and you need to edit a point or handle you've already drawn, press the Command (Control) key to toggle temporarily to the Selection tool. This will cause After Effects to think you're finished drawing, but never fear:

• If you accidentally deselect or otherwise interrupt the drawing of a mask shape before you've finished, you can continue where you left off. With the Pen tool active, press Command (Control) and select the last mask point you created (all other points should appear hollow), then continue drawing – the new point will be added onto the end of the path.

Editing with the Selection Tool

Once the path is drawn, we suggest you switch from the Pen to the Selection tool (shortcut: V) to edit it. The following builds on the tips in the earlier sidebar *Selection Moves* for selecting points and entire shapes. Note that some behaviors have changed in recent versions:

• Command+Option+click (Control+Alt+click) on a mask point to convert it from "corner" to "smooth" (pop out handles if they are retracted), or from smooth to corner (retract handles).

• To break the handles of a smooth point that has continuous handles, press Command+Option (Control+Alt) and drag a handle. To rejoin the handles, click and start to drag a handle, *then* press Option (Alt). Do not release Option (Alt) until after you release the mouse.

• When dragging a handle, add the spacebar to move the mask point.

• To add a point, press G and place the cursor along the line segment between two points. The cursor will change to the Add Vertex tool. Click to add a new point, release G, then drag it to a new position as required. *If the mask is animating over time, adding a point at one keyframe normally adds it to all points in time, but moving the new point will affect the current keyframe only.*

• To delete a point, click on it to select it and press Delete, or press G and click on it. *Be warned that if the mask is animating over time, by default this will delete the corresponding point and will normally reshape the mask at all keyframes.*

• To delete a mask, select its name in the Timeline panel (or select *all* points in the Layer or Comp panel) and press Delete.

• Only closed paths can create transparency. To close an open path, select Layer > Mask and Shape Path > Closed (you can also get this menu by right-clicking in the Comp or Layer panel). A line will be added connecting the last point drawn to the first point. To open a path, select the line segment you wish to remove, then choose the Closed menu item (which will have a check mark by it) – it will now "unclose" the shape, removing the line segment between the two points you selected.

Editing with the Pen Tool

If you prefer, you can create and then edit masks with the Pen tool. Instead of the above shortcuts, use the Add, Delete, and Convert Vertex tools found by expanding the Pen tool in the Tools panel. Be warned, though – simply clicking on a mask point with the Pen tool deletes it!

When you feel you're getting a handle on Bezier masks, practice cutting out the X in [**Ex.05b_Big X**]. For additional help with creating and modifying Bezier masks with the Pen tool, check out After Effects' online Help (F1 to open – search for "Pen tool"). Remember that these skills will also be put to use when drawing paths on shape layers (Chapter 32).

Delete or Move

If you place the Pen tool over a mask point, it changes to the Delete Vertex tool (a pen with a minus sign); clicking will remove that mask point. To move the mask point, press Command (Control) to toggle to the Selection tool.

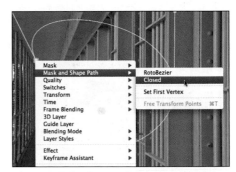

To close an open path, right-click in the Layer panel and select Mask and Shape Path > Closed (above). The path will close and create transparency (below). Footage courtesy Artbeats/Incarcerated.

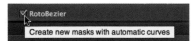

After you select the Pen tool, an option for RotoBezier masks will appear along the Tools panel; enable it before drawing the mask.

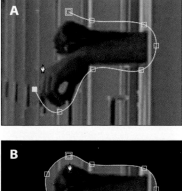

RotoBezier masks appear just as a series of points with no Bezier handles. When you create a new point, After Effects automatically calculates a smooth path between the adjacent points (A). Close the mask, and a smooth shape will be created (B).

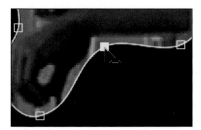

Holding Command+Option (Control+ Alt) allows you to adjust the tension (roundness) of a RotoBezier point.

RotoBezier Masks

An alternative to working with Bezier handles is to create RotoBezier masks. This type of mask – also created using the Pen tool – automatically calculates the curves leading into and out of mask points based on the positions of adjacent points. RotoBezier shapes can be easier to use for flowing, organic objects that feature curves rather than hard corners.

Click on the Comp panel's tab and select Close All. Open comp [**Ex.06_starter**] and select layer 1. Then select the Pen tool (shortcut: G). Along the Tools panel to the right the word RotoBezier will appear; enable it by checking its box.

Move your cursor to the Comp panel and click at a point a little bit above the hands to create your first point. Note that if you drag before releasing the mouse, Bezier handles do not appear; instead, you will move the point itself. Work around the hands, clicking to add points. As you click, you'll initially see a straight line segment between your two most recent points; as you continue adding points, After Effects calculates the curves between the earlier points. Don't sweat it if you're unhappy with the immediate results; you can edit your points later. When you have worked your way around the hands, click on the first point, and the mask will close.

After you have finished drawing a mask, press V to return to the Selection tool. Click and drag any point around, and watch as the curves before and after it automatically bend to follow. As with normal Bezier masks, temporarily holding G and placing the cursor over a line segment automatically switches to the Add Vertex tool; holding G and placing the cursor over a mask point switches it to the Delete Vertex tool. Unlike normal Bezier masks, dragging a line segment (with no modifier key) to adjust the curve also moves the mask points on either side.

You can adjust the otherwise-automatic tension of RotoBezier masks either after they're created or while you are drawing. Hold down Command+Option (Control+Alt) and click on a mask point to change it to a hard corner; doing so again returns its tension to 25%. Clicking and dragging with these modifier keys held allows you to adjust the tension of the imaginary Bezier handles running through the mask point; the Info panel updates the value between 0% and 100% as you drag. Note that these commands also work on all selected points, so be aware of what you have selected!

It takes some practice to develop a feel for the best places for RotoBezier points, especially if you are trying to create a tight outline around a shape. One approach is to place the points in the center of curved segments and let After Effects build the curves between them. Another approach is to place RotoBezier points at the very ends of straight-ish segments right before and after clear curves and let After Effects calculate the corners. The tighter the corners, the closer adjacent points must be. Of course, you can combine these two techniques on the same shape.

Converting between Bezier and RotoBezier

You can convert a RotoBezier mask to an ordinary mask: Select it and use the menu option Layer > Mask and Shape Path > RotoBezier to turn this feature off. For each point, After Effects will create handles that closely approximate the RotoBezier shape. You can use the same option to turn RotoBezier back on, but don't expect the resulting shape to match a carefully tweaked Bezier mask.

Colored Masks

Preferences > User Interface Colors > Cycle Mask Colors will draw each new mask outline in a different color rather than the default yellow.

Animating a Mask

Of course, Mask Paths can be animated. Practice this with [**Ex.06_starter**]. Press Home and create a mask shape you like around the hands. If the Mask Path isn't already visible in the Timeline, select the layer and press M. Then click on the stopwatch next to

To animate a mask, expose Mask Path and click on its stopwatch switch to enable keyframing.

Mask Path to enable keyframing. Scrub the current time indicator later in the Timeline until the hands have changed appreciably and modify the mask shape by moving the points (don't draw a new path from scratch). Moving even one point will automatically create another keyframe. Press 0 on the numeric keypad to RAM Preview your work.

Our version of the animated mask is in [**Ex.06-mask only**]. We didn't bother masking the hands too tightly, because in our final animation ([**Ex.06-final**]) we employed the trick of blurring the background to focus the viewer's attention. To do this we used two copies of the movie: The hands are masked in the foreground layer and remain sharp, while the Noise & Grain > Median effect was applied to blur the background layer. A large Mask Feather helps blend the two together.

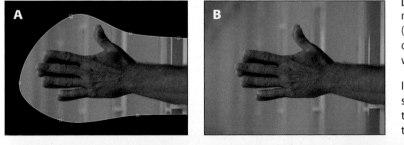

[Ex.06-final]: After animating a loose mask around the hands as they unfurl (A), a large feather was applied and the original movie added as a background with the Median effect applied (B).

In the Timeline panel (below), we smoothed the animation by selecting the Mask Path keyframes converting them to Auto Bezier (see Chapter 4).

The Mask Shape Dialog

If you need to create a mask shape with exact values, you can enter them in the Mask Shape dialog. Access this dialog by clicking in the Timeline on the word "Shape" beside the mask you wish to edit. You can also select a mask and choose Layer > Mask > Mask Shape from the menu or use the shortcut: Command+Shift+M (Control+Shift+M).

Specify the size of the mask by entering values for the bounding box (Top, Left, Right, and Bottom); the Tab key will move clockwise around the four entry boxes. The Units popup offers the option to enter values in Percentage of Source, handy if you want the same border on all four sides.

You can also reset the mask Shape to be a rectangle or ellipse that conforms to the size set in the Bounding Box above.

Mask Shape

Bounding Box

Top: 60 px

Left: 100 px   Right: 550 px

Bottom: 360 px

Units: pixels ▾

Shape

☐ Reset To: Rectangle ▾

○ **Rectangle**
Ellipse

Cancel   OK

FACTOID

Resizing the Layer

Changing a solid layer's size will resize any masks already applied. This behavior also applies to replacing the source of a layer (Chapter 6) or resizing a precomp (Chapter 19) when masks are applied in the top comp.

Masks and Velocity

One of the most common uses for animated masks is to "wipe on" or reveal an object. A typical approach is to create either a starting or final "at rest" shape, enable keyframing, then create a second keyframe by changing the shape of the mask by manipulating its points. The mask shape will interpolate over time between keyframes, just like any other property.

Open the [**Ex.07_starter**] comp where we've already created a final mask shape for the inset video. Note that we've also arranged a number of guides (View > Show Guides); these can be very helpful to ensure you're sticking to a design grid. Check that View > Lock Guides is toggled on so you don't accidentally move a guide while editing the mask.

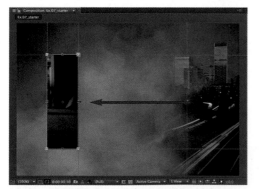

Step 3: The Free Transform Points boundary snaps to guides, making precise positioning easier. Background courtesy Artbeats/Timelapse Cityscapes.

Step 1: Move the current time indicator to 02:00; we want our final mask shape to hold from this time through the end of the comp. If Mask 1 > Mask Path is not visible, select **AB_BusExecutives.mov** and press M to reveal it. Then enable its keyframing stopwatch at this time.

Step 2: Move the current time indicator to 00:10, which will be the time of our initial keyframe. Select Mask 1 to highlight the mask in the Comp panel (Toggle Mask and Shape Path Visibility should be enabled). Note that the mask has a sub-dued outline; this indicates you are not currently located on a keyframe, and editing the mask shape will create a new one.

Step 3: With the Selection tool, double-click the mask path in the Comp panel to bring up Free Transform Points. Position the cursor over the middle handle on the right side and drag it left so that it snaps to the nearest guideline, which is at 200 pixels on the horizontal axis. Press Enter to turn off Free Transform Points.

If you'd like to try using the Mask Shape dialog to perform the same edit, Undo to remove the keyframe at 00:10 (or delete it), then click on the word "Shape" in the Timeline. The Bounding Box values state that the Left side of the mask is at 100 pixels and the Right side is at 550 pixels. Change the value for Right to "200" and click OK. The mask will now fill the space between the two guidelines. (If you want to close the mask shape entirely, reopen the Mask Shape dialog and set the Right value to equal the Left value.)

RAM Preview: The animating mask is nice, but the leading edge "strobes" a bit as it moves. It would be nice if you could blur just that edge, and none of the other edges, while the mask was opening. Well, we can, because Masks support Motion Blur!

Step 4: Enabling motion blur (above) for a layer with an animated mask will result in only the edges of the mask that are moving getting "feathered" (blurred) (left).

Step 4: Place the time indicator somewhere between 00:10 and 02:00. If the Switches column is not visible in the Timeline panel, press F4 to toggle it on. Enable the Motion Blur switch (under the icon with the echoed dots) for **AB_BusExecutives.mov**. Then click on the master Enable Motion Blur switch along the top of the Timeline. The animating edge of the mask will now be blurred; the blur disappears when the

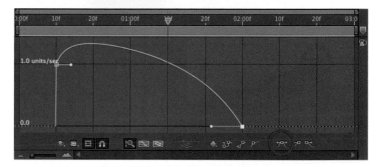

mask stops. You can change the amount of blur in Composition > Composition Settings under the Advanced tab; edit the Shutter Angle. (If you can't get enough of this trick, study [**Ex.08**] as well.)

Step 5: To refine the speed of our animation, open the Graph Editor – the shortcut is Shift+F3. Select the Mask Path parameter to reveal its speed graph. It's pretty simple right now: The white line rises suddenly and holds steady while it's moving, then drops back to zero. To craft something a bit more elegant, select the second keyframe and either click the Easy Ease button along the bottom of the Graph Editor or press F9. RAM Preview to see if you prefer this smoother stop.

Open [**Ex.07-final**] to see our slightly amped-up version of this composition. We had fun masking the various elements to control where they appeared in the final frame and used blending modes to mix them together in a subtle manner. RAM Preview, paying particular attention to the colored bars sliding on: Animated mask shapes, right? Wrong! For something as simple as solid lines, we merely animated the position of solids or shape layers. No sense making extra work for ourselves when a simpler solution would work just as well.

Step 5: After you apply Easy Ease to the final keyframe, the Speed Graph will indicate a gradual slowdown. (Note that you cannot edit mask values in the Graph Editor – only the speed of its animation.)

In [**Ex.07-final**], the blurred horizontal lines are solids that have feathered masks; we found it easier to move them across the screen by animating their position rather than their mask shape. Inset courtesy Artbeats/Business Executives.

When a rectangular mask shape is rotated using the Free Transform tool, the corners follow a straight line to their new positions, making the mask appear to shrink while it's interpolating. Preview this in **[Ex.09_problem]**. Movie courtesy Getty Images/Time Elements.

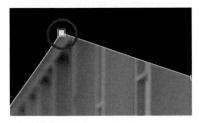

The First Vertex Point on one keyframe will always animate to the First Vertex Point on the next keyframe. If masks distort when they're animating, check that this "leader" point is set correctly.

Thinking Ahead

If you know you'll need to rotoscope (or even morph) footage ahead of time, try to shoot on 24- or 30-fps film or use a progressive scan camera. This will cut your workload in half compared with masking nearly 60 fields a second…

More Mask-Animating Advice

When you're animating mask shapes, and the mask shape needs to be precise, draw and edit the shape with the layer set to Best Quality (the default) and the composition set to Full Resolution and at least 100% Magnification. Watch out for these common gotchas:

- **Wotating Wectangles:** When mask keyframes are created by rotating a mask using Free Transform Points, the shape itself isn't rotated; instead, interpolation occurs between its individual points. This can yield some unexpected results – for example, the corners of a square will head straight to their new positions rather than rotating in an arc to these positions. You can review this anomaly in [Ex.09_problem].

There is a workaround of sorts: Copy the initial mask shape and paste it to a same-size solid layer. Then animate the solid layer using its regular Rotate property. Use the animated solid as an Alpha Track Matte (see Chapter 11) for the original layer. This is demonstrated in [**Ex.09-fix**].

- **The First Vertex Point**: When you select all points on a mask, have you noticed that one point is a bit larger than all the others? This is the First Vertex Point, and it controls how mask points interpolate. The First Vertex Point at one keyframe always interpolates to the First Vertex Point on the next keyframe – all the other points around the path follow their lead. When you're interpolating from very different shapes, you may need to manually change this "leader" point. Open [**Ex.10_twist**] and navigate to each of the four keyframes. Seems simple enough. But RAM Preview and see how the mask twists as it interpolates. The mask point at the top of the frame is the leader at the first keyframe; at subsequent keyframes, select this top point, right-click on it, and select Mask > Set First Vertex. The top point is now consistent, as shown in [**Ex.10-fix**].

- **Masking on Fields:** When you're masking interlaced footage where the fields have been separated in the Interpret Footage dialog (see Chapter 38), you will normally see only the first field of each frame in the composition. However, when you field render on output, both fields are used, and the mask will interpolate field by field. If the footage you're masking requires critical precision, you might want to check the mask on every field. To do this:

Change the comp's frame rate (Composition > Composition Settings) to double the existing frame rate: for NTSC, 59.94 frames per second (fps) is double 29.97, while 50 is double PAL's 25 fps rate. Don't use 60 fps to double 29.97 fps, however – tiny increments in time are very important to keyframe placement, and any slight difference can causes masks to appear to slip (discussed next).

Now when you navigate in time, you can check how the mask interpolates for each field, even setting keyframes on the second field if you need to. When you're masking field by field, you might want to place the footage being masked in its own precomp so you can change just this

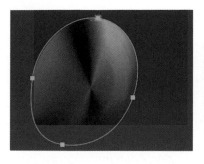

A mask is drawn to fit a movie running at 24 fps (left). When nested into a comp running at 29.97 fps, the mask will look correct only when it lines up with a keyframe (center). Interpolated frames will appear to slip (right). Pendulum courtesy Artbeats/Time & Money.

comp's frame rate. Then nest this precomp into the final comp (nesting is explained further in Chapter 18).

When it comes time to render, bear in mind that animated mask shapes will ultimately interpolate at the frame rate set in the Render Settings, not the comp's frame rate. (If you're masking field by field in an NTSC 59.94 fps comp, you don't need to return the frame rate to 29.97 fps before you render – just set it in Render Settings to 29.97 fps, with Field Rendering set to On.)

• **Masks not in sync with Source:** If a mask appears to be "slipping" in the rendered movie, even though it looks fine in the composition, there's another likely culprit: A mask is interpolating out of sync with the source frames. This is caused by a mismatch between the mask's keyframes and the frame (or field) rate of your footage. For example, if your footage has progressive frames (not interlaced frames), you would mask this layer on whole frames in a 29.97 fps composition. But if you field render the entire animation, the mask will now interpolate at 59.94 fps and appear to be out of sync with the source.

Similarly, if you remove 3:2 pulldown from a clip (see Chapters 38 and 41) to return it to its original 24 fps film frames, or if your footage is at 24 fps in the first place, then you should create your mask keyframes at 24 fps. However, if you then render at 29.97 fps (with or without fields), or nest it in another comp that's running at 29.97 fps, the mask will now interpolate at 29.97 fps and will appear to slip. This problem is shown in the next series of comps: In [**Ex.11-precomp@24fps**], the movie is masked at its native frame rate of 24 fps. This comp is then nested in [**Ex.11-final Comp@29.97fps**], where it now runs at 29.97 fps. Step through the **Final Comp**, and you'll see the mask is interpolating at the wrong frame rate (note how the 24 fps movie repeats frames, but the mask continues to move).

From the Comp panel's tab, select Close All and open [**Ex.12-precomp@24fps**]. We solved the problem in this series of comps by setting Preserve Frame Rate in the precomp's Composition Settings > Advanced tab. Now when you nest this precomp into the final comp, the nested comp's frame rate will be honored no matter what frame rate the final comp is rendered at. Open comp [**Ex.12-final Comp@29.97fps**] and preview; notice that the mask stays attached to the movie. For more on nesting compositions and the Preserve Frame Rate option, see Chapter 18.

Deleting Points

Whereas After Effects gracefully handles adding points to an animated mask, deleting a point from a mask is a different story. If you delete a point at one keyframe, it will remove it for all keyframes throughout the animation. This will reshape the mask, and you may lose valuable work. For this reason, the rule of thumb is to either start with the right number of points, or if the object you're masking changes shape, create the mask starting with the simplest shape. This way you'll be adding points as you create keyframes, not deleting them. (Note: If you require that the points you add or delete alter only the current keyframe, turn off "Preserve Constant Vertex Count when Editing Masks" in Preferences > General.)

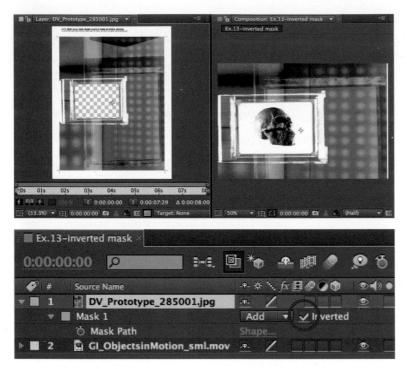

A mask is applied to a texture image in the Layer panel (top, left viewer), then Inverted in the Timeline panel (above) – which opens a window, revealing the skull movie layer behind (top, right viewer). Texture courtesy Digital Vision/Prototype; skull courtesy Getty Images/Objects in Motion.

When two identical masks align and one is inverted, a seam will be visible (A). Setting the layer on top to Alpha Add mode (center) will cure the problem (B). Footage courtesy Artbeats/Digidelic.

Inverting a Mask

Normally the image inside a mask appears opaque, and portions outside of the mask are transparent. It is possible to invert this behavior, however, so that the *inside* of the mask becomes transparent, as we did in [**Ex.13**]. In the Switches column opposite each mask is a checkbox that changes the mask to Inverted when it's selected. (No, you can't animate the Inverted option.) Meanwhile, the shortcut Command+Shift+I (Control+Shift+I) inverts a selected mask without having to hunt through the Timeline panel.

Inverting a mask is useful if you want to create a hole in a layer. For instance, if you draw a mask around a window, you can invert it to see through the window to the layers behind. Note that when you're using multiple masks, you'll need to use Mask Modes (our next major subject), rather than the Inverted option, to make one mask create a hole through another mask.

Fixing Seams with Inverted Masks

When a layer is set to Best Quality, mask edges are antialiased – even if Mask Feather is set to 0. In most cases, this is great. The one place where it can trip you up is if you have two layers with identical mask shapes arranged on top of each other and one is inverted – the two edges (with or without feather) will not add up to 100% opacity, creating a visible seam. The solution is very simple: Press F4 to expose the Modes column in the Timeline panel and set the Mode popup for the layer on top to Alpha Add (it's near the bottom of the list). This is demonstrated in [**Ex.14**] and discussed again at the end of Chapter 12.

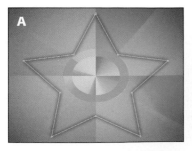

Multiple Masks

So far we've explored simple and Bezier masks, along with animating a mask over time. The final piece of the masking puzzle is how best to work with multiple masks. You can have an unlimited number of masks per layer; the Mask Modes control how masks interact with each other. Each mask has its own Mask Path, Mask Feather, Mask Expansion, and Mask Opacity controls, and we refer to these four values as a "mask group." In the Timeline panel, each mask group has its own twirly arrow as a subset of the main Masks section.

Mask Modes

When you create multiple masks on a layer, the first mask creates transparency by modifying the layer's alpha channel. Any subsequent mask(s) created on the same layer can add, subtract, intersect, or difference their transparency with the first mask, using the Modes popup associated with each mask group. You can also set a mask to None, which is very useful: You can draw mask shapes that don't affect the layer's alpha channel but which can still be used by effects (discussed later). Open path masks don't have a Modes popup, as they cannot create transparency. Also, Mask Modes can't animate over time.

Mask Modes can be a bit confusing at first, but let's run through a simple example and they should become clear. Open [**Ex.15_starter**], which consists of a red Solid layer with two masks: a square and a circle. Select the layer, and press M to twirl down Mask Paths. Masks are calculated from the top down as seen in the Timeline panel, so each mask operates based on the result of all the masks above it. New masks default to Add mode, so each shape adds its result to the previous shape. For this example, leave Mask 1 set to Add mode, and experiment with changing Mask 2 from Add to Subtract, Intersect, and Difference (Lighten and Darken are special modes, which we'll get to shortly). Of course, you can set Mask 1 to other modes besides Add, and you can invert mask shapes as needed. Just for fun, create a third mask shape that overlaps the other two, and experiment with Modes some more.

Each mask group has a Mode popup which determines how it interacts with the mask groups above.

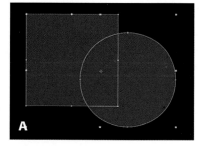

Two masks – a square and a circle – are applied to a red Solid layer. They default to Add mode (A); try changing Mask 2 to Subtract (B), Intersect (C), and Difference (D).

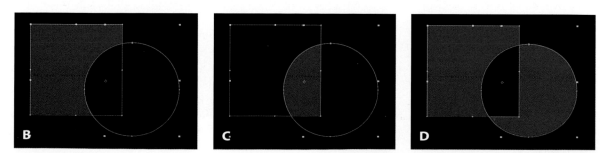

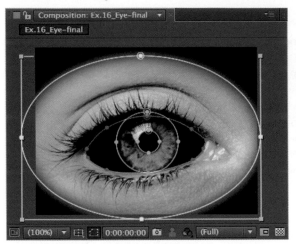

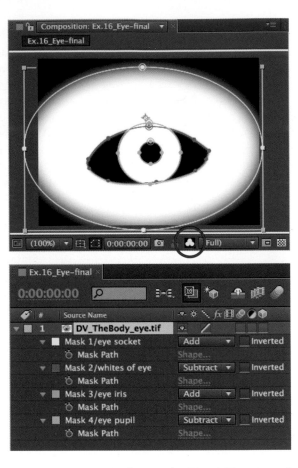

The combination of multiple masks and mask modes allows for great flexibility (above). **[Ex.16_Eye-final]** uses four masks to isolate different areas (right). The Comp's alpha channel shows which areas are opaque and which are transparent (above right). Eye image courtesy Digital Vision/The Body.

Pathfinder Envy

Mask modes affect how the alpha channel is calculated, but they do not combine multiple mask paths into a single shape. However, the Pathfinder panel in Illustrator excels at this task. So here is the workaround: Select the Mask Paths in After Effects and Copy them. In Illustrator, create a blank document and Paste. Use the Pathfinder panel to create a new single shape. Then Copy your new combined shape. Bring After Effects forward, select the path you want to replace, then Paste. Copying and pasting paths from Illustrator is discussed in detail later in this chapter. Using the Pathfinder panel is covered in detail in the Illustrator Help file.

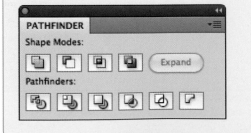

For a more practical example, [**Ex.16-Eye_starter**] has a layer already set up with several masks, all set to the default Add mode. Experiment with different modes for the masks, then different transparency and feather amounts per group. Our result is shown in [**Ex.16_Eye-final**]. If you make a mess, set Mask 1 to Add, and the others to None, then work on one mask at a time from the top down until you understand which mask is doing what. Remember the logic: Each mask operates on the result of all the masks above.

When you're working with Mask Modes, remember that the top mask sets the underlying shape for the other masks to intersect with, and it is usually set to Add mode or Add Inverted. Try to avoid inverting the other masks; you should be able to create the required result with just the Add, Subtract, Intersect, or Difference modes; inverting masks makes the logic harder to follow.

Problem-Solving Modes: Lighten and Darken

Mask Opacity refers to the opacity of the layer inside the mask shape. If you have multiple masks applied to a layer, each with a different Mask Opacity setting, the behavior of the alpha channel is such that the *overlapping* areas may appear more or less opaque. To solve this problem, there are two modes – Lighten and Darken – which come in handy.

When multiple masks with different opacity settings overlap in Add mode, the opacity of the intersecting area will appear more opaque than either of the individual shapes. For instance, if two masks in Add mode are both set to 50% Mask Opacity, the opacity of the intersecting area will be 75% (transparency scales rather than adds). When more than two masks overlap, as in [**Ex.17a**], it gets even more interesting.

The Lighten mask mode is designed to counteract this problem. Its rule is: The More Opaque Mask Wins. In [**Ex.17a**], leave the top mask set to Add mode, and change the other masks to Lighten. The order of the masks doesn't matter in this case; as long as the *modes* are in this order, the mask with the higher Mask Opacity percentage controls the resulting opacity where they overlap. Intersecting areas will never be more opaque than the most opaque mask. Our result is shown in [**Ex.17b**].

The opposite problem occurs when you set overlapping masks to Intersect: Their opacity values are scaled down instead of building up. For instance, in [**Ex.17c**], two masks set to 50% Mask Opacity overlap in Add mode. Change Mask 2 to Intersect, and the opacity of the intersecting area will be 25%, appearing more transparent than either of the individual shapes. The Darken mask mode is designed to counteract this reduction in opacity. Change the second mask from Intersect to Darken, and the opacity of the intersecting area will remain at 50%. Where Mask Opacity values differ, the lower number will be used.

If all that talk of lighten-darken jargon has your head spinning, bear in mind that you will rarely use these special-case modes. If after creating multiple masks you need only a *single, consistent opacity value*, leave all the Mask Opacity settings at 100% and use the regular Opacity property as a master transparency control.

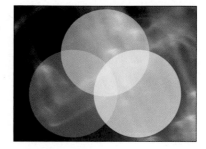

When overlapping masks have their own differing opacities, the overlapping areas appear more opaque than any individual shape. In comp [**Ex.17a**], Mask Opacity is set differently (30%, 50%, and 70%) for each circle. Background courtesy Artbeats/ Light Illusions.

Info in Percent

Set the Info panel's Option menu to Percent. Now you can move your cursor over the mask shapes and read the value of Alpha % in the Info panel.

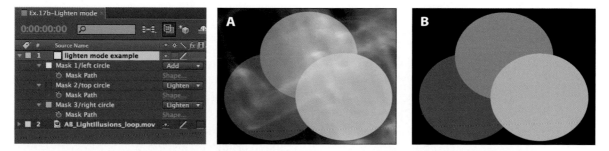

When three masks of varying opacities overlap each other and are set to Lighten mode (left), the overlapping region is only as opaque as the least transparent mask (A). The "lighten" logic makes sense if you turn off the background layer and look at just the resulting alpha channel (B): The "lighter" shapes in the alpha control the outcome.

Editing Multiple Masks

If you have multiple masks selected – even across multiple layers – editing any mask property other than Mask Path will affect all selected masks by the same relative amount.

You can reorder masks in the Timeline panel by dragging them up and down in the stack. A black line appears, showing you where in the stack you are dragging it to.

Mask Solo Keys

Shortcuts for revealing masking properties in the Timeline panel:

All Mask properties   MM
(two Ms in quick succession)

Mask Path   M

Mask Feather   F

Mask Expansion (no shortcut)

Mask Opacity   TT
(two Ts in quick succession)

Use the Shift key to add/sub-tract from a custom selection.

Management Advice

Following is a summary of tips for working with multiple masks:

• **Copying Masks:** You can copy and paste mask shapes from layer to layer, or within a layer. If you copy a mask shape you've selected in the Layer or Comp panel, you will copy only the Mask Path property. If you select the mask group name from the Timeline panel and copy, all four of the mask properties plus its mode will be copied. To copy the Feather, Opacity, or Expansion properties individually, click on the property name to select the value (and all keyframes on that track), and copy.

• **Pasting Masks:** When you select a layer and paste a Mask Path, if no masks are currently selected, a new Mask group will be created. If you first select an existing Mask Path in the Timeline or Layer panel, and then Paste, you will replace the selected mask. If the destination mask was animating, a new keyframe will be added (or the current keyframe replaced). Because you can easily replace a mask by accident, pay attention when you're pasting mask shapes. In a similar fashion, you can paste an entire mask group (Shape/Feather/Expansion/Opacity values) as a new mask group, or click on an existing Mask group name before you paste to replace all four values plus the mode. While you can copy multiple masks, you can paste multiple masks only as additional masks.

• **Reordering Masks:** When you have multiple masks on a layer, you can reorder them by dragging them up and down in the Timeline panel. This is useful when you use Mask Modes, as you may need to reorder the stack for masks to interact correctly.

• **Renaming a Mask Group:** You can rename a mask the same way you can rename layers. Select the mask group name in the Timeline panel, press Return, type in a new name, and press Return again. This comes in handy when masks relate to specific features, such as Left Eye, Right Eye, and so on. The new names appear in the Layer panel's Target menu also.

• **Color-Coding Masks:** When you're working with multiple masks, it's also helpful if each mask outline is a different color in the Layer and Comp panels. To change the color of a mask, click on the color swatch to the left of the mask's group name, and pick a new color from the color picker. A change in CS5 is that the next mask you create will use the new color.

• **Selecting Multiple Masks:** We saw earlier how you could select all the points on a mask by Option+clicking (Alt+clicking) the mask in the Layer or Comp panels. You can also select the entire mask shape by clicking on the mask group name, or just the Mask Path property, in the Timeline panel. This is a convenient way to select multiple mask shapes, as you can Shift+click to copy contiguous masks, or Command+click (Control+click) to select discontiguous masks. Remember that when you select the Mask group name and File > Copy, you're copying not just the Mask Path value, but the Mask Feather/Opacity/Expansion values and Mask Mode as well.

- **Deleting a Mask Group:** Select a Mask group name in the Timeline and press Delete to remove the mask group and all its keyframes. (If a keyframe is selected, it will delete the keyframe first, so you may need to press Delete a second time. Deleting a mask in the Comp or Layer panel works only if the entire mask is selected and no mask keyframes are selected.)

- **Locking and Hiding Masks:** When you're working with multiple masks, you can lock a mask to protect it from accidentally being edited. Just click the Lock box associated with each mask group in the A/V Features column. Masks will still appear in the Comp and Layer panels, but you won't be able to edit them or change any keyframes.

To hide locked masks from displaying, select Mask > Hide Locked Masks. To lock all selected masks, just click on the Lock switch for one of the selected masks. You can also right-click on a mask shape and select the Mask submenu to lock and unlock masks (plus perform other tasks).

- **Turning Off a Mask:** If a closed mask is being used by an effect, but is not meant to create transparency, change the Mask Modes popup in the Switches column from Add to None. The mask shape will still be available for editing, but it will not create transparency. If you want to hide a mask that's set to None, you must first Lock it, then Hide Locked Masks.

You can lock a mask to protect it from being edited accidentally; to reduce confusion, you can also select Layer > Masks > Hide Locked Masks to stop them from displaying while you continue to edit the unlocked masks.

Mask Target

In most cases, After Effects relies on the Mask Path you've selected to know if you want to edit, replace, or add a keyframe to a mask's shape. However, there is a case in which you need to use the Target menu in the Layer panel to determine which mask you're working on:

- Open [**Ex.18**] and double-click layer 1 to open its Layer panel. Select any mask tool and create a mask. Notice that as soon as you create a mask, the Target menu appears at the bottom of the Layer panel; it defaults to None.

- Press M to reveal Mask 1 in the Timeline panel and enable the stopwatch for Mask Path.

- Move the current time indicator later in time and use the same (or a different) Shape tool to start drawing a new mask shape. Note that even though you had Mask 1 selected, After Effects did not create a new keyframe – it created a new Mask 2.

- Undo until the new mask is gone and set the Target popup in the Layer panel to Mask 1. Now draw a new shape: It will create a second keyframe for Mask 1's Mask Shape.

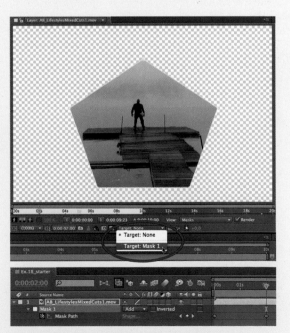

When drawing new shapes, select the mask being keyframed from the Target popup in the Layer panel to create new keyframes (otherwise, you'll create new masks).

Auto-trace

Auto-trace creates mask shapes based on the alpha, specific color channel, or luminance of a layer. It is an alternative to the new Roto Brush tool (Chapter 34), for those times when you really need a mask path – such as for effects that follow masks.

Step 1: Enable Preferences > User Interface Colors > Cycle Mask Colors. Auto-trace creates a lot of mask shapes; this will make it easier to tell them apart.

Step 2: Open **[Ex.19]**, and press 1 to move to 00:08; this reveals we need at least two mask shapes: the main outline, and the hole under the actor's arm.

Step 3: Select layer 1, then Layer > Auto-trace. Enable its Preview option to see preliminary results in the Comp panel. You will see mask outlines appear. To try to pull the actor out of the white background, set the Channel popup to Luminance. At the default Threshold of 50%, Auto-trace is trying to follow the squares in his jacket. Increase the Threshold (enter a new number and wait for the Comp panel to update) to reduce the number of spurious shapes – a value of 99 works well for this clip. Set the Time Span to Work Area to create masks for every frame of this movie. Click OK; wait a few seconds while After Effects works (the Info panel notes progress).

The Auto-trace dialog allows you to choose what channel to trace and how tightly to trace it. The Preview option makes it possible to tweak settings interactively.

Step 4: Press U to reveal the keyframes created. Auto-trace creates a new Mask Path whenever it sees a new feature it thinks it should follow, and keyframes Mask Opacity to turn it on and off. Spurious masks are easy to delete: Press Shift+F2 to deselect the masks, and select one at a time to see which is which in the Comp panel. Mask 1 should be the main outline; Mask 2 should be the hole under his arm; delete unnecessary shapes.

Step 5: Set Mask 1's mode popup (discussed earlier in this chapter) to Add. In this case, you will also need to enable Inverted. Set Mask 2's mode to Subtract to cut out the hole under the arm. Scrub the current time indicator and note the result; you judge if you'd be better off starting with this shape, or starting from scratch.

Our result is shown in **[Ex.19-final]**, where we added the Simple Choker effect to contract the edges.

Auto-trace is not exact – note the white edges, which are undesired snatches of the background – but it may be faster than starting from scratch. Footage courtesy Getty Images/Cool Characters.

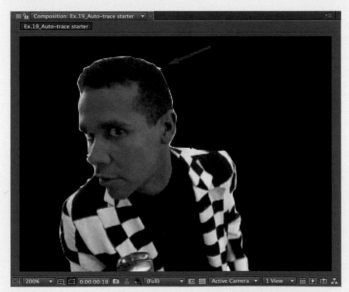

Rotoscoping Figures

While it is possible to create very complex shapes with the masking tools, masking moving figures out of a busy background (sometimes known as rotoscoping) is often a challenging task. If you have the luxury of planning ahead, shoot the action against a blue or green background and "key" it (Chapter 27). For footage that is already shot, After Effects CS5 introduced the Roto Brush tool (Chapter 34) which can intelligently differentiate between a foreground and background, but it has problems with footage where there is low contrast between the foreground and background – such as when an actor emerges from the shadows.

Therefore, some jobs require hand masking. Quite often, you don't want to approach the project by creating a single mask for an entire human figure or other complex shape. Instead, break the figure down into separate shapes for the head, torso, upper arm, lower arm, and so on. When the figure moves, you'll find it easier to keyframe the masks by concentrating on how each shape is changing. It may be possible to follow some of the shapes, such as the torso, by simply moving or scaling its respective mask.

Create your shapes just a little inside the shape being traced to get a clean edge that excludes the background. Objects that move or change shape quickly may need a keyframe every frame; others may be fine interpolating between shapes. Identify key points in the action, and create keyframes at these points in time first; then go halfway between these keyframes and adjust the mask as needed. Try to use RotoBezier masks, as they are known for interpolating more smoothly, and are often better suited for organic shapes. If the object was shot against a background with high contrast (such as a white seamless backdrop), you might try the Auto-trace tool to give you a starting point which you can clean up.

If you want to get a taste for what hand-rotoscoping entails, open comp [**Ex.20_starter**]. This is a relatively simple shot of a doctor staring at the camera, lowering his hand from his face. However, the similarity between the subject and the background causes fits for Roto Brush, Auto-trace, or any keying effect.

(Note: The footage was originally shot on film and telecined to 29.97 fps video, adding fields. We've already removed the 3:2 pulldown to revert the footage to its original 23.976 fps.)

mocha shape

The combination of mocha and mocha shape (Chapter 31) enables you to use motion tracking to adapt your shapes over time. You can also use Edit > Paste mocha mask to convert mocha shapes into masks.

To tackle this rotoscoping job, we've divided it into the head, shoulders, and hand, worrying about precision in just the areas where they don't overlap (above).

To keep the individual masks straight, color-code them by first enabling Preferences > User Interface Colors > Cycle Mask Colors, or change them yourself in the Timeline panel (below). This is the first frame; practice doing the entire shot – then you'll understand why you should charge so much for rotoscoping frame by frame. Footage from Artbeats/Retro Healthcare.

A Creative Alternative to Roto

You may come across a project in which a figure needs to be cut out of a background, but the budget doesn't allow for time-consuming precise masking. Rather than cut out the figure using a tight mask, create a funky mask outline loosely around the character. Animate the mask every few frames by moving the points. You might also try changing all the Mask Path keyframes to Hold keyframes for a really jumpy look. Add the Stroke effect to outline the mask shape, or add a Glow or Drop Shadow. An example of this is **[Ex.21a_funky mask]**. An alternative idea is to take advantage of the Wiggle Paths effect for a shape layer (see Chapter 32), then use it as a matte, as we did in **[Ex.21b_wiggle path]**.

Obviously, this doesn't suit every project – it works better when the subject matter is fun, or perhaps the audience is under the age of having taste. However, we once had a job that required *minutes* of footage to be cut out, and once the client agreed to go with this approach, it took us only days instead of weeks.

If it suits the job, consider wackier, creative solutions to otherwise tedious roto tasks. Here we're using a shape layer (with the "wiggle paths" effect) as a track matte.

Smoother Roto

RotoBezier masks interpolate more smoothly and with less "chattering" – because of this they are preferred for animated rotoscoping tasks.

The Pan Behind tool can be used to pan an image inside the mask directly in the Comp panel. It changes the values for Mask Path and Position in one step.

We've created a set of starter masks for the head, shoulders, and hand. They are set to Add mode, so they will add together to cut your final mask. Try animating the masks one at a time: First, do the head for the entire length of the clip, then the shoulders, then just where the hand and fingers appear outside the outlines of the head and shoulders – because they are all adding together, you don't need to be precise where they overlap. A fourth mask subtracts a hole between the hand and face. If you think this is the long approach, delete all the masks and start from scratch with one mask. We'll catch up with you later…

Panning a Layer Inside a Mask

Normally when you move a mask in the Layer panel, the "window" that reveals the image in the Comp panel moves across the frame. However, you may wish for this window to remain in a constant position in the Comp, and to pan the image inside the mask shape. To do this, After Effects needs to adjust two values: the position of the Mask Path (how the mask appears in relation to the layer in the Layer panel), and the value of Position (which is the position of the layer in relation to the comp). To make these two changes in one move, use the Pan Behind tool. We'll explore how it works, ending with a tease for an alternate way of working.

Open [Ex.22_starter] and notice the rectangular mask that's already created for layer 1. Select layer 1, and press M and Shift+P to reveal the Mask and Position properties in the Timeline panel. Select the Pan Behind tool (shortcut: Y), click *inside* the masked area, and drag the image to a new location. Notice that the mask stays stationary in the comp!

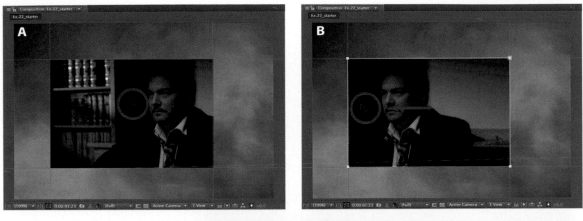

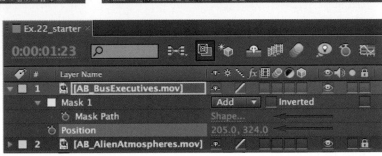

It achieves this feat by changing the values for both Position and Mask Path at the same time.

You can see what is going on more clearly by opening the movie in the Layer panel, and then placing the Layer and Comp panels side by side (as you did earlier in this chapter, on page 158). As you use the Pan Behind tool in the Comp panel, notice that the mask moved in relation to the image in the Layer panel, and that Position has changed by the same amount in the opposite direction. Press V to return to the Selection tool.

If that's all you plan on doing with Pan Behind, it works pretty well. But problems arise if you've already created a motion path for Position: The Pan Behind tool changes the value of Position only *at the current frame* – it can't offset all your Position keyframes at once. In a case like this, you'll have to move the mask using the regular Selection tool, then select all the Position keyframes and move the entire motion path so that the "window" moves back into position in the Comp panel.

Similarly, problems arise if you've animated the Mask Path (as we did for this layer earlier in [**Ex.07-final**]). Using the Pan Behind tool would only affect the position of the path at the current frame.

You can animate the Pan Behind effect, provided you turn on the stopwatch for *both* Mask Path and Position. Practically speaking, the Pan Behind feature is useful only if you're animating how the mask moves across the image and you don't need to have a separate Position motion path. Personally, we find animating Pan Behind cumbersome to use and prefer to set up this kind of effect using nested compositions. In this case, you would pan the image in the first comp, nest this in a second comp, and apply the mask (see *A Better "Pan Behind"* at the end of Chapter 18). You'll then be able to easily reposition the "window" in the second comp without having to move lots of keyframes.

With the Pan Behind tool active, drag the movie in the Comp panel from one position (A) to another (B) – the mask stays stationary in the comp. Note that both the layer's Position and Mask Path shape values change (above).

FACTOID

Triple Duty Tool

The Pan Behind tool performs two additional tasks: It edits the Anchor Point and Position together (Chapter 3), and it works as a Slip Edit tool for layer bars in the Timeline panel (Chapter 6).

Masks for Effect

Effects that include a popup called Path are capable of using a mask path to determine how they draw. This is discussed in more depth in Chapter 22; we'll touch on the basics here.

Some effects that use mask shapes include Audio Spectrum, Audio Waveform, Smear, Fill, Stroke, Scribble, and Vegas; Text layers (Chapter 21) can also follow mask paths. An example using the Stroke effect plus text is shown in **[Ex.23]**. To prevent the mask from creating transparency, set its Mode popup to None (this is the default for masks applied to Text layers).

Note that an effect can access only masks created on the same layer, and they see only the Mask Path – not the Feather, Opacity, or Expansion values. For example, in **[Ex.23]** select layer 2 and

Text layers plus effects such as Stroke can follow mask shapes. In **[Ex.22]**, masks are also used to isolate the singer and the circles. Image courtesy Digital Vision/Music Mix.

type MM to see its mask properties (if not already visible). Scrub Mask Expansion for Mask 5, which Stroke uses: The dotted lines are *not* offset to match.

TIP

Shapes Not Pasting?

When you're copying shapes from Illustrator, in Preferences > File Handling & Clipboard enable the AICB option. If you don't, and quit Illustrator before pasting, the masks won't paste into After Effects.

FACTOID

Text Outlines

In the most recent versions of After Effects, you may convert text layers (Chapter 21) either to shape layers (Chapter 32) or solids with mask paths. These options appear under the Layer menu when a text layer is selected.

Interchangeable Paths

After Effects considers mask paths, shape paths, and motion paths to be somewhat interchangeable. Thinking along the same lines will expand your bag of tricks! Here are some ideas of what you can do once you've created a path:

• Create a mask path for an effect to follow (see sidebar above) or as a path for text to run along (see Chapter 21). Note that effects and text can use only *mask* paths, not shape layer paths.

• Copy/paste paths between masks and shape layers (Chapter 32). Shape layers can create shapes with strokes, gradient fills, and more. If you are in the habit of creating solid layers, then creating a border with a mask and the Stroke effect, use a shape layer instead. Note that while shape layers offer shape effects such as zigzag and wiggle paths, these are post-processed; when you copy the shape layer's Path property to a Mask Path, the path loses its wiggle.

• Copy/paste between mask/shape paths and Paint Brush strokes (Paint is covered in Chapter 33).

• Copy paths from Illustrator or Photoshop, which you can then use for either a mask/shape path or a paint brush stroke.

• Copy/paste any paths to and from a motion path, which is covered in this section. This includes using Motion Sketch (Chapter 5) to create Position keyframes which can be pasted to any Path property.

• Use Expressions (Chapter 37) to have any path follow any other pen or brush-based path. (We used this technique in [**Ex.21b_wiggle path**].)

Working with Illustrator Paths

Although After Effects includes a Pen tool, many artists are more comfortable using the drawing tools in Adobe Illustrator. In addition to a full-featured tool set, Illustrator's Pathfinder panel can be used to create a new single shape from the interaction of multiple shapes, and it can use one shape to divide, trim, and crop any other shape. Illustrator also has automatic tools for creating spirals, artistic brush strokes, and various effects for distorting paths.

It's easy to copy and paste paths from Illustrator to After Effects. If you combine this technique with the Stroke effect, you'll find the result very handy for revealing curved lines or shapes in Illustrator files. To practice this technique, open [**Ex.24_starter**], where we've imported a layered Illustrator file. What were vector fills and strokes in Illustrator are now rendered as pixels in After Effects – *the underlying paths are not accessible.*

When you import a layered Illustrator file as a Composition, the vectors are converted to pixels – the paths themselves are not available in After Effects.

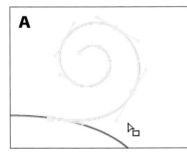

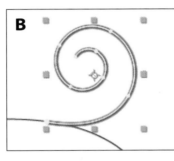

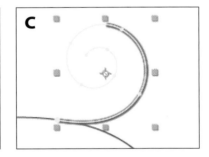

Step 1: Select layer 1 – **top spiral** – and press Command+E (Control+E) to open the **IllustratorShapes.ai** file in Illustrator. Select the topmost spiral path and File > Copy it.

Step 2: Bring After Effects forward and with the **top spiral** layer still selected, File > Paste to create a new mask. The path should paste in exactly the same place as the rendered stroke (if not, you may need to move or scale it using Free Transform Points).

Step 3: Now that you have a vector path to work with, apply Effect > Generate > Stroke; it will default to using Mask 1. The Stroke effect will *regenerate* the line, so set the effect's Paint Style popup to On Transparent so that the original pixels do not render. Now set the Color and Brush Size to taste. To animate the line, turn on the stopwatch for the End parameter and animate it from 0–100%. (Animating effects is covered in Chapter 22.) With a large Brush Size, the stroke may be clipped by the layer boundary: If so, apply Effect > Utility > Grow Bounds before the Stroke effect.

Repeat this trick with the **middle spiral** and **bottom spiral**; you can then offset the layers in time, as we did in [**Ex.24-final**].

Paste the path from Illustrator to the same layer in After Effects (A). Apply the Stroke effect and set the color and brush size to taste (B). With Paint Style set to On Transparent (below), animate the End parameter to draw on the line over time (C).

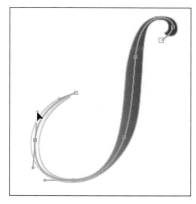

Step 1: With the Pen tool, draw a mask path through the centerline of your curved object.

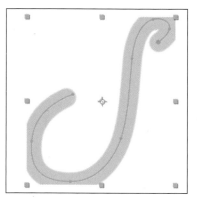

Step 2: Apply the Stroke effect and increase the Brush Size until the object is obscured.

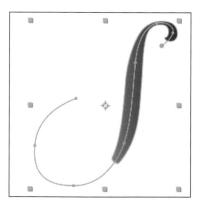

Step 3: Set the Paint Style to Reveal Original Image, then animate the Start or End parameters to wipe on the shape.

Wiping on Curved Shapes

If you've ever tried to animate a mask around a curved object, you know it is a frustrating experience. Here's a handy trick for using a mask path and the Stroke effect to do this more easily.

In [**Ex.24_starter**], select the **S-Shape** layer. Press Command+E (Control+E) to check out this shape in the Illustrator file; it does not have a "centerline" path like the spiral layers. However, there is nothing stopping you from creating this path directly in After Effects:

Step 1: In After Effects, select the Pen tool and draw a mask path *along the centerline* of the **S-Shape** layer, starting at either end. You don't have to be totally accurate, and you can tweak it later if need be.

Step 2: Return to the Selection tool and apply the Stroke effect. Increase the effect's Brush Size parameter until the underlying shape is completely obscured. (Any color stroke will do as we'll be using its alpha channel; also, don't worry if the stroke is clipped by the layer size.)

Step 3: Set the effect's Paint Style popup to Reveal Original image, then animate the Start or End parameter to wipe on or off the shape.

Note that if you use any of the artistic brushes in Illustrator to create objects, you will also need to use this alternate technique. Try it for yourself with layer 5, **art brush**. Select the layer and hot-key to Illustrator: Although the path looks simple and appears to have a "centerline," if you copy and paste it into After Effects, you'll end up with multiple mask paths.

More on Pasting Paths

You can also copy and paste multiple paths in one step. Closed paths are assigned the Difference Mask Mode as a default, but you're free to change the mode if you need some other behavior.

If you want to interpolate from one shape to another over time, you have to ensure that all the shapes are pasted to the same Mask Path track – otherwise, you'll end up with multiple masks that are independent of each other. After you paste your first shape, turn on the stopwatch for Mask Path; before you paste another shape at a different point in time, check that the Mask Path property remains highlighted. (You can also target this mask track using the Layer panel's Target popup.) If you're having problems interpolating between complex mask shapes, refer to the section *Mask Interpolation* (page 186).

Pasting paths from Photoshop is a very similar experience. However, newer versions of Photoshop offer Paths, Vector Masks, and Shape Layers. You will need to copy and paste Photoshop Paths to After Effects, as you did with Illustrator above. When you import the Photoshop file as a Composition (Chapter 38), Vector Masks and Shape Layers will convert automatically to After Effects' shape layers (Chapter 32).

Finally, copying paths is also a two-way street: You can copy path keyframes in After Effects and paste them to Illustrator as a path, or to Photoshop as either a path or a shape layer.

Mask Paths to Motion Paths

In After Effects, you can paste a mask shape into any parameter that has X and Y coordinates, such as a layer's Position or Anchor Point, a plug-in's Effect Point, or the Position or Point of Interest of a camera or light. The mask path will become a motion path for these properties. You can also reverse the process by pasting a motion path back to a mask (or shape layer) path.

To practice pasting a mask shape to Position, open [**Ex.25_starter**]. Layer 2 has a circular mask surrounding a circle in the image, and you'd like layer 1 to rotate along this circle:

Step 1: Select Mask 1 > Mask Path for layer 2 and File > Copy. Note that masks are always drawn in relation to the layer (known as *layer space*), and layer 2 is much larger than the comp's size.

Step 2: Select layer 1 – **CM_sensor_sqr.tif** – and press P if Position if not revealed. Click on the word "Position" in the Timeline to target this property and File > Paste. The path will appear as a motion path in the Comp panel and keyframes in the Timeline panel. Because Position keyframes are in "comp space," you will need to drag the motion path in the Comp panel until it lines up with the image in the background (repositioning motion paths was covered in Chapter 5).

You can paste a mask shape directly to Position, where it becomes a motion path with a duration of 02:00; you may need to reposition it in the Comp panel (above). Drag the first or last keyframe in the Timeline (below) to change the duration of the animation. Background courtesy Digital Vision/Data:Funk.

Note that the First Vertex Point (covered on page 170) of the Mask Path sets where the motion path begins and ends.

The timing of the animation defaults to two seconds, but since the middle keyframes are automatically converted to Roving keyframes, you can drag the last keyframe along the timeline to lengthen or shorten the animation. If the animation travels in the direction opposite to what you expected, select all the keyframes and apply Animation > Keyframe Assistant > Time-Reverse Keyframes (covered in Chapter 5).

Step 3: You can also have the sensor automatically rotate as it moves around the path. With the sensor layer selected, apply Layer > Transform > Auto-Orient, and select the Orient Along Path option (covered in Chapter 5). Our result is shown in [**Ex.25-final**], using two sensors.

The flexibility for copying and pasting opens up a whole host of new possibilities: For instance, a simple logo shape could be copied from Illustrator and pasted into an effect point path, such as a particle system, so that fairy dust could animate around the edge of the logo over time. Not that *you* would ever stoop to such a thing…

Free Transform Tips

When you're pasting paths from Illustrator or Photoshop for use as motion paths, first apply them to a solid layer of the same size, then transform the mask path using Free Transform. Then when you paste them to Position, the motion path will line up as Layer and Comp space will be the same (see [**Ex.26**]).

Of course, you can use this trick whenever you want to resize a motion path: Copy Position keyframes to a Mask Path on a full-frame solid layer, Free Transform it, then paste it back to Position!

▲ Default Interpolation ▲ Using Mask Interpolation

[Ex.27_Bottle-final] includes two mask path shapes – a champagne bottle and a martini glass. The red shape sequence shows the default mask interpolation at one-second intervals; the green shapes are the same two keyframes interpolated with Mask Interpolation.

Mask Interpolation

When After Effects interpolates between two very different mask shapes, the result often resembles blobs that only a lava lamp could love. The Mask Interpolation keyframe assistant (formerly called Smart Mask Interpolation) helps shepherd After Effects down more desirable paths.

To get a taste, close all comps and open [**Ex.27_Bottle_starter**], which animates a champagne bottle shape to a martini glass. RAM Preview; the bottle looks like it melts rather than morphs. Select layer 1, press M, and click on Mask Path to select its keyframes. Then open Window > Mask Interpolation. Click Apply, and After Effects will calculate new mask points and keyframes. Now RAM Preview again: The green bottle morphs in a much more orderly fashion. Try the same with the football-to-barbell morph in [**Ex.28*Football starter**]; Mask Interpolation means the difference between an orderly morph and one that resembles a prehistoric animal in the middle.

Mask Interpolation achieves these results by changing the points (vertices) along the mask, creating intermediate keyframes that use these extra points to keep After Effects on the desired path (below).

Quite often, the secret is setting the First Vertex Point to a mask point that makes sense. The area around this point tends to distort the least, so you may need to experiment to see which point works best. Indeed, picking a good First Vertex can cure problems with ordinary mask interpolation; in **Ex.29** Mask Interpolation buys very little improvement.

The Smart Approach

Now that you have a taste for its power, let's study the parameters in the Mask Interpolation panel in more detail and give it a more thorough workout. The parameters generally fall into three areas of control: frame rate, interpolation, and vertex placement.

Keyframe Rate: Controls how often new keyframes are created. The default is one per frame of the comp. More keyframes mean a more controlled interpolation; if you become overwhelmed, try reducing the rate. Regardless of this setting, Mask Interpolation will also always create additional keyframes just after the first and before the last keyframes you set, which it uses to establish its additional mask path vertices. If you plan to field render your final output, set Keyframe Rate to the frame rate you will use for rendering, and enable Keyframe Fields. Otherwise, you will get odd shape jumps at the start and end of interpolation.

There are three parameters which control whether Mask Interpolation follows a curvy, organic path or a rigid, geometric one:

Use Linear Vertex Paths: When this is enabled, Mask Interpolation will move all of the mask points in a straight line between its first and last keyframes. Disabling this option allows the interpolation to follow more organic curved paths. However, disabling it can cause wild swings in the mask shape; try for yourself with [**Ex.30_starter**] or RAM Preview the result in [**Ex.30-final**].

Bending Resistance: Decides how fluid the mask shape is during interpolation. Lower settings allow the shapes to bend more; higher settings maintain more rigid, geometric shapes. The default of 50% is a good compromise.

Matching Method: Leaving it at Auto works most of the time; change it only if you're having problems. Use the Curve setting for organic interpolations; Polyline for more rigid ones.

The other parameters control how many intermediate mask points (vertices) the assistant creates, and how it interpolates between them:

Add Mask Path Vertices: The more mask vertices, the more accurate the interpolation (and the longer it takes to compute). Enabling this allows Mask Interpolation to create additional vertices. To precisely set the number created, set the popup underneath to Total Vertices and adjust the number to its left.

Quality and **Use 1:1 Vertex Matches:** These decide how the rest of the mask vertices interpolate. You often want to let Mask Interpolation decide how to move one vertex to another; that means disabling Use 1:1 Vertex Matches, and optionally increasing Quality.

First Vertices Match: Keeping this enabled is crucial for having interpolations proceed in a predictable manner. Just as critical is where the first vertex is for each of your mask shapes. Set the first vertex (the one with a slightly larger square) to locations where you know you want "point A" to end up at "point B" (the first vertex tends to serve as the "anchor" for the interpolating shapes). To practice changing the first vertex for a mask shape, open [**Ex.31_mask shapes**], select a single mask point at the base of each shape, and choose Layer > Mask and Shape Path > Set First Vertex.

Window > Mask Interpolation needs to be set up differently depending on the type of animation you desire.

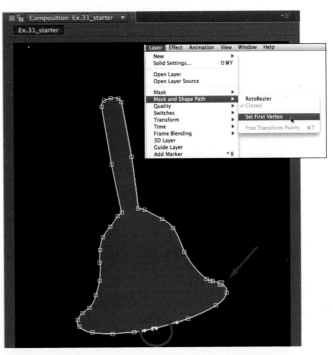

The current First Vertex Point (where the red arrow is pointing) needs to be set to a similar reference point on each mask path keyframe, such as a point centered on the top or bottom.

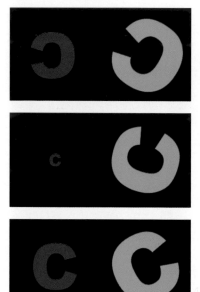

[Ex.32-final]: To allow shapes to rotate or otherwise follow more organic paths, disable Use Linear Vertex Paths. The blue shape is the result of a linear interpolation; the green shape rotates thanks to disabling this option.

TIP

Speed Shifts

Mask Interpolation ignores your original keyframe interpolation. To add ease in and out to the result, set the first and second-to-last keyframes to Hold, and precompose (with Move All Attributes on). Enable Time Remapping for the nested comp layer in the main comp. Use this to retime the shape morph. See **[Ex.35]** for more tips.

The red shape is the result of normal interpolation. The green shape uses Mask Interpolation with Use Linear Vertex Paths enabled; the top of the interpolated shape does not grow beyond the height of the original shapes (marked by the blue line). The blue shape has Linear Vertex disabled; it is more fluid, but does not stay "in bounds."

Along the Curve

Having shapes interpolate in a more curvy, organic fashion or rotate as they move requires deviating from the default settings. Close all open comps, open **[Ex.32_starter]** and RAM Preview. We started with a "C" character shape (keyframe 2) and rotated the mask 180° with Free Transform Points (keyframe 1). With the default interpolation, it inverts itself as it animates, looking not unlike a scale animation.

• Reveal the Mask Path keyframes for the second layer, select them, and apply Mask Interpolation with Use Linear Vertex Paths enabled. RAM Preview; you get a surprisingly similar result.

• Undo until the new keyframes are gone, disable the Use Linear Vertex Paths option, and click Apply again. RAM Preview; now the shape rotates instead of inverts, but the shape spins with an offset.

• Undo again and this time set the Add Mask Vertices popup to Total Vertices (the default of 100 is fine). Click Apply; with more vertices added for accuracy, the character stays centered as it rotates. The result is shown in **[Ex.32-final]**.

Straight and Narrow

When you have strong, angular geometric shapes, you need to set up Mask Interpolation to be stiffer to keep these shapes intact. Open **[Ex.33_starter]** and RAM Preview. Here we've set up three copies of the letter L morphing to the letter Z. Layer 1 is our reference of the normal interpolation, and so we've locked it for safekeeping. Select the Mask Path keyframes for layer 2 by clicking on the words "Mask Path," enable the Use Linear Vertex Paths option in Mask Interpolation, and apply. Scrub the current time indicator; the movement is pretty good!

Now select the Mask Path keyframes for layer 3, disable Use Linear Vertex Paths, and apply Mask Interpolation. As you scrub or RAM Preview, note how the top of the blue character grows as it morphs, extending above the pale blue guide line. Undo until your new keyframes are gone, try increasing Bending Resistance or setting the Matching Method to Polyline, and reapply: These "stiffen" techniques help, but unless Use Linear Vertex paths is enabled, the top of the character still wants to grow. The three results are displayed in **[Ex.33-final]**.

Inside-Out Interpolation

If a shape interpolates inside out (as is the case with [**Ex.34**]), you may need to reverse the path of the offending shape. Select the mask path keyframe, copy it, paste into Illustrator, use Object > Compound Path > Make, and reverse the path direction in the Attributes panel (see right). Copy and paste back to After Effects.

Smart Practice

We'll end by walking you through ideas that show some of the possibilities of combining Mask Interpolation with shape layers and track mattes (both discussed later in this book).

In [**Ex.36a_starter**], we want to use Mask Interpolation to interpolate from the bell shape to the guitar shape; we can then paste this mask to a shape layer to make the result more interesting. Before you start, remember to set the First Vertex for each keyframe's shape to the same relative point on both the bell and the guitar. We chose the bottom center (if you're stumped, we've already done this for you in [**Ex.36b**]).

Now practice using Mask Interpolation to create a smooth morph between these shapes. Our result is shown in [**Ex.36c**].

If you already have experience playing with shape layers (Chapter 32), copy your Mask Path animation. Create a new shape layer with the Pen tool and paste your animated mask keyframes into its Path parameter. We've done this in [**Ex.36d**]; while we were at it, we filled it with a gradient. We also used a gradient stroke, setting the Line Join to a Round Join to avoid spikes.

Now apply Add > Wiggle Paths to your shape layer. Wiggle automatically bends and moves path segments between vertices. Since the Mask Interpolation keyfame assistant greatly increases the number of vertices between the original keyframes, we deleted the original (first and last) keyframes to avoid "pops" in the wiggled outline. Our version is in [**Ex.36e**].

For a last example, composition [**Ex.37**] shows using an animated mask (layer 1) as a track matte for a video (layer 2). Track mattes are covered in the next chapter.

We hope you're now getting more ideas of your own!

Ex.36 starts with these two musical shapes pasted from Illustrator (**10_Chapter Sources > Shapes.ai**).

[**Ex.36e**] contains a smartly interpolated mask shape pasted into a shape layer, which then has its path wiggled.

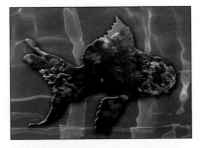

[**Ex.37**] uses a solid with a mask interpolation animation as a track matte for the video in layer 2. Footage from Artbeats/ Under the Sea and Water Textures.

CONNECT

Opacity and semitransparent layers: Chapter 3.

Easy Ease: Chapter 4.

Auto-orient rotation, moving and scaling motion paths using parenting: Chapter 5.

Motion blur: Chapter 8.

Track mattes: Chapter 11.

Nesting compositions, Preserve Frame Rate option: Chapter 18.

Text along a mask path: Chapter 21.

Mask shapes with effects: Chapter 22.

Keying: Chapter 27.

Time remapping: Chapter 28.

Masking with motion stabilization: Chapter 29.

mocha and mocha shape: Chapter 31.

Illustrator plus shape layers: Chapter 32.

Roto Brush: Chapter 34.

Interpreting footage with fields and removing 3:2 pulldown are covered in Chapters 38 and 41.

All About Track Mattes

Mastering track mattes is a prerequisite for creating complex multilayered compositions.

We've been reinforcing the idea throughout this book that managing transparencies is the cornerstone of creating composite images. But not all images come with their own transparencies – or ones we necessarily want to use. Sometimes, we'd prefer to borrow another image to create those transparencies. This second image is called a *matte*.

A matte can be a grayscale still image, another movie, or an animated graphic such as text. At the end of the day, After Effects sees it as a collection of grayscale levels which it uses to define the transparency of another layer. Understanding matte logic and how to use mattes in a hierarchy of comps is one of the keys to creating complex animations.

What's in a Matte?

Creating an alpha channel in Photoshop is often the best option for simple still image composites. But what if you need to create an alpha channel for a QuickTime movie? To achieve this effect, we use After Effects' Track Matte feature. This feature has two options: Luma Matte or Alpha Matte. Whether you use the Luma or Alpha Matte setting is determined by *where* the grayscale information you want to use as a matte resides; there is otherwise no real difference between the two. If you create a grayscale image to use as a matte, it's applied as a luma matte (see *Under the Hood*, page 193). But if the grayscale information resides in another layer's alpha channel, it's an alpha matte. Either way, you're giving your movie a new grayscale image (or movie) to use as a transparency channel.

No matter which variation of Track Matte you use, there are three simple rules to follow to make it behave in After Effects:

- The Matte layer must be placed directly on top of the Movie layer.
- Set the Track Matte popup for the Movie layer, *not* the Matte layer.
- The Matte layer's Video switch (the "eyeball") should remain off.

Creating a Luma Matte Effect

Let's jump in and set up a track matte. In this chapter's Example Project file (**11-Example Project.aep**), we've already imported a variety of sources and mattes for you to experiment with. We've also included a few final compositions for you to see how things should have turned out. First, let's practice creating a track matte effect:

Example Project

Explore the 11-Example Project.aep file as you read this chapter; references to [Ex.##] refer to specific compositions within the project file.

Step 1: Choose any D1-sized movie you want to use from the **Sources > Movies** folder in the Project panel and drag it to the New Composition icon at the bottom of the Project panel. This will create and open a new comp with the same size and duration as the movie; make sure it's set to 100% zoom and Full Resolution.

Step 2: From the **Sources > Mattes** folder, select **GrungeOval_matte.tif** to use as a matte. Press Command+/ on Mac (Control+/ on Windows) to add the matte to the comp; it should be on top of the movie.

Step 3: Make sure the Modes pane is visible in the Timeline panel. You can either use the Expand Transfer Controls button in the bottom left of the Timeline panel, or click the Toggle Switches/Modes button (shortcut: F4). The Track Matte, abbreviated to TrkMat, is the rightmost popup. For the movie layer, select Luma Matte from the Track Matte popup. Note that the name of the matte is included in the popup – this is a reminder that the layer *above* is being used as a matte. (Layer 1 has no popup available because there is no layer above *it* that could be used.)

As soon as you set the Track Matte popup, notice that the Video switch turns off for the matte layer. You will now see the movie you selected framed by the matte layer on top. If that's not the case, compare your results with ours in [**Ex.01-Luma Matte-final**]. You may need to turn the Video switch back on for the matte when you're applying effects or animating it, but the eyeball should remain off when it's time to render. Also, if you move the movie up or down in the layer stack, make sure you also select the matte layer so they stay together as a group.

As a clue that a Track Matte is in use, black-and-white icons are drawn directly to the left of both the matte and movie layer names, the eyeball

A movie (left) is dragged into a comp first, followed by a grayscale matte image (center) on top. When the movie is set to use a Luma Track Matte, the result is the movie being "cut out" by the matte layer (right). Underwater footage from Artbeats/Under The Sea 1.

FACTOID

Head Scratching…

Matte not working? Make sure that the matte is on top of the movie and that the popup is set for the movie layer, not the matte.

To tell the movie to use the layer above as a matte, the movie layer's Track Matte popup is set to Luma Matte, which then automatically turns off the Video switch for the matte layer on top.

After creating a track matte in **[Ex.01]**, areas in the comp where the background color is visible indicate transparency. You can also toggle on the Transparency Grid to view this transparency as a checkerboard pattern.

for the movie layer's Video switch is filled in solid, and the white line that ordinarily separates layers is even more subtle.

Just for fun, change the Track Matte popup to Alpha Matte. The movie appears full frame. Double-click the matte layer to open it in its Layer panel, and set the Show Channel popup at the bottom of this panel to Alpha. Since the matte layer was a grayscale image and had no alpha channel, After Effects filled the alpha channel with white (see *Under the Hood* sidebar). When you use this alpha as a matte, it displays the movie fully opaque. Return to the Comp panel and revert back to Luma Matte.

The comp's background at this point might look like it's just black (or whatever color the Background Color is set to), but if you click on the Toggle Transparency Grid button at the bottom of the Comp panel, you'll see that it actually represents transparency. This transparency means you can either composite another layer in the background, or render this comp with an alpha channel for compositing elsewhere.

Black Illustrator type against a black comp background can be hard to see. Option+click (Alt+click) on the Show Channel button at the bottom of the Comp panel to view the alpha channel and you'll see a matte in waiting.

Creating an Alpha Matte Effect

Creating a track matte using an alpha matte rather than a luma matte is very similar; the only real difference is the character of the source you're using for your matte. For example, Illustrator artwork usually works better as an alpha matte:

Step 1: Open comp **[Ex.02_starter]**. It may appear all black, even though there is a layer in it already. This is because the layer consists of black Illustrator text – not a very good luma matte, since it contains no luminance! To verify there is something there, either click the Toggle Transparency Grid button, or change the comp's background color (Composition > Background Color) to a color other than black.

Step 2: Select a movie from the **Sources > Movies** folder and add it to the comp as well; we designed this example around **AB_OceanWaterEffects.mov**, but feel free to try other sources, including your own.

Our movie (right) is set to use the text layer above as an alpha matte. The movie now plays inside the type (far right). Footage courtesy Artbeats/Ocean Water Effects.

Step 3: Use what you've learned so far to apply the text as an alpha track matte for the movie layer.

(Having a problem? Remember to place the matte layer above the movie layer, and set the Track Matte popup for the movie layer, not the matte.)

You should now see the movie cut out by the Illustrator text. Again, toggle the transparency grid to illustrate these transparent areas clearly. In contrast, try the Luma Matte settings: The image disappears. This is because the matte layer is black in color, which means totally transparent to a luma matte. Of course, if you filled the text layer with white (Effect > Generate > Fill), it would work as either a luma *or* an alpha matte!

Under the Hood

When you're deciphering how Track Mattes work inside After Effects, it may help to review how imported footage is treated. After Effects considers each footage item in a project as containing 32 bits of information: 24 bits of color information (Red, Green, Blue), and 8 bits of transparency information (Alpha). (When using 16-bit-per-channel sources, these numbers obviously double.) But that doesn't mean everything you import has to have four channels. If you import a regular QuickTime movie or any other 24-bit (RGB) source, the program will assign an alpha channel to it. Since it assumes you want the movie to be visible, this alpha channel will be completely white. Similarly, if you import a grayscale image, After Effects will place a copy of this image in each of the Red, Green, and Blue channels, then add a fully white alpha channel.

So just because your grayscale matte may look like an alpha channel to you, this does not mean it will be transparent when it's added to a composition – its pixels reside in RGB colorspace. However, if you were to instruct After Effects to look at this layer's luminance to use as a matte, it would collapse the RGB image back to grayscale and use what in essence is your original grayscale image for the matte.

In short, when you're using a grayscale image as a matte, select the Luma Matte option. You'll use the Alpha Matte option when the matte image is defined

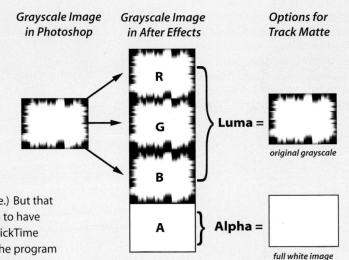

Grayscale Image in Photoshop *Grayscale Image in After Effects* *Options for Track Matte*

R

G

B   **Luma =**

original grayscale

A   **Alpha =**

full white image

Because After Effects always thinks internally in terms of R, G, and B color channels plus an alpha, even a grayscale image is divided into these channels (the same grayscale values are copied into each of the color channels), then its luminance is calculated.

by the alpha channel of the matte layer rather than by the luminance of its color channels, or when the matte is an Illustrator file.

Finally, a layer used as a matte should have its Video switch (the eyeball) turned off. You don't want to see this layer; it's only in the comp to provide information to the layer below. However, After Effects *does* see any masks, effects, or transformations you may have applied to the matte layer – it just uses them internally, rather than directly displaying them in the comp.

ORIGINAL IMAGE

A

ALPHA

B

LUMA

Some footage items work as either alpha or luma mattes. This microphone (above) has both an alpha channel (A) and its own interesting luminance (B). It therefore can be used as an alpha matte (C) or a luma matte (D). Gray luminance values create partial transparency. Microphone courtesy Classic PIO/Microphones.

C

ALPHA TRACK MATTE

D

LUMA TRACK MATTE

To Luma or To Alpha?

As you can see, alpha mattes behave just like luma mattes; they just look at different information in the source to create the matte. So how can you tell whether to use a luma or alpha matte? When you're starting out, you'll probably try one, and if that doesn't work, you'll try the other. Most of the time, the right choice depends on whether the transparency information in the matte resides in the color or alpha channels. The rest of the time, it is a creative decision.

[**Ex.03**] contains the **AB_UnderTheSea** movie that we used in an earlier example, a microphone for a matte, and a background layer. The microphone is from a still image "object" library, so it has an alpha channel cutting it out from its background – but the image can also be looked upon as a luma matte. Try both Track Matte options and compare the visual results.

Adding a Background

Once you've assigned a Track Matte, the matte will create transparent areas. You can then add a background layer by simply adding a new layer to the comp and sending this layer to the back. You don't need to also create an inverted matte for the background layer; the background will automatically fill the transparent holes.

An example of this is shown in [**Ex.04-Split Screen**]. Here, the matte is an animated "torn edge" (prerendered with the Roughen Edges plug-in), with the luma matte applied to the **AB_Gears** movie. The movie on

A half black/half white grayscale image is used as a matte to create a split-screen effect.

the right side is a background layer, and it comes through on its own in the areas where the matted layer above it is transparent.

Track Matte Inverted

So far, we've been applying mattes directly to movies to highlight a portion of them that we want to show through. However, it often makes sense to do the opposite: apply a matte inverted, so its white areas actually punch a hole through a layer, creating a picture frame effect. It now becomes easier to swap out movies behind this matted layer, or to use a composite of multiple layers inside the frame.

[**Ex.05-Inverted Luma_starter**] is an example of this. The layer to be matted is layer 2, **AB_Space_Planets.mov**. The matte layer (layer 1) has a white center with a black border.

To punch a hole through the center of the space movie with this matte, set the Track Matte popup for layer 2 to Luma Inverted. Now try adding other movies into this comp, dragging them below the space layer – they'll show through this rectangular hole. Switch this popup between Luma and Luma Inverted if you're not clear on what it is doing. Our version is shown in [**Ex.05-Inverted Luma-final**].

The same "inverted matte" concept applies to alpha mattes as well. Go back to [**Ex.02-Alpha Matte-final**] and try switching it to Alpha Inverted; the water movie will now appear outside the type.

When the split-screen matte is applied to the gears movie (left), the black areas become transparent, allowing a second movie (center) to show through (right). Footage courtesy Artbeats/Gears and Digital Web.

A typical matte has a white center and black border (above left). To punch a hole through another layer, set the Track Matte to Luma Inverted (below). Any footage placed behind this frame will show through the hole (above right). Footage courtesy Artbeats/Space & Planets and Retro Healthcare.

CLOCK OBJECT

LUMA MATTE

LUMA INVERTED MATTE

When our alarm clock object (A) is used as a luma matte (B), the gears movie shows through the light silver case but is transparent where the face is black or the clock's alpha channel cuts it out. If you want the clock face to be opaque, an inverted luma matte will do that – but since it inverts the *result* of the track matte, the area outside the alpha shows up (C). However, if you apply the Invert effect to the clock, this will invert its color channels (D). When used now as a regular Luma Matte (E), the result is that the clock's alpha is honored, and only the face area is opaque as desired. Clock courtesy Classic PIO/Sampler.

CLOCK WITH INVERT EFFECT

INVERT EFFECT + LUMA MATTE

Using the Invert Effect

There are occasions when using an inverted matte does not give the desired result. This occurs when you are using a layer as a luma matte, and it also happens to have an alpha channel. When a layer is used as a luma matte, any alpha channel the matte layer has is also factored into the equation. This means that regardless of the luminance values of the image inside the alpha, any area outside the alpha (where the alpha is black) is considered to be luminance = black.

Yes, it sounds confusing, so let's run through an example. [**Ex.06a-Inverted Track Matte**] contains an alarm clock object; it so happens that this clock has a black face – which means when used as a luma matte, the face would be mostly transparent. If you wanted the layer being matted to show through this face, your first instinct might be to use an inverted luma matte. However, that "black" area outside the hole cut by the alpha channel becomes "white" when inverted – causing the matted layer to be shown through as well. Try both Luma and Luma Inverted to compare.

If you want to invert the luma matte effect but still want the alpha channel of the layer being used as a matte to be obeyed, apply Effect > Channel > Invert to the matte layer; the default settings should work fine. This will invert the color channels of the matte (its luminance), but leave its alpha channel alone. This is shown in [**Ex.06b-Invert Effect**]; select the matte layer and open the Effect Controls panel (shortcut: F3) to see the Invert effect settings. Note that the movie is set to Luma Matte, not Luma Inverted, when the Invert effect is used.

TIP

Effect Controls

If a layer has effects already applied, select the layer and Effect > Effect Controls (shortcut: F3) to view the effect settings. To reveal the effect in the Timeline, select the layer and press E.

Project	Effect Controls: CP_AlarmClock.tif	
Ex.06b-Invert Effect • CP_AlarmClock.tif		
fx Invert	Reset	About...
Channel	RGB	
Blend With Original	0%	

The Effect Controls docks with the Project panel and may obscure it. To bring the Project panel forward again, press Command+0 (Control+0).

Increasing the Contrast of a Matte

When you're working with luma mattes, it is quite possible that the matte image you have does not contain quite the mixture of luminance values you want – for example, areas you want to be opaque may have some gray mixed in, resulting in partial transparency. Therefore, it is common to tweak the luminance values of a matte layer, using the Levels effect.

Open [**Ex.07_starter**] and study the layers. Layer 1 (**GI_TextFX.mov**) is footage of grungy black text on white, and this is being used as a luma matte for layer 2 (**AB_DigitalWeb.mov**):

Step 1: Turn on the eyeball for the matte layer and select it; to give the matte more contrast, apply Effect > Color Correction > Levels.

Step 2: When the Effect Controls panel opens, you'll see a histogram showing the range of luminance values that exist in the matte layer. Select the black (leftmost) triangle underneath the histogram and slide it to the right to adjust the Input Black point – this pushes dark grays into full black, filling in some of the holes in the text.

Alpha Levels

To adjust the contrast of a layer's alpha channel, set the Channel popup in the Levels effect to Alpha. Now the histogram controls and sliders adjust the alpha channel only.

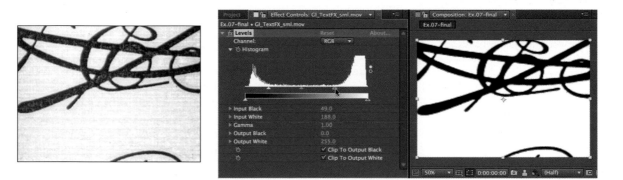

Step 3: Select the white (rightmost) triangle underneath the histogram and slide it to the left to adjust the Input White point – this pushes light grays in the background to full white.

Step 4: When you're happy with the result, run the cursor over the comp panel and read the RGB values in the Info panel (Window > Info to open). Black should read at 0 and white at 255.

Don't forget to turn off the eyeball for the matte layer when you're done. With the increase in the matte's contrast, note the difference it has in the final image: The text has much sharper outlines now, and more fully opaque areas. Check out [**Ex.07-final**] if you get lost.

If you need to increase the contrast of a matte's alpha channel, the Channel popup in the Levels effect can be set to modify the Alpha Channel only. For more control, check out the Effect > Color Correction > Levels (Individual Controls) effect, where each parameter can be animated.

When a grungy black-and-white (and gray) text layer (above left) is used as a luma matte, the light gray areas will not create full opacity. Increasing the contrast of the matte with Effect > Color Correction > Levels (center) will convert more partial blacks to full black and partial whites to full white (right). Footage courtesy Getty Images/TextFX.

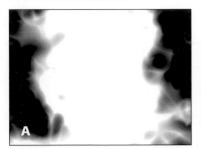

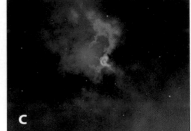

Soft-edged matte layers (A) can create very organic composites when they're used as a matte for our underwater scene (B). The background (C) matches the color palette well, resulting in a smooth blend (D).

Soft Mattes

While it's common to use text or other well-defined shapes as mattes, you can also use blurry images and movies. This creates a softer falloff to the image being matted, leading to more interesting blends.

In [**Ex.08-Soft Luma Matte**], we've prerendered a grayscale movie using the Fractal Noise effect that we will use as a luma matte. Many effects can create great grayscale patterns, and some are even loopable so you can render just a few seconds and loop it in After Effects. Notice how the soft edges of the foreground movie (the underwater scene) blend with the background movie (the space scene). When you're compositing soft mattes that are meant to blend together, you may need to spend some time color correcting one movie to match the other.

Specifying One Channel as a Matte

Sometimes it's better to use just one channel of an RGB file as a matte, rather than a grayscale representation. In [**Ex.09_starter**], the blue-on-white **GI_LiquidFX** layer is used as a Luma Inverted Matte, but if you view the comp's Alpha channel, you'll see that its luminance lacks contrast.

Rather than applying a Levels effect to increase the contrast, turn on the eyeball for layer 1, then select the Red, Green, and Blue channels in turn from the Show Channel popup at the bottom of the Comp panel, looking for a color channel with more contrast. In this example, the Red channel is very close to a pure black-and-white image and would make a better matte than collapsing the RGB channels to grayscale.

Our liquid matte movie (left), while colorful, does not have enough contrast if it's viewed as a grayscale image (center), resulting in a washed-out composite when used by the eye movie as a luma matte (right). Footage courtesy Getty Images/LiquidFX and iStockphoto, © HenryGrey, Image #9563051.

To use only the Red channel as a matte, you need to route the Red channel to the luminance. Fortunately, After Effects offers a number of effects for manipulating channels, so pick the approach you like best:

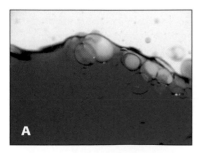

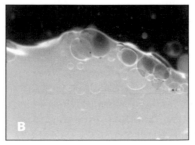

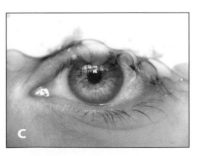

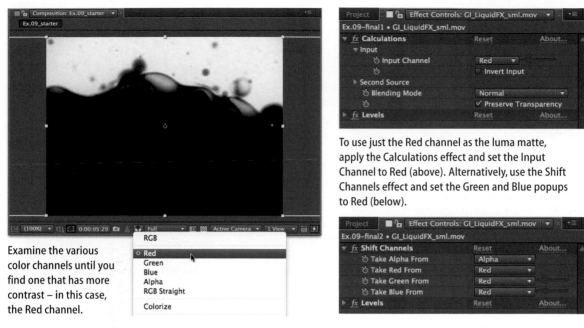

Examine the various color channels until you find one that has more contrast – in this case, the Red channel.

To use just the Red channel as the luma matte, apply the Calculations effect and set the Input Channel to Red (above). Alternatively, use the Shift Channels effect and set the Green and Blue popups to Red (below).

Option 1: Return the Show Channel popup to RGB, but leave the Video switch on for the matte layer. Select the layer and apply Effect > Channel > Calculations. In the Input section, set the Input Channel to Red.

To increase the contrast of the matte so that it's fully black and white, also apply Effect > Color Correction > Levels, as you did in [**Ex.07**]. Turn off the Video switch for the matte when you're done. Now when you set Show Channel to Alpha, you'll see that the luminance of the matte is represented by the original Red Channel with increased contrast. Our version is in [**Ex.09-final1**].

Option 2: An alternative to Calculations is to apply Effect > Channel > Shift Channels. Set the Take Green From popup to Red, and set the Take Blue From popup to Red. Now when After Effects reads the luminance values of the matte, it will collapse three Red channels down to one. (Note: While you could instead set the Take Alpha From popup to Red and use it as an Alpha Matte, you won't be able to view the matte as easily in the Comp panel.) Our version is in [**Ex.09-final2**].

Option 3: Yet another alternative is to apply Effect > Channel > Channel Combiner. Set the From popup to Red, and the To popup to Lightness only. Our version, using a different set of movie sources, is shown in [**Ex.09-final3**].

And if that wasn't enough choice, instead of using the Track Matte feature, you could instead apply the Set Matte effect to the fill movie (not the matte layer) and set the Use for Matte popup to the Red Channel. (See the sidebar on the next page for more on Set Matte.)

Once the matte is a nice high contrast black and white (top), you achieve a much better result (above).

Using the Set Matte Effect

Before the Track Matte feature was added in After Effects, the usual way to apply mattes was to use the Set Matte effect. These days it's included mostly so that legacy projects will be compatible. In fact, if you're still getting the hang of Track Matte, feel free to skip this section.

However, Set Matte has some advantages over Track Matte:

• Set Matte is applied to the movie layer, where it can select any channel from itself or another layer to use as a matte, regardless of its placement in the layer stack.

• Since the matte layer can reside anywhere in the layer stack, multiple layers can all point at a single matte layer. If you used Track Matte and need more than one layer to use the same matte, you would have to duplicate the matte layer for each movie, as the matte must always be on top of the movie.

• The Set Matte effect determines the transparency of the movie, so if you follow Set Matte with Drop Shadow, the shadow effect will work as expected. (With Track Matte, you need to apply edge effects in a second comp.)

The biggest drawback is that Set Matte is a *compound effect* (see Chapter 24), which means that any effects or animation applied to the matte layer must take place in a precomp. It's best if the matte and movie layers are also the same aspect ratio, so you may need to prepare the matte by sizing it in a precomp.

To see how Set Matte works, follow along (or skip to Step 8):

Step 1: Open **[Ex.10_starter]**. The *matte* is the **AB_Cloud-Fly-Thrus** layer, and the **iS_eyeblink** layer is the *fill*.

Step 2: When using the Set Matte effect, the matte layer can be placed anywhere in the layer stack, but do turn off its eyeball.

Step 3: Select the **iS_eye-blink** layer, and apply Effect > Channel > Set Matte. The Effect Controls panel will open. *Remember the Set Matte effect is applied to the movie, not the matte!*

Step 4: In the Effect Controls panel, set the first popup Take Matte From to be the **AB_CloudFly-Thrus.mov**. The effect will now look at the alpha channel for the matte layer – which happens to be a solid white rectangle, since it has no alpha.

Step 5: Just as in **[Ex.09]**, it turns out that the red channel will work best as a matte, so set the Use For Matte popup to Red Channel. The movie will show up wherever the red channel is white.

Step 6: Check the Invert Matte box so the opposite will be true.

Step 7: The other options in this plug-in are fine at their defaults. The Stretch Matte to Fit option determines what happens when the matte and the movie are different sizes (explore both options). The Premultiply Matte

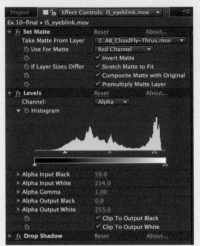

The Set Matte effect is a compound effect that uses either itself or another layer to determine the transparency of the layer it's applied to. In this example it's using the Red channel as a matte. The Levels effect then increases the contrast of this alpha channel. Since the transparency is created by the Set Matte effect, a Drop Shadow effect added later will work as expected.

Layer option is useful when the matte layer already has its own alpha channel; this factors it in.

Step 8: [Ex.10-final] is our version; select the **iS_eyeblink** layer and view the Effect Controls panel (F3) to see the effects applied. After the Set Matte effect, we added the Levels effect with its Channels popup set to Alpha to increase the contrast of the matte. We've also changed the background color to white and added the Effect > Perspective > Drop Shadow effect.

Creating Animated Mattes

It's possible to have an animated matte simply by using a movie as the matte layer. But the matte layer can also be animated inside After Effects just like any regular layer, with all the keyframe and velocity controls you're already familiar with.

In [**Ex.11_starter**], Illustrator text is panned from right to left using two Position keyframes. This animated layer is then used as an alpha matte. Another way to look at this effect is as a "window" moving across the movie, rather than moving the movie itself. In [**Ex.11-final**] we turned on Motion Blur for the matte layer. To finish off the composite, we also added an Invert effect to the movie, which gets applied to a movie *before* its track matte is calculated. We then composited the track matte result over the original movie using the Hard Light blending mode.

The movie is matted by animating text and has its own luminance inverted. The result is composited with a blending mode onto the original movie for the final effect.

Animating the Fill

Conversely, you can keep the matte stationary and animate the fill. In [**Ex.12**], a metal-toned gradient was created in Adobe Photoshop, at a size that's wider than the matte. The texture is panned from right to left so that it moves inside the type created in Illustrator.

To animate the movie and matte together as a group, you'll need to either use parenting or build a hierarchy of comps.

Parental Bond

Parenting (the subject of Chapter 17) can be handy for cases when you need the matte layer to follow the movie layer's animation exactly. If you're new to parenting, the most important concept is that while the child can be animated independently of the parent, the parent's animation is always applied to the child. Only Anchor Point, Position, Scale, and Rotation are handed down from parent to child – Opacity and Effects are not inherited. Let's run through a basic parenting example:

A larger layer is panned underneath its stationary matte, creating a moving texture through the title.

Step 1: Open [**Ex.13_starter**]. The **Liquid.ai** text layer is the matte, and the **AB_OceanWaterEffects.mov** layer is the fill. Practice scrubbing the Position, Scale, and Rotation values for the movie layer, and note how the matte remains unaffected. Be sure to Undo any transformations before proceeding.

Step 2: Press Shift+F4 to open the Parent column (you can also right-click on any column and select Columns > Parent). We prefer to position the Parent column to the right of the layer names.

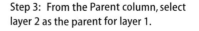

Step 3: Select the Parent popup for the matte (layer 1) and set it to use the fill movie (layer 2) as its Parent. Another way to set the parent is by dragging the pick whip to the parent's name (see figures on next page).

Step 3: From the Parent column, select layer 2 as the parent for layer 1.

Step 3 alternate:
To parent the matte to the movie, you can also drag the pick whip (circled in red) from the matte (layer 1) to the movie (layer 2).

Release the mouse when a box draws around layer 2's name, and Layer 1 will now use Layer 2 as its parent.

Step 4: Now scrub the Position, Scale, and Rotation values for the movie (parent) layer, and note that the matte (child) follows in sync. However, if you animate the matte layer, it will move independently of its parent. If you get lost, check our version [**Ex.13-final**].

The matte (text) selects the water movie as its parent (left). When the parent is scaled (center) or rotated (right), the matte layer follows along.

Of course, there's no reason the matte couldn't be the parent and the movie be the child. While a simple parenting setup like this can help with many animation tasks, you may find a need to animate the parent layer independently without also transforming the child. To the rescue comes the Null Object (Layer > New > Null Object). By using a null (or "dummy" layer) as the parent, you can control the transformations for both the movie and the matte as a group, while both children can also animate independently. [**Ex.14**] shows this arrangement. (For more on parenting and null objects, including some important gotchas, see Chapter 17, *Parenting Skills*.)

Options for Applying Effects

While Parenting is a welcome tool for animating the movie and matte as a group, it has one very important drawback. You cannot apply an effect to the parent and have it apply also to the child, since Parenting applies only to transformations.

Of course, you can apply effects to the matte layer or the fill layer individually; these are applied before the track matte is composited. In this case, you are making a choice of whether you want to effect the alpha channel (matte) or the image (the fill layer). If you want to apply the same effect to *both* the movie and the matte, you would need to apply duplicate effects to the two layers and remember to keep them in sync. However, with some effects, problems may arise if the movie and matte are not the same size or aspect ratio (for instance, the center of a Twirl effect would vary depending on the size of the layer).

Therefore, it often makes more sense to instead apply a single effect to the *result* of the track matte composite. Indeed, certain edge effects, such as drop shadows, glows and bevels, need to be rendered *after* the track matte has been composited so that the correct alpha channel is available. You can apply effects to your composite using one of these methods:

• If all you need is a drop shadow or bevel-type effect, apply one of the Layer Styles (Chapter 22); these are applied after the track matte is composited. Select the movie layer, and choose from the Layer > Layer Styles menu. This is shown in [**Ex.15a**].

• Add an Adjustment Layer (Layer > New > Adjustment Layer) above the movie and matte layers, and apply any effect from the Effects menu to the adjustment layer. Since After Effects renders from the bottom layer up, effects applied to an adjustment layer are applied to the *composite of the layers below*. This is shown in [**Ex.15b**]. The problem with adjustment layers is that if you add any background layers to this comp, they will also be effected. (For more on Adjustment Layers, see Chapter 22.)

• Probably the most flexible solution is to create the track matte in one composition, then "nest" this comp in a second composition where it appears as a single layer. This is shown in [**Ex.15c**]. Now you are free to apply masks, effects, and transformations to the group, and these will be applied after the track matte is composited. Note that Layer Styles applied in the second comp are applied after the group is transformed; if you are scaling the nested layer, you may wish to apply Layer Styles in the first comp.

We'll cover nesting comps in more detail in the next section (as well as in Chapters 18 and 19), as understanding how track mattes behave in a hierarchy of comps is extremely useful for creating certain effects. Also keep in mind that you can combine parenting and nesting if necessary.

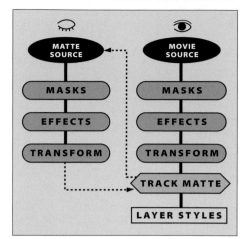

The movie and the matte each have their own set of Masks, Effects and Transformations, which are calculated *before* the Track Matte module. In addition, Layer Styles render after Track Matte.

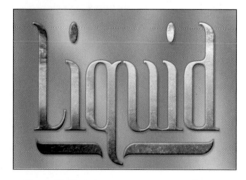

In [**Ex.15a**] (above), Layer Styles are applied after the track matte is composited, which allows for some edge effects to be applied all in one comp.

Using nested comps in [**Ex15c**] (below), you can apply any filter from the Effects menu as well as transform the composite as a group.

In our first comp, we set up our basic track matte. By nesting this inside a second comp, you'll have more flexibility in applying effects and animating the composite.

Building a Track Matte Hierarchy

One of the most powerful features of After Effects is its ability to create a hierarchy of nested compositions. Nesting is useful for project management and ease of editing, but it's also necessary to achieve specific effects. We'll cover the concepts of nesting and precomposing in detail in Chapters 18 and 19, but if you already know a little about nesting comps, you should be able to grasp the following specific information relating to track mattes. (If it proves too advanced, we suggest you complete Chapters 18 and 19, and return to this section later.)

Close all other comps and open [**Ex.16-Comp_1/matte**]. In this example, we've created a basic track matte effect. Note that in this composition you can easily animate the position of the matte independently of the movie (known as a *traveling matte*), and move the movie layer

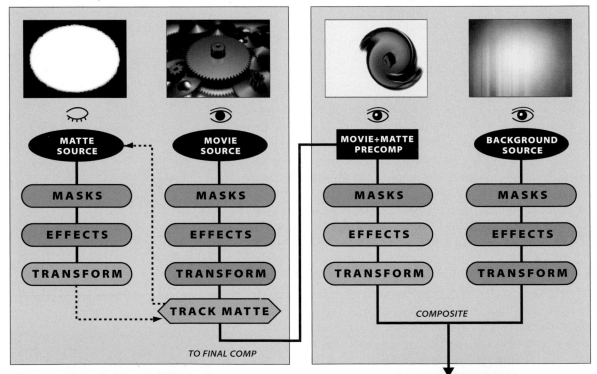

Comp 1: MOVIE + MATTE

MATTE SOURCE — MASKS — EFFECTS — TRANSFORM

MOVIE SOURCE — MASKS — EFFECTS — TRANSFORM

TRACK MATTE

TO FINAL COMP

Comp 2: FINAL COMP

MOVIE+MATTE PRECOMP — MASKS — EFFECTS — TRANSFORM

BACKGROUND SOURCE — MASKS — EFFECTS — TRANSFORM

COMPOSITE

In Comp 1, the matte layer is turned off. When it's used by the second layer as a track matte, the matte layer is triggered to run through its rendering order. Comp 1 is then nested in a second comp where a background is also added. The highlighted steps in the process are where editing has taken place: The matte animates in the precomp, and Track Matte is enabled for the movie layer. In Comp 2, the Comp 1 layer has been scaled and repositioned, and various effects have been added.

independently of the matte (pan the movie behind the matte shape). You can animate each layer using keyframes just like you would animate any other layer, and apply an effect to one layer or the other.

However, you cannot easily move and scale both layers together or apply effects to the movie if those effects need to render *after* it has been composited with the matte. The reason is that, according to After Effect's internal render order, effects are added to the movie *before* the matte has been composited (when it's still a plain, rectangular shape).

It's useful to use a separate comp to composite the movie with the matte. Once the track matte effect is complete, drag (or *nest*) this first comp into a second comp, where you can scale and position it as one layer, and apply any effect from the Effects menu to it.

[**Ex.16-Comp_1/matte**] is the first comp, where we applied the track matte. In this comp, we've scaled the matte to 90% and repositioned the movie inside the matte. This first comp should ideally be the same duration as the movie layer; if the movie is shorter than the comp, any blank areas will show up as "empty calories" (a ghosted bar with no content) in the second comp. Neither do you want to trim any frames by making the comp too short: trim out excess frames in the second comp *after* you nest.

Once the first comp was complete, we created a second composition, [**Ex.16-Comp_2/fx**]. We then dragged in the first comp (nested it) and animated Scale and Position, which are applied to the movie and the matte as a group. A Twirl effect is also applied to the group. Remember that many of the distortion effects, as well as edge-type effects (Roughen Edges, Drop Shadow, Glow, Bevel Alpha, and so on), need to be applied in the second comp to work as expected. Layer Styles can be applied in either comp; just remember that layer styles always render *after* the layer's transformations are calculated.

The hierarchy you've built is "live" until you actually render. The original movie and matte layers are still editable in the first comp. For more on nesting comps, check out Chapter 18.

Nesting Shortcut

Drag your first comp to the New Composition icon at the bottom of the Project panel to automatically nest it in a new comp with the same specs.

Synchronize Time

All comps in a nested chain will show the same frame thanks to the Preferences > General option "Synchronize Time of All Related Items." You can disable this preference if you need to see different points in time.

[**Ex.16-Comp_1/matte**] is nested in [**Ex.16-Comp_2/fx**], where it is now one easy-to-manage layer. In this second comp, the matte composite is further animated, various effects are applied, and a background layer is added. The result is a more complex yet manageable composite.

Precomposing After Track Matte

Nesting is by far the easiest way to set up a track matte hierarchy, but it does assume that you are planning ahead somewhat. What if you didn't plan ahead?

Let's say you built the track matte in one comp (let's call it "Final Comp"; it is [**Ex.17**] in this chapter's example projects), where you added a background and any number of other layers. Only afterward do you decide that you would like to move the movie and matte as one unit, and perhaps add a drop shadow. You can't nest this entire comp, as you would just be grouping *all* your layers – not just the two you need grouped. Don't panic: The Pre-compose feature lets you group the movie and matte layers together into their own comp (think of it as nesting backward). This new comp will then be rendered before your so-called Final Comp. Let's go through the actual steps involved:

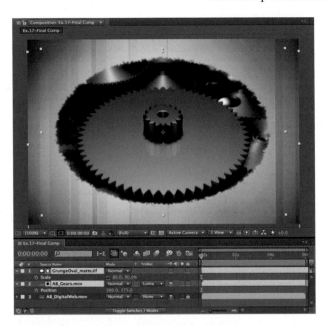

Step 2: Select the two layers that make up your matte composite (above) and select Layer > Pre-compose. In the Pre-compose dialog (below), if you'd like to open the precomp as tabbed panels, check the Open New Composition checkbox.

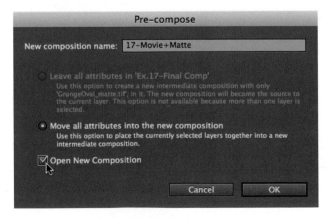

Step 1: Open [**Ex.17-Final Comp**], where we've built a track matte effect and added a background. There could be many other layers as well. Now we decide that the movie and matte need to be animated together and a drop shadow added. Rather than having to animate both layers, we'll group them using Pre-compose, then move them as a group.

Step 2: To precompose, select both the matte (layer 1) and the movie (layer 2), and choose Layer > Pre-compose (Command+Shift+C on Mac, Control+Shift+C on Windows). If you'd like to open the precomp as a tabbed panel, check the Open New Composition checkbox.

Step 3: Give the new comp a useful name, such as "**17-Movie+Matte**", and click OK. (If you checked the Open New Composition checkbox, the precomp will be forward, with movie and matte layers visible. If this is the case, click on the tab for [**Ex.17-Final Comp**] to bring this comp forward.) In the Final Comp, the two selected layers are replaced by one layer – the precomp – and this can be positioned and scaled as a group just as if you had nested it in the first place.

Step 4: Any keyframes or effects (attributes) that were applied to the precomposed layers have been moved to the precomp, where they are still live and editable. If the precomp is not

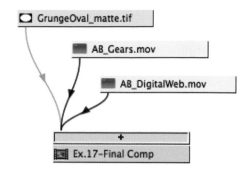

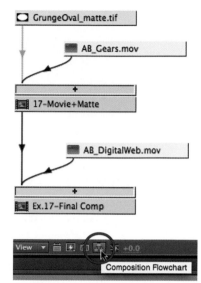

Before precomposing (left), all of our layers – matte, movie, and background – are in one composition. By selecting and precomposing the matte and movie layers, they are placed in their own comp, which then becomes a single layer in our original comp (right).

already available as a tab, double-click the new **17-Movie+Matte** layer in the Final Comp. Now you can toggle between the precomp and the original comp by clicking on the tabs. There's nothing special about this precomp; it's not much different from building the hierarchy by nesting.

The only drawback to precomposing the movie and the matte is that the new precomp will be the same size and duration as the Final Comp. This can be misleading if you have, say, a 20-second Final Comp, and you precompose two layers that are very short. The precomp will be 20 seconds in duration, and its layer bar in the Final Comp will indicate it's 20 seconds long – even though most of the precomp is empty (more empty calories). Chapter 19 covers precomposing in more detail and offers tips for addressing this problem. Below is another method of precomposing a track matte that avoids this problem altogether.

To open the Flowchart panel for your chain of comps, bring your Final Comp forward, and click on the Comp Flowchart Button, on the top right side of the Comp panel. (This is covered in detail in Chapter 18.)

Precomposing Before Track Matte

When you're building hierarchies of comps with track mattes, you can still think ahead even after you've already started. Close all comps and open [**Ex.18-Final Comp**]; this is a 20-second comp, with a background that spans the entire duration. The foreground movie is only six seconds long and has been scaled to 70%. We now decide that the foreground movie needs a more interesting torn-edge effect, which we'll create by using a track matte. However, rather than adding the matte to this comp, scaling the matte to fit, then finding out that we have to precompose to create a group anyway, we'll precompose just the movie layer:

Step 1: In [**Ex.18-Final Comp**], imagine you've just decided you need to create a track matte for layer 1, **AB_RetroHealthcare.mov**. At this point, select the foreground movie layer and then Layer > Pre-compose.

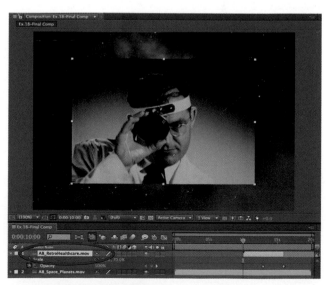

Step 1: Instead of creating a track matte composite in your current comp, select the movie layer and precompose it.

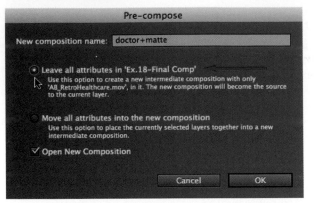

Step 2: Pre-compose using Leave all attributes. This will make a new comp that is the same size and duration as the movie, not the comp.

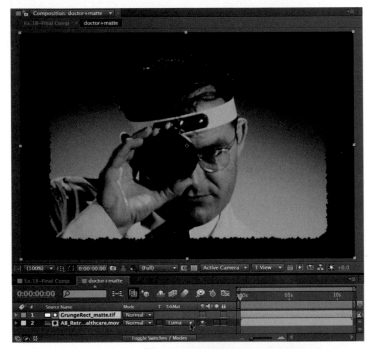

Step 4: In the precomp, we added the **GrungeRect_matte.tif** layer as a luma matte for a torn-edge effect.

Steps 5–6: Back in the Final Comp, the movie layer is replaced with the nested precomp where the track matte is composited. The advantage is that the layer has the same duration, size, position, and place in the timeline as the original movie. And now you can apply a glow too!

Step 2: In the Pre-compose dialog, make sure you select the *first* option, Leave all attributes. Don't forget to give the precomp a useful name, such as "**doctor+matte**" – we will be adding the matte in the next step. Be sure to check the Open New Composition option, and click OK.

Step 3: The precomp should be forward – if not, double-click the new precomp layer in the Final Comp. This precomp holds only the movie layer (at 100% scale) and is rendered before the Final Comp. Now is the time – *after* pre-composing – to create the track matte.

Step 4: From the Project panel's **Sources > Mattes** folder, select a matte of your choice and drag it into the precomp. With the matte above the movie, apply either Luma or Alpha track matte, depending on your matte. You can animate the movie and matte independently in the precomp.

Step 5: Bring the [**Ex.18-Final Comp**] forward. The movie layer has been replaced by a precomp with the same size and duration as the movie. Select it and press UU; any attributes that were originally applied remained in the original comp. (If we had "moved all attributes," this layer would now be as long as our comp, as opposed to our original movie, and the scale value would have moved down to the precomp.)

Step 6: You can now animate the movie and the matte as a group and apply drop shadow or glow effects as you desire.

This is the same hierarchy you would have created had you planned ahead and created the track matte in one comp and then nested it. If you get lost along the way, check out our comps in the [**Ex.18-result**] folder.

Effects in a Nested Comp Hierarchy

Creating a track matte and using two compositions will give you the most flexibility in picking and choosing how effects are handled. Effects that are capable of distorting pixels (blurs, scatter, wave warp, and so on) will give different results depending on what level of the hierarchy they are applied to, and whether they affect the movie, the matte, or both.

In the following series of examples, we've created a hierarchy you should be familiar with. The folders for [Ex.19], [Ex.20], and [Ex.21] consist of two comps per folder. The first comp in the chain (**movie+matte**) includes **AB_RetroHealthcare.mov** (layer 2), and an Illustrator shape (layer 1) which serves as an alpha matte. Each **movie+matte** comp is nested in a companion second comp (**Final Comp**), where a gradient background is added.

We have experimented with three different variations that demonstrate the options available for adding a simple blur (Effect > Blur & Sharpen > Fast Blur). These options include blurring the movie and the matte, blurring just the movie, or blurring just the matte.

You might want to close all open comps (select Close All from the Comp panel's Viewer menu) before opening a new pair of example comps, just to keep things simple. (To open a pair of comps more easily, drag a marquee around them in the Project panel, and double-click one of them. Both comps will open.)

TIP

Composition Relatives

You can navigate easily between nested comps by using the Composition Navigator along the top of the Comp panel. Another method is to select the Mini-Flowchart button in the Timeline (press Shift to open it centered on the mouse cursor's current location). These options will be covered in detail in Chapter 18.

Composition Mini-Flowchart (tap Shift)

The visual result of applying effects depends on where you apply them in the chain – for example, to a comp that contains both the movie and its matte (left), to just the inset movie but not its matte (center), or to just the matte shape (right). This applies to all effects, not just blurs.

▲ Effect Movie and Matte

Open the **[Ex.19-Final Comp]** and **[Ex.19-movie+matte]** comps. Notice the blur effect is applied to the *nested* comp layer in the second comp, after track matte is composited, and therefore blurs both the movie and the matte.

▲ Effect Movie Only

Open the **[Ex.20-Final Comp]** and **[Ex.20-movie+matte]** comps. Notice the blur effect is applied to the *movie* layer in the first comp. The blur is applied to the movie before the track matte is calculated, and therefore has no effect on the sharpness of the matte.

▲ Effect Matte Only

Open the **[Ex.21-Final Comp]** and **[Ex.21-movie+matte]** comps. Notice the blur effect is applied to the *matte* layer in the first comp. The blur is applied to the matte before the track matte is calculated, and therefore has no effect on the sharpness of the movie.

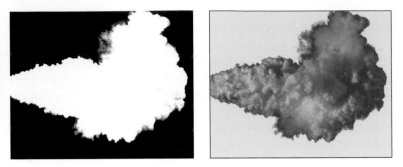

It is not uncommon for a special effects stock footage CD to supply both the image (left) and a separate matte created from the image (center). However, if you create a track matte using this matte pass, you may end up with fringing (right). Footage courtesy Artbeats/Cloud Chamber.

Unmultiplying a Separate Matte

After Effects' Track Matte feature assumes straight-style alphas. For instance, when using Luma Track matte, it expects the "fill" image will be larger than the matte, so when the track matte is applied, the edges will appear clean (the excess pixels will be outside the matte edge and therefore transparent). If you're outputting a separate fill and matte from another application, make sure you render with a Straight Alpha, not a Premultiplied Alpha.

Some special effects stock footage collections will supply separate mattes to use for their movies. They are separate files because the most common file format is JPEG, which doesn't support an alpha channel. However, these mattes are often derived from the original footage (such as an explosion), resulting in a premultiplied, rather than straight, alpha, because some of the background gets mixed in with the semitransparent parts of the image. An example of this is the Artbeats Cloud Chamber footage in [**Ex.22_Clouds-1/matte**].

This example uses a fairly common scenario in which the movie and the matte have been supplied as separate layers. In this case, the **AB_CloudChamber.mov** was shot on film against a black background. By modifying the original movie, Artbeats created an accompanying matte movie. However, because the fill and matte movies share the same edge, when a track matte is employed, the result shows a black fringe around the edges. It might be acceptable if you're compositing against a dark background, but not against a lighter background.

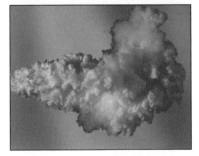

In a second comp, applying Remove Color Matting helps remove some of the fringe (top). Applying the Simple Choker effect with a value of +3 tightens up the matte (above).

To remove the black fringe, or "unmultiply" it, you need to nest this comp into a second comp [**Ex.22_Clouds-2/remove fringe**]. In the second composition, the Effect > Channel > Remove Color Matting effect is applied, which helps to remove the black fringe. You cannot do this all in one comp, as the Remove Color Matting effect must occur *after* the track matte is already composited together because it's an edge effect (see *Building a Track Matte Hierarchy* on page 204).

If the movie and matte were created precisely from a 3D program, it's likely that the edge would look fine at this point. But in this case, it helps to shrink the edge further. Therefore, we added Effect > Matte > Simple Choker with a value of positive 1.5 to "choke" the edge of the alpha channel. You could also use the more advanced Matte > Matte Choker.

For more problematic mattes, After Effects CS5 introduced a new Matte > Refine Edges effect. In addition to choking, feathering, smoothing, and color decontamination capabilities, Refine Matte tracks the motion in mattes to automatically add motion blur to moving edges or remove "chatter" from stationary edges of animated mattes.

Third-party vendors also provide tools for fixing edges in a composite. For example, BCC Alpha Process in Boris Continuum Complete includes edge blurring for a softer edge that composites better. The Key Correct Pro package from Red Giant Software has many useful edge tools, including Edge Blur, which you can apply after choking the matte.

Finally, instead of creating a Track Matte effect, and then trying to clean up the edge, we offer an alternative solution in [**Ex.22-Alt1_Screen mode**]. Use the original "fill" movie and simply composite it on top of the background using the Screen blending mode – this will drop out the black background. Although the result is quite different, it may be more pleasing, depending on the images being used. Movies for fire, explosions, lightning, and so on often look better when you simply composite them using Screen or Add mode. An example of compositing an explosion with Add mode is shown in [**Ex.22-Alt2_Add mode**].

There are other alternatives to dropping out footage shot against black such as using the technique described in the *Alpha Creation* sidebar in Chapter 22.

Fade the Movie or the Matte?

To fade in a movie with a track matte effect applied, you can fade up either the matte or the movie layer, as both will modify the transparency of the image. However, we suggest you apply Opacity keyframes to the *movie* layer. We demonstrate this in [**Ex.23-Fade Up Movie**]. Why? If you decide to remove the track matte, any opacity keyframes you applied to the matte layer will be removed too – meaning you just lost your fade.

If you create a track matte hierarchy (using nested comps, as discussed earlier in this chapter), we suggest you apply the Opacity keyframes in the second, higher-level composition – the idea being that you won't have to dig down into a precomp to edit the fade-up. And if you stay consistent, you'll always know where your Opacity keyframes reside.

Head Burn Fadeout

Most of our examples for track mattes so far have been using still, or otherwise slightly animating, sources for our mattes. However, animated mattes that change their luminance over time can also be used. And since luminance affects transparency, these can be used for more complex fade-in and fade-out effects.

In this vein, one of our favorite sources for transitions are film head and tail "burns" that go from black (unexposed) to white (fully exposed) in interesting ways. [**Ex.24**] demonstrates this technique – it makes the footage fade in a flickering manner, characteristic of an old movie. This technique is also great for nervous text treatments.

When an image was shot against solid black, an alternative to creating a matte is to use blending modes such as Screen or Add.

Slow Burn

To change the duration of "film burn" fades, change the Time Stretch value of the burn layer. Frame blending can smooth the result.

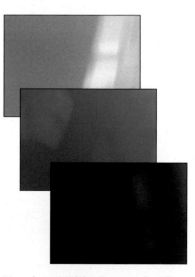

Matte layers with luminance values that change over time can make for interesting fades in an underlying movie file. Film burn courtesy Artbeats/Film Clutter.

Ex.24–HeadBurn Fadeout

0:00:05:07

#	Source Name	Mode	T	TrkMat			
1	AB_FilmClutter1.mov	Normal					
2	AB_Gears.mov	Normal		Luma			
3	AB_Gears.mov	Normal		None			

Toggle Switches / Modes

To use track mattes for fades, divide the movie into two segments at the point where the fade starts or stops. Apply the track matte only to the segment to be faded. This is shown in **[Ex.24]**.

To apply a matte transition such as this, you need to divide your movie into two segments, cutting it at the point where the transition is supposed to start or end. The Edit > Split Layer option is handy for this. Leave the portion of the movie that is not supposed to have fades alone – i.e., no matte. For a fade-out, align your fade matte movie to the start of the second segment, placed above this segment in the Timeline panel. Set this second segment to Luma Matte. Your specific circumstances – whether your matte moves from light to dark or vice versa, and whether you're fading up or off – will determine whether you use Luma Matte or Luma Inverted to create the transparency.

Custom Transition Mattes

You can use a matte as a transition, provided that you animate the matte layer in such a way that, at the beginning of the transition, the frame is completely black, and at the end of the transition, the frame is completely white (or vice versa to wipe an image off instead of on). The final examples in this chapter cover a variety of ways you can use mattes for transitions.

Depending on how you create the transition matte, you may need to apply the track matte only to the movie while it's transitioning on. Once the transition is complete, Edit > Split Layer and turn off the track matte for the rest of the movie that plays normally. This will save on rendering time; it also avoids having to extend a short matte.

A simple shape created in Illustrator is used as a matte; as the matte scales up to fill the frame, the movie is revealed. Background courtesy Artbeats/Digital Moods.

• [Ex.25] uses a shape created in Illustrator with the Star tool; you can use any shape, but those with a significant solid area in the center work best as a transition. The shape is scaled in After Effects from 0% to 222% to fill the frame and used as an alpha matte so that the movie is revealed as the shape scales up. We also turned on Continuously Rasterize for the Illustrator shape so it would rasterize at each frame and remain sharp when scaled above 100%. Motion Blur is turned on for the animated matte.

The matte is a movie from Getty Images/EditFX3 of white paint strokes (left); as the matte paints on, the foreground movie is revealed (right).

• [Ex.26] uses a movie of a paint brush filling a black frame with white strokes. When used as a luma matte, the movie appears to "paint on" a layer; when used as a luma inverted matte, it "paints off" a layer. Feel free to also time-stretch these transition matte movies as needed.

• **[Ex.27-final]** shows a similar setup. An animation of white shapes moves down and fills the frame; temporarily turn on this layer to preview if you need to. This is used as a luma matte to reveal the movie.

In this case we also needed to apply the track matte only to the transitioning section and allow the rest of the movie to play normally. If you'd like to practice splitting a layer:

White bars fill the screen from top to bottom (left) in an animation created using the Boris 2D Particles plug-in. When it's used as a luma matte, it serves as a transition (right) to wipe on our character. Footage courtesy Getty Images/Cool Characters.

Step 1: In **[Ex.27_starter A]**, select the matte (layer 1) and press O to jump to the out point at 05:13 where the matte is completely white. Advance one frame (shortcut: Page Down) to 05:14.

Step 2: Select the movie (layer 2) and Edit > Split Layer. In the Timeline panel, move the matte (layer 1) so it's above the first portion of the movie.

Step 3: Set Luma Matte for the first section of the movie. The background movie will now be visible during the transition. If you run into a problem, check out **[Ex.27-final]**.

After splitting the movie layer, set the first section to Luma Matte and the second section to Track Matte > None.

In **[Ex.27_starter B]**, we've given you an almost identical comp but with the addition of a foreground layer. However, in this case, the luma matte has already been applied to the movie layer, which results in some problems when the layer is split. To test this, move to 05:14 and split the movie (layer 3) as you did before. Notice that After Effects is smart enough to move the second half of the split movie *above* the matte layer, but it's not smart enough to disable its Track Matte popup. The result is that it now uses the layer above (the microphone in layer 1) as its matte! (This is true even if the second segment ended up at the top of the Timeline panel. In this case, even though the Track Matte popup would not be visible, it would become visible and active if you were to add a new foreground layer to the comp in the future.) So this is something to watch out for when splitting a layer.

Finally, **[Ex.28]** offers another transition flavor, using a movie and matte from Artbeats/Transitions. The foreground movie fills the frame with water bubbles, and the two movies in the background swap out.

CONNECT

Hot keying to external programs: Chapter 6.

Splitting layers: Chapter 7.

Nesting compositions: Chapter 18.

Precomposing: Chapter 19.

Applying effects: Chapter 22.

Layer Styles: Chapter 22.

Rendering with an alpha channel: Chapter 42.

12

Stencils and the "T"

Stencils are a great way to add transparency to multiple layers. And then there's that "T" switch...

The previous chapter was devoted to Track Mattes: having one layer create transparency for one other layer. Stencils, however, create transparency for *all* layers underneath. You can use a layer's luminance or alpha channel as a stencil, and invert it as well. This chapter also covers the Preserve Transparency switch, and an obscure but useful mode called Alpha Add.

Three layers have been blended with blending modes (left) with a matte (center) placed on top; this will become the alpha channel for all underlying layers when it's set to Stencil Luma (right). Background movies courtesy Artbeats/Digidelic and Starfields.

Stencil Luma

In our first example ([Ex.01_starter]) from this chapter's project file, we've composited three layers together using various blending modes and added a grayscale image on top, which we'll use as a stencil. Turn the top layer on and off to view the layers below.

To access the options for stencils, toggle the Switches/Modes column in the Timeline panel to Modes (shortcut: F4 to toggle). The plan is to use the luminance of the grayscale image, **GrungeRect_matte.tif**, to set the transparency of the composite of all the layers below:

Step 1: Unlike with track mattes, make sure the eyeball is *on* for the top layer, and select Stencil Luma from the Modes menu. The grayscale image will disappear, and where the matte was white, the layers below will appear opaque.

Step 2: The black background color that's visible denotes transparency. Confirm this by toggling on the comp's transparency grid.

You can add additional layers *above* the stencil layer, and they will be unaffected by the stencil below. To temporarily disable the stencil, turn off the layer's Video switch (the eyeball).

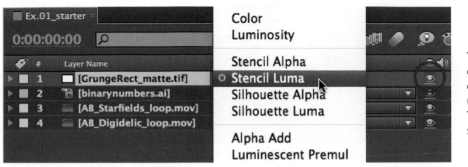

The Stencil layer goes on top, where it will cut out all the layers underneath. Unlike Track Mattes, its Video switch must be on.

Stencil Alpha

No prizes for guessing that Stencil Alpha (shown in [**Ex.02a**]) is practically identical to Stencil Luma, except that the transparency is dictated by the stencil layer's alpha channel, not its luminance. In this example, the alpha channel of an Illustrator file is used for transparency. You can animate the stencil which results in a moving window revealing the images below; in this case, the stencil layer scales up over time.

Just as with a track matte, you can apply effects directly to the stencil layer. For example, we added Effect > Blur & Sharpen > Fast Blur to the stencil in [**Ex.02a**].

When you apply effects to the stencil layer, they affect the stencil layer *only*, not the layers below. To apply an effect to all layers below, apply it to an adjustment layer (see Chapter 22), and place it below the stencil layer, as shown in [**Ex.02b**]. Place the adjustment layer above the stencil to also have it affect the stencil layer.

Layers with alpha channels – such as Illustrator logos and text layers – can be used in Stencil Alpha mode. Note that you can also animate the stencil layers to make the mask move. Effects applied to stencil layers, such as this Fast Blur shown in [**Ex.02a**], affect the edges of the matte only, not the layers underneath.

[**Ex.02b**]: For an effect to apply to all layers below, apply it to an adjustment layer placed below the stencil layer. To also affect the stencil, move the adjustment layer above the stencil.

Stencils 101

After Effects' stencils are akin to the stencils you buy in art stores: masks with cutout centers where the characters or images are supposed to show through. The "transparent center" of a real-life stencil is the equivalent of an opaque area in After Effects, which is defined by the areas where the stencil layer's luminance or alpha channel are white. Black areas in the stencil layer block out or remove the image underneath; gray areas are partially transparent. Silhouettes are the opposite, and could be thought of as simply inverted stencils: They block out the areas where the luminance or alpha are white and allow the underlying layers to show through where the matte layer is black. They are the equivalent of the Luma Inverted or Alpha Inverted choices for track matte types.

STENCIL ALPHA

STENCIL LUMA

Clock object: Choice between
ALPHA (left) or LUMA (right)

SILHOUETTE ALPHA

SILHOUETTE LUMA

If a layer has both interesting luminance and alpha channel information, such as many object library images (above), they can be used as either alpha or luma stencils or silhouettes. Experiment with **[Ex.03a]**, and compare the results of using this object as Stencil Alpha, Stencil Luma, Silhouette Alpha, and Silhouette Luma. Clock courtesy Classic PIO/Sampler; background courtesy Digital Vision/Beauty and Artbeats/ Digital Moods.

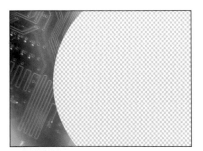

Arrange your stencil and the layers it is cutting out in their own composition. Footage courtesy Artbeats/Desktop Technology and Digital Moods.

Silhouettes and Alpha versus Luma

A *silhouette* is nothing more than an inverted stencil (it sure would be easier to understand if that's what they were called). The options offered are Silhouette Luma and Silhouette Alpha, based again on whether the luminance or alpha of the layer dictates the transparency.

Explore [Ex.03a] in this chapter's project. Just as with Track Matte, if the stencil layer has both an alpha channel and interesting luminance, it may work well set to either Silhouette Luma or Alpha. Using the alarm clock image as your stencil layer, compare the results of both stencil modes and their inverted silhouette counterparts. And just as with a track matte, applying the Invert effect to the stencil (see [Ex.03b]) will invert its luminance for another variation.

Adding a Background Layer

Layers render from the bottom up, so a stencil is creating transparency for the composite of all layers below. A shortcoming of this render order is that any background layer added to a comp will also become part of that composite and be cut out by the stencil. To add a background layer, therefore, you will need to use nested compositions. (We don't cover nesting comps in detail until Chapter 18. If the following proves too advanced, we suggest you return to this section at a later date.)

First, create your stack of images to be stenciled in one comp, with your stencil layer on top. Then, create a second composition and nest the first comp into it. Now you can add a background layer to the second comp that will remain unaffected by the stencil, which is already composited in the first comp. An example of this chain is shown in [**Ex.04-Comp-1/stencil**] and [**Ex.04-Comp-2/BG**].

As a bonus, you can now apply various edge treatments and effects to the stencil comp layer when it is nested in the second comp. For instance, we added Effect > Perspective > Bevel Alpha and Drop Shadow in our second comp. (Of course, you could apply these effects to an adjustment layer placed at the top of the stack in comp 1, but they are better applied in comp 2, where you can see how effects relate to the background image.)

In the second comp, add edge effects to the framing element. Footage of woman courtesy Artbeats/Business World.

Preserve Underlying Transparency

When the Preserve Underlying Transparency switch is turned on for a layer, the combined transparencies for all layers *underneath* affect the transparency of the layer you have turned it on for. This useful feature tends to get overlooked by many users. First, it shows up as a nondescript little T switch in the Modes column. Second, if one of the layers in the comp underneath the one getting preserve transparency is full-frame, this switch will have no effect, since there would be no transparency to borrow. Hence, you might have relegated it to the "I wonder what that switch *does*" category… That's about to change:

Step 1: Open the [**Ex.05_starter**] comp, which consists of three layers from an Illustrator file imported as a composition. Select Alpha from the Show Channels popup at the bottom of the Comp panel to view the sum of all alphas. The white areas show where the objects are opaque, and the black areas denote transparency. Return to viewing the RGB channels.

Step 2: Turn on the eyeball for the top layer, **AB_Digital Moods**, which obscures the layers below. Now turn on its T switch in the Modes column. The top layer is displayed only where the underlying layers are opaque. This is shown in [**Ex.05-final**], where some layers also animate.

The top layer can be animated just like any other layer. It must be noted that there is nothing you can do with Preserve Underlying Transparency that you couldn't do with a couple of comps and a track matte – it's just another tool to add to your growing arsenal of layering tricks.

GOTCHA

T Does Nothing

If the comp's alpha channel is fully white, Preserve Underlying Transparency will appear to do nothing.

Preserve Underlying Transparency is set using the T switch in the Modes column.

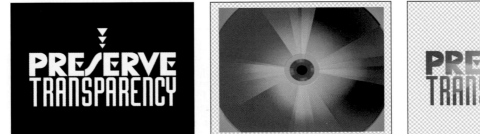

The alpha channel for all three text layers (left). Adding a video layer on top blots out those underneath (center). By switching on Preserve Underlying Transparency, the layer appears only inside the opaque areas of the alphas of the object layers below (right).

Glints, Backgrounds, and Effects

Preserve Underlying Transparency can also be used for adding glints and highlights to underlying layers. You can use After Effects to create soft-edged "glint" elements, then animate them across titles or objects to introduce subtle lighting effects. In [**Ex.06**] we moved a simple solid layer across the title and turned on Preserve Underlying Transparency.

If you add a background layer to a comp in which a layer has Preserve Underlying Transparency applied, any layers with the "T" switch on will become visible wherever the background is opaque. Try it in [**Ex.06**]: Turn on layer 3, the background movie, and notice that the glint is no longer confined to playing just inside the title layer.

Glint Effect

An alternative to the technique explained here is to use Effect > Generate > CC Light Sweep which can create a glint directly on layers with alpha channels.

An animated solid layer with a mask and feathered edge (left) serves as a simple glint for a title when Preserve Underlying Transparency is switched on (center). To add a background, nest this comp into a second comp (right). Footage courtesy Artbeats/Dreamlight 1.

In cases like this, you'll need to composite the glint within certain layers only in the first comp, then add background layers in a second comp (just as we did when we combined stencils and backgrounds earlier in this chapter). This is shown in the chain [**Ex.07-Comp-1/glint**] and [**Ex.07-Comp 2/BG**]. Notice that this setup also gives you the option to apply effects (such as bevels and drop shadows) to the title in the second comp, which are applied *after* the glint has been rendered.

Stencil versus Track Matte

The Track Matte and Stencil features can both accomplish the same results, but they go about it in different ways:

• Stencils can affect multiple layers, but a track matte can be applied to only one layer using one matte. If you need to apply a matte to multiple layers, you'll need to group layers in a precomp.

• You can have multiple stencils per comp, and you can create "doughnut" shapes or frames by combining stencils and silhouettes. Since After Effects renders from the bottom up, the lower stencil is calculated first, ending at the top stencil. You can't apply more than one track matte to a layer in one comp.

• Stencils affect all layers below them, so trying to add a full-frame background layer is futile – it will get cut out as well. You need to nest the stencil comp into a second comp and add the background there. However, you *can* add a background to a Track Matte comp, although you will have more flexibility if you also use a precomp (see Chapter 11).

• Track mattes and stencils can be mixed in the same comp so long as you keep track of their individual logic: A track matte takes its transparency data from the layer above, while stencils affect all layers below.

• Finally, with track mattes, the matte's Video switch (eyeball) should be *off*, but with stencils and silhouettes, the eyeball needs to be *on*.

When you're applying Preserve Transparency to multiple layers, you may occasionally run into fringing along alpha channel edges. This problem is shown in [**Ex.08**], where the top layer is darkening the edge of the title, despite its being set to Add mode. To fix this, composite the top two layers in a precomp, then set Preserve Transparency to the title in the second comp. This is shown in the [**Ex.09**] set of nested comps.

Finally, if you nest a comp that has a stencil or the preserve transparency option set, and then set the Collapse Transformations switch (Chapter 20), their effect will carry into the second comp as well.

Alpha Add with Stencils

Well, we promised you something obscure, and the Alpha Add mode is it. To keep track of what's going on, close all other comps, and open the [**Ex.10_starter**] comp. Preview the animation and note how the two sides of a torn-edge matte meet at 02:00 – but not exactly seamlessly. What's wrong?

The left side is using stencil luma, and the right side is the same image using silhouette luma (exactly like the left side, but inverted). Where the alpha channels meet along the seam, both antialiased edges have identical transparency values. But instead of adding these values together, the transparency of both layer edges are honored and factored together (50% opaque + 50% opaque = 75% opaque, not 100%). Since this fails to result in a fully opaque pixel, you get a seam. Note that this is not a problem with just stencils – you will see similar problems with track mattes and masking where identical edges meet.

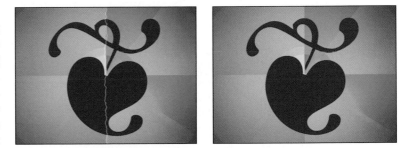

When any mask or matte edge is combined with its inverted cousin, a seam will appear where their partial transparencies meet (above left). By selecting the Alpha Add mode for the one on top (below), the complementary alpha values will be added together, and the seam will disappear (above right).

To fix this, select the top layer, and select the Alpha Add mode from the Modes column (it's the second-from-last item). The complementary alpha channels are now added together – as opposed to compositing on top of each other – and the seam disappears.

If you're curious as to how this animation was created, check out the precomps for [**Ex.10**]. The first comp, [**Ex.10_source layers**], composites the layers that will be sliced in two. This is nested in both the [**Ex.10-Stencil_Left**] and [**Ex.10-Stencil_Right**] comps, where the stencils are applied. Any changes made to the [**10_source layers**] comp will be reflected in both the left and right sides. The two sides are then nested in [**Ex.10-final**] and animated so that they join to form a complete image.

CONNECT

How transparency values add is also mentioned in the *Opacity* section in Chapter 3.

Alpha Add mode with masks: Chapter 10.

Track mattes: Chapter 11.

Nesting compositions: Chapter 18.

Adjustment layers: Chapter 22.

3D Space

Adding depth to your animations by mastering Z space.

One of the most important features in After Effects is the ability to move in 3D space. Layers do not need to be restricted to the left/right, up/down motions of the X and Y axes; they can also move closer or farther along the Z axis (think of a line extending from your computer monitor to your eyes), which relates to how close a layer is to you. This allows more for natural scaling, multiplaning, perspective changes, and depth sorting of layers – as well as 3D tumbles and rotations. 3D space extends to the use of cameras and lights, meaning graphic designers can build virtual sets, light them, and fly around them.

After Effects has implemented 3D space in a very flexible manner. Not all layers in a composition need to be in 3D; you can enable the 3D Layer switch just for those objects you want to add an extra dimension to, while keeping the others in familiar 2D space. You don't need to add cameras or lights either; a composition has a default camera which provides a head-on view, and a default light which illuminates all 3D layers evenly regardless of their orientation. (Of course, you can add and animate cameras and lights; this is covered in the next two chapters.)

These features can understandably cause trepidation among users not already fluent in 3D space. Even if you are, there are some features unique to After Effects' implementation of 3D – for example, the objects do not have true depth, which limits the illusion of 3D space. In the next four chapters, we will demystify working in 3D and uncover many of the creative options (and limitations) it presents.

This chapter will focus first on becoming familiar with how 3D space works, and how to view it. We will then progress to moving and animating layers through it, and then understanding the rendering issues involved when you mix 2D and 3D layers in the same comp.

Enter a New Dimension

In this section, we hope to give you a gentle introduction to working in 3D space. Even if you already have a good grasp of what 3D space is, working through the examples presented will show how to control it in After Effects and reinforce important concepts of how perspective causes 3D layers to appear to move differently than 2D layers.

TIP

OpenGL

OpenGL previewing greatly accelerates working in 3D space, with some tradeoffs. It is covered in depth in the *Preview Possibilities* sidebar at the end of Chapter 2; we recommend you read it before working in 3D.

Example Project

Explore the 13-Example Project.aep file as you read this chapter; references to [Ex.##] refer to specific compositions within the project file.

Postcards in Space

Layers themselves have not changed in After Effects – they are the same movies, still images, and vector artwork you are familiar with. A side effect of this is that they have no thickness, whether they are moving through 2D or 3D space. This is the main difference between After Effects and "real" 3D programs, in which you can create objects that have volume and depth.

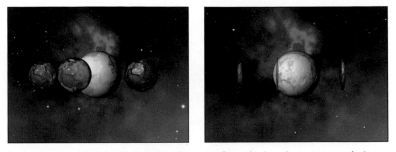

As the spheres move closer to and farther away from the imaginary camera during their orbits, they scale naturally, giving the illusion of depth (left). When the spheres turn on their sides (right), you can see that the layers themselves have no depth. Some refer to this implementation of 3D as "2.5D" or "postcards in space." Background courtesy Artbeats/Space & Planets.

Open the composition [**Ex.01**] in this chapter's Example Project and RAM Preview it: The first few seconds show spheres orbiting in 3D space, but the illusion is broken after the halfway point when they turn on their sides. Managing an object's position and orientation in 3D are two of the main subjects of this chapter.

The Z Factor

When you add a footage item to a composition, it defaults to using familiar 2D space. Open comp [**Ex.02a**], then select the footage item **SOURCES > Objects > CD_bikewheel** from the Project panel and press Command+/ on Mac (Control+/ on Windows) to add it to this comp. Type P to reveal its Position parameter, followed by Shift+S to also reveal Scale. Scrub its X and Y values in the Timeline panel; it should move as you would expect in two dimensions. Make a note of how far you have to scrub these values to push the wheel offscreen. Then scrub its Scale; the wheel gets smaller and larger. Return its Position to 360,243 and Scale to 100%.

Now let's place it in 3D space. Make sure the Switches column is revealed in the Timeline panel; if it isn't, press F4 to reveal it. The rightmost icon along the top of the Switches column looks like a cube – this is the 3D Layer switch. Click on the hollow box underneath it for **CD_bikewheel**. The already-exposed Position and Scale properties will each gain a third value: Z Position and Z Scale, respectively. (Rotation and Orientation values will also appear; we'll discuss those later.)

When you enable the 3D Layer switch (circled in red) for a footage item, it gains values for Z Position and Z Scale. The layer usually does not initially appear different in the Comp panel, except for the addition of a set of red, green, and blue axis arrows showing the X, Y, and Z orientation of the layer.

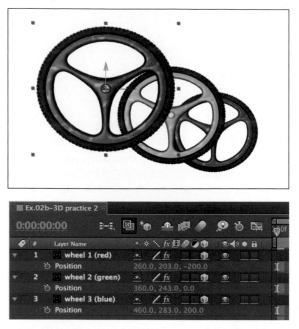

In **[Ex.02b]**, three wheels with the same scale value are offset from each other in Z space, resulting in different apparent sizes (top). The red and blue wheels have the same X and Y offset from the green wheel (above).

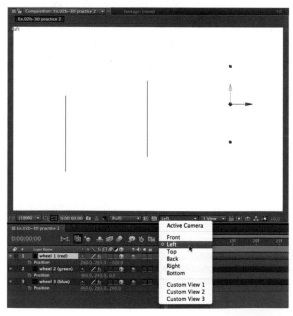

Click on the 3D View popup at the bottom of the Comp panel to view your layers from different perspectives. In the Left view, moving in the Z direction moves the layer left and right. Note you can now clearly see the blue Z axis arrow.

The **CD_bikewheel** layer will initially not look any different in the Comp panel. This is because a composition's default 3D camera is set up so that layers at Z Position = 0 have the same apparent size in 2D or 3D. However, you should notice a trio of arrows sticking out of the anchor point for the layer. These are the axis arrows, and they help you understand which way a layer is oriented in space. The red arrow represents the X axis, the green arrow Y, and the blue arrow Z. The blue arrow is hard to see right now, because it's pointing straight at you.

Scrub the value for Z Position (the rightmost value), and notice that the wheel gets smaller and larger, even though its Scale property remains unchanged. Set the Z Position to 300, and now scrub X and Y to see how far you have to move the wheel to push it offscreen – much farther than before. This is because 3D comes with *perspective*: An object's distance from the viewer changes how we perceive it. If you ever need a reminder of how this works, just wave your hand close to your nose, then an arm's length away from your face, noticing its relative size and how quickly it moves across your field of view compared with how fast you're moving your hand.

Open comp **[Ex.02b]**, which contains three of these wheels. Each wheel layer has the same Scale value (50%), but each is placed at a different distance in Z space. The Position property should be exposed (if not, select the layers and press P). Notice how Z distance relates to their relative size: Distance from the viewer acts as a natural version of Scale. The three wheels are also spaced the same distance from each other along X (the left and right axis). Scrub the Z Position for the left and right wheels (**wheel 1** and **wheel 3**), and notice how they drift around the Comp panel. In 3D space, objects that are not precisely centered in the view appear to drift in the X and Y axes as you move them in Z. The farther away they get, the more they appear to move toward the center; the closer they get, the faster they fly offscreen. This is also an example of perspective affecting how we see objects in 3D space.

If you're having a hard time visualizing what is going on when you scrub the Z axis, you can use an alternate 3D View. Click on the button along the bottom right of the Comp panel that currently says Active Camera: A popup menu appears with a list of alternative views. Select Top or Left, and scrub the Z Positions of the wheels to see how they move. Note that from these views, you can tell that all three wheels are still the same size. Select Custom View 3 (which gives you an angled perspective) and scrub all three Position axis values for the wheels. Once you feel you have a good grasp of the Z axis, return to the Active Camera view; we will explore these alternate views in greater detail later.

The three Custom Views offer a quick way to view a scene from different perspectives, without having to create a camera first.

Taking a Spin in 3D

Now that you've got the hang of moving objects in 3D, let's move on to rotating them. Open [**Ex.02c**]; it contains another copy of the now-familiar bike wheel, currently in 2D space. Select it and type R to reveal its Rotation property. Scrub this value; it rotates around its axle as you would expect. Leave this property at some value other than 0°.

Enable the 3D Layer switch for this wheel. There are now *four* Rotation parameters: Orientation, X Rotation, Y Rotation, and Z Rotation. Once you get over your initial surprise, you might notice that your previous Rotation value has been copied to the new Z Rotation parameter. Scrub the Z Rotation value, and the wheel will rotate just as it did before.

Now play around with scrubbing the X and Y Rotation values. You will notice that each causes the wheel to rotate around its corresponding axis arrow in the Comp panel. You will also quickly notice that rotating these axes ±90° results in the wheel disappearing as it is rotated on edge. As we mentioned earlier, *3D layers have no thickness.* Accidentally rotating a layer on edge and causing it to disappear is one of the most common "mistakes" when you're working in 3D in After Effects. Keep rotating past 90°, and you will see the back of the layer, which is a copy of the front – but it's backward now, as you have flipped it around.

Return to [**Ex.02b**], select all three layers, and press R to reveal their Rotation properties. With all three layers still selected, enter a Y Rotation value of 90° for one of the layers (they should all jump to this value). Notice that only the layer that was dead-center – **wheel 2** – disappears on edge; you can still see slivers of the other wheels. This is another manifestation of perspective. Select **wheel 1** or **wheel 3**, type Shift+P to also view its Position, and scrub its Z Position value, noting how you see more of the "side" of the layer as it moves closer to you.

3D layers have four – count 'em, *four* – Rotation parameters: Orientation, X Rotation, Y Rotation, and Z Rotation (this last value being the same as 2D Rotation). This may seem like overkill, but each has its purpose.

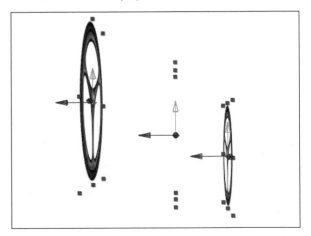

[**Ex.02b**]: Although all three wheel layers have been rotated "on edge" (90° around their Y axis), you can still see slivers of the layers that are not centered in the view. This is another example of how 3D perspective alters how layers are seen.

Quaternion Physics

The X, Y, and Z Rotation properties employ what is known as Euler rotation, which means they each do their own thing, regardless of what the other dimensions are doing. Orientation uses Quaternion rotation, which means the three axes coordinate to take the shortest path from value A to value B. (Remember those terms if you want to impress a client.) In general, use the Rotation values to animate a layer and Orientation to pose it.

Now go back to [**Ex.02c**], and return the X Rotation, Y Rotation, and Z Rotation parameters to 0°. Turn your attention to the Orientation property: It has three values. These correspond to X, Y, and Z Orientation. Scrub them; they will seem to have the same effect as scrubbing X, Y, and Z Rotation individually.

Why have two separate ways to rotate a layer? Because each animates differently. Open [**Ex.02d**], which contains two copies of the wheel. The Rotation values should be exposed. Press Home and End, and check out the keyframe values entered for the two wheels: They are essentially the same, except one wheel animates Orientation, while the other animates Rotation. RAM Preview the comp and notice how the two wheels animate quite differently. This is because Rotation always goes through the entire range of values you request, while Orientation takes a shortcut to reach its final pose with a minimum amount of fuss. The Orientation values are also limited to one revolution – unlike Rotation, you can't keyframe multiple revolutions with Orientation. *In general, it's better to use Orientation to "pose" a layer, and to use Rotation to animate it.*

Although you can rotate a layer with the Rotate tool, there is a nasty glitch: If Y Rotation goes beyond ±90°, the X and Z values flip by 180° (try it!). We recommend you scrub values directly in the Timeline panel.

The Hidden Effects of Z Scale

3D layers also have a Z Scale parameter. As layers in After Effects have no thickness, changing the Z Scale value will often appear to have no effect. However, if the Z value for a layer's Anchor Point is not zero, then Z Scale is multiplied by the Z Anchor Point to decide how far from this pivot point to draw the layer. You can observe this in [**Ex.04a**] by scrubbing **GI_goldfish**'s Scale and noticing it doesn't just get smaller and larger; it also moves closer to and farther away from its anchor.

The other exception is if a layer has a child attached to it (as discussed in Chapter 17, *Parenting Skills*). In this case, Z Scale factors into the "reality distortion field" that the parent casts over its children. In [**Ex.04b**], the parent layer is scaled 100% in X and Y, but 250% in Z. RAM Preview; notice how the child layer is distorted as it rotates into the parent's Z space.

In general, it's a good idea to leave Z Scale the same as X and Y Scale, unless you are consciously going after a certain effect.

The orange fish – the parent – is scaled 100% in X and Y, but 250% in Z. It still looks normal, as it has no thickness to begin with. However, the yellow fish – the child – stretches as it rotates into its parent's Z axis distortion field. Fish image courtesy Getty Images; background courtesy Artbeats/Liquid Ambience.

Anchors and Offsets

A layer's Anchor Point is the center around which it rotates and scales. This continues to be true in 3D. Click on the menu along the top of the Comp panel and select Close All to reduce the clutter, and open [Ex.02e]: **CP_Medical_arm** already has its 3D Layer switch enabled. Select the layer, and type Y to select the Pan Behind (Anchor Point) tool. In the Comp panel, place your cursor directly over the anchor – nicely illustrated by the 3D axis arrows – and move the anchor to the left end, near where the shoulder should be, which would be its natural pivot point. When you're done, type V to return to the Selection tool. With the layer still selected, type S followed by Shift+R to reveal its Scale and Rotation properties in the Timeline panel. Have fun scrubbing these values, confirming how transformations are centered about the anchor. Leave the arm skewed so that you can clearly see the blue Z axis arrow in the Comp panel.

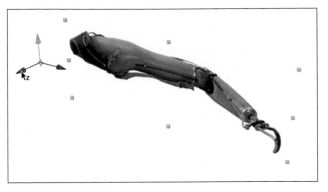

A layer's Anchor Point remains pivotal in 3D, acting as the center of Scale and Rotation transformations. The anchor can also be offset in Z from the layer itself. Arm from Classic PIO/Medical.

As with the rest of the Transform properties, placing a layer into 3D adds a Z dimension to the Anchor Point. With the layer still selected, press Shift+A to add Anchor Point to the list of revealed properties. Scrub the third Anchor Point value (its Z offset), and notice how the arm moves away from the axis arrows in the Comp panel. The Anchor Point does not need to be placed on the layer; the Z Anchor Point value becomes an invisible extension arm for the anchor's natural pivot point.

Open [Ex.03] and RAM Preview it: An arrow spirals in ever-widening circles. Select the layer named **arrow** and press U to reveal its keyframes. While it rotates on its Y axis, its Z Anchor Point animates outward, causing it to move farther and farther away from its pivot point. With the layer still selected, scrub the current time indicator along the timeline while watching the Comp panel – you will see the layer rotate around its green Y axis arrow at its Anchor Point, as it moves farther away from its anchor.

[Ex.03]: While the arrow rotates in Y around its Anchor Point (above), the anchor's Z value increases, causing the arrow to spiral outward away from the center (below). Background courtesy Artbeats/Gears.

The default 3D View for a comp is Active Camera (above). Click on it and select an alternate view, such as Front (below). The six orthographic views – Front, Left, Top, Back, Right, and Bottom – do not show any perspective, so all of the characters look the same size even though they are different distances from the virtual camera.

Working with 3D Compositions

You should now have a good feel for 3D space. However, it can be difficult to work in 3D with only a single 2D view. Fortunately, After Effects provides additional features to make life easier: The Comp panel can have alternate 3D Views as well as show multiple views at the same time; you can also open more than one panel to view the same composition.

3D Views

Open [**Ex.05**]: It contains three layers that spell the word "NOW" each placed at different Z positions, just as the three bike wheels were in [**Ex.02b**]. Along the bottom right edge of the Comp panel, you will see a button that says Active Camera; these words will be repeated in the Comp panel's upper left corner. This is the default "view" for a composition, and it means "use the current 3D camera to view 3D layers" (and if there isn't a 3D camera – as is the case here – use the comp's default camera). Viewing through a 3D camera introduces perspective; that's why the N in NOW – which is the closest to the camera – appears larger than the other characters.

Click on the 3D View popup; you will get a menu with nine additional choices: six *orthographic* views (Front, Left, Top, Back, Right, Bottom) and three "custom" views. You can think of your layers as floating in a very large room, with the six orthographic views as being the view from each of the six surfaces of the room, and the custom views being temporary cameras or viewing positions inside the room.

Select the Front view; the three characters will now appear to be the same size. Orthographic views do not show any perspective, which means distance from the viewer (Z Position values, in this case) has no effect on how the layers are viewed.

Now select the Left view. You will see only colored outlines of the layers. This is because you are viewing them directly on edge, and they have no thickness. If the Orientation parameter is not already visible in the Timeline panel for the text layer **N**, select it and type R. Scrub its Y Orientation value (the middle one); you should now see the letter N swing around. Return it to 0°, make sure its Position is exposed (shortcut: P), and scrub its Z Position value – you will see it move left and right.

The orthographic views often default to showing the layers too large. You can change their zoom level two ways. The obvious one – and the one you often *don't* want to use – is to change the Magnification of the Comp panel. Less obvious but more useful are the Camera tools, which allow you to change your view while leaving the Comp panel's settings intact.

While you're in Left view, locate the Tools panel along the top of the main Application window, and select the fifth tool from the left. These are the Camera tools. Click on the icon and hold down the mouse until a submenu of four tools pops out. For starters, select the Track XY Camera. Move your cursor over the Comp panel; the cursor will change to resemble its matching tool icon. Click anywhere in this panel and drag to the right until the edges of the three layers are centered in the Comp panel. Press C to toggle to the next tool in line: Track Z Camera. Now as you drag, you can zoom in and out on the layers. Zoom out a bit, and practice scrubbing the Z Position values for the three layers; toggle between the Track XY and Z tools to recenter your view. (The Orbit Camera tool has no effect in the orthographic views, as their viewing angle is fixed.) Try out the Top view – this is another good way to view what is happening along the Z axis. Note that its pan and zoom are separate from the Left view (it usually defaults to being too close); use the Camera tools to change it.

Unlike the orthographic views, the three custom views show perspective like a "real" camera does. They are great for looking at your objects from different angles without messing up their positions or a camera you may be animating (the subject of the next chapter). Select Custom View 3; it provides a good overview of how these particular layers have been arranged in space. Again, you can use the Camera Track tools to tweak the view; you can also use the Orbit Camera tool to swing around your layers.

If you have a three-button mouse, select the Unified Camera tool (the camera icon). When this is active, left-click to temporarily activate the Orbit tool, middle-click for Track XY, and right-click for Track Z.

All of your edits to these views are saved with your project. However, when you create a new composition, these views revert to their default settings. If you get lost in space, the menu command View > Reset 3D View can also be used to revert the current view to its default.

The function keys F10, F11, and F12 can be used to quickly switch between three different 3D Views. The default is Front (F10), Custom View 1 (F11), and Active Camera (F12), but you can easily assign these keys to your three favorite views. (Mac users will need to reassign Apple's Exposé, which uses these shortcut keys by default.) To assign a key, select the view you want, and use the menu item View > Assign Shortcut.

The best way to move around in alternate 3D views is to use the tools. They allow you to pan and zoom your view without changing the Comp panel's magnification settings or resizing the panel. Type C to toggle between them; type V to return to the normal Selection tool.

Use the Camera tools to customize your views to better frame the layers you are working with. Here we have chosen the Unified tool, and are right-clicking to select the Track Z tool which enables us to zoom in on the layers in Custom View 3.

 TIP

Look at Layers

To automatically zoom and center your view to see all of the desired layers, use View > Look at Selected Layers or View > Look at All Layers. If one of the Camera tools is selected, press F to Look at Selected Layers, and Command+Shift+F (Control+Shift+F) to Look at All Layers.

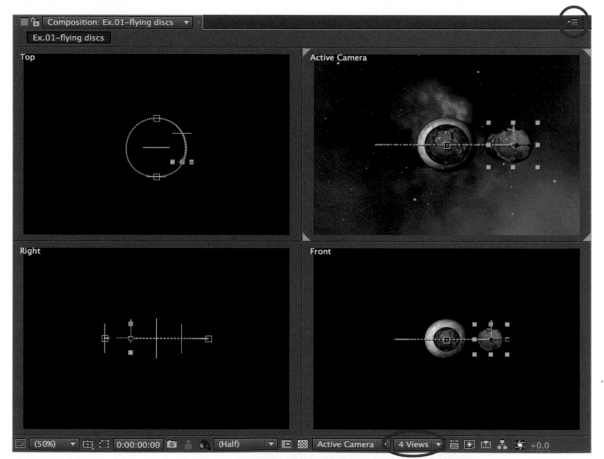

Choose from alternative layouts that offer multiple views inside a single Comp panel. To automatically assign changes to the Magnification, Resolution, and other View Options across all views, enable Share View Options.

View Layouts

Traditional 3D programs give you multiple views of the same workspace. You can leave one view showing the render camera's perspective, then use the others to arrange the objects in 3D space without having to move the camera to get a better look. Common arrangements include two views (one for the camera, and one to switch between alternate views) or four views (one for the camera, and one each for top, front, and right).

In this vein, After Effects has a Select View Layout popup along the bottom of the Comp panel. This popup provides a nice assortment of alternative layouts that offer multiple views inside the single Comp panel. This layout is set and remembered independently for each composition.

Reopen [**Ex.01**], then change Select View Layout from 1 View to 2 Views – Horizontal. The active view is noted by yellow triangles in its corners. Changes to 3D View as well as other options are applied to the

Change Select View Layout to 4 Views to re-create a common 3D arrangement in the Comp panel. The names of the views are displayed by default; these may be disabled in the Composition panel's Options menu (top right corner). Above is a common 3D workspace: one Comp panel set to the Active Camera to see how your layers will render (upper right), and three others showing the Top, Front, and Right orthographic views of your layers. Notice that a 2D background draws only in the Active Camera view.

selected view. Verify that one view is set to Active Camera. Then click anywhere in the other view to make it active and set its 3D View popup to an alternative such as Left.

Another approach is to add a second Comp panel to your workspace that looks at the same composition. Select View > New Viewer; an additional tab will appear in the same frame as your Comp panel. Each viewer can have its own settings. You can click on the tabs to toggle between viewers or drag one out to create a new frame for it (covered in Chapter 1).

Experiment with the other alternatives such as the 4 View options until you're comfortable with them. We will be using alternate views from here on. Select Close All from the top of the Comp panel before continuing.

When you have multiple views open, by default the view with the Active Camera will RAM Preview. If you want to change this behavior, disable Previews Favor Active Camera from the RAM Preview Options menu (above). Each viewer also has an Always Preview This View switch in their lower left corner (right).

The 2D Viewport

In earlier versions of After Effects, 2D layers were shown in all of the 3D Views, which was very distracting. Now, 2D Layers are only displayed in the Active Camera view, or if you have a specific camera selected (discussed in the next chapter).

However, one oddity that persists to this day is that the other views are still rendered inside a viewport which is controlled by the Composition's size.

To see this in action, open **[Ex.05]** and turn on the Video switch for **AB_LiquidAbstracts**. This is a 2D layer, which is supposed to serve as a background for our text. Note that it is rendered in Active Camera view, but not in any of the other views.

Select a view other than Active Camera (such as Custom View 3), and zoom in using the Track Z tool:

If a 3D layer is on the pasteboard, you will see only an outline of it; if it appears inside this 2D view area, then its image is displayed. Therefore, we often leave the comp's Magnification at 100% to maximize this render area, and then use the Camera tools to zoom and pan around our world (see page 227). Note that if you lower the Magnification of the viewport, you will restrict the area which is rendered, and – if you have Resolution set to Auto – also reduce the resolution the layers are rendered at.

Another side effect of this display method is that the optional rulers in the Comp panel are meaningless in the alternate views: They do not take into account how you may have panned, zoomed, and orbited the view.

In the Active Camera view, 2D layers are drawn in the same positions that they will render in (left), but are not visible in any of the alternate 3D Views (right). Background courtesy Artbeats/Liquid Abstracts.

Reducing the Comp's Magnification shrinks the "viewport." 3D layers outside the viewport are drawn as outlines.

When you move the cursor close to an axis arrow, a letter describing its dimension appears. Click and drag while this character is visible, and movements will be constrained to this axis.

RGB = XYZ

To remember which color arrow represents which axis, just recall that RGB (the three color channels) correspond to XYZ (the three axes).

Getting a Grip

Now that we have a handle on 3D space and how to view it, it's time to start moving layers around in it. We're going to assume you have Window > Workspace set to One Comp View; if you want to get some practice using the Two Comp View option, set Magnification for both Comp panels to Fit Up To 100%, leave one Comp panel set to Active Camera, and apply our instructions to your second Comp panel.

So far, we've been scrubbing transform properties in the Timeline panel to move 3D layers around, but you can also grab and move them directly in the Comp panel. Open [**Ex.06**] and verify that its view is set to Active Camera; it contains the same three characters you saw in [**Ex.05**]. Select text layer 1 **N**, press P to expose its Position, then V to make sure you are using the Selection tool. You should see the now-familiar red, green, and blue XYZ axis arrows in the Comp panel. Move your cursor near them, and the letter X, Y, or Z will appear next to your cursor arrow. If you click and drag when one of these letters is visible, your movements will be restricted to this axis. This is an expansion of the 2D trick of holding down the Shift key after you start moving a layer to constrain its movements to the X or Y axis.

By using this trick, you can even move the layer in an axis that would otherwise require you to push your mouse into the screen or select an alternate 3D View. Place your cursor near the stub of the blue Z axis arrow until the letter Z appears, and now click and drag. You should see the Z Position value update in the Timeline panel. If you click and drag without seeing one of these letters, you can now freely move the layer along the two axes determined by your current view. Practice this in a few different 3D Views, such as Top and Left.

Twirl versus Spin

In general, if we want to either pose or animate the rotation of a layer, we'll scrub the Orientation and Rotation values respectively in the Timeline panel. However, if you prefer to manipulate layers interactively, there's a Rotation tool – but it has a big gotcha.

When you have a 3D layer selected and choose the Rotation tool, you will see an extra popup menu toward the right in the Tools panel that allows you to choose if you are manipulating Rotation or Orientation. To decide which axis to rotate (or orient), place the cursor over the corresponding axis arrow until you see it change to an X, Y, or Z.

Make sure a layer in [**Ex.06**] is still selected, and reveal its Rotation properties by typing R. Select the Rotate tool (the shortcut is W). A popup will appear to the right of the tool icon in the Tools panel; select Orientation. As you move your cursor near the axis arrows in the Comp panel, you will now see the axis letter plus a circular icon. Click and drag while one of these letters is visible; note that rotations are constrained to this axis, and the corresponding Orientation value changes in the Timeline panel. Click and drag when an axis letter is not visible, and you can freely rotate the layer in any direction, updating all three Orientation values at once. However, if you drag Y Rotation or Orientation beyond ±90°, the X and Z values will jump 180°! This is why we don't use the Rotation tool in 3D – especially for animation.

Think Global; Act Local

Open comp **[Ex.99]**. The 3D View popup along the bottom of the Comp panel has been set to Custom View 3, and the radio layer has been tilted back in X so the image is at an angle. Select the radio layer, and note that its axis arrows are connected to the surface of the radio – this is the default. (The technical description is that the axis arrows are oriented in the layer's "local" coordinate space.)

• **Local Axis Mode:** This default behavior is selected by the first of three axis mode icons in the Tools panel. With the radio layer selected, reveal its Rotation and Position properties. Rotate the character slightly askew in X or Y; you'll notice the axis arrows rotate as well, as they are local to the layer. Drag the character with an axis letter visible; its movement will be constrained to the direction the arrow is pointing. However, all of the Position values will change, because the layer is now moving at an angle in the composition's overall space.

• **World Axis Mode:** Now select the middle icon: World Axis Mode. The axis arrows will snap around to orient along the composition's coordinate space. Drag them while an axis letter is visible, and you will notice that only one Position value updates at a time. This is a handy tool when you are using a perspective view like Active Camera, but want to

Axis Modes

Local   World   View

Along the right edge of the Tools panel are three small icons: These select the coordinate system for the axes. Left to right, they are: Local Axis Mode, World Axis Mode, and View Axis Mode.

move a layer precisely in X, Y, or Z without having to scrub it in the Timeline panel.

• **View Axis Mode:** Click on the icon at the bottom right; this is View Axis Mode. In the Comp panel, you will see that the axis arrows have snapped around to match your current view. Drag these arrows while an axis character is visible – now your movements are constrained to up/down, left/right, and in/out from the view's perspective. Watch the Position parameters in the Timeline panel, and you'll see that all values change – these reflect the layer's position in the composition's "world" coordinate space, not your view's. View Axis Mode is most useful when a layer (like a title) is centered in the view and you want it to move closer or farther away from the camera.

Reselect the Local Axis Mode again when you've finished experimenting.

Local Axis Mode   **World Axis Mode**   **View Axis Mode**

The Axis Modes determine if a layer's axis arrows are oriented according to the layer's local coordinates (the default), the comp's overall world space, or the current view. In the figures above, the layer orientations are identical (tilted back in X and centered in the Comp panel) – only the axis modes change. Radio courtesy Classic PIO.

3D Motion Paths

Once you can move layers through 3D space with confidence, it's a relatively short jump to start setting keyframes and animating them. The only tricky bit is trying to edit Bezier motion paths in 3D – you will need to work in multiple views to really understand what's going on.

Open [**Ex.07_starter**]: It contains the three characters that form the word NOW with their 3D Layer switches already enabled, plus a 2D background layer. The Comp panel should already be set to 2 Views – Horizontal; if not, choose this option from the Select View Layout popup. Set the left view to Left, and the right view to Active Camera.

The goal is to make each character fly into place:

Step 1: With many animations, it is easier to start with the final position and work backward; that's what we'll do here. Click on the time readout in the Timeline panel, type "**100**" and press Return to jump to the time 01:00. Then type Shift+1 to place a comp marker here, and press N to end the Work Area here as well. Select layer 1 (**N**), then press Option+Shift+P (Alt+Shift+P) to turn on the stopwatch and enable keyframing for Position. The Position property will twirl down in the Timeline, with the first keyframe set at 01:00. Press Home to return to time 00:00.

Step 2: We want the N to start far away in Z space, as well as down and to the left. Scrub the Z Position value to the right until it equals 1000 or so; you will see the character get farther away as well as move to the right (not left) as a natural result of 3D perspective. That's okay; just grab it in the Comp panel and drag it off the lower left corner, onto the pasteboard. If you need to, resize the Comp panel a bit larger to see the axis arrows. RAM Preview to get a feel for this straightforward move.

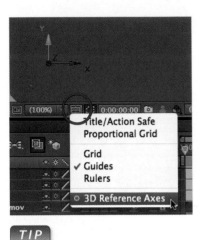

3D Reference Axes

For a quick visual reminder of the orientation of each of your views, click on the Choose Grid and Guide Options button in the lower left corner of the Comp panel and enable 3D Reference Axes (above).

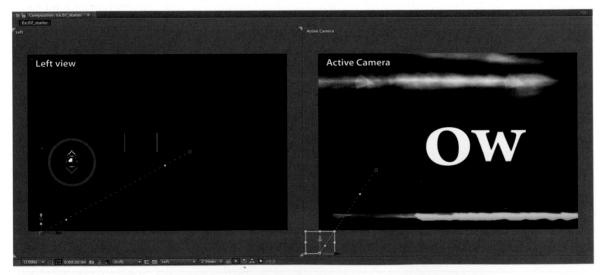

Steps 2+3: Start by setting two Position keyframes for the letter N: one at its final resting place, and one just off screen in the lower left corner. Note the default linear motion path. Press C to toggle through the Track Camera tools (inset) and center your layers in the Left view.

Step 3: This movement is okay, but it would be more dramatic if it swooped more quickly to the correct horizontal and vertical position, then came forward toward the viewer – while still moving from the lower left corner to its final resting place without wandering about the comp. There's no easy way to bend the Bezier motion path handles in a head-on view to accomplish this, so select the viewer in the Comp panel that is displaying the Left view. If the default view is zoomed in too much to see the entire motion path, select the Track Z Camera tool. Click and drag downward in the Comp panel until you can see the entire path. If you like, select the Track XY Camera tool and pan the view to the right to better center it. Press V to return to the Selection tool.

View Review

When you change 3D views, you can quickly return to your previous view by pressing the Esc key.

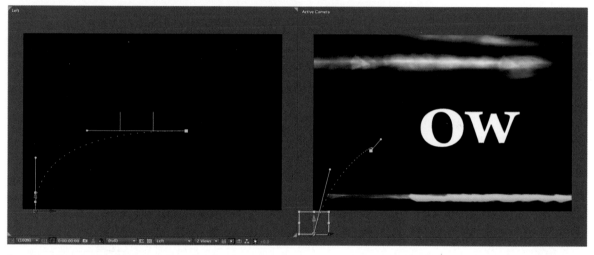

Step 4: To expose the Bezier handles for the layer, click on its Anchor Point icon, but not when one of the axis letters is showing (if you find this too fiddly, click on the word Position in the Timeline instead). While working in the Left view, drag the handle for the first (leftmost) keyframe upward and the handle for the second keyframe straight to the left. Turn your attention back to the Active Camera view and look at your motion path: Rather than moving in a somewhat straight line, it probably arcs upward. Editing a motion path in one view often has unintended consequences in another. Pull the handles for the two keyframes until they form a straight line in the Active Camera view. Then look back to the Left view, and make sure you still have the swoop in the Z dimension you intended. You may have to switch back and forth a few times to work out a compromise. Don't be surprised if the handles look unusually long or short in certain views, as you are seeing your handles (as well as your layers) from different angles.

Have fun coming up with alternate movements for the other two characters. If you get lost, study our motion path handles in [**Ex.07-final**] from a few different views.

Step 4: Edit the motion path to swoop along the Z axis (above left). While doing so, you may notice that you are affecting your formerly straight move from the lower left corner to the center (above right). Move between these views and refine your handles to get the final path you want (below).

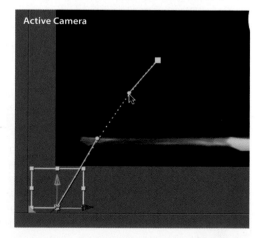

Work Smarter, Not Harder

Working in 3D is slower than working in 2D – in some cases, *much* slower. However, there are some techniques you can use to work faster, and leave the worst of the delays until the final render:

• The accuracy of motion blur (Chapter 8) for 3D layers is determined by the Samples Per Frame value in Composition Settings under the Advanced tab. Higher values are more accurate, but take longer to render; balance accordingly. Check the Motion Blur switch for only the layers that really benefit from it.

• Two of the most processor-intensive features in 3D are blurring the image based on a camera's depth of field, and calculating a light's shadows. We'll discuss both features in more detail in the next two chapters, but there is a handy button in the Timeline panel – Draft 3D – which temporarily disables depth of field and lights.

• OpenGL preview acceleration can greatly acceler-ate positioning layers in 3D. This uses hardware acceleration on your video card to interactively display a draft version of your composition as you edit parameters or drag the current time indicator. OpenGL is enabled via the Fast Previews popup menu along the lower right edge of the Comp panel. The button's icon will illuminate while OpenGL is engaged. OpenGL—Always On means always use OpenGL to render the image. OpenGL—Interactive means OpenGL will calculate the image only while you are moving it or updating a parameter; After Effects will revert to its normal software renderer

The Draft 3D switch temporarily disables lights (including shadows) and depth-of-field blur – two of the most render-intensive 3D attributes. Live Update toggles real-time updating on and off. Whether Motion Blur displays for layers with their corresponding switches set is determined by the Enable Motion Blur button.

when you are done (this is the preferred mode instead of Always On). OpenGL is discussed in detail in the *Preview Possibilities* sidebar in Chapter 2.

• Another option is working at a lower Resolution. Dropping Resolution down to Half means After Effects needs to calculate only one quarter of the pixels, as it is skipping every other pixel as well as every other line.

• If you have a large comp and want to focus just on action happening in a small area, the Region of Interest feature helps in some circumstances. Enable this button to the right of the Show Channel buttons in the Comp panel, and drag the mouse to select the area of the comp you are interested in viewing. This is the only section that will be rendered until you turn the switch off again. To reset the region, Option+click (Alt+click) on the Region of Interest switch.

And then there's always buying a faster computer…

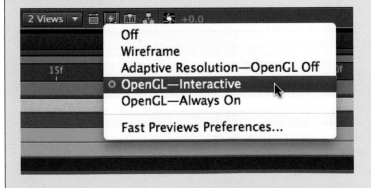

OpenGL preview acceleration provides much faster screen updates in 3D while scrubbing parameters or dragging the current time indicator. Selecting OpenGL—Interactive means that when you release the mouse, After Effects rerenders the frame using the normal software rendering engine, showing you what the final render will look like.

Auto-Orient Along 3D Path

In Chapter 5 we covered making a 2D layer auto-orient itself along its path – great for buzzing-fly animations and the like. This feature is even more powerful in 3D, but it does have a couple of gotchas.

To try this out, use either the animation you built in [**Ex.07_starter**] or our version in [**Ex.07-final**]. RAM Preview it so you are familiar with its current animation. Press 1 on the main keyboard (not the keypad) to locate to the comp marker at 01:00, then type Shift+F5 to save a snapshot of the current pose. Select text layer 1 **N**, and invoke the menu command Layer > Transform > Auto-Orient.

Auto-Orient works well in 3D, tilting the layer as it moves down its motion path as if on a string.

The default is Off; select Orient Along Path and click OK. The letter N will flip around backward! This is an example of a problem that occurs occasionally with Auto-Orient, as After Effects isn't sure which direction your layer is supposed to be pointing in. Stare at the axis arrows and think about which axis you need to flip it on. Then press R to reveal the Orientation property for **N**, and scrub this value to reorient the layer the way it's supposed to be facing. Worse case, scrub all three Orientation values until you figure out which one is right (the answer is Y, by 180°).

Toggle F5 on and off to compare your snapshot with the new pose; you might notice a slight shift. This is the second gotcha about Auto-Orient: Your motion path handles have to come into its final keyframe perfectly straight (in this case, along the Z axis) for layers to be oriented properly at rest. You can tweak your motion handles to get this right; move between the Left and Top views while you work. A cheat would be to adjust or animate the layer's Orientation settings so that the final "at rest" pose looks correct, and ignore the slight tilt during the actual move.

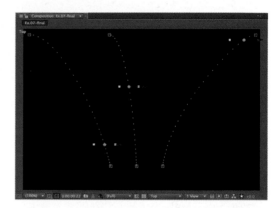

Study the axis arrows: When Auto-Orient is turned off (above), the layers face whatever direction they are pointed in, such as straight ahead. When Auto-Orient is set to Orient Along Path (below), the layers twist around to follow their motion paths.

Enough of the gotchas; RAM Preview and enjoy the new animation. You can also get a good idea of what Auto-Orient is doing by viewing your layer from the Left or Top view. Select the other two character layers, and use the keyboard shortcut Command+Option+O (Control+Alt+O) to open the Auto-Orientation dialog; choose Orient Along Path for them as well (note that you can set this for multiple layers at once). You can probably live with the 180° Y Orientation flip, as O and W happen to be symmetrical characters, but you might as well set them correctly to get in the habit of having to fix this for other layers in the future.

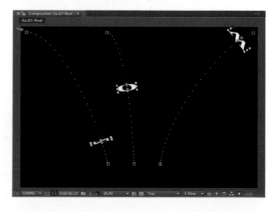

Our version is shown in [**Ex.07-final w/auto-orient**]. The third Auto-Orient option – Orient Towards Camera – will be put to use in the next chapter.

Rendering Orders

Now you know how to move and animate 3D layers, and have a feeling for how perspective distortion affects the way you view them. But we're still not quite done; we need to talk about how After Effects sorts out layers competing for the same space, combines 2D and 3D layers in the same comp, and how "2D" treatments such as blending modes and track mattes translate into 3D.

What a Difference a Dimension Makes

When After Effects renders a composition containing only 2D layers, life is easy: It takes the bottom layer in the Timeline panel and composites the next layer up the stack on top of it. If portions of the layer on top are transparent due to masking or alpha channels, portions of the layer underneath are revealed. This composite is saved in memory as a single image, and the process is repeated with the next layer up the stack. Exceptions are made along the way for blending modes, track mattes, stencils, and compound effects, but these are easily understood (especially after you've read the relevant chapters).

If the composition contains only 3D layers, stacking order in the Timeline is far less important. What matters now is how far away the objects are from the camera. If you're using the comp's default camera (as we have throughout this chapter), then a combination of the Z Positions and Anchor Points for the layers are a pretty good indicator of how they will be stacked in space, with larger Z values being further away and smaller ones (including negative values) being closer. If the layers are the exact same Z distance from the viewer and are oriented the same way, then the Timeline stacking order is used to sort them out.

To reinforce this, select Close All from the top of the Comp panel and open comps [Ex.08a] and [Ex.08b]. They contain the same collection of layers, stacked in the same order in the Timeline panel, but which is in front of which in the Comp panel is different. In [Ex.08a], all of the layers are in 2D space, which means reordering them in the Timeline will reorder them in the Comp panel – go ahead and play with swapping their positions. In [Ex.08b], all of the objects have their 3D Layer switch enabled, so now their Z Positions determine their stacking order: Scrub their respective Z Position values, and note how they both move and re-sort themselves in the Comp panel.

When all the layers are in 2D, their stacking order in the Comp panel is determined by their stacking order in the Timeline panel (above). When their 3D Layer switches are enabled, their stacking order is determined by their distances from the viewer (below). Note that because we had to place the background layer farther away in 3D, we also had to scale it up larger to fill the frame. TV courtesy Paul Sherstobitoff; other objects courtesy Classic PIO.

Intersections

By now you should be comfortable with the concept of 3D layers sorting themselves out according to their distance from the viewer or virtual camera. The next level of complexity comes when layers are at angles to each other, and cross in such a way that a portion of one layer should be in front of a second layer, while the rest of the first layer should be behind the second layer. This is referred to as *3D intersections*, and After Effects handles this situation automatically. (Indeed, Adobe has worked very hard on making sure the resulting line at the point of intersection is nicely antialiased, which can be a weakness in other programs.) The comps **[Ex.09a]** and **[Ex.09b]** show off a couple of fun examples that exploit intersections to create more complex composite objects.

After Effects automatically deals with layers that intersect each other in 3D space. You can exploit this to create some interesting constructs, such as the examples in **[Ex.09a]** (above) and **[Ex.09b]** (below).

Z Depth versus Scale

With 2D layers, you may be used to arranging your objects, then adjusting their Scale values to balance their relative sizes or to give the illusion of depth. However, placing 3D layers at different distances from the viewer also changes their apparent size, occasionally requiring you to readjust their Scale values.

For example, in **[Ex.08a]** we decided the 3D layer **CD_wc-blues** would be our background. We placed it at the bottom of the stack and scaled it to just fill the frame. However, when we started scrubbing the Z Positions of the layers in **[Ex.08b]**, any layer placed farther away than **CD_wc-blues** immediately disappeared behind it. When we placed **CD_wc-blues** farther away to make it the background again, it was too small to fill the frame – so we had to scale it up larger. Experience this yourself by enabling the 3D Layer switch for all the layers in **[Ex.08a]** and rearranging them from scratch. In general, if layers are going to be interacting with each other in 3D, it might be better to set their relative sizes by scaling them in 2D first, rather than using Z depth to size them. Then move them in 3D, and tweak their scale values only if needed.

As you tweak, you may find yourself scaling a layer beyond 100%, which is a major no-no in 2D as it inflates the pixels, reducing image quality. However, in 3D an object's distance is factored with its scale before it is rendered. If the result is less than 100% of original size, you're still safe. To test this, duplicate the layer in question, disable the 3D Layer switch for the duplicate, and set its Scale value to 100%. If the 2D version is larger than the 3D version, you're okay. If the 3D version was larger, you're inflating pixels and losing some quality; you may need to change your design or use a larger source file. Turn off or delete your 2D duplicate when you're done.

A typical arrangement is to keep background and foreground layers in 2D, with layers in-between in 3D.

3D Deployment

Red Giant Software PlaneSpace and Zaxwerks Layer Tools can help arrange selected layers into a variety of configurations in 3D space.

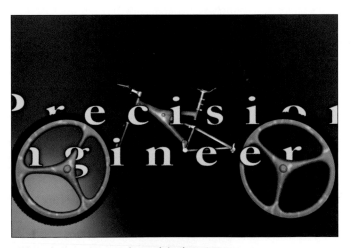

3D layer intersections can be exploited to create excitement with layers slicing through the title on their way to their final resting place.

Mixing 2D and 3D Layers

Life gets a little more complicated when you combine 2D and 3D layers in the same composition. In short, 2D layers act as "render breaks" between 3D layers. Groups of 3D layers that are stacked between 2D layers in the Timeline panel are internally flattened down to a 2D result, as if they were in a precomp by themselves. The entire composition is then rendered as if it consisted only of 2D layers, with each group of 3D layers being treated as a single 2D layer in the middle of the stack.

Open [**Ex.10a-2D title**] and RAM Preview it. This contains a typical arrangement of 2D and 3D layers in a composition:

• A full-frame background is left in 2D and placed at the bottom of the Timeline stack.

• A set of 3D layers interact in the middle of the Timeline stack (note how the bike wheels pop behind the bike frame as they settle into position).

• A 2D title that is supposed to sit on top of the entire composite is placed at the top of the Timeline stack. This is also where you would place lower thirds or 2D "bugs" (icons that go in a corner of the frame).

Keeping the background and title in 2D removes having to worry about their Z depths relative to the animating 3D layers, as they will render at the same depth no matter what happens in 3D. This 2D/3D/2D sandwich of layers will come in even more handy when you add 3D cameras and lights into the mix, as 2D layers are by definition not affected by cameras and lights.

On the other hand, interaction between 3D layers can add more excitement to a composition. Open the comp [**Ex.10b-3D title**] and RAM Preview it. Here we've enabled the 3D Layer switch for the title. As a result, the wheels slice through the title as they fly back into position (scrub the time indicator between 01:00 and 01:15 to study this more closely).

Breaking the Render Order

It is all too easy to break up groups of 3D layers, meaning those individual layers can no longer interact with each other (such as intersecting or casting shadows from one to another). Inserting the following types of layers between 3D layers will break up their groups:

• Any 2D layer, with the exception of Null Objects (covered in Chapter 17).

• Any Adjustment Layer (Chapter 22), even if its 3D Layer switch is enabled. The exception is an Adjustment Light (see Chapter 15).

• Any layer that has a Layer Style (Chapter 22) applied to it.

For example, say you wanted to use an adjustment layer to shift the hue of the bike wheels and background, but not the bike frame or title. Continuing with comp [**Ex.10b**], select Layer > New > Adjustment Layer. In the Timeline panel, drag it just underneath the **bike frame** layer, but above the **front wheel** layer. Preview the composition, and notice that the frame is now always in front of the wheels, even when the wheels are closer to the viewer in Z space. Delete the adjustment layer to return to normal. The workaround is to apply the desired effects to each layer individually.

To see another problem, still in [**Ex.10b**], select the first layer (**title – 3D**), and apply Layer > Layer Styles > Drop Shadow to help lift it visually away from the other layers. Preview, and you will notice that the wheels no longer slice through the title. To fix this problem, select Layer > Layer Styles > Remove All and apply Effect > Perspective > Drop Shadow instead.

Keep in mind that one person's curse can be another person's blessing. Say you wanted to keep the title in [**Ex.10b**] in 3D (it could be you used the Per-Character 3D feature mentioned in Chapter 21), but also wanted to keep the wheels behind the title. You could either work on rearranging their respective positions, scales, and animations in Z space…or you could merely insert an Adjustment Layer between the title and the other 3D layers to serve as a render break.

This is a core concept we mention throughout this book: Understanding the order that After Effects processes and renders layers is the difference between mastering this program and becoming baffled when it does "strange" or "unpredictable" things. Make sure you understand how 2D and 3D layers work together, and you will be able to easily craft complex compositions with subtle interactions between the layers.

Inserting an adjustment layer between 3D layers will break them into separate groups, and stop them from interacting with each other. (Turning on its 3D switch will not fix this.)

Applying a Layer Style to the title means it can no longer intersect with the wheels, even though all are in 3D.

Nesting in 3D

The output of a composition is a 2D image. If you nest one comp into another comp, the result of all of the layers in it – be they 2D or 3D – is considered to be a single 2D composite. The exception is if you Collapse Transformations for the nested comp layer. These subjects are discussed in detail in Chapters 18–20.

Warped 3D Layers

All layers in After Effects remain flat 2D planes, even when you use them in 3D space. Third-party plug-ins such as Digieffects FreeForm (Chapter 16) can give the impression that they are truly 3D.

Blending modes work in 3D, as long as the layer with the mode applied is in front of another layer. City footage courtesy Artbeats/Timelapse Cityscapes; data overlay from Artbeats/Digital Biz.

3D transformations applied to track matte layers affect the shape of the matte. Here, the video does not have any rotation, but the matte does. Footage courtesy Artbeats/Business Executives.

Other Layer Interactions

There are several features in After Effects – blending modes, track mattes, stencils, and adjustment layers, for starters – that rely on the interaction between layers. When these layers are in different locations in 3D space, the way these interactions work becomes less obvious.

Blending Modes

Modes work in 3D, which is exceptionally cool: Not only do you get perspective interactions between layers, but their colors can blend as well. Unlike 2D, the stacking order in the Timeline panel doesn't matter – how they sort in 3D space does.

To have a layer's blending mode affect another layer, the layer with the mode must be in front of the second layer in 3D space. Open comp [**Ex.11a**], and scrub the Z Position value for the **AB_DigitalBiz** layer, which has been set to Overlay mode. As long as its Z value is less than **AB_Timelapse-Cityscapes**, you will see the result of the mode. You can also play with **AB_DigitalBiz**'s Orientation. After you have dragged them to positions where you can see the result of the mode, reorder them in the Timeline panel to where **AB_DigitalBiz** is below **AB_TimelapseCityscapes**; the mode will still have the same effect.

Modes applied to 3D layers also affect 2D layers underneath them in the layer stack. Modes applied to 2D layers also affect 3D layers underneath *them* in the layer stack. Turn on the Video switch for the 2D layer **DV_InnerGaze** in [**Ex.11a**] and experiment with how it interacts with the 3D layers in the comp.

Track Mattes

Track Mattes also work in 3D, but with a couple of gotchas. You still need to place the matte above the layer to be matted in the Timeline, set the TrkMat popup for the layer to be matted, and make sure the Video switch remains off for the matte layer. Unlike blending modes, intersections and Z sorting *don't* matter when you're determining whether the matte will work, but the transforms applied to the matte layer in 3D space *do* affect the shape of the final matte – for example, pushing the matte layer farther away in Z space will make the matte smaller. Also, shadows don't cast properly; the matte is not taken into account.

Open [**Ex.11b**] and play around with the Z Position and Orientation of **matte layer** to get a feel for how these transformations affect the matte shape. You can also move the movie layer (**AB_BusExecutives**) in relation to the matte layer, just as with track mattes in 2D.

Just because you *can* do something doesn't mean you should: If you were to fly around these layers with a 3D camera, the perspective shifts between them will change which regions get matted. If you don't believe us, move these two layers to different positions in 3D space, choose a Custom View for the Comp panel, and use the Orbit Camera tool to see how the result changes with the view.

On the other hand, you can leave the movie layer in 2D, and transform the matte in 3D to create interesting animated matte shapes. Open [Ex.11c], select the **CD_goldspheremelt** layer (which is used as a matte), and scrub the time indicator to see how its animation affects the resulting matte shape.

Stencils

Stencils – which reside under the Mode popup – do not work in 3D. (They did in versions before CS3 if you used the Standard render engine, but alas, this render engine is no longer supported.) 2D stencils still work, and can cut out both 2D and 3D layers underneath them in the Timeline stack.

Stencils normally cut out layers underneath (left). However, if you enable their 3D Layer switch, they will no longer work (right).

As usual, we have provided a sample comp for your amusement: In [Ex.11d], note that the **stencil layer** on top initially has its 3D Layer switch enabled. It renders as just a white shape; the layers underneath render at their full size. Disable the 3D Layer switch for **stencil layer**; now it will cut out both the 2D and 3D layers underneath.

Adjustment Layers

You can enable the 3D Layer switch for adjustment layers. This means you can use 3D transformations to adjust the area of the overall frame affected by an adjustment layer (which are explained in more detail in Chapter 22).

The bad news – as mentioned earlier – is that adjustment layers break the 3D render order, and otherwise should not be thought of as normal 3D layers, even if their 3D Layer switch is enabled. The good news is that you can enable the Adjustment Layer switch for a 3D light, with interesting and useful results. We'll get to that in Chapter 15.

Compound Effects

We won't really discuss compound effects (in which one layer is used by an effect plug-in to treat another) until Chapter 24, but we wanted to reassure you that the 3D Layer switch has no negative impact on how compound effects work. Because compound effects look at the second layer at its source (before any transformations have been calculated), the 3D Layer switch is ignored.

TIP

Joined at the Hip

If you want one layer to reliably mode, matte, or stencil another in 3D space, either pair them up in a precomp or connect them using Parenting (Chapter 17).

CONNECT

Workspaces: Chapter 1.

OpenGL: *Preview Possibilities* sidebar, Chapter 2.

Motion paths and keyframing: Chapter 3.

Rotation and orientation: Chapter 3.

Motion blur: Chapter 8.

Blending modes: Chapter 9.

Track mattes: Chapter 11.

Stencils: Chapter 12.

Cameras: Chapter 14.

Lighting: Chapter 15.

Parenting: Chapter 17.

Nesting compositions: Chapter 18.

Precomposing: Chapter 19.

Collapsing transformations: Chapter 20.

Per-character 3D text: Chapter 21.

Compound effects: Chapter 24.

Cameras

Get new perspective on your 3D layers by placing cameras around them.

After Effects allows artists to decide just how much complexity they want to deal with in 3D space. You don't have to manage cameras and lights if you don't want to; each composition already has default versions of them. However, creating and animating your own cameras gives you much more creative control, including altering the sense of perspective, cutting between different views of the same set of layers, or re-creating an actual camera's parameters to match your graphics into a real scene.

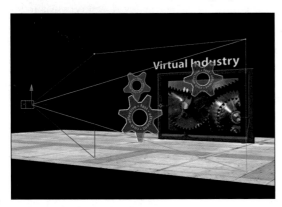

Cameras are used to view 3D layers in a composition. Footage courtesy Artbeats/Industry: Gears & Machines; sidewalk texture courtesy Artbeats/City Surfaces.

Shooting Script

Before we get into details, let's go over some general issues related to using cameras in After Effects.

Cameras only view 3D layers. If you enable the 3D Layer switch for an object, it will now be rendered in perspective based on how a camera is looking at it, with distance from the camera affecting how large the object appears. If the 3D Layer switch is off, the layer is rendered normally, regardless of the camera's settings or where it is pointing. This ability to combine 2D and 3D layers in the same comp is a real boon for a graphic artist: You can set up stationary background movies and foreground text or logo bugs in 2D, then fly around just the elements you need in 3D.

Cameras appear as layers in the Timeline panel. If there is no camera layer in a comp, After Effects uses an invisible default camera. You can have more than one camera in a comp; if you do, After Effects looks at the in and out points of the camera layers and notes which one is highest in the Timeline panel layer stack to decide which is the "active" camera at any given point in time. This means you can cut between alternate camera views (sorry; you cannot dissolve between them).

We're going to start by giving a taste for adding a camera to a scene and keyframing it. We'll then take a tour through pointing the camera, animating the camera including creating camera rigs and taking advantage of auto orientation, and showing how to cut between multiple cameras. We'll conclude by discussing the camera's parameters in more detail, including how to fake focus and depth of field effects.

Example Project

Explore the 14-Example Project.aep file as you read this chapter; references to [Ex.##] refer to specific compositions within the project file.

Instant Gratification

Let's start by getting a taste for where we're headed. Open this chapter's example project, then open composition [**Ex.01_starter**]. It contains a handful of 3D layers plus a full-frame 2D background. Since no camera has been created yet, the 3D layers in the scene are being viewed by the comp's default camera, which simulates a 50mm lens aimed straight ahead at the middle of the composition.

Step 1: Select Layer > New > Camera; the Camera Settings dialog will open. We'll discuss these parameters later; for now, locate the Preset popup and select 35mm. Smaller lens lengths represent wide-angle lens, while longer lengths represent telephoto lenses. Verify that the Type popup to the left is set to Two-Node Camera, and if necessary uncheck the Enable Depth of Field option underneath the camera diagram. Click OK to create a new camera layer. The video will appear to jump farther away, while the center gear appears to jump forward. This is because shorter lenses exaggerate perspective in 3D. Toggle the camera's Video switch off and on to compare the result with the comp's default camera.

Step 2: With **Camera 1** selected and its Video switch on, press P to reveal its Position, and Shift+A to reveal its Point of Interest. The Point of Interest is the second "node" of a two-node camera: No matter where you move the back of the camera (the Position), it will rotate to aim at this Point of Interest. (Later we'll work with a one-node camera as well.)

• Enable keyframing for Position and Point of Interest, and scrub these values to aim the camera and frame the scene as you like. Note that the 2D background layer does not move and remains full-frame: Again, 2D layers are not affected by 3D cameras (or lights).

• Move the current time indicator to the end of the comp, and edit the Position and Point of Interest values to create a nice second framing. If you would like to try a different method of moving the camera, select the Orbit Camera tool (the Camera tools are to the right of the Rotate tool), then click and drag around the Comp panel: This is a quick way to move the back of the camera around. Note that the camera continues to look at the Point of Interest, no matter where you orbit.

• Initiate a RAM Preview and enjoy your animation. The camera's Position and Point of Interest default to interpolating in a straight line between your two keyframes.

And that's how easy using cameras can be! But you can go much, much deeper. We'll start by getting a better grip on pointing the camera.

You can scrub the camera's Position (the back of the camera) and Point of Interest (where it is looking) in the Timeline panel (above) to frame a scene (below). Background footage courtesy Artbeats/Liquid Ambience.

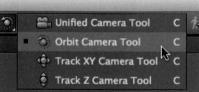

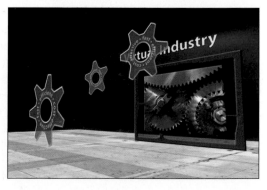

You can also use dedicated Camera tools (above) to aim a camera (below).

Step 2: By setting the Select View Layout popup to one of the 2 Views choices, you can position your camera in an orthographic view while checking the results in an Active Camera view. Objects courtesy Getty Images.

Pointing the Camera

After Effects allows you to position and animate cameras using *one-node* or *two-node* cameras. You can control them using a set of Camera tools, and see what you're doing with the aid of multiple comp views. Let's familiarize ourselves with these options:

Step 1: Select Close All from the top of the Comp panel and open comp [**Ex.02a**]. It contains a set of objects already arranged in 3D space. There is no camera layer yet in this comp, so you are currently viewing these objects using the invisible default camera.

Step 2: Positioning the camera is a perfect example of needing to view your overall world from different angles, while also seeing what the camera sees. Set the Select View Layout popup along the bottom of the Comp panel to 2 Views – Horizontal and drag the Comp panel wider if needed to see both images with at least 50% Magnification.

Click anywhere in the right portion of the Comp panel; yellow triangles will appear in its corners to show that this view is active. Set the 3D View Popup to Active Camera to monitor your results. Then select the left view and set the 3D View Popup to Left.

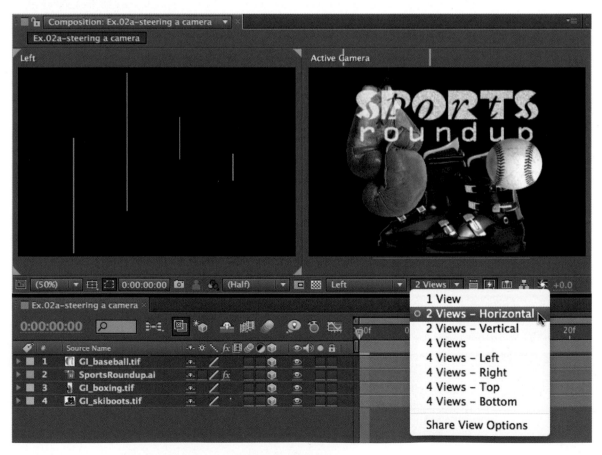

Step 3: In the Left view, you should see four lines representing your four 3D layers. If you don't, you will need to adjust this view. Select the Track XY Camera tool from the Tools panel and drag in the Left view until the layers occupy the left half of the view, leaving room for the camera on the right. If you are zoomed in too close or too far away, press C to toggle to the Track Z Camera tool, (or if you have a three-button mouse, take advantage of the Unified Camera tool – see the sidebar at the bottom of this page) then drag until all of the objects fit nicely. If necessary, switch back to the Track XY Camera tool to reposition your layers. Then type V to return to the normal Selection tool.

Step 4: Type Command+Option+Shift+C on Mac (Control+Alt+Shift+C on Windows) to create a new camera. Choose the 50mm preset, set the Type popup to Two-Node Camera, and uncheck the Enable Depth of Field option. Click OK.

Select all of the layers – including your new camera – and press P to reveal their Position properties. Deselect all, select just **Camera 1**, and press Shift+A to also reveal its Point of Interest property.

Two-node cameras have two location properties to manage: normal Position, which is where the camera lens is located in 3D space, and the Point of Interest, which is the spot where the camera is aimed. In the Left view, you can see this as a box with axis arrows that represent the camera's Position, and a line drawn to what looks like an Anchor Point icon – that's the Point of Interest. (If you can't see the entire

Step 3: The Camera tools can be used to move the camera's Position in Active Camera and the Custom Views, and to pan and zoom the image you see in the orthographic views (such as Top or Left).

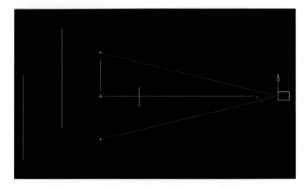

Step 4: Cameras are visible in the orthographic views; you need to select them to see both their "bodies" and their Point of Interest. The axis arrows are drawn from the camera's Position; dragging while an axis letter is visible constrains movement to that axis. One reason to resize the orthographic views with the Track Z Camera tool instead of the Comp panel's Magnification is that the camera icon will stay the same size, making it easier to see and grab.

Unified Camera Tool

If you have a three-button mouse, you may want to take advantage of the Unified Camera tool to move the camera and manipulate your 3D views. When it is selected, the left mouse button engages the Orbit Camera tool, the middle button engages Track XY, and the right button engages Track Z.

We will give directions based on selecting these tools individually, but if you have an appropriate mouse, feel free to use the Unified tool instead.

Look at Layers

To automatically zoom and center your view to see all of the desired layers, use View > Look at Selected Layers or View > Look at All Layers. If one of the Camera tools is selected, press F to Look at Selected Layers, and Command+Shift+F (Control+Shift+F) to Look at All Layers.

GOTCHA

When 3D Becomes 2D

Cameras cannot "see" 3D objects in precomps because the output of the precomp is a single 2D layer. Use Collapse Transformations (Chapter 20) for the precomp if you want the 3D layers inside it to interact with the camera in the master comp.

camera in Left view, zoom back a little more). Right now, the Point of Interest aligns with the **SportsRoundup.ai** layer because they both have the same Z value.

Step 5: Of course, you can always just scrub the Position and Point of Interest values in the Timeline panel, but often you'll want to grab the camera and position it directly. Moving a camera in 3D space is similar to moving an ordinary 3D layer (see the previous chapter), with a few differences thanks to the inclusion of a Point of Interest. To practice this, move the camera in the Comp panel view set to Left, and watch the results in the Comp panel view set to Active Camera. (You can also watch the parameters update in the Timeline panel for additional confirmation of what you are doing.)

Make sure the Selection tool (shortcut: V) is active. If you grab the camera icon when an axis letter (X/Y/Z) is *not* visible next to your cursor, you can freely move the camera around in space. In this case, you are changing just the camera's Position – not its Point of Interest.

If you try to move the camera when one of the axis letters is visible, your movements will be constrained to that axis. In this case, the Point of Interest will also move with the camera, maintaining its same relative position. To move Position constrained to a chosen axis *without* moving the Point of Interest, hold down the Command (Control) key as you drag.

Step 6: Moving just the Point of Interest is a bit more sensitive: If you don't click really close to the center of its crosshairs, the camera will be deselected, and the Point of Interest will disappear. To get a feel for how the Point of Interest works, drag it to the middle of one of the three layers, then drag the camera's body around – no matter where you move the camera, the layer you chose remains centered in its view.

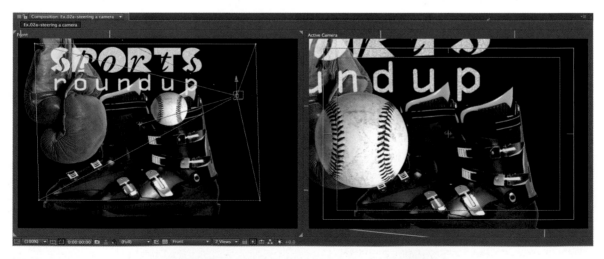

Step 6: Practice moving the Point of Interest from alternate views, such as Top and Front. Placing the Point of Interest in the center of a layer (left) keeps it centered in the Active Camera (right). To toggle on and off the Title/Action Safe guides, select a view and press the apostrophe key.

Step 7: Although we have been using the Orbit and Track camera tools to customize our views, their main purpose is to move the camera. Select your Comp panel view set to Active Camera. Position the cursor over it, and press C to enable the Camera tool. As you press C repeatedly, your cursor will toggle through Orbit, Track XY, and Track Z tools (or the Unified Camera tool – see the earlier sidebar on how to use it). Click and drag inside the Comp panel using each tool, watching what is happening to the camera's Position and Point of Interest in the Left view panel.

Step 7: The Orbit Camera tool (above) works only in the Active Camera and Custom Views.

Step 8: The Track tools change both Position and Point of Interest; the Orbit tool changes just the camera's Position. This distinction becomes important when you start keyframing animation. Although we will explore animation in more detail in just a moment, for now make sure Position and Point of Interest are exposed in the Timeline panel, and enable keyframing for both. Move later in time, and use the Orbit Camera tool to move the camera. Note that a keyframe will be created for Position, *but not for the Point of Interest*. This causes problems if you alter or keyframe the Point of Interest at a different point in time, as those changes may affect the framing you arranged here. (Relying too heavily on the Orbit Camera tool can cause other problems as well, which we'll discuss later.)

Step 8: Using the Orbit Camera tool alters Position, but not Point of Interest.

In short: With a two-node camera, if you are setting up a pose you want to keep, make sure you have keyframes for both the Position and Point of Interest at that point in time.

Hide and Seek

By default, when a camera is not selected, it is represented by a box. When it is selected, you will also see lines that represent its Angle of View and Zoom distance (and if you are using the two-point camera model, its Point of Interest), as well as Focus Distance if Depth of Field is enabled. If you find the Angle of View and Zoom lines particularly useful or distracting, you can change when they are visible by accessing View Options in the Comp panel's Options menu (click on the arrow in the upper right corner). Click on the popup next to Camera Wireframes, and choose When Selected (the Default), On, or Off. You can also set similar options for spotlights

(discussed in the next chapter), as well as if you want layers drawn as pixels or wireframes. These options can be set per Comp panel as well as per view; enable Share View Options from the Select View Layout popup to share options across views.

GOTCHA

Over-Eager Auto-Keyframe

If you have Auto-Keyframe mode enabled and the Rotate tool set to edit Rotation rather than Orientation, rotating one axis will set keyframes for all three axes.

One-Node Cameras

We personally prefer the two-node camera model, because it makes it easy to precisely aim the camera – just place the Point of Interest where you want to look. However, real cameras follow the one-node model: You orient the camera's body to decide where it is looking. It is also difficult to coordinate both Position and Point of Interest for some motion paths, such as flying around objects when you need to make multiple turns. Happily, After Effects supports one-node cameras as well.

Step 1: Open the comp [**Ex.02b**], which already has a group of 3D layers plus a two-point camera set up with a jaunty pose. Set your Comp panel to display the Left and Active Camera views as you did in Step 2 earlier in the previous exercise.

Step 2: Double-click **Camera 1** to open its Camera Settings dialog and drag it to a place where you can also see the Comp panel. Change the Type popup to One-Node Camera. If the Preview option is enabled, the line leading to the Point of Interest will disappear, and the camera will snap around to face straight ahead. Click OK.

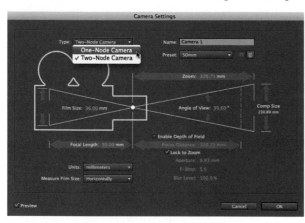

Step 2: Change the camera's Type to One-Node Camera. This causes it to no longer orient toward its Point of Interest. You can also choose One-Node Camera when you create a new camera. This setting can also be changed inside Layer > Transform > Auto-Orient.

Step 3: Make sure the Position property for **Camera 1** is visible in the Timeline panel (if it isn't, select it and type P), then type Shift+R to add the Orientation and Rotation properties.

There are two additional ways to aim the camera: Scrub the Orientation and Rotation properties in the Timeline panel, or press W to select the Rotate tool. The cursor will change to a circular arrow. Click near the camera and drag to orbit it; if you place the cursor near an axis arrow where an axis letter appears and then drag, rotation will be restricted to that axis. An additional popup near the center of the Tools panel sets whether the Rotate tool affects the Orientation or Rotation properties.

That said, be very careful using the Rotate tool to alter Y Rotation or Orientation: There is a nasty glitch that if you go beyond ±90°, the X and Z values flip by 180° (try it!). That's why we prefer scrubbing the values directly in the Timeline panel.

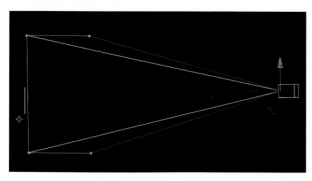

Step 3: In One-Node mode, you can scrub the Orientation and Rotation values in the Timeline panel, or use the Orbit Camera tool and Rotate tool to aim the camera. However, beware of the Rotate tool: If you rotate Y past 90°, unpleasant things happen to X and Z.

Step 4: Move the camera so you can see the layers in the Active Camera view. Then select the Orbit Camera tool, and drag in this view. With a one-node camera, the Orbit Camera tool rotates the camera rather than changes its Position value. Using the View > Look At menu options and corresponding shortcut keys alters just the camera's Position, taking into account its current rotation and orientation.

Animating Cameras

Everything you've learned about setting keyframes and animating properties elsewhere in this book (Chapters 3 and 4 in particular) apply to animating the camera. The only real trick is in coordinating keyframes for both the camera's Position and Point of Interest: If you get their keyframes out of sync, you might get some unanticipated results.

Close your previous comps, and open [**Ex.03_starter**]. This comp contains three still objects of musical instruments, four videos of musicians playing, and a two-point camera. Your task is to animate the camera to start with a good overview of all the layers, and end up isolating the video of the sax player (the layer farthest back). So let's get started:

Step 1: You'll want to jump back and forth between the Top, Left, and Active Camera views to help you create your camera path. If you haven't already set up keyboard shortcuts for these (explained in the previous chapter), select Top from the 3D View popup, then select View > Assign Shortcut to "Top" > F10. Do the same to assign F11 to Left and F12 to Active Camera. Now you can press F10, F11, and F12 to easily switch between these three views. As an alternative, you could also choose one of the 2 or 4 View options with the Select View Layout popup and set up the Comp panel's view ports to use a combination of these views.

Your goal in [**Ex.06**] is to fly a camera from a position overlooking the "set" to a close-up of the last video. Musician footage courtesy Lee Stranahan; additional objects courtesy Getty Images.

Step 2: Press Home to return to time 00:00. Make sure Position and Point of Interest are twirled down for **Camera 1** (P, then Shift+A), and turn on the keyframe stopwatch for both.

Step 3: Select the Left view. Pull the camera back (to the right) and up until you see a nice overhead view of all the layers in Active Camera.

Step 4: The camera is probably now aiming too low, and not at anything in particular. You can re-aim your camera using the Point of Interest: In Left view, drag the Point of Interest to the point in space you want centered in the Comp panel at the start of your animation.

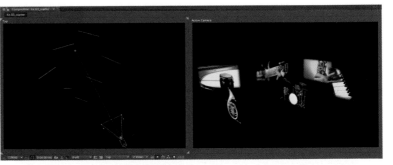

Step 5: Switch to the Top view. Pull the camera to one side to get more of an angle on the virtual "set" below. Go ahead and further tweak the Position and Point of Interest as desired, referring to the Active Camera view until you have a framing you like.

Steps 3–5: Take advantage of the alternate views to create a nice initial framing of the elements.

Step 6: Press End to go to time 04:19. You want to end up staring at the **LS_sax swing** layer; a good way to ensure this is to select it, press P to reveal its Position property, click on the word "Position" to select its value, and Command+C (Control+C) to copy. Then click the words "Point of Interest" for **Camera 1**, and Command+V (Control+V) to paste the sax's position into the point where your camera will be aiming.

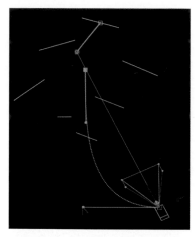

Step 7: Work with the motion path to create a nice swoop into your final pose.

Step 7: Move your camera back down and closer to the **LS_sax swing** layer until you are happy with your final framing in the Active Camera view. Tweak the Point of Interest as needed. RAM Preview your creation. Work with the Bezier handles on the camera's motion path to create a nice swoop into the final screen.

Step 8: It would be nice if the camera move eased into a stop at the end. Select **Camera 1**'s last Position keyframe, and press F9 to Easy Ease into it. RAM Preview: What's that weird sliding motion at the end of the move? It's a result of not applying Easy Ease to the Point of Interest as well. In general, if you want smooth, coordinated camera moves, make sure you apply the same velocity curves to both its Position and Point of Interest. Select the last Point of Interest keyframe, press F9, and RAM Preview again – much better.

Step 9: Then the client walks in, and says "Looks cool – but why do the conga and French horn look a bit warped during the move?" As you view what are inherently 2D layers at an angle, you will get perspective

Step 8: Ease into the final keyframes for both Position and Point of Interest to create a coordinated move.

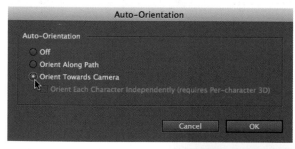

Step 9: Setting the objects to Orient Towards Camera (above) will reduce unusual perspective distortion (A is before; B is after).

distortion: It looks cool on the "video screen" movies, but not so cool on the other objects – it really points out that they don't have actual depth.

Press Home to return to 00:00. Select the three objects (layers 2 through 4), and select Layer > Transform > Auto-Orient. In the Auto-Orientation dialog, select Orient Towards Camera. Click OK, and note how they snap around in the Active Camera view to face toward the viewer. RAM Preview, and have a nice cup of tea as a reward.

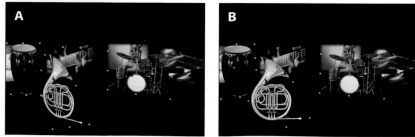

Auto-Orientation

In the previous exercise, you got a taste for how a layer's Auto Orientation property can come in handy with 3D cameras. To see another example, close the previous comps, and open **[Ex.04a]**. Select the Orbit Camera tool, and drag around the Comp panel, noting how the layers are often viewed at an unflattering angle. Then select the three non-camera layers, right-click on one of them, and select Transform > Auto-Orient from the contextual menu. Select Orient Towards Camera and click OK. All of the layers will now twist so that they face the camera. Use the Orbit Camera tool again, and note now the layers follow – with reduced perspective distortion.

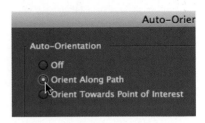

You can set a camera to Orient Along Path. This is much easier than keyframing such complex swoops.

Another trick involves having a camera auto-orient along an animation path. It can be hard to set up sweeping motions that don't appear to drift; this option points the camera for you.

Open **[Ex.04b]**, select a 2 Views layout, and set the views to Active Camera and Top. RAM Preview: The camera moves left and right as it travels. It's not bad, but it seems to drift more than swerve. You can see the camera's motion path by selecting the **Camera 1** layer and scrubbing the current time indicator as you watch the Top view.

With the camera still selected, open its Auto-Orientation dialog, choose Orient Along Path, and click OK. RAM Preview the Active Camera panel again, and note how the camera now appears to steer along its path. You can see this by studying the camera's path in the Top view. Note that when the camera is auto-orienting along a path, it might swerve more than you expect (we purposely simplified this camera's path); you may need to smooth out your path to avoid motion sickness. We also set the middle keyframes for the **Camera 1**'s Position property to rove in time (see Chapter 4) so that the speed would be fairly constant.

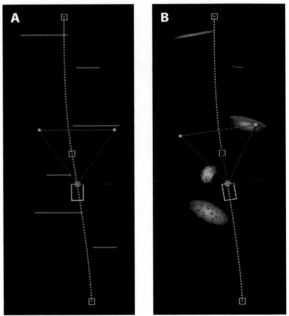

In **[Ex.04c]**, we've set up a variation of the above animations in which the objects auto-orient toward the camera, and the camera auto-orients along the path. We moved the objects in much closer to the camera's path to heighten the excitement of near-misses; the objects rotate out of the way as the camera moves by them. Notice how the objects keep their perspective throughout the flight. Again, choose the Top view and drag the current time indicator around, watching how the layers coordinate their movements automatically as the camera passes by.

The one shortcoming of Orient Along Path is that it does not cause a camera or layer to "bank" – rotate along its Z axis – while swooping about. Feel free to manually keyframe a little Z Rotation of your own to anticipate turns.

Normally, layers and cameras point where you tell them, which starts out as straight ahead (A). However, you can set layers to orient toward the camera (below), and also tell the camera to orient itself along its motion path (B).

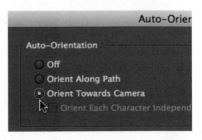

Camera Rigs

Sometimes, editing motion paths and keyframing the result is not the easiest way to create the desired camera animation. Many users prefer to create "camera rigs" where individual dimensions of the camera's movement are divided among a series of null objects. Parenting and null objects are discussed in Chapter 17; we'll give you a taste of their power here. First, let's work through a typical animation problem:

Step 1: Open the comp [**Ex.05a_starter**], which already contains a group of 3D layers and a camera. Select **Camera 1** and press U; we've already set up the first keyframe for you.

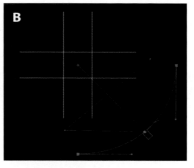

Step 2: Press End, select the Orbit Camera tool, and swing the camera around in the Active Camera view by a quarter-turn (90°). While using the Orbit Camera tool, you get the impression that you are maintaining a constant distance from the middle of the four layers. But RAM Preview, and you will find that the motion path that was actually created – which defaults to a linear interpolation – is causing the camera to pass too close to the layers during the middle of the move.

Steps 2–3: Even though the Orbit Camera tool gives the illusion of creating an orbital motion path, the reality is a straight path between keyframes that passes too close to the layers (A). Drag the Bezier handles to create a smooth arc (B).

Step 3: Switch to Top view, and pull out the Bezier handles on the camera's motion path to create a smooth arc. Work until you maintain a constant distance from the center of the layers throughout the move; it will take a bit of tweaking.

Orbit Camera Rig

For comparison, now try the same move using an orbit camera rig:

Step 1: Open the comp [**Ex.05b_starter**], which contains the same group of 3D layers plus a camera. No keyframes have been created yet.

Step 2: Create a New > Layer > Null Object. Enable the 3D Layer switch for this null. Press P to reveal its Position; it defaults to the center of the comp with Z = 0. You want the null to be in line with where the camera is initially pointing; in this exercise, it already is.

Steps 2–3: Create a null object at the point you want to orbit around, and parent the camera to this null.

Step 3: Right-click on any column header in the Timeline panel, and select Columns > Parent (the shortcut is Shift+F4). Set the Parent popup for **Camera 1** to be your new null object.

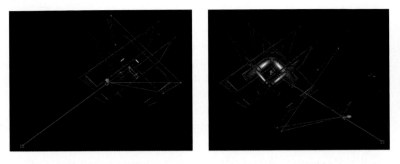

Step 4: Select your null object layer, and press R to reveal its Rotation and Orientation properties. Make sure you are at the start of the comp, and enable keyframing for Y Rotation. Then go to the end of the comp, and set Y Rotation to 90°. RAM Preview, and enjoy your perfect orbit animation, created without the need to tweak motion paths.

Step 5: To really appreciate the power of the camera rig approach, select **Camera 1** and press P to reveal its Position. Enable keyframing for its Z Position, and set different values for the start and end of the comp. RAM Preview, and enjoy the smooth arc animation. Try doing the same for Y Position to create an elevation move.

Because the camera is parented to the null, its position values are only in relation to the null. As far as the camera is concerned, it's moving in simple straight lines, while the null is in fact swinging it around as well.

Dolly Camera Rig

Another common camera rig re-creates a physical camera following a dolly track on the ground (movement in the X and Z dimensions), with a crane to provide elevation (movement in the Y dimension).

Step 1: Open the comp [**Ex.05c_starter**]. It contains a virtual room. Your plan is to swoop between the two cut-out actors.

Step 2: Create two Layer > New > Null Objects. Rename the one on top "**Floor Track Null**" and the one underneath "**Crane Null**".

Step 3: You want these two nulls to be placed in the same location as the one-node camera. Select **Camera 1**, press P to reveal its Position, and copy this value. Then select **Floor Track Null** plus **Crane Null** and paste.

Step 4: Time to assemble your rig. Make sure the Parent column is revealed (Shift+F4). Set the Parent popup for **Camera 1** to be **Crane Null**, and set the Parent popup for **Crane Null** to be **Floor Track Null**.

Step 4: Use parenting to mount your camera on its virtual crane, then mount the crane on its virtual dolly.

In [**Ex. 05b-final**] the null object swings the camera in an orbit around the 3D layers, while the camera independently pulls back from the layers in Z. Footage courtesy Artbeats/Virtual Insanity.

The Two Null Orbit Rig

In Step 5, you could create a second null object to animate Y Position separately from Z. Be sure to parent your first null to the second null to create the correct hierachy.

The virtual room you will be flying through. Textures courtesy Artbeats/Exteriors; actors courtesy Crowd Control.

Step 5: The camera is pulled through the room by the **Track Floor Null** (the red motion path). You can then animate the crane move independently.

Step 5: Let's work on the track move first. Make sure the current time indicator is at the start of the comp, reveal the Position value for **Floor Track Null**, and enable keyframing. Then jump to the end of the comp and scrub its Z Position value until you are positioned right in front of the ballerina. Ultimately, you want the camera to move around the ballerina rather than through her, so scrub **Floor Track Null**'s X Position value to the left until she's safely off to the side. Then set Z Position to 600, which is even with the ballerina.

Step 6: Scrub the current time indicator to where the frame is filled with the boy. You want to dodge him as well, so scrub **Floor Track Null**'s X Position to the right until you safely miss him. RAM Preview your move.

Step 7: Now you can work on the crane move. Animate **Crane Null**'s Y Position to create an elevation change; we started high enough to see the ballerina's head behind the boy, and ended scooting past the ballerina's toes. The advantage of separating these different movements between different nulls is that you can keyframe this smooth elevation change without worrying about affecting the track move.

Refine your animation to taste. In [**Ex.05c-final**], we eased into and out of the crane movement, roved the middle track move keyframe (Chapter 4), and added a 2D background.

Importing Camera Data

In Chapter 40, we discuss several ways to import camera animations from 3D programs. If you need to import keyframe information from an unsupported program or a motion control camera rig, you will probably need to massage the data in a spreadsheet program such as Excel to make it fit After Effects' keyframe format. Create a camera animation in After Effects, select the Position keyframes, copy, and paste them into a text document to see the format and header After Effects expects. Once you have formatted your data correctly, open it in a text document, copy it, select the camera's Position property in After Effects, and paste. Repeat as needed for Point of Interest, Orientation, or Zoom. (Be aware that motion capture data may require manual smoothing to achieve a good set of keyframes.)

To paste camera data from an unsupported application into the Position property of a camera in After Effects, it must fit its keyframe data format.

Adobe After Effects 8.0 Keyframe Data

Units Per Second	29.97
Source Width	720
Source Height	534
Source Pixel Aspect Ratio	1
Comp Pixel Aspect Ratio 1	

Position

Frame	X pixels	Y pixels	Z pixels
0	-1626.44	-1152.63	-3600.16
1	-1625.86	-1152.52	-3599.68
2	-1624.45	-1152.2	-3598.83
3	-1622.23	-1151.69	-3597.6
4	-1619.21	-1151.02	-3595.99
5	-1615.41	-1150.19	-3594
6	-1610.83	-1149.22	-3591.62
7	-1605.5	-1148.12	-3588.88
8	-1599.42	-1146.91	-3585.75
9	-1592.61	-1145.58	-3582.25
10	-1585.09	-1144.15	-3578.37

End of Keyframe Data

Animation Advice

Here are a few other tips to keep in mind while animating cameras.

• Resist the temptation to over-animate when you're in 3D; think of how a real camera moves in films. When you're using a two-point camera, sometimes all you need is to keyframe just the Point of Interest or just the camera's Position, and leave the other property stationary.

• Unless you have a specific plan choreographed in your head, it's a good idea to simplify things and choose between two different philosophies of movement: The camera is more or less locked down, and the layers provide the movement (as in [Ex.06a]), or the layers are arranged in a scene, and then the camera moves around them (the prior exercises, plus [Ex.06b]).

Right Side Up

If you animate the Position of the camera so it would be upside down, it will automatically orient right side up. If you want to flip the camera, use Rotation, or parent it to a null object that flips instead.

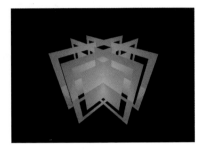

• After Effects will not allow cameras to fly upside down; it automatically rights them. Indeed, we had to be careful how we keyframed the move in [Ex.06b]: Go to the camera's keyframe at 03:02, and change its Z Position from –50 to 0, which would cause it to look straight down. RAM Preview, and you will see the camera wobble and try to flip over as it heads down between the layers. If you really want to turn the camera upside down, do it with Rotation, or parent it to a null object that flips over.

You don't *have* to animate the camera; you can leave it "locked down" and just animate the layers [Ex.06a]. Footage courtesy Artbeats/Digidelic.

• Roving keyframes (Chapter 4) can keep speed changes smooth during complex camera moves. Check them out in [Ex.06b]: Click on the Graph Editor button, then experiment with the final keyframe.

• As an alternative to the camera rigs demonstrated in the previous exercises, you can also take advantage of the Graph Editor and Separate XYZ option (both demonstrated in Chapter 4) to create precise, refined camera movements. We put these to work in [Ex.06c].

Separate XYZ (circled) allows you to perform dolly rig style movements without the need for parenting and null objects.

• A little humanization can go a long way to make your movements seem more realistic. To create a handheld or floating "Steadicam" look, add a wiggle expression (Chapter 37) to a camera's Position or Point of Interest. Select the camera in comp [Ex.06d] and press U to reveal the keyframes plus expressions.

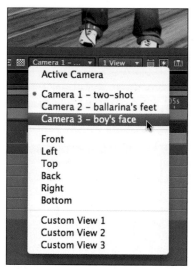

Use the Comp panel's 3D View popup to focus on a specific camera. Note that this popup does *not* determine which camera will render.

Editing Between Cameras

You can have multiple cameras in a composition. After Effects will use a combination of the camera layer in and out points plus the stacking order in the Timeline panel to decide which camera to render.

To experiment with multiple cameras, open [**Ex.07_starter**], which already has one camera. Create one or two additional cameras – perhaps using different presets – and create different poses or animations for them. (If you have a slow computer, you may want to enable OpenGL Fast Previews – see *Preview Possibilities* at the end of Chapter 2 for more details.)

Click on the 3D View popup along the bottom of the Comp panel. In addition to Active Camera, you will see the names of each of the cameras you created. Use this popup to make sure you are viewing the camera you plan to edit. (By the way, you will see the outline of any camera that's positioned in front of your selected camera.)

Once you have a few cameras in your comp, trim their in and out points or slide them along the timeline. Set the 3D View popup to Active Camera, and scrub the current time indicator while watching the Comp panel: As you cross an edit point, After Effects will display the visible camera ("visible" meaning the time indicator is between its in and out points, and its Video switch is on) that is highest in the layer stack. If

[**Ex.07-final**] contains an edit between three cameras plus the comp's default camera. Scrub the time indicator and rearrange the layer order of the cameras to get a feel for how they interact.

there is no visible camera underneath the current time indicator, After Effects will render the comp's invisible default camera.

The Active Camera view is always what will render; you cannot select a specific camera to render using the 3D View popup. If you want to render a specific camera, change the Video switches for each camera layer.

After Effects cannot crossfade between cameras; it only performs hard cuts at the in and out points. You can create a chain of nested and collapsed compositions (Chapters 18 through 20) and either crossfade between them or use the Blend effect; we've set up such a chain in the Ex.08 folder. However, this is a perfect example of when you shouldn't try to make After Effects do everything! Instead, also use other more appropriate tools such as a non-linear editor: Set up a series of camera moves in After Effects, render each one out to its own movie, then use an editing system to cut and crossfade between them. Indeed, this is the way many design houses split up the workload, with animators creating raw source material for editors to then cut into a final piece.

When Order Matters

The stacking order between a camera and 3D layers does not matter. However, the stacking order between cameras *does* matter; it helps determine which one to render.

Camera Settings

Many artists will be happy just using the different camera presets, choosing different presets or perhaps editing the Angle of View to alter the perspective. However, when you want to match an After Effects comp to a scene (either shot with a real camera or imported from another program), or otherwise customize or refine your look, you will need to understand and carefully set the parameters of After Effects' camera.

If you are new to working with cameras, do not be daunted by the large number of parameters in the Camera Settings dialog; many of them interact, providing different ways of answering two questions: What's my Angle of View? How far away are things supposed to be in focus?

Angle of View

Click on the popup menu that's in the tab along the top of the Comp panel, and select Close All to close your previous comps. Open [**Ex.09a**], and double-click on the layer **Practice Camera** to open the Camera Settings dialog. Make sure the Preview checkbox in the lower left corner is enabled, and drag the Camera Settings dialog to a location where you can also see the result of your changes in the Comp panel.

The Camera Settings dialog contains an illustration of a camera to give you an idea of how the different settings interact, but there are two deceiving things about this picture: The illustration doesn't animate as you change settings, and it always shows a picture of the camera from its side – even though the Measure Film Size option allows you to work in dimensions viewed from the top of the camera.

To give you an idea of how these settings relate to a real camera, set the Units popup in the lower left portion of the dialog to millimeters, and make sure the Measure Film Size popup below is set to Horizontally. You'll notice that the Focal Length parameter just above these two popups now reads 50, matching the 50mm lens preset we used when we created this camera. In After Effects, this number is the distance from the center of the imaginary lens to the center of the imaginary film. Above that is a parameter for Film Size; it will read 36mm – the horizontal image area for 35mm print film. If you prefer entering film sizes vertically or diagonally, you can change the Measure Film Size popup to match; we're going to stick with horizontal measurements for this chapter.

Last Settings = Default

Whenever you edit Camera Settings, those values will be used the next time you create a new camera.

You will practice manipulating the camera settings using this arrangement of 3D layers. Woman courtesy Digital Vision/Beauty; background courtesy Digital Vision/Naked and Scared.

To relate After Effects' camera to real film and lenses, change the Units popup to millimeters and focus on the Film Size and Focal Length parameters. These interact to determine the all-important Angle of View.

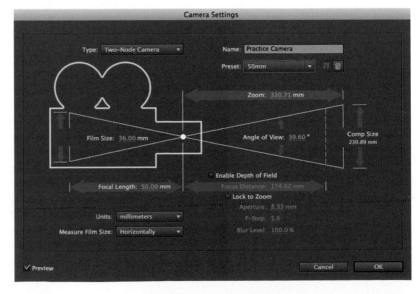

Units

After Effects uses pixels as its primary unit of measurement. Camera lenses and film sizes are usually given in millimeters; measurements on sets in the United States are usually taken in inches and feet. How are you supposed to translate between these different units, especially when you're trying to match the camera in After Effects to a scene from a 3D program or in real life? Here are some typical conversions to remember:

72 pixels = 1 inch
1 inch = 25.4 millimeters
1 millimeter = 2.8346 pixels

After Effects includes Units popups in the Camera Settings and Position dialogs to allow you to enter parameters in millimeters or

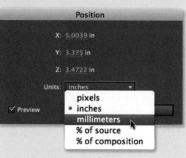

inches and have them automatically translated to its native pixels. To access the Position dialog, right-click on a Position parameter in the Timeline panel and select Edit Value, or use the shortcut Command+Shift+P on Mac (Control+Shift+P on Windows).

Type AA to reveal the Camera Options in the Timeline panel. These are the only camera parameters you can keyframe.

As you change the presets to different lenses, or manually enter your own Film Size or Focal Length values, you will notice the Angle of View value updates automatically (as does the resulting view in the Comp panel). If you edit the Angle of View parameter directly, After Effects calculates what focal length would be needed to get that angle for your chosen film size. The bottom line is always the resulting Angle of View: It is what determines the perspective your layers are rendered with.

Let's focus on the right half of this diagram. Change the Units popup to pixels, and look at the Comp Size value: It says approximately 654.5 pixels. Why not 720, as that's the width of our comp? After Effects is taking nonsquare pixels into account, multiplying 720 by 0.909 (the number it uses for NTSC D1/DV pixels).

Now turn your attention to the Zoom value: *This is the magic distance at which a layer is rendered the same size, whether it is in 2D or 3D.* Zoom updates automatically as you change Angle of View. Change Zoom directly, and the Angle of View changes to match (and the Focal Length in turn updates to match this new Angle of View). When you create a new camera, After Effects places it this same distance back in Z space, so layers at Z = 0 are not rescaled by perspective distortion. From then on, Zoom and Z Position are separate parameters; editing one does not update the other.

Although real film cameras don't have a Zoom parameter (it's more akin to a camcorder's Zoom control), Zoom is a handy way to relate a camera's settings to layer positions in After Effects, and animate the angle of view.

With our **Practice Camera** still selected, type AA (two As in quick succession). This will reveal the core camera settings in the Timeline panel: Zoom, the Depth of Field on/off switch, Focus Distance, Aperture, and Blur Level. You can scrub or type in their values here without having to open the Camera Settings dialog; these are also the only ones you are allowed to keyframe.

Press Shift+P to also reveal its Position. Play around with scrubbing the Zoom parameter while keeping one eye on the Comp panel and the other eye on the camera's Position (hold Shift while scrubbing to go faster). The objects in the Comp panel appear to get closer and farther away, but the camera isn't moving! Remember: *By editing Zoom, you are really changing the camera's Angle of View, which is how big a slice of 3D space is used to fill the Comp panel.* Zoom is *not* the same as Position, even if it occasionally seems to give the same results. (To compare Zoom with Position, Undo until the Zoom value returns to 909 pixels, and scrub the camera's Z Position value.)

Most of the time, the preferred approach is to set the Angle of View (Zoom) the way you want it, and to animate the camera's Position instead. However, there are exceptions to every rule. Open [**Ex.09b**] and RAM Preview it: This example illustrates a popular effect of moving a camera toward an object while changing the angle of view so that objects farther away seem to recede. This is tricky to pull off in real life; in After Effects, it's just a matter of simultaneously animating the camera's Z Position and Zoom parameters to balance one against the other, widening the angle of view (which normally makes objects become smaller) while also moving closer to them in space. If the camera's keyframes aren't already revealed, select the camera layer and press U.

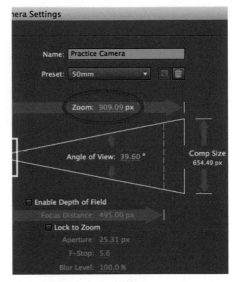

The Zoom value is automatically calculated from the Comp Size and Angle of View. It tells you the magic distance at which layers are not rescaled by perspective distortion.

In these frames from [**Ex.09b**], the layers aren't animating; the camera's Z Position and Zoom are being balanced off each other to make the "hero" layers come forward while the others recede. Chess pieces courtesy Digital Vision/Inner Gaze; background courtesy Artbeats/Digital Moods.

Presets, Defaults, and Reality

The camera presets in After Effects are based on popular lens lengths and 35mm print film. If you look closely at the Camera Settings after selecting a preset, you will find that After Effects enters a film width of 36mm, the horizontal image area for 35mm print film. When there is no camera in a comp with 3D layers, After Effects internally uses a default camera based on a 50mm lens and a 4:3 image aspect ratio, corresponding to a 36mm × 27mm "film plane."

If you are trying to match the physics of a motion picture camera, the ANSI standard for a 35mm non-anamorphic camera is an image width of 0.864 inches (21.95mm). You can find other common sizes in the *American Cinematographer Manual*. You can save your own presets (click on the document icon in the Camera Settings dialog), as well as delete existing presets.

Draft = No Blur

Enabling Draft 3D disables Depth of Field blurring, which speeds up previews.

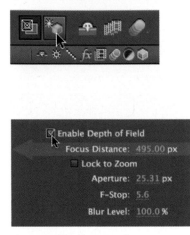

The second main group of parameters in Camera Settings decides how much 3D layers should be blurred, based on their distance from the camera.

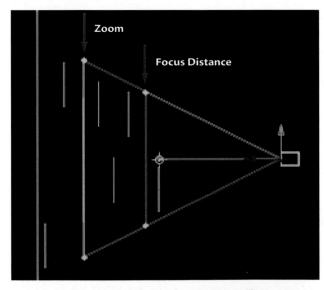

When you enable Depth of Field for a camera, you will see two lines in the camera display: the normal one that shows how far the Zoom parameter reaches from the camera, and a second line that shows where the center of focus is.

Depth of Field

Achieving sharp focus is one of the biggest challenges in using real cameras: The physics at work in a camera do not allow objects at different distances to all have the same degree of focus. By contrast, many software simulations of a camera – including the one in After Effects – support infinite focus, where everything is perfectly sharp regardless of its distance from the camera. As handy as this is, there are times when you want objects at different distances to have different amounts of blur, both because you want to make a creative statement and because it looks more natural.

To bring focus to your life, open [Ex.10a], select **Practice Camera**, open its Camera Settings, and click on the Enable Depth of Field checkbox. The Focus Distance parameter determines how far away layers should be from the camera to be in perfect focus. Any closer or farther away, and they will become progressively blurrier. The Lock to Zoom option causes editing the Focus Distance in the Camera Settings dialog to enter the same number for Zoom (and vice versa); this Lock has no effect outside of this dialog – ignore it for now.

The range of distances inside which images are reasonably sharp is known as the *depth of field*. After Effects gives you two different ways to affect this same property, both based on real cameras.

The Aperture setting is the size of the imaginary lens opening. Larger Aperture values result in a more shallow depth of field. Aperture's not-so-evil twin is F-stop: the ratio between Focus Distance and Aperture.

Many real-life cameras define the aperture size in F-stop units; therefore, this parameter might be more familiar to some users. Larger F-stop values result in smaller Aperture values, which in turn results in a more forgiving, greater depth of field.

The remaining value in this dialog is Blur Level. When it's left at its 100% default, depth-of-field blur in After Effects responds as a real camera should. If you find the results too blurry, you can reduce its effects by reducing this parameter. If you want to exaggerate the depth-of-field effect, you can increase this value to above 100%.

Click OK to close the Camera Settings dialog, make sure **Practice Camera** is still selected, type AA to reveal its Options in the Timeline panel, then Shift+P to also reveal its Position. Select layer 2, **DV_Beauty_eye**, and also reveal its Position value (Z = 250). For a layer to be in perfect focus, its Position (for example, Z = 250), minus the camera's Position (for example, Z = –400), must equal the Focus Distance (650, in this case).

Let's experiment with adjusting the options for depth of field:

• The image of the woman's eyes has been placed at the optimal Focus Distance from the camera; the spheres and background are varying distances closer or farther away. Scrub the value for Aperture; remember to hold the Shift key down to scrub in larger increments. As you scrub it to the right (increasing its value), the depth of field narrows, causing more of the other layers to go out of focus. Leave it at a value around 400.

• Now scrub the camera's Focus Distance parameter; you should be able to selectively place the other layers in and out of focus. Return Focus Distance to 650, where the eyes are back in focus.

• Finally, scrub the Blur Level parameter. You can think of this as a "scale" function for Aperture, increasing or decreasing the amount of blur caused by the Depth of Field effect. As a standard working practice, it's best to leave this at its default 100% and vary the Aperture setting; if you accidentally set Blur Level down to 0%, Aperture will have no effect no matter what value you set it to.

Depth Charges

We've set up two other sample animations based on depth of field that will hopefully kick-start your creative juices. RAM Preview them, select all the layers and type P to reveal their relative positions in 3D space, and press Shift+U to reveal the camera's animation:

• [**Ex.10b**] decreases the depth of field by animating the Aperture value. This draws the viewer's attention to one of the objects by blurring the others. In extreme cases (such as in this comp), the other objects are blurred so much they practically dissolve into thin air.

• [**Ex.10c**] is an example of the popular "rack focus" trick in which attention is directed from one layer to another by changing the Focus Distance. The depth of field is fairly narrow in this example as well, which exaggerates the blurring.

Depth of field takes longer to render, and the blur quality is not very good (akin to a "box" blur). If these are major issues for you, you might consider adding a normal blur plug-in to each layer and either manually keyframing the blur amount or using expressions (Chapter 37) to calculate the amount for you. This will result in higher quality, but you won't see varying amounts of blur across a layer (as with the floor in [**Ex.10c**]).

[**Ex.10b**]: By varying the Aperture setting, you can narrow the depth of field so that the camera focuses on one specific layer in the frame.

FACTOID

Blurless

OpenGL Fast Previews do not support Depth of Field.

[**Ex.10c**]: By animating the Focus Distance and setting the Depth of Field parameters appropriately, you can simulate "rack focus" effects.

CONNECT

OpenGL: Chapter 2.

Basic keyframe animation: Chapter 3.

Editing velocity, Graph Editor, and Separate XYZ transformations: Chapter 4.

Roving keyframes: Chapter 4.

Working in 3D, including 3D layers, perspective, and the alternate 3D Views: Chapter 13.

Lighting in 3D: Chapter 15.

Parenting and null objects: Chapter 17.

Nesting comps: Chapters 18 and 19.

Integrating with 3D applications: Chapter 40.

Lighting in 3D

We continue our exploration of 3D by discussing how to illuminate your layers.

TIP

C = Camera; L = Light

The shortcut to add a camera is Command+Option+Shift+C (Control+Alt+Shift+C); to add a light it is Command+Option+Shift+L (Control+Alt+Shift+L). Just remember "all those modifier keys, plus C for camera, L for light."

Example Project

Explore the 15-Example Project.aep file as you read this chapter; references to [Ex.##] refer to specific compositions within the project file.

You may have heard the expression "painting with light"; it's an appropriate description of what After Effects lets you do. You can illuminate layers, add colored casts to them, overlight them to add intensity or blow them out, vignette them, have them cast shadows…even cause layers to project their own images onto other layers. All of this comes with a price, of course: Lights are one of the deepest subjects in After Effects. We'll start with some basic concepts, progress through adjusting illumination and shadows, and end with advanced techniques such as creating virtual gels and gobos, plus faking reflections.

Lights and Surfaces

If there are no lights in a composition, when you enable the 3D Layer switch for a footage item, it will be rendered at 100% of its normal color value and brightness – just like a 2D layer. When you add a light, the comp's "default light" is disabled, and 3D layers are illuminated by your new light instead. You can add as many lights as you like, although each one will slow down your render. 2D layers ignore lights; they will render the same with or without them.

There are two basic types of light: *source* and *ambient*. Source lights may be placed in and moved through 3D space, just like footage layers. A source light's position relative to other layers determines how these layers are illuminated. By contrast, ambient lights don't have a position – they illuminate all 3D layers evenly regardless of where they are placed in space. The comp's default light is a form of ambient light.

Another popular expression is "it takes two to tango" – that's especially true when it comes to working with lighting in 3D. The lights are one half of the equation; the other half is how each layer reacts to those lights. In addition to a light's Intensity setting, several factors determine how strongly a 3D layer will be illuminated (the first five apply to source lights, while the last applies only to ambient lights):

- The angle between the light rays and the layer. If a layer faces a source light head-on, it can receive maximum illumination from that light.

- The angle between the active camera and the layer. This has less of an effect than the angle between a light and a layer, but as a layer turns on

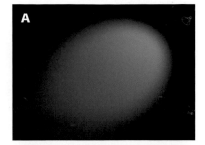

edge in relation to the camera, it does go dim. A good way to visualize this is that rays from a light must bounce off a layer and toward the camera to be visible.

• How efficiently a layer reflects light. This is referred to as its *diffuse value*. The angle between the light and the layer then affects how strong the diffuse illumination is, often causing illumination to fall off across the surface of a layer.

• How strong and broad the specular highlight is for the layer. This is the extra glint or "hot spot" you see on shiny objects; it is also affected by the angle between the light and the layer.

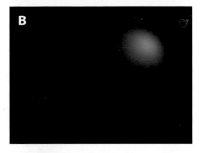

• Whether another layer blocks the light from reaching the layer you're looking at. Layers can be set to cast shadows onto other layers; they can even be set to project their colors onto another layer – but let's keep things simple for now...

• Whether there is also an ambient light in the scene. An ambient light adds illumination to a layer without considering the layer's position, angle, diffuse value, specular value, or shadow settings.

The final brightness of a layer is the sum of its diffuse, specular, and ambient illumination. The balance between these three can be set per layer by editing the layer's Material Options. The fact that these properties add to each other creates some interesting possibilities, such as the ability for a light to shift the original color of a layer, or create "blown out" looks (whether you intended this or not).

Lights don't have an Opacity parameter; instead, they have Intensity, which allows you to set their strength, plus fade them up and down over time. You can also trim the in and out points of a light's layer in the timeline, which controls when they are on and off. In most cases, lights do not care about layer stacking order; they illuminate all 3D layers in a comp based on their relative positions in 3D space. The one exception to this is an Adjustment Light, which we'll get to later.

Lights 101

First we will run through the basics of adding and positioning lights. Then we will cover a light's illumination properties: the type of light, its intensity, and its color. Next, we'll delve into a layer's Material Options – you can happily use its defaults, but if you're going after a special look (or trying to fix a specific problem), mastery of these will set your work apart. After that, we will discuss shadows, which involve both the Light Options

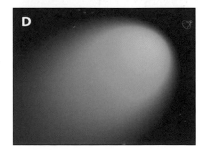

and the layer's Material Options to make them work properly. Finally, we'll conclude with a number of specialized lighting tricks, including light transmission, gels, gobos, reflections, and adjustment lights.

A layer's Material Options controls how it reacts to a light. Its diffuse (A), specular (B), and ambient (C) values are added to determine the final result (D). This is demonstrated in comp **[Ex.00]**.

We're going to assume you've read the prior two chapters, which means you're already familiar with the concept of 3D space, the different 3D views in After Effects, and moving 3D layers. Although we will recap some of these topics, in this immediate section we want to gain basic familiarity with how lights work and focus on how to add a light to a composition.

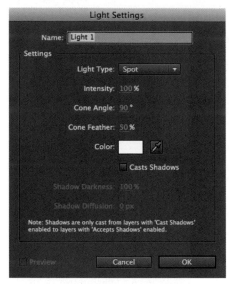

Step 3: The Light Settings dialog appears when you add a new light or edit an existing light. Use these settings to start with in comp [**Ex.01a**].

Step 1: Open the composition [**Ex.01a**] in this chapter's Example Project's [**Ex.01**] folder. It contains two 3D layers: an orange shape layer (**Orange Star**), and a colorful image (**CD_nature print leaves**). They are nice and bright because there currently is no light layer in the comp – so After Effects is using a default light, which illuminates all layers evenly to show their original colors.

Step 2: Make sure the Info panel is open (if it isn't open, press Command+1 on the Mac; Control+1 on Windows), and move your cursor over the orange star in the Comp panel – it should give a red ("R") value of 255, or 100% strength (use the Info panel's Options menu to change the display units). If you want to verify what's happening to the surface color of a layer as you experiment with lights, move the cursor around the orange star and watch the red channel's readout in the Info panel. If you want to just look at a pretty picture instead, turn off the Video switch for the **Orange Star** layer. We're going to assume you've left both layers on.

Step 3: Add a light to this comp by using the menu command Layer > New > Light or the shortcut Command+Option+Shift+L (Control+Alt+Shift+L). The Light Settings dialog will open. For now, choose a Light Type of Spot, set Intensity to 100%, Cone Angle to 90 degrees, Cone Feather to 50%, Color to white, and make sure Casts Shadows is disabled. Click OK, and a layer named **Light 1** will be added to your comp.

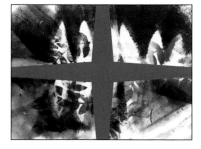
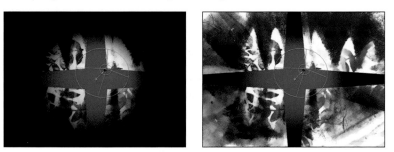

When no lights are present, 3D layers are illuminated evenly by a comp's default light (left). When you add a light, the characteristics of the light affect how the 3D layers are seen (center). 2D layers are not affected by lights; if you turn off the 3D Layer switch for the background in [**Ex.01a**], it returns to its normal color (right).

Step 4: You will notice that the images in your comp have become darker. Once you add a light to your comp, After Effects turns off its default light, and the two 3D layers are now relying on your new light for illumination. To verify that 2D layers do not interact with lights, turn the 3D Layer switch for **CD_nature print** off; it will return to its normal surface color and brightness while **Orange Star** will still appear incompletely illuminated by the light. Turn **CD_nature print**'s 3D Layer switch back on for the remainder of this exercise.

Step 5: Select **Light 1** and type P to reveal its Position, then Shift+A to reveal its Point of Interest. We chose a Light Type of Spot because it is arguably the most dramatic, and also because it offers the most control.

Spot lights can be aimed, just like a two-point camera. If you look in the Comp panel, the red/green/blue axis arrows show the Position of a light.

The wireframe cone represents the Cone Angle which you set to 90°; this wireframe helps give an idea of how light rays spray out from the light's Position. You should also see a line drawn to an anchor point icon; this is the light's Point of Interest, which is where it is aimed. Switch the 3D View popup to alternate views such as Left and Top to get a better look at the light; return to Active Camera when you're done.

Step 6: You can move a light three ways: Scrub its Position and Point of Interest values in the Timeline panel, use the cursor keys to nudge it (moving its Position and Point of Interest together), or grab these points individually and move them in the Comp panel.

First practice moving the light's Position in the Comp panel. The rules that you learned about moving 3D layers and cameras also apply to moving lights: If you can see a small X, Y, or Z next to your cursor, movements will be constrained to that axis. Like a two-point camera, when you move a light using axis constraints, the Point of Interest will come along for the ride; press Command (Control) as you drag an individual axis to keep the Point of Interest from moving. To move the light freely in any axis you want, while also leaving the Point of Interest where it is, click close to where the three axis arrows meet – but without an axis letter visible next to your cursor – and then drag.

Now practice moving the Point of Interest; note that it has no axis constraints. (You have to click very precisely on its icon to make sure you don't accidentally select one of the layers instead; if you are having trouble doing this, try locking the other layers for now.)

Have some fun steering both ends of the light around – you can even set up an animation if you like. Try to end up with a rakish angle across the layers – for example, we used a Point of Interest value of 250,330,0, and Position of 560,135,–200 for the next several figures.

Step 7: There are two ways to edit a light's settings after you have created it. To open the original Light Settings dialog, either double-click on the light layer, or select it and type Command+Shift+Y (Control+Shift+Y). To edit its settings directly in the Timeline panel, select the layer and type AA (two As in quick succession).

Select **Light 1** and type AA; make sure the Switches column is visible (press F4 if it isn't). Scrub the Intensity parameter: This controls how bright or dim a light is. Obviously, 0% is off; less obvious is that you can set Intensity above 100% – we'll get into the creative and practical uses of this later on. You can also set it to a negative value, to subtract illumination from a scene. For now, return Intensity to 100%.

Scrub the Cone Angle parameter, watching the Comp panel to note how the wireframe cone expands and contracts, while more or less of the layers are illuminated. Then scrub the Cone Feather angle, noticing how the light changes from a gentle falloff to a hard line where it either illuminates the layer or it doesn't.

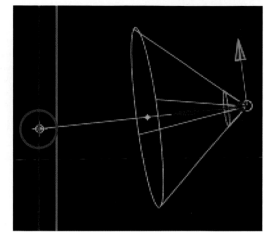

Step 5: Spot lights are like two-point cameras in that they have a Position (represented by the axis arrows) as well as a Point of Interest (where the cursor is pointing) that decides where the light is being aimed. The Cone Angle of a Spot light is also drawn as a wireframe in the Comp panel. (This image is from the Left view.)

Cone Angle or Position?

New Spot lights default to being positioned too close to layers. Instead of increasing its Cone Angle to illuminate the corners of the comp, try moving the light's Position back in Z.

Step 7: To reveal a light's Options in the Timeline panel, select it and type AA.

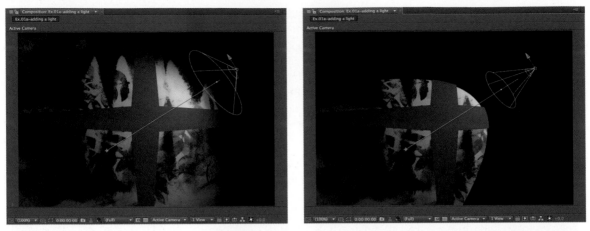

Step 7: Experiment with editing the light's Cone Angle and Cone Feather, from a wide angle and soft feather (above left) to a narrow angle and no feather (above right). The settings for the latter look are shown in the Timeline panel (right).

OpenGL Lights

When OpenGL is enabled, only the first eight lights are rendered.

In **[Ex.01b]**, select Top view to view the motion path for the light more clearly.

We'll cover both of these parameters in more detail later; after you get a general feel for them here, set the Cone Angle to 120° and Cone Feather to 50%.

Step 8: We want to conclude this quick tour of lights by reinforcing what we said about the angle between a light and a layer having an effect on how brightly the layer is illuminated. With the light still placed at the rakish angle we suggested in Step 6, press F2 to deselect the layers and simplify the Comp panel. Move the cursor over the **Orange Star** layer while watching the Info panel: The red channel's value doesn't quite make it to 100% (255) because the light is not facing the layer head-on.

Reselect **Light 1**, type P plus Shift+A, enter a Point of Interest of 160,120,0 and a Position of 160,120,–115 to center it directly over **Orange Star**. Press F2 and move your cursor over **Orange Star** again; at the center of illumination, its red channel is now at 100% strength.

To further reinforce how important the angle between the light and layer is, open **[Ex.01b]** and RAM Preview. In this comp, the two foreground layers are placed in 3D at a 90° angle to each other. A light animates from facing one layer head-on to facing the other layer head-on, resulting in the first layer becoming darker and the second layer becoming brighter. (Select **Light 1** and study its motion path using the Top view.) Playing

By animating a light to face first one layer, and then another, you can draw the viewer's attention between images in your comp. Here we animated the light's Position and Point of Interest to aim it, as seen from the Top view. Musician footage courtesy Lee Stranahan.

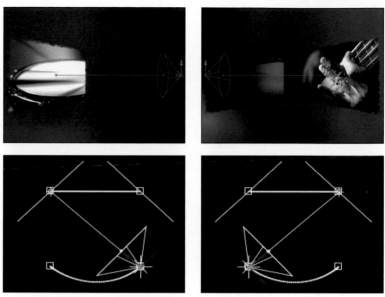

around with how a light is oriented toward various layers in a comp is an effective trick to draw interest from one layer to another.

Rotating a Light

Lights can also be rotated. Back in [**Ex.01a**], select **Light 1** and type R to reveal its Orientation and Rotation parameters. Experiment with scrubbing the X and Y values (all Z does is twirl a light along the axis it is aimed at, to no visual effect): These rotate where the light is aimed, *but do not move the Point of Interest*. If you rotate a light using the Rotation tool, After Effects will even warn you about this. You can use these two properties in concert with each other, by aiming the light using its Point of Interest, then using Rotation to offset its aim, cause it to spin around like a police light or wander like a searchlight.

If you are uncomfortable animating lights by coordinating their Position and Point of Interest, you can use Rotation and Orientation to aim them in space. First, select **Light 1** and type Command+Option+O (Control+Alt+O) to open its Auto-Orientation dialog. The default is Orient Towards Point of Interest; select Off and click OK. The Point of Interest property will disappear from the Timeline panel. You can now aim the light using a combination of Position and Rotation, without worrying about the Point of Interest.

Open [**Ex.01c**], and scrub the Timeline. You'll notice this is an animation similar to [**Ex.01b**], but this time it's created by animating Position and the Y Rotation. Select **Light 1** and study its motion path in the Top view.

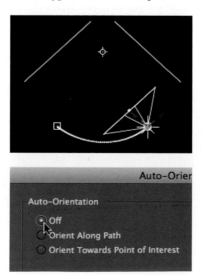

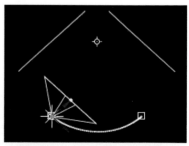

Once Auto-Orientation is turned Off (left), you can still aim a light by using the Rotation and Orientation properties. In [**Ex.01c**], the light rotates on the Y axis to aim first at the left video screen and then the right (above).

A Light Menu

Now that you have a feeling for how lights work in general, we can get into the specifics of the different Light Types, plus the Intensity and Color parameters. If you want to play around with these parameters as we describe them, use the popup menu along the top of the Comp panel to select Close All. Then open **[Ex.02a]**, which contains another pair of 3D layers and a light. If the light's parameters are not already revealed, select **Light 1** and type AA to reveal its Options in the Timeline panel. Also make sure the Switches column is open in the Timeline panel.

Falloff Lighting

Lights in After Effects do not diminish in strength over distance. To simulate this effect, check out Digieffects Falloff Lighting (*www.digieffects.com*).

Spot Light

We'll start with the Light Type of Spot, as you're already familiar with it from the previous section. All of the other Light Types are subsets of Spot in that they have fewer Options.

Spot lights are directional: Their rays start at their Position and are sprayed out in a cone centered around their Point of Interest. The distance between the Point of Interest and Position has no bearing on how far these rays shoot; all lights in After Effects extend an infinite distance (unlike some 3D programs, which allow you to control a light's falloff so that it can become weaker over distance).

The Cone Angle determines how widely the light rays are sprayed, with a maximum value of 180°. The farther a light is from a layer, the larger the cone of light will appear – think of aiming a flashlight toward objects farther away. The Cone Feather determines how quickly the effect of the light transitions from darkness (the area beyond the cone) to full illumination. Unlike Mask Feather, in which the feather is centered around the mask shape, a light's Cone Feather does not reach outside the Cone Angle – it only reaches inward. As a result, increasing the Cone Feather has the visual effect of reducing the amount of illumination a light contributes to a scene.

In **[Ex.02a]**, scrub the Cone Feather value between 0% and 100% to see how it softens the visual effect of the cone. Leave it at a low value (somewhere between 0% and 30%), and scrub the Cone Angle to watch the spot narrow and widen.

Spot lights are directional; they also have a cone that defines how wide an area they illuminate. Background courtesy Digital Vision/Inner Gaze.

A series of Spot lights with narrow cones, placed close to a layer, can create a nice effect. Animate each one's Point of Interest to create a searchlight feel. Image courtesy Digital Vision/Music Mix.

Wide Cone Angles make it easier to illuminate a large area of one layer (or even several layers) with one light. Conversely, you can use a series of lights with narrow Cone Angles to create a more mysterious look in which only select portions of your layers are illuminated. [**Ex.02b**] demonstrates using four lights with narrow cones placed very close to a layer to create slashes of light. Each one's Point of Interest is animated to create a "searching" effect.

Point Light

A Point light is essentially a Spot light that's not restricted by a cone. A good analogy is a light bulb, hanging in space, that does not have a lampshade directing where its light falls. Point lights are useful for adding broad illumination to a scene, while still retaining some natural falloff in brightness across a layer's surface.

Return to comp [**Ex.02a**], select **Light 1**, and make sure its Options are exposed (shortcut: AA). Look for the popup menu on the same line as the words "Light Options"; click on it and select Point. The parameters Cone Angle and Cone Feather will disappear from the Timeline panel. In the Comp panel, the wireframe representing the Cone Angle of a Spot light is gone; a much broader area of the image is illuminated as a result.

Point lights spray their rays out at all angles: Imagine drawing a line from various pixels on your layer back to the light, and think of the angle between your imaginary line and the layer. If you study the Comp panel, you will notice some lighting variation across the faces of the layers (move your cursor over the blue strip and watch its corresponding blue channel values in the Info panel for confirmation). Different portions of a layer are at different angles to the light; these varying angles result in the differences in illumination you see. The area of the layer that is closest to the light is the brightest, with a gentle falloff in illumination outward from this point.

To get a feel for how this works, change the 3D View popup to Custom View 1. Grab the light in the Comp panel; drag it toward and then around the faces of the layers to illuminate different areas. Then open [**Ex.02c**] and RAM Preview it: A Point light flies around very close to the surface of a layer, illuminating small areas of it; at the end, it pulls back away from the layer, resulting in the entire image being illuminated.

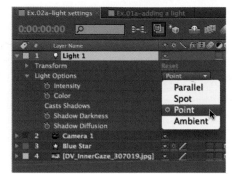

You can change the Light Type in the Light Settings dialog, or directly in the Timeline panel in the Switches column.

Point lights shoot their rays out at all angles, resulting in a natural falloff in illumination as pixels get farther away from the light.

As the Point light pulls back farther away from a layer, the layer becomes illuminated more evenly.

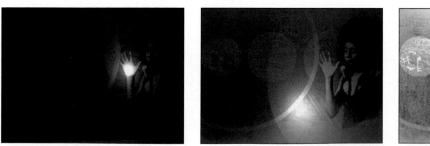

A Point light (above) generates a gentle falloff of illumination across a layer's face. A Parallel light (below) illuminates a layer more evenly and allows you to control the angle between the light and layer by moving the light (where the arrow is pointing) and the Point of Interest (circled).

Parallel Light

A Parallel light can be thought of as a variation on a Point light. The main difference is that you have control over which direction the light rays are aimed (therefore giving you more control over how a layer's surface is illuminated), rather than rays being shot out in all directions from the light's position. Parallel lights are used when you want the most even illumination but still want the angle between the light and a layer to make a difference in how brightly the layer is illuminated.

Return to [**Ex.02a**], and make sure the 3D View popup is set to Active Camera. Select **Light 1**, type P to reveal its Position, and enter the coordinates 450, 200, –300 to get you back where we started. Then type AA to reveal its Options again. With the Light Type still set to Point, type Shift+F5 to take a snapshot of what it looks like. Then change the Light Type to Parallel. Notice the change in the Comp panel (press F5 if you need a reminder of what the Point light looked like): The layer is more evenly illuminated, without the falloff you saw with the Point light.

The technical description of a Parallel light is that all of the light rays are pointing in the same direction. This simulates a distant light, akin to the sun; the result is you don't have the gradual falloff in illumination across the surface of a layer that you notice with a Spot or Point light. This also means that the distance between the light and layer does not affect how the layer is illuminated; Parallel lights act as if their real Position was infinitely far away.

Unlike the sun, you can aim a Parallel light. Look again at the Comp panel: In addition to the axis arrows surrounding the light's Position, you will also see a line drawn to the light's Point of Interest. With **Light 1** selected, grab and move the Point of Interest; you will notice the layer get brighter and dimmer. As you drag the Point of Interest farther to the left in the Active Camera view, the layer dims, as the light rays are hitting it at a more extreme angle. If the Position and Point of Interest are perfectly aligned to point straight at a layer, the layer will be at its brightest. (To ensure that the light is perpendicular to the layer, you can move the Point of Interest in the Top and Left views, then view the results in the Active Camera view.)

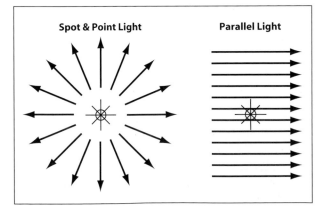

Spot and Point lights (far left) shoot their rays out at different angles from their source, which creates falloffs in illumination and causes shadows to grow larger over distance. Parallel lights (left) shoot all of their rays in the same direction, resulting in even lighting and sharp shadows (not always as desirable as it may sound).

Ambient Light

Ambient lights follow virtually none of the rules the other lights do. Ambient lights have no position, direction, or cone; they don't even cast shadows. They are omnipresent lights that evenly illuminate every 3D layer in a comp, regardless of where that layer is placed or how it is oriented. An Ambient light is used when you want to make sure all 3D layers are receiving some illumination, and you are unable to set up your normal lighting to accomplish this. They work as the ultimate "fill" light.

Back in [**Ex.02a**], make sure the Options are revealed for **Light 1**, and change its Light Type to Ambient. Assuming the Intensity is still set to 100% and the Color is still set to white, the layers will now be illuminated at their full brightness – move your cursor over **Blue Solid** and watch the color channel readouts in the Info panel to confirm this. Scrub the Intensity parameter; the layers will darken and brighten evenly.

Ambient lights can be useful problem solvers. Close your other comps to reduce clutter, and open [**Ex.02d_starter**]: It contains a woman's face vignetted by a Spot light. The client sees this, and says "I like what you're doing with the light – but can you make the dark areas less dark?"

To solve this Zen riddle, add a Layer > New > Light. Set the Light Type to Ambient, make sure the Color is white, change its name to "**Ambient Fill**" and click OK. The image will now be blown out, because you have two lights – including a full-strength, omnipresent Ambient light – adding together. With **Ambient Fill** selected, type T to reveal its Intensity (akin to Opacity), and scrub its value down until the dark areas of the layer are, to quote the client, "less dark." Note that the Ambient light is still brightening the portion of the face also illuminated by the Spot light; if any areas are looking blown out, you will probably need to reduce the Intensity for the layer **Spot Light** as well. Our results are in [**Ex.02d-final**].

Intensity

We've already played with the light's Intensity earlier in this chapter, but we wanted to re-emphasize one important point: *You can increase Intensity beyond 100%.* This has both corrective and creative uses.

We'll be going into a layer's Material Options in detail later in this chapter; their default values are set so that if a light is aimed perfectly at the layer (and the layer is facing the camera at a favorable angle), then the layer will be perfectly illuminated – its pixels will have the same color values as the original source. However, it's easy to introduce imperfections into this world: The light can be at an angle to the layer, the layer can be at an angle to the camera, et cetera. These result in the layer being rendered darker. This problem is multiplied if you have more than one layer to take care of. Rather than edit the Material Options for each layer, you can just crank up the light's Intensity value until the layers look natural again.

If a layer is over-illuminated, its color values are increased above their original values. This can look quite nice – almost like a form of glow – when the light has a natural falloff, as a Spot or Point light does.

Spot lights create nice vignettes, but they can leave areas outside the spot's cone too dark (above). Add an Ambient light, and balance its Intensity off the other lights to help fill in the dark areas (below). Image courtesy Digital Vision/Beauty.

TIP

T = intensiTy

To reveal just a light's Intensity parameter in the Timeline, select it and press T.

FACTOID

Below 0%; Above 100%

Intensity can be set above 100% to blow out a layer; it can also be set below 0% to remove illumination.

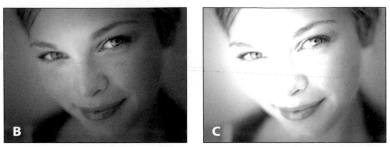

With no lights turned on, the comp's default light illuminates an image evenly (A). Adding just one light at 100% Intensity often results in a duller image than the original (B). Cranking the light's intensity beyond 100% can correct this problem, or take the image into new creative territory (C).

Step 1:   To see an example of over-illumination, open [**Ex.02e_starter**]: It contains a still image and a Point light. Turn off the Video switch for **Light 1**; this will allow you to see the image **DV_Beauty_eye** at its normal brightness. Press Shift+F5 to take a snapshot of what this looks like.

Step 2:   Turn **Light 1**'s Video switch back on, and make sure its Options are revealed in the Timeline panel (type AA). Gently increase its Intensity until the image seems to take on the same brightness as it had using the comp's default light. Press F5 to compare your results.

Step 3:   Keep increasing the light's Intensity while you're watching the Comp panel: Portions of the image will brighten until individual color channels clip at their maximum values. As you keep increasing Intensity, this clipping will result in a color shift in these portions of the image. Once you push through a certain undefined barrier, the result changes from looking like a mistake to a very creative treatment of the original image. Don't be afraid to keep pushing to see what happens (your monitor won't melt); you can animate this parameter to create some cool effects and transitions. RAM Preview [**Ex.02e-final**] to see a layer fade from almost total white to the normal image.

Color

Not wanting to dwell on the obvious, a light's Color is the color of the light. It tints the layers illuminated by the light.

An orange-tinted light can make a scene appear warm (above); a blue-tinted light can make the same scene cool (below).

Colored lights always seem like a good idea until you try to use them. Unless the layer is something simple like gray or white type, strong colors rarely work – they often interact with the colors of your source footage in unappealing ways. Also, saturated colors are less bright than the standard white light; you will need to increase a colored light's Intensity to get an acceptable brightness level in the final image.

Consider trying lightly tinted colors to change the mood of an image. For example, the sun's light is often attributed with a slight yellow/orange cast, which results in a warmer, more upbeat final image. Fluorescent lights can add a slightly bluish cast, which can make a scene seem emotionally cold. Open [**Ex.02f**] and RAM Preview it: Here, a Parallel light's Color animates from white to pale yellow to pale blue, resulting in the final image going from neutral to warm to cool. (If you try this trick with your own footage, remember that you must enable the 3D Layer switch for your footage to be affected by a light.)

The Material World

Before we discuss shadows, we want to cover the oft-overlooked Material Options for a layer. Material Options interact strongly with the lighting effects described above; you also need to be aware of these options when you start to work with shadows.

To reduce distractions, select Close All from the tab along the top of the Comp panel, and then open [**Ex.03a**]. It contains two lights – **Light 1/Spot** and **Light 2/Ambient** – and one 3D layer, **CD_CorvetteGrill**. The Video switch for **Light 2/Ambient** should be off for now. If you want to compare the original **CD_CorvetteGrill** photo with the lit result in the Comp panel, click on the Draft 3D switch in the Timeline panel to disable all lights (among other things); be sure to toggle Draft 3D back off again when you're done.

To check what the layer originally looked like, turn on the Draft 3D switch to stop lights from rendering.

If the Material Options are not currently visible for **CD_CorvetteGrill**, select it and type AA. We'll save the first three – Casts Shadows, Light Transmission, and Accepts Shadows – for later, and focus on the remaining six: Accepts Lights, Ambient, Diffuse, Specular, Shininess, and Metal.

Accepts Lights

This is a simple toggle for whether or not a layer interacts with lights. Still in [**Ex.03a**], Accepts Lights is currently On for the **CD_CorvetteGrill** layer; click on the word "On" to toggle it to "Off" and you will notice the layer reverts to its original colors, rather than being affected by **Light 1/Spot**. This is handy if you have an object you want to fly around in 3D space, but which you want to always be 100% illuminated regardless of what's going on with the lighting in the comp. Set it back to On for now.

Select a layer and type AA to reveal its Material Options in the Timeline panel. These determine how a layer reacts to lights in a composition. The defaults tend to underlight a layer, causing it to appear dull when light intensity is set to 100%.

Ambient

A layer's Ambient parameter decides how strongly it reacts to lights that have a Light Type of Ambient; the remaining Material Options decide how it reacts to the other Light Types.

The **Light 2/Ambient** layer is currently turned off, so it is not contributing to the layer's illumination. Turn on the Video Switch for **Light 2/Ambient**, and now **CD_CorvetteGrill** will be lit very brightly – it is reacting to both **Light 1/Spot** and **Light 2/Ambient**. Scrub the **CD_CorvetteGrill**'s Ambient parameter to the left to reduce how strongly it's reacting to **Light 2/Ambient**.

In the *Ambient Light* section earlier in the chapter, we suggested you vary the ambient light's Intensity parameter to decide how much it contributes to a scene. If all the layers have their Ambient parameter left at the default of 100%, they will all be affected equally by the ambient light. However, if you want individual layers to react differently to an ambient light in a comp, you can adjust their individual Ambient parameters.

For the remainder of our experiments here, turn *off* **Light 2/Ambient**.

GOTCHA

No Effects for Lights

You cannot apply an effect to a camera or light.

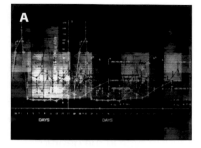

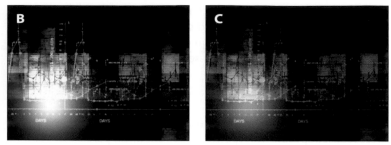

Dark layers are difficult to illuminate [**Ex.03b**]. Lights normally interact with a layer's surface color – and black doesn't leave much to interact with (A). Decrease the layer's Metal parameter, and the light becomes visible as a glare – even in black areas (B). Colored lights also show up better on dark layers with low Metal settings (C). Image courtesy Getty Images/Discovery.

Open [**Ex.03b**]; if the Material Options for **GI_Discovery_graph** are not visible, select this layer and type AA. Even though we have increased both its Diffuse and Specular values to 100%, and are using a Point light which normally gives very even illumination, this mostly black image is still very dark. Decrease the Metal parameter, and a glaring white hot spot will appear. Double-click **Light 1/Point** to open the Light Settings, and change its Color to something complementary such as orange: The hot spot will be orange as well. Then go back and scrub **GI_Discovery_graph**'s Metal parameter to reinforce how the light and layer interact. This is an important technique to remember when you want to have lighting effects on dark objects such as black text.

Out of the Shadows

Flying footage items, cameras, and lights around in 3D space is fun, but shadows – one layer blocking some of the light cast onto another – perhaps go the furthest in helping create the illusion of real objects interacting in real space. Managing shadows in After Effects takes a bit of thought, but the effort is handsomely rewarded.

For shadows to work, five requirements must be met:

• A nonambient light must be aimed so that it illuminates both the layer you want to cast a shadow and the layer you want to receive the shadow.

• The light must have its Casts Shadows option enabled (the default when you create a new light is the last value you chose).

• The layer casting the shadow must have its Casts Shadows Material Option set to On or Only (the default is *Off* – the most common gotcha).

• The layer receiving the shadow must have its Accepts Shadows Material Option set to On (fortunately, the default is On).

• There must be some space between the layer casting the shadow and the layer receiving the shadow.

Just to make life interesting, both lights and layers have additional options that affect how shadows are ultimately rendered. We'll start by learning how to enable shadows plus how they react to the relative position of the light, layers, and camera. Then we'll discuss the light's additional shadow parameters. After these are mastered, we'll move on to Light Transmission: a special case of shadows that allow one layer's image to be cast onto another.

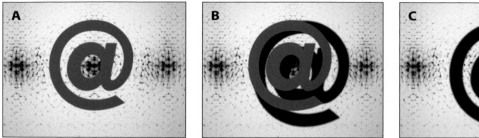

Shadows 101

Close any comps you may have been working with, and open [**Ex.04a**]. It contains a camera, a light, and two 3D layers placed at different distances from the camera and light. Right now, it just looks like a piece of 2D artwork, but we're about to change that…

Step 1: Select **Light 1** and double-click it to open its Light Settings dialog, or press AA to reveal the same parameters in the Timeline panel. Note its Light Type: It's currently a Point light; we'll experiment with the other types later. All of the lights we've used so far in this project have had their shadows disabled, and so does this one. If you opened the Light Settings dialog, enable the Casts Shadows option and click OK to close it; if you pressed AA, in the Timeline panel, click on the Casts Shadows parameter Off value to toggle it to On.

Step 2: Still no shadows…but that's because layers default to not casting them. Shadows take a lot of processing power (and extra memory) to calculate; that's why After Effects starts with them turned off.

Select the **at_symbol** layer and type AA to reveal its Material Options. Casts Shadows is currently set to Off; click on the word "Off" once to change it to On. A large black radial drop shadow in the shape of the @ symbol will appear behind it on the **GI_Discovery_circles** layer. Click on the word "On," and it will change to Only; in the Comp panel, the turquoise @ symbol will disappear and you will see just its shadow. Undo, or toggle Casts Shadows back to On.

Step 3: There was no need to enable **GI_Discovery_circles** to receive shadows, as this is the default for layers. Of course, you can set a layer to not receive shadows. Select **GI_Discovery_circles** and type AA to reveal its own Material Options; toggle Accepts Shadows to Off and back to On again to verify this.

Step 4: The light controls how strong the shadow is and how soft or sharp it is. With **Light 1**'s Options still exposed, scrub its Shadow Darkness parameter to lighten the shadow; notice that the Comp panel updates a little more slowly than you may be used to – that's the extra calculation time required by shadows. For now, leave it between 50% and 75%.

Now scrub **Light 1**'s Shadow Diffusion parameter. This controls how much "feather" there is to the shadow's edge (see the sidebar *Diffusion*

Step 2: A layer's Casts Shadows options may be set to Off (A), On (B), or Only (C), which means the original layer disappears and only its shadow remains. Background courtesy Getty Images/ Discovery.

Unaltered Shadows

Applying a Track Matte or certain effects to a layer will alter the layer's alpha channel, but not the shadow it casts – the shadow is based on the original layer. Precompose the layer (Chapter 19) for shadows to be based on the altered alpha.

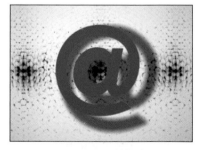

Step 4: You can soften a shadow's appearance by reducing a light's Shadow Darkness parameter (how strong, dark, or solid the shadow is) and increasing its Shadow Diffusion parameter (how blurry the edges are).

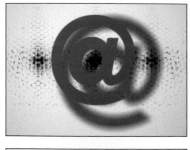

Step 5: If a Point or Spot light is closer to the shadow-casting layer than the camera, the resulting shadow will be larger than the layer itself (top). If the light is positioned farther away than the camera, the shadow is smaller than the shadow-casting layer (above).

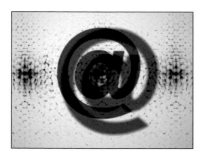

Step 6: If you apply a blending mode to the layer casting a shadow, the layer is blended using the mode, while the shadow is left unaffected.

GOTCHA

Out of Style

Applying a Layer Style (Chapter 22) eliminates a layer's ability to cast or receive a shadow.

Confusion for more details). A little Diffusion goes a long way toward softening a shadow's effect; set it to between 5 and 10 pixels for now.

Step 5: A shadow's position is controlled by the relative position of the light and the layer casting the shadow – no surprise there. (But go ahead and drag **Light 1** in **[Ex.04a]** around anyway, watching how the shadow moves in the opposite direction.) The shadow is also distorted in shape if one of the layers is tilted at an angle to the other.

The shadow's size depends in part on how far away the layer receiving the shadow is. Select all the layers and type P to reveal their Positions. Scrub **GI_Discovery_circle**'s Z Position, or type in a couple of alternate values such as 300 and 800. Point and Spot lights cast their rays in angles away from their Position. This means the farther away the background, the wider the rays spray out, resulting in a larger shadow. Leave its Z Position at 800 when you're done.

Just how large that shadow is can also be affected by the relative positions of the light and camera: With Point and Spot lights, if the camera is closer to the shadow-casting layer than the light, the shadow will appear *smaller* than the layer in the final result.

To see this in action, make a note of the Z Positions of **Light 1** (–300) and **Camera 1** (–400). The light is closer to the **at_symbol** layer (Z = 200) than the camera is, and in the Comp panel, the shadow appears *larger* than the layer casting it. Now change **Light 1**'s Z Position to –600 so it is farther away from the **at_symbol** than the camera is: As a result, the shadow will shrink to being *smaller* than the layer casting the shadow.

Step 6: Shadows are rendered separately from the layer that casts them. One of the advantages of this little piece of trivia is that you can apply blending modes to layers to blend them into their backgrounds, and not affect the shadow.

Press F4 to toggle the Switches column to Modes. Experiment with setting different modes for the **at_symbol** layer – start at Multiply and work your way down the list (the shortcut Shift + = will toggle down the list, Shift + – will go back up). Modes are one of the best features in After Effects; combining them with shadows presents even more creative possibilities. Set the Mode popup back to Normal when you're done.

Step 7: There's always an exception, isn't there? With the size of shadows, the exception comes with Parallel lights. This Light Type casts all of its rays parallel to each other, rather than spraying them out like Point and Spot lights do. The result is usually a smaller, tighter shadow. As the background moves farther away, the final shadow you see gets smaller, as it is getting scaled down by the increased distance you are viewing it at.

To see this behavior in action, double-click **Light 1**, change its Light Type to Parallel, and click OK. The shadow is now much smaller! Scrub **GI_Discovery_circles**'s Z Position to confirm that with Parallel lights, the shadow is never bigger than the layer casting it, and it only gets smaller as the receiving layer moves farther away. The farther away you move a Point or Spot light, the more it works like a Parallel light.

Diffusion Confusion

A light's Shadow Diffusion parameter defines how blurred a shadow is. The most obvious result of increasing Shadow Diffusion is that the shadow's edge (the transition zone between darkness and light) becomes more feathered.

Shadow Diffusion is specified as a number of pixels – but this does not mean that every shadow has exactly this many pixels of blur; the distances between the light, the layer casting the shadow, and the layer receiving the shadow come into play as well.

If the light is closer to the shadow-casting layer than the shadow-casting layer is to the layer receiving the shadow, then the diffusion amount will appear larger than the Shadow Diffusion parameter would suggest.

If the shadow-casting layer is moved closer to the layer receiving the shadow, the amount of perceived diffusion will be reduced. The proportions between these distances determine just how much diffusion is rendered.

To see this in action, open **[Ex.04b]**. The shadow-casting layer – **Solid 1** – has been set to Casts Shadows Only, so we can study its shadow without the layer getting in the way. **Light 1** has a Shadow Diffusion of 10 pixels. Select all three layers and type P to reveal their Positions. At time

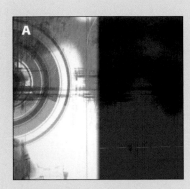

00:00, **Solid 1** is 400 pixels away from the background layer, and 800 pixels away from the light. The resulting shadow is not as blurred as you would expect from reading the Shadow Diffusion setting. Press End to move to 01:00; here **Solid 1** is 800 pixels away from the background and only 400 pixels from **Light 1** – and the result is that the shadow's edge is much more spread out.

For those who want to know the physics behind this, the Shadow Diffusion parameter is setting how large the virtual light is. If the light is infinitesimally small, all the rays shooting out from the light are coming from a single point, and the resulting shadow edges are cleanly defined. Larger lights have some rays shooting from their left edges, some shooting from their right edges, and some shooting from in-between. This means the edge of a shadow-casting layer is being hit by a number of light rays, all pointing in slightly different directions. When these spread-out rays hit the layer receiving the shadow, the result is a spread-out transition zone from darkness to light.

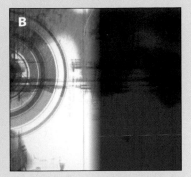

When a shadow-casting layer is closer to the shadow-receiving layer than the light, shadows appear tighter (A). As the shadow-casting layer moves closer to the light, the same Shadow Diffusion setting results in a much softer edge (B). Background courtesy Digital Vision/Data:Funk.

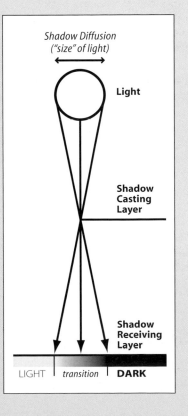

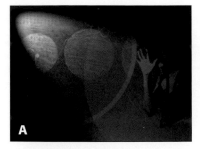

A

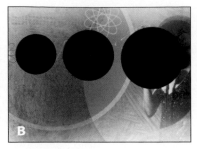

B

C

In **[Ex.06a]**, a moody spotlight illuminates the interior of our "building" (A). To give the impression of the sun shining through the circles in the design, we duplicated the image, cut out "windows" in the foreground copy (B), set the Light Transmission of the background copy to 100%, and placed an intense light behind these layers (C).

Light Transmission

One of the more interesting Material Options is Light Transmission, which opens a new set of creative possibilities.

When a 3D layer is hit by a Spot, Point, or Parallel light, the surface facing the light is illuminated, and normally the other side is rendered as black. This corresponds to a Light Transmission value of 0% (the default). As you increase Light Transmission, it mixes in more of the layer's own color; at 100%, the backs of layers are also illuminated by lights – as if they have become partially transparent. This solves the problem of a camera animation that results in a layer appearing between you and the light: If you don't want the layer to go black and disappear (and don't want to add another light to illuminate its back side as well), increase the layer's Light Transmission parameter.

The applications of Light Transmission can also be very creative, yielding "stained glass" types of effects. [Ex.06a] demonstrates a problem that would be difficult to solve without the Light Transmission parameter. We want the face of the layer to have a moody spotlight, as if artfully lit inside a building. This is provided by the layer **angled spot light**, which is placed in front of the image layers. But we also want the circles in the image to shine brightly, as if lit from the sun behind them.

To accomplish this, we made two copies of the image, and cut out holes in the foreground copy where we want the stained glass windows to show through. The foreground's Light Transmission is set to 0%; the background copy is set to 100%. Turn on the layer **animated backlight** – which has been placed *behind* the image layers – and you will see the windows come alive. RAM Preview to get the full effect; note that we cranked up the Intensity of **animated backlight** so it would slightly "blow out" the colors in the windows.

Before you ask: No, you can't see colored light beams being projected from the layer's surface. After Effects does not yet support the kind of "volumetric" lighting that real 3D applications offer. However, life gets more interesting when the layer is set to cast shadows. The default shadow color is black. As you increase the Light Transmission parameter, the shadow changes to represent the color of the layer. If the layer is a solid color, the shadow takes on that color: Open comp [Ex.06b], select the layer **at_symbol**, type AA to reveal its Material Options, and scrub Light Transmission to get a feel for how this works.

Shadow Detail

The sharpness of the shadows created by the Advanced 3D rendering plug-in depends on the size of its *shadow map*. Using too small of a map has exactly the same problem as using too small of an image: If it needs to get scaled up too far, it looks fuzzy and has artifacts. Larger map sizes create sharper shadows at the cost of exponentially increasing memory requirements and render times.

You can choose the map size by clicking on the Options button under the Advanced tab in Composition Settings. Deciding how large a shadow map you need depends on how far the shadows are being cast and how prominent they are in the comp. After Effects defaults the shadow map size to the same as the composition; this may or may not be optimal for your project – you really need to experiment with this setting on a case-by-case basis, taking snapshots and deciding how sharp you need your shadows to be. Practice using different settings with **[Ex.05]**.

The Advanced 3D plug-in's Shadow Map size is set by clicking on the Options button under the Composition Settings' Advanced tab.

The Advanced 3D plug-in creates a shadow map that is projected onto layers: small map sizes result in fuzzy shadows but shorter rendering times (A); large maps result in sharp shadows (B). Note you can still increase Shadow Diffusion to soften these more accurate shadows.

What if you want the shadow to be a different color than the layer? Then you will need two copies of the layer: one that does not cast shadows, and which is set to the layer color you want, and another set to Casts Shadows = Only, tinted to produce the shadow color you desire. This is shown in **[Ex.06c]**. For bonus points, we parented the shadow-only duplicate layer to the original layer so they could be animated easily as a group.

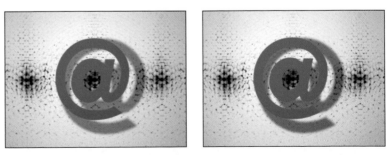

If Casts Shadows is set to On and Light Transmission is increased to 100%, the shadow is the same color as the layer (left). To create a shadow of a different color, duplicate the layer, change its color, and set Casts Shadows to Only (right).

Easy 2D Spot

To add a spotlight effect to 2D layers, apply Effect > Perspective > CC Spotlight. Its Render menu includes options for using a layer as a gel. Apply the effect to an adjustment layer (Chapter 22) to spotlight all layers below.

Layers can be used as gels for lights (left): Set Casts Shadows to Only, and Light Transmission to 100%. Adjust their Opacity to moderate their effect, or use a "fill" light to provide the remaining illumination needed (right). The colored gel pattern is featured in **[Ex.07b]** and is courtesy Artbeats/Light Effects.

Using Light Transmission results in the projected image interacting with the positions and orientations of the 3D layers that receive it. Hand courtesy Digital Vision/The Body.

Creating Gels

Life gets really interesting if the layer casting shadows has useful colors or shapes of its own, as these will now be projected onto the layers behind it. This is similar to placing a gel in front of a real light – except that the gel can be moving video, if you want.

Close the previous comps, open **[Ex.07a]**, and Option+double-click (Alt+double-click) **AB_SoftEdges_loop** to open it in the QuickTime player; play it to get a feel for how it animates. Close the player when you're done.

The **AB_SoftEdges_loop** layer has had its Material Options set to Casts Shadows = Only and Light Transmission = 100%. The resulting "shadows" are cast onto the background; RAM Preview to see them in action. Press P

to reveal Position, and scrub the layer's Z Position to see how its relative position between the light and background layer varies how its projected shadow is scaled by distance (closer to the light = larger shadow projected, blowing up its detail). The handles you see in the Comp panel of the layer's outlines are deceiving: What you end up seeing is its shadow – not the layer. Then scrub its Opacity to see how this affects how strongly it blocks the light.

A variation on this idea is used in **[Ex.07b]**. Here, the projecting movie is in color. (We've also used an ambient light to help fill in the dark areas of this background layer. Although many of our examples show using one light, on a real set it's more common to use at least one "key" light to light the main action and one "fill" light to make sure the rest of the set doesn't become too dark.)

Because the images projected by Light Transmission are really shadows, they interact with the positions and orientations of 3D layers, getting larger or smaller depending on their relative distances. Open **[Ex.07c]** and RAM Preview: Here, a still image of a hand (**DV_TheBody_hand.tif**) is projected onto a set of white squares that are rotating and moving through space. A camera orbits around the scene to provide additional perspective.

Why go through the trouble of using Light Transmission, when you could just use blending modes to "project" one image onto another? Open **[Ex.07d]**, which compares using the hand layer as a 2D layer, composited in Multiply mode on top of the animating 3D white solids. You can see that the effect is very different – and flat.

Another use of Light Transmission is to have a layer cast its image onto a floor, wall, or other surface as if light were emanating from a video or film projector. This same technique can also be used to make it appear as if you were seeing a type of reflection of a layer on a shiny surface, when in fact you are just seeing its shadow! (Reflections are not supported in After Effects, but they can be faked – more on that later.)

An example of this is demonstrated in [**Ex.07e**]. The Light Transmission value for the video image is set to 100%. One light (projection light) is behind the video and casts shadows, thereby casting the video image onto the floor; the second light is in front, just adding overall illumination to the scene. (Switch to Custom View 1 to get a good overview of the scene.)

[**Ex.07e**] contains an example of setting up a scene to cast light from a video screen onto a floor. The light on the right is casting the "shadows" (which is the video image, since this layer's Light Transmission has been set to 100%). Footage courtesy Artbeats/Animal Safari and Exteriors.

We've built a more complex example in [**Ex.07f**]. To get around the problem of the shadow-casting light (which is projecting our video) from illuminating the floor beyond the screen's image, we duplicated it and set the duplicate to have an Intensity of –100%, and not to cast shadows. This cancels out the illumination of the original light, leaving just its shadow. We also increased the Shadow Diffusion to get an out-of-focus projection, and added an Adjustment Light (discussed later) to add illumination to the floor.

Gobos

Shadows and Light Transmission can be used to create many interesting lighting effects, including *gobos* – blocking a portion of the light either to shape how it falls, or to project suggestive images such as sunlight through the leaves of a tree. Whereas Light Transmission projects the desired pattern as a colored shadow, another approach to creating gobos is to use the alpha channel of a layer to partially block a light.

The first task is finding or creating an image with an alpha channel to block portions of the light. If the layer you want to use as a gobo already has an alpha channel, such as an Illustrator file, you can use this layer directly. You can also use masks, or Shape Layers (Chapter 32). If your layer is a grayscale image, you can create an alpha channel from it by using it as a luma matte for a black solid. Since shadows do not work correctly with track mattes in 3D space, this often needs to be set up in a precomp. In the [**Ex.08**] folder, the **gobo precomp** was created to prepare our proposed gobo pattern. It is useful to make this comp's Background Color white (to represent the light that will shine through the gobo), and the matted solid's color black (to more easily see where light will be blocked). With other imagery, you may need to invert the matte, or use Effect > Color Correction > Levels to get the desired contrast for your gobo image.

[**Ex.07f**] is a more complex example, including using Shadow Diffusion to create a blurry projection.

An image is used as a matte in a precomp to create a gobo pattern in the alpha channel (left). A light is then projected through it onto a footage layer to create interesting light and shadow patterns (below). Gobo pattern courtesy Digital Vision/Quiet Form.

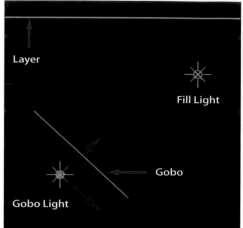

From the Top view, you can see how the gobo pattern is positioned between the gobo's light and the layer it's projecting onto.

2D Gobos

To create other lighting effects check out Composite Suite from Digital Film Tools. It comes with a library of gobo patterns. (*www.digitalfilmtools.com*)

To make it easy to reposition the gobo light and pattern together as a group, we parented the **gobo precomp** layer to **Gobo Light**. Moving the light (parent) will also move the gobo pattern (child), but you can still animate the child independently of its parent.

This gobo precomp is then nested into the composition where your 3D layers are arranged – [**Ex.08-Gobo Final**] in our case. The Material Options for the gobo layer should be set to Casts Shadows = Only; that way, you don't need to worry about accidentally seeing the image. Your choice of light to project your gobo pattern dictates the **gobo precomp**'s position and scale relative to the light. If you use a Parallel light, the **gobo precomp** can be placed at the same Position as the light. If you use a Point or Spot light (which will cause the gobo pattern to grow with distance – a more natural effect), you need to balance the distance between the light and gobo against the Scale of the gobo. We like to keep the gobo close to the light so there is less chance of accidentally positioning it behind the layer that is supposed to receive its shadow.

Feel free to adjust the Z Position and Scale of the nested **gobo precomp** layer and note how this changes the size of the gobo pattern in Active Camera. You might want to switch the Comp panel to 2 Views, with one view set to Top, to better see what is going on.

You can adjust how dark the shadows of the gobo are by adjusting the Opacity of the gobo layer or the Shadow Darkness of the gobo's light. Of course, you can also use a second light to act as a fill to further illuminate the scene. In [**Ex.08**], experiment with the Intensity of **Fill Light**, the Intensity and Shadow Darkness of **Gobo Light**, and the Opacity of the **gobo precomp** layer to get a feel for how they interact. If you want to blur the gobo pattern slightly, you can either apply a blur to the layer that creates the gobo pattern, or adjust the Shadow Diffusion parameter of **Gobo Light** (if the gobo image is a still, applying the blur in the precomp will render faster, as it will be rendered once and then cached).

Finally, we used parenting (discussed in Chapter 17) to attach the **gobo precomp** layer to the **Gobo Light**; press Shift+F4 if you want to view the Parent column. You can still edit the **gobo precomp** independently, but moving the **Gobo Light** will move both together as a group. Play with the Position and Orientation of the **Gobo Light** to reposition how the gobo's patterns cast across the woman's face. You can animate the light to move the group, or animate the Position, Scale, and Rotation of the **gobo precomp** to add life to the shadows it casts.

Close all of your comps when you're finished.

■ Ex.08–Gobo Final ×				

	#	Layer Name	Parent				
▶ ■	1	Fill Light (Point Light)	◎	None			👁
▶ ■	2	Gobo Light (Point Light)	◎	None			👁
▶ ■	3	[gobo precomp]	◎	2. Gobo Light (Point Light)			👁
▶ ■	4	[DV_Beauty_eye.jpg]	◎	None			👁

Fake Reflections

Although After Effects supports 3D shadows, it does not support 3D reflections. Third parties have created plug-ins to work around this: Zaxwerks Reflector is currently the most robust 3D solution, while Video Copilot VC Reflect and Red Giant Software RG Warp provide good 2D workarounds.

Many users have also developed techniques that do not require plug-ins; our version follows. Although ours is a touch more complex to set up, the trade-off is that it is much easier to alter and replace the sources after the fact – important for client changes or creating a reusable template. It relies on parenting, nested compositions, and precomps (the subjects of Chapters 17 through 20); if you get lost, come back later after you're comfortable with these subjects.

Step 1: Close all open comps and select the folder **Ex.09-Fake Reflections**. Type Command+N (Control+N) to create a new comp. For this exercise, use the HDV/HDTV 720 29.97 preset; in general, you want to make this comp large enough to hold any animation or elements you might want to add later. Name it "**Reflect Main**", set the duration to 05:00, and click OK.

Step 2: Drag SOURCES > Movies > **AB_Gears.mov** into [**Reflect Main**]'s Comp panel, placing it to the bottom of the frame to start. Feel free to add text or other elements if you wish.

Step 3: Open the comp [**Ex.09_starter**]. It currently has a floor placed in 3D. If Position is not revealed for the **Floor** layer, select it and press P. Note that its Y Position value is 500; this is the level of the floor that any new layers will sit on.

Step 4: Add [**Reflect Main**] to [**Ex.09_starter**] so it's the top layer. Enable the 3D Layer switch for **Reflect Main**. To make it sit on the floor, press A to reveal its Anchor Point. Right-click on the Anchor Point value and select Edit Value. Set the Units popup to % of Source, set Y to 100%, and click OK. This places the Anchor Point at the bottom of this nested comp layer, making it easier to place it at floor level. Then press P to reveal **Reflect Main**'s Position and set its Y Position value to 500; it should now sit correctly on the floor.

Step 5: Duplicate **Reflect Main** and rename layer 2 (the lower one in the stack) to "**Reflect Copy**". Press Shift+F4 to reveal the Parent column in the Timeline and set the Parent popup for **Reflect Copy** (layer 2) to be **Reflect Main** (layer 1). This means you can alter the Scale plus the X and Z Position of **Reflect Main**, and **Reflect Copy** will stay attached.

Step 2: Compose a scene in your **Reflect Main** composition.

Step 4: Set Reflect Main's Anchor Point to the bottom of the layer (above), then set its Y Position to be the same as the floor's (below).

Step 6: Press S to reveal **Reflect Copy**'s Scale, disable its Constrain Proportions switch (the chain link icon), and set just its Y Scale to –100%. An upside-down copy will just be visible below the floor.

Step 7: Drag **Floor** above **Reflect Copy** in the layer stack. Right-click on one of the column headers in the Timeline panel and select Columns > Modes. Set the blending mode for **Floor** to Screen; now the reflection will be visible – but it extends beyond the edge of the floor! Set the Track Matte popup for **Reflect Copy** to Alpha Matte. This will crop the reflection, but also turn off the floor; re-enable the Video switch for **Floor**. Finally, alter **Reflect Copy**'s Opacity to taste.

Step 7: At this point, you have your basic reflection relationship set up.

Feel free to increase **Reflect Main**'s Z Position to push the image plus its reflection further back on the floor, and to move the camera around the scene. Note that you can return to the [**Reflect Main**] comp and rearrange your sources; the reflection will update to match (a taste of the power of nested comps!).

There are many ways to enhance the reflection. The simple approach is to select **Reflect Copy** and add Effect > Transition > Linear Wipe. Set Wipe Angle to 180°, scrub Transition Completion to shorten the reflection, then increase Feather to smooth the transition. Then optionally add Effect > Blur & Sharpen > Fast Blur and increase Blurriness to soften the result. [**Ex.09-final1**] employs this approach. We also enabled shadows for the light and layers.

A more powerful alternative to Linear Wipe and Fast Blur is demonstrated in [**Ex.09-final2**]. Here, we duplicated **Reflect Copy**, renamed it **Gradient**, then used Layer > Pre-compose, selecting the Leave All Attributes option. In the precomp we created a gradient that will be our falloff map for the reflection. Back in [**Ex.09-final2**], we applied

Compound Blur (discussed in Chapter 24) to have the blur increase as the reflection trailed away, and used the Set Matte effect to fade it off. Both use the lightness of Gradient Precomp as their map; you will have to experiment with their Invert switches to get the desired result.

What if you want the layers in your [**Reflect Main**] comp to be separated in Z space? That requires a little more work, and is demonstrated in [**Ex.09-final3**]. We used the compound effects solution ([**Ex.09-final2**]) as a starting point and enabled the Collapse Transformations switch (Chapter 20) for the precomp layers **Reflect Main** and **Reflect Copy**. This allows the Z Position offsets for the layers in [**Reflect Main**] comp to come forward into the final comp. However, enabling this switch increases the effective size of these layers, meaning the gradient used by Compound Blur and Set Matte no longer lines up exactly with the reflection. This means you will have to tweak the starting and ending point of the gradient ramp based on the final camera position and other factors. The benefit of this approach is that it allows more complex interactions than is possible with VC Reflect or RG Warp, but it still doesn't equal the results you can achieve with Zaxwerks Reflector, which allows layers to reflect off each other.

Adding some blur and a fade enhances the appearance of the blur. This is demonstrated in [**Ex.09-final1**].

[**Ex.09-final3**] employs a more sophisticated approach, including Compound Blur plus the ability to preserve 3D depth from the main image's precomp. Woman courtesy Crowd Control.

Layers of Lights

Lights follow many of the same rules as other 3D layers – their order in the Timeline panel usually does not matter; it's their position in 3D space that counts. In contrast to normal 3D layers, placing 2D layers between lights does not break them into groups; they illuminate all 3D layers in the comp regardless. Unlike cameras, more than one light can be on at the same time; use a light's in and out points plus its Intensity parameter to affect when a light is on or off. Lights cannot "reach through" and illuminate layers in precomps unless you enable the precomp's Collapse Transformations switch (see Chapter 20). There are two exceptions to these general rules. One is that some effect plug-ins that simulate 3D effects can use the comp's camera and lights – but in some cases (such as Effect > Simulation > Shatter), they can use only the first light in the Timeline panel's layer stack. The other is that a light can also be an Adjustment Layer, which means it will illuminate only 3D layers that appear below it in the layer stack. You can use this as a tool to selectively light some layers and not others. (This is covered on the next page.)

Create a new light in **[Ex.10_starter]** using these settings.

When the Adjustment Layer switch is enabled for a light, it will illuminate only those layers below it in the Timeline panel.

Adjustment Lights

To get some practice with Adjustment Lights, open the composition **[Ex.10_starter]**: It contains a set of chess pieces cut out from a larger image, illuminated by a single Spot light. Our goal is to have different lighting treatments for the background pieces than for the two central "hero" pieces. To do this, we're going to employ an Adjustment Light, and play around with the layer stacking order so that this new light illuminates only some of the pieces.

Make sure that the Layer/Source Name column is set to Layer Name (click on it if it isn't), and that the Switches/Modes column is set to Switches (shortcut: F4). Type Command+Option+Shift+L (Control+Alt+Shift+L) to add a new light. Set the Light Type to Point, set the Intensity to a low value such as 50%, choose a mid blue color, and disable Casts Shadows. Give it a useful name such as "**Adjustment Light**" and press OK.

Initially, your results might not seem much better; now all the layers are merely brighter (and bluer). Drag **Adjustment Light** down the layer stack in the Timeline panel until it is below **hero 1** and **hero 2** – there's no change, as layer stacking order normally doesn't matter with lights. Now enable the Adjustment Layer switch (under the half-moon icon in the Switches column) for **Adjustment Light**; note that the pale blue light is now cast only on the layers underneath it (**piece 1** through **piece 10**).

Remember you can set a light's Intensity to negative values. This removes illumination, and is a good use for adjustment lights, as you can dim certain layers. Select **Adjustment Light**, type T to reveal its Intensity, and experiment with scrubbing its value below 0%.

You can experiment with dragging **Adjustment Light** further down the stack, noting how it illuminates fewer and fewer layers. To completely change the effect, return **Adjustment Light**'s Intensity to the original value you entered (such as 50%), drag it to the bottom of the stack, then drag **hero 1** and **hero 2** below this light – now only the hero layers get the additional illumination, which is perhaps the best solution in this case. This has been built in [**Ex.11-final**].

Our original lighting (A) does not differentiate the two middle "hero" layers enough from the others. We added a second light, turned it into an Adjustment Light, and had it illuminate only the background layers (B). We then rearranged the layer stack, making the Adjustment Light affect just the two hero layers (C). Image courtesy Digital Vision/Inner Gaze.

Light as a Creative Tool

Hopefully you now have a solid grasp of how lights work in After Effects. Mastery of 3D lights will go a long way toward setting apart your work from that of other users.

If you are already comfortable with animating a 3D camera, you will be happy to find that animating lights is very similar; you can even auto-orient lights along their motion paths, as we saw in the previous chapter on cameras (see the *Auto-Orientation* section in Chapter 14). Parenting a light to another object is a great way to move them together: Attach a light to a camera to make sure what the camera looks at is always well illuminated; attach a light to a layer to make sure that a particular layer is always well-illuminated. (Parenting is the subject of Chapter 17.)

But you don't have to animate lights to take advantage of them. You can also approach using 3D lights as akin to using color correction and other effects to enhance a scene. And on that note, we'd like to leave you with one of our favorite (and simplest to implement) uses for 3D lights: adjusting the lighting in footage that has already been shot. The precise steps will vary depending on the composition of the original shot and what you're trying to achieve, but this ending exercise should give you the general idea:

3D lighting can be applied to any 2D footage (above) to achieve dramatic (A) or subtle (B) vignettes, or to create an intense hot spot (C). Footage courtesy iStockphoto, © HenryGrey, Image #9563051.

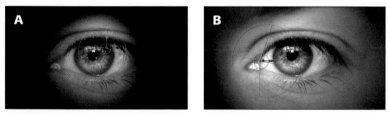

Step 1: Open [**Ex.11_starter**]: It contains an evenly lit close-up of an eye. We want to add more drama and mystery to the shot.

Step 2: Scrub the current time indicator to a point where the eye is open, and enable the 3D Layer switch for **iS_eyeblink.mov**. Note that the footage remains full-frame, as if it were still a 2D layer.

Step 3: Add a Layer > New > Light. To start, choose a Light Type of Spot, Intensity = 100%, Cone Angle = 90°, Cone Feather = 50%, and Color of white. Click OK. The result will be a dramatic vignette.

Step 4: With **Light 1** selected, press AA to reveal its parameters. Increase Cone Feather to soften the falloff, then increase Cone Angle until more of the eye socket is illuminated. Feel free to reposition the light to reframe the eye, and scrub Intensity to achieve the desired exposure. Toggle **Light 1** off and on to compare before and after.

Step 5: For a different look, change **Light 1**'s Type to Point. Then select **iS_eyeblink.mov** and type AA to reveal its Material Options. Increase Specular to 100% and increase Shininess to reduce the size of the hot spot. Reposition **Light 1** (including moving it in Z) to focus the hot spot where you want, and set Intensity to taste. That was easy, wasn't it?

CONNECT

OpenGL can accelerate working with lights: Chapter 2, *Preview Possibilities* sidebar.

Rotation and Orientation: Chapter 3.

Blending modes: Chapter 9.

Track mattes – useful for converting a grayscale image into an alpha-based gobo: Chapter 11.

Basics of 3D space, 3D views: Chapter 13.

Cameras: Chapter 14.

Parenting: Chapter 17.

Nesting compositions: Chapter 18.

Precomposing: Chapter 19.

Collapsing transformations: Chapter 20.

Compound effects: Chapter 24.

16

Parallel Worlds

***Combining 3D layers
from different sources.***

There are several ways to create 3D content for After Effects, including native 3D layers, 3D renders, and 3D effects. Unfortunately, not all of these are compatible with each other, resulting in problems – such as one "3D" layer not casting shadows onto or intersecting with another "3D" layer. Add that to the usual issues with combining 2D and 3D layers in the same composition, and it's no wonder some users are left confounded and confused.

In this chapter, we'll explain the issues with creating and using different 3D content, as well as how to overcome some of the resulting problems. Then we'll move onto creating 3D content with Adobe Photoshop Extended (including Vanishing Point Exchange, 3D model import, and the new Adobe Repoussé extrusion engine) as well as the newly bundled Digieffects FreeForm 3D warping and displacement effect. We'll end with a brief summary of useful third-party 3D plug-ins.

2D and 3D layers may peacefully coexist in the same comp. A benefit of this is that 2D layers – such as the title, bug, and background – stay in the same place as the 3D camera moves around the 3D layers.

Example Project

Explore the 16-Example Project.aep file as you read this chapter; references to [Ex.##] refer to specific compositions within the project file.

As some 3D effects are slow to preview, we suggest enabling Preferences > Memory & Multiprocessing > Render Multiple Frames Simultaneously.

2D versus 3D Layers

Interactions between 2D and 3D layers were discussed at the end of Chapter 13, but the subject is worth recapping here, as it provides the foundation for almost everything else we'll be discussing in this chapter.

Layers in After Effects normally exist in 2D space and are composited together to create a final 2D image. Enabling a layer's 3D Layer switch has two consequences: It allows the layer to be moved in three dimensions, but it also routes that layer off to a separate internal rendering engine. The output of that separate rendering engine is a *2D* layer, which is then composited with the other 2D layers inside a composition. This is how 2D and 3D layers can coexist inside the same comp: 3D layers must eventually be converted to 2D layers.

When multiple 3D layers are adjacent to each other in the Timeline panel's layer stack, they may interact by way of intersecting each other, casting shadows onto each other, and receiving shadows from each other. However, if a 2D layer appears between a selection of 3D layers, the 2D layer acts as a "rendering break" that separates adjacent 3D layers into their own groups. Although all 3D layers in a comp react to the same 3D lights and cameras in a comp, a particular 3D layer may interact only with adjacent 3D layers inside its group. Try this with [**Ex.01_2D+3D Layers**] in this chapter's example project: Drag one of the 2D layers (**2D Title** or **2D Bug**) between the 3D layers (the **pinwheel** and **bikewheel** layers) and observe how the shadow patterns change.

Why is this happening? 3D layers cannot cast "3D" shadows (those created by 3D lights) onto 2D layers – again, you will notice in [**Ex.01**] that the full-frame background video does not receive shadows from any of the 3D layers. A consequence of this is that if a group of 3D layers is collapsed internally into a 2D layer during compositing, a 3D layer in another group cannot cast 3D shadows onto this collapsed group, and vice versa. That's why some of the shadow patterns between 3D objects in [**Ex.01**] appear to toggle off and on as you drag 2D layers between them.

However, you can still use normal 2D compositing tricks. For example, a 2D shadow created using Effects or Layer Styles will "fall" from a 2D layer onto the 3D layer group underneath as well as other 2D layers (we used this trick in [**Ex.01**] for the title and bug); a blending mode set for a 3D layer will interact with both 2D and 3D layers underneath (try it with one of the 3D layers in [**Ex.01**]).

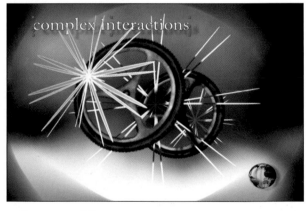

Placing a 2D layer between 3D layers in the Timeline panel (above) acts as a "rendering break" which disrupts how shadows fall between them (below). Note the lack of shadows on the front bikewheel.

Different Types of 3D Layers

Now that we have a handle on how 2D and 3D layers interact (or don't, in some cases), next comes understanding what is really a 3D layer, and what is really a 2D layer. There are a surprising number of ways to create 3D imagery that require 2D layers in After Effects. First we'll survey the different ways of creating 3D imagery, then demonstrate how to overcome some of the resulting limitations.

After Effects 3D Layers: If a layer has its 3D Layer switch enabled, it's a true 3D layer as far as After Effects is concerned. This includes any footage item you drag into a composition, as well as text layers, shape layers, and solids that you create inside a composition – as long as you enable their 3D Layer switches. The same applies to nested compositions: Interesting and useful things happen if you have a nested composition containing 3D layers, then enable both the 3D Layer and Collapse Transformations switches for that nested comp. All of the 3D geometry comes forward into the current comp, but you have only one layer to manage. This is discussed in more detail in Chapter 20, and is demonstrated in comp [**Ex.02a**].

A benefit of Per-Character 3D text is that shadows may be cast between characters in the same text layer as well as onto adjacent 3D layers. Be warned that applying an effect to the text layer will disable its shadows. Background courtesy Digital Vision/Prototype.

Per-Character 3D Text: Normally, text layers are rendered as 2D layers. If you enable the 3D Layer switch for a text layer, all of the text is manipulated in 3D as one flat plane. However, if you select the Animate > Enable Per-character 3D option for a Text layer, each individual character will be treated as a separate 3D layer, including the ability for characters in the same text layer to cast shadows onto each other. This is discussed in more detail in Chapter 21 and demonstrated here in comps [**Ex.02b**] and [**Ex.02c**]. The catch: If you apply any effect or layer style to a Per-Character 3D Text layer, it breaks the 3D interactions. Try applying Effect > Perspective > Bevel Alpha to the text layer in either [**Ex.02b**] or [**Ex.02c**] and note that the shadow interaction is lost.

Renders from a 3D Program: When you create a scene in a dedicated 3D program, it has its own camera and lights that are taken into account when the scene is rendered. Explore the various layers in comp [**Ex.02d_starter**]: The 3D-rendered room (layer 3) was imported into After Effects along with its camera and lights. As 3D perspective is already factored into the render, this layer must be treated as a *2D* layer – you don't want the layer reacting to both the 3D program's camera as well as the After Effects camera. This creates issues when you want to insert additional 3D elements in After Effects: The **wall texture** 3D

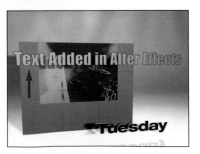

A project created in Maxon CINEMA 4D may be able to pass its camera and lights onto After Effects, but the 3D render will be a 2D layer (above). This means it will not accept shadows created by 3D layers added in After Effects (right). Fortunately, you're about to learn a trick to make those shadows work again. Wall texture courtesy Digital Vision/Naked & Scared.

layer added in After Effects catches shadows from the After Effects 3D text layer (notice they are adjacent layers so they are rendered as a group). However, the 3D-rendered room does not receive these shadows because it's a 2D layer. Chapter 40 on 3D Integration is dedicated to dealing with these issues; later in this chapter we will show how to cast shadows from 3D layers in After Effects onto other 2D layers (as employed in comp [**Ex.02d-final**]).

Layers with 3D Effects Applied: Many effects – from such classics as Shatter and CC Cylinder, to the newly bundled Digieffects FreeForm, to popular third-party effects such as Zaxwerks Invigorator, Trapcode Particular, and Boris BCC Extruded Text – create 3D imagery with depth and perspective. Most "3D" effects also have options to react to 3D camera and lights in After Effects. However, in reality these effects are miniature 3D programs residing inside After Effects: Rather than using the After Effects rendering engine, they have their own internal rendering engines that create their own imagery.

3D effects such as Shatter are normally applied to 2D layers (above). As a result, they do not cast nor receive 3D shadows (A); they also serve as render breaks to stop other 3D layers from rendering as a group. However, we'll show you a trick to regain some 3D interaction (B). Footage courtesy Getty Images/Discovery.

The result is a 2D layer – just like one produced by a dedicated 3D program – that does *not* interact with 3D layers in After Effects, as demonstrated in [**Ex.02e_starter**]. However, there is a trick you can employ that allows you to enable that 3D Layer switch and regain some interaction. This is shown in comp [**Ex.02e-final**] and will be demonstrated later in this chapter.

3D Imagery Imported from Photoshop Extended: Photoshop has been gaining 3D capabilities over time. Currently, it can create two types of 3D imagery which may then be imported into After Effects: Vanishing Point Exchange and Live Photoshop 3D. Vanishing Point Exchange files contain an arrangement of flat images with their 3D Layer switches enabled in After Effects. Live Photoshop 3D (also used by Adobe Repoussé) is like any other 3D effect mentioned above: The effect is doing the rendering, and the result is a 2D layer. Later in this chapter, we will work through exercises demonstrating these two ways of creating 3D imagery in Photoshop Extended, including how to bring the result into After Effects.

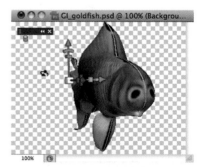

Any still image with an outline or alpha channel can be inflated by Repoussé into a 3D model, as in [**Ex.02f**].
(In Photoshop CS5, open any file in SOURCES > Objects, choose Select > Load Selection, then click OK. Now apply 3D > Repoussé > Current Selection and have fun!) Fish courtesy Getty Images.

To summarize: A surprising amount of 3D imagery, including that created by 3D effects, actually involve 2D layers. 3D layers do not cast 3D shadows onto 2D layers; 2D layers do not cast 3D shadows onto 3D layers. But it is possible to work around some of these limitations.

3D Shadows onto 2D Layers

There are many occasions where you may want 3D layers to cast 3D shadows onto 2D layers. For example, you may want 3D layers added in After Effects to cast shadows on a render from a dedicated 3D program. Or you may have a full-frame 2D background layer that you want your 3D layers to cast shadows onto.

There is more than one solution to this puzzle. After years of trying different approaches, we've settled on what we call the "shadow catcher" technique. With this approach, you place a white solid with its 3D Layer switch enabled at the location in 3D space where the 2D layers should be – this is what gives the shadows the correct size and perspective. You then adjust the Material Options for this layer so that it receives shadows but no other lighting effects, yielding pure shadows on a white background. Finally, you set the Blending Mode for this layer to Multiply so the shadows on this layer are blended onto the 2D layer(s) underneath. Let's walk through an example:

Step 1: Open [**Ex.03_starter**] and RAM Preview: The composition contains a set of 3D layers (the bike wheels and text) with an animated 3D camera move. The 3D layers are set to cast and receive shadows; you will see shadows falling from the forward wheels onto those behind. We've also created a background out of two pieces of full-frame 2D stock footage. We suspect this design might look better if all the elements appeared as if they were in the same room.

Step 2: Add a Layer > New > Solid. Change its name to "**Shadow Catcher**" and set its Color to white. Click OK.

Step 3: Drag **Shadow Catcher** down the layer stack to be just above the first 2D background layer (**AB_DigitalBiz.mov**) and enable its 3D Layer switch (if the Switches column is not visible, press F4 to toggle it forward). It will react to the 3D light in the scene and pop in front of most of the 3D elements.

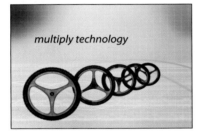

Step 1: The initial composition lacks something. The wheels are casting shadows onto each other, but the foreground elements aren't interacting with the background elements. Grid pattern courtesy Artbeats/Digital Biz.

Steps 3–4: Enable the 3D Layer switch for the Shadow Catcher layer; it will react to the light (A). Increase its Z Position to place it behind the text and wheels (B). Increase its Scale as necessary to fill the frame (C).

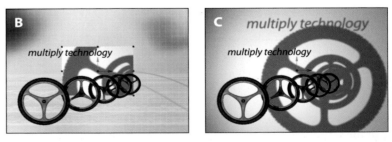

Step 4: Move to the end of the comp to view the elements in their "at rest" position. Press P then Shift+S to reveal **Shadow Catcher**'s Position and Scale. Increase its Z Position value until it moves behind all the wheels, and adjust until the size of the shadow feels right for your virtual room. As you do so, the layer will appear smaller as it recedes into the distance; increase its Scale value as needed until the entire frame is filled

again. (It's okay to scale shadow catcher layers beyond 100% – the layer's scale does not affect the resolution of the shadow it catches.)

Step 5: Press Home to return to the start of the composition. As the camera moves, **Shadow Catcher** might no longer fill the frame. Increase its Scale value until it does. To be safe, scrub the current time indicator to make sure **Shadow Catcher** covers the frame during the entire comp.

Step 6: Type AA to reveal **Shadow Catcher**'s Material Options. By default, Accepts Shadows is On, which is what we want. However, we don't want to pick up any shading falloff from the light – so set Accepts Lights to Off. The Shadow Catcher should now be evenly lit, except for the shadows.

Step 7: Press F4 to reveal the Modes panel. Set the blending mode for the **Shadow Catcher** layer to Multiply. The shadows will now appear on your 2D background composite! RAM Preview to verify that these new shadows react to the animating camera position and text layer.

There are a few ways to further tweak the result. With **Shadow Catcher** still selected, press T to reveal its Opacity; lower this value to reduce the strength of the shadows on the 2D background. Try a different blending mode such as Color Burn to create a more stylized look. Increasing the Light Transmission parameter will cause the 3D layers to be projected

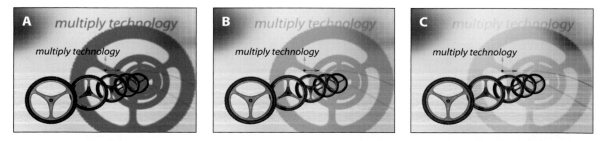

Steps 6–7: Set Shadow Catcher so that it no longer accepts lights and uses the Multiply blending mode.

onto the 2D background (try it with layer 4, the most prominent bike wheel). And as with ordinary 3D shadows, you can increase the light's Shadow Diffusion to soften the shadows, or increase Composition > Composition Settings > Advanced > Rendering Plug-in > Options > Shadow Map Resolution to sharpen the shadows.

You can create more complex shadow catcher arrangements to cast more complex shadows. For example, [**Ex.06**] in Chapter 40 demonstrates how to correctly catch shadows on multiple surfaces in a 3D render.

Casting shadows from the 3D layers onto the 2D background helps unify the scene (A). You can reduce the Opacity of the shadow catching layer to tone down the shadows (B), or even use a different blending mode such as Color Burn (C).

The 3D effect CC Cylinder renders perspective and follows a 3D camera correctly, but it does not cast or receive 3D shadows, and it breaks the rendering order between 3D layers.

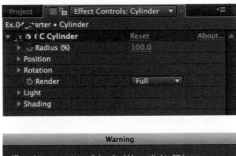

Step 2: The 3D Layer switch would normally be left off for the Cylinder layer (above), as it has a 3D effect applied (below).

Step 3: Enabling the 3D Layer switch for a layer with a 3D effect applied will elicit a warning (above), and its 3D icon in the Effect Controls panel will reflect its concern (right). Don't worry; in this case, two wrongs make a right…

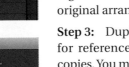

3D Shadows for 3D Effects

As noted earlier, 3D effects are usually applied to 2D layers. This is because the effect is already reacting to the 3D camera (and optionally, lights) in order to render the resulting image, and you don't want a second dose of camera perspective and lighting applied after the fact. However, this means layers with 3D effects normally cannot cast shadows onto or receive shadows from real 3D layers.

There is a workaround. It is imperfect, and requires some fiddling, but you may find the results justify the trade-offs. Here is an example using the CC Cylinder effect that ships with After Effects; the same general principles can be applied to other 3D effects:

Step 1: Open [**Ex.04_starter**] and RAM Preview: This scene contains a simple camera move around a text layer in 3D, a layer with the CC Cylinder effect applied, and a background layer also in 3D.

Step 2: Make sure the Switches column is exposed in the Timeline panel. Note that the layer **Cylinder** does not have its 3D Layer switch enabled. Select **Cylinder** and press F3 to reveal its Effect Controls: Since this effect automatically responds to 3D cameras in the composition, you will see a small 3D cube icon next to the effect's name.

Note that shadows are not currently visible in this scene. This is because the 2D **Cylinder** layer is arranged between the 3D foreground and background layers, breaking their interaction. Toggle **Cylinder**'s Video switch off, and you will see shadows from the text appear on the back wall. Turn **Cylinder** back on; the shadows disappear. (You can try reordering the layers, but no arrangement will result in both the correct layering order and shadows being cast. Return the layers to their original arrangement when you're done.)

Step 3: Duplicate the **Cylinder** layer so that you have a copy for reference. Enable the 3D Layer switch for one of the copies. You may see a warning dialog that 3D effects should be applied to 2D layers (in other words, we're breaking the rules); click OK.

The newly 3D **Cylinder** layer will jump to a different position, which is a problem with this technique: The 3D location and perspective is often calculated differently when the 3D Layer switch is enabled. For this exercise, press S to reveal Scale for the **Cylinder** copy with the 3D Layer switch enabled, and increase it to around 200%. (In the future, set up this workaround before you settle on a final arrangement. If you don't, you'll need to use a combination of the effect's and layer's position and scale values to get back to something close to your original arrangement, using the unaltered copy of the layer for reference.)

Step 4: Turn off or delete the unaltered copy. Shadows will appear! But if you RAM Preview, you may notice that **Cylinder** looks a bit flattened. This is caused by perspective distortion as you view the flat layer of a rendered 3D cylinder from an angle. To remove the distortion, you need the layer to always face the camera head-on, just as a 2D layer would appear.

Step 5: Press R to reveal both the Orientation and Rotation properties for the 3D **Cylinder** layer. Hold Option on Mac (Alt on Windows) and click on the animation stopwatch next to Orientation to enable expressions for this parameter; the words **transform.Orientation** will appear highlighted to the right. Expressions are discussed in more detail in Chapter 37 and Bonus Chapter 37B; for now, carefully replace the highlighted text with the following:

lookAt(thisComp.activeCamera.position, position)

Step 4: Enabling the **Cylinder**'s 3D Layer switch allows shadows to fall, but results in a perspective problem: Note how the cylinder appears flattened.

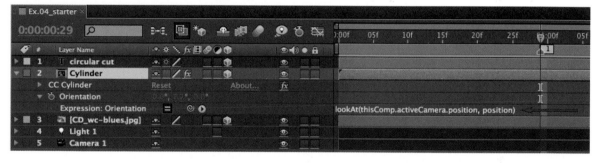

Then click in a blank area of the Timeline or Comp panels to accept this expression. The 3D **Cylinder** layer will shift subtly. RAM Preview: The flattening has been cured, and you have 3D shadows being cast and received by your layer with a 3D effect applied. (If you got lost, take a peek at [**Ex.04-final**].)

The shadows aren't perfect; for example, they don't wrap around the cylinder (remember: It's really just a flat layer being rendered by an effect), and the shadows cast by the cylinder shift as the layer orients toward the camera. There are also some issues with tracking the camera, especially if it gets too close. However, considering the alternative of no 3D shadows at all, it's a pretty good trade-off.

This technique works for virtually any 3D effect that can follow the comp's camera. There are still a few 3D effects – such as CC Sphere – that don't. This technique works for them too, as long as you make further adjustments: You need to offset the effect's internal rotation to compensate for the Orientation changes created by the **lookAt** expression. This is demonstrated near the end of Bonus Chapter 37B; a sneak peek is provided in [**Ex.04b-final**].

Step 5: After enabling the 3D Layer switch for Cylinder and entering an expression for its Orientation (above), 3D shadows appear, and proper 3D perspective is (mostly) maintained (below).

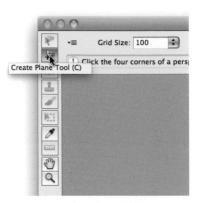

Step 1: Open your image and select Filter > Vanishing Point; the Create Plane tool should be selected.

Steps 2–3: Zoom in on the window – a perfect rectangle in real life – and click with the Create Plane tool to define its four corners (above). Then drag out the sides of the resulting grid to outline the wall (right). Adjust the corners until the lines in the grid run parallel to those in the wall. Photo courtesy iStockphoto, © jcarroll-images, Image #1741336.

3D Objects from Photoshop Extended

In the next several pages, we'll demonstrate different ways to create 3D objects in Adobe Photoshop Extended and import them into After Effects: Vanishing Point Exchange, 3D Model Import, and – new in CS5 – Adobe Repoussé. If you have a copy of Photoshop CS5 Extended, you can follow each exercise from start to finish; if you just have After Effects CS5, we'll provide half-baked compositions at a point after all the Photoshop work has been done.

Vanishing Point Exchange

This feature works best with images that can be broken down into a series of boxes and planes (such as most buildings and empty rooms). You arrange a series of grids in Photoshop Extended that match these planes, export the arrangement as a Vanishing Point Exchange (VPE) file, and import the result into After Effects as a composition. This provides a quick and dirty way to create virtual sets from still photographs. Here are the steps:

In Photoshop Extended:

Step 1: In Photoshop, open **16-Parallel Worlds > 16_Chapter Sources > building_starter.jpg**. Select Filter > Vanishing Point; the Create Plane tool will be selected.

Step 2: The most important part of this process is correctly identifying two rectangles in the source image that connect together, preferably at a right angle. The two visible walls of our building will serve that purpose nicely. Since we can't see the edges of walls, we'll start with a window on one of those walls as we know it should be a perfect rectangle in real life.

Hold Command (Control) and press = to zoom in closer; then hold the spacebar and drag the image to center the window in the display. With the Create Plane tool selected, click on each of the window's four corners in circular order. If the outline turns red, Photoshop was not able to detect a good plane to use – undo and start again, using different corner positions. If a blue grid appears, Photoshop is happy and you may continue.

Step 3: Drag out the sides of the blue grid to outline the entire left wall (we'll call this plane **A**). Adjust the corners to get the best alignment you can (again, zooming and recentering the image as needed while you work; if necessary, press V to reselect the Edit Plane tool). Compare the blue grid with the metal shingles to make sure you are matching the perspective correctly. Then extend the grid just beyond the left and bottom edges of the photo.

Step 4: Once you're happy with plane **A**, define the second wall by holding Command (Control) and dragging the handle in the middle of the right edge of the grid to the right. Drag the right-hand corners of your new grid to get it to fit better; this will be plane **B**.

Step 5: Plane **C** will define part of the overhanging roof, so Command-drag (Control-drag) the top of plane **B**'s grid to the right. Stop at the outer edge of the beige-colored braces. Finally, grab the middle left of plane **C** and extend it toward the upper left to the corner of the roof.

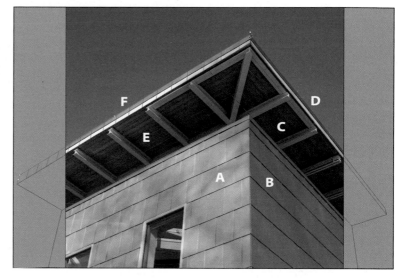

You will no longer be able to directly nudge the corners into place, but you can hold Option (Alt) and drag some of the handles to swivel plane **C** to a better fit. Due to the lens distortion in the original photo, it won't be perfect; this is just for practice anyway.

Step 6: Capture the vertical lip of the roof on the right side of the image by Command-dragging (Control-dragging) the top of plane **C** upward to create plane **D**.

Step 7: Hold Command (Control) to drag out new grid panels that define the roof.

Step 7: Finish defining the roof overhang on the left side by Command-dragging (Control-dragging) the handle on the top of your original plane **A** toward the upper left horizontal edge; we'll call this plane **E**. Then Command-drag (Control-drag) a final segment upward to cover the vertical lip. Finally, grab the right edge of this new plane **F** and drag it toward the upper right to the corner of the roof, meeting up with plane **D** created in Step 6. If needed, Option-drag (Alt-drag) its handles to get a better fit – but again, lens distortion is your enemy here.

Step 8: Click on the flyout menu arrow in the upper left corner of the Vanishing Point dialog, and select Export for After Effects (.vpe). Make a new folder to hold the multiple files that exporting creates and enter a file name. Photoshop will then automatically remove the perspective distortion to create a series of rectangular PNG files for each grid you defined, plus VPE and 3DS files which reassemble them into a 3D model.

Step 8: Export as a Vanishing Point Exchange file. A PNG file will be created for each plane, as well as 3DS and VPE files to reassemble them into your building.

Step 9: Click OK in the Vanishing Point dialog, then select File > Save As. Change the file type to Photoshop so it will remember your Vanishing Point grids and save it under a new name. Our version is saved as **building_final.psd**.

In After Effects:

Step 10: Return to After Effects, with **16-Example Project.aep** open. If you completed the prior steps using Photoshop, select File > Import > Vanishing Point (.vpe), navigate to the folder you created, and choose your VPE file. (If you don't have Photoshop Extended, we've saved our version as **16_Chapter Sources > Building VPE Files > building.vpe**; import that instead.) A folder with the PNG files as well as a comp will be created; we've also imported these into the **Ex.05** folder.

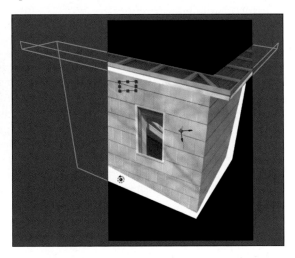

Step 11: Import the resulting VPE file results in a 3D composition in After Effects where you can pan and zoom around the building.

Step 11: Open the comp, and you will see your 3D scene. Use the Camera tools in the Comp panel to fly around your simple 3D building. If you want to animate the building, keyframe the **Parent** layer; this is a null object that all of the building planes have been parented to (press Shift+F4 to reveal the Parent panel).

Step 12: Precompose the planes and their null object. This groups the building parts into one layer. Then enable the 3D Layer and Collapse Transformations switches for this precomp layer.

Step 12: If you want just one layer to work with, select all of the layers except **Camera 0**, choose Layer > Pre-compose, give the precomp a name that makes sense (such as "**Building Parts**"), disable Open New Composition, and click OK. A layer named **Building Parts** will be created in place of all the component layers. Enable its 3D Layer and Collapse Transformations switches, and now you have just one 3D layer to manage. (Collapsing Transformations and working with 3D precomps are discussed in more detail in Chapter 20.)

There are several ways you can improve on the result. For example, double-click any of the individual building part layers to open it in its Layer panel. You can correct and extend these individual flat surfaces using the Paint tools in After Effects (Chapter 33) or Photoshop.

Live Photoshop 3D Layers

Adobe's Creative Suite 4 introduced a new way to use Photoshop Extended and After Effects together in 3D: importing a 3D model into Photoshop, then animating a camera to move around it in After Effects. There are some limitations to this technique, but it also offers some interesting possibilities.

In Photoshop Extended:

Step 1: Select the menu item File > New. In the Preset popup, choose Film & Video. Then in the Size popup, select either NTSC D1 Square Pixel or PAL D1 Square Pixel depending on the prevalent format in your country. Set Background Contents to Transparent, and click OK.

Step 2: Select 3D > New Layer from 3D File. Navigate to the **Chapter 16 > 16_Chapter Sources** folder, select **TV.3DS**, and click Open. After a pause, a stylized TV monitor will appear in the middle of your new document. Select the Object Rotate tool (shortcut: K) from along the toolbar on the left, then click and drag in your document window to move around your 3D model.

Step 2: After importing a 3D model into Photoshop Extended, you can manipulate it in 3D space. Model courtesy Wone Stone and 3dvia.com through Creative Commons License 2.5.

Step 3: Set Window > Workspace to 3D. The 3D and Layers panels will appear along the right side of your screen. The 3D panel makes it possible for you to modify the "materials" – surface color and other characteristics – originally assigned to the model.

Step 4: In the 3D panel, look under the group **Box01** and select the texture layer **N08_Default**. This is the material the model's creator assigned to the TV's screen. In the bottom half of the 3D panel, click on the color swatch for Diffuse and choose a different color. The 3D model's screen (as well as any other surface that has the material **N08_Default** applied) will update interactively. Change the color to black and click OK. (If you prefer the TV's shell to be a color other than white, change **N06_Default**. Reselect **N08_Default** when you're done.)

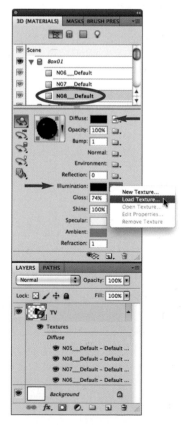

Step 5: TV and monitor screens project light. To assign an image to the screen to be projected, click on the popup menu to the right of the Illumination color swatch, and select Load Texture. In the Open dialog that appears, you can select any image – including a QuickTime movie. Navigate to the **SOURCES > Movies** folder that came from this book's accompanying disc, and select one of the files such as **AB_RetroHealthcare.mov**. Click Open. If a pixel aspect ratio correction dialog appears, click Yes. This movie will now appear on the TV's screen.

Step 5: In Photoshop's 3D panel, edit the texture **N08_Default** by setting its Diffuse color to black; load your own image or movie as the Illumination texture.

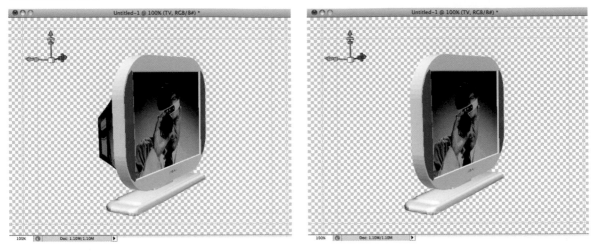

Steps 5–6: The movie loaded as the Illumination texture is applied to both the screen and the back of the TV (left). Disable the **Box02** group to turn off the back piece (right). Footage courtesy Artbeats/Retro Healthcare.

Step 6: Unfortunately, the same texture has been applied to both the screen and the back of this TV model! It is important to know that you are at the mercy of the model's creator when you're using this technique. Fortunately, we don't need the piece anyway (most TVs these days are flat). In the 3D panel, disable the group **Box02** by clicking on the eyeball to its left.

Step 7: Did you notice that the TV's outlines are rather jagged? That's because the default render quality for the model is set to Interactive (called Draft in CS4) in order to make Photoshop more responsive. In the 3D panel select the master group named **Scene**. Then in the Render Settings at the bottom of the panel, set the Anti-Alias popup to Ray Traced Draft (called Better in CS4).

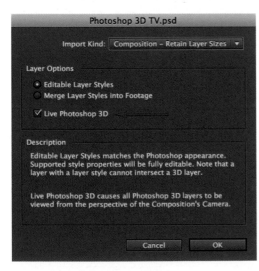

Step 8: Select File > Save As, name it "**MyTV.psd**", and make a note of where you are saving it. Before you click Save, make sure that the Format popup in the Save dialog is set to Photoshop and that Layers is enabled. If a Photoshop Format Options dialog opens after clicking Save, enable Maximize Compatibility and click OK.

In After Effects:

Step 9: Back in After Effects CS5 and the project file **16_Example Project.aep**, select the **Ex.06 Live Photoshop 3D** folder in the Project panel. Then choose the menu item File > Import > File and select the PSD file you saved above. (Our version is saved in the **16-Parallel Worlds > 16_Chapter Sources** folder as **Photoshop 3D TV.psd**.) After clicking Open, a second dialog will appear. Make sure that the Import Kind popup is set to Composition – Retain Layer Sizes, and that the Live Photoshop 3D option is enabled. Then click OK. Two items will be created in the Project panel: a folder and a composition, both named after your file.

Step 9: When importing a PSD file with a 3D layer into After Effects CS4 or later, make sure that you import as a composition and that Live Photoshop 3D is enabled.

Step 10: Double-click your Live Photoshop 3D comp to open it. (If you haven't completed the prior steps, open our starter comp: [**Ex.06_TV Import**].) In the Timeline panel, you will see four layers. Starting at the bottom:

Layer 1 is the background. As we defined the background to be transparent when we created the new file in Photoshop, you can delete this layer.

TV is the layer that contains a special Live Photoshop 3D effect that is rendering the 3D model. Select this layer and press F3 to see the effect in the Effect Controls panel. You can apply additional effects to this layer, as well as alter its Opacity, but any other animation should be applied to the **TV Controller** layer which is expressed to this layer (select **TV** and type EE to see the expression links).

If you applied a movie as a texture to the TV screen, the layer's duration will be truncated if necessary to match. Move the current time indicator and note how the image updates. Also note that this layer defaults to Draft Quality: Toggle its Quality switch to Best to render the TV more cleanly; toggle it back to Draft for more responsive updates.

[**TV Controller**] is a null object that controls the position and orientation of the layer. Twirl it open to reveal its Transform properties; these are what you should animate to move the 3D model. You can turn off its Video switch to hide its outline in the Comp panel.

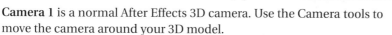

Camera 1 is a normal After Effects 3D camera. Use the Camera tools to move the camera around your 3D model.

Before you get too excited, we need to tell you that there are some important shortcomings with the current implementation of Live Photoshop 3D, including:

• The 3D model does not react to 3D lights created in After Effects, nor with other 3D layers (no intersections, no shadows, et cetera).

• You cannot assign After Effects layers as textures to your 3D model, nor animate those textures from inside After Effects.

• Any changes to the 3D model must be done back in Photoshop. Select the layer with the Live Photoshop 3D effect applied (**TV** in this example), choose Edit > Edit Original to reopen it in Photoshop, make your changes, save, and return to After Effects.

In general, we prefer third-party solutions such as Zaxwerks Invigorator Pro to Live Photoshop 3D. But if you already have an Adobe suite, and don't have the budget for extra plug-ins, Live Photoshop 3D gives you additional tools to work with.

Step 10: The resulting comp contains four layers. The **TV** layer contains a plug-in that does the rendering; the **TV Controller** layer is the layer you should use to animate the 3D object's Transform parameters. (After Effects automatically linked the controller to the 3D plug-in for you using expressions.)

Lights Not Live

Live Photoshop 3D layers do not react to lights created in After Effects. All lighting must be done in Photoshop. Scroll to the bottom of the 3D (Materials) list, select a light, and edit it in the panel below.

Step 3: In addition to adding extrusion depth, the Extrude section (below) also allows you to scale, twist, and shear the extrusion (above).

Adobe Repoussé

In Creative Suite 5, Adobe built on the concept of Live Photoshop 3D integration by adding Repoussé – a powerful extrusion and beveling tool – to Photoshop CS5 Extended. Layered Photoshop PSD files created with Repoussé can be imported into After Effects and animated in 3D (with similar limitations as other Live 3D layers). Repoussé is explained in detail in Photoshop's Help file; here is a quick tour:

In Photoshop CS5 Extended:

Step 1: Open file **16-Parallel Worlds > 16_Chapter Sources > Repousse Text.psd**. It contains a simple line of text created in Photoshop.

Step 2: Choose 3D > Repoussé > Text Layer. Photoshop will tell you it has to rasterize the text; click Yes. The Repoussé dialog box will open, and the text will be extruded in 3D. Click and drag the text downward slightly so you can better see the depth of the extrusion.

Step 3: First focus on the Extrude section. Experiment with Depth, Scale, Twist, and the Shear/Bend section. Depending on your video card, it can take Repoussé some time to calculate the results. Once you have a feel for how these parameters work, click on the Extrude preset in the upper left corner of the Repoussé Shape Presets, and reduce Extrude > Depth to a more discreet value between 0.2 and 0.5.

Step 4: Next, play with the Inflate settings. A good starting point is Angle = 90. Negative values cause the faces of your object to be hollowed out. Strength affects how the inflation is pulled out (or in), and is very sensitive – values well under 1.0 can introduce rendering anomalies with detailed selections.

Step 5: Reset Inflate > Angle to 0 for now, and have fun with the Bevel section. Setting Height and Width to 10 is a good starting point for this file; negative Height values cut into the face. The Contour popup gives you several different shapes to work with; the more detailed shapes work better on simpler sources with space between the outlines. Also beware of setting Width too high; thinner portions of the letters will overlap and cause artifacts.

Step 6: The Scene Settings are worth exploring. Under the Render Settings popup are several interesting choices, such as Wireframe and Shaded Illustration (return to Default when you're done exploring). Lights contains several default arrangements; Dawn works well with this example.

Step 7: Click OK to exit the Repoussé dialog. Make sure Window > 3D is open, and select **Scene** (it's at the top). In the Render Settings at the bottom, set Quality to Ray Traced Draft: The text will now render antialiased, with refined lighting effects like shadows. In the 3D window, you can again edit the materials applied to your object as well as the lighting. Note that you will *not* be able to alter the lighting in After Effects.

Step 8: Choose File > Save As; make sure that the Format popup in the Save dialog is set to Photoshop and that Layers is enabled. Rename your file "**My Repousse Model.psd**" and click Save. If a Photoshop Format Options dialog opens after clicking Save, enable Maximize Compatibility and click OK.

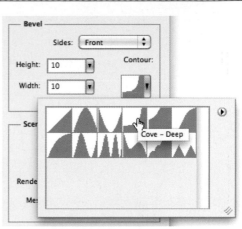

Steps 4–6: The Bevel section (above) creates the classic "beveled text" look; the Inflate section adds rounding to the faces (top left). The Scene Settings provide options for lighting and render styles (top right).

In After Effects:

Step 9: Back in After Effects CS5 and the project file **16_Example Project.aep**, select the **Ex.07 Adobe Repousse** folder in the Project panel. Then choose File > Import > File and select the PSD file you saved above (our version is saved as **16_Chapter Sources > Repousse Model.psd**). After clicking Open, a second dialog will appear. Make sure that the Import Kind popup is set to Composition – Retain Layer Sizes, and that the Live Photoshop 3D option is enabled. Then click OK. Two items will be created in the Project panel: a folder and a composition, both named after your file.

Step 10: Double-click the imported composition to open it (or our version [**Ex.07_starter**]). The layer arrangement is similar to the previous Live Photoshop 3D example, with a camera, controller, and layer with the Photoshop 3D effect applied. Press C to select the Camera tools and move around the text to verify it's not just another postcard in space.

Toggle the Quality switch for layer 3 (the one with the Live Photoshop 3D effect) to Best. The text will now be ray-traced, but the scene will also be a lot less responsive. Return Quality to Draft while you're posing and animating your scene, then make sure that the Render Settings popup for Quality is set to Best when you render (Chapter 42).

To edit a Repoussé layer, select the layer with the Live Photoshop 3D effect applied, choose Edit > Edit Original to return to Photoshop, then choose 3D > Repoussé > Edit in Repoussé. Save your file when done, and return to After Effects – the layer will update automatically.

Importing a Repoussé file as a composition results in three layers in After Effects (below). Toggle the Quality switch to Best for the layer with Live Photoshop 3D applied to see the ray-traced render (above).

Our final version – with lighting, and a bit more flare to the curl – is in comp **[Ex.08-final]**. Image courtesy Digital Vision/Music Mix.

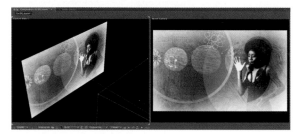

Steps 1–3: Apply Freeform to layer 1, then create a new camera. Set the Comp panel to 2 Views – Custom View 1 and Active Camera – and pull the camera back in Z space until you can see the entire image in the Active Camera view.

Steps 4–5: Increase DE_FreeFormAE > Grid > Columns to 4 (above), and have fun moving the grid points and tangents to warp the layer (right). We've changed the right viewer to Top to get an alternate perspective.

Digieffects FreeForm

A pleasant addition to After Effects CS5 is the 3D warping plug-in Digieffects FreeForm (formerly known as Forge FreeForm, created by Chris Bobotis of mettle.com). It offers two main features: the ability to warp any 2D layer in 3D space with a user-adjustable grid of points, and the ability to use a second layer to displace or extrude the layer FreeForm is applied to. In the next exercise, we'll introduce you to the warping feature, then give advice on using the displacement feature.

Warping Practice

To see where you're going, open **[Ex.08-final]** and RAM Preview (you might want to make a nice cup of tea while it renders). Now let's get to work recreating this 3D warping effect:

Step 1: Open the comp **[Ex.08_starter]**. It contains a still image you will be bending in 3D space. Select that layer, and apply Effect > Digieffects FreeForm > DE_FreeFormAE.

Step 2: It is easier to work in 3D space if you have multiple views. Set the View popup along the bottom of the Comp panel to 2 Views – Horizontal. Set the right view to Active Camera, and the left view to Custom View 1. Leave the left view selected for now (yellow triangles will appear in the corners of the viewer).

Step 3: At this moment, both views look the same. With some 3D effects (such as FreeForm), you need to add a 3D camera to the comp to take advantage of the 3D views. Add Layer > New > Camera, choose the 50 mm preset, and click OK. Press P to reveal its Position, and scrub its Z Position value to the right until you can see the entire image in the Active Camera view (around –1700 should work).

Step 4: Select the layer **DV_MusicMix_622018.jpg** and if necessary bring the Effect Controls panel forward (F3 is the shortcut). Select DE_FreeFormAE, and a yellow grid will be overlaid on the layer in the active viewer. Twirl open the Grid subsection to reveal its parameters and increase Columns to 4 to create more control points to work with.

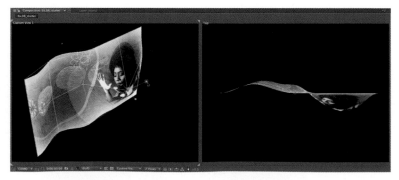

Step 5: In the left viewer, click on one of the grid intersections or corners: A blue vertex point with a set of green tangent handles will appear. Have fun pulling the blue vertex points around to displace the layer. Drag or even rotate the green tangent handles to further warp the layer. Set the right viewer to alternate views such as Top or Left to get a better idea of how the layer is being bent in 3D space. (Refer back to Chapter 13 on how to use the Camera tools to pan and zoom the views.)

Spend some time warping the layer to get a feel for how FreeForm works. Also experiment with the Editing Controls, seeing how the Manipulation and Tangent Alignment popups can constrain the way points and handles move.

Animating a Curl

Step 6: Once you've had your fun, click Reset (near the top of the Effect Controls panel). Set Grid > Rows to 1 to reduce the number of control points you need to edit. Keep the left viewer set to Custom View 1, and set the right viewer to Top.

Step 7: With the current time indicator at 00:00, enable keyframing for the Grid > Mesh Distortion parameter. Then press End to jump to the end of the comp (02:29).

TIP

Reselect the Effect

One of the most common sources of frustration with FreeForm is accidentally deselecting the effect. If the yellow grid disappears, reselect the effect (not just the layer, but the effect DE_FreeFormAE).

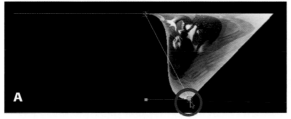

Step 8: In the left viewer, select the upper right grid point. Click inside the right viewer; the blue point control and green tangent handles should still be selected and visible. (If not, try again.) Pull the blue control point down – forward in Z space – and to the left toward the vertical center of the image. Then drag the green tangent handle back around to the right. The layer will bow like a sail.

Step 9: Click on the lower right control point (the one left behind in the Top view), and drag it to the same position as the previous control point. Bend its tangent handle back to the right as well.

Step 10: Return to the left viewer and select the upper left corner. Select the right viewer (the point should still be selected), and this time bend the corner behind the layer (above, in Top view). Do the same for the lower left corner as well.

Step 11: There may be a slight kink through the middle of the layer as the curl transitions between the two halves. Select the upper middle control point (it might take a little hunting), and drag its tangent handles longer to flatten out the kink. Do the same for the lower middle control point.

Step 8: To curl a layer over on itself, pull a corner control point forward (A) and bend its tangent back in the opposite direction (B).

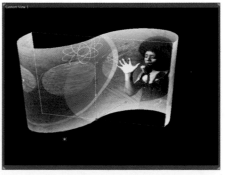

Step 11: At this point, your layer should be loosely curled into an "S."

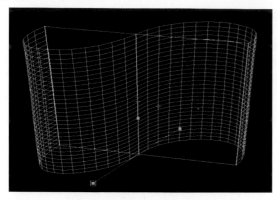

Step 12: The Mesh Subdivision determines how the layer is broken into pieces and rendered; higher values result in smoother images.

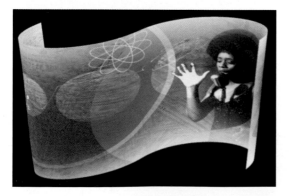

Step 13: Experiment with the values inside 3D Mesh Quality (above) to further refine your final image (below).

Return the right viewer to Active Camera and RAM Preview your work to this point: You should have a nicely animated curl, although the rendering will be a bit rough. Press End to view your layer at its most curled as you make the following adjustments.

Step 12: The Grid parameter in Freeform determines how many control points you have available to edit; the Mesh parameters determine how the image is interpolated between those grid points.

In the effect, twirl open the 3D Mesh Quality subsection and set the Rendering popup to Wireframe. The resolution of the wireframe determines how smoothly the layer is warped. Set Mesh Subdivision to a low value and return Rendering to Full: Your layer will look like it's folded rather than curled. Increase Mesh Subdivision, and the curl will be much smoother (and will take longer to render). The optimal setting depends on both the layer's resolution and how severely it is warped; values from 100 to 500 are common.

Step 13: Move to around 01:15; the microphone should be visible in Active Camera view. With Rendering set to Full, press Shift+F5 to take a snapshot of the layer in its current state. Then set the Antialiasing popup to Low: The layer should look even smoother. Press Shift+F6 to take a snapshot of this state, fix your attention on the microphone, and set the Image Filtering popup to On: Another slight improvement will be gained. Press F5 and F6 to recall your snapshots of the earlier states for comparison.

Then RAM Preview again: Notice how much better the image looks, but how much longer the preview took? FreeForm is powerful, but also render-intensive. In general, it is best to do all of your setup work and animation at lower quality settings, then increase these as necessary just before rendering.

There is more for you to explore inside Digieffects FreeForm:

• 3D Mesh Controls may be used to animate the layer as a whole in 3D space.

• Add a light and experiment with the Surface Controls, which respond differently than do a normal 3D Layer's Material Options (Roughness is akin to Shininess).

• Backside Controls determine what is seen on the back of the layer.

• Displacement Controls are used to extrude another layer through the FreeForm layer – see *Displacement Mapping* on the next page for pointers.

Displacement Mapping

Extruding layers with FreeForm is similar to using other compound effects such as Displacement Map and Compound Blur (both discussed in Chapter 24). The general procedure is to add a layer to act as your extrusion pattern, select this layer in FreeForm's Displacement Controls > Displace Layer popup, choose the highest contrast channel with the Use Layer's popup, set Displace Height to taste, and increase 3D Mesh Quality > Mesh Subdivision as needed. Following is a collection of tips to keep in mind when using FreeForm's displacement function; feel free to try some of these in our example comp [**Ex.09_FreeForm Displacement**]:

• You will need a 3D light to bring out the different shadings caused by the extruded shapes. Try toggling the light (layer 1) off and on in [**Ex.09_FreeForm Displacement**].

• If you see problems with displacement that look like aliasing artifacts (or don't see any displacement at all), try increasing the Mesh Subdivision. For standard definition video, a setting of 300 is barely adequate; 500–1000 is not uncommon.

• The displacement layer is stretched to fit the layer that has FreeForm applied. Therefore, it's a good idea to create a precomp the same size as the layer you intend to displace and to place your extrusion pattern in the precomp.

• Any effects or animation you wish to apply to the extrusion pattern must be applied in the aforementioned precomp (as we have done with precomp layers 4 through 6) – compound effects do not see effects or transformations applied to the modifying layer in the top-level comp.

FreeForm can also be used to extrude one layer based on another, including using that second layer's alpha channel to cut out the first layer. Footage courtesy Artbeats/Ocean Water Effects.

• If you use luminance or a color channel of a layer that also has an alpha channel, FreeForm takes the straight rather than premultiplied color (see the section on Alpha Channels in Chapter 38), which can result in some edge issues. Therefore, we prefer to use the alpha channel for the displacement map.

• If your extrusion pattern has an alpha, it can also act as a stencil: Try enabling Use Alpha as Mask under the effect's Displacement Controls.

• Sharp transitions in the extrusion pattern can cause tearing in the final displacement. Slightly blurring the extrusion pattern in the precomp will soften these artifacts. Add more blur to get sloped sides to your extrusions. In [**Ex.09_FreeForm Displacement**] compare setting the Displace Layer to the **5. Liquid Precomp – blur** layer versus **4. Liquid Precomp – no blur**.

• Banding in gradients and feathered alphas can cause "stepping" in the extruded shape. Set the Displace Layer to **6. Liquid precomp – gradient** and note the diagonal bands in the letter L. Set Project Settings > Color Settings > Depth to 16 bits to smooth these out.

CONNECT

3D space: Chapter 13.

Cameras: Chapter 14.

Lighting: Chapter 15.

Parenting: Chapter 17.

Collapsing transformations: Chapter 20.

Per-character 3D text: Chapter 21.

Expressions: Chapter 37, 37B.

Importing Photoshop files, alphas: Chapter 38.

3D integration: Chapter 40.

Render settings: Chapter 42.

Third-Party 3D Plug-ins

In this chapter, we focused on 3D layers created in After Effects, 3D plug-in effects that come bundled with After Effects CS5, and 3D elements you can create in Photoshop CS5 Extended. However, other companies also offer a variety of 3D effects that work inside After Effects. Here is a quick survey of some 3D effects worth checking out:

Boris FX

Boris Continuum Complete AE (*www.borisfx.com/after_effects/bccae*) is an extensive package of plug-ins for After Effects, including several dedicated 3D effects:

BCC Extruded Text. Image courtesy Boris FX.

BCC Extruded Text is a powerful 3D text engine with strong texturing capabilities, including reflection mapping. It can use an After Effects mask path as a bevel profile for the sides of your extruded characters. Its companion effect BCC **Type On Text** adds additional tricks for animating text reveals.

BCC Extruded Spline is similar to BCC Extruded Text, with the exception that you can use After Effects mask paths or a series of built-in primitive shapes as the outline to extrude (rather than text).

BCC Layer Deformer is akin to FreeForm. But rather than offset each vertex by hand, Layer Deformer offers a Shape popup that automatically creates planes, spheres, cylinders, page curls, and cubes, plus the ability to animate deformations including wraps, twists, curls, and ripples.

BCC 3D Extruded Image Shatter is akin to the built-in After Effects Shatter effect, with more control over how the resulting particles move.

Digieffects

In addition to FreeForm, Digieffects (*www.digieffects.com*) offers several inexpensive 3D effects that help create more realistic 3D scenes:

Camera Mapper replicates a popular trick in 3D software in which a camera is used to project a flat image onto a series of planes at varying distances. A second camera can then be used to animate around the resulting scene, creating the illusion of multiplaning with a flat 2D source image.

Falloff Lighting simulates the real world effect in which layers closer to a light are illuminated more strongly than those farther away. This also affects shadows and specular highlights.

Atmosphere adds fog-like effects in which portions of layers farther away from the camera appear more obscured than those closer to the camera. (The After Effects Fog 3D effect discussed in Bonus Chapter 40B works only on footage generated by dedicated 3D programs – not After Effects 3D layers.)

Camera Mapper + Atmosphere. Image courtesy Dustin Klein of Digieffects.

Trapcode

Trapcode – distributed by Red Giant Software (*www.redgiantsoftware.com*) – offers several plug-ins for creating realistic as well as purely graphical elements:

Trapcode Particular. Image courtesy Harry Frank of Graymachine.

Particular is a powerful 3D particle system that can be used to create everything from natural phenomenon such as explosions to fanciful graphical elements. Many After Effects artists consider it a must-have.

Form is a stylized spin-off from Particular that excels at creating grids and waves of particles and shapes, which react to audio.

Horizon allows you to create an infinite 3D environment by mapping images or gradients onto a giant sphere that contains your world. It tracks the After Effects 3D camera, allowing you to add other layers and 3D effects inside this environment and have them all work together.

Lux creates volumetric lighting effects from ordinary After Effects 3D lights. It's one of our secret weapons.

3D Stroke creates 3D paths from 2D mask shapes that may then be transformed in 3D space. Great for glowing line and logo treatments.

Echospace takes a 3D layer and replicates it in space with controllable offsets and transformations.

Zaxwerks

Zaxwerks (*www.zaxwerks.com*) excels at efficiently creating motion graphic elements. **ProAnimator** – available as a stand-alone as well as an After Effects plug-in – is its flagship, offering fancy 3D extrusions as well as easy animation templates and controls. It also has several plug-ins worth checking out:

Invigorator PRO takes text or Illustrator artwork and gives it depth with a huge variety of high-quality sweeps (akin to bevels, but more focused on edges than faces); it can also import 3D models. It has extensive material and lighting capabilities. It is the only "3D program" many motion graphics artists own.

Invigorator PRO + Reflector. Image courtesy Jason Hirsch of KUSA.

3D Flag performs the simple, useful task of making a layer behave like cloth in the wind.

3D Serpentine takes After Effects 3D motion paths and extrudes them into shapes including film strips, tubes, ribbons, and more.

3D Warps contains a pair of plug-ins and provides results similar to FreeForm and BCC Layer Deformer, further optimized for artists looking to create cool motion graphic elements.

Reflector enables After Effects 3D layers to reflect each other, plus it has the ability to exclude specific layers and more. It is more powerful than the reflection solutions we demonstrated at the end of Chapter 15.

17

Parenting Skills

The ability to group layers together greatly eases the creation of complex animations.

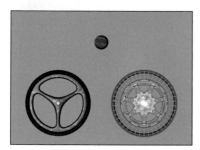

[Ex.01] contains three objects to help you practice your parenting skills.

TIP

Hide the Parent

Press Shift+F4 to show or hide the Parent column.

Example Project

Explore the 17-Example Project.aep file as you read this chapter; references to [Ex.##] refer to specific compositions within the project file.

Parenting allows you to group layers together and to treat them as one object. Any Position, Scale, or Rotation transformations applied to the parent are passed on to its children. Meanwhile, the children can still have their own animations, even as they get dragged around by the parent. Parenting can be used for anything from moving two layers at the same time to setting up complex coordinated animations.

Parenting, for the most part, works as you intuitively expect it should. After going over the basics, we'll focus on the creative applications of parenting. But there may come a time when you wonder why properties and keyframes are jumping to new values that don't seem to make sense, or why a child moves in an unexpected way. For a deeper understanding of what's going on when you parent or unparent a layer, see the sidebar *Parenting: Under the Hood*, which appears on page 316.

To get started, open this chapter's example project file (**17-Example Project.aep**) from the **Chapter Example Projects > 17-Parenting** folder.

Developing an Attachment

There are two ways to parent one layer to another; both are easy. To follow along as we explain the steps, open comp [**Ex.01**]. It contains three layers: **CD_peg**, **CD_bikewheel**, and **CD_tirewire**. Make sure the Position, Scale, and Rotation properties are exposed for all three layers (if they're not, select the layer or layers of interest, type P for Position, Shift+S to add Scale, and Shift+R to add Rotation).

A column titled Parent should be visible in the Timeline panel. If not, right-click on any other column, and select Columns > Parent from the menu that appears, or use the shortcut Shift+F4. You can rearrange the order of these columns by dragging them left and right; we prefer to place Parent just to the right of the Source/Layer Name column.

Parenting is performed by attaching a prospective child layer to its new parent layer. Say you want to attach **CD_bikewheel** to **CD_peg** so that **CD_bikewheel** becomes a child and **CD_peg** becomes its parent. Under the Parent column for **CD_bikewheel** is a popup that currently says None. Click on it and a list will pop up with the names of all the layers in the current composition. **CD_bikewheel** is grayed out, because you cannot attach a layer to itself. Select **CD_peg**, and it will become **CD_bikewheel**'s parent.

Scrub the Position, Scale, and Rotation properties for the **CD_peg** layer, and note how **CD_bikewheel** follows it around as if the two layers were part of one larger image. To break that illusion, scrub the Position, Scale, and Rotation properties of **CD_bikewheel**: No matter what the child layer does, its parent – **CD_peg** – remains unperturbed. (It's a shame all our parents weren't like that…)

Family Tree

A parent can have more than one child. Turn your attention to the **CD_tirewire** layer, and the spiral icon to the left of the parent popup. This is the *pick whip* tool. Click on it and start dragging – you will see a line extend behind, showing you are about to connect one layer to another. (Release it without selecting another layer, and enjoy the little "recoil" animation as the line winds back into its tool. Okay – recess over.) Drag the pick whip to the **CD_peg** layer name in the Timeline panel, and a box will appear around this layer's name. Release the mouse, and **CD_peg** will be assigned as the parent of **CD_tirewire**. Scrub the transform properties for **CD_peg**, and note how both layers now follow it around.

You can choose a new parent after you've already assigned one. A child can also be a parent. We'll continue to use [**Ex.01**] to demonstrate this. If **CD_bikewheel** and **CD_tirewire** are not already attached to **CD_peg**, do that now. Then use either the popup menu or pick whip tool for **CD_tirewire**, and select **CD_bikewheel** as its parent instead. Scrub the transform properties for **CD_tirewire**, and notice that it is the only layer that changes. Now scrub the transform properties for **CD_bikewheel**: Its child – **CD_tirewire** – follows along, but its parent – **CD_peg** – doesn't. Finally, scrub the transform properties for **CD_peg**, and note that both its child **CD_bikewheel** and "grandchild" **CD_tirewire** follow along.

Breaking the Bonds

To detach a child from its parent, click on the same popup under the Parent column, and select None. You can also set a child free by Command+clicking on Mac (Control+clicking on Windows) on the pick whip icon for a layer. If you have multiple layers selected, the parenting links will be broken for all the selected layers. Deleting a parent layer will also reset the Parent popup for its children to None.

When you break a parenting link, nothing should happen – the parent and child layers should remain at the position, scale, and rotation where you last left them (there are rare exceptions; we'll deal with those later). However, you can now transform the former parent and child layers independently from each other.

To attach one layer to another, select the prospective parent from the popup menu under the Parent column. You cannot attach a layer to itself; that's why the layer's own name in the list is grayed out.

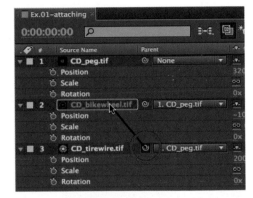

An alternate tool for assigning parents is the *pick whip*. Click its icon to the left of the Parent popup, and drag it to the new parent layer. You can change parenting relationships after you have set them up and assign a child of one layer to be a parent of another – that's what we're doing here.

Unparenting leaves things where they are now – it doesn't return you to where you started. If you think there is a remote possibility that you might need to return a child to its original state, you should duplicate the prospective child layer or the entire composition to keep a "fresh" copy you can return to. Another way back home is to set up parenting at a point in time where you have transform keyframes for both the parent and child, and you don't change the values of those keyframes. Return to these keyframes, then unparent.

Basic Parenting Lessons

Enough theory – time to put what you've just learned to work with some simple examples. These will illustrate using parenting as an easy way to group objects.

Saving Time

Open [**Ex.02_starter**]. In this first example, a clock and its two hands are provided as separate elements. You want to group them together so you can easily move and rescale them as a set. Thinking through the problem before you start animating will make your life much more pleasant later.

In this case, you will eventually want to rotate the clock's hands. This will require placing their anchor points at the spot where they should rotate. If you value your sanity, you should always place the anchor points *before* you animate or assign parents:

TIP

Individual Control

To attach individual parameters (such as Position, Rotation, and effect settings) between layers, use Expressions, which are covered in Chapter 37.

FACTOID

Opacity Ignored

Children are not affected by the opacity of their parent, or by any effects applied to it.

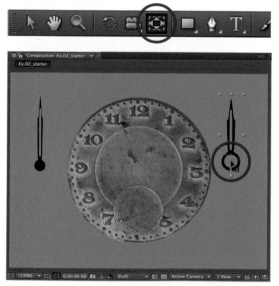

Step 1: Use the Pan Behind tool (circled in red, top) to reposition the anchor points for the clock hands over their proper pivot points (above).

Step 1: Press Y to select the Pan Behind tool (also known as the Anchor Point tool, as it allows you to edit the anchor point directly in the Comp panel without changing the overall position of a layer). Select the **hour hand** layer, and reposition its anchor over its pivot point. Do the same for the **minute hand** layer as well – look for the dot in its center. If you're having trouble positioning the anchor point precisely, zoom in for a closer look.

To verify that the hands will animate correctly, press R to reveal the Rotation parameters for the hands, and scrub them to make sure the hands rotate properly. Return Rotation values to 0° when you're finished testing. When you're done, press V to return to the Selection tool.

Step 2: The anchor point for the **clock face** layer is already set to its center, and the layer is positioned in the center of the comp. Next you need to place the two hands in position on the clock face. Since you have already placed their anchors correctly, you just need to make the Position value for all three the same. Select all three layers and press P to reveal their Position properties. Click on the word "Position" for **clock face** and type Command+C (Control+C) to copy its Position value. Then select the two hand layers and Command+V (Control+V) to paste the face's position to the hands. They should snap to the correct location in the Comp panel.

Step 3: Now it is time to group the clock pieces together using parenting. Make sure the Parent column is revealed in the Timeline panel. Select both of the hand layers, and either drag one of the pick whips to the **clock face** layer, or set their Parent popup to **clock face**.

To reposition or scale the entire clock, select just the **clock face** layer and manipulate it as you wish – the two hands will keep their correct placements.

At this point, you can safely animate the rotation of the hands; they will keep their same positions relative to the clock's face. Animate the Scale of the face, and the hands will scale with it. Check out [**Ex.02-final**] to see a finished version of this animation, complete with motion blur.

Step 3: Select the two hand layers and parent them to the clock face layer (left).

The [**Ex.02-final**] animation (above): The hands rotate independently of their parent (the face), while scaling the face also scales its children (the hands). Background courtesy Artbeats/Digidelic.

Move as a Group

The next example shows how parenting is useful when you need to move layers as a group. Open [**Ex.03_starter**], where we've set up a simple opening title for a program on boxing in prison.

Two of the graphic elements are a pair of handcuffs (the parent) and a pair of boxing gloves (the child). Since the gloves rotate back and forth, we moved the anchor point for this layer (**GI_boxing**) to the point where the gloves are tied together. Then we parented the gloves to the handcuffs. Notice that with the handcuffs layer as the parent, you can reposition the handcuffs and the gloves will dutifully follow.

Children and Effects

Still in comp [**Ex.03_starter**], select **GI_handcuffs** and apply Effect > Perspective > Drop Shadow. The child (the boxing gloves) did not get the drop shadow as well! This is because parenting affects just Position, Scale, and Rotation – *not* effects (or Opacity, for that matter).

To apply effects to a child/parent chain, apply the effect to each layer individually, or precompose the parent and children and apply the effect to the resulting nested comp (see Chapter 19).

You can turn this separation into an advantage; in comp [**Ex.03-final**] we applied an additional Levels effect to the handcuffs (select the layer and press F3 to open the Effect Controls) without having it affect the gloves layer.

Moving or rescaling the handcuffs (the parent) automatically affects the gloves (the child) as well. Objects courtesy Getty Images. Background courtesy Artbeats/Incarcerated.

Parenting: Under the Hood

When one layer is parented to another, the child's transform parameters reflect its placement relative to its parent – not its absolute location in the composition frame. After Effects combines the transform properties of the parent and child to decide where to render the child in the composition. To make this work, at the time a child is attached to a parent, After Effects alters the transform properties of the child to take the parent's transformation into account. We'll explain these alterations below. To practice these concepts, use the comps inside the folder **Ex.04-Under the Hood** in this chapter's Example Project.

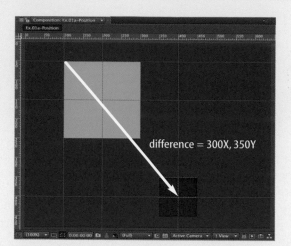

After parenting, the child's new Position value is the distance between its Anchor Point and the parent's Origin – not the parent's anchor point.

Position

When a child is attached to a parent, After Effects changes the child's Position values to reflect the distance between the Anchor Point of the child and the Origin of the parent. What is confusing is that the Origin is *not* the same as the Anchor Point – it is the upper left corner of the layer relative to the composition (just as the upper left corner of a composition has the coordinate 0,0).

Open **[Ex.04a]**, and make sure the Position and Anchor Point properties are revealed in the Timeline for all the layers (select them and type P, followed by Shift+A). **Layer 1** is a 100×100 pixel solid, with an initial Position of 400,400; **Layer 2** is a 200×200 pixel solid with an initial Position of 200,150. These position values show where their anchor points are located in the overall comp. By contrast, an Anchor Point's value reflects its distance from the layer's Origin in its upper left corner. Because the Anchor Points are centered for these layers, their values are 50,50 for **Layer 1** and 100,100 for **Layer 2**. *A layer's Origin is its Position minus its Anchor Point.*

When you parent **Layer 1** to **Layer 2** (which makes **Layer 2** the parent of **Layer 1**), **Layer 1**'s Position jumps to 300,350. If you were looking only at the difference between their original position values, you might expect **Layer 1** to move to 200,250 (400 – 200 = 200; 400 – 150 = 250). The added offset comes from **Layer 2**'s Origin being another 100 pixels up and to

the left compared with its anchor point. If you move **Layer 2**, **Layer 1** will follow, but **Layer 1**'s Position parameters will stay at their new values. In other words, *the child's Position is shown only as the offset from its parent's Origin, not its absolute position in the comp.*

Undo until the layers are back in their original states, before **Layer 1** was parented. **Layer 3** is a solid that is the same size as the composition: 640×480 pixels. It is centered in the comp, and its Anchor Point is centered in the layer, so both Position and Anchor Point have values of 320,240. When you parent **Layer 1** to **Layer 3**, **Layer 1**'s position value doesn't change! This is because the Origin of **Layer 3** is at 0,0 in the overall comp, and **Layer 1**'s new Position value is being calculated relative to **Layer 3**'s Origin.

This obscure bit of internal math explains why Null Objects have their Anchor Point at 0,0: so that their Position value is the same as their Origin, and there's no odd offset when you parent another layer to one.

Rotation

When a child is attached to a parent, its Rotation property is altered by subtracting the new parent's current Rotation. Rotation can also have an effect on a child's Position property.

Open **[Ex.04b]**, and make sure the Position and Rotation properties are exposed for **Layer 1** and

Layer 2 (if they aren't, select them and type P, followed by Shift+R). This comp is identical to **[Ex.04a]**, with the exception that **Layer 1** has been rotated by 35° and **Layer 2** by 25°. Parent **Layer 1** to **Layer 2**, and you will see **Layer 1**'s Rotation change to 10° (35 – 25 = 10). If you were to rotate **Layer 2**, **Layer 1** would swing around in space, but **Layer 1**'s Rotation parameter doesn't change, because its rotation relative to **Layer 2** stays the same.

As a side effect of **Layer 2**'s initial rotation, **Layer 1**'s Position will jump to 386.9, 242.1 (not 300, 350 as in the earlier Position-only example). This new Position takes into account that the child is also being rotated by its new parent in composition space. If you're having trouble visualizing this, try this exercise with **[Ex.04b]**: With **Layer 1** still parented to **Layer 2**, set **Layer 2**'s Rotation back to 0°. Then move **Layer 2** so its origin – its upper left corner – is in the upper left corner of the comp (its Position should now be 100, 100). If the Comp panel's Rulers aren't already visible, select this panel and use View > Show Rulers. You should be able to see that **Layer 1**'s Position is indeed right around 386.9, 242.1 in the comp – the same as its offset from **Layer 2** after parenting.

There is one more piece of unexpected behavior in Rotation, involving 3D layers. Open **[Ex.04c]**: It contains our now-familiar solids, but this time the 3D Layer switches for **Layer 1** and **Layer 2** have been enabled. Expose the Rotation and Orientation properties for both of these layers (shortcut: R); note that **Layer 2** has values of 15°, 40°, and 25° for its X, Y, and Z Rotation properties respectively. Parent **Layer 1** to **Layer 2**. **Layer 1**'s Rotation properties stay the same! However, its Orientation property is altered to take into account the new parent's initial rotation (below).

The concept of Orientation versus Rotation is discussed in Chapters 3 and 13; this is another example of where Orientation comes in handy: as a place to store offsets while the real animation work is done with the traditional Rotation parameters.

Scale

The concept behind how parenting and the Scale parameter interact is similar to the other transform properties. The extra twist is that the parent layer casts a "reality distortion" field around its children, causing some unusual behavior if you don't scale the parent uniformly in all of its axes.

Open **[Ex.04d]**, and make sure the Scale parameter is exposed for the bike wheels occupying the first two layers. **Layer 2** is scaled to 60%; **Layer 1** is scaled to 50%. Parent **Layer 1** to **Layer 2**: **Layer 1**'s Scale now jumps to 83.3%. Scrub **Layer 2**'s Scale parameter, and note how the layers change size together, while **Layer 1**'s Scale parameter stays the same.

(If you're curious to know how the math works internally, After Effects is taking the child's original Scale and dividing it by the parent's Scale to determine the child's new Scale: 50% divided by 60% equals 83.3%. When it comes time to render the child, After Effects then works the math backward: The child's new Scale times the parent's Scale equals how large to render the child, or 83.3% times 60% equals 50%.)

Note: It is generally a bad idea to combine non-uniform scaling and parenting; this is covered in the sidebar *A Skewed Perspective* on page 321.

One issue that may cause you concern is when children report high Scale values. However, this may be a false alarm. In **[Ex.04e]** the prospective parent, **Layer 2**, is scaled down to 25%, and **Layer 1** is currently at 100%. If you attach **Layer 1** to **Layer 2**, the child's scale will jump to 400% (400% times 25% equals 100%, the size it is actually rendered at). However, the image retains its original image quality, so this high scale value is not a cause for concern. To quickly check a child's true Scale, Command+click (Control+click) on the child's pick whip to temporarily unparent, check that Scale is at 100% or below, then immediately Undo.

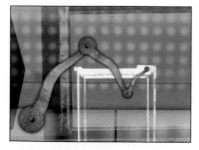

Parenting makes it easy to set up anthropomorphic constructions, such as this mechanical arm (above). Note the parenting chain (right), where each segment is connected to the next largest one. Background image courtesy Digital Vision/Prototype.

Family Selection

When you right-click on a parent, an option appears at the bottom of the list to select all of its children as well. This comes in especially handy when precomposing a group of layers.

Add a new null by selecting Layer > New > Null Object, using the keyboard shortcut, or right-clicking in the Comp panel's pasteboard.

Anthropomorphism

A common use of parenting is to set up multijointed objects that move like an arm or leg. This is particularly important for character animation. You will need to create separate layer objects for each independent piece of anatomy, such as upper arm, forearm, hand, and each segment of each finger. Move their anchor points to their natural pivot points, and align the pieces in a straight line (so rotation angles will make more sense later). Then build a parenting chain: forearm connected to upper arm, hand connected to forearm, and so forth.

Applying the basic concepts of character animation to mechanical-looking objects or abstract graphical elements is an effective way to create a spooky connection with viewers, who are often quick to imagine anthropomorphic connotations. **[Ex.05]** contains a simple example of such a construct. Experiment with the Scale and Rotation properties of the layers **segment 1**, **segment 2**, and **segment 3** to see how the sections of the extremities of the "arm" respond. Try an animation using rotation; add Ease In and Ease Out to the keyframes for more realistic motion.

Parenting with a Null Object

It's not always easy deciding who would make a good parent. There are occasions when you will want to edit the transform properties of the prospective parent without affecting the children. It is also often handy to have a child's coordinate system somewhat detached from its parent. In these cases, the perfect foster parent is a Null Object.

A Null Object is a special version of an ordinary solid: It never renders, even though it has an Opacity parameter. It also has its Anchor Point set to 0,0 – the upper left corner of the layer – so that its Position and Origin are the same, resulting in more intuitive Position coordinates for children. (See *Under The Hood*, page 316, for more on this.) To create a null, you can select the menu command Layer > New > Null Object, use the shortcut Command+Option+Shift+Y (Control+Alt+Shift+Y), or right-click in the gray pasteboard area in the Composition panel.

Open **[Ex.06_starter]**. You will see the handcuffs and boxing gloves from an earlier example, with their anchor points set appropriately.

What if you wanted to scale these together as a group, but also have the flexibility to animate each layer independently? Instead of designating one layer as the parent, use a null object as a parent for them both:

• Add a Layer > New > Null Object. A new layer named **Null 7** will be added to the Timeline. You should also see an outline of a 100×100 pixel layer in the Comp panel. This outline provides a handy way to grab a null and reposition, scale, or rotate it. If you find this outline annoying, turn off the Video switch for **Null 7** after you've set up your animation.

• Move the null in the Comp panel until its anchor in the upper left corner lines up with where the gloves meet the handcuffs. You don't have to precisely align the null, but doing so will make later transformations more intuitive.

• Parent both **GI_boxing** and **GI_handcuffs** to the null. With **Null 7** selected, press S to reveal its Scale and Shift+R to reveal its Rotation, and scrub these to confirm that both children follow this new parent. Now you can animate the group, but also animate each child independently of the other.

Getting a Handle

One of our favorite uses of nulls is as a "handle" with which to grab and move other layers that already have their own animation. A common application of this is for credits in opening titles: The client has approved a basic idea for how the credits animate; now you need to place these animating text layers into position over the different clips, repositioning them as needed to suit the background imagery.

An example of this is [Ex.07_starter]. The **first name**'s position animates, while **last name**'s scale animates. Trying to move both to a new position, with a new size, requires some gymnastics to make sure all the keyframes are correctly edited (go ahead – try it). Instead, take the easy route: Create a Null Object and attach the **first name** and **last name** layers to it. Now you can scale the null to resize the text, or use it to reposition the titles over the background footage. You can even go one step farther and create two Position keyframes to make the titles drift across the frame.

There are two refinements we added in [**Ex.07-final**]. When you're grabbing the null to reposition the text, you might occasionally grab the text layers by

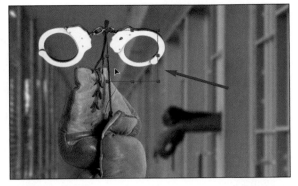

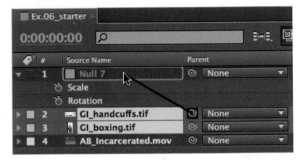

Null Objects display as an outline in the Comp panel (above). Select both objects and attach them to the null by pick whipping either one (below); now you can animate them independently, while still having master control over them through the null parent.

In [**Ex.07-final**], as the two text layers "Alan" and "Smithee" animate individually, a Null Object is used as their parent to make them drift across the frame as a group. Footage courtesy Artbeats/Business on the Go.

mistake. After attaching layers to a parent, turn on their Lock switch; they will still follow when you move the null (you just can't select them).

Another interesting note about nulls is that you can rename them just like a normal solid – either give them a new Layer Name directly in the Timeline panel, or select them and type Command+Shift+Y (Control+Shift+Y) to rename them in the Solid Settings dialog.

Local Coordinates

With a bit of preplanning, you can use parenting to help build complex arrangements of multiple layers by letting After Effects do the math for you. For example, [**Ex.08_starter**] has six spheres lined up in the same position. You've been asked to arrange them in a ring around a seventh central sphere. Quick: What are the Position coordinates for each outer sphere that would place them all the same distance away from the center? Okay; now let's do it the easy way…

To arrange children in a circle around a parent, rotate the parent, then attach a child. Background courtesy Digital Vision/Naked & Scared.

There are 360° to a full circle. Since you have six objects to spread around this circle, they need to be placed at 60° intervals (360 ÷ 6 = 60). We've already moved all the children to a good starting point in relation to the prospective parent, **center sphere**. Parent **outer sphere 1** to **center sphere**. Then rotate **center sphere** 60°, and use parenting to attach **outer sphere 2**. Rotate the parent another 60° (to 120°), and attach **outer sphere 3**. Keep going until all are attached. Our version is shown in [**Ex.08-final1**].

While this approach will work fine if all you need to do is rotate the spheres as a group, if you try to animate the Position for the children, most of them would not be moving in a straight line in relation to the Parent. Open [**Ex.08-final1**] and make sure the Position property is visible for all of the layers. Notice the odd values for the Position parameters; this is because After Effects is taking the rotation of **center sphere** into account when it's calculating the new relative positions for the child spheres. If you scrub the Y Position value for **outer sphere 1**, it moves closer to and farther away from the **center sphere**, but if you scrub **outer sphere 2**'s Y Position, it moves at an angle to its parent. To animate the children moving closer and farther away from the parent, you would need to animate the children first and *then* attach them to the parent, as we did in [**Ex.08-final2**].

An even better solution is to find a way to disconnect a child's coordinate system from its parent – and that's where the null object comes in. When you create a parenting chain that goes child > null > parent, the null's transform values are relative to the parent, while the child's parameters are relative to the null. This provides a layer of insulation between the parent and child, making transforms easier to manage.

To try this approach, open [**Ex.09_starter**], which is identical to the sphere example you used in [**Ex.08_starter**]. This time, create a new null, parent **Null 1** to **center sphere**, and **outer sphere 1** to **Null 1**. Rotate

Unparent Click

To quickly unparent a layer, Command+click on Mac (Control+click on Windows) on its pick whip tool.

A Skewed Perspective

After Effects does a good job of hiding any side effects caused by parenting. The one case where these side effects become obvious is when you have set up a nonuniform Scale for a parent (where the X and Y axes have different scale amounts) *before* you attach a child to it: The child will have its Scale parameter altered to reverse the effect of the Parent's scale. However, as you rotate the child, it will be distorted by the nonuniform scale of the parent. After Effects does not know how to compensate for this distortion, so it produces unexpected behavior when you parent and unparent rotated children.

You can observe this in [**Ex.10a**], where the prospective **Parent** layer has an initial Scale of 100%, 50%. Attach the **Child** layer with Scale values of 100%, 100% to this parent, and the child's Scale jumps to 100%, 200% (as 50% times 200% equals 100%). Rotate the **Child** layer, and you will see its shape distort as if a skew effect had been applied to it. Undo to the point before you parented, rotate the **Child** layer, and now parent it: Again, note how it jumps from being a square to a skewed shape.

This is another case in which a null object (or any other layer) placed between a parent and child can

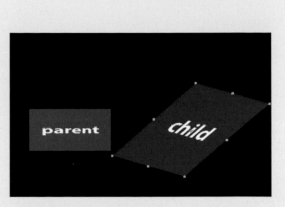

If a parent has been scaled nonuniformly, and a child is attached, the child's shape will skew when it's rotated. To fix this, place a null between the parent and child.

invisibly "soak up" transforms imposed by the parent. In [**Ex.10b**], a null has been placed between the **Parent** and **Child** layers in the parenting chain. The child's Scale is now 100%, 100% instead of 100%, 200% – the nonuniformity has already been adjusted for in the null's Scale – meaning the child can now rotate normally. So: Unless you want a nonuniformly scaled parent to skew a child, remember to put a null between them first.

---

center sphere 60°, create another null, parent **Null 2** to **center sphere**, and **outer sphere 2** to **Null 2**. Notice that the Position values for both **outer sphere 1** and **outer sphere 2** are 0,100: This is their Position relative to their nulls; the null objects are the ones that inherited the odd Position coordinates. Now you can scrub the Y Positions of these two spheres and both will work the same way, sliding in a straight line to and from **center sphere**. This means you can easily animate their positions after you've done all the parenting (unlike in [**Ex.08**]). Our version is comp [**Ex.09-final**], where each child moves into position while the center sphere rotates.

By using nulls to buffer the child spheres from their parent, they all have the same Position offset from their nulls, making it easy to animate them after the parenting has been set up.

#	Layer Name	Parent	
1	center sphere	None	0x +300.0°
	Rotation		
2	[Null 1]	1. center sphere	
3	outer sphere 1	2. Null 1	0.0, 325.0
	Position		
4	[Null 2]	1. center sphere	
5	outer sphere 2	4. Null 2	0.0, 325.0
	Position		
6	[Null 3]	1. center sphere	
7	outer sphere 3	6. Null 3	0.0, 325.0
	Position		
8	[Null 4]	1. center sphere	
9	outer sphere 4	8. Null 4	0.0, 325.0
	Position		
10	[Null 5]	1. center sphere	
11	outer sphere 5	10. Null 5	0.0, 325.0
	Position		
12	[Null 6]	1. center sphere	
13	outer sphere 6	12. Null 6	0.0, 325.0
	Position		
14	background	None	

In **[Ex.11]**, layers 2 through 6 are all part of a complex composite to build the TV image. Parenting them to a single null makes them easier to handle as a group. Footage courtesy Artbeats Business World and Space & Planets; television model by Paul Sherstobitoff.

The Face Inside the Window

Another good use of parenting and nulls is to group layers and track mattes to make sure they keep their correct alignment. [Ex.11] contains a complex hierarchy of images and track mattes that are carefully aligned so that the movie is centered in the TV screen, and the fake shadow is centered around the movie. Rather than individually managing the five layers that make up this composite, we've attached them to a null, which controls their final placement and size.

An alternative to using nulls to group layers is precomposing (discussed in detail in Chapter 19). Precomposing would send all the layers that make up a composite off into their own comp. Using parenting and nulls allows you to keep all the layers in the current comp, which comes in handy when you need to change one of those layers in relation to other layers in the current comp (such as trimming video in and out points). On the other hand, precomposing would leave you with just one layer to manage, and any effects applied would affect all the layers in the group.

Parents in Space

Parenting works with 3D layers just as well as it does with 2D layers. You can even parent a 3D layer to a 2D layer, or a 2D layer to a 3D layer – although be careful if you do, because the results can be a bit odd.

Open **[Ex.12_starter]**. It includes a simple 3D "model" we built out of four solids, with their 3D Layer switches turned on. The camera has been moved to view this model from an angle; the model itself is actually facing forward along the Z axis. It's important to start off prospective 3D children in a "clean" position where they're facing along the X, Y, or Z axis – this makes it easier to position and control their parents.

Create a new Null Object; note that it defaults to being a 2D layer. Select the layers **strut 1**, **strut 2**, **top plate**, and **bottom plate**, and parent any one of them to your new null – the rest will follow. With the null selected, press P, Shift+S, and Shift+R to reveal its Position, Scale, and Rotation properties. Scrubbing Position and Rotation will work as expected (with the exception of the null's outline being drawn straight-on, not taking the camera's angle into account), but as you scrub Scale, note the model keeps the same depth, even as you resize its height and width. Because 2D layers have no depth, 2D parents can't scale the depth of a group of 3D pieces. Enable the 3D Layer

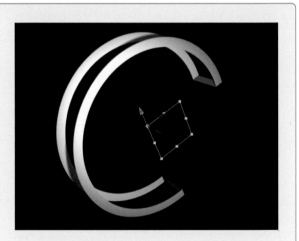

A null object in 3D space makes a good parent for the four layers that make up this model, transforming all as a unit.

switch for the null, and now all of its transforms – including Scale – will behave as expected.

Note that a 3D parent does not convert 2D layers into 3D layers. Open **[Ex.12]** and scrub **Null 1**'s Orientation, X or Y Rotation, and Z Position properties – the **AB_Digidelic** layer stays put, because 2D layers can render only in 2D space and ignore any 3D transforms they might otherwise inherit from their parent. Enable the 3D Layer switch for **AB_Digidelic** and now it can move in 3D as its parent does.

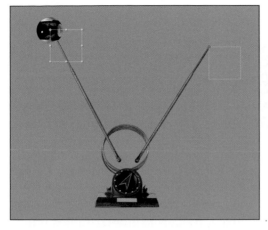

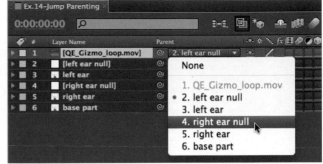

The **QE_Gizmo** layer is parented to the **left ear null** at the end of one antenna ear (left). If you hold down the Option (Alt) key while you're changing its parent to the **right ear null** (above), it will jump to the other ear (below), keeping the same relative animation. Gizmo courtesy Quiet Earth Design, antenna from Classic PIO/Televisions.

Jump Parenting

When you parent one layer to another, After Effects alters the child's transform parameters to take the parent's transformations into account. There is one case when this does not happen: If you hold down the Option (Alt) key when you parent or unparent, the child will assume the absolute position values. Normally, this would make a child jump to a perhaps unforeseen location in the comp. With a little planning, however, this becomes a vital trick when you want to move an animating child to a new parent.

In [**Ex.14**], a gizmo (**QE_Gizmo_loop.mov**) has been animated to wobble around one end of a pair of "rabbit ears" antenna. Note the parenting chain, because it is very important for this trick to work: A null object (**left ear null**)

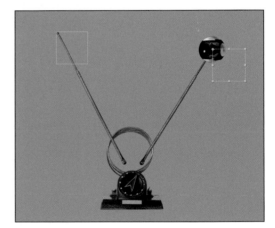

has been placed at the end of the ear, and has been parented to **left ear**. The gizmo was then centered around the null object and parented to **left ear null**. This results in the gizmo's initial Position being 0,0 – there is no offset between it and the null's origin. RAM Preview the comp, and note how the gizmo follows the waving antenna ear.

A similar null has been attached to the end of the right ear. Hold down the Option (Alt) key, and change the Parent popup for **QE_Gizmo_loop** from **left ear null** to **right ear null**. You will see the gizmo jump to the same relative position at the end of the right ear. RAM Preview, and the gizmo will now animate around its new parent. Edit > Duplicate the **QE_Gizmo_loop** layer, and Option+parent (Alt+parent) the copy back to **left ear null** to have a gizmo flying around each ear.

Parenting is a very powerful tool, useful for tasks ranging from "I'd rather just move one layer, thank you" to creating complex animations and coordinations between layers that might be too brain numbing or time consuming to perform otherwise. Just remember to practice safe parenting: Use a null whenever you intend to parent a child.

CONNECT

Animating position, scale, and rotation: Chapter 3.

Editing the anchor point: Chapter 3.

Parenting and track mattes: Chapter 11.

3D space: Chapter 13.

Parenting is an alternative to nesting compositions (Chapter 18) and precomposing (Chapter 19).

18

Nesting Compositions

Creating complex motion graphics that are easy to edit requires building a hierarchy of compositions.

Thisis the first of three chapters that show you how to build a hierarchy of comps. Here, our focus is on creating complex animations that are easy to edit. We also delve further under the hood of After Effects' rendering order: Understanding how data travels through the hierarchy will help you trouble-shoot if the result is not exactly what you expected…

This chapter includes many examples showing you the benefits of nesting 2D comps; the following chapter will cover *Precomposing* (sort of like nesting backward). If you are nesting comps with 3D layers, check out Chapter 20, *Collapsing Transformations*, which covers specific issues that arise when cameras and lights exist in the hierarchy.

Nesting 101

Graphics applications vary wildly, but advanced ones usually have one thing in common: a method of "grouping" items so you can transform multiple layers as easily as you can transform one layer. In After Effects, there are two main ways to edit layers as a group:

Parenting (the subject of Chapter 17): The parent layer controls the Position, Scale, and Rotation of any number of child layers in the same composition. Parenting is particularly useful for setting up a kinematic chain of layers, such as those used in character animation.

Nesting: By placing a group of layers in their own composition, then "nesting" this comp inside another, you can not only apply transformations, but also trim, fade, and apply effects to the group as if they were one layer. Another benefit is that you can create a *precomp* and nest it into multiple comps. This is useful when creating an animated element (like a logo) that may need to change; when you edit the precomp, its output will ripple through to all the other comps in which it is nested.

Nesting comps serves a second purpose: It allows you to override the default rendering order performed on a layer in a single comp.

In those cases where nesting is a better solution than parenting, the question becomes whether or not you were planning ahead. If you were, you'll find nesting comps to be quite straightforward and intuitive. However, if you discover a problem after the fact, you'll probably need to use the Precompose feature (which we cover in detail in the next chapter).

TIP

Double-clicking Duplicity

Double-click on a nested comp layer to open the original comp; add the Option (Alt) key to instead open its Layer panel. The opposite is true when the layer has Roto Brush or Paint applied (yes, this will drive you crazy).

Example Project

Explore the 18-Example Project.aep file as you read this chapter; references to [Ex.##] refer to specific compositions within the project file.

Nesting a Comp

If you are new to nesting, follow along as we run you through one example of nesting a small stationID bug comp into a D1-sized comp and positioning it into the bottom right-hand corner. Then we'll discuss how to create a more efficient workflow if you need to nest it multiple times.

Step 1: Open this chapter's project file [**18-Example Project.aep**]. In the **Ex.01-Nesting 101** folder, open the **stationID** comp and RAM Preview. This is a small comp (160×130 square pixels) with two layers: a text layer and an animated shape layer. Note that this comp is 30 seconds in duration, which is longer than it needs to be. Always err on the long side – trimming the out point for a nested comp layer is easy, but extending its duration will take more effort.

Step 1: The station ID bug is animated in the small **[stationID]** comp.

Step 2: Open the [**Ex.01-Weather**] comp, which is 08:00 in duration and 720×486 (D1, non-square pixels). It consists of one movie layer of a man shoveling snow.

Step 3: From the **Ex.01-Nesting 101** folder in the Project panel, locate the first comp, [**stationID**]. Just as you would drag in any source to become a layer, drag the [**stationID**] comp into the comp [**Ex.01-Weather**]. It will now appear as one layer, called **stationID**, starting at 00:00. Move to 02:00 or later so you can see the logo after it has built on, then move the layer around; notice how it moves as a group. Unlike parenting, you can apply effects to this group, or animate its opacity.

Now drag the **stationID** layer in the Comp panel to the bottom right-hand corner; as you drag, press Command+Shift on Mac (Control+Shift on Windows) and it will snap to the edges. Your trusty assistant has carefully created the size of the [**stationID**] comp so it doesn't need to be carefully positioned every time it is used – just snap it to any corner and it will appear in the correct position.

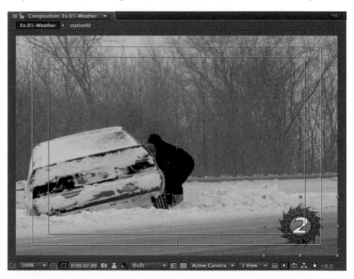

Step 3: Nest the small **[stationID]** comp into the D1-sized **[Ex.01-Weather]** comp and snap it to the bottom righthand corner (above). Note that it appears as one layer in the Timeline panel (below) and that the comp marker in the precomp appears as a layer marker when nested (Chapter 6).

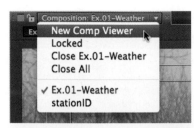

Note that the transparent areas of the first comp (where the background color is visible) are retained when the layer is nested. Changing the background color of the [**stationID**] precomp will not affect its transparency; set its color to whatever works best for display purposes.

You can reposition, scale, trim, and apply effects to the nested comp layer just as you would any single layer. In fact, the nested comp behaves just as if you had rendered the first comp and reimported it as a finished movie, with one very important difference: *The first comp is still "live"* – any edits to it appear immediately in the other comps.

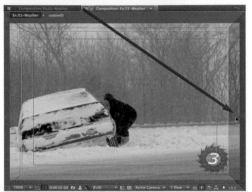

Step 4: In the first comp – [**stationID**] – double-click the text layer, type "**3**" then Enter to change the number. Press V to return to the Select tool. Notice how any change is reflected in the second comp.

Step 5: At this point, you may find it helpful to view both comps side by side. To do this, select New Comp Viewer from the Comp panel's menu, then drag the dotted area of the new viewer's tab and drop it on the right side of the Comp panel to achieve a side-by-side layout. The new viewer will be locked.

Better yet, use the "split frame" shortcut: Make sure the Comp panel is active, then press Command+Option+Shift+N on Mac (Control+Alt+Shift+N on Windows). This splits the frame containing the active viewer and creates a new viewer with opposite locked/unlocked states.

Step 5: To view two comps side by side, first create a New Comp Viewer (top), then drag one comp to the left or right side of the Comp panel (above).

Whichever method you use, the idea is to view [**stationID**] on the left side and [**Ex.01-Weather**] on the right. You can change which comp is displayed in each viewer by clicking the buttons along the top of the panels or by selecting them from the Composition menu. Now when you make changes to the precomp, you'll immediately see what effect this has in the second comp. The Timeline panel will reflect whichever Comp panel is forward. Close the second viewer when you're done.

Close all comps then check out our examples in the **Ex.01-Final Comps** folder. Note that our [**stationID_final**] precomp is nested

Step 5 *continued:* Click on the buttons (where the arrows are pointing) along the top of the Comp panels to determine which comp is shown in which viewer. The Always Preview This View button (circled in red) determines which comp renders when you RAM Preview. Footage courtesy Artbeats/Winter Lifestyles.

into three comps – [**Weather**], [**News**], and [**Sports**] – where it is locked to avoid accidental movement. The [**stationID_final**] precomp is D1-sized, and the text layer is a parent to the shape layer. Now if the client decides the bug should be in a different corner, we would have to edit only the precomp instead of the bug's position in all the comps it's nested into.

There is no one set of rules for how to set up your composition hierarchy, but try to predict which changes your client might make to a common element that is shared across multiple comps and see if you can create a hierarchy that will ease making those inevitable changes.

Easy Editing for Effects

Nesting a comp not only allows for animating multiple layers as a group, it's also a convenient way to apply an effect to a group of layers at once (as opposed to parenting, in which applying an effect to the parent layer does not also apply the effect to the children).

In [**Ex.02-Planet-1**], the planet movie and title animate independently of each other. In the second comp [**Ex.02-Planet-2**], the first comp is nested and the Effect > Perspective > Drop Shadow effect is added.

Because the shadow applies to both the planet movie and the planet text as a group, it's easier to edit it than if you applied it to the layers individually. Also, in the first comp, the planet movie is scaled 50%, while the type is at 100%. If you were to apply the drop shadow to each layer individually, the effect would be affected by the scale values, because Scale renders after Effects (more on the rendering order later in this chapter). Scaling down a layer with a Drop Shadow effect renders the shadow with less distance and softness, so the shadow on the planet movie would appear harder than the planet type, even with the same values for each parameter. This problem is not limited to the Drop Shadow effect – many other effects, along with Mask Feather, are affected by scaling.

We've also faded out the precomp as a group in the second comp – which again is something that cannot be achieved with parenting. Besides, it's easier than duplicating Opacity keyframes for multiple layers.

The more you start working with nested comps, the more opportunities you'll recognize for saving time and effort. But not only can you apply an effect to a nested comp for expediency, it may be the easier (or the only) way to create a certain look. In [**Ex.03-Distort-1**], two animated skulls are positioned side by side. This first composition (or *precomp*) is then nested in [**Ex.03-Distort-2**] where the Distort > Polar Coordinates effect is added. Because the effect is being applied after the two skulls have already been composited into one layer, the distortion effect is capable of blending together pixels from both skulls.

This would be practically impossible to achieve in one comp. It would not look the same if you applied the effect to both layers individually. You can work around it with Adjustment Layers (Chapter 22), but then you couldn't place a background in this comp without distorting it as well.

What's a Precomp?

A comp that is nested inside another comp is often referred to as a *precomp*, or *intermediate comp*, indicating that it is not the final output comp.

The Drop Shadow in the second comp applies to both the planet and title as a group and renders with a consistent effect, as they are both scaled 100% at this stage. Background courtesy Artbeats/Monster Waves.

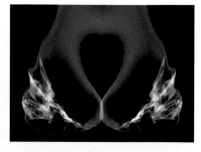

Two skulls are positioned side by side in comp 1 (left), then effected using Polar Coordinates in comp 2 (above).

Nesting can help you manage video sequences. The video edit is in the first comp, **[Ex.04-Editing-1]** (above and below).

Editing a Sequence of Clips

Using nested comps can also help you manage a sequence of video clips. In the first comp, edit several full-frame clips with fades or transitions in-between. Then nest this edited sequence in another comp, where you can mask, transform and apply effects to the video montage as a single layer. Of course, since the first comp is "live," you can re-edit or replace footage in the video montage without inflicting undue pain and suffering on the animation in the second comp.

For example, in **[Ex.04-Editing-1]**, a long clip of various skateboarders is chopped up into three segments, and fades are then added between each section.

The Composition Navigator (left).

Along the top of the Comp panel for the first comp, the Composition Navigator shows that this comp is nested into a second comp, [**Ex.04-Editing-2**] (circled in the figure to the left). Click on its name to open it, and its tab will be added to the Timeline. (You can also open it by double-clicking it in the Project panel).

In the second comp, an oval mask, animation, and the Stylize > Roughen Edges effect are applied to the sequence of clips as a group. Re-edit the video in the first comp and see how the changes ripple through to the second comp.

The edited sequence is nested into **[Ex.04-Editing-2]**, where you can animate and effect it as a single layer. Skateboarding footage courtesy Creative License; background from Artbeats/Virtual Insanity.

Size Doesn't Matter

You're already aware that layers can be larger, or have a different aspect ratio, than your comp. The same, of course, is true when you're nesting: Nested comp layers do not need to be the same size as the final output comp. This allows for lots of interesting animation possibilities.

A simple example of this is [**Ex.05**]. The first comp, [**Ex.05-Spheres setup**], consists of six spheres in a tall comp (200×1200 square pixels). This comp is nested in a D1 (720×486 non-square pixels) comp, [**Ex.05-Smoke Final**], where it is scrolled vertically. This makes animation easier, because we had to keyframe the animation for just the nested tall comp – not each sphere individually. It also made it easy to apply a blending mode and track matte to all the spheres as a group.

Just as you can pan around photographs documentary-style (Chapter 3), you can use the same motion-control technique for moving around a large composition. Compositions can be as large as 30,000×30,000 pixels (you'll need a lot of RAM, but hey). This gives you a lot of freedom to construct elaborate oversized comps, then nest them in a second comp where you can pan around the large layer looking at different areas of interest. This approach to animation is another way in which After Effects differs significantly from traditional editing systems.

[**Ex.06-Music-1/setup**] comp is 1160×714 pixels, about three times the required output size. A background still image from Digital Vision's Music Mix serves as a "stage" on which to arrange three objects (microphone, horn, and radio). This comp is nested in [**Ex.06-Music-2/final**], which is 320×240. RAM Preview this final comp and you'll see that the animation between both comps is coordinated; as each musical element has its one second of fame in the setup comp, it's timed to coincide with when the final comp is focused on that area. The Anchor Point – not Position – is animated for the nested comp layer. This ensures that when Scale is also animated to simulate a camera pushing in or pulling out, all scaling occurs centered around the area of interest (see Chapter 3 for more on animating the Anchor Point).

A series of six spheres in the first comp are easily panned as one unit in our final comp shown above. Background images courtesy Artbeats/Cloud Chamber and Soft Edges.

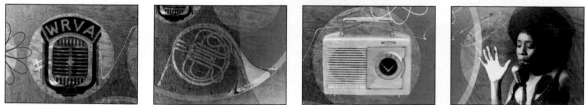

The images are set up and animated in the oversized first comp (top). This is nested in the final comp, where Anchor Point and Scale are animated "motion control style" (above). Images courtesy Digital Vision, Classic PIO, and Getty Images.

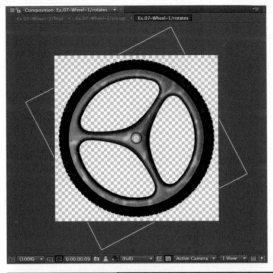

Repetition and Variation

Once you're familiar with nesting, you don't need to stop at just two. Building a complex animation may involve many nested comps. You should create as many levels in the hierarchy as necessary to make editing the animation easy and efficient. Managing an extra comp or two is usually easier than trying to keep layers in sync with each other. In the [Ex.07] series of comps, we use three compositions to create our animation. Before you proceed, first close any previously opened comps by selecting Close All from the Comp panel's dropdown menu.

Wheel-1/rotates: A small comp (400×400) is used to animate the wheel and is only as big as the wheel image. Two rotation keyframes turn the wheel counterclockwise. This comp is longer in duration (12 seconds) than required.

A chain of nested comps makes complex animations easy. First, a single wheel is rotated in comp 1 (above); this sets the master rotation speed for all the wheels in the later comps.

The first comp is nested six times in a wide second comp, and arranged and offset in time (below).

Wheel-2/six up: The first comp is nested in a second, wide comp (2400×400, eight seconds duration), where the rotating wheel is duplicated. Each layer is offset in time from the other to vary its appearance. Because we created the first comp with a longer duration than this comp (12 seconds compared with eight), the offset layers don't come up short in time.

Wheel-3/final: The second comp is then nested in a third comp, where it is duplicated. The foreground set of wheels is scaled down, panned from right to left, and a drop shadow is added. The larger background layer also pans, but more slowly. A blur effect has also been added to help it recede into the background.

The beauty of this hierarchy is that the rotation speed of all 12 wheels is controlled by just two Rotation keyframes in the first comp. Change the second keyframe in this comp to another value, and see how the edit ripples through the chain. Go one better, and replace the original wheel source with one of the sphere objects – now you have 12 spheres rotating. (Not that clients ever change their minds…)

The wide comp is used twice, at different scalings and animation speeds, in the final comp. Background courtesy Artbeats/Liquid Ambience.

Navigating Nested Comps

After Effects CS4 introduced several very useful enhancements for navigating chains of nested compositions: the Composition Navigator, the Mini-Flowchart, and expanded Edit This/Look At That functionality.

Composition Navigator

The Composition Navigator is a new user interface element that has been added to the top of the Composition panel.

Step 1: Open the comp [**Ex.07-Wheel-3/final**]. Look along the top of the Composition panel, just above the image area: You will see a string of comp names. These compositions are nested into each other.

Step 2: Click on the middle comp's name – [**Ex.07-Wheel-2/six up**] – in the Composition Navigator. This comp will open. Click on the third comp in the chain to open [**Ex.07-Wheel-1/rotates**]. (If the chain is too long to be displayed along the top of the Comp panel, you will see "…" at the left or right edge of the chain; click on the … or use your mouse's scroll wheel to navigate the entire chain.)

A shortcoming of the Composition Navigator is that it shows just one "thread" of a chain of nested comps. If there are more than two compositions nested into the currently forward comp, After Effects displays the name you opened most recently. If you don't see the comp you're looking for, try using the Composition Mini-Flowchart (coming up next).

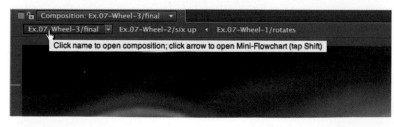

Instant Nesting

In the Project panel, drag a comp to the New Composition button to nest the comp into a new comp with the same specs as the comp being dragged.

The Composition Navigator is displayed along the top of the Comp panel. Click on a comp's name to jump directly to it.

Step 3: Click on the arrow to the right of a comp's name (circled in red, above) to open the Mini-Flowchart (below). Then click on the path arrow along the right edge of the Mini-Flowchart to reveal that chain's full path.

Step 4: Press the Shift key to have the Mini-Flowchart pop up centered on the cursor's location. When a comp is nested more than once into another comp, the number of times it is nested is displayed in parentheses after the comp's name (circled in red).

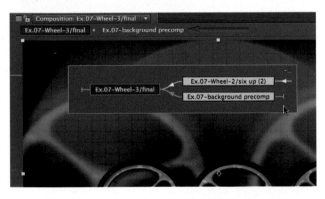

Step 5: After you replace the background layer with the comp [**Ex.07-background precomp**], the Mini-Flowchart will now display two nested comps in this hierarchy. Note that the Composition Navigator will display the precomp you opened most recently.

Composition Mini-Flowchart

Step 3: Click on the Composition Navigator button for [**Ex.07-Wheel-3/final**] to bring it forward again. Then click on the arrow to the right of its name in the Composition Navigator: The Mini-Flowchart will open. This shows all of the compositions connected to the currently selected comp. Click on the arrow along the right edge of the Mini-Flowchart to see the full extent of a specific branch of the comp chain. Click on a comp's name to open it.

Clicking anywhere outside the flowchart will close it without changing which composition is currently forward.

Step 4: The Mini-Flowchart opens centered on the mouse cursor's current location. To open the Mini-Flowchart somewhere other than the top of the Comp panel, make sure either the Comp or Timeline panel is forward, position your mouse, then tap the Shift key to open the Mini-Flowchart view.

Step 5: So far we've viewed a fairly simple chain of three comps. To make life more interesting, bring comp [**Ex.07-Wheel-3/final**] forward and select the background movie layer **AB_LiquidAmbience_loop.mov**. In the Project panel, select the comp [**Ex.07-background precomp**], press the Option (Alt) key, and drag this comp to the Timeline. The movie will be replaced with a nested comp layer.

Now press Shift to bring up the Mini-Flowchart and you'll see that multiple comps are nested into comp [**Ex.07-Wheel-3/final**]. Experiment with using the Mini-Flowchart to navigate up and down this chain of comps until you're familiar with how this works.

Note that you can also open the Mini-Flowchart by clicking its button along the top of the Timeline panel; it will open centered on the mouse cursor's current location.

Edit This, Look At That

After Effects CS4 also introduced enhancements to the "Edit This, Look At That" (ETLAT) behavior. Previously, you could lock the Effect Controls panel of a layer used in one comp, then bring another comp forward. This allowed you to edit an effect's settings inside a nested comp while viewing the results in a master comp downstream. You can now also lock the Comp panel for a master comp, then edit layers in the Timeline panel for a nested comp.

We know – that's a confusing statement to read. It's much easier to try it out for yourself in the following two examples:

Locking the Comp Panel

Step 1: Continuing from the prior exercise, make sure all three of the wheel comps in the [**Ex.07**] folder are open in the Timeline panel – the ETLAT behavior works best when all the comps you might edit are open!

Step 2: Bring [**Ex.07-Wheel-3/final**] forward and click on its lock icon to the left of its name along the top of the Comp panel. The lock will turn yellow.

Step 3: Select the tab in the Timeline panel for the nested comp [**Ex.07-Wheel-1/rotates**]. Its timeline will come forward, but the Comp viewer for [**Ex.07-Wheel-3/final**] will still be displayed.

Step 4: In the Timeline panel for [**Ex.07-Wheel-1/rotates**], select the layer **CM_bikelayer.tif**. This one layer is replicated numerous times in the comps downstream. Apply Effect > Distort > Twirl, and increase the Angle value in the Effect Controls panel. When you release the mouse, in the Comp viewer you will see that all of the wheels will have their spokes twirled.

Step 5: To return to normal behavior, click on the lock icon in the Comp panel to unlock [**Ex.07-Wheel-3/final**]. The comp you were working in – [**Ex.07-Wheel-1/rotates**] – will now be displayed in the Comp viewer.

This trick will save you from having to open two Timeline and Comp panels while working with tricky chains of nested comps. Note that in our example we first opened a series of nested comps, locked the master

TIP

Most Recent Comp

To open the most recently active nested composition without going through the Mini-Flowchart, hold Shift and tap Escape. Repeat to return to the previous comp.

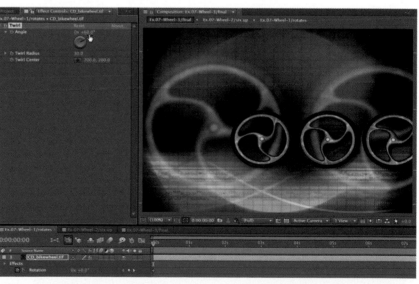

Click on the lock icon in the Comp panel to always view this comp while exploring the timelines of nested comps.

With the master comp's viewer locked, you can edit layers in nested compositions while viewing the result in the master comp. (If you RAM Preview, the master comp is what will be rendered.) Background footage courtesy Artbeats/Digital Biz.

Am I Being Used?

When you select a footage item or nested comp in the Project panel, you'll see a report at the top of the panel if it's "used x number of times." Click on the arrow to find out where it is nested; selecting one of the listed comps opens it.

comp, then used the tabs along the top of the Timeline panel to bring forward the timeline we wished to edit. Using the Timeline tabs is the most reliable method for getting this trick to work: If you switch to another comp using the Composition Navigator along the top of the Comp panel, the newly selected comp will then become the "locked" comp.

Note also that if you open a composition from the Project panel when one comp is locked, the new comp will open in a new Comp viewer docked inside the same frame (try this, and notice the additional tab at the top of the Comp panel). Even if a comp is already open, double-clicking it in the Project panel will open it in a new Comp viewer.

If you want to edit a precomp that is not currently open in the Timeline panel (such as the [**Ex.07-background precomp**]), return to the locked master comp, press Shift to open the Mini-Flowchart, and select the precomp. The precomp will become the locked comp, but at least it won't create a second comp viewer. Now you can reselect the master comp in the Composition Navigator to be the locked comp and use the Timeline tabs to edit the precomp.

To summarize: If you like the ETLAT behavior, for best results:

- open all the comps you might want to edit first;
- bring the master comp forward and lock its Comp panel; and
- to edit a precomp, click a tab in the Timeline to bring it forward.

Locking the Effect Controls Panel

To experiment with using ETLAT in the Effect Controls panel, make sure the Comp panel is *not* locked, then:

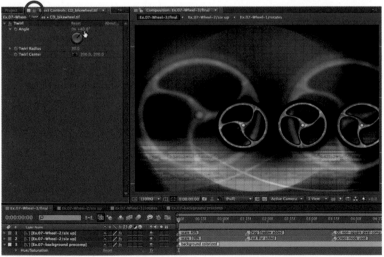

Steps 3–4: In the precomp, toggle on the lock icon in the Effect Controls panel (circled in red). Now when you bring the master comp forward, the Twirl effect will remain visible for editing.

Step 1: Bring [**Ex.07-Wheel-1/rotates**] forward, and select layer 1. The Effect Controls panel should be visible (if not, press F3) with the Twirl effect applied.

Step 2: To see the effect in context, bring [**Ex.07-Wheel-3/final**] forward. Now you can see the problem: The Effect Controls panel no longer shows the Twirl effect!

Step 3: Return to [**Ex.07-Wheel-1/rotates**] and in the Effect Controls panel for layer 1, toggle on the lock icon (in the top left corner).

Step 4: Now when you bring [**Ex.07-Wheel-3/final**] forward, the Twirl effect remains visible for editing.

There no doubt that the ETLAT behavior can be a little confusing at first, but it's well worth practicing as it's extremely useful when you're editing a complex chain of nested compositions.

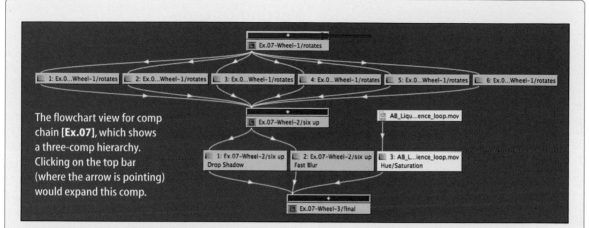

The flowchart view for comp chain **[Ex.07]**, which shows a three-comp hierarchy. Clicking on the top bar (where the arrow is pointing) would expand this comp.

Comp Flowchart View

The Flowchart View lets you see your chain of comps and layers within a comp in a diagrammatic way. This is helpful when you're trying to grasp a complex chain – particularly when someone else created a project that you now have to reverse engineer.

Comp Flowchart View shows the current comp and all its layers and nested comps, but not which comps use the current comp. The Flowchart View for the last comp in a chain (the one you will render) tends to be the most informative.

To practice using the Flowchart View, open comp **[Ex.07-Wheel-3/final]** and click on the icon (circled in red in the figure, right) in the lower right corner of the

Comp panel. The Flowchart View will open, docked in the Comp panel. In this view, comps and layers are drawn as bars, connected by wires with arrows. You can drag items to new positions to make the flowchart more legible, but you cannot change the "wiring" (or any other settings). Hold down the spacebar to access the Hand tool, which will move the entire flowchart around.

A gray bar along the top of a comp with a plus sign means the item is collapsed, hiding the hierarchy that made it; clicking on this bar exposes the hierarchy of layers and sources. The layer bars are numbered according to their order in the Timeline panel of the comp.

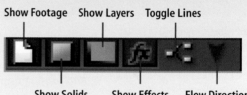

Show Footage   Show Layers   Toggle Lines

Show Solids   Show Effects   Flow Direction

The buttons at the bottom of the Flowchart View allow you to expose certain attributes and to customize the layout.

There are six option buttons in the lower left corner, identified from left to right as:

Show Footage, Solids, Layers, Effects: The first four buttons allow you to choose which attributes should be exposed.

Toggle Lines: Whether you prefer straight or curved lines to connect the items. Option+click (Alt+click) this button to clean up lines.

Flow Direction: The default for flowchart direction is top to bottom, with the "last" comp at the bottom; that's what we used mostly for this book.

Double-clicking on an item in the flowchart opens it. If it is a footage item, it opens in its own Footage panel; layers in comps bring their comps forward, with that layer highlighted. Selecting a layer with an effect applied and pressing F3 opens its Effect Controls panel.

Note that there is also a Project Flowchart View which shows the entire project file; you access it by clicking on the "picnic table" icon in the top right corner of the Project panel.

Composition Settings

Composition Name: Ex.07-Wheel-1/rotates

Basic | Advanced

Anchor:

Rendering Plug-in: Advanced 3D | Options... | About...

☑ Preserve frame rate when nested or in render queue
☐ Preserve resolution when nested

Motion Blur

Shutter Angle: 180°   Shutter Phase: 0°

Samples Per Frame: 16   Adaptive Sample Limit: 16

Samples Per Frame controls the number of motion blur samples for 3D layers, shape layers, and certain effects. 2D layer motion automatically uses more samples per frame when needed, up to the Adaptive Sample Limit.

☑ Preview   Cancel | OK

Check the Preserve Frame Rate switch in the Advanced tab of Composition Settings to force this comp to be sampled at its frame rate no matter what frame rate it is eventually rendered at.

Preserve Frame Rate can also be used for locking effects that randomize, such as Numbers, to a different frame rate than the comp they're nested into. Background courtesy Artbeats/Digital Biz.

TIP

Comp Won't Nest?

If a comp refuses to nest (it just bounces back to the project panel), chances are you're accidentally attempting to set up an "infinite loop" of comps that would use each other.

Nesting Options

Normally when you nest a comp, the second comp determines the frame rate that the precomp is sampled at; so if the final comp in the chain is set to 29.97 fps, all nested comps also render at that frame rate. Similarly with the Resolution setting: Changing the Resolution of the final comp would change the Resolution of any nested comps to match. At the end of the chain, resolution and frame rate are ultimately controlled by the Render Settings, which determine how the comp being rendered – and all comps nested within – actually renders.

There are exceptions to these rules. Two options found in Composition Settings – Preserve Frame Rate and Preserve Resolution – control how a composition behaves when it's nested.

Using the [**Ex.07**] series of comps, let's see the Preserve Frame Rate option in action:

• Open the [**Ex.07-Wheel-1/rotates**] comp, the first comp in the chain, and press Command+K (Control+K) to open Composition Settings.

• In the Basic settings tab, set the Frame Rate to 5 frames per second.

• In the Advanced tab, turn on Preserve Frame Rate. Click OK. RAM Preview to check that the wheel is indeed rotating at a low frame rate, as opposed to its previously smooth interpolation.

• Open the [**Ex.07-Wheel-3/final**] comp, and RAM Preview a few seconds worth. While the individual wheels rotate at 5 fps, the Position keyframes in this comp interpolate smoothly at the final comp's frame rate (29.97 fps).

Preserve Frame Rate is particularly useful when you want to "lock" animation keyframes to a movie's frame rate. For instance, if you're rotoscoping or masking a 24 fps clip shot on film, do the work in a precomp set and preserved to 24 fps. Nest this into your final 29.97 fps comp, and the mask keyframes will remain locked onto the film frames when you render.

Preserve Frame Rate is also useful when you need an effect that is capable of random output – such as Text > Numbers – to render at a low frame rate. In [**Ex.08-Numbers-1/setup**], we've created random numbers with the Numbers effect, and set this comp to 10 fps with Preserve Frame Rate turned on. When this is nested in [**Ex.08-Numbers-2/final**], it can be duplicated and time-stretched to create many other frame rates.

Preserve Resolution is less obviously useful. It can be used to force a precomp to a low resolution for a creative pixelated look, or to temporarily speed up workflow by locking an oversized precomp to a low resolution until you're ready to do the final render. Unlike Preserve Frame Rate, Preserve Resolution can be overridden in the Render Settings: If the Resolution popup is set to anything other than Current Settings, the Preserve Resolution option is ignored.

There are a couple of issues to watch for when using these options:

• A comp preserved to the same frame rate as the final output will only frame render, not field render (since field rendering samples a comp at twice the frame rate).

• Collapsing Transformations (see Chapter 20) for a nested layer will override any Nesting Options set for that precomp.

General Nesting Tips

• The biggest and best tip we can offer is to *give comps useful names!* Otherwise, we guarantee that you'll waste valuable time poking around and wondering which comp does what.

• If you find yourself duplicating keyframes so that multiple layers are in sync, stop and ask yourself whether you should be parenting or nesting comps instead, so you can manipulate multiple layers as a group.

• When building a hierarchy of comps, avoid scaling down layers until the final comp. Once you scale down layers, a smaller image is created and resolution is lost. (It's possible in some cases to recover resolution with Collapse Transformations – more on that in Chapter 20.)

• If possible, apply Opacity keyframes for fade up and downs in the final comp, so you don't have to hunt down keyframes in precomps.

• The Preferences > General, "Synchronize time of all related items" option means that when you move in time in one comp, all comps in the same chain will synchronize and park their current time indicators on the same frame. This makes it relatively easy to synchronize keyframes across multiple comps in a chain. This option defaults to on, but occasionally you may find it useful to turn it off temporarily.

• When you're reorganizing a chain of comps, you can copy and paste keyframes between layers (Chapter 5), including to and from layers in different comps. You can also copy and paste entire layers between comps (Chapter 6).

• If you need to create multiple animations that are related but otherwise unique, urge your client or boss to sign off on a sample animation before you duplicate comps and customize each instance.

• If an element – such as an animated logo layer – appears in multiple comps, animate the logo in its own precomp. Now if you update the logo animation, all uses will be updated.

• If you expect to make no further changes to a precomp, consider pre-rendering it and using it as a Comp Proxy (Chapter 44). This saves even more time if you're nesting the precomp more than once.

• If the Composition Navigator is not visible along the top of the Composition panel, click on the options arrow in the upper right corner of the Comp panel and enable Show Composition Navigator. Note that you can also use this menu to select which way the chains of comps flow in the navigator.

Opening Nested Comps in CS4/CS5

The shortcuts for opening nested comps have changed significantly in recent versions (and not necessarily for the better, in our opinion):

In all versions, if the layer is not a nested comp, double-clicking the layer opens the Layer panel (unless it has no source, such as a text layer or a solid layer). You also can't open the Layer panel for an Illustrator layer that is continuously rasterized (covered in Chapter 20).

In CS4 and later, double-clicking a nested comp layer in the Timeline opens the nested comp. (In earlier versions, it opened the Layer panel for the nested comp.) To open the Layer panel for a nested comp (to mask, motion track, and so on), hold Option (Alt) when double-clicking a nested comp layer.

In CS5, there is an exception to this rule: If the nested comp layer has Paint or Roto Brush applied, After Effects assumes that when you double-click the layer, you want to edit these effects – so the Layer panel comes forward. To open the precomp, hold Option (Alt) when you double-click.

Bottom line: Pay attention to what opens when you double-click a nested comp. The inconsistent behavior will keep you on your toes…

The Interpret Footage dialog (above): Here you can set how After Effects should treat the source's alpha channel (if applicable), conform a movie's frame rate, separate fields, and more. A second tab allows you to assign a color profile. To open this dialog, select a source in the Project panel then click the Interpret Footage button at the bottom of the panel (below).

After Effects' rendering order: masks, effects, transformations, and layer styles are calculated in that order.

The Rendering Order

If you've ever been frustrated when you're trying to achieve a specific effect, it's probably because After Effects has a mind of its own when it comes time to render. Unlike Photoshop, where the user mostly dictates the order in which effects and transformations are applied, After Effects processes layers based on its own internal *rendering order*.

The first rule to understand is that the order with which you apply effects and transform objects is not necessarily the same order that's used when rendering. By understanding the default rendering order, and how to manipulate it – including by nesting compositions – you'll be equipped to troubleshoot many of your visual problems.

When you import footage into a project, the source's first port of call is the Interpret Footage dialog (covered in Chapter 38). In this dialog, the layer's alpha channel type, frame rate, field order, and pixel aspect ratio is set. Interpret Footage is also where you assign the color profile when Color Management (Chapter 26) is enabled for the project. If you don't change these settings, the footage uses the defaults assigned to it.

When you drag this footage into a comp, the layer is sent through different stages before the final image is rendered to the Comp panel. Open comp [**Ex.09-Default Render Order**], select layer 1 and make sure it's twirled down. The default rendering order is listed in the Timeline panel:

Masks (if applied)
Effects (if applied)
Transform (always present)
Layer Styles (if applied)

If there are no masks or effects applied, only Transform will be listed. If a layer's Opacity is at 0% or its visibility is off, the layer is not rendered. If there are multiple layers in the comp, they are processed from the bottom up for 2D layers (rendering order for 3D layers depends more on distance from the camera, as covered in Chapter 13).

You can apply an unlimited number of effects per layer, which are processed from the top down. These are easily reordered by dragging them up and down in the Effect Controls or Timeline panels. However, *you cannot rearrange the main Masks > Effects > Transform > Layer Styles order within a comp.* Most of the time, the default order is the preferred choice, but there are times when you need to be able to reorder these events.

By trying to both mask and apply a Find Edges effect in one comp (right), we run into a problem – there's only one set of render order attributes. Since After Effects calculates Effects after Masks, the mask's "edge" is affected by Find Edges resulting in an ugly dark halo. Background courtesy Artbeats/Digital Moods.

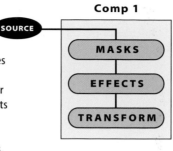

Existing render attributes

Consider the problem displayed in the [**Ex.09-Default Render Order**] comp. The **CM_Planet_loop.mov** layer has a circular mask applied to drop out the background. The Find Edges effect is then added, but because the effect considers the edge of the mask to be worth highlighting, an ugly dark line appears on the left side. (Don't worry; we'll show you how to fix that below.)

Two Comps Are Better Than One

If you work with a single layer across two comps, the layer will have two rendering orders: All attributes applied in the first comp are calculated first, and the result is passed to the second comp, where more attributes may be applied. This allows you to pick and choose which events happen in which order. Returning to the problem in [**Ex.09**], the solution is to override the default rendering order (Masks > Effects) by applying the Find Edges effect in Comp 1, and the mask in Comp 2. We've done that in [**Ex.10**].

In the [**Ex.10-Planets_pre**] comp, the planet movie has Find Edges applied. The first comp is the same size as the small planet movie, which conserves RAM. This precomp is nested into a second comp, [**Ex.10-Planets_final**], where it is masked to remove the dark edge and a drop shadow added. Transformations can be edited in either comp, but in this case you'd want to edit them in the second comp after the mask is applied.

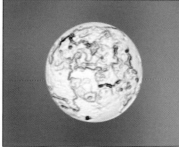

GOTCHA

Crossed Wires

Collapsing Transformations and Continuous Rasterization (Chapter 20) rewires the rendering order.

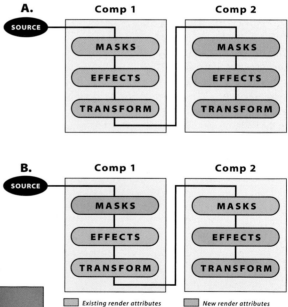

By nesting Comp 1 into Comp 2 (A, above), you'll have two render orders to work with and can pick and choose which attributes render in what order. By applying the Find Edges effect in the first comp and the Mask in the second comp (B), the default rendering order is reversed and the ugly edge is gone (left). In this case, animate transformations in Comp 2 (after the mask).

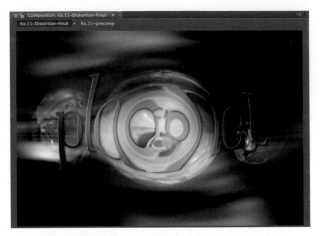

In **[Ex.11_precomp]**, a variety of layers including an animated title were composited. This was nested in **[Ex.11-Final]** where the CC Flo Motion effect was applied (above).

In **[Ex.12]**, we applied the regular Drop Shadow and Bevel Alpha effects to the globe on the left, and the equivalent Layer Styles to the globe on the right. Note that the Layer Styles light source remains consistent when the layer is rotated.

In **[Ex.13b]**, we placed the Transform effect before Drop Shadow.

Manipulating the Rendering Order

Creating a successful effect in After Effects often comes down to working around the rendering order, so that you are not constrained by the default order of Masks > Effects > Transform. Let's look at a few examples of how you can manipulate the render order to your advantage:

- One approach to distortion effects is using them to create "distortion fields" that objects are animated through. To do this, set up an animation in one comp. Nest this into a second comp and apply the distort effect of your choice to the nested layer. An example of this chain is demonstrated in [**Ex.11**]: The result is that the title appears to move through the distortion field created with Effect > Distort > CC Flo Motion.

- Effects that have a directional light source – such as Drop Shadow and Bevel Alpha – appear to behave oddly when the layer is also rotated. This is because rotation renders after effects, so the "light source" casting the shadow or creating the bevel appears to rotate around. While you can solve this by rotating in Comp 1 and applying the effect in Comp 2, you might find that applying Layer Styles is an easier solution. Besides offering some useful drop shadow, glow and bevel looks, Layer Styles (covered in Chapter 22) also offer the benefit of rendering after transformations, so they stay put when you rotate the layer, as demonstrated in [**Ex.12**].

- Another workaround for getting transformations to render before effects is to use Effect > Distort > Transform, which is capable of doing all the same tricks – and more – of the regular Transform properties. To give you an example of why this is so useful, comp [**Ex.13a**] uses regular Rotation keyframes: The light source appears to revolve around the object as the object rotates. In [**Ex.13b**], we instead animated the Rotation parameter in the Transform effect, and made sure it was placed before the Drop Shadow effect (see figure to the left). This thwarts the normal rendering order and fixes the rotating shadow problem all in one comp.

Problem Solving

At this point, we hope you're feeling pretty confident that you can troubleshoot visual problems in After Effects, armed with the knowledge that:

• Visual problems are often due to the rendering order of Masks > Effects > Transform, not user error.

• The answer to these problems is often to create the effect across two comps. If you think the problem can be solved by swapping a transform property with an effect, try using Layer Styles or the Transform effect instead.

We've shown how to solve a few common problems, but there are many others that will crop up in the course of a job. Instead of trying to show an example of every possible scenario we can think of, we'd rather arm you with the tools to troubleshoot *any* situation where you believe swapping attributes will help:

Step 1: DON'T PANIC, and Save your project.

Step 2: Get specific. Exactly which two properties are clashing? Until you narrow it down, you can't fix it. Consider [Ex.13a] in the previous section: The problem was not that "the drop shadow looks funny…" but that "the shadow is being affected by rotation."

Step 3: Note what order these properties are in now; it might even help to jot it down on paper: *1=Drop Shadow, 2=Rotation.*

Step 4: Reverse this order: *1=Rotation, 2=Drop Shadow.* This is your blueprint for fixing the problem. If you can solve the problem with Layer Styles or the Transform effect, use them. Otherwise, use the blueprint as a guide for what event needs to occur in the first comp, and what attributes need to be applied in the second comp. (If you slip up, File > Revert and try again.)

Remember that it's all too easy to identify the problem correctly, create two comps – and then re-create the problem! You must *reorder* the two properties that don't work in the current rendering order to actually fix the problem.

The Best Laid Plans

In this chapter, we've concentrated on building a chain of comps by nesting, which does entail some planning on your part. Of course, it's not always possible to preplan the perfect hierarchy, as the moment inspiration hits will dictate how comps are created and layers grouped.

When an additional comp needs to be added in the middle of the hierarchy (perhaps to fix a render order issue), you can create a new comp and shuffle things around and relink the chain. But the Precompose feature covered in the next chapter is designed specifically for adding comps in the middle of a hierarchy. It is a bit less intuitive than nesting, though, so we suggest you get a firm grip on nesting before moving on.

A Better "Pan Behind"

In Chapter 10 we discussed the ability of the Pan Behind tool to move an image inside a mask shape in the Comp panel. When we need to make a layer appear to pan "inside" or "behind" a stationary mask, we prefer to use nested comps. This is shown in [Ex.14]; the first comp of the chain contains the animation of the panning layer. It is then nested in a second comp, where it is masked and positioned. (This way, you can change the position or the panning motion independently, without one affecting the other. Using the Pan Behind tool, they are linked.)

If you just need a rectangular mask shape with no feathered edge, you don't even need to use a mask: Instead, let the size of the first comp (where the panning takes place) crop the image down to size. Then nest this comp in the second comp. This chain is demonstrated in [Ex.15].

CONNECT

Anchor point: Chapter 3.

Layer management essentials: Chapter 6.

Masking, Pan Behind tool: Chapter 10.

Parenting: Chapter 17.

Building a hierarchy of comps also comes up when working with track mattes (Chapter 11), and stencils (Chapter 12).

Collapsing transformations and continuous rasterization: Chapter 20.

Applying effects: Chapter 22

Interpret Footage dialog: Chapter 38.

Prerendering and proxies: Chapter 44.

Precomposing

Continuing our tour of After Effects' rendering order, we prove that precomposing is easy once you know how...

I n the previous chapter, we used nesting to group layers and fix visual problems caused by the default 2D render order. You'll find that nesting is an intuitive way to create a chain of comps when you're planning ahead. However, predicting exactly how many comps will be needed to build an animation is difficult; you may need to insert a comp in the middle of an existing hierarchy. That's where precomposing comes in.

We recommend that you complete Chapter 17 (*Parenting Skills*) and Chapter 18 (*Nesting Compositions*) before diving into precomposing so you'll be better able to compare the different approaches to grouping layers and solving render order problems. Once you're comfortable nesting and precomposing 2D layers, Chapter 20 (*Collapsing Transformations*) offers more advanced techniques for managing a hierarchy of comps, whether they include 2D or 3D layers.

You can learn many techniques by simply reading the words and looking at figures; precomposing isn't one of those. We suggest you either create some examples of your own or use our **19-Example project.aep**.

Precompose for Grouping

Precompose is used primarily for the same reasons you would use nesting – grouping layers and manipulating the rendering order. The difference is that nesting implies moving up the hierarchy; when you precompose, you're inserting an intermediate comp lower down in an existing hierarchy. You could think of it almost as nesting backward: The precomp created is always rendered first, before the original comp.

In this chapter's example comp [**Ex.01-Spheres_starter**], we've created a design with three spheres, a background, and a title. Let's say it's not until this point that you decide the three spheres should animate as a group (or have an effect applied to them as a group). It's a bit too late to nest, as you would bring the title and background along, so stand by to precompose:

Step 1: Select the three sphere layers (layers 2, 3, and 4), then select Layer > Pre-compose.

Step 2: In the Pre-compose dialog, give the new composition a useful name, such as "**Spheres Trio**". (Note that when multiple layers are select-

TIP

3D Exceptions

If you're nesting and precomposing 3D layers, refer also to Chapters 13 and 20 for how to manage 3D layers across a hierarchy of comps.

Example Project

Explore the 19-Example Project.aep file as you read this chapter; references to [Ex.##] refer to specific compositions within the project file.

ed, Move All Attributes is the only option available; more on this later.) Make sure the Open New Composition switch is *un*checked for now, and click OK.

Step 3: The three spheres will be replaced with one layer, a nested comp called **Spheres Trio**. You can now animate or apply effects to the spheres as a group; you can also trim or apply a blending mode or mask to the spheres as a group.

Just as with nesting compositions, all layers remain "live" for further editing. Simply double-click a nested comp layer to open it for further editing. You can switch back and forth between the precomp and the original comp using the tabs in the Timeline panel or by using the Composition Navigator (covered in Chapter 18). Note that if you need to open the Layer panel, Option+double-click on Mac (Alt+double-click on Windows) the nested comp layer.

The new precomp appears in the Project panel in the same folder as the original comp, and as far as After Effects is concerned, the hierarchy is the same chain you would have created by nesting if you had planned ahead. The precomp is rendered first, so any changes you make in the precomp will ripple up to the original comp. Another way to look at it is that the original comp is now the *second* comp in the chain. Check our **[Ex.01-Result]** folder if you want to compare your result with ours.

Step 1: Select the three sphere layers you wish to group (above), then select Layer > Pre-compose. After precomposing, the three layers will appear as one layer in the original comp (below). Background courtesy Artbeats/Digital Moods.

Precompose Options

Precomposing a single layer is used to solve the same sorts of often-unforeseen rendering order problems we looked at in the previous chapter. The solution to problems with the default rendering order is to reverse the order of some events by spreading the layer across two comps, so you can pick and choose which step happens in which comp. If there's only one layer in the current comp, you have the choice to either nest the current comp in a second comp, or to precompose the layer. If there are other layers in the comp, precomposing is your best option to rearrange the hierarchy, as nesting would bring all other layers along for the ride.

The Pre-compose dialog offers two options: *Leave all attributes in "current comp"*, or *Move all attributes to the new composition*. Attributes refers to the values and keyframes for masks, effects, transformations, blending modes, layer styles, trimming, and so on. For a single layer, both options are available.

TIP

Opening a Tab

Check the Open New Composition switch in the Pre-compose dialog to add the precomp as a tab in the Timeline panel and bring the precomp forward when you precompose.

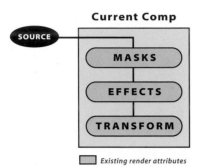

Current Comp

The basic default render order – Masks, Effects, Transform – is also spelled out in the Timeline panel.

To compare the results of each option, we've set up two example comps for you to practice on:

Option #1: Leave All Attributes

Select Close All from the Comp Viewer menu to close all open comps. Open the [**Ex.02-Option #1_starter**] comp. The **CD_planet_loop.mov** layer has attributes that include a Mask, a Find Edges effect, and Position keyframes. (Twirl the layer down if these are not visible.)

Step 1: Select the layer and precompose it, using the shortcut Command+Shift+C (Control+Shift+C). Name the new comp **Precomp with #1**. Be sure to select the *first* option, "Leave all attributes in [this comp]". The Open New Composition button should be *un*checked for now. Click OK and the layer will be precomposed.

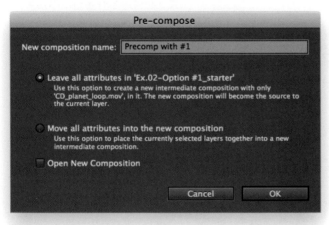

Selecting the first precompose option – Leave All Attributes – moves just the source of the layer into a comp of its own, leaving all masks, effects, and transformations in the original comp.

Step 2: The [**Ex.02-Option #1_starter**] comp should still be forward, but the layer's master twirly in the Timeline panel has rolled up. With the layer still selected, press UU (two Us in quick succession) to twirl down all changed properties, then Shift+E to also twirl down effects. Notice that the mask, effects, and transformation attributes remain in the original composition.

Step 3: Double-click the nested layer to open the new precomp, and notice that the size of the comp matches the **CD_planet_loop.mov** source (200×200 pixels), and it has the same duration (06:00). If you got lost, check out our version in the [**Ex.02-Result**] folder.

To summarize what happens when you use Option #1, Leave All Attributes:

• Option #1 is available for single layers only, including nested comps.

• After you precompose, the precomp will have one layer in it, and the size and duration of the precomp will be the same size and duration *as the original layer*.

• Any attributes (masks, effects, transformations, blending modes, trimming, and so on) applied to the layer before you precompose will remain in the *original comp*.

• The precomp will have a fresh render order, and any attributes applied to the layer in the new precomp will render *before* the attributes in the original comp.

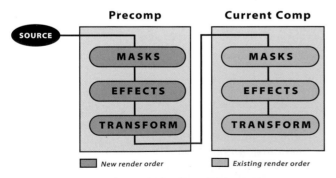

The result of precomposing is that you now have two full sets of attributes for the original source. By using the Leave All Attributes option, the existing attributes stayed in the original comp.

Option #2: Move All Attributes

Select Close All from the Comp Viewer menu. Open the next example comp, [**Ex.03-Option #2_starter**]. This is exactly the same animation as our [**Ex.02-Option #1_starter**] comp: The **CD_planet** movie has attributes that include a mask, a Find Edges effect, and Position keyframes.

Step 1: Select the **CD_planet** layer and precompose, using the shortcut Command+Shift+C (Control+Shift+C). Name the new comp "**Precomp with #2**". Be sure to choose the *second* option, "Move all attributes into the new composition". This time, turn on the Open New Composition checkbox (this will bring the precomp forward and add it as tabbed panels). Click OK.

Step 2: You should now have two tabs available in the Timeline – the original comp and the new precomp, with the precomp forward and the layer deselected. The layer's master twirly is rolled up, so select the layer and press UU and Shift+E – the existing attributes have been moved to the precomp. Notice that the size and duration of the precomp matches the original comp (720×486, 08:00 duration), not the source.

Step 3: Click on the tab for the [**Ex.03-Option #2_starter**] comp to bring the original comp forward. Twirl down this layer; this is a fresh render order (no mask or effects are applied, and the Transform properties are set to their defaults). Just as with Option #1, the precomp is rendered first, and its result is sent to the original comp for further processing.

(If you get lost along the way, check out our version in the [**Ex.03-Result**] folder.)

When you precompose multiple layers, only the second option, Move All Attributes, is available because the relationship between the layers can be maintained only if their attributes are kept intact. The layers that are precomposed will appear as one layer in the original comp so you can animate and effect them as a group, as in our spheres example earlier in the chapter.

To summarize Option #2, "Move All Attributes":

• Option #2 is available for both single layers and multiple layers, including nested comps.

• The precomp will be the same size and duration *as the original comp.*

• Any attributes (masks, effects, transformations, blending modes, trimming, and so on) applied to the layer(s) before precomposing will be moved to the *precomp.*

• The layer in the *original* comp will have a fresh render order, and any attributes applied to this layer will render *after* the attributes in the precomp.

The second option in the Pre-compose dialog – Move All Attributes – creates a new comp the same size and duration as the current one, with the selected layer(s) and all its attributes moved into the new comp.

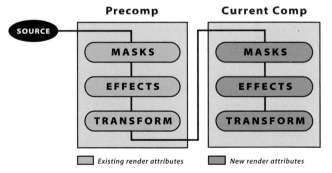

As before, the result of precomposing is that you now have two full sets of attributes for the original source. The main difference is that if you use the Move All Attributes option, the existing attributes have been copied into the new comp, and they are reset in the original comp.

Fixing Render Order Problems

When you precompose a single layer to fix a problem with the default render order, the option you choose depends on the problem and the solution you've devised to fix it. Let's run through one example.

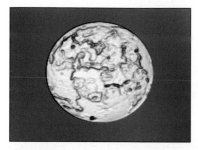

Select Close All from the Comp Viewer menu and open example [**Ex.04-Planet+BG_starter**]. You'll recognize this as the same rendering order problem we saw in [**Ex.10**] in the previous chapter: The planet image has a circular mask applied, but the Find Edges effect is finding the edge of the mask, resulting in a dark line around the edge. This, of course, is due to the default render order (Masks > Effects > Transform), which dictates that masks are rendered first, followed by effects. We have also composited the planet movie using the Hard Light mode and animated it with Position keyframes, just to make life more interesting.

We've created an animation and composite, with one rendering order problem: The fact that masking occurs before effects means that the Find Edges effect is finding the edge of our mask, which is not what we wanted.

Adjusted Rendering Order

Adjustment Layers (discussed in Chapter 22) can also fix render order problems by applying effects after all other attributes are calculated for the layer(s) below. (This is not a solution, obviously, if you have background layers that should remain uneffected.)

If we had foreseen this problem, we would have created a comp for the planet movie, with just Find Edges applied, nested it in a second comp, and added the mask there. Luckily, precompose allows us to fix this problem after the fact. As we saw above, precompose will spread a single layer over two comps. However, no matter which precompose option you choose, remember that the current render order remains *intact* – the mask will still render before any effects; it's just a matter of whether this all happens in the original comp or in the precomp. It's important to remember that neither precompose option will reverse the order of events and fix your problem *automatically*.

However, since both precompose options expand the layer across two comps, each with its own render order, *you'll have the opportunity to copy and paste attributes from one comp to the other*. In this case, so long as you end up with the Find Edges effect rendering first in the precomp, and the mask rendering in the original (now second) comp, it might not matter how you get there. So this is the question to ask before precomposing a single layer: Is there any advantage to having the current render order happen first or second? This will determine which precompose option you should favor.

Fixing the Edge

For fixing most render order problems with a single layer, we would usually pick the first option, Leave All Attributes. Since a layer's attributes include blending modes, which need to interact with layers below, we don't want to bury modes in the precomp. It's also more convenient to keep as many of the keyframes as possible in the final comp so that keyframes can be easily synchronized with other layers. So let's fix the ugly edge problem using Option #1:

Step 1: In the [**Ex.04-Planet+BG_starter**] comp, select the **CD_planet_loop.mov** layer, and Layer > Pre-compose. Name the new comp "**Planet_precomp**", and select Option #1, Leave All Attributes. Uncheck the Open New Composition switch, and click OK. The original comp should still be forward, and the movie layer will be replaced with a nested comp layer. All the original attributes remain in the current comp.

Step 2: With the nested comp layer selected, choose Layer > Effect Controls (shortcut: F3). Click on the name of the Find Edges effect (if not already highlighted) and press Command+X (Control+X) or select Edit > Cut.

Step 3: Now let's paste the effect to the image in the precomp. Double-click the nested comp layer to open the precomp. This precomp is a 200×200 comp, with just the **CD_planet_loop.mov** layer in it. Select the movie and paste (Edit > Paste) the Find Edges effect. Remember that this precomp will render first, before the original comp.

Step 4: Return to the [**Ex.04-Planet+BG_starter**] comp, and press UU to twirl down properties that have been changed from their original values. The mask you see here renders after Find Edges, and the ugly outline is gone. This comp has no knowledge of any effect in any earlier comp; it simply applies a circular mask to the 200×200 pixel image it receives from the precomp (note that the mask fits as before because the precomp and the movie are the same size). The blending modes and Position keyframes remain in the original comp and work as expected. Check our results in the [**Ex.04-Result**] folder if you got lost.

And what of Option #2? (We encourage you to try it out; we've repeated the starter comp in the [**Ex.04_why not try Option #2**] folder.) If you had instead used the Move All Attributes option when you precomposed, the existing render order would move down to the precomp. The first thing you would notice is that the Hard Light mode no longer works, as it's applied in the precomp where it has no effect (since there are no layers underneath). The original 200×200 planet layer would be replaced by a nested comp layer that's the same size as the original comp, 720×486. In order for the mask to render after the Find Edges effect, you would need to cut the Mask Shape from the precomp and paste it back to the layer in the original comp.

The problem with this method is that the mask was created to fit a specific layer, and when it's pasted to a different size layer, it may end up off center. Plus, the Position keyframes in the precomp are now moving the image *inside* the mask in the second comp. We think you'll agree that in this particular example, Option #1 is the better choice.

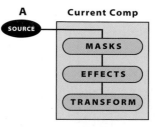

A single layer's render order (A, above) illustrating that the mask is followed by a Find Edges effect, which produces a dark edge which we find undesirable.

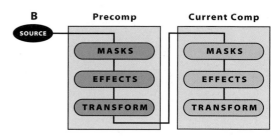

To fix the problem, the layer is selected and precomposed using option #1, Leave All Attributes (B, above). The Find Edges effect is then moved to the layer in the precomp (C, below).

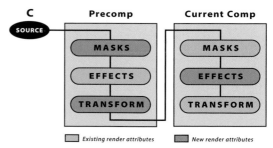

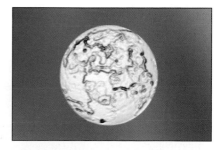

By precomposing and performing the Find Edges in the first comp, we can mask the planet movie cleanly in the second comp.

Fixing a Clipped Layer

Some effects – such as Simulation > Shatter or CC Pixel Polly – can't draw outside the layer's original boundary, and instead are clipped at the layer's edge. Fortunately most effects are now capable of drawing outside the layer's edge, but if you do come across this problem, there are a few workarounds, illustrated in the **[Ex.07]** folder of comps:

The CC Pixel Polly effect cannot render beyond the layer's original boundary, causing clipping problems.

[Ex.07a]: First, check if the effect has a Resize Layer option, as offered by the Radial Shadow effect.

[Ex.07b]: If not, apply Effect > Utility > Grow Bounds and make it the first effect in the stack. Then increase its Pixels parameter until the effect no longer clips.

[Ex.07c]: The third option is to place the layer (or layers) in a precomp; this comp should be whatever size you need the layer to be so that the effect has enough room to draw into. Nest this into a second comp and apply the effect. The effect will think that the layer is as large as the precomp. If the effect still clips, return to the precomp and increase its size. This method also allows you to animate the layer(s) in the precomp (this animation renders before the effect).

Trimming Out Empty Calories

One of the drawbacks to precomposing using Option #2, Move All Attributes, is that layers shorter than the current comp end up appearing longer when they're precomposed. To show you what we mean:

Step 1: Select Close All from the Comp Viewer menu, and open the **[Ex.05-Short Layers_starter]** comp. This comp is 10 seconds long. The three sphere layers are shorter than the full duration.

Step 2: Scrub along the Timeline to get a sense of the animation. The first sphere fades up starting at 01:00, followed by the other two spheres staggered later in time. The three sphere layers are trimmed out at 08:00. The beginning and end of the comp have no spheres visible.

Step 3: Let's say you want to rotate and fade out the three spheres as a group. Select the three spheres and precompose. Since you have selected more than one layer, your only choice will be Option #2 – Move All Attributes. Uncheck the Open New Composition switch, and click OK.

Step 4: The original comp should now be forward, and the layer bar for the nested comp appears to extend for the full duration of the comp.

Numbering Precomps

Don't name a precomp with a higher number, as you might do when nesting. If the current comp is Comp 2, the precomp will be inserted between Comp 1 and 2 (so it's a 1.5, not a 3!).

Step 1: Before deciding we needed to precompose the sphere layers, we animated them, slid them along the timeline, and trimmed their in and out points.

But scrub along the Timeline, and you'll see that the spheres are visible only between 01:00 and 08:00 seconds, as they were originally. The layer bar is misleading: The first second and last two seconds are "empty calories" (a layer bar with no imagery). This is not a problem – unless you later assume that more frames are available to work with than really exist.

Step 4: When you precompose with the second option (Move All Attributes), the resulting new layer seems to run the full length of the current composition, when in fact the layers in the precomp don't.

Removing Empty Calories by Trimming

An easy way around the misleading layer bar is to immediately trim the precomp layer's in and out points after precomposing, to match the first and last active frames in the precomp. When the empty calories are trimmed, the layer bar provides accurate feedback about which frames are "live." This solution is shown in the [**Ex.05-Result of Trimming**] folder, where we added rotation keyframes and faded the layers out as a group.

Removing Empty Calories by Moving Layers

Another solution involves a few steps but provides an even cleaner result. Close all comps and open the [**Ex.06-Short Layers_starter**] comp:

Step 1: Note where the first sphere layer starts in time (01:00, in this case) and where they end (08:00). Precompose the three spheres again.

Step 2: After precomposing, open the precomp, select all the layers, and drag layer #3 (the first layer in time) to the left so that it starts at 00:00; the other two layers will follow. Extend the out points for all three layer bars to the full length of the comp – you can trim unneeded frames in the original comp.

Step 3: Return to the original comp and move the in point for the nested layer to 01:00 (the original starting point) so that the first sphere starts fading up at 01:00 as it did previously. Trim the out point to 08:00.

The result is that any empty calories are removed from the head. You can also extend the nested comp layer at the tail knowing that the layer bar is not empty. Our results are in the [**Ex.06-Result of Moving**] folder.

Consider trimming the precomposed comp's layer bar to better represent its actual length; adding layer markers (see Chapter 6) helps to remind you which frames are active.

CONNECT

Masking: Chapter 10.

Nesting 2D comps, flowchart view: Chapter 18.

Nesting and precomposing rules for 3D layers: Chapters 13 and 20.

Applying effects, adjustment layers: Chapter 22.

20

Collapsing Transformations

Options for maximizing resolution also rewire the rendering order.

The Collapse Transformations switch in the default Off position (above) is empty; it fills in when it's On (below).

Now that we've discussed nesting and precomposing, we wrap up our focus on After Effects' rendering order by exploring the pros and cons of Collapse Transformations and its cousin, Continuous Rasterization. These powerful features open a door to higher quality and faster rendering, as well as enabling precomps with 3D layers to behave like complex 3D objects when nested. We consider this one of the more advanced concepts, so if you don't get it at first, don't panic. Skip ahead to some of the fun chapters on text, shapes and paint, and revisit Collapse Transformations when you feel more comfortable building hierarchies by nesting and precomposing.

Resolution Lost

If you've been with us for the previous two chapters, you know that After Effects renders in a series of discrete steps. The order of these steps is predetermined, so the order in which *you* apply effects and transformations is largely irrelevant. You're probably also aware that when a layer is set to Best Quality, After Effects antialiases it when an effect is applied that distorts pixels as well as when the Transform properties (position, scale, rotation, anchor point, and motion blur) are calculated. Each time a layer is antialiased, pixels are altered and the image appears slightly softer. However, if you change your mind about how a layer is effected or transformed, at least these values are reapplied to the original source, so the image is not degraded with every edit.

The ability to re-edit a layer while maintaining its original resolution can be lost when you start building a hierarchy of comps. When Comp 1 is nested in Comp 2, the nested comp is "rendered": Effects and transformations are applied to each layer, which are antialiased if necessary, and all layers in Comp 1 are composited together. Comp 2 receives *only* the composited frame (a "flattened" image) and has no history of the layers in the first comp.

At least, that's how it works if you don't know about the Collapse Transformations switch. This feature allows you to perform two sets of transformations without a loss in quality – the downside being a potential loss in sanity. Read on…

Example Project

Explore the 20-Example Project.aep file as you read this chapter; references to [Ex.##] refer to specific compositions within the project file.

In Comp 1, the image is scaled down to 10% and reduced to just a few pixels.

Then it's nested in Comp 2 and scaled 1000% for a truly ugly result.

However, when the Collapse switch is turned on, the original resolution from Comp 1 is restored, as the two Scale values are calculated in one step (10% × 1000% = 100%). Alarm clock from Classic PIO/Sampler.

Collapsing 101

At its simplest, Collapse Transformations allows you to scale a layer in one comp, scale it again in a second comp, and retain the same sharpness and resolution as it would have if you had scaled it just once.

In the **20-Example Project.aep** file, open the [**Scaling-1**] comp from the [**Ex.01**] folder. The **CP_AlarmClock** image is scaled down to 10%, where it's roughly 60 pixels wide. This comp is nested in [**Scaling-2**], where it's scaled back up 1000%. Open this second comp; select the nested comp layer and press S to twirl down Scale. The small image is blown up ten times – and looks as ugly as you might expect. The Collapse Transformations switch for the layer in the Timeline panel is set to Off (it appears empty), which is the default setting.

Time for some magic: Turn on the Collapse switch in [**Scaling-2**] for the nested [**Scaling-1**] layer. The lost resolution returns, as the Transform values applied in [**Scaling-2**] are combined with the values applied to each layer in [**Scaling-1**]. A calculator will tell you that 10% times 1000% equals the original value of 100%. Of course, applying scaling values that result in a value larger than 100% would introduce degradation – you can't improve on the resolution of the original image. (That *would* be magic…)

If you prefer to work in a square pixel composition, create your D1 comps at 720×534. Background courtesy Artbeats/Digital Moods.

Collapsing 102

Let's consider another example. Open comp [**Ex.02-D1 720×534**]. In this square pixel comp, you'll find a few animated layers. Some artists prefer to work in square pixels so round images and titles do not look distorted. But the D1 720×486 background movie needs to be scaled up to fit the comp size, which means this layer is degraded slightly.

To render the final movie, this comp is nested into [**Ex.02-D1 Final**], which is a non-square pixel 720×486 comp. The nested layer is scaled down to fit the D1 comp size. Normally, scaling this layer would add another antialiasing step, which would degrade the image. By collapsing the nested layer, the scale value of 91% is added to all the scale values in the precomp. Because the images are scaled once, you get better quality and faster rendering. Plus, the background movie is not scaled at all.

Before rendering, nest the square pixel comp into a D1 720×486 non-square pixel comp, and Fit To Comp Size. By collapsing transformations, an extra step of scaling and antialiasing is eliminated.

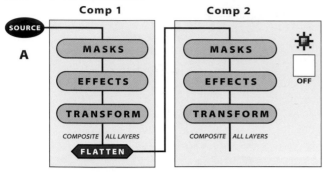

Figure A: With the Collapse switch off, layers in Comp 1 are composited together before flowing through to Comp 2's rendering order of Masks/Effects/Transform.

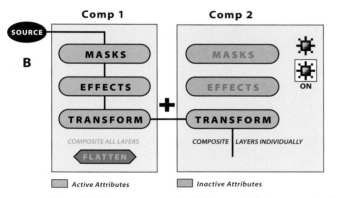

Figure B: When you turn on the Collapse switch in Comp 2 for the nested Comp 1 layer, the Transformations applied in Comp 2 are combined with the values applied to each layer in Comp 1.

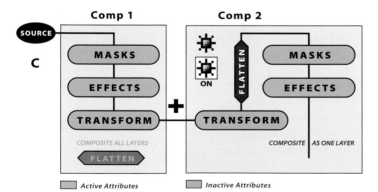

Figure C: When you turn on the Collapse switch in Comp 2 for the nested Comp 1 layer, *and* you apply a Mask or Effect to the nested layer, first the Transformations applied in Comp 2 are combined with the values applied to each layer in Comp 1. Then all the layers in Comp 1 are "flattened" or composited together. The Masks and/or Effects applied in Comp 2 are then applied to this flattened result.

Under the Hood

As we noted in the introduction to this chapter, Collapse Transformations rewires the rendering order After Effects follows when it is processing layers. Understanding what is going on inside After Effects is the secret to not being caught off guard when you engage the Collapse Transformations switch.

Under normal circumstances, After Effects processes the masks applied to a layer, followed by the effects, followed by the transformations. If you mask a layer, then apply an effect such as Perspective > Drop Shadow, the shadow will fall from the edge of the mask (combined with the layer's original alpha channel). If you then scale the layer down to 50%, the size of the mask and shadow will both be scaled 50% as well; rotate the layer, and the direction of the shadow will rotate.

Explore [Ex.03a] and note how the scale and rotation keyframes affects the vertical mask feather amount and the drop shadow parameters.

Figure A: If a number of layers reside in a precomp, they are composited together, resulting in a single 2D layer, the same size as the precomp. This result is then passed onto the next comp in the chain, where it is treated just like any other footage item. Once it's nested in this second comp, you can apply another set of masks, effects, and transformations to it, and these additional alterations will be applied in that same order.

When Collapse Transformations is enabled for a nested composition, *and nothing else is done to this collapsed layer*, After Effects essentially reaches back into the nested comp and brings all of those layers into the current comp – virtually placing them in the layer stack in the Timeline panel almost as if you copied them and pasted them in place of the nested comp's layer. If any of those layers had a blending mode applied, it would apply to all the layers underneath it in the current comp. Same goes if one of those layers was an adjustment layer or a stencil: It would treat all the layers underneath the collapsed composition as if everyone was in the same comp. (More on these features later in this chapter.)

Figure B: If you alter the transformations of the collapsed nested comp (for example, give it a Scale value other than 100%), After Effects combines these transformations with the transformations applied to each individual layer, and then performs one combined transformation on each layer, preserving quality and saving rendering time.

This is why in the earlier examples we could scale down a layer in a nested comp, then scale this comp back up again without any issues with aliasing and other ugliness. In [Ex.01], After Effects figured out internally that 10% × 1000% meant to scale the alarm clock once by 100%. In [Ex.02], After Effects scaled each sphere by 36.4% (the combination of 40% × 91%). In both cases, the combined scale was 100% or less, meaning we avoided the quality degradation that normally occurs when you scale a layer by more than 100%.

Figure C: Life gets considerably more complex when you apply a mask or effect to the collapsed nested composition. In this case, it becomes apparent that the rendering order for the collapsed comp's layer is actually wired differently than for a normal layer: Transformations are applied *first*, followed by masks and effects. After Effects performs the combined transformations as above (maintaining quality), but then it will composite ("flatten") all the layers inside the collapsed nested comp into one resulting layer, just as if you had nested the comp normally. The masks and effects are then calculated as with any other layer.

This rewired order has big implications for effects. Open [Ex.03b] where the TV layer has been replaced with a precomp that contains the TV. The layer is scaled and rotated as in [Ex.03a], and the layer has Collapse Transformations enabled. Scrub through the timeline and note that the drop shadow does not change apparent distance or direction; this is because it is now rendering after transformations. (In this case, it's actually a good thing that the direction is not animating!)

We've used a mask to crop off the bottom of the TV and applied a vertical mask feather to fade it out. Note that After Effects makes the vector-based mask paths behave normally: They scale and rotate along with the collapsed layer. The Mask Feather, however, is now calculated *after* transformations, and so does not rotate with the layer as desired.

This intermediate flattening also has huge implications for blending modes, adjustment layers, stencils, and 3D space: They are no longer passed onto the other layers that are in the same comp as the collapsed precomp. In other words, if you apply a mask or effect to a collapsed precomp, it behaves almost exactly like an uncollapsed precomp, with the exception that the transforms have been calculated together. In the next few pages, we'll explore these and other implications.

FACTOID

Concatenation

Some refer to the process of combining multiple transforms into a single step as "concatenation" of transformations.

In **[Ex.03b]**, if the Collapse switch is off, the drop shadow effect is scaled and rotated along with the nested layer. TV courtesy Paul Sherstobitoff.

In **[Ex.03b]**, if the Collapse switch is on, the Drop Shadow effect is not scaled or rotated, as it is calculated after transformations. While the Mask Path renders normally, the vertical Mask Feather (where the red arrow is pointing) animates oddly as it's calculated after rotation. Toggle the Collapse switch off and on again for the nested comp to compare the differences.

Problems and Opportunities

When you enable Collapse Transformations, the image is probably going to change. Sometimes this change will present new artistic opportunities; other times it will thwart your vision. Let's review a number of examples of how Collapsing can change your world…

Trial Run

If your animation relies on being able to collapse transformations (perhaps for an infinite zoom effect, along the lines of the classic "powers of ten" animation), do a trial run with dummy sources to confirm that the hierarchy will work as planned.

The Pasteboard

Once a layer's Masks, Effects, and Transform have been calculated, the rendering order includes a step we'll call "crop to current comp size" in which any pixels that end up on the comp's pasteboard are trimmed. After this stage, the layer is composited with other layers using blending modes, opacity, and track mattes.

[**Ex.04-Pasteboard-1**] has a large image panning across a 300×200 size comp. This is nested into [**Ex.04-Pasteboard-2**]. In this second comp, if you turn on Collapse Transformations, any pixels that spill onto the pasteboard in the first comp magically reappear outside the layer's boundary handles.

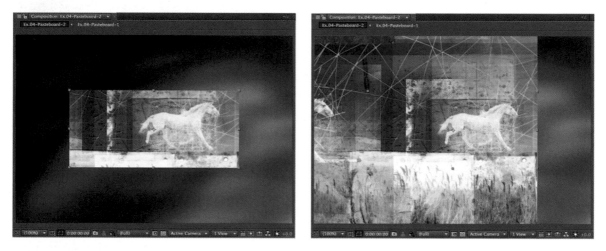

With collapse off (left), the image area outside the layer boundary handles is cropped by being on the pasteboard in the precomp, but collapsing the nested layer (below) reveals this area (right). Inset image from Digital Vision/Inner Gaze. Background courtesy Artbeats/Liquid Ambience.

If you need to collapse a comp and the excess imagery is a problem, you can mask it out. Select the collapsed layer and use Layer > Mask > New Mask to create a full-frame mask that will crop out the excess imagery. However, remember that this will flatten the layers before the mask is applied (as explained in Figure C on the previous page).

You could also use a track matte (Chapter 11) to crop any problematic layer in the precomp to the size of that comp. Create a full-frame solid as your track matte (use Layer > New > Solid, and click on the Make Comp Size button) and use this solid as an alpha track matte to crop the layer. Duplicate the solid and use it to matte other layers as needed.

Don't use a full-frame stencil in the precomp to crop layers, because collapsing in the top comp will bring this stencil forward, cropping any layers below (stencils are covered later in this chapter).

Blending Modes

When Collapse Transformations is enabled, blending modes applied to layers in the nested comp will be passed through to the current comp. This is usually a good thing, as you can group layers in a precomp for animation purposes and still have their individual blending modes apply through to the background layer(s) in the second comp.

As an example, in [Ex.05-Modes-1] the baseball layer is set to Screen mode and the clock layer is set to Overlay mode (it appears to have no effect, as there are no layers below to interact with). In the second comp, [Ex.05-Modes-2], turn on Collapse Transformations, and the modes from the first comp will react with the background in the second comp.

As soon as you apply a mask or effect to the collapsed comp, the blending modes in the nested comp are calculated only in that comp and do not pass through. Observe this by adding Effect > Blur & Sharpen > Fast Blur to the collapsed layer in [Ex.05-Modes-2]; the individual modes are not honored because the nested layer was flattened before the effect was applied (as shown earlier in Figure C). However, you will be able to select a single blending mode for the collapsed comp layer. Press F4 to toggle the Switches/Modes column to Modes if not already visible, and select Overlay mode for the [Ex.05-Modes-2] layer.

In the second comp, the modes don't come through with collapse off (above), but with collapse on, the images interact with layers underneath (below).

Motion Blur and Quality

After Effects does not give you a master Quality or Motion Blur switch for a collapsed nested comp that does not have masks or effects applied. Instead, it looks to the settings of these switches for each layer in the collapsed comp to determine how to process them.

Step 1: Open **[Ex.06a]**, which contains three spheres buzzing around (RAM Preview to verify their motion). In the Switches column, note that the Motion Blur switch has been enabled for layers 1 and 2, but not layer 3. Toggle on the Enable Motion Blur switch (along the top of the Timeline panel), and you will see that two of the three spheres are very blurred. Type Command+K (Control+K) and click on the Advanced tab; this comp's Shutter Angle has been set to 720°, which is quite high.

Step 2: Now open **[Ex.06b]**. It contains **[Ex.06a]**, scaled 200% and with added rotation. All three layers look fuzzy – not from motion blur, but because they've been scaled up too much. Enable the Collapse Transformations switch, and now they will be sharp.

Step 3: When you enabled the Collapse switch, bars appeared for the Quality and Motion Blur switches, as well as the T switch and Blending Modes popup. Click on them; nothing happens. But motion blur is still being passed through: Click on the comp's Enable Motion Blur switch, and two of the three spheres will be blurred, but less so. Type Command+K (Control+K) and click on the Advanced tab; note this comp has a much smaller Shutter Angle (180°). When collapsing, the master comp's Shutter Angle and Phase are used.

Note that although rotation has been added in the second comp, the additional "spin" motion blur is added only to the layers that have their motion blur switch enabled in the first comp.

Step 4: Now apply a mask or effect to the collapsed layer. The Motion Blur switch becomes enabled again – but even if you turn on the Motion Blur switch, it will impact only masks and effects applied to this layer, not Transformations!

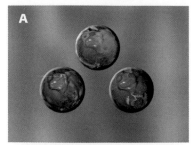

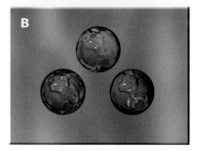

If you beveled the spheres with an adjustment layer in a previous comp, just the spheres would get the bevel (A). However, if you now collapse the nested comp layer, the underlying layers in the second comp get the effect of the Adjustment Layer – not quite what you intended (B).

Adjustment Layers

Another surprise awaits when you collapse a nested comp while the nested comp has an adjustment layer applied. In [**Ex.07-AdjustLayer-1**], our now infamous three spheres have an adjustment layer with the Bevel Alpha effect applied to it. The Bevel Alpha affects all layers below, after the spheres have been composited together.

When this comp is nested in [**Ex.07-AdjustLayer-2**], notice the result when you use Collapse Transformations. Effects applied as adjustment layers in the first comp now affect all layers below in the second comp. This behavior can be useful for applying common effects, such as color correction or noise, to multiple compositions simultaneously.

Applying a mask or effect to the collapsed nested layer will break this behavior, restricting the adjustment layer again to only affect the layers in its own comp. Another approach would be dispensing with the adjustment layer altogether, and applying the same effects to the collapsed layer instead. This is demonstrated in [**Ex.07alt**].

Opacity and Fade-Outs

When you use Opacity to fade down multiple layers at the same time, you end up with a "staggered" fade-out: As each layer fades, it reveals the layers below, which are also fading. Study [**Ex.08-Fade Out Staggers**] during the fade from 03:00 to 05:00, and note how messy it looks when each layer is semitransparent.

Normally, there are two solutions: Nest the comp with the images into another, and fade the nested comp (as in [**Ex.08a**]), or apply an adjustment layer above the images and use the Transform effect's Opacity parameter to fade out the composite of all the layers underneath. However, both of these solutions break if you nest the image comp into another and enable

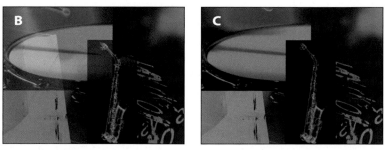

When you're fading a stack of layers (A), you don't want each one to become semitransparent (B). The solution is to fade a nested comp of these layers (C). Background from Digital Vision/Naked & Scared; drumming courtesy Lee Stranahan.

Collapse Transformations: Any Opacity keyframes applied to a collapsed nested comp are passed through to the individual layers (try this with [**Ex.08a-Opacity Fade**]), and as we've seen above, adjustment layers have unintended effects on layers in the master comp.

If you need to collapse the nested layer, one solution is to combine the two techniques: Nest the first comp, apply Effect > Distort > Transform to it, then keyframe the effect's Opacity parameter rather than the layer's own Opacity (as shown in [**Ex.08b-Transform Fade**]).

Nested Switches

In After Effects, some layer switches behave *recursively*, which means that changing their status in one comp changes the switch in the current comp and all nested comps. Switches that behave this way include the comp-wide switches Resolution*, Enable Motion Blur, Enable Frame Blending, Live Update, and Draft 3D, plus the Quality switch for the layer that represents a nested comp.

Whether switches are recursive depends on how the Switches Affect Nested Comps preference is set (Preferences > General). The preference is enabled by default – if it's off right now, turn it on for the following example.

In most cases, recursiveness is a good thing. For instance, if you change the current comp's resolution from Full to Half to save render time, you would want all nested comps to also change to Half so they're not wasting time processing a high-quality image. Close any open comps. Select the three example comps in the **[Ex.09-Recursive Switches]** folder, double-click to open all three, and check them out. Bring the final comp, **[Ex.09-Recursive-3]**, forward.

● Change this comp's Resolution from Full to Half – all nested comps change to Half also. You can check this by selecting their tabs in the Timeline panel.

● Change the top layer from Best to Draft Quality – all nested comps change their layers to Draft as well.

* If a precomp is set to Auto Resolution (Chapter 2), changing the top comp's resolution will change the nested comps under the hood. However, if you bring the precomp forward, it will use Auto Resolution.

This trick works because applying an effect flattens the layer, so the Transform effect is fading a single image. You can also force the flattening step by applying any effect, even a dummy effect such as one of the Expression Controls. Then you can fade out the layer using the regular Opacity property (as shown in [Ex.08c-Regular Fade]).

Stencils and Silhouettes

When you use a Stencil blending mode, as in [**Ex.10-Stencil-1**], the stencil will "cut out" all the layers below. When you nest a stencil comp and turn on Collapse Transformations, as in [**Ex.10-Stencil-2**], After Effects treats the stencil as if it were in the same comp as

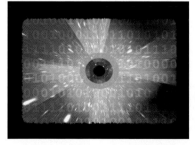

the layer that holds the nested comp. The result is it "reaching through" and stenciling all the layers in the current comp that are below the nested comp. To say the least, this is usually an unintended result. In short, stencils and silhouettes will probably wreak havoc when you turn on the Collapse Transformations switch.

As you might expect by now, applying a mask or effect to the collapsed layer changes this behavior: Stencils and silhouettes will no longer cut through from the nested comp into the higher-level comp. Try this with [**Ex.10-Stencil-2**] after you collapsed the nested layer **Ex.10-Stencil-1**. So if you need to collapse transformations but don't want stencils to pass through, apply a dummy effect (such as one of the Expression Controls).

A stencil was applied in the first comp (left), which cuts out all the underlying layers. When the stencil is composited in a second comp (right), you see the cut-out image over a new background. But if you turn on the Collapse switch for the nested comp, the new background will disappear, cut out by the stencil. Image composite includes Artbeats Starfields and Digidelic.

Collapsed Space

Collapsing also works with 3D layers. This can come in handy when you have a group of layers that need to be treated as a unit: Rather than have them clutter up your timeline, you can precompose them (resulting in one layer in your current comp), then use Collapse Transformations. The result is that they will continue to react to cameras and lights in the original comp. However, there are some gotchas that might not be immediately obvious – such as cameras and lights in the collapsed comp not coming through, and differences based on whether the 3D Layer switch has been set for the collapsed layer.

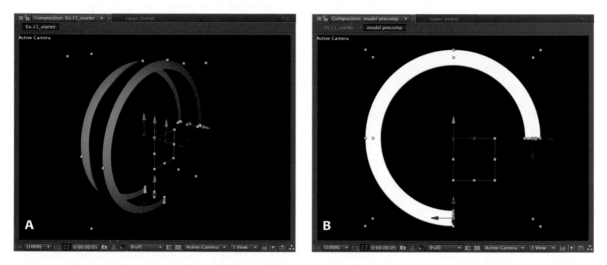

The initial model consists of four white solids and a null object, all in 3D space (A). The purple light provides all the color. When they are precomposed, the precomp renders them with a default camera and no light (B). Enabling the 3D Layer switch for the nested layer allows it to be affected by the main comp's camera and light, but it is still just a 2D composite moving in 3D space (C). Enabling the Collapse Transformations switch brings the 3D coordinates through, with the benefit of just one layer to manage (D).

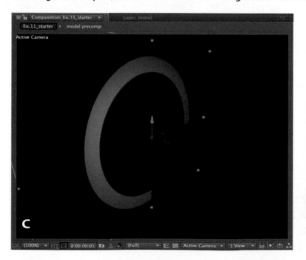
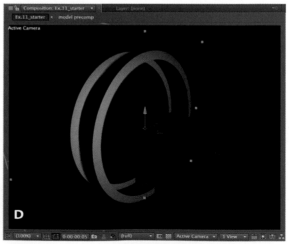

As always, the best way to understand these issues is to work through an example, referring to the figures on the previous page as you work:

Step 1: Open and RAM Preview [**Ex.11_starter**]: It contains a simple 3D "model" built out of four white solids plus a null object, which you may remember from Chapter 17 (*Parenting Skills*). (Figure **A**). It is illuminated by a purple-tinted light, and a camera animates around it. (Toggle off the camera and light to confirm where the perspective and color comes from; turn them back on when done.)

Step 2: Select layers 3 through 7, and select Layer > Pre-compose. Enable the Open New Composition option, enter the name "**model pre-comp**" and click OK. The precomp will open as commanded, yielding a brightly lit head-on view of the model – not the fancy lighting and camera move you had. (Figure **B**). Because

you didn't also precompose the camera and lights, this new precomp uses a default head-on camera view and no special lighting.

Step 2: Select the null object parent and the four model pieces and precompose. Note that the model pieces are made from solids, and have been continuously rasterized (covered later in this chapter) so that they render smoothly at any size.

Step 3: Switch back to [**Ex.11_starter**] – where you left your camera and light – and you get the same stark view. This is unusual, because pre-composing normally doesn't change the image in the main comp. However, the rendered result of a precomp is a flat 2D image, which by default is unaffected by 3D cameras and lights. You can turn on the 3D Layer switch for **model precomp**, but all you will get is a 2D version of your precomp treated by the nice lighting and camera move set up in the original comp. (Figure **C**).

To get back to where you started, turn on the Collapse Transformations switch for **model precomp**. Now you will see the original 3D model in all of its glory, using the camera and light in the current comp. (Figure **D**). Collapsing brings all the 3D geometry in the precomp through to the original comp – think of it as "half-

Step 3: For best results when dealing with a nested comp that includes 3D layers, turn on both the Collapse Transformations and the 3D switch for the nested layer.

baked" – where it now reacts to the original comp's Camera and Light. This is true whether or not the 3D Layer switch is enabled for the pre-comp (enabling the 3D Layer switch allows you to add further 3D transformations to the precomp – see [**Ex.11-final**]).

Discontinuous Space

As with so many of the previous examples using Collapse Transformations, as soon as you apply an effect or mask to the collapsed 3D layer, things change – namely, any interaction between 3D layers in the main comp and the nested comp is broken. The next example demonstrates this.

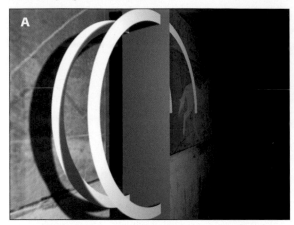

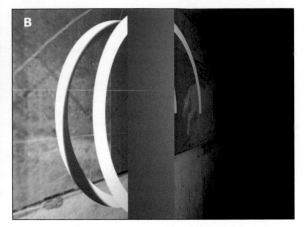

If you collapse a nested comp with 3D layers, they can still cast shadows on other layers in the main comp (A). However, if you apply a mask or effect to the collapsed comp, the rendering order is broken, and shadows can no longer be cast between nested layers and those in the main comp (B). Additionally, intersections are no longer possible between the layers in different comps.

Use the camera button at the bottom of the Comp panel to take a snapshot of the current scene. The button to its right displays the most recent snapshot.

GOTCHA

No Layer Panel?

You cannot open the Layer panel for a layer that has its Collapse Transformations or Continuously Rasterize switch enabled.

Open [**Ex.12_starter**]. This contains a similar arrangement of layers and nested comps as in [**Ex.11-final**], with the nested comp collapsed. Note that we've enabled shadows, which are being cast from the layers in the nested comp onto the 3D background that resides in this comp. Our nested 3D model pieces are also intersecting an additional 3D layer (**vertical bar**) we placed in this comp. Because all three layers are 3D and are adjacent on the timeline, they are rendered as a 3D group and can therefore cast shadows on each other as well as intersect if necessary.

Click the camera button to take a snapshot of the current scene. Then select the layer **model precomp**, and apply Effect > Blur & Sharpen > Fast Blur. Two things happen: The shadow interactions disappear, and the model pieces no longer intersect the layer **vertical bar**. Press the Show Last Snapshot button to compare the "before" snapshot to this result.

As you may remember from the earlier section *Under the Hood*, when you apply a mask or effect to a collapsed nested comp, After Effects flattens the contents of the nested comp into a single layer after the second round of transformations are calculated, but before the new masks or effects are applied. (If you want further proof of this, apply a mask to **model precomp** instead of an effect: You will end up with a masked window into your nested 3D world.)

A collapsed comp with masks or effects applied acts as a "render break" among 3D layers. Fortunately, After Effects passes along the result of the 3D transformations – as well as the current comp's cameras and lights – to the layers in the nested comp, but otherwise the nested comp will behave as a 2D layer stuck in the timeline among your 3D layers. You might to able to get away with applying the effect to each layer in the precomp instead of applying it to the nested comp layer. If not, try to mitigate the damage: Rearrange layers in the timeline so that the nested comp is not in the middle of the 3D group. That way, the other layers in the group will continue to interact with each other correctly. You can also use 2D drop shadow effects. However, you won't be able to fix the lost intersections. There are simply some issues that cannot be resolved when combining nested comps, Collapse Transformations, and 3D space.

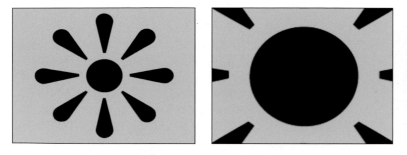

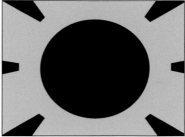

Continuous Rasterization

Continuous rasterization – rendering a vector-based layer at any size requested to maintain maximum sharpness – is closely intertwined with collapse transformations. For one, they share the same switch in the Timeline panel. Additionally, the render order is rewired as transformations are rendered before masks and effects are applied.

Many think of continuous rasterization as "the Illustrator switch" because in earlier versions, that was the only type of footage item it would work on. Now other types of layers (such as solids, PDFs, and SWFs) also have the option to be continuously rasterized, while text and shape layers are *always* continuously rasterized. These files are based on vectors rather than pixels: They have, in essence, infinite resolution. If continuous rasterization is off, they are converted into pixels at their "native" sizes (the document size of an Illustrator file, or the pixel dimensions in the Solid Settings dialog), and they are treated as any other pixel-based layer. If you enable continuous rasterization, the layer's transformations are calculated before it is converted into pixels, meaning its edges always stay sharp no matter what size you scale it to.

To see this in action, open comp [Ex.13] and RAM Preview. It contains an Illustrator file of an asterisk with continuous rasterization disabled (the default), animated from 10% to 300% scale. As it goes over 100%, it starts to get fuzzy: Press the End key to jump to the last frame of the comp and observe what the edges look like. Now enable the Collapse switch (also known as the Continuously Rasterize switch): The edges are rendered sharp again. Better yet, no matter what size you scale the layer, it remains crisp. This is because After Effects is applying the Scale value to the original Illustrator file, *then* converting the larger image to pixels.

Illustrator files are automatically rasterized at 100% scale (left). When they're scaled up to a larger value, such as 300%, they can look pretty soft (center). Enabling continuous rasterization causes them to be re-rasterized at their current scale value, resulting in crisp outlines at any size (right).

TIP

Vector Layers in 3D

When continuously rasterized layers have their 3D Layer switch enabled, they will appear sharp when a camera zooms in close.

When applied to Illustrator layers, the Collapse Transformations switch in the Timeline panel becomes the Continuously Rasterize switch.

Render Order Trickery

Before you think you just got a free lunch, it's worth spending a few moments understanding how the rendering order inside After Effects is being changed to accommodate this sleight of hand, as effects in particular behave differently when layers are continuously rasterized.

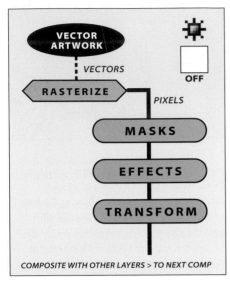

With continuous rasterization off (the default), the Illustrator file is converted to pixels at the source and is then treated like any other bitmap image.

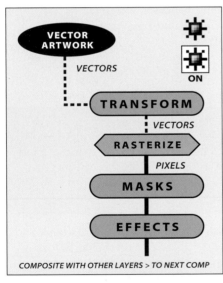

With continuous rasterization turned on, the Transform properties are calculated first, then the file is rasterized before being passed through Masks and Effects.

There are two points in the render order at which a vector-based file can be rasterized, and the Collapse switch toggles between them. When the Collapse switch is off (hollow), the file is rasterized at 100%, then these pixels pass through the regular Masks, Effects, and Transform stages just like any other bitmap image. This render order is shown in our first diagram at the left.

When the Collapse switch is turned on, the Illustrator outlines are passed directly to Transform, where Position, Scale, and Rotation are applied to the actual vectors. The transformed vectors are then rasterized, followed by Masks and Effects. So when you continuously rasterize an Illustrator or Solid layer, the render order is rewired internally so that Transform is processed *before* Masks and Effects. This is shown in our second diagram.

Thanks to some clever trickery, Mask Paths are affected by Transformations so that they scale and rotate normally. Mask Feather and Effects are not quite so lucky; the following examples demonstrate anomalies you might encounter when applying masks and effects to layers that continuously rasterize.

Incidentally, text and shape layers in After Effects continuously rasterize by default, so the behavior exhibited by Illustrator layers when they are collapsed always applies to text and shape layers.

Mask Feather Foolery

Open [Ex.14], where a rotating Illustrator layer has a vertical mask feather applied. With the Collapse switch off, preview the animation and notice that the feather behaves as you would expect (the mask feather rotates along with the object). Turn on the Collapse switch: You'll notice that while the mask path continues to rotate properly, the feather does not.

Text layers will always exhibit this odd mask feather behavior as they are always continuously rasterized.

[Ex.14]: You would normally expect the mask feather to rotate along with the object (above). But when the Collapse switch is on, Rotation is calculated before Mask Feather, potentially producing an undesirable result (below).

Eccentric Effects

Many effect parameters involve values based on pixels or angle of direction, so whether Effects are calculated before Scale or Rotation may have a large impact on how they appear.

You can see an example of this in [**Ex.15a**]: It contains our @ symbol again, this time with Tint, Bevel Alpha, and Drop Shadow effects applied. RAM Preview; note how the size of the bevel and shadow scale along with the layer. Now enable the Continuously Rasterize switch: Although the layer sharpens up at larger sizes, note that the bevel and shadow do not change in size as the layer animates, which can look rather odd.

If you want the scale of applied effects to change along with the layer, you may need to animate the effects. Another approach is to rasterize your artwork at a very large size in a precomp, then apply scaling and effects in a second comp. This chain is demonstrated in [**Ex.16**].

There is another issue that needs to be dealt with. Return to [**Ex.15a**], Press End, and toggle the Continuously Rasterize switch on and off. Note that when the switch is on, the portions of the @ symbol cut off by the comp's boundaries are also beveled, and the drop shadow is incorrect.

To solve these problems, in [**Ex.15b**] we applied Effect > Utility > Grow Bounds. The beveled, shadowed edges now look correct. This plug-in fakes After Effects into thinking the comp is bigger than it really is, so that edge-based effects such as bevels and shadows render correctly. Its Pixels parameter decides how much larger to grow the imaginary comp size by; use as small a number as you can get away with. *Note: Grow Bounds is usually placed before all other effects, but due to an anomaly, it needs to render after the Tint effect.*

We should also point out that unlike effects, Layer Styles always render *after* transformations, so the results will look the same whether or not the layer is continuously rasterized. Check it out in [**Ex.15c**]. Note that the edges of the comp do not suffer from the same problems as [**Ex.15a**].

In addition, this rewired render order may be welcome. In [**Ex.17**], our rotating graphics have drop shadow effects that stay put!

Finally, also be aware that Behaviors (Effects & Presets > Animation Presets > Behaviors) that use the Transform effect and the Wiggle expression behave in unexpected ways when a layer is collapsed. Instead of using the layer's anchor point, they rotate and scale around 0,0 in comp space. You can explore this behavior in [**Ex.18**].

[Ex.15a]: When the Continuously Rasterize switch is off, effects scale with the layer (left). When it is turned on, effects are calculated after transforms such as scale, which can change their look (center) as the layer animates.

[Ex.15c]: Layer Styles (right) are always rendered after transformations and so behave the same whether or not continuous rasterization is enabled.

Zoom, Zoom, Zoom

The Exponential Scale keyframe assistant makes zooming the scale of a layer look more realistic. Most footage looks bad at extreme scalings, but continuously rasterized vector-based files retain their sharpness, making them good partners for this assistant.

CONNECT

Motion blur: Chapter 8.

Blending modes: Chapter 9.

Track mattes: Chapter 11.

Stencils: Chapter 12.

3D issues such as Z space, cameras, and lights: Chapters 13–16.

Nesting compositions: Chapter 18.

Precomposing: Chapter 19.

Text layers: Chapter 21.

Applying effects, adjustment layers: Chapter 22.

21

Textacy

Mastering this powerful text animation engine is well worth the effort.

TIP

Quick Type

New in CS5: Double-clicking the Type tool creates a new text layer with the cursor centered in the Comp panel.

reating and animating text are among the most common tasks for motion graphics designers. Fortunately, After Effects allows you to create vector-based typography directly in the Composition panel; mix and match font styles, size, and color on one layer; then animate individual characters, words, or lines in dynamic ways.

In this chapter we'll cover the basics of creating and editing text, including text along a path. We'll then show how to use *text animators* to add sophisticated animation. You'll discover all aspects of animating text properties and Range Selectors, learn about the various selector Shapes, offset the characters in 3D space, and then use the Wiggly Selector to randomize properties. We will touch upon other topics, such as creating outlines from text layers, integrating with Photoshop's text engine, and outputting your animation as a SWF file.

The shortcut to select the Type tool is Command+T on Mac (Control+T on Windows); this also toggles between the Horizontal and Vertical Type tools. When Auto-Open Panels is checked in the Tools panel and you select the Type tool, the Character/Paragraph panels will open automatically. You can also use Workspace > Text.

The dynamic text animations you create can be stored as Animation Presets, so you can easily apply these animations to other text layers in future projects. After Effects ships with hundreds of text presets, which you can preview by using Adobe Bridge. These presets serve as an inspiration and as starting points for your own animations. (Saving and applying Animation Presets are covered in Chapter 25.)

The non-demo version of After Effects CS5 also installs a number of Adobe Open Type fonts during the installation process; some of these free fonts are used in this chapter's example project file. If you removed or otherwise don't have one of the fonts we've used, you will see a warning when you open the projet file. Don't panic: Either reinstall the free fonts or simply change an example to use a font of your choice.

Example Project

Explore the 21-Example Project.aep file as you read this chapter; references to [Ex.##] refer to specific compositions within the project file.

Creating Text

To get started, open this chapter's example project file (**21-Example Project.aep**, found in the **Chapter Example Projects > 21-Textacy** folder on the DVD), then open comp [**Ex.01_starter**]:

Step 1: Select the Type tool from the Tools panel; the Character/Paragraph panels should open automatically. The default Type tool is the Horizontal Type tool; the Vertical Type tool creates vertical type (the latter is covered in the *Horizontal/Vertical* sidebar on page 370).

Step 2: With the Type tool selected, click anywhere near the left side of the Composition panel; a new layer, **Text 1**, is added to the Timeline panel. Type as many words as you like, adding returns if desired, and press the Enter key. The name of the layer will be changed to whatever you just typed, and a bounding box will be drawn around your text to indicate that you are in *layer mode* (see figure to the right).

With the Type tool still selected, hover the cursor over your existing text; the cursor changes to indicate that clicking inside the existing text will put you back in *editing mode*. Click inside the text and note that the layer handles disappear in this mode.

Whenever the Type tool is active, you can press the Command key on Mac (Control on Windows) to switch to the Selection tool temporarily to scale or move the layer. While in editing mode, move the cursor well away from the text and the Move tool will also appear.

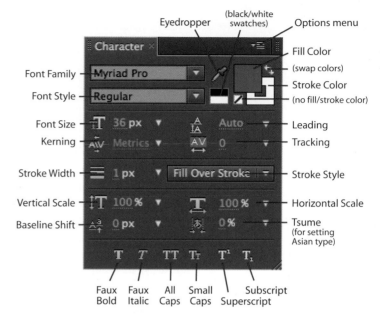

You can adjust values in the Character panel by scrubbing the icons to the left of their values. To cycle through the font menu, place the cursor in the Font name field and use the up/down arrow keys. You can also type a letter to jump to the first font that starts with that letter. Faux Bold and Faux Italic are handy if the font you choose has no true bold or italic styles.

Step 2: Text layers in the Timeline panel are named automatically based on the content, but you can rename them by pressing Return, typing a new name, and pressing Return again. Note how the cursor (circled in red) changes when it's moved away from the text; when it has a dotted outline, clicking will create a new Text layer.

Smarty Quotes

With Smart Quotes selected in the Character panel's Options menu, "tick marks" are automatically changed to proper "curly quotes" as you type.

"Not Smart"

"Smart"

Auto Kerning

High-quality commercial fonts usually include robust kerning pair specifications for automatically adjusting the spacing between two characters. To use these definitions, select your text and set the Kerning popup to Metrics.

After Effects also supports Optical Kerning, where the spacing between adjacent characters is adjusted based on their shapes. This might be a better default for text with a mix of fonts and sizes.

If the font you're using has inconsistent letter spacing, adjust the *Tracking* (the average spacing between characters) to get an overall improvement, then fix any problem character spacing by *Kerning* (using Option/Alt + left/right arrow keys).

Editing Type Attributes

Touring around the Character panel should be familiar territory if you've used other Adobe applications, and most of the shortcuts for editing and formatting text are the same as well.

Changes you make in the Character or Paragraph panels are applied to selected characters only. If the layer is selected and you're not in editing mode, changes apply to the entire layer. If nothing is selected, and you're in editing mode, changes apply to the next characters you type.

Using the Type tool, you can insert and delete text, and change existing text as you might expect. You can also freely change text

attributes so that different lines, words, or even characters have their own style, as shown above and in composition [**Ex.02**] .

• To change the color of your type, make sure the Fill color swatch is forward, then click on its color swatch to open the color picker. Select a new color and click OK. Note that even when the Selection tool is active, you can click on the black and white color swatches to quickly set the color to black or white; you can also use the Eyedropper tool to pick up a color from elsewhere on your screen.

• To add a Stroke, first set the Stroke Width value; click on the Stroke Color swatch to bring it forward, and change the Stroke Color as you did for Fill Color (if any text is selected, it will update as you pick your color). The Stroke Style popup defines how the fills and strokes are rendered together; the options are covered later in this chapter. To turn off the Stroke, select the None icon when the Stroke swatch is forward. To create outline text, set the Fill color to None and the Stroke Width to taste.

• Select the Font Family and Font Style from their respective menus. To get a live preview of the font, place the cursor in either field, and use the up and down arrow keys to cycle through your available fonts or weights. Click the arrow to the right to open a scrollable menu of your fonts.

• You can change the size of your text in various ways: Select a preset size from the Size popup menu, enter a size directly, or scrub the font size value in the Character panel. Add the Command (Control) key to scrub in finer increments. Once you get the hang of editing the font size, you'll find that the other fields work much the same way, including being able to scrub their values. If you make an unreadable mess, select Reset Character from the Character panel's Options menu.

• The shortcut for changing Tracking (the space between a group of characters) and Kerning (the space between two specific characters) is Option (Alt) + the left arrow/right arrow keys. Tracking works when a range of text is selected. To practice Kerning, select the Type tool, place the cursor between two characters, and use this shortcut; each click is the equivalent of 20/1000ths of an em.

Fill & Stroke Options

The Fill & Stroke options in the Character panel determine whether, within each character, the fill should render over the stroke, or the stroke over the fill. For thicker strokes, placing the fill on top usually works best. However, for cases when type is tightly tracked and characters overlap each other (see figures at right), you will want to explore the All Fills Over All Strokes and All Strokes Over All Fills options. Try them using **[Ex.03a]**. You can set these either from the More Options section in the Timeline panel or from the Character panel. These options override the fill and stroke properties of individual characters; to mix fill and stroke stacking orders, leave the popup in More Options set to Per Character Palette.

After Effects CS4 added the ability to change what happens to text strokes at sharp corners. Open comp **[Ex.03b]**. Note that the text outlines currently have very squared-off edges, both inside and outside the characters. Select the text layer **miter**, and open Window > Character. Click on the options arrow in the upper right corner of the Character panel and select the menu option Line Join: It is currently set to miter, which is the default. Choose the option Line Join > Bevel, and the squared-off edges will gain an extra "cut" to them. Choose the option > Round, and they will now have a soft rounding applied.

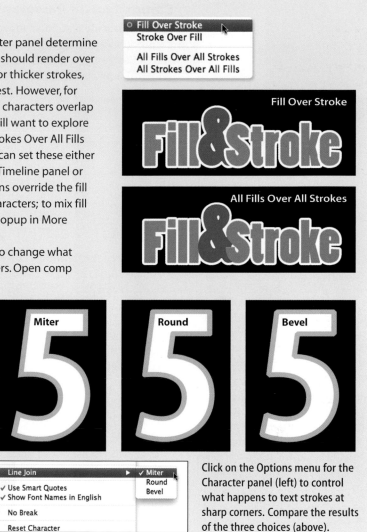

Click on the Options menu for the Character panel (left) to control what happens to text strokes at sharp corners. Compare the results of the three choices (above).

To quickly enter text editing mode, double-click the text layer; this brings the Comp panel forward with the text selected. More shortcuts for editing type are included under Help > Keyboard Shortcuts > Text. Note that some of these shortcuts work only when text is selected, not just when the layer is selected.

Text cannot be animated from the Character/Paragraph panels – note the absence of stopwatches alongside the parameters. Animation is applied using text animators (covered later in this chapter).

Finally, we remind you that when you scale a text layer using the Transform > Scale property, because text layers continuously rasterize (covered at the end of Chapter 20), the text will remain sharp at any size.

FACTOID

Text and Effects

You can apply effects to a text layer, such as glows or drop shadows, but only to the entire layer. Because text layers are continuously rasterized (Chapter 20), effects will render after transformations.

Composing for Paragraphs

When you create text, you can type directly in the Comp panel as you did earlier (this is called *point text*), pressing Return whenever you need to start a new line. Or, if you know you need a block of text, you can create *paragraph text* by defining the text box before you start typing:

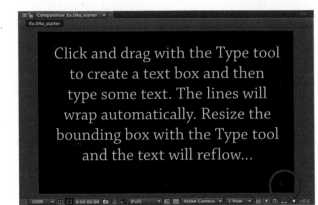

Click and drag with the Type tool to create a text box and then type some text. The lines will wrap automatically. Resize the bounding box with the Type tool and the text will reflow...

Drag the text box handles with the Type tool to reflow the copy. While you're dragging, add Shift to maintain the box's aspect ratio, or Command (Control) to scale from the center out.

The Paragraph panel's Options menu allows you to choose between the Adobe Single-line Composer (the default) or the Every-line Composer. The latter option will reflow text to even out the spacing within each paragraph.

No Break

New in CS5: If you don't want two or more words to split across separate lines, select the words and then select No Break from the Character panel's Options menu.

Explore the different Alignment and spacing options in the Paragraph panel; these can be set per paragraph. If you make a mess, select Reset Paragraph from the panel's Options menu.

Step 1: Open [**Ex.04a_starter**] and select the Type tool. Click and drag in the Comp panel to draw the text box, or press the Option (Alt) key before you drag to draw a box from the center out. Enter a few lines of text, or paste in some copy. If you enter too much text, it will overflow the box – drag the bottom right corner to enlarge the box; the text is not scaled when you resize the text box with the Type tool still selected.

Step 2: Press Enter to exit editing mode; note that now the layer handles will be visible and there is no box around the text. Press S to reveal Scale in the Timeline panel and switch to the Selection tool; now when you drag a corner you will edit the Transform > Scale property and resize the entire layer without reflowing the text. Add the Shift key after you start dragging to maintain the aspect ratio. Scaling in this manner always occurs around the layer's Anchor Point (Chapter 3).

You can convert text between point text and paragraph text. Select your paragraph text layer, and with the Type tool selected, right-click on the text in the Comp panel. Select Convert to Point Text from the popup menu. (*Gotcha: If you don't see this option, make sure you're not in text editing mode – press Enter prior to right-clicking so the colored layer handles are visible.*) Hard returns are added at each line ending when you convert. To convert in reverse, right-click and select Convert to Paragraph Text from the menu; you may need to delete any extra "hard returns" so text will reflow when you resize the text box.

To explore the Paragraph panel, open [**Ex.04b**], and select the text layer. Try the different alignment, indent, and space before and after options; they should be self-explanatory. Note that the layer's label color in the Timeline panel dictates the color of the layer handles in the Comp.

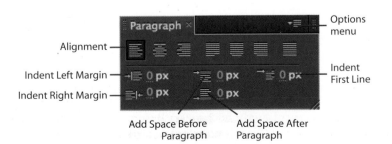

Text Along a Path

The Type tool can also be used to animate text along a path. Close your previous comps and follow these steps:

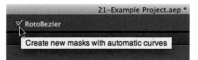

Step 1: Open [**Ex.05_starter**], where we've created some text, or create your own text layer. Select the Text layer – the mask you create must be applied to this layer! Then select the Pen tool (shortcut: G) and draw a curved mask path (masking was covered in Chapter 10). We used the RotoBezier option to create a smooth curve; for best results, avoid sharp angles so the text animates smoothly as it flows along its path.

Step 2: Return to the Selection tool, then expand layer 1's Text > Path Options section in the Timeline panel. Set the Path popup to Mask 1; a host of additional Path Options will be revealed. The text will now flow along the path, aligning to the left edge if the Paragraph alignment is set to Left (or centered if alignment is set to Center).

Step 3: To move the text along the path, either scrub the First Margin parameter or drag the text widget directly in the Comp panel (see figure, right). To animate the text along the path, turn on the stopwatch for First Margin at time 00:00. Move later in time and scrub this value to taste. RAM Preview to get a sense of whether the text is readable at that speed; turn on Motion Blur (Chapter 8) if the text is strobing. Our version is in [**Ex.05-final1**].

The other Path Options should be self-explanatory:

• Reverse Path draws the text on the opposite side of the path.

• Perpendicular to Path determines whether text is drawn straight up or perpendicular to the path.

• Force Alignment places the first character at the left side of the path (offset by First Margin, if non-zero) and aligns the last character with the end of the path (offset by Last Margin). It then evenly spaces out the characters in-between.

If you create a closed mask shape, the Mask Mode will revert to None (not Add) so that transparency is not affected. You can also copy and paste paths from Illustrator or Photoshop (see Chapter 10). Text on a path created in a Photoshop file can be converted to an editable text on a path in After Effects (covered at the end of this chapter).

Effects that can be applied to mask shapes – such as Stroke, Scribble, or Vegas – can also be added to the mix. In [**Ex.05-final2**], we used Vegas to animate the dotted line and Baseline Shift to raise the text above the path. A masked duplicate chimney layer hides the text as it disappears.

Steps 2–3: To animate the text along a path, set the Path popup to Mask 1, then set keyframes for the First Margin parameter. You can also edit the First Margin by dragging the widget (circled in red) in the Comp panel; press Shift as you drag and the widget will snap to mask vertices. New in CS5: The Path Options can be toggled off by disabling the eyeball. Background courtesy Artbeats/Industry Scenes.

Centered Text

Select Center Text in the Paragraph panel, then double-click the Type tool to create a text layer with the cursor exactly centered in the Comp panel.

Auto Range

If you select a range of characters before adding an animator, the Range Selector's Start and End parameters will automatically be set to match.

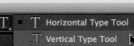

Horizontal/Vertical

The Vertical Type tool flows text from top to bottom (multiple lines flow from right to left). You can also convert existing text between Horizontal and Vertical. Open **[Ex.04c]** and select the horizontal text layer. With the Type tool active, press Enter to make sure you're not in text editing mode. Now right-click on the text in the Comp panel and select Vertical from the popup menu. To convert back, right-click and select Horizontal from the popup menu.

Text Animators

As we mentioned earlier, the properties of the Character and Paragraph panels cannot be animated over time. To bring your text to life, you need to add an *animator*. An animator is a group of *selectors* and *properties*. You start the process by choosing from a preset list of properties that can be animated, such as Position, Scale, Tracking, Fill Color, and so on.

Each animator group can include up to three different selector types: A *Range Selector* determines which characters will be affected by the animation. Range Selector 1 is added by default when you create an animator group. We'll look at the optional *Wiggly Selector* (to vary your text animation over time) later in this chapter. The *Expression Selector* is covered in the Expressions Bonus Chapter 37B.

All this power comes at the expense of a less-than-intuitive interface, so the following lessons are designed to build your skills gradually. We start with animating one property (Position) while we explore the basics; we'll then add on properties as we get deeper in the throes of textacy.

Creating a Typing On Animation

To get started, create some text or open our **[Ex.06_starter]** composition.

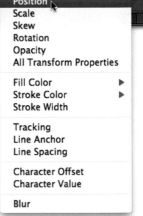

Step 1: Click on the Animate button in the Timeline, and select Position from the popup menu. The Animator 1 group will be added to the Timeline panel; it contains the default Range Selector 1 and the Position property (see figure next page). Twirl down the Range Selector to reveal its contents.

Don't confuse the Animator 1 > Position property with the regular Transform > Position property. Twirl down Transform and note that the only visual distinction is the amount of indentation. (It is easy to confuse the two, especially if one has keyframes and you use the U shortcut to twirl down only the properties that are animating.)

The initial value for Animator 1 > Position is 0,0, which means "no offset." Compare this with the value for Transform > Position, which refers to the distance of the layer's anchor point from the top left-hand corner of the Comp. All the properties you apply to an animator are modified relative to their current values. Twirl up the Transform group when you're done to avoid confusion. *Note: All references to properties from here on refer to properties added to an animator group.*

Step 2: Scrub Animator 1's Position value and notice how the text moves accordingly. You can also reposition text directly in the Comp panel: Make sure the animator's Position property is highlighted, then drag the text with the Selection tool (the cursor will change to a Move tool when positioned over text). Place the text below its original location at Position around X = 0, Y = 130.

• Range Selector 1 consists of three main parameters – Start, End, and Offset – plus an Advanced section which we'll explore later. The default values of Start = 0%, End = 100% mean that all characters are said to be *included* in the range. Slowly scrub the Start parameter – the beginning of the title jumps back up to its original placement in the Comp panel. When characters fall *outside* the range selection (also known as *excluded*), they are no longer affected by the Position offset value. Set the Start value to 100%; when Start = 100% and End = 100%, no characters are included in the range.

• Return the Start value to 0% and scrub the End parameter. The result is similar, but in this case the characters at the end of the title are excluded and return to normal.

• The selector bars (vertical lines plus arrows) in the Comp panel indicate the Start and End of the range selector. They are only visible when the animator group or one of its parameters (if it has only one Range Selector) is selected. Dragging the selector bars directly in the Comp panel also changes the Start and End values.

• Set Start to 0% and End to 33%, so only the first word is included. Slowly scrub the third parameter: Offset. This moves the Start/End range "through" the text, while maintaining its relative spacing.

Step 3: Let's set up a simple animation in which the characters appear to type on as they move up into position:

• Return Range Selector 1 to its default values: Start = 0%, End = 100%, and Offset = 0%. Position should still be set to 0,130 so the text is lower than its original position.

• At 00:00, turn on the stopwatch for Start.

• Move to 03:00 and scrub the Start value to 100%. RAM Preview and the text will animate into position.

Step 1: Select Position from the Animate popup to create Animator 1, and twirl down the Range Selector to reveal its options. Be aware that the two Position properties are easily confused! Remember that you can hide any properties in the Timeline panel that you're not using – just press Option+Shift (Alt+Shift) and click on them.

Step 2: Setting Position Y to 130 moves the text lower in the frame. As you scrub the Range Selector's Start value, the characters that fall outside the range return to their original position. You can also drag the selector bars directly in the Comp panel to change Start/End values.

Step 2 *continued:* Set Start and End to cover a percentage of the characters, then scrub the Offset parameter to move the range "through" the text. Offset saves you from having to move the Start and End values equally at the same time. To edit the Offset value directly in the Comp panel, press the Shift key as you drag the selector bars.

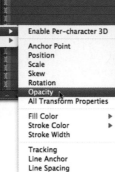

After animating Start from 0% to 100% in Step 3, select Add > Property > Opacity to add a second property to Animator 1.

Step 4: Set the Animator 1 > Opacity property to 0%; the characters will automatically become visible.

Add versus Animate

To add another property to an existing animator, select it from the Add menu. The Animate button adds a new text animator if no existing animator is selected; if one is selected, it behaves like the Add button.

Step 4: To make the text fade on as it animates, let's add the Opacity property to Animator 1. To the right of the Animator 1 group, click on the Add button (arrow); the popup menu shows the properties and selectors you can add to an existing animator. From the Add menu, select Property > Opacity.

• At time 00:00, scrub the Opacity value to 0%; the type will fade out. This is because the range currently includes the entire title. Scrub the time indicator later in time; as the Start parameter animates from 0 to 100%, the characters outside the range gradually move up and fade up. RAM Preview to see the full effect. Our version is shown in **[Ex.06-final1]**.

Randomize Order

For any text animation you create, you can have the characters animate in a random order instead of from Start to End. For instance, in comp **[Ex.06-final1]**, the characters are fading up as they move into position. To randomize the order in which they appear, twirl down the Advanced section of Range Selector 1. Click on the Randomize Order value to toggle it from Off to On, and RAM Preview. The characters still animate on from 0–100% over the same period of time, but they do so in a random order. Our example is shown in **[Ex.06-final2]**, where we've also enabled Motion Blur for the layer (covered in Chapter 8).

The Random Seed parameter "shuffles the deck." When set to 0 (the default), it is based on the animator number and layer index and selector index. To force different animators (even across layers) to behave the same, set Random Seed for all to a value other than 0.

Properties Parade

The previous examples introduced you to just a few of the properties that can be added to a text animator. Some of the others are self-explanatory (such as Stroke Width); the series of compositions in the [**Ex.07**] folder introduce some of the others. Remember you can turn on Randomize Order for any of these examples to add variety:

• [**Ex.07a-Rotation & Scale**] animates text rotating, scaling, and fading into place. Notice that the Anchor Point property can be used to move the origin of rotation (also see Anchor Point Grouping and Grouping Alignment later in this chapter). Motion Blur is enabled.

• [**Ex.07b-Skew**] is an example of words skewing as they move into place, also with motion blur; scrub the Skew Axis parameter to taste.

• [**Ex.07c-Fill Opacity**] starts with Vertical text that has no fill and a yellow stroke. By animating Amount down to 0%, the text returns to its original style. We also animated the Source Text (covered later in this chapter), customizing the number 8 in the final keyframe.

• [**Ex.07d-Tracking**] shows how easy it is to animate tracking. The twist is adding the Line Anchor property: At 0%, the tracking aligns left; 50% aligns center; 100% aligns right. When it's set to a specific value, you can manipulate tracking to center on a single character.

• When you're animating the Line Spacing property, it always anchors around the top line in a paragraph of text, but the Range Selector's Shape affects how the lines are spaced out. We use Ramp Up in [**Ex.07e-Line Spacing**], but try the others as well (more on shapes later in this chapter). We also set the Range Selector's Based On option to Words, reduced Opacity, and added a gold Fill Color. Turn on Randomize Order for a more interesting effect.

• [**Ex.07f-Character Offset**] shows how to offset characters by a specified number of Unicode values. For instance, ABC123 offset by 5 values would appear as FGH678. The Character Range popup lets you limit the results to Preserve Case & Digits (recommended), or the Full Unicode option (all characters and symbols in a font). Also of note is the Character Alignment popup: You can choose how to align the offset characters. Because the original text's alignment is used for the offset characters, the Center option can significantly reduce the jumpiness when characters are cycling in place. (See also the *Decoding Effect* sidebar on page 389.)

• [**Ex.07g-Character Value**] is akin to Character Offset, but instead of offsetting characters, all the characters are replaced with a specific Unicode value. We scrubbed Character Value until we arrived at an asterisk, which turns out to be 42 (*"the answer to life, the universe, and everything"*). Who knew.

As shown in [**Ex.07b**], including Skew can give the impression of speed, or animate characters from faux italics to normal.

When animating Tracking in [**Ex.07d**], keyframes are applied directly to the Tracking Amount property and the layer is faded up.

[**Ex.07e**] with Randomize Order Off (above) and turned On (below).

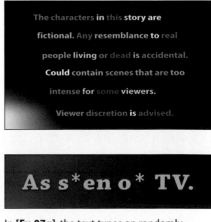

In [**Ex.07g**], the text types on randomly, replacing a string of asterisks.

Steps 1–2: Select Animate > Scale and set the Scale value to 300% (the characters will swell to a size where they overlap – that's okay). Then Add > Blur so the selected characters are blurred.

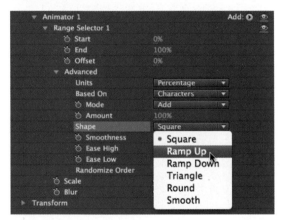

Step 3: Twirl down Range Selector's Advanced section and select the Ramp Up shape (above). In the Comp panel, the text will transition from the normal size/sharp at the Start to scaled and blurred at the End.

Step 4: Set the range to include 33% of the characters. (The text after the End parameter will be fully affected.)

Creating a Cascading Animation

A couple of pages ago, you learned how to make characters animate in one at a time, which we call a *typing on* style animation. In reality, most text animations look better when a series of characters *cascade* into position, as they do in [**Ex.08-final**]. This effect involves a recipe that includes animating Offset, using the Ramp Up shape, and the ubiquitous property, Opacity.

To create this style of animation, follow these steps:

Step 1: Open [**Ex.08_starter**]. We've already created a title for you to start with, but feel free to change the text or font style to taste. In the Timeline panel, twirl down the text layer and select Animate > Scale. This will create Animator 1 and Range Selector 1, with a Scale property. Change Scale to 300% (for now, don't worry about how the letters overlap!).

Step 2: Click on the Add arrow on the same line as Animator 1 and select Property > Blur. Blur will be added below Scale; set it to around 20 for now.

Step 3: Twirl down the Range Selector, then twirl down the Advanced section inside Range Selector 1 and take note of the Shape option:

• The default Shape is Square, which means that characters inside the range selector are fully affected by the Scale and Blur. We'll explain each Shape option in detail a little later; for now, select Ramp Up from the menu and twirl up the Advanced section.

• The Ramp Up shape uses the Start and End values to create a transition from the original text (normal size and sharp) at the Start of the range, to the fully affected text (scaled 300% and blurred) at the End. Move Start and End toward the center and notice that any characters beyond the End are also fully affected, as if they were inside the selection; any characters before the Start are not affected, as if they are outside the selection.

In short, Ramp Up *transitions* between selected and not selected. The size of this transition is determined by the number of characters between the Start and End points. Offset is then used to move the transition zone.

Step 4: In Range Selector 1, set the Start to 0% and scrub the End parameter to about 33%. This means that as the animation progresses, one-third of the characters will be included in the cascade.

Step 5: The Offset value is added to the values for Start and End. Since animating Offset moves both Start and End at the same time, the width of the selection will remain the same. Scrub the Offset parameter while watching the Comp panel and note how the transition area moves back and forth along the line of text.

• To create the cascading effect, press Home to return to 00:00 and enable the stopwatch for Offset. Set its value to –33%; this moves the transition completely to the left of the title. (Think about it: Start is now at –33% and End is now at 0%.)

• Move to 02:00 and scrub Offset to 100%; the transition will be pushed off to the right since you just added 100% to both Start and End.

Scrub the current time indicator along the timeline to get a feel for this animation.

Step 6: Notice that the scaling occurs around the baseline (bottom) of the text. What if you want the characters to scale from their centers? You can do this by changing the anchor point:

• Move to 01:00 to catch the animation mid-cascade. Select Add > Property > Anchor Point to add the Anchor Point property to Animator 1. Scrub the Anchor Point's Y value slowly to the left while watching the Comp panel; press the Command (Control) key to scrub in finer increments. A small negative Y value should center the characters vertically, but feel free to experiment with larger values to offset the text on the X and Y axes.

Step 7: The only missing ingredient in this recipe is to make the characters fade up as they cascade on:

• Select Add > Property > Opacity, then set Opacity to 0%. Because you're using the Ramp Up shape, the characters will transition from 100% opacity at the Start to 0% opacity at the End. Characters after the End will be fully transparent. RAM Preview and enjoy!

Remember that anytime you want the characters to transition into the frame without having to start them off screen, you need to add Opacity at 0%!

If you got lost, compare your results with our version in [**Ex.08-final**]. And don't forget that you can also toggle on Randomize Order for any animation (as explained in the sidebar on page 372).

Steps 5–6: Using the Ramp Up shape in combination with animating Offset results in our characters transitioning from being large and blurred to their original appearance. By adding the Anchor Point property to Animator 1 and offsetting its Anchor Point Y value slightly, you can center the expanded text vertically (above and below).

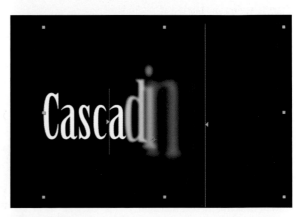

Step 7: Add Opacity at 0% and the characters will transition in because they fade from 100% at the Start to 0% at the End.

FACTOID

Text on a 3D Path

You can enable Per-character 3D for text along a path, but the mask path will still be aligned along a 2D "postcard in space."

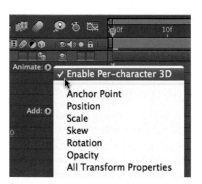

You can enable Per-character 3D for any text animation, even in a 2D comp.

Per-character 3D

The Per-character 3D option allows you to position and rotate the individual characters in a text layer through 3D space. Although you can enable Per-character 3D in a 2D comp, to get the most out of this feature you should be working in a comp that also has a 3D camera and lights. Working in 3D was covered in Chapters 13 through 16, so we will assume you're familiar with 3D workspaces and animating in Z. However, for simplicity's sake, we'll take advantage of Custom Views which already have dummy cameras set up for you.

Per-character 3D simply adds to all the other tricks you can do with text animators, so you can build on the recipes you've learned up to this point. Note that not all text properties are affected by Per-character 3D (for instance, Blur, Opacity, Skew, Fill Color, and Tracking appear the same whether or not it's enabled). However, Anchor Point, Position, Scale, and Rotation all will gain a third dimension: a Z parameter.

Text Position in Z

To get started, select Close All from the Comp panel's tab and open comp [**Ex.09_starter**]. A few words have already been typeset for you (feel free to change the words or restyle them if you like).

Step 1: In the Timeline panel, twirl down the text layer and select Animate > Position. This will create Animator 1 with the regular 2D Position property with values on X and Y.

Step 2: Now for the magic feature required to animate text in 3D space: Click either the Animate or Add button and select Property > Enable Per-character 3D from the top of the list. In the Timeline panel, the text's 3D Layer switch will sport two small cubes to show that Per-character 3D is enabled.

In the comp panel, the text layer now has a set of red, green, and blue 3D axis arrows that indicate how the layer is oriented in X, Y, and Z respectively. Their origin is where the layer's Anchor Point is located.

You will also notice that Position has three values: X, Y, and Z. Scrub the Z Position value (the third one) while watching the Comp viewer. Negative values bring the text forward in space (or closer to the front of an imaginary "stage"), while positive values send it farther back in space.

Steps 1–2: When you Add > Enable Per-character 3D for a text layer (top), you will see a special icon with two small boxes appear in its 3D Layer switch (above). The XYZ axis arrows show how it is oriented in the Comp view (right). New in CS5: When a text transform property is selected, the character's anchor point is shown as a small x.

Step 3: To better visualize what you are about to do, change the 3D View popup at the bottom of the Comp panel from Active Camera to Custom View 1. You should now see the text from above and at an angle. (If not, use the menu option View > Reset 3D View.)

Step 4: You can animate these characters to create a "type-on" effect similar to the method you learned earlier:

• Set Position to 0, –75, –350 to position the characters inside the Range Selector higher and forward in Z space compared with where the layer's axis arrows are.

• Twirl down Range Selector 1. At 00:00, enable the stopwatch for Start with a value of 0%.

Steps 3–4: Change the 3D View to Custom View 1 so you can see the text from above. As the Range Selector's Start animates from 0% to 100%, the characters will move from their offset position in 3D space back to their original plane.

• Move to 02:00 and change the Start value to 100%. RAM Preview and the characters will animate back to their original position.

• Return the 3D View popup to Active Camera and press Home to return to 00:00. Notice how characters that are closer to the camera appear to be larger, even though you haven't changed their scale value. They will remain sharp no matter how close they get to the camera because they are being continuously rasterized automatically (discussed at the end of Chapter 20).

• Click the Add button and select Property > Opacity. Set Opacity to 0% so that the characters will be invisible when they are outside the selector's range. Our version is shown in [**Ex.09-final**].

3D Text Rotation

To practice animating text using X, Y, and Z Rotation, open comp [**Ex.10_starter**] and RAM Preview it. To save time, we've already created a basic cascading type-on effect using the same technique you learned a couple of pages ago. Select layer 1 and press UU to see the relevant properties: namely, Opacity is set to 0%, the Shape is Ramp Up, and Range Selector 1's Offset is animated.

Step 1: In the Timeline panel, click the Add button for Animator 1 and select Property > Enable Per-character 3D. Then set the 3D View popup in the Comp panel to Custom View 1. You should now see the text from above and at an angle.

Step 2: Click on the Add button for Animator 1 and select Property > Rotation. Parameters for X, Y, and Z Rotation should appear.

Step 2: After enabling Per-character 3D, adding Rotation will yield three separate parameters.

X Rotation

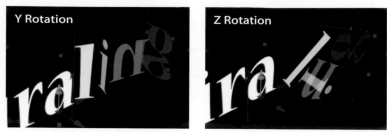

Y Rotation

Z Rotation

X Rotation swings characters around their baseline; Y Rotation twirls them around their vertical axis; and Z Rotation behaves the same as rotation in 2D.

Let's explore what happens when you rotate on each axis individually:

• Set X Rotation to 1 revolution and RAM Preview. The characters swing around their baseline as they fade up.

• Undo your X Rotation and set Y Rotation to 1 revolution. Now each character swivels around to face the viewer as it fades up. Try other values, then return Y Rotation to 0 when you're done.

• Set Z Rotation to 1 revolution: This parameter is equivalent to the rotation property when text is animating in 2D.

Explore combinations of X, Y, and Z Rotation. It doesn't take much before your characters are performing complex gymnastics – all with just two Range Selector keyframes!

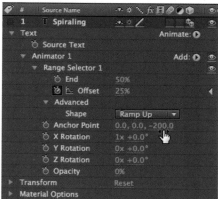

Step 3: Add > Property > Anchor Point and edit the Z value to offset the pivot point (above). Offsetting the Z Anchor Point causes the characters to spiral into place (below).

Step 3: Characters scale and rotate around their anchor point, which defaults to the text's baseline. Moving the anchor point when Per-character 3D is enabled can have a huge effect on how text rotates in 3D space. To see this in action:

• Set X Rotation to 1 revolution, and zero out Y and Z Rotation. Move to a time in the middle of the animation.

• Click on the Add button and select Property > Anchor Point. You will see three values, again corresponding to X, Y, and Z. These offset the pivot point for the characters. Scrub the third value (Z) and note how the characters move away from their baseline. RAM Preview to observe how they spiral into place.

• For more fun, try offsetting the X or Y Anchor Point and preview the result. Note that you don't have to view the text animation from a perspective view: Change the 3D View popup back to Active Camera, and you will still experience a sense of dimension. Per-character 3D can give you interesting results even while working in 2D comps! Our version is shown in **[Ex.10-final]**; we've enabled motion blur as well.

Per-character Align to Camera

A new Auto-Orientation option for Per-character 3D text automatically orients each character toward the camera, with each pivoting on its own anchor point.

Step 1: Open [**Ex.11_starter**]. It contains a text layer with its 3D Layer option enabled, plus a 3D camera. This composition has been created to default to Custom View 2, which provides an overhead perspective on both the text and the camera.

Step 2: Right-click on the text layer **Auto Orientation**, and select Transform > Auto-Orient. Enable the option Orient Towards Camera, leaving Orient Each Character Independently off for now. Click OK and note that the entire line of text pivots to face the camera.

Step 3: Right-click on the text layer and select Transform > Auto-Orient again. This time, enable Orient Each Character Independently and click OK. This will automatically enable Per-character 3D for the text layer. Now, instead of the entire line of text rotating, the line will return to its original orientation, and each character will orient around its local anchor point to face the camera. Drag the camera around the Comp panel, and note how the characters continue to automatically orient themselves; this behavior will track camera animations.

This auto-orientation behavior will also work if you animate the text. Any rotation animation you introduce will act as an offset to the rotation added by this auto-orient feature.

Later we will talk about the ability of the Range Selector to group the behavior of text based on individual characters, words, or lines. Per-character auto-orientation honors this grouping.

All 3D layers have a Layers > Transform option to orient toward the camera (above).

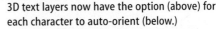

3D text layers now have the option (above) for each character to auto-orient (below.)

Degrees of 3D

It is important to understand that there is a big difference between enabling Per-character 3D for a text layer and merely enabling its 3D Layer switch: In Per-character 3D mode, each character is rendered as an individual element with its own 3D position and rotation offsets.

Compare the text in [**Ex.12a**] with [**Ex.12b**]: In [**Ex.12a**] the 3D Layer switch is on, but not the Per-character 3D option. This means the text elements exist only on a flat 2D plane, which can then only be animated as a whole in 3D space. The text will go around the rim of your circle (right) – but not stand up along its path, as they do in [**Ex.12b**]. The individual characters also will not cast shadows on each other.

Text Presets

To learn how to save and reuse
your text animations, don't miss
Chapter 25, *Presets & Variations*.
You can download additional
3D Text Animation Presets from
the After Effects section at
share.studio.adobe.com.

3D Text in a 3D World

If you want to get more ideas for what can be done with Per-character
3D, make sure you check out the Animation Presets that come with After
Effects. Either through Bridge (Animation > Browse Presets) or in the
Effects & Presets panel, open **Presets > Text** to access literally hundreds
of text presets; the **3D Text** folder contains 30 presets that show off
Per-character 3D.

We've used one of those Animation Presets – **3D Rotate around
Circle** – as our starting point in **[Ex.13]**. RAM Preview and note how the
text arcs from between the two hanging video screens, curling in front of
the gold screen. Select layer 1 and press UU to see what's been done to
this text layer to pull this off:

View your 3D composition from
different angles using multiple views
to get a better understanding of
how the layers interact. In **[Ex.13]**,
Per-character 3D and a mask path are
used to curve text between layers.
Footage courtesy Artbeats/Gears
and Industry: Gears and Machines.

• A circular Mask Path was added to the layer and assigned as the Path
for the text to follow. This makes the text arc around the rim of a circle.

• Per-character 3D was then enabled for the text, with Rotation added
as an animation property. Setting X Rotation to 90° stood the text up
along its circular path.

• The layer's normal Transform properties were then set and animated
to position and rotate the circle path. (You could also animate Path
Options > First Margin to push the text along a stationary path; that's
what the preset **3D Rotate around Circle** does.)

• As a finishing touch, Material Options > Casts Shadows was set to On
to help the text interact with the 3D light and layers in this comp. Note
that with Per-character 3D, characters can cast shadows on each other.

To get a better idea of how the text is arranged in relation to the other
layers, we've set the Select View Layout button along the bottom of the
Comp panel to 2 Views. The left view is set to Top to get a bird's-eye view
of the text's path.

Source Text Tricks

The actual text and attributes for the Character/Paragraph panels are contained in a property called Source Text in the Timeline panel. By animating Source Text, you can cycle words in place on one layer:

Step 1: Open [**Ex.80a_starter**]. Twirl down the text layer, then twirl down the Text properties. At 00:00, turn on the stopwatch for Source Text, which creates a Hold (noninterpolating) keyframe for the first word.

Step 2: Advance 10 frames, double-click the layer to select all; replace the text by typing "**Daytona**". Press Enter; another keyframe is created.

Step 3: Create as many keyframes as you like, and RAM Preview. Right-click a keyframe to view its source. When keyframes are selected, changes in the Character panel affect selected keyframes. To adjust the timing, click Source Text to select all keyframes then press Option (Alt) while you drag the last keyframe. Our version is [**Ex.80a-final**].

To create a list of words that cycle in place (above), animate Source Text in the Timeline panel (below). You can double-click a keyframe to edit its Source Text.

Expression enthusiasts should note that you can add expressions to the Source Text parameter. In [**Ex.80b**], we created a new Text layer and applied Animation Preset > Text > Expressions > Buzz Words. Press EE to reveal the expression. In the first line of the expression we entered the list of words to cycle through; note that the | symbol is used to signify new "keyframes." If you have a long list, prepare the text in a word processor. Adjust the frame rate in the Effect Controls panel or Timeline panel by changing the Effect > Buzz Frame Rate slider control.

The comps in the [**Ex.90**] folder use Expression Selectors (Add > Selector > Expression) and are covered in the Expression Bonus Chapter 37B.

In addition to using expressions, scripting (Bonus Chapter 37C) opens up numerous possibilities to interact with Source Text. A script we find particularly useful is **ptTextEdit** (*aescripts.com/pt_textedit*), which provides the ability to search a composition for occurances of a specific word (or even font!), and easily edit or restyle it. Visit *aescripts.com/tag/text/* for other useful texts scripts.

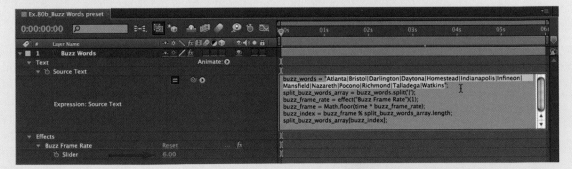

After applying the BuzzWords preset, edit the text between quotes in the expression's first line. The Buzz Frame Rate effect is used to adjust the frame rate. Another benefit of using the expression is that editing the Source Text affects all words.

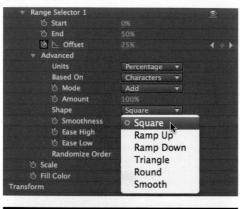

Animator Shapes

The Shape options in the Range Selector > Advanced section are key to customizing the look of your text animation:

Open [**Ex.14a-Shapes**]. Animator 1 includes the properties Scale and Fill Color (set to red); outside the range the text is its normal white color. We've set the Range Selector's Start to 0% and End to 50%, and animated Offset.

• Twirl down the Advanced section of Range Selector 1 and locate the Shape popup menu. The Shape defaults to Square, which gives a fairly abrupt transition zone at the start and end of the range. The Smoothness parameter directly below is available *only* when the Shape popup is set to Square. With Smoothness at its default 100%, RAM Preview or slowly scrub the timeline. The range moves through the text; there's a slight transition zone where about one character on either side of the range is partially affected by the Scale and Fill Color settings. Change the Smoothness value to 0% and slowly scrub the timeline; now characters are either completely included or excluded. Press 0 to jump to 01:15 when you're done.

• The Ramp Up and Ramp Down shapes affect the type differently from the other shapes and are often used when animating the Offset parameter. Select Ramp Up and note that the range selectors define the *transition zone* between the affected and unaffected characters. Before the Start value, the text is fully excluded (white and scaled normally); after the End value, the text is fully included (red and scaled 200%). The area between Start and End transitions from excluded to included. Change the Shape popup to Ramp Down and the opposite is true. Change the Start/End values to increase or decrease the size of this transition zone.

• The differences between the other shape choices – Triangle, Round, and Smooth – are easier to see if you set Start to 0%, End to 100%, and Offset to 0%. The Triangle shape transitions evenly between fully unselected/excluded and fully selected/included and back again within the start/end range. Round renders the characters at the extremes of the range closer to their affected style (redder and larger, in this case). Smooth has a different tendency – it renders the characters close to the start and end of the range closer to their original size and color.

Remember that these shapes apply to all the properties that can be added to a text animator, not just Fill Color and Scale. Try adding other properties and see how they behave. As we'll see next, the Ease High and Ease Low parameters can be used to further customize how text transitions between being selected and unselected.

The Lowdown on Ease High and Low

Perhaps the least understood parameters in the Advanced section are Ease High and Ease Low. These refine the shape between characters being fully included (the *high* point) and fully excluded (the *low* point) and thus ease the transition between selected and unselected states.

Open [**Ex.14b-EaseHighLow**]. The series of dollar signs has one animator, with Position, Scale, and Fill Color properties added to it and the Triangle Shape is used. RAM Preview; Offset is animated through the text.

In the Advanced section, the two ease parameters appear below the Shape popup; they both default to 0%:

• Press 0 to jump to time 01:06, and scrub Ease High from 0% to 100%. As the value increases, the influence of the high point in the animation (fully green, raised 50 pixels on Y, and scaled 200%) expands to affect more of the characters to each side. At –100% only the center character is fully included. Set Ease High back to 0% when you're done.

• Now consider the Ease Low parameter. Scrub its value from 0% to 100%: The characters at the low points in the animation (close to the gray arrows) ease more gradually from being unselected to being partially selected.

• Change the Shape from Triangle to Ramp Up; the low point is at the start of the transition and the high point is at the end. Experiment with changing the Ease High and Ease Low values.

The best way to understand how the ease controls work is to see how they affect characters as they animate. Open comp [**Ex.14c**]. RAM Preview to view the characters fall into place thanks to the Ramp Up shape and Offset keyframes. Adjust the Ease High to 100%; characters now ease away from their high point (where they are "most selected"). Undo. Set Ease Low to 100%; characters now fall gently into position as they move toward the low point of their range.

In [**Ex.14d**] the Ease High and Low values control whether the spiralling characters speed up or slow down as they approach their landing time. Experiment and set to taste.

Note that using Ease for the Shape is different than easing the Range Selector's Start, End, or Offset keyframes in the Graph Editor (Chapter 4). In that case, you are changing the speed that the range selector moves across the characters, without control over how each character behaves. This is still useful; for example, adding an ease in to the last keyframe of a text animation (as we have in [**Ex.14d**], shown in the Speed Graph at right) gives a sense of finality, and also forces the viewer to pause and ponder the last few characters or words.

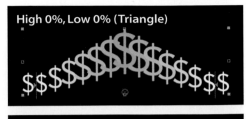

High 0%, Low 0% (Triangle)

High +100%, Low 0% (Triangle)

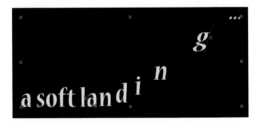

High 0%, Low +60% (Ramp UP)

In [**Ex.14b**], explore the Ease High and Ease Low parameters and see how they affect the transition between selected and unselected states.

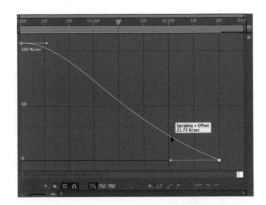

In [**Ex.14c**], adjust the ease parameters to affect the speed at which individual characters fall down into place. Setting Ease Low to 100% gives a soft landing.

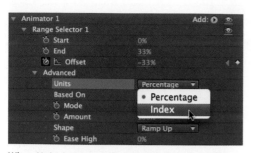

When Units is set to Index, the Start, End, and Offset parameter values are based on the number of characters. (Be aware that if you change the Based On popup to Words or Lines, the Index values will now refer to words or lines, not characters.)

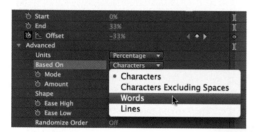

The Based On option determines if the Range Selector animates by character, word, or line. The default is to animate individual characters (**A**), but you can also set text to exclude spaces, or to animate using Words (**B**) or Lines.

More Options

The Range Selector > Advanced section includes more options that are well worth exploring. Try these out using [**Ex.15a**]:

Units: The Units popup can be set to Percentage or Index values for the Start, End, and Offset parameters. The advantage of Percentage is that if you change the content (and potentially the number of characters in it), the animation will likely work as expected. This is particularly important when you're saving and applying Animation Presets. Change Units to Index, and the Start, End, and Offset parameters will show the number of characters in the text block instead. This can be useful when you need to set the range selectors to include specific characters.

Based On: The default is to animate individual characters (spaces are considered as a character), but you can change the Based On popup to use Characters Excluding Spaces, Words, or Lines. *Gotcha:* If Units is set to Index, changing the Based On popup will *not* update the Start/End/Offset values to match. It's best to switch Units to Percentage before changing Based On, then switch the Units popup back to Index.

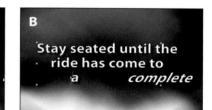

Mode: The properties you add to an animator group normally apply to text defined by the Range Selector, but if you change the Mode popup from Add to Subtract, characters outside the range are affected. Only Add and Subtract modes are useful when there are no previous selectors. The other modes come into play when you add more Selectors (covered later in this chapter).

In [**Ex.15b**], the Amount parameter is animated from 100% to 0% (above sequence); this fades out the effect of the Scale, Fill Color, and Tracking properties. To have these properties fade on or off at different rates, leave Amount at 100% and animate the properties, as shown in [**Ex.15c**].

Animating Amount & Property Values

Amount: When you've added multiple properties to an animator, the Amount parameter allows you to fade the entire "effect" up and down. At 100% (the default), the properties are applied at their full values; at 0%, their effect is reduced to zero. The title in comp [**Ex.15b**] has multiple properties applied – Scale, Fill Color, and Tracking. The Amount parameter is animating from 100% to 0% so that the effect of the three properties fades away over time.

The Amount parameter is handy for controlling the impact of all properties at once, but you can also set keyframes for the properties. Open [**Ex.15c**], which again has text that is scaled, colored, and tracked. The Amount is set to 100%, and the property values are animated. This approach allows for each property to animate at different points in time. (Note that you're still free to animate the Start, End, and Offset parameters as well; the two approaches are not mutually exclusive.)

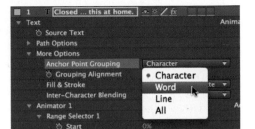

Anchor Point Grouping and Alignment

When characters are rotated and scaled in an animator group, they default to using their own baseline as an anchor point. Anchor Point Grouping lets you specify the anchor point per Character, Word, or Line.

To try this out, close all previous comps, open [**Ex.16**], and make sure the Text > More Options section is twirled down. RAM Preview to see the underlying animation (per Character). Change the Anchor Point Grouping popup to Word, then Line, previewing as you go.

The Grouping Alignment control lets you offset the placement of the anchor point; positive values means text will originate from below and to the right. The Grouping Alignment values are based on a percentage of the text size (not pixels). This means you can change the type size without having to tweak these values. To center the anchor point in all capital letters, try values for X and Y of 0%, –50%; for lowercase letters, try 0%, –25%.

A welcome improvement in CS5 is that when you select transform properties applied to a text animator in the Timeline panel, the anchor point is now visible in the Comp panel. In previous versions it was different to know where the anchor point was located, particularly in 3D.

Note that if there are multiple animators applied (as we show later in this chapter), the More Options section will apply to all of them.

In [**Ex.16a**], change the Anchor Point Grouping in More Options (top). The default is to rotate and scale around each character's anchor point (**A**).

Don't confuse the Anchor Point Grouping setting with the Range Selector's Based On popup (which specifies whether text is "selected" based on characters, words, or lines). In [**Ex.16b**], where the animation cascades in, change the Anchor Point grouping to Word (**B**). Because the Range Selector's Based On popup is still set to Character, the Rotation and Scale values are being applied to characters inside each word at a different rate, creating an unwanted bend. Set Based On to Word for a simpler result (**C**).

Inter-Character Blending

Also included in More Options is the Inter-Character Blending popup. This allows overlapping characters within the same text layer to composite using blending modes, as shown in [**Ex.17**]. All the regulars are here – Multiply, Add, Overlay, and so on. You can also set the layer's regular blending mode (Chapter 9), which sets how the text layer blends with layers below.

Random vs. Wiggly

Randomize Order changes the order in which the Range Selector selects characters. The Wiggly Selector randomizes the property values added to the animator.

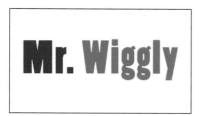

The original text (above) and after the Wiggly Selector was added (below). Position is set to 0,50, Scale to 150%, Rotation +30°, and Opacity 0%.

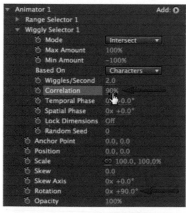

To best understand the Wiggly Selector, offset just one property at a time and then try each Wiggly option separately.

Adding a Wiggly Selector

Not to be confused with the Wiggler keyframe assistant, the Wiggle Paths shape operator, or the wiggle expression, the Wiggly Selector proves that there is no end of possible variations on the word "wiggle" that Adobe can conjure up. The optional Wiggly Selector can be added to an animator group to randomize the values of the properties associated with that group. Note that the Wiggly Selector affects *all* properties included in an animator group, so if you want to wiggle just certain properties, you will need to create multiple animator groups (coming up shortly).

The Wiggly Selector allows for lots of control over how things randomize. Open [**Ex.18_starter**], where we've created the "Mr. Wiggly" text layer, or design your own title to wiggle:

Step 1:   So that you'll have some properties to wiggle, create an animator group with all the Transform properties applied at once by selecting Animate > All Transform Properties. Animator 1 is created, along with all the Transform properties applied at their default settings.

Step 2:   Once you have created an animator group, click the Add button and choose Selectors > Wiggly. Wiggly Selector 1 is added below Range Selector 1. Nothing will happen yet because the property values are not offset. Edit the following properties, RAM Previewing as you go:

• Scrub the Position values to start; the characters wiggle left or right when X is changed, and up or down when Y is changed.

• Scrub the Scale value – whether it's above or below 100%, some characters get larger and others get smaller. Aspect ratio is not maintained unless Lock Dimensions is toggled On in the Wiggly Selector (see below).

• Set Rotation to +30 degrees; characters wiggle to a max of ±30 degrees.

• Set Opacity to 0%; characters are now varying degrees of transparent.

The result of this silliness is shown in [**Ex.18-final**]. Note that the Wiggly Selector also works with Per-character 3D, as shown in [**Ex.19b**].

Wiggly Options

Twirl down the Wiggly Selector and explore the various options. (Toggle the Wiggly Selector eyeball on and off if you need to check what the property is doing without the wiggle applied.)

• Mode determines how the Wiggly Selector should be combined with any selectors placed above it (see the *Modes of Confusion* sidebar).

• Max Amount and Min Amount specify the amount of variation. If you need to fade up or down the wiggle amount, set keyframes for Max and Min Amounts. To better see their influence, simplify the animation by offsetting just one property at a time (reset the others to their defaults).

For example, if just Rotation is set to offset +90 degrees, using the default values (Max Amount at 100%, Min Amount at –100%), the characters can rotate up to 90° clockwise and counterclockwise. However, if you change Min to 0%, the layer would rotate only clockwise (positive). Or you could

Modes of Confusion

An animator can have more than one Selector. Each selector has a Mode parameter which determines how the ranges are combined in the resulting animation. If you follow one Range Selector with a second Range Selector, the default Mode is Add. This means two ranges can be used to select words or characters that are not adjacent, as demonstrated in **[Ex.22-final]**.

More interesting is following a Range Selector with a Wiggly Selector. The default Mode in this case is Intersect, which means the second selector only operates on the range set by the first selector; the

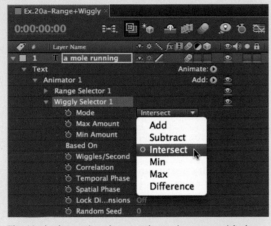

The Mode determines how a selector interacts with the one above it, creating more interesting selections.

depth of its effect is scaled by the range. This is demonstrated in **[Ex.20a]**, where a rounded Range Selector moves through characters in a line of text and is followed by a Wiggly Selector which randomizes how their positions are offset. To better understand what each selector is contributing, toggle the "eyeballs" for the Range and Wiggly Selectors to isolate each one's animation.

Intersect is the Mode you will use most often with the Wiggly Selector. The other Modes are less intuitive; we've set up **[Ex.20b]** as a practice comp for you to play with. Try different Modes for the Wiggly Selector, toggling the Range and Wiggly Selectors on and off to isolate what each is adding to the final animation. In all cases, the result cannot exceed the property's maximum offset value, which can cause a "clipping" style behavior.

Add Mode adds the result of the Range and Wiggly Selectors as if you'd applied them individually. Min and Max take either the smallest or largest offset per character. Difference gives the characters outside the first range the opposite animation as characters inside that range. Subtract inverts the behavior of the selector, so that if its value would be near +100% or –100% amount, the result is close to 0% (no offset). As the selector's value nears 0%, its result nears 100% offset; as it moves from –1% to +1%, the offset suddenly jumps from –99% to +99%.

---

set a range from –50% to +50% to randomize up to half the property value (±45°). In other words, the Max and Min Amounts scale (or attenuate) the property offset value, and set the range that it wiggles within.

Now let's say Position is offset 100, 100: Another way of explaining it is that a positive Max Amount value takes you toward the "goal" (100 pixels down and right), while negative Min Amount moves the type in the opposite direction (up and left). Note that Scale is a bit of a brain twister: If Scale is set to 0%, then Max Amount at 100% will vary scale between 100% down toward the "goal" of 0%, while setting Min Amount to –100% will actually scale it larger (up to 200%), or away from the goal.

Note that some properties, such as Opacity, cannot animate to illegal values (such as 200%); if Opacity is set to 0% and the Min Amount is –100%, half of the random values will be clamped at 100%.

GOTCHA

Wiggly Reseed

The Wiggly Selector seed is based on layer order. If you change the layer order and then edit the layer, the Wiggly pattern will change.

[Ex.19c] uses two animators (for Scale and Position) and animates Temporal and Spatial Phase with Hold keyframes to create a "slamdown" effect. Wiggles per second is set to 0.

[Ex.19a] is set up to help you understand the difference between Temporal and Spatial Phase. Correlation is set to 95% so the characters are wiggled similarly (but not identically).

TIP

Textacy Blur

Motion Blur (Chapter 8) looks great applied to animating text, particularly if it's wiggling.

[Ex.19e] uses a Wiggly Selector to randomize the initial position of characters, then animates the position offset to 0 to settle them into place. Notice how 3D drop shadows are cast and received between characters when Per-character 3D is enabled. Image courtesy Digital Vision/Prototype.

- Based On: Similar to the popup of the same name in the Range Selector, Based On lets you apply wiggle values based on characters, words, or lines.

- Wiggles/Second is self-explanatory; set it to a very low value for a nice slow wiggle. This parameter can animate only with Hold keyframes.

- Correlation controls whether the individual character offsets are very different (0%) or all wiggled the same (100%). Temporal Phase changes the seed in time, giving different results for the same animation values. Spatial Phase moves the pattern through the text like a wave.

To understand these three parameters, open **[Ex.19a]** where we've added Position and Fill Hue to Animator 1. The Wiggly Selector is using default values. Scrub Correlation and watch the results, then set it back to 95% so characters are similar but not identical. Scrub Temporal Phase: The variations are changed as if you're moving in time (not unlike Evolution in other effects). Set it so that you see a distinctive pattern, then scrub Spatial Phase and watch this pattern move through the text.

- Lock Dimensions is useful when wiggling Scale; turn it On to wiggle Y the same as X, thus maintaining the aspect ratio.

To review: The Wiggly Selector churns out random values that can be applied to any of your animations. These random values change based on the number of wiggles per second and the Temporal Phase. You can also control how the wiggles affect individual characters differently by modifying the Correlation and the Spatial Phase options.

Note that you can set Wiggles/Second to 0 and just animate Temporal and Spatial Phase. This is used in **[Ex.19c]** to create a "slamdown" effect; Hold keyframes are used so that the phase values don't interpolate between the "freeze frames."

Another option is to set Wiggles/Second to 0 and instead animate a property value such as Position. The characters will start in randomized positions, then elegantly resolve into place as demonstrated in 2D in **[Ex.19d]** and in 3D in **[Ex.19c]**.

Decoding Effect

The Wiggly Selector can be used in combination with animating the Character Offset property to create some classic decoding effects:

• **[Ex.21a]** shows text that has been scrambled with Character Offset (almost any value except 0 will do as a seed), then wiggled. Start is animated to reveal the original text. Reduce the Wiggles/Second value to swap letters more slowly.

• To scramble from one word to another, create a Source Text keyframe for the first word, then wiggle Character Offset. While the characters are busy scrambling, add a second Source Text keyframe for the second word (you'll need to temporarily turn off Animator 1 so you can see what you're doing). Animate Offset to move the scramble through the type, revealing the target word. Refer to **[Ex.21b]**.

• **[Ex.21c]** shows how the decoding effect can be coupled with a typing on effect for a nice title reveal (below). As the title types on, the characters at the leading edge do a quick fade up and descramble.

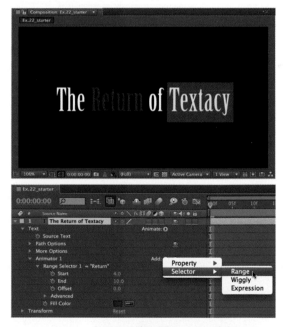

Multiple Range Selectors

An animator group can have multiple Range Selectors in order to select discontiguous ranges (for instance, only the second and fourth words in a title). To see how this works:

Step 1: Open **[Ex.22_starter]**. Animator 1 has one property applied – Fill Color – and the Start and End values for the first Range Selector have been set to contain the second word, "Return". The Units are set to Index.

Step 2: You would like the fourth word, "Textacy", also to be colored red. Select "Textacy" with the Type tool, then select Add > Selector > Range. Because you preselected a range of characters, the second range selector will be set automatically to affect only these characters. Note that the Units popup for this Range Selector is also set to Index; if you preselect characters when first creating an animator, the Units will also default to Index, not Percentage.

The Modes popup in the Advanced section come into play when you have more than one Range Selector in the same animator group. The default is to Add to the selections made in earlier Range Selectors (see the sidebar, *Modes of Confusion*, on page 387). *Gotcha:* Randomize Order applies globally – it does not follow the limits set by each Range Selector.

Each Range Selector can animate independently, so you can set property values to apply to different words at different points in time, as in **[Ex.22-final]**. But if you need to treat characters differently (for instance, have one red word that scales and one blue word that rotates), you'll need to create multiple animators instead (coming up next).

Step 2: Select "Textacy" in the Comp panel (top), then select Add > Selector > Range (above). The Start/End values for the new Range Selector are set automatically (below).

In **[Ex.23a]**, Position in Animator 1 is keyframed to type on the characters. Scale and Fill Color are applied in Animator 2 but do not animate. The Ramp Up shape creates the gradient effect.

Custom Layer Name

If you rename a text layer, the custom name will be retained even if the content is subsequently changed.

Having two animators allows for different properties to have varying shapes, wiggly values, and so on. In **[Ex.23d]**, Position and Opacity are animated Based On > Character, while Fill Color is Based On > Word.

In **[Ex.23c]**, a Wiggly Selector does the descrambling while a normal Range Selector expands the tracking.

The Case for Multiple Animators

Up to now we've worked primarily with a single animator, adding a Wiggly Selector for variety. (And just like you can add more Range Selectors, you can add more Wiggly Selectors to the same animator.) But once you start building more complex animations, you'll often find you need to use more than one animator.

For instance, you may want to animate some properties but not the others, as in **[Ex.23a]** where one animator provides the gradual change in scale and color fill across the text, while a second animator slides the individual characters into place.

You can also animate Wiggly and Range Selectors independently for different properties, as in **[Ex.23b]** and **[Ex.23c]**. In **[Ex.23c]**, a Wiggly Selector scrambles the characters, then a normal Range Selector opens up the tracking while the Wiggly resolves. Getting more complex, you can also use multiple animators to apply different Wiggly Selector values to different properties, as in the slamdown trick back in **[Ex.19a]** where Scale and Position are in separate animators so each can have different phase values.

Using multiple animators also allows more subtle control. In **[Ex.23d]** we use one animator with its Based On popup set to Character to rain down the characters individually, and a second with Based On set to Word to change the color of whole words at a time. You can use different Shapes for different properties, or even have different Smoothness values for the Square shape. For instance, in **[Ex.23e]** the Character Value has its Smoothness set to 0% so that it doesn't interpolate as it resolves. On the other hand, the animator containing the Position property needs Smoothness set to 100% to prevent visual "pops."

This is just a short list of ideas – try not to be overwhelmed by the possibilities! Start with one animator and the most obvious property ("I know I want Position to animate like this"), then add properties as ideas come to you. At some point it'll become clear that you can't do everything with a single animator (such as having the Fill Color – but not Position – affected by a Wiggly Selector). Just create a second animator, then copy and paste properties between them as necessary.

Adding and Managing Animators

Once you determine that a second animator is required, the process couldn't be easier: First, make sure no existing animator is selected, then click on the Animate button and select the property you want to animate. (Note that if an existing animator is selected, the Animate button behaves like the Add button.) Animator 2 will be added to the Timeline. If you preselect some characters before clicking the Animate button, only those characters will be included in the new Range Selector.

Once you've created two or more animators, here are some tips to help you manage and keep track of everything:

• To move properties or selectors between animator groups, click on their names to select their properties and any keyframes associated with them, and Edit > Cut. Select the animator group you wish they belonged to instead, and Edit > Paste.

• Range or Wiggly Selectors can also be moved between animator groups by dragging and dropping them onto a different animator.

• Both animator groups and selectors can be renamed: Select one, press Return, and type a useful name (such as "Anim1/Position+Scale" or "Anim2/Offset+RampUp"), then press Return again to accept.

• If you're using the Range Selector at its default values, you can delete it to simplify the Timeline. Any properties applied to the animator group can still be animated and will apply to all characters.

• There are individual eyeballs to toggle on and off each animator group, Range Selector, and Wiggly Selector. If you get confused, toggle them off and on again to see what each group is contributing to the animation.

• To simplify the Timeline, hide properties you're not using by pressing Option+Shift (Alt+Shift) and clicking on them.

• There are many reasons for placing properties in multiple animator groups, and this may require having two Range Selectors, or other parameters, that need to stay in sync. While you can copy and paste keyframes, a simple expression (Chapter 37) can keep them in sync, as shown in [**Ex.23g**].

To create this expression, open starter comp [**Ex.23f**]. Option+click (Alt+click) on the stopwatch of the Offset parameter that is the *follower*, drag its pick whip to the *master* parameter (see figure), and press Enter to accept. The follower's value appears in red to indicate that its value is the result of an expression. When you edit the master keyframes, both parameters stay in sync. You can also use this simple expression technique to link effects (such as blur, bevel and glow amounts) to text animation values, modifying the results if needed.

One Per Customer

You can use the same property in multiple animators, but only once per animator. Enabling Per-character 3D applies to all animators.

R U a Picky Selector?

To reveal only the parameters you wish to work with, select them in the Timeline and press SS (two Ss in quick succession) to Solo the Selected parameters.

TIP

Hide Selection

Selected type appears highlighted with the layer label's color. If you find this distracting, you can hide the selection by pressing Command+Shift+H (Control+Shift+H).

Use the pick whip to create an expression for the second Offset value in [**Ex.23f**]; after selecting the master Offset, press Enter.

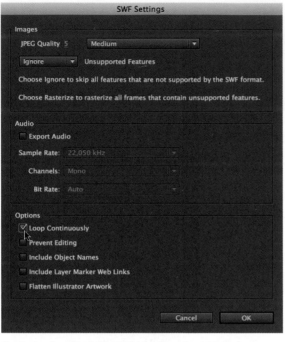

Exporting Text to SWF

Your 2D text animations can be exported as a vector-based Adobe SWF file for incorporating into a web page. To see how easy this is, open [**Ex.24**] which includes a web-sized animation that loops. Select File > Export > Adobe Flash (SWF) and choose a destination on your drive. In the SWF Settings, set Unsupported Features to Ignore to help you check which features (such as Drop Shadow effects) are unsupported and would be rendered as JPEG images instead of vectors. Set other options to taste, and click OK. Two files are saved to disk: the SWF file, and an HTML file that saves a report on which features were unsupported.

After Effects CS4 and later can also export an animation as a Flash Professional project file. This feature is covered in Chapter 39, *Integration 101*.

The text animation in [**Ex.24**] (right) can be exported as a SWF (above) and set to Loop Continuously; Unsupported Features are set to Ignore.

Drum image courtesy Getty Images.

Photoshop Text Integration

After Effects' text engine uses the same core technology as Adobe Photoshop, and so there is some integration between the various apps. You can copy text from Photoshop and Illustrator, and paste it into After Effects; basic styling is retained as much as possible.

More useful is that Photoshop files including vector Text layers (not rasterized text) that are imported into After Effects as a Comp can be converted to a Text layer. Even text on a path and rotated text layers are supported. To try this, open [**Ex.25_starter**], which is a PSD file imported as a comp. Select Layer 1 and use Layer > Convert to Editable Text. The path is converted to Mask 1, and automatically set in Text > Path Options. At this point, you can animate the type as if it originated in After Effects. Our interpretation (shown at left) is in [**Ex.25-final**].

Unfortunately you can't convert Illustrator text layers to editable text. A workaround is to export the Illustrator file as a PSD [File > Export > Photoshop (psd)] and then import this PSD file as a Composition in After Effects. The artboard size seems to be ignored, but you should be able to convert text layers. However, while text on a path seems to work, text that is rotated in Illustrator converts incorrectly. A workaround is to undo the rotation in Illustrator and rotate it later in After Effects. All in all, if you have a trusty assistant creating sources for you to animate, the advantage goes to Photoshop text layers as they convert with less hassle.

Create Outlines

Text animators allow you to create some crazy animations, but if you want to change the shape of the characters by editing points on a Bezier curve, you'll need to create outlines from your text layer.

The Create Outlines feature has had a hard time making up its mind in recent versions. In After Effects version 7, you could convert a text layer to a solid that contained a series of masks that corresponded to the characters in the text. This allowed you to animate the individual vertices of the character shapes. (Animating Masks was covered in Chapter 10.)

In After Effects CS3 – where Shape Layers were introduced – this feature changed so that Create Outlines created a shape layer with a series of shape paths that corresponded to the individual characters.

With version CS4 and later, you now have the option to create *either* solids with masks or to create shape layers. Select a text layer (such as the layer in [**26a-Create Outlines**]), choose either Layer > Create Shapes from Text or Layer > Create Masks from Text. Some of the fun you can have with this feature is demonstrated in more detail in the *Shapes from Other Places* section in Chapter 32, page 550.

The Shapes option has the advantage that more of the styling of the original text (such as its stroke) remains intact. On the other hand, the Masks option allows you to apply effects that use mask shapes such as Audio Waveform, Scribble, Vegas, and Stroke (see Bonus Chapter 23B).

Remember that either type of path can also be copied and pasted as a motion path to Position or Effect Point properties. This allows you to start with a character and then have another object or light follow along its motion path, or have particles whizz around the shape of the letter.

Closing Characters

Per-character 3D text moves flat characters through 3D space, but it does not give the text any thickness. For true 3D text you'll need to purchase a third-party plug-in. Check out the summary of third-party 3D plug-ins at the end of Chapter 16; Zaxwerks Invigorator PRO and ProAnimator or the Boris Continuum Complete package are probably your best bets. Adobe Repoussé, which is part of Photoshop CS5 Extended, can also create 3D extruded elements and is also covered in Chapter 16.

Text can be converted to either Shape Layers or mask shapes applied to a white solid. The Shapes option retains the original color and stroke of the text plus allows you to apply Shape Effects (Chapter 32).

TIP

Expressive Text

You can add Expression Selectors to a text animator (Add > Selector > Expression) in the same way you add a Range or Wiggly Selector. This is covered in the Expressions Bonus Chapter 37B.

CONNECT

Keyframing: Chapters 3 and 4.

Motion blur: Chapter 8.

Masking: Chapter 10.

3D space: Chapters 13 through 16.

Continuous rasterization and text rendering issues: Chapter 20.

Animation Presets, text presets: Chapter 25.

Shape layers: Chapter 32.

Expressions: Chapters 37 and 37B.

Additional Photoshop issues: Chapter 38.

To find more tips on good typography practices, enter "rules of typography" in your favorite web search engine. (Typoholics can browse the Upper & Lower Case archives at *www.itcfonts.com/ulc/*.)

3D text rendered with Zaxwerks Invigorator PRO. Courtesy Joe Mason.

Example of Boris Extruded Text. Courtesy BorisFX.

22

Applying and Using Effects

After animating layers comes treating their images with special effects.

O ne of the richest areas for exploration in After Effects is its "effects" side. The variety of effects supplied with After Effects ranges from the extremely utilitarian to the extremely wild, each with anywhere from one to over 100 parameters you can adjust. Fortunately, virtually all effects share the same basic methods of adjusting and animating those parameters.

In this chapter, we will start with an overview of how to apply and edit effects. We'll then move onto some more sophisticated tricks using effects, such as animating their Effect Point, using adjustment layers, exploiting mask paths, and adding blending modes. We'll end with Layer Styles: a powerful alternative to common effects such as bevels, glows and shadows, borrowed from Photoshop.

Applying an Effect

Each layer has a master effects on/off checkbox under the *"fx"* column in the Timeline panel. Twirl the effects down for the layer (select it and press E on the keyboard), and each individual effect will be revealed, with its own on/off switch underneath the Video switch (the eyeball icon).

There are two approaches to applying an effect to a layer: using the Effect menu, or using the Effects & Presets panel. To use the traditional Effect menu, select the layer or layers you wish to effect in either the Comp or Timeline panel, and click on the Effect menu heading. You will be presented with a list of categories representing general classes of effects; if you have any third-party effects, you may also see categories based on the vendor's name. Mouse down to the category you want, and a hierarchical menu will appear with all the effects in that category. Select the specific effect you want and release the mouse button – it is now applied to all the currently selected layers.

After an effect has been applied, the layer will gain a new checkbox under the "*fx*" column in the Timeline panel. This *fx* switch is the master effects switch, and if an *fx* appears in this box, all effects that are enabled will be processed. Click on the master *fx* switch to turn off all effects for that layer. With a layer selected, press E, and the names of the effects applied to that layer will automatically twirl open. Each individual effect also has its own *fx* switch under the Video column (the eyeball icon) in the Timeline panel; here, you can turn individual effects on and off.

Composition **[Ex.01]** in this chapter's project (**22-Example Project.aep**) consists of a single layer (a "sunprint" created by Trish); select it, and add Effect > Blur & Sharpen > Sharpen. In addition to the *fx* column becom-

Example Project

Explore the 22-Example Project.aep file as you read this chapter; references to [Ex.##] refer to specific compositions within the project file.

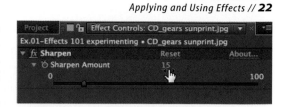

ing active in the Timeline panel, the Effect Controls panel automatically opens. This panel lists all the effects applied to a layer, as well as checkboxes to enable or disable each one individually. You can hide or show each effect using the main "twirly" to the left of its name.

If you close the Effect Controls panel and need to edit the effect further, select the layer, then reopen this panel with Effect > Effect Controls – the shortcuts are F3, or Command+Shift+T on Mac (Control+Shift+T on Windows). You can also double-click the name of the effect in the Timeline panel. Remember, if you want to re-edit an already applied effect, don't select it again from the Effect menu, or you'll just reapply it.

To delete an effect, select it in the Timeline or Effect Controls panel and press the Delete key.

The Effect Controls panel lists all effects applied to a layer and is the best place to edit their parameters. Values may be scrubbed directly; here, the user interface element for the Sharpen parameter (a slider) has been twirled open as well.

Effects & Presets Panel

The often-preferred way to apply effects is to use the Effects & Presets panel. It provides several ways to organize and search for effects and gives more flexibility in applying them.

The Effects & Presets panel has its own frame in the Standard workspace. If it is not visible, it can be opened using Window > Effects & Presets; the shortcut is Command+5 (Control+5). Of course, you can dock it into another frame if you wish; it's best to display it as tall as possible so you can better see the choices available.

At its default, the Effects & Presets panel presents a list view of the same effects folders you find under the Effect menu item. Rather than navigating through a hierarchical menu to select effects inside a particular category, you twirl open these same category folders in the panel.

Double-clicking on an effect in this panel adds it to the currently selected layers. You can also drag an effect directly to a layer (currently selected or not) in either the Timeline or Comp panel; the Info panel tells you which layer will receive the effect. Even better, if you have a layer's Effect Controls panel open or have its effect stack twirled down in the Timeline panel, you can drag your new effect to exactly the place in the stack you want to insert this effect, just as you can drag new footage items from the Project panel to the desired place between layers in the Timeline panel.

TIP

Preset Power

Animation Presets are a great way to save your favorite effect settings, and are the subject of Chapter 25.

The Effects & Presets panel provides a list view of the installed effects and saved Animation Presets, with several options for how to sort and view them. Note that Show Animation Presets has been disabled for now.

You can drag a new effect directly from the Effects & Presets panel to any place between already-applied effects in the Timeline or Effect Controls panel. You can also reorder effects by dragging them up and down in these panels.

To search the names of currently installed effects, type a few characters of the word you are looking for in the Contains field of the Effects & Presets panel, and all matching effects will be revealed. (If Show Animation Presets had been enabled, presets with "color" in their name would also have been revealed.)

Practice this in [**Ex.01**]: After adding the Sharpen effect, select the **PS_Axis** layer in the Timeline panel and type E to reveal the effect applied to it. Also make sure the Effect Controls panel (F3) is open. In the Effects & Presets panel, twirl open the Color Correction category. Either double-click the Color Balance (HLS) effect or drag it to the **PS_Axis** layer in the Timeline or Comp panel. Then twirl open another category and practice dragging a third effect to different locations in the effect stack in either the Timeline or Effect Controls panel.

The Search Party

Where the Effects & Presets panel comes into its own is in searching for a specific effect. Sometimes it's hard to remember which company made which effect, or which category to look inside to find a stock Adobe or Cycore CC effect – particularly since some effects change folders in new versions of the program (which happens periodically). This is where the QuickSearch field (labeled "Contains:") along the top comes in handy. Type a word – or even a few characters – of the name of the effect you are looking for, and After Effects will automatically present you with a list of matching Effects and Animation Presets while you type, as well as presets that use an effect with a matching name.

The Options menu at the top right of the Effects & Presets panel (the arrow circled in red in the figure on the left) lets you view effects in various ways. If your main viewing option is set to Categories, then when you perform a search, the folders that contain the searched-for effects will also appear, twirled open to reveal those effects inside. Can't remember which effect package or folder had that color effect you were looking for? Type "**color**" and every effect installed with the word "**color**" in its name will appear. You still have to remember some part of the name of an effect to find it, but it's better than randomly searching a long hierarchical menu when you can't remember what category an effect is in.

There are other options, of course. Switching the view from Categories to Alphabetical removes the folder distinctions and shows all installed effects as a simple list; switching to Finder Folders re-sorts them by the folders they reside in on your drive, rather than the category folders they are preprogrammed to appear in.

You can create and name your own folders inside the application's Plug-ins folder and re-sort individual effects into these new folders as you see fit. Duplicating effects and dragging the copies into your folders will cause After Effects to complain that it doesn't know which duplicate to use, and only one instance of the effect will appear in the Effects & Presets panel. Bear in mind that reorganizing effects in the Plug-ins folder will not change the categories they appear in, just how they sort when you're viewing the Effects & Presets panel by Finder Folders. Also, re-sorting third-party plug-in packages will make it trickier to update them.

Effect Controls

There are several ways to edit the parameters of an effect. These parameters appear in both the Effect Controls and the Timeline panel; you may need to twirl it open (click on the arrow next to the effect's name) to reveal the parameters. Effects can also have subsections; click on the arrow next to a subsection's name to reveal more parameters. Hold Command (Control) when you click to open all the nested subsections.

Effect parameters that have numeric values are easy to adjust. The most common way is to click on its value while also dragging the mouse to "scrub" its value. For finer control, press Command (Control) while scrubbing; to scrub values faster, press Shift while scrubbing. If you know the precise value you want, click on the value to highlight it and type in a new value. Alternatively, you can right-click on a value to open a dialog where you can also edit it.

While scrubbing a parameter of a calculation-intensive effect, you may notice that the image in the Comp panel becomes pixelated. Depending on how you have Preferences > Previews and the comp's Fast Previews popup set, After Effects may be employing "adaptive resolution" and temporarily switching to a lower resolution to keep up with your scrubbing. As soon as you release the mouse, the frame will render normally. If you find this annoying, set the Fast Previews popup along the bottom right side of the Comp panel to Off. (For more information, refer to the *Preview Possibilities* sidebar at the end of Chapter 2.)

If you prefer a more graphical user interface, edit effects inside the Effect Controls panel. Click on the arrow next to a parameter's name to reveal a user interface element such as a slider to manipulate it. Most effect parameters use the same set of user interface elements – we'll go through this next.

Stacking Effects

You can apply an unlimited number of effects to each layer in a comp. The effects are processed in top-to-bottom order, as viewed in Effect Controls or the Timeline. To reorder them, drag them by their names up and down the list.

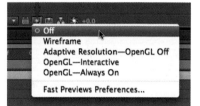

When Fast Previews (the icon with the lightning bolt located in the lower right corner of the Comp panel) is set to either Adaptive Resolution or OpenGL, the image in the Comp panel may temporarily become pixelated while you edit a slower effect's parameter. If this is too distracting, set Fast Previews to Off.

Sliders

The most common effects parameter controller is the Slider. It gives you quick access to a range from a minimum to a maximum value, such as 0% to 100%. Sliders have been all but replaced by directly scrubbing parameter values, but some of you may still prefer to drag a slider for the visual feedback it provides while setting a value, or because you can customize the parameter ranges it can access. To use a slider in the Effect Controls panel, twirl down the arrow to the left of a numerical parameter and drag the slider's knob along its track.

The numbers at the left and right ends of a slider are not necessarily the minimum and maximum values – they are just the end points of the effect creator's idea of what would be a useful range. Right-click on a numeric value, and from the popup menu that appears, select Edit Value. This opens a dialog box where you can directly type in the number you want and edit the slider's minimum and maximum ranges.

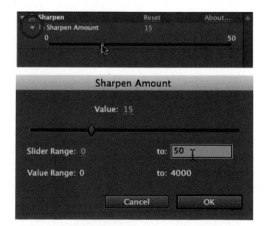

To reveal the slider, twirl down the arrow to the left of a numerical value (top). A slider's range can be changed; try reducing the maximum value for more precise control (above).

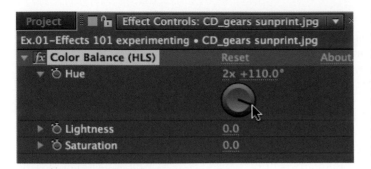

Rotary dials are used to adjust angle parameters. To edit the value with more precision, drag the mouse further away from the dial.

Scrubbable Swatches

If a color swatch is revealed in the Timeline panel, you can click and drag the swatch to interactively "scrub" its color.

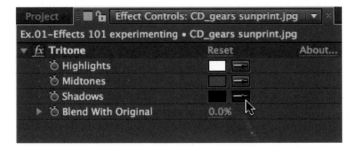

Tritone is an example of an effect that allows you to pick colors to use in a treatment. You can click on the swatches to edit the color, or use the eyedropper to pick a color from elsewhere on the screen.

Rotary Dials

In [**Ex.01**], select layer 1, and make sure its Effect Controls panel is open (F3). Delete any effects you have applied to it (Effect > Remove All), and apply Effect > Color Correction > Color Balance (HLS). It has sliders for Lightness and Saturation. The Hue parameter has another type of user interface, which we call the rotary dial.

Most parameters that adjust an angle – such as rotation, drop shadow direction, or even color hue angle – use this circular controller. To adjust it graphically, click anywhere inside or along the edge of the dial and it will jump to this position; to further tweak it, hold the mouse down and drag it around the circle. To drag with more precision, hold down the mouse, then move the cursor farther away from the dial's center – now as you rotate around the dial, you will have more control because you are using a longer "lever" to tweak it with. You can also scrub its numeric value.

Most effects with angle parameters allow you to enter multiple revolutions. For visual confirmation, look at the leftmost component of the rotary dial's numeric value – a number other than zero in front of the "x" means there is more than one revolution applied. While the value 110° may look visually identical to 2 × +110°, this feature allows you to smoothly animate changes in values that "go through zero."

Color Swatches

There are many effects that allow you to colorize an element, and After Effects gives you two ways to set colors. Still in [**Ex.01**], delete any effects you have applied, then add Effect > Color Correction > Tritone. It has three colors to set, which affect the blacks, whites, and midtones. These default to black, white, and a sepia color.

Click on the color "swatches" – the small rectangles of color – for Midtones to open the color picker for that swatch. (The default is the Adobe Color Picker; if you prefer the system default picker, enable Use System Color Picker in Preferences > General.) Select your color; edits performed in the Adobe Color Picker will interactively update the image in the Comp panel as you edit.

The other method is to click on the eyedropper next to the color swatch, then click on a color you want that is visible somewhere on the screen. If you have the Window > Info panel open, it will update the color values it "sees" – both numerically and with a temporary swatch of its own – as you move your cursor around. Note that it picks an average color of pixels around your cursor position.

Popups

Some effect parameters have discrete choices rather than continuous numeric ranges. These are usually represented as popup menus. The most common menu choices are Horizontal and Vertical for blur directions and their ilk. To experience a moderately more complex set of popups, add Effect > Channel > Minimax to our test layer in [**Ex.01**], set a small value for Radius, and try out the various menu options.

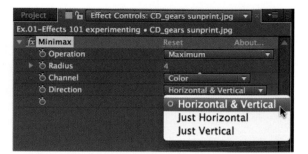

Effect Points

Several effects have specific points that they are centered around or that otherwise define the area the effect takes place over or between. Examples include the center of a lens flare or particle system effect, the center of a twirl, or the two points that define a lightning bolt. These are known as effect points and are represented by a crosshair icon in the Effect Controls panel.

Popup parameter menus, shown here in Minimax, cannot interpolate between values, though they can be animated using Hold keyframes.

In our trusty comp [**Ex.01**], select Effect > Remove All, and then apply Effect > Generate > Lens Flare. In the Effect Controls panel, click on the crosshair icon next to Flare Center; your mouse cursor will change to a live set of crosshairs. Click on the point in the Comp panel where you want the lens effect centered.

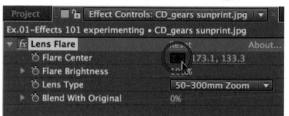

The effect point can also be spotted and edited directly in the Comp panel. Select the effect in the Timeline or Effect Controls panel; the effect point symbol will then appear in the Comp panel. It is identified as a small circle with a + symbol inside it (in contrast with the anchor point's registration symbol). Click and drag to edit its location. If you can't see the effect point, check that the effect name is indeed highlighted, and make sure that Effect Controls is enabled in the Comp panel's View Options (accessed by the options wing menu in the upper right corner).

The effect point's parameter has a value on the X and Y axes that is in relation to the *layer*, not the overall composition. You can animate the layer's position without messing up your effect points. However, this distinction can be a problem if you copy and paste values between effect point and position keyframes: Unless the layer and comp sizes are the same and the layer is centered in the comp, the same raw numbers will be describing different points in space.

Finally, if the effect point is animated, it will have a motion path that can be edited in the Layer panel (see *Animating Effects*, later in this chapter).

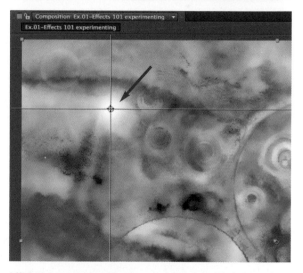

Effect Points are identified by a crosshair icon (circled in red) in the Effect Controls panel (top). They can be moved either by directly grabbing this icon in the Comp panel, or by clicking on this icon and then "placing" the crosshair center in the Comp panel (above).

Now You See It...

...now you don't. Crosshairs, or any special interfaces for an effect, are displayed in the Comp panel only when the name of the effect is highlighted in the Effect Controls or Timeline panel.

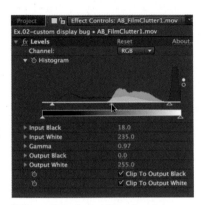

Effect > Color Correction > Levels is an example of an effect with a custom interface; the "histogram" shows you the luminance distribution in the image.

Option Dialogs

Some effects have special Options dialogs or related additional choices (such as Choose LUT) along the top of their Effect Controls panel.

• They don't always open automatically when the effect is applied.

• You can edit them later by clicking on the word Options (or their equivalent, such as Choose LUT for the new Apply Color LUT effect) to the right of the effect's name in the Effect Controls panel.

• You *cannot* undo them; you will need to manually change them back to their previous values.

• When you copy and paste, not all of the values in the Options dialog are necessarily included. Check to be sure.

Custom Interface Items

Beyond the standard user interface items mentioned above, many effects – especially those from third parties – will have custom user interface elements. Some are intuitive; for those that are not, you can always consult the online help or the user's manual.

There is unfortunately an "issue" (we call it a bug) with the way custom interface elements interact with the RAM caching scheme in After Effects. If the custom interface draws a graphic based on the underlying image (such as the Histogram in Levels), and the underlying image changes from frame to frame (for example, a movie), it will not get redrawn if you go back to a frame that has already been stored in After Effects' image cache.

To see this in action, open [**Ex.02**], select the layer in it, and open its Effect Controls panel. Note the shape of the Histogram display. Step forward a few frames (Page Down); notice how it changes to show the luminance values of each new frame. Step back (Page Up); notice it doesn't change back to its previous shape. Turning the effect on and off refreshes the cache and therefore the display for the entire layer. If you're setting values based on how these elements draw, toggle it off and on again to be sure you're getting the right information.

Lost and Found

If you open a project that uses an effect that you do not currently have loaded, you will see a warning dialog. To locate missing effects, open each composition and press FF (two Fs in quick succession) to reveal missing effects in the Timeline.

After Effects will keep a placeholder for the missing effect, including all of its keyframes. You will see the word "Missing" next to the effect's name in the Effect Controls and Timeline panels.

If you install the missing effect, relaunch After Effects, and reopen the problematic project, the effect will be relinked, and everyone will be happy again. If the project used an older version of the effect that is no longer compatible with an updated effect, you still have all of its parameters and keyframes available to copy and paste to the new effect.

Animating Effects

Animating effect parameters is very much like animating any other property of a layer – all the rules and tricks you've already learned in the earlier chapters about the stopwatch, keyframes, and velocity controls apply. However, there are a few additional tricks for creating and navigating between keyframes from the Effect Controls panel that are worth learning.

Tricks to Click

First, turn on the stopwatch to the left of any effect parameter's name to turn on animation for that parameter and set the first keyframe. The stopwatches are available in both the Effect Controls and Timeline panels. Option+clicking (Alt+clicking) on the *name* of any effect parameter in the Effect Controls panel sets a keyframe for that effect. If that parameter has no keyframes yet, this is the same as turning on the stopwatch. Be aware, though, that if you're parked on an existing keyframe, Option+clicking (Alt+clicking) will remove the keyframe.

Right-clicking on an effect parameter's name in the Effect Controls panel offers several handy shortcuts for creating, deleting, and navigating between keyframes.

The second trick is to right-click on a keyframeable parameter's name. With most effects, this brings up a contextual menu that allows you to set a keyframe (or remove it, if it has already been set), jump to the next or previous keyframe, copy an expression applied to that parameter, or reset just this parameter to its initial value. If the parameter has already been enabled for keyframing, note that Reset will set a keyframe at the current time with the reset value. Finally, Reveal in Timeline will reveal the parameter in the Timeline if it's not already revealed. (If the layer is twirled up, the parameter will be revealed with the last twirled-down state of the layer, so don't expect it to solo just this one parameter.)

Of course, remember the trick of selecting a layer and pressing U to twirl down just the properties currently being animated; again, this is a real boon with effects that can have up to 127 parameters. Press UU to twirl down only properties that have changed from their default values.

Effect Point Animation

While you can edit an effect point in the Comp panel and set keyframes, you can't see the motion path it creates. This has led many to believe you can have only linear movements with effect points. As it turns out, since the effect point has a value on the X and Y axes in relation to the layer (just like the Anchor Point), access to the motion path is in the Layer panel.

To see this in action, in [**Ex.03**] we applied the Effect > Generate > Lens Flare effect and animated the Flare Center parameter so that the lens flare moved around the frame. Double-click the layer to open the Layer panel, and select the Lens Flare effect from the View menu (bottom-right corner). The motion path will now be visible. The spatial keyframes default to Auto Bezier, but you can edit the handles just like the motion path for Position (as covered in Chapter 3). The Layer panel shows only the motion path; the result appears only in the Comp panel.

A New View

To view a layer in isolation, double-click it to open its Layer panel. The Render checkbox allows you to view it with or without effects; the View popup enables you to choose where in the render pipeline you preview the result.

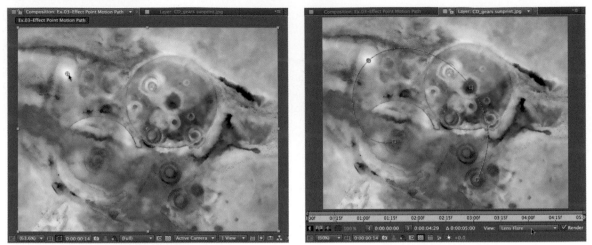

You can see an effect point in the Comp panel (above); to edit its path, select it from the Layer panel's View (right).

Expressive Effects

You can also use expressions (Chapter 37) to link effect parameters. If you already know how to use expressions, try linking the Flare Brightness to the gizmo's Scale in [**Ex.04**].

Remember that the effect's name must be selected in the Effect Controls panel to also see the effect point(s) in the Comp panel.

Pasting Position and Masks to Effect Point

Just as you can copy and paste mask paths into position-related properties to create animations that follow their paths (as covered in Chapter 3), you can also paste either Position animations or mask paths to the effect point to animate it.

Pasting a mask path to an effect point to create a motion path will come in handy if you've already traced an object or path in a layer, and now want to animate an effect such as a Lens Flare or a particle system to follow it. The generic steps are:

Step 1:   Select the mask path in either the Layer or Timeline panel.

Step 2:   Command+C (Control+C) to Copy.

Step 3:   Select the effect point parameter name in the Timeline panel you want to paste into.

Step 4:   Command+V (Control+V) to Paste.

To practice pasting a Position path to an effect, open [**Ex.04_starter**] and RAM Preview: It features a timelapse shot of a freeway, plus a UFO flying through it using Position keyframes. Say you wanted to add a lens flare behind the UFO to make it pop out more from its background:

Step 1:   Select the **AB_TimelapseCityscapes.mov** layer and apply Effect > Generate > Lens Flare.

Step 2:   Make sure the Position keyframes for the **QE_Gizmo_loop** layer are exposed in the Timeline panel. If they aren't, select the layer and type P to reveal them. Click on the word "Position" to select its keyframes, then type Command+C (Control+C) to copy them.

Step 3:   In its Effect Controls panel for **AB_TimelapseCityscapes**, right-click on the words "Flare Center" and select Reveal in Timeline from the

You can paste one layer's Position animation into an effect point parameter – such as Flare Center (left) – to make an effect follow an object animation (right). For this to work, the layer with the effect must be the same size as the comp, since you are pasting from "comp space" (Position) to "layer space" (the effect point). Gizmo courtesy Quiet Earth Design; background courtesy Artbeats/Timelapse Cityscapes.

popup menu. With the time indicator at 00:00, click on the words "Flare Center" in the Timeline panel (it will be highlighted, see figure above) then Command+V (Control+V) to paste.

RAM Preview your animation – the Lens Flare effect will stay centered behind the moving gizmo. If you got lost, check our result [**Ex.04-final**].

Unfortunately, these tricks will not work if the layer and comp sizes differ and if the layer is not centered in the comp. Effect points are defined by their position in the layer, not the comp (since the layer might also be moving in the comp). Those with a 3D background might know this problem as a difference between "local" and "global" coordinates. These two coordinate systems are the same only if the layer and comp are the same.

Copying and Pasting Effects

You can copy and paste effects between layers, but there are a few behaviors you should be aware of:

• If you select the effect's name in the Effect Controls panel, copy it, and paste it to a layer that does not have this effect, the entire effect will be pasted, including any keyframes. Remember that the first keyframe copied will be pasted starting at the current time, so pay attention to where the time marker is parked before you paste.

• In the past, some parameters inside an effect's Options dialog have not been reliably copied and pasted. After pasting, double-check any settings you changed inside Options for an effect.

• If you paste an effect to a layer that already has the same effect applied, it just pastes its values, rather than a duplicate of the effect.

• You can duplicate a selected effect in the Effect Controls panel using Command+D (Control+D)

to Edit > Duplicate, which is handy for effects like Stroke, where you might want to apply different effect settings to each mask path (as in [**Ex.05-final**]).

• If multiple copies of the same effect are applied to a layer, the behavior is such that if no effect is selected when you paste, another instance of the effect will be applied. To copy values to a specific effect, select it first to "target" it, then paste.

• You can select individual effect parameters by clicking on the parameter name in the Timeline panel. If you copy these parameters and paste to another layer that already has the same effect applied, just the values (or keyframes) for the selected parameter(s) will get copied across. If the effect is not already applied, the default values will be used for any parameters that are not part of the copy/paste process.

• To save a complex animated effect to reuse in future projects, save an Animation Preset (Chapter 25).

The Stroke effect can follow any mask path currently applied to a layer, and even animated along the path, as with the purple lines in [**Ex.05-final**]. Image courtesy Digital Vision/Music Mix.

Masks as Paths

Several effects let you create an effect that follows the outline of a mask. The parameter you need to set is called *Path* – this tells the effect which mask path to look at. Examples of effects that can use a mask path include Generate > Audio Spectrum, Audio Waveform, Fill, Stroke and Vegas. In fact, some effects (such as Stroke) do nothing unless the Path popup points to a mask.

To practice, open comp [**Ex.05a_starter**] and double-click the layer **DV_MusicMix** to open its Layer panel. Note the four mask paths that are already created. If these masks are not already revealed in the Timeline panel, select **DV_MusicMix** and press M to reveal them. If you have enabled Toggle View Masks along the bottom of the Comp panel, you will also see them outlined in the Comp panel. Back in the Timeline panel, note the names of the masks and the fact that they are set to None (off): We don't want them to create transparency.

Now, apply Effect > Generate > Stroke. Notice that its first effect parameter is a popup called Path. Click on it, and you get a list of available masks. Select each one in turn, and note that a different outline will now get the stroke. For additional fun, animate their Start and End points to draw these stroked paths. Our version is shown in [**Ex.05a-final**].

A more fun example of using mask paths for effects is demonstrated in [**Ex.05b**]. Select the layer **AB_EstabUrban**; if the Toggle Layer Masks switch is on, you will see we carefully outlined the skyline of buildings with a mask. We then applied Generate > Audio Spectrum, set its Path popup to use our mask path, enabled it to Draw on Original (so we could see the original footage underneath), and set the Audio Layer popup to use **TU_WSBump1Bounce**. RAM Preview: The result is an animated line that traces the skyline and bounces along with the music.

Generate > Audio Spectrum is set to follow the mask path we drew along the skyline in this footage, resulting in a fun animated outline. Footage courtesy Artbeats/Establishments: Urban.

Render Settings

Most effects take little to no rendering time when the effect has zero effect on the image. So when you animate a blur effect down to zero, the effect is essentially turned off from that point forward. If an effect is slowing down rendering even after the effect hits the last keyframe, split the layer (Edit > Split Layer) and delete the effect where it's not needed. Also, non-animating effects applied to still images should cache after the first frame rather than reapply themselves on every frame in the composition.

When it comes time to render your comp, the Render Settings includes a menu for Effects. The options are Current Settings, All On, and All Off. (More on Render Settings in Chapter 42.)

Generally, rendering with Current Settings is the safest option: Any effects that are on will render, and those that are turned off won't be processed. However, if you've turned off an effect while you're editing because it's too slow, make sure you turn it on before you render.

The second option, Effects > All On, will turn on all effects, whether they're currently enabled or not. The danger here is that you will not only turn on that slowpoke effect you turned off temporarily, but other effects that you didn't want that you'd forgotten all about. In general, if an effect experiment failed, delete the effect rather than turn it off. That allows you the option to turn off slow effects temporarily and have Render Settings override current settings with the All On option.

The Effects menu in Render Settings controls whether effects that are turned off are processed.

CC Composite

Many effects have a Blend With Original or similar parameter. This allows you to tone down the strength of an effect by blending together "before" and "after" versions of the image.

However, not all effects have this parameter. Also, Blend With Original is slightly misnamed; what it really means is "blend with what the image looked like right before this effect." If you have more than one effect applied to a layer, the Blend With Original parameter for the later effects don't reach all the way back to the original image.

The solution to both of these problems is Effect > Channel > CC Composite. Apply it after any effect,

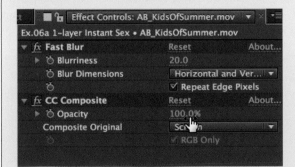

CC Composite's Opacity provides a "blend with original" feature for whatever effects are applied before it.

CC Composite makes it possible to create "instant sex" treatments without having to duplicate the original layer. Footage courtesy Artbeats/Kids of Summer.

and its Opacity parameter will blend between the processed image and the original, unaltered image, no matter how many effects you have applied. As a nice bonus, its Composite Original popup has a long list of blending modes to create different types of looks. If the prior effects altered the alpha channel of the image, the RGB Only switch decides whether the new alpha should be applied to the copy of the original image as well.

In **[Ex.06a]** we combined Fast Blur plus CC Composite to create a version of the "instant sex" look we mention in Bonus Chapter 23B.

In **[Ex.06b]**, we added Color Key to key out the grass, then disabled CC Composite's RGB Only switch. This left the grass unaffected while just the kids and sky got the "instant sex" treatment.

The "half moon" icon in the Timeline panel is the switch that changes any ordinary layer into that superhero known as an Adjustment Layer. In **[Ex.07]** we've applied a Gaussian Blur effect to blur the composite of all layers below – the layer above is unaffected.

Adjustment Layers

An alternative way to use effects is to apply them to *adjustment layers*. All the layers below an adjustment layer in the Timeline panel are composited together, then the effects applied to the adjustment layer are applied to a copy of this composite. The original and effected versions are then blended together.

Any content in an adjustment layer is ignored. What is important is its alpha channel, as this determines which portions of the underlying composite receive the effects. A full-frame adjustment layer means the entire frame is treated. To apply effects to selected areas, you can crop the adjustment layer using masks and mattes; to blend in an adjustment layer's changes at less than full strength, reduce its opacity. Blending modes further affect how the treated and untreated versions of the image are combined. You can also animate the adjustment layer as well as the applied effects. We'll illustrate all of these features in the next few pages.

Adjustment Logic 101

To practice using adjustment layers, select Close All from the tab along the top of the Comp panel, then open comp **[Ex.07_starter]**. It contains a simple composite of several layers: a text layer, two object layers, and a pair of backgrounds, many of which use blending modes to mix them together. Say you wanted to give the same amount of blur to all the images except the foreground text layer. You could add a blur effect to each of the background layers individually (remembering to alter the blur amount per layer to compensate for how much each layer is scaled), or you could precompose these layers and apply the blur to that. Or, you could use an adjustment layer.

To try this out, select Layer > New > Adjustment Layer. A solid that is the size of the comp will be created with a default name and with its "half moon" Adjustment Layer switch turned on in the Switches column of the Timeline panel. This switch indicates that the image information in the layer should be ignored as it is going to be used only for adjustments.

An adjustment layer does nothing on its own – so let's apply an effect to it. Add Effect > Blur & Sharpen > Fast Blur and set the Blurriness slid-

Ex.07_starter					
0:00:00:00				0f	10f
#	Source Name				
1	SportsRoundup.ai	fx			
2	Adjustment Layer 1	fx			
	Fast Blur	Reset	fx		
3	GI_boxing.tif				
4	GI_baseball.tif				
5	AB_NatureAbstracts_loop.mov	fx			
6	DV_Electro_ex_sml.mov	fx			

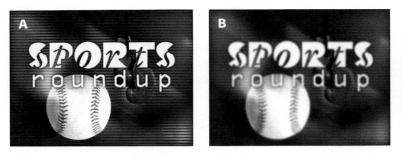

er to a value of 6. Note that all layers below are now blurred. Drag the adjustment layer down one layer in the Timeline panel so it is below the **SportsRoundup.ai** layer. This text remains sharp because it is above the adjustment layer, while layers below are blurred. Experiment with reordering the layers to reinforce this idea. If you get lost, check out our comp [**Ex.07-final**], where we also animated the Blurriness parameter.

Edited Sequence

Adjustment layers are also useful for treating a sequence of edited layers. In [**Ex.08**] we've given a sequence of movies a rich blue cast using Effect > Color Correction > Tritone. The effect is applied only in proportion to how opaque the adjustment layer is, so edit the adjustment layer's Opacity value (press T to reveal) to mix back in the color from the original footage. This is a great way to give a set of disparate shots the same overall "look."

Additional Adjusting Tricks

Adjustment layers are easy – and fun – if you just keep their logic in mind: They are a region of a comp that you can apply effects to (but not Layer Styles). You can also apply multiple effects to a single adjustment layer and multiple adjustment layers in a single comp (these are processed from the bottom up, with each adjustment layer sending its result to the adjustment layer above).

The sections of the adjustment layer that are opaque determine what portion of the underlying image is affected. The adjustment layer's in and out times are also obeyed. Apart from adjusting the Opacity value, there are other tricks for modifying the opaque areas. The following examples employ techniques covered in detail in other chapters, as noted:

Simple Selections

The simplest example of limiting the scope of the adjustment layer is to transform it (Scale, Position, or Rotation) – the layers below are affected only directly under the adjustment layer, as shown in [**Ex.09a**]. Because this layer is simply a white solid that happens to have the adjustment layer switch on, you can also open the Layer > Solid Settings dialog (Command+Shift+Y on Mac, Control+Shift+Y on Windows) and rename or change the size of the solid.

The "before" image of a stack of layers (A). A new adjustment layer was created and the Fast Blur effect was applied; this affects all layers (B). To keep the foreground text layer "in focus," we moved it above the adjustment layer (C). Sports images courtesy Getty Images; backgrounds from Digital Vision/Electro and Artbeats/Nature Abstracts.

An adjustment layer can treat a sequence of edited layers with the same effect if it is applied on top of all of the clips [**Ex.08**]. Musician footage courtesy Lee Stranahan.

Placing the adjustment layer along the bottom of the frame limits the Channel > Invert effect to just this area. Footage courtesy Creative License.

In **[Ex.09b]** a circular mask (the yellow outline) applied to the adjustment layer causes the Mosaic effect to be limited to that region around the woman's head. Footage courtesy Artbeats/Business World.

In **[Ex.10-final]**, the title layer and goldfish image are both used as adjustment layers. Fish courtesy Getty Images; ocean footage from Artbeats/Monster Waves.

We applied Find Edges and composited the result in Screen mode.

Masking Shapes

For more interesting shapes, applying a mask (Chapter 10) to the adjustment layer will limit effects to the masked area. In [**Ex.09b**], an oval mask was created so that the effects would apply to the masked area only (the adjustment layer is now transparent outside the mask). The Stylize > Mosaic effect was applied to blur the woman's face, and a generous mask feather fades out the edges of the effected area. Additional mask examples for you to explore are included in the [**Ex.09**] folder, including a mask pasted from Illustrator.

Any Alpha Will Do

Any layer can become an adjustment layer if you turn on its adjustment layer switch, although images with interesting alpha channel shapes work best. The original image will disappear, but effects applied to it will modify all layers below based on that layer's alpha channel. To practice this, open [**Ex.10_starter**] and turn on the adjustment layer switch for the **SharkAttack.ai** title layer (the image will vanish – that's okay). Apply Effect > Channel > Invert. The effect will be applied to the water texture below, using the title's alpha channel to limit its area of effect. The goldfish layer can also be an adjustment layer – we used it to darken the background footage in [**Ex.10-final**]. Multiple adjustment layers are rendered from the bottom up. You can also use Shape Layers (Chapter 32) as Adjustment Layers.

Animating Adjustments

An adjustment layer can also be animated using the regular Transform properties. This applies to both simple solids and layers with alpha (see image to the right). Try animating the position of the title and fish layers in [**Ex.10**] and see how the effects now move across the background. You can also ani-

Comedian courtesy Getty Images/Cool Characters.

mate effect parameters, as well as animate the mask path when you're creating selections with masks. The [**Ex.11**] folder includes examples of adding animation to solids, alpha shapes, masks, and effects.

Blending Modes

Effects applied to an adjustment layer can also be reapplied to the original image using a blending mode (Chapter 9) and Opacity to further refine the mix. This is particularly useful for more subtle effects when mixing in the original image with just the Opacity parameter doesn't cut it. The [**Ex.12**] folder includes some examples, including compositing just the edges found by the Find Edges effect, plus two variations on the classic "instant sex" effect.

Luma Track Mattes

Any footage with an interesting alpha channel could make a good adjustment layer, but what if the footage is grayscale? In this case, create a new adjustment layer, then apply the grayscale footage as a luma track matte (Chapter 11) for the adjustment layer. Make

sure the grayscale footage is on top of the adjustment layer, then set the adjustment layer to Luma Matte (or Inverted Luma Matte) in the track matte (TrkMat) column. Effects will now apply to all layers below as dictated by the matte. Try this in [**Ex.13_starter**]; check out our version in [**Ex.13-final**].

In [**Ex.13**] a matte movie (left) is used as an inverted luma matte to modify a solid adjustment layer; the areas that are black in the matte are then blurred and washed out (right). Matte courtesy Artbeats/Cloud Chamber; footage courtesy Artbeats/Business Executives.

Transforming Adjustments

The Transform effect (Effect > Distort > Transform) may also be applied to an adjustment layer, allowing you to scale, rotate, reposition, skew, and fade the *contents* of the adjustment layer – i.e., the stack of all the layers underneath. By comparison, the adjustment layer's regular Transform properties change only the shape of the *region* that will be adjusted. Experiment with comp [**Ex.14**], adjusting the Scale, Position, and Rotation parameters of the Transform effect in the Effect Controls panel (select the layer and press F3). The Transform effect is particularly handy for fading a stack of layers to avoid opacity artifacts.

In addition, we created three animations in the [**Ex.15**] folder for you to explore. These put to use the various techniques discussed above.

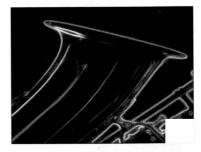

[**Ex.15a-Edgy Musicians**] (above) further refines the Find Edges effect applied to the sequence of musician clips. [**Ex.15b-Recital**] (below) uses an animated Illustrator text layer as an adjustment layer to invert the layers below. The Distort > Transform effect then fades out all layers as a group. Footage courtesy Lee Stranahan.

Adjusting in 3D

The order of 2D layers in the Timeline panel decides how they are composited, with layers being composited from the bottom up. By contrast, 3D layers are rendered depending on how far they are from the comp's active camera. While you can combine 2D and 3D layers in the same composition, these 2D layers act as "rendering breaks" which divide and group the 3D layers in a composition. Adjustment layers also act as rendering breaks – *even if their 3D Layer switch is enabled*. If an adjustment layer exists between groups of 3D layers, one 3D group cannot interact with another 3D group, even if the adjustment layer is in 3D as well. This includes casting and receiving shadows and intersecting layers between groups. These rendering order issues are covered in detail in Chapter 13, *3D Space*.

When working in 3D, there's an additional use for the Adjustment Layer switch: When it's enabled for a 3D light layer, that light will illuminate only 3D layers below it in the Timeline panel's stacking order. This is covered in detail in Chapter 15, *Lighting in 3D*.

TIP

Renaming Effects

You can rename any effect in the Effect Controls panel by selecting it, pressing Return, typing in a new name (such as Blue/Orange Duotone), and pressing Return again.

Alpha Creation

An alternative to using modes to blend black solids or shape layers on top of other layers is to create an alpha channel for the black solid or shape layer. To do this, apply the Channel Combiner effect, change the From popup to Max RGB and the To popup to Alpha, then apply the Remove Color Matting effect. This converts the RGB levels of the image to corresponding amounts of transparency. We have saved this as an Animation Preset in the **Goodies** folder as **Unmultiply Black.ffx**.

Effects and Solids

It's common to think of effects as filters that treat an image. However, many effects – such as stroked lines and lens flares – create their own images. Although you can apply them directly to footage, it is usually more powerful to apply them to their own separate layer so that you can then perform additional compositing tricks. And the best layer to apply them to is often a simple black solid.

Dropping Out the Black

Lens flares are a classic example of when using a black solid is the best solution. Here is an example to try:

Step 1:   Open [**Ex.16_starter**]: We've set up a Lens Flare to follow the light in the upper left corner of the frame. Select the layer and press F3 to open its Effect Controls. Although you can change the Lens Type and Flare Brightness, you still don't have much control over the color of the flare or how it interacts with the image. Select the Lens Flare effect, and Edit > Cut it.

Step 2:   Choose Layer > New > Solid, name it "**Lens Flare solid**" and click the Comp Size button to make sure it covers the entire frame. Make the color black, and click OK to create the solid.

Step 3:   With the black solid positioned above the image layer, select Edit > Paste. The Lens Flare plus its settings are applied to the solid. (Because the movie and solid are the same size, the Flare Center's position will appear in the same place. If they were different in size, masks or effect points may shift.) The flare appears in isolation against a black background.

Step 4:   A great way to composite images – especially those on black – is to use blending modes. Make sure the Modes column is visible in the Timeline panel (F4 is the shortcut), and experiment with different blending modes: Screen gives the most natural look for lens flares; Add and Color Dodge give more blown-out looks.

 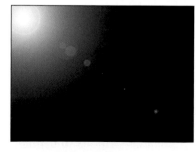 

A lens flare applied directly to an image (left) limits your compositing options. Instead, apply the effect to a black solid (center). Use the Screen blending mode to drop out the black background and change the flare color (right) or add other effects. Footage courtesy Artbeats/Family Life.

Step 5: As the lens flare now exists separate from the underlying image, you can apply additional effects to just the flare. For example, Effect > Color Correction > Hue/Saturation lets you change the color of the flare. If you do this while it is applied to the underlying image, this effect would alter both the flare and the image. An example of using blending modes plus color adjustments is shown in [**Ex.16-final**].

Note that the black solid does not need to be the same size as the composition or underlying layers. You can gain extra flexibility by making the solid larger than your comp. This way, you can transform the solid (and therefore, the effects applied to it), including scaling or rotating it.

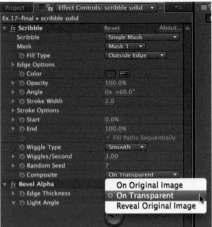

Effects such as Generate > Scribble can offer options as to how they composite with the image they are applied to.

Divide and Conquer

Some effects can create their own alpha channels, either providing a matte for (or out-and-out replacing) the layer they are applied to. The most common manifestations of this option are a Composite on Original checkbox or a popup menu at the bottom of the Effect Controls (which may be named Paint Style, Render Options, or something similar).

As flexible as this is, there are still times when you'll want these effects on their own layer so you can take advantage of applying additional

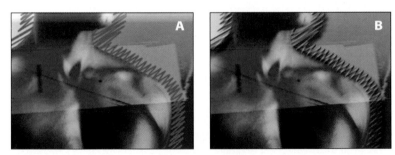

When a stack of effects are applied directly to the image, they affect the entire image (A). If they are applied to their own layer instead, you have much more control over how they interact (B). Image composite from Digital Vision's The Body plus Naked & Scared.

effects or using blending modes. For example, in [**Ex.17_starter**] we've masked the outline of a figure and applied Generate > Scribble. It's a good start, but we think it would look even better if the scribble was more dimensional, perhaps using the Bevel Alpha and Drop Shadow effects. Unfortunately, applying these all directly to the figure layer bevels the entire layer – not just the scribbling (see [**Ex.17_wrong**]).

To get our desired result, we need to make a black solid that's the same size as the underlying layer, cut the mask and Scribble effect from the original layer, and paste them onto our new solid. Now we can apply more effects, and even use blending modes to create more interesting composites. This is demonstrated in [**Ex.17-final**].

Rather than cutting and pasting mask paths and effects from an image to solids, it might be better to duplicate the original image and apply the effects to the duplicate. The advantage is that you now have the image as a reference in the Layer panel. Two examples of this approach using the Stroke and Write-On effects are contained in the **Ex.18** folder.

CONNECT

Layer Styles

In addition to plug-in effects, After Effects also supports Photoshop Layer Styles. Layer Styles are a set of editable effects, textures, and gradients that create interesting bevel, shadow, emboss, and glow treatments. These treatments are more sophisticated than their normal After Effects counterparts. If you've seen text or a logo from Photoshop that looks like it was made of metal, plastic, or glass, chances are it was built using Layer Styles.

When you import a Photoshop file that includes Layer Styles, you have the option to keep them live and editable – which means all of their parameters are available in After Effects to tweak or even keyframe. (If you accidentally flattened them on import, in After Effects you can use Layer > Layer Styles > Convert to Editable Styles to get them back.)

You can also apply Layer Styles to any layer in After Effects. The catch is that the user interface is a bit hidden (it's in the Timeline panel, not Effect Controls), and is not as sophisticated as Photoshop's.

Styled Layers

The folder **Ex.19** contains a set of compositions with text and logos that already have Layer Styles applied. These styles were created by Andrew Heimbold at Reality Check (*www.realityx.com*), a studio that creates a lot of broadcast sports packages.

Open the composition **[Reality_1]**. It contains two layers: a solid white background and a layer called **Reality 1**. Twirl **Reality 1** open, and you will notice a new entry in the Timeline panel just below Transform: Layer Styles. Twirl Layer Styles open, and you will see a series of special Layer Effects. The top one – Blending Options – is a set of global controls. In addition to providing one set of global controls for lighting angles for all Layer Effects used in this layer, the Advanced Blending section has a Fill Opacity parameter that can fade out the source layer and keep just the result of the styles to create "ghosted"

Layer Styles and the Layer Effects they contain appear in the Timeline panel in After Effects. Note that Layer Styles always render *after* transformations are calculated.

looks (leave it set to 100% for this exercise).

Now twirl open Drop Shadow. You will see this is far more sophisticated than Effect > Perspective > Drop Shadow, allowing you to highly tune the look of the shadow; there's also a blending mode for just the shadow effect. Then twirl open Bevel and Emboss, which has even more parameters including

Photoshop Layer Styles are often used to create metal, glass, and plastic looks. These examples are in the **Ex.19** folder; they were created by Andrew Heimbold of Reality Check.

popup menus for different bevel contours. Take a few minutes to explore the parameters for these two Layer Effects. Also note that each Layer Effect has its own visibility switch (the eyeball icon), making it easier to isolate the contribution of each effect.

Explore the other comps inside this folder. Some of the more complex examples employ multiple layers, such as **[Reality_6]** which has layers for the metal bevel, plastic inserts, and center button. (Note: If you'd like to import these styles and more into Photoshop, they are included in the **Goodies** folder on the DVD.)

Adding Style

As mentioned, you can add Layer Styles to any layer in After Effects. **[Ex.20_starter]** contains a simple Text layer: Brand X. Select **Brand X** and apply Layer > Layer Styles > Drop Shadow. Layer Styles will appear in the Timeline panel; twirl it open, then twirl open Drop Shadow. Experiment with its parameters – for example, set Distance to 0 and Size to 15. This creates a soft, broad, centered shadow that's hard to create with the normal Drop Shadow effect. Increase Spread to alter its density. Note that each Layer Effect, as well as the overall Layer Styles group, has its own Reset option in the Timeline.

Next, apply Layer > Layer Styles > Inner Shadow. This instantly creates a cutout look that is hard

to re-create using standard effects. Have fun experimenting with the other styles as well – there is a lot of depth here. Also try copying and pasting Layer Styles from the **Ex.19** examples to your sample text.

Layer Styles make it easy to add soft shadows, inner shadows, rounded bevels, and gradient fills to After Effects text.

Caveats

Here are a few things to watch out for when using Layer Styles:

• If Layer Styles are applied to a 3D layer, it will lose its ability to interact with other 3D layers.

• You cannot completely delete Layer Styles by deleting all the individual Layer Effects. To remove all traces, click Reset for each individual layer effect, then use Layer > Layer Styles > Remove All.

• Unlike normal effects, you cannot reorder Layer Effects.

• There is no Effect Controls panel for Layer Styles; you have to edit them in the Timeline panel.

• You have to import a Photoshop file as a composition, not footage, to get access to its Layer Styles. (Importing Photoshop files is covered in more detail in Chapter 38.)

• You cannot add Pattern Overlay in After Effects; you need to set it up inside Photoshop, then import the file.

• There is currently no way to load Layer Style ASL files. Load your styles into Photoshop, apply them to a dummy layer, import that layer into After Effects, then copy and paste the style to your desired layer. Note that you can then save the Layer Styles as Animation Presets (Chapter 25).

Resources

There is also a wealth of styles available on Adobe Exchange (*share.studio.adobe.com*). Note that most Layer Styles have been created for print work, which often has a larger file dimension than video work; if needed, use Layer > Layer Styles > Scale Effects in Photoshop before moving to After Effects.

The After Effects help file contains relatively little information on Layer Styles and what each parameter does. If you have Photoshop installed, you are better off opening its own Help file, then following the links for Layers > Layer Effects and Styles > Layer Style options.

There are also numerous Photoshop books available; Andrew suggests the *Photoshop Wow!* series by Jack Davis, while we also suggest *Photoshop for Video* by Richard Harrington.

23

Effects Roundup Overview

Where to find tips on our favorite effects.

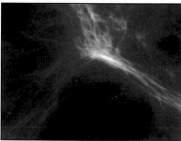

Here are but a few of the looks you can create with effects. These are demonstrated in Bonus Chapter 23B on the DVD-ROM.

After Effects CS5 comes with literally hundreds of effects plug-ins – and just for good measure, it also installs third party plug-ins from Cycore (CC FX), Digieffects (FreeForm), The Foundry (Keylight), and Synthetic Aperture (Color Finesse). So – where do you learn how to use them?

One place not to overlook is the built-in Help file, accessed by pressing F1 while inside After Effects. Select Effect Reference from the Contents list down the left side of the Help Viewer, and you will be presented with options to see both picture galleries and text explanations of the stock effects.

But knowing what an effect does in the abstract doesn't tell you how you might actually use it on a real project. Therefore, the **Bonus Chapters** folder on the DVD-ROM that comes with this book contains a large PDF file plus an After Effects project that goes over many of our favorite effect groups by categories, and tells you how we might use them. If there's a useful feature that's not obvious, or a certain trick required to get an effect to work, we'll tell you that, too. Note that it doesn't cover every single effect in After Effects; after all, we don't use them all ourselves!

Several other chapters in this book and on the DVD also cover specific families of effects. They include:

Chapter 8 – *Motion Blur and More:* Includes a handful of effects that simulate motion blur-like looks, including echoes.

Chapter 16 – *Parallel Worlds:* Demonstrates how to best work with effects which create the illusion of 3D (including Digieffects FreeForm).

Chapter 24 – *Compound Effects:* These effects look at a second layer to determine what to do, such as use the grayscale pattern in one layer to displace the position of pixels in another.

Chapter 27 – *Keying:* Effects that can be used to create an alpha channel for footage shot against a particular color backdrop, such as green or blue. Includes a tutorial on the popular Keylight effect.

Chapter 36 – *Working with Audio:* This chapter, as well as Bonus Chapter 36B on the DVD, discusses effects that manipulate sound.

Chapter 37 – *Expressions:* Expression Controls help you create user interfaces for expressions.

Chapter 40B – *3D Effects:* This special category of effects takes advantage of additional information that is sometimes included in 3D renders, such as depth maps. This bonus chapter can be found on the DVD.

If you're unsure which chapter would discuss a particular effect, look in this book's Index – there is a special section dedicated to effects. In some cases, effects that have special applications (such as reducing interlace flicker in video frames) are also mentioned in other chapters.

Getting More from Effects

Just slapping an effect on a layer is not always the best way to use it. If you zoomed straight to this chapter, we encourage you to take some time to read the previous chapter on applying effects; it includes tips on using adjustment layers as well as applying effects to their own solid layers and then using blending modes to finish the composite.

Chapter 25 (*Presets and Variations*) tells you how to save your favorite combinations of effects as animation presets so you can reuse them later. Adobe also supplies hundreds of presets of its own, many of which employ effects.

Despite all the advice the Help file or we may give you, sometimes you will still hit a creative block while using an effect. In these situations, you might want to try Brainstorm. This module randomizes any collection of parameters you select, helping you discover new combinations and introducing you to new ideas. Brainstorm is discussed in Chapter 25 as well.

Third-Party Effects

We know many of you are on a budget, so the idea of having to buy even more effects is not exactly at the top of your list. But there are reasons other companies make effects: because users have asked them to create a particular plug-in, or because a company feels it can do a particular job significantly better than Adobe does. An example would be the wonderful plug-ins from Trapcode (*www.trapcode.com*) – such as Shine, Starglow, Particular, Form, and Lux – which excel at creating cool lighting and particle effects. Or the 3D plug-ins from Zaxwerks (*www.zaxwerks.com*) – such as Invigorator and ProAnimator – which make it possible to extrude and texture 3D objects inside After Effects. We discussed some of these and more back in Chapter 16.

In general, if you see a look on television that everybody is using but that you can't seem to re-create yourself, chances are there's a third party plug-in that does it.

The place to start with your hunt for plug-ins is *www.toolfarm.com*: It carries plug-ins from many different third parties (many with free demo versions available), plus it has several handy charts, making it easier to find a particular plug-in.

Effects can be accessed through the Effect menu (shown here) or the Effects & Presets panel (Chapter 22). Related effects are grouped into categories.

Bonus Chapter 23B

On the DVD, we've included a bonus chapter called **23B-Effects Roundup**. Look for it in the **Bonus Chapters** folder; it includes a PDF and its own Example Project file.

Compound Effects

Compound effects may seem nonintuitive at first, but they require learning only a few simple rules.

A *compound effect* is one that looks at a second layer to decide exactly how to treat the layer it is applied to. Examples of these vary from Compound Blur – which can selectively blur one layer based on the varying luminance values of another – to Texturize, which is great for simulating those embossed station identity bugs most networks use these days, among other things.

The "modifying" layer that a compound effect points to can range from a simple gradient to a second movie or composition. In most cases, the information being passed is the brightness values of each pixel of a grayscale image, or the luminance values in a color image. These gray levels are then used by the effect to determine which pixels in the first layer are blurred, faded, displaced, and so on.

By pointing to a second layer, compound effects sidestep the normal rendering pipeline order of bottom layer to topmost layer. As a result, mastering these effects requires a little forethought in preparing your sources, and quite often requires that you create the effect using more than one comp.

In this chapter we'll focus on three of these compound effects: Compound Blur, Texturize, and the versatile Displacement Map. These cover the gamut from fairly straightforward to fairly complex. Once you understand the logic behind compound effects, you should be able to adapt the techniques to any effect (including third-party effects) that uses a second, modifying layer.

The power of compound effects comes in selecting a second layer to modify the one the effect is applied to. If the default is None, no matter how many other parameters you change, the result will still be "no effect." Don't forget to select a modifying layer.

That Other Layer

Compound effects are easy to spot because they have a popup for you to select a second layer to work with. Most of these effects either default to None (which results in no effect, because no layer has been selected) or use themselves as the modifying layer. This popup menu automatically lists all layers in the current composition.

The modifier layer does *not* need to be turned on in order to be used by a compound effect. In fact, if its image is not being used directly in the comp, it's best to turn it off to ensure it does not appear accidentally.

Example Project

Explore the 24-Example Project.aep file as you read this chapter; references to [Ex.##] refer to specific compositions within the project file.

Size Matters

The way compound effects work is to line up the modifying layer with the effected layer, pixel by pixel, and decide how to treat each pixel in the effected layer based on some property (usually luminance) of the modifier layer. If both layers are the same size, life is more straightforward. But what if the modifying layer is not the same size or aspect ratio as the layer the effect is applied to? For example, if you were to take a logo or bug that is, say, 200×200 pixels, and emboss it into a movie layer of 720×486, After Effects needs to know if it should:

• *Stretch to Fit*, which would stretch and distort the logo to 720×486 before applying it as a texture;

• *Center* the smaller logo in the 720×486 area; or

• *Tile* the logo, so that you see multiple logos, some of which may be incomplete if the two sizes do not match up nicely.

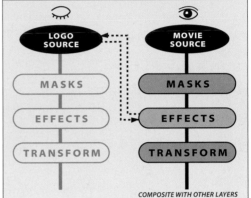

Short Circuit

While these options are often valid, they don't allow for the logo to be scaled and placed in the lower right corner of the screen akin to a network ID bug.

The reason for this is the rendering order inside After Effects: When an effect is applied to the movie, and that effect is told to refer to a second "map" layer for data, it's capable of seeing the modifying layer only at its "source" – *before* any masks, effects, or transformations have been applied to it. In other words, it uses the modifying layer as it would appear in its own Layer panel with View set to None – *not* in the Comp panel. Hence, no scaling or positioning of the logo layer is taken into account by the compound effect.

When a compound effect, such as Texturize, is applied to a layer, the effect looks at just the source of the modifying layer and ignores any masks, effects, or transformations that may be applied to the "map" layer.

Longer (and Better) Circuit

The trick, then, is to present the effect module with a modifying layer that's the same size (or at least the same aspect ratio) as the layer being effected, and with any attributes already applied to the modifying layer. You do that by preparing the map in a precomp that is the same size as the layer being effected. You can position, scale, and otherwise transform – as well as animate, mask and effect – the modifying source in this precomp, and the result will then be applied faithfully by the compound effect in the main comp.

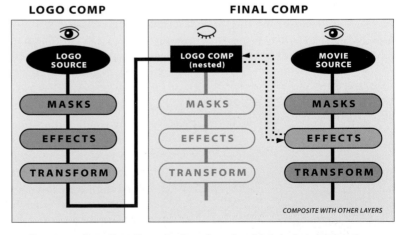

Apply any transformations (for example, scale and position the logo bug) to the modifying layer in its own precomp, and nest this into the comp with the layer that gets the compound effect (Texturize in this example). Now the effect will take the transformations applied to the bug into account when it processes.

Smooth Blur

If Compound Blur is too "boxy" for you, try the SmoothKit > Gaussian effect from RE:Vision Effects (demo available at *www.revisionfx.com*). It's a true compound blur with a smoother look.

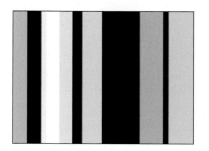

Take a footage layer, apply Compound Blur, and direct it to use a movie of animated lines as a blur map (above). The result is selective blurring of the original image (right), based on the luminance values in the modifying layer.

Now that we have a general understanding of how compound effects work, let's look at a few in detail:

Compound Blur

This effect can be thought of as a variable blur, with the amount of blur controlled by the luminance of the modifying layer it points to. The amount of blur is calculated on a pixel-by-pixel basis: The brighter a pixel is in the modifying layer, the more blurred the corresponding pixel will be in the layer Compound Blur is applied to.

In the **24-Example Project.aep** file (from the **Chapter Example Projects > 24-Compound Effects** folder), open the [**Ex.01_starter**] comp, which contains some text and a few sources for you to use as blur maps.

> even the clearest thoughts and ideas can become blurred when subjected to random disturbances from outside forces – especially when one appears to have no control over these events.

Step 1: Select the text (layer 1) and apply Effect > Blur & Sharpen > Compound Blur. The Effect Controls panel will open.

Step 2: The modifying layer is set to itself (**clear_ideas.ai**). Change the Blur Layer popup to the **_white background solid** layer. The text will now appear at its maximum blur value, since the modifying layer is solid white. The default Maximum Blur value of 20 is usually too high – reduce it to around 5.

Step 3: Change the Blur Layer popup to **autobars.mov**, and now the blur varies across the text in proportion to the luminance values of the **autobars** movie. Double-click the **autobars.mov** layer to open it in its own Layer panel and compare how it looks with the blur pattern. Bring the comp viewer forward, and experiment with other Compound Blur parameters, such as Invert Blur (means black areas in the modifying layer get maximum blur and white areas no blur), and the Maximum Blur amount. Try the other blur map movies (layers 3–5) for comparison.

Finally, compare Compound Blur with Effect > Blur & Sharpen > Lens Blur; use its Depth Map Layer parameter to set the modifying layer.

A compound effect works best when the two layers are the same size or aspect ratio. If they aren't, it needs to know how to interpret the modifier layer.

Texturize

Many will feel this effect should have been named Emboss, because that better describes the end result: It looks like an object has been embossed into the layer it was applied to. We'll use the Texturize effect to create a bug embossed in the corner of our footage. Close all comps and open [**Ex.02a_Aqua Main**] so that you know what the end result should look like. As noted earlier in this chapter, Texturize is a prime example of a compound effect in which you may need to prepare the modifying layer in another composition so you can control the position and scale of the bug. You can take two different approaches to get there – *nesting* or *precomposing*. We'll try it both ways:

Texturizing by Nesting

If you're the type who likes to plan ahead, you would create an embossed effect by preparing the bug in its own precomp, then nest this precomp with the movie to be embossed in a second comp. Apply Texturize to the *movie* layer, using the bug precomp as the texture map layer. To recreate our [**Ex.02a**] example, follow these steps:

Step 1: From the Comp viewer menu, select Close All. In the Project panel, select the **My Comps** folder, then make a new composition and name it "**bug precomp**". It should be the same size and duration as the movie you'll be effecting (720×486 D1 NTSC if you're using our sources).

Step 2: Add the **Aqua2000Bug.tif** logo from the Project panel's **Sources** > **Text** folder to your comp. Our logo is a grayscale file with *white text on black*, which is ideal for the Texturize effect as it looks only at high-contrast edges, *not* the alpha channel.

Step 3: Resize and position the bug in the bottom right-hand corner.

Step 4: Make a second composition in which you'll create the actual effect. Do this by dragging the movie you want to effect to the New Comp button at the bottom of the Project panel. We used **Sources** > **Movies** > **AB_MonsterWaves.mov**. The new comp will open and contain the movie layer. Select Composition > Composition Settings, rename your new comp "**Texturize Comp**", and click OK.

Step 5: Add [**bug precomp**] from the Project panel to this new comp.

Step 6: Turn off the Video switch (the eyeball) for the **bug precomp** layer, as it is not supposed to be visible.

Step 7: Select the movie layer (*not* the bug layer) and apply Effect > Stylize > Texturize to the movie; select **bug precomp** in the Texture Layer popup. Because the movie and precomp layers are the same width and height, the Texture Placement popup is now irrelevant. With all comps set to Full Resolution and Magnification set to 100%, edit the Contrast slider to taste. Sharp horizontal lines may flicker when they're field rendered, so we tend to use the 0.3–0.7 range for a softer effect. (If you got lost, compare to [**Ex.02a_Aqua Main**] and [**Ex.02a-bug precomp**].)

Safe Bugs

When you're creating logo bugs, keep any "lower-third" graphics away from the bug zone, or verify that the bug will be placed elsewhere (such as the upper left corner).

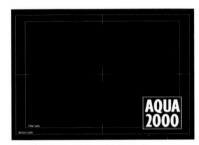

Steps 1–3: Our bug is prebuilt in one comp, where it is sized and positioned.

Steps 4–7: The logo bug is applied to our video layer in the second comp, resulting in an embossed effect. Background footage courtesy Artbeats/Monster Waves.

Step 7: The Timeline panel of the second comp, where you can see how the Texturize effect has been set up.

Step 1: The animated Recital title is a black Illustrator title. The idea is to emboss it into the background layer. Footage courtesy Lee Stranahan.

Texturizing by Precomposing

If you forgot to plan ahead and already started to create the effect all in one comp, the following steps using precompose show you how to successfully build an animated texturize effect. It will also reinforce some important concepts. So let's start over again with a second scenario:

Step 1: Close all comps, then open [**Ex.02b_Recital Main**]. Layer 1, **Recital.ai**, is a black title created in Illustrator and animates from right to left. Layer 2, **piano group**, is a precomp consisting of two layers composited together. The idea is to apply the Texturize effect to the **piano group** layer using the animated Recital title as the texture layer.

Step 2: Turn off the Video switch (the eyeball) for the **Recital.ai** layer, as it is not supposed to be visible.

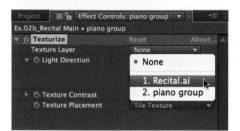

Step 3: Apply the Texturize effect to the **piano group** layer and set the Texture Layer to **Recital.ai**.

Step 3: Select the **piano group** layer (*not* the title layer) and apply Effect > Stylize > Texturize. For the Texture Layer popup, select the **Recital.ai** as the texture. Nothing happens. A bit of sleuthing is in order…

Double-click the **Recital.ai** layer to open its Layer panel, which displays the layer's source. The image in the Layer panel tells you what's being fed to the Texturize effect applied to the piano group layer. All you can see is black! Toggle on the Transparency Grid and you will see the black title, but it is not animating from right to left.

You have just uncovered two separate problems: First, the effect is not receiving an animated layer, because the Position keyframes are not taken into account by the effect. Second, the Texturize effect doesn't use a layer's alpha channel; it depends on receiving a high-contrast image (black on white, or white on black) – and right now it is receiving a black on black image!

The first problem can be solved by precomposing the title so the Transform properties are calculated in a precomp:

Step 4: After precomposing, the **Recital.ai** layer and its keyframes will be moved to the precomp.

Step 4: Select the **Recital.ai** layer, then choose Layer > Pre-compose. In the Pre-compose dialog, name the new precomp "**title precomp**" and be sure to select the second option, "Move all attributes into the new composition". This option will send the Position keyframes down to the precomp and create a precomp with the same size, duration, and frame rate as the current comp. Be sure to also turn on the Open New Composition switch – that way the precomp (not the original comp) will be forward. Click OK and **title precomp** will be created. Initially you will see a black composition; toggle on the Transparency Grid to view the animated title.

The new precomp has one layer in it, the original **Recital.ai** layer, animating from right to left. Notice anything strange? You had turned off the Video switch for the title layer in Step 2, but the precomposing step automatically turned back on its visibility. After all, unless it renders in the precomp, it's not going to show up in the main comp!

Tap Shift to bring up the Mini-Flowchart and select [**Ex.02b_Recital Main**]. The Texturize effect has correctly figured out that the name of its Texture Layer has changed – but the effect still doesn't work! Although *you* can see the title against the transparency grid, Texturize considers "transparency" to be black. Even changing the precomp's background color to white will not solve the problem – no matter what color you make a comp's background, it will always indicate "transparency," which is considered to be "black" by an effect.

There are two solutions to giving your title the necessary contrast. One is to place the text over a white solid in the precomp, since solids exist in RGB space. Alternatively, use the Fill effect to fill the layer's RGB channels with white, but remember to apply the Fill effect in the precomp so that the source Texturize receives in the main comp is already white. (If you apply the Fill effect in the main comp, it will be ignored by Texturize.) We'll use the latter technique:

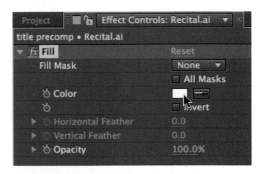

Step 5: Apply the Fill effect to the **Recital.ai** layer in the precomp. If you apply the Fill effect to the title in the main comp, it will be ignored by the Texturize effect.

Step 5: Tap Shift again and select [**title precomp**]. Select the **Recital.ai** layer and apply Effect > Generate > Fill. The Effect Controls panel will open. Click on the Color swatch and change the color to white. Toggle off the Transparency grid, and you will see white text on black.

Step 6: Return to [**Ex.02b_Recital Main**] and now the Texturize effect will be working as expected. Adjust the Texture Contrast to taste. Set the Texture Placement popup to Center Texture to reduce edge artifacts.

Note that the **title precomp** layer will still be turned off in this comp, which is what you want. To summarize: The Video switch for the title should be *on* in the precomp so that its data is sent to the main comp, but it should be *off* in the main comp as you don't want it to appear in the render.

If you'd like to compare your results with ours, check out our versions in the [**Ex.02b-Final Comps**] folder.

Step 6: Now that the Texturize effect is receiving animated white text from the precomp, which is the same size as the piano group layer, you get the correct result.

Displacement Map

A *displacement map* displaces pixels – in other words, moves them up or down and to the left or right – depending on the luminance values of the modifying layer. It's great for creating warped effects, as well as making one layer appear as if it has been projected or painted onto an uneven surface. To see how this works, close all comps to reduce clutter. Open [**Ex.03_starter**] comp. Layer 1 is a grayscale displacement map, and layer 2 is the movie layer that will be displaced:

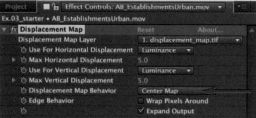

In [**Ex.03**], the displacement map (top) is 1440 wide by 480 high. When we applied it to the 720×486 movie, we used the Center Map setting (above).

Step 1: Turn off the Video switch for the map in layer 1.

Step 2: Select the movie in layer 2 and apply Effect > Distort > Displacement Map. The Effect Controls panel opens automatically; resize it so you can read the full parameter names. The Displacement Map Layer popup defaults to using itself as a map, so change this to point at layer 1: **displacement_map.tif**.

Step 3: Choose what channel you want to use for Horizontal Displacement in the next popup; because the map is grayscale, you can use any of the Red, Green, Blue, or Luminance settings. Set the Maximum Horizontal Displacement with the slider below. The next popup and slider control the Vertical Displacement in a similar way.

Step 4: The Displacement Map Behavior parameter kicks in when the map is not the same size or aspect ratio as the movie it's displacing. Our map is 1440×486, and the movie is 720×486, so compare the Center Map and Stretch Map to Fit settings. The latter uses the entire map scaled to 720×486, so it has more extreme results.

Step 5: The final trick to Displacement Map is the checkbox for Edge Behavior. If you displace pixels away from an outer edge of the layer, what fills in the space they left behind? Checking Wrap Pixels Around borrows part of the image from the opposite edge to fill in the gaps. If the layer has a fairly consistent color around its edges, this works well, as the borrowed pixels will match.

Step 5: Note the edge artifacts with Wrap Pixels Around turned off. Expand Output is on, allowing the result to extend beyond the layer boundary. Footage from Artbeats/Establishment – Urban.

To not displace an image, the modifying map needs to be 50% gray (RGB values 128/128/128), or its alpha channel must be transparent. Darker areas displace in "negative" directions (up and to the left), and lighter areas displace in positive directions (down and to the right), with the maximum amount controlled by sliders in the effect. You can select any number of characteristics of the modifying image to provide the map, such as the strength of a specific color. In contrast to Texturize, slightly blurred maps tend to work better than sharp ones; sharp contrasting edges result in disjointed displacements (or "tearing") along those edges.

Animating the Map

Displacement maps often look good when they're animating, and this is where the concept of preparing the map in a precomp comes up yet again, just like with the Texturize effect earlier.

Close all comps and open [**Ex.04_starter**]. Here's the same movie displaced by the same wavy map, and if you scrub the Timeline, you'll notice that the displacement isn't moving. But turn on the Video switch for layer 1, and you'll see that the displacement map is panning from right to left (if the Position keyframes aren't visible, select layer 1 and press P). Remember that a compound effect sees the map layer at its *source* – *before* any masks, effects, or keyframes have been applied. (If you view the map layer in its Layer panel, with the View popup set to None, you can verify that the effect sees the original map image, not an animation.)

To have the map animate while it's displacing the movie, the Position keyframes need to be moved down to a precomp so that the layer is already panning by the time it hits the Displacement Map effect. Follow the steps for precomposing detailed earlier in *Texturizing by Precomposing* to move the animated map down to the precomp. (When you're done, check the Layer panel for the map precomp layer – you should see it panning and, more importantly, so should the effect.)

If you get lost, compare your results with our two comps from the [**Ex.04-final comps**] folder.

Different Sizes

We've seen how you need to animate a displacement map in a precomp. But what if the image or movie you're displacing is also animating? Or what if you have a stack of layers you want to displace as a group?

In this case, you'll need to animate the movie (or group the images) together in a second precomp that's the same size as the map precomp. In the third and main comp, you nest both precomps, then create the displacement map effect.

You could think of these precomps as two sides of a sandwich. When they come together in the main composition, the Displacement Map Behavior popup will be irrelevant because both precomps are the same size. This gives you the opportunity to create the precomps a little larger than the main comp so that any edge artifacts are cropped off by the pasteboard in the main comp. Explore our sample comps in **Ex.05**.

Slice 'n' Dice

We usually suggest that displacement map sources not have sharp transitions in luminance because these could cause sudden shifts in the positions of the displaced pixels. Of course, there are exceptions to every

What's My Source?

A compound effect sees the modifying layer at its source. To check what this source looks like, double-click the layer to open it in its Layer panel, and set the View popup to None. This is what the effect sees too!

[**Ex.05**] consists of a precomp where the map pans right to left; a second precomp where the images animate; and a third, main comp where the displacement map effect is created.

The [**Ex.05_Main Comp**]. The edge artifacts still exist, but since they're out on the pasteboard area they won't be visible in the final render.

The autobars movie is used to both blur and displace the skyline in **[Ex.06]**.

rule. Open [**Ex.06**], and you'll see the same animated grayscale bars used earlier in this chapter now used to displace slices of the movie in the vertical direction.

We also applied Compound Blur to the movie so that some of the slices will be more or less blurred, and inverted the blur so that black in the map would be maximum blur, not white. (Compound Blur is best applied after the Displacement Map effect so that the blurred and displaced slices line up.)

The Mirror Cracked

Taking this idea to another level, [**Ex.07**] simulates a cracked reflective surface, such as a broken mirror. A movie of some gears is displaced by a map where each faux mirror shard is given a different gray value, which results in a different amount of displacement per shard.

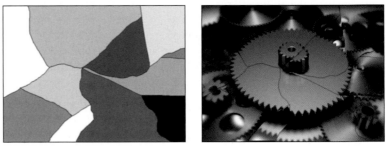

[Ex.07] uses a displacement map to simulate a cracked mirror effect; the lines in the map also serve as an alpha matte. Movie courtesy Artbeats/Gears.

We included black separation lines to help cover for the artifacts that result along sharp displacement edges – they serve as an alpha matte to make the pieces look like they are separated slightly.

Why Isn't It Working?

The techniques you've learned in this chapter apply to all compound effects, including Card Dance, Caustics, Wave World, and others. If you're still having problems, here is a summary of the most common reasons compound effects don't seem to work initially:

• The modifier layer has been left at None, or it defaults to using itself; set the Layer popup to the desired layer.

• The modifier or map layer is not the same size as the layer the effect is being applied to, so the aspect ratio is being distorted. Solution: Place the map in a precomp the same size as the layer to be effected, and use this precomp in place of the original map layer in the Effect Controls.

• The modifier layer has effects or animation that is being ignored by the compound effect. Remember that the compound effect takes the map at its source *before* mask, effects and transform. Precompose the map layer, being sure to check the Move All Attributes option.

• The precomp has a white background color, but the precomp's background color is always considered as "black" (zero alpha) by a compound effect. If this is causing a problem, use a white Solid layer instead.

CONNECT

Blending modes: Chapter 9.

Track mattes: Chapter 11.

Nesting compositions: Chapter 18.

Precomposing: Chapter 19.

Applying effects: Chapter 22.

Lens Blur effect: Chapter 23B.

Brain Tickler: *Walk on Water*

If you've read this chapter carefully, you should have a pretty good idea of what's involved in creating a displacement map effect. So now we'd like to challenge you! Close all comps and open the **[Ex.08]** folder and play the **Walk on Water.mov**: The text "Liquid" animates from right to left and appears to be at the bottom of a swimming pool. Open **[Ex.08_starter]**, and see if you can re-create this movie using the following outline:

• Layer 1 is the black text **Liquid.ai**. This needs to be animated from right to left and then displaced with the water texture.

• Layer 2 is a movie of water ripples that will be used as both a background and a displacement map. Rather than use the background movie directly as the displacement map, create a special grayscale version so you'll have more control.

• Due to the inherent video noise in the water texture movie, you'll notice some slight "tearing" when the text is displaced; you might want to lightly blur the grayscale version for a smoother result.

• When you apply the Displacement Map effect, make sure that the distortion in the text layer synchronizes with the highlights in the water (it's possible that they won't match if you don't build the effect correctly).

• To fool the eye into thinking the text is at the bottom of the pool, change the color of the text to a light blue (like the highlights in the water) and apply a blending mode so that the **Liquid.ai** layer interacts with the water texture in an interesting way.

• Create as many precomps as you think you'll need to achieve the look of our finished movie. (Check the section *Why Isn't It Working?* if you get stuck.) When you've given it your best shot, come back here to compare results.

The Solution

How did you do? There are a few variations you could have chosen to complete the above task; our version is in the **[Ex.09]** folder. The hierarchy of comps is the most important part:

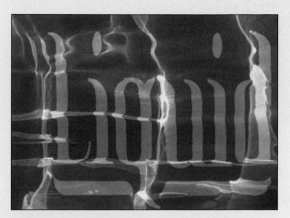

Use your newfound knowledge about displacement mapping to re-create this animation using the sources in the **[Ex.08_starter]** comp. No peeking at the solution until you've given it your best shot! Footage courtesy Artbeats/Water Textures.

• **[Ex.09-map precomp]:** Using the Shift Channels effect, we used the Red channel to create a grayscale movie to use as a luminance displacement map. Adding Levels increases the contrast, and Fast Blur reduces the video noise.

• **[Ex.09-text precomp]:** We animated the text from right to left in a precomp, because otherwise the Displacement Map effect would render *before* the Position keyframes. In order to keep the edges of the text from appearing distorted later on, this precomp is slightly larger than the main comp (740×500 as opposed to 720×486).

• In the main comp, **[Ex.09_Walk on Water-final]**, both precomps are nested and the background movie added. The Displacement Map effect is applied to the **text precomp**, and the map layer set to look at **map precomp**. The ripples in the distorted text line up with the ripples in the background movie even though the layer sizes differ, because the Center Map option is used. Any other strangeness at the left/right edges of the text fall outside the comp's image area. Wrap Pixels Around was turned off.

To make the type interact with the background, we used the Fill effect to color it a pale blue and then set it to Overlay mode.

25

Presets and Variations

Alternatives to reinventing the wheel every time you use an effect.

If you can copy and paste it, you can save it: That is the philosophy behind Animation Presets. Presets allow you to save static values or keyframed animations for text, masks, effects, layer styles, and transformations. These presets are saved to individual files on disk and presented in the Effects & Presets panel for later application to any layer in any project. You can later edit these values to suit their new application.

In addition to being able to create your own presets, Adobe provides hundreds of factory presets that include effects, text, and shapes. Later in this chapter we will focus on some of our favorite categories, including Behaviors, which allow you to animate layers without applying keyframes or expressions. Finally, we'll explore an intriguing feature called Brainstorm. This allows you to select any combination of effects, keyframes, and parameters and have After Effects automatically generate variations for you to check out.

Presets in Action

Perhaps the easiest way to learn about Animation Presets is to use them. In this chapter's Example Project, open comp [**Ex.01_starter**] and RAM Preview: It includes a simulation of a show's opening title, using a sequence of three video clips plus a text animation. The first video transitions on in an interesting fashion by animating a combination of Scale, Opacity, and the Box Blur effect. Say the client likes this, and now asks you to apply it to every transition. No problem:

Step 1: Select the layer **AB_UnderTheSea1.mov** (the earliest clip in the sequence, which already has the transition the client likes) and type UU – two Us in quick succession – to reveal all properties that have been changed from their defaults. You will see keyframes for Scale, Opacity, and the Box Blur effect's Blur Radius.

Step 2: Click on the word Opacity; this will select all of its keyframes without requiring you to select them individually. Shift+click on the word Scale to add its keyframes. Then Shift+click on the words Box Blur to highlight the effect's name. By selecting the entire effect, you'll make sure you capture all of its parameters as well as any keyframes or expressions that have been applied.

GOTCHA

Presets versus Styles

Unlike "styles" in other applications, resaving an Animation Preset will not dynamically update layers that you had previously applied the preset to.

Example Project

Explore the 25-Example Project.aep file as you read this chapter; references to [Ex.##] refer to specific compositions within the project file.

Ex.01_starter

0:00:00:10

#	Layer Name
1	T Natural Wonders
2	[AB_EstablishmentsMixedCuts.mov]
3	[AB_AnimalSafari.mov]
4	[AB_UnderTheSea1.mov]

Effects
  Box Blur   Reset
    Blur Radius   36.2
    Blur Dimensions   Horizontal
    Repeat Edge Pixels   On
  Transform   Reset
    Scale   108.1, 108.1%
    Opacity   100%

Steps 1–2: Reveal all modified properties by typing UU, then Shift+select their names in the Timeline panel. Selecting an effect's name will grab all of its parameters and keyframes, even though they are not highlighted. Footage courtesy Artbeats/Under the Sea 1.

By the way, when you save a preset, you don't have to include every parameter you've changed. You can Shift+click or Command+click on Mac (Control+click on Windows) to select just the properties you wish to save. The same goes for keyframes: Just select those you wish to save and apply later. To be clear as to what is and isn't selected, it's a good idea to first press F2 to deselect all, then select just the properties you wish to save.

Step 3: There are several ways to save an Animation Preset; the following methods all have the same result – so decide which is the easiest for you to learn and remember. Most of these require the Effects & Presets panel to be open and forward; if it isn't, first type Command+5 (Control+5).

Method 1: Select the menu item Animation > Save Animation Preset.

Method 2: Drag one of your selected items to the Effects & Presets panel and release the mouse.

Method 3: In the Effects & Presets panel, click on the page icon in its lower right corner.

TIP

Natural Deselection

To make sure you don't have any twirled-up keyframes, masks, or properties accidentally selected, type Shift+F2 to deselect everything except the layer itself.

Where to Save Presets

You can save a preset anywhere; the default is in the **Adobe > After Effects CS5 > User Presets** folder After Effects creates inside your main user documents folder. This makes your presets easy to find should you want to exchange them with others; the downside is that they don't appear in Adobe Bridge alongside the Adobe-supplied presets. Personally, we suggest you save them inside the **Adobe** folder, which appears inside **User Presets** – this takes you

into the **Adobe After Effects CS5 > Presets** folder. You can create your own subfolders to keep your presets organized. Saving somewhere inside **User Presets** (or **Adobe After Effects CS5 > Presets**) will result in your new presets appearing in the *** Animation Presets** folder in the Effects and Presets panel. If you save them anywhere else, they won't appear in this panel, although you can still open them from the Animation menu.

To select all the parameters for a mask, be sure to select the Mask group name, not the Mask Path property. Footage courtesy Artbeats/Establishments: Urban.

TIP

Solo Selected

To view only a desired set of properties in the Timeline panel, reveal them, select them by Shift+clicking or Command+clicking (Control+clicking), then type SS to hide all the other unselected properties.

GOTCHA

Null and Void

Remember, parents do not pass effects along to their children. Therefore, Animation Presets that use effects do not work when applied to null objects or other parents. This includes the Behavior presets, as they rely on effects to make them tick.

Precut Masks

So far we've focused on keyframes and effects; a preset can also contain masks. Open [**Ex.02_starter**] and RAM Preview: The first video clip (**AB_EstablishmentsUrban.mov**) is revealed through a set of rectangular masks that have their individual opacities animated. Practice saving a preset of this:

- In [**Ex.02_starter**], select the layer **AB_EstablishmentsUrban**; if the names of the mask are not already visible, type M to reveal them. Click on **Mask 1**, then Shift+click on **Mask Final** – this will select all four masks. (Be sure to select the Mask group name, not just the Mask Path or Mask Opacity properties, so that all mask parameters are saved.)

- Save the preset using any method you prefer and give it a name you'll remember, such as "**4 mask fade up.ffx**".

- Select the second layer (**AB_LosAngelesAerials.mov**), type I to locate to its in point, then type Command+Option+Shift+F (Control+Alt+Shift+F) to apply the preset you just saved. RAM Preview, and now both clips will be revealed in the same way.

Remember that you can then edit the mask paths to better suit the new video without losing the Mask Opacity animations. Our more elaborate version, with a Stroke effect that animates around the mask outlines plus some additional layering, is shown in [**Ex.02-final**].

Presets and Effects

Animation Presets are particularly well-suited to saving favorite combinations of effect parameters. Additionally, the Effect Controls panel has an option where it can display presets that employ already-applied effects. Here is an example:

Step 1: Open [Ex.03a], select the layer **AB_EstablishmentsUrban.mov**, and press F3 to reveal in the Effect Controls panel the two effects applied to it. Click on Minimax (which has two keyframes for its Radius parameter), then Shift+click on Channel Mixer to select both effects. Save a preset using the method of your choice, naming it "**minimax cubes.ffx**".

Step 2: Animation Presets are searchable in the Effects & Presets panel, just as are normal effects, but the search criteria are based on the characters you type being contained in the preset or effect name. Type "**minimax**" into the Contents field of the Effects & Presets panel; you will notice that the name of your new preset appears in the Animation Presets folder as well as under the effects it uses. As you can see, in general it is a good idea to use names that include the name of the effect, such as "Warp + Blur" instead of "Molten Mess".

Step 3: Open [**Ex.03b**], which has similar but different video clips from [**Ex.03a**]. At time 00:00, select layer 1, then double-click **minimax cubes** in the Effects & Presets panel. Both the effects and associated keyframes are applied, as you would expect.

Click on the arrow in the upper right corner of the Effect Controls panel to open its Options menu, and enable Show Animation Presets. You will now see an Animation Presets popup at the top of each effect. These popups display a list of all presets saved in the Presets folder that use the corresponding effect. You can also save a preset of selected effects through this popup. However, be aware that selecting a preset from the Effect Controls panel gives a result different from the methods described previously:

Step 4: Select layer 2, **AB_LosAngelesAerials.mov**, then press I to jump to its in point. The Minimax effect is already applied to this layer using its default values; if necessary, press F3 to bring the Effect Controls panel forward. Select **minimax cubes** from the Animation Presets menu for Minimax: The Radius keyframes are applied to this effect (press U to verify), but the Channel Mixer effect is not. Selecting a preset in this popup will update the parameters of *just the matching effect* – it won't apply any other effects, masks, or properties that may be part of the preset!

Scaling Presets

Applying a preset to a layer that is of a different size than the layer it was saved from does not automatically scale up all of its parameters to match the new size – you may need to do some work to change the motion path, scale parameters in effects (many of which are based around a number of pixels), resize masks, and so forth. If you often work in different formats, consider appending the format size to a preset's name – such as "widescreen DV" or "1080" – or save them to specific folders.

Steps 4: The Effect Controls panel's Animation Presets popup shows which presets use the selected effect. Choosing one loads the parameters for just this effect, replacing any existing keyframes. Underlying footage courtesy Artbeats/ Los Angeles Aerials.

Another difference between using the Animation Presets popup in the Effect Controls panel versus applying presets in the normal fashion is that any previous keyframes for the effect are removed before the new preset is applied. This eliminates some of the problems experienced in Step 7 of our first example.

Note that you cannot clear out any keyframes you applied from this menu – selecting None from the Animation Presets popup does nothing; clicking Reset for the effect restores its parameters at the current point in time but does not disable keyframing. Undo if you need to go back to where you were before applying the preset.

Here's Looking at UU

To reveal all properties, keyframes, and expressions that have modified values, select a layer and type UU.

Quick Navigation

In Adobe Bridge, hold Command (Control) and use the up and down cursor keys to quickly move up and down through levels of nested folders.

Search for Presets

If you know a word in the name of a preset you want to apply, enter it in the Contains field of the Effects & Presets panel. For example, type "**inset**" and you will see the Adobe presets that can convert a full-frame footage layer into a picture-in-picture inset, as well as the subfolders they reside in.

Adobe's Presets

In addition to being able to save and apply your own presets, After Effects ships with hundreds of ready-made presets for you to explore, employ, and tweak for the task at hand. These are great for beginners who need to crank out work quickly or for veterans in need of inspiration. They're also a great learning tool: Apply a preset, type UU to reveal what parameters the preset added or changed, and reverse-engineer it to learn how a particular trick was done.

We'll start our study by using Adobe Bridge (originally discussed in Chapter 1) to help us explore and apply presets, then focus on a pair of our favorite categories: Text and Behaviors.

Browsing Presets

In this next exercise, we will explore some of the provided presets, choosing one to tint the first clip in an edit, and another to transition the second clip on over the first.

Step 1: Open [**Ex.04a**] and select the second clip (**AB_RetroTransportation.mov**). Choose Browse Presets from either the Animation menu or the Effects & Presets Options menu. This will launch Adobe Bridge: a central application for exploring and importing media.

Step 2: You will be taken directly to the **Presets** folder, where you will see a selection of subfolders that correspond to the subfolders listed under Animation Presets in the Effects & Presets panel. Double-click

Image – Creative to open it. This subfolder contains a number of colorization presets, lighting effects, masks, and other tricks. Select individual presets to view them in the Preview panel. Select one of the mood lighting presets near the bottom, and you will see the preview animates.

Step 3: Double-click the preset named **Colorize – sepia.ffx**. You will be returned to After Effects, and this preset will be applied to your selected layer. Hmm…this old postcard look isn't quite what we had in mind. No problem: Undo (making sure the second layer is still selected) and switch back to Bridge by pressing Command+tab (Alt+tab). This time double-click **Colorize – sky blue.ffx**. Now this more subtle effect will be applied.

Step 3: Select a clip, then choose Browse Presets either from the Effects & Presets panel or the Animation menu. This will launch Adobe Bridge. Double-click the **Image – Creative** folder and explore some of the presets inside. The chain of folders is listed along the top, making it easy to get back to the other category folders. Double-click a preset to apply it.

Step 4: There are many different categories of presets. Select layer 1 – **AB_Transportation.mov** – and press I to locate to its in point. Rather than keep this hard cut, let's select a transition to more gracefully move into the second cut. Switch to Bridge and click on the **Presets** folder icon along the top of its application window. Double-click one of the **Transitions** folders, and preview a few of the choices available. Once you find one you like (we used **Transitions – Dissolves > Dissolve – vapor.ffx**), double-click it for this preset to be applied in After Effects. RAM Preview to check the result.

Expression Containers

Presets also remember Expressions – pieces of JavaScript code that tie parameters together – applied to the properties you copy, which makes presets a great tool for saving and reusing expressions. Expressions are covered in user-friendly depth in Chapter 37; the biggest gotcha here is if you save a preset with an expression that refers to another effect, layer, or comp by name, After Effects will complain when you apply this preset if it cannot find the same name it is looking for. You can usually just relink the expression to make After Effects happy again.

Quick Tasks

To get a better idea of the breadth of presets provided, open comp [**Ex.04b_starter**] which contains an edited skateboard montage. Say you wanted to place this clip in a picture-in-picture box, then fill the background with some abstract texture. Select the clip **CL_Skatesequence_DV.mov** and choose Animation > Browse Presets. This will take you back to Bridge and place you at the top level of the **Presets** folder. Double-click **Transitions – Movement**, then double-click **Fly to Inset.ffx**. Once you are returned to After Effects, RAM Preview: The full-frame video will animate down to a third of its original size in the upper right corner of the frame, with a border and drop shadow already applied.

Press F3 to open the Effect Controls panel: Some of Adobe's presets have special controllers that make it easier to keyframe or modify a preset that relies on a series of effects. If the names of some effects are surrounded by parentheses, the intention is that you can leave these alone and edit just the top effect. In this case, most of the parameters you need – transition completion, size, position, and the color of the frame – are included in the custom effect controllers named Fly to Inset.

Now for that background. Move the time indicator to some point after the transition has completed, and be sure to press F2 to deselect all layers. Return to Bridge, navigate to the **Backgrounds** subfolder, and browse the available choices. Double-click one you like. Since you didn't have a layer selected, After Effects will create a new solid for you and apply the preset to it. Drag this solid below **CL_Skate-Sequence.mov** and preview the result! All that's left is for you to place your keyed "talking head" commentator on top (Chapter 27). Our version is in [**Ex.04b-final**].

Some presets come with custom controllers to make them easier to modify. If the names of effects are in parentheses, focus on the controller effect at the top of the Effect Controls panel.

[**Ex.04b-final**]: Adobe's animation presets make it easy to place video in a picture-in-picture inset and add an abstract background. Skateboarders courtesy Creative License; commentator courtesy Photron.

Exchanging Presets

Adobe has posted over 300 additional Shape and 3D Text presets for After Effects on its Exchange website: Visit *share.studio.adobe.com* and go to the After Effects section.

Text Presets

Back in Chapter 21, we covered After Effects' powerful but complex text engine. Fortunately, After Effects comes with hundreds of Text Animation Presets that you can use (as well as learn from!).

Browsing, applying, and modifying a text preset is no different from working with any other Animation Preset. Close any previously opened comps, then open [**Ex.05**]. It contains some text for you to play with. (We duplicated the same layer several times and turned off the Video switch for the duplicates; the idea is if you find a preset you like – or make a hopeless mess – you can turn off that layer and use one of the duplicates.)

Step 1: Select the first layer, then choose Browse Presets from either the Animation or Effects & Presets Options menu. This opens Adobe Bridge, placing you in the **Presets** folder. Double-click the **Text** sub-folder, and you will see another group of subfolders showing the many different categories of text presets (hey, there are over 300 of them; better than throwing them all into the same folder!). If you feel like playing, go ahead and spend some time opening differ-ent subfolders and previewing their animations.

Step 2: Navigate to the **Animate In** subfolder and double-click the **Fade Up Characters** preset. You will be returned to After Effects and this preset will be applied to your text layer. RAM Preview: The characters fade in one by one in a softened "typewriter" fashion.

Step 3: Undo to remove the pre-set and return to the original text, then press Home to return to 00:00 (remember: presets apply their keyframes starting at the current time). Return to Bridge and double-click **Animate In > Raining Characters In**. (If you don't need to preview it first, you can also locate and apply it from the Effects & Presets panel.)

Step 1: You can also browse text presets using Adobe Bridge.

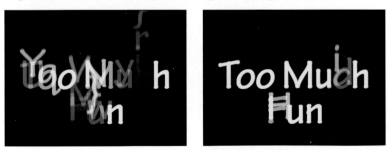

Step 3: The **Raining Characters In** preset is an interesting combination of animation, randomized text, and the Echo effect.

RAM Preview: This is a far flashier preset that randomizes the characters, drops them in from the top of the composition, and echoes them as they fade up. To figure out how it was done, type U to see which parameters are animated, or UU to check which parameters have been changed from their default values.

Step 4: Many of the text presets provided by Adobe – such as the **Raining Characters In** preset – employ effects in addition to animating type. The Effect Controls panel should have opened when you applied this preset; press F3 if it isn't visible. In this case, a Text Animator slides the characters down into position and offsets the characters used, while the Echo effect adds to the complexity. Move to 02:05 on the timeline and turn off the Echo effect by clicking on the stylized "*fx*" in the Effect Controls or Timeline panels to see the underlying text animation.

Step 5: Since Animation Presets create normal keyframes, you can customize them any way you like by editing those keyframes – for example, by moving them closer together to speed up the animation, changing their values, adding eases (Animation > Keyframe Assistant > Easy Ease), or deleting keyframes or effects that aren't needed or desired.

When you apply an Animation Preset, the first keyframe starts at the current time. If you accidentally pasted a preset later in time than desired, just drag the keyframes back.

You can also change the underlying Source Text at any time by double-clicking the layer and replacing the text. You may need to temporarily turn off any Text Animators so you can see the text clearly: This can be done by twirling open their layers and clicking on their respective "eye" icons in the Timeline panel.

Experiment with applying more Text Animation Presets. Remember that presets add to properties and keyframes already applied; applying a preset does not delete one you applied before. For instance, try applying a preset from the **Animate In** folder at time 00:00, then later in time apply a preset from the **Animate Out** folder. (If you make a big mess that you can't Undo out of, you can turn off the layer you are working with in [**Ex.05**] and use one of the duplicate layers instead.)

Mo' Blur

Most text animations look better with motion blur (Chapter 8), although it will take longer to render.

The Click That Refreshes

If you drag preset files into the **Presets** folder while After Effects is open, they will not immediately appear in the Effects & Presets panel. Select Refresh List from the panel's Options menu.

Step 5: Animation Presets create ordinary keyframes that you can edit as needed. Here we're sliding the Offset keyframes to start at time 00:00.

Saving Text Styles

When you're saving a text animation as a preset, selecting the Source Text property will save the settings from the Character and Paragraph panels. This is a good way to store "style" templates for font, size, color, and so on. However, be aware that saving Source Text will also save – and later apply – the underlying text as well. If you want to save just the text *animation* so you can apply it to different text in the future, select only the text Animator groups (plus the More Options section if used) when you save the Animation Preset. You will note that nearly all of the text presets Adobe provides save the Animators, but not the Source Text. In addition, if you don't have a layer selected when you apply a text preset, dummy text will be created for you; simply double-click the new layer to replace the source text.

Bad Behavior

The Wiggle and Scale Bounce Behavior animation presets do not get along with any layer that is continuously rasterized, including all text and shape layers. If you enable the Continuous Rasterization switch for a layer that has one of these Behaviors attached, they will transform around the upper left corner instead of their anchor point.

The Autoscroll behaviors duplicate a layer and can animate it horizontally or vertically. Arm courtesy Classic PIO/Medical.

The Fade Out Over Layer Below behavior automatically fades the layer on top based on the length of time it overlaps the layer underneath (above and below).

Behaviors

One of our favorite categories of presets is Behaviors. These use a combination of effects and expressions to automatically animate a layer without the need for keyframes – instead, you set general values such as "move the layer in this direction at this speed." Try them out for yourself:

Step 1:   Close all comps, then open [**Ex.06a**] and select the **CM_bike-wheel** layer.

Step 2:   In the Effects & Presets panel, clear out the Contains box, twirl open Animation Presets > Presets, and twirl open Behaviors. Double-click **Rotate Over Time** to apply it.

RAM Preview; the wheel will slowly rotate. The Effect Controls panel should have opened when you applied this preset (if not, press F3); at the top is a custom Rotate Over Time effect control. Edit its Rotation value and preview again.

Step 3:   Some behaviors can be combined. For example, double-click **Behaviors > Fade In+Out – frames** to add it to the wheel. RAM Preview; the wheel will fade in and out at the ends of the comp without having to set any opacity keyframes. Go ahead and edit the Fade In and Fade Out Durations in the Effect Controls panel.

Step 4: With the Effect Controls panel active, type Command+A (Control+A) to select all effects and press Delete. Then apply **Behaviors > Wiggle – rotation**. RAM Preview; now the wheel rocks back and forth randomly, without having to apply Wiggler (Chapter 5) or write your own wiggle expression (Chapter 37).

Feel free to experiment with applying behaviors to other layers! For example, add **Drift Over Time** to one of your text layers in [**Ex.05**] so that your title doesn't have to stop moving after it's animated on. In [**Ex.06b**], select layer 1 and try out the **Autoscroll** behaviors; RAM Preview to see an endless succession of arms marching across your screen. Undo to delete this preset, and apply **Wigglerama** instead to make it reach about the frame. Then open [**Ex.06c**] and add **Opacity Flash – random** or **Scale Bounce – random** to its spheres for automatic "nervous" animations.

In addition to the **Fade In+Out** behaviors where you can define the fade times in frames or seconds, the **Fade In** and **Fade Out Over Layer Below** behaviors automatically adjust their fade times based on how much a layer overlaps the next one in the timeline – this is demonstrated in [**Ex.06d**]. We show you how to create your own variation on this idea at the end of Chapter 37B – check out *Just a Fade We're Going Through*.

Brainstorm

Ever reach a mental block on how to make a piece of footage look more interesting? Or ever become daunted by the number of parameters an effect has, or not know where to start? Or maybe you already have a look you like, and just need to create some variations on that theme.

This is where the Brainstorm feature comes in. What it does is take any effects, keyframes, and other parameters you have selected (including Transforms and Layer Effects); randomize their values; and present you with nine variants to look at. If you see something you like, you can apply it to your current composition, save it to a duplicate comp, or use it as a "seed" for more exploration. Or, discard them all and keep generating new ideas until you find one you like. As with many things concerning effects, it's best to see it in action, so close your previous comps and let's jump in:

Step 1: Open [**Ex.07a**] and RAM Preview – this comp contains footage of a camera panning by a bank of sunflowers.

Step 2: Let's say you've heard that there's this Cycore effect – Flo Motion – that works like a cross between a kaleidoscope and black hole, but you've never used it. So select the layer **Sunflowers** and apply Effect > Distort > CC Flo Motion.

Nothing happened! At its defaults, CC Flo Motion does not distort the image. You could start experimenting with its parameters…or you can sit back and let After Effects do the heavy lifting:

Step 3: Make sure the effect CC Flo Motion is selected in either the Effect Controls or Timeline panel. Then click on the Brainstorm icon along the top of the Timeline panel (it looks like a light bulb).

A dialog will open with nine copies of your comp, distorted in various ways. (The first cell contains your original comp, as it is the "seed" for the variants.) Click the Play button or tap the spacebar; After Effects will start rendering motion previews of each variant. It will be slow; after all, it's rendering the comp nine times for each frame! After a couple of seconds have rendered, press the spacebar again and these will start playing back in real time. Press the spacebar again to stop playback.

TIP

Brainshapes

Brainstorm works particularly well with shape layers and effects. We explore this more in Chapter 32.

FACTOID

Random Masks

Brainstorm cannot randomize a mask path. But it can still create variations on Mask Feather, Opacity, and Expansion.

Step 3: Select the items you want randomized, click the Brainstorm icon in the Timeline panel (above left), and a new window will open showing nine variants on your composition (above). Footage courtesy Kevin Dole.

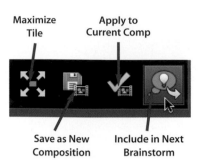

Maximize Tile · Apply to Current Comp

Save as New Composition · Include in Next Brainstorm

Step 5: Select a variant you like, and either save it to its own comp or use it as a seed for future variants.

Replacing Brain Cells

Brainstorm replaces only selected parameters and keyframes; it does not create new keyframes.

Step 4: Let's say you don't like any of these variants: Just click on the big Brainstorm button, and nine more ideas will be generated. Keep going until you find one you like; if you think you preferred a variant in an earlier attempt, use the cursor buttons to the left and right of the Brainstorm button to navigate through your previous attempts.

Step 5: Hover your cursor over one of the variants that you like best; a set of four buttons will appear in its lower right corner. Click on the second one from the left: A new composition will be created using these parameters while allowing you to stay inside Brainstorm. You can do this as many times as you like while exploring ideas. Then click on the switch on the right (the one that looks like the original Brainstorm icon); this means to use it as a seed for your next attempt. You can pick more than one variant to use as a seed.

Step 6: Click the Brainstorm button again, and another set of variants will be generated using your chosen seeds. You can select new seeds if you like. If you feel you're getting close, reduce the Randomness value before clicking Brainstorm to create variants that are more similar to your seed(s); if you aren't seeing enough variety, increase Randomness.

Step 7: Once you find a variant you want to use, click on the third icon from the left that looks like a checkmark. This will apply these settings to your currently selected layer(s).

Step 8: Bring the Project panel forward. You will see additional comps that start with "Ex.07a-Brainstorming" and include a number at the end; these are the variants you saved as comps while experimenting. Feel free to open any of these as well.

In [Ex.07b], use Brainstorm to try out different text treatments with the Box Blur and Roughen Edges effects.

More Brainwaves

You can use Brainstorm in subtle or wacky ways. We've created a few other comps for you to experiment with before heading off to try your own ideas:

- [Ex.07b] contains some text with Box Blur and Roughen Edges applied. Select the text layer and, if effects are not already visible, press E to reveal them. Select both effects and brainstorm them. This is an example of an effect that works better with high Randomness values to get more interesting results. Once you find something you like, reduce the Randomness value to hone in on the final look you want.

- Open [Ex.07c], which contains a simple logo with Layer Styles added. If it's not already visible, twirl open the layer in the Timeline panel and select Layer Styles, then click the Brainstorm button. This is an example where smaller Randomness values may give more useable results.

Brainstorm can be used with Layer Styles such as Gradient Overlay plus Bevel and Emboss – try it yourself in **[Ex.07c]**. Background courtesy Artbeats/Digital Aire.

• **[Ex.07d]** contains the ever-popular – but ever-daunting – Fractal Noise effect. We've added a couple of keyframes to its Evolution parameter so it will animate over time. If it's not already twirled open, select the solid layer and press E to reveal both Fractal Noise and a Tritone effect we applied to colorize the result. With Tritone, we prefer to leave black and white alone, and vary the midtones. To do this, twirl open Tritone and select just Midtones. Then shift+click the name of the Fractal Noise effect (which will select all of its parameters including keyframes) and brainstorm away!

• Brainstorm can be used on normal transform properties as well as multiple layers. Open [Ex.07e], which contains three identical copies of a satellite streaking across the universe, auto-orienting along its path. Type Command+A (Control+A) to select all the layers, then type E (Effects) followed by Shift+P (Position) and Shift+S (Scale). Shift+click on the words Tritone, Position, and Scale for every layer to select all of their values and keyframes. Then brainstorm, making sure you render animated previews to see how their paths and scales are altered. Even though all three started with the same flight path, you can see that each is randomized individually, creating a swarm of satellites darting about.

By now, ideas should be popping into your head about effects and animations you might like to apply Brainstorm to. If nothing else, it's a good way to blow off some steam and have some fun in the middle of all the other serious work you have to do.

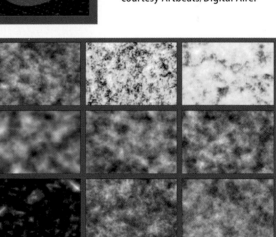

Fractal and Turbulent Noise are good candidates to Brainstorm. **[Ex.07d]** includes an example with Tritone to colorize it.

CONNECT

Adobe Bridge: Chapter 1.

Keyframing: Chapter 3.

Auto-orient rotation: Chapter 5.

Masking: Chapter 10.

Parenting: Chapter 17.

Text animation: Chapter 21.

Effects, Layer Styles, and the Effects & Presets panel: Chapter 22.

Shape Layers: Chapter 32.

Expressions: Chapter 37.

Color Management

Preserving your colors through your workflow.

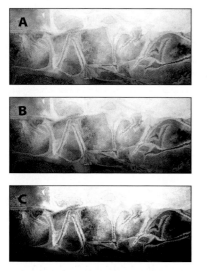

Without color management, images might look slightly washed out (A); using color management allows them to be displayed correctly (B). The wrong color profile can misrepresent an image's internal colors (C).

Example Project

This chapter employs several different example projects, all located in the 26-Color Management folder on the accompanying DVD-ROM. We will instruct you on which project to load for each major section of this chapter.

If you've ever noticed that a video played back on television looks different when played back on a computer, wondered why your photos don't look the way you remembered them, or mused how colors on video look different than they do on film, you've experienced issues related to color management.

The subject of Color Management in After Effects is ever-evolving; the first half of this chapter provides a snapshot of suggested video-centric workflows as of After Effects CS5 version 10.0.0 (note: you should always run your own tests to verify what works for you). We will then discuss the related subjects of working in a linear working space (also known as 1.0 gamma), floating point (including high dynamic range imagery), and Cineon (a logarithmic color space that is common for film work).

Color Management Overview

Motion graphics imagery may come from a wide range of sources, including photographs, video, film, and illustrations. The delivery options are equally wide-ranging. Unfortunately, each of these options may have its own idea about how color should be represented. Some have a limited *gamut* (range of colors) they can represent; others may have differences in contrast or an overall tint.

Color management is based on the idea that if we know what these various idiosyncrasies are, we can translate between them so that "lime green" as captured by one device is correctly stored as "lime green" in your chosen file format, which can then be displayed as that exact same "lime green" by your chosen output device (gamut permitting).

Your main weapon to make this happen is the *color profile*: a description of the idiosyncrasies of each device and file format you'll be using or rendering to. Select the correct color profile for each source footage item in your project, choose a profile as your *project working space*, set the correct profile for the file format or device you are rendering to, and After Effects will perform all of the necessary translations for you.

Ahhhh…if it were only that simple. It *can* be, but there are also a number of exceptions, special cases, and unknowns (such as exactly where a file came from or whether it was tagged with the correct profile) that can throw you off track. In the next few pages, we'll discuss each step of the process including the most common traps and pitfalls you may encounter.

Project Working Space

To use color management, first you must select a Project Working Space (PWS for short). This is the central color space that all footage files are translated into before compositing and that is then translated via an output profile into the desired color space upon rendering. All content generated directly inside After Effects – such as solid, text, and shape layers, as well as colors specified in a color picker – are also created in this space.

New projects have color management disabled by default. To enable color management, open File > Project Settings and select a color profile other than "None" from the Working Space popup.

Of course, now the question becomes: Which profile should you select? There are two schools of thought on this subject.

The most common approach is to select a color profile that matches your intended render target (and, hopefully, most of your source material). If your footage, PWS, and output module all use the same color profile, no color translation is required as an image moves through these stages, reducing the potential for color shifts or math errors. For example, common choices would include:

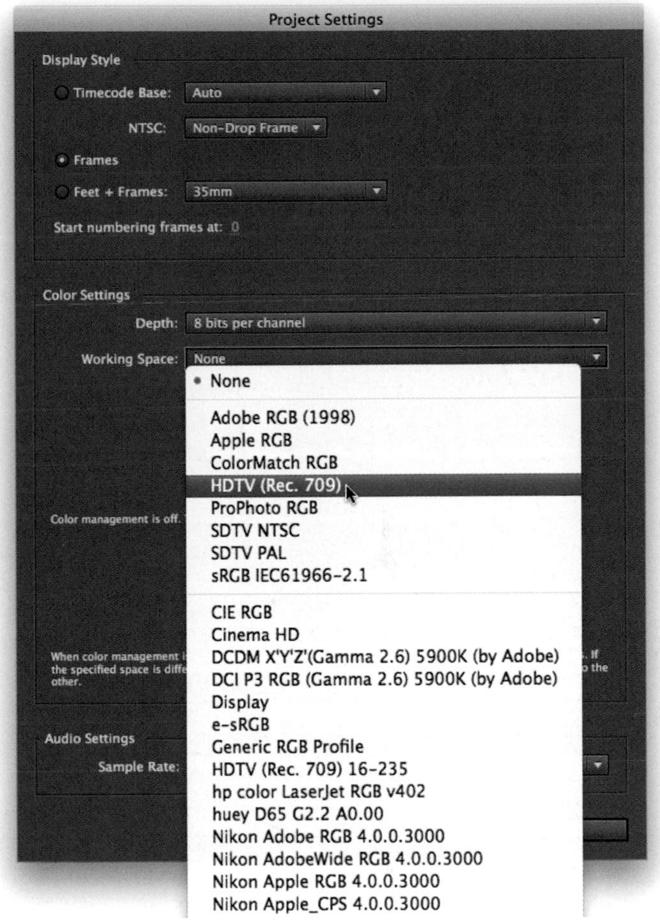

- For DV and other standard definition formats (including uncompressed YUV), choose SDTV NTSC or SDTV PAL depending on the prevailing format in your country.

- For high definition, choose HDTV (Rec. 709).

- If the movie or graphic is to be displayed on a web page, select sRGB IEC61966-2.1.

The alternate school of thought is to pick a color profile that has a very large gamut to minimize the possibility that colors may be "clipped off" because they exceed the color gamut of a more specific profile. For example, when working on film or any project that requires 32-bit floating point color (discussed later in this chapter), a good choice would be Kodak's ProPhoto RGB profile.

We will discuss the Linearize, 1.0 Gamma, and Match Legacy Gamma checkboxes that appear below the Working Space popup later in this chapter. By the way, the area below these checkboxes often contains very useful feedback connected to your color management choices; make sure you read the fine print!

To enable color management, open File > Project Settings and select a color profile for your Working Space. You can also open Project Settings by clicking on the project color depth button at the bottom of the Project panel.

Keeping Up with Changes

We anticipate future updates to After Effects may affect color management workflows. For the most recent information, check the book errata for Creating Motion Graphics on our website, *www.crishdesign.com*.

RED Codec

Make sure you install the RED QuickTime codec, available from *www.red.com/support*.

When color management is enabled, selecting footage items in the Project panel will result in their input profile being displayed next to their thumbnail (above). These can be verified and changed in their Interpret Footage dialog under the Color Management tab (below). These choices will be grayed out if you don't have color management enabled for the project.

Input Profiles

The next step on the road to color management bliss is to correctly assign profiles to all of your source footage. After Effects first checks to see if a color profile has been embedded in the source file, then consults its user-modifiable Interpretation Rules (see Chapter 38). Failing that, it assigns the default profile sRGB IEC61966-2.1. This default is correct for most digital photos and web content (and is the default in Photoshop as well), but is wrong for most video and film content.

First, let's see how big an impact color management can have. Open the project file **26a-Input Profiles.aep**. It should have color management turned off; open File > Project Settings and make sure Working Space is set to None. Click OK, then open comp [**Ex.a01**] which contains what initially looks like a washed-out image of a car (see **A**). This image was saved using a particular color profile, but currently After Effects doesn't know what to do with the embedded profile.

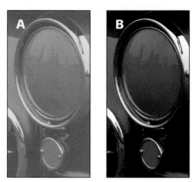

Open the Project Settings dialog again; the shortcut is to click on the bit depth indicator at the bottom of the Project panel. Set the Working Space popup to HDTV (Rec. 709) and click OK. Now the true colors lurking inside this photograph have been revealed (**B**).

Right-click on the layer **CM_Corvette_e-sRGB.psd** and select Reveal Layer Source in Project. Its thumbnail will appear at the top of the Project panel. The bottom line of text in this area reads "Profile: e-sRGB" which indicates the input profile that After Effects is using.

With this file selected in the Project panel, choose File > Interpret Footage > Main (there is also an Interpret Footage button in the lower left corner of the Project panel), then click on the Color Management tab. In the Profile section you will notice that the first line says "Embedded Profile: e-sRGB." This indicates that After Effects found a profile embedded in this footage item and is therefore going to use it. The Assign Profile popup can be used to override this setting; notice that the first two choices are the project's working space and the embedded profile. (These choices will be grayed out if you don't have color management enabled for the project.)

Some Examples

Let's work through some common footage examples. Open comp [**Ex.a02**] and solo the respective layers to view them in the Comp panel. Changes made in the corresponding Interpret Footage dialogs will appear immediately in the Comp panel.

CL_SkateSequence_DV.mov: This movie was captured with a DV camera and saved using the DV codec, which After Effects decodes itself. Therefore, a profile of SDTV NTSC Y'CbCr is automatically assigned.

AB_coast_1080i.mov: This high-definition stock footage clip was also saved using the PhotoJPEG codec. After Effects CS5 auto-detects the codec and the image size, and automatically assigns the profile HDTV (Rec.709) Y'CbCr. (By the way, After Effects CS3 and CS4 displayed some PhotoJPEG footage too bright; this has been fixed in CS5.)

hcw_godiva_close.png: This image sequence was captured with an HD camera, but does not employ a file format that After Effects decodes natively – so it assigns the default profile sRGB IEC61966-2.1. Go into this file's Interpret Footage dialog and change the profile to HDTV.

CD_finchbath.mov: This HD movie was captured with a Canon 5D mk2 DSLR camera, which saves files using the H.264 codec and RGB color space. In 10.0.0, After Effects assigns this variant the default profile of sRGB IEC61966-2.1. Go into this file's Interpret Footage dialog and change the profile to…not HDTV, but SDTV NTSC, which is the profile Canon uses internally in the 5D.

AEA2_Effects & Presets.mov: This is a Mac-based screen capture, saved using the H.264 codec. After Effects 10.0.0 assumes H.264 movies (other than those from a 5D) are HDTV and assigns this profile, causing it to appear too bright. As of 10.0.0, you can't change this profile in Interpret Footage – so select this clip in a comp and apply Effect > Utility > Color Profile Converter. Change the Input Profile to HDTV, the Output Profile to Apple RGB, and set Scene-ref. Output Compensation to On.

A001_C031_0924MQ_001.R3D: For video workflows with RED clips, it is best to assign the HDTV (Rec. 709) color profile. (It defaults to sRGB in AE 10.0.0; we expect this to be fixed in an update.)

CD_metrowide.mov: We created this animation using a Mac 3D program that was not color managed. In this case, the most accurate color profile is that of the computer monitor it was created on. Therefore, change its color profile to Apple RGB.

AB_ReelTextures.mov: When you don't know how a footage item was created, assigning the correct input profile is more of a judgment call. As this clip was intended to be used as video stock footage, a good first guess would be SDTV NTSC – but experiment and see which looks the most "correct."

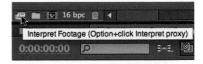

To change the color profile for a footage item, select it in the Project panel, then click the Interpret Footage button at the bottom of the Project panel.

After Effects internally decodes many video formats. As a result, it will assign a color profile automatically, and may not allow you to change that profile (note that the Assign Profile popup is grayed out in the dialog above). If you need to change it, apply the Color Profile Converter effect, set Input to the incorrect choice, and Output to the correct profile.

CD_columbine.jpg and **CD_Bosque_ARGB.jpg: :** Most digital still image cameras default to using the sRGB profile; some higher-end cameras offer the option of using the larger-gamut Adobe RGB profile. These profiles are embedded in the image file. After Effects will detect it, and use the embedded profile as the default.

DV_NakedScared.tif: This composited still image was not saved using color management, so you have no embedded profile to rely on. If no profile is detected for a still, After Effects will assign the current Project Working Space as the input profile. As with computer-generated video, the most accurate profile to select would be the monitor the artist was looking at when they created it. Good first guesses are Apple RGB for a Mac, or sRGB for Windows.

Autumn Leaves: This shape layer was created inside After Effects, and does not have an Interpret Footage dialog. Text, shape, and solids created in After Effects use the Project Working Space as their profile, and any colors you eyedropper will be matched to the PWS at the time you eyedroppered them. If you change the PWS later, beware that their colors will also change!

Changes in CS5

After Effects version 10 (CS5) has taken over the decoding of many video formats, improving color management fidelity. However, as of version 10.0.0, you cannot change the profile auto-assigned to these formats. Use the Color Profile Converter effect to correct any cases of mistaken identity.

Open the Output Module by clicking on its template name in the Render Queue (above right). Each Output Module may have its own target color profile, selected under its Color Management tab (above). The default is the same as the project's working space profile; change as needed for your target format (such as sRGB for web video). As with other color management dialogs, the text underneath explains precisely what is going to happen.

Output Profiles

Just as it is important to assign the correct color profile for every footage item on the input side, you must also select a color profile for every movie or image you render when using color management. You do this in the Output Module under the Color Management tab. After Effects will then translate colors from the Project Working Space into the output profile's space before saving the file. Every Output Module has its own profile, and each render can have multiple Output Modules – meaning you can render to more than one target at once!

In the project file **26a-Input Profiles.aep**, open Window > Render Queue, where we've already set up a composition to render. Click on the text to the right of the first Output Module menu arrow to open its related dialog, then click on the Color Management tab. The default output profile is the same as the working space – remember earlier where we said your planned output format makes a good PWS! Click on this popup to select a profile that matches your planned file format. For example, if you are rendering to the FLV or F4V formats for the web (as is the case with our second Output Module in this example), sRGB IEC61966-2.1 would be the correct profile.

Display Management

When color management is enabled, there is one more translation to make: from the Project Working Space to the color profile for your monitor. This helps eliminate the idiosyncratic color cast your particular brand and model of monitor may have.

After Effects does this for every Comp, Footage, and Layer panel. The menu item View > Use Color Management toggles display compensation on and off independently for each view (it defaults to on); the shortcut is to hold Shift and press / on the numeric keypad. When color management is enabled for a particular view, a small "+" icon will appear in the Show Channel switch along the bottom of its panel.

When display management is enabled, the computer's operating system tells After Effects which color profile to use for the translation. Your monitor's profile is set in System Preferences > Displays > Color on the Mac; the location on Windows may vary depending on the operating system and display card – Control Panel > Display > Settings > Advanced > Color Management is a typical path. The Mac usually detects which monitor you are using and loads a profile for it. Under Windows, sRGB is used if a matching profile is not available; many monitors can be set to sRGB from their own front panel menu.

Note that a cheap monitor may have a limited color gamut or a shift that cannot be completely fixed by using a standard color profile. There can also be variations between individual copies of otherwise identical monitors. To get closer to that elusive perfection, it is a good idea to buy or borrow a monitor calibrator to create a custom profile for your specific monitor.

To toggle display management on and off for the current view, use the View menu or hold Shift and press the / key on the numeric keypad. If it is enabled for the current view, a + icon appears in the middle of the Show Channel icon along its bottom. Click this icon for Display Management options.

FACTOID

Video Preview Not Managed

The Video Preview output is not color managed – no translation takes place from the Project Working Space to this output. This is a good thing: If you are using a true video monitor for this output and have set the PWS to a corresponding video format, the result will be an accurate preview of your video.

Output Simulation

What if you want to see what your image would look like through a specific playback device other than your current monitor? In this case, After Effects needs to know the output profile you plan to render with, as well as the color profile of your intended target device. The result of these two conversions are then translated to your own monitor.

Presets for several common scenarios (including video, film, and web pages viewed on different platforms) are available under the View > Simulate Output menu. To see how these were built, first select the desired preset such as SDTV NTSC, then select View > Simulate Output > Custom. Study the Output Simulation dialog that opens: Rather than just send the project working space's profile directly to your monitor, these presets typically use special "presentation environment" profiles. For example, TV and film are often viewed in much darker rooms than they were shot in; presentation environment profiles such as SMPTE-C take this into account. You can change these settings and save your own custom presets.

To simulate what your images will look like through a different playback chain, use View > Simulate Output. For more information on how to exploit this, search for Output Simulation in the After Effects Help Center.

445

Apply Color LUT

A new feature in After Effects CS5 is the ability to read and apply color look-up tables (LUTs) stored in the 3DL and CUBE file formats by using the Utility > Apply Color LUT effect. Color LUTs are an alternative to using standard ICC color profiles (which also contain LUTs); ICC profiles often represent specific devices, while LUTs are used to accomplish specific tasks. Some of those tasks include:

• You have created a color treatment in Color Finesse (which is bundled with After Effects), and you wish to share this treatment with another user on a different system. Or, you might prefer to apply just the resulting LUT to other clips inside After Effects rather than reapply the entire Color Finesse effect.

• Someone has created a specific color treatment or "look" in another system, and you wish to apply this treatment to footage in After Effects.

• Someone has created a LUT that represents how a particular display device or film stock will change the colors of sources you output to it, and you want to preview the resulting transformations in After Effects.

Let's get a quick taste for how to accomplish those tasks. Open **26b-Color LUTs.aep**, then the comp [**Ex.b01_starter**]. Select the clip in this comp, and apply Effect > Synthetic Aperture > SA Color Finesse 3. In the Effect Controls panel, click the Full Interface button; Color Finesse will be launched.

Create a color treatment in Color Finesse, or load one of their presets (click the Gallery tab along the left side of the interface, open Settings

LUT Formats

After Effects can read 3D LUTs in the 3DL or CUBE formats, with the technical restriction that all three axes have the same number of points, with each axis containing 64 or fewer points. A common format is a 17x17x17-point LUT.

Presets (System), and double-click the desired treatment). Then choose File > Export > Settings to Autodesk 3D LUT > Smoke. Name your file, choose a location to save it, and click Save. Then click OK to exit Color Finesse. You can now give the resulting LUT to the operator of another system, or reuse it inside After Effects.

Back in After Effects, open [**Ex.b02_starter**], select the sole layer in this comp, and choose Effect > Utility > Apply Color LUT. A file dialog will open; choose the LUT you just saved, or navigate to **26_Chapter Sources > LUTs** and select **CF Bleach Bypass.3dl**. Click Open, and this LUT will be applied to your selected layer. You may also apply it to an Adjustment Layer placed above an edit or a composite. If you want to change the LUT, click on Apply Color LUT > Choose LUT in the Effect Controls panel.

If you are simulating an output device, don't apply the LUT directly to the footage; apply it temporarily to an Adjustment Layer above your composite. Open comp [**Ex.b03_starter**], and create a Layer > New >

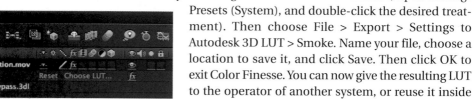

Apply Color LUT provides a quick way to apply a color treatment to a clip. Footage courtesy Artbeats/Transportation.

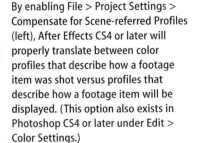

When you're simulating a particular display environment, use Apply Color LUT on an Adjustment Layer for proofing, and set it to be a Guide Layer so the treatment will not render.

Adjustment Layer. Then choose Effect > Utility > Apply Color LUT, and select your simulation LUT – such as **26_Chapter Sources > LUTs > CF Fuji 8583 Eterna 400T.3dl**. To ensure that this simulation won't render (the output device or film stock is already going to make this adjustment – you don't want to perform it twice), choose Layer > Guide Layer. Then make corrections in your sources underneath this adjustment layer to achieve the desired final look.

Scene-Referred Profiles

Color management has been improved in After Effects and Photoshop so that they both recognize and compensate for the differences between "scene-referred" and "display-referred" color profiles. The short explanation is not to worry – After Effects is merely more accurate now. Leave the option File > Project Settings > Compensate for Scene-referred Profiles enabled when using color management, and in some scenarios your output will now be even more accurate than it was before. For a longer explanation, read on.

By enabling File > Project Settings > Compensate for Scene-referred Profiles (left), After Effects CS4 or later will properly translate between color profiles that describe how a footage item was shot versus profiles that describe how a footage item will be displayed. (This option also exists in Photoshop CS4 or later under Edit > Color Settings.)

Image States

Some color profiles – such as SDTV, HDTV, Camera Raw, plus many film-based profiles – are based on how an image appeared when it was originally captured, and therefore are known as *scene-referred*. Other color profiles – such as sRGB, Adobe RGB, Apple RGB, SMPTE C, and others – are based on how an image is to be displayed, and are therefore known as *display-referred*.

If you think of a typical video workflow, you shoot footage outdoors in sunlight or with the assistance of additional lighting, and the contrast (or "dynamic range") between the brightest light and darkest shadow is considerable. However, a typical television does not have nearly the dynamic range available on a set, so the final image will inevitably be displayed with reduced contrast and potentially altered colors. As a result, when you shoot a scene on a high definition camera (for example), its output – which is in the HDTV Rec. 709 color space – will be "tone mapped" (have its dynamic range reduced) by a high definition television so that the source image can be displayed in the high-def TV's own sRGB color space. A side effect is that the image will typically appear darker on a TV than it was on the set.

This becomes an issue when you're viewing HD (and other scene-referred) sources on your computer monitor in After Effects: You would prefer to see it as it would ultimately appear on its corresponding display device (in this case, a high-def TV). To accomplish this in CS3, you would use the View > Simulate Output > HDTV (Rec. 709) option to perform the tone mapping. In After Effects CS4 and later, instead you can just enable File > Project Settings > Compensate for Scene-referred Profiles. When enabled, this adjustment will take place automatically regardless of which combination of scene- and display-referred profiles you are using.

Continuing with our example, HDTV source material will now appear darker on your computer monitor while working with it in After Effects, matching what an HD television would do to the image. An important under-the-hood detail is that the underlying pixel values will *not* be changed, which means you don't have to worry about color shifts in sources passed straight through After Effects.

Mixing Profiles

The second major issue involving Scene versus Display Referred Profiles comes up when you're combining output-referred source material – such as digital photographs that have already been saved in the output-referred sRGB or Adobe RGB color space – with source material that has a scene-referred profile, such as SDTV or HDTV footage. As these additional sources already exist in an output-referred space, unlike your video they do *not* need additional adjustment to compensate for how they will ultimately be displayed (aside from any necessary translation from one output-referred space to another, such as from Adobe RGB to sRGB).

FACTOID

Adobe White Paper

Adobe has created a document that further explains the "image state adjustment" that After Effects performs between scene- and display-referred color profiles. Go to *www.adobe.com/go/learn_ae_ sceneoutputreferredpaper*

GOTCHA

QuickTime Options

QuickTime Player 7 is preferrable over QuickTime Player X (and neither is accurate all the time). In QuickTime Player 7, open Preferences and turn on Enable Final Cut Studio Compatibility.

To see this in action, open the project file **26c-Scene Referred.aep**, then open File > Project Settings. Under Color Settings set Working Space to HDTV (Rec. 709) NTSC, and for now *disable* Compensate for Scene-referred Profiles. Click OK; color management will be enabled, and you will be working in a mode similar to After Effects CS3 with Output Simulation turned off.

Open the comp [**Ex.c01_starter**]. It contains two sources: **hcw_godi-va_close**, keyed video footage that has been assigned a color profile of HDTV (which is scene-referred), and the still image background **CD_Bosque_ARGB.jpg** which has been assigned a color profile of Adobe RGB (which is output-referred). You might notice that the actress looks a little bright or washed out in this composite. That's partially because you are viewing her as she was shot on the set. In a normal broadcast chain, a television set would display her darker than that.

Reopen File > Project Settings, and enable Compensate for Scene-referred Profiles. Click OK; now the actress will appear darker in the Comp panel. After Effects is compensating for how she will appear to a viewer on a properly calibrated television set (in this standard definition case, one that conforms to the sRGB color specification).

Why didn't the background photograph get darker as well? Because it is already output-referred, meaning it has been pre-compensated for how it will appear when displayed. You don't want After Effects to throw a second output compensation on top of that; the result would be wrong. Instead, all After Effects has to do in this situation is translate the source's Adobe RGB color space into the desired output space.

Yes, this is a confusing subject – but it is an important issue, and one that After Effects is now taking into account for you automatically (as long as you have the Project Settings option set to Compensate for Scene-referred Profiles enabled!). In addition to the SDTV and HDTV cases, this scene- versus output-referred compensation will also take place for color-managed film projects.

In After Effects CS3, video-sourced footage (such as the keyed woman in the foreground here) will be displayed using its scene – rather than output – profile, causing it to appear artificially bright (A). In CS4 and later, the Compensate for Scene-referred Profiles option will display scene-referred video footage darker, while maintaining output-referred sources such as the background photo here (B). Woman courtesy Hollywood Camera Work.

ProRes Codec Settings

When rendering to the ProRes 4444 codec, change Format Options > Codec Settings > Gamma Correction to None.

Disabling Management

To disable color management on a specific footage item, open its Interpret Footage and enable Preserve RGB under the Color Management tab.

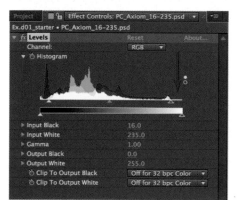

If footage looks a touch washed out, chances are its codec is passing its internal 16 to 235 luminance levels directly to After Effects. Verify this by applying Color Correction > Levels and studying the Histogram for gaps at the left or right extremes (above).

Setting Input Black to 16 and Input White to 235 will stretch the luminance back out to its full range (right). Footage courtesy Perception Communications and American Isuzu Motors Inc.

Luminance Range Issues

When talking about color, we are used to 0 equaling black and 255 equaling white, or full strength for a specific color channel. (These are the 8-bit-per-channel values; scale up accordingly if your project is in 16-bit mode.) However, most digital video formats use an internal system where 16 – not 0 – equals black, and 235 – not 255 – equals white. This gives them some extra wiggle room to capture over-bright hotspots and to create rough "superblack" keys where opaque black is at 16 and transparent areas are at 0.

Most of the time, this bit of trivia is hidden from us: When decoding digital video files, many codecs rescale the luminance range to place black at 0 and white at 255. When they write one of these files, they do the opposite, scaling 0 up to 16 and 255 down to 235. However, some systems (such as digital disk recorders) pass these internal luminance ranges to After Effects in their unaltered state.

If you notice that a piece of footage seems to have less than ideal contrast, you need to study its luminance. To practice this, open the project file **26d-Luminance.aep**, then open comp [**Ex.d01_starter**]. For reference, press Shift+F5 (or click the camera icon in the Comp panel) to take a snapshot of what its image looked like originally.

Select the layer **PC_Axiom_16-235.jpg** and apply Effect > Color Correction > Levels. The Effect Controls panel will open (press F3 if you don't see it); drag this panel wider so you can see the full width of its Histogram display. You may notice gaps at the left (black) and right (white) edges of the display, which indicate this clip is not using the full luminance range available to it.

Set Input Black to 16 and Input White to 235, which are the magic numbers to stretch out the internal video luminance range to full RGB range. Press F5 to compare the adjusted image with the snapshot of the original; it looks much better now! You can now apply effects, blending modes, and other operations to this clip while working with the full luminance range available.

Deciding whether a clip is displaying a 16 to 235 or a 0 to 255 range can be a bit of a judgment call. For example, you may have noticed in this example that there is a peak in the Histogram to the left of the Input Black pointer's new location. This corresponds to the fringe you see around the clip in the Comp panel (a side effect of the transfer process) and is not unusual to see. If portions of the image were overexposed, you may see some activity in the Histogram to the right of the Input White pointer's new location. You may have to use your aesthetic sense to judge if most of the useful image information is happening between 16 and 235 or is already spread across the full luminance range.

Match Legacy Gamma

Previous versions of After Effects had some issues accurately "round tripping" colors between different platforms or applications. The old advice was to disable Match Legacy Gamma when moving between Mac and Windows, and to enable it when moving between Apple software and After Effects.

Gamma handling in After Effects CS5 has been substantially rewritten, and now most codecs round-trip between After Effecs and Apple software without issues. Therefore, it is best to disable Match Legacy Gamma. When opening an old project with Match Legacy Gamma enabled, it is best to disable it, save the project, and restart After Effects.

There is still a problem trusting QuickTime Player to "proof" your colors, as QuickTime Player may introduce gamma errors, even when you have turned on Enable Final Cut Studio Compatibility. Don't rely on it for the final word on color. For the most up-to-date information on this topic, visit: *www.adobe.com/go/learn_ae_quicktimegamma*

If you are using color management in your project (as we are in this one), and you know a clip is giving you a 16 to 235 luminance range rather than 0 to 255, you can use color profiles to perform this adjustment for you. Open composition [**Ex.d02_starter**], which contains the same original image as in the previous example; press Shift+F5 to take a snapshot of it.

Right-click the layer **PC_Axiom_16-235.jpg** and select Reveal Layer Source in Project. Select File > Interpret Footage > Main to open the Interpret Footage dialog, then choose the Color Management tab. The SDTV NTSC profile has already been embedded into this clip. Click on the Assign Profile popup and instead select SDTV NTSC 16–235 (it's farther down the list). Click OK and return to your comp. The car should look better now; press F5 to compare the result with your snapshot.

What if you need to render back to a codec that is expecting a 16 to 235 luminance range instead of your now-expanded 0 to 255? If you have color management enabled for your project, you can make this adjustment in the Output Module when you render. Select one of your comps and press Command+M (Control+M) to add it to the Render Queue. Click on the text to the right of Output Module to open its settings dialog, then select the Color Management tab. Click on the popup menu for Output Profile and change it from the Working Space to SDTV NTSC 16–235.

If you are not using color management, the workaround is to add a Layer > New > Adjustment Layer to the top level of your final composition, then add a Levels effect to it. This time, set the Output (not Input) Black to 16 and Output White to 235. Now you will have done the same levels of compression as the output color profile would. This is demonstrated in composition [**Ex.d03**].

You can change the color profile of a footage item to expand the 16 to 235 levels to full range for you. Note that there are 16–235 choices for SDTV NTSC and PAL as well as for HDTV. Incidentally, the 16 to 235 luminance range is sometimes referred to as "601" luminance, named after the ITU-R 601 digital video specification.

Linear Blending and Gamma

Related to color management is how to treat the distribution of color and luminance values inside a source image or working space. You may be used to the typical computer representation where a 50% luminance value (such as RGB 127) results in an image that appears to be 50% gray on screen. However, this is not how our eyes work; they are much more sensitive to low lighting conditions. An example of this is the "18% gray card" that photographers may be familiar with: A paint chip that reflects only 18% of the light that hits it is perceived by our eyes to be 50% gray.

Therefore, After Effects offers an alternative way of working where internal calculations are "linearized" to match the way our eyes would perceive luminance levels. This approach is sometimes referred to as *gamma 1.0* or *linear light* (the latter not to be confused with the blending mode of the same name). The Project Settings contain two checkboxes that are connected to this:

Linearize Working Space: When enabled, all image processing – including color profile conversions, masks, effects, 3D lighting, and the way layers are blended together – are performed in a gamma 1.0 space.

Blend Colors Using 1.0 Gamma: This option can be thought of as "Linearize Working Space Lite." When enabled, only the blending together of layers is performed in a gamma 1.0 space, not effects or other processing. You can enable this even when color management is disabled. It is enabled by default when Linearize Working Space is enabled.

Linear Blending Examples

The effects of linear blending become apparent when a partially transparent object is mixed with an image behind: The brighter areas will be favored. To see examples of how linear blending affects your work inside After Effects, open the project file **26e-Linear-Blending.aep** and verify that Linearize Working Space as well as Blend Colors Using 1.0 Gamma are *disabled* in File > Project Settings.

Motion Blur: One of the reasons visual effects artists prefer to work with a gamma of 1.0 is that blurred objects blend more naturally. Open [**Ex.e01**], verify that the master Motion Blur switch is enabled in the Timeline panel, and RAM Preview: It contains a pair of planets – one light, one dark – whizzing across space. Move the current time indicator to 00:20 and press Shift+F5 to take a snapshot of this scene. Open Project Settings and enable Blend Colors Using 1.0 Gamma. Select the Comp panel to bring it forward again and press F5 to compare the results: With 1.0 gamma, the brighter motion blur streaks are more prominent, corresponding to our eyes' sensitivity to light.

The Project Settings dialog contains a pair of options that change how images are composited inside After Effects.

PWS and Gamma

It is generally a bad idea to enable or disable linear blending in the middle of a project, as the change in internal gamma will affect how layers are blended together. Even when Linearize Working Space is disabled, changing the Project Working Space will still affect how layers are blended together as different color profiles have different gammas.

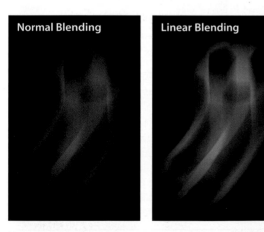

Linear blending has an impact on motion blur, as brighter blurred areas are more prominent than before. Photo courtesy iStockphoto, © Deejpilot, Image #10467200.

Opacity Fades: Disable Blend Colors Using 1.0 Gamma and open [**Ex.c02**]: This comp contains a simple crossfade from one clip to another. RAM Preview, paying attention to how the fade progresses in the light and dark areas. Locate to 01:00 and press Shift+F5 to take another snapshot. Re-

Normal Blending

Linear Blending

enable Blend Colors Using 1.0 Gamma in the Project Settings, bring the Comp panel forward, and press F5 to compare before and after: The brighter areas are favored when 1.0 gamma is used. RAM Preview and note how the bright areas in the second clip are the first to appear, while the bright areas in the first clip are the last to disappear. This result is sometimes referred to as an *optical fade*.

Linear blending also has an impact on how objects blend when they are faded. Footage courtesy Artbeats/Sky Effects and Establishments: Urban.

Linearize Working Space versus Blend Colors

When you enable Linearize Working Space (which also enables Blend Colors Using 1.0 Gamma by default), more operations inside After Effects – such as the processing of 3D lights and effects – will also take place with a 1.0 gamma. The implications can be subtle or enormous.

The following examples are also in **26e-LinearBlending.aep**. Make sure both Linearize Working Space as well as Blend Colors Using 1.0 Gamma are *disabled* in File > Project Settings when you first open these comps:

3D Lights: Open [**Ex.e03**] which uses a combination of lights to project video onto the floor as well as to light the front of the screen. Enabling just Blend Colors Using 1.0 Gamma will not change the appearance of this scene. However, try enabling Linearize Working Space: Now the lighting appears brighter (see figure right) because fainter areas are being emphasized.

Effects: Disable Linearize Working Space and open comp [**Ex.e04**]. Select **AB_EstablishmentsUrban.mov** and press F3 to open its Effect Controls; we've already applied the common effects Levels for you. Play with decreasing Levels > Input White, getting a feel for how it affects the image (particularly the gradient in the sky). Now enable Linearize Working Space: The Levels Histogram will change quite a bit. Many other effects also behave differently when Linearize Working Space is enabled.

TIP

Linear RED

To work with RED footage in a linear working space, under the Color Management tab (in its Interpret Footage dialog) set the Interpret as Linear Light popup to On, and change Main Options > More Options > Gamma to Linear.

GOTCHA

Managed Snapshots

Snapshots are affected by the project working space. Therefore, you cannot rely on snapshots to give you accurate comparisons of the effects of changing the PWS. Snapshots can still be used to compare the use of different color profiles on individual footage items.

Linearize Working Space affects how effects are calculated. For example, note how the Levels Histogram changes with Linearized disabled (far left) or enabled (left).

A project's bit depth is indicated at the bottom of the Project panel. You can Option+click (Alt+click) on this indicator to change the bit depth or click normally to open the Project Settings dialog.

With the project set to 32-bit mode, dragging the cursor across hot spots in an HDR image (above) results in color channel values greater than 1.0, where 1.0 equals white (above right). Image courtesy HDR-VFX (*www.hdrvfx.com*).

Non-32 Bit Effects

If you apply an effect that is not compatible with 32-bit float mode, a yellow caution symbol will appear next to it in the Effect Controls panel. This means it will clip under-range or over-range colors. The cure is to apply the Animation Preset > Image – Utilities > **Compress-Expand Dynamic Range**, place your problematic effect between the two new effects this preset adds, and adjust the Gain and Gamma values until you are pleased with the result.

32-Bit Floating Point

The default 8-bit-per-color channel mode in After Effects uses 0 RGB to represent pure black or the absence of a given color in a pixel and 255 to represent pure white or a 100% contribution of a given color. 16-bit mode provides 256 times finer resolution (at the cost of more RAM and processing time) but otherwise keeps the pure black to pure white limits.

32-bit-per-channel mode (also known as *32-bit float* or *floating point* mode) provides two additional features: even more resolution as well as the ability to represent colors darker than black and brighter than white.

This may sound frivolous, but in fact it is very handy to keep track of these colors rather than clip them off as you pile on the processing and effects.

For a taste of this, open the project file **26f-Floating Point.aep** and verify that the project's bit depth is set to 8- or 16-bit mode by checking the indicator at the bottom of the Project panel – you can Option+click (Alt+click) on this indicator to toggle through these modes. Then open [**Ex.f01**] and RAM Preview: It contains a fade-out of an image of a sunrise. Note how the sun's hot spot goes gray as it fades.

Open File > Project Settings, change Depth to 32 bits per channel (float), and click OK. Make sure the Window > Info panel is open with its Options set to Auto Color Display (the default). Press Home and move your cursor around this image while watching Info: The range of values displayed has changed. In floating point mode, 0 still represents black, but 1.0 represents white. As you move across the sun, you will see values higher than 1.0 where the sun is blown out. This sunset is an HDR (high dynamic range) image that was captured in a way so that very bright (and very dark) values were preserved, with the results saved as floating point values.

RAM Preview while in 32-bit mode and observe how the sun fades: Rather than a gray blob, the overexposed "blooming" effect in the clouds around the sun shrinks until you see the sun at its normal size, which then fades out. The final appearance is much more akin to "turning down the sun" than a normal video "fade to black."

Note that merely switching to 32-bit float mode will not recover color information from files that did not contain it in the first place! [**Ex.f02**] contains a split screen with the HDR image on the left (**A**), and a JPEG version of the image on the right (**B**). JPEGs cannot store floating point information, so the sun still turns gray during the fade.

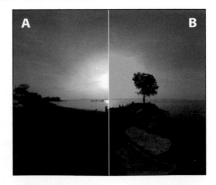

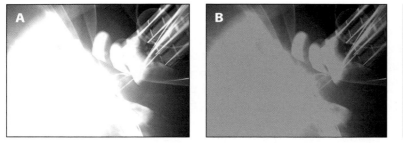

That being said, you don't need to use floating point sources to create values higher than 1.0 (or lower than 0.0) in a composition – blending modes such as Add as well as glows, lens flares, and other effects can also create these out-of-range values. The reason to preserve them is so you can retain the detail when you fade out or add lighting to an image, or otherwise cause the values to be shifted so the clipped values return to the legal range.

In [**Ex.f03**] we've created an over-bright composite by stacking layers in Add mode (note that this comp would look the same in 8-, 16-, or 32-bit mode). We then nested this composite into [**Ex.f04**] where we faded out its end. RAM Preview [**Ex.f04**] in 32-bit float mode and compare it with the results you see in 8- or 16-bit mode – a lot of "lost" detail is maintained during the fade in 32-bit mode.

An over-bright composite (A) turns to muddy gray when you fade it out in 8- or 16-bit mode (B). However, in 32-bit mode details reappear in the bright areas during the fade (C). Bassist courtesy Lee Stranahan; lighting courtesy Artbeats/Light Alchemy.

Camera Raw Files

Some high-end digital still image cameras can save images in *camera raw* format (CRAW for short; the file type is .crw or .cr2), which captures all of the information presented to the image sensor at the time you shot the image. When you import a CRAW image into After Effects (or Photoshop), you will first get a special dialog where you can alter the exposure, tint, sharpness, and numerous other details on the image. You can return to this dialog by selecting the file and using Edit > Edit Original in After Effects.

Although camera raw (as well as the .dng Digital Negative format you can save to from the CRAW dialog in Photoshop) is a High Dynamic Range Image format, After Effects does not pass floating point values into a composition – your black and white points are clipped by the settings in the CRAW dialog. We often set the Exposure value in the CRAW dialog to a negative value to

The Camera Raw dialog is your digital darkroom to expose your image before passing it onto After Effects.

retain the over-bright whites, then use the Exposure effect to restore the image's intended brightness. The RED R3D Settings dialog has the same limitation, except its exposure setting does not respond the same as the Exposure effect; you will need to make additional tweaks with Levels.

The Levels effect works in 32-bit mode , allowing you to recapture over-bright values and tame them back into the visible range. (See **[Ex.f05_final]**.)

Altering Exposure

Working in floating point mode also lets you use effects to recover or rebalance the potentially blown-out results of using lens flares, Add mode, and the like. While still in 32-bit float mode, open **[Ex.f05_starter]** which contains a copy of our earlier over-lit composite. Select **Adjustment Layer 1** which already has Levels applied. Press F3 to open its Effect Controls: The Levels Histogram will go off the chart to the right, reflecting the high brightness levels present. Note that the Levels parameters are now defined by the floating point range of 0 to 1. Increase Input White until detail reappears in the blown-out areas. Then edit the Gamma value to get the overall luminance balance you desire.

For those with photographic and film experience, After Effects also features Exposure controls. Still in 32-bit float mode, open composition **[Ex.f06_starter]**. Along the bottom right edge of the Comp panel is a camera shutter icon with a value to its right (see figure). Scrubbing this value alters the exposure (in "stops") of how you are viewing the current panel. *This does not affect your final render –* just the way you are viewing the composite so you can see if there is any visual information you wish to recover. Click on the shutter icon to return this value to 0. This control appears in the Comp, Layer, and Footage views, even if you are not in 32-bit mode.

Highlight Compression

One of the main attractions of high dynamic range files (including Cineon film scans) is that they contain detail in "over-bright" areas such as light sources. If your final destination does not support over-range color values (such as ordinary standard- or high-definition video), you can significantly improve the appearance of some shots by taming these hot spots so their hidden detail is visible in the normal color range.

In the project **26f-Floating Point.aep**, open the comp **[Ex.f07]** which contains an image of a sunrise. The sun creates a wide hot spot in the clouds (**A**). Make sure the project's bit depth is set to 32 bpc, select **HD_sunrise_float.exr**, and apply Effect >

Utility > HDR Highlight Compression. Now the sun will be reduced to its normal size and the clouds around it will no longer be blown out (**B**), while the remainder of the image remains mostly unchanged. Experiment with this effect's Amount parameter to tweak the appearance of each HDR scene that is destined for the web or video.

To recover visual information for your final render, select the layer and apply Effect > Color Correction > Exposure. This will give you control over exposure, brightness offset, and gamma adjustments. Indeed, keyframing Exposure provides an alternate way to fade an HDR layer in or out, as we have in [**Ex.d06_final**].

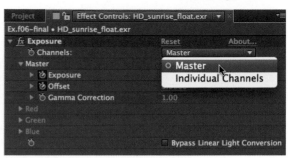

Creative Float

The overexpose-and-recover nature of working in 32-bit float mode lends itself to creative applications as well. Any overexposed image will start to return to its underlying color when darkened or made partially transparent. This can be used to create the impression of a colored glow around the layer. Here is the recipe:

* Make sure your project is in 32-bit float mode.

* Pick the glow color you want to reveal. There should be a bit of red, green, and blue all mixed into your color; otherwise, you will not be able to push all of the color channels over 1.0, preventing you from achieving pure white.

* Over-expose the layer by some means, such as by using Effect > Color Correction > Exposure.

* Make the layer partially transparent. Feathered masks and blurs (including motion blur) will help create a fringe; fading the entire layer will make it transition from white to your glow color.

To practice this, open composition [**Ex.f08_starter**] in **26f-Floating Point.aep**. RAM Preview: It includes some text which is fading and blurring on.

Move the current time indicator to a point where you can see some blurred characters as well as some unblurred (at rest) characters. Select the text layer **smokin' grooves...** and apply Effect > Color Correction > Exposure. Increase the Exposure value until the "at rest" characters just barely turn white or a nice tint of the original color. If there is a big difference in the underlying red, green, and blue channel values, it can be hard to do this by increasing the Exposure value alone; add a small amount of Offset to help push it into white. RAM Preview, and you will see the text dissolve from the original glow color to white as the characters settle into place.

Note that if you push the Exposure and Offset values too far, the antialiased edges around the layer may start to look crunchy; the cure is to pick an underlying "glow" color that has more of each primary color mixed in. We have chosen a golden color for the text's glow; try changing it to a different color (select the text layer, open Window > Character, and click on the Foreground color swatch).

This trick does not need to be restricted to text – you can use it for shape layers, solids used as "chasers" or underscores, particle systems, or virtually any other graphics that you can make semitransparent.

Use Effect > Color Correction > Exposure if you want to alter the exposure of an HDR image in a composite or render.

[Ex.f08]: Apply Exposure to a colored layer and increase its Exposure and Offset values to push its color toward white. Then when you fade, feather, or blur this layer in 32-bit mode, the original color will appear as a glow (above). This glow will not be visible in 8- or 16-bit modes (below).

A raw Cineon file captures a wide dynamic range with logarithmic encoding, resulting in what appears to be a washed-out image (A).

Converting it to the PWS and tweaking the Cineon Settings brings it into a normal viewing color space (B).

Best is if you can assign it a color profile that matches its film stock; the initial results will be even closer to true color (C). Image courtesy Cinesite Los Angeles (*www.cinesite.com*).

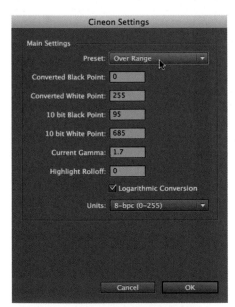

Even if color management is disabled, under the Color Management tab you can access the Cineon Settings dialog where you can customize how the file's values are translated. There is also a Utility > Cineon Converter effect.

Cineon Log Color Space

Film is the original high dynamic range image format – it too can capture color values brighter than can be represented on videotape or on most computer displays. To digitize film accurately, Kodak designed the Cineon format (file type .cin; it is also often encoded as .dpx and .exr files). The Cineon file format represents each color channel with 1024 values spread across a special logarithmic range. When neutral test cards are shot on film and scanned into this format, "film black" is set at a Cineon value of 95, 2% reflection (scene black) at 180, 18% reflection (neutral gray) at 470, and 90% reflection (stark white) at 685. This leaves extra room to capture (and recover) darker or brighter than normal portions of a scene. This has several uses – for example, in the case where film was purposely overexposed to trade off reduced highlights for less noise in the shadows, increasing the exposure on the film one "stop" raises all these values by 90.

When working with film, it is a good idea to work in 32-bit float mode, and to choose a PWS such as ProPhoto RGB that represents a wider color gamut. Also enable either Linearize Working Space or Blend Colors Using 1.0 Gamma to better emulate how light behaves in the real world.

Open the project file **26g-Cineon.aep**, which has already been set to 32-bit float mode. We've imported a Cineon source file and placed it in composition [**Ex.g01**]. The image in this comp initially looks washed out; by default, After Effects is showing us the entire 0–1023 range of the Cineon file uncorrected for exposure.

In the Project panel, select **CineonGirl.cin**, open File > Interpret Footage > Main, and click on the Color Management tab. When After Effects does not detect a color profile embedded in a Cineon file, it uses the Project Working Space. Click on the Cineon Settings button to the right; here you can manually map internal Cineon values to the corresponding values you wish to use inside After Effects. The default is to present the Full Range of values with no gamma adjustment. From the Preset popup, select the Standard or Over Range presets; we prefer Over Range as it sets the Highlight Rolloff value to 0, allowing you to manually adjust the highlights (see the sidebar *Highlight Compression*, page 456). Click OK for the Cineon Settings and Interpret Footage dialogs; the image in the Comp panel will look much more realistic (if a bit oversaturated).

A better way to handle Cineon files is to assign a film input color profile. Again select **CineonGirl.cin**, open Interpret Footage, and click the Color Management tab. Click on the Assign Profile menu and pick Kodak 5229/7229 Printing Density – this is the closest match for how this scene was shot. Click OK: Now the Comp panel will show a more realistic color interpretation. From this point on, a Cineon file can be treated just like any other 32-bit float source. With Window > Info open, move the cursor over the Comp panel; you will notice some over-range values (color channels over 1.0) in the highlights in the background. Experiment using effects such as Exposure or Levels to improve the brightness and contrast in this scene. You can also composite other layers – such as film titles – on top of your footage.

As long as you keep the project in 32-bit float mode and render back out to a floating-point file format, the over-brights in the scene will be maintained. If your final destination is video or the web, you may want to use Effect > Utility > Highlight Compression to damp down some of the hot spots. You can also use Cineon files in 8- or 16-bit mode as well; you'll just lose the ability to manage your over-bright areas unless you spend some quality time with the Cineon Settings dialog or Effect > Utility > Cineon Converter.

Rendering a Cineon file isn't much more difficult. Add your comp to the Render Queue (as we have with [**Ex.e01**]); open the Output Module; and select DPX/Cineon, OpenEXR, or Radiance Sequence from the Format popup. Then click on the Color Management tab. For the output profile, pick the film stock that your images will be printed to (usually the same as your source footage). If you want to manually manage the Cineon conversion, select the Working Space for your Output Profile, click on the Cineon Settings button, and tweak the parameters as desired (a good starting point is to use the same Preset as you did on the input side).

If you are rendering a video proof, you can scale down your final comp to video size and pick a corresponding video codec in the Output Module. If your project is in 32-bit float mode, a small amount of your over-range colors will be mapped into the 235 to 255 luminance values inside the video file (discussed earlier). In 8- or 16-bit modes, they will be clipped to what you see in the Comp panel.

If you'd like to learn about the Cineon format, the **Goodies** folder on the DVD includes white papers on the Cineon file format, courtesy Cinesite Los Angeles (*www.cinesite.com*).

The preferred workflow is to select a color profile that best matches the film stock the footage was shot on.

TIP

Workflow White Paper

This document explains color management, including case studies for three common workflows plus descriptions of the Adobe-supplied color profiles. Download it from *www.adobe.com/go/learn_ae_colormanagementpaper*. There is also a wealth of information in the online Help for After Effects: Press F1 and search for "color management."

RED R3D Settings

In addition to setting the color profile for RED footage (HDTV is recommended for video workflows), at the bottom of the Interpret Footage dialog's Main Settings panel is a More Options button. This opens the RED R3D Settings dialog where you can change many parameters of how the footage is converted. The "correct" settings depend on your footage, application, and how much color correction you plan to perform; *www.reduser.net* is a good place to compare notes. In general, setting both Color Space and Gamma Curve to REDspace approximates the LCD viewfinder while shooting and is considered a good default correction. Rec. 709 is often a more neutral starting point for your own corrections; start by changing the Gamma Curve.

Broadcast Safe Colors

Related to both color management and video issues (Chapter 41) is the matter of "legal video" or "broadcast safe" colors. It is possible to create combinations of color and luminance values that, when they're modulated together to travel down a video cable or to be broadcast by a transmitter, would create out-of-range electrical values. Although this is becoming less of an issue with time, sometimes the engineering department of the facility that may duplicate or broadcast your final project will check your colors to make sure they stay within proper ranges. You can leave it to them to color-correct your imagery after you're done with it – or, you can pre-emptively try to correct the colors yourself before you hand over your final work.

After Effects has a Broadcast Colors effect that you can apply directly to suspected offending layers, and have it automatically reduce either the saturation and luminance of the offending areas of an image. However, we don't recommend you use it that way – aesthetic control is taken out of your hands, and there can be a bit of posterization as you transition from legal colors to the selectively treated illegal colors. Instead, we apply it to an adjustment layer that resides above our final composite, use this effect to help us see where the offending areas are, and then adjust just those layers (using whatever tools we prefer) until they are legal.

To practice this yourself, open the project file **26h-Broadcast Safe.aep**, and then open the comp [**Ex.h01_starter**]. It contains DV video of a bright yellow motorcycle shot with a DV camera plus some fairly ugly text (sorry; we needed the color to make a point). You may assume that

The bright motorcycle and text have areas that are not broadcast legal.

Color Finesse

After Effects comes bundled with a great color correction tool: Effect > Synthetic Aperture > SA Color Finesse 3. It can correct luminance separately from color, which helps in solving broadcast safe issues. See Bonus Chapter 23B for more info.

The motorcycle and text turn black when we apply an adjustment layer with the Broadcast Colors effect set to Key Out Unsafe (left). We selectively tweaked the colors of the motorcycle and text to make them legal (right).

anything you can shoot with a video camera must be video legal, but unfortunately you'd be wrong!

Add a Layer > New > Adjustment Layer to the composition, and select Layer > Guide Layer – this will make sure it does not appear in your final render. Then apply Effect > Color Correction > Broadcast Colors to this adjustment layer. You will immediately notice a portion of the motorcycle's gas tank turns grayish-yellow. This is the result of Broadcast Colors trying to fix your problems for you. Locate Broadcast Colors in the Effect Controls panel and set the How to Make Color Safe popup to Key Out Unsafe; now a portion of the tank – along with the center of the red text – will go transparent, showing the comp's black background color behind.

Let's fix the motorcycle first. Select **CM_motorcycle_full.jpg** and apply Effect > Color Correction > Hue/Saturation. Play with the Master Hue, Saturation and Lightness controls to get an idea which approach returns the yellow tank to being visible with the least displeasing shift in color. Then click Reset at the top of Hue/Saturation's Effect Controls, and focus your color correction by setting the Channel Control popup to Yellows. Widen the range of colors to include some oranges as well by using the Channel Range controls that reside between the two horizontal color bars.

Now turn your attention to the text layer (**can you handle it?**). Select this layer, and expose Window > Character. Click on the red color swatch in Character to open the Text Color dialog, alter the color of the text as needed to make the black "keyed out" sections disappear, and click OK. One potential solution is demonstrated in [**Ex.h01_final**].

If this is an issue for your work, stay away from deeply saturated pure colors, such as hot reds and yellows. Reducing saturation moves a color toward gray; reducing its brightness moves it toward black. To our eyes, yellows usually correct better if you desaturate them rather than reduce their brightness. Conversely, reds usually look better if you reduce their brightness closer to a blood-red than reduce their saturation, which can shift them toward a salmon pink. Don't use the same "rules" in every circumstance; see what looks best for the specific image you're working on.

The Hue/Saturation effect allows you to target a specific color range to alter. The upper bar shows the original color range; the lower bar shows the result of your corrections.

CONNECT

Comp, Footage, Layer panels: Chapters 1 and 2.

Adjustment Layers: Chapter 22.

Effects: Chapters 22 and 23B.

Interpret Footage: Chapter 38.

Video issues including interlacing: Chapter 41.

Video Preview output: Chapters 2 and 41.

Output Modules, rendering in general: Chapter 42.

Preferences > Display > Hardware Accelerate Composition, Layer, and Footage Panels allows OpenGL to accelerate drawing images when color management is enabled: Chapter 45.

Many thanks to David McGavran, Todd Kopriva, Peter Constable, and Vladimir Potap'yev for their help in constructing this chapter.

Keying

Effectively removing a color background requires attention throughout the chain.

Paint Me Down

Use paint, tape, and fabrics that have been specially formulated to be keyed, such as the Rosco DigiComp, Chroma Key, and Ultimatte lines (*www.rosco.com/us/scenic/index.asp*), plus fabric and lights from Composite Components Company (*www.digitalgreen-screen.com/prodindex.html*).

Example Project

Explore the 27-Example Project.aep file as you read this chapter; references to [Ex.##] refer to specific compositions within the project file.

Compositing images shot against one background over a new background is one of the trickier visual effects tasks you will encounter. It requires separating the foreground elements from the original background they were shot against. Even if the foreground comes with its own alpha channel (the result of a 3D render), getting it to blend nicely with its new background can still be a challenge.

Time for the bad news: Not all images can be cleanly separated from their background. Neither can you assume that all images can be seamlessly blended with a new background. But with some preplanning and patience, you should be able to produce professional images. This chapter will give you an overview of the keyers After Effects offers, then go into detail on using the preferred Keylight plug-in. We'll end by giving you some advice on how to further improve your results.

Keying 101

The process of *keying* footage means creating an alpha channel that isolates (or "pulls") the objects or actions you want (usually referred to as the "foreground") from the background they were originally shot against. You can use a number of techniques to accomplish this separation.

The most common technique is based on *color keying*. The action is shot against a solid-color background. This color is preferably one that does not appear in the foreground – for example, blue or green are good when people are your subject, because skin tones tend to be shadings on red. You then instruct your software or hardware to remove this background color by making the alpha channel transparent where the background is visible, and to keep whatever is not the same as the background color by making its alpha channel opaque in these areas.

In addition to keying, other terms you may hear include *chroma keying* (chroma meaning color), *Ultimatte* (synonymous with one of the oldest companies creating keying equipment), and *bluescreen* or *greenscreen* (describing the background color). A related technique is *luminance keying*, which creates an alpha channel based on the relative brightness present in a scene rather than just its similarity to one color. "Luma" keying works well for white text on black title cards, or for objects shot against a seamless white or black set.

Although the basic concept may sound easy, things rarely work out so neatly in practice. Real images often contain a mixture of colors rather than pure ones. It is hard to evenly paint and light a background screen or set. Chances are strong that the light hitting this background is reflecting ("spilling") onto the foreground, and as a result it will take on some of this unwanted color. Then there's the issue of how to handle semitransparent parts of an image, such as wispy hair, shadows, and smoke. And those are just the obstacles in creating a key – now you have to convincingly blend the object into another world…

That's why any keying job should be treated in three phases: shooting the best quality (in other words, least-compressed), highest-resolution footage you can; keying; then compositing. Throughout this chapter, we'll make the assumption that you are shooting against green; the same ideas apply to blue or other colors.

Approaches

In this chapter, we will discuss the keying plug-ins that are included with After Effects. In most cases, we will provide two sample clips for you to practice with (shown above): a head shot that should be reasonably easy, and one involving transparent fabric which is considerably more difficult – indeed, many keyers won't provide useable results with this clip. Both were shot in high definition using the DVCPRO HD format; make sure you zoom in to check details as you key. This chapter's example project file is also set to 16 bits-per-channel resolution for enhanced color fidelity; if you see a yellow warning symbol next to an effect, it is processing the footage at 8 bits per channel, which is a lower quality. Each comp will also have a background image you can toggle on and off, so that you can check your work in context.

Virtually all of these keying effects must be followed by spill suppression and color correction, which are discussed later in this chapter. Although most of them have some way to soften and clean up the edges of the key, you may consider using additional tools, such as the matte chokers discussed later in this chapter, the new Refine Matte effect (discussed in Chapter 34, *Roto Brush*), or third-party solutions. Another approach is using the keying effect just to create a good alpha channel, and to use the result as a track matte for a copy of the original footage.

Hollywood Camera Work generously supplied these two high definition greenscreen shots for you to practice with. The second image with the transparent fabric is particularly challenging. (*www.hollywoodcamerawork.us*)

Green or Blue?

In many digital video formats, the blue channel tends to have less useful information and more noise. As a result, you may have better results shooting against a green background. The one exception is shooting blondes, which many say key better against blue.

GOTCHA

Unwanted Enhancements

When you're shooting for keying, turn off edge enhancement options at the camera or during the telecine transfer from film.

Taking Out the Garbage

Use masks outside your foreground as "garbage mattes" to remove unwanted areas of the background. Many of our final comps use garbage mattes.

Trial Run

Try to key samples of the footage before you sign on to do the whole job. Some footage simply cannot be keyed; a one-day bid for keying can easily turn into a week of rotoscoping hell (this is what Roto Brush is for).

Setting Off Fireworks

If you are compositing fire or explosions shot against black, please don't use the Luma Key. Try a blending mode such as Add or Screen.

A Box Full of Keys

As the Help file that comes with After Effects contains quite a few details on its various keying effects, we're going to give just a brief overview of the keying plug-ins found under the Effect > Keying menu. We will then focus on Keylight, which is the most professional choice.

As noted in the introduction, we've set up some examples for you to experiment with. Begin with the "a_starter" composition, and then after you're comfortable using the effect, try your hand at the "b_starter" comp. We've provided "-final" versions which reflect where you should be after about a minute of work; see if you can improve upon these results.

Color Key

The simplest of the keying effects, this is a "binary" key where you eye-dropper a color representative of your background, and the plug-in decides whether other pixels in the image match this color or not.

Use its eyedropper to select the green background (closer to the actress is better). Then increase the Color Tolerance until enough similar colors disappear (the default value is 0, which is far too low). Further shrink the mask using Edge Thin, then try to soften the damage with Edge Feather. This key tends to have a blobby look, which is particularly bad on wispy edges like hair. You will see it is completely useless on the transparent fabric in [**Ex.01b**].

Luma Key

Use this tool when footage has been shot against black or white. The Threshold defaults to an intolerant 0; increase it to see results, tweak Edge Thin to shrink the matte, and use Feather to expand it back out softly. Use the Tolerance parameter instead of Threshold when you're using the Key Type options Key Out Similar and Dissimilar.

In [**Ex.02a**], Luma Key works fairly well for dropping out the white seamless background behind the actors – although the white shirts are a challenge. We have a similar issue in [**Ex.02b**]: the black background keys out easily, but the dark center of the skateboard wheel keys out as well. In both cases, we fixed them by placing a copy of the original layer underneath, and masking it just to the area required to fill in the holes.

Use the Luma Key when the action is shot against white or black. When the foreground is too similar to the background (such as the white shirts here), you may need to duplicate the layer and use masks to fill these holes back in. Footage courtesy iStockphoto, © simonkr, Image #11942172.

Color Range Key

Color Range is an improvement on binary keyers, in that you get to define a "bounding box" in color space of what colors to remove, rather than picking just one color and adjusting a Tolerance slider. This is helpful when you have uneven color or luminance in the background.

Open either [**Ex.03a_starter**] or [**Ex.03b_starter**] and apply Color Range Key. Use the normal eyedropper to select the green background near the actress. Then use the eyedropper followed by a + symbol to select additional ranges of the background which should be transparent. If part of the foreground goes transparent as well, use the eyedropper followed by the – symbol to put those colors back. Then increase the Fuzziness parameter until the edges crop in nicely. Don't go so far that you start to eat away semitransparent details such as hair; remember that you can use spill suppression later to remove the color tint in these areas (in the "-final" versions, toggle Spill Suppressor on and off to see how much it helps). If you still have trouble getting acceptable results, click on Reset and set Color Space to RGB or YUV before proceeding.

The Color Range key uses a system of three eyedroppers to define which colors are transparent and which are opaque. Its Preview shows you the resulting alpha channel. You can eyedropper its Preview, or the Comp panel.

Linear Color Key

Linear keys are more sophisticated than binary keys: Rather than simply keeping or matting out a color based on whether it matches a color you choose, linear keys alter the transparency of pixels based on how closely they match the color you choose. This makes them better at dealing with semitransparent areas, such as smoke.

Try the Linear Color Key with the footage in [**Ex.04**]. Use the main Key Color eyedropper to select the green background, then use the + and – eyedroppers to fine-tune the Matching Tolerance range (akin to Color Range). Use Matching Softness to expand the matte's range.

An important feature of Linear Color Key is the Key Operation popup, which you can set to Key or Keep Colors. The preferred workflow is to apply this effect multiple times, using one copy to remove the background, and other copies to keep regions of the foreground that were accidentally removed by the first copy of the key. For example, in [**Ex.04a-final**] (pictured at right) the first effect (with Match Colors set to Using RGB) keys the green, the second (with Match Colors set to Using Hue) keeps the skin tones, and the third (set to Using Chroma) keeps the jacket. Toggle the second and third effects off and on to see their individual contributions.

Color Difference Key

This complex effect used to be the most powerful keying plug-in that came with After Effects. It has since been surpassed by Keylight, which we will discuss in more detail later. In the name of completeness, we included examples using Color Difference Key in [**Ex.05**]. A tutorial on using the Color Difference Key is included on this book's DVD as Bonus Chapter 27B.

Multiple uses of Linear Color Key are shown in [**Ex.04a-final**].

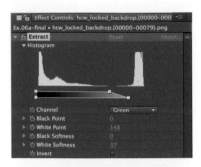

The Extract keyer allows you to select a specific channel to work on, then adjust the Transparency Control Bar (the gray region underneath the Histogram) to decide what luminance range of this channel to keep and remove.

Inner/Outer Key may require a number of animated masks to use it effectively with moving footage – but the result can be quite good. Footage courtesy Desktop Images.

Combination Lock

For challenging keys, try keying multiple copies of the image, each with a different feature – such as clean-edged clothing or wispy hair – isolated with masks, so you can tweak the keyer for each feature.

Extract

This enhancement on a straight luminance keyer focuses on a single channel of information: alpha, overall luminance (good for black or white backgrounds), or just red, green, or blue (the background color you wish to remove). It gives you a visual reference of the luminance values active in this channel (the histogram), and a Transparency Control Bar underneath where you can decide what ranges of this color to key.

In [**Ex.06a_starter**], select the clip and apply Extract. Set the Channel popup to Green; most of the greenscreen will disappear. The luminance range histogram shows two distinct active regions: dark greens (the actress) and light greens (the bright greenscreen). Turn your attention to the Control Bar underneath the histogram, and drag the upper right control point to the left until just before her nose starts to disappear. Then drag the lower right control point to the right to restore more of her hair, stopping before the greenscreen background starts to reappear. Note where these points ended up in relation to the histogram…

Now try Extract with [**Ex.06b_starter**]: the semitransparent areas in her shawl make the difference between foreground and background a lot less distinct. Removing the background with Extract creates holes in her dress and shoulder, requiring some time-consuming repair work: You would need to duplicate the clip, then create animated masks to restore these missing areas. (Go ahead – try it with [**Ex.06b-final**].)

Inner/Outer Key

This plug-in works differently from any of the keyers featured here. Instead of picking colors, you create mask shapes: an inner shape for what you want to keep, and an outer shape for what you want to lose. The plug-in then calculates transparency for the color transition between these shapes. The closer the mask outlines are to the object's edge, the better. The results on a still (see [**Ex.07a**]) are spooky-good; more work is required with moving footage (note all the mask keyframes in [**Ex.07b**]).

Difference Matte

Use this effect when you have shot two passes of your footage: a clean background plate that does not have your action present, and a normal pass that includes the action you wish to isolate from this background. If the camera is locked down, you don't need a long clip for the clean background plate; even a still will do.

In theory, Difference Matte can be used to key action out from any background – not just a solid color backdrop – as After Effects is matching the color of each respective pixel between the two passes and showing only the pixels where it finds a difference. However, anything that contaminates or adds noise to the background – video noise or film grain, dust, water, or camera shake – will make it harder to get a good key. The Blur Before Difference parameter will help reduce some of the problems caused by video noise or film grain.

Keylight

After Effects comes bundled with a very powerful third-party keying plug-in: Keylight from The Foundry (*www.thefoundry.co.uk*). Keylight handles creating a matte, edge enhancement, and color correction. It allows you to pull satisfactory keys quickly and to improve them without much effort; it also contains a lot of power underneath the hood to take on challenging tasks or to further finesse the result.

You can download the Keylight user guide plus additional practice materials by visiting The Foundry's website, following the menu for Plug-Ins > for After Effects > Keylight, and looking under the Support & Training header. For those who resist cracking open manuals (you know who you are), we're going to give a quick overview of how to apply Keylight and make quick tweaks that will cover the majority of the situations you should encounter. If you need to dive deeper, crack open that manual; it's very useful.

To reduce the clutter, select Close All from the Viewer menu along the top of the Comp panel, then open [**Ex.08b_starter**].

• Select layer 1, and apply Effect > Keying > Keylight. In the Effect Controls panel that opens, click on the eyedropper for Screen Colour, then click on the green background near the actress. Boom – you've already got a pretty good key! But you can refine it from here…

• To see the alpha channel being created by Keylight, change its View popup to Combined Matte. We have some nice grays around the hair and shawl, which indicate they will be semitransparent (as they should be); you can also see that other parts of her body – particularly the bottom half of her arms – are being eaten away a bit by the key.

• To see these details more clearly, change the View popup to Status: This gives an exaggerated display where the foreground is white, the background is black, and the gray areas show the partially transparent areas. Now's when you realize that you have some more work to do!

After applying Keylight and using the Screen Colour eyedropper to select our green background (above), we already have a pretty good key (below).

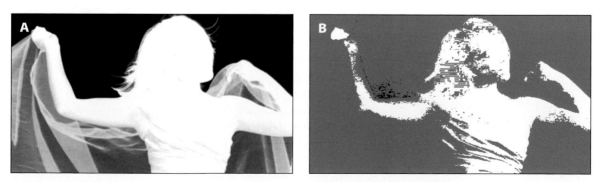

Setting the View popup to Combined Matte displays the alpha channel that will be generated (A). Changing it to Status gives an exaggerated view that more clearly shows problems as gray (partially transparent) pixels where they aren't supposed to be (B).

With View set to Status, we've used a combination of Screen Strength and Clip Black to get rid of the noise above her head, and Clip White to fill in her arm and eyes.

TIP

Video Training

To watch a video we created on using Keylight, visit *www.adobe.com/go/vid0229*

Setting View to Intermediate Result shows the image keyed, without any color correction (A). Changing View to Final Result shows the effects of Keylight's built-in spill suppression (B).

• There are a few ways to improve the matte. For starters, with View still set to Status, slowly increase the Screen Gain parameter until the gray noise above her head disappears; be careful not to erode too much of the semitransparent areas around the fringe of her hair. Hold Command on Mac (Control on Windows) while scrubbing to change this parameter in finer increments.

• To try an alternative approach, reset Screen Gain to 100. Twirl open the Screen Matte section, and slowly increase Clip Black until the gray noise along the top of the frame erodes away, noticing how the noise to the left of her head disappears more quickly than with Screen Gain.

The best approach is usually to balance Screen Gain and Clip Black. In general, we suggest using Clip Black to get rid of the worst of the problems, then Screen Strength to deal with what's left:

• Reset Screen Gain to 100 and Clip Black to 0. Slowly increase Clip Black until the noise along the top left of the frame disappears. Then slowly increase Screen Gain until the rest of the noise along the top disappears, remembering you can use a garbage mask to later get rid of the noise in the upper right corner. You can check your results any time by setting View to FinalResult.

• Next, you need to fill in the semitransparent (gray) areas in the body. With View set to Status, slowly decrease Clip White until these areas fill in. The pale green areas that appear in the Status view are a warning that we may have some color issues in these fringes; we'll tackle spill suppression soon.

• Change the View popup to Intermediate Result: This displays the footage with its new alpha channel, but without any color correction or spill suppression. Then change the View popup to Final Result, which shows the image with spill suppression applied. Take a snapshot (Shift+F5) to remember what this stage looks like.

Use the Despill Bias eyedropper to sample her skin tone (left). This will restore some of her original color to the shot (right). If needed, set the Screen Softness popup to Hard Colour for more natural, less noisy results.

• If you want to remove more green spill, select the Despill Bias eyedropper and click on a light area of her skin – such as by her collarbone. Press F5 to compare the result with what the image looked like before using Despill Bias. If the coloration is too strong, slightly reduce the Screen Balance value, or try altering the Despill Bias color.

You might have noticed that Alpha Bias defaults to the same color as Despill Bias. Keylight often edits both the alpha channel and color correction to the edges in concert with each other, and therefore defaults to locking these two parameters together. If you find that editing Despill Bias is causing unwanted erosion to your edges, disable the Lock Biases Together checkbox underneath, and tweak Alpha Bias to achieve the degree of softness you want in the edges.

• One side effect of Despill Bias is that it may introduce some noise in the skin tones – RAM Preview to verify this. Changing Screen Matte > Replace Method to Hard Colour often cures it.

• This DVCPRO HD footage has some additional issues with artifacts around the edge of her arm on the right side half of the frame. This can be cured with a small amount of Screen Matte > Screen Softness.

Issues with rough edges (above) can be cleaned up with judicious application of Screen Softness and Screen Shrink/ Grow (below).

• Turn on the background (layer 2) and RAM Preview; you might notice a dark outline around the right edge of her shawl. This can be cured by decreasing Screen Matte > Screen Shrink/Grow. Just make sure you don't erode away too much of her hair or the rest of her shawl!

Keylight offers many other powerful features, including color correction of the foreground and edges, choosing what color to factor into the edges when they've had spill removed, the ability to select mask shapes to keep or remove areas in the original image regardless of their color, and other parameters to smooth, expand, or erode the matte. Again, we encourage you to check out its manual: The explanations are good, and the tips are exceedingly useful.

Fixing It in the Mix

If you pulled a good key, you have reason to be happy. But it's no time to quit: That final bit of polish comes in blending your newly keyed foreground into its new background image. The following exercises will give you some practice color-correcting the results of your keys. (For your convenience, we've saved copies of our already-keyed footage.)

A dead giveaway a scene has been composited – aside from a bad key – is when the foreground and background images have different contrast and tonal ranges. You will see this sin left uncured even in feature films.

In [**Ex.09_starter**], the water fountain footage is too green for the red sky (left) – an obvious giveaway. Color correct to taste, to better match the red sky (right). Foreground courtesy Photron (creators of the excellent Primatte keyer); background courtesy Artbeats/Sky Effects.

Careful use of color correction can greatly aid in compositing disparate images, or further correcting a color cast in the foreground object caused at the lighting stage.

Close all other comps, and open [**Ex.09_starter**], which contains a water-drenched statue composited against a red evening sky. The statue, although very saturated, has a different tone than our sunset. You'll need to fix that. Experiment with different color correction effects to try to push the statue's color more toward its new background. Again, there is more than one right answer; in [**Ex.09-final**], we used the Effect > Color Correction > Channel Mixer to reduce the strength of the green cast in the original key, then added a slight master hue shift with the Color Correction > Hue/Saturation effect to move the entire foreground more toward red.

Other problems to watch out for are the black-and-white tones and the overall contrast. For example, in [**Ex.10_starter**] we took our statue and moved him out into the snow. He is way too dark for this scene, and needs lightening. With this vintage background shot, we also have a less saturated palette of colors to match. A good place to start for these adjustments is Effect > Color Correction > Levels. Gamma is usually the first parameter we grab – it leaves the black-and-white points intact and changes the gray levels between them. If the image

The dark statue is out of place in this snow scene (left). Applying Levels and tweaking its Gamma helps brighten it up, and Hue/Saturation helps desaturate and shift its color to better match the scene (right). Background courtesy Artbeats/Retro Transportation.

needs more contrast, squeeze the Input Black and Input White arrows closer together; if it needs less, squeeze the corresponding Output arrows.

For additional practice, try blending the water fountain with other backplates – the basic project is set up in [**Ex.11a**] with a pair of backgrounds to choose from. We've also placed an actress shot against blue over a new background in [**Ex.11b**], but be careful when color correcting not to change her skin tone to something too sickly!

Refine Matte

An alternative to using the Spill Suppressor, Matte Choker, Simple Choker, and related effects is to apply the new Refine Matte plug-in. Use your keying effect of choice just to create a hard-edged alpha channel, and then apply Refine Matte to smooth, choke, and feather the edges, remove ("decontaminate") the spill color, and create partial transparency where edges should be motion blurred from movement in the underlying shot. For more details, refer to the last two pages of Chapter 34 – the Refine Matte effect is derived from the Refine Matte section in Roto Brush.

Living on the Edge

The last frontier we'll explore in this chapter is improving the edges of your keyed objects. If nothing else, you need to reduce or eliminate any leftover garbage around the edges. Ideally, you want the colors and apparent light from your new background to appear to illuminate and wrap around the edges of your foreground image. These techniques apply to compositing synthetic objects, such as 3D renders, as much as for bluescreen work.

The Matte Effects

The plug-in Effect > Matte > Matte Choker effect was designed to help clean up problematic color keys where there may be holes or tears in the edges. The idea behind Matte Choker is to first spread the edges to fill in the holes, then choke the joined edge back in.

Unfortunately, its default parameters are not ideal for what you usually need to do. For example, if you want to spread the matte first (which is what negative choke values do), the first Choke parameter should be negative, not positive. Second, the higher the Gray Level Softness parameter, the less effect the Choke parameter has – and since the second Gray Level is set to 100%, you may think its Choke parameter is broken. Third, the Geometric Softness parameter is set a bit high for the first set of parameters (the spread pass) and low for the second set of parameters (the choke pass); try 2.0 as a starting value for both instead.

This effect can be used for softening edges, even if they are already clean. In this case, you can almost ignore the Choke parameters and treat Geometric Softness as an "amount of blur" parameter, with Gray Level Softness setting the blend. This application is demonstrated in [**Ex.12**].

For cleaning up less-tattered alpha channels, we use Simple Choker, particularly in cases where even correctly interpreting the alpha channel as Premultiplied still leaves a lingering black fringe or white halo around an object. This is a common problem with photos shot against a white background in which the alpha isn't cut quite tight enough. A value of up to 1.0 is usually a good starting point for Simple Choker.

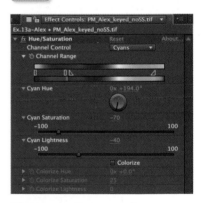

TIP

Alternate Suppression

An alternative to using the Spill Suppressor effect is to use Hue/Saturation: Restrict its Channel Range to the color of the spill, and then desaturate or hue shift the spill as desired. This is demonstrated in [**Ex.13**].

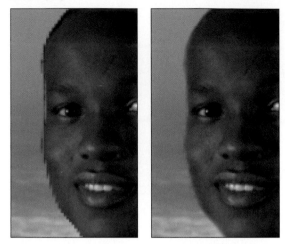

This well-shot bluescreen footage was unfortunately mangled during the video transfer, resulting in rough edges (left). To fix this, first blur the alpha, then choke it back in size. The result is a more acceptable edge (right). Test footage courtesy Artbeats.

Blurring the Lines

Another common trick for blending images into their backgrounds is to blur their edges so more of the background image will seem to leak around the foreground. This can also help repair bad edges of mattes that otherwise can't be pulled cleanly.

One tool for accomplishing this is Effect > Blur & Sharpen > Channel Blur, which can blur each color channel, as well as the alpha channel, individually. This means that we can leave the color information sharp and smear just the matte. The downside of this is that the matte usually spreads out wider as a result of being blurred, revealing more of the background. You can rein the edge back in using Effect > Matte > Simple Choker – positive values shrink the matte back down in size. Depending on your specific problem, you might have better results by reversing the order of the effects so that you choke the edge first, then apply Channel Blur.

Backgrounds for Bluescreen

If you are creating backgrounds for keyed footage, and the key is less than satisfactory, you'll make your life a lot easier – and make the composite more believable – by designing the backgrounds using the same general color range as the color you keyed.

Let's say you're keying a talking head, and the subject is wearing glasses, has wispy hair, and there's lots of spill on the shoulders – *and* the key is less than perfect. Instead of choking the key to death, design an animated background with hues from the quarter of the color wheel centered around your screen's color. For bluescreen, you can use the range from purple to blue to blue-green. Greenscreen, unfortunately, forces you to design in the less desirable and more challenging yellow-green range.

When you add some fake lighting effects to the background, the mind is fooled into thinking that behind your subject is a live source that was casting

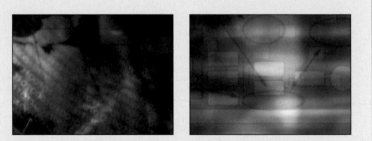

Examples of bluescreen (left) and greenscreen (right) backgrounds we created for one of our clients, Xerox Media West. We combined numerous stock library movies and stills with elements created in Illustrator and 3D programs to create something appropriate for each project.

bluish or greenish light onto the person being interviewed. Remember that unless the background looks like it emits some kind of light, the mind will find no explanation for color spill.

Chapter 9 (*Blending Modes*) includes tips for using "lighting" movies composited on top of the other layers using the Overlay or Soft Light blending modes. If possible, create looping backgrounds and animations so you can repeat them for as long as needed to go behind any shot either in After Effects or in your editing system.

Compositing Tools

If you do a lot of compositing, there are a couple of excellent third party effect packages you should check out. Our favorite is Key Correct Pro, distributed by Red Giant Software (*www.redgiantsoftware.com*). This package includes plug-ins for edge treatments including repairing holes in alpha channels, color matching, color spill removal, and light wrap.

Additionally, Boris Continuum Complete from Boris FX (*www.borisfx.com*) also contains a good number of useful key, matte, and color correction effects. Both sets would make excellent additions to your toolbox. (The "light wrap" effects in both sets are designed to easily create the technique shown below in *Seeing the Light*, below.)

Seeing the Light

Light naturally wraps around the edges of an object in a scene – such as the blue spill we've been working so hard to remove. To really sink an object into its new background, you have to make it appear as if light from this new background is wrapping around your keyed foreground or 3D render. To do this, you need to create a matte that is just a blurred edge of your foreground object, but that doesn't extend beyond your foreground's edges. You then use this as a matte for a blurred copy

The edges around this actress are too sharp to convincingly blend her into the new background image. We created a blurred matte that sits inside her edges (left), and used that to blend in a blurred version of the background, making it seem like she is affected by the colors of this image (right). Woman courtesy Photron.

of your background. Place this blurred edge on top of your original foreground, and now the background will seem to seep around its edges.

[**Ex.14a**] shows one way to build this. It contains two copies of footage, already keyed. The copy on top has been blurred; the amount of this blur controls how much wrap will take place. The copy underneath uses this blurred version as an Alpha Inverted matte. The result is a blurred edge that's *inside* the keyed footage's original edge. We also filled the result with white so you can see it more clearly (and use it as a luma matte if needed), but this is not necessary.

Now open [**Ex.14b**]. It contains [**Ex.14a**] as a precomp (layer 1), which acts as a matte for a blurred version of our background (layer 2). These are then placed above our normal composite of the keyed foreground and new background. Turn the Video switch for layer 2 on and off to see its contribution; you can also alter its Opacity to blend it in more subtly.

Try different modes for layer 2: Screen makes the edges really glow; Overlay results in darker areas of the background darkening the corresponding edges of your foreground layer – almost as if they were in shadow.

Mastering Keying

The Green Screen Handbook by Jeff Foster is an exhaustive resource on all things keying.

CONNECT

Blending modes: Chapter 9.

Masking: Chapter 10.

Track mattes: Chapter 11.

Applying effects: Chapter 22.

Effects such as Hue/Saturation: Chapter 23B.

Color Difference Keyer: Chapter 27B.

Roto Brush, Refine Matte: Chapter 34.

Frame Rate Manipulation

Time Stretch, Reverse, and Remap, plus smoothing the result with Frame Blending.

Reality is fine, but it's not always what you want. Sometimes you need a captured movie to play back more quickly, more slowly, or backward, or to stop altogether. After Effects has options to Time Stretch a clip, which gives it a new constant speed, or Time Remap it, which allows the speed to change over time. Both often result in staggered motion compared with the original clip, so at the end of this chapter we will discuss Frame Blending which can help smooth out the result.

Time Stretch

The Time Stretch feature can be used to speed up or slow down video, audio, and nested comp layers. Time stretching affects any animation already applied to masks, effects, and transformations, so speed changes also apply to keyframes.

When you speed up a movie (a stretch value of less than 100%), frames in the movie will be skipped in order to keep pace. Likewise, when you slow down a movie (a stretch value of more than 100%), source frames will be duplicated as necessary to pad out the new duration.

If you'd like to ensure that frames are duplicated in a consistent fashion, use a multiple of 100%. For example, a stretch value of 400% will play each frame four times. To blend the frames rather than simply duplicate them, enable Frame Blending, which is covered later in this chapter.

If a movie layer contains audio, the audio will also be time stretched and resampled. If you don't want to time stretch the audio, before stretching duplicate the layer, then turn Audio off for the original and Video off for the duplicate. The original layer will play just video and can be time stretched, while the duplicate layer will only play the audio, unstretched.

You can approach entering a time stretch value from three angles:

- you have a stretch value that you'd like to use;
- you know what duration the layer needs to be; or
- you know where you'd like the in or out point to extend to (but don't necessarily know what the duration should be).

You can experiment with these options in comp [**Ex.01**]. Reveal the In/Out/Duration/Stretch columns in the Timeline panel by clicking on

TIP

Keyframes Only

To reverse only keyframes, not the entire layer: Select the keyframes, right-click on any selected keyframe, and choose Keyframe Assistant > Time-Reverse Keyframes.

Example Project

Explore the 28-Example Project.aep file as you read this chapter; references to [Ex.##] refer to specific compositions within the project file.

the expand/collapse button (the icon of two brackets) in the lower left corner, or right-click on the top of any other column and select Stretch. Then click on the value for Stretch for **AB_SkyEffects.mov**. This opens the Time Stretch dialog, which can also be accessed via the menu item Layer > Time > Time Stretch.

You can enter a value for New Duration, or a value for Stretch Factor in % (higher numbers being slower). Notice that when you change the Duration, the Stretch Factor updates accordingly, and vice versa. The Hold In Place option sets the point in time around which the stretching occurs (the layer's in point, current frame, or out point). Hold In Place defaults to Layer In-point, which is often the most useful.

You can also scrub the Stretch value directly in the Timeline panel. Scrubbing the Duration value will result in Stretch also being changed.

There are also some great shortcuts to precisely time stretch a layer so that it starts or stops when you want, while keeping the other end at the same place in time:

Right-click on any column and select Stretch to add it to the Timeline panel (above). Click on the Stretch value to open the Time Stretch dialog (below).

- To stretch the in point of the layer to the current time, Command+click on Mac (Control+click on Windows) the value in the In column, or use the shortcut:

Stretch in point to current time   **Command+Shift+, (comma) (Control+Shift+,)**

- To stretch the out point of the layer to the current time, Command+click (Control+click) the value for Out in the Out column, or use the shortcut:

Stretch out point to current time   **Command+Option+, (comma) (Control+Alt+,)**

Stretching Animations

Time stretching a movie results in either skipping or repeating frames in that movie. However, this does not mean that any processing added to the movie – such as transform keyframes or effects – also skips frames. For example, if you have an effect that's applied to the movie and that normally reprocesses every frame (such as Effect > Noise & Grain > Noise), the effect will still be processed every frame of the comp, even if frames of the source are being repeated. If this is not what you want, apply the effect in a precomp and enable the Preserve Frame Rate when Nested option in Composition Settings > Advanced (see *Nesting Options*, Chapter 18).

If the time stretched layer is a nested composition, stretching it will have the appearance of stretching all the layers in the nested comp. Any keyframes applied to layers inside the precomp will be adjusted accordingly, retiming the animation. This is a handy way to adjust the speed of an animation containing graphics and type animation; if any of the layers in the nested comp are movies, however, you may want to avoid time stretching them, and stretch just their actual keyframes.

GOTCHA

Stretching Stills

Don't stretch stills: Keyframe precision will be compromised, and other anomalies may occur. If you need to extend a still, drag the end of its layer bar to extend its length. Then stretch selected keyframes by Option+dragging on the Mac (Alt+dragging on Windows) the last keyframe.

When a layer is reversed, the layer bar will display red hash marks along its lower edge. Both the Stretch and Duration values will be displayed as negative numbers.

When you reverse a layer, keyframes are also reversed; because they were attached to the beginning of a frame in time, they now align to the end of a frame – so they appear to be one frame off.

Step 2: Precompose the movie using the Leave All Attributes option. Check the Open New Composition option so that the precomp comes forward when you click OK.

Going in Reverse

If you need a movie to play from back to front, you can easily reverse the playback direction using the following shortcut:

Reverse Layer   **Command+Option+R** (**Control+Alt+R**)

Practice using [**Ex.02**]. After reversal, the layer bar will show red hash marks along its bottom. All keyframes applied to the layer will also be reversed. This shortcut will apply a time stretch value of negative 100%, while also moving the in and out points so that the frames play in the same position of the timeline as before. (If you don't use the shortcut and manually time stretch by negative 100%, the layer will reverse itself around the in or out point or current frame, usually resulting in the layer moving in time.) To return the layer to regular playback, reverse the layer a second time using the same shortcut.

Backward Logic

Once a layer is reversed, pressing I will still jump to the earlier point in time in the comp's overall timeline, and O to the later time. However, navigating in the Layer panel is a little more confusing: Going forward in the source now goes backward in the comp. More of an annoyance is that keyframes will appear to be off by one frame in the timeline: Because keyframes are normally attached to the beginning of a frame in time, after reversal they will now be attached to the end of a frame, which makes them appear to be one frame late.

As a result, you may find it less confusing to reverse your footage in a precomp, and then do any editing or keyframing in a master comp. This example will demonstrate:

Step 1: Open [**Ex.03_starter**]. Select **AB_RetroHealthcare.mov** to be reversed, and select Layer > Pre-compose.

Step 2: Give the precomp a more useful name (such as "**Movie Reversed precomp**"), and select option #1: Leave All Attributes (see figure, left). Make sure the option Open New Composition is checked, and click OK. A new comp that contains only the original source movie will be created and opened automatically. All keyframes will remain in the original comp.

Step 3: With the new precomp still forward, select the movie layer and reverse it using the shortcut Command+Option+R (Control+Alt+R).

Step 4: Return to the original comp. Select the layer in it (which is now the nested precomp) and press U to reveal its keyframes. The layer will now play backward, but the keyframes will not be affected, and navigation shortcuts will work as expected. If you need to also reverse the keyframes, select them and use Animation > Keyframe Assistant > Time Reverse Keyframes. (If you get lost, check out the [**Ex.03-final comps**] folder.)

Slipping into Reverse

The drawback to the "reverse in the precomp" technique is that you may lose your edit points for the segment of the movie you wanted to see.

If you have trimmed the in and out points of a layer, then precompose it, the precomp will contain the entire source – not just the trimmed portion. Reverse this clip in the precomp, and the segment used in the main comp will probably be different. To see this in action, open [**Ex.04_starter**] and scrub the time indicator: We've trimmed this movie to use the middle segment of the patient's arm. Say you wanted to reverse this action. Precompose the movie as above, and reverse the movie in the precomp. Return to [**Ex.04_starter**] and you'll see a different segment.

You can fix this using the Slip Edit tool. Press I to locate to the in point, locate the cursor over the empty layer bar to the left until it turns into a double arrow with vertical lines at the ends, and drag the clip until you see the first frame of the arm. Check the other end of the clip if you want to make sure the out point is correct. Compare your results with our comps in the **Ex.04-final comps** folder.

Keyframe Behavior Tips

When you time stretch or reverse a layer, any keyframes already created are also time stretched. Here are some workarounds:

• Before you stretch the layer, select any keyframes you do not want to have stretched. Cut these keyframes, then stretch the layer. Paste the keyframes back to the now-stretched layer.

• Apply the time stretch in a precomp (see *Backward Logic*). This will stretch the movie before the keyframes, not after, and the keyframes will remain untouched in the original comp.

• The built-in frame rate of the movie can be overridden with the Conform Frame Rate setting (select movie in Project panel and File > Interpret Footage > Main). If you enter a lower or higher value, you'll slow down or speed up the movie before it even reaches the comp, meaning your keyframes are unaffected. A 30 fps movie conformed to 10 fps will play every frame three times – equivalent to time stretching by 300%.

• Time Remapping (covered next) is like time stretching on steroids; plus it does its magic *before* Masks, Effects, and Transform keyframes.

• If you forget to work around the problem, stretch or squash selected keyframes back to their original timing by Option+dragging (Alt+dragging) the first or last keyframe.

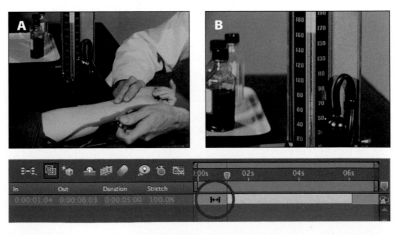

If you trim a movie to isolate a specific piece of action – such as the patient's arm (A) – you may find you see a completely different segment after performing the reverse-in-precomp trick (B).

It is simple enough to use the Slip Edit tool in the original comp's Timeline panel (right) to re-edit the clip. Footage courtesy Artbeats/Retro Healthcare.

Time Remapping

Beyond Time Stretching is Time Remapping (TR, for short). It allows you to keyframe which frame of your source plays at a specific time in your overall timeline. After Effects then stretches the clip between keyframes as necessary to make this happen, even playing the clip backwards if an earlier keyframe has a lower value (i.e. frame number in the source clip) than the one before it. The concept of keyframing time can take a bit to get your head around, but once you do, you'll see it has a lot of potential.

A natural result of this capability is that the stretch value can be different between keyframes, allowing you to create speed changes during the life of the clip. And because you're working with regular keyframe interpolation types, you get the benefit of velocity curves for ramping speed up and down. You can also easily create freeze frames, and even make a movie play backward. And did we mention that you can do all of this to nested comp layers as well?

You will not see Time Remapping listed as a default property of a layer when you reveal it in the Timeline. It needs to be enabled by selecting the layer and invoking the menu item Layer > Time > Enable Time Remapping. It will then be the first item in a layer's list of properties, because it happens before Masks, Effects, and Transform. You can then keyframe it just like any other property. Unlike Time Stretching, Time Remapping keyframes does *not* affect the timing of other keyframes already applied to a layer – it behaves as if you time stretched the clip in a previous composition.

Getting Started (and Stopped)

A common use for Time Remapping is to make a clip longer than it originally was. Therefore, it's a good idea to start with a practice composition that's substantially longer than the clip you will be working with. To get started, close all comps and open [**Ex.05_starter**]. It contains a movie clip of a dancer with some distinctive moves. Double-click the clip to open its Layer panel and play it until you're familiar with its action.

Add a few new dance steps to this dancer movie using Time Remapping. Footage courtesy Getty Images.

Close the Layer panel, and with the layer still selected, select Layer > Time > Enable Time Remapping. The Time Remap property is added to the layer (if you twirl up the layer and twirl it back down, you'll see that Time Remap appears in the Timeline panel above Transform). The shortcut to twirl down just Time Remapping is RR (two Rs in quick succession).

When you enable Time Remapping, two default keyframes are automatically created: one at the start of the clip, and another one after the

clip's out point (see the sidebar *The Real Out Point*, page 488). To disable Time Remapping and delete all keyframes, turn off the stopwatch to the left of Time Remap in the Timeline panel. You can also use the shortcut Command+Option+T (Control+Alt+T) to toggle on/off Time Remapping. If you make a big mess as you learn how to time remap, toggle Time Remapping off and on again to start over.

Freeze Frames

With Time Remapping enabled, you can extend the duration of a clip by dragging its out point to the right. The clip will be frozen on its last frame. Try it in [**Ex.05**] by extending layer 1 and previewing the result.

To freeze on the first frame before the movie starts, click on the words Time Remap to select *both* default keyframes, then drag the first keyframe to its new time. The second keyframe will move by the same amount. For example, moving the first keyframe from 0:00 to 02:00 will produce a two-second freeze frame at the beginning of the clip. Note that you're moving its *time* keyframes, *not* the layer bar. To create only freeze frames, be certain to always move both keyframes together to keep their relationship the same as they slide along the timeline. Should they drift together or apart from each other, you will be introducing either a speedup or a slowdown of the movie, not just a simple freeze frame.

If you want to create a freeze frame during a more involved time remap animation, use hold keyframes (Chapter 4).

When you enable Time Remapping for a clip, it gets two default keyframes, marking its normal start and end. The second keyframe is placed just after the original end of the clip. Drag on the end of the clip to extend its length.

TIP

Easy Single Freeze Frame

To convert a movie to a still image, place the current time indicator at the desired frame of the source and use Layer > Time > Freeze Frame. This will enable Time Remapping with a single keyframe at this time.

The Graph Editor (also covered in Chapter 4) also comes in very handy for understanding what is happening to a clip during time remapping.

To start with a hold, then play at normal speed, make sure you drag *both* Time Remap keyframes – not just the first one (above). While working in the Graph Editor (right), double-click the words Time Remap to select the keyframes and then press Shift while moving the selection left and right.

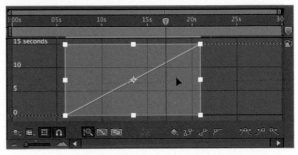

Doing Time

To add a Time Remap keyframe, move somewhere to the middle of the clip, click on the underlined value in the Timeline panel, and enter a new frame number. You can also click the Add/Remove Keyframe switch in the Timeline panel's keyframe navigator to set a new keyframe at the current source frame's value.

Once you've created a TR keyframe, there are a couple of ways to interactively edit the keyframe. Practice both of these in [**Ex.05**], RAM Previewing the results as you go, until you start to feel comfortable:

• Scrub the Time Remap frame number in the Timeline panel while watching the Comp panel.

• Enable the Graph Editor either by clicking on its icon along the top of the Timeline panel or by using the keyboard shortcut Shift+F3. Move the current time indicator to the overall time in the comp you're interested in. Then drag the Time Remap keyframe you wish to edit inside the Graph Editor while watching the result in the Comp panel. If you've enabled Show Graph Tool Tips, a box will also appear by your cursor while you're dragging, showing you the source time in the clip (bottom number) and the new time in the composition (top number). You can hold Shift while dragging to constrain your movements, or to snap to other events such as other keyframes.

If you enable Show Graph Tool Tips (under the circled Choose Graph Type button), dragging a Time Remap keyframe in the Graph Editor allows you to set both the source frame number (the bottom value) and the overall composition time (the upper value). The Time Remap value to the left (circled in red) shows the source frame number at the current time in the comp. Press and hold the G key and click on the graph to create a new keyframe.

Giving you an idea of how this might work, [**Ex.06**] is an example of a movie that has been time remapped. Open it and RAM Preview to see how the action plays out. The Time Remap parameter and the Graph Editor should both be visible in the Timeline panel; if they aren't, select the layer, type RR, then press Shift+F3. Select Time Remap to see its values in the Graph Editor. We'll explain what's going on:

For the Graph Editor's Graph Type, we've selected Edit Value Graph; that's the white line you see with the little keyframe nubbins. We've also enabled Show Reference Graph to show us the playback speed; that's the gray line without the nubbins. Finally, we've enabled Show Graph Tool Tips. This means you can see a graph's or keyframe's current value

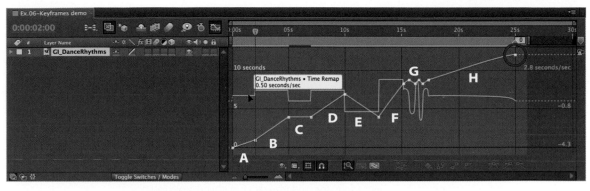

by hovering your cursor over it. Let's analyze the implications of our keyframes in more detail:

• In [**Ex.06**], hover your cursor over the gray Graph Editor line between keyframes (KF) 1 and 2 (**A** in the figure above): The movie plays at half speed, which is displayed as 0.50 seconds/sec in the tool tip. This means through this section, After Effects will play one second of source material over two seconds of time, duplicating each frame to do so.

• Between KF 2 and 3 (**B**), the movie plays at a normal speed of 1.00 seconds/sec (for every one frame of source, you have one frame in the timeline in which it plays). Note that the white value graph has a steeper upward slope, and the gray speed graph is higher – both indicators that the clip is playing faster than between the previous two keyframes.

• Between KF 3 and 4 (**C**), the movie freezes for 2 seconds, on frame 04:00 into the clip (note we're at 05:00 in the timeline because we played the first portion of the movie at half speed). The value graph stays flat, and the speed graph line displays 0.00 seconds/sec. The third keyframe was changed to a hold keyframe to accomplish this, which we recommend to ensure a solid freeze, especially if you're also frame blending the layer (frame blending is covered later in this chapter).

• Between KF 4 and 5 (**D**), the movie plays forward at normal speed.

• Between KF 5 and 6 (**E**), the movie plays backward at –1.00 seconds/sec. The value graph has a strong downward slope, and the speed graph is below the horizontal center of the Graph Editor display – both indicators that the clip is playing backward.

• Between KF 6 and 7 (**F**), the movie plays forward, this time faster at 2.00 seconds/sec.

• The sequence of six keyframes (7–12) (**G**) is set so that just a few frames are repeated back and forth, and Auto Bezier keyframes help smooth out the jarring changes in direction – you can see this reflected in the wavy gray speed graph.

• The final keyframe has a value of 12:04, well before the last frame of the movie (14:29). An ease in was added to slow down the movie as it enters the last keyframe, at which point it holds on that frame.

A set of Time Remap keyframes have been set to manipulate the speed of the clip. Enabling Graph Tool Tips allows us to see the values of the keyframes and the graph lines that connect them.

You can edit the current source frame interactively by scrubbing the current value, just as with any regular keyframe. You can also drag the keyframe nubbin (circled in red) to edit the keyframe value.

Between KF 5 and 6 (**E**), the downward Value line indicates the movie is playing backward (a negative velocity value).

TIP

Trimmed Time

If you have trimmed a movie, then enabled Time Remapping, immediately go to the new in point, click the TR keyframe checkbox, and do the same for the out point. Now delete the two default keyframes. This will keep only the trimmed frames in play for freeze frames and editing.

Time Remapping to Music

The **Goodies** folder on the DVD contains an article titled **Varispeeding** that we wrote for Artbeats on how to use Time Remapping to make action in a movie more closely match a soundtrack.

In **[Ex.07]**, you'll use time remapping to extend the time spent circling this side of the skyscraper. Footage courtesy Artbeats/Los Angeles Aerials.

Start playing around with the keyframes yourself, sliding them to different points in the timeline. Observe how the Value and Velocity graphs change, and Preview to reinforce what's going on. Add some new keyframes and play around until you get a good feeling for the graphs. When you're adjusting TR graphs, be careful that your velocity does not go negative – this means your clip will back up.

You don't need to edit Time Remap keyframes in the Graph Editor; return to the normal timeline and simply slide keyframes left and right. Dragging keyframes with the Window > Info panel open gives you feedback as to precisely which point in time you are dragging to.

Now disable and re-enable Time Remapping, and start over with your own ideas for how the dancer should perform.

Repairing Shot Timing

We often use Time Remapping to alter a section of a clip to make it work better with the music or voiceover. In the following example, we'll show you how to "pad" time into the middle of a clip. Close the previous comps, open [**Ex.07_starter**], and preview the **AB_LosAngelesAerials** movie in it of a helicopter flying around a skyscraper. At around 05:00, the view into the building is what's important to the story, but the pilot flew by these windows too fast. Let's take this section of the clip and slow it down, leaving the beginning and ending untouched:

Step 1: In [**Ex.07_starter**], select the clip, and then select Layer > Time > Enable Time Remapping.

Step 2: Extend the layer bar's out point so that it extends to the end of the composition.

Step 3: Move to 03:00, where the helicopter is about to move around the side of the building we're interested in. Click the keyframe diamond to add a TR keyframe at 03:00 with a value of 03:00. This anchors the first three seconds of the movie so that it will continue to play at normal speed.

Steps 3–4: Create new Time Remap keyframes at 03:00 and 06:00. The section in-between these two keyframes will be extended in Step 5.

Step 4: Move to 06:00 and add another TR keyframe with a value of 06:00. This will allow the last portion of the movie, from 06:00 to the end, to also remain unaffected.

Step 5: The idea is to take the portion of time between the two new keyframes and spread it out over a longer period of time so the three seconds of source movie (between 03:00 and 06:00) will play from 03:00 to 08:00. To do this, move the time indicator to 08:00, select KF 3 and 4, and drag KF 3 to the right. Both keyframes should move together, meaning that the playback speed will remain at 100% for this ending section. Press the Shift key as you approach 08:00 in the timeline, and KF 3 will snap to the time indicator. Press Shift+F2 to deselect all keyframes.

Step 6: Reveal the Graph Editor (Shift+F3), then enable Edit Speed Graph plus Show Reference Graph using the Graph Type popup. Hover your cursor over the flat speed graph line between 03:00 and 08:00; it will read 0.60 seconds/sec. The sudden jumps in level in the speed graph indicate that the speed changes around our keyframes will be abrupt.

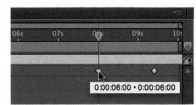

Step 5: Move keyframes 3 and 4 so that the third keyframe starts at 08:00.

Step 6: The speed for the middle section is 0.60 seconds/sec. The Speed Graph indicates sudden changes in speed at 03:00 and 08:00 (left).

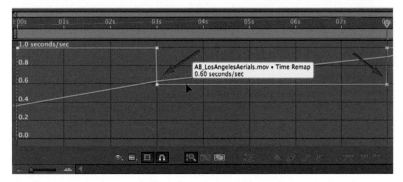

Step 7: Let's refine the velocity curve by adding some eases to smooth out the sudden drop between the different speeds. Grab the outgoing velocity handle for KF 2 at 03:00 and drag it higher until it snaps together with the incoming handle; the tool tip should read Speed 1:00 seconds/sec. Also drag this handle to the right until Influence reads about 30% or so. The velocity curve should now ramp smoothly from normal speed to the slower speed, and the value reference graph should also show a smooth transition through this keyframe.

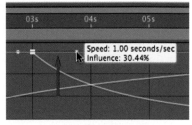

Step 7: Drag the outgoing velocity handle higher for the keyframe at 03:00 (above) so that it ramps smoothly from normal speed to the slower speed.

Step 8: You can also edit speed transitions numerically. In the Graph Editor, double-click on the third keyframe at 08:00 to open its Keyframe Velocity dialog. Change the Incoming Velocity to "1" seconds/sec (one second of source plays for one second in the timeline), and enter 30% for the Influence. Be sure to leave the Outgoing Velocity untouched, then click OK. Feel free to also enter the velocity for the keyframe at 03:00 numerically if you weren't happy with your first edit, remembering that you need to change the Outgoing Velocity for that keyframe. In the Graph Editor, you will see smooth speed curves around your keyframes. RAM Preview and adjust to taste.

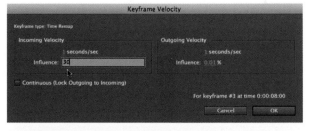

Step 8: Ease into the third keyframe at 08:00 by entering values in the Keyframe Velocity dialog (above). The incoming handle will now smoothly transition into the keyframe (below).

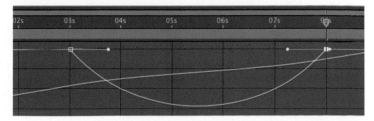

So why didn't we use the Easy Ease keyframe assistants? Because they would bring the speed down to 0.00 seconds/sec at the keyframe – try it if you don't believe us! These keyframe assistants are still useful, however, when you need a Time Remap keyframe to slow down a clip to a smooth stop.

Step 9: The last trick is enabling Frame Blending for the layer and the comp. We're going to discuss frame blending in more detail in just a few

pages, but if you're already familiar with it, enable the Frame Blending switch for the layer, and the Enable Frame Blending button along the top of the Timeline panel. Frame

Step 9: Turn on the Frame Blending switch and Enable Frame Blending to help smooth out the motion.

blending is a useful partner to "selling" time remapping, as it helps by creating artificial frames between the original ones as you vary the speed. Preview your animation again and check out [**Ex.07-final**] if you got lost along the way.

Adding Handle

In [**Ex.08**], time remapping extends the "handle" at the beginning of this clip (above) by slowing down the first few frames in the Graph Editor (below).

Another practical use for time remapping is to add more handle to the beginning or end of a clip by, say, stretching the first 10 frames out to 30 frames. With a longer handle, you can create a slower crossfade between clips in a sequence. The technique is similar to that shown above: Enable Time Remapping for the layer, create a new keyframe at 00:10, then drag both the new keyframe and the last keyframe 20 frames later in time. This is shown in [**Ex.08_Adding Handle**].

Because frame blending (discussed later in this chapter) incurs a render hit even when the playback speed is normal, you might want to split your layer after remapping and turn off blending on the sections where it is playing at normal speed, as shown in [**Ex.08_Split Layer**]. Also, if time remapping is affecting only a small section at the beginning or end of a layer, you can remap just this section, leaving the second layer to play the rest of the movie in its original state.

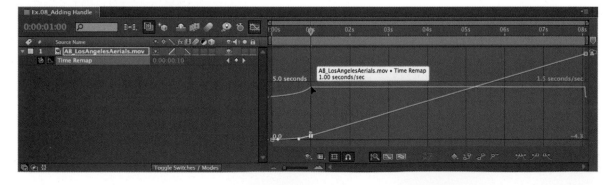

Two Timelines

You can also create and edit Time Remap keyframes in the Layer panel, which is useful if the key "frames" are easier to select visually than by timecode. The Layer panel has additional features when Time Remapping is enabled:

With **[Ex.09]** open, double-click the layer **GI_DanceRhythms** to open the Layer panel, and you'll notice two timelines. The upper time ruler (labeled Source Time) scrubs through the movie frames and sets or edits a TR keyframe, while the lower ruler corresponds to the layer bar in the Timeline panel. Press the spacebar to play the movie from the Layer panel and watch how the top time indicator scrubs back and forth (kinda spooky!) while the bottom time indicator makes steady progress.

To edit an existing TR keyframe, step to a keyframe in the Timeline panel. Now, in the Layer panel, drag the *upper* time indicator around to identify which frame of the source you want on this keyframe. To create a new keyframe, move the comp time indicator (the lower one in the Layer panel) to the desired point in time, then drag the upper time indicator around. The timecode readout on the left is the current time in the clip; click it to enter a new Go To time. The timecode readout on the right

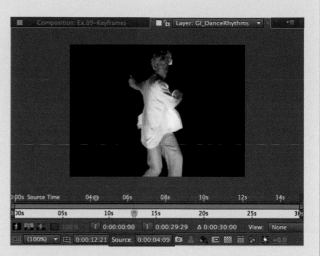

When Time Remapping is enabled, the Layer panel boasts a second time indicator above the regular one. The red box highlights the source time (04:09) that is being played back at time 12:21 in the remapped layer.

represents the time remapped value; click it to enter a keyframe value numerically.

When Time Remapping is enabled, we suggest you create masks in a precomp or in a second comp. Otherwise, when you try to edit or animate masks in the Layer panel, you'll inevitably add or edit TR keyframes accidentally as you navigate the timeline.

Remapping a Comp

Time Remapping is not limited to movie sources – you can also apply it to a nested comp layer. For instance, let's say you have spent a significant amount of time choreographing a dozen or so layers in an animation, only to have the client ask for the entire animation to happen in less time. And could it start and end a little faster, while slowing down in the middle? There's no need to redo the animation. By nesting the animation into another comp and applying Time Remapping, you can adjust the timing to taste. This is shown in [**Ex.11-Picasso-1/animation**], where the animation takes place, and [**Ex.11-Picasso-2/remap**], where the speed is adjusted with time remapping.

If you're unclear how this works in practice, close your previous comps and open [**Ex.12-Practice Comp**]. The layers are already animating over a background layer when the client delivers the bad news. Notice that the animation finishes at 06:10.

> "Art washes away from the soul the dust of everyday life."
> — Pablo Picasso

You can time remap a nested comp layer, which is a handy technique for retiming a complex graphical animation. Background courtesy Artbeats/Alien Atmospheres.

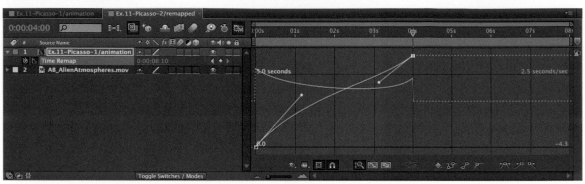

Above is our final time remapped title. You can practice re-creating this example in **[Ex.12-Practice Comp]** by following the accompanying steps.

Step 1: Go to time 06:10; here the animation ends. Press Shift+0 (on the keyboard) to place Comp Marker 0 at this frame as a reminder.

Step 2: Select layers 1–11 (select layer 1 and Shift+click layer 11).

Step 3: Select Layer > Pre-compose to send these layers to their own precomp. In the Pre-compose dialog, name the new comp "**Quote precomp**". Leave Open New Composition *unchecked* – you don't need to edit this comp. Click OK. The **[Ex.08-Practice Comp]** should still be the forward comp, and the selected layers are now replaced with a single nested comp layer.

Step 3: Precompose the selected layers (1–11) so that you will have a single layer to time remap.

Step 4: Select Layer > Time > Enable Time Remapping; the default keyframes should be visible.

Step 5: Still at time 06:10, check the keyframe checkbox to create a Time Remap keyframe with a value of 06:10.

Step 6: Select the last Time Remap keyframe at 08:00 and delete it. There is no need to interpolate between the last frame of the animation and the end of the layer. Deleting this keyframe will save rendering time because the frame at 06:10 will be cached and repeated. If you don't delete the keyframe, the precomp will continue to be sampled at each frame, even though no change is occurring in the animation.

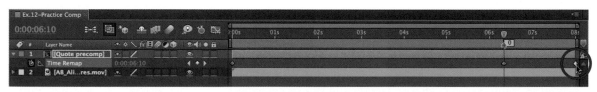

Step 6: Select the last keyframe at the end of the layer and press Delete. Now the keyframe at 06:10 will be cached and repeated, saving rendering time.

Step 7: Now you can drag the new keyframe at 06:10 earlier in time, and apply Easy Ease (or for bonus points, create your own velocity curves to taste). Create a couple of variations and RAM Preview to see how easy it is to change the timing. You could even add hold keyframes to freeze on certain words if needed.

Of course, if the animation consists of movie layers, you probably won't be able to avail of this shortcut, as time remapping the nested comp will affect the speed of the movie sources also. But this is still a great time-saver for retiming graphical animations. Now that you know how easy it is to time remap a nested comp, let's offer a couple of variations on the theme.

Remapping Sequenced Layers

The Sequence Layers keyframe assistant (Chapter 7) can be used to distribute layers in time and create automatic crossfades between layers. In [**Ex.13-Numbers-1/sequence**], a series of 10 images (the numbers from 1–10) were trimmed to 01:20 in length, and sequenced in time with 10-frame crossfades. The end of the sequence occurs at 12:10. If you RAM Preview, you'll see that the pace of the sequence is constant.

This comp is then nested in [**Ex.13-Numbers-2/remapped**], where time remapping is applied in the same fashion as in Steps 4–7 above. A keyframe was created at 12:10 which represents where the number "10" is fully on, and then this keyframe can be moved around at will to retime the animation. By moving it to 10:00 and adjusting the Velocity graph, the numbers start counting more slowly and finish counting quickly, stopping exactly at 10:00. RAM Preview to see the difference. Now imagine trying to create this animation by carefully timing out each number!

Remapping Exponential Scale

When you scale up a layer by a large amount using linear keyframes, the visual result is that the layer appears to scale quickly at first, then slow down as it gets larger. You can preview this problem in [**Ex.14a-Linear Scale**].

To the rescue comes the Exponential Scale keyframe assistant (Chapter 5). By selecting the current Scale keyframes and applying this assistant, the scale will have a constant pace. (It does this by creating keyframes at every frame, forcing a change in velocity too extreme for the velocity controls to achieve on their own.) Preview the results in [**Ex.14b-Scale-1/exponential**].

If you find that Exponential Scale is *too* smooth, no points for guessing that you can apply Exponential Scale in a precomp and use Time Remapping in a second comp to retime the motion. This is shown in [**Ex.14b-Scale-2/remap**]; feel free to experiment, previewing as you go.

Simply Sequenced

If you drag multiple items to the New Composition button at the bottom of the Project panel, an options dialog will open. Provided you select Create Single Composition, you can also choose to Sequence Layers (with the same options as the keyframe assistant).

After you apply the Exponential Scale keyframe assistant, the layer (above) will scale at a consistent pace, despite how the curve may initially appear (below). You can tweak the pacing by time remapping in a second comp.

The Real Out Point

If you use the default Time Remap keyframes and apply velocity curves, you may not achieve a smooth entry into the last keyframe, particularly if you use a very long ease in. Because the second default keyframe is created one frame *after* the last real frame of the movie, the last real frame of the movie appears in the comp *before* the last keyframe is reached and is then repeated if you freeze the end of the movie.

For example, in **[Ex.10a]**, our 15-second movie **GI_DanceRhythms** starts at 00:00. The last frame is 14:29 and it appears at 14:29 in the timeline. But when you enable Time Remapping, the second default keyframe is created at 15:00 – *one frame later*.

The reason for placing the keyframe one frame after the end is that After Effects assumes your source is an interlaced movie, whereby you would be viewing only the first field of frame 14:29 at time 14:29. If the default Time Remap keyframe was created at 14:29 also, any freeze you create at the end of the movie would freeze on the first field of this frame. As a result, you would never see the second field. By placing it at 15:00, the idea is that you would freeze on the second field of the last frame.

This is a nice feature in theory, but the reality is that not all sources are interlaced (this one isn't), so the actual image data from the last frame (or field 2 in an interlaced movie) appears *before* the keyframe icon. This is a problem only if you have a slow ease into this keyframe. Let's say the image on the last frame is supposed to freeze at the big finale audio sound effect at 24:00. So you drag the second default keyframe from 15:00 to 24:00 and apply Easy Ease In so that the movie slows down and stops at 24:00. The problem is that the image from the last frame will appear in the comp at 23:09, well ahead of the theoretical audio, as shown in **[Ex.10b]**.

Our preference is to always re-create the last keyframe so that it freezes on the first field of the last frame, as shown in **[Ex.10c]**. Now when you move the last keyframe later in time to slow it down, rounding errors are less likely to occur **[Ex.10d]**.

The workaround we used to fix this "feature" is fairly simple. Practice the following steps in **[Ex.10e]**:

• *Before* you enable Time Remapping, select the layer and press O to jump to the real out point (at 14:29 in this case), select Layer > Enable Time Remapping. Press the ; (semicolon) key to zoom in closely in time so you can see some detail.

• Check the keyframe box to create a new keyframe for the real last frame, at time 14:29. *Note: Don't just drag the default keyframe back to 14:29.*

• Press Page Down to advance one frame and uncheck the second default keyframe created at 15:00 to remove it, or select it and press Delete. Press the ; key again to zoom out, and continue to work normally with Time Remapping.

TIP

J & K Keys

When keyframes are exposed in the Timeline panel, you can press J and K to jump to the previous or next keyframe, respectively.

Remapping a Sequence of Frames

Time Remapping can also be used as a "sequencer" of sorts for individual frames, such as you might have with cel animation. Import the frames as a sequence, and use Time Remapping to control how the frames play back.

This concept is shown in [Ex.15-Frame Sequencer], where the comp is set to 12 frames per second (fps). The series of numbers from 1–10 has been imported as a "sequence" by selecting the first frame in the folder, and checking the Illustrator/PDF/EPS Sequence checkbox in the Import File dialog. The footage is added to the composition, where it appears as one layer. (Alternatively, this layer could be a nested precomp in which multiple layers are sequenced in time using Sequence Layers.) By

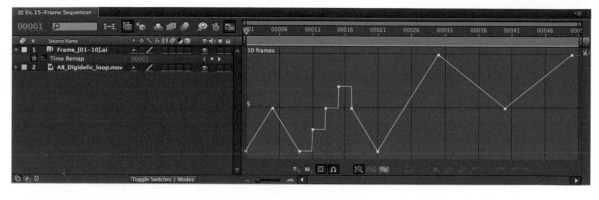

enabling Time Remapping and setting keyframes appropriately, you can force the individual frames (or images) to play forward and backward, or freeze on a frame using hold keyframes.

When you're working with frames, you will probably want to set your project to count in frames, rather than SMPTE. You can do this from File > Project Settings, where you can also set the "Start numbering frames" to 1 if that's more intuitive to you. You can also toggle between SMPTE, Frames, and Feet+Frames by Command+clicking (Control+clicking) on the current time readout in the Comp, Timeline, or Layer panels.

In **[Ex.15]**, time remap keyframes control how cel animation frames play back. Note we've toggled the Timeline panel's time readout to be in frames. We've told After Effects to start numbering frames at 1 to make the timeline match our footage.

Stepping Out with Time Remap

One popular trick is to create a step-time feel by reducing the frame rate of the comp. However, a drawback of this technique is that you don't get to pick and choose exactly which frames are displayed. For example, RAM Preview **[Ex.16-Step Frame]**, which has a frame rate of 2.25 fps. At this slow frame rate, less desirable frames may be held for many frames, while more attractive frames are skipped. It also took us some time to find a frame rate that worked with the music track. Close all comps and take a tour through a different approach, using time remapping:

Step 1: Open [**Ex.16a**]. Time Remapping was enabled for the movie in this 29.97 fps comp. We then stepped through the comp frame by frame, and added a new Time Remap keyframe whenever a frame was deemed "attractive" (frames with too much motion blur or strange facial expressions were skipped). Note that the timing of the keyframes at this point is irrelevant. Also, because the keyframes interpolate, the movie plays back normally when it's previewed.

Step 1: Time Remapping was enabled for the Cool Characters movie (below), and keyframes created only where frames were deemed "attractive" (above).

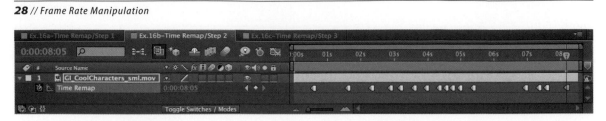

Step 2: After applying Time Remapping and creating keyframes for the most attractive frames, toggle all the keyframes to hold keyframes so they don't interpolate.

Step 2: Open [**Ex.16b**]. The second step was to select all the Time Remap keyframes and invoke Animation > Toggle Hold Keyframe. This ensures that only the desirable frames will appear, with no interpolation in-between. As we didn't want the two default Time Remap keyframes (denoting the first and last frames of the movie), these were deleted.

Step 3: The final step is to drag the Time Remap keyframes to synchronize with the music beats, adjusting the animation as needed to match the music. One keyframe was changed back to linear.

Step 3: Open [**Ex.16c**]. The music track was added, and the beats were marked out with layer markers (Chapter 36). We then dragged the Time Remap keyframes to each music beat (pressing the Shift key will make the keyframes stick to layer markers as you drag). The result is that only attractive frames are used, and the timing to the music is exact. Not only that, but by using Time Remap keyframes, you're not locked to a fixed frame rate – you can play a few frames at a faster rate, hold on one frame for longer, or play back frames out of order or backward. You can also repeat sections or change some keyframes back to linear, as we did toward the end of the animation.

Frame Blending

As mentioned earlier, any time footage is played back at speed other than its original pace, frames must be skipped or duplicated. This results in staggered motion. Frame blending offers some potential solutions to this problem.

After Effects offers two types of frame blending:

- *Frame Mix*, where adjacent frames are crossfaded to create new in-between frames. Even when footage is sped up, a small percentage of adjacent frames are blended into the result.

- *Pixel Motion*, where After Effects attempts to track the motion of similar pixels from frame to frame, then creates new pixels where it guesses they should be at an intermediate point in time. This general technique is often referred to as *optical flow*.

You don't have to time stretch to use frame blending. You can frame blend any movie layer that does not have an original frame for every

---

FACTOID

Always Calculating

When Frame Blending is enabled, it is always calculating, even when playing back at normal speed or when the current time indicator lands on what should be a perfect frame of the source. This results in an altered image and longer render times. Therefore, enable it only when needed!

composition frame. Some use this to conform 29.97 fps interlaced sources for 23.976 fps output, for example. There are also creative applications, which we'll demonstrate in *Blending Steps* (page 492).

Although frame blending often improves the look of footage that has been time stretched or remapped, sometimes the visual artifacts it creates outweigh its benefits. You should always carefully preview the results before committing to a final render with frame blending.

In the [Ex.17] folder, we've set up some side-by-side comparisons so you can see what Frame Mix, Pixel Motion, and the third-party solution RE:Vision Effects' Twixtor look like when speeding up and slowing down the same shot. Although they will take some time to render, RAM Preview them at 100% Magnification so you can see that whereas a given solution may look good on some frames, it may look terrible on others. In particular, jump to the comp markers in [Ex.17a] to see cases where Pixel Motion scrambles portions of the image.

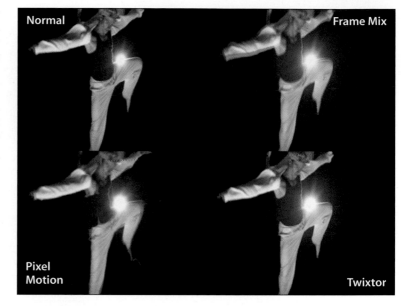

[Ex.17] contains side-by-side comparisons of no frame blending (upper left), Frame Mix mode (upper right), Pixel Motion mode (lower left), and RE:Vision Effects' Twixtor (lower right). Preview the comp; differences are visible on the forearm to the right.

Applying Frame Blending

Frame blending is set on a layer-by-layer basis. Make sure the Switches column is visible in the Timeline panel (press F4 if it isn't), and search for the icon that looks like a series of overlapping film frames. An empty box means Frame Blending is off for the layer. Clicking once in this box enables Frame Mix mode (noted with a dotted backslash inside this box); clicking again enables Pixel Motion mode (noted by a solid forward slash). Click again to turn Frame Blending off again. The switch will be unavailable if the layer is a still image or nested composition; you can frame blend only a movie or sequence of stills.

Once Frame Blending has been checked on for a layer, you can choose whether to display the result in the Comp panel as you work and perform previews. To do this, you need to toggle on the master Enable Frame Blending switch along the top of the Timeline panel. It's common to check on Frame Blending for a layer, but leave the Enable Frame Blending button off in the comp to avoid the rendering hit while you work. If you do turn on the comp's Enable Frame Blending and find the slowdown unacceptable, be

To enable Frame Blending per layer, click in the row of boxes under the film icon in the Timeline panel's Switches column. The backslash indicates Frame Mix mode; the forward slash is Pixel Motion mode. To see the results displayed in the comp, also turn on the Enable Frame Blending button (the larger film frame icon along the top of the panel).

Timewarp

If you want to use Pixel Motion but are experiencing unacceptable artifacts on some frames, you may want to try Effect > Time > Timewarp instead. Internally, this plug-in works similarly to Pixel Motion, with the difference being that it exposes several of its internal parameters for you to tweak.

To use Timewarp, disable Frame Blending for a layer, as you will be duplicating the plug-in's efforts. You should also disable Time Remapping and set the layer's Stretch value to 100%. Instead, use Timewarp's Speed parameter to varispeed the footage. Note that Speed is the inverse of a layer's Stretch value: 200% Stretch = 50% Speed. Timewarp also has an Adjust Time By option that allows you to directly set which source frame happens at what point in time, akin to Time Remapping.

Timewarp is based on the Kronos technology from The Foundry. The Foundry has written detailed instructions for Kronos. You can download it by going to *www.thefoundry.co.uk*, navigating to Plug-Ins > Final Cut Pro > FurnaceCore, and clicking on the

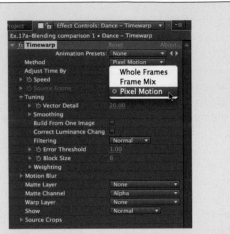

Unlike Pixel Motion, Effect > Time > Timewarp lets you go "under the hood" and tweak the parameters used to perform optical flow frame blending.

link for User Guide. In general, we find the Vector Detail and Block Size parameters inside the Tuning section to be the quickest path to solving problems in "torn" frames. Also handy is the Motion Blur section, where Timewarp can create multiframe blur for any footage (see Chapter 8).

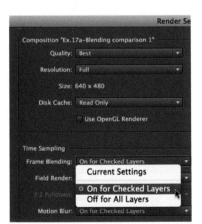

When you're rendering a comp that includes frame blended layers, make sure your Render Settings have the Frame Blending option set to On For Checked Layers. The Current Settings option obeys the comp's Enable Frame Blending switch, which may have been turned off to speed up your workflow.

sure to turn off this button rather than uncheck the frame blend switch for the layer!

The Enable Frame Blending button behaves *recursively:* By default, it also turns on the Enable switch in all nested compositions. You can turn this behavior off by unchecking the Switches Affect Nested Comps option in Preferences > General. (An obscure Mac-only shortcut: To temporarily override the preference's current setting, hold the Control key when you select Enable Frame Blending.)

Rendering with Frame Blending

When you render your composition, make sure that On For Checked Layers is set in Render Settings for the Frame Blending menu. This will ensure that all layers that have their frame blend switch checked on will render with frame blending, regardless of whether a comp's Enable button is on.

It should be obvious that the per-layer frame blend switch is what's really important – the Enable button is for display only and can be over-ridden easily in Render Settings. The other options available for Frame Blending when rendering are Current Settings, which indeed follows the status of the Enable switch, and Off For All Layers, which is useful for rough proofs, as it will render all layers without frame blending.

Blending Advice

The number one tip we can give you about frame blending is to always, always, *always* audition it before committing to a render you're going to hand a client. Weird artifacts can pop up suddenly in the middle of a clip, especially in Pixel Motion mode. With Frame Mix mode, you may notice some "strobing" between soft and sharp frames, especially if you choose a mathematically clean Stretch value such as multiples of 100%; we often use "irrational" Stretch values (such as 311%, instead of 300%) to make sure Frame Mix is always blending between adjacent frames.

In general, soft imagery frame blends much more readily than sharp imagery. Well-defined edges that move are prone to showing echoes, especially in Frame Mix mode. In Pixel Motion mode, these edges may become wavy if they cross in front of another shape that is either stationary or moving in the opposite direction – After Effects doesn't know which pixels are moving in which direction, so the image often appears to "tear" as a result. New objects appearing on screen (such as an eye when a person turns his or her head) will also confound Pixel Motion. In these cases, you may want to try using Timewarp (see the associated sidebar) or a third-party solution. For example, RE:Vision Effects's Twixtor Pro lets you use mask paths to define edges, helping its internal motion detection algorithm.

You can frame blend only footage items – not compositions. When one comp is nested inside another, it is sampled at the second comp's frame rate (and ultimately, by the frame rate it's rendered at). To frame blend a time stretched nested comp, prerender the comp, import it as a movie, and replace the nested comp layer with the rendered movie. The drawback is that keyframes in the nested comp are now set in stone.

Blending Steps

We'll leave you with a fun little special effect, using what you've learned in this chapter. It's ironic that now we've achieved full-motion playback from the desktop, we're eager to drop frames for that neat jerky look. While you can use step framing "dry," you can achieve some interesting variations if you add Frame Blending to the mix. There are two basic approaches:

• **Preblend:** In [Ex.18a], the **GI_CoolCharacters** movie is placed in a 10 fps comp, and Frame Blending is turned on. Because all the original frames are available to the comp, the blending results in multiple intermediate "ghost frames."

• **Postblend:** In [Ex.18b], the same movie is first prerendered at 10 fps without frame blending, then re-imported and placed in a 29.97 fps comp. When frame blending is applied, the steps are more pronounced as there are fewer source frames to blend together, resulting in a harder look with fewer ghost images to bridge the gap.

Remember that you can also use Time Stretch values to speed up or slow down the movies, in addition to step framing.

CC Time FX

Effects that can smear frames across time include Effect > Time > CC Time Blend and CC Wide Time, both of which are discussed in Chapter 8.

Enabling Frame Blending for the original movie in a 10 fps comp (above) results in more ghost images than if you apply blending to a prerendered 10 fps movie in a 29.97 fps comp (below). Footage courtesy Getty Images.

CONNECT

Graph Editor, Easy Ease, hold keyframe: Chapter 4.

Time-Reverse Keyframes, Exponential Scale keyframe assistants: Chapter 5.

The Slip Edit tool, trimming, split layer, and the Sequence Layers keyframe assistant: Chapter 7.

Motion blur: Chapter 8.

Nesting and precomposing: Chapter 18–19.

Effects: Chapters 22–25.

Interpret Footage: Chapter 38.

Render Settings: Chapter 42.

Motion Stabilization

After Effects includes the ability to stabilize wobbly footage. Mastering this is also the key to having one object track another.

Motion Stabilization and Motion Tracking – the subjects of this chapter and the next – sometimes seem like magic…magic that you often can't quite get to work. Some of the problems come from improper preparation of footage (not all shots can be stabilized or tracked), some with how the tracker's options have been set, and some with just a lack of practice and experience.

The key to both Stabilization and Tracking is learning how to track the movement of a visual feature from frame to frame in a footage item, and that's what we'll focus on here. We'll then show how to use the Stabilize option of this tool. In Chapter 30, you'll learn how to have one object track the movement of another, and in Chapter 31 you'll move onto mocha: an advanced motion tracking tool bundled with CS5.

Stabilizing 101

The point of Motion Stabilization is to remove drift, wander, zoom, or rotation in a footage item, making it appear as if the camera and action were solidly locked down. This drift might have come from a camera that was not perfectly steady – perhaps because it was handheld – or an object that was drifting off its mark.

To stabilize a footage item, the item needs to have some feature with an identifiable edge or shape with a strong contrast in color, brightness, or saturation from its immediate surroundings that can then be recognized and followed by the software. Dots are great; sharp corners also work well. Continuous edges or lines, or otherwise indistinct features, do not work for a "point" motion tracker like the one built into After Effects.

You point After Effects at this identifiable feature, and After Effects tracks the feature by looking for a similar feature in subsequent frames of the layer. It will then create new Anchor Point (and optionally, Rotation or Scale) keyframes to offset the apparent image center of the layer in a way that makes the overall image seem stable.

First we will discuss setting up a layer to be stabilized. We will then cover the stabilizer's all-important options, and finish by performing motion stabilization with a series of examples.

To practice motion stabilization, we will use the comp [Ex.01a_starter] in the file **29-Example Project.aep** – if you have your computer handy,

FACTOID

Third-Party Trackers

Not everyone relies on the tracker built into After Effects. The powerful mocha (Chapter 31) is now bundled with After Effects. Also check out SFX Silhouette Roto, Andersson Technologies SynthEyes, 2d3 Boujou, or Pixel Farm's PFTrack, and The Foundry's new Camera Tracker plug-in.

Example Project

Explore the 29-Example Project.aep file as you read this chapter; references to [Ex.##] refer to specific compositions within the project file.

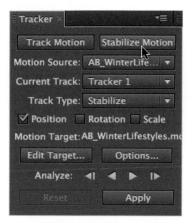

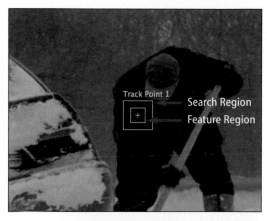

Select the layer to track and open the Tracker panel (left). Choose the Track Type you want to perform (Stabilize, in this case), and what type of motion you want to stabilize – Position, Rotation, Scale, or any combination. Then click on the button Stabilize Motion. This opens the selected clip's Layer panel (right) and adds a set of Tracking Region boxes.

open this project and comp now. The footage you will be stabilizing is **AB_WinterLifestyles.mov**: a pretrimmed, handheld shot of a person trying to dig their car out of the snow.

You can stabilize a piece of footage only if it's already a layer in a composition. The user interface for the Motion Tracker and Stabilizer is a special panel that can be opened by selecting Window > Tracker, or setting the Workspace to Motion Tracking. In [**Ex.01a_starter**], select the **AB_WinterLifestyles.mov** layer to stabilize, open the Tracker panel, check that only Position is selected (not Rotation or Scale), then click on its Stabilize Motion button. This will open the footage in its Layer panel.

In the Layer panel, you will see a set of Tracking Region boxes automatically named **Track Point 1**. The inner box – the Feature Region – needs to be centered and resized around the feature you have decided will make a good target to lock onto. The outer box – the Search Region – is how large an area After Effects will search beyond the inner box for each frame to find a matching feature from frame to frame.

In this example, you can choose to enlarge the Tracking Region boxes to track a large feature such as the taillight, or reduce them to track a smaller feature such as the orange sticker on the license plate. As you move the cursor around the boxes to different target areas, the cursor will change to reflect what you are about to move:

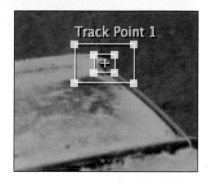

An example of making the Tracking Region boxes snugly fit our feature to track, with enough room to follow its movements from frame to frame (above). The Feature Region is automatically magnified 400% when you move the boxes, allowing you to more clearly see the detail you are tracking (below). Footage courtesy Artbeats/Winter Lifestyles.

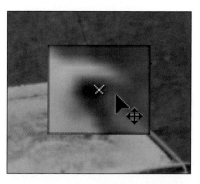

Target Area	Cursor	Behavior
Region Handle		Resize Feature or Search Region
Within Track Point		Move All
Feature Region Edge, or hold Option (Alt) key down		Move All except Attach Point
Search Region Edge		Move Search Region independently
Attach Point		Move Attach Point Independently

Set the corresponding checkboxes below the Track Type popup if you want to track Rotation and/or Scale instead of Position (above). Rotation and Scale each require two Tracking Regions to calculate, called Track Point 1 and 2 (below). If you track Position in addition to Scale and/or Rotation, the Attach Point (the + symbol that defaults to the middle of Track Point 1's Feature Region) becomes the Anchor Point and therefore the center around which the stabilized layer rotates or scales. Footage courtesy Artbeats/Lifestyles: Mixed Cuts.

To move both boxes together, grab them in the middle of the inner box. After you start to move them, the Feature Region will appear magnified 400% to help you see details. To resize the boxes, grab their handles on their respective sides or corners. You will probably find it easiest to hold the Command key on Mac (Control key on Windows) as you drag; otherwise, the other side of the box will automatically move in the opposite direction as you drag, which can cause it to go offscreen. Dragging the Feature Region larger than the Search Region "bumps" the Search Region larger as needed.

Minimizing the size of both the Search and Feature Regions will speed up tracking, but going too small will make After Effects lose the track. Make the Feature Region just large enough to enclose the feature you are tracking, with at least a pixel of contrasting image around the edges. Make the Search Region just big enough to follow the frame-to-frame movement of the object – not how much the feature moves over the entire clip. After the software finds the feature being tracked in a frame, it will update the position of these regions to match the feature's new location. It is a good idea to preview your footage before setting this box so you have a feeling for how much your feature to track will move and change size, and in what direction.

The + symbol that is initially placed in the middle of the Feature Region is called the Attach Point. This point is important when you're tracking, as it says where you want the anchor point of a second layer to be placed when you're finished. It is also important when you're stabilizing position in addition to scale and/or rotation, as this is where the layer's Anchor Point will be placed, becoming the center of the layer's Scale and Rotation. You can move the Attach Point independently of the track regions, if you want to relocate it to a better place to scale and rotate around.

The tracker will default to using the layer's in and out points. Trim the in and out if you plan to use less than the entire clip in this comp; there's no point spending time tracking more of the clip than you'll need. Normally the Layer panel's Time Ruler is the same color as the layer bar in the Timeline panel. When the tracker/stabilizer is active, the Layer panel's Time Ruler will turn gray. Trimming the Ruler's in and out points while this bar is gray will edit the piece of time in the clip you are stabilizing, but will not change the clip's in and out points in the composition's overall timeline.

Back in the Tracker panel, note the Track Type popup: Leave it at Stabilize to perform motion stabilization; the other options are for tracking (the subject of the next

chapter). Beneath it are a set of checkboxes to determine what property you will be stabilizing (or tracking): Position, Rotation, Scale, or any combination of these. To stabilize rotation or scale, you need two points to track, and you will see in the Layer panel two Tracking Regions connected by a line with arrows. The arrow travels from the anchor point to the second reference to decide how much the layer has rotated or scaled. The farther apart these two regions are, the more accurately rotation or scale will be stabilized. Note that you can stabilize rotation in only two dimensions; After Effects' tracker cannot stabilize imagery that appears to tilt in 3D space.

Essential Options

Exploring the Motion Tracker/Stabilizer Options dialog is the secret to getting a good stabilization or track in difficult situations. There is no one setting that works for all situations; you may need to experiment with different settings to see which gives you the best results.

Channel helps give After Effects a better scent to track. If the detail you are tracking has a strong change in brightness compared with its surroundings (such as a white table tennis ball on a dark wall), use Luminance. Luminance is the default, but note that it is not always the best choice! When the difference is more in color than in brightness (for example, a red dot against a green background), use RGB. Saturation is the option you will use the least; it comes in handy for rare cases, such as a bright red tracking point against a dull, rust-colored background.

In the case of [**Ex.01a_starter**], if you were tracking the dark window trim against the white snow of the car's roof, luminance would be your choice. If instead you were to track the orange tag on the blue license plate, RGB may be a better choice.

Process Before Match helps occasionally with some problem footage. If the object being tracked is out of focus and therefore soft, but the footage is otherwise clean, check this box and try the Enhance option – it runs the equivalent of a "sharpen" filter on the layer just during the tracking stage. If the footage is noisy or grainy, use the Blur option (lest a speck of dust or noise gets mistaken for a detail in the image to track).

If the Tracking Region boxes are not visible, verify that the tracker/stabilizer is active by checking the status of the View popup along the bottom of the Layer panel.

When you have problematic tracks or stabilizations, you will need to tweak the Motion Stabilizer Options for best results. The first section to experiment with is Track Options. The Adapt Feature section is also important.

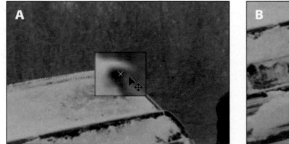

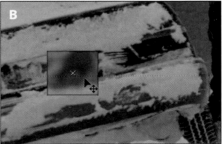

When tracking a detail with a large amount of contrast (A) set Channel to Luminance. When the detail has a different color than its surroundings (B), try setting Channel to RGB instead.

Stabilize, Then Move

There are times when you will want to offset or reanimate a stabilized layer – for example, to remove the effects of a shaky camera move, then reintroduce a smoother one. A universal cure-all is to parent the tracked layer to a null object (Chapter 17), and then transform the null as needed. Or, you can try one of these alternative approaches:

Tweaking Stabilized Position

Stabilize Position animates the Anchor Point, not the Position of a layer. Therefore, you can edit or animate the layer's Position property to recenter or further animate your tracked footage.

Tweaking Stabilized Rotation

After Effects remembers the initial Rotation value of a layer before stabilizing, then keyframes the Rotation parameter as needed to stabilize it (if the 3D Layer switch has been enabled, the Z Rotation value is keyframed). Therefore, it is best to orient your layer before stabilizing. If you forgot, you can enable the 3D Layer switch and use the Orientation property to reorient your layer.

If your source material has interlaced fields (as much video does), and the feature you are tracking has sudden or unpredictable motion, try enabling the Track Fields option to catch this motion. If the feature you are tracking moves slowly and smoothly, try leaving this option off: Your track will run faster, and won't be thrown off by the data interpolated between fields.

You will want to leave Subpixel Positioning enabled 99.9% of the time. When this option is enabled, After Effects attempts to locate the feature being tracked within 1/256th of a pixel. When it is off, After Effects will correct the position of a layer only to whole pixels.

The Adapt Feature On Every Frame option asks "Should I match what this thing looked like on the first frame of the track? Or should I match the most recent frame I just tracked?" If the feature is going to change radically over the course of the track – for example, if the object is coming toward you – then enable it (and make sure your Feature Region is large enough to capture this change in size). Otherwise, disable it, and set the popup below it to Adapt Feature: This will cause After Effects to try to match the look of the initial feature until it is too different to comfortably match (this threshold being set by the If Confidence Is Below number to its right); once the feature has changed too much, After Effects will then adapt to what the feature looked like on the previous frame and use that as a guide for the following frames. This is the combination we use most often.

The rest of the options in the popup below Adapt Feature give After Effects further instructions on what to do if it has trouble matching the feature being tracked. If the feature has changed considerably since the track started (again, the threshold being set by the If Confidence Is Below number  to the right of this popup), the Continue and Stop options decide whether to keep tracking regardless, or to stop so you can inspect what's gone wrong and possibly choose a new Feature Region to track. If the object you are tracking gets obscured by another object during the course of the track (for example, a car temporarily goes behind a utility pole), or the track otherwise seems to randomly jump on a few frames, try the Extrapolate Motion option: This will tell After Effects that if it is not very confident of the feature match on a given frame, it should keep moving in the same direction as the feature was previously moving, then see if it can find that feature again on a subsequent frame.

After Effects notes how accurately it matched the feature it was tracking in each frame; this is the If Confidence Is Below number. The default of 80% is pretty good. If you find After Effects is breaking off the track too often, try lowering this number; if you feel the track isn't tight enough, try raising it. The Confidence values are saved with each track as keyframe values in the Timeline panel after a track, so you can inspect them later.

Track and Apply

Once you have set your Tracking Regions, Options, and the in and out points of the segment of time you want to track, click on the Analyze Forward or Analyze Backward buttons in the Tracker panel (depending on whether you are starting at the beginning or end of your track). You will see After Effects walk through your footage frame by frame, attempting to follow the item highlighted in your Feature Region.

A Closer View

If you're having trouble adjusting the Feature and Search Region boxes around small details in the image, increase the Magnification of the Layer panel.

To initiate a track, click on the appropriate Analyze button in the Tracker panel (above).

After a track is finished, you will see the motion path for the tracked feature in the Layer panel (right).

If you see the Tracking Regions wander off from the feature you are tracking, stop and re-tweak your settings. [**Ex.01a_starter**] is pretty easy to track; if you are having a problem with it, your Feature or Search Regions are probably too large, and After Effects is mistaking a nearby feature (such as another specular highlight) for the feature it is supposed to be tracking. Once the analysis stage is finished, you will see the motion path of your track in the Layer panel.

Once the tracking is finished, you will also find the layer has a new set of keyframes in the Timeline panel: Select the layer and press U to reveal them, or twirl down Motion Trackers > Track Point 1 to reveal all of the parameters associated with the track (see figure, next page).

If you want to try multiple variations of a track, just create a new tracker by clicking on the Track Motion or Stabilize Motion buttons: The first set of keyframes will be preserved, and a new set of Tracking Points will be created for you to experiment with.

Faster in RAM

The analyze step of tracking and stabilization will go much faster if the clip has already been cached into RAM – for example, if you've recently RAM Previewed the footage.

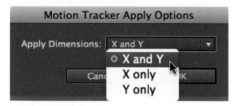

After Effects saves the results of a track or stabilization analysis as a series of parameters and keyframes attached to a layer. You can save multiple tracks per layer. This makes it easy to experiment, check on how accurate the track was (by looking at the Confidence value), and apply a track or stabilization later.

When you click on Apply, After Effects will ask you which dimensions you want to stabilize.

TIP

Track Names

You can rename your individual Tracker data sets, as well as Track Points, in the Timeline panel by selecting them, pressing Return, typing in your new name, and pressing Return again. You can also rename a Tracker in its Options dialog.

When you are ready to apply a stabilization, verify in the Tracker panel that you have the right layer selected under Motion Source, and that you have selected the Tracker data you want to use under Current Track. Then click the Apply button. A dialog will appear asking you if you want to apply both the X and Y dimensions of the track, or just one of the dimensions. Applying a single dimension comes in handy in special situations such as when you want to preserve the original left-to-right (X axis) movement of an object but stabilize its up-and-down (Y axis) movement. In the case of [Ex.01a_starter], use the default of applying both dimensions.

Bring the Comp panel back forward by clicking on its tab. Press U until all of the layer's keyframes are revealed; in our example here where you stabilized just the position, you will see Anchor Point keyframes for the layer. (If you were to track Rotation or Scale, you would see keyframes for these applied as well. Feel free to try this yourself with comp [Ex.01b_position+rotation].)

RAM Preview your stabilized comp and note that the car stays in the same location in the comp's overall frame – although the edges of the footage now wander in relation to the comp (we'll discuss fixes and workarounds for that later).

The cold, hard truth about motion stabilization is that the results are seldom perfect. Don't rely on it for miracles; in some cases, you may have to accept "good enough." In this example, there is some optical distortion caused both by the camera focusing, and the snow passing in front of the camera. This results in the car seeming to shimmer on occasion, even though it is stabilized. Try stabilizing the alternate edit of the car in [Ex.01c_starter]; the greater distance and poorer focus results in a less-stable result. And if the object you're tracking had inherent motion blur, the object would also appear to strangely blur in place even though it appears to be stabilized.

Masking and Motion Stabilization

When you crop footage down to a small feature – such as the head and shoulders of a person for a picture-in-picture effect – wobbles in the camera become more obvious. For example, open and RAM Preview **[Ex.02_mask only]**. This shot employed a handheld camera, and the camera shake results in the head wobbling slightly inside the masked area.

After reading this chapter, you might think "no problem – I'll just stabilize the footage." But because stabilizing animates the Anchor Point, and transforms such as Anchor Point are calculated *after* masks, your mask will bounce along with the person, as demonstrated in **[Ex.02_wobble mask]**. It doesn't matter if you stabilize first or mask first; the render order will remain the same if you use only one comp.

To mask footage that is stabilized, you'll need to use two compositions so you can reverse the default render order. The idea is to stabilize the footage in the first comp and apply the mask in the second comp. If you want some practice:

Step 1: Open **[Ex.02 starter]**, which contains the footage to be stabilized. Consider which feature would be best to use. We tried his watch and then his eye, but realized that as he shifted his body, the wall then moved behind him. In the end, we used a feature on one of the books behind him. After you Analyze and then Apply the Motion Stabilization, this layer's Anchor Point will be animated.

High Tech Crime

The original source movie is stabilized in one comp, then masked in a second comp. Now the mask is unaffected by the Anchor Point keyframes. Edge effects have been added to the picture-in-picture layer, plus a background and title layer. Footage courtesy Artbeats/Business Executives and Digital Aire plus Digital Vision/Electro.

Step 2: Create a new comp **[Ex.02-final]** and nest **[Ex.02 starter]** into it. Now apply a rectangular mask to the head and shoulders.

Step 3: *Optional:* You can also feather the edges or apply a bevel, drop shadow, or other edge effects to finish off the picture-in-picture effect, and add a background movie of your choice.

Our two compositions appear in the folder **[Ex.02-final versions]**.

Broken Tracks

You do not have to track an entire clip with one Tracking Region definition. The best feature to track might change during the course of a shot. Or, you might not have tracked enough of the original shot, and need to add onto a track you've already performed.

If you need to pick up a track in the middle, the most important thing is to not accidentally move the Attach Point: Otherwise, your track or stabilization will have a discontinuous jump in the middle. In case you forget, first save your project to make it easy to revert back to the track's previous state.

Make sure that the clip you need to continue tracking is open in its Layer panel (double-click it if it isn't), and that the Tracker panel is also

FACTOID

Saving Tracks

After Effects saves tracking and stabilization data as keyframes for a layer. You can save multiple sets of tracking data for the same layer, and later apply whichever one you choose.

Stabilizing 103

Time for a more challenging stabilization. Open comp [**Ex.04_starter**] and RAM Preview it. This close-up of a moving peacock was shot at a distance with a handheld camera at high zoom – understandably, it has a good amount of wobble that needs to be removed.

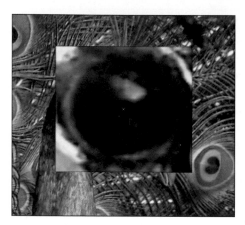

Double-click the layer **HM_peacock1.mov_DV**, open Window > Tracker, click on Stabilize Motion, and enable just Position under Track Type. As for a feature to track, the eyeball of the peacock is an obvious choice. Place your Tracking Region boxes appropriately to track this feature; keep in mind there is a lot of motion from frame to frame, so make your Search Region larger than you did for the previous example. Open the Options, and decide if RGB is the best Channel to track, or if you should try Saturation or Luminance. Turning on Process Before Match and selecting Enhance might also accentuate the edge of the eye socket for tracking; try it if you have trouble getting a good track.

Setting up the Tracking Region around the eye of the peacock – include some of the color outside the eye to get better edges to track. Peacock footage courtesy Harry Marks.

Analyze, Apply, then RAM Preview. Note that the head of the peacock now stays centered in the screen. With the background moving so much, you might experience the optical illusion that your tracked object is moving. Place your cursor over the eye for reference, then preview again to check that the tracked area is indeed stable.

Note that stabilizing this footage requires moving the layer quite a bit – too much to use the "scale up" or "rely on safe areas" solutions suggested in the previous example. In [**Ex.04-final**], we used a track matte to crop down the image to a reliably useable area.

Go ahead and experiment with alternate Tracking Regions. For example, the spurs around the large white region behind the eye are good high-contrast regions. Using the leftmost one will offset the pivot point around which stabilization occurs, which results in less neck movement at the expense of more beak movement after stabilization – perhaps a

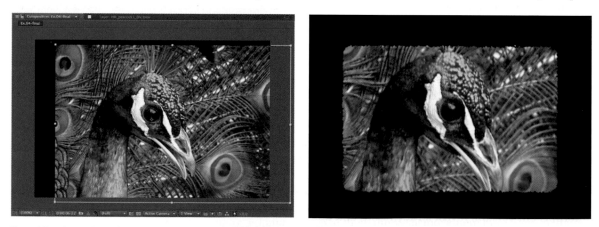

If an object is moving relative to its background and you stabilize the object, the background will usually move out of frame (left). To avoid seeing wandering edges, use a matte to crop the peacock down to a usable, stable region (right).

better trade-off. This is shown in comp [**Ex.04-final_alt**]. The end of the beak, on the other hand, would be a poor choice to stabilize – you don't want the entire head and body pivoting around the end of its beak as it opens and closes!

By the way, this source footage contains fields. Enable Track Fields in the Motion Stabilizer Options and see if this improves your track.

Stabilize Position & Rotation

Comp [**Ex.05_starter**] shows a different perspective on our peacock. Preview it to again note the camera wobble; also note there is a slight rotation, as the right side seems to dip down slightly toward the end. This is a good example to try stabilizing both position and rotation. Lucky for you, a male peacock in display has built-in tracking dots: the "eyes" on its feathers.

Select the layer **HM_peacock2.mov_DV**, open Window > Tracker, and click on Stabilize Motion. This time, enable the Position and Rotation checkboxes. Note that two Track Points now appear. Also note the

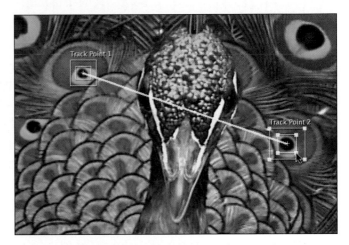

Peacocks, fortunately, have built-in tracking dots on their feathers. Look closely and notice the Tracking Regions around them.

arrow on the line that joins them: The arrow is coming away from the Track Point that surrounds the feature that will be stabilized; the other Track Point determines how much rotation correction is necessary. Select a pair of "eyes" on the feathers to track. Remember that the farther apart they are, the more accurate the rotation will be; the smaller they are, the faster they will track. For example, you might lock onto the two small

eyes to the left and right above its nostrils, but feel free to experiment.

Analyze, Apply, and RAM Preview. Select the layer and press U to note that both the Anchor Point and Rotation are being animated. As you step through the composition, note that the rotation value is changing; you can also see this from the edges of the original layer as they creep into the composition. Again, you can mask this and recenter the layer's position in the comp; just note that After Effects adds an unneeded Position keyframe at the start of the track – remove this so you can change the layer's position at any time in the composition without introducing unwanted animation.

Our peacock after stabilizing Position and Rotation. Note from the outlines of the original layer how it has been rotated to keep the bird stable.

CONNECT

Rotation, orientation, anchor point: Chapter 3.

Subpixel positioning: Chapter 3.

Masking: Chapter 10.

Track mattes: Chapter 11.

Nesting compositions: Chapter 18.

Precomposing: Chapter 19.

Video safe areas: Chapter 41.

Motion Tracking

Motion Tracking allows you to add an object to a scene after it was shot – if you're both lucky and good...

In the last chapter, we covered the core concepts behind using the Motion Tracking and Stabilization engine. In this chapter, we will cover the additional features required to make one layer follow a feature in another layer, making them appear they were originally shot together, or just to coordinate their actions. We have included several realworld examples for you to practice with.

Tracking 101

Everything you learned in the previous chapter relating to Motion Stabilization applies to Motion Tracking (so make sure you read and understand that chapter first). With Stabilization, the inverse of the tracking data is applied to the Anchor Point of the layer you tracked to make it appear stable. With Tracking, the tracking data is usually applied to a second layer, hopefully making that layer move as if it were pinned to a feature in the layer you tracked. With simple tracking, the Position, Rotation, and/or Scale of the second layer is keyframed; with Perspective tracking, a Distort > Corner Pin effect is applied to the second layer, and its corners are keyframed to give it motion. You can also choose to apply the tracking data to an Effect Point of an effect.

Tracking Regions and Attach Point

To practice how this works, open the project **30-Example Project.aep**, and start out by opening comp [**Ex.01_starter**]. It contains some text you want to attach to the head of a wheelchair racer. Select the second layer – **AB_Recreation&Leisure.mov** – as it is the one we want to track.
Step 1: Open Window > Tracker and click Track Motion. Its Layer panel will open, showing a set of Tracking Regions.

Displaying Track Keyframes

Preferences > Display > Motion Path determines how many keyframes you see at any one time in the Comp and Layer panels. If you find your track keyframes "disappearing," select the All Keyframes option; if your display is getting too confusing, choose one of the "No More Than" options.

Example Project

Explore the 30-Example Project.aep file as you read this chapter; references to [Ex.##] refer to specific compositions within the project file.

Ex.01_starter			
0:00:00:00			
#	Source Name		
1	text precomp		
2	AB_Recreation&Leisure.mov		

In [**Ex.01_starter**] you'll track the movie, then attach the **text precomp** layer to it.

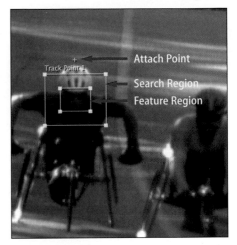

Steps 1–3: To track a layer, select it, open the Tracker, and click Track Motion (left). The Layer panel will open with a set of Tracking Regions, given the default name Track Point 1. Because you'll be tracking in reverse, press O to jump to the out point, and move the regions into place around the feature you wish to track (right). Footage courtesy Artbeats/Recreation & Leisure.

Step 2: Our goal in this example is to track the helmet or face of one of the racers, and place a "thought bubble"(text) above his head. It is easier to track an object as it goes from large to small than to track it going from small to large, and the racers come toward us during the clip – so press O to locate to the out point of the clip before setting up your Feature and Search Regions.

We chose to track the face of the red racer (the sun glinting off the helmet can cause false tracks). Resize the center Feature Region to enclose his face, and set the outer Search Region to be a few pixels larger. Remember that you can hold Command on Mac (Control on Windows) to move the region corners and sides independently of each other.

Step 3: In the middle of the Feature Region you will see a + symbol. This is the Attach Point: the spot that will be used to define the Position value of a second layer (in this case, our text). You might need to pin the second layer onto one particular feature, but another feature in the shot might be better to track. Fortunately, the Attach Point can be moved. For our purposes here, place the Attach Point just above the helmet so that the text will float above the racer's head.

Clicking and dragging somewhere inside the Feature Region but not on the Attach Point itself moves both regions as well as the Attach Point as one unit. Holding Option (Alt) and dragging inside the Feature Region moves both regions while leaving the Attach Point where you put it. Because moving the regions can accidentally move the Attach Point – but not vice versa – get in the habit of setting your Tracking Region(s) first, then placing your Attach Point (as you have here).

Step 4: Click on Options to optimize the tracking process. For this clip, set Channel to RGB, enable Adapt Feature on Every Frame (as he steadily gets smaller), and the popup underneath to Extrapolate Motion. Then click Analyze Backward in the Tracker, and see if the track looks acceptable. (If not, undo, tweak the Feature Region or Options, and try again.)

TIP

Adjust Separately

Option+dragging (Alt+dragging) inside the Tracking Regions moves them without moving the Attach Point; Command+drag (Control+drag) the corners to selectively reshape the regions. Dragging the Attach Point does not move the Tracking Regions.

TIP

TrackerViz

There are numerous scripts available to enhance the power of the After Effects Tracker. One of the best is TrackerViz: *aescripts.com/trackerviz*

Step 4: After setting up the Tracking Regions, Attach Point, and Options, click Analyze Backward to perform the track.

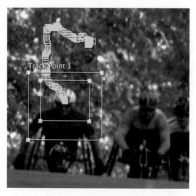

Step 5: After you finish tracking, you will see the motion path for your track in the Layer panel (above). Choose which layer to attach this motion to by clicking Edit Target (below). Then click Apply, and accept both X and Y dimensions.

After applying your track, bring the Comp panel forward again (above): The track data will now be the motion path for the chosen layer. In the Timeline panel (right), the layer being tracked will have keyframes which store the tracking data, while the layer being attached has its Position animated.

Step 5:   If you realize you set up the Attach Point in the wrong place after you performed the track, you can fix it using the Motion Trackers > Tracker 1 > Track Point 1 > Attach Point Offset parameter. This offset is used only when you click Apply (which you'll do next); it does not fix the motion path after you've already applied it.

Once you're satisfied you have a good track, click on Edit Target in the Tracker panel. It defaults to the layer above the one you are tracking (which is what we want in this case); you can change that default here. Click OK, then click Apply. As with stabilization, you have the option to apply either or both of the X and Y dimensions; use the default of both, and click OK. Bring the Comp panel back forward, and RAM Preview. The text and pointer will now follow the red racer's head.

Step 6:   We did some work for you ahead of time by moving the Anchor Point of **text precomp** to the bottom of the pointer. By doing so, when you attached this layer the text already appeared to float above the head, with the pointer starting where you placed the Attach Point. But you may not always be thinking this far ahead.

There are a couple of ways to tweak the results after you've applied the tracker. Select the layer that has had the track applied to it (**text precomp**, in this case) and press U to reveal its keyframes. Click on Position to select all of the keyframes, and make sure the time indicator is parked on one of them (the keyframe navigator box will have a check mark in it). Use the cursor keys to nudge the layer directly in the Comp panel. You can also offset the Anchor Point of the tracked layer to change its relationship to the master layer it follows, which is particularly useful if you need to change the center around which it scales and rotates. (For bonus points, animate the Anchor Point in this example to keep the thought bubble a more consistent distance above his helmet throughout the shot.)

The object you attach using the motion tracking data can have its own animation – especially if that layer is a precomp. In [**Ex.01-final**], we animated the text in a precomp to come on while the racer was getting up to speed.

Tracking Scale and Rotation

You can track properties other than Position; you will notice there are checkboxes for Rotation and Scale as well. You can select any combination of these three properties. As was the case with stabilization, tracking rotation or scale requires having two features to track: One serves as the anchor point, while the other is used as a reference to decide how much the object has rotated or scaled.

To practice tracking scale, open [**Ex.02a_starter**] and RAM Preview. The camera zooms in on the motorcycle; you want the text to zoom by the same amount. In the Tracker, select **CM_motorcycle_zoom** in the Motion Source popup, click Track Motion, and verify Track Type is set to Transform. Below this popup, enable Scale, then disable Position.

As the cycle zooms toward you, it's better to start this track at the end, where the features to track will be their largest. Press O to go to the trimmed end of the clip, and pick two features to track that are as far apart as possible – we chose the front reflector and the rear taillight. Inside the Tracker Options, enable Adapt Feature on Every Frame so After Effects can keep up with the scale changes in the Feature Regions. Then click on Analyze Backward. Note that the track does not need to be perfect; we're just trying to get the Scale close.

Verify that the Motion Target is set to the text layer **terrorize your neighbors**, then click Apply. RAM Preview: The type should scale up as the camera zooms in on the bike, as it does in [**Ex.02a-final**].

Tracking Rotation or Scale requires setting up two track points to analyze.

To track scale changes in a layer, select this property in the Tracker (left) and set up two Tracker Regions. In [**Ex.02a-final**], we made the scale of a text layer follow a camera's zoom on this motorcycle (above, left and right).

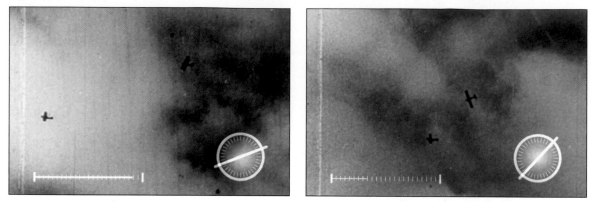

In **[Ex.02b]**, we tracked scale and rotation to animate a pair of control panel elements that measure how far apart the two planes are as well as the angle between them. Footage courtesy Artbeats/Early Flight.

Next, open [Ex.02b_starter]. We've used shape layers (covered in Chapter 32) to build a control panel element, and we want to track the two dogfighting airplanes in the shot to control the rotation of the horizontal bar.

Select **AB_EarlyFlight** and click Track Motion in the Tracker. Enable Rotation, then disable Position. Set up the two track points over the two airplanes in the shot. As the planes change perspective throughout the shot, we made the Feature Regions a touch larger than normal and set the Tracker Options to Adapt Feature On Every Frame.

After you analyze the track, make sure the Motion Target is set to **Shape Layer 1 – level**, then apply the track. RAM Preview the result. Our version is in [Ex.02b-final]; we added a second indicator to show how far apart the planes were. Try it yourself using [Ex.02b_starter 2] and tracking scale to apply to **Shape Layer 3 – distance**.

Effect Track

The Motion Tracker also allows you to have an Effect Point – such as the center of Distort > Bulge – follow a feature of the layer you are tracking. First apply the effect you want to the layer, then use the Tracker.

To practice this, open **[Ex.03_starter]** where Bulge has been applied to our hapless peacock from the previous chapter. Track the peacock's eyeball using what you learned in **[Ex.01]**, placing the Attach Point at the center of the eye. After analyzing, click on Edit Target, and select Effect Point Control instead of Layer for the Apply Motion To option. Note that its popup will already be set to Bulge/Bulge Center (if you have multiple valid effects, you can choose between them here). Click OK, then Apply, choosing both dimensions. Bring the Comp panel forward and RAM Preview the result. Check out **[Ex.03-final]** to compare your work.

Motion Tracking can also apply to effect points, such as having the center of a Bulge track this peacock's eye. Experiment with this for yourself in **[Ex.03]**. Peacock courtesy Harry Marks.

Realworld Examples

Every motion tracking case is different; that's why it is better to work through some actual examples. Here are three examples of projects you could expect to be asked to do.

Multipart Track

Open [Ex.04_starter] and RAM Preview. In this shot, the camera pans down from the cymbal to the snare drum, then back up again. The client has an idea that some text should follow this motion. The problem is, no one feature to track stays in frame for the entire shot! You have three choices: talk the client out of his idea, hand-keyframe portions of the animation, or find another feature in the shot to continue tracking. Let's try the third option.

In [**Ex.04_starter**], you'll need to track the movie in two parts. Applying the track to a null object which serves as a parent for the text layer will make it easy to reposition the text.

Step 1: Since we're not sure yet where the text is going to go, first create a Layer > New > Null Object to apply your track results to; you can parent the text to it and offset it later.

Step 2: Select the layer **LS_hi-hat_snare.mov**, make sure the Tracker panel is open, and click Track Motion. The Layer panel will open and Track Point 1 will appear. Study the first three or so seconds of the shot, looking for something to track. The top of hi-hat cymbal won't work, as it's moving while the camera is stationary; however, there's a green glint lower down the cymbal stand that looks like a possibility.

Press Home to make sure you start at the beginning of the clip. Center the Feature Region over the glint you identified. Make the Search Region a bit taller than its default to capture the camera's fast movement.

Your Friend, the Null

Many advanced users prefer to initially apply the result of a track to a Null Object. You can later attach the real layer to the null using parenting, offsetting the layer as needed. Get in the habit of adding a Layer > New > Null Object to your comp before starting a track.

Step 2: Set the initial Feature Region around the glint on the cymbal stand. Footage courtesy Lee Stranahan.

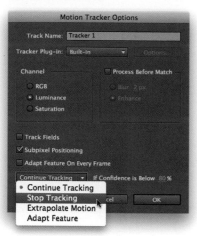

Step 3: Set the Motion Tracker Options to Stop Tracking when After Effects can no longer follow this glint.

TIP

Averaging Tracks

You can use expressions to average together multiple tracks. For the Position of the "follower" layer, inside parentheses add together the Attach Point values of the tracks you want to average (use the pick whip to select them), then divide the total by the number of tracks you are averaging: **(track1 + track2) / 2**.

Steps 5–6: After the green glint goes off screen, hold down Option (Alt) and adjust the Track Point to pick up another feature (right). Analyze Forward again, and the track will continue with this new feature (far right).

Step 3: Open the Tracker Options. Set Channel to Luminance (which should work fine for the glint) and set the popup at the bottom to Stop Tracking when it can't find the feature it's tracking. Disable Adapt Feature on Every Frame – the feature stays the same size throughout this shot.

Step 4: Click Analyze Forward. If the analysis stops before the glint goes out of frame, your Search Region is too small; undo, make it larger, and try again. If the analysis continues after the glint goes out of frame (a known weakness in the tracker), press any key to stop the analysis.

Step 5: Scrub the current time indicator back in time while watching the Layer panel, until you pick up the last good track frame. Now study the image for another feature to track, such as some of the chrome glints lower down the stand.

The secret to continuing a track with a new feature is to hold down the Option (Alt) key while adjusting the Track Point. This will leave the Attach Point (the + symbol) in its current position. You will see the track motion path extending from the old track keyframes to your new position. Once you have set the new Feature and Search Regions, click Analyze Forward again. The same tips apply about the analysis stopping too soon or too late.

Step 6: Scrub the current time indicator to the last good track point before the original green glint reappears in the frame. *Hold down Option (Alt)*, and adjust the Track Point again to pick up the green glint. Click Analyze Forward one last time to finish the track.

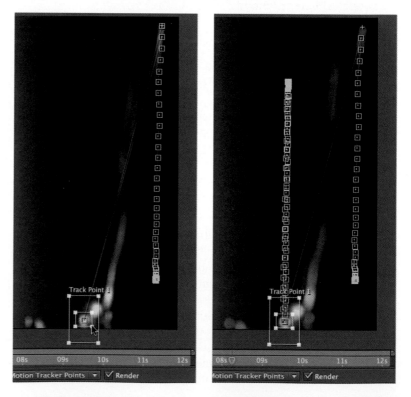

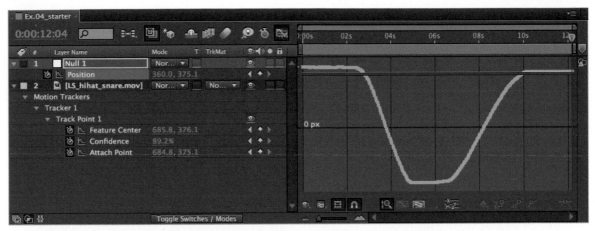

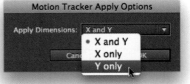

Step 7: To apply your resulting track, click Edit Target and make sure your null object is selected. Click Apply and think about Apply Dimensions for a second: If all you want to keep from this track is the up/down movement and not any incidental left/right movement, set the Apply Dimensions popup to Y Only before clicking OK.

Step 7: When you apply the track, choose Y Only (below) to get just the up and down movement. The result is a lot of keyframes, with some jitter (above).

Step 8: The cymbal stand was also vibrating a lot during the shot; since this is a case in which the general move is more important than a precise track, you could artificially smooth them: Select the null's Position keyframes, open Window > Smoother (Chapter 5), and click Apply.

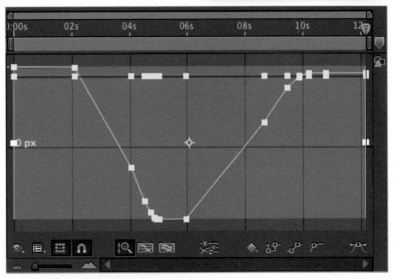

Step 8: To reduce the number of keyframes, you can apply the Smoother keyframe assistant (above) to greatly simplify the Position path (right).

Step 9: Finish this example by creating some text of your own and parenting it to your null to have it follow the camera's motion. Remember that you can also add further animation to your text. In [**Ex.04-final**], we added some keyframes to make the text return to the picture after it gets carried out of the frame.

Motion Blur

One of the secrets to making motion tracked objects work in a scene – particularly when there is a lot of movement – is to use Motion Blur. Most footage of moving objects captured on film or video exhibit motion blur; you will need to have After Effects add blur to objects tracking a feature in your footage to make it appear as if they were shot at the same time.

To add this blur to your objects, enable the Motion Blur switch for the "applied to" layer, turn on the Enable Motion Blur switch in the Timeline panel, and RAM Preview to see if it helps. The Motion Blur Shutter Angle has a large effect on how well it works: too much angle, and the object will seem to over-shoot its movements, even if the shot was tracked perfectly. You can change this in Composition > Composition Settings under the Advanced tab.

If you need this angle to be different for every other layer in the rest of your comps, consider using the Distort > Transform Effect for your movement. It has its own shutter angle, which can override the program's default. Copy and paste your Anchor Point, Position, and/or Rotation keyframes from the normal layer properties into the Transform effect's properties. Of course, remember to go back and delete the original keyframes and reset their values to a good starting point, or else you will get twice the motion.

Each composition also has its own motion blur shutter angle setting, so another method for getting different motion blur values per layer is to select the tracked layer and the layer that's following it, Layer > Pre-compose, then set the desired motion blur shutter angle in the precomp.

Note that Motion Blur often may not work as well when you use one of the Corner Pin options. This is because Motion Blur is only looking to the Position keyframes to decide how to blur the layer, but the layer itself is being "moved" by a combination of Position and the Corner Pin effect. You may need to manually keyframe a blur effect to get the best final result.

A common use for Corner Pin tracking is to paste a new message on a sign. In this example, because no tracking dots were provided, you would try tracking the corners, or use a planar track such as mocha (Chapter 31). You would also need to mask around the fingers in a shot such as this. Faux footage from Digital Vision's Blank Message.

Corner Pin Choices

As we mentioned earlier, there are also two Corner Pin tracking options, found under the Track Type popup. These add the Perspective > Corner Pin effect to the second layer, and create keyframes for the corners based on the Attach Points as well as Position keyframes for roughly the center of what is being tracked.

In the next couple of pages, we offer a pair of examples you can work through to practice corner pinning with the tracker. But first, we need to define the difference between Affine and Perspective pinning.

Normally, you will want to use Perspective Corner Pin, which tracks all four corners and does whatever is necessary to fit your new layer over your tracked points, including bending it into all manners of trapezoidal shapes. By contrast, Parallel Corner Pin keeps the opposing sides of the pinned layer parallel to each other, resizing and skewing the layer only as needed – akin to using a shear or skew tool in Illustrator or Photoshop. To accomplish this, only three of the four corners are tracked, as the fourth corner has to be calculated in a way to keep the sides parallel. Use this option only if the layer is not supposed to take on an angled, perspective look.

Close your previous comps before moving on.

Tracking with Dots

For motion tracking jobs, you really want to consider placing tracking dots on the object to be tracked – even if the object is a 3D render. Many 3D programs can now export their camera data for use in After Effects (discussed in Chapter 40), but for those that don't, you can still use this tracking trick.

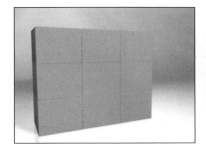

In [**Ex.05_starter**], we rendered a 3D videowall box on a virtual stage with a simple camera move around it. The face of the wall was left blank so we could apply different movies later in After Effects; this renders much faster than having to render the video directly in the 3D application. To make this easier, we rendered a second pass in 3D, with virtual table tennis balls stuck on each corner of the face of the box. This technique gives us a far cleaner set of features to track than trying to follow the corners of a gray box against a gray backdrop. If you are doing a live shoot with a motion control camera that can automatically perform the exact same move over and over, you might consider shooting a separate take for just the tracking dots; this will come in handy as any other activity (such as an actress walking across a stage) might obscure the dots during the shot.

Select the layer **CM_stagedots** (layer 3), and click on Track Motion in the Tracker panel. Set the Track Type popup to Perspective Corner Pin; you should now see four Tracking Regions in the Layer panel. The order of the regions is very important! Place Track Point 1 on the upper left dot, 2 on the upper right, 3 on the lower left, and 4 on the lower right – otherwise, the wrong corners will be pinned.

You can leave the Attach Points at their default positions of centered in their respective Feature Regions. As you adjust each Feature Region, place the X icon in the middle of the dot. Where you place these points is where the corners of your video will be pinned. Check the Options (Luminance is an obvious choice for Channel; you can leave Adapt Feature off), and click Analyze Forward. Click on Edit Target and choose **AB_EstablishmentsUrban.mov** as the target layer, click OK, and then click Apply. Bring the Comp panel forward and RAM Preview: The movie layer will now be pinned onto the videowall front.

The final trick in a job like this is to clean up the edges. Most motion tracks still end up with some jitter, which gives the game away – particularly as the edges wander in relation to their frame. Layer 1, **CM_stageface.mov**, is a matte for just where your tracked image is supposed to end up. To use it, set the TrkMat popup for layer 2,

A virtual stage rendered in 3D (left), along with virtual tracking dots that were placed on the corners of the box and rendered as a second pass (right). This is a good technique to use with real sets and motion control cameras as well.

*Select Perspective Corner Pin for Track Type (above); set Motion Target to **AB_EstablishmentsUrban.mov**. Then center each Tracking Region over its respective dots, centering the crosshair in the dots (below).*

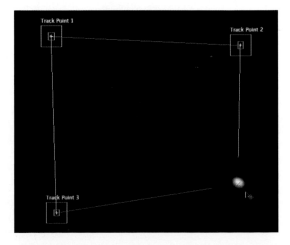

After tracking the dots, the video is perfectly pinned onto the front of our virtual videowall (A). To clean up the edges, we rendered a separate 3D pass of just the front face of the wall (B) and used that as a track matte for the video, as shown in **[Ex.05-final]**. We also used a Hard Light blending mode to allow the creases and shadows of the wall to show through the video. Footage courtesy Artbeats/Establishments: Urban.

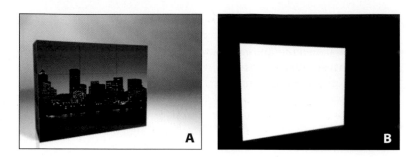

AB_EstablishmentsUrban.mov, to Luma Matte, as we did in [**Ex.05-final**]. Of course, in 3D, it's easy to render a separate high-contrast pass of just the face that is supposed to receive the tracked image; on a video shoot, perhaps paint this surface green or blue and key it later as your matte. In either case, set your Attach Points slightly outside the area where the image will get matted to so you have some spill to crop off.

A Challenging Replacement

A common motion tracking task, from corny in-house videos to serious feature films, is to replace a sign or billboard in a shot with something more appropriate to the storyline. This requires using the Perspective Corner Pin option for the tracker.

In comp [**Ex.06_starter**], we have a rather challenging example for you: motion tracking an interlaced DV NTSC shot of a street sign in France we want replaced. Problem is, it's a handheld shot (lots of wobble), and the camera also zooms out – so the features we want to track change over the course of the shot.

This shot of the sign changes from a close-up to a zoom-back, adding to our challenge. (By the way, the reason the sun and shadow patterns are so strange on the wall is that this was taken during a solar eclipse, turning the gaps between a tree's leaves into numerous pinhole cameras.) Footage courtesy Kevin Dole.

Fortunately, the sign practically has tracking dots built in: the blue dots of paint in its corners. The sign corners are also fair game, though the sunlight patterns occasionally wash them out in contrast to the pale wall.

The biggest challenge is the camera pullback during the shot, because this means the size of the features we want to track is going to change during the track. You can try tracking the shot in multiple segments (such as before, during, and after the pullback), enabling Adapt Feature On Every Frame, or leave Adapt off and set the popup below it to Adapt Feature.

3D Tracking

After Effects can track in 2D only. It fakes 3D perspective by using the Corner Pin effect to distort the layer that is being applied on top of another. However, there are applications that can track a scene and derive 3D movement information from it. On the high end is Boujou from 2d3 (*www.2d3.com*), which can transfer this info directly to After Effects through a plug-in it provides. Another popular (and much more affordable) tracker is SynthEyes by Andersson Technologies LLC (*www.ssontech.com*). SynthEyes can export a Maya ASCII (.ma) format file, which contains 3D camera data that can be imported by After Effects. See Chapter 40 for more on integrating with 3D programs.

While you're in the Motion Tracker Options, you may consider enabling the Track Fields option. However, the upper and lower fields of deinterlaced video interpolate into slightly different images from each other, which can confuse a highly adaptive track. To see for yourself, try this track with and without the field option checked, and render an interlaced movie for playback. You will have other decisions to make, such as whether to try either of the Process Before Match options, and whether to set the Channel to RGB or Luminance.

Expect to need to make several attempts before you get an acceptable result! Don't forget you can save multiple track attempts per layer, and to set the Attach Points just beyond the outer corners of the sign (so that it will be completely covered by the new sign). If you become exasperated, consider hand-tracking the sign by manually keyframing the Corner Pin effect – or learn mocha for After Effects, which is discussed in the next chapter.

After you have successfully tracked the old sign and corner-pinned on our new one (which says "Your Name Here" in French), you might notice it looks a bit flat and artificial. The unspoken second half of every motion tracking job is making the new object look like it actually belongs in the original scene.

For clues, look at the sign on the original video clip. Notice it has some thickness and a shadow where it does not mount perfectly flush against the wall. Perhaps it would be best to simulate these in the new sign. Try a couple of the Perspective effects, such as Bevel Alpha and Drop Shadow. Eyedropper colors from the original scene and adjust intensities to help improve the blend. A little blur might help as well, to match the camera focus. Our attempt is included as [**Ex.06-final**]. As you can see, there's no one answer to making a tracking shot "work." But start to view these tasks with an artist's eye, and it will be easier to solve their puzzles.

In addition to setting up the Tracking Regions, think about where to place the Attach Points. The exact corners of the sign might not be a good idea, as the color of the sign bleeds into its surroundings (a result of both the focus and the color undersampling inherent in DV). Remember to set the Attach Points out far enough that your new sign will cover this bleed.

Our improved version of this shot is in [**Ex.06-final**] and includes Bevel Alpha and Drop Shadow to help make the new sign look more real. Place them before the Corner Pin effect so they get the same perspective distortion as the shot animates. Good luck trying to duplicate the lighting effects…

CONNECT

Anchor point: Chapter 3.

Motion blur, which helps match an object with the natural camera blur in the original shot: Chapter 8.

Blending modes: Chapter 9.

Track mattes: Chapter 11.

Animating effects: Chapter 22.

Setting up the motion tracker/stabilizer engine: Chapter 29.

mocha: Chapter 31.

Integrating 3D renders with After Effects: Chapter 40.

mocha

Advanced motion tracking using mocha for After Effects plus mocha shape.

Step 1: mocha will fill out the settings in the New Project dialog based on the clip you import. Be sure to set the frame rate and field order options before clicking OK.

Example Project

Explore the 31-Example Project.aep file as you read this chapter; references to [Ex.##] refer to specific compositions within the project file.

After Effects CS4 and CS5 come with a powerful third-party motion tracking system: mocha for After Effects. Rather than tracking individual points, with mocha you define a "plane" – a flat surface with obvious features – for it to follow, often yielding better results. From this, mocha can create transform or corner pin data as well as mattes that may be exported for use in After Effects. After Effects CS5 also comes with the mocha shape effect, which makes it easier to transfer complex mattes from mocha into After Effects.

mocha for After Effects is a deep, versatile application. It comes with an 80-plus page Quick Start guide accessed by pressing F1 while in mocha; also, Imagineer Systems hosts helpful video tutorials on its website (*www.imagineersystems.com/support/mocha/tutorials/*). The intention of this chapter is to get you up to speed quickly and to demonstrate some good working practices for using mocha.

Perspective Tracking with mocha

We'll start where the previous chapter left off: tracking and replacing a sign shot with a handheld camera. The steps include creating a mocha project, tracking an object, refining the track, and transferring the corner pin data to After Effects.

Preparing a Project

The first trick is finding mocha for After Effects: It's a stand-alone application inside the **Adobe After Effects CS5 > mocha** folder. To make it easier to find in the future, you may want to create an alias, Dock, or Start item for it. Launch mocha now.

If you have not yet registered mocha, you will be asked to do so. The start-up screen then has two options: View Manual and Start. Click Start.

Step 1: Select File > New Project. A dialog that requires you to make some important decisions will open:

• In the New Project dialog, click Choose to the right of the Import Clip box. Select **31-mocha > 31_Chapter Sources > KD_streetsign_DV.mov**.

• mocha will fill out the Project information below based on the clip you choose. It defaults to naming the project after the clip and saving

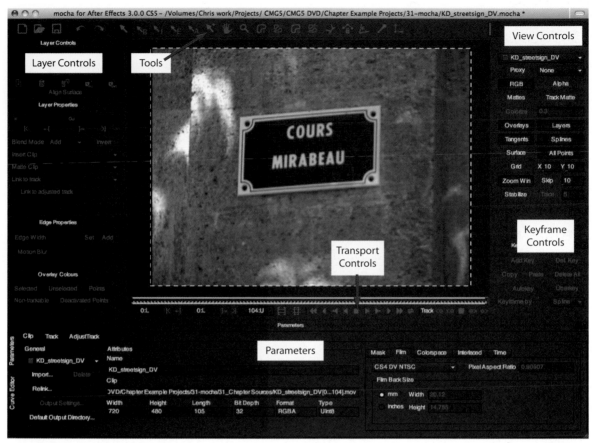

the project file alongside the clip. Change the Project > Location to a location you prefer.

- mocha will detect the frame rate from a movie file. If you're importing an image sequence, it is crucial that you enter a Frame Rate in the Options tab that equals the footage's rate in your After Effects composition.

- For this clip, set the Separate Fields popup to Lower Field First.

Click OK when done. (If you get an error message saying you don't have permission to save the project inside the clip's location, select Save Project As and save in a different location.)

Step 2:   Select the Clip tab along the bottom. A yellow dashed outline will appear around the clip. Drag these borders to crop off any junk that may surround the clip (so as not to throw off tracks that go off screen). You can also click on the Mask tab along the right side of the Clip section to manually crop the clip. For this clip, set the left and right values to 4.

Explore the other tabs and fields inside the Clip panel. Note that you can change other clip parameters such as frame rate or pixel aspect ratio (but not the field order) at any time, even if you missed them when importing the clip.

mocha's user interface is divided into a series of panels that may be resized and rearranged, similar to After Effects (mocha's equivalent of workspaces appear under View > Layout).

With Layout 1 at its original settings, the clip is in the center with transport controls underneath; panels relating to the tracking layers are along the left; View options and Keyframe Controls are along the right; Parameters tabs to modify the Clip and the Track and to Adjust Track (along with a Curve Editor for keyframed values) are along the bottom; a toolbar is along the top.

Hovering the cursor over the icons and most parameters reveals helpful tooltips. Footage courtesy Kevin Dole.

Step 3: Scrub the small black current time indicator to find a good representative frame to start the track from.

Step 4: Use the Create X-Spline Layer tool (above) to create a loose mask around features on the same plane to track (right). The length of the blue handles determines the sharpness of the bend. mocha displays a Zoom Window for the point you are editing; you can disable this in the View Controls panel.

Excluding Regions

Spline shapes may be used to define areas you don't want mocha to track, such as a person walking in front of a sign, a hand that moves in front of a data screen, et cetera. If you draw multiple splines on the same layer, the area where they overlap will be excluded. It is also common to draw exclusion splines on a separate layer above the layer you wish to track; disable the Tracking switch – the gear icon – for these exclusion layers. In either case, the splines may be keyframed to follow moving objects.

Performing a Track

Step 3: Just as with the normal After Effects tracker, mocha can track forward or backward from a reference frame. It is best to choose a frame in which the area to track is clear, unobscured, and large. Drag the small black current time indicator along the timeline to scrub through the footage; anywhere in the first half of this clip will work. For simplicity, we'll start at frame 0.

Step 4: Next is defining which portion of the image mocha is to track. Rather than precisely placing track regions, with mocha you draw a loose mask around a flat, relatively unobscured section of the object. You may use Bezier splines (similar to drawing mask shapes in After Effects), but many prefer mocha's X-Splines, especially for organic shapes.

For this tutorial, select the Create X-Spline Layer tool. Click four points comfortably outside the edges of the sign. (You could draw around just a portion of the sign, but the more unobscured image on the same plane that you give mocha, the better.) To close the path, either click on the first point, or right-click anywhere. Click and drag points to reposition them; drag the ends of the blue tension handles to alter the curve of the spline near that point. Although not necessary with this clip, you can use the Add X-Spline or Add Bezier Spline tools (to the right of their normal counterparts) to draw multiple shapes on the same layer. This will give mocha more areas to track. If needed, splines may be keyframed to encompass new regions to track while regions are obscured or go off screen.

When you create a spline, a new layer will be created for you automatically. Rename it to suit in the Layer Controls panel in the upper left corner of the user interface.

Step 5: The Track panel in the Parameters section along the bottom of the user interface is where you set up tracking options. The defaults are good; if you are tracking a larger area that has a strong perspective shift during the shot, also enable Motion > Perspective. If the area is small, in low detail, or there is minimal perspective shift, leave Perspective off.

Underneath the timeline you'll find a series of buttons; the rightmost one is the Track Forwards button (hover over a button to see its tooltip). Click on the Track Forwards button; mocha will automatically search each frame for the region you defined with your spline(s). When done, you can either manually scrub the time indicator or press the spacebar to preview the track (press the spacebar again to stop). mocha typically does an excellent job on the first attempt; if your track wanders excessively, undo and try tracking a different region.

Step 5: Click Track Forwards to perform the track. If you started from a point other than the first frame, after the track is finished move the time indicator to that starting frame and click Track Backwards.

The track's motion path does not appear by default; to reveal it, enable both the Surface and Trace options in View Controls. However, the preferred way of working is not to edit the track, but to offset the track only as needed. We'll tackle that in the next few steps.

Step 6: To define the area you wish to corner pin a new graphic to, enable Surface under View Controls along the right. Move the time indicator to the start of the clip where the sign is the largest and use the Zoom tool to zoom in if necessary. (If you don't see the spline handles or the Surface corners, reselect Layer 1 under Layer Controls.) Select the Pick tool (it looks like a Selection tool), then drag the corners of the blue Surface outline to just enclose the sign plus any color bleed or shadow. These corners are the equivalent of your Attach Points.

Step 6: Enable Surface (top), select the Pick tool, and drag the corners of the blue Surface rectangle to just enclose the sign (above). If you don't see the blue Surface corners, reselect Layer 1 under Layer Controls. If you don't see the helpful Zoom Window, enable it in View Controls.

Step 7: Enable View Controls > Grid, which will help you check if your corners are forming a proper rectangle in perspective. Increase the X and Y settings to the right of Grid to 12 to better align with the edges of this sign. Tweak your Surface corners as needed for the grid to align with the sign.

Step 8: To check your proposed new sign in context, make sure your tracking layer is still selected under Layer Controls, then click on the menu to the right of Layer Properties > Insert Clip. Here you may select between a variety of grids or the mocha logo to stand in for your new sign, or import your own image.

Select Import, navigate to **31_Chapter Sources**, choose **VotreNomici.tif**, and click Open. You don't need to worry about the Import Clip Wizard settings for this simple still, so click Next twice then Finish. (If you see just the sign and not the original footage, re-select the clip **KD_streetsign_DV** from the popup just under the header View Controls.)

Preview your track to see how well it works. You can turn off View Controls > Grid, Surface, and Layers if you find them distracting.

Step 7: The Grid helps you align your Surface corners and check the integrity of your track.

mochaImport

Mathias Möhl has created a very useful shareware script and set of tutorials to help automate common workflows using mocha for After Effects: visit *aescripts.com/mochaimport/*.

Perfecting the Track

At this point, you should have a pretty good track; enable Grid and scrub the time indicator through the timeline to verify how accurate the track is. If you're satisfied, you can jump straight to the section *Exporting to After Effects*. If you're not, you can adjust the track – but be careful that you don't make it worse! Indeed, it's a good idea to save your mocha project now in case you want to revert back to this pre-adjust stage. For clarity, select Layer 1, set Insert Clip back to None, and optionally re-enable the Grid.

Step 9: In AdjustTrack mode, define your Master Frame by dragging the red markers to good reference points near your original Surface corners.

Step 10: If you see that your reference point has drifted from its position on the Master Frame (above), you can either manually drag them or use the Nudge section of the AdjustTrack panel (right) to select which reference corner you are editing (the brown brackets) and to adjust its position.

Step 9: Move the time indicator to the latest point in time where the track looks correct (the frame where you started the track is always correct). This will be the master reference frame for your adjustments.

Select the AdjustTrack tab in the Parameters section along the bottom. You will see four red crosses at the corners of your Surface rectangle. Drag these to nearby, sharp reference areas in the underlying footage, such as the corners of the blue outline stroke in the original sign. mocha will use these points as references to help you adjust the track.

Step 10: Choose one of the corners, and make sure View Controls > Zoom Window is visible. Slowly drag the time indicator while watching the Current Frame display, comparing it with the Master Frame. If you detect drift, stop and click the Auto button in the center of the AdjustTrack > Nudge section. This will create a keyframe (a green marker) in the timeline. If this does not properly recenter your reference point, you can use the Up/Right/Down/Left nudge buttons or manually drag the reference point as needed. To confirm you aren't making things worse, make sure the grid still aligns well with the sign.

Repeat this procedure as needed for the other corners. Double-check your work between keyframes, keeping in mind that more keyframes increase the chances of unwanted jitter in your final track – which can look worse than the drift did! Use the Keyframe Controls to the right of the timeline to delete unwanted keyframes. Return to the Track tab when done.

Exporting to After Effects

Next you'll export your track to After Effects. (Feel free to use our project to perform these last steps using our track. Double-click the file **31-mocha > 31-streetsign-finished.mocha** to open it in mocha for After Effects CS5. If you see a warning message that the associated clip could not be found, click OK. In the next dialog, click on the brown folder icon and navigate to the clip **31-mocha > 31-Chapter Sources > KD_street-sign_DV.mov**. Then click Finish.)

Step 11: To export your tracking data, make sure your tracking layer is selected under Layer Controls (our layer is called **sign track**), and choose File > Export Tracking Data (or, click on the button by the same name on the right side of the Track panel). In the dialog that appears, set the Format popup to After Effects Corner Pin (*.txt) [supports motion blur]. Then click Copy to Clipboard. Alternately, you can click Save to store your tracking data in a text file, which you could then later copy and paste into After Effects.

Step 12: If you haven't already, open **31-Example Project.aep**. Then open the comp [**Ex.01_starter**], which contains copies of the clip you tracked plus your new sign.

Step 13: Select the new sign layer – **VotreNomici.tif** – and Paste. Press U: You will see that the Corner Pin effect plus numerous keyframes have been applied to this layer.

Step 14: As the sign and tracked footage have different sizes, their initial positions do not line up after pasting. To cure this, press A to reveal its Anchor Point, and carefully scrub its coordinates until your new sign covers the original.

RAM Preview, and mentally compare this with your result at the end of Chapter 30; chances are good that the mocha track is better. As before, you can finish this off by applying a bevel and drop shadow, plus enabling Motion Blur as we have in [**Ex.01-finished**]. For best results, the motion blur's Shutter Angle (set in Composition Settings > Advanced) should match the shutter angle used by the camera.

 TIP

Editing Values

By default, scrubbing values in mocha works differently than in After Effects: Rather than dragging left and right, you drag in a circle as if turning a dial. If this drives you crazy, open Preferences > System and change the setting under UI Look and Feel from Rotational to Linear Controls.

TIP

Pinning Already Positioned Graphics

If the new graphic you wish to corner pin has already been saved presized and transformed to match the first frame of the tracked footage, skip the steps for resizing the Surface. Instead, right-click the tracked layer in mocha and select Reset Layer Surface before you export.

Step 14: After pasting, the new sign will not line up with the old (below left); scrub its Anchor Point values to line them back up. Use effects plus Motion Blur to yield a more realistic composite (below right).

The plan in this second exercise is to track the center of the sunflowers in mocha (left) and to use this information to colorize them in After Effects (right). Footage courtesy Kevin Dole.

No Splines?

If you don't see your shape splines in mocha, chances are you accidentally deselected the layer – reselect it in the Layer Controls panel. Another possibility is that the layer has been trimmed shorter than the clip; check the in and out values immediately underneath the Layer Properties header. Finally, make sure the Track tab is selected in the Properties section.

Step 2: The Layer Controls includes two tracking layers with their visibilities turned off.

Mattes with mocha shape

A significant addition to After Effects CS5 is the inclusion of the mocha shape effect. This allows you to use splines to define shapes inside mocha and paste them onto layers in After Effects, controlled by a plug-in effect. These shapes may be different from your tracking Surface, and offer features such as the ability to define a different feathering amount for each spline vertex. They may also be animated beyond following a motion track. In the following exercise, we'll use mocha shape to create a simple matte to help color correct a moving region in a video clip – but the same techniques may be used for far more advanced applications, including tracking-assisted rotoscoping.

Creating a Shape

Step 1: Double-click the file **31-mocha > 31-sunflowers_starter.mocha** to open it in mocha for After Effects CS5. When the first screen of the Open Project Wizard appears, click Next. If you see a warning message that the associated clip could not be found, click on the brown folder icon near the bottom of this second screen and select the clip **31-mocha > 31-Chapter Sources > KD_Sunflowers1_DV.mov**. Then click Finish.

We've already performed loose tracks of the centers of a pair of sunflowers that pan past the camera. As color correcting a region of footage is often less critical than sign replacement or other motion tracking assignments, we didn't spend too much time perfecting the tracks, but we did have to make sure we tracked the center of the head rather than the entire flower. The petals and outer portions of a head are on different planes than the raised center; the resulting parallax means the center drifts in relation to its surrounding petals during the course of the shot.

Step 2: Two tracking layers should be visible in the Layer Controls panel in the upper left (with their visibilities turned off); if not, make sure the Track tab is forward under Parameters along the bottom and/or increase the height of the mocha application window. Move the current time indicator to around frame 60:L, where the right sunflower is centered in the shot.

Step 3: Select either the X-Spline or Bezier tool, and draw a spline shape following the intermediate ring of the sunflower head. This will create a new layer. Spend a few moments smoothing out the profile of the shape; sharp corners will result in spikes later when you feather it. If you are not happy with the position or size of the spline, the three rightmost tools along the top may be used to rotate, scale, and move the entire shape (if you find only one point is moving, double-click the layer name and try again).

Step 4: Click twice on your new layer in the Layer Controls panel and rename it "**R Head Shape**". Make sure it is selected when you're done; this will also select all of its vertices.

Step 5: Locate the Edge Properties panel (underneath Layer Properties in the default layout). Set Edge Width to around 35, and click Set: This will set the feather amount for all selected vertices to this value.

Step 6: Since the sunflower head is not perfectly symmetrical, you will need to alter the location of this outer edge spline. Select the Pick tool and then the Move Edge Points tool (the arrow with an E). Hover over a handle until the move tool appears, then right-click and choose the Selection > Select All in Spline from the contextual menu. With the move tool still visible, drag the outer edge spline downward to better capture the rest of the flower head. You may also edit vertices individually.

Step 7: Enable View Controls > Mattes and disable Colorize to test how your shape matte looks.

Step 3: Draw a spline shape to encompass the center of the sunflower head. With no individual point selected, you can use the Rotate, Scale, and Transform tools along the top to alter the spline as a whole.

Steps 5–6: Use Edge Properties > Edge Width (inset) to set an initial wide feather for all of the vertices. Then use the Move Edge Points tool (circled in the toolbar) to move the outer spline to properly encompass the rest of the head.

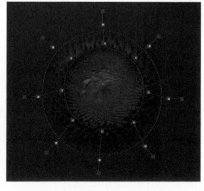

Step 7: Temporarily enable Mattes and disable Colorize to preview your shape matte.

Step 8: Link your shape layer to follow its corresponding tracking layer.

Step 9: If your outer spline shape drifts away from the edge of the sunflower head (A), use the Move Edge Points tool to adjust it (B). With Autokey enabled, your adjustment keyframes (the green markers in the timeline) will be placed automatically (below).

Linking a Shape to a Track

Step 8: Make sure **R Head Shape** is selected in the Layer Controls. Then under Layer Properties, change the Link To Track popup to R Head Track. This will make your shape follow the track we previously performed, complete with shearing and transformations.

Step 9: Disable View Controls > Mattes to get a better look at the underlying footage, and scrub the current time indicator to see how well the track works. The outer edge of your shape will probably appear to drift near the start or end of the track; this is partially caused by looking at the raised sunflower head from the side.

With Keyframe Controls > Autokey enabled (the default), go to the earliest and latest frames where you can still see a portion of the head (such as 0:L and 118:U). Adjust the outer edge vertices as needed using the Move Edge Points tool you employed in Step 6. (If both inner and outer vertices move together, Undo, select another tool, reselect Move Edge Points, and try again.) Keyframes will be placed automatically, and the outer edge shape will interpolate between these keys. Disable View Controls > Zoom Win if these displays get in your way.

Exporting Shape Data to After Effects

The final part of the process is transferring the shape data from mocha to the mocha shape effect in After Effects.

Step 10: Once you're finished tweaking your splines, Save your project. With the layer R Head Shape selected, choose File > Export Shape Data. (A corresponding button also exists in the Track panel.) In the Export Shape Data dialog that appears, choose the Export option Selected Layer, and click Copy to Clipboard.

Step 11: Return to After Effects project file **31-Example Project.aep**. Open the comp [**Ex.02_starter**].

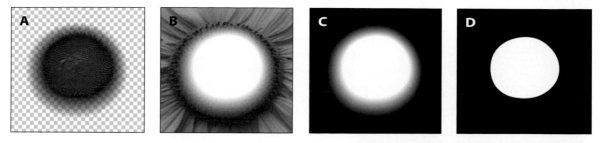

Step 12: Select the layer **KD_Sunflowers1_DV.mov** and duplicate it. Select the copy on top and Paste. Press F3 to reveal its Effect Controls panel: A copy of the mocha shape plug-in – automatically renamed **R Head Shape** to match the name of your shape layer in mocha – will be applied.

Experiment with the different options for the Render Type popup and the Render Edge Width checkbox; you can see how mocha shape can be used either to create a matte, or to "mask" the layer it is applied to. When applying effects that alter the alpha channel of an image after mocha shape, you may want to use a copy of the layer with mocha shape applied as a track matte (Chapter 11), and then apply your additional effects to a copy of the original layer underneath.

The Blend Mode popup comes into play when you have more than one copy of mocha shape applied to a layer: It controls how these multiple copies interact. Normally, the effect on top is set to Multiply, and additional shape effects underneath are set to Add. Or, you can duplicate the original layer, and apply one instance of mocha shape to each layer (as we have in [**Ex.02-finished_2**]).

As you will be applying a simple color correction effect to one shape, set Blend Mode to Multiply, Render Edge Width to On, and Render Type set to Shape Cutout (the defaults).

Step 13: Apply Effect > Color Correction > Hue/Saturation (or any other effect of your choosing) to the layer on top. Scrub Master Hue to change the color of the center of the sunflower's head.

Step 14: RAM Preview to check your result.

Our results are shown in [**Ex.02-finished_1**]. For a final challenge, create and export the shape for the left sunflower as well. Our versions are contained in the mocha project **31-sunflowers-finished.mocha** and the After Effects comp [**Ex.02-finished_2**].

Although mocha is initially daunting to learn, we hope these two exercises have shown you some of the power it contains and have helped get you over that steep first step in its learning curve. Again, we encourage you to take advantage of the numerous resources Imagineer Systems (*www.imagineersystems.com*) offers, including videos, an online FAQ, and the Quick Start manual installed with After Effects.

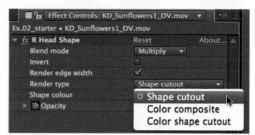

Step 12: mocha shape (above) has several options for how it renders the resulting shape matte (A–C above), including the ability to ignore the per-vertex feathering (D).

Step 13: The center of the sunflower head on the right has been tracked and colorized using mocha for After Effects CS5 plus mocha shape (the head on the left is untreated).

CONNECT

Masking: Chapter 10.

Precomposing: Chapter 19.

Motion tracking and stabilization in After Effects: Chapters 29 and 30.

Interlacing: Chapter 41.

Special thanks to Martin Brennand and Ross Shain of Imagineer Systems for their assistance.

32

Shape Layers

These new vector-based layers open a multitude of graphic possibilities.

Shape layers can create anything from simple lower thirds to full-blown cartoons. They are particularly strong at creating graphical elements and abstract backgrounds akin to the Shape Presets shown here.

Shape layers are one of the most versatile graphic creation tools inside After Effects. Shapes may be created using simple primitives, the Pen tool, or copied from masks as well as other programs. They can be cleanly scaled to any size, as well as filled and stroked with solid, semi-transparent, or gradient colors. A single layer can contain multiple individual shapes which can be grouped, merged, and intersected in a number of ways. They can be modified using a large selection of shape effects, including the Repeater which quickly creates grids and constellations of shapes. And of course, shapes – including most of their parameters – may be animated; some shape effects auto-animate as well.

Explaining all that can be done with shapes is akin to describing what you can do with a pencil. In this chapter we aspire to acquaint you with the basics of creating, combining, and modifying shapes. Our focus will be on creating graphical elements; those who are familiar with Adobe Illustrator or have a cel animation background will quickly see that the possibilities go far beyond what we can cover in these few pages.

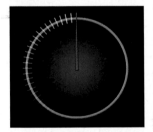

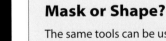

Mask or Shape?

The same tools can be used to create shape layers as well as mask out portions of any layer. So how does After Effects know which it is you want to do? By following these rules:

• If no layer is selected, After Effects assumes you want to create a shape.

• If a non-shape layer is selected, After Effects assumes you want to create a mask.

• If a shape layer is selected, the Tool Creates switches determine whether the Shape and Pen tools will create a mask or a new shape path.

Example Project

Explore the 32-Example Project.aep file as you read this chapter; references to [Ex.##] refer to specific compositions within the project file.

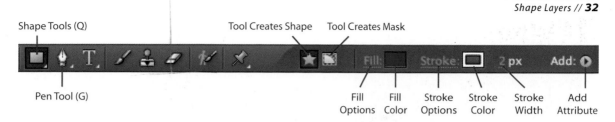

Shape Tools (Q)   Tool Creates Shape   Tool Creates Mask

Pen Tool (G)

Fill Options | Fill Color | Stroke Options | Stroke Color | Stroke Width | Add Attribute

Shape Tool Overview

Before we start creating shapes, first let's quickly review what the various Shape tools and options do. Open **32-Example Project.aep** followed by the comp [**Ex.01_starter**] and make the following adjustments and explorations:

Shape tools: The former Rectangle and Ellipse mask tools were replaced in After Effects CS3 with a longer menu of core "parametric" shapes. You can edit and animate several aspects of these shapes. Choose the Star tool for now, as it has the most parameters to play with.

Pen tool: The same tool you used to draw mask, motion, and graph editor paths can also be used to draw shapes. We'll use it later; leave it unselected for now.

Fill Options: Here you decide if the fill is enabled or disabled and whether the fill is a solid color or a gradient. You can also set the blending mode and opacity for the fill. Click on the word Fill and choose a type of Solid Color, Normal mode, and 100% Opacity. To cycle through the Fill or Stroke type options without having to open their respective dialogs, press Option on Mac (Alt on Windows) and click on the Fill or Stroke color in the Tools panel.

Shape Fill Color: Click on this swatch to open a standard color picker; choose any color you like for now. If you set the fill type to gradient, a gradient editor will appear instead.

Stroke Options: You have the same options for strokes as you do for fills. We will discuss Stroke and Fill operators in much greater detail later in this chapter; for now select a Solid Color type, Normal mode, and 100% Opacity.

Shape Stroke Color: Click on this swatch to open a color picker, just as for Shape Fill Color. Change it to white for now.

Stroke Width: You have great control over the appearance of strokes. For now, set the width to 2.0 pixels.

Add: This menu allows you to add attributes to a shape layer; it is grayed out if a shape layer is not currently selected. An identical menu appears for a shape layer's Contents in the Timeline panel.

When you select the Shape or Pen tool, additional options for Fill and Stroke appear to their right in the Tools panel (above). Click on the Shape tools icon to reveal the basic parametric shapes (below).

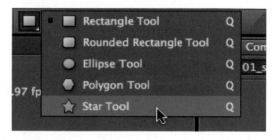

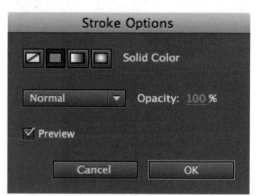

Both Fill and Stroke allow you to choose between solid colors and gradients (above). You can also use blending modes to mix together colors and shapes. Solid colors use the standard Adobe color picker (below); gradients employ an expanded dialog we'll discuss later.

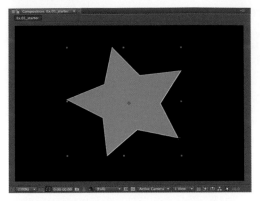

With any Shape tool selected (and no other layer currently selected), click and drag in the Comp panel to create a parametric shape.

Simple stars can quickly evolve into more complex shapes (above) by manipulating Polystar Path 1's parameters (right).

Creating Parametric Shapes

Assuming you've opened [**Ex.01_starter**] and selected the Star tool, click in the middle of the Comp panel and drag: A star shape will be drawn from the center out as you drag (see figure to the left). Release the mouse and turn your attention to the Timeline panel: **Shape Layer 1** will appear, twirled open to reveal the shape group Contents > Polystar 1. Contents is a master group that contains however many shape groups you may have added to a layer.

Twirl open Polystar 1 so we can study the hierarchy of a shape layer. (By the way, it's called a "polystar" because this same shape path operator can be used to create polygons or stars.) A basic shape group typically consists of a shape path, Stroke and Fill operators, and a set of Transform properties.

Now twirl open Polystar Path 1: A lot of flexibility is contained inside this deceptively simple shape. For example, scrub the Inner and Outer Roundness values to create some interesting pinched or looping shapes; you can create sunbursts by increasing the number of Points. Add Inner and Outer Radius to the mix to create shapes that resemble flowers with rayed petals.

Transformations

Each shape group has its own set of transform properties. It is important to understand the difference between the transform properties for a shape path, a shape group, and a shape layer:

• Parametric shapes have simple transform properties of their own. To reveal the transforms for this shape path, twirl open Polystar Path 1. The polystar path's initial Rotation reflects where your mouse was released when you dragged out the shape. Its local position defaults to 0,0. Note that it has no Scale property – just its parametric dimensions (Inner and Outer Radius). Editing a parametric shape's parameters will not change the thickness of its Stroke. Shape paths also do not have their own Opacity.

Parametric shape paths have their own Position and (optionally) Rotation parameters, which are separate from the shape group's Transform parameters below. The entire shape layer also has its own set of transforms (the last line for the layer in the Timeline panel).

- To reveal the transform properties for your initial shape group, twirl open Transform: Polystar 1. The group's initial Position equals the center of the shape path you created in relation to the center of the comp. To center your shape, set the group's transform (Transform: Polystar 1) to 0,0. Note that in addition to the normal transform properties such as Scale and Opacity, you also have Skew. If you add multiple shape paths to a group (we'll get to that shortly), the group's transform affects all of these paths as if they were a single complex shape.

- The shape layer's main Transform section (which exists outside of the shape layer's Contents) is just like the transform properties you're used to for any other layer.

Centering Shapes

To center an existing shape in the comp, set the group's transform (Transform: Polystar 1 for example) to Position 0,0.

When you drag out a new shape path for a layer, a new shape group is created for it (above). Each group has its own visibility switch, Transform properties, and Fill plus Stroke.

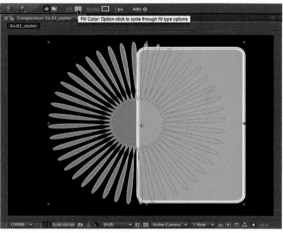

Multiple Shapes

Twirl up Polystar 1 to simplify the Timeline panel.

With **Shape Layer 1** still selected, choose a different Shape tool such as the Rounded Rectangle (Q is the shortcut to cycle between these tools). Click and drag in the Comp panel to add your second shape to this layer. In the Timeline panel, note that a second shape group called Rectangle 1 has been added: *Whenever you add a new shape path by dragging or drawing in the Comp panel, a new shape group will be created – even if an existing shape group was already selected.*

Each shape group has its own visibility switch (the eyeball icon). (Other attributes inside the group – such as the Path, Stroke, and Fill – have their own switches as well.) You can also reorder which shapes draw on top of which by dragging one above the other in the Timeline panel.

Twirl open Rectangle 1, and you will see that it has its own Path, Stroke, Fill, and Transform. Twirl open Rectangle Path 1: Note that as with your star, it defaults to a local Position of 0,0. It has no Rotation parameter of its own; to rotate it, use Transform: Rectangle 1 > Rotation.

With both shape paths visible in the Comp panel, select one of them by selecting its group in the Timeline panel. (You can also press V to return to the Selection tool and double-click its shape in the Comp panel.) Then change its Fill or Stroke Color: Note the other one keeps its original color. This is but a taste of the power behind individually grouping shape paths; we will discuss managing multiple shapes later.

Shape Presets

Select Browse Presets from the Effects & Presets Options menu; when Bridge opens, look inside the Shapes folder. Download hundreds more presets for free from *share.studio.adobe.com*.

Expressive Shapes

The expression pick whip (Chapter 37) may be used to link together mask paths, paint strokes, and shapes that were created with the Pen tool. Parametric shape paths cannot be pasted or expressed to other path types.

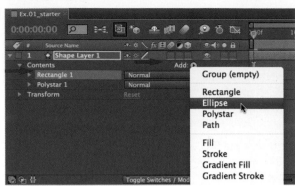

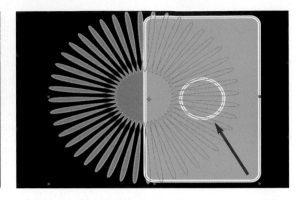

To add a path to an existing group, select the target group and use the Add menu (above). It will be added to the center of the existing shape group (above right).

If you find yourself distracted by the thin line outlining your shape, disable the Toggle Mask and Shape Path Visibility button along the bottom left of the Comp panel (above).

What if you want to have multiple paths take on the same color and transformations? First select the group (such as Rectangle 1), then click on the arrow next to Add in either the Timeline or Tools panels, selecting a new parametric shape such as Ellipse. A circle will be added to the center (as defined by the group's Transform > Position) of the selected shape group. It will have the same fill and stroke color as the original path in this group, although it may be smaller and therefore enclosed by the original shape (see figure above).

Note that if you select the word Content or the overall layer instead of an existing shape group, you will create a new shape group (not add a path to an existing group) when you click the Add arrow.

Have fun creating multiple shape paths, groups, and layers; feel free to delete or turn off the visibility of previously created shapes. Be sure to twirl open the parameters for the different parametric shape path types such as Rectangle and Ellipse and play with these values as well.

Shaping as You Drag

While dragging out a parametric shape in the Comp panel, you can press the following keys *before releasing the mouse* to alter some of the shape paths:

Shape type	up/down cursor keys	left/right cursor keys	page up/down
rounded rectangle	corner roundness	toggle rectangle/ellipse	
polygon	number of sides	outer roundness	
star	number of points	outer roundness	inner roundness

You can also change the outer radius of the Star by pressing Command on Mac (Control on Windows) when dragging to create a shape.

If you have a mouse with a scroll wheel, it will have the same action as the up and down cursor keys. You can also reposition any parametric shape before releasing the mouse by holding the spacebar and dragging. These helpers can be used while drawing mask paths as well.

Pen Path Shapes

The weaknesses of the parametric shape paths you've been playing with so far is that there is a limited number of them, and they're always symmetrical. If you want to create freeform shapes and paths, you're better off using the Pen tool. Fortunately, virtually everything you've learned in other chapters about using the Pen tool to create masks and motion paths can be applied to shape layers as well.

Open [**Ex.02_starter**] and select the Pen tool. Set the Stroke and Fill Options and Colors as you like; uncheck the RotoBezier option for your initial experiments. Click and drag in the Comp panel to pull out a Bezier handle for your first point. As you click and drag your second point, the line between these vertices will be stroked, and the area "enclosed" by this still-open path will be filled with your chosen color. When you want to close off the path, hover the pen cursor over your first point; a circle will appear next to the base of the cursor. Click (and optionally drag, to control the Bezier handles) on this last point to seal the deal.

Twirl open **Shape Layer 1**, then Contents, then Shape 1 to reveal the contents of this group. Path 1 is the Bezier path you just drew, followed by the same Stroke, Fill, and group Transform attributes you're now familiar with from parametric shapes. If you twirl open Transform: Shape 1, you will note that its default Position is 0,0; the position of a pen-based shape path relative to its group and layer are determined by the location of its vertices in the Comp panel. Indeed, twirl open Path 1 and you will see no parameters other than an animation stopwatch for Path.

Editing Pen Shapes

To edit your shape, press V to switch to the Selection tool and make sure the Toggle Mask and Shape Path Visibility button is enabled along the bottom left of the Comp panel. If Path 1 (but not Path) is selected in the Timeline panel, you should see vertex squares along the path. Click on one to select it (the hollow square turns solid when selected); this also reveals the Bezier handles for that vertex as well as the adjacent vertices. Editing individual points is simple:

- To move a vertex, drag it or use the cursor keys.

- To alter the path between vertices, drag the Bezier handles or click on the line segment and drag to reshape.

- To toggle between a "corner" point (no handles) and a Bezier point, hold Command+Option (Control+Alt) to get the Convert Vertex tool and click on a vertex.

- To break the Bezier handles and move them independently, hold Command+Option (Control+Alt) and drag a handle.

- To delete a vertex, press and hold down G (to temporarily switch to the Pen tool) and click on the vertex.

- To add a vertex, hold down G and click on the path between vertices.

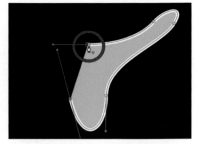

Click and drag to create vertices and extend the Bezier handles for these corners. To close a shape, click on the first point you drew – a special cursor with an "O" at its base will confirm you're about to close a path.

TIP

RotoBezier Paths

When the Pen tool is selected, the RotoBezier option appears to the right along the Tools panel. RotoBezier paths do not have Bezier handles – instead, After Effects automatically calculates a smooth path between vertices. Drawing RotoBezier paths was discussed in Chapter 10.

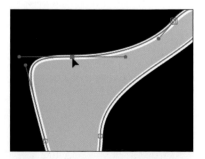

Click on an individual vertex to edit it. To enter this mode, either click on Path 1 in the Timeline panel (clicking on Path selects all points) or double-click the shape to select the group, then select an individual point.

Transforming Shapes

There are three methods for transforming a shape in the Comp panel. With the Selection tool active, press F2 to Deselect All, then:

- Click once on the shape; colored layer boundary handles appear with *no connecting line*, and only the name of the layer is selected in the Timeline. Move, scale, or rotate the shape in the Comp panel and note how this affects the layer's overall Transform properties.

- Double-click the shape in the Comp panel; *a dotted line connects the handles*, and the shape group is selected in the Timeline. (You can also select a group's Transform property in the Timeline directly.) Transforming the shape in this mode affects the group's Transform properties. Press and hold down Y to move the group's anchor point when in this mode. (From this mode you can also select an individual vertex in a Pen path for editing.)

- Double-click a Pen path in the Comp panel; *a solid white line will connect its handles*. This is Free Transform mode; transforming in this mode affects the path rather than any transform properties. You can also enter this mode directly *by selecting the Path property in the Timeline* and pressing Command+T (Control+T). Press Enter to exit this mode.

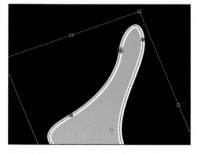

To transform a Pen path shape as a unit, double-click the path (not the shape's filled area) to enter Free Transform mode. (If you see *dotted lines* connecting the boxes, the shape group is selected, but you're not in Free Transform mode. The *Transforming Shapes* sidebar above discusses these modes.)

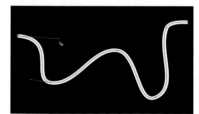

To draw an open path shape, set the Fill type to None (right), then draw your path in the Comp panel without bothering to close it (above).

Free Transform Points

Shapes can also be altered as a group. Double-click on a freeform path (one created with the Pen tool) and handles connected by *a solid white line* will appear. This is Free Transform mode: Drag on any of these boxes to stretch and squish the shape; the rotate cursor appears when you hover along the white line. To change the center around which the shape is rotated, drag the crosshair icon that defaults to the middle of the shape. To also Scale around this point, press Command (Control) as you drag the handles. To exit free transform mode, press Enter.

Go ahead and alter your shape. Click on the stopwatch for Path 1 > Path to enable keyframing, press End, and alter it again. Press 0 on the numeric keypad to RAM Preview your shape path animation. Feel free to practice creating other shapes with the Pen tool.

Open Paths

Not all shapes need to enclose a space – you can also create open paths to use as strokes, map lines, and other graphical elements.

Open [**Ex.03_starter**] and select the Pen tool. Click on the word Fill to open its Options and select a type of None (or press Option (Alt) and click on the Fill Color swatch until it changes into an empty box with a red slash). Now draw your path in the Comp panel. When you've drawn your last point, rather than clicking on the first point to close the path, press V to switch back to the Selection tool. With this path still selected, feel free to alter its Stroke color and size. Unfortunately, you cannot vary the width of the stroke over its path.

Stroke Over Fill Over Stroke

We're going to devote the next few pages to some of the options available in the Fill and Stroke operators. We'll start with the question of whether the fill is on top of the stroke, or underneath it. Open [**Ex.04_starter**] and choose one of the Shape tools (we'll use Rounded Rectangle). Open the Fill Options, set its type to Solid Color, and set the Opacity to 50%. In Stroke Options set the type to Solid Color and the Opacity to 100%. Choose different colors for Fill and Stroke, and set Stroke Width to a generous number such as 12 pixels.

Drag out a shape in the Comp panel. For new shapes, the default is stroke over fill. Twirl down **Shape Layer 1** > Rectangle 1 (or whatever shape type you created) in the Timeline panel and confirm that the Stroke 1 operator appears above Fill 1. Reorder these by dragging Fill 1 above Stroke 1: In the Comp panel, the fill now partially overlaps the stroke; since the fill is partially transparent, you can also see the stroke through the fill.

You can have multiple strokes and fills in the same group. Make sure the group header Rectangle 1 is selected, click on the arrow next to Add in the Timeline panel and select Stroke – a second Stroke will be added above the existing Stroke and Fill

operators. Twirl open Stroke 2 and change its Color to be different from your current fill and stroke, keeping its Stroke Width lower than Stroke 1's: You will now see a narrower stroke inset on top of the first stroke. We have set this up in [**Ex.04-final**] (see figure, left).

Gradients

When motion graphics artists hear the word "gradients" they often visualize boring business presentations. But gradients can be used in far more subtle and interesting ways.

Open composition [**Ex.05_starter**] which contains a rounded rectangle already placed over some footage in a typical lower third position. Select **Shape Layer 1** and click on the word Fill in the Tools panel to open its Options: We're currently using a Solid Color fill type with Opacity set to 75%. Select the Linear Gradient fill type and click OK. The fill will change to a gradient, still partially transparent.

In the Timeline panel, twirl open **Shape Layer 1** > Contents > Rectangle 1 > Gradient Fill 1. Make sure the Selection tool is active, and select Gradient Fill 1. In the Comp panel you will see a pair of dots joined by a thin line (see figures on the next page): These denote the gradient's overall start and end points. Drag these dots to extend over the horizontal length of the bar; you can also scrub their Start and End Point values in the Timeline panel.

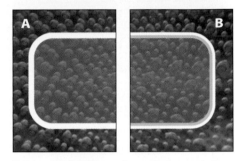

The default order is stroke over fill (above and A).

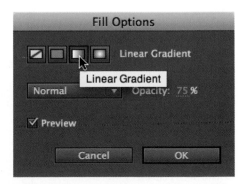

You can set the fill over the stroke by reordering them in the Timeline panel (below); the fill's Opacity being set to 50% makes it more obvious (B). Background courtesy Artbeats/Digital Web.

TIP

Shape Blending Modes

Each Stroke and Fill operator has its own blending mode popup, as does each group.

In Fill Options, set the fill type to Linear Gradient.

Select Gradient Fill in the Timeline (left) and edit the Start and End Points of the gradient either in the Timeline or in the Comp panel (above). Footage from Artbeats/Business World.

To edit the gradient's colors, either click on the Fill Color swatch in the Tools panel or on the words Edit Gradient in the Timeline panel. The Gradient Editor will open. The bottom portion looks like an ordinary color picker, but the top contains a bar with pointers ("stops") that determine what happens along the gradient. The opacity stops are on top, with the color stops underneath.

In the Gradient Editor, the points ("stops") along the top of the bar determine opacity along the gradient, while the pointers along the bottom determine color.

Start by selecting the bottom left pointer – the first Color Stop – and choose a new color in the picker below. Assuming you have the Preview switch enabled, the Comp panel will update while you work. To add a new color, click just underneath the bar (a finger icon will appear) to create a new stop. You can slide this stop or numerically edit its Location value below.

Turn your attention to the Opacity Stops above the bar. Click on the stop in the upper right and set the Opacity value (below the bar, to the left) to 0% to have the fill fade out completely. Then drag the leftmost Opacity Stop to the right so that the fade does not start until somewhere around the middle. (Note that the fill's maximum opacity is still being determined by the Fill 1 > Opacity parameter!) Click OK when you're done.

Strokes can have their own gradients; try it out here, having the stroke fade out toward the right as well. Also experiment with editing the gradient Start and End Points to create a vertical gradient and fade, as we have in [Ex.05-final] (see figure to the left).

Note: If you place Gradient Fill or Stroke outside of a shape group, their user interface elements for Start and End Point will disappear in the Comp panel. Make sure they are enclosed inside a group with the shape paths they are coloring. Also make sure the Selection tool (V) is active.

[Ex.05-final]: We edited the gradient's direction, added Layer Styles, and then parented the text layer to the shape layer so we could move them as a group.

Corners and Caps

Strokes can be customized in a few different ways. Open comp [**Ex.06_starter**] which contains a sharp-edged crosshair. Twirl open **Shape Layer 1** > Polystar 1 > Stroke 1 and focus your attention on the Line Cap and Line Join parameters. Line Join defaults to Miter Join, which results in a pointed corner here; if the corner angle was more severe or the Miter Limit was reduced, it would change to a bevel. Change the Line Join popup to Bevel Join, and the corners take on a bevel at all angles. Try Round Join; now they are rounded.

The way stroke lines end and form corners ("cap" and "join") can be altered (left) to create softer or harder shapes (above). Footage courtesy Artbeats/Business Executives.

Press Shift+F2 so you can see how the line elements end without being obscured by the selection box. Change the Line Cap popup to Round Cap and press Shift+F2 again; they will be subtly rounded. Projecting Cap squares them up again, but now they extend slightly beyond the ends of the original lines.

Dashed Lines

Another significant feature is the ability to convert a stroke into a dotted or dashed line. Open [**Ex.07_starter**] where we've already created a map route using a shape layer that employs a stroked open pen path. Twirl open **Shape Layer 1** > Contents > Shape 1 > Stroke 1. Click on the + symbol to the right of Dashes in Stroke 1: The line will become segmented in the Comp panel, and Dashes will twirl open in the Timeline panel revealing Dash and Offset parameters. Scrub the Dash value to change the length of the dashes as well as the spacing in-between.

Want independent control over the length of the dashes and the length of the spaces? Click the + symbol again: A Gap parameter will appear; scrub it to taste. Click + two more times, and now you have control over an alternating pattern of two pairs of dashes and gaps. (Click the – symbol if you got carried away and created too many segments!)

Set the Line Cap popup to Rounded Cap: The dash segments will get longer as rounding is added to their ends. Set one Dash value to 0, and you will have alternating dashes and dots (as we've created in [**Ex.07-final**]). The Offset parameter can be used to choose where in this pattern the line starts; animate Offset to move the line along the path.

Clicking on the + symbol in Stroke > Dashes (above) adds alternating Dash and Gap segments, which are then repeated for the length of the stroke (below). To animate the "drawing on" of a stroke, use the Trim Paths operator (discussed later in this chapter). Map from Duruy's *History of the World* published in 1898.

Intersections and Holes

When you have two shape paths that overlap inside the same group, you have some control over how the fill is drawn without having to resort to a Merge Paths operator.

Open **[Ex.08_starter]** which already contains a star with its Roundness values cranked up to create a looping symbol. Twirl open **Shape Layer 1** > Contents and select Polystar 1, then Add > Ellipse:

You will initially see the stroked outline of this circle, but that's it. Twirl open Fill 1 and change the Fill Rule from its default Non-Zero Winding to Even-Odd, and now Ellipse Path 1 will punch a hole out of Polystar Path 1. Twirl open Ellipse Path 1 and scrub its size larger; the Fill Rule popup continues to determine whether the center is punched out. Its effect may change with other combinations of shape paths.

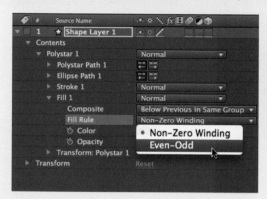

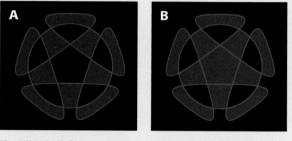

The Fill Rule (left) has an effect on how shape paths in the same group interact. In general, Even-Odd (A) creates more holes at intersections than Non-Zero Winding (B).

TIP

Quick Grouping

To group selected shapes, press Command+G on Mac (Control+G on Windows). To ungroup selected shapes, add the Shift key: Command+Shift+G (Control+Shift+G).

GOTCHA

Invisible Attributes

If you add a shape path, fill, or stroke and it is not immediately visible, chances are you either did not add it into the intended group, or it landed in a place where it will not render (such as after the group's fill and stroke). Just drag it into its desired location in the attribute stack.

Managing Multiple Shapes

Creating multiple shape paths as part of the same shape layer has many advantages over creating multiple layers. For example, you can divide shape paths among groups to give them the same or different stroke and fill treatments. The Merge Paths operator gives additional control to craft more complex composite shapes out of individual component paths.

Each shape group usually has its own Stroke, Fill, and Transform attributes. When you add shape paths to a group, they take on the group's attributes.

To see this in action, close the other comps and open **[Ex.09_starter]** which contains three parametric shapes we dragged out in the Comp panel. Each time a shape path is added in this fashion, a new shape group is created. You can clearly see we gave each a different fill and stroke; if you like, double-click a shape to select it independently and change its Stroke and Fill Colors from the Tools panel. What's less obvious is that we also altered the Transform values of each shape group: In particular, the location where we created the shape path determined the initial Transform > Position value for that group.

Now let's add a shape path to an existing group. Twirl open **Shape Layer 1** > Contents and select one of the Polystar shape groups. Select Add > Rectangle: The selected shape group will twirl open, and Rectangle

Comp **[Ex.09_starter]** contains three shape groups. We selected one of the shape groups and used the Add menu to add another shape path to it – in this case, a Rectangle Path was added to the group Polystar 1 (above and below).

Drag Rectangle 1 into another shape group, and it will take on the color and transformations of that group (above). Make sure you position the path above the group's Stroke and Fill (below), or it will not be visible!

Path 1 will be added to it. (If you didn't select an existing group, then a new group will be created instead; undo and try again.)

Twirl open another Polystar group, and drag Rectangle Path 1 into that group below its Polystar Path but above its Stroke. The rectangle will change position, color, size, and angle as it takes on the attributes of its new group.

You can combine multiple shape paths and fills in the same group. For example, drag Rectangle Path 1 after Fill 1 – it will disappear, as it is no longer getting stroked or filled inside this group. With its group selected, use Add > Fill and drag this new Fill 2 below Rectangle Path 1: The rectangle will reappear behind this group's star. Twirl open Fill 2 and use it to give the rectangle its own color. Select both Rectangle Path 1 and Fill 2 and drag them just above this group's Polystar Path – now the Rectangle will appear on top, still with its own fill color. Change the blending mode popup for Fill 2 to alter how the rectangle blends with the star underneath.

You can combine multiple shape paths and fills inside the same group (above); this means the paths will still use the exact same transformations including Position (left). Note that you can also rename virtually any shape attribute, which is helpful for keeping shape paths straight in more complex layers.

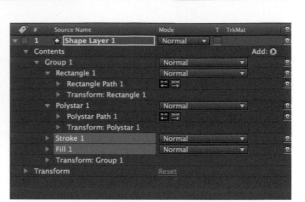

To position parametric shapes independently, give them their own subgroups; you can then enclose these inside a master group to give them the same master transformations (left). If you also want them to take on the same color, move Fill and Stroke out of the subgroups and into the master group (above right).

When you add Fill and Stroke to the master group, pay attention to how the Composite popup is set; the default is to composite them below the existing subgroup's fill and strokes.

Grouping

If your goal is to give individual shape paths their own strokes and fills but otherwise transform them together, you're better off creating a new group that encompasses your components. Select the shapes you wish to group together and press Command+G (Control+G) to enclose them in a new master Group with its own Transform: Group properties.

For additional flexibility, you can Add > Fill and Stroke properties to the master group. You can then choose whether the new master Fill and Stroke properties replace or blend with the individual shape colors:

- To have the new master Fill and Stroke be *shared* by all the shape paths, delete or toggle off the individual Fill and Strokes in each shape subgroup.

- To *mix* the new master Fill with the existing colors in the subgroups, place it *after* the subgroups in the Timeline and change its Composite popup to Above Previous in Same Group. At 100% the master Fill color takes over; reduce the Opacity or use a blending mode to mix colors.

Note that if you use Composite > Below Previous in Same Group, then the individual Fills will need to have reduced opacity or a blending mode applied to mix with the master fill below them. The Composite popup is similarly important if you wish to add a master Stroke to the group and mix it with previous strokes.

Merge Paths

Multiple shape paths inside a group will all receive a stroke. However, sometimes you want just the outline of the *composite* shape to be stroked, or you want more control over intersections and fills than what's provided by the Fill operator's Fill Rule popup. This is where the Merge Paths operator comes in.

Open [**Ex.10_starter**] which contains a sunburst shape. Our goal is to crop it to create a symbol that might appear in the corner of a logo or business card. Select **Shape Layer 1** to add a new shape path to this layer (rather than create a new shape layer). Then choose the Rectangle shape tool and verify that Tool Creates Shape is checked in the Tools panel.

Make sure the shape layer is selected and Tool Creates Shape (circled) is enabled before drawing the rectangle.

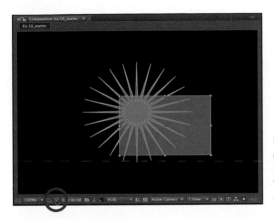

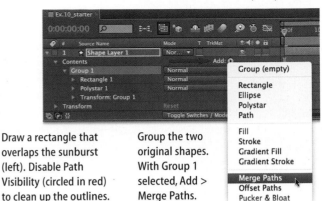

Draw a rectangle that overlaps the sunburst (left). Disable Path Visibility (circled in red) to clean up the outlines.

Group the two original shapes. With Group 1 selected, Add > Merge Paths.

Drag out a rectangle that encloses roughly a quarter to a third of the sunburst, then press V to return to the Selection tool. Disable the Path Visibility switch along the bottom of the Comp panel to better see the outlines of each shape. Initially you will see one shape on top of another, as dragging a new shape path creates a new shape group.

Select Rectangle 1 and Polystar 1 and press Command+G (Control+G) to group them into a master group. Twirl open Group 1 and check that Rectangle 1 is on top.

With Group 1 selected, select Add > Merge Paths. Merge Paths, Stroke, and Fill operators will be added to Group 1 below the two shape path subgroups they will be modifying, and the two shapes will now be joined together in the Comp panel. Twirl open Merge Paths 1 and experiment with its Mode popup: Intersect gives you the look we were going for, but the other options (such as Subtract) are also interesting.

Note that these new Stroke and Fill operators for the master group take their colors from the current Fill and Stroke colors in the Tools panel, and they now override those contained inside the shape subgroups! To reduce potential confusion, it's a good working practice to delete operators that are not contributing to the overall shape. Twirl open Rectangle 1 and Polystar 1 and delete the Stroke and Fill operators inside there. We've done this in [**Ex.10-final**].

You can still manipulate the relationship between the sunburst and rectangle by altering their respective path and transform parameters. You can then use either the Transform: Group 1 or the layer's Transform properties to reposition and resize the composite shape.

Merge Paths requires that you pay particular attention to the order in which shape paths and groups are arranged in a shape layer (for example, with the Merge Paths > Mode set to Subtract, try dragging Polystar 1 above Rectangle 1 in [**Ex.10**]). Unexpected results can often be cured by rearranging the order of paths or groups or by isolating shapes and their Merge Paths operator into their own shape group where they can then merge in peace before being composited with other shapes and groups. [**Ex.11-Gear**] demonstrates such a chain of merged shape paths that create a complex final shape.

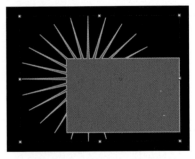

After Merge Paths is applied, the two shapes are added together – note the stroke outline.

Change the Merge Paths 1 > Mode popup to Intersect (above) to create a new shape where the rectangle crops the sunburst (below).

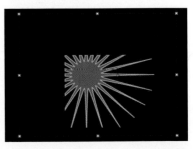

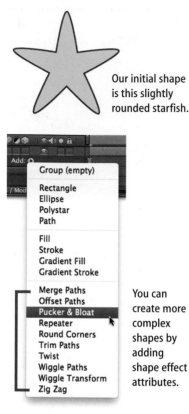

Our initial shape is this slightly rounded starfish.

You can create more complex shapes by adding shape effect attributes.

Shape Effects

Next we'd like to introduce you to the set of shape layer attributes known as *path operators*; we personally refer to them as *shape effects*. These attributes alter parametric or pen-based shape paths to create new shapes. They can be keyframed to create anything from mechanical to organic animations. If you include several shape paths or groups inside of another group, and then apply a shape effect after these paths or subgroups, all of the shape paths will be effected as a group.

To experiment with these, open [**Ex.12_starter**] and twirl open **Shape Layer 1** to reveal the shape group Polystar 1 which we've initially set up to resemble a starfish. As you move through these examples, select Polystar 1, open the Add menu, and select the suggested shape effect from the list. Twirl this shape effect open in the Timeline and explore its parameters. Then toggle its visibility switch (the eyeball icon) off before moving on to the next effect.

Merge Paths: This was discussed in detail in the Merge Paths section earlier in this chapter.

Offset Paths: This expands or contracts shape paths. Note that it does not work exactly the same as scaling a path: As you reduce Offset Paths > Amount for our rounded starfish, the shape will contract into a pointy star. Results can be unpredictable when combined with more complex shapes that have substantial rounding.

Pucker   Bloat

Pucker & Bloat: This effect is a great way to quickly make a simple shape become complex. It takes the line segments between the vertices of a shape path and either curves them inward (pucker) or bends them outward (bloat). At extreme positive or negative values, the shape path will cross over itself.

Repeater: The richest of the shape effects, Repeater takes the underlying shape and repeats it as many times as desired with each repeat offset by a series of transformations. The last few pages of this chapter are devoted to it; skip it for now.

Round Corners: This effect adds rounding to the corners of a path. Use it after some of the more angular shape effects to soften up the results.

Trim Paths: Use this effect to wipe shapes on and off. When applied to an open path shape, or if Fill is set to None, this effect can also be used to draw a stroke on and off (as we did in [**Ex.07-final**]). Use Offset to "chase" a stroke around its path. Note the Trim Multiple Shapes popup: If Trim Paths follows multiple shapes inside a group, this determines if all shapes are wiped and stroked together or in succession. To reverse the direction of a path, click on the Reverse Path Direction buttons that appear on the top line of a path in the Timeline panel.

Trim

When the shape group contains multiple paths, each path gets twisted individually (A). To twist the group as a whole, add Merge Paths before Twist (B). (These are in **[Ex.13]**).

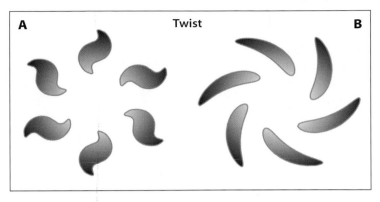

A   **Twist**   B

Twist: Twirls each shape above it in the group around that shape's anchor point, which defaults to its center. The amount of rotation is more severe in the middle than at the outer reaches.

Wiggle Paths: This shape effect is related to the Wiggly Selector in text layers, and is the only shape effect that auto-animates (RAM Preview after you apply it; we also used it subtly in **[Ex.12-final]**). It is more complex than most of the shape effects:

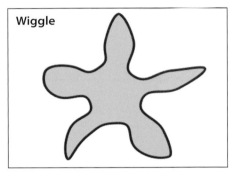

Wiggle

• Size determines how far the path is bent; Detail sets how big or small the undulations are (higher values equal more closely spaced ripples). The Points popup decides if the deflections are smooth or if they add sharp corners to the shape.

• Wiggles/Second sets the animation speed; Correlation decides if all the sides do their own thing (low values) or if they inflate and deflate together (high values).

• Temporal Phase and Spatial Phase affect the pattern of the random waves that pass through the wiggled shapes. You can set Wiggles/Second to 0 to stop the auto-animation, then use these Phase controls to strike poses or otherwise manually animate the wiggles. Random Seed makes quick wholesale changes to the pattern of the wiggles; the seed is also affected by layer order.

To auto-animate other shape parameters and operators, you can use the Wiggle Transform effect (discussed later in this chapter), or the wiggle expression (Chapter 37).

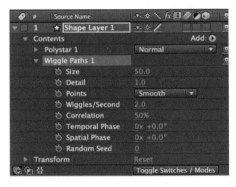

Zig Zag: Adds jagged or rounded ripples to the shape path. As with Pucker & Bloat, you can crank Zig Zag's Size parameter to extremes to create complex overlapping shapes.

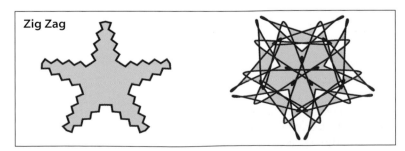

Zig Zag

TIP

First Vertex

When you create a new shape, the top-most vertex (denoted by a larger square) is the first vertex where strokes plus effects such as Trim Paths originate. To change the first vertex for a path created with the Pen tool, right-click on the desired vertex and choose Mask and Shape Path > Set First Vertex.

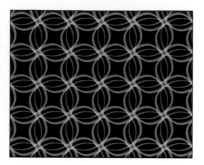

The Repeater can be employed to create anything from geometric logos to random backgrounds from just a few initial shapes.

The Repeater

The most interesting shape layers contain multiple paths. Fortunately, there's a quick way to create multiple paths: the Repeater. It takes the shape paths that appear above it in a shape layer's hierarchy and makes copies of them. Each successive copy is offset in space, scaled, and rotated by the amount you specify. Exactly what the result looks like depends a lot on where the Repeater appears in the shape hierarchy – for example, before or after a shape group's Transform properties. Let's explore a bit of what's possible by using the Repeater.

Close your prior comps and open [**Ex.14_starter**] which contains a simple oval (ellipse) centered in its shape group, the shape layer, and the composition. We've reduced the Opacity of the ellipse's Fill so you can see through it to the other copies you will be creating.

Select the shape group Ellipse 1 and Add > Repeater. It should appear in the Timeline panel below Fill 1 and above Transform: Ellipse 1. (If it appears below Transform: Ellipse 1, the group was not selected; just drag it into the desired position in the hierarchy.) You will now see three ellipses in the Comp panel, marching off to the right of the screen.

Twirl open Repeater 1: You will see that Copies is set to 3.0; the initial shape is considered to be the first "copy." Increase it to about 6 so that you'll have more copies to play with. Then twirl open Transform: Repeater 1 and note its Position is set to 100,0. This means each copy will be offset from the previous copy by 100 pixels in the X direction. Reduce this value by scrubbing it in the timeline so that all of your copies appear on screen.

Experiment with the Transform: Repeater 1 parameters to get a feel for how they work. Note that they are recalculated for each copy: For example, if you set Scale to 125%, each copy is scaled to be 125% larger than the previous copy.

After you've toyed around a bit, let's walk through setting up some common arrangements using this shape as a starting point. Before trying each of these, zero out Transform: Repeater 1's Anchor Point, Position, and Rotation, and set its Scale, Start Opacity, and End Opacity to 100%.

The Repeater's position in the shape layer hierarchy can have a big impact on the result. For these initial explorations, add it to the Ellipse 1 group, positioned above Transform: Ellipse 1. The Repeater's Transform values (above) are added or multiplied to each copy created, yielding results that appear to cascade (below).

Flowers, Pinwheels, and Tick Marks

The Repeater creates copies around the center of the group or layer. If you increase Transform: Repeater 1 > Rotation, the petals will just rotate around this center, creating an atomic symbol. However, flower petals are not centered in the flower; they are offset from its center. Therefore, twirl open Ellipse Path 1 and scrub its Y Position to offset it from the center point.

Creating perfectly spaced petals requires just a little math: Take 360°, divide it by the number of Copies (which will be the number of petals), and the result is your desired Rotation value. Or you can just eyeball it: Create the desired number of copies, then press Command (Control) to scrub Rotation in fine increments. To add a center to the flower, create a second ellipse in its own shape group after Repeater so it won't be repeated.

Stroke Scale

If the Repeater is placed after a Stroke operator, the stroke size of each copy will be affected by Repeater > Transform: Repeater > Scale. If you want the stroke to remain the same width for each copy, drag the Repeater above Stroke.

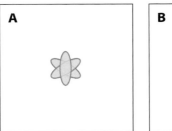

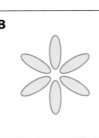

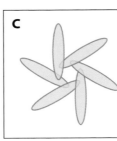

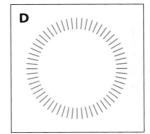

To create variations on this basic shape, scrub Ellipse Path 1's X Position as well; the result is a pinwheel. You can animate these values to create some interesting converge-then-fly-apart movements. For a related effect, scrub or animate Transform: Repeater 1 > Anchor Point to make the petals appear to fly in from and off to the sides or top.

You can alter Ellipse Path 1 > Size to change the underlying shape and therefore the pattern of the shapes. Larger ellipses create interesting abstracts. Reducing the X Size of the ellipse to 0% creates tick marks; increasing its Y Position and the number of copies creates the tick marks that go around the rim of a clock. Each of these shapes are built in comp [**Ex.14a-final**].

If your initial shape is centered, using Repeater to offset Rotation will rotate copies stacked on this point (A). Offsetting the Position value for the initial shape will create flower (B) and pinwheel (C) patterns. Alter the underlying shape to create tick marks (D).

Spirals

Creating spirals requires a slightly different logic than flowers. Starting with the initial centered shape, increase Rotation to 60°, but this time offset Transform: Repeater 1 > Anchor Point. At this point, it will look like the pinwheel you created above, but offset from the center of the comp. Now increase Transform: Repeater 1 > Scale to create the spiraling effect; if the shapes overlap, set Repeater's Composite popup to Above for the copies to stack correctly. To create a busier spiral, reduce Ellipse Path 1 > Size (as well as its Stroke Width), increase Repeater 1 > Copies, and tweak Anchor Point plus Scale to get the arrangement you want. One example is saved in [**Ex.14b-final**].

To create this spiral, we offset the Repeater's Anchor Point, added Rotation, and increased Scale above 100%.

Twisted Repeats

If you add the Twist effect after a Repeater, each individual shape will be twisted – not what you might expect. To twist the repeated pattern as a whole, add Merge Paths between the Repeater and Twist effects.

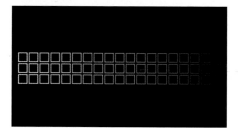

The Repeater can be used to quickly create lines and grids out of a single shape (above). The source and the repeats can both be modified to create more complex patterns (below).

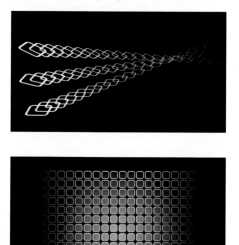

Gradient Fills and Strokes – applied *after* the Repeaters – can also be used to fade patterns on and off.

Lines and Grids

The Repeater makes it very easy to create lines and underscores out of core elements; grids are only slightly more difficult to make. With a little planning, you can also make these lines and grids fade on and off.

Open [**Ex.15_starter**] which contains a small rectangle with no fill as our seed shape. Twirl open **Shape Layer 1** and Add > Repeater. This will place the Repeater *after* the rectangle's shape group; that's okay as we can then take advantage of the rectangle group's Transform properties to alter the original shape.

Twirl open Repeater 1, then Transform: Repeater 1. To create a horizontal line, decrease X Position until the squares are more closely spaced, then increase the number of Copies. Scrub Offset to the left (negative values) to help center the line. To make the line fade on or off, play with Start and End Opacity. (We'll show you a trick for getting the line to fade on then off again in just a second.)

To create a grid of these squares, add a second Repeater to **Shape Layer 1**. Set Repeater 2 > Transform: Repeater 2 > X Position to 0 and increase Y Position to add vertical rows. Again, Copies controls the number of rows, and Offset will help center the layout of the grid.

Once you have a grid set up, changing the seed shape will automatically result in the grid being drawn with this new shape. For example, twirl open Rectangle 1 > Rectangle Path 1 and experiment with Size and Roundness. Then twirl open Transform: Rectangle 1 and experiment with Skew and Rotation. You can also change the basic shape path by selecting Rectangle 1 and using the Add menu to add a new shape.

A lot of fun can also be had altering the other Transform properties of the Repeaters. For example, experiment with Transform: Repeater 1 > Scale or > Rotation. If you have entered a negative value for Repeater 1 > Offset, study the results in the Comp panel: Copies on the "positive" side of the grid will get the expected change, while copies on the "negative" side of the grid will exhibit the opposite effect (such as growing larger instead of smaller if Scale is below 100%).

There are some limitations in the current implementation of the Repeater. For example, you cannot randomize the transformations of each individual copy. Another is the aforementioned problem of getting repeated elements to fade on, then fade off. One approach is to create multiple groups: one that repeats to the left and fades off in that direction, and another that repeats to the right and fades off in this other direction (built in [**Ex.15a-final**]). Another approach is to delete the Fill and Stroke for the original shape and instead follow the shapes and Repeaters with a Gradient Stroke or Fill. You can then use Opacity Stops to perform the fades (this is built in [**Ex.15b-final**]).

Wiggle Transform

After Effects CS4 introduced a very nice update to shape layers: the Wiggle Transform shape effect. This effect randomizes and auto-animates the transform properties – Anchor Point, Position, Scale, and Rotation – of the components of a shape group. It works particularly well in conjunction with the Repeater shape effect. However, there are a couple of things to be aware of when you're using Wiggle Transform that we'll cover in the next two exercises.

First, let's gain some familiarity with how Wiggle Transform works internally. Once you understand this, it will be much easier to apply and use it on your own projects.

Step 1: Open [**Ex.16_starter**]. It contains a single shape layer named **Jellybean**. Your goal is to make **Jellybean** wander automatically around the screen.

Step 2: Twirl down **Jellybean** > Contents to reveal the shape group named Shape 1. Select Shape 1 to ensure your shape effect will be placed inside this group, and choose Add > Wiggle Transform.

Step 3: Twirl down Wiggle Transform 1 > Transform. All of its transform offsets default to zero, which means it initially appears to have no effect. Set Wiggle Transform 1 > Transform > Position to X = 300, Y = 0 and RAM Preview: The shape will slide back and forth horizontally.

Step 4: Set Wiggle Transform 1 > Transform > Rotation to 1x +0.0°. RAM Preview, and carefully note **Jellybean**'s behavior: As it moves to the left (negative X direction), it rotates counter-clockwise (negative rotation); as it moves to the right (positive X direction), it rotates clockwise (positive rotation).

FACTOID

Just a Phase We're Wiggling Through

The Wiggles/Second, Correlation, Phase, and Random Seed parameters for Wiggle Transform work the same as the identically named parameters in a text animator's Wiggly Selector (Chapter 21).

Steps 2–3: Add the Wiggle Transform effect to **Jellybean**'s Shape 1 group, and set its X Position to 300.

Here is what is going on underneath the hood: Wiggle Transform internally generates a single random value, ranging from –1 to +1. This internal value is then multiplied by the Transform offsets you've entered. If you enter offsets for more than one parameter, they will all change in concert with one another, as they are being driven by the same underlying random value.

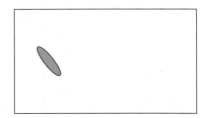

Step 4: When the same Wiggle Transform effect is used to wiggle both Position and Rotation, these parameters move in concert with each other.

What if you want to randomize, say, Position differently than Rotation? That will require more than one Wiggle Transform shape effect:

Step 5: First, set Wiggle Transform 1 > Transform > Rotation back to 0x +0.0°. Then select Add > Wiggle Transform again. Twirl down Wiggle Transform 2 > Transform, and set Rotation for this second instance of the effect to 1x +0.0°.

RAM Preview; the rotation will happen independently of the horizontal movement.

Now that you have two Wiggle Transform effects, you have the additional flexibility of setting different speeds (Wiggle/Second) for each instance. Go ahead and experiment; if you get lost, our result is in composition [**Ex.16-final**].

Step 5: By dedicating separate Wiggle Transform shape effects to Position and Rotation (left), these two parameters will now wiggle independently from each other (below).

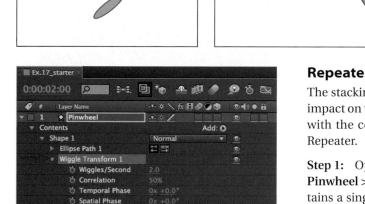

Repeater + Wiggle Transform

The stacking order of shape operators often has a big impact on the resulting image. This is particularly true with the combination of Wiggle Transform and the Repeater.

Step 1: Open comp [**Ex.17_starter**], then twirl open **Pinwheel** > Contents > Shape 1. This shape layer contains a single ellipse shape that has been repeated to create a pinwheel.

Step 2: Select the group Shape 1 and Add > Wiggle Transform: It will be added to the shape group after Ellipse Path 1 and well before Repeater 1.

Step 3: Twirl open Wiggle Transform 1 > Transform and enter some values. The exact numbers don't matter; we used Y Position = 20, Scale = 50%, and Rotation = 30°.

Step 2: When you Add > Wiggle Transform, note that it is placed before Repeater 1.

RAM Preview: Note that all of the petals in the pinwheel pulse in unison and that the entire pinwheel shape rotates as a whole. This is because you are currently wiggling the transform values for the initial ellipse *before* it is repeated to create multiple shapes.

Step 3: When Wiggle Transform is before Repeater, all of the repeated shapes will wiggle in unison.

Step 4: Drag Wiggle Transform down the list so that it is after Repeater 1 and just before Transform: Shape 1. The pinwheel will take on a disheveled appearance!

RAM Preview, and each petal will scale, rotate, and move independently of the other petals. This is because you are first repeating the ellipse to create multiple petals, *then* wiggling the transform of each of those petals. (Wiggle Transform wiggles each component shape of a shape group.)

Step 4: When Wiggle Transform is after Repeater (left), each repeated shape is wiggled individually (below).

Step 5: Correlation controls how much each wiggled shape resembles or varies from another, with higher values for Correlation resulting in a higher degree of resemblance. Increase Wiggle Transform 1 > Correlation to 90%. RAM Preview, and note how much more coordinated the actions of the individual petals appear to be. [**Ex.17-final**] contains two copies of **Pinwheel**, with low correlation (left) and high correlation (right).

Step 5: Increasing Correlation results in the repeated shapes wiggling in a wave, rather than in a random pattern.

Shapes from Other Places

In addition to creating paths using the Pen and Shape tools, After Effects provides several other ways to create or borrow shape paths from other sources such as text layers, masks, or Illustrator files:

Create Outlines

Text layers can be converted into shape layers (similar to how Illustrator can create outlines from text). Each character is converted into a path or combination paths, which can then be edited and animated.

Open comp [**Ex.18_starter**], select the text layer **flow**, then choose Layer > Create Shapes from Text. The text layer's Video switch will be turned off, and a new shape layer called **flow Outlines** will be created with the same fill and stroke colors as the original text.

Twirl open **flow Outlines** > Contents: You will see four shape groups, each named after a character in the original world. Twirl open the "o" group and study it: It contains two shape paths followed by a Merge Paths operator (useful in case you apply a shape effect such as Trim Paths). This is how After Effects creates a compound path to cut the center out of a letter such as o.

To edit a character, make sure Path Visibility is enabled and double-click one of the character shapes – a dotted rectangle will appear; vertices will be visible around its outline. Click on one of these points: Bezier handles will appear for you to edit. If you want to animate the path, type SS (Solo Selected) to reveal that character in the Timeline panel; twirl it open until you reveal its Path parameter, then enable its animation stopwatch. (We animated the paths in **flow Outlines** for your amusement in [**Ex.18-final**].)

Masks to Shapes

Jeff Almasol of redefinery has created a "beta" script to convert masks applied to a layer into a corresponding shape layer. After running it, you need to manually Add > Fill and/or > Stroke. Download it from: *www.redefinery.com/ae/view.php? item=rd_MasksToShapes*

After you Create Shapes from Text, a shape layer will be created with one shape group per character (left). When a character is created by a compound shape (one path cutting out another), both paths plus a Merge Path operator will be created. You can then modify or animate the paths for each individual character (above). Background footage courtesy Artbeats/Ocean Effects.

Masks into Shapes

Mask paths can be pasted into shape paths. This is handy if you have a tool that creates interesting mask paths, but not shapes.

For example, open [**Ex.19_starter**]: The layer **silhouette** should have a set of nine Masks (select the **silhouette** layer and type M to reveal them). These were created by taking a piece of video footage and applying Layer > Auto-trace (Chapter 10).

Choose one of the masks to copy (say, Mask 7), select its Mask Path, and Edit > Copy. Then press F2 to deselect the layer.

Next, create a "dummy" shape layer you can paste to by selecting the Pen tool and clicking once in the Comp panel. Press V to return to the Selection tool. Twirl open **Shape Layer 1** > Contents > Shape 1 > Path 1. Select the word Path (not the higher level Path 1) and Edit > Paste – the shape path will now match the mask path you copied.

To move additional masks into the same shape layer, first copy the desired Mask Path. Then in **Shape Layer 1** select the desired group and use Add > Path. Twirl open the new path, select its Path property, and paste. You can do more than one at a time: Create or duplicate enough dummy shape paths to accept them, copy your multiple mask paths, select your multiple shape paths, and paste. (Also see the Tip on the previous page for a handy script.) If you employed Mask Modes to create compound mask shapes, use the Merge Paths operator to reconstruct them.

Select the Mask Path and copy (above). Create a dummy shape using the Pen tool, expose its Path property, and paste (below).

In [**Ex.19-final**], we added the Wiggle Paths shape effect to add some fun automatic animation to our resulting shapes.

Note that out of all the items in After Effects that have paths, only shape layers have the ability to automatically wiggle. You cannot copy and paste or express the result of a shape effect such as Wiggle Paths back to a mask shape or paint stroke.

In [**Ex.19-final**], we've pasted all the shapes over, wiggled their paths, and applied gradients and effects.

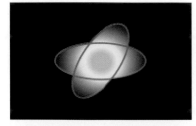

If you attempt to copy and paste multiple shapes from Illustrator into After Effects one at a time, they will be centered on top of each other.

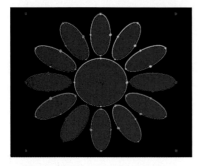

To paste multiple paths from Illustrator to mask paths, select the group of paths (or the entire layer) in Illustrator, copy, then paste to a layer in After Effects. Pasting them to a Shape Layer, however, involves a few more steps.

Illustrator Paths into Shapes

With just a bit more effort, you can also copy paths from Illustrator and paste them into shape paths in After Effects.

If you have a copy of Illustrator, return to the Project panel in After Effects and twirl open **Sources > 32_Chapter Sources**. Select **flower_layers.ai** and type Command+E (Control+E) to edit it in Illustrator. In Illustrator, open Preferences > File Handling & Clipboard and verify that Copy As: AICB is enabled. Then select one of the petals and Edit > Copy.

Return to After Effects and open [**Ex.20_starter**]. Select the Pen tool and click in the Comp panel to create a pen path shape (one click will do).

In the Timeline panel, twirl open **Shape Layer 1** > Shape 1 > Path 1, *select the Path parameter*, then Edit > Paste. The petal will appear as a shape – with a catch: If you paste a *single* path, it will be centered in the Comp panel rather than offset to its relative position as in the Illustrator document. If you were to then copy and paste another petal into a second path, it would appear centered on top of the first one.

Pasting a group of paths from Illustrator to After Effects as mask paths is easy: Just select the whole layer in Illustrator, switch to After Effects, select a layer, and paste.

However, if you want to paste a group of paths directly to a shape layer all at once, you need to do some preparation:

• In Illustrator, select as many paths as you plan on bringing across into After Effects, count the number of paths, then copy.

• In After Effects, with no layers selected, select the Pen tool and click once in the Comp panel to create a new shape layer to paste to. In the Timeline panel, twirl open **Shape Layer 1** > Shape 1 and select Path 1. Press Command+D (Control+D) to duplicate it as many times as you have paths to paste (in our example, you'll need Path 1 through 13).

• Now here's the trick: Twirl open each Path group and Shift+click to select each Path parameter (see figure, below left), then paste. The group of shapes will maintain their relationships. Style Shape Layer to taste.

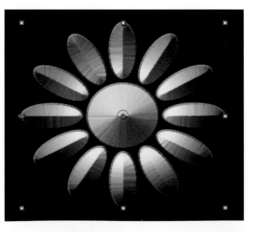

To paste a group of paths from Illustrator to shape paths, first create the correct number of dummy Pen paths, then select *the Path properties* and paste (left). We applied layer styles to add more dimension in comp [**Ex.20_final**] (right).

Brainstormed Shapes

The Brainstorm module (Chapter 25) is a great tool to help you explore what can be done with shape layers. Click on Contents to select all of the shape layer's properties (excluding the layer's overall transformations). Or select specific properties such as the parametric shape path, Fill and Stroke, shape effects, or any combination of these. Then use Brainstorm to generate variations.

You can also use Brainstorm to create shape layer animations. Set up a basic shape you like – perhaps using the Repeater – then set keyframes at the start and end of the comp for some of its properties. You can build a simple animation or set the start and end keyframes to the same values – Brainstorm will randomize the start and end keyframes differently anyway.

We've set up a simple animation for you to experiment with in **[Ex.21]**. Select **Shape Layer 1** > Contents, then click on the Brainstorm icon along the top of the Timeline panel. Click the Play button to see how your potential animations will move.

Brainstorm can be used with shape layers to quickly develop new ideas – especially when shape effects such as the Repeater are involved!

If you find an idea you like, move your cursor over that cell and click Save as New Composition. Keep clicking the Brainstorm button to generate as many new ideas as you like!

Closing Shapes

Before we wrap up our discussion of shape layers, we want to mention one additional trick using the Repeater that may not be obvious from scrubbing its Copies and Offset values directly in the Timeline: When you animate these values, they interpolate. If you animate Offset, the repeated shapes will appear to move along their "repeat path" rather than pop on and off. If you animate Copies, each new copy will fade on or off rather than pop on and off. To simulate what this means before setting up an actual animation, hold down Command (Control) and scrub to alter these parameters in finer increments.

We have but scratched the surface of what can be done with shape layers. For instance, a common result of using Repeater is creating overlapping shapes. Take advantage of the blending mode popups for Stroke and Fill to make these copies blend in interesting ways.

Also note that you can enable Motion Blur (Chapter 8) for shape layers. This is particularly useful when animating multiple copies of shapes with the Repeater.

There's a lot of power inside shape layers; experiment and have fun!

GOTCHA

Not so SWF

As of After Effects CS5, shape layers still cannot be exported as SWF vector objects.

CONNECT

Keyframing: Chapters 3 and 4.

Drawing with the Pen tool: Chapters 3 and 10.

Masks, RotoBezier paths, Set First Vertex Point: Chapter 10.

Layer Styles: Chapter 22.

Animation Presets: Chapter 25.

Paint: Chapter 33.

Wiggle expression: Chapter 37.

Paint and Clone

A painting workout in After Effects using the Brush, Erase, and Clone tools.

Example Project

Explore the 33-Example Project.aep file as you read this chapter; references to [Ex.##] refer to specific compositions within the project file.

After Effects offers a set of paint tools for painting directly on layers. You can use vector-based paint tools accessed from a pair of dedicated panels to retouch footage and create animated graphical elements, plus use cloning to remove unwanted elements and replicate areas of a layer. The brush strokes are nondestructive. Individual brush, clone and eraser strokes can be edited and animated in the Timeline.

In this chapter we'll explore using the Paint tools and cover the basics of painting, erasing, and cloning. We will also explore the various methods for animating strokes, and walk you step by step through automating a repair task using motion tracking and expressions. Along the way we'll also present tips for incorporating other effects with Paint, as well as saving custom brushes and clone presets.

Getting Started with Paint

Open the [**Ex.01-Doodling_starter**] comp from this chapter's example project, where we've created a solid layer for you to practice with. There are three paint tools that we'll be using: Brush, Clone Stamp, and Eraser. You can select them from the Tools panel and toggle between them using the shortcut Command+B on Mac (Control+B on Windows). If Auto-Open Panels is checked in the Tools panel, selecting one of the paint tools will open the Paint and Brushes panels.

Brush Tool   Clone Stamp Tool   Eraser Tool   Toggle the Paint Panels

If Auto-Open Panels is checked in the Tools panel, the Paint and Brushes panels will open when any of the paint and clone tools are selected. The panels button toggles the Paint and Brushes panels open and closed.

It's important to remember that the paint tools work only in the Layer panel – attempting to paint in the Comp panel will result in an error message. So to start painting, double-click your layer to open it in the Layer panel. If you like, you can select the Paint workspace from the Workspaces popup at the top right of the Application window. This will

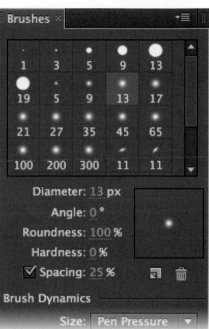

The Paint and Brushes panels at their default settings. Changing any of these settings affects new strokes only; existing strokes must be edited in the Timeline panel.

The Clone Options section (left) is grayed out unless the Clone Stamp tool is selected. The Brush Dynamics section in the Brushes panel (right) has options for pressure-sensitive tablets.

X is the shortcut for toggling the Foreground/Background colors. Press D to reset the Foreground/Background colors to Black/White.

arrange the Layer and Comp panels side by side, which is handy as you can see the results in context. We'll leave it up to you to set up your workspace to taste.

To create a few practice strokes on our **Black Solid 1** layer, check that the Layer panel is forward, select the Brush tool, check that the color in the Paint panel is something other than black (it defaults to red), verify that the Duration popup is set to Constant, then paint a stroke or two to get started. The default settings for the Paint panels are shown in the figures above, if you need to reset any of the parameters.

Go ahead and try a few strokes using a variety of Foreground colors and brush tip sizes. You can select a new brush from the Brushes panel or by creating a new brush interactively. To resize a brush interactively, press the Command (Control) key and drag in the Layer panel to set the diameter; release the modifier key and continue to drag to set the feather amount.

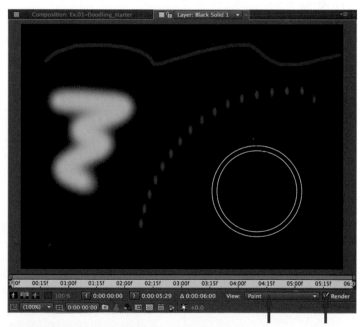

The Paint tools can be used only in the Layer panel. You can also create a new brush by interactively dragging in the Layer panel (see instructions to the left). If you're having trouble seeing your strokes, make sure the View popup is set to Paint, and the Render box is checked.

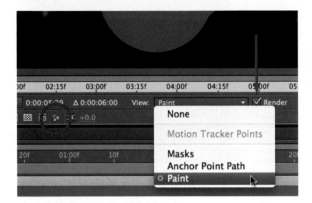

Paint is an "effect," although the only option in the Effect Controls panel is Paint on Transparent; check this option to render the paint strokes only (the underlying layer will be transparent).

The Layer panel's View menu shows the render order for this layer; other effects applied could appear before or after Paint. Make sure the Render checkbox is enabled to see the brush strokes. Click the Comp button (circled in red) to bring the Comp panel forward.

Expressive Strokes

You can use expressions to link together paint strokes, mask paths, and shape layer paths created with the Pen tool. You can animate a shape or mask path, then express it to your paint stroke.

A few more important concepts coming up:

• Paint is considered to be an "effect," so it appears in the Effect Controls panel. The only parameter you can edit there, however, is Paint on Transparent, which determines whether the underlying layer (the solid in our example) is visible or not.

• Because Paint is an effect, you can use multiple instances of Paint as well as interleave other effects with your paint strokes. See the *Effects and Paint* sidebar, page 567, for details.

• The Layer panel includes a View popup and a Render checkbox. The View menu allows you to pick and choose which part of the rendering order appears in the Layer panel (the original source, after Masks, or after each individual effect). The Render checkbox determines whether the current view is rendered (you will always want to render the Paint effect).

• Changing any of the settings in the Paint and Brushes panels affects only new strokes – if you need to edit an existing stroke, you'll need to use the Timeline panel. So without further ado…

Editing Existing Strokes

In the Timeline panel, expand the solid layer and twirl down Effects > Paint to see your strokes, or use the shortcut PP (two Ps in quick succession) to reveal the Paint properties. Expand Paint to reveal the Paint on Transparent parameter plus a twirly for each Brush stroke created, numbered sequentially.

To the right of each brush stroke section is a popup menu for setting the Blending Mode per stroke; this mirrors the Mode popup in the Paint panel. Each brush stroke breaks down further into three sections: Shape, Stroke Options, and Transform (not to be confused with the regular Transform settings):

• The Path can be animated over time. Unfortunately, you can't reshape the path by manipulating handles as you can with a mask path or a shape layer path, but you can paste or express a mask path or shape layer path to a Paint stroke's Path property, and vice versa (see *Random Paint Splatters* at the end of this chapter).

• Stroke Options allow you to edit and animate most of the brush characteristics found in the Paint and Brushes panels; it also includes Start and End parameters for animating on a stroke. The Channels popup mirrors the Channels menu in the Paint panel (more on this in a bit).

• You can reposition, scale, and rotate each stroke using its Transform settings.

Some of these parameters are self-explanatory; we'll explore the others as we go. The most important thing to remember is that you don't need to sweat setting up the Paint and Brushes panels properly to begin with, as you can edit the mode, color, size, opacity, and so on for each stroke in the Timeline panel after the fact.

Note also that each brush stroke in the Timeline panel has a duration bar: A brush stroke can be moved in time as well as have its in and out points moved (without the limitations that movie layers encounter). If the Duration popup in the Paint panel was set to Constant, each brush stroke will extend for the duration of the layer (we'll cover the Duration options shortly).

Managing Your Strokes

You can name brush strokes to keep track of which one is which. To rename a stroke, select its name (Brush 1, for instance), press Return, type a new name, and press Return to accept it.

The order of the strokes in the Timeline panel also sets their rendering order; brush strokes render from the bottom up. Drag strokes up and down in the stack to change their render order.

To delete a brush stroke, select it in the Layer or Timeline panel and press Delete. You can also temporarily hide it by turning off the eyeball for individual strokes.

Practice editing your existing strokes by scrubbing the values in the Timeline, then create additional strokes and practice renaming and reordering them. *Be warned that creating a new stroke while an existing brush stroke is selected will replace that stroke;* get in the habit of pressing F2 to Deselect All before creating a new stroke.

Paint on Transparent

The Paint on Transparent option can be found in both the Timeline and Effect Controls panel; it determines whether the underlying layer is opaque or transparent when composited over other layers. Toggle Paint on Transparent to On and the black solid in our example comp will disappear, revealing the Background Color (white in this case) in the Layer panel. The background color is for display only; you can change this color by opening Composition > Composition Settings.

If you need to check whether the color you're seeing is transparent, toggle on the Transparency Grid at the bottom of the Layer panel.

Most of the settings from the Paint and Brushes panels are editable – and animatable – in the Timeline panel after the fact. You can also rename strokes and change their rendering order by moving them up and down in the stack.

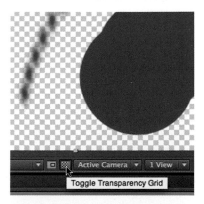

If the Paint on Transparent option is on, the solid will disappear, revealing the composition's background color. To display the background color as a grid instead, enable the Toggle Transparency Grid button.

You can drag a path to reposition it (top) as well as use shortcuts to scale and rotate it interactively. Each Brush stroke has its own set of Transform properties for finer editing (above).

The Channels popup in the Paint panel determines which channels are affected.

Transforming Brush Strokes

Select one of your strokes and note how it appears in the Layer panel: The stroke's Anchor Point appears at the start of the path, and a line runs through the center of the stroke. Explore the Transform properties in the Timeline panel to edit the path:

• The Anchor Point is the origin around which the stroke scales and rotates. Note that if you edit the anchor point value, the anchor point remains in the same place while the stroke offsets its position.

• You can move the Position of the stroke by simply dragging it with the Selection tool. If the Layer panel is forward, you can also use the up/down/left/right arrow keys to nudge the path one pixel at a time; add the Shift key to nudge times 10.

• Changing the Scale value affects the size of the stroke path as well as the brush diameter (the width of the stroke). If need be, edit the Diameter in the Stroke Options section to counteract this. To scale interactively, first select the stroke in the Layer panel (the Layer panel must be forward), then press Option (Alt) and the + and – keys on the numeric keypad (not the regular keyboard) to scale in 1 percent increments. Add the Shift key for times 10.

• Use Rotation to rotate the path around the stroke's anchor point. To rotate interactively, first select the stroke in the Layer panel (the Layer panel must be forward), then press the + and – keys on the numeric keypad (not the regular keyboard) to rotate in 1 degree increments. Add the Shift key for times 10.

Of course, all of these properties can also be animated, so you have an enormous amount of control over every single stroke.

Choosing Channels

The Channels popup in the Paint panel determines whether Brush strokes (including Clone Stamp and Eraser strokes) affect the RGB+Alpha channels, RGB only, or the Alpha channel only.

To compare these options, select an image with an obvious alpha channel, such as the picture frame in [**Ex.02-Frame_starter**]:

• Double-click layer 1 to open the Layer panel, and select the Brush tool. In the Paint panel, select a large brush and a blue Foreground color. Check that Mode is set to Normal, Channels is set to RGBA, and Duration is set to Constant.

• Paint over the left side of the frame (see first figure on the next page).

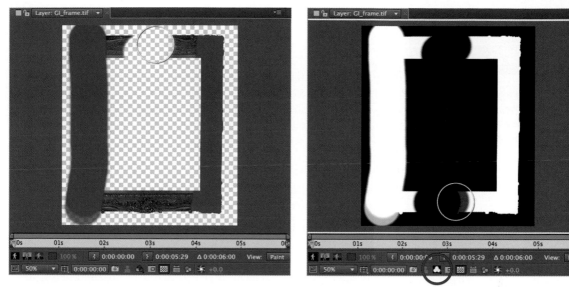

The blue stroke on the left was painted with Channels set to RGBA; the blue stroke on the right was painted in RGB mode. Painting in Alpha mode with black paint makes the top of the frame invisible. Frame courtesy Getty Images.

When the Paint panel's Channels is set to Alpha, only the alpha channel is affected when painting. Option+click (Alt+click) the Show Channel button to toggle between viewing RGB and Alpha. Feel free to paint with Alpha Channel enabled (above).

The stroke affects the RGB channels but also affects the layer's alpha. Select Alpha from the Show Channel button at the bottom of the Layer panel to view the alpha channel only (you can also paint in this mode).

• Return to viewing the RGB channels. In the Paint panel, set the Channels popup to RGB and paint another blue stroke on the right side of the frame; the color appears only where the alpha channel is opaque (i.e., the transparency is preserved).

• Set the Show Channel popup to Alpha; the Foreground/Background colors change to black and white, respectively. Press X to switch the Foreground and Background colors. Painting with a Foreground color of black will render the corresponding pixels in the alpha channel as transparent; painting in white will render them as opaque; shades of gray will be more or less transparent.

Painting with Modes

Each individual brush stroke includes a blending mode setting to control how it interacts with the underlying layer and other paint strokes that are rendered before the current stroke. You can set the Mode popup in the Paint panel before you paint, or set it at any time in the Timeline panel.

[Ex.02_Frame-final2] shows an example of using the Color mode to colorize the frame; remember that these colors can be animated if you feel like going a little crazy.

This frame was painted with different colored strokes all set to the Color blending mode.

When the Eraser tool is selected in the Tools panel (above), the Erase popup in the Paint panel is active (below). *Note that the options in the Paint and Brushes panels are remembered separately for each of the three tools – so be sure to select the Eraser tool first, then set options accordingly.*

Eraser Logic

Our next guided tour is of the Eraser tool, with which you can zap image pixels and paint strokes then unzap them at will. Erasing in After Effects is particularly stress-free because not only can you erase any unwanted paint strokes, you can also delete strokes created with the Eraser tool. Depending on how the Paint panel's Channels and Eraser popups are set, you can erase back to the background color, erase only paint strokes, or erase the last stroke only. Let's explore the various options:

Open the [**Ex.03-Erasing_starter**] comp. Select the Eraser tool first, then double-click the **microphone precomp** layer to open its Layer panel. (Having trouble? If a paint tool is not active, double-clicking a nested comp layer opens the precomp, not the Layer panel.)

• The Paint and Brushes panels remember a separate set of options for each tool; be sure to select the Eraser tool *before* you select a brush or set other options in the Paint panel. We'll start by erasing the bottom portion of the microphone, so select a large brush, make sure Channels is set to RGBA, Duration is Constant, and the Erase popup is set to Layer Source and Paint. The Opacity and Flow settings in the Paint panel also affect the characteristics of the Eraser tool – set them both to 100%. Erase the bottom of the microphone.

• Press PP (two Ps in quick succession) to reveal the Paint section in the Timeline panel; your stroke appears as Eraser 1. Although it lacks Mode and Channels popups, or a Color swatch, all other parameters of an Eraser stroke can be edited and animated just like the Paint strokes you created earlier.

• Select Eraser 1 and press Delete to remove it. Set the Channels popup to RGB, and again paint over the base of the microphone. Instead of making the pixels transparent, they erase to the Background color in the Paint panel (not the comp's Background Color). The alpha channel is not affected.

• Setting the Channels popup to Alpha mode with a black Background color is similar to erasing in RGBA mode; when it's set to white, you can extend the alpha channel. (You could also achieve a similar result using the Brush tool to paint in the alpha channel.)

Using the Eraser tool with the Channels popup set to RGBA and the Erase popup set to Layer Source and Paint will erase portions of the image (above). The Eraser strokes appear in the Timeline panel (right) just like Brush strokes.

Erasing the Paint Only

Still using the same microphone layer in [**Ex.03**], select the
Brush tool and verify that the Channels popup is set to RGBA
and that the Mode is Normal. Paint a few colorful brush
strokes around the microphone in the Layer panel; make
sure some of them overlap the image itself (see figure).

Once you're happy with your paint strokes, select the
Eraser tool and verify that Channels is set to RGBA; set the
Erase popup to Paint Only and erase the portion of the
strokes that overlaps the image. In Paint Only mode, the
image is not affected – only the strokes are erased.

Erase Last Stroke

You can also erase a portion of the last stroke painted,
which is useful when you make a mistake and the last
stroke you painted overlapped other strokes you were
happy with. You can erase portions of the last stroke using
one of two methods:

• Select the Eraser tool, then set the Erase popup in the
Paint panel to Last Stroke Only.

• Press Command+Shift (Control+Shift) when using the
Brush or Clone Stamp tools; this will temporarily toggle the
current brush to Erase Last Stroke Only mode.

An eraser stroke made with the Last Stroke Only option is
permanent – it does *not* create an item and duration bar in
the Timeline panel that you can later delete, edit, or animate.
On the other hand, you end up with a less cluttered stack
in the Timeline panel.

Remember that no matter what settings you use, you are
never destroying the original RGB pixels; After Effects'
painting tools create nondestructive vector paths that can
always be deleted to restore the original image.

Finally, just as with brush strokes, you can rename,
reorder, and delete eraser strokes.

Our version is in [**Ex.03-Erasing-final**],
where we added a Drop Shadow effect and a
background layer. RAM Preview; we wiggled
the microphone layer and the individual
paint strokes using expressions (Chapter
37). Select the microphone layer and press
F3 to open the Effect Controls panel; play
with changing the position and rotation
wiggle amounts using the sliders in the
expression controllers.

When the Erase popup is set to Paint Only, the
underlying image is not affected. Note that you
can erase across multiple strokes at the same time.
Image courtesy Classic PIO/Classic Microphones.

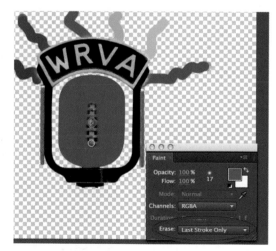

A hole was created in the orange stroke by erasing in
Last Stroke Only mode.

Our final version (left)
includes a randomly moving
microphone with jiggling
strokes thanks to the
wiggle expression.

Animating Strokes

There are various ways to animate the drawing of your brush strokes: You can animate the Start or End parameters, or you can paint in Write-on mode. You can also paint frame by frame, or use a single brush stroke and interpolate the shape of the stroke over time. And, of course, you can move the duration bar for a series of strokes to have them start at different points along the Timeline and trim their in and out points. We'll look at these options in this section.

Start Here, End There

Close all open comps to reduce clutter, and open [**Ex.04-Smoke_starter**]. An industrial smokestack belches smoke, but the color of the smoke closely matches the sky. Double-click the **AB_IndustryScenes.mov** layer to open it in the Layer panel, and let's colorize the smoke:

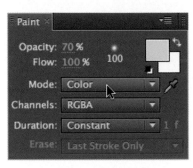

Step 1: The yellow stroke will colorize the layer when Mode is set to Color.

Step 1: Select the Brush tool, and use a soft brush a little larger than the width of the chimney. Check that Channels is set to RGB or RGBA, Duration is Constant, and change the Mode popup to Color (to colorize the footage). Set the Foreground color to yellow; the luminance of the color you choose isn't important, only the Hue and Saturation will be used in Color mode. Reducing the Opacity value to 70% will make the new color blend more naturally.

Step 2: At time 00:00, paint a swirly brush stroke coming out of the chimney (see figure). The resulting color will take on the Hue and Saturation of the yellow color, but will retain the luminance of the underlying smoke.

Step 3: To animate on the stroke, press PP (two Ps in quick succession) to reveal the Paint property in the Timeline, and expand it to reveal Paint > Brush 1 > Stroke Options. Scrub the End value to 0% and turn on the animation stopwatch.

Step 4: Move to a point later in time, like 03:00, and set the End value back to 100%. RAM Preview and the stroke will wipe on over time.

Step 2: Paint a squiggly yellow stroke in the Layer panel (above). To see the stroke's path, select Brush 1 in the Timeline panel. Footage courtesy Artbeats/Industry Scenes.

Steps 3–4: Animate the stroke by setting keyframes for the End parameter in the Timeline panel (right). Remember that you can also change the mode, color, diameter, hardness, and other characteristics of the stroke at any time.

Using Write On Mode

Painting in Write On mode sets the End keyframes for you automatically, so let's try this alternate approach:

Step 1: With the Brush tool still selected, change the Foreground color to green and set the Duration popup to Write On.

Step 2: Press 3 to jump to the marker at 03:00 so that the new stroke starts here, and press F2 to Deselect All (if your first stroke is selected, you will replace it unless you deselect first).

Step 3: Paint another squiggly stroke coming out of the chimney over the course of a few seconds. When you release the mouse, the stroke won't be visible as the End parameter is at 0%, but if you press Play or RAM Preview, you'll see it draw on in real time starting at 03:00.

Step 4: Press U to reveal all animated properties for the layer, and you'll see that After Effects automatically added two End keyframes to Brush 2, ranging from 0% to 100%. You can move the location of the second keyframe to retime the stroke's animation.

Note: If you were a really slow squiggler, the second End keyframe may be located past the end of the comp! To gain access to the second keyframe, you can either drag the stroke's duration bar earlier in time, or temporarily extend the comp's duration.

Step 5: Strokes extend to the end of the layer's duration. So if you move the duration bar for Brush 2 earlier in time, the layer bar no longer extends to the end of the comp. However, unlike a movie's layer bar, you can extend the out point for a stroke's bar past its original length.

Note that whether you create the End keyframes manually or use Write On mode, the stroke itself will retain all the inherent timing nuances (speed ups and slow downs) of your hand's movement.

Step 1: With Duration set to Write On, paint strokes will be recorded in real time.

GOTCHA

Replacing Strokes

If a brush stroke is selected in the Timeline panel and you paint a new stroke, you will overwrite the selected stroke. If you don't want that behavior, press F2 to Deselect All before painting a new stroke.

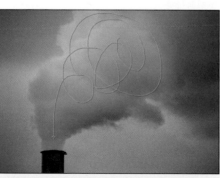

Step 3: After pressing F2 to Deselect All, paint a squiggly green stroke in the Layer panel (left).

Steps 4–5: Press U to reveal all animated properties. The two Brush 2 > End keyframes were created automatically by Write On.

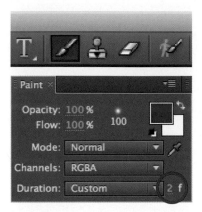

Set the Duration popup to Custom, then set the value immediately to its right to the stroke's duration. Of course, you can actually paint on any frame you like, or change the Custom frame duration value at any time. For instance, you might want to animate some sections "on 1s" and other areas "on 2s".

In **[Ex.05-Roto-final]** (above), we painted musical notes and flourishes at two-frame increments. Note that you can add multiple brush strokes at each frame (below). Footage courtesy Lee Stranahan.

Rotoscoping Frame by Frame

A common rotoscoping task involves painting a series of individual frames by hand. It can be a tedious undertaking, but After Effects offers both Single Frame and Custom options in the Duration popup as well as some keyboard shortcuts to help automate this task.

Open comp [**Ex.05-Roto_starter**]. Layer 1 is a movie of a saxophone player; let's add some paint strokes emanating from the bell of the sax:

Step 1: Select the Brush tool and double-click to open the movie in the Layer panel. In the Paint panel, pick a brush and color of your choice, set the Opacity to 100%, Mode to Normal and the Channels to RGBA.

Step 2: If you were to set the Duration popup to Single Frame, your strokes would be one frame long. This would result in a frenetic animation, plus it would be time-consuming to paint. Instead, set the Duration popup to Custom; this automatically sets any stroke you create to a custom duration as set by the value immediately to the right of the popup. The default is 1 frame, so change this value to "**2**".

Step 3: At time 00:00, paint a stroke. Press PP to see this stroke in the Timeline; note that it is two frames in duration. Advance the current time indicator to 00:02; then paint another stroke.

To quickly move the current time indicator forward and backward by the exact increment you set in the Paint panel (*n*), use the following shortcuts:

- 1 (on the regular keyboard) advances forward by *n* frames
- 2 (on the regular keyboard) jumps backward by *n* frames

RAM Preview at any time to see how your animation looks. Our version is shown in [**Ex.05-Roto-final**].

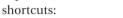

Brushes and Tablets

A brush stroke is actually created by many individual brush marks, and the settings in the Brushes panel control their Diameter, Angle, Roundness, Hardness, and Spacing. Furthermore, the Opacity and Flow settings in the Paint panel set the maximum paint coverage and how quickly paint is applied, respectively.

You can customize a preset brush in the Brushes panel and then save your new brush as a preset. These presets are saved in a Preferences file. To create a custom brush, select any existing brush and change the value for the various options: Diameter, Angle, Roundness, Hardness, or Spacing. These should be self-explanatory, but if not, check out the *Brushes and Brushes Panel* section in Help > After Effects Help > Drawing, Painting, and Paths > Paint Tools.

To save your customized brush, click on the icon in the Brush Tips panel (see figure). Your new brush will be named automatically based on its hardness, roundness, and size.

From the Brushes Options menu (top right of panel), you can also Rename or Delete an existing preset, view the brushes in various ways, and Reset the panel to the default set of preset brushes.

If you use a pressure-sensitive tablet (such as a Wacom tablet), you can set how the pen's pressure, tilt or stylus wheel affects the brush's characteristics dynamically. For instance, less pressure could decrease the diameter and opacity. Expand the Brush Dynamics section and set your own preferences for how to dynamically control the Minimum Size, Angle, Roundness, Opacity, and Flow. These settings are not saved when you change from one brush to another, so you may want to save a set of custom brushes.

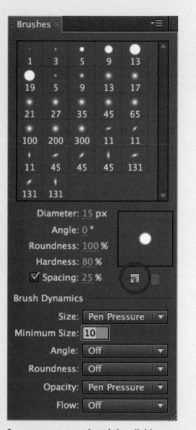

Save your custom brush by clicking on the icon (circled in red).

Interpolating Brush Strokes

If you animate the Path property, After Effects will interpolate between different brush strokes. Open comp [**Ex.06-Science-final**] and RAM Preview to get a sense of how you might embellish the section where the middle scientist stares at his container. Let's practice this technique:

Step 1: Open comp [**Ex.06-Science_starter**], move in time to 03:00 and double-click **AB_RetroScience.mov** to open it in the Layer panel.

Step 2: Select the Brush tool, and set the Duration popup to Constant. The Channels should be RGBA and the Mode set to Normal. Using a small brush and any color, draw a stroke emitting from the bottom of the blue container (don't worry if it covers the scientist's hand).

Step 3: Press PP to reveal Paint in the Timeline panel, and twirl down Brush 1. Turn on the stopwatch for the Path property to create the first keyframe at 03:00 (see figure to the right).

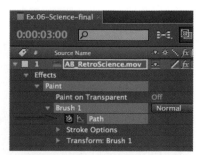

Step 3: To interpolate between brush strokes, draw the first stroke, then turn on the stopwatch for the Path property in the Timeline panel.

TIP

Focused RAM Preview

Press Option (Alt) when starting a RAM Preview to preview 5 frames up to and including the current frame. The number of frames previewed may be changed in Preferences > Previews > Alternate RAM Preview.

Step 4: Keep Brush 1 selected for the following steps: Advance to 3:15 and paint another quite different stroke. *Provided that Brush 1 remained selected*, the second shape will replace the first one and create a second keyframe for the Path property. Scrub the timeline to see the first shape interpolating to the second shape.

Step 5: Repeat Step 4 to create additional strokes every 15 frames, finishing up at 06:00. If you don't like one of the shapes, return to that point in time and – with Brush 1 still selected – paint a replacement stroke. If you change any of the settings in the Paint panel, when you create a new stroke, the new settings will apply to all previous shapes as well (think about it – all the shapes belong to a single brush stroke).

Step 6: The advantage to creating all the paths on Brush 1 is that you have only one set of Stroke Options and Transform settings, so you can easily animate parameters such as Diameter and Opacity across all the interpolating shapes. You can also tweak the Anchor Point's Y to move all the strokes up and down. Be aware that once you've turned on the stopwatch for any other parameters, adding a new Path keyframe to Brush 1 will add keyframes to these other parameters as well.

Our version is in [**Ex.06-Science-final**], where we first created our strokes, then animated a few parameters including Diameter, Opacity, and Scale. Note that scaling is applied after the stroke is rendered which will effect the Hardness value (the softness of the stroke).

By animating Path, a series of brush strokes appears as a single interpolating stroke (above). We then further animated the "blue smoke" by keyframing Brush 1's Diameter, Opacity and Scale (below). Footage courtesy Artbeats/Retro Science.

Effects and Paint

Paint is an effect that appears in the Effect Controls panel. Once you've created some paint strokes, any effect you apply will render after Paint. However, you can easily reorder the effects in the Effect Controls or Timeline panel, and even create multiple Paint effects.

Open **[Ex.07-FX Stack]**, where we've painted "clues" on a calendar and added various effects to tint and distort it. Double-click the calendar layer to open the Layer panel, and verify that the View pop-up is set to Roughen Edges (the last effect in the stack). Press F3 to open the Effect Controls panel.

There are two instances of Paint. The first instance writes "April" at the top of the calendar; because it's first in the rendering order, it's affected by the Noise HLS and Tint effects that follow, creating a parchment look to the paper. The second Paint effect creates the clues in blue paint, then the entire composite is distorted with Turbulent Displace. Roughen Edges affects the layer's alpha channel, and would have the same effect no matter where you placed it in the effect order.

This stack of effects is also reflected in the View popup at the bottom of the Layer panel; selecting any item from this list will display the composite at that point in the render order.

Try reordering the effects in the Effect Controls panel so you get a sense of how important the rendering order is. For instance, moving Turbulent Displace to the top distorts the source image but not the paint strokes. After moving an effect, check that the View popup is displaying the desired view.

To add another instance of Paint, select a view you want to paint, such as Tint. A new Paint effect will be added directly after the current effect. (If the current view is a Paint effect, new strokes will be added to it.)

In **[Ex.07-FX Stack]** we've added a number of effects in addition to two instances of Paint: The first instance creates the word "April" at the top of the calendar, followed by Noise HLS and Tint effects to add a parchment look to the paper. The second instance of Paint adds the "clues" in blue, followed by Turbulent Displace and Roughen Edges. When you're reordering effects, check that the View popup is set to the desired view and that the Render switch is on.

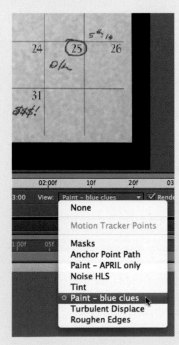

The View popup at the bottom of the Layer panel determines the point in the rendering order that is being displayed. For instance, selecting the "Paint – blue clues" effect shows the layer before Turbulent Displace and Roughen Edges are factored in. If you reorder effects in the Effect Controls or Timeline panels, the View menu will immediately update to reflect the changes. Calendar courtesy Getty Images.

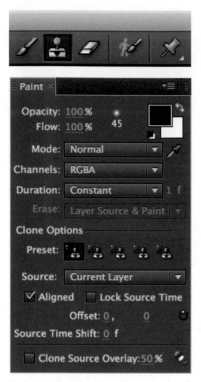

Step 1: Select the Clone Stamp tool and make sure the Clone Options section is visible in the Paint panel.

Using the Clone Stamp Tool

The Clone Stamp tool samples pixels on a source layer, then applies the sample to another part of the same layer or a different layer in the same comp. To Photoshop users, cloning is a familiar friend for repeating sections of an image and repairing flaws; in After Effects, you can also clone from a different point in time.

In this section we'll start with the basics, such as Clone Presets, Overlay mode, and cloning from a different layer. You'll then learn how to automatically clone out a problem area in a movie using a combination of Motion Tracking and Expressions.

We assume you've worked through this chapter from the start, as this section builds on concepts that were previously introduced. To get started, close all other comps and open [**Ex.08-Cloning_starter**].

Step 1: Our comp includes two movies; we'll start with layer 1, a clip of colorful boats in a harbor. (We'll use layer 2 in the next section.)

Double-click **AB_FrenchCountryside_exc.mov** to open it in its Layer panel and select the Clone Stamp tool. Make sure the Clone Options section is revealed in the Paint panel. Choose a soft brush around 45 pixels in size, and verify that the Paint panel is using default values for the other parameters (see figure to the left) – particularly Mode = Normal, Channels = RGBA, and Duration = Constant.

If you've ever cloned in Photoshop, you know there are two methods of repeating the sampled area: aligned (where the first stroke you make determines the offset for subsequent strokes), and not aligned (where every stroke starts from the same origin point). We'll explore both options.

Step 2: In the Layer panel (above), Option+click (Alt+click) on the red boat (circled in red) to set the source point, then clone a second boat in the bottom right corner. Clone strokes in the Timeline sport extra parameters (right). Footage courtesy Artbeats/French Countryside.

Clone Presets

The Clone Options settings can be saved in one of five Clone Presets. All you need to do to save a preset is first select its slot; any changes you then make will be stored in that preset. Get in the habit of picking the next Clone Preset button when you're working on a complicated job: This allows you to return to the Clone Options used earlier by reselecting that preset. The shortcuts for recalling Clone Preset 1 through 5 are the numbers 3 through 7 on the regular keyboard.

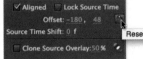

Clone Presets are convenient for storing the settings of the Clone Options section. Option+click (Alt+click) on a different Clone Preset to duplicate the current settings.

Step 2: Select the first Clone Preset in the Paint panel and verify that Aligned is enabled.

• Press the Option (Alt) key (the cursor will change to a "bull's eye" icon) and then click on the front of the red boat to set this pixel as the clone source. The Source Layer popup in the Paint panel will update to reflect the name of this layer (we'll explore using different layers in a moment).

• Release the Option (Alt) key. As you move the cursor, the Offset value in the Paint panel updates to reflect how far you are from the source pixel. You can either begin cloning now, or press Option+Shift (Alt+Shift) to temporarily see an overlay of the offset image. Move your cursor to reposition this overlay; this also updates the Offset value. To begin cloning, release any modifier keys and click to paint a clone of the red boat elsewhere on the frame.

You can also scrub the Offset values directly in the Paint panel. When you do, the overlay will also appear temporarily as a guide.

If you paint again somewhere else, this time you will *not* get another red boat, as the same *absolute* offset will be used.

Step 3: Select Clone Preset 2; verify that the Source Position for this preset is at 0,0. Disable the Aligned switch.

• Press the Option (Alt) key and click on the white buoy (the ball) at the rear of the yellow boat. This sets the Source Position around X = 383, Y = 388.

• Release the Option (Alt) key and clone the white buoy behind the red boat. Try another stroke somewhere else. With Align off, every stroke you make is sampled from the original clone source, not an offset from the cursor position.

To reset the Offset value, either repeat the Option+click (Alt+click) step to pick a new origin point, or click the Reset Offset button along the right side of the Paint panel to change the values to 0,0.

Step 3: When Aligned is off, every stroke is sampled from the same Source Position.

Set the Mode to Hard Light, then set the Clone Options as shown above. The Clone Source Overlay displays an overlay of the source as a guide; set its transparency interactively by scrubbing the % value. (The button to the right toggles the overlay to Difference mode.)

Clone Source Overlay

Let's add a little color to the gray clouds in [Ex.08] as we introduce two more features: Clone Source Overlay and Lock Source Time.

Step 1: Double-click layer 2 – **AB_SkyEffects.mov** – to open it in its Layer panel and preview it: It contains a big yellow sun setting over a warm sky. If you were to use this movie to colorize layer 1, the color would fade out as the sun sets, so let's clone from only a single frame.

Step 2: Press Home to make sure the time indicator is at 00:00. Bring the Layer panel for **AB_FrenchCountryside_exc.mov** forward again, and with the Clone Stamp tool selected, click the third Clone Preset button.

- Set Opacity to 50% and set the Mode popup to Hard Light.
- For the Source popup, select the **AB_SkyEffects.mov** layer.
- Turn on Lock Source Time so that the same frame is used throughout, and verify that Source Time is set to 0f (the frame at 00:00).
- Check that the Aligned switch is on and that Offset is set to 0,0.

Step 3: Enable Clone Source Overlay in the Paint panel. The clone source will appear as an overlay when you move over the Layer panel.

- Scrub the value for Source Time to pick a different source frame (if you use a later frame, the sun appears to be setting above the buildings).

Step 4: With a large soft brush (at least 100 pixels), clone the sky area in one continuous stroke (so you'll only have one set of parameters to manage later). If you don't like the result, Undo and clone again.

The original sky and water is rather gray (left). By selecting a different layer to clone from (center), you can add a little color to the movie (right). We created two clone strokes: a 50% Opacity stroke for the sky area, and a 30% Opacity clone for the buildings and water. Footage courtesy Artbeats/Sky Effects.

If the color is too strong, reveal the stroke in the Timeline panel and set the Stroke Options > Opacity value to taste. Try other Modes as well.

Note that as the sky is quite colorful, the water may look unrealistically gray. Create a second clone stroke for the buildings and water, but reduce the Opacity so it appears as a reflection of the sky.

Our version is shown in comp [**Ex.08-Cloning-final**].

Note: You can change the Clone Time in the Timeline panel, but you must toggle on Lock Source Time before you clone as this option is not editable in the Timeline. If you need to lock the source frame after the fact, use Time Remapping to create a freeze frame of the desired clone source frame. Select the clone movie and go Layer > Time > Freeze Frame.

Shifting the Source Time

Close [**Ex.08**], and open [**Ex.09-CloneTime_starter**]. For your next trick, you'll clone the flag on top of the building. When you're cloning identical objects, you'll often need to also shift the timing of the duplicate:

Step 1: Double-click **AB_FrenchTowns_exc.mov** to open it in its Layer panel. Select the Clone Stamp tool, and pick the fourth Clone Preset.

• In the Paint panel, set Opacity to 100% and Mode to Normal.

• Set the Clone Options as per the figure to the right.

• Create a brush suitable for cloning the flag (we edited the soft 21-pixel size brush in Brushes so that it had a Hardness value of 50%).

Step 2: Zoom in 200%. Press Option (Alt) and click on the base of the original flag to set the source point. Move the cursor to the top of the leftmost flagpole; the Clone Source Overlay will follow the cursor. Clone to create a second flag, then RAM Preview to see the result.

Step 3: Notice anything odd? Both flags are flapping exactly the same, which gives the game away. Rather than offsetting the Source Time Shift in the Paint panel and redoing the stroke, it's easier to press PP then twirl until you see Stroke Options in the Timeline and scrub Clone Time Shift's value. The image will update in the Layer panel. (Be aware that the footage is wrapping around itself. For instance, if you offset time by one second, the clip will wrap around to the head of the clip one second before the end.)

Step 4: This second flag is supposed to be in the rear, so reduce its size using Clone 1 > Transform > Scale.

Step 2: Zoom in and sample the base of the original flag (red circle to the right), then clone a copy on top of the leftmost flagpole. Footage courtesy Artbeats/French Towns & Villages.

Steps 3–4: In the Timeline panel (above), the cloned stroke was shifted in time and scaled down to push it to the rear (right).

The white boat in **[Ex.10]** is distracting and needs to be removed. Footage courtesy Artbeats/New York City Aerials.

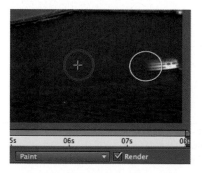

Step 1: Select Clone Preset 5 and pick a brush large enough to cover the boat (above). In the Layer panel (below) select the water to the left of the boat (see red circle) as the clone source point, then remove the boat.

Tracking the Clone

While you can animate the position of a stroke as well as the clone source position, it's not easy to clone out an object that is moving at an irregular speed by simply setting keyframes. However, Motion Tracking excels at tracking an object from frame to frame. By combining both techniques, you can easily and accurately remove or duplicate a moving object.

Open the [**Ex.10-Tracking_starter**] comp and RAM Preview. The aerial footage of the Statue of Liberty is exactly what the clients want, but they find the white boat distracting and want it removed. In this section, you'll use motion tracking to determine the boat's location on each frame, then use a simple expression to make the clone stroke follow the tracker data. We hope we've included enough instructions so you can follow along even if you're unfamiliar with Motion Tracking or Expressions (if not, please revisit this section after you've read Chapters 29–30 and 37 respectively; it should then make more sense).

Be aware that if you can't successfully remove or clone the object on a single frame, throwing the motion tracker at it won't help. The tracker excels at following a pattern of pixels – but it can't work miracles and make unsuitable footage suddenly easy to clone!

Creating the Dummy Clone Stroke

In order for the Clone stroke to follow motion tracking data, you first need to create a stroke that is the right size to remove or clone your object:

Step 1: Double-click layer 1 – **AB_NewYorkCityAerials_exc.mov** – to open its Layer panel, select the Clone Stamp tool, then select the fifth Clone Preset. You should know by now how to set up the Paint panel and Clone Options to create a simple clone stroke (if you don't, see *Using the Clone Stamp Tool* earlier in this chapter, page 568).

Note that the boat gets bigger before it exits the frame around 06:00, so select a brush that's a little larger than you need at time 00:00. We used a 50 pixel size brush with a 50% Hardness value. (Remember that you can save your current brush settings as a new brush by clicking on the "new document" icon at the bottom of the Brushes panel.)

At time 00:00, press Option (Alt) and click on an area of clear water to the left of the boat to select a good source point, then clone some of this water over the boat. Make the stroke a little longer than you need, to account for the fact that the boat will be bigger later on.

Tracking the Boat

The next step is to motion track the movement of the boat:

Step 2: Return to the Selection tool (shortcut: V). Select Animation > Track Motion; this creates Tracking Region boxes in the Layer panel, and the View will be set to Motion Tracker Points. The Tracker Controls panel will open, and a Motion Trackers section appears in the Timeline.

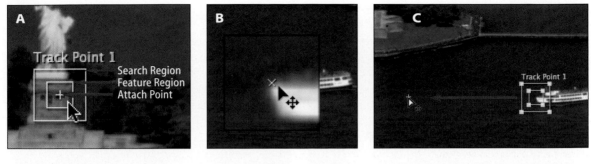

Step 3: Track Point 1 defaults to the center of the Layer panel (see **A** above). The inner box is the Feature Region (the "pattern" of pixels to be tracked); the outer box is the Search Region (the area to be searched for the defined pattern); the + symbol in the center is the Attach Point.

Zoom in, click inside the inner box (the Feature Region will zoom up), and drag the Feature Region so that it centers on the front tip of the boat (see **B** above). This takes a little practice; if you end up moving the Attach Point or enlarging one of the boxes, Undo and try again!

Step 4: Motion tracking is normally used to attach a second layer to the footage being tracked, in which case the Attach Point (the + symbol) would be moved to where the anchor point of this second layer should be positioned. In this case, the Attach Point data will be used for the Clone Position, so move the attach point to the water to the left (see also caption for **C**). You can also set this value numerically by editing the Attach Point value in the Timeline.

Step 5: Still at 00:00, click the Analyze Forward button in the Tracker Controls (see figures below). Although you can hit the Stop button in the Tracker Controls when the boat disappears off the bottom of the frame, we let it track to the end; you can always trim the out point for the clone stroke. When the track is done, keyframes will be created for each frame.

A: The default position for Track Point 1.

B: Moving the Feature Region.

C: Dragging the Attach Point to the left. This point will be the area of the water used for the start of the clone stroke; because the boat moves off the bottom of the frame, be sure the attach point is no lower in the frame than the tip of the boat, or it will move out of frame earlier.

TIP

Who's Up First

If you create the tracker first, the Layer panel will be filled with tracker points when you try to clone. To see an obstructed image, set the View menu to None.

Step 5: Once the Feature Region and the Attach Point are in place, click the Analyze Forward button.

Step 5 *complete:* When the track is complete, the Layer panel (above right) will show the path of the track (don't worry about the end where the boat dipped out of the frame). The Timeline panel (above) will show the data captured for Track Point 1.

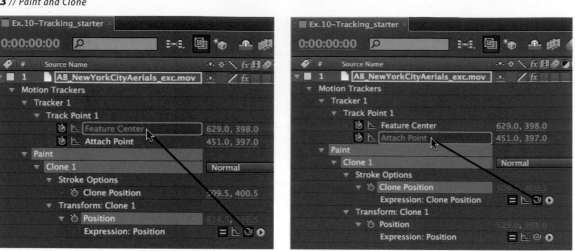

Step 6: Express the clone stroke's Position parameter to Track Point 1's Feature Center (left). Then express the Clone Position parameter to the tracker's Attach Point (right).

Hide Parameters

To simplify these figures, we hid unused parameters by pressing Option+Shift (Alt+Shift) and clicking on their names in the Timeline panel.

Expressing the Clone Stroke

Step 6: Now it's time to make the clone stroke follow the tracker data. Reveal the Clone 1 and Tracker Point 1 sections in the Timeline panel so you can see all of their parameters. With the Selection tool still active:

• Option+click (Alt+click) on the stopwatch for the Clone 1 > Transform > Position parameter to start the expression, click on the pick whip (the spiral icon) and drag it to the Feature Center parameter in Track Point 1, then release the mouse. Press Enter to accept the expression.

• Option+click (Alt+click) on the stopwatch for the Clone 1 > Stroke Options > Clone Position parameter, select its pick whip and drag it to the Attach Point parameter in Track Point 1. Press Enter to accept.

Bring the Comp panel forward and RAM Preview; the boat should be removed throughout. If you find the edge of the boat is visible in places, increase the Diameter of the stroke to 60px.

We finished off our version [**Ex.10-Tracking-final**] by fading out the stroke at 06:00 and trimming the end of the Clone 1 stroke.

Step 6 *complete:* The expressions linking Clone 1's parameters to Track Point 1. The Clone stroke is faded out by animating Stroke Options > Opacity from 100% to 0%, starting at 06:00 when the boat disappears. The end of the stroke can also be trimmed.

Random Paint Splatters

We'll finish our tour with a smattering of other issues and ideas for getting the best from Paint and Clone:

Painting in a Straight Line: To paint, erase, or clone in a straight line, click once at the start of the stroke, hold down the Shift key, move (don't drag) your mouse to where the line should end, and click again. A straight line stroke will be created. Continue holding Shift and clicking to paint additional straight line segments. Cloning in a straight line is handy for removing film scratches and so on. Practice this in **[Ex.11-StraightLine_starter]**, where we've added a fake scratch at 02:00. (Tip: Set the Duration popup to Single Frame to create a one-frame stroke.)

Copy and Pasting Strokes: You can copy and paste mask paths and shape layer paths to and from a stroke's Path property. One example of animating a star-shaped brush stroke is in **[Ex.12]**. To do this trick: Select the Mask Path property in the Timeline and Copy, click on the stroke's Path property and Paste.

Cloning the Clone: The Clone Stamp tool samples from the cloned image. To use the original source, add a duplicate copy of your layer to the comp and select it in the Clone Options > Source popup.

Motion Tracking in Time: In **[Ex.10]**, we showed using motion tracking and expressions to automate removing the boat by replacing it with the water texture. In other situations, such as removing a bird flying across the sky with a locked-down camera, you might be better off cloning from the same area of the sky but right before or after the bird flew by. To do this, in Step 6 express both the Position and Clone Position parameters to the Feature Region, then edit the Clone Time Shift value.

Revealing a Title: To use Paint to write on a layer with an alpha channel (such as a solid text layer or logo), paint over the text in Write On mode, enable Paint on Transparent, then apply Effect > Channels > Set Matte (at default settings) to reapply the original alpha channel. This is shown in **[Ex.13]**. (Note: If the text is textured, not solid, use the painted layer as an alpha track matte; see **[Ex.14]**.)

Eyedropper Toggle: When the Brush tool is selected, press Option (Alt) to toggle to the eyedropper tool, then click anywhere in the Layer panel to sample a new foreground color from a single pixel. To sample from a 5×5 pixel area, press Command+Option (Control+Alt) then click.

Opacity and Flow Shortcuts: Press a number from 1 through 9 on the keypad to set a painting tool's Opacity from 10% to 90%, respectively; press the decimal key for 100%. Add the Shift key to adjust Flow instead.

To repair this (fake) film scratch, create a straight line clone stroke with a slight horizontal Offset value or one-frame Source Time Shift.

Paint Shortcuts

For a full list of shortcuts for Paint and Clone, select Help > Keyboard Shortcuts > Shortcuts for working with paint tools.

CONNECT

Blending modes: Chapter 9.

Masking: Chapter 10.

Applying effects: Chapter 22.

Motion Tracking: Chapter 30.

Shape layers: Chapter 32.

Expressions: Chapter 37.

34

Roto Brush

A new tool for separating foregrounds from backgrounds.

The Roto Brush is a new tool introduced in After Effects CS5 that helps automate creating a matte to separate a foreground from a background, such as isolating an actor from the room around him. To accomplish this, you draw brush strokes to teach After Effects the difference between the two. After Effects uses this information in conjunction with edge detection, motion tracking, and optical flow technologies to follow the changes in foreground and background over time. You can then touch up any remaining problem areas with the paint and masking tools. It's not perfect, but it's a lot easier than hand drawing and animating precise mask shapes.

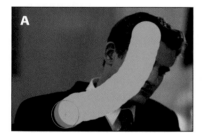

The Roto Brush allows you to paint relatively loose strokes to define the foreground (A) and background of an image (B). The result is an alpha channel for the foreground portion of the image (C). Footage courtesy Artbeats/Business Executives.

In this chapter, we will guide you through a preferred workflow for achieving good results with Roto Brush. We will also discuss Refine Matte: a section of the Roto Brush effect that greatly improves the matte edges created by Roto Brush. Refine Matte is also available as a stand-alone effect that can be used to clean up mattes created through conventional keying, masking, or painting techniques.

Roto Brush Workflow

Of course, every project is different, and as you become more familiar with using Roto Brush you will gain a better understanding for how to tackle varying tasks. But in general, this is a good workflow for using Roto Brush:

• If your footage has interlacing and/or pulldown, make sure you first Separate Fields and Remove Pulldown (covered in Chapter 41).

• Choose a representative frame where the maximum amount of the foreground is clearly visible. This will be a Base frame.

Example Project

Explore the 34-Example Project.aep file as you read this chapter; references to [Ex.##] refer to specific compositions within the project file.

- Create broad Foreground and Background Strokes.

- Use smaller strokes to define the Base frame as best as you can.

- Move a few frames away from the Base, and tweak the Propagation parameters to optimize Roto Brush's tracking of the shot.

- Step away from the Base a frame at a time, adding Foreground and Background Strokes as needed.

- Tweak the Smooth, Feather, and Choke parameters to get a good rough outline.

- Enable the Refine Matte section to further tweak the final result.

We're going to follow the above steps as we work through this chapter's exercise; we'll also note where you might need to take deviations for your own footage.

Creating a Base Frame

Roto Brush starts with the strokes you define on your Base frame, then attempts to propagate the resulting criteria backward and forward through adjacent frames. As a result, it's important that you create the best Base possible to start.

Step 1: Open [**Ex.01_starter**]. You must perform your Roto Brush work in the Layer panel. Therefore, double-click the layer **AB_BE120_ex.mov** to load it into the Layer panel.

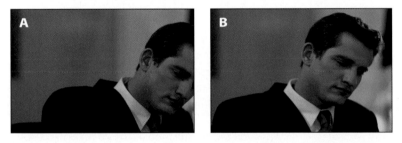

Step 2: Scrub the current time indicator through the clip to find a good starting frame. The section where the actor's head is partially off screen would be a bad choice, as Roto Brush would have a harder time tracking changes in his head's shape as it re-entered the frame. A good candidate is frame 00:16, as the actor's shoulder and chair have come on screen from the left, while his head has not yet exited the screen on the right.

Step 3: Select the Roto Brush tool (it's between the Eraser and Puppet Pin tools). Position the cursor over the actor's head; a green circle will appear representing the brush size. Resize the brush to roughly the size of his eye socket by pressing Command on Mac (Control on Windows) and dragging. Brush size is not critical at this stage, but a larger brush will yield slightly better results for these initial strokes than a tiny brush will.

TIP

Full Resolution

For good results, you should set the composition to Full Resolution when using Roto Brush, even if Magnification is set to a value other than 100%.

Step 2: Image A would make a bad Base frame, as the actor's head is cropped off. Image B (at 00:16) is a much better candidate, as his head and shoulder are at their most visible.

TIP

Painting Inside the Lines

If you accidentally cross over to the background while painting a Foreground Stroke (or vice versa), don't paint an opposing stroke to compensate; instead, undo and repaint the stroke.

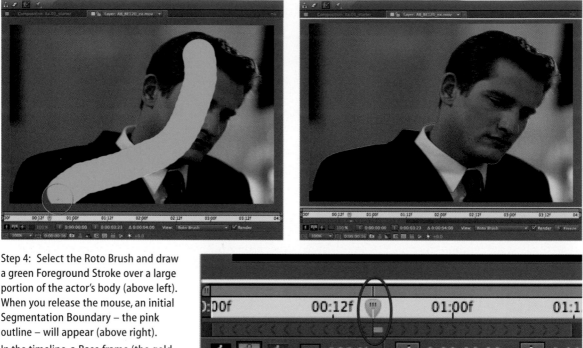

Step 4: Select the Roto Brush and draw a green Foreground Stroke over a large portion of the actor's body (above left). When you release the mouse, an initial Segmentation Boundary – the pink outline – will appear (above right).

In the timeline, a Base frame (the gold bar in figure, right) will be created, along with gray arrows showing the length of the initial Roto Brush Span.

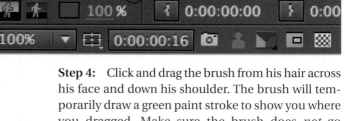

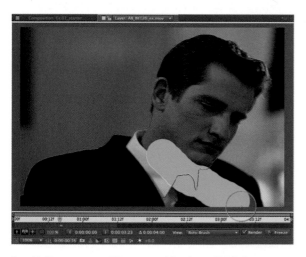

Step 5: Draw a second Foreground Stroke to finish the rough selection of the actor's body.

Step 4: Click and drag the brush from his hair across his face and down his shoulder. The brush will temporarily draw a green paint stroke to show you where you dragged. Make sure the brush does *not* go beyond the outline of his body; if it does, undo and try again.

After you release the mouse, the green brush stroke will disappear, and a pink outline will appear around a portion of his body. This is the *Segmentation Boundary*, which shows the line between foreground and background. In the timeline for the Layer panel, you will see a short gold bar extending from the current time indicator; this denotes a *Base frame*. The gray arrows extending before and after the Base show the extent of the current *Roto Brush Span*: how far the Roto Brush will attempt to track the shot on its own before it requires additional clues.

Step 5: Draw a second Foreground Stroke starting on his shirt collar and dragging across his tie and down his other shoulder. The Segmentation Boundary should now encompass most of his body.

Step 6:   Hover your cursor over the wall behind the actor, and press the Option (Alt) key: The brush will change from a green circle with a plus sign to a red circle with a minus sign. Red indicates you are about to draw a Background Stroke. Drag across the back wall to teach Roto Brush what to exclude in the frame. You may optionally draw additional Background Strokes over the bright sections on the right.

Step 7:   Now that you have taught Roto Brush what to do in broad terms, it's time to work on the details. Zoom in to 200% Magnification or more, and pan around the clip looking for places where the Segmentation Boundary does not quite follow the actor's outline. (You can hold down either the space-bar or the H key to temporarily engage the Hand tool, allowing you to drag the footage around inside the Layer panel.) The goal is to define the Segmentation Boundary to within a pixel or two of the foreground's actual outline.

Once you find an area where the foreground is not properly enclosed, with the Roto Brush selected press Command (Control) and drag to create a small brush; use this brush to paint over the areas you wish to include in the foreground. A good technique is to start or end your stroke over a section already included to tie the areas together.

Move around the frame, adding details around the actor's hair, ear, and eye as needed. If you accidentally brush into the background area, undo and try again. If you brushed within the foreground but Roto Brush selected part of the background, *don't* undo; teach Roto Brush the difference by pressing Option (Alt) and drawing a new Background Stroke to exclude the area Roto Brush grabbed by mistake. In general, don't worry about giving Roto Brush too much information; just worry about giving it *bad* information.

Although it's not an issue with this clip, if you have holes – often caused by arms or legs creating enclosed spaces around background areas – which have accidentally filled in, use Background Strokes to exclude these areas from your matte.

Save your project. If you want to check your work, our progress at this point is saved in [**Ex.01a-Base Frame**]. If you'd prefer to use our version, remember to open the clip in the Layer panel.

Step 6: Hold Option (Alt) and draw a Background Stroke to teach Roto Brush which areas to exclude.

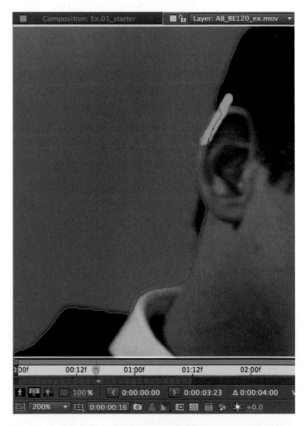

Step 7: Perfect the Segmentation Boundary by drawing more detailed Foreground and Background Strokes.

Focused RAM Preview

Press Option (Alt) when starting a RAM Preview just a few frames from the current time indicator in the direction of the Roto Brush Span arrows. The number of frames defaults to 5; this may be changed in Preferences > Previews > Alternate RAM Preview.

.

Propagation

Roto Brush attempts to detect movement from frame to frame, and uses that information to determine where the Segmentation Boundary should be on those adjacent frames. You can optimize how good a job Roto Brush does.

Step 8: Twirl open Roto Brush's Propagation section in the Effect Controls panel, and enable View Search Region. A yellow outline will appear in the Layer panel indicating how far Roto Brush is searching for movement, and the image will turn black and white. Ideally, Roto Brush should search far enough to capture any movement from frame to frame, yet narrow its search for portions of the foreground that aren't moving as much. If the Search Region is too loose, the result can be "edge chatter" in which Roto Brush mistakenly assumes stationary edges are moving. If the Search Region is too tight, Roto Brush may miss some movement.

Step 8: Twirl open the Propagation section in Roto Brush and enable View Search Region (above). It will appear as a yellow outline around your foreground object (right).

Explore the frames adjacent to your Base; the green bars extending from the gold Base frame marker (below) indicate which frames Roto Brush has calculated and cached.

Press Page Up and Page Down (or click the Previous Frame and Next Frame buttons in the Preview panel) to explore the frames adjacent to your Base. There will be a slight pause as Roto Brush detects the movement and calculates the new Segmentation Boundary. Note how the yellow Search Region adapts from frame to frame. (There is no time savings in jumping ahead several frames at once; Roto Brush has to calculate all of the intermediate frames to get there.)

Step 9: First, let's explore the parameters Roto Brush uses to detect the underlying motion:

• Search Radius is a general number for how far Roto Brush searches for movement from frame to frame. Since the motion is not too fast in this clip, you can reduce the Search Region slightly to tighten up the detection. Check adjacent frames to make sure Roto Brush does not lose track.

• Motion Threshold affects how Roto Brush determines if an edge is moving. You will notice that the yellow Search Region is thinner around the shoulder on the left (which moves less) compared with the head (which moves more). Set Motion Damping to 0%, then increase Motion Threshold: If you go too far, the Search Region will disappear around the shoulder – which is not good, as the shoulder does move a little. Decrease it until you get at least a few pixels of yellow across the entire edge for each frame.

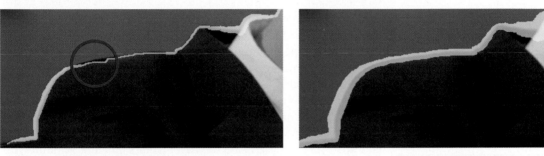

• Motion Damping controls how tight Roto Brush makes the Search Region for edges that are moving slowly. Once you have a good Motion Threshold setting, increase Motion Damping and observe how the Search Region narrows around the slow-moving shoulder. If the yellow Search Region no longer encompasses the foreground's outline, you've gone too far and Roto Brush is losing the track; decrease it until the Search Region continues to encompass the proper edge between the foreground and background across adjacent frames.

Once you have the Propagation values optimized, toggle View Search Region off.

Step 10: Next, let's explore options that affect how tightly the Segmentation Boundary follows the actual edge between foreground and background:

• Edge Detection determines how Roto Brush calculates the Segmentation Boundary for frames other than the Base frame you defined. The Favor Current Edges option puts an emphasis on edges found in the current frame in isolation, which may be more accurate if the image changes a lot from frame to frame. The Favor Predicted Edges option tries to predict where the edge should be based on the location of those edges in adjacent frames (which helps when the footage is noisy, or the foreground and background are very similar). Balanced considers both equally.

Try the different options on this shot while stepping through adjacent frames. We found that Favor Current Edges tended to leave out areas like the hair below his ear, whereas Favor Predicted Edges looked a little loose on some frames – so Balanced was our best choice for this shot.

• Use Alternate Color Estimation alters the internal algorithm used to determine what is foreground and what is background. In this shot, we found that enabling it helped track some details such as the eye.

Again, save your project. Our work to this point is saved in comp **[Ex.01b-Propagation]**.

Step 9: If Motion Damping is too high, Roto Brush may get lost searching for moving edges (left). Decrease Motion Damping until the yellow Search Region encompasses the correct edges over several frames of movement (right).

GOTCHA

Retro Roto!

If your image is black and white and you don't know why, check to see if View Search Region is still enabled!

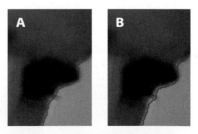

Step 10: Roto Brush might lose track of fine details, such as the outline of the actor's eyelash (A). In these cases, try enabling Use Alternate Color Estimation to see if it helps – which it does in this case (B).

Tracking the Rest of the Shot

At this point, you've created a good Base frame and refined Roto Brush's ability to track movement away from this frame. Now it's time to step through the rest of the frames and make any necessary corrections.

Note that *while the Roto Brush tool is active*, you can press 1 and 2 to step backward and forward one frame at a time, respectively. You can also use the shortcuts Page Up and Page Down.

Step 11: Return the current time indicator to your Base frame at 00:16. With the Layer panel forward and the Roto Brush selected, press 1 to step backward toward the start of the clip. Carefully study each frame before moving on; if the Segmentation Boundary no longer correctly follows the edge between your foreground and background, add corrective Foreground or Background Strokes. Any corrections you make will then propagate from this frame onward in the direction indicated by the gray Span arrows underneath the Layer panel's timeline. With this clip, chances are good that you won't have to make any corrective strokes.

Step 12: Again, return to your Base frame at 00:16. This time, press 2 to step forward a frame at a time, studying and correcting each frame before you move on. For example, you may encounter a problem at frame 01:00 where the actor's motion-blurred hand rises into the frame and is not automatically captured inside the Segmentation Boundary – include it by painting a Foreground Stroke from his suit across his hand. This action will also extend the forward Span to be 20 frames from your most recent adjustment.

Step 13: We noticed another interesting issue at frame 01:01 where the actor is holding a pen in the lower right corner of the frame. Ideally, there should be a hole formed by the actor's hand and the pen he's holding (it may even appear as a small hole in your version). The hole is missing (or appears too small) for a few reasons:

• Roto Brush is trying to preserve as much of the hand as it can, even though it is heavily motion blurred.

• The Segmentation Boundary is just a rough representation of the final matte; it may look better when we toggle on Refine Matte later.

• The Roto Brush > Matte > Smooth parameter defaults to a value of 2.0, which attempts to round out the features of the hole.

Step 12: Use a Foreground Stroke to add the hand to the foreground selection inside the pink Segmentation Boundary.

Step 13: If the hole between the pen and the body is ill defined (A), reduce the Matte > Smooth value (B) and draw a Background Stroke (in red) to open it up (C). The result is a better defined hole (D).

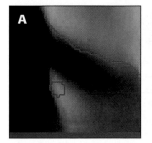
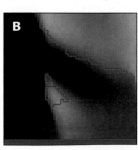
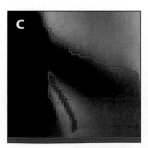
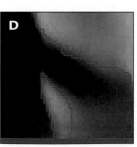

To create or improve the hole, follow these steps:

- Temporarily set Matte > Smooth to 0.0 to see more detail in the hole.
- Zoom in to a Magnification of 400% or so.
- Hold Command (Control) and drag to make a very small brush.
- Hold Option (Alt) and draw a Background Stroke in the area where the hole should be transparent. The Segmentation Boundary will be better defined now. If needed, draw additional Foreground or Background Strokes to improve the hole's definition.
- Set Matte > Smooth back to 2.0 for now.

Step 14: Proceed in this manner through the rest of the clip, keeping your eye on the relationship between the current time indicator and the gray Span arrows along the bottom of the timeline. If you step more than 20 frames beyond your last adjustment, you will be beyond the end of the Span, and the Segmentation Boundary will select the entire frame. If this happens, you have a few choices:

- If Roto Brush was doing a good job, you can extend the Span by dragging the last arrow in the span to the right.

- Alternatively, you can back up to a frame inside the Span, then draw an additional Foreground or Background Stroke to refresh the track.

- Or you can move to a time beyond the current Span (the entire frame will then be outlined) and start a second Base frame by drawing new Foreground and Background Strokes. Indeed, in this shot where the actor pulls away from the edge of the screen later in the clip, a good approach is to jump to a representative frame during the second half of the clip, create a new Base frame, and work backward from there to join up with your previous Span.

We took the third approach when working through our version of this example. Our results to this point are saved in [**Ex.01c-Segmented**].

Go ahead and spend some time improving your Segmentation Boundary across the entire clip. It may take a bit of work, but it is usually far less than if you had to precisely mask every frame by hand. When you're done, press V to return to the Selection tool.

Deleting Strokes and Spans

If you have created multiple Base frames and corresponding Span, and are unhappy with one of them, right-click on it and select Remove Span – this deletes the span, but leaves the strokes. Note that if you have only one Base frame, Remove Span will be grayed out.

To delete all strokes on the frame you are viewing in the Layer panel, press Command+A (Control+A) to select all, then press Delete. To delete a specific stroke, type PP to reveal the strokes in the Timeline.

TIP

Lock Segmentation

You can click the Freeze button in the lower right corner of the Layer panel to lock the Segmentation Boundary in place, save it with your project, and prevent time-consuming recalculations later. Just remember to unfreeze if you want to make a correction to the segmentation!

Step 14: If you haven't drawn a corrective stroke for more than 20 frames, you can either extend the Span or start a second Base frame and Span.

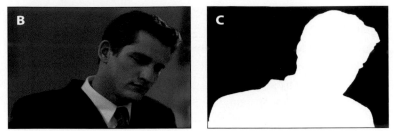

A series of buttons have been added to the Layer panel in After Effects CS5 that control its view modes (below). With these you can view your matte against the Transparency Grid (A) or the comp's Background Color, with an alpha overlay color (B), or as a high-contrast matte (C).

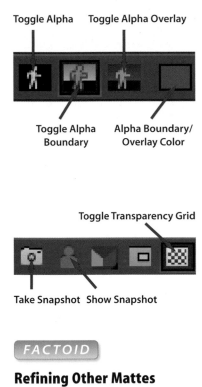

Toggle Alpha   Toggle Alpha Overlay

Toggle Alpha   Alpha Boundary/
Boundary   Overlay Color

Toggle Transparency Grid

Take Snapshot   Show Snapshot

Refining Other Mattes

The Refine Matte section of Roto Brush also exists as a standalone effect under the Matte category. It can be applied to other problematic mattes and alpha channels, including those created by a bad color key.

Refining the Matte

The pink Segmentation Boundary you've been looking at so far is but a crude representation of the final matte. Roto Brush is capable of creating an antialiased matte with feathering and motion blur; it can even color correct the areas around the edges.

Before moving on, become acquainted with the new view modes added in CS5. Along the bottom left corner of the Layer panel is a series of three buttons that change how the image in the Layer panel is displayed; explore the different looks they provide.

Step 15:   Toggle the Alpha Boundary off and the Transparency Grid on. Study the area where the actor's chin crosses over his shoulder, as well as where his eyelash extends beyond his face. The areas around these features are probably rounded rather than sharp, revealing part of the background. You can reduce Roto Brush > Matte > Smooth to tighten up these corners. If the result is a jagged outline elsewhere, counterbalance it by increasing Matte > Feather. If the background is visible as a colored fringe (look at his shirt collar), increase Choke to clean it up, being careful not to eat away too much of the detail in his hair. Revisit these parameters later and keep balancing them against each other to perfect your edges.

Matte		
▸ ⏱ Smooth		1.0
▸ ⏱ Feather		50.0%
▸ ⏱ Choke		50%
⏱ Refine Matte		☑
▸ ⏱ Reduce Chatter		50%
⏱ Use Motion Blur		☑

Step 16:   Click the Take Snapshot button (the camera icon, see figure to the left) along the bottom of the Layer panel to remember what your matte looked like. Then enable Matte > Refine Matte. Your matte edges should improve considerably; click the Show Snapshot button to compare before and after. Enabling Refine Matte also gives you access to additional parameters.

Step 17:   Move the current time indicator to around 02:19 where the actor's head is moving the fastest. You will notice that the matte around his head is softer than around his relatively stationary shoulders – this is an example of Motion Blur being calculated. Toggle Roto Brush > Matte > Use Motion Blur on and off to compare.

To further tweak how Motion Blur is rendered, twirl open the Matte > Motion Blur section. Here you can tweak the Samples Per Frame and

Step 17: Roto Brush's Matte > Motion Blur section (left) controls how fast-moving edges are rendered (above).

Shutter Angle (discussed in Chapter 8). The Higher Quality switch trades off additional quality for additional render time; toggle it and see if you notice an appreciable difference.

Step 18: Finally, Roto Brush's Refine Matte section has the ability to reduce color spill from the background onto the edges and foreground, including partially transparent motion-blurred edges. This correction is enabled or disabled using Matte > Decontaminate Edge Colors; the depth is controlled with Matte > Decontamination > Decontamination Amount. This shot was well-lit and does not contain much contamination to remove, although you may notice a slight improvement around the edges.

Twirl open the Matte > Decontamination section, and enable View Decontamination Map. The white outline shows the area where Roto Brush is performing color correction. This area changes size depending on how fast the foreground is moving. If visible color spill extends beyond this area, use Increase Decontamination Radius to correct a wider zone.

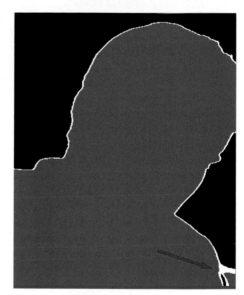

Step 18: The white zone in the Decontamination Map shows the areas that will be automatically color corrected. Here on frame 01:01, notice the large white area in the lower right corner around the fast moving (and partially transparent) hand and pen.

If your foreground isn't moving, but the matte around its edges is changing from frame to frame anyway, increase Roto Brush > Matte > Reduce Chatter. By contrast, if Roto Brush seems to be ignoring slight movements or if it erodes fast-moving edges, try decreasing Reduce Chatter. The Extend Where Smoothed switch comes into play only when Matte > Reduce Chatter is greater than 0. If an edge must be moved to "dechatter" it, and Extend Where Smoothed is enabled, the area around these edges is more thoroughly color corrected. Toggle to see if you notice an improvement; leave it off if you don't.

If you've worked all the way through this example, then you have a good idea how to employ Roto Brush on other shots. Not all clips will be as easy to clean up as this one; you may need to create more corrective strokes on more frames, or use the Paint tools (Chapter 33) on the alpha channel to clean up problem areas. However, Roto Brush can often create very useable mattes in a fraction of the time of traditional painting or masking techniques, which is particularly useful in less critical applications such as color correcting just a region of an image.

CONNECT

Motion Blur: Chapter 8.

Masking: Chapter 10.

Paint: Chapter 33.

Interlacing and Pulldown: Chapter 41.

The Puppet Tools

A fun way to organically warp and animate layers.

One of the most fun areas to explore in After Effects is using the Puppet tools. These provide a new way to warp layers, including shape and text layers created inside After Effects. Applications include creating character animation or just imparting fun movement to otherwise inanimate objects.

Previously, the best tool in After Effects for character animation was parenting (the subject of Chapter 17). Parenting requires setting up a hierarchy of layers that correspond to the individual body parts, and carefully arranging their pivot points by relocating the Anchor Point for each layer. Once this is done, you can animate the rotation of your "limbs" around their joints, and the attached parts will follow.

Puppeting takes a different approach. Rather than working with a rigid bone analogy, puppeting is more akin to working with a sheet of rubber. You place pins in this sheet where you want sections to stay put or at points where you want to pull and deform the rubber. All the pixels in-between flex as needed to accommodate your movements. There are optional tools for setting stiffness as well as making sections of a layer pass in front of or behind others.

To give you a basis for comparison, open this chapter's example project, then open the comp [**Ex.01**]. It includes vector artwork of a marionette where we have separated a hand, forearm, and upper arm onto their own layers apart from the rest of the body. We have already moved the anchor points of each limb to a logical pivot point, then set up a parenting chain where the hand is connected to the forearm and so forth.

Expose the Rotation parameter for each of the layers and scrub these values in the Timeline panel while watching the Comp panel to get an idea for how such a parenting chain works. (By the way, the original layered vector file – **Marionette_deconstruct.ai** – is in the **35_Chapter Sources** folder if you want to continue with this approach.)

Now let's try the puppeting tools:

Puppet Pins

Open comp [**Ex.02a**] which contains another copy of our marionette – but this time, he's a single layer rather than a collection of limbs. Puppeting works by creating a mesh based on the alpha channel of a single frame of your image, *so the outline of the layer must not change over time.*

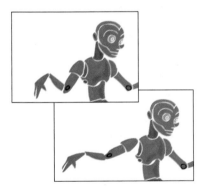

Parenting – the normal approach to character animation – requires setting up a hierarchy of separate layers to animate. Puppet courtesy iStockphoto, © FeralMartian, Image #2184370.

Example Project

Explore the 35-Example Project.aep file as you read this chapter; references to [Ex.##] refer to specific compositions within the project file.

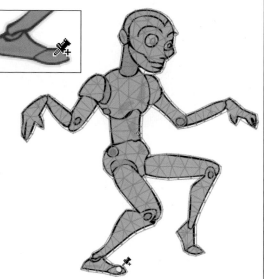

Select the Puppet Pin tool from the Tools panel along the top of the Application Window (above); the shortcut is Command+P on Mac (Control+P on Windows). A series of options will appear to the right along this toolbar. To start out, Enable Mesh: Show, set Expansion to 1 and Triangles to 350. Press Home to return the current time indicator to 00:00.

As mentioned, puppet pins represent points you want to grab and move or you want to stay in place. To keep our marionette firmly rooted on the ground, click once on his toes on the left. After Effects will pause for a moment as it auto-traces the layer's alpha channel, then a mesh of triangles will appear overlaid on top of the character. The Triangles parameter determines how fine this mesh is: Higher values result in more accurate distortions at the cost of taking longer to render. Expansion resizes the mesh around the alpha to make sure it captures the finer details on the underlying layer. Set this number too low, and bits of the layer may be cut off; too high, and independent limbs may get woven together. (We'll go into these issues in more detail in the *Mesh Issues* sidebar later in this chapter.) We suggest you leave the mesh on while becoming familiar with the Puppet tools; you can disable it at any time if you find it's obscuring the underlying image too much.

When you add your first Deform Puppet Pin to a layer (above, inset), After Effects will auto-trace its alpha channel and create a mesh of triangles based on the result (above).

The color of the mesh is based on the layer's label color; change this color if the mesh color is too similar to the image.

Add two more Deform Puppet Pins – one on the fingers of each hand. Hover your mouse over one of these new pins until it changes to a cursor with a four-headed arrow as its tail, then click and drag the pin: It's easy to bend the marionette into all sorts of crouching and reaching poses by moving just this one point! Undo to return this pin to its original location, then have fun dragging the pin on the other hand. Note how much more fluid the result is – for better or worse – compared with the parenting approach.

If you like, add pins to other parts of the marionette (such as its raised toe or the middle of his head) and practice dragging them about. Adding more pins is certainly a double-edged sword: It will give you more control over how sections of the layer move, but it also means you have to take responsibility for moving several other nearby pins to achieve more realistic poses.

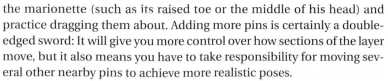

Just dragging one of three Deform Puppet Pins on a shape can quickly yield a wide variety of poses. A cursor with a four-headed arrow at its tail indicates you are about to move an existing pin rather than create a new one.

TIP

Puppet Path Clarity

If you have a busy composition which makes it hard to see the Deform Puppet Pin paths, double-click the layer to open its Layer panel and edit the path there. Remember to set the View popup to Puppet and enable the Render checkbox along the bottom right of the Layer panel to see the Puppet effect.

Keyframing Puppets

While dragging pins around is fun, it's even more useful to animate these movements. Use our pre-pinned puppet in [**Ex.02b**] to give it a try.

When you place a Deform Puppet Pin on a layer, After Effects applies an effect named Puppet. It can be revealed just like any effect: by selecting the layer and pressing E. The shortcut to reveal pins is to select the layer and press PP. Even more revealing is to select the layer and press U, which exposes all keyframes for a layer – you will see that a first keyframe has been created at the location of the current time indicator each time you add a Deform Puppet Pin to a layer. Note that this is the only parameter in After Effects that behaves this way; every other parameter requires you to enable its keyframing stopwatch first.

Press V to return to the Selection tool (this will also hide the mesh overlay if it was visible). Move the current time indicator to 01:00. Select the Puppet effect to reveal its pins in the Comp panel, then drag the pin on one of the hands to strike a new pose: A new keyframe will be created in the timeline for that Puppet Pin, and you will see a motion path drawn in the Comp panel indicating its movement. Go ahead and move the other hand – notice that the motion path is displayed for the selected pin only.

Now move to 02:00 in time and drag these pins again to create a third pose. Press N to end the work area at this point, and press 0 on the numeric keypad to RAM Preview your animation.

You can edit the motion path created by animated Deform Puppet Pins similar to other motion paths:

- By default, Auto Bezier keyframes are created: Click on a keyframe in the Comp panel to select it, and you will see dots on either side of it. Drag one of these dots, and influence handles will appear as the keyframe converts to Continuous Bezier; reorient the handles to change how the pin's animation flows into and out of that keyframe.

- To break handles and create discontinuous motion, hold down Option (Alt) and drag a handle.

- To retract the handles, *make sure the current time is not set to the time of that pin* (move the time indicator if so), then Command+Option+click (Control+Alt+click) on the keyframe in the Comp panel. To drag out handles again, repeat this shortcut and the Auto Bezier dots will reappear.

Of course, you can edit the velocity of Deform Puppet Pins as well. For example, select the first and second keyframes for Puppet Pins 2 and 3, then press F9 to apply Easy Ease to them. RAM Preview: The marionette will ease away from its first pose, hesitate at its second pose, and move quickly into its third pose where the keyframes are still linear. Of course, you can also tweak a pin's Speed Graph in the Graph Editor

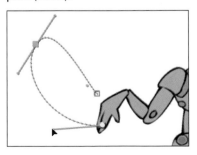

Puppet Pins are automatically enabled for keyframing in the Timeline panel as soon as you create them (above). Their paths can be edited in the Comp or Layer panels similar to other motion paths (below).

(you might want to toggle off Show Animated Properties if you have a lot of pins, so only selected pins are displayed).

Motion Sketching Pins

Puppet animation is something that lends itself particularly well to "motion sketching," in which After Effects records your movements as you drag the cursor around the Comp panel. You don't have to use the Motion Sketch panel to do this; the Puppet effect has this capability built in.

Select Close All from the Comp panel's tab to clean up the display. Open [**Ex.02c**] and make sure Puppet is exposed in the Timeline panel – select the layer and press E if it isn't. Select Puppet to see the already-placed pins in the Comp panel. Then select the Puppet Pin tool. To the right along the Tools panel you will see the words Record Options; click on them to open the Puppet Record Options dialog:

- The Speed parameter controls how fast your sketching relates to real time – for example, 50% means your sketching will be recorded at half the speed it will ultimately be played back at (set it to 100% for now).

- Smoothing controls how much your sketching is simplified when the corresponding keyframes are created – lower values create more keyframes and are better for catching frenetic movements; higher values create fewer keyframes and are better for capturing flowing movements (set it to 16 for now).

- We tend to enable Use Draft Deformation to see an outline of the mesh while recording, but we turn off Show Mesh. Click OK.

Animation is recorded from the current time forward (the work area is ignored); press Home to return the time indicator to 00:00. Select the Puppet effect to reveal the pins. Hold down the Command (Control) key and hover the cursor over a pin (try the hand on the left first); it will change to a stopwatch icon. When this icon is showing, recording will begin as soon as you click – even if you haven't started moving the cursor yet. Have fun dragging the hand around the screen; a yellow outline will show you roughly how the layer is being warped. Recording stops either when you release the mouse or reach the end of the timeline.

After you are done, you will see a Bezier motion path in the Comp panel for the deform pin you dragged, which you are free to edit. RAM Preview (and have patience – Puppet is rather computer-intensive); if you're not happy with your initial results, you can always Undo and try again! Feel free to press Home (to return to 00:00) and animate the other hand.

The Puppet Record Options control how fast and how smoothly your sketchings are recorded.

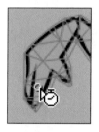

With the Puppet Pin tool selected, press Command (Control) to get the stopwatch icon when you hover the cursor near a Deform pin.

With Command (Control) still held, drag this pin to record your animation. The result is a Bezier motion path in the Comp panel (above) and a number of linear keyframes in the Timeline panel (below). You can edit both freely.

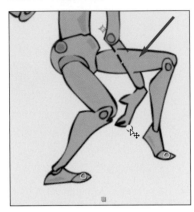

Before you define the Overlap weighting of the triangles in a puppet mesh, After Effects can be uncertain as to which triangles are supposed to pass in front of or behind the others. Note the outlines on the forearm: One line is in front of the thigh, while the other is behind.

The Overlap tool (right) is used to define the front/back weighting of a portion of your layer. Each Overlap pin has its own In Front % (weighting), plus an Extent value that determines how far the pin's influence reaches (far right).

TIP

Renaming Pins

Deform, Overlap, and Starch pins may be renamed in the Timeline panel by selecting their name and pressing Return.

TIP

Solo Selected

To edit a specific pin's values such as Extent, select it in the Comp panel and scrub its values in the Tools panel above. Or, press SS to reveal the selected pin in the Timeline panel, then twirl it open to reveal its parameters.

The Overlap Tool

One of the best features of Puppet is the ability for portions of the layer to pass in front of or behind other portions. However, a layer does not instinctively know which portion is supposed to be in front – you have to set this up yourself.

Open [**Ex.03_starter**], which contains our familiar marionette with a few more pins added to help keep the body more stationary. Press V for the Selection tool, make sure the Puppet effect is exposed in the Timeline panel (select the layer and press E if it isn't), and select Puppet. Click and drag the pins on the hands or feet so that they overlap the other limbs and notice how they initially cross over. There are problems in particular with the hand on the right: As its forearm crosses the leg below, portions of its outline draw in front while others draw behind. Undo to return to your original pose.

This can be resolved by using the Puppet Overlap tool. Select this from the popup that appears when you click on the Puppet Pin tool in the Tools panel, or type Command+P (Control+P) to toggle through the Puppet tools until it is selected. Two new parameters will appear to the right along the toolbar: In Front, which "weights" portions of the layer to

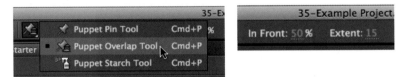

be more in front or more behind, and Extent, which defines how far the influence of each Overlap pin reaches. Segments with higher In Front values will be drawn in front of segments with lower values. Any segment of the mesh without an Overlap pin applied is assumed to be at a value of 0%; In Front defaults to a value of 50%.

You will also notice in the Comp panel that the marionette is now outlined in gray. If you have left a Distort pin in a new position, this gray outline will show the original undistorted outline of the layer – *you need to place Overlap pins according to the undistorted shape, not a distorted pose.*

Start by clicking on the elbow or forearm on the right side of the marionette. A pin will appear, along with a white overlay around the pin. This overlay fills in the adjacent triangles based on the Extent value (enable Show Mesh to see this more clearly). Use an initial In Front value such as 50%. Then scrub the Extent value until the entire arm fills in (see figure A, next page). If the white overlay starts to creep into the body, you can drag the blue Overlap pin further down the arm to recenter the extent region. (Try not to add more Overlap pins – the fewer pins you have to manage, the easier it is to use puppeting.)

To see the result of adding the Overlap pin, either toggle back to the Puppet Pin tool or press V to switch to the Selection tool. Drag the yellow Puppet Pin on the right side hand across the leg on that side:

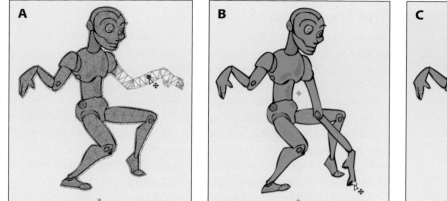

The arm will now pass in front of the leg with no artifacts, as in figure B. (If you still see artifacts, press UU to reveal the Overlap parameters in the Timeline and increase the Extent values as needed.)

Let's say you want the arm to pass behind the leg rather than in front. There are two ways to accomplish this. One is to select the Overlap pin on the forearm and set its In Front value to a negative number (remember, the rest of the mesh defaults to a value of 0%). When the Overlap tool is selected, the forearm will be shaded black to reflect the negative value.

The other approach would be to add an Overlap pin to the shin on the right side, increase its Extent to cover the entire leg, and give this segment a higher In Front value than the forearm.

You can also add other Overlap regions to define more complex interactions. For example, reduce the Extent on the shin, place an Overlap pin on the thigh, and give this new pin a lower In Front value than the arm. The arm will now pass in front of the thigh but behind the shin.

You cannot animate the location of Overlap pins, but you can animate their Extent and In Front values. An application for this would be allowing the arm to pass in front during one point in an animation, and to pass behind later. Hold keyframes work well for this application.

Use an Overlap pin to define the arm to have a postive In Front value, shown by the white overlay (A). It will pass in front of the leg without breaking up (B). Assign the arm a negative In Front value, and now it will pass behind the leg (C).

Dueling Overlaps

When Overlap regions overlap each other, their In Front values are combined, weighted by the strength of their Extent at the triangles in question. You can tell the relative in front/behind value of a polygon by how strong the white or black overlay is, respectively.

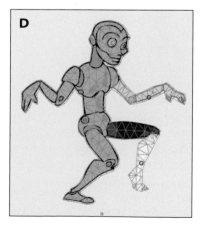

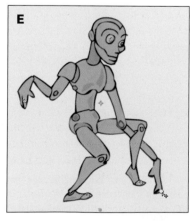

In **[Ex.03-final]**, we defined the shin to be more "in front" than either the thigh or the arm (D); their relative shadings give clues to their relationships. Now the arm passes in front of the thigh but behind the shin (E).

The Puppet Starch tool is used to define which portions of the layer's mesh should be stiffer or looser than the others.

Too Much Starch

If a Starch pin creates a very stiff area, you can loosen up an adjacent area by adding another Starch pin with a negative Amount value.

Scratchy Starch

Although you can keyframe a Starch pin's Amount and Extent, these values don't animate very smoothly over time; the layer will jump and jitter as you do so.

The Starch Tool

As you drag around puppet pins, you will probably notice that portions of your layer may deform in ways that are unattractive. In contrast to other distortion-based effects, Puppet allows you to define the relative stiffness or looseness of specific portions of the layer, akin to the way you defined their overlap priorities above.

To get some practice with this tool, open [**Ex.04_starter**] which includes a rabbit that has four Deform pins already placed. Reveal and select the Puppet effect to see the location of the pins on the hands and feet. Drag the hand on the left far out to the side: The body will exhibit some unusual kinks where the arm connects to it.

With the rabbit in this distended state, click on the Puppet Tools popup menu or type Command+P (Control+P) to toggle to the Puppet Starch tool. A gray outline will appear in the Comp panel that shows the rabbit in his pre-deformed state (if you have Show Mesh enabled, you will see the mesh triangles as well): As with the Overlap tool, you need to define which triangles get starched *based on the original shape of the layer*.

Hover your mouse inside this gray outline where the arm you dragged meets the body; a cursor that looks like a spray bottle will appear. Click to set a Starch pin and scrub the Extent value in the Tools panel above the Comp panel until a few triangles around the arm/body junction are filled with gray. Then adjust Amount % (to the left of Extent): You need only a small amount such as 1% to 15% to have a large impact on the result. Be patient, and After Effects will update the Comp panel to show you the result of edits to the Starch pin's location, Amount, and Extent. In this case, you should see the body return to a more rounded shape, repairing the angular kink you saw earlier. As with Overlap pins, you can drag Starch pins after you've created them to see if a different position would work better.

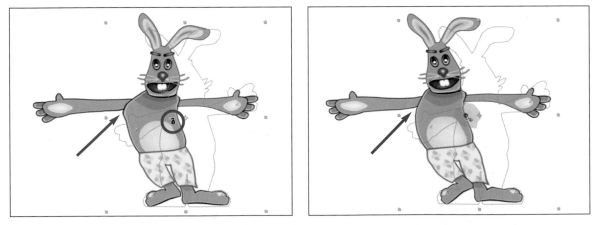

The Puppet Starch tool's cursor looks like a small aerosol can. Click it on the area that needs loosening or stiffening based on the layer's gray outline in the Comp panel, *not on its currently deformed state* (left). A little starch goes a long way in smoothing out kinks (right). Rabbit courtesy iStockphoto, © AdiniMalibuBarbie, Image #2188406.

Mesh Issues

The Mesh Expansion and Triangles parameters play a very important role in determining how a layer's outline is auto-traced and how smoothly it will deform. You generally want to set these values as low as you can get away with to improve rendering times and reduce the chances that appendages accidentally get stitched together. But set them too low, and visual artifacts will result.

Open **[Ex.05a]** which contains the rabbit we used in the Starch tool example. We initially set Mesh Expansion to 0 and Triangles to 350, added pins to his hands and feet, and animated the hands away from the body. RAM Preview and look closely at the Comp panel: Those little black flecks aren't dirt on your monitor; they're pieces of the rabbit's hands and whiskers that are being left behind as the layer is deformed (figure A).

Press End to make sure the rabbit is in a deformed pose, then select Mesh 1 in the Timeline panel (select the layer, press E to reveal the Puppet effect, and twirl it open to reveal Mesh 1). Make sure Show Mesh is enabled in the toolbar. Study the mesh in the Comp panel: Its low resolution is causing the stroke around the hands to be chopped off.

One solution is to increase the Mesh Expansion parameter. As you do so, the mesh will extend beyond the rabbit's outlines, fully enclosing the hands. However, if you go too far you will notice that the gap between the legs disappears as the mesh outlines overlap (figure B). If this happens, you can no longer move the legs independently from one another. Reduce Mesh Expansion to where the leg gap is maintained while the hands are still fully enclosed; hold Command (Control) to scrub in finer increments.

C

Setting Expansion to around 1.0 and increasing the Triangles value until the layer's alpha is fully enclosed is a good – if CPU-intensive – approach to creating clean puppet animations.

Another approach is to increase the number of triangles used to define the mesh. Reduce Expansion to 1 and try higher Triangle values (figure C). Note that After Effects will be slow to update (especially at higher numbers), and that you often have to double the number of triangles or more to get meaningful changes. The trade-off is that higher triangle counts allow After Effects to trace the layer more accurately which usually results in smoother deformations.

The more detailed the alpha channel of your layer, the higher Triangle or Expansion values you will need. You will experience this with **[Ex.05b]** which contains a version of this rabbit with "fur" added to its outline. When creating your own layers to deform, try to simplify their outlines and create additional space between limbs you wish to deform independently – you can always deform them to be closer together later.

A

If the Mesh Expansion and Triangles are set too low, the result can be pieces of the layer left behind when you try to deform it.

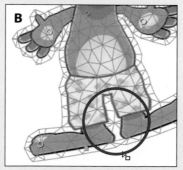

B

Higher Mesh Expansion values remove artifacts from portions of the layer being cut off, but may accidentally join other portions together (such as the legs here).

In **[Ex.06-final]** we separated the puppeted characters on their own layers so we could add individual shadows and bevels to them. This is necessary to manage overlaps between multiple meshes. Photo courtesy Digital Vision/All That Jazz. Font is Adobe Eccentric Std (previously installed free with After Effects).

Motion Blur

Puppet movements respond to motion blur (Chapter 8).

Deforming Text

We'll end your study of the Puppet Tools with an exercise in which you will deform some text to match a soundtrack.

Step 1: Close all previous comps and open [Ex.06_starter]: It contains a text layer plus a soundtrack. Press Home to make sure the current time indicator is located at the start of the timeline. Then press the period key on the numeric keypad to audition the soundtrack and get a feel for it.

Step 2: Select the Puppet Pin tool; remember the keyboard shortcut is Command+P (Control+P) to toggle between its related tools. Click once on the top of the J. A mesh will be created for just this character – After Effects traces the alpha channel of just the object you click. Chances are this mesh is very fine as this layer contains a small area; go ahead and reduce the Triangles count to 100 or so, making sure you still contain the entire character (an Expansion value of 1 will help).

Multiple Shapes in a Mesh

When a layer contains multiple disconnected shapes such as the individual characters of a text layer, by default you'll be creating one mesh per shape. If you want to deform the entire layer as a unit, first draw a mask that encompasses all of the shapes. Then place a Puppet Deform Pin somewhere inside the mask, but *not* on one of the shapes. This will create a mesh that fills the mask. This is shown in **[Ex.07]**, and in the figure to the right. Add additional pins as you like; you can delete the mask at this point if you wish.

If you want to deform just a portion of a layer rather than the whole thing, you can also use a mask to enclose an area smaller than an entire layer before you create a mesh. (Change the Mask group popup to None so that it doesn't create transparency, or delete the mask after you create the mesh.)

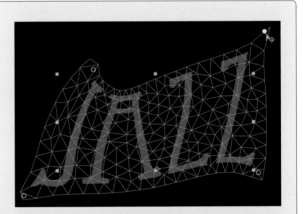

Important Warning: Continuously rasterized layers – including shapes and text – cannot be safely transformed (scaled, rotated, or moved) after you have created a puppet mesh. The workaround is to do the puppeting in a precomp, or use Effect > Distort > Transform to alter the layer after puppeting.

Step 3: Try placing a second Deform Puppet Pin somewhere lower down on the J. Drag it around to make sure it's going to deform in a way you like. If you're not happy with your tests, undo and try a different location for the pin (we found a location just above the hook in the J works well). Worse case, you can use the Starch tool to firm it up.

Step 4: Click on Record Options in the Tools panel (to the right of the Puppet Tools). Verify that the Speed is set to 100% and set smoothing to a moderate value (10 to 20 will work well).

Step 5: Hold down Command (Control) and start dragging one of the pins on the J. The soundtrack will start playing back automatically. Drag the J around in time with the music, perhaps following the bass line. You can reduce the amount of your dragging later in the song; you're going to be animating the other characters when the piano and trumpet come in, and you don't want the J hogging the spotlight the entire time! If you're not happy with your animation, just undo and try again. If you're close, you can go back later and tweak the timing of the keyframes to better match the peaks in the audio's waveform.

Step 6: Move the time indicator to a little before 06:00, just before the trumpet comes in (you can verify this by pressing period on the numeric keypad to audition it). Make sure you give yourself enough time to feel the music before the trumpet starts. We're doing this first because After Effects creates Deform pin keyframes at the current time as soon as we create a new pin. Press B to begin the work area here, making it easier to RAM Preview what you're about to do.

Step 7: Place a pair of Deform pins on the first Z, again testing how they work before you commit to animating with them. Note that your last settings for Mesh Expansion and Triangles will be used for this new shape as well. (The same Record Options will also be used.) You may also notice that this created Mesh 2 in the Timeline panel. You can click on the names of the meshes in the timeline to select their corresponding shapes.

Step 8: Hold down Command (Control) and animate the Z in time with the music, this time reacting to the trumpet line. RAM Preview; undo and try again if you like. In our case, we were mostly happy, but didn't like the way our animation started; we just pressed U to reveal the keyframes and slid the first keyframe for this Deform Puppet Pin later (to about 06:00, with an Easy Ease Out) to better time with the first note. You can also edit the motion path if you have a stray keyframe or two.

Feel free to animate the other characters to taste! In our version **[Ex.06-final]** we added a few other touches, such as separating each character out onto its own layer and applying Layer Styles (Chapter 22) to them to give them added dimension. The Puppet Tools open a lot of possibilities for creative animation; we expect you will have a lot of fun with them.

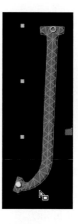

Try a few different ideas for Deform Puppet Pin locations on the J. Here we tried the lower extent of the J but found we didn't like how the hook in the J deformed as a result.

Sketchin' to the Music

A pen tablet such as a Wacom is an excellent tool for motion sketching puppet animations.

Command+drag (Control+drag) a Deform Puppet Pin on the J in time with the music to create a fun motion path.

CONNECT

Previewing audio: sidebar at the end of Chapter 2.

Editing motion paths: Chapter 3.

Easy Ease, roving keyframes, and the Graph Editor: Chapter 4.

Motion Sketch: Chapter 5.

Masking: Chapter 10.

Continuous rasterization: Chapter 20.

Text layers: Chapter 21.

Layer Styles: Chapter 22.

Timing animation to audio: Chapter 36.

Working with Audio

An overview of handling audio in After Effects, including how to "read" audio as clues for editing and animation.

After Effects has never made audio one of its strong points. If you need to seriously rework a soundtrack, do it in a dedicated audio program. But if you just need to edit, mix, and do some basic improvement or "sweetening" to your soundtrack, After Effects already has the tools you need.

Audio is also an important guide for making animation decisions, plus it can drive some effects. But first, we need to get a handle on how sound itself works – after that, everything else makes a lot more sense.

Seeing Sound

To best handle audio, you have to become familiar with how to "read" its graphic waveform display. You can't look at a waveform and know *exactly* what the sound is, but it will give you enough important clues – such as where beats of music land, or where individual words in a sentence start.

To get some practice with this, open the project file **36-Example Project.aep** from the **Chapter Example Projects > 36-Example Project** folder on the DVD. Open comp **[Ex.01]**. It includes a short piece of music we created called **CD_Inglemuse**. Or, if you like, import a piece of your own audio into this project, drag it into a new composition, and follow along.

All layers with audio, including any comps that have layers with audio, will have a speaker icon in the Timeline panel's Audio/Video switches column; clicking on this turns the audio on and off. Twirl open the layer's parameters in the Timeline panel. If the clip contains both video and sound, you will see a new category called Audio: Twirl that open as well to reveal the properties Audio Levels and Waveform. If the clip contains only audio, all the normal masks and transformations will be missing, and Audio will be the only category you see.

Click on the twirly to the left of the word Waveform. See all those squiggles that appeared in the timeline? That's a visual representation of your sound. As mentioned, **[Ex.01]** contains the **CD_Inglemuse** music file for you to look at. Let's discuss where those squiggles came from, and what they mean.

The eyeball (Video switch) and speaker (Audio switch) icons in the Timeline panel indicate whether a layer has image or audio data, or both. Here, the first layer has video and audio; the second has audio only (circled in red).

Example Project

Explore the 36-Example Project.aep file as you read this chapter; references to [Ex.##] refer to specific compositions within the project file.

Good Vibrations

For there to be a sound, something must vibrate. This vibration could be a guitar string swaying back and forth, a speaker cone pumping in and out, or pieces of glass shattering as you throw your phone through the window after the client's most recent round of changes. These motions vibrate the air, pushing it toward you and pulling it back away from you. This in turn pushes your eardrum around, causing it to flex in sympathy. This stimulates nerves in your ears, which ultimately convince your brain that a sound has occurred.

The pattern and nature of these vibrations affect the character of the sound we perceive. The stronger the vibrations, the louder the sound. The faster the fundamental pattern of vibrations, the higher the apparent "pitch" of the sound. Humans can perceive vibrations from a speed of 20 back-and-forth cycles per second to as high as 20,000 cycles per second – a lot faster than the frame rate of video or film.

Sound is recorded by intercepting these vibrations in the air with a device akin to our eardrum – typically, a microphone – which converts them into electrical signals with a similar vibrational pattern. In a computer environment, these vibrations are frozen by *digitizing* or *sampling* that electrical signal. When sound is digitized, its instantaneous level (how strongly the air has been pushed toward or pulled away from the microphone) is measured (sampled) and converted into a number (digitized) to be stored in the computer's memory. A very short instant later, the signal is measured again to see how the air pressure changed since the last measured moment in time. This process is repeated very quickly over a period of time to build up a numeric picture of what the pattern of vibration was.

The speed at which it is performed is called the *sample rate*, which is roughly equivalent to frame rate. The higher the sample rate, the more accurately high frequencies – which help make sounds more intelligible – are captured. Professional digital video cameras sample audio at

Those squiggles in the Timeline panel are the "waveform" of the audio, indicating how loud it is at each point in time.

Instant Waveform

To directly access Levels and the waveform twirly, select the layer in the Timeline panel and type L for Levels. To see the waveform, type LL (two Ls) quickly.

TIP

Waves to Keys

Animation > Keyframe Assistants > Convert Audio to Keyframes creates keyframe values that match the combined amplitude of the audio waveforms in a comp. This is great for driving expressions (Chapter 37).

Here are two simple waveforms displayed in an audio editing application, zoomed in the same amount. As the curve of the wave goes above the centerline, air is being pushed toward you; as it goes below, air is being pulled away. Time passes from left to right; the markings along the bottom of this particular display are in 10-millisecond (hundredth of a second) increments – giving an idea of how fast sound vibrates. Since the up and down excursions for the second waveform are not as tall as for the first, you know the second sound is relatively quieter; because its up and down excursions are also happening faster, you know it is higher in pitch.

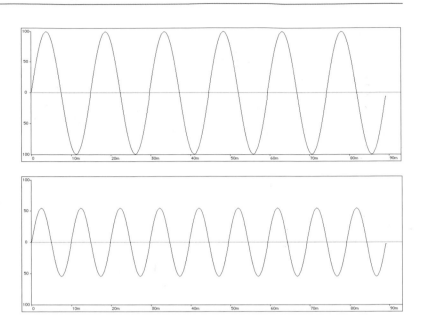

Inaccurate Waveforms

Most programs do not display every sample of a waveform, so the same waveform looks different at different zoom levels. For critical edits, zoom in to single frame view (in After Effects, type ; on the keyboard) for the highest display accuracy.

48,000 times a second, usually expressed as 48 kHz (Hz = Hertz = cycles per second; kHz = thousands of cycles per second). Audio CDs use a sample rate of 44,100 (or 44.1 kHz); consumer DV uses a rate of 32 kHz. Professional audio can use rates as high as 96 kHz or 192 kHz.

The resolution at which these samples are digitized is defined as the number of bits per sample (akin to bit depth of a color image). Higher resolutions result in less *quantization distortion*, which is often heard as noise. Professional quality gear uses 16-bit or 24-bit resolution, while some audio programs process sound internally at 32-bit resolution. 8-bit resolution sounds very noisy and should be avoided. The 12-bit format used by consumer DV is just short of the 16-bit format in quality.

This resulting *waveform* is typically displayed on a computer screen by drawing a point or line that represents the air pressure at one point in time, followed by additional points or lines that represent succeeding points in time. As a result, you can "read" a waveform from left to right to get an idea of the vibrational pattern. No one can look at the resulting squiggles and tell you what the sound was, but you can pick up some clues: Louder points in time will be drawn taller than quieter points in time; cycles that take relatively longer to fluctuate up and down are lower in pitch than ones that fluctuate more quickly.

Sample Rate Management

The final audio sample rate and resolution is determined by your Render Settings after you have queued a comp to be rendered. You can combine files with multiple sample rates, and After Effects will perform the sample rate conversion automatically.

If you're a real stickler for the absolute best quality, try to capture all of your audio at the final sample rate you need. If you must mix rates, before you import your audio into After Effects, use a dedicated high-quality audio program to convert the sample rates of the deviant files to be the same as your final render target.

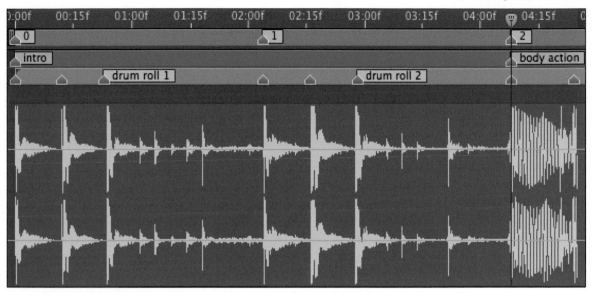

Spotting Audio

When we are animating or editing visuals to sound, the most interesting points in the audio tend to be the loudest ones: the moment a door slams, lightning cracks, a drum is hit, or a client's wails crescendo. By looking for these *peaks* – taller points in the audio waveform, going in either the upward or downward direction – we have a tremendous head start in finding the more interesting audio events, which we can then use as a reference point for visual edits and effect keyframes. Strong drum beats produce these peaks, as do syllables in words. Areas with no peaks or other visible waveform indicate pauses between words and sentences.

Comp and layer markers (Chapter 6) can be used to mark important beats in the music or words in the voiceover. We often use the comp markers to mark the major sections in the music or animation. Note that since comp markers are connected to the comp's timeline, they will no longer line up if you move the audio track in time. Layer markers, on the

Starting the process of spotting important points in a piece of music. We've used both numbered comp markers along the top, plus named layer markers. Comp markers have the advantage of letting you jump directly to the first 10 numbered markers by using the numbers on the regular keyboard. You can have any number of comp or layer markers, and add your own comments.

Our audio after spotting. We've marked every major beat, plus added comments to a second layer that indicate where major sections of the music begin or end.

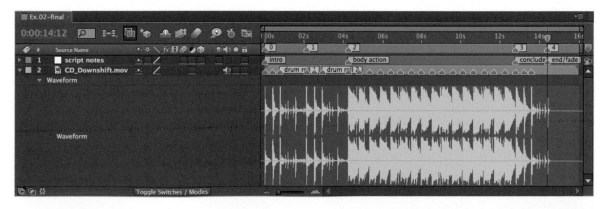

TIP

Audio Guide

If you are using the same audio track in a precomp as well as a later comp, click on the copy in the precomp and select Layer > Guide Layer. This will prevent it from also playing in the later comp, which may result in overloading and distortion.

Place the Audio panel in a tall frame for finer control; resize if needed. The meters display the instantaneous level of audio being previewed. If the bars at the top are red, the volume was maxed out, possibly distorting. These "clip" indicators reset each time you preview; you can also reset them by clicking on them. The sliders on the right are used for setting Levels values.

other hand, are attached to the layer. Use these to mark your musical beats and script highlights. Practice this with [**Ex.02_starter**].

If the audio layer fills up with markers, make a Layer > New > Null Object; give it a suitable name such as "**script notes**" in Layer > Solid Settings. Now you can add markers to the null layer with your more prosaic descriptions, and place markers for the music beats on the audio layer itself.

Our process is to view the waveform, locate these peaks both visually and by listening to the audio, and set layer markers to remind us where they are. Then we twirl up the waveform display (which takes both time and room to draw), and animate based on the position of the markers.

For quickly adding layer markers, use the "tap-along" method. Select the layer you want to place the layer markers on (the layer with audio, or a dummy solid layer as mentioned above), set the current time indicator to the start of the section you want to spot, preview the audio by pressing the period key on the keypad (the duration is set in Preferences > Previews), and press the keypad's asterisk key in time with the music. (New in CS5: MacBook owners can hold Control and tap 8.)

Don't be surprised if you tapped slightly late. When you're done tapping, study the relative location of your markers and the waveform's peaks, and slide the markers back until they line up. If the marker wants to land just before or just after a peak (based on the timeline's frame increments), it is usually better to err on the early side.

Once the music and script layers have markers, you can copy and paste these layers into precomps for easy animation decisions. Just make sure that only one audio layer is rendered (multiple audio layers will probably result in distortion as the combined sound is now too loud). You can either set the audio switches to off in the top comp for these nested precomps, or set the audio tracks in the precomps to be Guide Layers (Layer > Guide Layer) so that they don't render in subsequent comps.

On the Level

In After Effects, all layers with audio are assumed to be in stereo, containing left and right channels in the same layer. If the source file was mono (one channel of audio), After Effects internally duplicates the audio so that the same sound is in the left and right channels.

You can alter or keyframe the Audio Levels of a layer. These values react differently from a normal linear parameter: Most of the useful values for Levels exist in a small area around the 0 mark. Unlike a parameter such as Scale or Opacity, 0 means no *change*, rather than nothing rendered.

There are four ways to edit this value: Scrub it in the Timeline panel, enter it directly in the Timeline panel, move the sliders in the Audio panel, or enter it directly in the Audio panel. We'll assume you already know how to scrub or enter values in the Timeline panel, so we'll focus on the Audio panel.

The shortcut to expose Audio Levels in the Timeline is to select the layer and type L. The Audio panel is usually tabbed together with the Info panel; you can also drag it out to be its own panel. If it is currently

Previewing Audio

Unlike video, audio cannot be previewed by pressing the spacebar unless you have opened a source in QuickTime Player. Otherwise, you will need to either preview it or scrub it.

There are several ways to perform a RAM Preview for audio inside a composition. The easiest is to set the current time indicator to where you want to start, then press the decimal point key on the numeric keypad (MacBook owners can hold Control and press period). Pressing any key will stop playback.

If you want to preview your images with audio playing, make sure the speaker icon in the Preview panel is switched on, then click on either the RAM Preview button or press 0 on the numeric keypad (MacBook owners can press Control+0). The preview will obey your work area and Loop setting. On rare occasions, After Effects cannot play your video at normal speed, causing it to lag behind the

audio; if so, the frame rate display in the Info panel will turn red during playback.

Finally, you can "scrub" audio by holding down the Command (Control) key while you're moving the time indicator with your mouse. This works in the Footage, Layer, and Timeline panels. Scrubbing will play a single frame of audio for each frame you move the time indicator to. If you hold the cursor in place without moving, after a pause After Effects will start playing a one-third second loop of the audio, starting at the current location of the time indicator.

The sample rate used is set in File > Project Settings > Audio Settings. The best choice is to use the same sample rate and bit depth as used by most of your source layers.

If you have audio effects applied, there may be a pause before audio previews as After Effects renders the

To play back audio while you're previewing your visual animation, make sure the speaker icon is turned on in the Preview panel, and then start a RAM Preview.

final sound. The Stereo Mixer effect – as well as any animation of the Levels setting – will play back in real time as soon as you initiate an audio-only preview.

closed, open it using the menu item Window > Audio or the keyboard shortcut Command+4 on Mac (Control+4 on Windows). To edit the Levels in this panel, move the sliders: Dragging one changes just the channel it is associated with; dragging the bar between the sliders alters both the left and right channels together (keeping their same relationship). You can also directly enter values in the numeric boxes along the bottom of this panel.

One of the main reasons to edit the Audio Levels for a layer is to balance the relative volume between multiple sound tracks. Focus on which is the most important sound at any given time that the viewer should be listening to: Make sure that layer is the loudest, and reduce the level of the other audio layers so that they contribute but do not detract.

TIP

Maximum Viewing

After Effects draws the audio waveform after it has been processed with the Levels parameters. Spot your audio first, perhaps even with Levels set artificially high (to better see details in the waveform), then set your final Levels later.

TIP

Audio Bonus Chapter

This book's DVD-ROM contains a Bonus Chapter (36B) on audio effects such as Tone, Reverb, Echo, and equalization options.

The Audio Options dialog is opened by clicking on the arrow in the upper right corner of the Audio panel. These affect how you enter and view Levels parameters using the panel's sliders. As most Levels adjustments take place in a small range around 0 dB, you might consider setting the Slider Minimum to a range between –12 and –36 dB.

You've Got the Power

You have two ways of viewing and entering Levels parameters in the Audio panel: as a *percentage* of full scale volume, and in *decibels* (units of loudness). You can switch between these two methods by selecting the Audio Options (the menu arrow in the upper right corner). These changes affect only the Audio panel; the Timeline panel always shows Audio Levels in decibel (dB) units.

Unless you have a background in audio, you will probably be most familiar and comfortable with the percentage scale. When we're reducing the volume of a music or sound effects track behind a narration track, we usually start at 50% volume for the music track and preview to make sure the voice is intelligible.

Decibels is a *power* scale that more closely relates to the way we perceive loudness. When we're reducing the volume of music to help make any simultaneous narration clearer, we start at –6 dB from where the normal level was; it is not unusual to use values of –12 to –16 to really clear the way for more intelligible speech. To fully turn off the volume of a clip with audio, you need to set its Levels parameter to –96 dB for a 16-bit resolution clip. When you're trying to even out the volume of a narrator that may be fluctuating from soft to loud on individual phrases, changes in the range of 0.5 to 1.5 dB are often sufficient; quick dips of 12 to 64 dB are useful for removing coughs and other unwanted sounds. You might want to set the Slider Minimum to –12 or –24 dB in the Audio Options dialog to facilitate making smaller adjustments, then manually type in larger values such as –96 when you want to set a track to silence.

You can increase the volume of clips by setting their level above 0. You may need to do this if the original audio was recorded too softly, but be careful: It is easy to scale the audio samples to the point where they exceed their maximum value and "clip" – resulting in nasty distortion. The same goes for mixing together several loud clips in a comp or project. If you preview audio for the comp and the volume meters in the Audio panel light up the top red indicator, you are clipping; reduce the volume of the audio track(s) slightly.

Speed Shifts

You cannot conform the "frame rate" of an audio file in the Interpret Footage dialog. If you conform the rate of a video file that has audio attached, the audio will *not* be altered to match. To speed up or slow down an audio layer, use Time Stretch or Time Remapping.

A better way to do this is to use a dedicated audio processing program. Many of these have dedicated time-stretching routines, with an option of preserving the original pitch of the file. If your audio program doesn't have time-stretch capabilities, convert the sample rate to a new rate that is slowed down or sped up by the speed shift you need (for example, to slow down 0.1%, increase the sample rate 0.1% – from 48,000 to 48,048), then edit the file's header info back to its original sample rate.

Clipping Distortion

If you boost the loudness through a combination of Audio Levels and the Stereo Mixer, its waveform may exceed its maximum possible range. Mixing together multiple layers with audio will also increase the overall loudness. Some plug-ins create additional copies of or boost certain portions of the original sound, also potentially increasing its overall volume. If any of these go too far, After Effects may have to "clip" the waveform at its maximum value, resulting in audible distortion.

If you're not sure whether you have a problem with clipping, look at the top of the signal level meters in the Audio panel during or just after a preview: Red bars at the top indicate clipping has occurred. You'll have to reduce the loudness of some or all of your layers to fix it.

Audio Levels is calculated on a per-layer basis after the effects have been calculated. If reducing Audio Levels does not fix your clipping problem, then reduce the Dry and Wet amounts some plug-ins offer, or place a Stereo Mixer effect first in the chain and reduce the volume before the other effects are calculated.

If your audio is distorted before applying effects or increasing its volume, you will need to repair it before using it in After Effects. Programs such as Adobe Audition and Soundbooth or Apple Soundtrack Pro have options that can smooth out some distortion.

If one or both of the two red bars at the top of the Audio panel's level meters are lit up, you clipped during your most recent preview.

Mixing Audio

Remember that Audio Levels *modifies*, rather than *sets*, the volume of an audio layer. Don't get hung up on leaving its value at 0 dB, as you might leave Opacity at 100%. If the audio was recorded too soft, increase Audio Levels; if it was recorded too loud, reduce it. You can animate a layer's audio level to make it fade in or out. Additionally, if the volume varies in a distracting way – such as a given word that is too loud or too soft – you can animate it to compensate.

After Effects interpolates between Levels keyframes using the power-oriented decibel scale, not normal percentage. This results in fade-downs that can range from natural to slightly abrupt. Fade-ups sound very unnatural, seeming to linger at the lower volume, then suddenly rushing up to the higher volume. Given this problem, we take a two-step approach to mixing audio in After Effects:

• Use the Stereo Mixer effect to animate fades and other temporary dips or boosts in loudness.

• Use the Levels parameter to then tweak the overall level of a track, to balance it against other tracks or to avoid clipping.

Handling Dual Mono

Some programs capture "stereo" audio as a pair of individual monophonic files – one for the left channel, one for the right. You may find this arrangement easier to handle if you reassemble the stereo track in a precomp. This is demonstrated in **[Ex.03]**.

This may seem like more work initially, but it will save your sanity later. For example, if you already keyframed fade-ups and fade-downs using Stereo Mixer, then later decided the entire track needed to be louder or softer (but wanted to keep the fades), you could just alter the layer's Levels parameter and leave your keyframes alone.

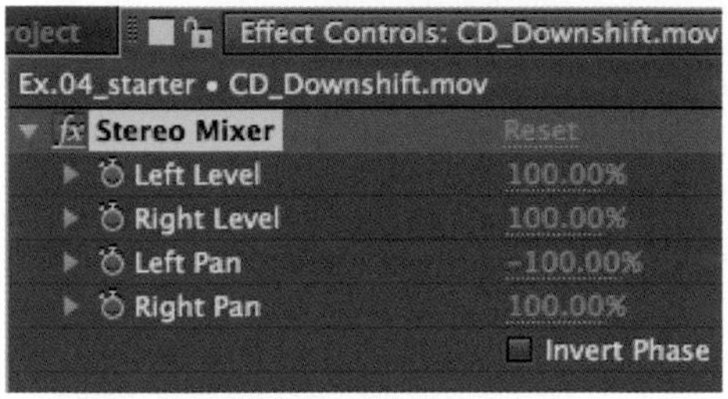

The Stereo Mixer effect provides a great alternative to Levels.

Stereo Mixer

This workhorse effect provides an alternative to a layer's Levels parameter. The advantage is that it works in a linear scale that is easier to grasp and allows you to create smoother fades.

To get some practice with Stereo Mixer, open [**Ex.04_starter**], select the audio layer **CD_Downshift.mov**, and apply Effect > Audio > Stereo Mixer. The Effect Controls panel should open; press F3 if you don't find it. You can see there are separate controls for Left and Right Level, as well as for Left and Right Pan (each channel's position in the stereo field). Feel free to experiment with these if you like. When you're done, click Reset along the top of Stereo Mixer's Effect Controls to return to the default settings.

Quite often, you want to adjust the Left and Right Levels by the same amount. Unfortunately, there is no "link" switch for them (as you would expect for X and Y Scale, for example). However, you can create an expression (Chapter 37) – and save it as an Animation Preset (Chapter 25) – to create your own link:

Use the pick whip to create a simple expression that links Right Level to Left Level. (After you release the mouse, the expression text shown here will appear in the timeline to the right.) This way, you need to keyframe only Left Level; Right Level will follow along.

With **CD_Downshift.mov** still selected, type E to reveal Stereo Mixer in the Timeline panel, then twirl down the parameters for Stereo Mixer. Option+click (Alt+click) on the stopwatch icon to the left of Right Level to enable expressions for it. Then drag the pick whip that appears in the Switches column for Right Level to the words Left Level. Release the mouse, then press Enter to accept this expression. Now, as you scrub (or keyframe) Left Level, the Right Level will follow automatically. The result is demonstrated in [**Ex.04-final**]. If you then need to balance the left and right channels, use the sliders in the Audio panel.

Rather than having to re-create this expression every time you want to use Stereo Mixer, you can save an Animation Preset for it. After you've created the expression, but before you've added any keyframes, select Right Level and use Animation > Save Animation Preset. We've saved this preset for you in the DVD's **Goodies** folder: **StereoMixer_link.ffx**.

If you have a mono sound that you want to pan around, set Left and Right Pan to be the same value. Again, you can use a simple expression to link them together: Enable expressions for Right Pan, then drag its pick whip to Left Pan. Try this out in [**Ex.05_starter**]; the result is demonstrated in [**Ex.05-final**]. This is saved as the preset **StereoMixer_mono.ffx**. As this doubles up the volume of the sound, you should reduce the Left and Right Level by 50% to avoid clipping when you use it.

More Natural Fades

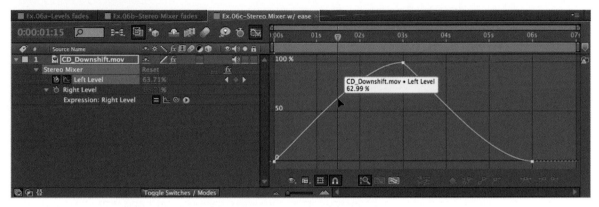

As we mentioned, Stereo Mixer gives linear fades rather than the exponential fades that the Levels parameter yields. The linear fades will sound more natural in most cases. To improve on this, we ease into the second keyframe of a fade. To compare these, RAM Preview [**Ex.06a**] (exponential fades using Levels), [**Ex.06b**] (linear fades using Stereo Mixer), and [**Ex.06c**] (linear out/ease in fades using Stereo Mixer).

Trimming Layers with Audio

Quite often, events in audio are much shorter than a single video frame. This can make it difficult to trim out small noises such as lip smacks and plosive consonants. The workaround is to temporarily increase the composition's frame rate (the maximum is 99 frames per second), make your edit, then return the comp's frame rate to the normal video rate.

Another issue that comes up with trimming audio layers is the addition of effects. A side effect of some common audio effects such as Echo and Reverb is that they produce altered versions of the sound that are supposed to exist after the original sound is finished. However, if you have trimmed an audio layer to end as soon as the original sound had stopped, the plug-in will stop there too: An effect cannot render audio that plays past the end of the trimmed layer. When you're working with effects that create trailing versions of the processed sound, select the layer and apply Layer > Time Remapping. Effects are applied after a clip has been remapped. Therefore, you can then extend the last "frame" of the audio layer as long as needed by dragging its out point (*not* the last Time Remap keyframe). This is demonstrated in the comp [**Ex.07**].

Often, the smoothest-sounding fades come from animating Effect > Audio > Stereo Mixer instead of Levels, using linear keyframe interpolation at the start of the fade, and Easy Ease In (or its equivalent) at the end of the fade. The Value graph shows the softened exponential fade shape that results.

CONNECT

RAM Previewing: Chapter 2.

Keyframe interpolation: Chapters 3–4.

Easy Ease keyframe assistants: Chapter 4.

Comp and layer markers: Chapter 6.

Nesting compositions: Chapters 18.

Precomposing: Chapter 19.

Audio effects: Chapter 36B.

37

Expressions

Expressions hold the key to animating repetitive tasks or complex relationships.

TIP

Revealing Expressions

To reveal expressions, select one or more layers, and type EE (two Es in quick succession). Typing U reveals both keyframes and properties with expressions.

Example Project

Explore the 37-Example Project.aep file as you read this chapter; references to [Ex.##] refer to specific compositions within the project file. Enable Preferences > General > Expression Pick Whip Writes Compact English while working through this chapter.

Creating expressions – the ability to tell one parameter to follow another, stay at a constant value, or create new values as the result of ingenious calculations – is one of the most powerful features in After Effects. For many, it is also one of the most daunting: To get the most out of it, you have to deal with math and what looks suspiciously like computer programming. But it's not that bad! In this chapter, we'll show you how to make expressions work for you with minimal effort (and math); a bonus chapter on the DVD dives in deeper for those who want to move to the next level.

If you're an artist with an aversion to math and technical issues, you should not shun expressions because of their technical nature: They can save you time and help you avoid tedious tasks. The most common uses require no knowledge of computer programming and only the most basic math skills, such as "times 2" and "divided by 100."

If you are a programmer who can't wait to dig deeper, you will be interested to know that expressions are based on the JavaScript language – including many of JavaScript's methods – with extensions that take After Effects properties into account. As there are many books thicker than this one dedicated strictly to teaching JavaScript, it is not our intention to provide a computer programming manual here, but to explain uses for some of the more interesting pieces of the Expressions language.

Our study of expressions will be broken into three sections:

Introductory Expressions: What expressions do, how to apply (and remove) them, and some of their more common applications, presented in a tutorial manner. If you already have experience using expressions, you can probably skim or skip this section.

Deeper Modes of Expression: Bonus Chapter 37B (a PDF on the DVD) dives into more detail, highlighting some choice sections of the expression language and demonstrating how you might use them. Bonus Chapter 37C contains an overview of Scripting in After Effects. If you like, you can set this section aside until later.

Expressive Tricks: Bonus Chapter 37B also contains several practical examples that pull together the different concepts explained in this chapter and in the bonus chapter.

Introductory Expressions

Expressions can be thought of as an alternative to keyframes. You can apply an expression to virtually any property that you can keyframe. The expression will then create a value for this property, often by looking at the values of other properties (such as basing the scale of one layer on its own rotation, or on the opacity of another layer). You can also combine expressions and keyframes – say, to add a slightly random wiggle to an already-keyframed motion path.

Expressions are very flexible, and are especially useful when you want to set up master/slave relationships between multiple layers – for example, to be able to change one master color, and have it affect several other layers or effect properties at once. Think of expressions as tireless assistants helping you on your project: Teach them once what it is you need done, and they will copy your work or follow your instructions for as many other layers or effects as you need. In general, this is the trade-off expressions present: If you can spare the extra time up front needed to create them, they'll save you time later.

Enabling and Disabling

First, let's go through the basics of creating, enabling, and disabling expressions. Open the project file **37-Example Project.aep**, twirl open the folder **Ex.01** in its Project panel, then double-click [**Ex.01_starter**]. It contains two wheels, one of which has already been keyframed to rotate. Select both layers, and type R to reveal their Rotation properties in the Timeline panel – note that Rotation keyframes have been set for the **Wheel 2** layer, but not for **Wheel 1**.

Before we show you how to make **Wheel 1** follow **Wheel 2**'s rotation using an expression, first you need to learn how to apply and disable expressions, and what to do when they break.

There are three ways to enable expressions for a property. Try any of these on Rotation for **Wheel 1**:

- Select the property (not just the layer) by clicking on it in the Timeline panel, and use the menu command Animation > Add Expression.
- Select the property, and type Option+Shift+= (equals sign) on the Mac (Alt+Shift+= on Windows).
- Option+click (Alt+click) on the property's animation stopwatch in the Timeline panel. (This is the one we use most often.)

After you have done any of the above, the value for this property will turn red (see figure on the next page). A line will be added that has the words "Expression: Rotation". An equals sign (=) will appear to the right of this text; this shows an expression has been enabled. To the right of this in the timeline, you will see a line of text has appeared that says "transform.rotation" – this is a default expression that says you have now made Rotation equal rotation. Press Enter on the numeric keypad to accept this expression. You can also click almost anywhere else in the

More Expressions

For those who want to learn more about expressions, we've included a Bonus Chapter 37B on your DVD called *Deeper Modes of Expression*. Look for it in the **Bonus Chapters** folder; it includes a PDF file and its own Example Project. This bonus chapter examines important sections of the expression language in greater detail. Many of the tricks demonstrated there are then put to work in the advanced examples at the end of that chapter. Even if you don't have a desire to write code, there are a number of useful expression "modules" and Animation Presets discussed in the bonus chapter that you can reuse in your own projects.

Beyond using expressions is writing scripts to control what After Effects does. This is discussed in Bonus Chapter 37C, *Scripting Overview*, by Dan Ebberts.

37B

Deeper Modes of Expression

In this bonus chapter, we'll examine different sections of the expression language in greater detail. By no means is this guide exhaustive; our goal is to show advanced tricks and techniques we personally find useful.

A large collection of useful concepts, presets, and techniques to expand your mastery of expressions.

Mucho Gracias

Other Useful Math Expressions ... 3

Interpolation Methods ... 9

A useful method for matching different ranges of values, plus a sidebar on saving expressions as Animation Presets.

Deeper into Arrays ... 11

Space Conversions ... 16

Example Project

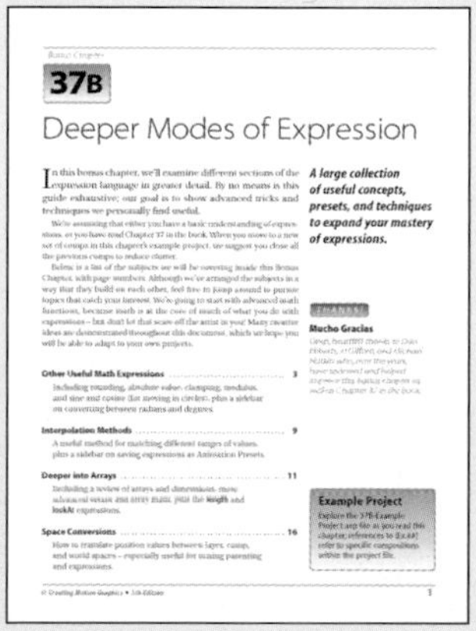

panel, and it will have the same effect. Don't press Return; it will just start a new line for you to write a more detailed expression.

Rotation = rotation is a pretty boring expression; let's work on that. To edit an expression, select the expression's text – in this case, the words **transform.rotation**. The text defaults to being highlighted when you create a new expression, or first click on the expression text. Type in a number that you want Rotation to equal, such as "**45**", and press Enter. (Don't type "**= 45**" – the equals sign is assumed, and you'll get an error.) **Wheel 1** will jump to a 45° angle in the Comp panel, and you will see that its value has changed to 45 in the Timeline panel. Note again that the property's value is displayed in red: This is a clue that an expression is setting this parameter.

When you first enable expressions for a property, After Effects automatically writes a default expression that makes the property equal to itself – in this case, Rotation = rotation. To accept an expression, press Enter (not Return).

To disable an expression, click on the = sign; it changes to a ≠ symbol. As you do this for **Wheel 1**, note how the wheel jumps back to its original rotational value before you applied an expression, and that the color of this value returns to yellow. Click on the ≠ symbol, and the expression is enabled again. Most expressions *replace* the value normally assigned to a layer, although it is possible to write ones that *add* to this initial value – we'll discuss that later.

You can apply expressions to properties that have keyframes, as well. Try the above tricks with **Wheel 2**. Many people like to use simple expressions just like this one to temporarily override a layer's keyframes with a single value (such as Rotation = 45° here, or Opacity = 100% for a layer that's fading in and out) to help them sort out what's happening in a complex project.

Click on the = symbol to temporarily disable an expression. The = will change to a ≠, and the property's value will revert from red to yellow. Click again to re-enable the expression.

If you want to hide an expression, twirl up its property in the Timeline panel. To reveal it again, select the layer and type either EE (two Es in quick succession) to reveal just expressions, or U, which reveals keyframes plus any properties that have expressions attached.

To delete an expression, do the same thing as you would to create one: Option+click (Alt+click) on either the stopwatch or = sign, select the property and use the command Animation > Remove Expression or type Option+Shift+= (Alt+Shift+=), or delete the expression text and hit Enter.

Click Anywhere

To accept an expression, clicking almost anywhere has the same effect as pressing Enter. This is handy if you're using a laptop without a dedicated Enter key.

Breaking Expressions

Expressions are easy to break. You will encounter this often, so let's get over the shock factor now. All that happens when you break an expression is that it is disabled; you can fix it and re-enable it. You won't crash; you won't lose any work.

Convert Audio to Keyframes

A popular animation trick is to make an animation seem to follow the beats in the music. There is not yet an expression that can directly read audio, but there is a keyframe assistant – Convert Audio to Keyframes – that can. Combine this with expressions, and many animation possibilities open up.

To use this assistant, open a composition that features audio, and choose Animation > Keyframe Assistant > Convert Audio to Keyframes. There is no need to select a layer first; After Effects mixes the audio for all of the layers in the composition, and then creates keyframes based on this final mix. If you have more than one layer with audio in a comp, and don't want to convert the audio levels of all of them, turn off the Audio switch for the unwanted layers before running this assistant.

Try this for yourself in [**Ex.99_starter**]. A null object named **Audio Amplitude** will be added to your comp; select it and press U to reveal its keyframes. It will have Slider Controls that represent the left channel, right channel, and left+right mix of the audio in your composition.

In [**Ex.99-final**], we've tied the resulting keyframes to the Scale of a rotating gizmo, and the Opacity of one of the background layers.

You may notice that the resulting animation has a "nervous" quality from trying to follow the volume changes very closely. You can try running Window > Smoother on the keyframes, or use Trapcode's SoundKeys (*www.trapcode.com*), which is a more sophisticated tool for converting sound to keyframes, including the ability to smooth the result.

First, a gotcha: Still in [**Ex.01_starter**], with an expression enabled for **Wheel 1**'s Rotation to set it to 45°, try to scrub or edit its red parameter value. It appears you can edit it, but as soon as you are done, Rotation's value will change back to 45°. Guess it had no effect, eh? Not quite: Click on the = sign to temporarily disable the expression, and you will see that After Effects remembered the new value you entered. This is a feature, as expressions can modify a parameter's original or keyframed value; just make sure you don't accidentally edit a value you wanted to keep! Re-enable the expression by clicking on the ≠ symbol.

Let's do something more problematic: Select the expression text, and instead of typing in a number, type in a word such as "**ten**" and press Enter (not Return). You will get an error dialog, with a warning that is probably incomprehensible to most nonprogrammers. The clues to look for are words in single quotation marks (in this case, it mentions the 'ten' you just typed), and the line number the error occurred on (which will help later as you write more complex multiline expressions).

Click OK; the expression will be disabled; it can't be re-enabled until you fix your error. Either replace **ten** with a value like **10**, or press Command+Z (Control+Z) to undo until you are back to where you were before creating the error.

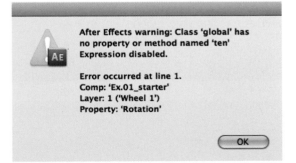

After Effects warning: Class 'global' has no property or method named 'ten' Expression disabled.

Error occurred at line 1.
Comp: 'Ex.01_starter'
Layer: 1 ('Wheel 1')
Property: 'Rotation'

OK

Expression error dialogs can be baffling to nonprogrammers at first. Major hints include words inside quotes, and the line number the error happened on. You can always undo back to where you were before making the error.

Pick Whipping for Pleasure

After Effects does what it can to make writing expressions easier. The best tool for this is the *pick whip*, which allows you to literally connect one property to another.

To reduce the potential for distraction, close comp [**Ex.01_starter**] and open [**Ex.02_starter**], which is essentially the same composition. Select the two layers and type R to reveal their Rotation properties. Rotation has already been keyframed for **Wheel 2**; say you want **Wheel 1** to have the same animation. You could copy and paste keyframes from one to the other, or you could use expressions.

Option+click (Alt+click) on the Rotation animation stopwatch for **Wheel 1** to enable expressions (remember, the expression is applied to the layer that will be the slave, not the master). Note that three additional icons appear in the Timeline panel to the right of the = sign. The middle one (which looks like a spiral) is the pick whip tool. Click on it, and with the mouse held down, drag to the word "Rotation" for **Wheel 2** (remember you want the property name, *not* the layer name). An outline box will appear around the word "Rotation", confirming you have selected it. Release the mouse, and After Effects will write the resulting expression for you:

thisComp.layer("Wheel 2").rotation

Seems like a lot of text, but actually it is quite logical: It states that in this comp, there is a layer called Wheel 2, and we want to use its Rotation. Some may find this easier to read backward: Take the Rotation, of a layer called Wheel 2, that is in this comp. Either way, the periods mark

TIP

Frozen Expression

Using expressions to temporarily set an animating property to a constant value is a handy tool when you're trying to sort out a complex animation.

To link one property to another, enable expressions for a layer, and use the pick whip tool (the spiral icon) to connect it to another property (below). After Effects will automatically write the correct expression to link the two (bottom).

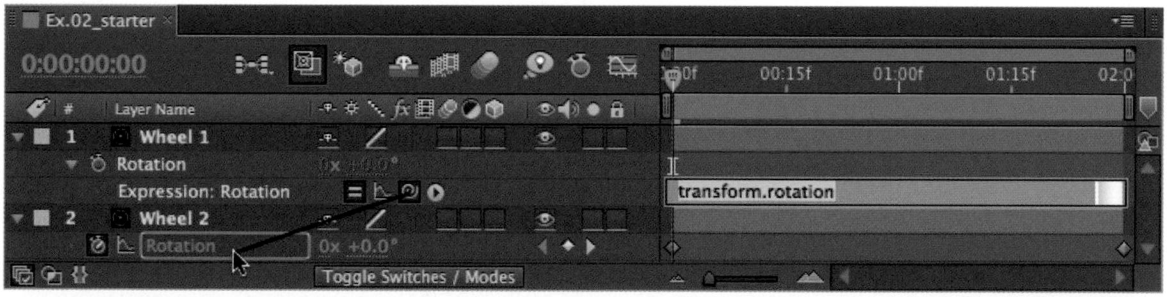

important breaks in the syntax as you read an expression. Using the pick whip tool relieves you of having to type this in yourself, avoiding both tedium and the chances for typos or other errors.

Press Enter to accept the expression and either scrub the timeline or RAM Preview; both wheels will now rotate the same. The advantage of expressions over keyframing is you can now change the keyframe values of **Wheel 2**, and **Wheel 1** will automatically follow without needing to copy and paste keyframes again; also, editing velocity curves for the master layer will update the slave layer. Go ahead and try this yourself.

That's a nice time-saver, but there's a problem: If two wheels touched – as they do in this composition – they would rotate in opposite directions from each other. Also, because **Wheel 1** is twice the size of **Wheel 2**, **Wheel 1** should rotate only half as fast as **Wheel 2**. If you were keyframing normally, it would be time to drag out the calculator. With expressions, you can let After Effects be the calculator.

Select the expression text field for **Wheel 1**, and place the cursor at the end of the line (pressing the down arrow is a good shortcut). Then add to the end of the text:

* –1 / 2

The * –1 means times minus one, which will make **Wheel 1** go in the opposite direction. The / 2 means divided by two, which will make it rotate half as fast. Press Enter and RAM Preview; the resulting animation should now look correct. The finished version is shown in [**Ex.02-final**]. Again, you can edit the Rotation keyframes for **Wheel 2**, and **Wheel 1** will automatically adjust itself to match. Try it and see!

Math Symbols

Expressions use slightly different math symbols than those on a calculator. The first column is the standard symbol; the second is what to use for expressions:

+	+	add
–	–	subtract
×	*	multiply
÷	/	divide

More complex math operations, such as "add-and-increment" or "modulus," are discussed in Bonus Chapter 37B on your DVD.

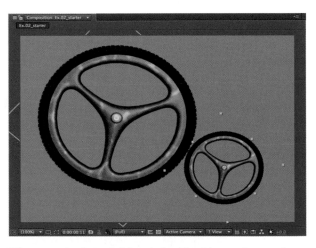

When two wheels touch (above), they should rotate in opposite directions, with their speed depending on their relative sizes. It's easy to have expressions do this math for you (below).

Ex.04_starter

0:00:01:11

#	Source Name
▼ ■ 1	CD_bikewheel.tif
▼ Ö Direction	1x -572°
Expression: Direction	transform.rotation * –1 + value
Ö ᒪ Rotation	1x +132.0°

The above expression rotates the shadow's Direction in the opposite direction as Rotation is animating, keeping the shadow stationary.

Shadow Fix Options

The *Rendering Order* section in Chapter 18 includes a few more solutions for fixing the rotating shadow problem, such as using Layer Styles instead of the Drop Shadow effect.

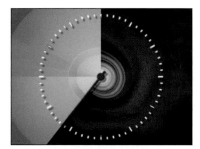

In [Ex.05b], a Radial Wipe effect is tied to the stopwatch hand's rotation. This requires additional scaling to match 360° rotation to 100% effect completion. Footage courtesy Artbeats/Digidelic and Virtual Insanity.

In [Ex.05c], expressions automatically tie blur amount and wave warp height to the tracking between characters.

Option+click (Alt+click) on the stopwatch for Direction; this will enable expressions and reveal this property in the Timeline panel.

In the Timeline panel, drag the pick whip for Direction to Rotation. You need the shadow to rotate in the opposite direction, so type " * –1" at the end, and press Enter. RAM Preview; the shadow remains stationary, but it's in the wrong place! This is because expressions normally *replace* a parameter's original value: in this case, 135°. To fix this, add " + 135" onto the end of the expression. Or, instead of manually entering the value for the direction angle, type " + value" which tells After Effects to add the parameter's original value to the result. This way, you don't have to remember what the original value was; you can even keyframe the value, and the expression will automatically take this offset into account. The result is shown in [Ex.04-final], with some parentheses added to make the expression easier to read.

Using expressions to tie together disparate properties is a great technique to make an overall animation seem more cohesive. Once you've set up a relationship between properties, you can edit the master and have the rest follow along automatically.

A few additional ideas are included in the **Ex.05** folder:

- [Ex.05a] ties the center of a Spherize effect applied to one layer to the location of a second layer which contains a magnifying glass. If the keyframes and expressions are not visible, select **magnifier** and type U, then **background** and type EE.

- [Ex.05b] ties a Radial Wipe effect applied to **AB_Digidelic** to the rotating second hand on a stopwatch. Note that we had to add some simple math modifiers to scale 360° of rotation to equal 100% of transition completion. As a bonus, select **hand** and type EE: We used the trick learned in [**Ex.04**] to counter-rotate the Bevel Alpha and Drop Shadow angles as the hand revolves to keep their perspectives intact.

- [Ex.05c] is the classic example of tying blur amount to the tracking parameter of text (a very popular look for a while), with a Wave Warp thrown in for good measure. Note that in the case of [**Ex.05c**], the expressions link together different effect parameters; remember that Animation Presets allow you to save multiple effects – and their expressions!

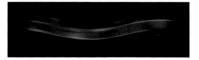

Moving Between Dimensions

So far, we've discussed using expressions to link similar properties, such as a layer's Rotation and an effect's Angle. However, there are numerous occasions when you will want to link together incompatible properties. For example, if you want to link Rotation to Position, do you mean the X Position or the Y Position? This is going to require diving a bit deeper into the expression language.

After Effects is concerned about how many *dimensions* a property has. Opacity has one value, so it has one dimension. 2D Position has two values – X and Y – so it has two dimensions; 3D Position has three dimensions (X, Y, and Z). Although you may be used to thinking of Scale as a one-dimensional value, in reality it also has two or three dimensions (depending if the layer is in 2D or 3D space), as each dimension of a layer can be scaled independently. A clue that a property has multiple dimensions is if its values are separated by commas in the Timeline or Effect Controls panel.

The values of a multidimensional property, taken together, are described as an *array* or *vector*. Expressions group together the values of an array inside square brackets, separated by commas: For example, a Position of X = 360, Y = 243 would be represented as **[360, 243]**.

If an expression is trying to link together two properties that have different numbers of dimensions, After Effects needs to know how to fill in the holes. One way it does this is by referring to individual dimensions inside an array: The first dimension is identified as [0], the second dimension as [1], and so forth. For example, if an expression wants to refer to the X Position value, it identifies it as **transform.position[0]**.

The pick whip tool does what it can to help resolve differences in the number of dimensions between properties. To see this in action, close all the prior comps, and open **[Ex.06_starter]**. Select **CM_curvedarm** and type P followed by Shift+R to reveal its Position and Rotation properties. Enable expressions for Position – a property with two dimensions – and drag its pick whip to the word "Rotation", a property with one dimension. After Effects resolves this difference by creating a two-line expression that copies Rotation's value into a variable called **temp**, and then by using **temp** for both dimensions in an array for the value of Position. Press Enter to accept the expression and scrub the Rotation value; note how Position updates: Both values (dimensions of its array) are always equal to Rotation.

Delete the expression for Position, and enable expressions for Rotation. Drag the pick whip from Rotation – a property with one dimension –

FACTOID

Brackets and Dimensions

When a property has more than one dimension, its value is contained inside square brackets – for example, **[360, 243]** for the position X = 360, Y = 243.

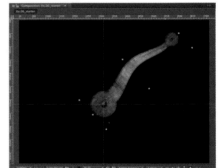

When you use the pick whip to connect Position to Rotation, Rotation is copied to a temporary variable, which is then used for both values of Position's array (below) (if needed, drag the expression text area larger to read both lines of the expression). As you scrub Rotation, both the X and Y Position take on the same value (above).

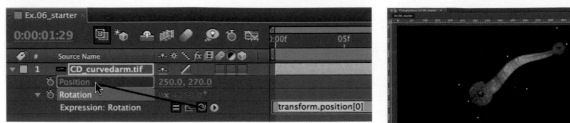

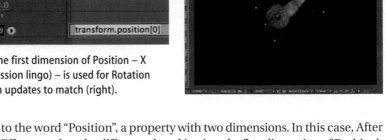

If you pick whip from Rotation to Position, the first dimension of Position – X (defined as **transform.position[0]** in expression lingo) – is used for Rotation (above). As you alter the X Position, Rotation updates to match (right).

to the word "Position", a property with two dimensions. In this case, After Effects resolves the difference by taking just the first dimension of Position's array (the X value), as noted by the expression **transform.position[0]**. Press Enter to accept this expression, and scrub the Position values for **CM_curvedarm**: Scrubbing X Position causes the arm to also rotate; scrubbing Y Position does not affect the rotation of the arm.

What if you want Rotation to be tied to the Y Position, not X? There are a couple of ways to do this. You can manually edit the expression to use a different dimension – in this case, change the expression text for Rotation to be **transform.position[1]**, and the second dimension – Y –

You can also pick whip to specific dimensions. Here, we are connecting Rotation to the Y Position value (known as **transform.position[1]** in expression language).

will be used. (Many computer languages start counting at 0, not 1. Programmers are used to this, although many artists aren't.) Another approach is to use the pick whip more selectively: Delete the current expression applied to Rotation and re-enable it, and this time drag the pick whip for Rotation to one of the individual Position values in the Timeline panel. A box will draw around the value to show you which one you are about to select. Drag the pick whip to the second value (Y), release the mouse button, and press Enter – the expression will be changed to **transform.position[1]**.

Each value inside an array is fully independent of the others; the only reason they're inside brackets is to make it clear they are part of the same property. Delete the expression for Rotation, re-enable it for Position, and again drag Position's pick whip to Rotation; After Effects will create the expression **temp = transform.rotation; [temp, temp]**. ("**temp**" is what's called a *variable*; we'll discuss those later.) Say you wanted just X Position to equal Rotation, but Y Position to keep its original value. Select the last **temp** in the expression text, and drag the pick whip to its own Y Position value. The expression will change to **[temp, transform.position[1]]**. This means the first value in the array – X Position – equals Rotation, and the second value in the array – Y Position – equals Y Position. Press Enter, and test it out by changing the value for Rotation.

Array Math Basics

Because each value inside an array is its own value, you can treat each one just as you would any single value you are calculating in an expression. For example, in the [**Ex.06_starter**] exercise on the previous page, you can replace any of the values inside an array with a constant, or add additional modifiers such as **transform.rotation * 2** (demonstrated in [**Ex.06-final**]). If your calculations get complex, you might want to surround them with parentheses to make them easier to read. Just don't delete the comma that separates the values inside an array; you will get either an unexpected result or an error message.

It is possible to perform math operations on an entire array, but it is often not as straightforward as you might expect. Open [**Ex.07_starter**] where we have two arms. Select both, and type S to reveal their Scale.

In [**Ex.07**], if we add a value to a two-dimensional array such as Scale (below), this value is added only to the first dimension of the array (X Scale). The lower arm distorts as a result (above). Arm image courtesy Classic PIO/Medical.

Enable expressions for the Scale property of **arm 2**, and drag its pick whip to the word "Scale" for **arm 1**. Press Enter to apply the expression. Now scrub Scale for **arm 1**; **arm 2** reacts as you would expect, scaling to match.

Click on the expression text for the **arm 2** layer, press the down arrow to move to the end of the text, type "*** 2**", and press Enter. As you scrub Scale for **arm 1**, both the X and Y Scale dimensions of **arm 2** change to be twice **arm 1**'s Scale – makes perfect sense.

Select the *** 2** you entered, delete it, replace it with **+ 20** and press Enter. You might think this would add 20% to both the X and Y dimension of Scale, but it adds 20 to just the first dimension of **arm 2**'s Scale (scrub **arm 1**'s Scale to confirm this). You can multiply and divide arrays by a single number, but you need arrays with the same number of dimensions to add or subtract. For example, **position + scale** is a valid expression, but if you want to add 40 to both the X and Y Position, you need to write **position + [40,40]**. Both of these are shown in [**Ex.07-final**]. See the section *Deeper into Arrays* in Bonus Chapter 37B for more details.

Group Therapy

After Effects provides three different ways to group layers and their actions: Expressions, Parenting, and Nesting/Precomposing. They differ in how inclusive or selective they are.

Nesting/Precomposing allows you to treat a group of layers as one layer in the next comp up the chain, including adding masks, effects, and transformations to the group.

Parenting allows transformations applied to the parent layer to be reflected in the child layers. However, masks, effects, and opacity are not transferred from parent to child.

Expressions transfer only one property at a time between layers. You need to create an expression for each transform or effect property you want transferred. Expressions can be used to link different properties, such as Rotation to Scale.

FACTOID

Resolving Conflicts

When you pick whip from a two-dimensional property to a one-dimensional property, the one-dimensional property is repeated. When you pick whip from a one-dimensional property to a property with more than one dimension, only the first dimension is used – for example, **position[0]**.

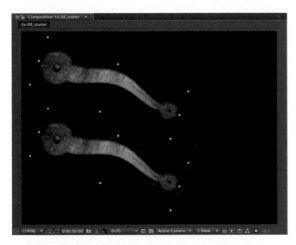

Null Objects are good masters for expressions: Using them eliminates some confusion as to which visible layer is a master and which layers are slaves.

Controlling Expressions

So far, we have experimented with using expressions to link one layer to another, or to link different parameters for the same layer. You can also link expressions to layers or effects that don't appear in the final render. This can make projects easier to organize, as it's clear who is the master controller for a group of layers.

Null Objects – which are useful as master "containers" when you're working with parenting – are equally useful as master controllers for expressions. Close any lingering comps, and open [**Ex.08_starter**] which contains the two arms we used earlier. Add a Layer > New > Null Object to this comp. Type Command+A (Control+A) to Select All, then type S followed by Shift+R to reveal their Scale and Rotation properties.

Enable expressions for **arm 1**'s Scale, drag its pick whip to the word "Scale" for **Null 1**, and press Enter. Do the same for **arm 2**. Scrub **Null 1**'s Scale, and the two arms will follow. (Note that unlike parenting, the arms do not move closer to and farther away from **Null 1**, because you are not scaling all the layers as a group around the null's anchor point; you're using expressions to modify the Scale of each layer individually.) Now repeat the same trick for Rotation, linking **arm 1** and **arm 2** to **Null 1**. Scrub Rotation for **Null 1**, and the two arms will rotate around their own anchor points (*not* around **Null 1**).

Bonus Points for Fun: Duplicate the arm layers, and move them to another area of the Comp panel. Expressions are copied when you duplicate a layer, so **Null 1** will still act as a master for all of these duplicates. You can also add modifiers to the end of the Scale expressions (such as *** 0.75**) for each arm to make them different sizes, but all still controlled by the same master layer. This result is shown in [**Ex.08-final**]. Note that you can turn off the Video switch (the eyeball) for the **Null 1** layer to remove its bounding box in the Comp panel – the expressions continue to work.

Null layers are good for controlling transforms; the Expression Controls are good for nearly everything else. These effects include Angle, Checkbox, Color, Layer, Point, and Slider Controls. These interface elements don't do anything by themselves, but they can be used to control expressions. You

Saving Expressions as Animation Presets

Expressions cannot be saved by themselves. Instead, you will need to copy and paste them between After Effects and a text document, or import projects that contain expressions you want to reuse.

A better way to save expressions is to use Animation Presets (originally discussed in Chapter 25). Expressions applied to effects – or ordinary parameters – can be saved along with the effects as Presets. Simply apply your expressions to effects, select the effects in the Effect Controls panel, and use Animation > Save Animation Preset to store the result as a preset. Select a new layer and use Animation > Apply Animation Preset to recall the effects with their settings, keyframes, and expressions intact. (Note that if these expressions referred to other layers or comps, then you will need to re-enter the new layer and comp names). If you save Presets inside the default folder After Effects points you to, they will show up in the Effects & Presets panel where they are even easier to apply.

We like to use Expression Controls and the Distort > Transform effect (which gives you a second set of Position, Scale, and Opacity controls for a layer) to write self-contained expression modules.

Expression Controls can also provide a simplified "user interface" to a complex expression or effect. Here are the naming conventions we use when we're building these expression presets:

- **in_** is used for controls that need to be pick whipped to another property – for example, the Position of a master layer.

- **set_** is used for controls that are intended to be adjusted by the user. They set parameters for an expression, such as the number of frames.

- **out_** is used for controls that contain the results of our expressions. The expressions are applied to these elements, and then we pick whip the layer properties we want to control to the **out_** elements.

We will use these naming conventions in the examples that appear throughout the bonus chapter on the DVD. The Expression Presets we saved for you all have the prefix **exp_** and are saved in the **Goodies** folder on your DVD; don't forget to copy them into your **After Effects > Presets** folder. If After Effects is currently open, select Refresh List from the Effects & Presets panel's Options menu and they will appear in the Animation Presets listing.

---

can apply Expression Controls to any layer; they won't affect its appearance. We like to apply them to null objects to keep it clear who the master is.

To get a quick feel for these, open [**Ex.09_starter**]. It looks just like [**Ex.08_starter**], with a null object already added (which we've named **Master Null**). Select **Master Null**, and apply Effect > Expression Controls > Angle Control. Type E to reveal it in the Timeline panel, then twirl it open. Select **arm 1** and **arm 2**, type R to reveal Rotation, and use the pick whip to hook up expressions between the Rotation properties of the arms and the Angle value of your new Angle Control. You can drag the pick whip to the word "Angle" in either the Timeline or Effect Controls panel (remember to drag to the parameter name "Angle" – not to the effect's name "Angle Control"). Press Enter, and when you scrub Angle, both arms will rotate as before. You can also rotate the Angle dial in the Effect Controls panel. (For bonus

The Expression Controls provide user interface elements to hook expressions to.

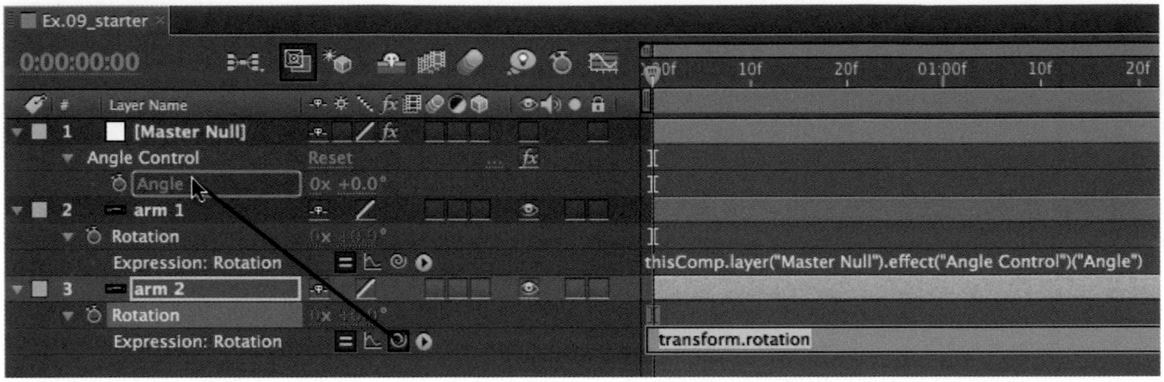

[Timeline panel showing:]

Ex.09_starter

0:00:00:00

#	Layer Name
▼ ■ 1	[Master Null]
▼	Angle Control Reset fx
	Ŏ Angle 0x +0.0°
▼ ■ 2	arm 1
▼ Ŏ	Rotation
	Expression: Rotation thisComp.layer("Master Null").effect("Angle Control")("Angle")
▼ ■ 3	arm 2
▼ Ŏ	Rotation
	Expression: Rotation transform.rotation

After you apply the Expression Control you want, twirl it open in the Timeline panel, and use the pick whip to hook other properties to it.

points, add Effect > Expression Controls > Slider to Master Null, and hook up expressions for the Scale of **arm 1** and **arm 2** to this new controller. The result is shown in [**Ex.09-final**].)

The expression After Effects created when you hooked up these controls is a bit longer than what you've seen so far, but can still be read just the same as other expressions. Let's break it down:

thisComp.layer("Master Null").effect("Angle Control")("Angle")

What this expression says is that in this comp, there is a layer named Master Null, which has an effect named Angle Control, and we want to use its parameter named Angle.

Note that the name of the effect is called out explicitly. To keep your expressions shorter and easier to read, give your Expression Controllers short names that match what you intend to use them for.

Other Controller Ideas

We've created a pair of additional comps for you to explore, to give you more ideas of what can be done with Expression Controllers:

- [**Ex.10a**] contains one layer – **Master Color** – which controls the Fill effect for a number of other layers in the same comp. Select **Master Color**, press F3 to open its Effect Controls panel, and edit the swatch for Color Control; note how all of the text layers update. Select any of these text layers and type EE to see their expressions. Remember that you can use the pick whip to connect expressions across multiple comps; this means one color swatch could control an entire project, making it easier to accommodate last-minute client changes.

- [**Ex.10b**] contains a more advanced example of the master color concept. Select **Text Master** and press F3 to open its Effect Controls: It contains Expression Controls for the color, shadow distance and softness, and the light angle for the Drop Shadow and Bevel Alpha effects applied to each of the text layers (select any of them and type EE). This is a great way to simplify control of a complex effect, even if applied to a single layer: Create Expression Controls for just the parameters you know you'll be tweaking, and twirl up the effect itself.

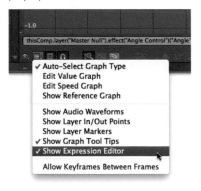

TIP

Expressions in the Graph Editor

To view expressions while the Graph Editor is active, click on the Graph Type and Options button and select Show Expression Editor from its popup menu.

Also note in [**Ex.10b**] that we used **Text Master** as a parent for the text layers; this makes it easy to position and scale them. Don't be afraid to mix and match parenting, nesting, precomposing, and expressions, using the strengths of each. Just because you *can* create an expression to control a parameter, doesn't mean you *have* to!

Variables and Multiline Expressions

So far, most of the expressions we've seen can be contained on one line, and are pretty explicit: Make this number equal that number. However, it doesn't take much before expressions can start getting long and messy. It is a good idea to break them down into easier-to-read chunks whenever possible. To do that, we'll add another tool to our arsenal: *variables*.

Say you wanted the width and height of a layer to be controlled by a pair of Slider Controls. In [**Ex.11_starter**], we've given you a head start by adding these controls to the layer **master_scale**, giving them the names "width_slider" and "height_slider". Select **master_scale** and type E to reveal its effects in the Timeline panel, and then twirl these open. Then select the layer **blue_sphere** and if necessary, type S to reveal its Scale. Enable expressions for **blue_sphere**'s Scale, and do the following:

Step 1: Type "[" (open bracket, without the quotes).

Step 2: Drag the pick whip to the word "Slider" under the effect name "width_slider" in the Timeline panel. This links the X Scale.

Step 3: Type a comma to separate the X and Y Scale dimensions in the array.

Step 4: Drag the pick whip to the word "Slider" under the effect name "height_slider", linking the Y Scale.

Step 5: Type "]" (close bracket).

Step 6: Press Enter to accept the expression. If you like, scrub the two sliders to make sure they work as expected.

The result is the following none-too-short expression, appearing all on the same line:

```
[thisComp.layer("master_scale").effect("width_scale")("Slider"),
thisComp.layer("master_scale").effect("height_scale")("Slider")]
```

Expression Controls allow you to have one parameter control a number of layers, and to simplify effects by exposing just the parameters you need to edit. Here, a Null Object called Text Master is used as a parent (top left), with Expression Controls (top) set up for color, shadow distance, shadow softness, and the bevel's light angle for a set of effects applied to a group of text layers (above). Remember that you can rename effects! Image courtesy Digital Vision/All That Jazz.

TIP

Across Panels

You can drag the pick whip to a parameter in the Effect Controls panel, or even to the Timeline panel belonging to another comp.

That long expression is hard to read; it might even extend past the right edge of your Timeline panel. This also makes it hard to edit later – for example, if you wanted to select just the Y Scale portion of this expression, you need to grab a large line of text buried in the middle of an array.

Let's rebuild this expression in a friendlier way. Select the expression text for **blue_sphere**'s Scale, delete it, and with the cursor at the start of the expression text line, follow these steps instead:

Step 1: Type a name you will find easy to remember, such as "**my_X**" (again, without the quotes), followed by an equals sign. This word is a *variable*: a temporary value you can make up to store values in during an expression.

Step 2: Drag the pick whip to the word "Slider" under the effect name **width_slider** in the Effect Controls panel. This links the X Scale.

Step 3: Type a semicolon; this tells After Effects you have finished one line of an expression. Press Return (*not* Enter) to start a new line in the expression text.

Step 4: Type a second name, such as "**my_Y**" followed again by an equals sign.

Step 5: Drag the pick whip to the word "Slider" under the effect name **height_slider**, linking the Y Scale.

Step 6: Type a semicolon and press Return.

Step 7: Type "[**my_X, my_Y**]" and press Enter to accept the expression. If you like, scrub the two sliders to make sure they work as expected.

```
my_X = thisComp.layer("master_scale").effect("width_slider")("Slider");
my_Y=thisComp.layer("master_scale").effect("height_slider")("Slider");
[my_X, my_Y] // our final answer
```

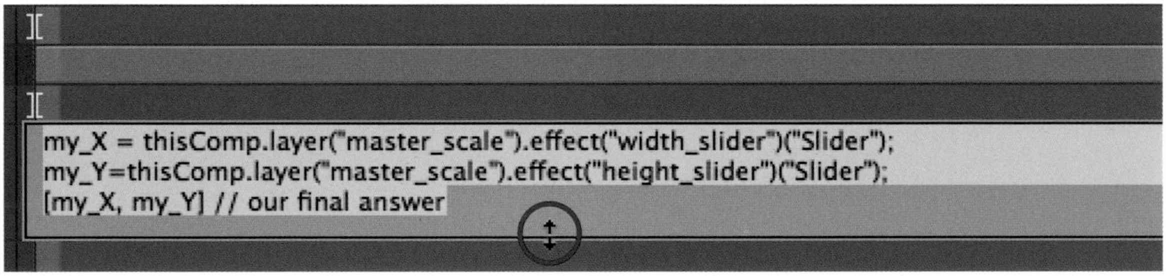

Multiline expressions that use temporary variables are often easier to break down, read, and edit. If necessary, drag the expression text box larger to read them (the special resizing cursor is circled in red). Note how we've added a comment (signified by the characters //) to the last line of this expression as well.

The result is the following multiline expression:

```
my_X = thisComp.layer("master_scale").effect("width_scale")("Slider");
my_Y = thisComp.layer("master_scale").effect("height_scale")("Slider");
[my_X, my_Y]
```

Although it uses more words and lines, the result is an expression that is neater and easier to read. For example, if you want to assign Y Scale to a different value, it is clearer what you need to select and edit. The last valid line of a multiline expression usually provides the final answer.

Every line or "phrase" of your expression – except the last line executed – should end with a semicolon. This tells After Effects that this piece of the expression is finished, and that the next text it encounters is a new piece of the expression. Often, a return at the end of a line works as well, but there is less ambiguity with the semicolon. We often use both to avoid errors and to make the final expression easier to read.

If you want to add comments to your expression to remind yourself later what each line is doing, type // (two slashes), then whatever comment you want. After Effects will not try to execute anything after // and before the next Return. When you enter a Return, this tells After Effects the line is over, and it can start executing the expression again from the start of the next line. If you want to write a long comment that requires more than one line, or sneak a comment into the middle of a line, surround your comment with the characters /* and */. To wit:

> **// this is a comment**
> **/* this also works**
> **as a comment*/**

Expression Language Menu

In addition to the pick whip, a second way After Effects helps write expressions for you is the *expression language menu*. It exists to the right of the pick whip icon: Click on the menu arrow, and you will be presented with a hierarchical list of many of the expression properties, attributes, and methods available to you. Using this menu helps avoid typos; it also provides important reminders of the format used by expression attributes and methods.

Each method (an expression piece that requires additional numbers to be entered inside parentheses afterward) contains abbreviated hints as to what values this method needs. For example, if you need a reminder as to what interpolation methods are available and how to write them, click on the expression language menu arrow, and select the

submenu Interpolation. You can see that these methods have options where you can define the minimum and maximum range for "t", or ignore it (in which case it will then use a range of 0–1).

Select the method you want, and After Effects will type this text in for you. You can then select the text for "tmin" or "value1" and either type in the number or variable you want, or use the pick whip to select another property or an Expression Control.

The expression language menu resides under the arrow icon to the right of the pick whip.

The expression language menu reminds you what attributes and methods are available, and what form they take – including hints as to what values they need. Select one, and After Effects types it in for you.

The Wiggle Expression

Even if you believe your adventures will never wander beyond a few simple pick whips, there is one advanced expression method that is well worth learning: wiggling a value.

You may be familiar with the Wiggler keyframe assistant (discussed in Chapter 5). In short, it randomizes the values of keyframes it is applied to, yielding anything from subtle human imperfection to in-your-face jumpiness. The wiggle expression creates similar effects and in many ways it is easier to control because you don't have to create new keyframes every time you want to adjust its operation.

The Wiggler keyframe assistant (above) and the basic wiggle expression (below) perform the same basic function. Wiggler's Frequency and Magnitude values correspond to the two values in parentheses for the wiggle expression.

The simplest way to add the wiggle expression to a property is to enable expressions for that property, type "**wiggle**(", enter a number for how many times per second you want the wiggle to jerk around, add a comma, enter a second number for how wide a value swing you want to wiggle by, type ")", and press Enter. To try this out, close all other comps, open [**Ex.12_starter**], select the baseball layer, type P to reveal its Position, enable expressions, and enter:

wiggle(5,10)

RAM Preview, and watch the baseball wiggle in space. Change the first number to slow down or speed up the wiggling; change the second to vary how far the baseball wiggles.

The wiggle expression works with any keyframes a property may have. Click on the = symbol to temporarily turn off this expression, click on the stopwatch for Position to enable keyframing, then animate a simple movement. Then click on the ≠ symbol to turn your expression back on, and RAM Preview: Note how the baseball wiggles around the path you keyframed.

To get an idea of how this expression is modifying your

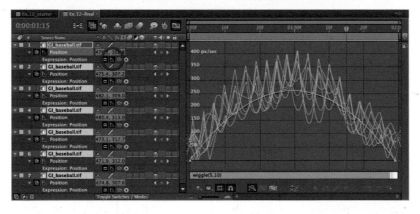

The wiggle expression wanders around any keyframed animation you have set up. The smooth line is the keyframed velocity curve before the expression; the squiggly line represents the curve after the expression. Wiggles are randomized based on layer number; that's why you see multiple squiggles.

path, open the Graph Editor, select Position, and click on the graph icon to the left of the pick whip tool. In the resulting graph, the gracefully arcing line is your original velocity curve; the squiggly line that moves above and below it is the curve after the expression has been calculated. If you have the layer selected in the Timeline panel, exposing the expression graph also draws the wiggled path in the Comp panel. Toggle the graph icon to see the difference.

The wiggle expression randomizes its path depending on its layer number in the timeline. Duplicate the baseball layer a few times, and note how you now have a flock of baseballs, each wiggling independently of each other. This is shown in [**Ex.12-final**].

The wiggle expression can be applied to virtually any property, including Rotation, Scale, and Opacity – go ahead and try this in [**Ex.12_starter**] for practice; we've also included some alternate examples – [**Ex.13a**] through [**Ex.13c**] – for your perusal.

The problem with the wiggle expression is that it keeps wiggling – even if your layer is supposed to be motionless (for example, when it reaches the final Position keyframe). However, it is easy to keyframe the wiggle amount; you just need to add an Expression Control.

Open [**Ex.14_starter**]: It contains an alarm clock that we want to wiggle as if its alarm is going off. Select the clock, type R to reveal its Rotation if not already visible, enable expressions for Rotation, type in the expression **wiggle(10,30)**, and press Enter. RAM Preview; the clock shakes for the entire comp.

With the clock still selected, apply Effect > Expression Controls > Slider Control. In the Timeline panel, twirl down Effects, then Slider Control to reveal its Slider parameter. In the expression text, select *just the second number* in the wiggle method (**30**, which is your wiggle amount) and drag the pick whip to the word "Slider" under Slider Control. Press Enter to apply. At this point the clock's not wiggling because Slider Control defaults to a value of 0, which is no wiggle amount. Increase its value, and note how it controls how much the clock wiggles.

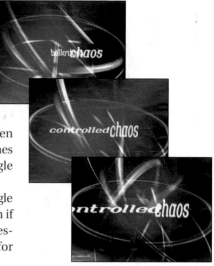

[Ex.13b]: Applying extreme amounts of wiggle to Scale creates jumpy, nervous animations. Background courtesy Artbeats/Virtual Intensity.

To keyframe the wiggle amount, select its value in the expression text (circled in red), and use the pick whip to connect it to a Slider Control.

Press Home to return to 00:00, and turn on the stopwatch for Slider Control in the Effect Controls panel. Press U to expose its keyframes in the Timeline, and set the Slider value to 0. Move to 01:00 and ramp up the value to around 30, then at 02:00 return to 0. RAM Preview again; note how the clock's shaking follows your keyframed values. Our version is contained in [**Ex.14-final**].

This is a very handy technique for controlling the wiggle expression. We will expand on this technique further in the expressions bonus chapter on your DVD – including a great little Animation Preset to add to all your motion control camera moves to make them look more realistic.

CONNECT

Wiggler keyframe assistant: Chapter 5.

Parenting and null objects: Chapter 17.

Nesting compositions: Chapter 18.

Precomposing: Chapter 19.

Animation Presets: Chapter 25.

Spotting audio: Chapter 36.

In Search of the Lost Codec

You open a movie in After Effects or QuickTime Player, and instead of the desired image, you get a white screen and an error message. You select it in After Effects' Project panel, and all it says is "Unknown Compressor." This means you don't have its codec installed. Don't panic; you can often find out what the missing codec is. Inside After Effects, Option+click (Alt+click) on its name in the Project panel to display both the file type and codec codes.

If the four-character codec code is too obscure, open the movie in Apple's QuickTime Player 7. Type Command+I (Control+I) to Get Info; the Format section will spell out the codec used. Also, QuickTime Player will give you an option to visit an Apple support page that provides links to many third parties who have created their own codecs.

On the Windows side, open the AVI movie with the missing codec in the Windows Media Player. In the Now Playing pane, enable the Playlist display. Right-click on the movie file and select Properties. This will tell you (in some cases) the codec being used.

WS_hummingbirds.mov – Inspector	
WS_hummingbirds.mov	
Source:	/Volumes/RAID/Wildscaping/ ! WS videos/WS_hummingbirds.mov
Format:	H.264, 1920 x 1080, Millions 16-bit Integer (Little Endian), Stereo (L R), 44.100 kHz
FPS:	30
Playing FPS:	(Available while playing.)
Data Size:	71.66 MB
Data Rate:	45.49 mbits/s
Current Time:	0:00:00:00.00
Duration:	0:00:00:13.21
Normal Size:	1920 x 1080 pixels
Current Size:	1920 x 1080 pixels (Actual)

To tell what codec a movie uses, open it in Apple's QuickTime Player, and type Command+I (Control+I) to Get Info. The lines next to Format explain the respective audio and video codecs and their settings as used by this movie.

Once you know which codec is missing, you can go back to either the person who provided you the file or the codec's manufacturer to get the correct codec, or request that the movie be provided using a different format. Note that a few video cards and nonlinear editing systems insist that you have their hardware installed to be able to render a movie to their codec. Also, many of these manufacturers are slow to update their codecs when a new operating system comes along. In either case, be proactive and tell them what their user base requires – and in the meantime, consider using a more universal codec.

Swiss Codecs

When there is concern over sending out or receiving a movie with a codec that either we or our clients do not have, a neutral codec supported natively by QuickTime is usually the best choice.

If 8 bit per channel (bpc) quality is acceptable, we use the Animation codec, set to Millions of Colors for RGB movies or Millions of Colors+ for those with alpha channels. We set the Quality slider to 100 for lossless output; in this case, the Animation codec uses lossless run-length encoding. We also turn off any keyframing in the QuickTime dialog. (Keyframing, which stores a whole reference frame at desired intervals and then just the data that changed between the intervals, may not update reliably as you jump around in time in an editing application.)

If the resulting Animation movies are too large, we'll use the Photo JPEG codec with quality set in the range 95 to 99. It should be perceptually lossless. The downside is that you lose alpha channel capabilities and will have to output the alpha channel as a separate movie.

If higher quality is required, we use image sequences instead of QuickTime movies. For 16 bpc quality, PNG sequences with Depth set to Trillions or Trillions+ colors is good; for 32 bpc, we use OpenEXR sequences with Depth set to Floating Point or Floating Point+.

Import Specifics

Now that we've covered the basic issues of bringing sources into After Effects, let's focus on more specific issues with each file type:

Movie Issues

A movie can consist of just video, audio plus video, or just audio. The video portion of a movie is actually a series of still images known as frames. The most common format for movies is QuickTime. QuickTime is just a container for media; After Effects can import and use any format of movies, stills, and audio that can be contained inside a QuickTime file.

The video portion of many movie files have been data compressed in some way. Even so-called lossless files have some specific data format or packing. The compression or packing method is usually referred to as a movie's *codec* (which stands for compressor/decompressor). QuickTime supports several different codecs natively; many video cards and non-linear editing systems also employ their own proprietary codecs, even though their data is stored inside a QuickTime file container. To use a movie that has a non-native codec, you need to add the codec to your operating system (see the sidebar *In Search of the Lost Codec*).

After Effects also supports some non-QuickTime movie formats. Some of these formats present you with multiple files including video content and metadata; you may need to do some searching to figure out which file to "import." For footage from a RED camera, import the .R3D file (not the lower resolution .MOV versions); for footage from some Panasonic cameras, import the .MXF file.

Movie files, along with all other footage items, are then processed by their Interpret Footage settings. These settings affect how alpha channels are interpreted, what frame rate is used when the individual image frames within a movie are accessed, and so on. We will discuss the Interpret Footage dialog in detail later in this chapter.

Audio Issues

After Effects also supports audio. In many cases, audio is embedded in a movie file along with the image, but QuickTime movies can contain just audio. After Effects supports any audio file format QuickTime supports, as it essentially reads it by using QuickTime's own "import" routines to internally turn it into a movie.

In contrast to being able to conform a movie's frame rate in the Interpret Footage dialog, After Effects does *not* allow you to conform the

Forced Induction

Ever have a file that you know is compatible with After Effects, but you can't select it in the Import dialog? You can force After Effects to accept it by setting the Enable popup to All Files, then setting the Format pop-up to the file format you think it is. If you're wrong, you'll merely get an error dialog. For example, to import an AVI file on the Mac, use this trick with Format set to QuickTime.

TIP

FLV Files

After Effects can import (as well as render) FLV and F4V format files. However, note that as of CS5, the Sorenson Spark codec is no longer supported for these files.

To change the playback speed of an audio clip, use Stretch, not the Interpret Footage dialog.

TIP

Scaling Up

After Effects is notorious for being poor at scaling up images cleanly. If you need to scale a movie or still larger than 115% or so, you will get better quality using a third-party plug-in such Red Giant Software's Instant HD.

GOTCHA

No Speak CMYK

With the exception of PSD and Illustrator files, After Effects will not import a still image file that uses CMYK color mode – change it to RGB or resave it as a PSD file.

sample rate. If a movie has audio attached, conforming the frame rate of the movie does not change the sample rate of the audio. This means the audio will continue to play back at its original speed, causing it to fall out of sync with the video. Therefore, it is better to use time stretching (discussed in Chapter 28) to change the playback speed of an audio track, or a layer that contains both audio and video.

To hear the audio after you import it, double-click it to open it in the Footage panel and press period on the numeric keypad. Previewing audio was covered at the end of Chapter 2; working with audio was covered in more detail in Chapter 36.

Still Issues

After Effects works internally at 8, 16, or 32 bit per channel resolution, assigning that number of bits to the red, green, blue, and alpha (RGBA) channels of every source. If the native color space of an image is less, such as grayscale, or uses an 8-bit color lookup table, After Effects will convert it to full RGBA when it displays it. If there is no alpha channel present, After Effects will automatically create a full white (opaque, or full-visibility) alpha channel for it.

After Effects does not look at the ppi (pixels per inch) setting for a still image – all it cares about is how many pixels are in it. A still image should have enough pixels that you don't have to scale it up past 100% when you're using it in a comp; otherwise, you may see unwanted artifacts. (Note that zooming in on a layer in 3D space may have the same result as scaling beyond 100%.) If you must scale up a still image, it is better to do it in a program such as Adobe Photoshop.

Conversely, you do not want your still images to be unnecessarily large, or you will waste processing power and RAM manipulating them inside After Effects. As a rule of thumb, if we expect to never scale an image larger than 50% in After Effects, we will create a scaled-down version of it in Photoshop and replace the source.

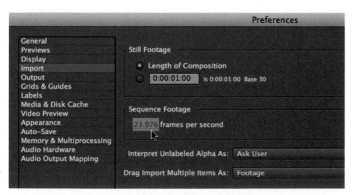

How stills and sequences are handled is also affected by the Preferences > Import dialog. These parameters are not set in stone; you can retrim a still's duration in a comp, and change a sequence's frame rate in its Interpret Footage dialog.

After Effects has a footage and comp size limitation of 30,000 pixels by 30,000 pixels. Some still image file formats may have size limitations smaller than this.

Still images have infinite duration in After Effects, and may be trimmed as desired. When you add a still to a composition, its default length is set in Preferences > Import > Still Footage. The default setting is Length of Composition, which means they will be automatically trimmed to equal each comp's duration. An alternative is to specify a time in this preference, which may be useful if you know you will be building a sequence out of a set of disparate images.

Sequences Issues

An alternative to movies is importing a series of still image files as a continuous sequence. While in the Import File dialog, if you select a valid still image, a checkbox will become active in the lower left quarter of the dialog with the file type (TIFF or PNG, for example) followed by the word "Sequence." Check it, click Open, and After Effects will now try to match up the rest of the files in the same folder to see if it can build a sequence.

All of the files for a sequence must be in the same folder, and they must be of the same file type. If the file you select does not contain a number in its name (as in **Filename.tif**), After Effects will use all the files in the folder of the same type to make the sequence, arranged in alphabetical order. If the files are of different sizes, the size of the file you select will be assigned to the sequence.

If the file you select has a number in its name, an additional option – Force Alphabetical Order – will become available. If you check this option, all of the files in the same folder will still be used to make the sequence. If you leave this option off, After Effects will use only the files with the same prefix before the number, creating a sequence of a duration that corresponds to the difference between the first and last number it finds. If the numbers increment continuously, everything's cool. If there are gaps between the numbers, After Effects will give a warning, and substitute color bars for the frames in the sequence where numbers are missing; check the Force Alphabetical Order option if you intended for numbers to be skipped.

You can also import just a section of a properly numbered sequence. Select the first file in the sequence you want, enable the Sequence checkbox, then Shift+click the last file you want. The range of files you've selected will be noted in the Import File dialog just below the Force Alphabetical Order option. Click Import, and just the portion of the sequence from the first to last file you clicked will be imported.

When you import a sequence of stills, After Effects automatically assigns it the frame rate set in the Preferences > Import dialog. We suggest you set this Preference to 29.97 fps (frames per second) for NTSC video sequences; 25 fps for PAL; 24 or 23.976 fps for digital cinema. You can change the preference before importing the sequence, or change the frame rate later in the source's File > Interpret Footage > Main dialog (discussed in more detail later in this chapter).

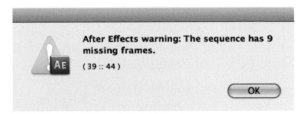

When you select a still image in the Import File dialog, you can check a box to treat it as a sequence. The files that are used to build this sequence depend on matching file types, file names, whether you select one file or a range, and whether you check the Force Alphabetical Order option.

If you attempt to import a sequence in which numbers are skipped in the file names, After Effects will give you a warning about how many numbers were missing, and substitute color bars for these frames in the sequence.

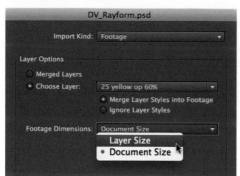

If you import a layered Photoshop or Illustrator file as a footage item, you will be presented with a second dialog in which you can choose to import either an individual layer or all of the layers flattened down to a single image. If you choose a single layer, you can decide whether to automatically crop it (the Layer Size option).

Supported Features

When you import a layered file as a composition, a number of features in Photoshop are translated into equivalent features in After Effects (note that some of this behavior changes if you save the file to a format other than PSD):

Photoshop	=	After Effects
Transparency	=	Alpha Channel
Opacity	=	Opacity
Blending Mode	=	Blending Mode
Layer Mask	=	Alpha Channel
Vector Shape	=	Shape Layer
Layer Styles	=	Layer Styles
Layer Groups	=	Nested Comps
Video Layers	=	Layers
3D Layers	=	Layers + 3D Effect
Editable Text*	=	Rasterized Text

* To convert Photoshop's Editable Text into text you can edit and animate inside After Effects, select the layer, and use Layer > Convert to Editable Text.

Photoshop Issues

When you create an Adobe Photoshop file, you can create it either as a single image or as a layered file. A single image, such as a scan, would normally consist of a sole flattened "background" layer; however, it could be a logo design created on a single transparent layer that has its own alpha.

Files with one or more transparent layers should be saved using the Photoshop file format. If you do this, After Effects can then import each of the component Photoshop layers as an individual image, merge (flatten) all the layers down to a single image, or import all the layers as separate footage items and create a comp for you that includes them in the correct stacking order and positioned as they were inside Photoshop. Video layers will also be imported as normal layers; 3D layers receive special treatment (see Chapter 16). The Photoshop layer names are used by After Effects, so try to give your layers useful names.

To import either a single layer or a flattened version of a layered file, select it in the Import File dialog, make sure the Import As popup is set to Footage, and click Import. You will be presented with a second dialog where you can either pick a single layer or choose to merge all of the layers into a flattened file. If you choose a single layer, an additional Footage Dimensions popup either crops the imported file to just the layer's dimensions or uses the overall image's dimensions with the layer properly positioned inside. (We prefer the Layer Size option, as the pretrimmed layers are faster to work with; plus, the anchor point will be in the layer's center.) There is also an option to either ignore any Photoshop Layer Styles used in the file or to render them into the imported layer.

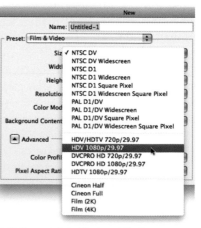

Photoshop can create new documents at standard video sizes using its Film & Video presets. Photoshop supports non-square pixels, although you might want to toggle off the View > Pixel Aspect Ratio Correction for best quality. The advantage of using these presets is that Photoshop will automatically create guides for you that outline the Action and Title Safe areas (see Chapter 41); these guides come along for the ride when you import the resulting PSD file into After Effects as a composition.

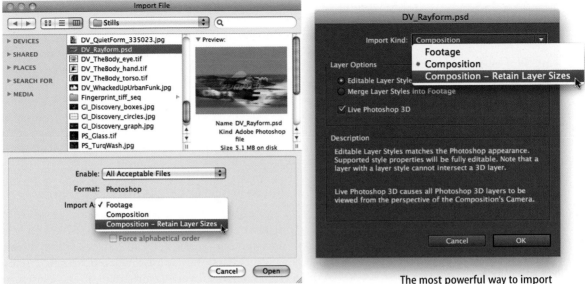

The most powerful way to import a layered Photoshop file is as a composition. This gives you additional choices on how to handle Photoshop Layer Styles and Photoshop 3D layers, plus whether or not to pre-crop the layers (Retain Layer Sizes). The result is a folder containing the layers, and a composition with them properly stacked and arranged. Layered Photoshop file from Digital Vision/Rayform.

If you wish to import all of the layers, you can go down one of two paths. The first is to set the Import File dialog's Import As popup to either Composition or Composition – Retain Layer Sizes, then click Open. Any Photoshop Layer Styles will be converted into After Effects Layer Styles (discussed in Chapter 22). The second path is to set the initial Import As popup to Footage and click Open. In the second dialog that opens, set its Import Kind popup to either Composition or Composition – Retain Layer Sizes. The rest of the options in this dialog will then change to give you a choice of whether to render any Photoshop Layer Styles into the footage items that are imported, or to keep the Layer Styles "live" and editable inside After Effects.

After importing, After Effects will create two items in the Project panel: a folder that contains all of the layers as individual footage items, and a comp that has all the layers in the correct stacking order. Both the folder and the comp will have the same name as the layered file. If the layered Photoshop file does not include a video layer, the comp's initial frame rate and duration are determined by the last comp you created. (If one or more video layers are present, the frame rate of the first layer added to the file is used.) You can change the comp's rate and duration after importing.

There are numerous rules and exceptions to importing layered files, depending on the tools you used inside Photoshop. See the sidebar *Supported Features* on the previous page for a quick summary; these are explained in more detail in the After Effects Help file.

If you create a Layer Group inside Photoshop, the contents of this folder will be grouped into its own precomp in After Effects. This precomp will then appear as a layer in place of the Layer Group in the resulting layered composition, and will be stored in the same folder as the other layers.

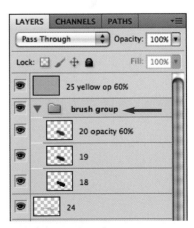

When you create a Layer Group inside Photoshop and import the file as a composition, the contents of the Layer Group will be placed in their own precomp in After Effects.

"Hot Key" to Edit Source

The Edit > Edit Original feature (see Chapter 6) allows you to hot key from After Effects to Photoshop, Illustrator, and other applications to edit a file.

If you merge a layered Photoshop or Illustrator file when you import it, you can change your mind and convert it to a layered comp without having to re-import it. Add the merged footage item to a comp, select it, and either right-click it or use the Layer menu and choose Convert To Layered Comp. The layer will be replaced with a precomp that contains the component layers.

To create a new Photoshop file that has the same dimensions as your current composition as well as the same bit depth as your project, use File > New > Adobe Photoshop File. This file will already be set up with safe area guides in Photoshop and will be imported automatically into your After Effects project.

Anywhere that's "paper" in Illustrator is automatically transparent in After Effects. Click on Toggle Transparency Grid along the bottom of the Footage or Comp panel if in doubt.

You can import Illustrator files as Footage or as a Composition.

Illustrator, PDF, SWF, and EPS Issues

After Effects will automatically rasterize (convert to pixels) vector-based Illustrator, PDF, SWF, and EPS files into bitmaps as needed, with very clean edges. Unlike bitmap-based artwork, you can safely scale vector-based artwork beyond 100%; in this case, turn on the Continuously Rasterize switch for the layer to have the vectors rerendered on the fly. (Be warned that enabling Continuous Rasterization does change the internal rendering order; read the *Continuous Rasterization* section in Chapter 20 for more details.)

Create your artwork in RGB color in Illustrator (although After Effects will import a CMYK file, the conversion may not always be accurate). Save your file in AI format and enable Create PDF Compatible File in the Illustrator Options dialog box.

When you import an Illustrator file, areas that would be considered the "paper" in Illustrator will be converted to an alpha channel in After Effects. Text and outlines will be rasterized; more recent versions of Illustrator now embed fonts in the document, so it is no longer necessary to convert text to outlines. However, unlike Photoshop text, you cannot convert Illustrator text into editable text inside After Effects.

You can import layered Illustrator files in three ways, similar to the way you import Photoshop files: as Footage (a merged composite of all layers), by choosing a single layer from the file, or as a composition that contains all of the individual layers that make up the file. As with Photoshop, the comp's initial frame rate and duration are determined by the last comp you created. Both can be edited after importing.

When you import a layered Illustrator file as a comp, After Effects creates a folder that contains each layer as an individual footage item, and a comp that

Import and Interpret // **38**

Import and Interpret // **38**

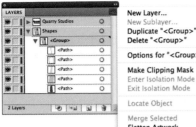

After Effects reads only the top layer hierarchy in an Illustrator file; you may need to move sublayers up to the top level. Our logo had five elements grouped inside a layer called **Shapes**. We selected **<Group>** (not the layer), and selected Release to Layers (Sequence) from the Layers panel's Options menu (left). The five path elements were converted into real layers, which we then dragged up to the top level and renamed (right).

contains those layers. As of CS5, After Effects does not read embedded color profiles from Illustrator files; you will need to assign the color profile (Chapter 26). It also doesn't read guides or blending modes. To improve the rendering of color gradients, open the Interpret Footage dialog, click on More Options, and set the Antialiasing popup to More Accurate.

The Illustrator Artboard

The way that "document size" is handled for Illustrator files has changed considerably in recent versions. Illustrator CS4 introduced the concept of Artboards to represent regions that can contain artwork. While Illustrator can create multiple artboards per document, After Effects will use Artboard 01 (the default when you create a new file) as the Composition size when you Import As Composition. To edit the dimensions, double-click the Artboard tool to open the Artboard Options.

Illustrator also includes a set of film and video document profiles. An advantage of using these presets in CS5 is that if you create a new Illustrator file using one of the Video and Film presets, in addition to creating Artboard 01 at the appropriate size, it also creates a second artboard that is much larger (14,400 × 14,400 to be exact). Provided you import your file into After Effects as a Composition (and you have at least two layers), any imagery that falls outside Artboard 01 isn't cropped off or lost – it will reside outside the composition frame, ready to be animated onto the stage.

If the file was created without using a CS5 preset, create a second artboard at 14,400 × 14,400 – this magic size will trigger After Effects to behave the same way.

After importing a layered Illustrator file, you'll have a composition and a folder of individual footage items; change the Composition Settings as needed.

Double-click the Artboard tool (circled) to open the Artboard Options dialog. (Note the "Video Ruler Pixel Aspect Ratio" option; we recommend you set it to "1".)

Importing Projects

You can import entire After Effects projects into your current project. The entire project, with all of its comps and sources, will appear in a folder with the project's name inside your current project (and inside whichever folder was selected when you imported). This works particularly well if you've set up a template for a specific effect as a standalone project: When you want to use that technique or template again, import the whole project.

You can also import the current After Effects project back into itself. This is handy when you have a chain of comps that you need to duplicate to create a variation of your animation. If you duplicate individual comps, you will have to relink nested comps to create a duplicate chain, but by re-importing the project back into itself, you have a second chain of comps ready to tinker with. Of course, you can also import prior versions of a project you are working on, just to remind yourself what you were doing previously.

Many use this feature to set up a batch of projects to render overnight. Set up the Render Queue with the desired comps in each of the original project files. Start a new "render" project, then import the set up projects. All of the items in their Render Queues will be added to the queue in your new render project.

All this project merging might mean you end up with multiple references to the same sources inside your project – which is unnecessary, because After Effects can reuse a source limitless times. To clean up organizational messes like this, use the File > Consolidate All Footage command. It will search for identical sources, link all references to one copy of the source, and delete the duplicates; if common sources won't consolidate, chances are they are being treated differently in the Interpret Footage dialog, or they are the same movie imported from different locations on disk. This command is undoable, but it's a good working habit to remember to save before doing anything this drastic, regardless.

Inverted Alphas

Some files have inverted alpha channels: black represents visible or opaque areas; white represents transparent areas. Examples of this include mattes created by some hardware keyers and film systems.

Opening Old Projects

New versions of After Effects introduce new features, which requires an updated Project format. When you're opening an old project in a new version, After Effects creates a new project with appropriate version translations.

The oldest project format After Effects CS5 can open is AE 6.0; CS4 is the most recent embedded format supported. When you archive a project, make a note of which version and fonts were used. Unfortunately, you usually cannot open a project created in a newer version of After Effects in an older version.

When you upgrade After Effects, consider "mothballing" the old version (freeze it at that point in time, and don't update the third-party plug-ins in that folder). Try to keep one computer around that can run your previous version – it will come in handy in the event you need to open an old project which uses effects you have not updated or other unsupported features.

> **AE** After Effects: this project must be converted from version 8.0.1 (Macintosh PPC) and will open as an untitled project. Standard Definition pixel aspect ratios will be updated for compatibility and improved accuracy. The original file will be unchanged.
>
> OK

When opening an old project, After Effects will warn you that it has to convert it to the new project format. You will not see this warning if you import (rather than open) an old project.

Interpret Footage

The Interpret Footage dialog is where you can indicate how After Effects handles your source files as it hands their images off to your comps. To open it, *you must select the footage item in the Project panel*, then either select File > Interpret Footage > Main, or click on the Interpret Footage icon in the bottom left corner of the Project panel. You can change the interpretation of any footage item at any time.

We discussed alpha channels in detail earlier in this chapter in the context of importing a file; you can change those settings here in Interpret Footage. The remainder of the parameters in this dialog – pixel aspect ratio, fields, pulldown, and in many cases frame rate – become issues when you're working with film and interlaced video. These issues are covered in Chapter 41; we will give an overview of them here and discuss some of the most common reasons for editing these parameters.

Alpha

The top portion of the box is a repeat of the alpha channel dialog that usually pops up while it's importing files that have alphas. If you feel you might have made a mistake with your initial alpha interpretation, you can go back and change it any time here. If you are having problems with colored fringes on objects with alphas, there's a good chance that changing alpha type from straight to premultiplied with black or white will clean it up.

If the file does not have a premultiplied color saved with it, the color will default to black. However, some source material – such as that found in still image object libraries – is originally shot on white. If the masks were cut right on the edges of the objects, chances are some of the white background got mixed in; selecting Premultiplied and changing the Matted With Color swatch to white will usually improve them. If a different background color was used, temporarily set the Alpha to Ignore, open its Footage panel, and eyedropper the real background color.

The settings in the File > Interpret Footage > Main dialog sit between your source and every comp you may use it in. You can set alpha interpretation, frame rate, and how interlaced video frames are treated.

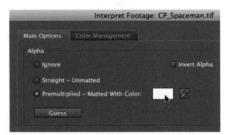

Object libraries with alpha channels that are shot against white are usually incorrectly guessed as having a straight alpha, which may result in white fringing around the object. Set the alpha type to premultiplied with white (above), and the fringe will go away. Notice the effect alpha channel interpretation has on semitransparent areas (left), as well. Spaceman from Classic PIO/Nostalgic Memorabilia.

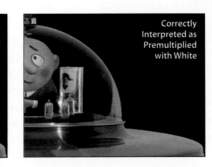

Wrongly Interpreted as Straight

Correctly Interpreted as Premultiplied with White

Color Management

The Color Management tab in the Interpret Footage dialog is discussed in detail in Chapter 26. If the Project Settings > Working Space is set to None, the parameters under the Color Management tab have no effect.

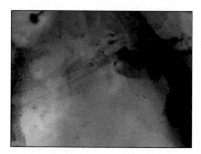

This movie (**GI_PaintFX.mov**) from Getty Images/PaintFX consists of rapidly changing random frames. Slow down the frame rate, and it becomes less nervous; turn on Frame Blending, and the interpolated frames become downright dreamy.

Frame Rate

The next pane is dedicated to frame rate and applies only to movies or sequences of stills. Movies come in with a rate already embedded in them; sequences have their default rate set via the Preferences > Import dialog. However, you can change or conform that rate to a new one inside After Effects for either practical or creative reasons.

You also may need to change the frame rate because it was mislabeled. For example, NTSC video runs at 29.97 fps, but many people render 3D animations and label stock footage at 30 fps. Leaving these sources at 30 while you build your comps and render at 29.97 fps will result in skipped frames, because your source will be feeding frames at a faster rate (30.00 fps) than they are being requested (29.97 fps) by the comp or rendering engine. These frame jumps will occur every 33.33 seconds, and may even start with the second frame. If you are separating fields, the frame rate effectively doubles, and a field (a half-frame) will slip every 16.67 seconds.

Other corrected frame rates that are of importance are conforming 60 fps to 59.94 fps (NTSC's field rate), 24 fps to 23.976 fps (the real speed telecined film is run at, and used for most digital cinema), and 24 fps up to 25 fps, since many films are simply sped up for playback on PAL video.

There are also creative uses of frame rate manipulation, such as faking staggered and other similar looks. One trick is to bring in a sequence of stills, set a low frame rate such as 1 fps (you can go as low as 0.01), then frame blend between them to create a dreamy background. Higher frame rates can be used for nervous grunge sequences and treatments.

Changing the frame rate of a source in Interpret Footage is also a handy way to "time stretch" footage – with an advantage: Conforming the frame rate happens *before* any other attributes, so keyframes remain in their original positions. If you use the regular Time Stretch feature, you will also stretch any keyframes applied to the layer in the comp. These tricks are discussed in more detail in Chapter 28.

Fields and Pulldown

Behind door number three are different ways to pull apart the separate fields that often make up a video image. Most single frames of video consist of two "fields" or are partial images taken at different points in time. They are woven into one frame through a process known as interlacing. You usually want to unweave them into the separate images that they came from, for maximum processing flexibility and quality. This popup is where you help After Effects figure out how to unweave or separate them.

If you have selected one of the popup options for separating fields, an additional popup under-

In most cases, you want to separate the fields of interlaced video so that After Effects can handle each field as its own image.

neath – Remove Pulldown – activates. When 24 fps film is transferred to nominally 30 fps video (or video is shot in "film mode"), a special process called *pulldown* is used to spread four film frames across five video frames. It is often desirable to remove this pulldown and get back to the original film frames. Clicking on the Guess button underneath has After Effects try to detect if pulldown was used in the movie under inspection and to set the field order and pulldown sequence accordingly; if not, no settings are changed. If the Guess fails, try each of the phases individually; when you've found the correct phase, no interlaced frames will be visible in the After Effects Footage panel.

Pixel Aspect Ratio

The fourth section is Other Options, which includes the very important Pixel Aspect Ratio popup. Although most computer displays tend to be based around square pixels (they are as wide as they are tall), many video and film formats project pixels differently, resulting in what initially appears to be stretched or squashed images when they are viewed on a computer. For example, "anamorphic" film images are only half as wide on the film than they ultimately appear on the screen; in this case, a special lens is used to stretch the image back out upon projection. In video, the issue becomes how many pixels are spread across one horizontal scan line of a video monitor.

Things can get really confusing when you try to combine images with different pixel aspect ratios, or try to do something as simple as draw a "perfect" circle with squashed pixels. By telling After Effects how the image was originally captured or created (with normal square pixels, or with a particular non-square pixel aspect ratio), it will handle these differences internally and protect you from a lot of potential confusion. You can even mix and match sources with different individual pixel aspect ratios.

Most artwork you scan in or create on your computer uses square pixels, so this setting is left at its default. However, After Effects keys off of certain "magic numbers" (such as DV 720×480 and D1 720×486) for image size when sources are imported, and it will automatically set the pixel aspect ratio if the image matches one of these magic numbers. Some image sizes can have more than one valid pixel aspect ratio (normal TV versus widescreen); the software often assumes the nonwidescreen case – but you can always set the popup to the widescreen case.

It is a good idea not to create square pixel images at these magic sizes in programs like Photoshop, because After Effects will assume that it must treat them as non-square, causing image distortions. (You can always set them back to square in the Interpret Footage dialog if so.) Note that you can create additional Interpretation Rules (see next page) to accommodate more ratios, or to override After Effects' guesses.

More on Fields and Pulldown

We have created in-depth online training modules on the subjects of interlacing and 3:2 pulldown. For information on where to get them, visit *www.crishdesign.com/ online_training.html*

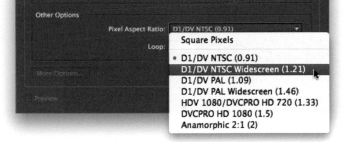

After Effects looks at tags saved with a footage item to see if its pixel aspect ratio is already known. If it can't find these tags, it guesses the aspect based on certain frame sizes – such as assuming 0.91 for 720×486 pixel movies. This is not infallible; for example, anamorphic widescreen video uses the same frame size. In this case, manually change the Pixel Aspect Ratio in the Interpret Footage dialog.

Grayed Out?

The Interpret Footage menu item will be grayed out unless you select the footage in the Project panel.

Live Preview

New in CS5: If a footage item has already been added to a composition, most changes made in the Interpret Footage dialog will immediately be reflected in the Comp panel, without having to first close the Interpret Footage dialog. Unfortunately, as of CS5 (version 10.0.0) these updates do not appear in the Footage panel until you close the Interpret Footage dialog.

Copy and Paste Interpretation

If you have a number of footage items that all need to have their Interpret Footage parameters set the same – such as Straight Alpha, 29.97 fps, Lower Field First, SDTV NTSC color profile – you can copy and paste from one item to many. Set up one the way you want, select File > Interpret Footage > Remember Interpretation or use the keyboard shortcut Command+Option+C (Control+Alt+C), select the other items to receive these parameters, then select File > Interpret Footage > Apply Interpretation or use the shortcut Command+ Option+V (Control+Alt+V). This can save you countless keystrokes early in a project.

Looping

You may loop any movie or sequence to repeat more than once – in fact, up to 9999 times. This is great for extending the running time of stock movies and other animations that have been built to loop seamlessly.

More Options

A few formats have additional settings hiding under the More Options button. For example, if you've imported footage from a RED Camera, click More Options to access a dedicated RED R3D Settings dialog, which provides a large amount of control over how a raw RED file is interpreted.

The More Options button provides access to how RED R3D files are interpreted. Footage courtesy Pixel Corps.

More Options may also be used to access the Camera Raw dialog for still images (discussed in Chapter 26, *Color Management*).

It is important to be aware that even though Camera Raw and RED R3D are high dynamic range formats (meaning they can access over-value colors), any out-of-range values are currently clipped once they leave these dialogs and cannot be recovered inside After Effects.

Therefore, our preferred floating point workflow with these file formats is to eliminate any overexposure issues inside these source dialogs, and then reshape the highlights as desired using Exposure, Levels, Curves, or similar effects inside an After Effects composition.

Interpretation Rules

When you import footage items into a project, After Effects makes several guesses on how to set the Interpret Footage parameters for an item. Some guesses are based on tags embedded in certain files; as discussed earlier in this chapter, you are also given the opportunity to set or have After Effects guess the alpha channel type.

When it can't find an information tag, After Effects looks at a text file of Interpretation Rules. This employs a simple form of scripting in which the program looks at certain parameters of a file, compares it with a set of rules in the file *interpretation rules.txt* that resides in the same folder as the program, and automatically sets many of the Interpret Footage parameters based on these rules if it finds a match. Of course, you can always override these automatic settings later in the Interpret Footage dialog.

The default rules that After Effects ships with include some helpers for a few common file types. To modify and write your own rules that can filter specific file types and image sizes, open the **After Effects CS5 > interpretation rules.txt** in a text editor, and save a copy to make sure you can get back to the original file if needed. Then add your own rules (or modify the rules already in the file), and save it back over the original.

The file contains extensive comments that help explain how it works, which we won't repeat here. However, let's work through an example:

Blackmagic 10-bit 720 x 486 is D1-pixel-aspect, lower-field first

720, 486, 29.97, "MooV", "v210" = 10/11, L, *, *, r6nf, 0

This means look for an NTSC D1 sized file (720×486), running at NTSC rate (29.97), that is a QuickTime movie (MooV) and is saved using Blackmagic's 10-bit YUV codec (v210). If the footage file being imported matches, set its pixel aspect ratio to be the standard 10/11 that After Effects now uses, with lower field first (L). The next two asterisks mean don't bother changing the frame rate (it's already correct) or alpha channel (it doesn't have one, anyway). The final two values are for the ICC color profile to use (r6nf means SDTV NTSC with black at 0 and white at the highest RGB value), and to leave linear light – an indicator of the internal gamma – off. And the # symbol at the start of the description is used to designate a comment that does not need to be interpreted.

While poking around the Interpretation Rules file, make sure you go to the very end: It describes how to create custom popups for pixel aspect ratios which will then appear in the Interpret Footage and Composition Settings dialog.

Immigration

If you regularly need to import large numbers of files (particularly image sequences), check out Immigration (*aescripts.com/immigration*) by Lloyd Alvarez. It is much more efficient at opening large folders of files, plus contains other intelligent sorting and batch replacement features.

To identify the file type and codec codes used by a footage file, import then Option-click (Alt-click) it in the Project panel. The four-character code for its file type is appended onto the front of the codec's name in the information to the right of the file's thumbnail; the four-character code for its codec will be appended onto the end.

Integration 101

Going beyond the simple exchange of rendered movies and images.

Surprisingly few jobs both start and end inside After Effects. More often than not, After Effects is used to add production value to a job started in a non-linear editing (NLE) program, or to create elements for a DVD or the web. And then there's the entire world of using After Effects to enhance 3D renders or to add new elements into 3D scenes.

Being smart about dividing up your work between applications allows you to shift the workflow to the best tool for the job, improving the result – while making you more efficient in the process.

In this chapter, we will give you an overview of how After Effects can be used with other programs in various environments. We'll also discuss issues pertaining to web and NLE integration, as well as authoring for DVDs and mobile devices. In the next chapter, we will focus on integrating 3D applications with After Effects.

Web Integration

After Effects is a great tool to create elements for web pages, ranging from animated ad banners to keying or rotoscoping live actors to superimpose on a web page. Also, as web animation design has influenced broadcast design over the past few years, you often need to bring web elements into After Effects. Here are some issues to watch out for:

GIF and PNG

Imported GIF and PNG-8 (8-bit indexed color) files will lose any embedded transparency, with transparent areas being filled with white. This is related to After Effects' inability to recognize transparency in any file that uses indexed color. A workaround is to first open them in Adobe Photoshop, then change their Image > Mode to RGB color. Keep the image as a transparent layer; do not flatten it. Save under a new name, using either PNG-24 or PSD formats with transparency. Import this new file into After Effects, and its transparency will appear as a normal alpha channel. (After Effects can render to PNG-24 files, but not PNG-8.)

Animated GIF is no longer supported as a render file format. The new suggested workflow is to render a QuickTime movie from After Effects, import it into Photoshop Extended, and export to animated GIF using Save For Web & Devices.

SWF

After Effects can both import and render SWF files. On the input side, the vector-based symbols in SWFs can also be continuously rasterized (Chapter 20), allowing you to scale them up cleanly.

After Effects recognizes the transparency in a SWF movie; just remember to set your background in Flash to be transparent before you export! To do this, you need to create a custom background color in Flash: In the Color panel, create a new color with Alpha set to 0%. Then bring the Swatches panel forward, and click along its bottom to add this color to your palette. It will be identified with a graph paper pattern. Then in the Properties Inspector, select this transparent swatch for the Stage color.

To give you a feel for working around issues with SWF files provided by others, [**Ex.01**] contains an example where we exported a simple animation of a television set as a SWF file and imported it into After Effects. Double-click the layer **SB_TV.swf** to open it in a Layer panel, and enable the Toggle Transparency Grid to see its alpha channel: The outside is transparent, but the oddly shaped screen in the middle isn't. For this, we exported just the screen symbol as a second SWF and used it as an alpha matte for the inset video (bring the Comp panel back forward to see the result). We also used a copy of screen matte to create an inner shadow around the screen bezel. The FLA (Flash project) files for the television elements are saved on your DVD, inside the **39_Chapter Sources** folder.

Elements created in Flash usually have square pixels and frame rates that are whole integers – such as 30 frames per second (fps), instead of 29.97. Remember to conform these frame rates inside After Effects as necessary in their File > Interpret Footage dialog.

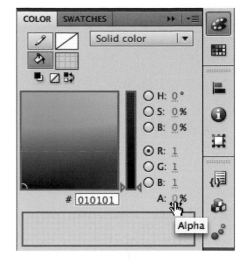

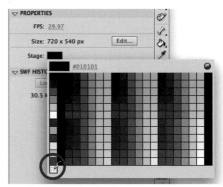

In Flash's Color panel, create a color that has its Alpha set to 0% (above), and click along the bottom of the Swatches panel to make a new swatch. Then assign this as your background color (below).

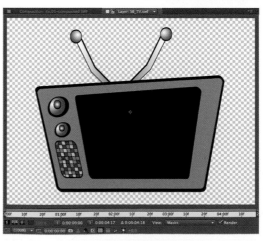

Alpha channels of SWF files are honored in After Effects (right). Here we show using an animation and matte created in Flash as part of an After Effects animation (above). TV courtesy Richard Fenton; background courtesy Artbeats/Digital Web.

SWF Settings

Images

JPEG Quality 5   Medium

Rasterize   Unsupported Features

✓ Rasterize
Ignore   ...ip all features that are not supported by the SWF format.

Choose Rasterize to rasterize all frames that contain unsupported features.

Audio
☑ Export Audio

Sample Rate: 44,100 kHz

Channels: Stereo

Bit Rate: Auto

Options
☐ Loop Continuously
☐ Prevent Editing
☐ Include Object Names
☐ Include Layer Marker Web Links
☐ Flatten Illustrator Artwork

Cancel   OK

If an After Effects layer cannot be exported as a vector object, you must decide whether you want it ignored or rasterized to an image.

F4V Options

Video

▼ **Basic Video Settings**

Codec: MainConcept H.264 Video

Profile: High

Level: 5.1

▼ **Bitrate Settings**

Bitrate Encoding: ● CBR   ○ VBR, 1 Pass

Bitrate [Mbps]: ——————————————— 0.19

▼ **Advanced Settings**
☐ Set Key Frame Distance

Adobe Flash Video is now supported in the Render Queue. Click on Format Options to customize how the FLV or F4V is created.

On the export side, only certain After Effects layers – such as text, solids, and Illustrator artwork – can be exported as vector symbols; the rest are rasterized into pixels and saved as JPEG images (or if you choose, ignored altogether). Note that applying virtually any effect results in a layer being converted to pixels.

Nested comps are always processed as pixels when exporting to SWF, even if the precomp contains vectors and the nested comp is collapsed. Try to work in one comp, using nulls as parents for grouping (see Chapter 17).

To export a composition to SWF, select File > Export > Adobe Flash (SWF). After Effects will create the requested SWF file, plus an HTML document that contains your SWF and a report of your settings and what unsupported features – if any – were rasterized on each frame. Practice exporting [**Ex.02**] with both the Ignore and Rasterize choices, open their respective .htm files in your web browser, and compare the results. (More details are contained in the After Effects Help file.)

If you have Adobe Flash CS4 or later, you may find it far more convenient to export your After Effects project as an XFL format file, and import that into Flash for further manipulation. We'll discuss that workflow starting on the next page.

FLV and F4V

After Effects can both import and render to the Adobe Flash Video format. Add your composition to the Render Queue, open the Output Module (discussed in more detail in Chapter 42), and set Format to either FLV or F4V. Click Format Options to set the target bit rate (and in the case of F4V – which is based on the H.264 codec – the encoding Profile and Level).

Although you can render FLV and F4V files directly from After Effects, for the best results you should export a high-quality movie from After Effects, and then use either Adobe Media Encoder or the third-party encoder of your choice in order to better fine-tune your compression settings.

Flash Professional

After Effects now has the ability to export an After Effects composition as an XFL format project, which can then be opened by Adobe Flash Professional CS4 or later. You may then trim, transform, or add interactivity to them within Flash; you may also insert new symbols in-between these layers in Flash.

During export, each After Effects layer is usually rendered to its own FLV movie or PNG sequence which is then used by Flash. Under certain circumstances, your sources may be passed directly through to Flash, along with any 2D transform properties (Scale, Position, Rotation, Opacity) that were altered or keyframed in After Effects. Some of these special circumstances include:

Our goal is to export this animation from After Effects into Flash Professional. Background courtesy Digital Vision; video insets courtesy Getty Images.

- The underlying footage must employ a format natively used by Flash (such as a PNG or JPEG still image, or an FLV movie or PNG sequence).

- No effects may be added to the layer. Likewise, the layer cannot use a Blending Mode; may not be time stretched; and cannot employ motion blur, frame blending, 3D, or be matted or stenciled.

- The layer's duration must not be trimmed. (Note that if the source footage is longer than the composition, this counts as trimming!)

Let's work our way through an example to get a better idea of how this works.

Flash Catalyst

After Effects CS5 does not integrate in any special way with Adobe Flash Catalyst.

Step 1: Open the comp [**Ex.03-XFL Export**]. We've done some work ahead of time to make this composition more Flash-friendly: The video thumbnail layers (**GI_WaterElements.flv** and **GI_CyberTechnology.flv**) are already compressed as FLV files, and the background layer – **DV_InnerGaze_307019.jpg** – is already in the supported JPG format.

Step 2: RAM Preview the comp to become familiar with its animations. Select **DV_Inner-Gaze_307019.jpg** and press U; notice that its Position parameter has keyframes. Then select **GI_WaterElements.flv** and press UU to reveal its animating property (Opacity) as well as its other transform properties that have been edited from their defaults (Position and Scale).

Step 2: FLV and JPG files are supported formats and therefore may be exported intact into Flash, even though their transform properties are animating or otherwise altered from their defaults.

The layer **GI_CyberTechnology.flv** has the same properties edited. Since these layers are already in Flash-friendly formats, and have no other effects or modes applied to them, these transform properties should be preserved during the XFL export.

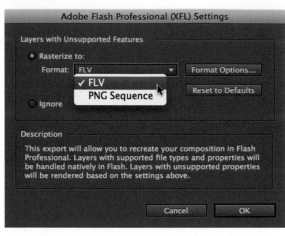

Step 3: Choose File > Export > Adobe Flash Professional, enable Rasterize, set the Format to FLV (above), then set your desired bit rate (right).

XFL = XML FLA

An XFL file is a compressed archive folder that contains a Library folder and an XML document (DOMDocument.xml) that describes the FLA file.

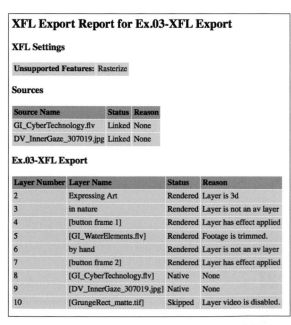

Step 5: After Effects will generate a report stating which layers were linked to, and which needed to be rerendered.

Step 3:   Select File > Export > Adobe Flash Professional (XFL). Enable the Rasterize option, and set the Format popup to FLV. Then click on the Format Options button, which will open the FLV Options dialog discussed earlier. The default bit rate of 1,280 kbps is fine for this exercise; set Quality to Best, and click OK.

Step 4:   Back in the XFL dialog, click XFL to start the exporting process. Choose where you want to save this project, and click OK. Pay attention to the Exporting dialog that appears next, as well as the Video switch (the eyeball icon) for each of the layers in the Timeline panel: These will indicate which layer is currently being processed. Alpha channels will automatically be created for the layers that need them. You will notice that After Effects will render most of the layers, but will skip over the JPG layer plus one of the FLV layers.

Step 5:   After Effects will generate an HTML-format report file and save it next to your XFL project. This contains information on which layers were rerendered (and why), as well as on which layers were okay in their current state and are therefore merely linked to. Double-click this file to open it in a web browser. Among other interesting details, it tells you that it had to rerender one of the supposedly Flash-friendly FLV layers because its length was trimmed (it extended beyond the end of the comp).

Step 6: If you have a copy of Flash CS4 Professional or later, open the XFL project file you saved in Step 3. The Scene panel should resemble your Comp panel in After Effects; the main difference is that you will see the entire background image – it will not be cropped by the composition's boundaries. (If you want to crop a single layer, create a comp-sized solid and use it as an alpha matte. To crop all layers below, use the solid as a stencil alpha; note that this will cause all of the layers below to be rendered upon export.)

Toggle the layers' Show/Hide switches (under the eyeball in the Timeline) and scrub the time indicator to confirm that these layers and their animations came across intact. Look closely, however, and you will notice that one layer from the After Effects composition has disappeared: **TU_Manzanita.mov**. Unfortunately, audio is currently not exported to XFL projects.

Step 7: Select **GI_Cybertechnology.flv** – a supported layer that was not rasterized on export – and click on the Motion Editor tab. Scroll through its Basic motion, Transformation, and Color Effect parameters: You will see that it retained its Scale and Position values along with its Opacity (Alpha Amount) animation, meaning you can resize and reposition them inside Flash without rerendering or loss of quality. Unfortunately, a keyframe has been created for every frame of the animation. Adobe does this to ensure accuracy, but it comes at the cost of editability.

Step 6: Flash will contain a re-creation of your After Effects composition.

Step 7: Simple transformations are retained for supported layers. However, keyframes are generated for every frame of an animation.

Despite its obvious shortcomings (lack of audio support and an overabundance of keyframes), we still feel this new feature goes a long way toward aiding After Effects artists who wish to create content for the web.

Reference Copy

Many transitions, text elements, and effects will not translate from your NLE into After Effects. In addition to the project file, ask to get a rendered version of the project for visual reference.

GOTCHA

The Codec Chase

If you run After Effects on a computer other than the one that has the NLE installed, you may need a codec that matches the NLE's hardware in order to read its files. Some companies offer software versions of their codec; others make them available only to registered owners of their hardware.

Non-Linear Editing Systems

A common workflow is to edit a program in an NLE, then have an After Effects artist generate new elements (such as an opening title or lower thirds) or enhance some scenes that have been temporarily cut in (special effects and informational graphics being two common examples). In the former case, it's often enough for the editor to just tell you what they need and how long it should be. In the latter case, it's a good idea to get a copy of the program the editor is working on, so you can see exactly how your bit is supposed to fit in. You can get a render of the edited sequence…or even better, get a copy of the entire timeline, edits and all.

Adobe Premiere Pro

Since Adobe makes both After Effects and Premiere Pro, it is only natural that they integrate very tightly. You can import a Premiere Pro project into After Effects, as well as export an After Effects project as a Premiere Pro project file. Additionally, if you have the CS5 Production Premium or Master Collection bundle, you can also transfer the following:

• Footage items – as well as compositions and sequences – can be copied and pasted between the Project panels in both programs.

• Footage items can be copied from an After Effects comp's timeline into a Premiere sequence's timeline. You can also copy nested comps, solids, Photoshop layers, and audio tracks.

• Virtually any track item can be copied from a Premiere timeline and pasted into the After Effects timeline.

If any of the layers involved in any of these commands use effects that are shared by both programs, the effects will make it across intact. More

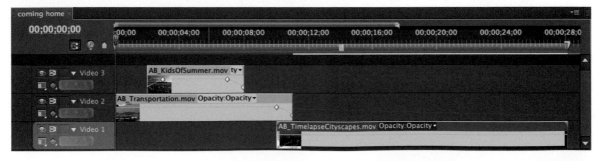

If you have the Production Premium bundle, you can copy and paste compositions and sequences between After Effects (above) and Premiere Pro (below). All associated footage items will be pasted as well, automatically.

advanced After Effects layer types – such as text, shape, and adjustment layers – will not make the transition. Same goes for Premiere-specific items such as transitions, titles, bars, and tones. The Help documents for each program contain additional details on how items are translated between the two applications.

For advanced integration – such as incorporating a "live" After Effects composition inside a Premiere Pro timeline without rendering – explore Dynamic Link, which is discussed later in this chapter.

Apple and Avid

If your editor (which may be you) uses an Avid system, Apple Final Cut Pro, or Apple Motion, you should know about Automatic Duck's Pro Import AE. This plug-in set makes it possible to export timelines from these three programs and import the result into an After Effects composition.

By using File > Import > Automatic Duck Pro Import, you will be presented with a special import dialog with additional options such as whether to automatically separate fields and how to handle audio. Pro Import AE will build you an After Effects comp that attempts to create the timeline as closely as possible, including the ability to retrim the footage if you had any handle left over. Of course, there are a lot of ins and outs of what gets translated and what doesn't; for more details, visit Automatic Duck's website: *www.automaticduck.com*. Its documentation and support are also excellent.

FACTOID

One-way Street

No one provides a way to bring After Effects compositions into non-Adobe editing systems. You will need to render your comps and import the results into these other systems just like any other footage item.

Using Automatic Duck's Pro Import AE plug-in set, sequences can be exported from NLEs such as Apple Final Cut Pro (below) and imported into After Effects, where a composition will be created to re-create the original sequence (bottom).

Dynamic Link

For those who own the CS5 Production Premium or Master Collection bundles, an additional level of integration may be achieved by taking advantage of *Dynamic Link.*

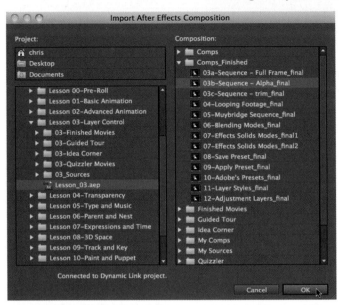

To defer rendering until you actually need to see a frame, import an After Effects project into Premiere Pro or Encore using Dynamic Link and choose which comps you want to bring in as footage items or assets.

One of the most common bottlenecks during a project is waiting for a program to render the files you need. Dynamic Link allows you to skip the wait-while-rendering step. Instead, you can link an After Effects composition into Adobe Premiere Pro or Encore in its unrendered state and use it as a footage item; these applications will render the comp "on demand" to display a specific frame.

To take advantage of Dynamic Link, you need to save your After Effects project at least once so that you have a file the other programs can see. If you like, you can leave the project open in After Effects. Then in either Premiere or Encore, open or start a new project, and choose File > Adobe Dynamic Link > Import After Effects Composition. Choose the project file you saved, then choose one or more comps presented on the right side of the dialog. (You can also drag and drop comps from the After Effects Project panel into the Premiere or Encore Project panels, or use the normal Premiere File > Import menu command.)

After you've set up this link, you can use the result as you would any other footage item, including trimming and otherwise processing it. You can also use a linked comp as a motion menu in Encore. Aside from not having to wait for the initial render, the second main benefit of Dynamic Link is that you can return to After Effects (whether or not Premiere or Encore are still running) and update the composition there; the "footage" will automatically update in Premiere or Encore without having to save the After Effects project! (When you do save, use the same file name or the link will be broken.)

Dynamic Link works both ways: You can also import a Premiere Pro sequence into After Effects, and treat it like an ordinary footage item. If you update the edit in the Premiere Pro project, these changes will be reflected in the corresponding "footage" in After Effects.

The After Effects Help file contains exhaustive information on Dynamic Link, including how to optimize performance and manage your files. Keep in mind that Premiere or Encore have to rerender the After Effects comp every time they need to use it (unless they manage to cache the result); if you feel you're done altering the After Effects comp, it is more efficient to render the comp and import the resulting movie into Premiere or Encore.

Shared Media Cache

When After Effects imports certain footage types such as MPEG, it caches optimized versions of these files so that it can more quickly generate previews. These files are saved in the place specified by Preferences > Media & Disk Cache > Conformed Media Cache. Managing this cache is discussed in Chapter 45 on Preferences.

Buttons for Adobe Encore

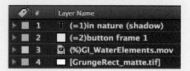

Among the many uses of layered Photoshop (PSD) files is exchanging files between After Effects and Encore. For example, PSD files are used to hold the different elements that make up a DVD button. You can start a menu design in Encore, then use its command Menu > Create After Effects Composition. Encore will save a layered PSD file of the menu elements and create an After Effects project that has these layers already imported and arranged in a composition. You can then modify or create buttons from scratch in After Effects, and save each button as a layered PSD file to import back into Encore. You could also animate these elements to create a movie that plays before the menu elements settle into place. Render this movie and bring it back into Encore, resolving into the menu's layout.

Encore requires very specific naming conventions to know which layer is supposed to be which element in a button. To practice this, open **[Ex.04_starter]**. For each button, we want to identify a video thumbnail, as well as a pair of "subpictures" (color channels to be used in the button's subpicture layer): the outline frame and a glow for the text (which is actually an overlay that will appear on top – the text itself is an element in the final background plate). To save one of these buttons with the naming conventions Encore requires, select the layers that make up the button elements: Click on **GI_WaterElements**, then

After you design a DVD menu in After Effects, you need to save the button elements as layers with special names in a PSD file to be used by Encore.

Command+click on Mac (Control+click on Windows) **in nature (shadow)** and **button frame 1**. Next, choose the menu item Layer > Adobe Encore > Create Button. In the dialog that opens, give your button a name (such as "**NatureButton**"); set the popups for Subpicture 1 to **in nature (shadow)**, Subpicture 2 to **button frame 1**, and Video Thumbnail to **GI_WaterElements**.

Click OK, and After Effects will nest the selected elements into a new composition that has the button's name, with **(+)** appended to the front which tells Encore this is a button. Option+double-click (Alt+double-click) this new layer in the current Timeline panel to open the new comp, and you will see the Subpicture 1 layer has **(=1)** appended to the front, Subpicture 2 has **(=2)**, and the Video Thumbnail has **(%)** – more Encore clues. The **GrungeRect_matte** layer was also copied to this new comp, as two of the layers use it via the Set Matte effect.

Select your button element layers, then choose Layer > Adobe Encore > Create Button to assign these layers as Subpictures or a Video Thumbnail.

After Effects automatically adds to layer names the prefix Encore needs to identify the button elements.

Select Composition > Save Frame As > Photoshop Layers, and save the file to your drive keeping the **(+)** at the front of the file's name. After Effects will automatically render the effects – including Set Matte – needed by each layer to create a clean PSD file. You can inspect this file in Photoshop or use it in Encore as a button.

If you have already created a composition specifically for a button, you can also rename your layers directly without going through the Create Button dialog: Just select the layer in After Effects, select the menu item Layer > Adobe Encore, then use the appropriate submenu item to assign a Subpicture or Video Thumbnail. The required characters will then be appended to the front of the layer's name.

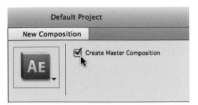

Step 1: Enable the Create Master Composition option: This will allow you to create content in one comp that is then automatically routed to multiple output comps.

Step 2: Click the Add button at the bottom of the Test Devices panel to create a new group.

Step 5: All of the devices you add to your device group will be visible in the Device Library panel at right. Select an individual device in your group to see its details.

Mobile Media

Creating content for mobile devices is an important new business segment. The problem is that there are a number of devices out there, and many have different specifications and requirements. This process has been greatly simplified by the new ability to use Device Central to automatically build a chain of After Effects compositions. Try it for yourself:

Step 1: Open the Adobe Device Central CS5 application. In the welcome screen that appears, click on Create New Mobile > After Effects Composition. Under the New Composition tab that opens, enable Create Master Composition – this will come in handy back in After Effects.

Step 2: Along the bottom of the Test Devices panel, click the + icon and select Add New Group. A new folder will appear; select its name, rename it "**Mobile Project**", and press Return.

Step 3: Time to add some devices to your group. If you do not have an internet connection, a small number of Flash Lite and Flash Player devices will already be available for you to use in the Test Devices panel. To view a profile of one of these devices, select it from the Test Devices list.

If you do have an internet connection (highly recommended), click on the Browse button in the upper right corner to open the Device Library, then click on the Home button (the house icon) underneath the Device Library tab. This will load the profiles of all available devices. Select a device, and click the View Details button at the bottom of the Device Library panel. Click Home or the nearby Back button to return to the full list.

Step 4: Select several different devices – choosing a variety of screen sizes and aspect ratios – and drag them to your **Mobile Project** folder. If they were available online, they will be downloaded and installed into the Test Devices panel.

Step 5: Select the **Mobile Project** folder in the Test Devices panel to see an overview of all of the devices in your set in the Device Library panel at right. Click on the individual devices in **Mobile Project** to see their details. In some cases, you will see a graphic of the actual phone.

Step 6: Click the Create button in the upper right corner of the Device Central window; this will reveal the New Composition tab again. Verify that the Create Master Composition option is enabled. Then select each of your devices one at a time to make sure Device Central has enough information to create a composition for it (otherwise, the display will read "No device selected").

Step 7: Select your Mobile Project folder and click the Create button in the lower right corner of the New Composition panel. You will be returned to After Effects, and a new folder named **Device Central Comps** will be created in the Project panel for you.

Step 8: Twirl open the **Device Central Comps** folder and open the comp [**Device Master**]. It will contain an empty stage with red bars down the sides. The red bars indicate the area that will be cropped by different cell phones. Solo the guide layers in the [**Device Central**] comp to see how much each one will crop your universal master image; disable all the solo switches when you're done.

Step 9: Drag a source file or comp – such as the high-definition, widescreen movie **SOURCES > Movies > CD_finchbath.mov** – into [**Device Master**] and place it below all of the nested guide comps. Scale and position it to fit inside [**Device Master**] so that it is nicely framed, taking the red cropping bars into account.

Step 10: Tap the Shift key to open the Mini-Flowchart. You will see that a number of "guide" comps – one per device in your set –

FACTOID

Scaled Playback

A mobile device's screen size does not always equal its recommended video size. For example, many devices with a 640x480 screen will take only 320x240 video, which is then scaled up by the device.

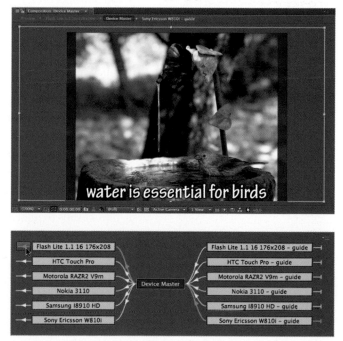

Step 9: Scale and position your source (above) to neatly fit inside [Device Master], taking the red cropping guides into account (below).

Step 10: [Device Master] is Grand Central Station in your mobile device project: It contains nested guide layers that display each device's cropping area, then feeds comps to render for each individual device.

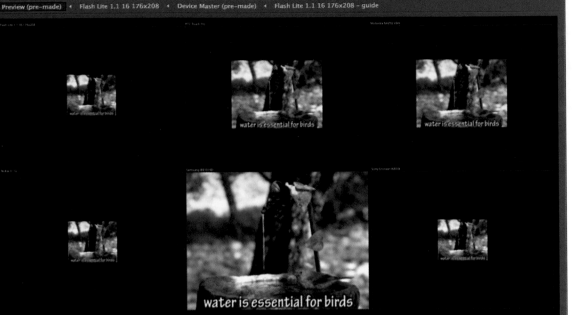

Step 11: [Preview] displays all of your device output comps side by side, so you can check their relative size and cropping. This helps you make adjustments to font sizes and layer positions to ensure that your content will look good on all of your requested devices.

CONNECT

Parenting, null objects: Chapter 17.

Continuous rasterization: Chapter 20.

Keying: Chapter 27.

The Interpret Footage dialog – as well as importing layered Photoshop and Illustrator files: Chapter 38.

Integrating with 3D applications: Chapter 40.

Video issues such as pixel aspect ratios and frame rates: Chapter 41.

Rendering: Chapters 42–43.

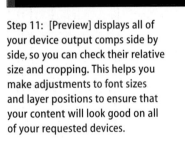

are nested into [**Device Master**]. [**Device Master**] then flows into one output composition per device in your set.

Step 11: Click on one of the arrows exiting to the left out of any of the device rendering comps (not the guide comps). This will reveal that all of the device comps also feed a master **Preview** comp. Select [**Preview**]; this displays the output of all of your device comps side by side to give you an idea of how they look relative to each other. Resize the Comp panel larger as needed to get a good look; if necessary, go back to [**Device Master**] to reframe your source to achieve the best compromise across your selection of devices. Note that text is particularly challenging with small target device sizes!

The result of our trial is saved in the folder [**Ex.05**]. The only thing missing is rendering your individual device comps. Check the video format required by each (detailed in Device Central), and adjust the lengths of your comps to match your source.

3D Integration

Here's one of the key secrets that sets motion graphics professionals apart: Virtually no 3D scene is finished inside the 3D program in which it was created. Instead, the 3D renders are massaged and enhanced inside programs such as After Effects. Simple elements can also be added in After Effects, avoiding the need to rerender the original 3D scene. So even though it requires a fair amount of work on your part, it is very useful to learn how to integrate 3D applications with After Effects – and that is the subject of the next chapter.

Integrating with 3D Applications

Real 3D programs have several advantages over After Effects: For example, their objects have real depth, and the texturing and lighting options are far more advanced. However, this power often comes with a significant speed penalty, which can be a problem when accommodating client changes. After Effects is also the better tool in which to refine the final look of your 3D worlds. Offloading portions of the work from your 3D program to After Effects will save time while giving you more power and flexibility – but it requires some planning to set up.

Techniques to get more information from your 3D program into After Effects.

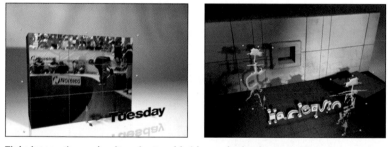

Tight integration makes it easier to add video and other layers to 3D environments in After Effects. Video courtesy Creative License; textures courtesy Artbeats.

In this chapter, we will give advice on how to successfully integrate your 3D program with After Effects. We will then work through a pair of case studies: Adding 2D video to the face of a 3D object, and integrating lights and shadows between After Effects and your 3D render. The DVD also contains a bonus chapter which covers the 3D Effects that can access additional information saved with some 3D renders such as the Z buffer (how far objects are away from the camera).

Unfortunately, there is no one universal file format to bring information from a 3D application into After Effects. In our case studies, we are going to focus on using Maxon Cinema 4D as it currently has the tightest integration with After Effects, plus is the 3D program we personally use. However, many of the concepts we'll be covering are universal and can be applied to other programs as well. We will also include some specific advice for programs such as Autodesk Maya and 3ds Max.

FACTOID

3D Channel Effects
Bonus Chapter 40B on this book's DVD covers the special 3D Channel effects such as Depth of Field and Fog 3D, as well as how to replicate their results with 3D programs not directly supported by these plug-ins.

Example Project
Explore the 40-Example Project.aep file as you read this chapter; references to [Ex.##] refer to specific compositions within the project file.

TIP

Motion Blur

If you rendered your 3D scene with motion blur enabled, you should also enable motion blur for the 3D layers you add in After Effects. Don't forget to match the blur's shutter angle you used in your 3D program.

GOTCHA

Maya Camera Import Bug

There is a known issue where some older Maya .ma projects may import at the wrong size. For example, **Maya_camera.ma** included on this book's disc imports as 540x486 pixels, when it should be 320x240.

3D Advice

The next few sections include topics to keep in mind as you work on a project that will flow from a 3D program to After Effects. This includes getting the camera move across, lining up world coordinates between the two programs, and creating mattes so that select objects in the 3D world will appear to pass in front of layers added in After Effects.

The Camera Move

A typical workflow will include finalizing your camera move in the 3D program, rendering the 3D scene, then bringing the camera move and render into After Effects. Your render will be a 2D layer in After Effects, as it already has the camera move calculated into it; you can optionally enhance the render using After Effects' tools. You can then add new 3D layers on top of this render in After Effects, using the camera data you moved across. For example, you can add text, video, and other objects to your scene in After Effects without having to go back into your 3D program for another potentially lengthy rerender.

It is a really, really good idea to finalize the camera move before bringing it into After Effects. Changing the camera move means having to re-render the 3D scene as well as replace the camera move in After Effects. Do a few rough renders and get the client to sign off on the general idea and movement before putting in too much work.

The way you move camera data from a 3D application into After Effects varies from program to program. Here are some of the more common options:

- Export your project to the .ma – Maya ASCII – format. After Effects can then import this project through its normal File > Import menu command; it will extract the camera movement from this file along with the movement of any null objects that explicitly have the word "NULL" or "null" in their name. An example of the result is demonstrated in this chapter's example project in the comp [**Ex.01-Maya Import**]. If your project uses non-square pixels, a square pixel precomp will also be created which contains the actual camera animation.

- Embed the camera move in a .rla or .rpf frame sequence when you render. Bring this sequence into an After Effects comp, select it, and use Animation > Keyframe Assistant > RPF Camera Import.

Maya ASCII (.ma) project files may be imported directly into After Effects. The result is a comp with the Maya camera, any null object with "null" in its name, parenting chains including cameras and nulls, and their animation.

Programs such as 3ds Max can embed their camera move in an RPF file sequence during their render. After Effects can extract this data to create a matching camera of its own.

After Effects will then create its own camera with the same movement. You can practice this with the comp [**Ex.02_starter**]; the result – along with some additional compositing tricks using 3D Effects – is demonstrated in [**Ex.02-final**].

• Cinema 4D has the ability to save an .aec project file which contains the camera move and much, much more (which we will discuss in detail in the upcoming case studies). After Effects can then import the .aec file with a Maxon-supplied plug-in.

• If the functionality you need isn't built into your 3d program of choice, you may be able to write a spreadsheet or script that converts keyframe data from your 3D program into After Effects keyframe data, and paste that into a new camera created in After Effects; see the *Camera Data Translation* sidebar for leads on others who have already.

• Worst case, create an object in your 3D world in the same location as layers you would like to add in After Effects, with obvious markers in its corners. Make a separate render pass of this object, and use Motion Tracking in After Effects to corner pin your new layer into the position and perspective you had in mind. This was demonstrated in Chapter 30's [**Ex.05**]; another example is included in this chapter's [**Ex.03**].

Sometimes, your imported camera move will not appear to match the motion in your 3D render. The most common problem is that the Angle of View for the After Effects camera is wrong. Verify the value for this parameter (also known as Field of View) in your 3D program, and enter this value manually in the Camera Settings dialog in After Effects.

Some 3D programs also do not take into account any curves you may have applied to the camera's path or speed. Therefore, you will often need to "bake" the camera move in the 3D program to create a keyframe for every frame of your timeline before exporting its move. For example, in Maya use Edit > Keys > Bake Simulation in Maya.

Camera Data Translation

Several users and third parties have created plug-ins and scripts to help move camera data and related information between After Effects and select 3D programs that may not have broad After Effects support built in:

• MAX2AE from Boomer Labs (*www.boomerlabs.com*) allows you to import a scene from After Effects into 3ds Max 6 or later. It also provides a nice alternative to importing Max scenes into After Effects, including support for lights and "helper planes."

• 3DMation's MoCon (*www.3dmation.com*) is a collection of scripts to transfer 3D motion to and from After Effects, Maya, Nuke, SynthEyes and Electric Image, including going from After Effects into Modo.

• Several useful scripts reside on the essential AE Enhancers site (*www.aenhancers.com*), including getting an After Effects camera move back into Cinema 4D or 3ds Max, plus exporting a simple representation of your scene from After Effects to Maya, Max, and LightWave.

• Byron Nash has created a Softimage|XSI script that exports cameras, lights, nulls, and polygons from XSI to After Effects. It's available at: *armoredsquirrel.com/blog/?page_id=69*

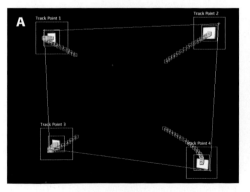

If there is no way to import the camera data from your 3D program into After Effects, you can create a 3D model with dots to track in After Effects (A), and corner pin a new layer in After Effects to their location (B). 3D renders courtesy Reject Barn.

TIP

The 50 Percent Solution

If we know we will be compositing a layer in After Effects onto the surface of a 3D model, we usually try to make that surface average 50% luminance (gray) after it has been textured and lit. If we composite the new layer in After Effects using modes such as Overlay or Hard Light, it will pick up the lighting and shadows that fall across the 3D surface without unduly changing the appearance of the new layer.

When Worlds Align

When you try to place a new object in After Effects into your already-rendered 3D world, the next question becomes: How big should everything be? It can be quite disconcerting to, say, add a video capture to a scene only to find it is several times bigger than everything in the 3D render – or at the other extreme, is just a few-pixel speck to the 3D camera.

In an ideal world, you should first decide on the sizes of the objects you will be adding in After Effects – such as 1080-line tall HD video, or a 72-pixel tall text caption – and construct your 3D world so that its models have a good size relationship to these layers.

For example, if we know we will be compositing standard definition video onto 3D videowalls we're about to construct, the first thing we'll do in our 3D program is create a plane that is the same number of "world units" as our video is in pixels, and then build the rest of our world based on that reference. If you were not fortunate enough to plan this out ahead of time, or run into common issues such as the world units are in meters but the camera position translation is in centimeters, just increase or decrease the Scale value of the new layers in After Effects to resolve the difference.

In addition to the size of objects, you also need to know where they are located! If you're lucky, your 3D program of choice translates the position of objects other than just the camera. For example, importing a Maya .ma file will also bring across any null objects with NULL in their name. Place a null object where the face of your videowall or line of text should be, and you can use the resulting coordinates to copy and paste to your new object in After Effects. In Cinema 4D, you can add an External Compositing tag to an object, which will cause a null object or solid to be created at the same place in After Effects. Dummy lights or cameras are also sometimes used in other programs for this purpose.

Worst case, you can write down those coordinates and manually type them in. Just be aware of where the anchor point of your 3D object is: Quite often, it may be in the middle of the model, rather than on its

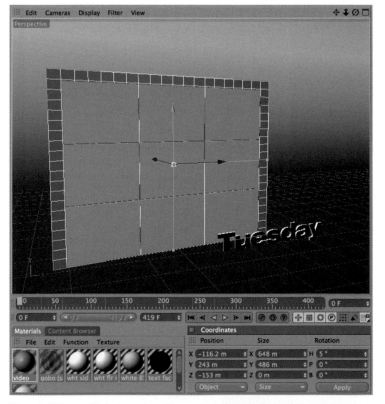

When building a video screen in a 3D program, we start by creating a dummy plane (the green rectangle) that corresponds to a square pixel size for the video we later plan to place on it. We then make our video screen (the gray boxes) slightly smaller so we can later crop off the Action Safe area of the video.

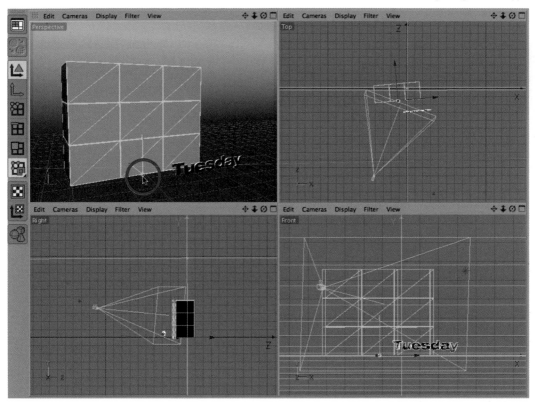

face. Make sure the anchor is in the same relative position between the two programs, such as the bottom of the 3D object and the After Effects layer.

On occasion, you may find that some of the axis units are reversed between your 3D program and After Effects. For example, After Effects considers a positive Z Rotation to be clockwise; some programs think a positive Z Rotation means counterclockwise. It is easy to change the sign of a value for an object's location; it is a little trickier when this translation is already factored into, say, the camera's keyframes. Fortunately, you can use fairly simple expressions to perform the reverse translation. In our hypothetical example, you would merely assign the expression **–value** to Z Rotation; the resulting expression for Position would be [**value**[0], **value**[1], **–value**[2]].; modify as needed for other dimensions.

And remember, you might also need to throw in an additional multiplier for world unit translation issues, such as ***10** or **/10** for the difference between meters and centimeters.

Place your object's anchor point at the location where you plan to place the corresponding layer in After Effects – such as on the face (not in the middle) of a videowall (above). Then either write down its coordinates, or find a way to export its position such as using an External Compositing tag in Cinema 4D (below).

Context-Sensitive Cinema Help

In later releases of Cinema 4D, make sure you download the Help system from Maxon's website (under Downloads > Documentation) and install it following their instructions. Open the dialog you have a question about and press Command+F1 (Control+F1) to open Help to the relevant page. It contains a lot of useful information on tags and multipass rendering.

Case Studies

So far we've been talking about integrating 3D applications with After Effects in fairly general terms. In the remainder of this chapter, we're going to work through a pair of typical tasks using Cinema 4D and After Effects. Since we can't assume you own Cinema, we'll describe the steps to be taken in Cinema 4D Release 11.5 and include the results on the book's disc; you can execute the After Effects portion yourself in this chapter's accompanying project. Even if you don't own Cinema, we think you'll find that the concepts discussed in these studies will help prepare you for issues you may encounter in your own 3D program of choice.

Study #1: Videowall

To create a series of promos for NBC, we crafted a simple 3D environment to replicate a videowall sitting on a seamless white cyclorama stage. We then planned to composite video edits made in After Effects onto the face of this wall. Additional 3D elements included the NBC Peacock, the name of the show, and the day of the week it was on; we've included the day of the week to give an example of a 3D object that needed to appear in front of the video we're going to composite in After Effects.

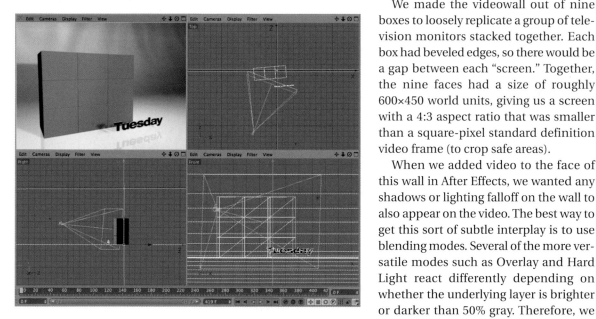

We made the videowall out of nine boxes to loosely replicate a group of television monitors stacked together. Each box had beveled edges, so there would be a gap between each "screen." Together, the nine faces had a size of roughly 600×450 world units, giving us a screen with a 4:3 aspect ratio that was smaller than a square-pixel standard definition video frame (to crop safe areas).

When we added video to the face of this wall in After Effects, we wanted any shadows or lighting falloff on the wall to also appear on the video. The best way to get this sort of subtle interplay is to use blending modes. Several of the more versatile modes such as Overlay and Hard Light react differently depending on whether the underlying layer is brighter or darker than 50% gray. Therefore, we

In this first case study, we're going to prepare this scene in Cinema 4D to make it easy to composite video on the front of this videowall and behind the 3D day of the week.

took care when texturing and lighting the wall's face to make sure it averaged about 50% luminance during the course of the camera movement.

Now that you know what we were thinking when we created this scene, let's move on to the steps needed to get this world into After Effects. For those of you with Cinema 4D Release 11.5, we've included the project file on your DVD in the **40_Chapter Sources > Cinema 4D Projects > C4D videowall** folder.

Step 1: First, we wanted to know where the face of the **box group** model was located in the 3D world. We placed its anchor at the bottom of its face. We selected **box group** in the Object Manager and noted its coordinates: –116.2, 0, –153.5 with a 5° rotation in Y (known as H – heading – in Cinema).

A great feature in Cinema is the ability to have it create a null object or a solid to appear in After Effects that contains this coordinate data, as well as any animation it may have. To take advantage of this, we selected box group and added Tags > Cinema 4D Tags > External Compositing, and set the Tag Properties to taste.

Step 2: We want to crop our video to the face of the videowall and to cut out our video where the word Tuesday appears in front of it. Therefore, we need to create a matte that matches the face of the wall. We lumped together all of the videowall cube faces into one group called **box faces**, selected it, and in Cinema added Tags > Cinema 4D Tags > Compositing. In the Attributes panel for Compositing, we selected the Object Buffer tab and clicked on Enable for Buffer 1. If we wanted, we could have selected our **box bevels** group and done the same, but in this case we wanted clear breaks between the box faces.

Step 1: Place the object's anchor on its face and note its coordinates. In Cinema, you can add an External Compositing tag to have a null object or solid created in After Effects at this position (see figure on page 662).

Step 2: To create a matte that represented the box faces, we selected this model group, added a Compositing tag (left), and enabled Object Buffer 1 for this group (right).

Step 3: Time to export the render and accompanying information. In Cinema, we opened the Render Settings dialog and made the following adjustments:

• In the Output panel, we set the Resolution to 720×534 (the new square pixel size for NTSC video, as of After Effects CS4) and the Frame Rate to 29.97 (note that earlier versions did *not* support fractional frame rates).

C4D AE Training

We have created extensive video training on integrating Cinema 4D with After Effects. It is available from both *cineversity.com* and *lynda.com*.

Step 3: In the Render Settings dialog, we told Cinema to export an After Effects project file with 3D data for the camera and lights (left); we also set it up to render the object buffer that contained our screen's matte (right).

• We enabled both Save and Multi-Pass along the left side of the dialog.

• We then clicked on the Multi-Pass button below and selected Object Buffer. In the Object Buffer Pass panel that opens to the right, we selected Group ID 1, as that's what we assigned the **box faces** group to. (If we wanted to create a multipass render to alter more characteristics of the render after the fact, we would have added more Channels via the Multi-Pass button.) In the Multi-Pass panel, we set Separate Lights to None.

• In the Save panel, we made sure Save was enabled for both the Regular Image and Multi-Pass Image, and set up our file type and path.

• Lower in the Save panel under Compositing Project File, we enabled Save, and selected After Effects as the Target Application. We also enabled 3D Data, which means information for cameras, lights, and objects will be exported.

Finally, we closed the Render Settings, and selected Render > Render to Picture Viewer. The result is three files: The normal RGB render, the Object Buffer, and the .aec file.

Alpha Interpretation

Most 3D programs generate premultiplied alpha channels by default; some give you a choice (straight is preferred). When in doubt as to what type was rendered, try both settings in File > Interpret Footage. If neither looks right (as is the case with many post-processed renders, such as glowing objects rendered from Maya), set the alpha interpretation to Straight and use the blending mode Luminescent Premultiply when compositing the 3D render over another object.

Step 4: In order to import the resulting .aec file with our 3D data into After Effects, the Cinema import plug-in has to be installed. You will find it in the **Cinema 4D R11.5 > Exchange Plugins > aftereffects** folder or on Maxon's website (*www.maxon.net*) under Downloads > Updates > Plugins; place it in the **Adobe After Effects CS5 > Plug-ins > Format** folder and restart After Effects.

Step 5: Time to import the 3D data: In After Effects, type Command+I (Control+I) to import, and select the .aec file. We have saved our version as **40_Chapter Sources > videowall > Videowall.aec**. If you do not have access to the Cinema plug-in, the result of this import is in this chapter's example project in the [**Ex.04 Videowall_starter**] folder.

After you import the .aec file, you will see three folders: **C4D videowall.c4d** (the main render plus the After Effects composition), **Solids** (the null objects or solids for any objects that had an External Compositing tag applied), and **Special Passes** (the object buffer matte). Twirl open the first folder and double-click [**C4D videowall.c4d**] to open it. It contains a camera and three lights matching those in the Cinema scene, a solid layer named **box group** positioned over the videowall's face, and the render of the 3D scene.

Step 6: Import a video you wish to place on the face of the videowall, and select it. (You will find a few to choose from in the Project panel's **Sources > Movies** folder; we used **AB_Seascapes1.mov**.)

Step 7: Next is replacing the placeholder solid with the real video. Return to the composition [**C4D videowall.c4d**] and select the layer **box group**. Type Command+Option+/ (Control+Alt+/) to replace it with your selected footage item.

Step 8: The video will be positioned a little low in the frame; this is because the solid's Anchor Point is located in its center rather than the lower middle, as was the case with the videowall face.

With the video layer still selected, type A to reveal its Anchor Point. Right-click on one of its values and select Edit Value. In the Anchor Point dialog that opens, first set the Units popup to % of source, then type in 50 for X-axis (centered) and 100 for Y-axis (the bottom of the layer). Click OK; the video should now be better centered on the videowall's face. You can tweak the Anchor Point value later if you need to move it.

RAM Preview and observe that your video is now perfectly tracking the videowall as the camera moves around it.

To finish off the animation, we'll matte the video so that it just fits the face of the videowall, employ blending modes so that it will appear to have the same lighting and shadows as the video-wall's face, and conform our comp's size and frame rate for a proper video render.

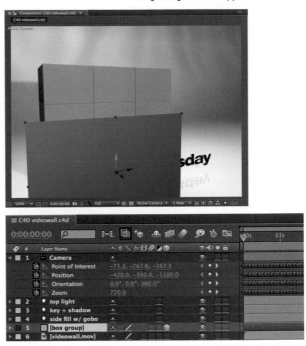

Step 5: Importing the .aec file will result in a composition with the render of the videowall, a solid placed over the face of the videowall, and copies of the camera and lights from Cinema 4D.

Steps 7–8: After replacing the solid with our video and offsetting its anchor point to the same relative position, it now covers the face of the videowall. Video courtesy Artbeats/Seascapes 1.

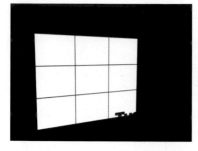

Step 9: Add the videowall's matte pass to the comp (above) and set it to be a track matte for the new video layer (above right) – the video will be neatly trimmed (including around the "day of the week" text) (below).

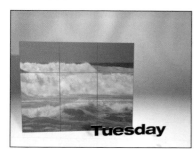

Step 11: A combination of blending modes plus lighting allows the new video layer to interact with the 3D scene as if it was originally rendered inside the 3D program.

Step 9: Our new video blots out the entire videowall as well as part of the "day of the week" text; we need to add our matte pass to trim it into place. In the Project panel, twirl open the Special Passes folder and drag the matte pass **CM_videowall_object_1.mov** into the comp just above the video layer. Make sure the Modes column is visible in the Timeline panel (press F4 if it isn't), then set the TrkMat popup for the video layer (not the matte layer!) to Luma Matte.

Step 10: We mentioned that we often design the face of our videowalls to have an average luminance of 50% to take advantage of blending modes. Set the Mode popup for your video layer to a mode such as Overlay or Hard Light. The luminance of the video will now vary across the videowall's face. You will also notice how the shadow from the word Tuesday appears to fall on your video. These are the advantages of using modes.

Step 11: The video is still a bit under-lit by the existing lights imported from Cinema. There are three different ways to fix that:

• Select the **key + shadow** light, press T to reveal its Intensity, and increase it until you are happy with how the video looks; around 100% should do.

• Or, select your video layer, type AA to reveal its Material Options, and increase its Diffuse and Specular values so that it will react more strongly to the lights hitting it.

• Or, turn off the Video switches (the eyeball icons) for the three lights imported from Cinema, and the video will take on its original luminance.

Step 12: The last step is conforming this composition to a size that matches the target video standard:

• Create a New Composition. Select the NTSC D1 or DV preset, give it a duration of 14:00, name it "**Videowall Final Render**", and click OK.

• In the Project panel, drag and drop [**C4D videowall.c4d**] onto the [**Videowall Final Render**] comp to nest it.

• Select the nested layer **C4D videowall.c4d**, and choose Layer > Transform > Fit to Comp Width to shrink it to fit its new home.

And you're done! If you like, RAM Preview your final result. Our version is in the [**Ex.04 Videowall-final**] folder.

Multipass Rendering

There are other ways to combine 3D programs and After Effects into an overall workflow. For example, as an alternative to creating object buffers, some like to render 3D objects (such as logos) as individual elements with alpha channels, then composite them in After Effects.

Many 3D artists like to render individual aspects of their scene – for instance, diffuse color, specular high-lights, shadows, reflections – as independent "passes" to be reblended in After Effects using a combination of alpha channel and blending modes (Multiply for shadows, Add or Screen for reflections and other color passes). This results in a high degree of control, such as being able to change the strength or blurriness of a reflection map or darkness of a shadow without having to go back into the original 3D project.

Most 3D programs require you to set up and render each of these passes individually. If you are trying to isolate specific properties perhaps on just a few objects in your scene, you can tweak your project file as needed between renders. If you know you will be tweaking a multi-pass render later in After Effects, it is a good idea to "overdo" properties such as shadow darkness, specular highlights, and reflections so that you have some latitude to decrease the opacity of these layers (and therefore, their contribution to the final composite) without having to render the scene over from scratch.

In the **[Ex.05]** folder, we have included a render from Cinema 4D that demonstrates some of this power. Cinema is the current king of integration with After Effects: It has a dedicated Multi-Pass render section where you can set which properties will be rendered to their own files simultaneously with the main render, and it will create an After Effects project with all of these properties already arranged in a composition using the correct modes.

Multipass rendering gives you the power to adjust the strength of shadows, highlights, and reflections after the fact. Experiment for yourself with **[Ex.05]**; the original Cinema project is **C4D videowall_multipass.c4d**.

Have fun playing with the opacities of the various layers. We've increased the shadow darkness and amount of reflection in the original Cinema project to give you a wider value range to play with.

Another option offered by Cinema is the ability to separate the contributions of each individual light in the scene – even the diffuse, specular, and shadow properties of each light! In addition to controlling their relative strengths inside After Effects, this also allows you to change the color of the light by applying a hue shift or other color correction to the nested composition that contains the light's contributions after the fact.

This feature is set up in Render > Render Settings inside the Multi-Pass panel. Remember to set these parameters *before* you render.

Study #2: Shadow Trickery

One of the more challenging areas of integrating a 3D render with After Effects objects is handling the shadows. You'd like for any new objects you add in After Effects to cast 3D shadows onto objects in the original 3D render. However, the 3D render must be imported as a 2D layer, and 3D layers cannot cast 3D shadows onto 2D layers. Your choices? Do without, fake it with an ordinary 2D Drop Shadow effect, or do a little extra work: Add 3D layers in After Effects to mimic objects in the original 3D scene which can then catch the 3D shadows. Let's try this last approach.

Open [**Ex.06_starter**]; it contains a more complex room with a window in the back wall to worry about as well as a table. Here are the steps needed to make it shadow-friendly in After Effects:

Follow Along

For those with Cinema 4D, our original Cinema project file for Study #2 is on this book's disc in **40_Chapter Sources > Cinema 4D Projects > C4D Room**.

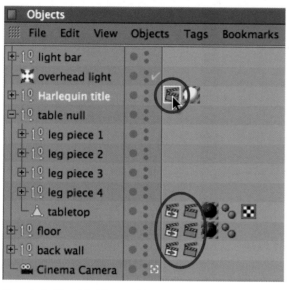

Steps 1–2: We added Compositing and External Compositing tags to the **tabletop**, **floor**, and **back wall** models to generate null objects and mattes for them in After Effects. We also added a Compositing tag to generate a matte for the **Harlequin title** model.

Step 1: The wall, floor, and table are candidates to catch shadows, so we need to know where to place their stand-ins in After Effects. We made a note of their sizes and where their faces were located in 3D space. In Cinema, we set their anchors to the center of their faces, then applied External Compositing tags (discussed in the previous section) to these models. This resulted in null objects being created for them in the corresponding .aec file.

Step 2: To crop our stand-in layers, we needed to render mattes that corresponded to just the visible portions of the faces of these models. In Cinema, we applied Compositing tags to these objects and assigned them to individual Object Buffers. We did the same for the Harlequin title so we could place layers in After Effects "between" the title and the wall.

Step 3: Once these 3D passes were rendered, we imported them along with the camera and light data into After Effects. We've already done this for you in [Ex.06_starter].

Open the composition that was created and note the three null objects **back wall**, **floor**, and **tabletop**. You need to replace these with solids. Here are the steps for one; the others are done the same way:

Step 4: The face of the **back wall** model piece is roughly 3110 wide × 1050 high in "world units" in Cinema, so create a Layer > New > Solid of this size, using square pixels and colored white. Name it "**wall shadow**" and click OK.

Step 5: Next, you need to move this shadow catcher into the same position as the wall. To do this, enable the 3D Layer switch for **wall shadow**. Select **back wall** (the null object created by Cinema) and type P followed by Shift+R to reveal its Position and Rotation parameters. Copy these, and paste them to **wall shadow**.

More on Multipass

Check out dvGarage's Multi-Pass Render Lab for a set of in-depth training materials on enhancing renders using a multipass approach (visit *dvgarage.com* and look under Products > 3D Development).

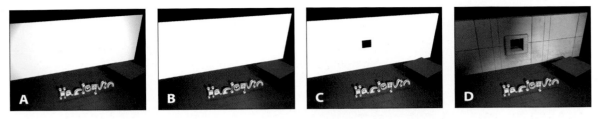

Steps 4–8: Create a white solid the size of the back wall, put it in the same position (A), set its Material Options > Accepts Lights to Off (B), crop it by its corresponding matte (C), and set its Mode to Multiply (D) so it blends into the original 3D render.

Step 6: We want this layer to receive our new shadows, but not otherwise be affected by lights in this scene. With **wall shadow** still selected, type AA to reveal its Material Options in the Timeline. Leave Casts Shadows = Off and Accepts Shadows = On (their defaults), but set Accepts Lights to Off.

Step 7: The shadow catcher needs to be matted to match the visible portions of the 3D wall. In the **Special Passes** folder, locate **AEA Room_object _2.mov** and drag it into your comp just above wall shadow. Reveal the Modes column (F4) and set the TrkMat popup for **wall shadow** to Luma Matte.

Step 8: To composite just the dark shadows – not the wall's white color – onto the back wall, set the Mode popup for **wall shadow** to Multiply.

After you're done, new 3D layers added in After Effects can cast shadows on the wall, floor, and table. If you have Cinema and are up for a challenge, use our projects to also create a shadow catcher for the Harlequin title…

Step 9: Add a layer to the scene in After Effects, enable its 3D switch, and enable Cast Shadows. Its shadow will appear on the back wall of the original 3D render. Feel free to tweak the color, intensity, and shadow darkness of the lights originally created in Cinema to work best for your new layers in After Effects, but keep their positions if you want the new shadows to match the original render.

If you want to cast shadows on the floor or table, repeat steps 4–9 above and use these parameters:

• The floor is about 3100×2050 pixels in size and uses Object Buffer 3. You will need to set its X Orientation to 270° to flip it down horizontally.

• The tabletop is approximately 512×512 pixels and uses Object Buffer 4. Due to differences in how the object was created in Cinema, disable keyframing for the three Rotation values, zero out Y Rotation and instead set Z Rotation to –17°, and set X Orientation to 270° to flip it down.

The comp **[Ex.06-Shadow Trickery-composite]** has these three shadow catcher layers set up, with some new objects casting shadows. Adding 3D elements from After Effects into a fully rendered 3D world creates an interesting hybrid look in its own right; you can also gain substantial flexibility from distributing your workflow between the programs.

Blending modes: Chapter 9.

Track mattes: Chapter 11.

Working in 3D: Chapters 13–16.

Null objects and parenting: Chapter 17.

Time stretching: Chapter 28.

Corner pin motion tracking: Chapter 30.

Expressions: Chapter 37.

Importing files and the Interpret Footage dialog: Chapter 38.

Pixel aspect ratios and frame rates: Chapter 41.

Video Issues

An overview of all those pesky technical issues you need to keep straight when you're working with video.

Just because we can edit and create video content on our computers doesn't mean video is like any other computer artwork. There are a number of nonintuitive technical issues – including interlaced fields, frame rates, frame sizes, pixel aspect ratios, safe image areas, and color spaces – that differentiate video and that must be handled properly to ensure your final work appears on television as you intended. We will give an overview of these topics here.

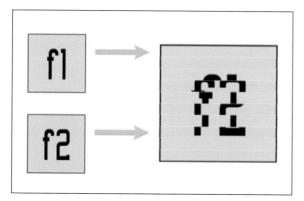

A video frame often contains two fields – subimages captured at different points in time – that have been interlaced into a full frame. Fortunately, After Effects knows how to pull these fields apart and reassemble them later.

Example Project

Explore the 41-Example Project.aep file as you read this chapter; references to [Ex.##] refer to specific compositions within the project file.

Fields and Interlaced Frames

Much video employs a trick in which each frame of the image contains visual information from two different points in time. The two subimages that represent these different points in time are known as *fields*. These two fields are combined into a single *frame* through a technique known as *interlacing*: The first horizontal line for the full frame is taken from the first line of one field, then the next horizontal line for the full frame is taken from the first line of the other field, then the next line for the full frame is taken from the second line of the first field, and so forth. Which field comes first is known as the *field order* of the footage, which is important to know to keep time straight when you pull the lines apart again.

Whenever an object in the frame is moving, that object will be in two different positions at the two different times the individual fields were captured. This often results in a visual "comb teeth" effect in a whole frame that was built from interlaced fields. To see this, open this chapter's project file **41-Example Project.aep**, and in the Project panel look inside the folder **Ex.01**. Double-click the comp **[Ex.01-Deinterlacing]** to open it; you should see this comb effect.

In the same folder is a footage item named **CL_SkateSequence_DV**: Select it and choose File > Interpret Footage > File. Drag the Interpret Footage dialog to a location where you can also see the Comp panel clearly, and make sure Preview is enabled. Set the Separate Fields popup to Upper Field First: Note in the Comp panel that the teeth have disappeared, and that you see the skateboarder in one position. Set Separate Fields to Lower Field First, and the teeth will still be gone, but the skateboarder will now be in a different position.

How can you determine the correct field order? Pick one, close Interpret Footage, double-click the clip to open it in its Footage panel, and step through the clip a field at a time using Page Up and Page Down. If the motion staggers back and forth while stepping in the same direction, you picked wrong; just change it to the other. DV is lower field first; HD is upper field first; D1 NTSC can vary depending on the system used to capture the clip (but it's usually lower); D1 PAL is upper. Some other programs use the terms *even* and *odd* for field order; you may need to test these to be clear exactly what they're doing.

When you have set the Interpret Footage dialog correctly, After Effects is able to pull apart ("separate") the lines of a frame to reform the original fields. After Effects can then work internally at the field rate of the footage (double the frame rate) and reinterlace these fields back into frames when saving a render to disk. When the resulting file is played back through a matching video system, motion will be smoother, as it has been sampled at twice the current frame rate.

Interlaced video frames that contain motion often appear to have "comb teeth" – this is caused by fields showing two different points in time being interlaced on alternating lines. Footage courtesy Creative License.

When converting interlaced footage between different formats, you need to pay attention to field order. This chapter's example project folder contains a PDF with advice on moving between NTSC DV and D1.

Note that if your source footage does *not* have interlacing (such as progressive scan captures or web animations created in Flash), you must set Separate Fields to Off, or you will lose half your resolution.

Field Flicker

A side effect of the interlaced, alternating-line nature of video playback is that thin horizontal lines are prone to flickering when shown on interlaced displays such as television sets. This won't be visible on a normal *progressive scan* (noninterlaced) computer monitor. That's why we recommend you view your work through a true video chain – see the section *Monitoring Your Work* at the end of this chapter for more details.

We've included some examples of graphics that cause problems in the **Ex.02** folder. If you have a true video monitoring setup, open the comp that matches the resolution of your monitor and display it through that chain. The two thin grids are particularly prone to flickering, but even the text can vibrate around the horizontal portions of its characters.

The cure for interlace-based field flicker is to soften the transition from horizontal lines to their adjacent pixels. Glows or shadows often help. Usually, you will need to add a small amount of blur: You'll lose some sharpness, but overall the image will be easier to view. After Effects has

The thin horizontal lines in the grids in **[Ex.02]** are prone to flickering on interlaced monitors. Even the horizontal bars on some fonts can shimmer slightly.

a special Reduce Interlace Flicker effect; it is also okay to use Fast Blur, Gaussian Blur, or Directional Blur set to blur in only the vertical direction. Use the least amount of blur you can to remove the flicker. We've set up adjustment layers with blurs in the **Ex.02** comps for you to try.

Rather than blurring the entire image, the best fix is to blur just the elements that are causing problems. Open [**Ex.03-selective blurring**], and if necessary, change the Preset in Composition > Composition Settings to match your monitoring chain. The horizontal elements of the grill in this radio flicker. Then turn on layer 1: We've isolated (masked) and blurred just these problem areas. This way, the rest of the radio's details remain sharp.

Only the horizontal grill elements in this radio flicker. To cure this, we made a copy of the layer, masked out just the problem areas (outlined here in blue), and gave them a slight horizontal blur. Radio courtesy Classic PIO/Classic Radios.

TIP

Preserve Edges

When separating fields, we usually enable the Preserve Edges option in the Interpret Footage dialog – especially if we are treating the footage or plan to output without fields.

TIP

Conforming Frame Rates

If your source has an incorrect frame rate, you can change it in the Interpret Footage dialog. This is also the cure for footage that mysteriously repeats or skips frames: reconform it to what its rate is supposed to be.

Frame Rates and Timecode

The most common frame rates for video in North America are 23.976 or 29.97 frames per second (fps). Don't be tempted to round these numbers to 24 or 30 fps: The difference sounds tiny, but it adds up to a frame every 33.3 seconds (or a field every 16.7 seconds), which quickly becomes noticeable. Mismatches in frame rates between 30 and 29.97 can cause audio/video synchronization errors, as well as skipped or repeated images.

Along with the oddball frame rate of 29.97 comes two different ways to number the frames: *drop-frame* timecode and *non-drop* timecode. Drop-frame alters the counting sequence so that for long continuous pieces of video, the number assigned to the frames in an editing program or on tape matches a normal realtime clock. To do this, it skips the first two frame numbers (not *frames*; just the *numbers* assigned to frames) every minute, except for the multiples of 10 minutes.

Confusing? Yes. That's why most After Effects users (us included) use the non-drop counting method: Every frame is given a sequential number, and you rarely will have a project long enough in After Effects for the running time versus realtime discrepancy to become an issue. This is set in File > Project Settings.

Those who live in places where PAL-spec video is the norm (virtually everywhere outside North America and Japan) have life easier, as they use a clean 25 fps as their standard. We here in NTSC-land are jealous of you.

High-definition video that conforms to the ATSC specifications (used in North America and elsewhere) can be any one of a smorgasbord of frame rates: 23.976, 24, 29.97, 30, 59.94, or 60 fps, including the potential for pulldown on a tape tagged as 29.97 or 30 fps. Making life even trickier, not all cameras or decks tell you the original frame rate when you capture the footage into your computer. Always verify what the original frame rate of the footage was, especially if it's a question between 23.976 and 24 fps. In reality, most non-European hi-def production is being done at either 23.976 or 29.97 fps.

Film Rates and Pulldown

Film usually runs at 24 fps. When film is transferred to NTSC video, it is slowed down by 0.1% to 23.976 fps, and every four frames of film are distributed across five frames (ten fields) of video through a process known as *pulldown*. Some video cameras also shoot at this rate and add pulldown to simulate film-like motion. You can treat the result as normal interlaced footage, but it is preferred to remove the pulldown sequence so that you are working with the original source frames inside a composition.

To see if a source has pulldown, double-click it to open it in the Footage panel – do this with **Ex.04 > AB_BusinessontheGo.mov**. Use Page Up and Page Down (or the buttons in the Preview panel) to step through the footage. If you have not yet separated its fields, look for a pattern where some frames are interlaced and some are not. If you have separated fields, look for fields being repeated for varying numbers of steps as you progress through the clip. Both are signs of a pulldown sequence being present in the footage.

After Effects can remove the most common "3:2" pulldown sequences where source frames are spread across two or three fields of video in a specific pattern. Select the footage and click the Interpret Footage button at the bottom of the Project panel. Then click Guess 3:2 Pulldown. If After Effects thinks it has found the right sequence, the Separate Fields and Remove Pulldown popups will be set automatically, and a line of text will appear stating the footage now has an effective frame rate of 23.976 fps (its original rate). If After Effects has not found a sequence, try clicking on the Guess 24Pa Pulldown button.

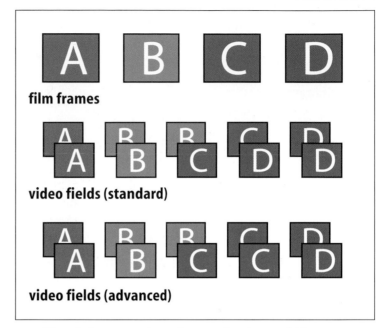

film frames

video fields (standard)

video fields (advanced)

3:2 pulldown is the process of spreading every four frames of video across a sequence of ten video fields.

After Effects can usually guess the correct sequence and remove 3:2 pulldown from footage, returning it to its original frame rate.

More on Fields and Pulldown

We have created in-depth online training modules on the subjects of interlacing and 3:2 pulldown. For information on where to get them, visit *www.crishdesign.com/ online_training.html*.

p and i

When a frame rate or frame size is followed by the letter *p* – for example, 24p – it means it was captured with progressive scan, with no interlacing of fields. When it is followed with an *i* – for example, 1080i – it means the frame has two fields that have been interlaced.

Converting Between Formats

When scaling up standard definition sources to fill high definition frame sizes, plug-ins such as Red Giant Software's Instant HD are preferable to normal scaling in After Effects.

When converting between frame rates (such as 29.97 fps interlaced to 23.976 fps), try Pixel Motion or other "optical flow" effects (see Chapter 28).

After Effects occasionally guesses wrong, so always test your footage after removing pulldown: Return to the clip's Footage panel and step through the frames. If you see interlacing artifacts on any frame, then verify that Separate Fields has been set correctly (see the previous section on fields) and manually try different pulldown sequences in the Remove Pulldown popups until all signs of fields have disappeared. If nothing works, then the footage contains a pulldown sequence After Effects does not recognize; set the Separate Fields popup correctly, but leave Remove Pulldown set to Off.

When film is transferred to PAL video, it is either sped up to 25 fps or transferred through a more complex pulldown sequence that distributes 24 frames of film across 25 frames (50 fields) of video.

Also note that film can be shot at virtually any rate, including 25, 29.97, or 30 fps; this is not a bad idea if you know a project is going to end up only on video.

Frame Sizes

With video, there are two overall image aspect ratios you will be dealing with: normal standard definition television, which has a 4:3 width/height relationship, and widescreen or high-definition television (not always the same thing), which has a 16:9 image aspect ratio. The frame sizes in pixels that various video formats use to fill these overall images are often different from the computer monitor resolutions you are used to.

When you are working under the NTSC standard, the professional D1 frame size is 720×486 pixels; the DV frame size is 720×480 pixels – the same as D1, but with six lines cropped off. These same sizes are used whether the overall image is to be displayed at a 4:3 aspect ratio or a 16:9 aspect ratio; the individual pixels are scaled horizontally as needed to fill the frame. (We'll get to the issue of non-square pixels next.)

When PAL is the standard you are working under, both D1 and DV frames are 720×576 pixels. As with NTSC, this same size is used whether the overall image is to be displayed at a 4:3 aspect ratio or a 16:9 aspect ratio; the individual pixels are scaled horizontally as needed.

The ATSC standard for hi-def video in the United States supports several frame sizes. When the final image is supposed to have a 4:3 aspect, the frame size may be 704×480 or 640×480 pixels; these are the *standard def* sizes inside the ATSC standard. When the final image is supposed to have a 16:9 aspect, the recognized sizes are 704×480 (standard def), 1280×720 (hi-def), or 1920×1080 pixels (also hi-def, and the more common of the two hi-def sizes). In reality, the 704×480 size is rarely used, while many hi-def cameras use *anamorphic* frame sizes that are smaller than the ideal.

Those who have already whipped out a calculator will have noticed some discrepancies, such as whereas $4 \div 3 = 1.33$ (the overall aspect ratio of a normal television image), $720 \div 486 = 1.48$. Why? The difference is that in most video formats – including anamorphic hi-def – not all pixels are intended to be perfect squares. We'll discuss that little piece of mental torture next.

Non-square Pixels

Up until now, all that's been special about video are a few relatively trivial technical details, such as its frame size or frame rate. But now we have to tackle a subject that's not at all trivial or intuitive: non-square pixels and pixel aspect ratios.

In a computer, each picture element (pixel) that makes up a file is assumed to be square. Create a file that is 100 pixels tall and 100 pixels wide, and the computer assumes it will be displayed as a perfect square on your computer monitor. These same assumptions are made when the computer processes an image – for example, rotate this file 90°, and it should still be displayed as a perfect square.

For reasons far too convoluted to bore you with here, professional digital video systems *don't* treat pixels as perfect squares. In the case of 4:3 images, D1 and DV pixels in NTSC systems display their pixels to be roughly 90% as wide as they are tall. If you look at a D1 or DV NTSC capture on a computer monitor that displays pixels as squares, your video captures will look about 10% wider than normal. D1 and DV pixels in the PAL world are distorted in the opposite direction, intended to be displayed about 7% wider than they are tall. To get an idea of what this looks like, open the folder **Ex.05** inside this chapter's project, and double-click on the two files inside – **AB_IndGearMach_NTSC** and **AB_IndGearMach_PAL** – to view them on your computer monitor. They will look out-of-round.

You can get used to viewing out-of-round images on your computer monitor. (If you can't, we'll get to a couple of workarounds.) However, problems can arise when you don't take into account the pixel aspect ratio of your sources versus how they will be displayed. For example, if you send a computer-native square pixel image out through a D1 or DV NTSC video card or converter without compensation, that image may appear on the video monitor about 10% skinnier than you would expect.

Compression Artifacts

Be aware that if your video format of choice compresses the image too much, synthetic graphics – such as text – can have chewed-up edges. This is common with the DV format. DV also undersamples the color, resulting in banding on color gradients.

A round wheel appears correct when it's displayed in the environment it was created for. If you correctly tag both the image and the composition you place it in, the wheel will be distorted as needed to stay round when it's displayed in either world.

Non-square D1 and DV NTSC pixels make round objects appear "fat" when they're displayed on a square pixel computer monitor. This is okay; they will be round again when they're displayed on a video monitor through a D1 or DV chain.

Images captured using PAL D1 or DV systems will look skinny when they're displayed on a computer monitor – this is correct. (By coincidence, *improperly* tagged square pixels will look like this when they're displayed in NTSC.)

This skateboard wheel, shot using the DV NTSC format, looks out-of-round on a computer screen. However, as it rotates it doesn't wobble – it remains stretched horizontally. With non-square pixel sources, the image itself isn't distorted; just the way it is being displayed. Footage courtesy Creative License.

This would all be reason for despair…if After Effects didn't have the capability to track these pixel aspect ratios throughout a project and make adjustments under the hood as needed to translate between them. You just have to do two things for this to happen:

• Set the Pixel Aspect Ratio (PAR) popup correctly for all your sources in their respective Interpret Footage dialogs. This means keeping track of the system they came from – NTSC, PAL, or a computer.

• Set the Pixel Aspect Ratio popup in the Composition Settings dialog to match the way the output of this comp will be displayed. For example, if you are working in a 720×480 pixel comp that will be rendered and played back on an NTSC DV system, set the comp's PAR to D1/DV NTSC (0.9).

If you want to verify this piece of magic, open comp [**Ex.05-rotation distortion**]. The comp has been set up to the DV NTSC frame size and pixel aspect ratio; it also contains DV footage of a skateboard wheel. The wheel looks out of round on a computer monitor because these pixels expect to be displayed through a chain that will eventually show them skinnier than this. RAM Preview; note that the rotating wheel doesn't wobble – it keeps the same distortion. With non-square pixels, *it's not the original image that's distorted – just the way it is being displayed.*

Now turn on the Video switch for the layer **CM_bikewheel** – it looks stretched, just like the skateboard wheel. Double-click it to open it in its Layer panel; it now looks perfectly round. This is because it was created in a 3D program using square pixels. Since it has been tagged as such, After Effects knows to stretch it when it's placed in a D1/DV NTSC comp. Bring the Comp panel forward, and scrub its Rotation value in the Timeline panel. Note that just like the skateboard wheel, it doesn't wobble; it remains stretched horizontally regardless of its angle of rotation.

Anamorphic Widescreen

High-definition television has adopted a widescreen overall image aspect ratio of 16:9 and usually square pixels. However, most hi-def cameras don't use the same number of pixels as described in the specification; this would require too much data to fit onto tape. Plus there are many who want the widescreen look without having to upgrade to hi-def equipment. Therefore, fiendishly clever video engineers figured out a way to give us widescreen images using less expensive equipment: They take a widescreen image, squish it horizontally until it fits into a smaller frame size, and save that image to tape, disk, or DVD. On playback, compatible televisions or video monitors can be set to restretch the image back out to fill a 16:9 aspect ratio. This technique is referred to as *anamorphic widescreen.*

The secrets to successfully working with anamorphic widescreen footage are:

- Make sure the pixel aspect of the source is tagged correctly in its Interpret Footage dialog.

- Make sure the pixel aspect ratio of your composition is labeled correctly. If you are working at the original anamorphic size, use that pixel aspect ratio in the Composition Settings. If you are working at the normal square pixel size, make sure you pick Square Pixels from the Pixel Aspect Ratio popup.

In the Interpret Footage dialog, make sure the Pixel Aspect Ratio for your source is tagged correctly.

- Make sure your final render is at the anamorphic frame size required by the format. If necessary, squeeze it horizontally using the Resize portion of the Output Module dialog.

Standard definition widescreen footage is tricky to handle inside After Effects, as it has the same frame size in pixels as normal 4:3 footage. As a result, in many cases After Effects cannot automatically tell the difference. This often leaves it up to you to manually tag the Pixel Aspect Ratio of widescreen footage in the Interpret Footage dialog. Look at the image and see if something strikes you as funny – like the unnaturally thin surfer in the footage inside the [**Ex.06**] folder in this chapter's project. (Both NTSC and PAL widescreen will look skinny, just by different amounts.) If you're not sure, ask the cameraperson who shot the footage. Once you tag it correctly, again, After Effects will handle the rest.

As mentioned, many hi-def formats also use non-square pixels. HDCAM and HDV stretch a 1440×1080 source frame size to fill a 1920×1080 image (with a pixel aspect ratio of 1.33:1). DVCPRO HD uses a 1280×1080 source frame to fill 1920x1080 final frame (PAR = 1.5:1), and a 960×720 source to fill 1280×720 frame (PAR = 1.33:1). There is even an anamorphic film format that uses a 2:1 pixel aspect ratio!

The anamorphic widescreen technique takes widescreen images (above) and squishes them horizontally to fit into a standard 4:3 frame (below). Note that you cannot always tell footage has been squished just by eyeballing it! Footage courtesy Artbeats/Surfing.

To view your non-square pixel comps as square pixels while you're working, enable the Pixel Aspect Ratio Correction switch along the bottom of the Composition panel.

Working Square

If viewing distorted images drives you mad, and you don't have a way to preview your comps through a real video monitor (discussed later in the section *Monitoring Your Work*), After Effects provides a fix. You will find the Pixel Aspect Ratio Correction switch along the bottom of the Comp, Layer, and Footage panels. Click on it to toggle correction on and off. When on, it will now rescale the *display* of your comp panel to simulate square pixels. Don't worry – sources still aren't being altered, and this feature is ignored during rendering.

Generally, when we're designing for a 4:3 image, we work at the native D1/DV sizes with Aspect Ratio Correction turned off, and view our work through a native D1/DV display chain – or just live with the distortion on our computer screen, compensating mentally. If we find there are some graphic elements that beg for straightforward square pixels (creating graphics on grids, using certain effects that work only in square pixels, and so on), we'll create these elements at their square pixel sizes (see table below), then nest this comp into the final D1 comp, scaling the nested layer to fit.

On the other hand, if we are designing for anamorphic 16:9 playback, we tend to do all of our work in square pixel comps, as the pixel aspect distortion is too great to ignore on a computer screen. Also, anamorphic widescreen formats tend to sacrifice resolution, which is not preferable.

Below is a table of common non-square pixel source sizes along with their corresponding square pixel sizes. If your final render is going back to the same format as the source, remember to render at the required size by either nesting and scaling in a final comp or, if you are not field rendering, by scaling in the output module.

Better Quality

To improve the image quality when Toggle Pixel Aspect Ratio Correction is enabled, set Preferences > Previews > Viewer Quality > Zoom Quality to More Accurate.

Converting between D1 and DV

If you are working with interlaced sources and need to convert between DV and D1, refer to the recipes in the PDF included in this chapter's folder.

Format	Source Size	Square Pixel Size
D1 NTSC 4:3	720x486	720x534
D1 NTSC 16:9	720x486	872x486
DV NTSC 4:3	720x480	720x528
DV NTSC 16:9	720x480	864x480
D1/DV PAL 4:3	720x576	788x576
D1/DV PAL 16:9	720x576	1024x576
HDCAM/HDV 1080	1440x1080	1920x1080
DVCPRO HD 1080	1280x1080	1920x1080
DVCPRO HD 720	960x720	1280x720

Clean versus Production Aperture

The frame sizes defined for standard definition video have a quirk: They contain more pixels than are supposed to be used. When engineers designed these formats, they built in a few extra pixels along the edges to allow for artifacts caused by video processing algorithms and the like. The full captured frame is referred to as the Production Aperture; the smaller area inside which refers to the actual image is referred to as the Clean Aperture.

For many years, video hardware and software ignored this difference, using just the Production Aperture size for everything. A side effect of this choice was that they also used very slightly wrong pixel aspect ratios to make the math work – otherwise, the extra pixels in the Production Aperture made it look like the frames were wider than 4:3 or 16:9.

The Gory Details

If you want to know the story behind Clean and Production Apertures – and why pixels aren't square to begin with – we wrote a detailed online article on the subject: *tinyurl.com/par4course*

As of Creative Suite 4, Adobe decided to rectify this and started using the technically correct pixel aspect ratios in After Effects and other products. The suggested square pixel sizes on the previous page encompass the entire Production Aperture; that's why they have image aspect ratios wider than 4:3 or 16:9 (for example, 720 ÷ 534 = 1.348; not the expected 1.333).

What does this mean for you? Less than you might expect:

• None of the square-pixel frame sizes have changed. This means you can interchange files with other programs without worry.

• When you create imagery using the new, correct square pixel frame sizes, be aware that a few pixels on the left and right sides are extra. For example, the Clean Aperture area for 4:3 D1 NTSC is 712 x 486, meaning four pixels along each edge will be ignored when displayed.

When you add a square pixel source that used the old (incorrect) common sizes to a non-square pixel composition that uses the correct pixel aspect ratios, the least-fuss approach is to match their widths (select the square pixel source and choose Layer > Transform > Fit to Comp Width), and allow pixels on the top and bottom to be cropped.

• When using square pixel compositions or artwork created at the "old" sizes, scale the width to match the target non-square pixel comp, and allow those extra pixels on the top and bottom to be cropped off. This is demonstrated in [**Ex.07**]. (Alternately, you can match their heights and live with some pixels missing from your source along the sides.)

• Know that from now on, your "perfectly round" circles will actually be perfectly round.

This issue does not affect any of the anamorphic HD formats; in all of their cases, Clean and Production Apertures are the same.

Viewing the Comp panel on a computer monitor can lull you into a false sense of security, as it will show you more of the image (above) than will eventually be visible on TV (below).

Safe Areas

When television was first being worked out, there was a lot of concern over the quality and repeatability of the image that would be projected on the screens. Picture tubes were prone to shift the image off-center, shrink the size of image they were projecting with age, and cause visible blurriness and distortion around their edges. Therefore, television was defined as an *overscan* system: The image frame extends beyond the visible portion of the television screen, cropped by the bezel that runs around the picture tube. This is in contrast to the typical computer display, which is *underscanned* – there is a black border around the edge of the picture before you reach the bezel to make sure no important information is cut off.

A region inset 5% from each edge of the frame is defined as the *action safe* area. It is assumed that any action beyond this area could be cut off by a television set's bezel. Therefore, 10% of the height and width of the frame could potentially not be seen by the viewer. You should still put some image (such as an extension of your background) in this area, because you have no idea how much of it will truly be visible or will be cut off by any given TV set. But don't put anything in this region that you need your viewer to see. One positive side effect is that the bezel crops off a lot of junk – such as black borders and half-field scan lines – that you *don't* want to see!

Action and title safe areas – shown here as the white lines inside the borders of the image area – reduce the cumulative width and height of the frame you can work with by 10% (for design elements) to 20% (for readable text). Footage courtesy Artbeats/Business on the Go.

A second region inset an additional 5% along each side from action safe (taking another 10% overall from the edges, consuming a total of 20% of the width and height of the frame) is referred to as *title safe*. It was assumed that picture tubes would distort the image too much for text to be readable beyond this area. Therefore, it is common practice to keep all text you expect your viewer to read inside the title safe area.

The design implications of this are that you have far less area of the screen you can use for supposedly visible elements than if you were designing for multimedia or other computer-based playback. Design using the entire screen, and your compositions will appear zoomed up and cropped off when they're played back on a video monitor.

Over time, picture tubes improved to have less distortion. Of course, now most new televisions have plasma or LCD screens, greatly reducing or eliminating issues with the bezel cutting off part of your image. As a result, we have all seen news and sports broadcasts using the lower portion of the action safe area to display stock market tickers, sports scores, and news updates. Despite this, you must still assume that at least some of your image will be cropped. Also, some broadcasters and disc duplicators will still reject your submissions if you do not respect the traditional safe area zones.

Fortunately, After Effects can display safe area overlays in the Comp, Layer, and Footage panels. These may be selected from the Choose Grid and Guide Options popup along the bottom of these panels, and may be quickly toggled on and off by pressing the apostrophe key. A nice recent addition is that 4:3 "center cut" safe area guides are also displayed in widescreen comps (more on that below).

You can adjust the size of the safe area zones in Preferences > Grids & Guides. Ask your client what are the safe area percentages they use, and enter these numbers in the preferences before you begin designing.

Moving Between Aspect Ratios

For the next several years, there is a good chance that the graphics you create will be used for both normal 4:3 as well as widescreen 16:9 video. Therefore, an important question is how do you make the same piece of video work in both of these formats?

From 16:9 to 4:3

When trying to make a widescreen image work in a 4:3 frame, the central question becomes: How much of the image are you going to cut off? It is very common for prime-time television programs and graphics to be prepared at 16:9 for high-def broadcast, but then to have the left and right sides cut off for 4:3 standard definition broadcast, with no blank spaces left over above and below. This technique is known as *center cut*, and results in a lot of image area being lost (remember, you lose the Action Safe area as well). It is demonstrated in [Ex.08] and [Ex.09a].

Need to put text here to be safe!
Text placed here would get cut off in 4:3 version

When working on your 16:9 widescreen master composition, make sure all important action and text stays inside 4:3 safe areas as well. Footage courtesy Artbeats.

Center cut requires extra diligence when shooting footage and creating graphics – you have to make sure nothing you need to see is outside the center 4:3 area. Some widescreen cameras have a center cut overlay to aid you while you're shooting. After Effects also now displays 4:3 action and title safe center cut overlays when you create a widescreen composition.

At the other extreme, you can scale down the widescreen version so that all of its image is contained inside a 4:3 screen. The trade-off is large *letterbox* bars above and below with no image. This is done by some

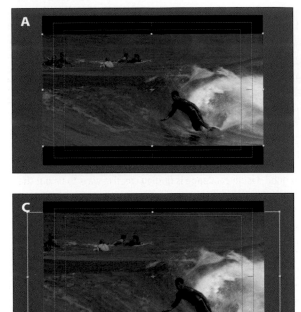

A 16:9 letterbox keeps the entire image but results in large empty bars above and below (figure A). Common compromises are 15:9 (figure B) or 14:9 (figure C) letterboxes; the yellow outlines indicate how much image is being lost. Also watch for any pieces of action – such as the swimmers in the upper left – also appearing outside of Action Safe.

FACTOID

Correct Center Cut

The center cut guides in After Effects CS4 defaulted to the wrong location. This has been corrected in CS5.

Scaling 4:3 footage wider to fill a 16:9 frame usually looks immediately wrong – especially if it contains circular objects. Footage courtesy Artbeats/Industry – Gears and Machines.

purist film channels and is demonstrated in [**Ex.09b**]. More common is a compromise in which part of the image is cropped off the left and right sides with smaller letterbox bars above and below. Common aspect ratios for the visible image area are 15:9 (commonly used by PBS) and 14:9 (BBC). These are demonstrated in [**Ex.09c**] and [**Ex.09d**]. Finally, there is the *pan and scan* technique where you actively move and scale the footage to keep the most important subjects centered – this is shown in [**Ex.09e**]. These same issues exist if you are shooting anamorphic standard definition video for display on both widescreen and 4:3 displays. The various letterboxing options are demonstrated in the **Ex.10** folder.

This issue also comes up when working on a "film" using high-def video equipment: widescreen may be fine for theatrical release, but what are you going to do for the standard definition television and DVD versions? To avoid problems later, you need to settle on your output workflow *before* you shoot footage and spend time creating graphics.

From 4:3 to 16:9

There are similar issues when trying to make 4:3 content and designs work for 16:9 output. The wrong solution is to place your 4:3 clip in a 16:9 composition and use Layer > Transform > Fit to Comp. The result is a distorted image that everyone can immediately see is incorrect – compare the two comps in the **Ex.11** folder yourself.

The easy solutions are either to place the 4:3 clip in the middle of the 16:9 comp with black bars filling out the left and right (known as a *pillarbox*) or to scale the clip up to fill the comp's frame. These are demonstrated in **Ex.12**. Note that if you plan to scale up the footage, you will need to shoot it protected in a different direction, making sure nothing important exists along the top or bottom of the frame.

The better solution is to find creative ways to fill in this extra area, perhaps by using copies of the original footage (creating a multi-display effect) or using it for complimentary images and supporting text. A couple of these ideas are presented in the **Ex.13** folder. Another common solution is to create an animated "wallpaper" to sit behind – and act as a frame for – the 4:3 footage.

A related issue is that film is usually shot on a roughly 4:3 frame (2048 × 1556) that is then cropped top and bottom for widescreen theater presentation. In this workflow, you will need to center your titles vertically to ensure they will be safe for the theater and for when they're reformatted for video.

A good design challenge is finding creative ways to fill out the remaining area in a widescreen frame when your sources are 4:3. Footage courtesy Artbeats/Incarcerated.

faster
cheaper
high-tech
cutting edge
internet
direct
revolutionary
future
digital
personalized

Safe Colors and Video

Images viewed on a video monitor often appear different from those on your computer monitor. One reason is that video uses a different gamma curve for luminance than some computers. You have to keep on eye on the shadows and highlights in particular.

Another reason is that video uses a different color space – YUV – than computers, which prefer RGB. The two color spaces do not completely overlap, so it is possible to create RGB colors that do not translate directly into YUV. Also, video has certain restrictions in that it must be encoded for broadcasting or recording on tape, which creates a further restriction in what colors are wise to use. For example, it is advisable to stay away from deeply saturated pure colors, such as hot reds and yellows.

This is why we recommend that if you are working in video, you should add to your After Effects workstation a card or converter with video out capabilities – it is the best way to preview how your colors, gray level balance, safe areas, and more will actually look when you output your work to video.

Chapter 26 discusses strategies for checking and correcting colors to make sure they are broadcast safe. There are also some great third-party tools to help you tweak your colors, such as Color Finesse from Synthetic Aperture (*www.synthetic-ap.com*), bundled free with After Effects.

Practice Safe Color

Chapter 26 demonstrates how to use the Broadcast Colors effect to make sure your colors are video legal.

FACTOID

Illuminated

Another important video issue is the luminance range of your source footage. This, as well as overall color management, is discussed in Chapter 26.

Color bar test signals show a weakness of the composite video format: Contrasting colors can cause dots to appear along their borders.

Composite Dot Crawl

Related to the "safe color" issue are artifacts that can appear when certain colors are placed side by side, then displayed through composite video systems (the lowest common denominator, and how many televisions are still connected to DVD players and the like).

When you're viewing a video image sent through a composite connection on a video monitor, you might notice a series of dots crawling vertically along high-contrast edges at a rate of about one line per video field (roughly 60 pixels a second for NTSC). This artifact is caused by the way composite video is encoded. Reducing the amount of contrast on sharp vertical edges – for example, by feathering or blurring the edge – will reduce this artifact.

Similarly, sharp transitions between saturated colors that have large differences in YUV colorspace can also cause a dot pattern to appear along a shared horizontal edge (from scan line to scan line), especially on higher-resolution studio monitors. Ironically, lower-quality consumer TVs and VTRs may not show this particular flaw; record a tape or burn a disc and play it back on a normal TV before completely freaking out or changing the color scheme of your design. (Note that this problem is *not* related to the field flicker issues discussed earlier.)

Monitoring Your Work

Many of the issues raised in this chapter – non-square pixels, interlaced fields, safe areas, color spaces, and such – are the reasons we suggest you strongly consider adding real video output capabilities to your After Effects workstation. Viewing your work through an actual video chain is the only way to really see how it will look in the real world. Looking at a computer display and trying to make judgment calls about how much pixels will stretch, thin lines will vibrate, colors will shift, and how much of the image will be chopped off, just doesn't cut it.

Your preferred choice would be to add to your computer a display card that features direct video output. We highly recommend cards such as the AJA Kona or Blackmagic DeckLink, which have the ability to function as a second desktop screen: Create a View > New Viewer, undock the panel to be its own

TIP

Preview Current Frame

Instead of using Video Preview, you can set Output Device to Computer Monitor Only and use the / key on your numeric keypad to send just the current frame to your monitor.

You can create a second viewer for your composition, and place this viewer on a dedicated video monitor.

window, drag it to your second screen, and press Command+\ (Control+\) twice in order to center then resize it to fit.

Alternatively, open Preferences > Video Preview and set the Output Device to match your card or a device on your FireWire port. Then set Output Mode to match the format you wish to display such as NTSC or PAL (often, the trick is to pick an "RGB" option, or the display may remain blank). A series of options underneath then allow you to choose what you see and when, as well as any scale compensation such as for a 4:3 or 16:9 monitor.

The next step up from Video Preview is using Synthetic Aperture's Echo Fire software suite. It adds a host of useful features to the equation, such as deciding how odd-sized comps are scaled to fit the video display, providing transport controls, playing from disk (instead of just RAM), a standalone video previewer, optionally overlaying a waveform monitor and vectorscope, and previewing Photoshop documents or the computer's desktop to video through devices that don't support independent desktop display. EchoFire also tends to support additional video cards the stock Video Preview function doesn't. For more information on Echo Fire, visit *www.synthetic-ap.com.*

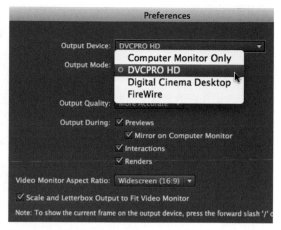

You can set up Preferences > Video Preview to echo your Comp panel through a compatible video device.

Creating Good Web Video

These days, it is quite common to take video originally intended for broadcast and to create a version to be played from a website. Many just take their final render and send it off to encoding (using a program such as Adobe Media Encoder, installed with After Effects) to create the web version – but the results may be less than optimal. Before you encode, make sure you take the following into account:

• Deinterlace any field-based sources, or create progressive scan versions of those sources. Interlaced material looks terrible when played back on a computer. You can deinterlace the final render, or if you are the creator, consider making a special progressive scan version of your project. (Many like to use the Fields Kit plug-in set from RE:Vision Effects to deinterlace field-based footage.)

• Convert the final movie to a square pixel format. Computers can't compensate for non-square pixels or anamorphic video formats.

• Crop the edges to simulate how much a TV bezel would crop the image (in other words, beyond Action Safe). The imagery was composed taking Action Safe areas into account; your job is to present a web version that represents the original intentions of the cameraperson or motion graphics artist. An example of this is demonstrated in [**Ex.14**]. At the very least, crop off any gunk that might exist around the edges.

• Consider color-managing your render to convert it to the sRGB color space that is the standard for web-based imagery. (Color Management was discussed in detail in Chapter 26.)

USEFUL LINKS

If you are interested in additional technical information, here are some excellent websites:

lurkertech (*www.lurkertech.com*) – Contains the now-legendary *Lurker's Guide to Video* that Chris Pirazzi wrote while at SGI. Also contains a pointer to the Apple specification for uncompressed video (which Chris also wrote).

Adam Wilt (*www.adamwilt.com*) – Highly useful ruminations on a wide assortment of video gotchas, particularly in the area of the myths and realities of dealing with the DV format, as well as color and text issues.

Synthetic Aperture Tips and Articles (*www.synthetic-ap.com/tips/index.html*) – Articles on selecting a FireWire-to-Video converter, choosing and calibrating a video monitor, and using QuickTime and AVI codecs.

High-Definition Specifications (*www.atsc.org/standards.html*) – ATSC document A/53 describes the ATSC specs for hi-def television; Table A3 is the money box with the frame size and rate specs.

Render Queue

The Render Queue is where you set up and manage the creation of your final work.

To create a movie or still image from your animations and arrangements, you have to render a file. After Effects is very flexible in allowing you to set up and override certain parameters when you render, as well as to create multiple files with different aspect ratios and file formats from the same render pass. You can also create and save templates of these render and output settings.

Internally, After Effects treats rendering a movie as a two-step process: Calculate an image, then decide how to save it to disk. These two steps are presented to the user as two different sets of options for each comp in the Render Queue: *Render Settings* and *Output Modules.* You can twirl down the arrows to the left of these tags to see the parameters that have been set, or click on the name to the right to open a dialog to change these settings.

Caps Lock

Engaging Caps Lock stops After Effects from updating the Comp panel, which can save time during rendering.

A comp in the Render Queue, with the Render Settings and Output Module details twirled down for inspection (they default to twirled up). After clicking the Render button to start the render, twirl down the Current Render (circled in red) to see how long each stage is taking – great for spotting a slow effect – and how large the final movie will be.

Example Project

Explore the 42-Example Project.aep file as you read this chapter; references to [Ex.##] refer to specific compositions within the project file.

Rendering 101

There are several ways to prepare to render a file. The most common way to render a composition is to open it and press Command+M on Mac (Control+M on Windows). To render a still, locate the time indicator to the frame you want and type Command+Option+S (Control+Alt+S).

You also need a name for the file. After Effects can name your render for you (if the Use Default File Name and Folder option is enabled in Preferences > Output); you can also take advantage of Name Templates (see Chapter 43). You can change the name and file path any time before rendering.

You must then click on the Render button in the Render Queue (or press Return or Enter) to start rendering. The settings used will be those in the default templates (see the section *Creating and Editing Templates* later in this chapter). You can also choose a new template or modify the current one. You can tweak the render settings and output module before you click Render; the exception is with Save RAM Preview, which launches the render as soon as you've named it.

Multiple comps can be dragged to the Render Queue, which After Effects will then render one after another as a batch. The batch in the Render Queue is saved with the Project, so you can Save, Quit and render later. While you can't render multiple projects at once, you can create a new project and

use File > Import > File to merge other projects and their Render Queues into your new project.

Compositions are rendered in their current state – not the state they were in when queued up. You cannot change the contents of the project or a comp while you are rendering. If the composition being rendered is open and in a different frame than the Render Queue, it will come forward and update as it renders. Press the Caps Lock key to stop the Comp panel updating (saves time).

Renders can be paused or stopped. If you click on Stop, After Effects will create a new item in the Render Queue for the comp that was interrupted, set to render just the segment of time not yet finished. If you Option+click (Alt+click) on Stop instead, After Effects will use the same duration as originally set for the comp.

The basic size of the frame that will be rendered is set by the comp's size, so try to build it at the correct size to begin with. If that's not possible, you can alter it in another comp and render this new composition instead, or scale plus crop it in the Output Module.

Conversely, the frame rate of a comp can be overridden during rendering. (The exception to this rule is if you enabled the Preserve Frame Rate option under the Advanced tab in a comp's Composition Settings.) Render Settings defaults to the same

rate as used by the queued comp, but you are free to change it.

Changing the render frame rate does not speed up or slow down the speed of the *motion* in the comp or any of the source material used in it; it merely changes the *intervals of time* at which the rendering engine steps through the comp to decide what to render next. You will find many advantages to this scheme, such as the ability to field-render without having to work at the field rate, or to work at 24 fps in a comp, and then introduce 3:2 pulldown later when you render.

A number of composition switches – such as whether or not effects, proxies, frame blending, and motion blur are rendered – can be set or overridden at the render stage. It can often be useful to work with processor-intensive enhancements such as frame blending turned off as you build a composition, then turn them on at the rendering stage. You still need to preset the layers in your compositions with your intentions; the render modules can do only large-scale overrides such as *ignore all effects*, *set all layers to Best Quality*, and *turn on frame blending for all checked layers*. Note that the Collapse Transformations/Continuously Rasterize switch must be set manually per layer – there is no Render Settings override to continuously rasterize all Illustrator files, for instance.

TIP

Redirection

To change the folder that multiple renders will be saved in, select them by Shift+clicking or Command (Control)+clicking on their Output Modules (not the Render Queue items themselves), and change the file path for any one.

Queue ≠ Freeze

After Effects renders the queued compositions in their current state when you click the Render button – not the state they were in when you added them to the Render Queue. If you queue up a comp, After Effects does not memorize the state of the comp when you queued it – so be careful of any additional changes you make between queuing and rendering. A common mistake is to queue a comp, turn on a layer, queue it again, turn on another layer, queue it again, and *then* render, thinking you're rendering three variations of the same comp (you know who you are). In fact, you are rendering only the comp in its most recent state, three times. Either render one version at a time, or duplicate the comp to create variations.

In this chapter, we will first discuss the general difference between rendering a still image, a movie, and a RAM Preview. Then we'll go over the two parts involved in rendering a movie: the Render Settings and the Output Module. Finally, we will cover making templates for the Render and Output sections, so you don't have to set them up manually.

There are several other useful features in After Effects related to the render process. For example, you can prerender portions of a comp chain to save time later and distribute renders across multiple machines. The Collect Files feature, which was created to help set up distributed renders, also makes it easier to gather just what is needed to render a composition – this is a great aid in backing up or handing off a project to someone else. We'll discuss prerendering and proxies as well as advanced rendering techniques in the next two chapters.

Movies

The item you will want to render most frequently is a movie (including a still image sequence) of your composition. To do this, you need to add it to the Render Queue. You can do this several ways: The most common is to select or bring forward the comp you want and use either the menu command Composition > Make Movie or the keyboard shortcut Command+M (Control+M). You can also drag comps or footage directly from the Project panel to the Render Queue, or select them in the Project panel and type Command+Shift+/ (Control+Shift+/). If you do this with a footage item, After Effects will automatically create a comp for it, as if you had dragged it to the New Composition icon.

Adding an item to the queue will automatically open the Render Queue panel. You can then change the render and output parameters, queue up other comps, or go back to work – just don't forget to eventually click Render! In the Render Settings, you can also define the time segment you want rendered: the entire comp, the already set work area, or a custom-entered region of time.

By default, After Effects automatically names the movie it will create (we'll discuss other options in a moment); you can always rename it before rendering. If a comp does not have a file name assigned – indicated by the file name appearing in italics in the Render Queue – you must assign it one for it to render (see *Names and Paths* on the following page).

Stills

To render a still of a frame in a composition, locate to the desired time in the comp with the time indicator; use either the menu command Composition > Save Frame As > File or the shortcut Command+Option+S (Control+Alt+S). Give it a file name, then click on the Render button in the Render Queue to render it. You can change the time the still will be taken from after queuing, but it is good to get in the practice of locating to the correct time as a confidence check before you queue it. Again, you can batch up multiple stills before you render; just be careful not to accidentally change a comp you haven't rendered yet.

Another option is saving a still in the form of a layered Photoshop file: First set all layers to Best Quality and Full Resolution, then select Composition > Save Frame As > Photoshop Layers. Effects, masks, and most transformations will be precomputed; blending modes and opacity settings will be carried through to the new layered file. Track mattes will not be computed, but the track matte layer will appear in the Photoshop file, turned off, for you to convert to a layer mask.

RAM Preview

You can queue up your most recent RAM Preview and save it to disk as a movie. To do this, select Composition > Save RAM Preview, or Command+click (Control+click) on the RAM Preview button in the Preview panel. If the current work area has not already been previewed and cached to RAM, After Effects will cache it as if you invoked a RAM Preview first. If you already RAM Previewed the work area, the rendered frames will already be cached. After Effects will then automatically open the Render Queue, ask you for a file name, and save the preview to disk using the default RAM Preview Output Module template (templates are discussed later). RAM Previews are not field rendered; saving a RAM Preview will not allow you to interlace a movie or add pulldown.

Names and Paths

By default, when you add an item to the Render Queue, it will be named after its composition, with the file type appended onto the end. As for where on the disk to save it, After Effects remembers the last path you set up. You can always change the file name or path by clicking on its name, which appears in the Render Queue on the same line as the Output Module next to the words Output To. If you prefer to manually name each file as you add it to the queue, go to Preferences > Output and disable the option Use Default File Name and Folder. If you disable this and either duplicate an item in the queue or add it to the queue directly from the Project panel, it will get the name *Not yet specified* (you will need to rename the item before rendering).

In the next chapter we discuss File Name Templates. Briefly, there is a popup menu arrow between the words Output To and the file name. Click on it, and you will see a list of name templates that include combinations and variations on the comp's, project's, and output module's name, the file's dimensions, and the range of frames requested.

If none of these strike your fancy, you can create your own template by selecting Custom from this list. A dialog will open that will allow you to modify the existing presets or build your own from scratch. Click on the Add Property popup to select what bit of information you want After Effects to automatically insert into the name for you; it will appear inside square brackets [like this] inside the Template area of the dialog. You can add your own characters such as spaces, underscores, dots, and the like between these elements. Click on the document icon to give your new template a name, and it will now be added to the list.

Files Missing

When you initiate a render, if any files used by the selected comp are missing, After Effects will warn that there are indeed missing files. However, it does not tell you the names of the missing items. Note that After Effects does not look at the section of time you are rendering – the files could be used before or after the work area you might be rendering. Any missing items will appear as color bars in a comp; if you see such a layer, right-click it and select Reveal Layer Source in Project. Missing footage will appear *in italics* in the Project panel. (Another way to identify missing items

is to type "**missing**" into the QuickSearch dialog at the top of the Project panel and press Return.) Once you find the missing footage, double-click it and relink to the source on your disk. In most cases, After Effects will automatically find other missing footage in the same directory.

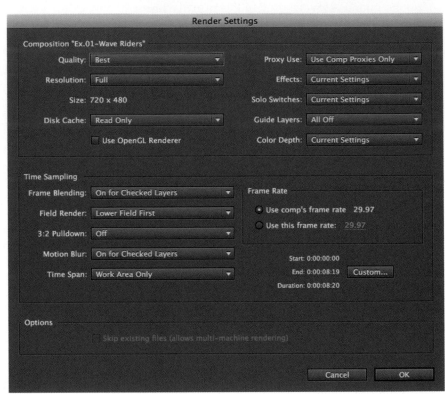

In the Render Settings dialog, the Composition section interprets or overrides various comp and project switches; the Time Sampling section determines which points in time to render. The result is an RGB+Alpha uncompressed frame that is then sent to the Output Module for saving.

Click on the downward-pointing arrows to see all available templates.

Render Settings

These parameters decide how the composition is processed when After Effects renders – basically, you enter all the information After Effects needs to create an uncompressed frame (RGB and Alpha channels). Some may appear to just be duplicates of other switches available in the program, but in fact the ability to reset them during rendering can greatly enhance your workflow. To access Render Settings, click on the underlined text to the right of the words Render Settings. The settings default to those of the current template as selected from the Render Settings popup menu in the Render Queue (click on the arrow to see all available templates). Let's go over each one of the parameters and their settings, including tips on when to use which option, and the gotchas associated with some of them.

Quality

Quality affects how each layer is calculated. You usually want this set to Best, which means that every layer is forced into Best Quality during rendering. If it's set to Current Settings, it obeys the current Quality switch for each layer, be it Best, Draft, or Wireframe. This is useful on those occasions when you purposely switch some layers to Draft Quality to exploit artifacts and the lack of antialiasing.

Resolution

This is identical to the Resolution settings for comps. For a final render, you will want Full, as it will force every comp in the chain to Full Resolution. Choosing a lower resolution renders less than every pixel and produces a smaller sized movie – for example, a 1920×1080 comp set to Half would render a 960×540 image. The size of the image that will be rendered is displayed in parentheses under the Resolution menu as a quick confidence check.

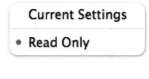

It is quite common to set various nested comps to different resolutions while you're working; if you use Current Settings, those settings would *not* be overridden, and each comp would render using the resolution you'd set for it manually.

If you are rendering a lower-resolution proof (Half for high-def video, Quarter for film), in most cases these menus will override the current settings in the comp chain and drastically reduce rendering time, as a quarter or a sixteenth of the actual pixels would be computed.

Disk Cache

While rendering a preview, if the RAM cache is full, and Preferences > Memory & Cache > Disk Cache is enabled, After Effects calculates if it would take longer to rerender an already cached frame than to save it to disk and read it back later. If yes, then After Effects copies it from RAM to disk for later use. The Read Only option allows After Effects to use already cached frames during the render, saving time. The Current Settings option looks at the Enable Disk Cache preference to decide whether to cache *new* frames. If a comp or layer is used multiple times during the course of a render, caching can save you time; if not, caching frames that are not used again will cost you time.

Use OpenGL Renderer

If you have a high-performance video card, OpenGL will render very quickly (perhaps good for rough proofs), at the cost of not rendering some features – see *Preview Possibilities* at the end of Chapter 2 for details. If you want to ensure the highest quality render, leave this off.

Proxy Use

Proxies are prerendered stand-ins for footage files or entire compositions. They are usually created either to save time (by prerendering an otherwise time-consuming comp that will need to be rendered time and time again), or as lower-resolution placeholders for footage items to make the program more responsive while you're animating.

The setting Comp Proxies Only will use proxies applied to comps but not to footage. If you are using proxies strictly as placeholders, you can choose Use No Proxies; if you're using them as prerenders, Current Settings should work fine. Proxies and prerendering are explained in detail in Chapter 44.

TIP

Where to Go?

Feel free to dock the Render Queue panel into a frame with more room to view its contents, such as with the Comp panel. Some users undock it into its own floating window, so they can move it out of the way and see the Comp during rendering.

Effects

When this option is set to Current Settings, What You See Is What You Get: an effect has to be enabled to be rendered. If you are the type to stack up three or four different effects on a layer to quickly compare their results and then forget to delete the unused ones before rendering, selecting All On will turn on all effects in the final render. Naturally, this leads to much confusion and wasted rendering time. However, some effects are so processor intensive that they drastically slow down navigating around a comp, so you might turn these off when you're working. Select the All On setting, and they will be used for the final render. All Off is used only to blast out a quick proof and is less useful.

Try to be consistent in how you work with effects. If you prefer to not delete unused ones, Current Settings would work better; if you tend to temporarily turn off slow ones, All On would be best.

Solo Switches

Typically, you'll use Solo switches to quickly isolate a layer while you're working. During a render, you usually want to ignore Solo and let all the layers follow their normal settings – if that's the case, set this to All Off. If you're using Solo as a way to render only a select number of layers, use Current Settings.

Guide Layers

Guide Layers appear in the composition in which they are placed, but become invisible or silent when you nest their comps into another composition (unless you Collapse them – see Chapter 20). To keep this behavior, set this option to Current Settings. However, if you render a comp that contains a Guide Layer, Current Settings will mean that the guide will appear (as it hasn't been nested into another comp). To ensure all guides stay invisible and silent, set the Guide Layers popup to All Off.

Color Depth

This popup allows you to override the project's color depth setting at the time you render. This is handy for two reasons: You cannot otherwise set color depth on a per-comp basis, and it is often more efficient to work at a lower bit depth in the name of speed and then render at a higher bit depth while you eat or sleep. However, don't just blindly change this setting and hope for the best; changing the color depth can change the appearance of your images, especially when floating point (32 bits) mode is involved. Change it first using File > Project Settings and make sure you see what you expect. (Color Depth is explained in more detail in Chapter 26.)

Frame Blending

Frame Blending (Chapter 28) falls into that category of a great-looking treatment when you want it, but is too slow to leave on while you're working (especially Pixel Motion mode). We usually turn it on for the layers we want blended, but leave Enable Frame Blending off at the comp level for speed, then set this render parameter to On For Checked Layers to calculate it in the final render. If you're just blasting out a rough proof, use Off For All Layers. Current Settings will render according to which comps (not just individual layers) have Enable Frame Blending turned on.

Field Render

Video issues such as interlacing, field rendering, and 3:2 pulldown were covered in the previous chapter. We'll give a quick summary here:

When it's enabled, Field Render effectively doubles the frame rate but outputs the same number of frames. One entire frame is rendered at the start of the frame; After Effects then moves forward a half-frame in time and renders another complete frame. These two frames are then interlaced into a single frame, taking alternating lines from each. The order of the lines taken is determined by the Upper and Lower Field First choices. If you are delivering the final tape, set this popup to match your playback hardware; otherwise, set it as needed by your client.

Field rendering does not create new frames if they did not exist in the source. For example, if you had rendered a 3D animation at 29.97 frames per second, selecting field rendering here will not magically give it fields – the rendered frames will look the same as they did before (exception: enabling Pixel Motion for those layers, or using an optical flow effect). Field rendering works when the source material was interlaced and has had its fields separated, or if you want your keyframed animation moves created inside After Effects to look smoother on video playback.

3:2 Pulldown

Pulldown is a special technique of interlacing frames that is relevant only when your source material originates on 24 fps film (or you are trying to simulate the "motion" of 24 fps film), but you need to render a file for NTSC video playback. If you're not doing this, leave it off. Otherwise, work at 24 or 23.976 fps in your comps, set the Field Render order your hardware needs, then pick one of the five pulldown phases from the popup. (All phases render essentially the same; the only time you need to pick a specific one is if you are trying to exactly match the pulldown phase of a scene you will be splicing this render back into.) Make sure the Frame Rate parameter below is set to 29.97 fps; if not, enter it.

If Pulldown is enabled, After Effects will then render the comp at 23.976 fps, saving a considerable amount of rendering time, and updating keyframed animations only at the film rate. These rendered frames will then be split across video frames and fields as they are saved to disk. Note that if you field-rendered the same comp at 29.97 fps, the same result will occur for 23.976 fps source material; however, all of your animation moves will be sampled at 59.94 fps (the field rate) instead, and rendering overall will take longer because more points in time are being calculated.

Current Settings

• On for Checked Layers
  Off for All Layers

Off

  Upper Field First
• Lower Field First

TIP

Out in Left Field

Field render only if you are creating full-frame video that is supposed to be interlaced. Web video, film, and progressive scan video formats should not have interlacing introduced.

• Off

  WSSWW
  SSWWW
  SWWWS
  WWWSS
  WWSSW

You can set a custom time span to render sections of a comp independently of the work area, or to "lock in" the work area.

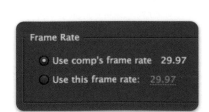

Motion Blur

This switch works similarly to the Frame Blending setting mentioned earlier: Because Motion Blur (Chapter 8) takes longer to calculate, it is usually checked for individual layers, but Enable Motion Blur is turned off at the composition level so you can work faster. When it comes time to render, you can override the comp switches and render with it on (without having to manually enable it in all precomps) by setting this menu to On For Checked layers. Current Settings will render each comp according to whether Enable Motion Blur is on or off.

As the amount of blur is related to a frame's duration, changing the frame rate or enabling field rendering in Render Settings changes the length of blur you will see in the final render. You may need to double the blur angle in Composition Settings before field rendering.

Time Span

As we mentioned earlier in this chapter, you can direct After Effects to render the entire queued comp, the work area set in that comp, or another section of your choosing. The first two choices are obvious from the menu; the third choice can be invoked either by selecting Custom or by clicking on the Custom button. Clicking this button will open a new dialog where you can enter the time range desired. Entering a number in any one field automatically updates the other two; the timebase set under Display Style in File > Project Settings is used. A duration of one frame in essence means render a still, at the Start time specified.

Note that if you select Work Area from the popup, After Effects will look at the work area as defined at the time you click on the Render button, not the work area set when you queued up the comp to render. This is pretty slick if you know what it is doing, and another gotcha if you don't – you might end up rendering a different time span than you intended! To "lock in" the intended work area, click Custom, then click OK.

Frame Rate

A crucial concept about rendering in After Effects is that a comp's set frame rate can be overridden at render time by the value chosen here in Render Settings. This does not change the *speed* of anything, just the increments of time at which new frames are calculated.

The exception to this is if a comp has the Preserve Frame Rate option enabled under the Advanced tab in the Composition Settings dialog. If this is the case, the rendering frame rate is ignored in lieu of the comp's rate. If you have a chain of nested comps, only the comps that have this option enabled will ignore the render frame rate. This is useful for forcing a "stop motion" look for a particular precomp.

The comp's frame rate is chosen as the default, but you can type in a new number here. If you need a quick proof of a 29.97 fps comp, set the frame rate to 10 or 15 fps – don't change the comp's frame rate in Composition Settings, as keyframes will shift slightly if you edit them.

Skip Existing Files

There are a couple of approaches to having multiple machines render the same movie in order to save time. One is to copy the entire project and its media to a second computer, set up both machines to render a different Custom segment of time (that you will later splice end to end), and hope you balanced the load evenly between them.

Another approach is to copy your projects and media to more than one machine, but network them and point them at the same folder on one of the machines to render to. Render as a sequence of stills rather than as a movie (discussed later in this chapter in the section *Output Module Settings*) with Skip Existing turned on. Each machine will now look at this one folder, check for the next frame number that does not already exist, create a placeholder for that next frame, and start rendering it. The end result is a nicely load-balanced network render, since each machine can proceed at its own pace and the final render will be built sequentially in one folder without having to marry segments together later. Note that Skip Existing is available only when you render a sequence of stills – it does not work for movies.

This feature is also a good trick to fall back on if your render crashed and you don't want to calculate what time to enter to restart it, or if you (accidentally or intentionally) trashed some already-rendered frames. It just requires that you render a sequence of images, rather than one already-appended movie.

Options

☑ Skip existing files (allows multi-machine rendering)

The Skip Existing Files option is only available if you have set the Output Module's Format popup to render a still image sequence.

FACTOID

No More Overflow

The Use Storage Overflow option has been removed as of After Effects CS5.

XMP Metadata and Markers

As noted on page 699, After Effects now supports reading and writing XMP metadata. One everyday use of this feature is to embed comp and layer markers in the rendered movie so they appear when you reuse the rendered file.

In this chapter's example project, open **[Ex.01]** and examine the markers in its timeline. Press Command+M (Control+M) to add it to the Render Queue. Open its Output Module settings, and enable the option Include Source XMP Metadata. Close the Output Module and render.

When the render is finished, click on the words "Output Module" in the Render Queue and drag to the Project panel – the rendered movie will be imported. Drag this movie to the New Composition icon at the bottom of the Project panel, and observe

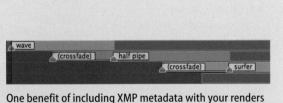

One benefit of including XMP metadata with your renders is that markers from the original composition (above) are saved with the newly rendered movie (below).

that this movie contains all of the comments that were entered in the original comp. (If you do not see these markers, make sure Preferences > Media & Disk Cache > Create Layer Markers from Footage XMP Metadata is enabled, then try again.)

The Output Module Settings dialog is where you decide what to do with your rendered frame: what format to save it in, what to do with the color and alpha channels, whether or not you want audio, and if you need to do any scaling and cropping to the image as it is saved.

AIFF
DPX/Cineon Sequence
F4V
FLV
H.264
H.264 Blu–ray
IFF Sequence
JPEG Sequence
MP3
MPEG2
MPEG2 Blu–ray
MPEG2–DVD
MPEG4
OpenEXR Sequence
PNG Sequence
Photoshop Sequence
• QuickTime
Radiance Sequence
SGI Sequence
TIFF Sequence
Targa Sequence
WAV

Output Module Settings

Now that After Effects has rendered a frame, it has to do something with it – namely, save it. Sounds simple, but there are a number of decisions that have to be made before that happens, such as file format, color depth, whether you want audio and/or video, if you need to do any scaling or cropping to the image, and if you want the finished movie re-imported when it's done or assigned as a proxy for an existing composition. These parameters are set up in the Output Module.

One of the best features in After Effects is that *a single render can have multiple Output Modules*. Every render must have at least one, and it gets one as a default when queued; to add more, select the comp in the Render Queue, then select Composition > Add Output Module. For example, some editing systems require that audio and video be separate; you can render video with one module and audio with the other.

In these cases, you have to render (which is your big time-killer) only once, but multiple output modules can take the render and save it in as many formats as you need. However, since the frame rate and field rendering decisions have already been made in Render Settings, in some cases you may need to render two different versions – for instance, a 720×486 interlaced movie at 29.97 fps would have to be rendered again if you also needed a 320×240 15 fps version without fields.

There is also a Color Management tab in the Output Module Settings. (Color Management was the subject of Chapter 26.) Selecting a Format of DPX/Cineon Sequence automatically opens the Color Management tab, which is where the Cineon Settings button resides.

To change the settings of any of the modules, click on the underlined text to the right of the phrase Output Module in the Render Queue.

Format

After Effects can render to any of a number of formats, which can be self-contained movies (QuickTime for most nonlinear editing systems) or a sequence of still images, one for each frame (SGI RGB or Cineon files for film). You select the basic format here and set its parameters in the Format Options section below. The best format depends completely on where your renders are going when you're done – choose the one preferred by the application that will be reading your files.

Include Project Link

After Effects has the ability to embed into a rendered movie a pointer to the project that created it (referred to as a "link"). When you later import this movie, look at the Import As option at the bottom of the the Import dialog: You can choose whether to import the render or the project. Make sure you regularly Save As, using different names to keep project versions straight (especially whenever you create a new render).

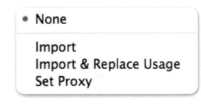

Include Source XMP Metadata

A relatively new feature in After Effects is support for XMP metadata. Footage items with metadata contain information on how the footage was created, copyright ownership, and the like. (To view this, select a Footage item and open Window > Metadata.)

If you enable the Include Source XMP Metadata option when you render a composition, After Effects will add to the resulting movie all of the XMP metadata from the footage items used in that comp, as well as any project-level XMP metadata that exists. Additionally, metadata will be created from the composition and layer markers in the comp, plus from the Comments column in the Timeline panel as well as comments in the Project panel for the footage items used. If you have nested compositions, metadata from those precomps will be copied as well.

Marker Metadata

The next chapter contains an example where marker metadata is saved with a render, and imported with the resulting footage item.

Post-Render Action

This option also appears in the Render Queue panel when you twirl open the Output Module. Normally, you would leave this set to None. If you want to perform a quick confidence check on a file you just rendered, set it to Import: When the render is finished, After Effects will automatically import it. This is handy for checking your renders without leaving the program, but make sure you remove files from the project before archiving if you've trashed them – they'll just create confusion later on.

The other options are a bit more advanced, and occasionally dangerous – for example, Import & Replace Usage replaces all instances of a comp or footage item in the current project with the rendered movie, removing any links to the original item. We prefer to use the Set Proxy option instead as it preserves the existing comp hierarchy and just temporarily (rather than permanently) replaces a precomp with a Comp Proxy (which can be toggled on or off in the Project panel). These options plus advanced rendering in general are explored further in the next two chapters.

Drag to Import

If you forgot to set Post-Render Action to Import, you can drag the Output Module of a finished render to the Project panel. This will import the rendered file.

Video Output

Do you want the visual portion of the render saved with this Output Module? If yes, check this; if you are rendering just the audio portion of a comp, uncheck this. Don't worry about wasting rendering time; After Effects is smart enough to look first if any of the Output Modules have Video Output checked before bothering to render any images.

Constrained Output Formats

Some output formats and codecs (such as DV, HDV, MPEG2-DVD, et cetera) have restrictions as to what frame sizes and/or frame rates they will accept – for example, a DV frame is always either 720×480 or 720×576 pixels.

> Settings mismatch...   Cancel
>
> Warning: Output file will be resized from 872 x 486 (1.00 PAR) to 720 x 480 (1.21 PAR) to meet format constraints.
>
> Warning: Frame rate of output file will be adjusted from 30 to 29.97 fps to meet format constraints. Audio may not synchronize.

If you try to render a composition with incorrect specifications to one of these "constrained" formats without first resolving the differences yourself, After Effects will automatically scale the output and/or conform the frame rate as needed. If the comp's settings do not match the requirements of a constrained format you choose in the Output Module, a small warning icon with the text "Settings mismatch" will appear in the lower left corner of the Output Module. Click on this icon or hover your cursor over it to see a summary of what After Effects is going to do to resolve the issue. Note that (as of After Effects CS5 version 10.0.0) you will *not* see this warning in the Render Queue panel. This is an issue if you choose an Output Module template that would create a mismatch and don't open the Output Module to double-check its settings.

If your comp settings do not match the requirements of a specific codec, you will see a Settings Mismatch warning icon along the bottom of the Output Module dialog. Click on it or hover your cursor over it to read what actions After Effects is going to take to resolve the differences.

Sometimes, this automatic resolution is handy: For example, square pixel widescreen comps will automatically be scaled horizontally to fit the needs of anamorphic widescreen codecs such as DV, HDV, and DVCPRO HD. Other times, this behavior is deadly: For example, field-rendered material may be scaled vertically (a big no-no) to fit the needs of a given codec. So keep an eye out for the Settings Mismatch icon in the Output Module, and try to resolve any mismatches yourself.

TIP

The Lost Render

Twirl open the Output Module's settings in the Render Queue panel, and you will see the directory path for the rendered file. Clicking on it will take you to that folder on your drive and select the file.

Format Options

Depending on what format you chose above, any options it may have can be accessed under this button. If you selected QuickTime movie, the standard QuickTime codec dialog will be opened. Other typical options include bit depth, whether or not to RLE or LZW encode the file to save disk space (check with the people receiving the file to make sure they can read these encodings), and other operating system-specific features (such as PC versus Mac byte order).

Not all formats have Format Options; if they don't, this button is grayed out. The first time you select a Format that has options, After Effects will automatically open its Format Options dialog. From then on, the program remembers your last settings for that format.

Changing the Format Options can automatically change the Channels, Depth, and Color settings that reside elsewhere in this dialog – for example, changing the Format Options for a QuickTime movie to Millions of Color+ will update Channels to RGB + Alpha.

Starting

This parameter appears only if you have selected a format that is a sequence of still images, such as a TIFF sequence. The successive rendered frames will get auto-incremented numbers, starting at the number you enter here. The Use Comp Frame Number will automatically compute the start number for whatever work area you may have set to render.

When you select a format of sequential frames, After Effects will automatically add _[#####] to the name of the file entered. You must have this somewhere in the name and before the file extension in order for frames to be numbered predictably. The pound symbols (#) indicate how many digits you want in the number; the program will automatically pad with leading zeroes. You can remove or add pound symbols if you want. Because After Effects thinks only file extensions should start with a period (.), by default it uses an underscore (_) to separate the number from the rest of the name.

Channels

The Channels, Depth, and Color menus are all somewhat interrelated; together they control which channels (RGB, Alpha, or both) are saved and whether the alpha is straight or premultiplied. If you need to save an alpha channel, select RGB + Alpha, but make sure to select a 32-bit file format in Format Options (QuickTime Animation at Millions of Colors+, for instance). If your nonlinear editing system doesn't support embedded alphas, you will need to use two output modules: One module renders Channel > RGB only with Color set to Straight, and the other renders Channels > Alpha only.

Note that changing the Format Options can result in the Channels setting (as well as Depth and Color) being changed automatically, so verify these settings after you edit Format Options.

Depth

What bit depth of color do you want the file saved at? Different file formats will give you different choices, and setting the Channels will often limit the Depth choices. Usually, you will want Millions (8 bits per channel) or Trillions (16 bits per channel), although you could also specify 256 Grays if you are just creating a matte. If you are also saving an alpha channel, you must choose an option with a + symbol at the end, such as Millions of Colors+ (24-bit color plus an 8-bit alpha).

Only a few formats and codecs support 16 or 32 bit per channel color. If your chosen file format has this capability, the menu items Trillions of Colors or Floating Point will become available (and if an alpha channel is available, you will again see a + symbol at the end). Note that After Effects will not automatically recognize all compatible formats or codecs! If this is the case, your vendor will usually supply instructions on how to modify the Preferences text file to enable this feature.

GOTCHA

Alpha Output

Remember: You must choose a codec or file format that actually supports an alpha channel in order to select Channels > RGB+Alpha.

- **RGB**
  Alpha
  RGB + Alpha

256 Colors
Millions of Colors
Millions of Colors+
- **Trillions of Colors**
Trillions of Colors+
Floating Point
Floating Point+

256 Grays
Floating Point Gray

Straight (Unmatted)
• Premultiplied (Matted)

Hidden Color

Premultiplied alpha channels are multiplied against the comp's background color. If you intend this color to be black, make sure you set Composition > Background Color to black. FLV files are automatically premultiplied with black.

Color

This deceptively named popup does not have color choices. Instead, it determines how the RGB channels should be rendered if there are also transparent areas in the alpha channel. The alpha type choices are Straight (in which the color information extends, full strength, past the edges of the alpha) or Premultiplied (in which the color information extends only as far as the alpha).

If you select Channel > RGB+Alpha, you will normally want the Color menu set to Straight (Unmatted) so that the background color is not premultiplied into the image. If you are rendering Channels > RGB only, be sure to set the Color menu to Premultiplied to composite the color channels over the comp's background color. Be warned that if you change the Format or Format Options, After Effects resets the Color popup to Premultiplied: annoying at best, as most applications prefer Straight alpha channels.

If you select both Channels > RGB and Color > Straight, the Settings Mismatch icon will appear in the lower left corner of the Output Module dialog, suggesting "you should also output an alpha channel to use

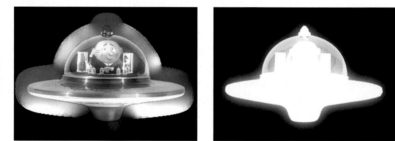

The Channels/Depth/Color menus control which channels are saved and whether the alpha is matted or unmatted. We applied Effect > Stylize > Glow effect to the spaceman, and rendered using the following variations: RGB with alpha premultiplied (left), RGB with straight alpha (center), and alpha channel (right). Spaceman courtesy Classic PIO/Nostalgic Memorabilia.

Stretched Fields

If you selected Field Rendering in the Render Settings, do not ever, ever, *ever* set the Resize Height to anything other than 100%. Doing so would cause the already-interlaced fields to get scrambled between lines, resulting in "field mush."

straight color." Heed this warning – otherwise, your color channels will have an image area extending beyond the alpha area, but you will have no alpha channel to cut it out. The only time you should ignore the warning is if you are outputting the RGB and Alpha channels separately using two Output Modules.

Resize

We're going to treat all the parameters in this section of the Output Module as a whole, since they interact so strongly. This is where you can resize your rendered composition before you save it to disk.

The *Rendering at* line shows the original size of the comp you rendered, factoring in any Resolution reductions you may have selected in the Render Settings. In the *Resize to* section, you can type in the new size you want, larger or smaller than the original. To facilitate typing in numbers, you can check the *Lock Aspect Ratio* box to make sure you don't distort your image, or select a preset size from the popup to the right of these boxes – it contains the same list of sizes as in the Composition Settings dialog. The *Resize %* line underneath shows you how much you stretched by; the *Resize Quality* popup determines how smooth the scaling is (leave this at High for best results, obviously).

Note that changing the size here does not change the size your original comp will be rendered at – by the time the image gets to this setting, it has already been rendered; we're just resizing it here.

Common uses for Resize are to translate between video sizes with different horizontal dimension (for example, squash an 864×486 square-pixel widescreen comp down to a 720×486 anamorphic widescreen NTSC file), or to create a scaled-down proof of a noninterlaced film-size render in a second module.

Crop

In addition to, or as an alternative to, resizing an image is just chopping parts of it off. This is done by the Crop parameters. You can set the number of pixels that get chopped off the Top, Left, Bottom, and Right of the already-rendered image before it is saved to disk. Your final size is updated automatically, as a confidence check that you've entered the right parameters. These are often used in conjunction with Stretch to resize between video standards – for example, resizing and cropping a frame-rendered 720×486 D1 NTSC comp down to 320×240 for the web. There is also a checkbox to automatically crop to a comp's Region of Interest.

A not-so-obvious trick is that you can use negative numbers to pad extra pixels around the image. The added pixels will be black in both the alpha and color channels. This is commonly used for resizing video. For example, you can pad the 480-line NTSC DV format up to 486-line NTSC D1 format by adding two lines above and four lines below; you would do this by cropping Top –4 and Bottom –2.

Audio Output

This section will also be discussed as a group. If you want audio saved with the file, check this option.

Note that some video file formats (such as OMF or the old Media 100) require the audio to be in its own file rather than interleaved with the video; in this case, add a second "Audio Only" output module.

The Format Options change depending on what file format you have chosen. In most cases, you will get the standard system audio options dialog box. Some codecs, such as MP3, have additional settings.

Odd Lines Flip Fields

If you are cropping lines from the top or bottom of an already-interlaced render, be careful: Even numbers of lines keep the same field order, where odd numbers of lines reverse the field order. For example, if you rendered a 720×486 composition Lower Field First and are saving the file to the DV 720×480 lower field first standard, don't crop three lines off the top and bottom – crop four off the top and two off the bottom. (A PDF of common cropping sizes is included with Chapter 41.)

Audio Tips

QuickTime interleaves audio and video into the same stream. How often a chunk of audio is stored is set by the Audio Block Duration parameter inside Preferences > Output. The default of one second works well. If the block size is longer than the movie, all the audio will be stored first in the file – good for some multimedia applications.

If any of your sources have a different sample rate than your planned output, or if you have time stretched any layers with audio, render at Best Quality to improve how After Effects sample rate converts the files. For the absolute highest audio quality, perform this processing in a dedicated audio program.

TIP

Duplicating Queued Items

To rerender a comp, or duplicate an already-queued item, select it and press Command+D (Control+D) to duplicate it, using the default name. Command+Shift+D (Control+Shift+D) duplicates the render item, using the Output To name you gave it.

After Effects provides a long list of common sample rates; choose the one that matches your desired target system – typically 44.100 or 48.000 kHz for higher-end video. Available bit depths are 8, 16, and 32 bit. Almost no one uses 8 bit anymore because of its high levels of quantization distortion; 32 bit is overkill for video delivery and is usually just used during audio production. After Effects does not support the special 32 kHz 12-bit format used by consumer DV.

You can select Stereo or Mono. All of the audio tracks inside After Effects are inherently stereo; mono sources are automatically converted to stereo, centered in their pan position. If combined to mono, the levels of the left and right channel are scaled by 50% before mixing down to one, in order to avoid potential clipping. This may result in a slight perceived loss of volume. After Effects does not directly support the "dual mono" format used by some systems.

In the past, you could run into trouble if you rendered audio and video together to the same file while Preferences > Output > Segment Movie Files was enabled. If the Audio Block Duration (see *Audio Tips*, left) did not match the segment lengths, movies could be padded out with white frames to fill the rest of the audio block. As a result, After Effects no longer allows you to segment files that have both audio and video. Instead, use one Output Module just for video, and a second just for audio.

The Render Queue Panel

Now that we've covered what goes on when After Effects renders, and the parameters you can set to customize the rendering process, let's talk about managing renders in the Render Queue panel.

As alluded to earlier, a single queued composition may have multiple Output Modules: just click the + button to the left of the Output To line to add more. This comes in handy (and saves a lot of rendering time) when you need to deliver multiple formats, or want to try several different render quality settings to see which yields the best results.

You can queue up as many compositions as you want to render. They will be rendered in top-to-bottom order in the queue. To reorder items in the queue, grab them by their comp names and drag them up and down the list, but you must do this before you start rendering the first item. You can twirl down the Render Settings and Output Module displays to check their settings before you render, as well as during rendering.

There is a bar of column headers between the render details portion of the panel above and the queued renders below. Most of the fields can be reordered by dragging, as well as resized, just as panels in the Project and Timeline panels can. Right-clicking on these panels allows you to hide some or reveal an additional Comments panel (useful for handing a project over to someone else to render).

After Effects will render only the comps that have a check in the box in the Render column and a legal name (if the name is in italics, click on it and enter a name and destination). Only items that are "Queued" in the Status column will be rendered when you click the Render button.

After a render finishes, the Status will change to either Done, User Stopped (if you clicked on Stop before it was finished), Unqueued (if you stop an item with multiple Output Modules), or Failed (if a problem arose during rendering). In any of these states, you can still twirl down the settings sections, although you can no longer edit them. A render item remains in the queue until you select and delete it.

If a render did not finish successfully, an unqueued copy of it will be made and appended to the end of the Render Queue. If it was stopped by you, its Time Span (in Render Settings) will be automatically updated to cover the unrendered portion; if you held down the Option (Alt) key when you stopped it, then the original Time Span will be used. If the render failed, you can't count on the Time Span being correct; check it before proceeding. These partial renders will not be appended onto the end of the previous file (unless it was a sequence of numbered stills); enter a new name before rendering the remainder.

When a render fails, you may prefer to rerender the entire composition – not just the unfinished portion. To do so, select the original queued item and type Command+Shift+D (Control+Shift+D) to duplicate it while keeping its original name. It will now overwrite the original render.

Render Progress

While After Effects is rendering a composition, it keeps you informed about its progress. Twirl down the Current Render Details section of the panel to see which step of which layer of which comp After Effects is currently on, plus how long each frame took. This is a good way to see if a particular layer or effect is bogging things down. Be warned that the Estimated Time Remaining is a best guess and is based only on the average time previous frames took to render multiplied by how many frames remain to be processed. If the layers and effects are fairly balanced from start to finish in your animation, this estimate is pretty accurate.

If you have multiprocessor rendering enabled (in Preferences > Memory & Multiprocessing), there will be a pause before a comp starts to render as the project data is copied to the additional instances of After Effects. If your comps are very short on average, it may be faster to disable multiprocessing – otherwise, it's a great help.

The Current Render bar shows you how far along the current render you are. When it's done (or if the current render fails), After Effects will automatically start the next render in the queue. When all queued renders are finished, you will hear a chime. To be safe (in the event an error occurred while you had your back turned), always check the individual comps' Status and the Message bar along the top

The Current Render Details also tracks file sizes and free disk space, so you can tell ahead of time if you're going to run out of room. This section does take time to update during a render, slowing things down a bit; twirl it back up when you are done watching the paint dry, or it will automatically twirl back up after a certain period of time. If you don't want it to time-out in this way, press Option (Alt) when you twirl it down.

TIP

Stop Press!

When a render is in progress, Option+click (Alt+click) on the Stop button to stop the render and leave the original Time Span settings in place.

The Render Log

- Errors Only
  Plus Settings
  Plus Per Frame Info

After Effects can create a text log file of how your rendering progressed. What is saved is set by the Log popup in the Render Queue.

The default is Errors Only, which creates a document only when something goes wrong. If you render more than one item, After Effects will also create a log file explaining when each started and ended. These logs are in a folder alongside the project.

If you select Plus Settings, this log file will contain all of the parameters in the Render Settings and the Output module(s). The Plus Per Frame Info selection saves the render settings, as well as how long each single frame took to render. This allows you to go back later and see if there was a particular stretch of frames that was killing your overall render time, but this information is overkill for most cases.

Memory Loss

Templates are stored in the Preferences file on your drive; creating new prefs deletes them.

Creating and Editing Templates

Render Settings and Output Modules contain a large number of parameters to set every time you render. Fortunately, you can create as many preset templates as you like for both and assign them to any item in the Render Queue. Both are accessed under the menu item Edit > Templates. If you disagree with the templates, go ahead and edit them. For example, we usually change any of the templates that save an alpha channel to create a straight rather than premultiplied alpha.

In the Edit > Templates > Render Settings Template dialog you can create templates and choose which ones are used as defaults. Note that there are separate defaults for saving a movie versus saving a frame, as well as RAM Previews, prerenders, and proxies.

Creating a useful set of templates is another way to streamline your After Effects workflow. We suggest you create templates for each of the codecs you regularly render to, as well as your preferred data rates for web video. This will save time (as well as reduce mistakes) when it comes time to render.

The Render Settings templates and Output Modules templates behave pretty much the same. They are both just copies of the parameters you would normally set in their respective dialogs. The Output Module templates even remember the Format Options settings, including file encoding for stills and codecs, quality settings, and codec data rates for QuickTime movies. The differences are that you can create and edit them without having a composition in the Render Queue. You can then give them names, and save them for later use. To change their settings, open them from the Edit > Templates menu and click on New or Edit; you will get the same editing dialog as if you had a composition in the Render Queue. The current templates are selected by a popup in their respective dialogs; select one to see its settings, duplicate it, or edit it.

Very handy is the ability to set the template Defaults: the template that will be used whenever you add a still or movie to the Render Queue, or ask for a RAM Preview to be saved to disk. There are also templates for creating prerenders and proxies. Be aware that changing the default template does not change the settings for any currently queued items!

Using Templates

After templates are created, they are selected in the Render Queue by using the menus that appear directly to the right of the Render Settings and Output Module titles for a queued item. Templates are automatically sorted by name in alphabetical order.

Edit > Templates > Output Module Templates has separate defaults for saving a movie versus saving a frame, as well as for RAM Previews, prerenders, and proxies.

Once in the Render Queue, you can still pick another template from the menu (the current Default is at the top of the list), edit the current template for this one instance (either by clicking on the template name or choosing Custom from the list of available templates), or save current settings you may have just created as a new template (the Make Template choice at the bottom of the popup).

Holding down Command (Control) while you select a new Render Settings or Output Module template will automatically change the default to the selected template, which saves a trip to the Edit menu. You can also change multiple comps in the Render Queue to the same Render Settings at the same time: Command+click (Control+click) or Shift+click on their names to select them, and pick a new template; all selected comps not already rendered will now use this template. To change multiple items to have the same Output Module template, select them by clicking on the words "Output Module" in the Render Queue, not the comp names themselves.

Template sets can be saved to disk or loaded from previously saved files. Note that Load is actually a merge; all of your current templates plus the templates you loaded will appear in the list. If there are templates with the same name, After Effects will give you a warning message and not load these duplicates.

We depend on a variety of templates: The Render Settings templates are set up for rendering proofs or final renders, field rendered or not, work area or length of comp. The Output Module templates are even more numerous, and take into account many different hardware devices and video formats we might output to and need to convert between.

Pressing Command (Control) while selecting a template will make it the default for the next time you add a comp to the Render Queue.

CONNECT

RAM Preview: Chapter 2.

Motion blur: Chapter 8.

Frame blending: Chapter 28.

Working with audio: Chapter 36.

Alpha channels: Chapter 38.

Field rendering and 3:2 pulldown: Chapter 41.

Advanced rendering: Chapter 43.

Proxies: Chapter 44.

43

Advanced Rendering

Network rendering and project management features.

When projects get big, you need help. That help may come in the form of cleaning up your project by removing duplicate or unused sources. Or stripping out everything except what is needed for selected comps so you can pass a portion of your project onto another artist. Or collecting all of your source footage to one folder for backup or transport. Or even enlisting the aid of multiple copies of After Effects to help you render a particularly intensive comp.

After Effects can provide all of these forms of help, and we'll review them in this chapter. We're going to start with general file management issues, then proceed to the ability to distribute a render across processors as well as a network of machines. We'll also touch on saving XMP metadata along with your render.

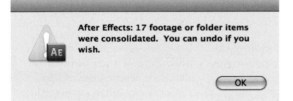

Consolidate All Footage removes duplicate sources in a project and relinks comps to use the consolidated sources that remain.

Streamlining Projects

After Effects offers several options under the File menu to help you reduce the clutter in a project:

Consolidate All Footage looks for duplicates of footage in a project, and removes the duplicates. If a comp used one of the duplicates, these layers will be relinked to use the single copy of the footage item that remains. This feature comes in handy when you've imported multiple projects or folders or source materials, and there are overlaps in the sources. (Note that if footage doesn't consolidate, chances are that the interpret footage settings are set differently for each item.)

Remove Unused Footage looks for source items that are not used by any of the comps in your project and deletes them. This is particularly helpful when you've imported a large number of source files early on during a job while you were still deciding which sources to use, and now want to reduce a project down to the sources actually used.

Reduce Project looks at the comps you have selected in the Project panel, keeps these comps, any precomps and source material used by those comps, then deletes the unselected comps and all other unused footage. This is good for reducing a complex project just to the comp or comps a coworker may need to work on. The one occasion when this function can trip you up is if an expression in a comp you kept referenced a comp you did not select before running Reduce Project: The referenced comp will still get deleted.

All of these commands exist under the File menu. Fortunately, all can be undone. Still, it is a good idea to save your project to a new name *before* performing one of these commands, in the event you accidentally selected Save instead of Save As.

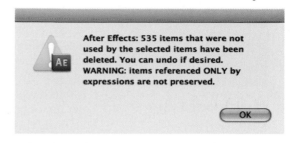

Reduce Project keeps only the comps you selected in the Project panel along with any sources used by those comps.

Collect Files

The File > Collect Files command has several uses. One is to take a project that may reference source items spread out across several folders and drives, and consolidate all of this footage into a single new folder, complete with a new copy of the project file that links to these copied sources. This is handy for archiving, or moving a job and all of its assets to another computer. Note that in the Collect Files dialog, the Collect Source Files popup has options to either collect just the sources used in the project (akin to running Remove Unused Footage, mentioned above), or copy all sources whether or not a comp currently uses them.

Another way to use Collect Files is as a variation on the Reduce Project command discussed above. First, you select the comps you want to collect, then select File > Collect Files. Set the Collect Source Files popup to For Selected Comps, and click Collect. Rather than delete the unused comps and sources from your project (which is what Reduce Project will do), all of the comps and source files referenced are left in the current project, and only the sources used by the selected comps will be copied to their new location.

A third use for Collect Files is to set up a multimachine network render, which we'll discuss later in this chapter.

Be aware that Collect Files does not collect everything you need to recreate a project: Fonts, effects, and codecs are *not* copied. Instead, Collect Files creates a text file named **xxxReport.txt** (xxx is the name of your project) that gives you statistics on which files are used by the current project or the selected comps in that project, plus a list of fonts and effects used. If you are archiving a project, or moving it to another machine, it is up to you to make sure a copy of the fonts and effects you need make the trip as well. Note that you can also add your own hints, reminders, and comments to the Report file; just click on the Comments button in the Collect Files dialog before collecting.

Collect Files allows you to be selective in deciding how much source footage you want to copy to a new location. A Report file is also generated listing the fonts and effects used.

Back to the Future

When backing up a major project, create a simple text file (or use the Comments option in Collect Files) to annotate what version of the program created the project, as well as the version number of any critical third-party plug-ins.

Multiprocessor Rendering

Before you resort to network rendering, make sure you are taking full advantage of your existing single computer. If your machine has multiple processors or cores, try enabling Preferences > Multiprocessing > Render Multiple Frames Simultaneously. After Effects will launch clones of itself in the background to speed up RAM previews as well as renders, in essence executing a network render on one computer without any additional work on your part. There are two catches: There will be a delay the first time you render as After Effects launches these additional copies, and you will need lots of RAM to take advantage of this feature – at least one gig per CPU, and preferably more.

Also less than obvious are the various proxy options. Proxies are discussed in the next chapter, but to summarize: If you are using proxies as low-resolution or still-image placeholders, definitely disable the Obey Proxy Settings option when you're collecting. This way, both the original sources and their proxies will be copied. However, if you prerendered some comps and set proxies, and are now collecting files simply to render on a separate machine, you might consider checking Obey Proxy Settings. This will copy the currently enabled proxies, but *not* the source material used in the comps that the proxies are standing in for. This means fewer files will be collected, but you won't be able to turn off the proxy later, as the sources that created it would not have been copied.

Network Rendering

"Network" or "distributed" rendering can be as simple as setting up a second computer to render a project while you continue to work, or as advanced as having a render farm of multiple machines all pitch in. The network can be as simple as wired local ethernet, or even encompass the internet (for example, using the *Dropbox.com* file sharing service).

First, an overview: To set up a distributed render you need a copy of After Effects installed on each computer you want to enlist as a render slave. If you don't have enough activations (the limit is two per serial number), perform a normal install, but don't activate the copy. Launch these activation-less copies using the **After Effects Render Engine** shortcut in the **Adobe After Effects CS5** folder. You will also need a central "Watch Folder" that the render slaves can look at.

At your main computer, queue up the comp you need rendered. Save your project, and then use the Collect Files feature to place a copy of this project and its source materials in the Watch Folder and to create a **Render Control File**: This tells the slaves the status of the project (in other words, whether it has already been rendered).

If you select an output format of a sequence of still images, multiple computers can work on the same comp, each taking a different frame to work on. If you render to a movie-based format, only one computer can work on a comp, because there is no easy way for multiple computers to insert frames into the middle of a movie file. Only one computer can work on an individual frame.

Cloning

As mentioned, Collect Files does not copy fonts, effects, or codecs. Therefore, you need to make sure matching sets of fonts and effects are installed on your render slaves, as well as any codec your files may be compressed with or that you want to write to. If a particular effect needs a hardware key or is serialized to a single machine, you may need multiple keys; some vendors supply render-only versions of their plug-ins. Otherwise, prerender those sections (discussed in the next chapter) so that you no longer rely on these effects.

Setting Up a Distributed Render

Create a folder that will act as Grand Central Station for your distributed render, and mount it on the computers that will be using it. This is referred to as your Watch Folder. In the slave copies of After Effects, choose File > Watch Folder and select this folder. The slave copies will close any open projects, and start checking the Watch Folder every ten seconds for new or updated Render Control Files.

Next is queuing up a comp to render. When you're network rendering, there are a couple of settings you need to pay additional attention to. If you want more than one render slave to work on the same composition, in Output Settings you must choose an output file format that is a sequence of still images. Once you have set this up, go to the Render Settings and enable "Skip existing files" in the Options box at the bottom. This prevents multiple computers from trying to render the same frame – they will look to see which frames have already been rendered, and start on the next one that hasn't been rendered. After Effects provides Multi-Machine templates for the Render Settings and Output Module that set this up for you; change the Format in the Output Module to the file type you prefer.

Rendering comps as a sequence of stills may not be optimal for your situation if, for example, you require an embedded audio track or you need to re-import the files into an editing system that does not support sequences. Options include rerendering the sequence as a movie (discussed later), or breaking a longer render into segments. This will allow the job to get distributed while still writing movies, and it is a good practice even with a single machine so that one bad disk sector does not trash many minutes worth of frames.

Next, you need to decide where the rendered files are written to. This must be a shared disk or folder so all the slaves can access it as well. Either mount the

When a render slave has been assigned a File > Watch Folder, it will look inside it every ten seconds for a new Render Control File.

To have more than one computer work on the same comp, render to a sequence of stills, and enable "Skip existing files" in the Render Settings.

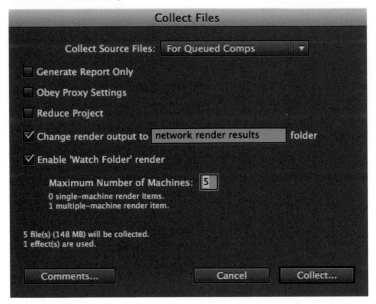

To Collect Files for a distributed render, make sure you check the option Enable "Watch Folder" render. For efficiency, collect sources just For Queued Comps; for safety, check the option "Change render output to".

Nucleo Pro

An alternative to multiprocessor and network rendering is to use GridIron Software's Nucleo Pro plug-in. It also optimizes use of multiple processors and cores, plus it offers unique features such as "speculative rendering" and a background render queue where Nucleo renders comps while you continue working.

shared drive and aim the Output To pointer in the Output Module to a sub-folder in this shared folder or drive, or enable the option "Change render output to" in the Collect Files dialog, which creates a subfolder inside the one used for your collected project. We prefer the latter approach, as it creates a new folder with each render; this eliminates potential confusion with overwriting or skipping an already-rendered version of the project.

Speaking of File > Collect Files, this is your next step. Check the option Enable "Watch Folder" render; this is what writes the all-important Render Control File. To save on the amount of data that is collected, select For Queued Comps in the Collect Source Files popup. Then click Collect. You will be prompted to choose where to write the collected files; choose your Watch Folder. Note that Collect Files will not allow you to overwrite folders; you must give each collect-ed project a new name. After Effects will then write the sources, project, and **Render Control File** into this folder.

When the slave renderers check the Watch Folder and find a **Render Control File** that points to a comp that has not yet been rendered, they will open the collected project and start rendering it. Each slave renderer also updates an HTML file in the Watch Folder called **watch_folder.html** which details its history and progress – open this in any web browser to check its status or perhaps to see why a render failed.

Although there is a Maximum Number of Machines parameter, there is no limit to the number of machines that can pitch in on a network ren-der; the bottleneck tends to be network activity as multiple machines work on the same project.

Recovering from Failure

Once a render engine records a failure (such as from a missing file), the entire project will be tagged as failed. This means that none of the render engines will start work on the remaining queued items. If one machine has already started to render an item and a second machine gets an error, the currently rendering item will finish rendering, but subsequent items won't. Open the HTML log file created to see what went wrong and fix it – these problems unfortunately don't disappear on their own.

Your collected project has not been damaged or changed; however, its Render Control File now thinks there's a problem with it and won't allow it to be rendered. To start rendering a previously collected project that didn't complete rendering:

Step 1: Open the copied project (*not* the original!).

Step 2: Select File > Collect Files with the Collect Source Files popup set to None.

Step 3: Save the new project; this will create a new collect folder.

This process allows you to create a new project with the path to already collected source files intact. You should delete all partially rendered files to remove any potential confusion as to which files are the "real" ones.

It is not uncommon to need to render a project again, perhaps to accommodate a client correction. If you had to copy a large amount of source material to the Watch Folder, you may understandably want to avoid doing this again. Just collecting files again will either copy all of the sources again, or create a project that doesn't point to the old sources. Users have come up with different techniques to hack the Render Control File to force a rerender; sometimes they just manually reload the render on the slave machines. Here's the technique we suggest for rerendering a project without having to recopy the sources:

Step 1: Collect Files – sources included – to a shared folder, *without* checking the Enable "Watch Folder" render option.

Step 2: Then Collect Files to the Watch Folder with Collect Source Files set to None (Project only) and with Enable "Watch Folder" render checked.

Step 3: If you need to rerender, repeat Step 2.

TIP

The Watch Project

If you open an After Effects project file named **Watch This Folder.aep**, it will automatically launch After Effects into Watch Folder mode, looking at the folder this project was in. Place an alias of this project file in the **Startup** folder, and your render slaves will automatically start up in Watch Folder mode.

Name Templates

After Effects offers the ability to use a file name template when you're naming a render. This helps you keep your renders organized, particularly when you will be handing them off to another person. You may select a new file name template from a popup menu in the Render Queue's Output Module section – look between the words Output To: and the file name. Selecting a new template automatically renames your render.

Adobe provides a number of useful templates, many of which are based on the Comp's name (which in turn relies on you giving your comps meaningful names – no more Comp 1, Comp 2, et cetera). You can also create your own templates: Select Custom from the popup, string together whatever properties you want (such as frame number or field order) from the popup menu next to the Template dialog, and add your own characters (such as underscores) between these properties.

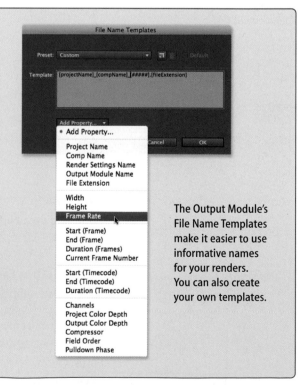

The Output Module's File Name Templates make it easier to use informative names for your renders. You can also create your own templates.

Render Scripts

Scripting – discussed in Bonus Chapter 37C on this book's DVD – may be used to extend the rendering options After Effects offers. For example, After Effects ships with a script that can send a brief email letting you – or a coworker, or client – know when a render is finished. Here are the steps:

- Queue up your comps to render.

- Enable Preferences > General > Allow Scripts to Write Files and Access Network (you need to do this only once).

- Select File > Scripts > Render and Email.jsx. The first time you run this script, it will guide you through the process of setting up your email. You need to know the address of your outgoing email SMTP server and log-in information required by that server (such as log-in ID and password), the email address you wish to use as the "reply to" address, and the email address you wish to send the notice to.

Once this above information is entered, selecting the script will start the queued renders, and – after a slight pause – send the requested email when finished.

To change the email settings, select File > Scripts > Run Script File, and navigate to the After Effects application folder. (On Windows, you will then need to open the Support Files folder.) Choose Scripts > (support) > Change Email Settings, and go through the setup procedure again.

Other useful rendering scripts created by After Effects users include:

Background Renderer *(aescripts.com/bg-renderer/)*: This much-loved script by Lloyd Alvarez will render already-queued comps in the background so you can keep working.

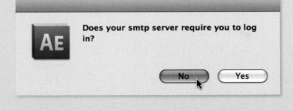

Before attempting to run the Render and Email.jsx script, enable the General > Preference that allows scripts to access the network (top), and have your SMTP email server and login information handy (above).

If you regularly check email on the same computer, chances are you'll already be logged in when After Effects tries to send email, meaning you can answer "no" when asked if your server requires you to log in (below).

Render Layers *(www.redefinery.com/ae/view.php?item=rd_RenderLayers)*: This script by Jeff Almasol renders selected layers in a comp individually.

Render Multiple Sections *(www.crgreen.com/aescripts/)*: This script by Christopher Green will queue multiple "work areas" to render based on the span of Guide Layers.

Converting Sequences to Movies

Network rendering is most efficient when you render to a file sequence with Skip Existing enabled. However, most editing systems prefer to import movies instead of sequences, with a codec matching their timeline and perhaps with any audio already embedded. You can automate this by taking advantage of Proxies, which are discussed in the next chapter. But as long as you're here, we'll give you the formula for how to pull this off.

Take your "final" comp – the one you plan to queue up for network rendering – and drag it to the New Comp icon at the bottom of the Project panel. This nests it into a new comp that has the same dimensions and duration. If your final comp had audio, add a copy of this audio to your new "convert to movie" comp as well. Give these two comps unique names to help distinguish them from each other.

Add your final render comp to the Render Queue first. In its Output Module, make sure you set the Format to your preferred still image sequence format and set the Post-Render Action popup to Set Proxy. (Don't forget to go back to the Render Settings and enable Skip Existing Files!) Then add your "convert to movie" comp to the Render Queue. Set its Output Module to your desired movie format, such as QuickTime, AVI, Windows Media, or Adobe Flash Video.

When you network render this project, your original "final" comp will render first, being worked on by all available render slaves to speed things up. After it is done, the still image sequence that was created will be assigned as a proxy for this comp. This proxy will be used in the next comp, which will then be processed by the next render slave that's free to create your movie. (Remember: Still images don't contain audio; this is why you had to include a copy of your audio in the second comp.)

Another time-saving trick involves a similar workflow: If you have a render-intensive background or animation that is used as a precomp in several other comps, first queue the precomp to render, then use Post-Render Action > Set Proxy to assign the result as a proxy for itself. The remaining comps will use the proxy movie, speeding their own renders.

When you set up the first comp to be network rendered as an image sequence, set the Post-Render Action to Set Proxy. This way, the already-rendered proxy will be used by the next comp, which will then take much less time to render the final movie.

Merging Projects for Render

If you import a project (File > Import > Project), not only will it add all the comps and source material to the current project, it will also merge all of the items in the imported project's Render Queue into the current project's queue.

If we are working with several different project files but want to render them as a batch, we'll set up their respective Render Queues the way we want, create a new project, import all the projects we want to render, open the Render Queue, and click Render to do the entire batch.

CONNECT

RAM Previewing: *Preview Possibilities* sidebar at the end of Chapter 2.

Layer and comp markers: Chapter 6

Video luminance ranges: Chapter 26.

Render queue and output module settings: Chapter 42.

Proxies and prerendering: Chapter 44.

Prerendering and Proxies

Planning ahead can save time later.

One of After Effects' strengths is that you don't have to pre-render anything: All of your sources, layers, and manipulations are "live" all the time, allowing you to make unlimited changes. However, calculating everything all the time can slow down both your work and your final render. Newer versions of After Effects have gotten much better about internally caching the results of comps and frames it calculates (especially if you enable Preferences > Memory & Cache > Enable Disk Cache), but you will still find yourself spending a lot of time waiting.

In this chapter, we'll explain how prerendering complex comps can speed up your workflow, and using proxies for footage and comps can streamline that process further. Then we'll work through an example so you can see this in action.

Prerendering

Prerendering is the practice of creating a movie or still of an intermediate composition, or one that you intend to reuse as an element. You then swap this rendered movie into a project in place of the comp that created it. The reason is you save processing time while you're working, as well as rendering time later on. You can create prerenders for various reasons and purposes, but you should be clear on whether the prerendered element is temporary, or whether it could be used to speed up the final render:

• When you're satisfied that a precomp is final, you could render it at this point to save processing time later. This really adds up if it is nested multiple times, or if you expect to be rendering a lot of proofs. This precomp might contain, say, a stack of background movie layers with blending modes, masks, and blurs; when it's nested it might be colorized or manipulated further, but the basic precomp design is locked down. Or, you may have spent a lot of time keying some footage, and now you're done – you don't need to keep rerendering the key. Once you've prerendered this comp and swapped in the resulting movie, only one movie needs to be retrieved and no further processing is needed. If you're prerendering a logo or element that will be manipulated further in other comps, be sure to save the prerender with an alpha channel.

TIP

Temporary Freeze

If you don't have time to prerender a slow precomp that's not changing much, find a representative frame and use Time > Layer > Freeze Frame. This will use Time Remapping to pause on the selected frame, while all of your other effects and transforms applied to the layer continue to work. Just don't forget to disable Time Remapping before you render!

Example Project

Explore the 44-Example Project.aep file as you read this chapter; references to [Ex.##] refer to specific compositions within the project file.

• You might have one layer that has a very slow effect applied (such as a particle system or a large radial blur). Prerender this one layer, with an alpha channel if needed, and re-import the movie. Turn off the original layer (don't delete it), and use the prerendered layer instead.

• Optical Flow effects such as RE:Vision's Twixtor or the built-in Pixel Motion (Chapter 28) are notoriously slow. The powerful 3D warping and displacement effect FreeForm (Chapter 16) is also render-intensive. These are prime candidates to prerender, both to get client approval and to replace slow comps.

In all cases, you can import the prerendered element normally and use the prerender in place of the original. To swap in the prerender where the original comp was nested, use Replace Source (covered in Chapter 6). However, there is a slicker way to manage these stand-ins: Proxies.

Proxies

A *proxy* is a file that is designed to stand in for a footage item or an entire composition. It can be used temporarily to speed up editing, or as part of the final render. This is particularly becoming an issue with new cameras which can shoot frames that are 4096 pixels wide or larger.

It is easy to turn proxies on or off on an individual basis, or on a project-wide basis when you render. After Effects will also automatically scale a lower resolution proxy to match the size of the footage or comp it is standing in for. When it comes time to archive the project, you can trash the proxies without ruining your hierarchy – just remove the proxies to return the project to its original structure.

There are several situations where we use proxies, some of which are the same as the reasons we create prerenders:

• Prerender a composition, to save time during both working and rendering. This prerender is created at the full size of the composition, interlaced if necessary, and referred to as a *Comp Proxy*.

• Prerender a still of a comp, to save time while you're working. This is also considered a Comp Proxy, though you would not use it during final render.

• Create reduced resolution versions of movies, to save time while working; these are referred to as *Footage Proxies*. You can prerender footage proxies in After Effects or another program, taking care that they are the same length as the original movie. The original footage would be used during final rendering. Creating smaller-sized versions of movies is recommended only when the original footage is at hi-def or film resolution, where the savings would be significant. Otherwise, the comp's Resolution setting is designed to drop all footage to Half or Quarter Resolution on the fly.

• If you have an extremely large background still image that's slowing you down, create a low-res proxy for just the background layer (for example, open a hi-res image in Photoshop, scale to 25%, and save under a new name). Now you can work at Full Resolution to design the foreground layers, while the background layer alone is at "quarter resolution."

High Quality Prerenders

If you prerender elements that will later be used in the final render, you do not want to lose any image quality in the process. For video work, many have been happy with Apple's ProRes codecs (installed with Final Cut Studio). For the highest in both quality and compatibility, consider using image sequences of PNG or ProEXR format files, which are good for 16 and 32 bit per channel projects, respectively.

If you are creating field rendered materials, consider rendering your proxies at double the frame rate (for example, 59.94 frames per second for NTSC). This way, you'll have the extra visual information you need when you transform later. If you are prerendering a full-frame layer that will not be scaled or animated further, and your output will be field rendered, you can safely field render the prerender; there is no point in rendering and saving more data than you need.

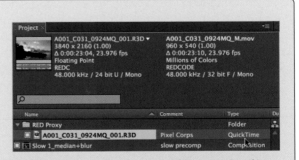

After you have assigned a proxy, a white box (the proxy on/off switch) appears to its left, and two sets of information appear overhead – the right one is for the proxy. The item whose name is in bold is the one that's active.

Layer Proxies

After Effects cannot create or assign a proxy for a single layer in a comp – proxies apply to entire compositions only.

Applying Proxies

After you have prerendered your proxy, in the Project panel select the footage item or composition it is supposed to stand in for, select File > Set Proxy > File, and locate your proxy file. Two things will change in the Project panel: A white box will appear next to the comp or footage item in the list, and when you select this item, two sets of information will appear along the top of the panel. The left one is for the original file/composition; the one on the right is for your proxy. (You may need to widen or scroll the Project panel to see both.)

If you rendered the full length of a selected comp to create its proxy, their size and duration will match. If the proxy's size was smaller, After Effects would automatically scale it up so it appears to be the same size as the original. If you need to change any of the Interpret Footage settings for the proxy (for example, to separate its fields or set it to loop), select File > Interpret Footage > Proxy.

The white box next to the item is the Proxy Switch. Click on it to toggle usage of the proxy off and on. The current status is echoed in the top of the Project panel: The source being used – original file/comp or proxy – will have its name in bold. To change the proxy file, use Set Proxy again; don't use File > Replace Footage. To remove a proxy, use File > Set Proxy > None. When it comes time to render, the Proxy Use menu in the Render Settings determines whether proxies are rendered at their current settings, globally turned on or off, or set to render Comp Proxies only.

RED Proxies

The RED camera creates its own .R3D format raw files, as well as a set of QuickTime movie proxies at full, half, quarter, and eighth resolution that are calculated from the .R3D file. To take advantage of these in After Effects, first you must install the RED QuickTime codec (download it from *www.red.com/support;* currently only a Mac version is available).

Then in this chapter's example project, twirl open the **RED Proxy** folder, and double-click **A001_C031_0924MQ_001.R3D** to open it in the Footage panel. Set Magnification to 25%, and press the spacebar to get a feel for how slow it is to load and play.

Return to the Project panel, and with the original RED clip still selected choose File > Set Proxy > File. Navigate to **44_Chapter Sources > RED Footage** and select **A001_C031_0924MQ_M.mov.**

The RED Camera creates its own QuickTime proxies of its captures. You may use these to speed up your work in After Effects. Footage courtesy Pixel Corps.

Return to the Footage panel and attempt to play the clip: You won't get realtime playback (it is still being calculated from a 3840-pixel-wide file), but it will be much more responsive. Toggle the proxy on and off, or experiment with the other resolutions.

Proxy Behavior

When a proxy is assigned to a footage item or comp, it is as if you replaced that item. The exception is that low-res proxies will be scaled to the original dimensions of the item they are standing in for. Low-res proxies may look a bit pixelated, but the autoscale feature has a great advantage in that all your transformations and effects settings will work the same for the proxy as for the original file. If you had simply replaced the file with a smaller one, this would not be the case as you would have had to scale up the stand-in (perhaps in a precomp) to match the original's size.

When a proxy is used for a comp, stepping through time in the comp steps through the prerendered proxy. Editing layers in the comp the proxy is applied to will not change what you see in the Comp panel, which can be disconcerting. A red bar across the bottom of the Comp panel tips you off that you are viewing a proxy, not the comp's contents. Of course, further comps that use this comp won't care if the layer they are accessing is a comp or a prerendered image or movie, and navigating higher up the chain will be much faster.

You can, of course, turn off the proxy in the Project panel, which will now make the comp "live" again. Make your changes, and observe the effects downstream in the comps that use this comp. If you prefer your new variation, render a new proxy and swap it in, or simply remove the proxy and work normally.

Working with Proxies

Let's get some practice creating and using proxies. We'll take advantage of the Post-Render Action option in the Output Module Settings. Originally mentioned in Chapter 42, these make creating prerenders and proxies much easier.

Open the project file **44-Example Project.aep** that goes with this chapter. It contains a chain of three comps that nest into each other. Open Preferences > Display, and enable Show Rendering Progress in Info panel. Then make sure the Info panel is visible; if not, select Window > Info Panel and position its panel where you can see it.

Open [**Slow 3_final composite**] and move the current time indicator around, or attempt to preview the comp. Notice how slow the Comp panel updates, particularly closer to the start of the comp. If no frames have been cached yet, the Info panel will tell you that the Median effect in [**Slow 1_radial blur**] is the culprit.

(If you've already cached a preview, use Edit > Purge > All to clear any cached frames.)

Archiving Proxies

Because proxies are just stand-ins, you could archive your project without saving the proxies.

Drafty Proxies

You can also select a comp in the Project panel and use the menu command File > Create Proxy, which will automatically set the Post-Render Action option to Set Proxy. However, the default Render Settings for proxies is the Draft Settings template; change this default under Edit > Templates > Render Settings to Best Settings.

TIP

Nucleo Pro

GridIron Software's Nucleo Pro takes prerendering to the next level, offering options to create proxies for selected layers and to "speculatively" create RAM Previews or final renders.

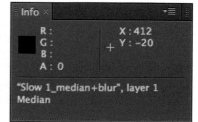

When Preferences > Display > Show Rendering Progress option is enabled, the Info panel lets you know what's taking so long as you move from frame to frame. Here, the Median effect is causing the delay. Images from Digital Vision/Inner Gaze plus Getty Images.

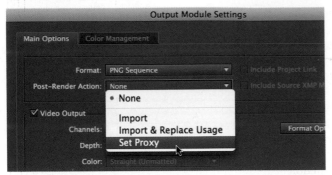

Set the Post-Render Action popup in the Output Module Settings (above). Using Set Proxy means After Effects will automatically assign the rendered file as a proxy for the comp you are rendering. You can also access these options by twirling open the Output Module in the Render Queue (below), which has the added feature of allowing you to pick whip to another footage item or comp in the Project panel to assign this proxy to.

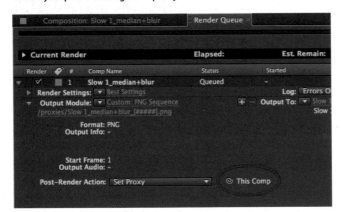

Collapsing and Proxies

The one instance where behavior of a comp and a comp proxy differ is if you enabled Collapse Transformations for this comp layer in another comp. Collapse looks beyond the frame size of a nested comp and can access images on the pasteboard; a comp proxy does not have this information anymore. If you're depending on using Collapse Transformations, you may not be able to use a comp proxy.

Now open the nested comp [**Slow 2_clock sweep**]. Move the time indicator; this comp is almost as slow, as After Effects is still calculating the Pixel Motion and Median effect. You can turn off the Frame Blending switch in this comp's Timeline panel to temporarily disable Pixel Motion, but the Median effect in [**Slow 1_radial blur**] is still making things sluggish.

Open the nested comp [**Slow 1_radial blur**], and move its time indicator or RAM Preview to get a feel for how slow the Median effect is. This precomp is a good candidate for a proxy. If you are in a hurry, you can make a still image proxy for this comp. Type Command+Option+S on Mac (Control+Alt+S on Windows) to render the current frame. Bring the Render Queue forward, give the file a name that you will be able to find later, and twirl down the Output Module section. At the bottom of this section is a popup labeled Post-Render Action: Change its setting from None to Set Proxy. This means After Effects will automatically assign the rendered file as a proxy for the comp you are rendering. Click the Render button and a single frame will be rendered and saved to disk.

When the render finishes, look at the Project panel: The item [**Slow 1_radial blur**] has a white box to its left, indicating a proxy has been assigned. Select this comp, and the Project panel will display details of the comp and its proxy (you may need to drag the panel wider).

Return to [**Slow 1_radial blur**]. A red bar is drawn along the bottom of its Comp panel, with the words Proxy Enabled in the lower left corner. Move the time indicator or RAM Preview, and note how quickly it responds: All After Effects is doing is displaying the still image you rendered, rather than calculating Radial Blur. You can even toggle the Video switch for **DV_InnerGaze** off and on; the image will still be visible in the Comp panel. Toggle the Proxy switch off in the Project panel and select Edit > Purge > All to clear the caches; life is slow again. Turn the Proxy switch back on for now.

Open [**Slow 2_clock sweep**] again, and RAM Preview. It should be more responsive now – especially if the Frame Blending switch is still off! But there's a slight problem: The Radial Blur and Media effects were animating in [**Slow 1_radial blur**], and we don't get to see that progression now, as a still image is standing in for the animation.

Return to the Project panel, select [**Slow 1_radial blur**], and select File > Set Proxy > None. This removes the link to the proxy (but does not delete it from your hard drive – you can select File > Set Proxy > File and use it again later if you wanted). With this comp still selected, type Command+M (Control+M) and this time render a movie of it. In the Output Module, set the Post-Render Action popup to Set Proxy. We have set this project to 16 bits per channel; if we want to preserve all of that quality in the proxy (and we do, if we intend to use it as a final render),

When a proxy has been assigned to a comp and is enabled, the Comp panel has a red bar across the bottom. Edits to the comp's layers will not be visible in the Comp panel, as After Effects is looking to the proxy instead.

pick a higher quality format such as a QuickTime movie using ProRes 444 or a PNG Sequence set to Trillions of Colors. Click the Render button, and go make yourself a nice cup of tea while you're waiting… When the render is done, the new proxy will automatically be assigned. Return to [**Slow 3_final composite**]. It should be much more responsive, especially if Frame Blending is still off for [**Slow 2_clock sweep**].

You can use a proxy for [**Slow 2_clock sweep**] as well – just queue it up to render. Remember to set the Post-Render Action to Set Proxy. Also open its Render Settings, verify Frame Blending is set to On For Checked Layers, and change the Proxy Use popup to Use Comp Proxies Only to take advantage of the proxy we already rendered for [**Slow 1_radial blur**]. Since we need an alpha channel for this precomp, choose a file format that saves one, such as a PNG Sequence set to Trillions+. After the render finishes, note how much zippier [**Slow 3_final composite**] is.

Rendering with Proxies

When it comes time to render, you can use or ignore proxies. This is determined in Render Settings under the Proxy Use menu. You want to ignore proxies if they were low-resolution versions of your footage; you want to render the proxies that are prerenders standing in for computationally intensive compositions.

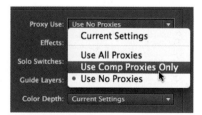

You can override your proxy switches in the Render Settings dialog.

A common choice is Current Settings, which means obey the current status of the proxy switches in the Project panel. This means the final comp will render exactly as you are viewing it. The other choices override the Project panel settings.

If you were using low-resolution footage proxies, but the prerendered comps were final versions, choose Use Comp Proxies Only for your final render. This will use the original footage, but still use any composition proxies you may have prerendered to save time. This is our usual default.

If you used stills to stand in for comps, remove these proxies in the Project panel before the final render, or select Use No Proxies. Of course, if you've already prerendered horribly slow comps, Use No Proxies will start rendering everything again from scratch (been there, done that…).

CONNECT

Collapsing transformations: Chapter 20.

Importing footage: Chapters 1 and 38.

32-bit floating point: Chapter 26.

Fields: Chapter 41.

Rendering: Chapters 42 and 43.

What's Your Preference?

Setting preferences to optimize your workflow.

TIP

Fresh Preferences

Press Command+Option+Shift on Mac (Control+Alt+Shift on Windows) while launching After Effects to delete the preferences file and restore the settings to their defaults.

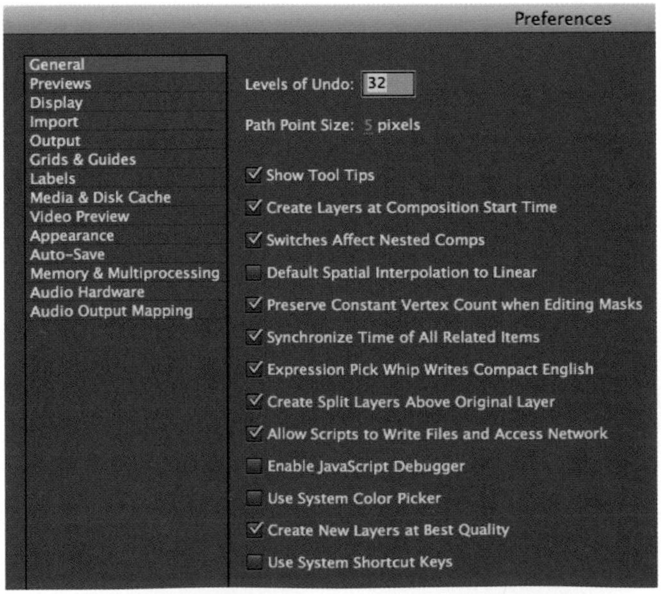

After Effects features a variety of settings that control importing files, opening multiple compositions, previewing audio, the appearance and interactivity of the program, plus numerous other details. In this chapter, we'll give an overview of what these settings mean and what they do, highlighting those settings that we find aid our efficiency.

There are 14 individual Preferences panes. To access them, select the main Preferences item under the After Effects menu on OS X, or under the Edit menu on Windows. You can also open the General preferences by typing Command+Option+; on Mac (Control+Alt+; on Windows). After you choose one pane (which also opens the main Preference dialog box), you can access any of the other panes either by clicking the Previous and Next buttons in the upper right corner, or choosing your desired category from the list along the left. To accept your changes to Preferences, click on OK (which is also the default if you press Return); to ignore them click on Cancel.

We'll go through each Preferences pane, discussing what the options control and how we personally set them. If you want to learn more about a specific preference, search for its name in the After Effects Help.

General

Levels of Undo: This controls how many of your last steps After Effects remembers. Some actions are not stored in the Undo buffer, such as – ironically – editing the Preferences.

Path Point Size: Controls the size of the verticies and Bezier handles for masks, shapes, and motion paths. Increase it if you're having trouble grabbing these points.

Show Tool Tips: Ever wonder what a funky tool or button does? Enable Show Tool Tips (the default), hover your cursor over it, and After Effects will tell you.

Create Layers at Composition Start Time: When enabled (the default), any new layer you add to a comp will snap to start at the beginning of the comp. The exception is if you drag it directly into the timeline and drop it at the time you want it to start. If you disable it, you can still use Option+Home (Alt+Home) to send a layer to the comp's start.

Switches Affect Nested Comps: Also known as recursive switches. Setting the comp-wide switches for Resolution, Wireframe Interactions, Draft 3D, Frame Blending, and Motion Blur cause the corresponding switches to be set the same way in any nested comps. Also, changing the Quality of a layer that is a nested comp sets the Quality the same for all layers in that nested comp. We leave this enabled.

Default Spatial Interpolation to Linear: If this is disabled, spatial interpolation between Position keyframes defaults to Auto Bezier, which we prefer. Spatial interpolation is discussed in Chapter 3.

Preserve Constant Vertex Count when Editing Masks: If this is enabled and you add or delete a mask point for one keyframe on an animating mask shape, that point (or one After Effects thinks is like it) will be added or deleted from all other keyframes.

Synchronize Time of All Related Items: Enabling this means that as you move the current time indicator in one comp, the time indicator is moved to a corresponding point in any nested comps. You may experience odd behavior when the same comp is nested more than once with the copies offset in time, or when a layer has been time remapped. In general, though, this is a hugely useful feature worth the slight slowdown it entails.

Expression Pick Whip Writes Compact English: When enabled (the default), expressions are created using wording that can be transferred across multiple language versions of After Effects.

Create Split Layers Above Original Layer: This option decides if the second half of a split layer appears above or below the first half.

Allow Scripts to Write Files and Access Network: Allows scripts to write files, create folders, and access the network. Disabled by default for security.

Enable JavaScript Debugger: An essential tool when creating scripts. See Adobe's *After Effects Scripting Guide* which can be found online at *www.adobe.com/devnet/aftereffects*.

Use System Color Picker: After Effects defaults to using a Photoshop-style color picker. Enable to use the System Picker instead.

Create New Layers At Best Quality: If you have a very, *very* slow computer, disable this and new layers will be created set to use Draft Quality. Remember to render using Best!

Use System Shortcut Keys (Mac only): When enabled, Command+M, Command+H, and Command+Option+H are taken away from After Effects for use by the system; add Control to them for the normal After Effects use. (You may need to toggle it a couple of times for it to work.)

Switches Affect Nested Comps applies only to the comp-wide Wireframe Interactions, Draft 3D, Frame Blending, Motion Blur, the Quality setting of layers that are nested comps, and (not pictured here) the Resolution switches for nested comps.

FACTOID

Templates are Prefs Too

The Render Settings and Output Module templates (Chapter 42) are also saved in the Preferences file.

The Previews preferences. Clicking Open GL Info button in Preferences > Previews allows you to verify your video card's level of support in the OpenGL Information dialog.

Previews

Fast Previews: This feature is discussed in more detail in the *Preview Possibilities* sidebar at the end of Chapter 2. In short, the preferences under this heading determine what actions After Effects will take to accelerate rendering the display in the Composition panel as you edit parameters or scrub the current time indicator in a render-intensive composition. In general, we leave the master Enable OpenGL switch enabled (unless we're experiencing problems with OpenGL), and then set the Fast Previews popup as desired on a per-comp basis.

Viewer Quality: This new section introduced in After Effects CS5 controls whether additional smoothing is performed for Color Management (the subject of Chapter 26) and for "zoom." By "zoom" After Effects means when you have the Magnification popup set to Fit and the display is being scaled to an in-between value (for example, 137% instead of 100% or 200%), or when Pixel Aspect Ratio Correction is enabled. The choices are Faster, More Accurate Except RAM Preview (which means previews will be displayed more quickly, but the display will revert to More Accurate when the preview is stopped), or More Accurate. We prefer to set these to More Accurate so that the display while we're working will most closely resemble what our final render will look like. Try the other settings if you are stuck with a particularly slow computer.

Alternate RAM Preview: This feature was also introduced in CS5: If you press Option (Alt) when initiating a RAM Preview, After Effects will play just a few frames preceding the current time indicator. This is handy for quickly checking how well a motion track, animated mask, key, or Roto Brush matte is working, or if you have issues with edge chatter or a tracking mismatch. The default is five frames; you can change the value here.

Audio Preview: The Duration setting controls the length of audio playback when you initiate an audio-only preview (press the numeric keypad's period key). The Sample Rate used is set in File > Project Settings.

Display

Motion Path: Determines how many keyframes of a selected layer's motion path are displayed in the Comp panel. We prefer to see the entire path (the All Keyframes option), but you can opt for less to cut down on visual clutter when you're focusing on a complicated path.

Disable Thumbnails in Project Panel: Normally, After Effects displays a thumbnail of the selected footage file at the top of the Project panel. It also creates thumbnails for comps, rendering the first frame to do so. These can slow down the responsiveness of the program, particularly with high-resolution sources or complex comps. If we are familiar with our sources, we will turn this off to buy some extra speed.

Show Rendering Progress in Info Panel & Flowchart: This shows you what's taking so long (such as a slow effect) each time you move to a new frame. There is a slight performance penalty, but we like the information.

Hardware Accelerate Composition, Layer, and Footage Panels: Enable to use the graphics processing unit on your video card to accelerate the sending of images to these viewers. You only need to disable it if you are having OpenGL driver crashes or related issues.

Import

Still Footage: When you add a still to a comp, does it default to the comp's length, or a predetermined length? We prefer the former, as it is easy to trim the duration of individual or multiple stills in a comp.

Sequence Footage: Not to be confused with Sequence Layers, this sets the default frame rate of an image sequence when you import it. To save on headaches later, you usually want to set this to equal your working frame rate (such as 23.976 frames per second for film-rate video).

Interpret Unlabeled Alpha As: We set this to Ask User. It's always safest to have After Effects ask you how you want your alpha interpretation set when you import footage, because it sometimes guesses wrong. However, if you drag and drop items to the Project panel, it will always guess regardless of this preference (see Chapter 38 for details).

Drag Import Multiple Items As: When you drag multiple layered Photoshop or Illustrator files directly to the Project panel, do you want them flattened into normal footage items, or imported as compositions? If you do set this preference to Composition, we recommend using the Composition – Retain Layer Sizes option.

Output

Segment Sequences At: Some computers really…slow…down when there are too many files in a single folder. If you encounter this problem when you're rendering long image sequences, enable this option and set it to a few hundred or so. It's often faster to merge together the files later.

Footage as Composition

For more on importing layered files as compositions, refer to the sections on Photoshop and Illustrator in Chapter 38.

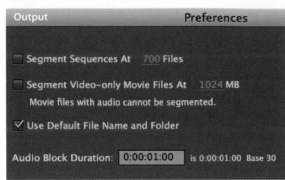

Segment Video-only Movie Files At: Some file systems and media have limitations as to how large a single file can be. To avoid exceeding these limits, enable this option and set a size limit a few megabytes smaller than the maximum size. (Ignored if audio is embedded; render audio separately.)

Use Default File Name and Folder: When you queue up a comp to render, do you want After Effects to automatically make a file name out of the comp's name, and save it to the last place you saved a render? If not, disable this option, and After Effects will ask for the file name and destination every time you add an item to the Render Queue.

Audio Block Duration: Audio data is typically not saved for every frame of video, as it is usually so tiny compared with the video data in a frame. Realtime playback often works better if audio is saved into medium-sized blocks, such as every half or full second.

Grids & Guides

Grids, Rulers, and Guides were discussed in Chapter 2. You can toggle the display of these on and off from the Choose Grid and Guide Options menu from the Comp, Layer or Footage panels. Note that objects can snap to Grids and Guides, but not the Proportional Grid.

Grid: This is an overlay for the Comp panel that can consist of lines, dashed lines, or dots, spaced by the number of pixels specified.

Proportional Grid: An overlay for the Comp panel that does the math for you, automatically spacing out lines depending on how many divisions you want for the comp, regardless of its size.

Guides: This controls the color and drawing style of the guide lines you can drag into the Comp panel from the rulers (View > Show Rulers).

Safe Margins: This is another Comp panel overlay, this time telling you where the Action and Title Safe areas are. The defaults are the typical standard definition video values; After Effects CS4 added the display of 4:3 center-cut safe zones for widescreen compositions.

Labels

Quite simply, this is where you get to create and assign the default colors to be used for footage items in the Project and Footage panels, layers in the Timeline and Layer panels, and comps in the Render Queue, Composition, and Timeline panels. You can also rename the colors. In most cases, you can change the color assigned to these items after they are created or imported by clicking on the swatch next to them – a great way to help visually organize a complex Timeline in particular.

Media & Disk Cache

Disk Cache: If the RAM Preview buffer is full and you request new frames to be cached, normally After Effects will determine which previously cached frames are needed the least and delete them to make room. If you check Enable Disk Cache, instead frames which took awhile to render will be copied to the location specified in this section. If you then later perform a RAM Preview or a final render that can reuse those frames, After Effects retrieves them from disk rather than rerenders them. These files are deleted when you close a project. (This is also discussed in the *Preview Possibilities* sidebar at the end of Chapter 2.)

Conformed Media Cache: To improve performance, After Effects (as well as other programs in the CS5 Production Premium bundle including

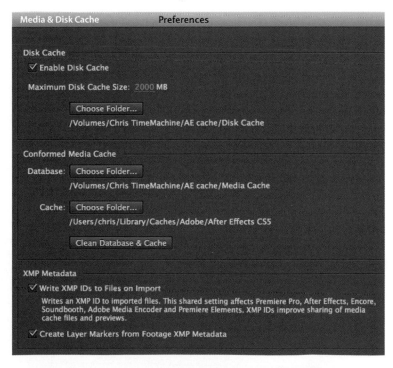

Adobe Premiere Pro, Encore, and Soundbooth) converts some CPU-intensive footage file formats such as MPEG to a faster, uncompressed internal format. There is a slight delay when you first import one of these files, but they will be much faster to access afterward. These files are saved in the Cache location, which should be a large, fast drive.

The Database is smaller and can exist on your main drive. The Production Premium programs share the same database so that each can take advantage of the decompressed files, even when they exist in another program's cache. If the original source file is no longer available, it's a good idea to click the Clean Database & Cache button so the other applications don't go looking for a missing file.

Video Preview

These settings are discussed at the end of Chapter 2 plus mentioned again in Chapter 41, so we won't go over them again here. The most common gotcha: When you're previewing through a video card such as AJA Kona or Blackmagic DeckLink, you need to set Output Mode to RGB, not the 8-bit or 10-bit YUV modes you would normally render to.

Note that cleaning the database is *not* the same as deleting the cached file! If you are running out of disk space, manually delete items in the Cache folder, then click Clean Database & Cache.

XMP Metadata: The After Effects Help file contains a thorough explanation of metadata. In short, files can contain additional information concerning how they were created, who owns the original content, and many other details. In some workflows, it is highly desirable to keep track of this information through a project. The two options in this section – in conjunction with the related Output Module preference demonstrated in the *XMP Metadata and Markers* sidebar in Chapter 42 (page 697) – control how metadata flows through an After Effects project.

The Write XMP IDs to Files on Import option creates unique IDs for files that don't already have XMP metadata attached, making it easier to track these files through the production chain (even if you change their names). The Create Layer Markers from Footage XMP Metadata option will translate time-based metadata into markers inside After Effects, which may then be viewed and edited in a composition – plus copied to the resulting file upon rendering. (Again, see the example in Chapter 42.)

Appearance

This pane allows you to customize the user interface's appearance:

Use Label Color for Layer Handles and Paths: Makes it easier to relate paths and outlines in the Comp panel to layers in the Timeline panel.

Use Label Color for Related Tabs: New in After Effects CS5 is displaying label colors in the Comp, Timeline, Layer, and Footage panels.

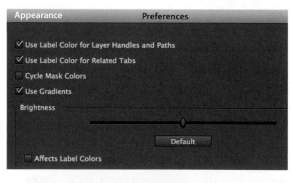

Cycle Mask Colors: Enable for each mask outline to be a different color; disable for them to be the last color set. (You can change them later.)

Use Gradients: Purely cosmetic; adds a slightly dimensional look to the user interface. Disable on slower computers to speed up screen redraws.

Brightness: Alters how dark or bright the surrounding user interface is drawn. The Affects Label Colors checkbox determines if the label colors also shift to match.

Auto-Save

Decides whether you want After Effects to keep saving copies of your project automatically while you work. You can determine how often projects are saved and how many versions are kept around. The downside of enabling this feature is that the program may briefly appear sluggish without warning as it saves the project file. We personally leave this off, and regularly use the keyboard shortcut Command+Option+Shift+S (Control+Alt+Shift+S) to save our current project (while automatically incrementing its version number) as we go.

Memory & Multiprocessing

Memory: This is the section where you balance the amount of memory used by After Effects versus your system and any other programs that may be running. While it is tempting to reduce the "reserved for other applications" number as low as possible, if you go too far performance will suffer as the operating system swaps elements in and out of RAM.

If you have CS5 Production Premium or Master Collection, the video family of applications can share memory between themselves. This is done automatically for you (but if you're curious, click the Details button near the bottom of this dialog).

After Effects Multiprocessing: If you have a multiprocessor or multicore computer, as well as a lot of RAM, enabling this option can significantly speed up RAM Previews and final renders. With it enabled, After Effects will launch multiple copies of itself in the background, copy your project's elements as needed to these copies, and order these background copies to render frames. During RAM Previews, as memory starts to fill up, the background processes will "go quiet" and release their RAM. The main foreground copy will then continue rendering frames until memory is exhausted or all of the preview frames have been rendered.

On a multiprocessor desktop computer, we tend to reserve two CPUs for other applications (particularly if we want to keep working in another program while rendering in the background).

If the current composition is using an effect which relies on OpenGL (such as Cartoon), multiprocessor rendering will be temporarily disabled.

Clicking on Details in the Memory & Multiprocessing preference pane (above) will open a second dialog (below) where you can observe how the programs are automatically allocating the available RAM between themselves.

Preferences

Memory & Multiprocessing Details

Installed RAM: 2.00 GB   Current RAM Usage: 0.93 GB   Allowed RAM Usage: 1.48 GB

Proces... ▲	Application Name	Min Needed Memory	Max Usable Memory	Max Allowed Memory	Current Memory	Current Priority
276	Premiere Pro	0.55	2.00	0.55	0.41	3 – Low
345	After Effects	0.40	2.00	0.40	0.15	2 – Normal
500	Adobe Media En...	0.52	2.00	0.52	0.37	3 – Low

The Text Preferences

Your preference settings are saved in a text file called **Adobe After Effects 10.0-x64 Prefs**. This file is updated each time you quit After Effects. Many instances of mysterious behavior can be attributed to the preferences file getting corrupted or your forgetting you changed a preference long ago.

If you want to return to your default preferences, search your system drive for a file named "**Adobe After Effects 10.0-x64 Prefs**" and save a copy of it in a safe place in case you want to go back to them someday. Then hold down Command+Option+Shift (Control+Alt+Shift) while launching the program to delete the preferences file and restore the settings to their defaults.

In extreme cases, another associated preferences document may also be damaged; if you suspect this is the problem, you may want to trash the entire preferences folder (after making a safe copy, of course). Here is where that folder can be found:

MacOS 10.6:

Drive\Users\<your user name>\Library\ Preferences\Adobe\After Effects\8.0

Windows 7:

C:\Users\<your user name>\AppData\ Roaming\Adobe\After Effects\10.0

The text preferences file contains a lot of additional internal switches and settings which are not exposed to the user. If you're feeling brave, quit After Effects, make a safe copy of the **Adobe After Effects 10.0-x64 Prefs** file, open the original in a text editor, and look around. Most of this file will read like gibberish, but there are a few gems hidden inside.

For example, say you checked the Enable Disk Cache preference, but feel After Effects is too quick to delete cached frames rather than copy them to disk. With this preference enabled, quit After Effects, open the text preferences, and search for the phrase "Proclivity Multiplier" (we warned you about gibberish). Set its value to something lower (say, 1.2 instead of 1.5), save the prefs file, and relaunch After Effects.

In the same folder is the **Adobe After Effects 10.0 Shortcuts** file that maps keyboard shortcuts to functions inside After Effects. If you are using a foreign language keyboard, and need to remap a shortcut to a special key, find that key's Unicode character (such as U+00A7 for §), and replace the current assignment inside parenthesis with the Unicode value.

For more conventional reassignments, you don't need to edit this file by hand: Use Jeff Almasol's "KeyEd Up" script, which is available as part of a collection of Additional Scripts in the After Effects section on *share.studio.adobe.com*.

CONNECT

Audio Hardware

Default Device: Where you want your audio routed while working in After Effects. It is usually set to your computer's built-in audio; change this popup if you want to route it instead to your video card.

Buffer Size: This Mac-only value can be tweaked to optimize performance in spooling chunks of audio to the selected device. Smaller is better; increase it if the audio drops out during previews.

Settings: On Windows, opens a dialog to adjust the settings for your sound card, including Buffer Size. (For Mac users, audio hardware parameters may be edited with the Audio MIDI Setup utility.)

Audio Output Mapping

Some audio and video cards have multiple audio outputs. You can use this dialog to determine which outputs After Effects routes its previews to.

Media Credits

We would like to acknowledge and thank the companies and artists who provided the media we used in the illustrations and projects throughout this book. To find out more about these folks and what they have to offer, check out the **Credits and Info** folder on the DVD and log onto their respective websites.

Artbeats offers a unique variety of royalty-free stock footage, at a quality that you won't find anywhere else. Their library encompasses an extensive array of NTSC, PAL, Hi-Definition, and RED Hi-Res clips.

iStockphoto is the internet's original member-generated image and design community. Get easy, affordable inspiration with millions of safe, royalty-free photographs, vector illustrations, video footage, audio tracks and Flash files from $1.

Please read and understand the End User License Agreements (EULAs) included on the DVD-ROM; you are agreeing to abide by these whenever you use the content on the DVD.

Stock Footage Suppliers:

AB	**Artbeats**	www.artbeats.com
CC	**Crowd Control**	www.toolfarm.com
CP	**Classic PIO Partners**	www.rcnainc.com
DV	**Digital Vision**	www.gettyimages.com/digitalvision
GI	**Getty Images**	www.gettyimages.com
iS	**iStockPhoto**	www.istockphoto.com

Additional content providers:

CL	**Creative License**	www.creative-license.com
CD	**Crish Design**	www.crishdesign.com
DI	**Desktop Images**	www.desktopimages.com
HCW	**Hollwood Camera Work**	www.hollywoodcamerawork.us
HD	**HDR-VFX**	www.hdrvfx.com
HM	**Harry Marks**	www.harrymarks.com
KD	**Kevin Dole**	www.kissthefrogmovie.com
KS	**Keith Snyder**	www.woollymammoth.com
LS	**Lee Stranahan**	vfxfilmmaker.com
PH	**Photron**	www.photron.com
PS	**Paul Sherstobitoff**	homepage.mac.com/sherstobitoff
QE	**Quiet Earth Design**	www.quietearth.net
SH	**Shelley Green**	shelley@shetlandstudios.com
SS	**Smart Sound**	www.smartsound.com
TU	**Giovanna Imbesi**	www.tuttomedia.com
VS	**Pixélan Software**	www.pixelan.com
—	**Pixel Corps**	www.pixelcorps.com

All images in the book not explicitly credited were created by Crish Design.

Index

Adobe Effects

3D Channel Extract, BC40B

Add Grain, BC23B

Advanced Lightning, BC23B, BC37B

Alpha Levels, BC23B

Angle Control, 619

Audio Spectrum, 404, BC23B

Audio Waveform, BC23B

Auto Color, BC23B

Auto Contrast, BC23B

Auto Levels, BC23B

Bass & Treble, BC36B

Bevel Alpha, BC23B

Bezier Warp, BC23B

Black & White, BC23B

Blend, BC23B

Block Dissolve, BC23B

Box Blur, BC23B

Broadcast Colors, 460

Calculations, 199, BC23B

Card Dance, BC23B

Card Wipe, BC23B

Cartoon, BC23B

Caustics, BC23B

CC effects. *See Third-Party sidebar*

Change Color, BC23B

Change to Color, BC23B

Channel Blur, 472

Channel Combiner, BC23B

Channel Mixer, 470, BC23B

Checkbox Control, BC37B

Cineon Converter, 459

Colorama, BC23B, BC40B

Color Balance, BC23B

Color Balance (HLS), BC23B

Color Control, 620, BC37B

Color Difference Key, 465, BC27B

Color Key, 464

Color Profile Converter, 443, 444, BC23B

Color Range Key, 465

Color Stabilizer, BC23B

Compound Blur, 418, BC23B, BC40B

Corner Pin, BC23B

Curves, BC23B, BC40B

Delay, BC36B

Depth Matte, BC40B

Depth of Field, BC40B

Difference Matte, 466

Directional Blur, BC23B

Drop Shadow, 327, BC23B, BC37B

Dust & Scratches, BC23B

Echo, 136–37

Exposure, 457

Expression Controls, 618–21

Extract, 466

Eyedropper Fill, BC23B

Fast Blur, BC23B

Fill, BC23B, BC37B

Flange & Chorus, BC36B

Foam, BC23B

Fog 3D, BC40B

Fractal Noise, 439, BC23B

Gaussian Blur, 406, BC23B

Glow, BC23B

Gradient Wipe, BC23B

Grow Bounds, 363, BC23B

HDR Highlight Compression, 456, 459

High-Low Pass, BC36B

Hue/Saturation, 461, 471, BC23B, BC40B

ID Matte, BC40B

Inner/Outer Key, 466

Layer Control, BC37B

Leave Color, BC23B

Lens Blur, 418, BC23B, BC40B

Lens Flare, 399, 401–2, 410–11

Levels, 197, 199, 200, BC23B, BC40B

Levels (Individual Controls), BC23B

Linear Color Key, 465

Liquify, BC23B

Luma Key, 464

Match Grain, BC23B

Matte Choker, 471

Median, BC23B

Mesh Warp, BC23B

Minimax, 430–31, BC40B

Modulator, BC36B

Mosaic, BC23B

Motion Tile, BC23B

Noise, BC23B

Noise Alpha, BC23B

Noise HLS, BC23B

Noise HLS Auto, BC23B

Numbers, 336, BC23B, BC37B

Offset, BC23B

Optics Compensation, BC23B

Paint, 554–75

Parametric EQ, BC36B

Photo Filter, BC23B

Point Control, BC37B

Polar Coordinates, BC23B

Puppet, 586–95

Radial Blur, BC23B

Radial Shadow, BC23B

Radio Waves, BC23B

Ramp, BC23B

Refine Edges, 211

Refine Matte, 471, 584

Remove Color Matting, 210, 410

Remove Grain, BC23B

Reshape, BC23B

Reverb, BC36B

Ripple, BC23B

Roughen Edges, BC23B

Scribble, 411, BC23B

Selective Color, BC23B

Set Channels, BC23B

Set Matte, 199, 200, BC23B

Shadow/Highlight, BC23B

Sharpen, BC23B

Shatter, 287, 293, BC23B, BC37B

Shift Channels, 199, BC40B

Simple Choker, 210, 471, BC40B

Slider Control, 625, BC37B

Smart Blur, BC23B

Spill Suppressor, 471

Stereo Mixer, 603–5

Stroke, 403, 404, BC23B

Texturize, 418–21

Timewarp, 135, 492

Tint, BC23B

Tone, BC36B

Transform, 340, 341, 409, 619, BC23B

Tritone, 398, 439, BC23B

Turbulent Displace, BC23B

Turbulent Noise, 439, BC23B

Unsharp Mask, BC23B

Vector Paint, 554

Vegas, BC23B, BC37B

Vibrance, BC23B

Warp, BC23B

Wave Warp, BC23B

Wave World, BC23B

Write-on, BC23B

Note: BC = Bonus Chapter on DVD-ROM

Third-Party Products

Note: BC = Bonus Chapter on DVD-ROM

Credits

Acquisitions Editor
Dennis McGonagle

Publishing Services Manager
George Morrison

Project Manager
Anne McGee

Marketing Manager
Amanda Guest

Production Credits

Cover & Interior Design
Trish Meyer

Page Layout
Trish Meyer

Copy Editor
Mandy Erickson

Proofreader
Sam Molineaux-Graham

Indexer
Ken DellaPenta

Printed in the United States of America by RR Donnelley.

Only two names end up on the cover, but in reality, scores of people are involved in the creation of a book like this. We greatly appreciate everyone who worked with us on this revised edition of Creating Motion Graphics.

RESOURCES

Some of our favorites places to learn more about motion graphics and After Effects:

Our own website is full of information about our video training, what we write and where we speak. Key pages to visit include:
articles.crishdesign.com
books.crishdesign.com
training.crishdesign.com

We maintain a pair of blogs for ProVideo Coalition. One is an archive of useful articles (*cmgkeyframes.provideocoalition.com*), while the other contains commentary and general chatter about motion graphics (*cmgblog.provideocoalition.com*).

We've also written a series of articles for Artbeats. You'll find them in their Written Tutorials section (*www.artbeats.com/written_tutorials*).

These are some of our favorite blogs, forums, web sites, and user groups when we need to find answers to questions on After Effects:
blogs.adobe.com/toddkopriva
blogs.adobe.com/keyframes
media-motion.tv/ae-list.html
www.adobeforums.com
www.aenhancers.com
www.aescripts.com
www.motionscript.com

When you need to feed the other side of your brain, also visit:
www.motionographer.com

Here are good sources for software and plug-ins (including freebies):
www.toolfarm.com; www.redgiantsoftware.com

DVD Tech Support

If your DVD becomes *damaged*, contact Focal Press Customer Service at: usbkinfo@elsevier.com

The phone number is: 1 (800) 545-2522 inside North America and +44 (0) 1865 474010 in Europe.

If you have trouble *operating* the DVD, contact Focal Press Technical Support at: technical.support@elsevier.com

The phone number is: 1 (800) 692-9010 inside North America and +1 (314) 872-8370 from overseas.